D1378214

FAMOUS FIRST FACTS ABOUT AMERICAN POLITICS

Other H. W. Wilson titles by Steven Anzovin & Janet Podell

Facts About the Presidents, Seventh Edition (forthcoming)
Famous First Facts, Fifth Edition
Famous First Facts, International Edition
Old Worlds to New: The Age of Exploration and Discovery
Speeches of the American Presidents

Other titles in the Wilson Facts Series

Facts About American Immigration (forthcoming)
Facts About the American Wars
Facts About the British Prime Ministers
Facts About Canada, Its Provinces and Territories
Facts About China (forthcoming)
Facts About the Cities, Second Edition
Facts About the Congress
Facts About Retiring in the United States (forthcoming)
Facts About the Supreme Court of the United States
Facts About the Twentieth Century (forthcoming)
Facts About the World's Languages
Facts About the World's Nations
and
Famous First Facts About the Environment (forthcoming)
Famous First Facts About Sports

STEVEN ANZOVIN & JANET PODELL

FAMOUS FIRST FACTS
ABOUT
AMERICAN POLITICS

The H. W. Wilson Company
New York • Dublin
2001

Library of Congress Cataloging-in-Publication Data

Anzovin, Steven.
    Famous first facts about American politics / by Steven Anzovin and Janet Podell.
        p. cm.
    Includes bibliographical references and indexes.
    ISBN 0-8242-0971-0 (alk.paper)
    1. United States—Politics and government—Miscellanea. 2. United States—History—Miscellanea.
I. Podell, Janet. II. Title.
    E183 .A64 2000
    973—dc21   00-49960

Printed in the United States of America

The H. W. Wilson Company
950 University Avenue
Bronx, NY 10452

Visit H.W. Wilson's Web site: www.hwwilson.com

Contents

Preface

Famous First Facts About American Politics is the latest volume in the series inaugurated by the H.W. Wilson Company in 1931 with the publication of Joseph Nathan Kane's classic reference book, *Famous First Facts*. Our goal has been to afford readers a new way of understanding the rich history of elections, parties, and governments in the United States.

Famous First Facts About American Politics contains more than 4,000 entries under subject headings ranging alphabetically from the American Revolution to the White House. It covers the political history of the United States from the founding of the Iroquois Confederacy by Haionhwat'ha and Deganawidah sometime before the year 1550 to the ground breaking events that took place at the end of the millennium, including the first grand jury testimony delivered by a sitting president (1999) and the first campaign by a First Lady for election to public office (2000). The reader's attention is directed to the section on the next page entitled "How to Use This Book," which describes in detail the classification scheme and the indexing system.

We would like to express our thanks and appreciation to Michael Schulze, Gray Young, and Lynn Messina of the General Publications division of the H.W. Wilson Company. Thanks are also due to Lawrence Podell; to Diane Kopperman Podell of the C. W. Post Library, Greenvale, NY; and to the many libraries and Web site sponsors where we did our research. Our special gratitude goes to our children, Hannah, Miriam, and Rafael Anzovin, for their patience and helpfulness.

Readers who would like to make suggestions for firsts to be included in future editions of this book are invited to send them to Editor, *Famous First Facts About American Politics*, H.W. Wilson Company, 950 University Avenue, Bronx, NY 10452.

Steven Anzovin and Janet Podell
Amherst, MA
January 2001

How to Use This Book

Related entries are grouped together under main subject categories, which are arranged alphabetically. When necessary, the main categories are divided into subcategories, likewise alphabetically arranged. For example, the main category **CONGRESS** contains a large section of general entries, followed by the subcategories **HOUSE**, **PAGES**, **SALARIES**, **SENATE**, and **SESSIONS**. The subcategory **HOUSE**, in turn, contains the further subcategories **REPRESENTATIVES** and **SPEAKERS**. Within this structure of classification, the entries are arranged chronologically.

Each entry begins with a four-digit indexing number, starting with 1001, and an introductory phrase, referred to here as the first line, in boldface (for example, **1023. Colony to declare its independence**). Please note that the four-digit indexing number does not indicate the year in which an event took place; the date can be found in the text of the entry.

History is a complicated subject, and classification is an inexact science. In many cases, entries were classifiable under more than one subject category. To find a specific entry, the reader may turn to one of the five indexes printed at the back of the volume: the comprehensive Subject Index, which alphabetically lists all major topics mentioned within entries; Years, in which entries are arranged chronologically by year; Days, in which entries are arranged by date (for example, January 1); Names, which lists the names of all the persons mentioned in the book; and Geographical, which indexes all locations by city and nation. All indexes refer not to a page number but to the entry's indexing

Famous First Facts
About American Politics

A

AMERICAN REVOLUTION

1001. Plan for the union of the British colonies to be given formal consideration was the Albany Plan of Union, drafted by Benjamin Franklin and presented to representatives of the colonies of New York, Pennsylvania, Maryland, Massachusetts, Connecticut, Rhode Island, and New Hampshire at the Albany Congress, held at the Albany Courthouse in Albany, NY, from June 19 to July 11, 1754. Franklin urged the colonies to form a self-governing federation under a president-general appointed by the British crown, with a grand council of representatives chosen by each province. His plan may have been modeled on the government of the Iroquois Confederacy, which was represented at the Congress by a Mohawk delegation led by Hendrick (Tiyanoga), who addressed the participants on July 9. Though accepted by the Congress, Franklin's idea was turned down by both the American colonial legislatures and the British. An earlier suggestion for a confederation was made by William Penn, the founder of Pennsylvania, whose "Plan for the Union of the Colonies in America," composed in 1697, called for a central conference on matters of commerce and defense to which each colony would send two delegates.

1002. Committee of correspondence formed in a British colony in America was authorized on June 13, 1764, in Boston, MA, by the provincial House of Representatives, following a proposal made at a Boston town meeting. Its purpose was to stay in contact with the political leadership of the other provinces in order to achieve a united plan of action against oppressive British laws. In 1772–74, as the political crisis intensified, standing committees of correspondence were set up in most of the British colonies.

1003. Colonial boycott of British goods began in Boston, MA, in August 1764, when the city's merchants committed themselves not to wear lace and ruffles manufactured in Britain until Parliament eased its tough trade laws. In late 1767, after Parliament imposed a set of new import duties (the Townshend Acts), a Boston town meeting extended the boycott to other British products. The idea was quickly taken up in other provinces. Nonimportation pledges and outright bans on British goods cost Britain nearly £1 million in 1769 and led to a partial repeal of the Townshend Acts.

1004. Orator of the Revolution was Patrick Henry of Virginia. As early as 1765, speaking before the Virginia House of Burgesses in Williamsburg, Henry publicly set himself in opposition to the colonial power as he brilliantly denounced the British Stamp Act, a law requiring colonial citizens to pay for a special stamp on legal publications and documents. In asserting the right of the Virginia assembly to pass its own laws and not merely to enact those of a distant Parliament, he appeared to threaten the crown itself. "Caesar had his Brutus, Charles the First his Cromwell, and George III—" he began, but when interrupted by shouts of "Treason! treason!" he continued: "—may profit by their example. If this be treason, make the most of it."

1005. Direct tax on Britain's American colonists without their consent was the Stamp Act, enacted on March 22, 1765, by Parliament. It required colonists to buy revenue stamps for every pair of dice, every pack of playing cards, and every newspaper, pamphlet, and document, including charters, legal papers, licenses, and college diplomas. The purpose of the tax was to raise funds to pay for the upkeep of the British army in America. The act was repealed in March 1766 after the colonists mounted a sustained boycott of British goods. It was replaced the following year by the Tea Tax, which taxed various articles of everyday use, in addition to tea.

1006. Local government to refuse to obey the Stamp Act was Frederick County, MD. On November 23, 1765, twelve judges of the Court of Frederick County declared that "all proceedings shall be valid and effectual without the use of stamps." Courts in many other cities and counties followed suit.

AMERICAN REVOLUTION—*continued*

1007. City to be occupied by the British before the Revolution was Boston, MA, where resentment against British taxes and Parliamentary authority was threatening to lead to insurrection. British troopships carrying two infantry regiments and supporting artillery arrived in the harbor on September 28, 1768. On October 1 the troops entered Boston and occupied the main public buildings, including the courthouse and the statehouse.

1008. Attack on British soldiers by civilians in the Revolution was made in New York City on January 18, 1770, by the Sons of Liberty, a crowd of Americans who attacked a group of 40 to 50 soldiers because they had cut down the liberty poles that the Americans had erected. The soldiers used their bayonets and dispersed them. No one was killed, but several persons on both sides were seriously injureds. The mob fight has been termed the Battle of Golden Hill.

1009. Americans killed by British soldiers in the Revolution were shot on March 5, 1770, at Boston, MA, when British soldiers of the 29th Regiment of Foot fired at a taunting crowd, killing Crispus Attucks, James Caldwell, Patrick Carr, Samuel Gray, and Samuel Maverick. The incident became known as the Boston Massacre. The soldiers were tried for murder and were defended by John Adams and Josiah Quincy, Jr. Two soldiers were found guilty, branded on the hand, and discharged. Six other soldiers and an officer were acquitted. Attucks, the first American to fall, was an African-American whalerman.

1010. Protest against British taxation of tea shipments occurred in October 1773, when a delegation of Philadelphians invited the agents of the East India Company, which had a monopoly on the sale of British tea, to resign their commissions or risk the consequences. Some of them complied. Intimidation of tea agents in port cities continued over the next few months, along with mass protest meetings.

1011. Destruction of British tea shipments was the "Boston Tea Party," which took place on December 16, 1773. Colonists enraged by the high British tea tax disguised themselves as Mohawks, boarded three ships (the *Dartmouth,* the *Beaver,* and the *Eleanor*), and dumped 342 chests of tea into Boston Harbor. Many other colonies held their own "tea parties." In April 1774, 18 boxes of tea were dumped into New York Harbor at the "New York Tea Party." On October 19, 1774, patriots in Annapolis, MD,

forced the owner of the ship *Peggy Stewart* to burn his cargo of taxed tea. On October 25, 1774, 51 women of Edenton, NC, burned their tea in support of the colonies' cause. And on December 22, 1774, a "Tea Party" was held at Greenwich, NJ, in which tea was taken from the British ship *Greyhound* and burned.

1012. Association of British colonies in America was the Continental Association, proposed on October 18, 1774. It was joined over the course of the next six months by twelve of the colonies and to a limited extent by Georgia, the 13th. They agreed on a program of nonintercourse with Britain, including withdrawal from the slave trade, a trade embargo, and refusal to use British products. Any province that reneged on its promises in this regard was itself to be subject to a boycott by the others. Cooperation with the agreement was enforced on individuals by local committees.

1013. Attack against the British by a state militia occurred in New Hampshire on December 13, 1774, when Major John Sullivan led 400 men of the Granite State Volunteers in an attack on Fort William and Mary, a British garrison on the island of New Castle in Portsmouth harbor. They bound the commander of the fort and frightened the soldiers away, capturing 100 casks of powder and small arms. This attack took place some four months before the battle of Lexington.

1014. Reconciliation plan to end the rebellion of the British colonies in America was proposed to the British Parliament by Prime Minister William Pitt on February 1, 1775. Parliament was in receipt of resolutions from the Continental Congress protesting the Intolerable Acts, economic and political sanctions that Parliament had enacted the previous spring to retaliate against Massachusetts for the Boston Tea Party. Pitt's plan included Britain's recognition of the Continental Congress, colonial recognition of Parliament's superior authority, Parliament's pledge to obtain the assent of the colonial assemblies before levying taxes, and Congress's pledge to forward revenue to Britain. The plan was defeated in the House of Lords. Another reconciliation plan, put forward by Lord North on February 20, was rejected by the Continental Congress on July 31.

1015. Clash of arms in the Revolutionary War was the Battle of Lexington, a skirmish at Lexington, MA, on April 19, 1775, between 70 Minutemen volunteers under Captain John Parker and about 700 British regulars under Major John Pitcairn, who were on their way to destroy illegal military stores at nearby Concord. The Americans were ordered to disperse. As they were doing so, one of them fired a shot. The British returned fire, killing eight Minutemen and wounding ten.

1016. War hero was Captain John Parker of Lexington, MA, a farmer and mechanic who was the leader of a local volunteer militia group, the Minutemen. At midnight on April 18, 1775, the Boston silversmith Paul Revere reached Lexington on horseback with a warning that British troops were coming to destroy a supply depot at nearby Concord. The force of 700 British soldiers, led by Major John Pitcairn, reached the Lexington town common at dawn on April 19 to find the Minutemen waiting for them. Parker told his men, "Stand your ground. Don't fire unless fired upon, but if they mean to have a war, let it begin here." The first shots of the Revolutionary War were fired shortly after, leaving one British soldier and ten Americans wounded and eight Americans dead. Parker himself died the following September, of illness.

1017. Mobilization of American troops in the Revolutionary War was ordered on April 23, 1775, by the Provincial Congress in Massachusetts. Some 13,600 American volunteers were called up from all over New England. The first major action of American forces was to lay siege to Boston, which was held by the British.

1018. Call for troops to fight in the Revolutionary War was made on May 10, 1775, at Philadelphia, PA, on the opening day of the second session of the Continental Congress. The delegates passed a resolution calling for 20,000 men to serve in the armed forces.

1019. Naval battle in the Revolutionary War took place on June 12, 1775, when Captain James Moore of the British schooner *Margaretta* arrived in the harbor of Machias, ME, and ordered the inhabitants to take down a liberty pole they had erected. The townspeople, led by Jeremiah and John O'Brien, set out in a confiscated sloop, the *Unity,* and in a hand-to-hand encounter captured the *Margaretta* and confiscated her cannons. The captured crew was marched overland to Cambridge, MA, where they were turned over to General George Washington. The American loss was four killed and eight wounded.

1020. Major battle of the Revolutionary War was the Battle of Bunker Hill, fought on June 17, 1775, at Breed's Hill (the actual location) in Boston, MA. More than 2,000 British soldiers under General William Howe mounted an assault against American volunteer forces dug in around the crest of the hill. Ordered not to fire on the enemy until they could see "the whites of their eyes," the Americans waited until the British frontal assault was only 15 paces away, then opened with a withering volley that halted the British advance. A second British attack also failed, but a third sally overwhelmed the American troops, who had run out of ammunition. The battle resulted in more than 1,000 British and about 400 American casualties, including the American commander, General Joseph Warren.

1021. Royal proclamation declaring Britain's colonies in America to be in open rebellion was issued by King George III on August 23, 1775, after he rejected the Olive Branch Petition, sent to him by the Continental Congress the previous July. The petition, written by John Dickinson, was a statement of loyalty to the crown and a request for the king's assistance in resolving the conflict.

1022. American prisoners of war were captured by the British between 1776 and 1783 and held on prison ships anchored in New York Harbor. More than 11,000 American soldiers died in captivity during the war and were buried in a crypt in Fort Greene, Brooklyn, which is now marked by the Prison Ship Martyrs' Monument.

1023. Colony to declare its independence was New Hampshire, which issued its own Declaration of Independence from Great Britain in 1776, several months before the signing of the Declaration of Independence on July 4, 1776.

1024. Models of republican liberty for the architects of the American Revolution of 1776 were the Jews of the Bible, the ancient Roman republic, and the Native American tribes, whose egalitarian and collegial political traditions were observed at first hand by many of its leaders.

1025. Public call for independence to be published was *Common Sense,* published on January 9, 1776, in Philadelphia, PA. The 50-page pamphlet, written by the Anglo-American revolutionary Thomas Paine, attacked the concept of monarchy and provided reasoned justification for American independence. With sales of 100,000 copies in three months, it was the first bestseller of American political thought.

AMERICAN REVOLUTION—*continued*

1026. Major battle lost by American forces was the Battle of Long Island, fought on August 27, 1776, between soldiers under British general Lord William Howe, commander in chief of the British Army in North America, and the Continental Army under George Washington. The American forces, outnumbered two to one, were outflanked by Howe, who took 1,200 American prisoners and inflicted about 400 casualties. However, rather than pursue a complete victory, Howe elected to lay siege, allowing Washington and his remaining men to escape to Manhattan under cover of fog.

1027. Peace conference during the American Revolution was held on Staten Island (now a borough of New York City) on September 11, 1776. The American delegates—Benjamin Franklin, John Adams, and Edmund Rutledge—met with the British admiral, Lord Richard Howe, who offered pardons for American rebels in return for the voiding of the Declaration of Independence. They turned him down.

1028. American executed as a spy was Nathan Hale, a young schoolteacher from Connecticut. Hale joined the Connecticut militia in July 1775 and was promoted to captain under Thomas Knowlton's Rangers. Volunteering in August 1776 to observe British troop movements on Long Island, he crossed the British lines posing as a Dutch schoolteacher. On September 21, as he made his way back to the American position at Harlem Heights, he was betrayed and captured. Hale was hanged the next morning without a trial by order of General William Howe, the British commander. His famous last words—"I only regret that I have but one life to lose for my country"—were adapted from *Cato,* a play by Joseph Addison.

1029. Traitor to the American cause during the Revolutionary War was William Demont (or Dement), a member of the 5th Pennsylvania Battalion, who was appointed adjutant in Colonel Robert Magraw's battalion on February 29, 1776. He deserted on November 2, 1776, and notified the British of the position of Fort Washington (now a neighborhood in New York City). Demont's act enabled the British general Sir William Howe to conquer the fort with a force of 8,900 men on November 16, 1776. They captured 2,818 American officers and men, 43 guns, and 2,800 muskets.

1030. Foreign officers recruited to the cause of the American Revolution were recruited in Europe in 1776–77 by Silas Deane of Connecticut, who had been charged by the Continental Congress with finding military experts willing to lend their assistance. Most of them were not of high caliber. Among the foreign military leaders who received officers' comissions in the Continental Army were Tadeusz Kósciuszko and Kazimierz Pulaski of Poland, Johann de Kalb and Baron von Steuben of Germany, and the Marquis de Lafayette of France. Pulaski and de Kalb both lost their lives in battle.

1031. Major American victory in the Revolutionary War occurred at the Battle of Saratoga, actually a series of battles fought in 1777 in upstate New York. The British general John Burgoyne was pushing down from Canada along the Hudson River with an army of 6,000 regulars and auxiliaries with the plan of cutting off New England from the rest of the colonies. Ranged against him was a smaller American force commanded by General Horatio Gates. After several failed British assaults, Burgoyne made a last attempt at a breakthrough at the Battle of Bemis Heights, also called the Second Battle of Freeman's Farm, fought on October 7, 1777. Gates's forces threw back the British, killing some 700 men, about four times the American losses. On October 17, 1777, Burgoyne and his remaining army surrendered to Gates at Saratoga. The victory, a turning point in the war, prevented the British from pursuing a divide-and-conquer strategy and encouraged the French to offer aid to the new nation.

1032. Framework for a national government was contained in the Articles of Confederation. The idea for a confederation of states was suggested to the Continental Congress by Richard Henry Lee of Virginia on June 7, 1776. A congressional committee headed by John Dickinson of Pennsylvania drafted the "Articles of Confederation and Perpetual Union," which were adopted on November 15, 1777, submitted to the state two days later, and declared ratified on March 1, 1781. The Articles established a loose federation of sovereign states under a weak national government that lacked a chief executive and a judicial system. Congress, the only institution of the national government, could pass no laws without the consent of nine states, which was attained only rarely, and it had no power to levy taxes or to enforce treaties. The result was political and financial instability. On June 26, 1786, Congress began debate on a motion by Charles Pinckney of South Carolina to reorganize the Articles of Confederation. Eight months later, Congress agreed that the states should hold a convention to revise the plan of government. The Constitutional Convention opened in Philadelphia on May 25, 1787.

1033. State to ratify the Articles of Confederation was South Carolina, on February 5, 1778. The last of the 13 states to ratify them was Maryland, which withheld its ratification until Virginia ceded to the United States the western lands it claimed. Maryland ratified the Articles on February 27, 1781, and Congress declared them fully ratified on March 1.

1034. American general to engage in treason was Benedict Arnold, the Connecticut-born Revolutionary officer whose defection to the British has made his name, among Americans, a synonym for a traitor. Arnold was a courageous and capable battlefield commander whose hastily improvised navy won a key victory over a superior British fleet on Lake Champlain on October 11, 1776. However, Arnold's efforts in Canada proved a failure, and the Continental Congress viewed him as untrustworthy. In February 1777 he was passed over for promotion. Believing that he would receive better treatment from the British, Arnold contacted British secret service chief Major John André in May 1779 and indicated that he was willing to shift his allegiance. In September 1780 Arnold promised to deliver the important garrison at West Point, NY, to the enemy in return for £20,000, plus a lifetime stipend of £500 per annum, but the plot was revealed when André was captured with incriminating documents. Arnold fled on a British ship, leaving André to the hangman's noose, an act that earned him the enmity of many Loyalists. After leading a raid on New London, CT, in September 1781, Arnold moved permanently to England in 1782, where he died in 1801.

1035. Naval hero was John Paul Jones, the Scottish-born captain who led a series of spectacular actions against the British during the Revolutionary War. The most famous took place on September 23, 1779, when Jones, commanding the *Bonhomme Richard* at the head of a four-ship squadron, captured the warship *Serapis* and its convoy of merchant vessels in a three-hour battle off the coast of Britain. He won the victory despite long odds, and his retort to the enemy's call for his surrender—"I have not yet begun to fight"—was made part of American folklore. He was decorated by the United States and the king of France, became a rear admiral in the Russian Navy after political infighting put an end to his American career, and died in obscurity in Paris.

1036. Centennial celebration of the Revolution was held at Lexington and Concord, MA, on April 19, 1875, to commemorate the 100th birthday of American liberty. The participants included President Ulysses Simpson Grant, three cabinet secretaries, and many state governors.

AMERICAN REVOLUTION—CONTINENTAL CONGRESS

1037. Call for a congress of the American colonies was made by colonial leaders in Providence, RI, on May 17, 1774, in reaction to the enactment by Britain's Parliament of the Coercive Acts and other punitive laws. It was supported by their counterparts in Philadelphia and New York. All the colonies with the exception of Georgia—which eventually changed its mind—agreed to choose and send delegates to a Continental Congress, which convened in Philadelphia the following September. (Earlier intercolonial congresses, including the Albany Congress, held in Albany, NY, in 1754, and the Stamp Act Congress, held in New York City in 1765, had narrow goals and involved only a few of the provinces.)

1038. President of the Continental Congress was Peyton Randolph, a delegate from Virginia, who was elected on September 5, 1774, the day the Congress assembled. He resigned on October 22, 1774, to attend the Virginia State Legislature, and his place was taken on the same day by Henry Middleton of South Carolina.

1039. Seat of the Continental Congress was Philadelphia, PA, where the first session of the Continental Congress opened on September 5, 1774, presided over by Peyton Randolph of Virginia and Henry Middleton of South Carolina. It ended on October 26. The second session, from May 10, 1775, to December 12, 1776, was also held in Philadelphia. From December 20, 1776, to March 4, 1777, Congress met at Baltimore, MD; from March 4 to September 18, 1777, again at Philadelphia; on September 27, 1777, at Lancaster, PA; at York, PA, from September 30, 1777, to June 27, 1778; in Philadelphia from July 2, 1778, to June 27, 1783; at Princeton, NJ, from June 30 to November 4, 1783; at Annapolis, MD, from November 26, 1783, to June 3, 1784; and at Trenton, NJ, from November 1 to December 24, 1784. The four final session of the Continental Congress were held at New York City (January 11 to November 4, 1785; November 7, 1785, to November 3, 1786; November 6, 1786, to October 30, 1787; and November 5, 1787, to October 21, 1788). After the adoption

AMERICAN REVOLUTION—CONTINENTAL CONGRESS—*continued*

of the Constitution, Congress remained in New York, meeting there from March 4, 1789, to August 12, 1790. It met in Philadelphia from December 6, 1790, to May 14, 1800, after which it moved permanently to Washington, DC.

1040. Session of the Continental Congress began on September 5, 1774, at Carpenters' Hall, Philadelphia, PA. The participants were 44 delegates from eleven colonies, including John Adams and Samuel Adams of Massachusetts; John Jay of New York; Roger Sherman from Connecticut; and George Washington, Patrick Henry, Richard Henry Lee, and Benjamin Harrison, from Virginia. (Delegates from Georgia and North Carolina did not attend until later sessions.) The Congress adjourned on October 26, 1774, recommending another session to begin on May 10, 1775, in Philadelphia.

1041. Chaplain of the Continental Congress was the Reverend Jacob Duche, rector of Christ Church, an Episcopalian church in Philadelphia, PA, who was elected chaplain by the Continental Congress on September 6, 1774. The election of a chaplain was the first act undertaken by the Continental Congress after the presentation of credentials and the adoption of rules of order. The chaplain offered his first prayer at a meeting of Congress on September 7.

1042. Objection to opening a congressional session with prayer was made on September 6, 1774, by John Jay of New York, delegate to the first session of the Continental Congress, which had assembled at Philadelphia, PA. Once the delegates had presented their credentials and adopted rules of order, they entertained a proposal to elect a chaplain who would offer prayer at the beginning of each session. Jay objected, citing the variety of religious views held by the delegates. He was countered by Samuel Adams of Massachusetts, who replied that he "was no bigot and could hear a prayer from any gentleman of piety and virtue who was also a friend of his country." A chaplain was elected and the first prayer was offered on the following day.

1043. Prayer offered at a session of Congress was offered on the morning of September 7, 1774, the third day of the first Continental Congress, at Carpenters' Hall, Philadelphia, PA. The Reverend Jacob Duche, who had been elected chaplain the previous day, read the morning service of the Episcopal Church, with his clerk making the responses. He also recited a prayer that began: "O Lord our Heavenly Father . . . look down in mercy, we beseech thee, on these our American States, who have fled to thee from the rod of the oppressor and thrown themselves on Thy gracious protection, desiring to be henceforth dependent only on Thee. To Thee have they appealed for the righteousness of their cause; to Thee do they now look up for that countenance and support, which Thou alone canst give; take them, therefore, Heavenly Father, under Thy nurturing care. . . . "

1044. Major action taken by the Continental Congress was the endorsement on September 17, 1774, of the Suffolk Resolves, four resolutions authored by Joseph Warren of Massachusetts that took an aggressive stance towards Britain's attempts to impose punitive economic and political sanctions on its rebellious American colonies. They denounced the Intolerable Acts enacted by Parliament, encouraged Massachusetts residents to defy the British by refusing to do business with them or pay taxes to the crown, and recommended the formation of a militia. The resolutions were unanimously adopted on September 9, 1774, by a group of Massachusetts political leaders who convened after the abolition by Parliament of the colony's representative legislature. They were carried by Paul Revere to Philadelphia, PA, where Congress voted to endorse them.

1045. Medal awarded by the Continental Congress was granted to General George Washington for his exploit of March 17, 1776, in compelling the British forces to evacuate Boston, MA. The date of the resolution authorizing the medal was March 25, 1776. It was struck in Paris. The obverse showed Washington in profile. The reverse showed Washington and his officers on horseback viewing the town of Boston in the distance with the British fleet in view under sail. The medal was not actually presented to Washington until 1786.

1046. Lottery held by the Continental Congress was held on April 10, 1777, in Philadelphia, PA, for the purpose of raising funds. The lottery was approved on November 1, 1776, and seven managers were appointed to conduct it. Treasury bank notes were awarded as prizes, payable at the end of five years. Funds were obtained by lottery by individual colonies at various times prior to this national lottery.

1047. Medal awarded by the Continental Congress to a foreigner was a silver medal presented to Lieutenant Colonel François Louis Teisseidre de Fleury, who commanded the first of the storming parties in the assault upon Stony Point, NY, on July 15, 1779. He was the first man to enter the main fort and strike the

British flag with his own hands. Fleury, who had been in the French military service, joined the Continental Army in 1777. The date of the congressional resolution was July 26, 1779, and the presentation was made on October 1.

1048. Congress to call itself "The United States in Congress Assembled" was the seventh session of the Continental Congress, which met at Philadelphia, PA, from July 2, 1778, to June 27, 1783. Midway through the session, on March 1, 1781, the Articles of Confederation establishing a national government were declared in force, having been ratified by all 13 states between February 5, 1778, and February 27, 1781. On March 2, 1781, the Continental Congress adopted the title "The United States in Congress Assembled." Samuel Huntington of Connecticut continued as its president.

1049. Complete edition of *Journals of the Continental Congress* was not published until 1904–1937 by the Library of Congress. This edition includes the confidential records, as well as the official records kept of the daily proceedings of the First and Second Continental Congress.

AMERICAN REVOLUTION—DECLARATION OF INDEPENDENCE

1050. Declaration of independence by citizens of an American colony was formally made on July 12, 1774, in the First Presbyterian Church in Carlisle, PA, at a meeting of freeholders and freemen from the several townships. The Reverend John Montgomery presided. A similar statement was the Mecklenburg Declaration of Independence, adopted by local citizens on May 20, 1775, in Charlotte, Mecklenburg County, NC.

1051. Declaration of rights was passed by the First Continental Congress in Philadelphia, PA, on October 14, 1774, and was known as the "Declaration and Resolves of the First Continental Congress." It stated that the the colonists "are entitled to life, liberty and property; and they have never ceded to any foreign power whatsoever a right to dispose of either without their consent."

1052. Proclamation of the unification of the colonies was a resolution adopted by the Second Continental Congress on June 7, 1775: "On motion, resolved, that Thursday, the 20th of July next, be observed throughout the Twelve United Colonies as a day of humiliation, fasting and prayer." Only twelve of the 13 colonies were represented because Georgia did not send delegates to the First and Second Continental Congresses.

1053. Declaration of independence by a British colony was made by New Hampshire, whose provisional government announced its independence from Britain on January 5, 1776, six months before the signing of the national Declaration of Independence.

1054. Colonial government to instruct its delegates to the Continental Congress to proclaim independence was North Carolina. In April 12, 1776, the Provincial Congress in session at Halifax, NC, by unanimous action empowered its delegates to the Second Continental Congress to concur with delegates of other provinces in declaring independence from Great Britain. The declaration is known as the "Halifax Resolves."

1055. Statement of the principle of inalienable rights was formulated by George Mason of Virginia in his *Declaration of Rights,* adopted on June 12, 1776, by the Virginia Convention and incorporated into the state constitution. The first article reads: "That all men are by nature equally free and independent, and have certain inherent rights, of which, when they enter into a state of society, they cannot by any compact deprive or divest their posterity; namely, the enjoyment of life and liberty, with the means of acquiring and possession property, and pursuing and obtaining happiness and safety." Thomas Jefferson drew on this model when he drafted the Declaration of Independence.

1056. Congressional vote on a declaration of independence took place in Philadelphia, PA, on July 1, 1776, after the delegates, meeting as a committee, debated a resolution that had been introduced on June 7 by Richard Henry Lee of Virginia and seconded by John Adams of Massachusetts. The first part of this resolution read: "RESOLVED. That these United Colonies are, and of right ought to be, free and independent States, that they are absolved from all allegiance to the British Crown, and that all political connection between them and the State of Great Britain is, and ought to be, totally dissolved." The motion was carried, but not unanimously; negative votes were cast by Pennsylvania, South Carolina, and some of the delegates from Delaware. On the following day, Congress, meeting in formal session, took a second vote, with twelve states in favor, one abstaining, and none opposed. The delegates then debated the document written by Thomas Jefferson, which they adopted, with amendments, on July 4.

AMERICAN REVOLUTION—DECLARATION OF INDEPENDENCE—*continued*

1057. Signer of the Declaration of Independence was John Hancock of Massachusetts, president of the Continental Congress, who signed it on July 4, 1776, in Philadelphia, PA. It was also signed by secretary Charles Thomson, who was not a delegate. The parchment copy was signed by the delegates on August 2, 1776.

1058. Printing of the Declaration of Independence was done on July 5, 1776, in Philadelphia, PA, by John Dunlap in a folio broadside and distributed the same day. On July 4, Congress, acting as a Committee of the Whole, approved the Declaration and ordered that it be printed and that copies be "sent to the several assemblies, conventions and committees or counsels of safety and to the several commanding officers of the Continental troops that it be proclaimed in each of the United States and at the head of the army."

1059. Newspaper to publish the Declaration of Independence was the *Pennsylvania Evening Post* of Philadelphia, PA, which printed the text in its edition of July 6, 1776.

1060. Public reading of the Declaration of Independence took place on July 8, 1776, when Colonel John Nixon, delegated by the high sheriff of Philadelphia, read it in the old State House yard (now Independence Square). The Liberty Bell, which bears the biblical inscription "Proclaim liberty throughout all the land unto all the inhabitants thereof," was rung to call the citizens together to hear the reading.

1061. Publication of the Declaration of Independence in another language took place in Philadelphia, PA, on July 9, 1776, when a translation of the Declaration was published in the *Staatsbote,* a German-language newspaper.

AMERICANA

1062. Use of "America" as a geographical designation was in the *Cosmographiae Introductio,* a world map by the geographer Martin Waldseemüller (also called Ilacomilus or Hylacomylus) of Württemberg (now Germany). In April 1507, at St. Díe in the Vosges Mountains of Alsace, Waldseemüller printed one thousand copies of the map using twelve woodcut blocks. The book contained an account by the Italian explorer Amerigo (Americus) Vespucci of his discoveries in South America. Waldseemüller labeled the New World "America" in his honor.

1063. Political document printed in America was the "Oath of a Free Man," printed in March 1639 by the Stephen Day Press, Cambridge, MA. It was a one-page sheet that read: "I doe solemnly bind myself in the sight of God, that when I shall be called to give my voice touching any subject of this State, in which Freemen as I shall be to deal, I will give my vote and suffrage as I shall judge in mine own conscience may best conduce and tend to the publick weal of the body, without respect of persons, or favour of any man."

1064. Use of the name "United States" instead of "United Colonies" was authorized on September 9, 1776, by the Second Continental Congress: "That in all continental commissions and other instruments where heretofore the words, 'United Colonies' have been used, the style be altered, for the future, to the 'United States.'"

1065. Map of the United States engraved in America was a wall map, 41 by 46.5 inches, made by Abel Buell in New Haven, CT, in 1783, after the Treaty of Paris. It was a line engraving and was advertised for sale in the *Connecticut Journal* of March 31, 1784: "As this Map is the effect of the compiler's long and unwearied application, diligence and industry, and as perfection has been the great object of his labors, and it being the first ever compiled, engraved, and finished by any one man, and an American, he flatters himself, that every patriotic gentleman, and lover of geographical knowledge, will not hesitate to encourage the improvement of his country. Every favour will be most gratefully acknowledged, by the public's most obedient and very humble servant."

1066. Use of the term "Era of Good Feelings" to describe the administration of President James Monroe occurred in the pages of the *Columbian Centinel,* a Boston newspaper, in the spring of 1817, shortly after his inauguration. The disappearance of the Federalist Party had left Monroe's Democratic-Republicans without an opposition, giving the nation a temporary sense of unity.

1067. National hall of fame was National Statuary Hall, formerly the Hall of the United States House of Representatives in the Capitol at Washington, DC, which was established by act of Congress of July 2, 1864. Each state was invited to contribute marble or bronze statues of its most distinguished citizens.

1068. Use of "American" as an adjective instead of "United States" was officially recommended by John Hay, secretary of state, who instructed American diplomatic and consular officers under date of August 3, 1904, to adopt it. The adjective form of designation is not used in strictly formal documents and in notarial acts performed by consular officers; instead, the full name of the country is given (for example: the Government of the United States of America; Embassy of the United States of America).

1069. Museum devoted solely to American political memorabilia was the Museum of American Political Life, which opened in 1989 at the University of Hartford campus in West Hartford, CT. The museum's mission was to collect, preserve and exhibit artifacts and other materials relating to presidential campaigns, presidents and the electoral process. The core of the museum's holdings were donated by collector J. Doyle Dewitt and included 60,000 artifacts, such as posters, buttons, banners, textiles, prints, medals, fine pottery, glassware, snuffboxes, ribbons, torchlights, and a variety of other electoral paraphernalia.

AMERICANA—BOOKS

1070. Book describing the government of a British colony in America was A True Relation of Such Occurrences and Accidents of Noate as Hath Hapned in Virginia Since the First Planting of that Collony, by Captain John Smith, one of the leaders of the British settlement at Jamestown, VA. It was published in London in 1608.

1071. American woman to write political satire and history was Mercy Otis Warren, sister of the revolutionary leader James Otis and wife of Major General James Warren. Her books included two political satires (The Adulateur, published in 1773, and The Group, published in 1775). Her History of the Rise, Progress, and Termination of the American Revolution, Interspersed with Biographical, Political and Moral Observation, a three-volume narrative history of the Revolutionary War, was published in Boston, MA, in 1805.

1072. Political satire was a 16-page pamphlet by Francis Hopkinson entitled A Pretty Story, Written in the Year of Our Lord 1774 by Peter Grievous, Esquire, ABCDE. Velunti in Speculo. It was a political satire on the administration of the British colonies in North America and the causes of the American Revolution. It was printed in Williamsburg, VA, in 1774 by John Pinkney, for the benefit of Clementine Rind's children.

1073. Comic political history of the United States was A Diverting History of John Bull and Brother Jonathan, a 135-page book by Hector Bull-Us, the pseudonym of James Kirke Paulding, author of the novel Westward Ho!, who also served as secretary of the Navy from 1837 to 1841. It was published in 1812 in New York City by Inskeep and Bradford. The work portrays the United States and England as a father and son who begin amicably but soon become engaged in an acrimonious family feud.

1074. Scholarly political history of the United States was A Political and Civil History of the U.S.A. from the year 1763 to the close of the administration of President Washington in March, 1797 including a summary view of the political and civil state of the North American colonies, prior to that period, by Timothy Pitkin. It was published in two volumes by Hezekiah Howe and Durrie and Peck in 1828 at New Haven, CT.

1075. Reference book of American political history was Hill's Political History of the United States: A Condensed Summary of the Important Political Events in United States History, from the Founding of the Government to the Present Time, with Forms of Naturalization, Directions Relating to Australian Ballot, Qualifications in Order to Vote, Etc. The compiler was Thomas E. Hill. The book was published by Hill's company, the Hill Standard Book Company, Chicago, IL, in 1894.

AMERICANA—FLAGS

1076. Flag flown by the Continental Army under Commander-in-Chief George Washington was the Grand Union Flag, also called the Continental Flag, which was flown for the first time on January 1, 1776, at Washington's headquarters at Cambridge, MA. It was similar to the Stars and Stripes, except that instead of the current field of stars, the flag showed in its upper left corner Britain's Union Jack (the superimposed crosses of St. George and St. Andrew). The 13 stripes symbolic of the 13 colonies, alternating red and white, were the same as they are now. The flag was made to Washington's specifications by Rebecca Young of Baltimore, MD, the mother of Mary Young Pickersgill, who later sewed the flag that inspired "The Star-Spangled Banner."

AMERICANA—FLAGS—*continued*

1077. American flag saluted by a foreigner was the Continental Union flag flown by the brig *Andrea Doria* at St. Eustatius, Dutch West Indies, on November 16, 1776. It was saluted by Johannes de Graeff, governor of the colony. The brig was captained by Nicholas Biddle, who had been sent to St. Eustatius to transport arms and ammunition for the American army.

1078. National flag to represent the United States was the design adopted in Philadelphia, PA, on June 14, 1777, by the Second Continental Congress of the United States of America, during its war of independence against Britain. The resolution, read by John Adams of Massachusetts, declared: "Resolved, that the Flag of the thirteen United States shall be thirteen stripes, alternate red and white; that the Union be thirteen stars, white on a blue field, representing a new constellation." The first specimen is said to have been stitched by Betsy Ross (Elizabeth Griscom Ross) in her shop at 239 Arch Street, Philadelphia, PA, at the request of George Washington, Robert Morris, and Colonel George Ross, for the Continental Congress. The design of the flag remains unchanged, except for the adding of a new star for each newly admitted state.

1079. American flag displayed on a warship was flown in Portsmouth Harbor, NH, when a group of young women presented to Captain John Paul Jones a flag they had made, using cloth taken from their own and their mothers' gowns. Captain Jones raised it to the mast of his ship, the *Ranger,* on July 4, 1777.

1080. American flag flown in battle was carried on September 3, 1777, by a detachment of light infantry and cavalry under General William Maxwell at Cooch's Bridge, DE, where they met an advance guard of British and Hessian troops under Generals Richard Howe, Charles Cornwallis, and Wilhelm von Knyphausen.

1081. American flag flown on the high seas was carried by Captain Thomas Thompson of the American sloop *Raleigh,* who engaged a British vessel on September 4, 1777.

1082. American flag saluted by a foreign nation was flown from the top mast of the *Ranger,* under the command of Captain John Paul Jones. The *Ranger* sailed for France on November 1, 1777, with dispatches announcing the surrender of British general John Burgoyne. On February 14, 1778, the *Ranger* saluted the French flag in the harbor of Quiberon, France, with 13 guns. The salute was returned by Admiral La Motte Piquet with nine guns, the same salute authorized by the French court to be given in honor of an admiral of Holland or of any other republic.

1083. Map to show the American flag was *A New and correct Map of the United States of North America Layd down from the latest Observations and best Authority agreeable to the Peace of 1783,* drawn by Abel Buell and published in 1784. The flag was part of an elaborate display of symbols, including the eagle and the rising sun, that were used to decorate the title.

1084. Ship to carry the American flag around the world was the *Columbia,* a 212-ton vessel under Captain Kendrick that sailed from Boston, MA, on September 30, 1787, on a fur-trading mission to Canada. It was accompanied by the sloop *Washington,* under Captain Robert Gray, who exchanged commands with Captain Kendrick and completed the trip, returning to Boston on August 9, 1790. The trip took nearly three years and covered a distance of 41,899 miles. The crew explored the Queen Charlotte Islands and discovered the straits of Juan de Fuca and the mouth of the Columbia River.

1085. Changes in the American flag to be authorized by Congress were passed by Congress on January 13, 1794, an "act making an alteration in the flag of the United States" and providing "that from and after the first day of May 1795, the Flag of the United States be fifteen stripes, alternate red and white; and that the union be fifteen stars, white, in a blue field." The change was made so that Vermont and Kentucky would be represented on the flag. A law passed on April 4, 1818, reduced the number of stripes to 13 to represent the original 13 states, as in the first American flag, and provided one star for each state. A new star was to be added on the Fourth of July following the admission of each new state.

1086. American flag flown over a fortress of the Old World was flown on April 27, 1805, when Lieutenant Presley Neville O'Bannon of the Marines raised the colors over the harbor fortress stronghold of Derna (Tripoli) in the First Tripolitan War. It is this action that is commemorated on the Colors of the Corps and in the Marine Corps' hymn with the words "to the shores of Tripoli." For his bravery in battle, O'Bannon was presented with the "Mamaluke sword" by Hamet Karamanli, the deposed brother of the pasha of Tripoli. A replica of this sword is carried by every Marine officer today.

1087. American flag flown over a schoolhouse was flown in May 1812 over the log schoolhouse at Catamount Hill, Colrain, MA. It was cut and made by Rhoda Shippee, Mrs. Lois Shippee, Mrs. Sophia Willis, and Mrs. Stephen Hale at the home of Captain Amasa Shippee, who instructed the women in the arrangement of the stars and stripes.

1088. Star-Spangled Banner was sewn in the first two weeks of September 1814, during the War of 1812, by Mary Young Pickersgill, a seamstress in Baltimore, MD, with the assistance of her daughter and two nieces. The commission came from Commodore Joshua Barney and Brigadier General John Strickland of nearby Fort McHenry, who ordered a giant flag that would be visible to the British in Chesapeake Bay. Mrs. Pickersgill's flag, made from more than 400 yards of wool bunting, measured 30 feet by 42 feet. It was flying above Fort McHenry on September 13, 1814, when 16 British warships began a bombardment that lasted until dawn the following day but failed to dislodge the Americans. This episode, witnessed by a young American lawyer, Francis Scott Key, was the inspiration for his poem "The Defense of Fort McHenry," which was later set to music as "The Star-Spangled Banner" and adopted as the national anthem. Mrs. Pickersgill was paid $405.90 for her work on the flag, which is now on display at the Museum of History and Technology of the Smithsonian Institution in Washington, DC.

1089. Federal flag act officially establishing an American flag was passed by Congress on April 4, 1818, "an act to establish the flag of the United States." It authorized a flag with 13 horizontal stripes, alternating red and white, to represent the 13 original states, and a union of 20 white stars in a blue field, one star to be added to the flag for each new state on the Fourth of July succeeding such admission.

1090. Stars and Stripes with the number "76" is held in the collection of the Bennington Museum in Bennington, VT. It has 13 stripes and a canton with 13 stars in a semicircle over the numerals "76." Although an oral tradition holds that this flag was flown at the Battle of Bennington on August 16, 1777, it is more likely to have been made for the 50th anniversary of the Declaration of Independence in 1826 and mistaken by later scholars for a Revolutionary War artifact.

1091. National flag to become a state flag was the flag of Texas. The area that is now Texas was a province of Spain from 1691 until 1821, when it was joined to the newly independent country of Mexico. The successful rebellion of white Texan settlers against Mexico in 1836 produced the independent Republic of Texas. Its flag, a design of red, white, and blue rectangles with a white star on the blue field, became the state flag of Texas on December 29, 1845, when Texas became the 28th state.

1092. American flag made on the Pacific Coast was carried by Ernest Haskell, manager of the Adams Express Company of San Francisco, CA, in that city's Admission Day parade, held on October 26, 1850. It had been stitched together from pieces of silk and satin.

1093. Confederate States flag legally established was the "Stars and Bars," adopted by the Convention of Confederated States at Montgomery, AL, on March 4, 1861, the same day Abraham Lincoln became president of the United States. It was designed by Major Orren Randolph Smith of Louisburg, NC, and was reported to the convention by William Porcher Miles, president of North Carolina College. It consisted of three bars and a field of seven stars, one for each of the Confederate States at that time. A star was added for each additional seceding state. During the First Battle of Bull Run (July 16–21, 1861), the soldiers were confused by the similarity between the Confederate flag and the Union's Stars and Stripes. The Confederacy consequently adopted another design, with a blue St. Andrew's Cross and 13 stars set against a red field, the battle flag that came to symbolize the Confederacy.

1094. American flag made of American bunting to fly over the Capitol in Washington, DC, was hoisted on February 24, 1866. It was 21 feet by 12 feet and was made by the United States Bunting Company, Lowell, MA. It was presented to the Senate by the company.

1095. Foreign city with the Confederate flag in its coat of arms was the city of Villa Americana (now Americana), Brazil, located about 100 miles from São Paulo, Brazil's largest city and the capital of São Paulo State. It was founded circa 1868 by ex-Confederates (called Confederados), of whom about 9,000 emigrated to South America after the Civil War, hoping to build a new cotton plantation culture in the Amazon basin.

AMERICANA—FLAGS—*continued*

1096. Flag salute was written for Flag Day, June 14, 1889, by Colonel Balch, a kindergarten school principal in New York City, who had his students recite it every day. The words were: "We give our heads and our hearts to God and our country; one country, one language, one Flag."

1097. Pledge of allegiance to the flag was created in August 1892 by Francis Bellamy and James Upham, writers for *The Youth's Companion,* a patriotic magazine for children. The original text of the Pledge of Allegiance was: "I pledge allegiance to my flag and to the Republic for which it stands; one nation, indivisible, with liberty and justice for all." The words were written by Bellamy, who based them on elements of the Preamble to the U.S. Constitution and on the American Flag Salute written in 1889 by one Colonel Balch, a New York City school principal. Upham added the idea of physically saluting the flag by standing at attention and stretching out the right arm with palm upraised. The modern salute, with palm over heart, was adopted during World War II, when the upraised palm became identified with the Nazi salute. The words "under God" were added to the pledge in 1954.

1098. American Flag Association was founded in New York City in 1897. The association's mission was to preserve and honor the flag and to promote knowledge of and respect for it.

1099. President's flag was adopted on May 29, 1916, by Executive Order No. 2390 of President Woodrow Wilson. It showed the president's seal in bronze on a blue background, with a large white star in each corner. Previous presidents had had flags, but they were more or less individual emblems. President Harry S. Truman, by Executive Order No. 9646 of October 25, 1945, made several further changes and increased the number of stars to 48, one for each state. The flag now has 50 stars, as decreed by Executive Order No. 10,860 of February 9, 1960, effective July 4, 1960.

1100. American flag displayed from the right hand of the Statue of Liberty in honor of an individual was flown on June 13, 1927, designated as Lindbergh Day, in honor of Charles Augustus Lindbergh's transatlantic solo flight. The flag was hoisted to the peak of the right arm of the Statue of Liberty in unison with the raising of the Post Flag and the discharge of the Morning Gun at Governors Island, and was lowered in unison with Post Retreat ceremonies.

1101. Vice president's flag was established on February 7, 1936, by Executive Order No. 7285. It contains the seal of the United States and a blue star in each corner on a field of white. The Navy had previously created a naval flag for the vice president.

1102. American flag to orbit the earth was carried in the capsule of the satellite *Discoverer 8,* which was launched on August 10, 1960, by the Air Force at Vandenberg Air Force Base, CA. A 300-pound reentry capsule was ejected on August 11, 1960, on the 17th orbit and was recovered the same day by the U.S.S. *Haiti Victory,* whose frogmen used a helicopter. The flag was presented to President Dwight David Eisenhower on August 15, 1960. The orbital time of the satellite was 94.1 minutes; its perigee was 161 miles, its apogee 436 miles.

1103. Official etiquette for handling the American flag was the Flag Code of The United States (Public Law 94–344), enacted by Congress on July 7, 1976. The Code formalized the etiquette for displaying the flag outdoors, raising and lowering the flag, displaying the flag indoors, parading and saluting the flag, pledging allegiance, playing the national anthem, and displaying the flag in mourning. It also specified the conditions under which the flag is not to be used or displayed.

AMERICANA—GREAT SEAL

1104. Proposals for the design of the Great Seal of the United States were made in July 1776 by Benjamin Franklin, Thomas Jefferson, and John Adams, all of whom were members of the congressional committee charged with producing the seal. Franklin's design showed, in his words, "Moses standing on the Shore, and extending his Hand over the Sea, thereby causing the same to overwhelm Pharaoh who is sitting in an open Chariot, a Crown on his Head and a Sword in his Hand. Rays from a Pillar of Fire in the Clouds reaching to Moses, to express that he acts by Command of the Deity." The motto, taken from the biblical Book of Maccabees, read: "Rebellion to tyrants is obedience to God." Adams offered a design based on Simon Gribelin's rendering of the "Judgment of Hercules," a Greek fable in which Vice and Virtue attempt to influence the young hero. Jefferson also suggested an allegorical design based on the Exodus for the front of his seal. On the reverse, he proposed an image of Hengist and Horsa, the legendary brothers who led the first Anglo-Saxons in Britain.

1105. Artist's design for the Great Seal of the United States was revealed on August 20, 1776. The rendering, by artist Pierre Eugène Du Simitière, showed a shield with emblems of the six European cultures that migrated to America: three for Britain (English rose, Scottish thistle, Irish harp) and three for continental Europe (French fleur-de-lis, German eagle, Belgic lion). Supporting the shield were the Goddess of Liberty wearing the Phrygian cap and holding a spear, and the Goddess of Justice with her balance. The Crest was described as "the Eye of Providence in a radiant Triangle whose Glory extends over the Shield and beyond the Figures." The reverse combined elements from Thomas Jefferson's and Benjamin Franklin's designs; it showed the Children of Israel crossing the Sea of Reeds, with Moses, illuminated by rays of light from a Pillar of Fire, raising his hand to cast the waters over Pharoah.

1106. Design for the Great Seal of the United States that was accepted was made by Charles Thomson and adopted by Congress on June 20, 1782. Thomson's design, which differs slightly from the present-day seal, showed an "American eagle on the wing and rising" (not regnant with spread wings, as in the official die), bearing on its breast a shield with 13 red and white stripes, with an olive branch in its right talon and 13 arrows in its left. In its beak was a ribbon bearing the legend *E pluribus unum* ("from many, one"). Over the head of the eagle was a golden light breaking through a cloud surrounding 13 stars that formed a constellation on a blue field.

1107. Impression made by the Great Seal of the United States was made on September 16, 1782, on the upper left corner of a document authorizing General George Washington to negotiate and sign an agreement with the British for the exchange, subsistence, and better treatment of prisoners of war. The document bore the signatures of John Hanson, president of the Continental Congress, and Charles Thomson, secretary.

AMERICANA—LIBERTY BELL

1108. Casting of the Liberty Bell was made in 1751 by the Whitechapel Bell Foundry in London, England, having been commissioned by the Pennsylvania Provincial Assembly, to whom it was delivered on September 1, 1752. The cost to the assembly was about £500. The bell was cracked by a stroke of its own clapper while it was being tested for the first time. It was melted and cast again in Philadelphia, PA,

by Charles Pass and John Stow, but the second casting sounded harsh. The third casting, also by Pass and Stow, succeeded, and the bell was hung in the steeple of the State House (now Independence Hall) in 1753.

1109. Tolling of the Liberty Bell for an event of political importance took place in February 1757. The bell was rung to announce the gathering of Pennsylvania's colonial assembly, which met to consider the significant question of how to raise revenue for the defense of the western frontier. The legislature decided to do so by levying taxes on the estates held by the colony's proprietors, the Penn family, and sent Benjamin Franklin to London to negotiate with them.

1110. Tolling of the Liberty Bell to announce a battle took place after news reached Philadelphia of the Battle of Lexington on April 19, 1775, the first clash of arms in the War of Independence.

1111. Use of the name "Liberty Bell" was made in 1839, when a poem entitled "The Liberty Bell" appeared in the *Liberator*, the magazine of Boston abolitionist William Lloyd Garrison. The bell had been a symbol of the abolitionist movement since 1837, when a picture of it had appeared in the New York Anti-Slavery Society's publication *Liberty*.

1112. Cracking of the Liberty Bell after its final casting took place at an unknown date. A Philadelphia newspaper article from 1914 stated that it cracked in 1828 when it was rung to announce the signing of the Catholic Emancipation Act, but there is no contemporary evidence to confirm this. Evidence is also lacking for the traditional story that the bell cracked in 1835 as it was tolling for the funeral of John Marshall, the chief justice of the Supreme Court. What is known for certain is that sometime before 1846 it acquired a crack that did not interfere with its sound because the edges were kept filed. At noon on February 22, 1846, after pealing all morning to celebrate the birthday of George Washington, the bell sustained a jagged crack that silenced it permanently.

AMERICANA—SONGS AND MUSIC

1113. Patriotic song to achieve popularity during the Revolution was "Yankee Doodle," written in 1755 by Dr. Richard Shuckburgh, regimental surgeon to General Edward Braddock, commander in chief of the British forces during the French and Indian War. The verses were written at Albany, NY, and set to an ancient English tune, "The World Turned Upside Down." Shuckburgh intended to ridicule the

AMERICANA—SONGS AND MUSIC—*continued*

"homely clad colonials," but the song was taken up by the colonists themselves, and was played at the victory celebration in Yorktown in 1781 when Lord Cornwallis surrendered at the end of the Revolutionary War.

1114. Patriotic song by an American was "The Liberty Song," also known as "In Freedom We're Born," published by John Mein and John Fleming in July 1768 in Boston, MA. The lyrics were by John Dickinson, set to the tune of "Hearts of Oak" by William Boyce of London. The words were published in the *Boston Gazette* of July 18, 1768.

1115. Patriotic war song by an American was "Chester," composed in 1778 by William Billings of Boston, MA. The song was published in Billings's *The Singing Master's Assistant, or Key to Practical Music,* printed by Draper and Folsom, Boston, in 1778. "Chester" contains the following chorus: "Let tyrants shake their iron rod; / And Slav'ry clank her galling chains, / We fear them not; / We trust in God, / New England's God forever reigns."

1116. Patriotic song to achieve national popularity was "Hail, Columbia," written in 1798 by Joseph Hopkinson, a young lawyer in Philadelphia, PA, to awaken "an American spirit which should be independent of and above the interests and passions and policy of both belligerents [England and France, then at war], and look and feel exclusively for our own honor and rights." It was sung at a concert in Philadelphia and became immediately popular. The song begins: "Hail, Columbia! happy land! / Hail ye heroes! heaven-born band! / Who fought and bled in Freedom's cause, / And when the storm of war was gone, / Enjoyed the peace your valor won."

1117. Performance of "Hail to the Chief" took place in New York City on May 8, 1812, as part of a dramatic production of Sir Walter Scott's poem "The Lady of the Lake." The song had been written circa 1810 by English composer James Sanderson. The tune was quickly adopted for military and processional use. It is not known when "Hail to the Chief" was first played at a presidential inauguration.

1118. Performance of "America the Beautiful" was given by Boston schoolchildren on July 4, 1832, in the Park Street Church, during an Independence Day celebration. Its author was Dr. Samuel Francis Smith, a Baptist minister, who wrote it down on a scrap of paper in half an hour. The original manuscript is in the Harvard University Library.

1119. Song used as an anthem by the Confederacy was "Dixie," or "I Wish I Was in Dixie's Land," written and composed by Daniel Decatur Emmett, a songwriter and performer from Ohio who organized one of the earliest minstrel show troupes, the Virginia Minstrels. On April 4, 1859, while performing with Bryant's Minstrels in New York City, he introduced "Dixie" as the show's final number. The song was published by Firth Pond and Company. It became widely popular in the South and was sung at the inauguration of Jefferson Davis as president of the Confederate States at Richmond, VA, on February 22, 1862.

1120. Performance of *The Stars and Stripes Forever* by John Philip Sousa took place at the Academy of Music in Philadelphia, PA, on May 14, 1897. Sousa's greatest march was such a smashing success that the audience asked to hear it twice more. One newspaper account praised it as "stirring enough to rouse the American eagle from his crag and set him to shriek exultantly while he hurls his arrows at the aurora borealis." Some musicologists believe the march was first performed in public in Augusta, ME, on May 1, two weeks earlier.

1121. Performance of "God Bless America" took place on November 11, 1938. The Jewish-American composer Irving Berlin wrote the song for the entertainer Kate Smith, who performed it during her regular radio program. The song became a patriotic favorite.

1122. Civil rights anthem to achieve fame was "We Shall Overcome." The song was originally published in Chicago, IL, in May 1945 as a gospel song, "I'll Overcome Someday," with music by Atrong Twigg and revised lyrics and music by Kenneth Morris. The tune was based on the melody of a hymn dating from the colonial era. The words were adapted from another hymn that included the line: "If in my heart, I do not yield, I'll overcome some day." African-American workers sang the song on a picket line in Charleston, SC, in 1945. The song became the anthem of the civil rights movement in the 1960s.

AMERICANA—STATUE OF LIBERTY

1123. Design for the Statue of Liberty was developed by French sculptor Frédéric-Auguste Bartholdi for another project, a giant lighthouse in the form of a statue to be erected at the entrance to the Suez Canal. In 1867, as the canal neared completion, Bartholdi submitted plans for "Egypt Carrying the Light to Asia," the robed figure of an Egyptian woman wearing a headband and holding a torch, to the Egyptian ruler, Isma'il Pasha. The project was never commissioned, but it formed the basis for Bartholdi's later design of "Liberty Enlightening the World."

1124. Exhibition of part of the Statue of Liberty in the United States took place in August 1876 at the International Centennial Exhibition in Philadelphia, PA. French sculptor Frédéric-Auguste Bartholdi had planned for the upraised arm of Liberty to arrive in America from France, where it had been assembled, in time for the opening of the Exhibition on July 4, 1876, but the arm was not completed in time and arrived the following month. A 50-cent admission was charged for visitors, who could climb a ladder inside the arm to the torch balcony.

1125. Act in the construction of the Statue of Liberty was performed by the American ambassador to France, Levi P. Morton, who drove the first rivet into the statue on October 24, 1881, in Paris.

1126. Organization in charge of the Statue of Liberty was the Lighthouse Board, a federal agency. Between 1886 and 1902, the board administered the statue and Bedloe's Island in conjunction with the Army and the American Committee. Authority was transferred to the War Department in 1901. President Calvin Coolidge declared the Statue of Liberty to be a national monument on October 15, 1924. Administration and maintainence of the park site was taken over by the National Parks Service in 1933.

1127. Construction of the Statue of Liberty on site at Bedloe's Island (now Liberty Island) in New York Harbor began in May 1886. The disassembled statue had arrived from France on June 19, 1885, packed in 214 wooden crates. It took six months to assemble the huge copper statue on its massive base. The Statue of Liberty was unveiled for public view on October 28, 1886. The bronze plaque with Emma Lazarus's poem "The New Colossus" was not added until 1903.

1128. Dedication ceremony for the Statue of Liberty took place on October 28, 1886, during a dedication ceremony at Bedloe's Island (now Liberty Island) in New York Harbor. Twenty thousand people headed for the Battery in a ticker-tape parade, the first ever held. The harbor was crowded with ships of the United States and France. The festivities were attended by President Grover Cleveland, French prime minister Jules Ferry, and sculptor Frédéric-

Auguste Bartholdi, who waited in the head of the statue. At a signal from a boy on the ground, Bartholdi was to pull a rope that would drop the huge French flag that veiled her gleaming copper face. The boy's cue was the completion of a presentation speech by Senator William M. Evarts, known to be an orator of exceptional long-windedness. Evarts began, paused to take a breath, and the boy signaled Bartholdi, who dropped the flag, setting off a thunderous cacophony of cannon blasts, whistles, shouts, and applause.

AMERICANA—SYMBOLS

1129. Character personifying the United States was the figure of a Native American, sometimes drawn as a man but more often as a woman. This figure appeared in numerous illustrations and political cartoons from the Revolutionary era, including several by Paul Revere. One famous example, published in the *Royal American Magazine* (Boston, MA) of June 1774, was "The Able Doctor, or America Swallowing the Bitter Draught," which showed the British prime minister pouring the hated British tea down an Indian woman's throat while other British officials look on with glee. By the War of 1812, this image had largely given way to that of "Brother Jonathan," a cleanshaven American countryman, often depicted in a farmer's hat and coat, who eventually evolved into "Uncle Sam."

1130. Native American symbols adopted for political purposes by colonial Americans included the Great White Pine, or Tree of Peace, symbol of the Iroquois Confederacy, which helped give rise in the Revolutionary era to liberty trees and liberty poles; the Mohawk costume worn by the Sons of Liberty in their raids on British tea imports beginning in 1775; the calumet (peace pipe) and tomahawk as denoters of peace and war; the bundle of arrows to signify individuals or groups united for some purpose; and the bald eagle, another Iroquois symbol.

1131. Use of the term "Uncle Sam" as a reference to the United States appeared in an editorial in the *Troy Post* of Troy, NY, in the issue of September 7, 1813. "Uncle Sam" was originally Samuel Wilson, a Troy meatpacker who was employed by a government contractor as a food inspector during the War of 1812. Barrels that met with his approval were stamped "U.S.," for "United States." Local pundits said that the initials actually referred to Wilson, a famously honest fellow who was known as Uncle Sam. A congressional resolution passed in 1961 gave official recognition to Wilson as the source of the Uncle Sam symbol.

AMERICANA—SYMBOLS—*continued*

1132. Character symbolizing the American people was Jack Downing, who appeared in numerous political cartoons after 1830. He was originally Major Jack Downing, a Yankee character created by the Maine humorist and newspaper editor Seba Smith, whose *Portland Courier* began publishing "letters" from Downing beginning in January 1830. He was replaced as a symbol in the late 1880s by Mr. Common People, a baldheaded, bespectacled, timid man in a tiny top hat who was invented by the cartoonist Frederick Opper, and who himself was replaced in the mid-20th-century by cartoonist Vaughn Shoemaker's John Q. Public.

1133. Popular image of the Minute Man was the work of sculptor Daniel Chester French. His bronze "Minute Man" of 1875, musket at the ready, was cast for the town of Concord, MA, and is now located on Liberty Street within Minute Man National Historic Park (founded 1959). Versions of the figure appeared on posters, stamps, war bonds, and other government materials from World War II.

1134. Portrait of Uncle Sam to become famous appeared on the cover of the magazine *Leslie's Weekly* for July 6, 1916, during World War I, and afterwards as a widely circulated poster. It showed the traditional image of Uncle Sam—a stern-looking old man, white-bearded and white-haired, in an old-fashioned coat and a hat decorated with stars and stripes—pointing his forefinger at the viewer and asking "What Are You Doing for Preparedness?" The face of Uncle Sam was a self-portrait of the artist, James Montgomery Flagg, who used his own likeness to save the cost of hiring a model. A virtually identical portrait, again with Flagg as Uncle Sam, appeared in 1917 on a military recruiting poster, with the legend "I Want You for U.S. Army."

1135. Public service symbol of the federal government was Smokey Bear. During World War II, the Forest Service sought advertising help to educate the public about the danger of forest fires. On August 9, 1944, Albert Staehle, an illustrator of animals, came up with the image of a fire-fighting bear. The slogan "Only you can prevent forest fires" was coined by a Los Angeles ad agency in 1947. Smokey Bear appeared on posters and comic books distributed to schoolchildren and on television commercials. In 1950, a bear cub rescued from a forest fire in New Mexico was dubbed "Smokey Bear." He was exhibited in the National Zoo in Washington, DC, and died in 1976.

C

CABINET

1136. Proposal for a presidential cabinet modeled on the privy councils of European monarchs was formally put forward during the Constitutional Convention on August 20, 1780, by Gouverneur Morris, delegate from New York. He introduced resolutions proposing the creation of a Council of State, composed of the chief justice of the Supreme Court and five departmental secretaries or department heads, whom the president could consult on any matter. The Committee of Detail, to whom the plan was referred, specified that the five departments should be Foreign Affairs, Domestic Affairs, War, Marine, and Finance, and added two additional members, the speaker of the House of Representatives and the president of the Senate. After this revised plan was rejected by the Committee of States, George Mason of Virginia introduced a motion to establish an executive council with six rotating members, two from each region. Though Mason's proposal had the support of Benjamin Franklin and James Madison, it was defeated.

1137. Cabinet comprised the five top officers of the federal government, appointed by President George Washington during his first term. Its members were Thomas Jefferson of Virginia, secretary of state; Alexander Hamilton of New York, secretary of the treasury (the first to be appointed, on September 11, 1789); Henry Knox of Massachusetts, secretary of war; Samuel Osgood of Massachusetts, postmaster general (unofficial member); and Edmund Jennings Randolph of Virginia, attorney general. The use of the term "Cabinet" to designate the President's advisory council of federal officers did not come into use until circa 1793.

1138. Secretary of the treasury was Alexander Hamilton of New York City, who was appointed by President George Washington on September 11, 1789, and who served until February 1, 1795. His salary was $3,500. The Treasury Department, authorized by Congress on September 2, 1789, was the third executive department to be created.

1139. Attorney general was Edmund Jennings Randolph of Virginia, appointed by President George Washington on September 26, 1789, who took office on February 2, 1790, and served until January 1, 1794. The office was created by the Federal Judiciary Act of September 24, 1789. The officeholder received a salary

$1,500 a year but was required to provide his own quarters, law books, fuel, furniture, and stationery, and to pay a law clerk. Although Randolph and his successors as attorney general were members of the president's cabinet, the Department of Justice, of which the attorney general is the head, was not established by Congress until June 22, 1870.

1140. Secretary of state was Thomas Jefferson, who was appointed by President George Washington on September 26, 1789. He took office on March 22, 1790, at a salary of $3,500 a year. The State Department had been established on July 29, 1789, as the Department of Foreign Affairs, the first executive department authorized by Congress. John Jay, who had served as secretary for foreign affairs under the Continental Congress, continued to act as secretary until Jefferson took office, at which point the department's name was changed to the State Department; thus Jefferson, rather than Jay, is considered the first secretary of state. The secretary of state is the senior member of the President's cabinet.

1141. Secretary of war was Henry Knox of Massachusetts, who took office on September 12, 1790. The Department of War, established by Congress in New York, NY, on August 7, 1789, was the second executive department to be created. The secretary's salary was $3,000 a year.

1142. Difference of opinion among members of the cabinet appears to have developed in February 1791 over the question of whether the Constitution would permit the creation of a proposed Bank of the United States. The proposal was supported by Alexander Hamilton, the secretary of the treasury, and by Henry Knox, the secretary of war. It was opposed by Thomas Jefferson, the secretary of state, and Edmund Randolph, the attorney general. President George Washington requested written opinions from each of them.

1143. Cabinet meeting took place in April 1791, though it was not a formal meeting conducted by the president. The heads of the three executive departments were called together by the secretary of state, Thomas Jefferson, so that he could inform them of the contents of a letter written by President George Washington. The president, who was about to leave Philadelphia for a fortnight's trip through the South, instructed the three secretaries that if any pressing matters came up during his absence, they were to consult with one another and with the vice president, John Adams.

1144. Use of the term "cabinet" to refer to the secretaries of executive departments (and other top federal officers) acting as an advisory council to the president was initiated by James Madison, Thomas Jefferson, and Edmund Randolph circa 1793. By 1806 the term was common enough to be used in a congressional debate. Its first appearance in a statute occurred in the General Appropriation Act of 1907.

1145. Regular cabinet meetings did not take place until April 1793, when a political crisis was precipitated by the arrival of the French chargé d'affaires, Edmond-Charles-Édouard Genet, who came to enlist American support for France's war with England despite the opposition of President George Washington. The president, who had previously preferred to consult individually with his advisors, began to summon them as a group to frequent meetings.

1146. Cabinet member to serve in two or more cabinet posts was Timothy Pickering of Pennsylvania, who served in the cabinets of President George Washington. Pickering became postmaster general on August 12, 1791, and was recommissioned on June 1, 1794. On January 2, 1795, he was sworn in as secretary of war. From December 10, 1795, to February 5, 1796, he served as secretary of war ad interim (temporarily). Meanwhile, on August 20, 1795, he also took office as secretary of state ad interim, and on December 10, 1795, he became the secretary of state.

1147. Test of presidential authority over the cabinet secretaries took place in 1797, at the beginning of the administration of John Adams. The cabinet then consisted of the heads of the departments of State, Treasury, and War (respectively, Timothy Pickering, Oliver Wolcott, Jr., and James McHenry), as well as the attorney general and the postmaster general. All five officeholders had been appointed by Adams's predecessor, George Washington, and were allowed to continue in office. The ability of the three secretaries to work under President Adams was somewhat compromised by their loyalty to Alexander Hamilton, the former secretary of the treasury, who was Adams's political antagonist, though both were Federalists. They refused to approve the President's choice of Elbridge Gerry as one of three commissioners to France (though Gerry was ultimately appointed, on May 31), joined with Washington to force the president to change the ranking of major generals in the provisional army so that

CABINET—*continued*

Hamilton would be listed first, and tried unsuccessfully to defeat the appointment of three new commissioners to France who had been nominated by the president without the knowledge of the cabinet.

1148. Secretary of the navy was Benjamin Stoddert of Maryland, who was appointed to the post by President John Adams. He took office on June 18, 1798, and received an annual salary of $3,000. The Department of the Navy was established by Congress on April 30, 1798. Since 1789 the Navy had been the responsibility of the Department of War.

1149. Cabinet secretaries to be fired were Thomas Pickering of Pennsylvania, the secretary of state, and James McHenry of Maryland, the secretary of war. Both, on several occasions, opposed decisions that had been made by President John Adams and actively sought to have them reversed. On May 10, 1800, the president asked for their resignations. McHenry complied and was replaced on June 12 by Samuel Dexter of Massachusetts, with Benjamin Stoddert, the secretary of the navy, serving ad interim. Pickering refused to comply and was dismissed by the President on May 12. He was replaced by Charles Lee of Virginia, the attorney general, ad interim until the appointment of John Marshall of Virginia.

1150. Cabinet appointee to be rejected by the Senate was Henry Dearborn of Massachusetts, who was nominated in 1815 by James Madison to serve as secretary of war, a post he had already held (1801–09) under Thomas Jefferson. Because Dearborn, as a major general in the Army, had done a mediocre job as commander of the country's northern border during the War of 1812, the Senate immediately voted against him. The vote was quietly expunged from the record, however, because Madison had already made it known that he intended to withdraw Dearborn's nomination.

1151. Child of a president to serve in a presidential cabinet was John Quincy Adams, the son of John Adams, who joined the first cabinet of James Monroe as secretary of state beginning on September 22, 1817, and continued in that post during Monroe's second administration. He was elected to the presidency himself in 1824. Other children of presidents to serve in Cabinet posts were Robert Todd Lincoln, secretary of war under President Garfield; James Rudolph Garfield, secretary of the interi-

or under Theodore Roosevelt; Herbert Clark Hoover, Jr., under secretary of state under President Eisenhower; and Franklin Delano Roosevelt, Jr., under secretary of commerce under Lyndon Baines Johnson.

1152. Kitchen cabinet of unofficial presidential advisors was assembled by President Andrew Jackson during his first term in office, which began on March 4, 1829. Within a short time, he found himself at odds with his vice-president and his cabinet members over the refusal of their wives to confer social acceptance on Peggy Eaton, a former barmaid who was now the wife of Secretary of War John Henry Eaton. The "kitchen cabinet" included Amos Kendall and William B. Lewis, both of whom were Treasury auditors; journalist Duff Green and Francis P. Blair; and the President's relative and private secretary, Andrew Jackson Donelson.

1153. Cabinet member who was Catholic was Roger Brooke Taney of Maryland, attorney general in President Andrew Jackson's cabinet from July 20, 1831, until September 23, 1833, and secretary of the treasury from September 23, 1833, until June 25, 1834.

1154. Cabinet appointee on record as having been rejected by the Senate was Roger Brooke Taney of Maryland, President Andrew Jackson's attorney general, who was appointed by the president on September 26, 1833, to become secretary of the treasury. While he was awaiting confirmation, Taney carried out the president's policy of removing public funds from the Bank of the United States and depositing them in state banks. The Senate voted on June 24, 1834, not to confirm him. The following year, Jackson nominated Taney to become an associate justice of the Supreme Court. Again, the nomination was killed by the Senate, not by a vote of rejection, but by a decision to postpone a vote indefinitely. Some months later, Taney was nominated to succeed John Marshall as chief justice of the Supreme Court, and he was confirmed.

1155. Secretary of state to serve in the State Department simultaneously with his son was Daniel Webster, secretary of state from 1841 to 1843 and again from 1850 to 1852. His eldest son, Daniel Fletcher Webster, served as chief clerk of the State Department from March 6, 1841, to April 23, 1843. The chief clerk was at this time the second-ranking officer in the department.

1156. Secretary of the interior was Thomas Ewing of Ohio, who was appointed by President Zachary Taylor on March 8, 1849, and who served until July 23, 1850. The department was then known as the Home Department. It was established by Congress on March 3, 1849.

1157. Secretary of state to serve more than once was Daniel Webster of New Hampshire. He served from March 5, 1841, to May 8, 1843, under William Henry Harrison and John Tyler, and from July 22, 1850, to October 24, 1852, under Millard Fillmore.

1158. Attorney general to fill the position on a full-time basis was Caleb Cushing of Massachusetts, who served from 1853 to 1857 in the administration of Franklin Pierce. Previously, attorneys general often maintained an outside law practice.

1159. President whose cabinet remained unchanged during his term in office was Franklin Pierce. None of his cabinet members resigned or died during the four years of his administration, which ended on March 3, 1857.

1160. Secretary of state to travel outside the United States while in office was William Henry Seward, who served as secretary of state in the Lincoln and Johnson administrations. Vacationing in the Caribbean between January 1 and January 28, 1866, Seward met with Danish colonial officials in the Virgin Islands, with the presidents of the Dominican Republic and Haiti, and with Spanish colonial officials in Cuba.

1161. Secretary of state to serve less than two weeks was Elihu B. Washburne. He occupied the post from March 5 to March 16, 1869, thereafter serving as the minister to France.

1162. Attorney general to head the Department of Justice was Amos Tappan Akerman of Georgia, who was appointed attorney general on June 23, 1870, and took office on July 8. During his term in office, on July 1, 1871, the Department of Justice was established, with the attorney general (formerly a Cabinet member without a department) as its head, charged with enforcing the laws made by Congress and carrying out the policies of the president.

1163. Cabinet officer impeached by the House of Representatives was President Ulysses S. Grant's secretary of war, William W. Belknap. In 1875, charges surfaced that he had accepted bribes tied to military acquisitions, and in March 1876 he tearfully resigned. However, the House unanimously sent the impeach-

ment to the Senate, where Belknap was acquitted on August 1, 1876, primarily on the grounds that he was no longer a federal official and therefore not within the Senate's jurisdiction.

1164. Cabinet member who had served as a Confederate officer was David McKendree Key, a senator from Tennessee, who served from March 12, 1877, to August 24, 1880, as postmaster general in the cabinet of President Rutherford Birchard Hayes. He had been a lieutenant colonel in the 43rd Regiment of Tennessee and had been wounded and captured at Vicksburg.

1165. Secretary of agriculture was Norman Jay Colman of Missouri, the former commissioner of agriculture, who was appointed on February 13, 1889, by President Grover Cleveland, who had only three weeks left in his term. Colman served until March 5, 1889.

1166. Cabinet in which two secretaries had the same last name was the cabinet of Benjamin Harrison. John Watson Foster of Indiana served as secretary of state from June 28, 1892, through February 23, 1893. Charles Foster of Ohio served as Secretary of the Treasury from February 24, 1891, until the end of Harrison's administration on March 3, 1893.

1167. Secretary of commerce and labor was George Bruce Cortelyou of New York, who was appointed by President Theodore Roosevelt to head the Department of Commerce and Labor, established by Congress on February 14, 1903. Cortelyou took office on February 16. In 1913, commerce and labor were given separate cabinet-level executive departments.

1168. Secretary of state to travel outside the United States on official business was Elihu Root, secretary of state under President Theodore Roosevelt. On July 4, 1906, Root departed the United States to attend the Third International Conference of American States in Rio de Janeiro, Brazil. After the conference, he traveled in Uruguay, Argentina, Chile, Peru, Panama, and Colombia.

1169. Cabinet member who was Jewish was Oscar Solomon Straus of New York, who was secretary of commerce and labor during President Theodore Roosevelt's second administration. He was appointed on December 12, 1906, and served from December 17, 1906, to March 3, 1909.

1170. Cabinet secretary to share the same last name as the president was William Bauchop Wilson of Pennsylvania, who took office on March 5, 1913, as secretary of labor in the cabinet of Woodrow Wilson.

CABINET—*continued*

1171. Secretary of commerce was William Cox Redfield of New York, formerly the secretary of commerce and labor. Appointed by President Woodrow Wilson, he became secretary of commerce on March 5, 1913, the day after Congress authorized the division of the Department of Commerce and Labor into two departments. He served until March 5, 1921.

1172. Secretary of labor was William Bauchop Wilson of Pennsylvania, who served from March 5, 1913, until November 1, 1919. He was appointed by President Woodrow Wilson. Congress created the Department of Labor on March 4, 1913, when it abolished the old Department of Commerce and Labor.

1173. Cabinet member to serve in five successive administrations was James Wilson of Iowa, who was appointed secretary of agriculture by President William McKinley. He took office on March 5, 1897, and left it on March 6, 1913, having served 16 years plus one day. After President McKinley was assassinated during his second term, Wilson was asked to remain in his post by McKinley's successor, Theodore Roosevelt. He continued as secretary of agriculture after President Roosevelt was elected to a full term in 1904 and was kept on by President William Howard Taft after his election in 1908.

1174. Subcabinet member who was a woman was Annette Abbott Adams, who was appointed assistant attorney general on June 26, 1920, by President Woodrow Wilson. She resigned on August 15, 1921.

1175. Father and son to occupy the same cabinet post were Henry Cantwell Wallace, secretary of agriculture under Presidents Warren Gamaliel Harding and Calvin Coolidge from March 5, 1921, to October 25, 1924, and Henry Agard Wallace, secretary of agriculture under President Franklin Delano Roosevelt from March 4, 1933, to August 26, 1940.

1176. Secretary of state to receive the Nobel Peace Prize was Frank Billings Kellogg of Minnesota, secretary of state under President Calvin Coolidge from 1925 to 1929. He received the 1929 Nobel Peace Prize for his work in negotiating the Kellogg-Briand Pact, which was signed by the representatives of 15 nations on August 27, 1928. The agreement, authored by France's foreign minister, Aristide Briand, required signatories to renounce war as an instrument of foreign policy. It was not enforceable, and it eventually failed in its purpose. A

previous secretary of state, Elihu Root of New York, who served from 1905 to 1909 under President Theodore Roosevelt, was awarded the prize in 1912 for his work as president of the Carnegie Endowment for International Peace.

1177. Cabinet member convicted of a crime committed during his tenure was Albert Bacon Fall, secretary of the interior in President Warren G. Harding's cabinet, who was tried in the District of Columbia Supreme Court in 1929. He was charged with accepting a bribe of $100,000 from Edward Laurence Doheny of the Pan-American Petroleum and Transport Company, who wanted Fall to grant his firm valuable oil leases in the Elk Hills Naval Oil Reserve in California. Fall was found guilty by Justice William Hitz on October 25, 1929. On November 1, he was sentenced to one year in prison and was fined $100,000.

1178. Cabinet in which all members were sworn in at the same time and place by the same official took office on March 4, 1933, when Justice Benjamin Nathan Cardozo of the Supreme Court swore in nine men and one woman as President Franklin Delano Roosevelt's cabinet in the library on the second floor of the White House.

1179. Woman to serve in a presidential Cabinet was Frances Perkins, appointed secretary of labor by President Franklin Delano Roosevelt. She served from March 4, 1933, to June 30, 1945, the only cabinet member who served throughout all four terms of Roosevelt's administration. She had been state industrial commissioner for New York prior to this appointment.

1180. Cabinet member to address a joint session of Congress was Secretary of State Cordell Hull, who reported on November 18, 1943, that the tripartite conference at Moscow pointed toward the maintenance of peace and security in the postwar world. The two houses, being in recess, assembled to hear him, but technically it was not a "joint session."

1181. Woman cabinet member to serve under two presidents was Frances Perkins of New York, who served as Secretary of Labor for four terms under President Franklin Delano Roosevelt and who continued to serve for three months into the term of his successor, President Harry S. Truman, who took office on April 12, 1945.

1182. Secretary of defense was James Vincent Forrestal of New York. He was sworn in on September 17, 1947. The Department of Defense, which combined all executive departments governing the armed forces, was authorized by Congress under the National Security Act of July 26, 1947.

1183. Secretary of health, education, and welfare was Oveta Culp Hobby of Houston, TX, who was sworn in on April 11, 1953, as the tenth officer in President Dwight David Eisenhower's cabinet. Previously, she had been administrator of the Federal Security Agency. The Department of Health, Education, and Welfare was split into the Department of Health and Human Services and the Department of Education on May 4, 1980, by the Department of Education Organization Act.

1184. Cabinet conference to be televised was presented on June 3, 1953, from the White House, Washington, DC. President Dwight David Eisenhower conferred for half an hour with Oveta Culp Hobby, secretary of health, education, and welfare; George Magoffin Humphrey, secretary of the treasury; Ezra Taft Benson, secretary of agriculture; and Herbert Brownell, attorney general. The telecast was carried by four networks.

1185. Subcabinet member who was African-American was James Ernest Wilkins of Chicago, IL, who was appointed assistant secretary of labor for international affairs by President Dwight David Eisenhower on March 4, 1954, and sworn in March 18, 1954, in Washington, DC. On August 18, 1954, when Secretary of Labor James Mitchell and Under Secretary Arthur Larson were out of town, he became the first African-American representative of a department to attend a cabinet meeting. (William Henry Lewis, an African-American attorney, was special assistant attorney general from March 26, 1911, to April 1, 1913, but the "special" in his title deprived him of subcabinet rank.)

1186. Cabinet session to be broadcast on radio and television was recorded at the White House, Washington, DC, on October 25, 1954. The telecast showed a special meeting to hear the report of Secretary of State John Foster Dulles on agreements in regard to West Germany signed in Paris on October 23, 1954. All the members of President Dwight David Eisenhower's Cabinet were present, with the exception of Vice President Richard Milhous Nixon. The report was broadcast over the ABC, NBC, and CBS radio and television networks.

1187. Secretary to the cabinet and presidential assistant was Maxwell Milton Rabb of Boston, MA, appointed on November 22, 1954, by President Dwight David Eisenhower "to organize the work, keep the records, follow through on decisions, etc."

1188. Cabinet session held at a place other than the seat of the federal government was held on November 22, 1955, at President Dwight David Eisenhower's farm at Gettysburg, PA. It was attended by the president, the vice president, the ten cabinet officers, and four other government officials.

1189. Cabinet member who was the brother of the president was Robert Francis Kennedy, who took office as attorney general in the cabinet of President John Fitzgerald Kennedy on January 21, 1961, in Washington, DC.

1190. Cabinet meeting attended by a foreign national was held on April 20, 1965, at Washington, DC. At the invitation of President Lyndon Baines Johnson, the meeting was attended by Aldo Moro, the visiting Italian premier; Amintore Fanfani, the Italian foreign minister; and Dr. Sergio Fenoaltea, the Italian ambassador to the United States.

1191. African-American to serve in a presidential cabinet was Robert Clifton Weaver of Washington, DC, who was nominated by President Lyndon Baines Johnson on January 13, 1966, to become the first secretary of housing and urban development.

1192. Secretary of housing and urban development was Robert Clifton Weaver of Washington, DC, who took office on January 18, 1966. He resigned in 1968 to become president of Baruch College in New York City. The Department of Housing and Urban Development had been authorized by Congress on September 9, 1965.

1193. Secretary of transportation was Alan Stephenson Boyd of Florida, who took office on January 16, 1967. He had been nominated by President Lyndon Baines Johnson. Congress authorized the creation of the Department of Transportation on October 15, 1966.

1194. Attorney general whose father had also served as attorney general was William Ramsey Clark of Texas, sworn in on March 10, 1967, at Washington, DC. His father, Thomas Campbell Clark of Texas, who had served from June 30, 1945, to August 22, 1949, administered the oath to his son.

CABINET—*continued*

1195. Cabinet member to serve in four different capacities was Elliott Lee Richardson of Massachusetts, who was sworn in on June 24, 1970, as secretary of health, education and welfare; February 2, 1973, as secretary of defense; May 25, 1973, as attorney general; and February 2, 1976, as secretary of commerce. The first three posts were in the cabinet of President Richard Milhous Nixon, the fourth in the cabinet of President Gerald Rudolph Ford.

1196. Attorney general to plead guilty to a criminal offense was Richard Gordon Kleindienst of Arizona, who served in the administration of President Richard Milhous Nixon from June 12, 1972, to April 30, 1973, when he resigned, along with two other close associates of the president, as a result of the Watergate scandal. On May 18, 1974, in Federal District Court, Washington, DC, he pleaded guilty to charges that he had given inaccurate testimony before the Senate Judiciary Committee in March–April 1972, during its investigation into an antitrust settlement involving the International Telephone and Telegraph Corporation. He was convicted of a criminal misdemeanor.

1197. Woman to serve as secretary of housing and urban development was Carla Anderson Hills of California, who was appointed by President Gerald Rudolph Ford. She was sworn in on March 10, 1975.

1198. African-American woman to serve in a presidential cabinet was Patricia Roberts Harris of Washington, DC, the former ambassador to Luxembourg, who was appointed secretary of housing and urban development by President Jimmy Carter. She was sworn in on January 23, 1977. She served as secretary of health, education, and welfare from August 3 to September 27, 1979, when she became secretary of the newly created Department of Health and Human Services.

1199. Woman to serve as secretary of commerce was Juanita Morris Kreps of North Carolina, appointed by President Jimmy Carter and sworn in on January 23, 1977. An economist, Kreps was also the first woman public director of the New York Stock Exchange (1972) and the first woman to become a vice president of Duke University (1973).

1200. Attorney general to be incarcerated was John Newton Mitchell, attorney general during President Richard Milhous Nixon's first term in office, who was convicted on January 1, 1975, of perjury, conspiracy, and obstruction of justice in connection with the Watergate burglary and cover-up. He entered the federal minimum security prison at Maxwell Air Force Base, near Montgomery, AL, on June 21, 1977. He was the 25th person convicted of crimes in connection with the Watergate scandal, which had forced the resignation of President Nixon in 1974.

1201. Secretary of energy was James Rodney Schlesinger of Virginia, who was appointed by President Jimmy Carter and was sworn in on October 1, 1977. The Department of Energy had been authorized by Congress on August 4, 1977. Schlesinger had previously served as secretary of defense under Presidents Richard Nixon and Gerald Ford.

1202. Secretary of health and human services was Patricia Roberts Harris of Washington, DC. She had been appointed secretary of the Department of Health, Education, and Welfare by President Jimmy Carter in August 1979. On October 17, the department was split into the Department of Health and Human Services, with Harris in charge, and the Department of Education. Harris first entered President Carter's cabinet in 1977, when she was appointed secretary of housing and urban development.

1203. Secretary of education was Shirley Mount Hufstedler of California, formerly a circuit court judge. She took office on December 6, 1979, joining the cabinet of President Jimmy Carter. The department was created by Congress on October 17. A federal agency known as the Department of Education had existed from 1867 to 1869, but it did not have cabinet status.

1204. Woman to serve as secretary of transportation was Elizabeth Hanford Dole of Kansas, who was nominated by President Ronald Reagan. She took office on February 7, 1983. She served in the cabinet of President George Herbert Walker Bush as secretary of labor, beginning on January 30, 1989.

1205. Cabinet member indicted while in office was Raymond L. Donovan, secretary of labor under President Ronald Wilson Reagan from 1981 to 1985. Facing a trial for larceny and fraud in New York, Donovan resigned on March 15, 1985. He was acquitted of all charges on May 25, 1987, after an eight-month trial in New York City.

1206. National security advisor forced to resign was Rear Admiral John M. Poindexter, who announced his resignation on November 25, 1986. Poindexter left office following news reports of the Iran-Contra affair, in which a secret, illegal deal was struck by National Security Council officials to supply Iran, then on a

U.S. list of terrorist states, with advanced weapons in return for aid in obtaining the release of American hostages held by Iranian-backed terrorists in Lebanon. Some of the money paid by Iran for the arms was diverted to the Contras, a rebel group seeking to overthrow the Marxist Sandinista regime in Nicaragua. U.S. military aid to the Contras was forbidden under the Boland Amendment, passed by Congress in 1984. Poindexter had approved the transactions, which were carried out by his subordinate, Lieutenant Colonel Oliver North.

1207. Cabinet nomination by a newly elected president to be rejected was made in January 1989 by President George Herbert Walker Bush, who sought to appoint as secretary of defense John Tower of Texas, a 24-year Republican veteran of the Senate (1961–85) and the former chair of the Senate Armed Services Committee. On March 9, 1989, the nomination was rejected by a vote of 47 to 53 after Senate Democrats publicly aired a series of allegations about Tower's moral fitness for the job (he was accused of being an alcoholic and a womanizer, and of having profited from shady defense contracts). On March 21, 1989, the Senate approved Richard Bruce "Dick" Cheney for defense secretary.

1208. Secretary of veterans affairs was Edward Joseph Derwinski of Illinois, who took office on March 15, 1989, on the same day that Congress elevated the Veterans Administration to cabinet status as the Department of Veterans Affairs. He served through October 26, 1992.

1209. Secretary of state who was a former member of the Foreign Service was Lawrence Sidney Eagleburger, secretary of state from December 8, 1992, until January 19, 1993, under President George Herbert Walker Bush. A protégé of Henry Kissinger, Eagleburger served as ambassador to the former Yugoslavia under President Jimmy Carter. With the election of Ronald Wilson Reagan in 1980, he was appointed assistant secretary of state for European affairs. On August 23, 1992, Eagleburger became acting secretary of state when James A. Baker 3d stepped down as secretary of state to run President Bush's reelection campaign.

1210. African-American to serve as secretary of agriculture was Mike Espy, sworn in as the 25th United States secretary of agriculture in the Clinton administration in January 1993. Espy was also the first Southerner to hold the post. Espy previously served as a member of Congress from a poor farming district in Mississippi.

1211. Woman to serve as secretary of energy was Hazel O'Leary of Minnesota, who was nominated by President William Jefferson Clinton. She took office on January 21, 1993.

1212. Woman to serve as attorney general was Janet Reno of Miami, FL. She took the oath of office on March 12, 1993, after quick confirmation by the Senate on March 11. Reno had earned a law degree from Harvard University in 1963 and had been elected state attorney for Dade County, FL, in 1979.

1213. Woman to serve as secretary of state was Madeline Korbel Albright, born in Prague, Czechoslovakia, in 1937. Albright served as ambassador to the United Nations during the first administration of President William Jefferson Clinton. After a 99–0 vote of confirmation by the Senate, she was sworn into office by Vice President Albert Gore, Jr., on January 23, 1997, at the White House, Washington, DC.

1214. African-American to serve as secretary of labor was Alexis M. Herman of Mobile, AL, whose appointment was approved by the Senate in an 85–13 vote on April 30, 1997. She had previously served in the Carter administration.

CAPITOL

1215. Designs for the building of the Capitol were submitted in 1792 to the Commissioners of the District of Columbia, in response to an advertisement dated March 14 announcing a competition for the best design. The prize was $500 and a building lot in the city of Washington; second prize was $250. The announcement specified a brick edifice containing five rooms at full elevation and twelve others at half elevation. Sixteen entries are known to have been submitted, but none of them met with the approval of President George Washington and Secretary of State Thomas Jefferson. (Jefferson, himself a distinguished architect, designed a building modeled after the Pantheon of ancient Rome, but he did not enter it in the contest.) The winning entry was a low-domed Palladian design by a young physician and painter, William Thornton, who turned in his plan in 1793 and was named to the post of Architect of the Capitol.

1216. Architect of the Capitol was William Thornton, who in 1793 had submitted the winning entry in the competition for the design of the Capitol. A naturalized citizen (he had been born Jost Van Dyke in the British West Indies), Thornton was trained as a physician rather than an architect, but he had already designed a building for the Library Company of Philadel-

CAPITOL—*continued*

phia and had worked with the American engineer John Fitch on the invention of the steamboat. In 1794 he resigned as Architect to become one of the three Commissioners of the District of Columbia, in which post he continued to supervise the Capitol construction project until Benjamin Henry Latrobe was appointed as Architect in 1803. Thornton also served from 1802 to 1828 as the first superintendent of the Patent Office.

1217. Dome on the Capitol was designed by William Thornton in 1793 as part of his original plan for the Capitol. A low dome of copper-covered wood, it was completed by Charles Bulfinch in 1829. When the building was expanded in the 1850s, the dome appeared ridiculously small. A design for a bell-shaped dome of cast iron, influenced by the domes of St. Paul's Cathedral in London and St. Peter's Cathedral in Rome, was prepared by the fourth Architect of Congress, Thomas Ustick Walter. Construction went on slowly but almost continuously during the Civil War, at the insistence of President Abraham Lincoln, who noted: "If the people see the Capitol going on, it is a sign that we intend the Union shall go on." The dome, 135 feet 5 inches wide at the base and weighing 8 million pounds, was completed in 1863.

1218. Superintendent of construction of the Capitol was a French-born architect, Stephen Hallet. In 1792 Hallet entered the competition for the design of the Capitol building. Though he came in second to William Thornton, in 1793 he was appointed superintendent of the construction project. He was dismissed the following year for making unauthorized changes in Thornton's design. He was replaced by George Hadfield and then by James Hoban, the architect of the White House.

1219. Ceremony at the Capitol took place on September 18, 1793, when the cornerstone was laid by President George Washington. A procession of Masons and members of the Alexandria Volunteer Artillery accompanied him. Washington, a Mason since 1753 and the acting grand master of Maryland's Grand Lodge, wore the apron, sash, and collar of a Master Mason. According to a contemporary newspaper report, "the ceremony ended in prayer, Masonic chanting Honours, and a fifteen volley from the Artillery." A barbeque followed, featuring a 500-pound ox "and every abundance of other recreation."

1220. Commemorative tree planted on the Capitol grounds was an American elm that was planted in honor of George Washington sometime before 1800, under the sponsorship of the state of Virginia. The first commemorative tree on the Capitol grounds that was planted in honor of a group of people, rather than of an individual, was the Mothers' Tree, a white birch that was planted on May 9, 1925, in honor the mothers of America. It was also the first tree to be sponsored by all the states together, rather than by one state.

1221. Section of the Capitol to be completed was the north wing. Both houses of Congress met there beginning in 1800. In December 1802, the House of Representatives moved into the south wing, which then consisted of a temporary brick structure, a sweltering oval-shaped room known as the Oven. This was demolished in 1803 by the Architect of the Capitol, Benjamin Henry Latrobe. By 1811, when construction work on the Capitol was halted by the preparations for war with Britain, Latrobe had finished the House wing and rebuilt the leaky Senate wing. After the Capitol was burned by the British in 1814, its reconstruction was overseen by Latrobe until 1817 and by Charles Bulfinch, his successor, from 1818 until 1829, when the project was completed.

1222. Historical paintings in the Capitol were commissioned by Congress in 1817 from artist John Trumbull, who filled four of the eight niches in the rotunda with paintings of episodes in the Revolutionary War.

1223. Architect of the Capitol who was born in the United States was Charles Bulfinch, a native of Boston, MA, and a graduate of Harvard College, who was appointed to the post by President James Monroe on January 8, 1818. He finished the reconstruction begun by his predecessor, Benjamin Henry Latrobe, in accordance with the design drawn up by the first Architect, William Thornton. (Latrobe had been born in England, Thornton in the West Indies.)

1224. Landscaping of the Capitol grounds was the work of the third Architect of the Capitol, Charles Bulfinch, who served from 1818 through 1829. In addition to building the central unit of the original Capitol, together with its dome, Bulfinch produced landscaping designs, including earthen terraces for the west side. Most of the surrounding land was left untouched, and cattle often wandered through it until the grounds were comprehensively redesigned in 1874 by the eminent landscaper Frederick Law Olmsted, the designer of New York City's Central Park.

1225. Sanitary facilities in the Capitol were incorporated as part of the new design drawn up by Benjamin Henry Latrobe in 1814 and completed by Charles Bulfinch in 1829.

1226. Telegraph message sent from the Capitol was the famous message "What hath God wrought," transmitted from the Supreme Court chamber by Samuel Finley Breese Morse on May 28, 1844. The message, selected by Annie Ellsworth, daughter of the commissioner of patents, was taken from the biblical book of Numbers, the 23rd verse of the 23rd chapter. It was received at the Mount Clare station of the Baltimore and Ohio Railroad Company in Baltimore, MD, by his associate, Alfred Vail, whose reply was: "What is the news in Washington?" The exchange of messages inaugurated commercial telegraph service. The Baltimore–Washington line had been built with a $30,000 appropriation from Congress.

1227. Photograph of the Capitol known was probably made by John Plumbe, Jr., circa 1846. A daguerrotype, it shows the east front of the building, with a large water cistern at the foot of the steps.

1228. Gaslight illumination in the Capitol took place during the 1840s. The gaslight in the Senate chamber was activated on December 3, 1847. Previously, candles had been used to provide lighting for sessions that lasted into the evening hours.

1229. Expansion of the Capitol was approved by Congress in September 1850, when funds were appropriated for the design and construction of two additions to the building. Since the original plans were drawn up by William Thornton in 1793, the Senate had grown from 30 to 62 members and the House from 106 to 237 members. A competition was held for a new design. The winner, Thomas Ustick Walter of Philadelphia, PA, was named the fourth Architect of the Capitol on June 11, 1851. Over the next 14 years he oversaw the construction of the new wings and the reconstruction of the Capitol's dome. At the laying of the cornerstone for the additions, on July 4, 1851, President Millard Fillmore wore the Masonic apron that had been worn by George Washington at the laying of the original cornerstone. The new chamber of the House of Representatives was occupied on December 16, 1857, and that of the Senate on January 4, 1859. The former House chamber was used as a storage room until 1864, when it was renovated as National Statuary Hall. The former Senate chamber became the new hall of the Supreme Court.

1230. Person to lie in state in the Capitol rotunda was that of Senator Henry Clay, who died in Washington, DC, at the age of 75 on June 29, 1852. His funeral was held on July 1, 1852, in the old Senate Chamber, after which he lay in state for the remainder of the day in the rotunda, prior to interment in Lexington Cemetery, Lexington, KY.

1231. Frescoes in the Capitol were painted in the Agriculture Committee Room in 1855. They were the work of the Italian-born artist Constantino Brumidi, a refugee from political persecution, who spent the next 25 years painting frescoes throughout the building, fulfilling his intention "to make beautiful the Capitol of the one country on earth in which there is liberty." When he died, he left unfinished a circular frieze in the rotunda, showing important episodes in the history of the United States. The work was carried on by Filippo Costaggini until 1888. The frieze was brought up to date and completed in 1953 by Allyn Cox.

1232. Design for a statue for the raised Capitol dome was made by the sculptor Thomas Crawford in 1856. Entitled *Freedom*, it was a woman's figure, wearing the conical "liberty cap" that was worn by emancipated slaves in ancient Rome and that symbolized opposition to tyranny during the French and American revolutions. Jefferson Davis of Mississippi, secretary of war under President Franklin Pierce, objected to the liberty cap as an inflammatory symbol in the context of the nation's regional conflict over slavery. Crawford substituted an eagle-headed helmet decorated with feathers and stars. The statue, 20 feet high and weighing 15,000 pounds, was modeled in plaster in Rome, Italy, and shipped to New York to be cast in bronze. On December 2, 1863, it was hoisted into place.

1233. Bathtubs in the Capitol were marble tubs that were installed in the basement in 1859 for the use of congressmen and senators whose temporary lodgings did not provide bathing facilities. Modern plumbing was completed in the building in 1894.

1234. Use of the Capitol as a war facility took place in 1861, at the beginning of the Civil War. The rotunda, though cluttered with scaffolding to support the raising of the Capitol dome, was employed as a barracks for men who came to Washington to volunteer as soldiers in the Union Army. The lawns were used for military drill, provisions were stored in the corridors, and bread ovens were installed in

CAPITOL—*continued*

congressional committee rooms. The following year, the Capitol was temporarily turned into a military hospital for soldiers wounded in the Second Battle of Manassas and the Battle of Antietam.

1235. Statue installed in National Statuary Hall in the Capitol was a bust of Nathanael Greene of Rhode Island, the Quaker general who commanded the American army in Georgia and the Carolinas during the Revolutionary War. The hall was formerly the old chamber of the House of Representatives. On July 2, 1864, following a suggestion by Justin Morrill, representative of Vermont, it was dedicated as a place of commemoration, with the various states invited to contribute statues of people to be honored. So many statues were donated that in 1933 some of them had to be moved elsewhere because their collective weight was threatening to buckle the floor.

1236. President to lie in state in the Capitol rotunda was Abraham Lincoln, who died from an assassin's bullet on April 14, 1865. His body was moved to the White House and remained there until April 18. It was then moved to the Capitol rotunda, where it lay in state on a catafalque on April 19 and 20. On April 21 Lincoln's body was taken to the railroad station and put aboard a train that conveyed it to Springfield, IL. Lincoln was buried on May 4 in Oak Ridge Cemetery, near Springfield.

1237. Member of the House of Representatives to lie in state in the Capitol rotunda was Thaddeus Stevens of Pennsylvania, an abolitionist before the Civil War and a leader of the Radical Republicans during Reconstruction, who served in the House from March 4, 1849, through March 3, 1853, and from March 4, 1859, until his death on August 11, 1868. He lay in state on August 13–14, and his funeral was held in the rotunda.

1238. Elevators in the Capitol were installed in 1874.

1239. Vice president to lie in state in the Capitol rotunda was Henry Wilson (born Jeremiah Jones Colbaith), who served as Republican senator from Massachusetts from January 31, 1855, through March 3, 1873, and thereafter as vice president in the second term of Ulysses S. Grant, having been elected on November 5, 1872. He died on November 22, 1875, in the Vice President's Room of the Capitol and lay in state on November 25–26, after which his funeral was held in the Senate Chamber.

1240. Electric power in the Capitol was installed in the Senate cloakroom in 1885. By 1900, electric wiring was installed throughout the building.

1241. Office buildings for U.S. senators and representatives were built in the first decade of the 20th century to accommodate the growing numbers of members of Congress (96 senators and 435 representatives), whose space needs could no longer be met within the Capitol. Two identical buildings, designed by John Carrere and Thomas Hastings, were constructed on Capitol Hill. The Cannon House Office Building, completed in 1908, was named for Joseph G. Cannon of Illinois, who was then speaker of the House (1903–11). The Russell Senate Office Building, completed in 1909, was named for Richard Russell, senator from Georgia. Four additional office buildings have since been built.

1242. Naturalized citizen to lie in state in the Capitol rotunda was Pierre Charles L'Enfant, the French-born architect, engineer, and soldier who came to colonial America in 1776 to join the Continental Army during the Revolutionary War, rising to the rank of major, and afterward was commissioned by President George Washington to design the new federal city of Washington, DC. He died on June 4, 1825, and was buried in Maryland. His body was exhumed in 1909 and lay in state in the Capitol on April 28 prior to reinterment in Arlington National Cemetery, Arlington, VA.

1243. War hero to lie in state in the Capitol rotunda was Admiral George Dewey, who led American naval forces against the Spanish at Manila Bay, the Philippines, on May 1, 1898, during the Spanish-American War. He died in Washington on January 16, 1917, and lay in state on January 20 during his funeral service. James Abram Garfield, who had served in the Civil War as major general of volunteers, had lain in state in the rotunda on September 21–23, 1881, but the honor was accorded him because he was an assassinated president.

1244. Unknown soldier to lie in state in the Capitol rotunda was an American soldier who died in Europe during World War I. His body lay in state from November 9 to November 11, 1921. Unknown soldiers who died in World War II and the Korean War lay in state in May 1958, and another who died in the Vietnam War was honored in May 1984.

1245. Air-conditioning in the Capitol was installed in 1929. By 1932, the Capitol had what was then the world's largest air-conditioning unit.

1246. Chief justice of the Supreme Court to lie in state in the Capitol rotunda was William Howard Taft, who was both president of the United States (March 4, 1909, through March 4, 1913) and chief justice of the Supreme Court (July 11, 1921, through February 3, 1930). He died in Washington on March 8, 1930, and lay in state on March 11. His son, Robert Alphonso Taft, who served as senator from Ohio from 1939 through 1953, also lay in state in the rotunda, on August 2–3, 1953.

1247. Terrorist shootings in the Capitol Building took place on March 1, 1954, when four Puerto Rican nationalists, shouting "Freedom for Puerto Rico!" fired more than 30 rounds at the floor of the House of Representatives from a visitors' gallery. Alvin Bentley of Michigan, George Fallon of Maryland, Ben Jensen of Iowa, Clifford Davis of Tennessee, and Kenneth Roberts of Alabama were all wounded. The nationalists—Lolita Lebrón, Rafael Cancel Miranda, Andrés Figueroa Cordero, and Irving Flores—served 25 years of their 50 year sentences before they were pardoned on September 6, 1979, by President Jimmy Carter.

1248. Prayer and meditation room in the Capitol was opened in April 1955 in a small room that had formerly been part of the office space of Speaker of the House Joseph W. Martin, Jr. It was furnished with a stained-glass window showing George Washington praying on bended knee beneath a banner reading "One nation under God," with the words of the 16th Psalm surrounding him: "Preserve me, O God, for in Thee do I put my trust." Its use was intended to be nonsectarian. The proposal for such a room was made by Brooks Hays, representative from Kansas, and A. S. Monroney, senator from Oklahoma.

1249. Federal agency chief to lie in state in the Capitol rotunda was John Edgar Hoover, who was director of the Federal Bureau of Investigation (FBI) from 1924 until his death on May 2, 1972. A memorial service was held in the rotunda on May 3, after which he lay in state until the following day.

1250. Policewomen to serve on the Capitol police force were hired in 1974.

1251. Capitol Police Officers killed in the line of duty were Special Agent John Michael Gibson, 42, and Police Private First Class Jacob Joseph Chestnut, 58. Both were shot on July 24, 1998, by a deranged Montana man named Russell Weston, Jr. Weston entered the Capitol and shot Chestnut point blank, then exchanged fire with Gibson, killing him before collapsing of his own wounds. The bodies of the two officers were displayed in the Capitol Rotunda on July 27, and were then buried in Arlington National Cemetery.

CITIES AND COUNTIES

1252. Chartered city in the United States is York, ME. It was founded as Gorgeanna in 1641 by William Gorges, governor of New England, who held a grant from the English crown to the territory that later became Maine.

1253. City incorporated in the British colonies was Georgeana (now York), ME. On December 2, 1631, Sir Ferdinando Gorges received a grant of 24,000 acres on both sides of the Agamenticus, or York, River and founded a town named after the river on April 10, 1641. The name was changed to Georgeana when the city was incorporated on March 1, 1642, and was later changed again to York. The charter embraced a territory of 21 square miles and the inhabitants were formed into a body politic. This was the first English charter for a city in America. Kittery, ME, was the first and oldest town in the state, but Georgeana was incorporated as a city rather than as a town.

1254. Public library in an American city was established in Charleston, SC, in 1698 through the efforts of Thomas Bray (later the representative in Maryland of the Bishop of London), who in 1696 forwarded religious books to the clergy. On November 16, 1700, Charleston passed an act "for securing the Provincial Library of Charlestown, by which commissioners and trustees were appointed for its preservation." The act authorized any inhabitants to "have liberty to borrow any book out of the said provincial library, giving a receipt."

1255. Town built by free African-Americans in an area now in the United States was Fort Mose, near St. Augustine, FL. In 1738, Spanish authorities established a free militia of 100 former slaves, including men, women, and children, who had escaped from British territory in what is now Georgia. They built Fort Mose, a 65-foot-square structure in the salt marshes north of St. Augustine. They were driven away by a British attack in 1740 but rebuilt and enlarged the fort in 1752. In 1763, when Spanish Florida was ceded to England, the residents of Fort Mose moved to Cuba. The fort was declared a national historic landmark in 1994.

CITIES AND COUNTIES—*continued*

1256. Town named for George Washington was a North Carolina town originally known as Forks of Tar River, which had been founded on November 20, 1771, by James Bonner. It changed its name to Washington in 1775 and was incorporated in 1782.

1257. Town to be incorporated under the name of Washington was a town in Wilkes County, GA, that was incorporated on January 23, 1780.

1258. Town known to have been founded by a woman was Tangipahoa, LA, settled in 1806 by Rhoda Holly Singleton Mixon, who came from South Carolina accompanied by her daughters and slaves. Her grandchildren sold their property in 1869.

1259. Public library established after the Revolution was founded in Peterborough, NH, on April 9, 1833. The funds for its creation came from state monies that had originally been appropriated for a state university and were then distributed to towns to use for educational purposes. The library was maintained by a public tax, controlled and managed by town vote, and open to all community members without restriction. An earlier but unsuccessful attempt to establish a free public library was made in New Orleans, LA, by the philanthropist Judah Touro, who founded the Touro Free Library Society in 1824.

1260. Town founded by African-Americans after the Civil War was Princeville, NC, founded in 1865 by a group of newly freed slaves. The town was located on swampy ground on the southern side of the Tar River, across from the white settlement of Tarboro. Continuously occupied from that date, the town was chartered by the state in 1885, becoming the first municipality in the United States to be chartered and governed solely by African-Americans. Princeville was washed away in the massive floods of summer 1999.

1261. Major city to be unincorporated was Seattle, WA. Originally, Seattle was incorporated as a town on January 14, 1865, by act of the Washington territorial legislature. However, following submission of a petition by several citizens, the town was unincorporated on January 28, 1867. Little is known of this two-year-period of Seattle government because the municipal records were destroyed or lost. Seattle was reincorporated as a city on December 2, 1869.

1262. African-American town in continuous existence west of the Mississippi is Nicodemus, KS. A tiny settlement with 50 permanent residents, it was founded in 1877 and was named after an African prince who was reputed to be the first slave to buy his freedom. The town was designated a national historic landmark in 1976.

1263. County created by federal law was Latah County in Idaho, authorized by Congress in a bill enacted on May 14, 1888. The bill set aside a portion of Nez Perce County in Idaho to become Latah County, with the county seat at Moscow.

1264. Major American city founded in the 20th century was Las Vegas, NV, which was founded on May 5, 1905, and incorporated in 1911. A gambling mecca from its earliest days, the city grew rapidly after World War II. In 1946, mobster Benjamin "Bugsy" Siegel inaugurated the modern Las Vegas gambling industry by building the Flamingo Hotel and Casino on a strip of Las Vegas desert (the future intersection of Las Vegas Boulevard and Flamingo Road), with financing by Murder Incorporated co-founder Meyer Lansky.

1265. City to run an airport was Hartford, CT, which purchased Brainard Field near the Connecticut River in 1920.

1266. City to own a National Football League franchise was Green Bay, WI, whose Green Bay Packers were incorporated by the city in 1923 to save the team from bankruptcy. According to the corporation bylaws, no individual shareholder in the franchise is allowed to purchase more than $5,000 in shares.

1267. Urban renewal program in the nation was begun in Boston, MA, in 1958, with the controversial demolition of the old West End neighborhoods to make way for the construction of the Charles River Park complex. With a new building code in hand that allowed buildings higher than the old limit of 125 feet, the Boston Redevelopment Authority oversaw several large developments in the central city, including the Government Center, containing the new City Hall, which was completed in 1968, and the renewal of the downtown waterfront.

1268. Municipal air-raid shelter was the Highlands Community Shelter, Boise, ID, which could accommodate 1,000 people. A membership fee of $100 per family was charged. The shelter, completed on July 1, 1961, cost $142,000, of which $122,000 was government research funds obtained from the Office of Civil Defense.

1269. City occupying more than 1,000 square miles was Juneau, the capital of Alaska. In 1970, Juneau merged with the city of Douglas, on an island across the Gastineau Channel, forming a municipality of 3,108 square miles. The next largest city in area, Los Angeles, CA, occupies less than 500 square miles.

CITIES AND COUNTIES—COURTS

1270. Women to serve as jurors took their seats under oath in 1870 in Laramie, WY.

1271. Woman to serve as justice of the peace was Esther Hobart Morris, a suffragist who was appointed on February 17, 1870, in South Pass, Wyoming Territory. She was empowered to commit cases for trial, perform marriages, judge misdemeanors, and administer oaths.

1272. Juvenile court was the Juvenile Court of Cook County, known as the Chicago Juvenile Court, authorized on April 21, 1899, and opened on July 1, 1899, with Richard Stanley Tuthill as judge. This was the first juvenile court in the world. During the first year, about 2,300 cases were heard. Cases involving girls were tried by a female judge, Mary Margaret Bartelme, beginning on March 3, 1913.

1273. Night court was opened in New York City on September 1, 1907. It was a magistrates' court, the Jefferson Market Court at Ninth Street and Sixth Avenue, presided over by Charles Nathan Harris. Sessions were held from 8 P.M. to 3 A.M. until September 1, 1910, when the closing hour was fixed at 1 A.M.

1274. Municipal small claims court was the Conciliation Branch of the Municipal Court of Cleveland, OH, established on March 15, 1913. The complainant could not be represented by counsel but had to present his own case. Strict rules of evidence and procedure were waived. The judgment rendered had the same force and effect, and was as binding, as a judgment rendered in any court of record.

1275. County public defender was Walton J. Wood, who assumed his duties on January 7, 1914. The office of public defender had been established by Los Angeles County, CA, on June 13, 1913. Wood's salary was $200 a month. He had three deputies, one secretary, and one assistant secretary.

1276. African-American woman to be appointed a municipal judge was Jane Matilda Bolin, who on July 22, 1939, was appointed judge of the Court of Domestic Relations by Mayor Fiorello La Guardia of New York City. She was also the first African-American woman to graduate from Yale Law School and the first to be admitted to the New York City bar.

1277. African-American woman to be elected to a judgeship was Edith Spurlock Sampson, elected associate judge of the Municipal Court of Chicago, IL, on November 8, 1962, and sworn in on December 3, 1962. She became an associate judge of the Circuit Court of Cook County, Chicago, IL, on January 1, 1964.

1278. Judge who had served time in prison was Robert A. "Bob" Young, who was elected to serve the term from January 3, 1977, to December 31, 1983, as judge of the Justice Court, Loomis, CA. He had been convicted at the age of 19 of stealing a credit card out of the mail and had served 20 months in federal prison and four years on parole. He was graduated from law school in 1970 and after a two-year investigation was admitted to the bar.

CITIES AND COUNTIES—ELECTIONS

1279. African-American to hold elective office was John Mercer Langston, who was elected town clerk by the voters of Brownhelm, OH, in 1855. Langston, the son of a plantation owner and a freed slave, was an Oberlin-educated lawyer. He went on to serve as law professor and dean of Howard University, minister to Haiti and chargé d'affaires to Santo Domingo (1877–85), and president of the Virginia Normal and Collegiate Institute. He was the first African-American to represent Virginia in the House of Representatives, in 1890–91.

1280. Secret ballot was adopted by Louisville, KY, in 1888. The system, developed in Australia and now current throughout the United States, requires the government to provide each voter who arrives at the polls with a printed ballot showing the names of all the candidates and a private place in which to mark his or her choice.

1281. Voting machines used in an election were used on April 12, 1892, at Lockport, NY, where 3,271 votes were cast for the office of mayor and other town offices. The invention of Jacob H. Myers, a safemaker from Rochester, NY, they were manufactured by the American Ballot Machine Company, which was later absorbed by the Automatic Voting Machine Corporation of Jamestown, NY. Myers said that his machine was designed to "protect mechanically the voter from rascaldom, and make the process of casting the ballot perfectly plain, simple and secret." Use of the machine, then called a voting cabinet, was authorized by the New York State legislature on March 15, 1892, by an act "to secure independence of voters at town meetings."

CITIES AND COUNTIES—ELECTIONS—
continued

1282. Election using the preferential ballot system took place in Grand Junction, CO. The charter that contained the preferential ballot provision was adopted on September 14, 1909, and the first election using the system took place on November 2. Opposite the name of each candidate were three columns headed "First Choice," "Second Choice," and "Third Choice." Any person receiving more than half of all the votes cast for first choice was elected. If no one received more than half the first choices, the lowest candidate was dropped and the first and second choices were added together. If any remaining candidate received a majority of the combined votes, that candidate was elected; if not, then the lowest candidate was again dropped, and all choices for each candidate were then added together, with the victory going to the person receiving the largest total vote. In case of a tie, priority in choice determined election.

1283. Election using proportional representation was held on November 2, 1915, in Ashtabula, OH, to elect seven council members. The votes were counted so that each group consisting of one-seventh of all the voters secured a representative.

1284. Local election results to be announced on radio were the results of congressional and county primaries, broadcast on August 31, 1920, by station 8MK (later WWJ) in Detroit, MI.

1285. Openly homosexual individual to run for public office was probably the drag performer José Sarria, who in November 1961 ran for a seat on the Board of Supervisors of San Francisco, CA. He received nearly 6,000 votes.

1286. Openly homosexual politican to win a municipal election was Kathy Kozachenko, who was elected to the City Council of Ann Arbor, MI, in November 1973.

CITIES AND COUNTIES—GOVERNMENT

1287. Use of the word "caucus" originated in the local politics of Boston, MA, in the mid-18th century. In February 1763, John Adams, the future president, made the following entry in his diary: "This day I learned that the caucus club meets at certain times in the garret of Tom Dawes, the adjutant of the Boston regiment. . . . There they smoke tobacco till you cannot see from one end to the other. There they drink flip, I suppose, and there they choose a moderator who puts questions to the vote regularly; and selectmen, assessors, collectors, wardens, fire wards and representatives are regularly chosen before they are chosen in the town."

1288. City government using the commission plan originated in Galveston, TX, in 1901 as an emergency measure following a disastrous flood. The legislature granted Galveston a charter on April 19, 1901, and the system went into operation on September 18. Under this form, large powers both legislative and executive are vested in a single group of officers, elected by the whole body of voters within the city without regard to political party.

1289. City government run by a city manager originated in Staunton, VA, whose city council elected Charles Edward Ashburner general manager on April 2, 1908. His first year's salary was $2,000; the second year's, $2,500. He served until July 1911.

1290. City government using the manager plan was adopted by Sumter, SC, in June 1912, when the voters, in a regular election, adopted the manager-commission form of government. The commission was composed of a mayor and two councilmen, all elected at large. The commission employed a city manager to whom active administration of the affairs of the city was entrusted and who was accountable to the commission.

1291. Zoning ordinance was put into effect in New York City on July 25, 1916, in the wake of concern over the unprecedented size of the 39-story Equitable Building, erected in lower Manhattan in 1915. The ordinance restricted the height and mass of skyscrapers and required buildings to be set back from the street, with the amount of setback calculated from the height and area of the building site. The total floor area of skyscrapers was also limited to no more than twelve times the area of the building site.

1292. Nationwide municipal reform organization was the National League of Cities, founded in 1924 as the American Municipal Association by ten state municipal leagues. The goal of the NLC is "to strengthen and promote cities as centers of opportunity, leadership, and governance." By the 1990s, the NLC represented 49 state municipal leagues, more than 1,500 member cities, and more than 18,000 cities and towns in total.

1293. City council composed entirely of Libertarian Party members was the city council of Big Water, UT, after elections in 1987. The Libertarian Party's political base has traditionally been strongest in the western states and at the level of municipal councils and state legislatures.

1294. City council with a majority of Green Party members was elected in November 1997 by voters in Arcata, CA, a former logging town with a reputation as "the greenest town in the United States." The five-person council consisted of three members of the Green Party, including the town's vice mayor, Jason Kirkpatrick, and two Democrats.

CITIES AND COUNTIES—MAYORS

1295. Mayor of New York, NY, was Thomas Willett, who was appointed in 1665 by Richard Nicolls, the English colonial governor. New York's mayors continued to be appointed until 1820, when Stephen Allen was elected by the city's Common Council. The first mayor of metropolitan New York City, formed from the consolidation of the five boroughs of Manhattan, Queens, Brooklyn, the Bronx, and Staten Island on January 1, 1898, was Robert van Wyck, who had been handpicked by Richard Croker, the head of Tammany Hall, the city's powerful Democratic machine.

1296. Mayor of Philadelphia, PA, was Humphrey Morrey, appointed in 1691 by William Penn, Proprietor of the colony of Pennsylvania. Edward Shippen was the first mayor named under the provisions of the Charter of 1701; he served for one year. Beginning in 1702, the Common Council of Philadelphia elected a mayor from among its members. This practice lasted until 1836, after which any citizen of the city was allowed to run for the office. In 1840, John Swift became the first mayor who was elected directly by the people of Philadelphia.

1297. Mayor of Norfolk, VA, was Samuel Boush, appointed mayor on September 15, 1736, the year Norfolk and its suburbs were incorporated under charter from King George II. Boush died before the first council meeting in November 1736 and was replaced with George Newton on November 18.

1298. Mayor of Schenectady, NY, was Joseph C. Yates. He was elected on March 26, 1798, when Schenectady was incorporated as a city. Yates later became the eighth governor of New York.

1299. Mayor of Augusta, GA, was Thomas Cumming, elected intendant of the Augusta City Council on March 31, 1798. He gave his name to Augusta's Cumming Street, now called Tenth Street.

1300. Mayor of New Orleans, LA, was James Pitot, who served as the first mayor of the incorporated city of New Orleans (at that time the economic center of the Louisiana Territory) from 1804 to 1805.

1301. Mayor of Cleveland, OH, was Alfred Kelley, elected in 1815, when Cleveland was still a village (although it had already been selected as the county seat). After Cleveland's incorporation as a city in 1836, the first elected mayor was John Willey.

1302. Mayor of Boston, MA, after its incorporation as a city by the state legislature in 1822 was John Phillips, who was sworn in on May 1, 1822.

1303. Mayor of St. Louis, MO, was William Carr Lane, who served from 1823 to 1829 and again from 1837 to 1840. Carr was briefly governor of New Mexico Territory from 1852 to 1853.

1304. Mayor of Memphis, TN, was Marcus Winchester, who was elected as the town's first mayor in the spring of 1827, shortly after the Tennessee State Legislature granted Memphis a charter of incorporation in December 1826. The land on which Memphis was built was co-owned by Andrew Jackson, who purchased it in a parntership with James Winchester (Marcus's brother) and John Overton in the late 1790s.

1305. Mayor of Buffalo, NY, was Ebenezer Johnson, a medical doctor and the city's wealthiest citizen. He was appointed by the Common Council in 1832. Immediately after Johnson assumed office, the city was struck by an epidemic of cholera.

1306. City mayor elected by popular vote was Cornelius Van Wyck Lawrence, a Democrat, who defeated Gulian Crommelin Verplanck, a Whig, in the three-day election held on April 8–10, 1834, in New York City. There were 34,988 votes cast, of which 17,573 were for Lawrence, 17,393 for Verplanck, and 22 for others. Seven other municipal officers were also elected. Previously, mayors had been chosen by a board of the Common Council.

CITIES AND COUNTIES—MAYORS—continued

1307. Mayor of Chicago, IL, was William B. Ogden, chosen in the election of May 2, 1837, the first held following Chicago's incorporation as a city. Isaac N. Arnold was elected clerk, and Hiram Pearsons was made treasurer. In September 1839, Ogden purchased a share of the Hass and Lill brewery, the city's oldest, thus inaugurating the long-lasting connection between beer and Chicago politics.

1308. Mayor of Austin, TX, was Edwin Waller, a signer of the Texas Declaration of Independence. A native of Virginia, Waller was elected Austin's first mayor on January 13, 1840, but resigned before his term expired. On August 12 of that year he took part in the battle of Plum Creek.

1309. Mayor of Hannibal, MO, was James Brady, who became the city's first mayor upon its incorporation in 1845.

1310. Mayor of Peoria, IL, was William Hale. The city received its charter to incorporate in 1845, and Hale was elected as Peoria's first mayor in April of that year.

1311. Mayor of Milwaukee, WI, was Solomon Juneau, head of a French-speaking trading family that settled in the Milwaukee area in the 1830s. He was elected in 1846, the year Milwaukee adopted a city charter. The original aldermen numbered 15, from five districts, and received no salary.

1312. Mayor of New Bedford, MA, was Abraham Hathaway Howland. He was elected mayor of the fishing and whaling town in 1847, the year it was granted a city charter by the Massachusetts legislature.

1313. Mayor of Syracuse, NY, was Harvey Baldwin, elected in 1848, the year that the villages of Salina and Syracuse merged to become the City of Syracuse.

1314. Mayor of Independence, MO, was William McCoy, who took office on July 20, 1849. The first city council included J. V. Hovey, B. F. Simpson, Robert Duke, John W. Modie, T.J. Shaw, R.D. Green, Robert Stone, Porter McClanahan, and Abslom Wray.

1315. Mayor of San Francisco, CA, was John White Geary, elected San Francisco's last American alcalde in August 1849 and its first mayor on May 1, 1850. Geary had been a member of the State Constitutional Convention at Monterey. He served one year, then returned to his home state of Pennsylvania. Geary was later governor of the Territory of Kansas (1856).

1316. Mayor of Corpus Christi, TX, was Benjamin F. Neal, elected in 1852, the year in which Corpus Christi's streets were laid out and named and the first jail was built.

1317. Mayor of Kansas City, KS, who was eligible to serve was Johnston Lykins, a Virginian by birth, who was a Baptist missionary and physician. In 1853, William S. Gregory won the first mayoral election, but it was later discovered that he was not qualified for the post because he had not lived in town long enough. Lykins, who was city council president, completed Gregory's term.

1318. Mayor of Los Angeles, CA, was Benjamin D. Wilson, also known as Don Benito Wilson. Wilson was a wealthy rancher and vintner whose landholdings included much of what is now Alhambra, San Marino, South Pasadena, and Pasadena. He was appointed by President Millard Fillmore in 1852 as an Indian agent, and in 1855 became the mayor of Los Angeles, then a small town.

1319. Mayor of a major city to fire the entire police department was John Wentworth of Chicago, IL. In 1861, he fired the entire Chicago Police Department when his term ended. Some 60 patrolmen, three sergeants, three lieutenants, and one captain were let go. The city was without police protection for twelve hours until the Board of Commissioners swore in new officers.

1320. Mayor of Minneapolis, MN, was Dorilus Wilson. He was sworn in as mayor in 1867, the year the city of Minneapolis was incorporated.

1321. Mayor of Seattle, WA, was Henry A. Atkins, appointed by the Washington territorial legislature following the incorporation of the City of Seattle on December 2, 1869. Atkins was elected to a second term in July 1870.

1322. Mayor of Abilene, TX, was D. B. Corley, who was chosen on January 2, 1883, the date that Abilene residents voted to incorporate the city.

1323. Woman elected mayor of a town was Susanna Medora Salter, elected mayor of Argonia, KS, on April 4, 1887, shortly after Kansas women had gained the right to vote in city elections. She was the daughter of the town's first mayor and the daughter-in-law of Melville J. Salter, a former Kansas lieutenant governor. Her name was submitted without her knowledge by the Woman's Christian Temperance Union, and she did not know that she was a candidate until she went to the polls and found her name listed on the ballot. Although only 27 years of age, she received a two-thirds majority of the votes. She served one year for $1.

1324. Woman mayor with a town council consisting entirely of women was Mary D. Lowman, elected in April 1888 in Oskaloosa, KS. Her council consisted of Sadie Balsley, Millie Golden, Emma Hamilton, Carrie Johnson, and Hannah Morse.

1325. Mayor of Fairbanks, AK, was Captain E. T. Barnette, who established the first American trading post in the area in 1901. Gold was discovered nearby in 1902, and the trading post rapidly grew into a town to accomodate the needs of thousands of prospectors. In 1903, the seat of the Third Judicial District was moved from Eagle to Fairbanks, the town was incorporated as the City of Fairbanks, and Barnette was elected the first mayor.

1326. Socialist mayor of a major city was Emil Seidel, who served as mayor of Milwaukee, WI, from April 1910 to April 1912.

1327. City commissioner of Salt Lake City, UT, was a socialist, Henry Lawrence, elected in 1911, the year the city adopted the commission form of government.

1328. Woman mayor elected west of the Rocky Mountains was Clara Munson, who served as mayor of Warrenton, OR, from January 6 to December 1, 1913.

1329. Major American city to elect a woman as mayor was Seattle, WA, where Bertha Knight Landes was elected mayor in 1926. She served one two-year term and was defeated for reelection in 1928.

1330. Mayor of a major city to be recalled was Frank Shaw, elected mayor of Los Angeles, CA, in 1932, and head of what is usually considered the most corrupt government in the city's history. A county board of supervisors inquiry indicated that Shaw, as the board's former chairman, had taken kickbacks from state-run food services and cafeterias. A subsequent grand jury investigation of the Shaw administration found that 1800 bookies, 600 brothels, and 200 gambling dens were paying graft to city officials, mainly the mayor. Shaw was recalled in 1937 and replaced with reform candidate Judge Fletcher Bowren, who had overseen the grand jury proceedings.

1331. Mexican-American mayor of El Paso, TX, was Raymond Telles, elected in 1957.

1332. African-American to serve as chief executive of a major city was Walter Edward Washington, formerly an official with the municipal housing authorities of Washington, DC, and New York City, who took office on September 28, 1967, as commissioner and chief executive of the District of Columbia, the equivalent of its mayor. This was not, however, an elected post; it was filled by an officeholder appointed by the president of the United States. In 1972 Congress reorganized the government of the capital city and replaced the commissioner with an elected mayor. The first mayoral election, held in November 1974, was won by Walter Edward Washington, who took office on January 2, 1975.

1333. Major city to elect an African-American as mayor was Cleveland, OH, whose voters elected Carl Burton Stokes, a Democrat, on November 7, 1967. He was sworn in on November 13, 1967, in the City Council Chamber.

1334. African-American mayor of a major Southern city was Charles Evers, brother of the slain civil rights leader Medgar Evers and his successor as Mississippi field director for the National Association for the Advancement of Colored People. On May 13, 1969, Evers, a Democrat, was elected mayor of the small, rural community of Fayette, MS. He went on to serve four terms.

1335. African-American mayor of a major Eastern city was independent Democrat Kenneth A. Gibson. He was elected mayor of Newark, NJ, in a runoff election held on June 16, 1970, defeating incumbent Hugh J. Addonizio by 55,097 votes to 43,086.

1336. Woman to serve as mayor of Oklahoma City, OK, was Patience Sewell Latting, sworn in on April 13, 1971, as mayor of Oklahoma City, OK. Her salary was $2,000 a year. The city's population exceeded 366,000.

1337. African-American mayor of Atlanta, GA, was Maynard Jackson, Jr., who was elected Atlanta's first African-American mayor on October 16, 1973. Inaugurated on January 7, 1974, he served three terms before announcing his retirement in 1993. Jackson was the first African-American to serve as chief executive of a major Southern city in the United States

CITIES AND COUNTIES—MAYORS—_continued_

1338. African-American mayor of Detroit, MI, was Coleman A. Young. Previously a combative union organizer, Young was on the ballot in 1969 and was elected mayor of Detroit in 1973. He served a record five terms in office before retiring in 1993.

1339. African-American mayor of Los Angeles, CA, was Democrat Thomas Bradley, elected in 1973 after defeating Sam Yorty. A former policeman, the son of a sharecropper and the grandson of slaves, Bradley served a record five terms as mayor of Los Angeles before announcing he would not seek reelection when his fifth term expired on June 30, 1993.

1340. Woman to serve as mayor of a major city with a population over 500,000 was Janet Gray Hayes of San Jose, CA, elected on November 6, 1974, on the Democratic ticket.

1341. African-American militant to be elected mayor of a major American city was Marion S. Barry. Barry was elected the first national chairman of the Student Nonviolent Coordinating Committee (SNCC) in 1960 and organized protests in Washington beginning in June 1965. In the 1970s, he turned to more mainstream forms of political activity and in 1978 announced his candidacy for mayor. He was elected chief executive of Washington, DC, on November 7, 1978. The inauguration took place on January 2, 1979, when Barry took the oath of office from Thurgood Marshall, associate justice of the Supreme Court.

1342. Woman mayor of San Francisco, CA, was Dianne Feinstein, born Dianne Emiel Goldman, a Democrat. In 1969 she became the first woman to be elected president of the San Francisco Board of Supervisors. After failing twice in her bid to become mayor, Feinstein announced on the morning of November 27, 1978, that she planned to retire from politics. Later that day, she automatically became acting mayor of San Francisco when former supervisor Dan White assassinated Mayor George Moscone and another supervisor, Harvey Milk. Her installment as mayor was formalized by the Board of Supervisors on December 4, 1978. Feinstein served in the post until 1988.

1343. Woman mayor of Chicago, IL, was Jane Margaret Burke Byrne, elected in 1979. A protégé of former mayor Richard Daley who had never before held elective office, Byrne had recently been fired by incumbent mayor Michael A. Bilandic from her post as commissioner of consumer sales. Byrne took political advantage of a harsh winter that had brought the city nearly to a standstill and made Bilandic's administration appear unresponsive and arrogant. She defeated Bilandic in Chicago's Democratic party primary on February 27, 1979, and won a crushing victory in the general election held on April 3, 1979, taking 82 percent of the vote to Republican candidate Wallace Johnson's 16 percent.

1344. Mayor of a major American city who was of Mexican descent was Henry Gabriel Cisneros, who was elected mayor of San Antonio, TX, on April 4, 1981. Cisneros was the first Mexican-American to lead the city since 1842, when Texas was not yet part of the United States.

1345. African-American mayor of Chicago, IL, was Democrat Harold Washington. While serving as U.S. representative from a Chicago district, Washington upset incumbent Jane Byrne for the Democratic nomination in 1983, then narrowly defeated white Republican candidate Bernard Epton in the general election. Washington served as mayor until his death on November 25, 1987.

1346. Latino mayor of a city without a large Latino population was Federico Fabian Peña, mayor of Denver, CO, from 1983 to 1991. Peña, descended from an old Tejano family, defeated Dale Tooley in a June 1983 runoff election with 51 percent of the vote. Latinos comprised only 18 percent of Denver's population.

1347. African-American mayor of Philadelphia, PA, was Democrat W. Wilson Goode, elected on November 8, 1983, as Philadelphia's 126th mayor. He served from 1984 to 1992.

1348. African-American mayor of Baltimore, MD, was Kurt L. Schmoke, elected in November 1987 to succeed William Donald Schaefer. Schmoke defeated his Republican opponent, Samuel A. Culotta, by 74,111 votes, garnering about 65 percent of the white vote and 95 percent of the African-American vote.

1349. Incumbent African-American mayor of a major city to lose to a white candidate was Eugene Sawyer, an alderman who had been named by the City Council of Chicago, IL, to succeed to the mayor's office after the death of Harold Washington. In the 1989 Democratic primary, Sawyer was defeated by Richard M. Daley, son of the Windy City's late political patriarch, Richard J. Daley. In a special election held on April 11, 1989, Daley defeated challenger Timothy Evans of the Harold Washington Party with 55 percent to 41 percent of the vote.

1350. African-American mayor of Seattle, WA, was Norman Rice. He won election in November 1989, defeating a white opponent in a city that was only 10 percent black. His tenure began January 1, 1990. Prior to his election, Rice had served on the Seattle city council for eleven years.

1351. African-American mayor of New York City was David N. Dinkins, the Manhattan borough president and a Democrat, who was elected on November 7, 1989. He served one term. He was defeated in his 1993 bid for reelection by Republican candidate Rudolph Giuliani, whom he had beaten in 1989.

1352. Mayor of a major American city arrested on drug charges was Marion Barry, mayor of Washington, DC. On January 18, 1990, Barry was arrested at the Vista International Hotel in downtown Washington and charged with drug possession and the use of crack cocaine. He had been the subject of a sting operation mounted by FBI agents and District of Columbia police. Barry was sentenced on September 28, 1991, to six months in prison, but his political base in the city remained strong, and in 1994 Barry was reelected to the mayor's office. He was stripped of his powers in 1997 when control of the city government was transferred to Congress.

1353. Muslim mayor of an American city was Charles Bilal, elected mayor of Kountze, TX, in 1991.

1354. African-American mayor of Kansas City, MO, was the Reverend Emanuel Cleaver, who defeated city councilman Bob Lewellen in the mayoral election of March 1991. Cleaver had served for three terms on the city council and was endorsed by organized labor and top business leaders, as well as a broad segment of the city's white population.

1355. African-American mayor of Denver, CO, was Wellington E. Webb, a Democrat, who was elected on June 18, 1991. Webb, a former city auditor, mounted a grassroots campaign in which he walked back and forth across the city talking with voters. He won handily over his opponent, District Attorney Norm Early, taking 58 percent of the vote. At the time of Webb's election, Denver's population was 68 percent white, 12 percent African American, and 20 percent Hispanic.

1356. Mayoral election in a major city in which both candidates were African-Americans was the 1991 contest for mayor of Denver, CO, in which Democrat Wellington E. Webb, a former city auditor and state legislator, was matched against Republican District Attorney Norm Early. Early ran a standard campaign and raised about $1 million in contributions; Webb ran a grassroots effort in which he walked the city talking to voters and staying the night in their homes. Webb won the election on June 18, 1991, with 58 percent of the vote.

1357. Woman mayor of Orlando, FL, was Glenda Hood, elected in 1992 after serving on the Orlando City Council for ten years.

1358. African-American mayor of St. Louis, MO, was Freeman Bosley Jr., elected with 67 percent of the city's vote in the election of April 1993. Bosley ran a grassroots campaign based on the themes of racial harmony, neighborhood redevelopment, combating crime, and improving public schools. Bosley served until 1997, when he was unseated by Clarence Harmon, Jr., another African-American.

1359. Woman to serve as mayor of Minneapolis, MN, was former Minneapolis city council president Sharon Sayles Belton, elected in November 1993. She was also the first African-American to serve as the city's mayor.

1360. African-American mayor of Dallas, TX, was Democrat Ron Kirk, formerly the Texas secretary of state. He won the election of May 6, 1995, with 62 percent of the vote. Kirk was the first African-American mayor of any major Texas city.

1361. African-American mayor of Savannah, GA, was Floyd Adams, Jr., who defeated Susan Weiner, the Republican incumbent, and was inaugurated on January 2, 1996. He ran on a platform stressing unity among the city's residents. A Democrat, he served for 13 years as a member of the City Council. In 1991 he became the first African-American elected to townwide office in Savannah when he won the office of alderman at large. In 1992 he became the first African-American to be elected vice mayor. He was also the editor of the *Savannah Herald,* a weekly newspaper for Savannah's black residents.

CITIES AND COUNTIES—MAYORS—_continued_

1362. Executive Mayor of Miami–Dade County, FL, was Alex Penelas, elected on October 1, 1996. Penelas was responsible for the largest metropolitan government in the southeastern United States, exercising authority over the county's $4.1 billion budget and representing its 2.1 million residents. Penelas was previously a member of the Miami-Dade Board of County Commissioners and served as Councilman for the City of Hialeah from 1987 to 1990.

1363. African-American mayor of Jackson, MS, was Harvey Johnson, elected on a racial unity platform in June 1997. The election was especially notable because of the city's long history of racial hatred and division.

1364. African-American mayor of Houston, TX, was Lee Patrick Brown, elected in a runoff contest held on December 6, 1997.

CIVIL WAR AND CONFEDERACY

1365. Secession act at the start of the Civil War was the Ordinance of Secession, passed by the legislature of South Carolina on December 20, 1860, in reaction to the election on November 7 of the Republican presidential candidate, Abraham Lincoln. It declared that "the Union now subsisting between South Carolina and other states, under the name of the United States of America, is hereby dissolved."

1366. State to secede from the Union was South Carolina. On December 20, 1860, the state legislature passed the Ordinance of Secession, declaring: "We, the people of the State of South Carolina, in convention assembled, do declare and ordain, that the ordinance adopted by us in convention on the 23d day of May, in the year of our Lord 1788, whereby the Constitution of the United States was ratified, and also all acts and parts of the General Assembly of this State ratifying amendments of the said Constitution, are hereby repealed; and that the Union now subsisting between South Carolina and other States, under the name of the United States of America, is hereby dissolved." On December 24, the South Carolina delegation in Congress offered its resignation, but it was not accepted by the speaker of the House. A new state constitution was ratified on April 3, 1861, by a vote of 114–6. The secession of South Carolina was followed by those of Mississippi, Florida, Alabama, Georgia, Louisiana, Texas, Virginia, Arkansas, Tennessee, and North Carolina.

1367. Slave state to reject secession was Delaware, whose legislature voted on January 3, 1861, to remain in the Union. The vote was unanimous. Three other slave states declined to join the Confederacy and contributed troops to the Union side: Maryland, which was kept out by a federal purge of Confederate sympathizers in the state government; Kentucky, whose legislature voted to remain neutral; and Missouri, whose population was so divided that martial law had to be imposed. In addition, the people of the western region of Virginia, a slave state that left the Union on April 17, themselves seceded from their seceded state and organized a Union government, eventually to be admitted to the Union in 1863 as the state of West Virginia.

1368. Northern city to consider secession during the Civil War was New York City, whose mercantile and financial interests resented the interruption of business with the Southern states. On January 6, 1861, Mayor Fernando Wood wrote to the city's Common Council, suggesting that the citizens of New York City should withdraw from the Union and set themselves up as a free city, retaining the revenue that they formerly contributed to the state and federal governments. In this course, he said, the city "would have the whole and united support of the Southern States, as well as all the other States to whose interests and rights under the Constitution she has always been true." The mayor stopped short of advocating an armed rebellion to achieve his goal.

1369. Act inaugurating the Civil War took place on January 9, 1861, when a detachment of Confederate forces at Morris Island, in Charleston Harbor, Charleston, SC, fired upon the _Star of the West,_ a merchant steam vessel. The vessel had been chartered by the federal government to convey supplies and men to reinforce Major Robert Anderson at Fort Sumter, Charleston Harbor, although the announced destinations were Savannah, GA, and New Orleans, LA. It left New York harbor January 5, 1861, and was fired on within two miles of Forts Sumter and Moultrie. Its captain, John McGowan, retired from the scene after 17 shots had been fired at his ship. The first shot was fired by Cadet George E. Haynesworth of Sumter, SC, who was ordered to fire by Major P.F. Stevens.

1370. Capital of the Confederate States of America was Montgomery, AL, where a provision government was established in February 1861. The capital was moved in July to Richmond, VA, where it remained until the city was captured by the Union Army in 1865, after which the executive branch relocated in quick succession to Danville, VA, Greensboro, NC, and Charlotte, NC, where the cabinet had its last meeting.

1371. Session of the Confederate Congress took place in Montgomery, AL, from February 4, 1861, to March 16, 1861. Delegates from South Carolina, Mississippi, Florida, Alabama, Georgia, and Louisiana were present. The legislature's official title was Congress of the Confederate States. The president of the Senate was Alexander Hamilton Stephens of Georgia, the president pro tempore was Robert Mercer Taliaferro Hunter of Virginia, and the secretary of the Senate was James H. Nash of South Carolina. The House of Representatives under the permanent constitution convened on February 18, 1861, in Richmond, VA, where Emmet Dixon of Georgia was elected clerk and Thomas Salem Bocock of Virginia was elected speaker. The session adjourned on April 21, 1862.

1372. Confederate constitution was a provisional constitution, adopted on February 8, 1861, at Montgomery, AL, by the Congress of the Confederate States. It was superseded on March 11 by a permanent constitution, which was closely modeled on that of the United States of America. Slavery was given legal protection, as was the return of fugitive slaves to their owners, but the importation of slaves was prohibited, since this was a condition of good relations with France and Britain, on whose material support the Confederacy relied. The preamble states: "We, the people of the Confederate States, each State acting in its sovereign and independent character, in order to form a permanent federal government, establish justice, insure domestic tranquillity, and secure the blessings of liberty to ourselves and our posterity—invoking the favor and guidance of Almighty God—do ordain and establish this Constitution for the Confederate States of America." The first signature on the document was that of Howell Cobb, president of the Confederate Congress.

1373. Confederate cabinet was appointed on February 9, 1861, at Montgomery, AL. It consisted of Robert Toombs, secretary of state; Leroy P. Walker, secretary of war; Stephen R. Mallory, secretary of the Navy; Christopher G. Memminger, secretary of the treasury; Judah P. Benjamin, attorney general; and J.H. Reagan, postmaster general.

1374. President of the Confederacy was Jefferson Davis, born in Todd County, KY, on June 3, 1808. A Democrat from Mississippi, he was a graduate of the United States Military Academy at West Point and combined an intermittent career in the army with service in the House of Representatives (1845–46), the Senate (1847–51, 1857–61), and the cabinet of President Franklin Pierce, in which he was secretary of war. He resigned from the Senate when Mississippi seceded from the Union. Chosen to be provisional president by the Confederate Congress on February 9, 1861, he was inaugurated at Montgomery, AL, on February 18, and was inaugurated again at Richmond, VA, on February 22, 1862, after he was elected to a six-year term by popular vote. He served until the Confederacy was defeated in 1865.

1375. Vice president of the Confederacy was Alexander Hamilton Stephens of Georgia, former member of the U.S. House of Representatives, who was elected provisional vice president on February 9, 1861, at Montgomery, AL. He remained in the post until the collapse of the Confederacy in 1865. In 1866 he was elected to the U.S. Senate, but the senators refused to allow him to take his seat. From 1873 to 1882 he served in the U.S. House of Representatives, and in 1883, the year of his death, he became governor of Georgia.

1376. First Lady of the Confederacy was Varina Howell Davis, the second wife of Jefferson Davis. Born on May 7, 1826, at Natchez, MS, she was 19 years old and 18 years Davis's junior when they married in 1845. After Davis was inaugurated president of the Confederacy on February 18, 1861, she became known as the First Lady of the Confederacy. She was Davis's close advisor, serving as his personal secretary, and was at his side when he was captured on May 10, 1865, in Irwinville, GA. After his death she wrote a two-volume biography of him. She died on October 16, 1906.

CIVIL WAR AND CONFEDERACY—*continued*

1377. State to hold a public referendum on secession was Texas, which did so on February 23, 1861. The vote was 34,792 in favor of secession to 11,255 against it, thus ratifying the decision made by the state legislature on February 1. Other states to hold referenda were Virginia, on May 23, and Tennessee, on June 8. Both states had already formally seceded, and in both cases secession was favored by a large majority.

1378. Presidential call for volunteer troops to fight in the Civil War was made by Abraham Lincoln on April 15, 1861, two days after U.S. troops in Fort Sumter, SC, surrendered to Confederate forces after a 34-hour bombardment. He issued a call for "the Militia of the several States of the Union to the aggregate number of 75,000" to aid the federal government in its "effort to maintain the honor, the integrity, and existence, of our national Union, and the perpetuity of popular government, and to redress wrongs already long enough endured." The first task of these troops, he said, "will probably be to repossess the forts, places, and property which have been seized from the Union." At the same time, he called for the assistance of all loyal citizens, ordered rebellious citizens "to retire peacefully to their respective abodes," and summoned Congress to a special session to consider a course of action. Shortly before this call went out, the District of Columbia mustered ten companies of militiamen, who were put to work guarding government buildings from possible attack.

1379. Union troops to arrive in Washington, DC, entered the city at noon on April 25, 1861, eleven days after the fall of Fort Sumter and ten days after President Abraham Lincoln issued his call for volunteers. They were the members of the 7th New York Regiment, who were followed a few hours later by the 8th Massachusetts Regiment. The 6th Massachusetts had been on its way to Washington on April 19 when it was assaulted by a mob in Baltimore, MD. Southern sympathizers in Baltimore subsequently cut the rail and telegraph lines, leaving Washington isolated until these first Northern regiments marched in. During the next few weeks, the District of Columbia was turned into an armed camp, with tent cities, military hospitals, and a network of forts.

1380. Suspension of habeas corpus in wartime was authorized by President Abraham Lincoln for selected areas beginning on April 27, 1861. The suspension was extended by the federal government to the entire nation on September 24, 1862. Under the suspension, as many as 13,000 arrests were made without warrant. Lincoln's decree paved the way for other abridgements of individual rights during the World Wars.

1381. Major battle of the Civil War was the First Battle of Bull Run, fought on July 21, 1861, along a stream named Bull Run outside Manassas, VA, an important rail junction. About 37,000 Union soldiers led by General Irvin McDowell attempted to break through the 35,000-man Confederate line, which was under the leadship of General P. G. T. Beauregard. Arrival of Confederate reinforcements forced the retirement of McDowell's troops, resulting in the first important Confederate victory of the war.

1382. Federal law to emancipate slaves during the Civil War was the confiscation act passed on August 6, 1861, which gave immediate freedom to slaves whose owners had assigned them to work for the Confederate war effort. Further congressional action taken in 1862 abolished slavery in the District of Columbia (April 16) and in United States territories (June 19) and liberated the slaves of rebellious citizens (July 17).

1383. African-American to enlist in the United States armed forces during the Civil War was probably James Stone, who enlisted on August 23, 1861, in the 1st Fight Artillery of Ohio. He had escaped from slavery in Kentucky. African-Americans were not allowed to enlist in the Army until the following year, but Stone, who had fair skin, was accepted as white. He died in 1862.

1384. African-American unit organized during the Civil War was the 1st South Carolina Volunteers, who enlisted at Leavenworth, KS, on July 17, 1862, under Major General David Hunter. Other African-American regiments to enlist during 1862 were the 1st and 2nd Kansas Colored Volunteers and the 1st Louisiana Native Guards. The first African-American regiment raised among Northerners was the 54th Massachusetts Volunteers, organized on January 26, 1863. General Order 143 of the War Department, issued in May 1863, established the United States Colored Troops to oversee African-American regiments. African-American soldiers and their officers who were captured by the Confederates were likely to be executed, rather than taken prisoner.

1385. Military service by African-Americans to be authorized by Congress was authorized by an act introduced on July 16, 1862, by Senator Henry Wilson of Massachusetts and signed on July 17, 1862, by President Abraham Lincoln. It empowered the president to accept "persons of African descent, for the purpose of constructing intrenchments or performing camp competent."

1386. African-American unit to fight in the Civil War was the 1st Kansas Colored Volunteer Infantry, a regiment of escaped black slaves. They were recruited beginning in 1862 by Kansas senator James H. Lane, and first went into combat at the Battle of Island Mounds on October 28, 1862. In 1863, the 1st Kansas, led by a white officer, James M. Williams, fought alongside white Union troops at Cabin Creek in Indian Territory. The regiment was renamed the 79th U.S. Colored Infantry in December 1864 and was discharged at Fort Leavenworth in October 1865.

1387. Oaths of allegiance to the United States taken by civilians were administered to Southerners during and after the Civil War, before they were given full political rights. Abraham Lincoln penned what is perhaps the earliest in 1863. It began: "I, _____, do solemnly swear, in presence of Almighty God, that I will henceforth faithfully support, protect, and defend the Constitution of the United States and the union of the states thereunder; and that I will, in like manner, abide by and faithfully support all acts of Congress passed during the existing rebellion with reference to slaves . . . "

1388. Offer by a foreign power to mediate the Civil War was made on February 3, 1863, by the Emperor of the French, Napoléon III. William Henry Seward, the secretary of state, declined the offer, with the support of Congress. The following June, France sent an army to occupy Mexico City with the intention of establishing an empire there. France and Great Britain also intervened in the American conflict by selling naval vessels to the Confederacy until the fall of 1863, when they were dissuaded from continuing by the threat of war with the United States.

1389. Peace conference during the Civil War took place aboard a steamer, the *River Queen,* at Hampton Roads, VA, on February 3, 1865. Three commissioners representing the Confederacy—Alexander Hamilton Stephens, the Confederate vice president; John Archibald Campbell, the Confederate assistant secretary of war; and Confederate senator Robert Mercer Taliaferro Hunter—met with President Abraham Lincoln. The four-hour conference, held at Hampton Roads, VA, turned on the issue of whether the South had to accept Federal authority before an armistice could be arranged, as Lincoln insisted, or whether an armistice could take place without such an acknowledgement. No agreement was reached. The participants convened a second time on March 23, also aboard the *River Queen,* which had been rented to the federal government at a daily cost of $241.

1390. Capture of an American president by enemy troops took place on May 10, 1865, when Jefferson Davis, the president of the Confederacy, was arrested by Union cavalrymen near Irwinville, GA. With the Confederates defeated in battle, Davis was on his way from Richmond, VA, the Confederate capital, to the east coast of Florida in the hope of escaping by sea to Texas to establish a government in exile. He was taken by sea to Fort Monroe, VA, where he was imprisoned on charges of treason for two years before being released on bond. He was not brought to trial.

1391. Trial of a war criminal by the federal government was held in Washington, DC, from August 23 to November 4, 1865. The defendant was Captain Henry Wirz, superintendent of the Confederate prison at Andersonville, GA, who was accused of conspiring to torture, injure, and murder Union prisoners. He was tried under 13 separate specifications by a military commission presided over by General Lewis Wallace, U.S. Volunteers. Wirz was convicted and sentenced to death by hanging. He was executed on November 10, 1865, and buried in Mount Olivet Cemetery, Washington, DC.

1392. State readmitted to the Union after the Civil War was Tennessee, on July 24, 1866. A new constitution was adopted on January 9, 1865, and ratified on February 22.

1393. Drama about the Civil War was *Held by the Enemy,* written by William Gillette, which premiered in Brooklyn, NY, on February 22, 1886. Another play by Gillette, *Secret Service* (1895), also had a Civil War plot.

COLONIAL GOVERNMENT

1394. Spanish colonial settlement was attempted by Juan Ponce de Léon, who sailed from Puerto Rico on February 20, 1521, at the head of a 200-man expedition. Their settlement, thought to have been near Charlotte Harbor, FL, lasted only a few months before Native American attacks drove them away; Ponce de

COLONIAL GOVERNMENT—*continued*

Léon died of wounds he received there. Another failed colony was San Miguel de Guadalupe, founded in 1526 by Lucas Vazquez de Ayllón in North Carolina with 500 settlers who were quickly decimated by an epidemic of fever. The lack of success of additional colonizing efforts led King Philip II to ban them in 1561.

1395. French colonial settlement was founded in 1562 by a group of Huguenot (Protestant) settlers under Jean Ribaut, who sailed to Florida under the sponsorship of Admiral Gaspard de Coligny in the hope of finding a haven from religious persecution. Their settlement, at Port Royal, in what is now South Carolina, failed in 1564 for lack of supplies, but a second one was founded later that year at Fort Caroline. Its residents were massacred four years later by a Spanish army under Pedro Menéndez de Avilés.

1396. Permanent Spanish colonial settlement was established on September 8, 1565, when Pedro Menéndez de Avilés landed on the shore of the Matanzas River and founded St. Augustine, FL, now the oldest city in the United States.

1397. English colonial settlement was Fort Raleigh on Roanoke Island in North Carolina's Pamlico Sound, where Ralph Lane and a group of settlers arrived in August 1585. The colony failed, and in July 1587 a second party of 150 men and women under John White landed at Roanoke to reestablish it. White sailed back to England later that summer; when he returned in 1590 the Roanoke settlers had vanished without a trace, and their fort was in ruins.

1398. Letters written by an English colonial governor in America are claimed to be the four letters of Ralph Lane, the first governor of Raleigh's first colony at Roanoke Island, NC. The letters were written on August 12, 1585, from Porte Ferdynando. They were not published until 1860.

1399. Spanish governor-general of New Mexico was Juan de Oñate, the grandson-in-law of the conquistador Hernán Cortés. In 1595 Oñate received permission from the authorities of New Spain to establish and govern a colony in the north. His group of 400 settlers and soldiers crossed the Rio Grande in July 1598 and founded a colony at San Juan Pueblo, near present-day Espanola, NM. Failing to find gold in the area, he led sorties as far as central Kansas (1601) and the Gulf of California (1604) before resigning his governorship in 1607. He was exiled in 1614 after being convicted of cruelty, immorality, and false reporting.

1400. Colonial council was held in Jamestown, VA, on May 13, 1607. Its members were Bartholomew Gosnold, Edward Maria Wingfield, Christopher Newport, John Smith, John Ratcliffe, John Martin, and George Kendall. They had been selected for the council by King James I, who had placed their names in a sealed box that was not to be opened until the colonists sponsored by the London Company arrived in America. The council elected Wingfield as the first president.

1401. Permanent English settlement was established at Jamestown, VA, on May 13, 1607, with the arrival of the colonists who had been sent out by the London Company from Blackwell, England, on December 19, 1606. A total of 105 colonists arrived on the *Susan Constant,* 100 tons, under Captain Christopher Newport; the *Godspeed,* 40 tons, under Captain Bartholomew Gosnold; and the *Discovery,* 20 tons, under Captain John Ratcliffe.

1402. Rebellion in a British colony took place in December 1607 at Jamestown, VA. George Kendall, one of the original first councilors appointed in England, "was put off from being of the Council, and committed to prison; for that it did manyfestly appear he did practize to sew discord between the President and Council." He was condemned for mutiny and shot.

1403. Public building in the United States that has been continuously occupied is the Palace of the Governors in Santa Fe, NM. Built by Governor Pedro de Peralta in 1610, the Palace has variously housed the Spanish governors, a Pueblo tribal community, the territorial governments under Mexico and the United States, a federal post office, the Santa Fe Chamber of Commerce, the School of American Research and, since 1909, the Museum of New Mexico.

1404. Colony financed by a lottery was Jamestown, the first permanent English settlement in America, founded in what is now Virginia in 1607. Its sponsor, the Virginia Company of London, raised funds for the struggling colony by running lotteries in English towns, after receiving the crown's permission in 1612.

1405. Dutch colonial settlement was a trading post set up in 1614 at what is now Albany, NY, following the explorations of the Dutch explorer Henry Hudson in 1609. The Dutch West India Company established Fort Orange at Albany in 1624.

1406. Colonial law mandating Sabbath observance was promulgated in Virginia in 1610. It read: "Every man and woman shall repair in the morning to the divine service and sermons preached upon the Sabbath day, and in the afternoon to divine service, and catechising, upon pain for the first fault to lose their provision and the allowance for the whole week following; for the second, to lose the said allowance and also be whipt; and for the third to suffer death." The first such law to be enacted by a colonial legislature was passed by the Virginia House of Burgesses at its first session in 1619. The law provided that "all persons whatsoever upon the Sabbath days shall frequent divine service and sermons, both forenoon and afternoon." The Anglican Church was made the sole legal religion, and the creed of the church was the rule of the colony.

1407. Permanent Dutch colony was New Netherland, founded in what are now the states of New York and New Jersey by the Dutch West India Company, which received a charter from the States General of the Netherlands on June 3, 1621. The colony, stretching along the Hudson River from New York Bay to Albany, had its capital at New Amsterdam, on Manhattan Island. Lack of interest by Dutch people in emigrating to New Netherland forced the company to recruit volunteers from Belgium, France, Sweden, and other Western European countries. About 30 families, the majority Walloons from Belgium, arrived in the spring of 1624. Cornelis Jacobsen May, the first director, was replaced in 1625 by Willem Verhulst, who himself was quickly replaced by Peter Minuit.

1408. Town meeting of record took place in Dorchester, a town in Massachusetts Bay Colony, in 1633. Town meetings were eventually held throughout New England to settle disputes.

1409. Board of selectmen was formed in Charlestown, in the Massachusetts Bay Colony, in 1634.

1410. Colonial ban on clergymen in the legislature was observed in Maryland, which, from its settlement in 1634, excluded all ministers, preachers, and priests from serving in the Assembly.

1411. Colonial treason trial was held on May 7, 1634, when the Virginia Assembly heard complaints against Sir John Harvey, governor of Virginia. On April 28, 1635, he was removed from the governorship as a traitor and replaced by Captain John West. Harvey was returned to England, where his case was considered. On April 2, 1636, he returned to assume his post, which he held until November 1639.

1412. Sabbath laws published by a colony appeared in New Haven, CT, in 1638. They established Sunday as the day of rest and restricted various activities on that day in accordance with biblical teachings.

1413. Colonial ban on convicts holding public office was passed on March 2, 1642, by Virginia. It stated: "Be it also enacted that no person or persons whatsoever for any offence already committed or to be committed shall be hereafter adjudged to serve the collony."

1414. Confederation of English colonies was the United Colonies of New England, a union of the four colonies of Plymouth, Massachusetts, New Haven, and Connecticut. It was founded at Boston on May 19, 1643, to allow better communication between the colonial governments and better coordination of their efforts. Each colony agreed to send two commissioners, appointed by the general court, to an annual meeting, at which they would consult on declarations of war, relations with the Native Americans and foreign nations, capture of fugitives, and mutual disputes. The sessions became intermittent after 1664, and the confederation ceased in 1684.

1415. Statement of legislative independence by a colony was delivered in 1646 by the General Court of Massachusetts. Replying to criticism that its law code, the Body of Liberties (adopted in 1641), relied too heavily on Mosaic law rather than English law, the Court said, "Our allegiance binds us not to the laws of England any longer than while we live in England."

1416. Colonial statute establishing religious qualifications for public office was passed by the General Court of Massachusetts on October 18, 1654. Citing the necessity to ensure "the safety of the Commonwealth, the right administration of justice, the preservation of the peace, and purity of the churches of Christ therein, under God," the law stipulated that no man "shall be accepted as a deputy in the General Court, that is unsound in judgment concerning the main points of the Christian Religion as they have been held forth and acknowledged by the generality of the Protestant Orthodox writers, or that is scandalous in his conversation, or that is unfaithful to the government."

1417. Rebellion by colonists against an English governor took place in Delaware against Governor Francis Lovelace and was led by Marcus Jacobson, "The Long Finne," who claimed to be the son of the Swedish general Hans Christoph Konigsmark. He was trapped and turned over to the English commandant.

COLONIAL GOVERNMENT—*continued*

On December 20, 1669, he was condemned for insurrection in the first trial by jury in Delaware. He was lashed in public, branded with the letter *R,* and sold in chains as a slave in Barbados.

1418. Colonial statute establishing religious toleration in public office was passed in 1681 by West New Jersey. It stated that the province's freemen could not be "rendered incapable of office in respect of their faith and worship."

1419. Colony requiring rotation in public office was Pennsylvania. The colony's original Frame of Government, composed by William Penn and instituted on May 5, 1682, provided for the election of legislators to the Provincial Council for three-year terms. Once a member completed his term, he was rendered "uncapable of being Chosen again for one whole year following that so all may be fittest for the Government and have Experience of the Care and burthen of it."

1420. French governor of the Louisiana Territory was Antoine Le Moyne, sieur de Sauvolle, appointed in 1699 at Fort Maurepas (now Ocean Springs, MS), the first French settlement in the region.

1421. Maces as symbols of royal authority were used in the colonial legislatures, admiralty courts, and city governments of Britain's colonies. The use of a mace to represent the British monarch dates from the 14th century, when the king would send one of his weapons—his sword or his mace—to a session of the House of Commons if he was unable to attend in person. The oldest colonial American mace still in existence is a silver mace in the shape of an oar, crafted circa 1725 by Charles LeRoux, a New York City silversmith, for the Vice-Admiralty Court of the Province of New York. The mace, 22 inches long, displays an engraving of the royal coat of arms on the blade.

1422. Mason known to hold high government office in the colonies was Jonathan Belcher, a citizen of Boston, MA, who was made a Mason in England in 1704. Belcher, the first mason born in the New World, served as royal governor of the Colony of Massachusetts Bay from 1730 to 1741 and royal governor of New Jersey from 1746 to 1757.

1423. Colonial congress was the Albany Congress, which met at Albany, NY, from June 19 to July 11, 1754, to consider adopting a plan of union. Seven colonies attended, together with an Iroquois Confederacy delegation. Massachusetts Bay sent four representatives, New Hamp-

shire four, New York four, Pennsylvania four, Connecticut three, Maryland two, and Rhode Island two. The delegates approved the Albany Plan of Union, drafted by Benjamin Franklin, which would have united them under a grand legislative council and an executive officer, both subject to the British crown.

1424. Spanish governor of the Louisiana Territory was Antonio de Ulloa, appointed by King Charles III of Spain after the French surrendered control of the region to Spain in 1764 in order to keep it out of the hands of the British. Ulloa served from 1766 until 1768, when he was ordered to leave by the Superior Council. Spain ceded Louisiana back to France on October 1, 1800, under the secret Treaty of San Ildefonso, and France sold it to the United States on April 30, 1803, for $15 million.

1425. Spanish governor of California was Gaspar de Portolá, who served from 1767 to 1770 as the military governor of Las Californias, both Alta (upper) California, in what is now the United States, and Baja (lower) California, now part of Mexico. He spent much of his tenure on a long march of exploration, during which he founded the cities of Monterey and San Diego.

1426. Independent civil government in America was the Watauga Commonwealth, an independent civil government. By the treaty of Fort Stanwix in 1768, the Iroquois Confederacy agreed to surrender all the lands between the Ohio and Tennessee rivers to the British. Inasmuch as there was some misunderstanding because the Iroquois had ceded land to which they had no legal right, the settlers organized a civil government of their own in May 1772 and drew up the "Articles of the Watauga Association," the first written constitution ever adopted by a community of American-born freemen. The settlers elected a representative assembly of 13 men, which in turn elected a committee of five—John Sevier, James Robertson, Charles Robertson, Zachariah Isbell, and John Carter—who were vested with judicial and executive authority. This was the first free and independent community of settlers other than Native Americans to be established on the American continent. The area was in North Carolina and the mountains of Tennessee.

1427. Jewish person elected to a public office in the New World was Francis Salvador, a Jew of Sephardic descent, who on January 11, 1775, took his seat on the South Carolina Provincial Congress. Salvador was prominent in the defense of Charleston, SC, and in 1776 became the first American Jewish soldier to die in the Revolutionary War.

1428. Independent government in an American colony was formed in March 1776 in Charleston, SC. John Rutledge was elected president, Henry Laurens vice president, and William Henry Drayton chief justice. An army and navy were created, a privy council and an assembly were elected, and the issue of $600,000 of paper money was authorized, as well as the issue of coin.

1429. Russian colonial settlement was established on March 15, 1812, at Cazadero, 18 miles north of Bodega Bay on the Russian River in California. The party consisted of 95 Russians and 80 Aleut hunters from Sitka, AK, under the command of Ivan Alexandrovich Kuskof. They built Fort Rumiantzof, a compound of nine buildings surrounded by a twelve-foot spiked stockade, as well as 50 buildings outside the stockade. The fort was dedicated on September 11, 1812. On April 15, 1839, the Russians decided to abandon it, and it was sold to the German-American pioneer John Augustus Sutter for $30,000. The Russians evacuated the fort in December and sailed from San Francisco on January 1, 1842. The Spaniards called the settlement Fuerto de los Rusos, the Americans, Fort Ross. Sutter built a trading post there called Sutter's Mill, the site of the 1849 Gold Rush.

1430. Russian colonial governor of Alaska was Aleksandr Andreyevich Baranov of the Russian-American Fur Company, founded by Gregory Shelikhov, which was chartered in 1799 with a fur-trade monopoly in the region. Baranov founded Fort St. Michael (now Sitka) in July 1799.

1431. Governor of California under Mexican rule was Pablo Vicente Solá. He took office in 1815, when California was still ruled by Spain. Mexico won its independence from Spain in 1821, and Governor Solá made a formal act of affiliation with Mexico in April 1822. Later that year he was replaced by Luis Antonio Arguello, the first native-born Californian to serve as governor (1822–25).

1432. Government on the Pacific Coast was authorized by the people of Willamette Valley at Champoeg, OR, on May 2, 1843, when American and Canadian residents met in a field to consider the report of an organizational committee that had been appointed the previous month. A committee of nine was chosen on July 5, 1843, to devise a plan of civil government. The first governor was George Abernethy, who served from June 12, 1845, to March 3, 1849, when the United States took over jurisdiction of the Oregon territory.

COLONIAL GOVERNMENT—CHARTERS AND CONSTITUTIONS

1433. English colonial charter was granted by King James I of England in April 1606 to two groups of merchants who had formed joint stock companies and had petitioned the crown for a patent giving them settlement rights in America. The Virginia Company of London, also known as the London Company, was authorized by the charter to the land between latitude 34 degrees N and 41 degrees N. The Virginia Company of Plymouth, also known as the Plymouth Company, was authorized to settle the land between latitude 38 degrees N and 45 degrees N. The overlapping area was to constitute a buffer zone. The grant of land extended westward from the Atlantic coast for a distance of 100 miles. The following year, the companies sent out two groups of settlers, one to Jamestown, VA, and another to the Kennebec River in Maine.

1434. British colony whose charter guaranteed representative government was Maryland. The charter was issued by King Charles I on June 20, 1632, to Cecilius Calvert, the second Lord Baltimore, whose father, George Calvert, had applied to the king for a grant of land north of the Potomac River, having already tried in vain to establish a colony in Newfoundland called Avalon. Section VII of the charter gave Lord Baltimore "free, full, and absolute Power . . . to Ordain, Make, and Enact Laws, or what kind soever, according to their sound Discretions, whether relating to the Public State of the said Province, or the private Utility of Individuals, of and with the Advice, Assent, and Approbation of the Free-Men of the same Province, or of the greater Part of them, or of their Delegates or Deputies, whom We will shall be called together for the framing of Laws, when, and as often as Need shall require." The Maryland legislature, with Lord Baltimore's agreement, interpreted this clause as giving it the the power to initiate laws, as well as to approve them.

1435. Colonial constitution was the first constitution of Connecticut, known as the "Fundamental Orders." Written by Roger Ludlow, magistrate of Connecticut from 1639 to 1654, it was adopted on January 14, 1639, in Hartford, CT, by representatives of the towns of Wethersfield, Windsor, and Hartford. Ludlow was influenced by a sermon delivered on May 31, 1638, by the Reverend Thomas Hooker at Hartford's Center Church.

COLONIAL GOVERNMENT—CHARTERS
AND CONSTITUTIONS—*continued*

**1436. Colonial charter of religious freedom
for Christians** was the Act Concerning Religion (also known as the Act of Religious Toleration), passed in 1649 by the Colonial Assembly at St. Mary's (now St. Mary's City, DE), at the urging of Cecil Calvert, Lord Baltimore, who was a Catholic. The Act stipulated that no Trinitarian Christian "shall from henceforth be any waies troubled, molested, or discountenanced, for, or in respect of his or her religion nor in the free exercise thereof within this Province."

**1437. Colonial charter of religious freedom
for all faiths** was the royal charter issued by King Charles II in 1663 to Roger Williams's colony of Rhode Island. The charter guaranteed that "no person within the said colony, at any time hereafter shall be any wise molested, punished, disquieted, or called in question, for any differences in opinion in matters of religion, and do not actually disturb the civil peace of our said colony; but that all and every person and persons may, from time to time, and at all times hereafter, freely and fully have and enjoy his and their own judgments and consciences, in matters of religious concernments." The charter was in effect from July 8, 1663, until the state constitution, adopted in November 1842, became operative on the first Tuesday of May 1843.

**1438. Concealment of a colonial charter to
prevent its revocation** took place on November 1, 1687, at Hartford, CT. Sir Edmund Andros, sent to New England by King James II to reorganize the colonies as a single royal dominion and to impose religious and political restrictions on their inhabitants, came to Hartford to seize its charter, which had already been annulled by the king together with those of the other colonies. To prevent this, Captain Joseph Wadsworth is said to have concealed the charter in an oak tree, afterwards known as the Charter Oak. Andros nonetheless succeeded in taking over the government of Connecticut. He was arrested and deported in 1689, after Britain's Glorious Revolution ended the rule of King James.

**1439. Written constitution adopted by a
community of American-born freemen** is known as the "Articles of the Watauga Association." It was written in May 1772 by colonists from North Carolina and Tennessee who formed an independent civil government called the Watauga Commonwealth.

COLONIAL GOVERNMENT—COURTS

**1440. Colonial court to hear testimony from
an African-American** was a court session held in 1624 at Jamestown, VA, at which an African-American named John Phillip gave evidence against an English colonist.

1441. Grand jury convened on September 1, 1635, at New Towne (now Cambridge), MA, to investigate accusations against persons charged with crimes and indict them for trial before a petit jury if there was sufficient evidence. The magistrates received from the grand jury a list of 100 indictments.

**1442. Colonial trial for slander against the
government** took place in Virginia in 1640. Francis Willis, the Gloucester county clerk, was brought to trial for criticizing the local judges and the General Assembly. He lost both his job and his license to practice law, was fined £28, received a jail term, and was publicly humiliated by being forced to stand in front of the courthouse with a sign on his head.

1443. Jury composed of women was ordered by the General Provinciall Court at the session held on September 22, 1656, at Patuxent, MD. The jury was composed of seven married women and four single women who tried Judith Catchpole for the murder of her child. The order read: "Whereas Judith Catchpole being brought before the Court upon Suspicion of Murdering a Child which She is accused to have brought forth, and denying the fact or that She ever had Child, the Court hath ordered that a Jury of able women be Impannelled and to give in their Verdict to the best of their Judgment whether She the said Judith hath ever had a Child or not." The jury's verdict was "not guilty" and the court ordered that "the said Judith Catchpole be acquitted of that charge unless further evidence appear."

1444. Court martial in a colony was held on August 24, 1676, in Newport, RI, by Governor Walter Clarke, Deputy Governor John Crayton, and their assistants. Edmund Calverly was the attorney general. Quanpen, a Native American sachem also known as Sowagonish, was found guilty of participation in King Philip's War against the colonists and ordered shot on August 26. Others who had participated in the war were sentenced to various penalties.

1445. Judge to be impeached was Nicolas More, chief justice of colonial Philadelphia. He fell under such displeasure that the assembly on May 15, 1685, presented ten charges of impeachment against him to the council. Among other offenses he was charged with "assuming to himself an unlimited and arbitrary power in office." He was expelled on June 2, 1685, but the council refused to sanction the impeachment proceedings.

COLONIAL GOVERNMENT—ELECTIONS

1446. Voting requirements were enacted at Boston in 1631 during the second General Court of the Massachusetts Bay Colony. A law was passed declaring membership in a church as a requirement for both citizenship and suffrage.

1447. Election held in a colony took place on May 18, 1631, when John Winthrop was elected governor of Massachusetts. It is believed, however, that in 1619 the Virginia Assembly was selected by means of votes.

1448. Paper ballots were employed in the general election of 1635 by the Massachusetts Bay Colony.

1449. Colonial election held in defiance of the Royal Courts was held on April 11, 1640, in Wethersfield, CT, when Matthew Mitchell was elected recorder. The King's Court at Hartford refused to recognize the election and penalized Wethersfield £5 and the recorder 40 nobles. The fines were not paid.

1450. Contested election in a colonial legislature of record took place in Massachusetts in 1644. On May 30 of that year the House of Deputies took up a case from the town of Gloucester, whose freemen had elected a man named Steevens to represent them and then had withdrawn their support and substituted a man named Bruin. The General Court insisted that Steevens take his seat as a deputy.

1451. Colonial law to control corrupt election practices was passed on May 22, 1649, by the General Court in Warwick, RI. It provided that "no one should bring in any votes that he did not receive from the voters' own hands, and that all votes should be field by the Recorder in the presence of the Assembly." A committee of four freemen was authorized to determine violations of the law and "to examine parties and present to this court what they find in the case."

COLONIAL GOVERNMENT—GOVERNORS

1452. Virginia colonial governor was Edward Maria Wingfield, one of the recipients of the Virginia Company charter of 1606, who came to Jamestown with the first settlers in 1607 and was made president of the council on May 13. He was deposed in September, replaced by John Ratcliffe, and repatriated. The last of the company governors was Sir Francis Wyatt (1621–24), who became the first royal governor (1624–26) after the company was dissolved and who served again from 1639 to 1642.

1453. Governor of the colony of Virginia was Thomas West, Baron De La Warr, appointed governor and captain general of Virginia in 1610. De La Warr rebuilt Jamestown after it had been abandoned by the first colonists and served until his death in 1618. West also gave his name to the state of Delaware.

1454. New York colonial governor was Cornelis Jacobsen May, a sea captain and a director of the Dutch West India Company, who brought the first settlers to the Dutch colony of New Netherland in 1624. After the Dutch gave up control of the colony to the English in 1664, it was governed by Richard Nicolls (to 1668). Dutch rule was briefly restored in 1673–74.

1455. Governor of the Massachusetts Bay Colony was the Puritan leader John Winthrop, the principal shaper of the Bay Colony as a biblical community. A country squire in England, Winthrop lost a court post and much of his income during the anti-Puritan reign of Charles I and traveled to the newly chartered New England colony with the first large group of Puritan emigrants. Winthrop had arranged to be made governor before embarking for America, and after the colonists' arrival was formally elected on May 18, 1631. He served as governor in 1629–33, 1637–40, 1642–44, and 1646–49. The first governor of the Plymouth Colony was John Carver, who died shortly after his arrival in 1621 and was succeeded by William Bradford, Plymouth's leader for most of the years until 1656.

1456. Maryland colonial governor was Cecilius Calvert, the 2nd Lord Baltimore, who ruled the colony as Lord Proprietor from 1632 to 1675 through a series of proprietary governors, of whom the first was his younger brother, Leonard Calvert (1634–47). In 1692, after three years under the control of Puritan leaders, Maryland was made a royal colony and Sir Lionel Copley was appointed its first royal governor. The proprietary governors were restored in 1715.

COLONIAL GOVERNMENT—GOVERNORS—*continued*

1457. Delaware colonial governor was Peter Minuit, governor of New Sweden in 1638. Delaware shared colonial governors with Pennsylvania from 1638 to 1655, with New York from 1655 to 1682, and again with Pennsylvania from 1682 to 1776.

1458. Pennsylvania colonial governor was Peter Minuit, governor of the West India Company's colony of New Sweden in 1638. Pennsylvania shared governors with New York from 1655 to 1681, when William Markham became the colony's first provincial governor. At the same time, Pennsylvania also had proprietors, of whom the first was William Penn (1681–1718).

1459. Colonial governor of Connecticut was John Haynes, whose first term was 1639–40. He continued to serve one-year terms until 1654, rotating in office with Edward Hopkins and George Wyllys. From 1639 to 1664, when it merged with Connecticut, New Haven Colony was a separate political entity; its first governor was Theophilus Eaton, who served until 1658.

1460. Rhode Island colonial governor was Benedict Arnold, the great-grandfather of the Revolutionary War traitor of the same name, who administered the colony from 1657 as its first president. He had the title of governor in his subsequent terms (1663–66, 1669–72, and 1677–78).

1461. North Carolina colonial governor was William Drummond, who was appointed in October 1664 to be governor of the province of Albemarle (renamed North Carolina in 1691). Eight English noblemen had been granted proprietary rights to the area in 1663 by King Charles II.

1462. South Carolina colonial governor was William Sayle, proprietary governor of both Carolinas from 1669 to 1671. The first proprietary governor of South Carolina after it was separated from North Carolina in 1712 was Charles Craven (1712–16). In 1719 the proprietors were overthrown by the colonists and South Carolina became a royal colony, with James Moore as its first governor (1719–21).

1463. Colonial governor who was born in America was Josiah Winslow of Plymouth, MA. He was elected governor of New Plymouth Colony in 1673 and served until his death in 1680. In 1675–76 he led the United Colonies forces against the Wampanoags and their allies in the conflict known as King Philip's War. His parents, Edward and Susanna Winslow, were the first English colonists to be married in New England.

1464. New Jersey colonial governor was Edward Byllinge, who served as governor of West New Jersey from 1680 to 1685. East New Jersey was a part of Pennsylvania from 1682 to 1702, when the two Jerseys were united as a royal English colony. Its first governor was Edward Hyde, Viscount Cornbury, already the governor of New York, who took office in 1703.

1465. Colonial governor of Georgia under the Georgia Trustees was James Edward Oglethorpe, founder of the Georgia colony, who served from 1733 to 1743. In 1754, Georgia became a royal province under Governor John Reynolds, with a council and an elected house of commons.

1466. Governor of the republic of Vermont was Thomas Chittenden, a popular local farmer and statesman. He set up the seat of government at Arlington in 1778, after Vermont declared itself an independent republic, and served until 1789.

COLONIAL GOVERNMENT—LEGISLATURES

1467. Fines levied on colonial legislators for lateness or absence were imposed circa 1619 by the assembly of Virginia, which assessed a fine of one shilling from any member who did not take his seat at the beginning of the session, when prayers were read.

1468. Prayer offered at a session of a colonial legislature was read at the first one ever held, the meeting on July 30, 1619, at Jamestown, of Virginia's House of Burgesses. The session was opened with prayer by a Mr. Bucke. According to the official report, "Prayer being ended, to the intente that as we had begun at God Almighty, so we might proceed with awful and due respect towards his Lieutenant, our most gratious and dreade Soveraigne, all the Burgesses were intreatted to retyer themselves into the body of the Churche, which being done, before they were duly admitted, they were called to order and by name, and so every man (none staggering at it) tooke the oathe of Supremacy and then entred the Assembly."

1469. Representative assembly in colonial America was the House of Burgesses, which met in Jamestown, VA, on July 30, 1619, with John Pory as speaker. The location was the Old Church, a wooden structure 50 by 20 feet. The men sat with their hats on, following English custom. It was decided that the new governor, Sir George Yeardley, was to summon a "General Assembly" consisting of 22 members elected by the inhabitants, two from each borough, with every free man voting. The first laws enacted were prohibitions against idleness, drunkenness, and gambling.

1470. Colony to give its legislators immunity from arrest was Virginia, whose General Assembly enacted a law on March 5, 1623, barring the arrest of members of the House of Burgesses (the Assembly's lower house) during the legislative session and for one week before and after it. The intention was to prevent legislators from being arrested by creditors to whom they owed money, not to protect them from criminal arrest.

1471. Law code of an American colony was a set of laws established on October 4, 1636, by the General Court of the Plymouth Colony in Plymouth, MA. Among its provisions was a guarantee that the consent of the colony's freemen would be required for new legislation. Citizens were also guaranteed a jury trial. The code was published in 1671 as *The Book of the General Laws of the Inhabitants of the Jurisdiction of New-Plimouth.*

1472. Pay for colonial legislators was offered by Massachusetts. Expenses for food and lodging incurred by the representatives were originally recompensed by the colony, then by the towns from which they were elected. In March 1638, the General Court ordered "that every towne shall beare the charges of their owne magistrates & deputies, & to alow for a magistrate 3s. 6d. a day, & for a deputy 2s. 6d. a day, from the time of their going out to the Court until their returne, for their dyot & lodging."

1473. Colony with a bicameral legislature was Massachusetts Bay Colony. The legislature, known as the Great and General Court, had been established in 1630 by the Puritan leader John Winthrop. Originally it consisted of the governor and 18 assistants. In 1634, it was enlarged to include deputies chosen by the freemen of the various towns. In 1644, the General Court, having become embroiled in a public dispute over its handling of the case of a stray sow (*Shearman v. Keayne*), was divided into an upper house (the assistants) and a lower house (the deputies, two from each town).

1474. Smoking ban in a colonial legislature was imposed by the House of Deputies of Massachusetts Bay Colony on November 4, 1646. The penalty was a fine of sixpence for every pipe of tobacco smoked "within the roome where the Courte is sitting." The fine was doubled for second offenses.

1475. Colonial ban on lawyers in the legislature was passed in 1663 by the General Court of Massachusetts, which declared "that no person who is a usuall & common attorney in any inferiour Court shall be admitted to sitt as a deputy in this Court." At that time, the General Court served as an appeals court as well as a legislature. The exclusion of lawyers grew out of concern the General Court would not be an impartial judiciary if it had to decide a case in which one of its own members took a lawyer's role.

1476. Colonial legislature whose upper and lower houses had terms of differing lengths was that of Pennsylvania. Under William Penn's Charter of Liberties of 1682, the members of the lower house, the Assembly, were elected annually; those of the upper house, the Provincial Council, were elected for three-year terms. These terms were staggered, with a third of the seats coming up for election each year.

1477. Colonial legislature to use a mace as a symbol of authority was the Maryland House of Delegates (then called the Lower House of the General Assembly), whose speaker received a ceremonial mace on April 3, 1698, as a gift from Governor Francis Nicholson, to be delivered "to the person that should be appointed to attend this House, in the nature of a Sergeant att Armes, who by bearing the same, should have authority to take such persons and bring them before Mr. Speaker, as Mr. Speaker and the House should direct him." The mace is now lost, but Maryland's current mace, an ebony staff 2 feet long, may have been part of the original. On December 7, 1700, Nicholson, now governor of Virginia, presented a mace to that colony's House of Burgesses.

1478. Colony to change from a bicameral to a unicameral legislature was Pennsylvania, whose legislature was divided into a council and an assembly in the Frame of Government which it received from William Penn in 1682. The Charter of Liberties, which replaced the Frame of Government on November 8, 1701, placed all the legislative power with the assembly, relegating the council to an administrative and advisory role.

COLONIAL GOVERNMENT—LEGISLA-TURES—*continued*

1479. Colonial legislature's mace still extant is that of South Carolina, which was made in London, England, by a woman, Magdalen Feline, who belonged to the London goldsmiths' guild. It is scepter of solid silver, burnished with gold and topped by a miniature version of the English crown, and decorated with four panels showing the colony's seal, scenes of agriculture and trade, and a picture of a woman, the personification of South Carolina, curtsying to the king. It was purchased for 90 guineas by order of the Commons House of Assembly dated March 8, 1756.

CONGRESS

1480. Meeting place of Congress was Federal Hall in New York City, located on Wall Street, at the intersection with Broad Street. It had been built in 1699 as the city hall, and had since been used as a courthouse, prison, and provincial capitol. In 1788, after New York City was chosen to be the temporary home of Congress, the building was renovated for its use, with $32,000 of financing donated by wealthy New Yorkers (another $33,000 was later raised from taxes and a lottery). The architect was Pierre Charles L'Enfant, soon to be famous as the architect of Washington, DC. The renovations included the addition of a second-story balcony, where George Washington took the oath of office as president on April 30, 1789. Congress assembled there for the first time on March 4, 1789. The building reverted to its use as City Hall when Congress left for Philadelphia in 1780 and was torn down in 1812.

1481. Joint committee of the House and Senate was created on April 7, 1789, the day after the Senate, delayed by the lack of a quorum, was finally able to start business. The committee was charged with establishing a set of rules under which the two houses would work together.

1482. Joint rule of both houses of Congress was a rule that provided for creation of conference committees to resolve procedural differences between the House and the Senate. It was enacted on April 17, 1789.

1483. Contact between the president and the Congress took place on April 23, 1789, a week before George Washington was inaugurated as president. As Washington embarked from Elizabeth Town, NJ, to cross New York Harbor on the way to his future home in New York City, he was escorted by an eight-member joint congressional committee, including three senators and five representatives. A similar committee, composed of two senators and three representatives, greeted John Adams, the vice president-elect.

1484. Ceremony proposed for transmitting bills between houses of Congress was recommended in a report made by a House committee assigned to devise "a mode of communication to be observed between the Senate and the House of Representatives with respect to papers, bills, and messages." The committee proposed a ceremony in which the members of the receiving house would rise from their seats and receive "obeisances" made by the presenters from the other house. The Senate's version of the report allowed for a less complicated ceremony. The Senate's debate over the report on April 30, 1789, was interrupted by the arrival of the members of the House of Representatives to attend the inauguration of George Washington as president. Simpler rules were eventually adopted.

1485. Form of the enacting clause used in congressional bills was "Be it enacted by the Congress of the United States." The Senate, mindful of its dignity, required that this be changed to read "Be it enacted by the Senate and Representatives of the United States of America in Congress assembled." The debates over the proper wording of this clause took place in May 1789.

1486. Congressional act was "An Act to regulate the Time and Manner of administering certain Oaths," which was approved by President George Washington on June 1, 1789. The law formulated the language of the oath of office as follows: "I, A.B., do solemnly swear or affirm (as the case may be) that I will support the Constitution of the United States!" This oath was ordered to be administered to members of Congress, federal officers, and state lawmakers, executives, and judges.

1487. Party tactics in Congress were developed by the Federalists beginning with the first session of Congress, which lasted from March 4 to September 9, 1789. Congressmen with Federalist views were invited to caucus meetings in which matters of policy were discussed and bills were drafted, often under the tutelage of the secretary of the treasury, Alexander Hamilton. This practice, not envisioned in the Constitution, gave the executive branch considerable power in developing a legislative agenda and influencing its passage.

1488. Congressional act declared unconstitutional by the Supreme Court was Section 13 of the Judiciary Act of September 24, 1789, which authorized the Supreme Court to issue writs of mandamus (written orders on matters outside constitutional law) to American courts and public officials. On February 24, 1803, the Court, ruling in *Marbury v. Madison,* held that this statute extended the Supreme Court's powers beyond what was specified in the Constitution. No other act of Congress was found unconstitutional until 1857, when the Supreme Court, in *Dred Scott v. Sandford,* overturned the Missouri Compromise on the ground that the property rights of slaveowners were protected by the due process clause of the Fifth Amendment.

1489. Year in which the Federalist Party won control of both houses of Congress was 1790, in the elections for the Second Congress, when it took 16 seats in the Senate and 37 in the House, compared to 13 and 33 for the Democratic-Republicans. However, though the parties had not yet fully formed when the First Congress was elected in 1788, the members of Congress already subscribed to two competing philosophies, and of these two, the one that was to emerge in the Federalist Party enjoyed a majority in both the Senate (17 seats, to nine for the opposition) and the House (38 seats, to 26 for the opposition).

1490. Meeting place of Congress that is still in existence was Congress Hall, a two-story brick building at the corner of Sixth and Chestnut streets in Philadelphia, PA, near Independence Hall. In July 1790, Congress voted to move the seat of federal government from New York City to Philadelphia for a ten-year period while a permanent federal city was constructed. The Philadelphia County Commissioners offered Congress the use of their new courthouse, refitted the courtrooms for its use, and hired a local cabinetmaker, Thomas Affleck, to make chairs, writing desks, and other items of furniture. Congress began meeting there on December 6, 1790, the Senate occupying a courtroom on the second floor and the House a larger courtroom, which had a spectators' gallery, on the ground floor. When the House, reapportioned after the 1790 census, grew from 69 to 105 members in 1793, the building was enlarged to accomodate them. Congress continued to meet there until May 4, 1800, after which the hall became a courthouse again. It was restored in 1912–13 and again in 1962 and was incorporated into Independence National Historic Park in 1951.

1491. Congressional investigation was authorized on March 27, 1792, to uncover the facts behind the military defeat of November 4, 1791, when more than 600 federal troops and militiamen under the command of General Arthur St. Clair were killed in the Northwest Territory, near what is now Fort Wayne, IN, by a Native American army led by Chief Little Turtle (Michikinikwa), comprising men of the Chippewa, Miami, Shawnee, Ottawa, Delaware, and Potawatomi tribes. The House of Representatives, by a vote of 44–10, resolved "that a committee be appointed to inquire into the causes of the failure of the late expedition under Major General St. Clair; and that the said committee be empowered to call for such persons, papers and records as may be necessary to assist their inquires." The seven-member committee, which was headed by Thomas Fitzsimons, a Federalist of Pennsylvania, found that the Army camp had been inadequately guarded at night, but absolved St. Clair of responsibility and ruled that his defeat "can in no respect be imputed to his conduct either at any time before or during the action." St. Clair nonetheless resigned his army command, but retained his post as governor of the Northwest Territory.

1492. Year in which the Democratic-Republican Party controlled both houses of Congress was 1800, the year of Thomas Jefferson's election to the presidency. The party won 18 seats in the Senate and 69 seats in the House, compared to 14 and 36 for the Federalists. The Democratic-Republicans continued to control both houses of Congress until 1824, when the party began to break up into conflicting factions, eventually to evolve into the Democratic Party.

1493. Latino to serve in the House of Representatives was Joseph Marion Hernández, a Whig elected in 1822 as a delegate from the Territory of Florida. Born in St. Augustine, FL, in 1793, when Florida was still a Spanish colony, he served in the 17th Congress from September 30, 1822, to March 3, 1823. In 1837 Hernández commanded the expedition that captured the Seminole leader Oceola, and in 1845 he made an unsuccessful bid for the Senate as a Whig candidate

CONGRESS—*continued*

1494. Issue of *Register of Debates in Congress* was published by two brothers-in-law, Joseph Gales and W.W. Seaton, on December 6, 1824. Prior to that time, there was no consistent record of debates in the Senate except for the accounts that appeared in the main Washington newspaper, the *National Intelligencer*. The *Register* ceased operations in 1836. Transcriptions of debates continued to appear in the *Congressional Globe* until 1873, when an official publication, the *Congressional Record*, took over.

1495. Foreigner to address a joint meeting of Congress was a French nobleman, Marie-Joseph-Paul-Yves-Roch-Gilbert du Motier de Lafayette, the Marquis de Lafayette, who had volunteered to serve in the Continental Army during the Revolutionary War and, as a major general, had helped lead the attack on Yorktown that resulted in the American victory. In 1824–25, towards the end of a long career as a statesman in France, he paid a visit to the United States. He addressed the assembled senators and representatives in the House chamber on December 10, 1824, remarking: "Sir, I have been allowed, forty years ago, before a Committee of a Congress of thirteen states, to express the fond wishes of an American heart. On this day I have the honor, and enjoy the delight, to congratulate the Representatives of the Union, so vastly enlarged, on the realization of those wishes, even beyond every human expectation, and upon the almost infinite prospects we can with certainty anticipate."

1496. Year in which the Democratic Party controlled both houses of Congress was 1828, the year of Andrew Jackson's election to the presidency. In the Senate, the Democrats had 22 seats, the National Republicans 22. In the House, the Democrats had 139 seats, the National Republicans 74. The Democrats continued to maintain control of both houses until 1840, when they were eclipsed by the Whigs.

1497. Use of the term "lobbyist" took place circa 1830. Close by the House and Senate chambers in the Capitol are anterooms, known as lobbies, where legislators can have private meetings. The word "lobbyist" denotes a person who visits congressmen and senators for the purpose of persuading them to take a particular position on a particular issue.

1498. Congress in which 1,000 bills were introduced was the 22nd Congress, held from December 5, 1831, to July 16, 1832 (226 days) and December 3, 1832, to March 2, 1833 (91 days). Of the 976 bills and 24 joint resolutions introduced, 462 were passed, comprising 175 public acts, 16 public resolutions, 270 private acts, and 1 private resolution.

1499. Volume of *Debates and Proceedings in the Congress of the United States* was published in Washington, DC, in 1834 by Joseph Gales and W. W. Seaton. The *Debates and Proceedings*, better known as the *Annals of Congress*, contained the text of speeches given on the floor of the House, beginning with the First Congress in 1789 and continuing through the first session of the 18th Congress in 1824. Most of the texts were reprinted from transcriptions made by newspaper reporters. The final volume of the *Debates and Proceedings* appeared in 1856.

1500. Year in which the Whig Party controlled both houses of Congress was 1840, the year of William Henry Harrison's election to the presidency. In the Senate, the Whigs received 28 seats, the Democrats 22, with two seats held by neither. In the House, the Whigs received 133 seats, the Democrats 102, with eight seats held by neither. This was the only year in which the Whigs had a double majority.

1501. Congressional lobbyist who was a woman was Dorothea Lynde Dix, who in the 1840s and 1850s championed the care of the indigent insane. On June 23, 1848, she presented a petition to Congress for a grant of 5 million acres for "the relief and support of the indigent insane in the United States." By courtesy of Congress, a special alcove in the Capitol Library was set apart for her use, where she could converse with members.

1502. Clerical help for congressional committees was introduced in 1856, when Congress appropriated money to hire full-time clerks for the House Ways and Means Committee and the Senate Finance Committee. Committee chairmen had received funds for clerical help since the beginning of Congress.

1503. Federal law compelling the testimony of witnesses before the House and Senate was enacted in 1857, after a witness refused to answer questions put to him by a House investigating committee. The law declared that refusal to testify constitutes a misdemeanor "punishable by a fine of from one hundred to one thousand dollars and imprisonment in the common jail from one to two months."

1504. Congressional medal awarded to a physician was presented to Frederick Henry Rose of the British Navy. In April 1858, in Jamaica, yellow fever broke out on the U.S.S. *Susquehanna*. Rose offered his services and sailed to New York with the stricken crew. On May 11, 1858, Congress authorized a gold medal to be presented to him for his kindness and humanity to the officers and crew.

1505. Year in which the Republican Party controlled both houses of Congress was 1860, the year of Abraham Lincoln's election to the presidency. In the Senate, where the Republicans had their first majority, the ratio was 31 seats for the Republicans, 10 seats for the Democrats, and 25 vacant, mostly because they belonged to Southern states that had withdrawn from the Union. In the House, the Republicans had 105 seats, the Democrats 43, and there were 33 seats held by other parties (or vacant) and 56 seats vacated by secession. The Republicans maintained control of both houses until 1870, when the resurgent Democrats gained a majority in the House.

1506. Officer to preside over both of the branches of Congress was Schuyler Colfax of Indiana, who served as speaker of the House of Representatives in the 38th, 39th, and 40th Congresses (March 4, 1863–March 3, 1869), and who presided over the Senate as President Ulysses Simpson Grant's vice president (March 4, 1869–March 3, 1873).

1507. African-American allowed to enter the grounds of Congress was the Reverend Dr. Henry Highland Garnet, pastor of the 15th Street Presbyterian Church, Washington, DC, who gave a sermon to Congress on February 12, 1865, at the invitation of the chaplain of the House, the Reverend William Henry Channing.

1508. Congressional directory published by the federal government was authorized by act of February 14, 1865, and published in 1865 for the first session of the 39th Congress. It was compiled by Benjamin Perley Poore. In addition to a roster of congressmen, the 57-page directory contained information about Washington banks, insurance companies, hotels, express offices, churches, railroads, steamboats, and mail service.

1509. Congressional campaign committee was organized in 1866 by the Democrats in both houses of Congress to manage the party's upcoming election campaign and to provide Democratic congressional candidates with staffing and financial help. Beginning in 1882, the Democrats formed separate committees for the House and the Senate. This useful arrangement was eventually adopted by the Republicans as well.

1510. Voting machine was devised by Thomas Alva Edison, who was then a young freelance inventor living in New York City. In 1869 he took out a patent on the machine, the first patent of his career. A congressional committee witnessed a demonstration of its powers but declined to purchase it, and Edison went on to make his first fortune as the inventor of the Edison Universal Stock Printer.

1511. Issue of the *Congressional Record* covered the proceedings of December 1, 1873 (the first day of the first session of the 43rd Congress), and was published in Washington, DC, by the Government Printing Office. This was the first official record of congressional proceedings. The GPO continues to issue the *Congressional Record* daily.

1512. Congress to appropriate $1 billion was the 52nd Congress, which lasted from March 4, 1891, to March 3, 1893. It appropriated $507,376,398 in the first session for the fiscal year 1893 and $519,535,293 in the second session for the fiscal year 1894. The appropriations included funds for the postal service, payable from postal revenues, and estimated permanent annual appropriations, including sinking-fund requirements.

1513. Secretarial help for congressional representatives at public expense was authorized by Congress in 1893.

1514. Political cartoon entered in the *Congressional Record* was a drawing of an enormous cow standing with its hindquarters in New York and New England and its forelegs on the western side of the Mississippi River. Midwestern farmers stuff its mouth with alfalfa, corn, and wheat while a banker in a top hat milks the cow into a bucket labeled "Wall Street." The cartoon was drawn by Tom Fleming from an idea provided by Senator Benjamin Tillman of South Carolina, better known as "Pitchfork Ben." It was published in the *New York World* on March 1, 1896. Tillman entered it in the *Congressional Record* for October 3, 1913.

CONGRESS—*continued*

1515. Federal statute to be printed on paper rather than parchment was Public Law 66-190, issued on March 1, 1920.

1516. General Accounting Office was established by the Budget and Accounting Act of June 10, 1921, as the investigative and auditing arm of the Congress, charged with examining all matters relating to the receipt and disbursement of public funds. Its first chief was John Raymond McCarl, who served simultaneously as the first comptroller general of the United States.

1517. Congress to enact more than 1,000 laws was the 70th Congress, which met from March 4, 1927, to March 3, 1929. It enacted 1,722 acts, comprising 1,037 public acts, 108 public resolutions, 568 private acts, and 9 private resolutions.

1518. Physician to Congress was Dr. George Wehnes Calver, a retired rear admiral. He reported for duty at the Capitol in Washington, DC, on December 8, 1928, in response to a resolution of the 70th Congress, passed December 4, requesting the secretary of the Navy to detail a medical officer to be in attendance at the sessions of Congress. His title was "the attending physician."

1519. Convening of Congress under the 20th Amendment to the Constitution took place on January 3, 1934. Section 2 of the 20th Amendment reads: "The Congress shall assemble at least once in every year, and such meeting shall begin at noon on the 3d day of January, unless they shall by law appoint a different day." Before the amendment was adopted, the Constitution had required Congress to "assemble at least once in every Year, and such Meeting shall be on the first Monday in December, unless they shall by law appoint a different day."

1520. Two joint sessions of Congress held on one day took place on January 6, 1937. Congress met to count the electoral votes for the presidential election in which Franklin Delano Roosevelt was elected to his second term, and then met again in joint session to receive President Roosevelt's Annual Message.

1521. Law requiring registration of congressional lobbyists was the Federal Regulation of Lobbying Act of 1946. Under the act, professional lobbyists must register with the secretary of the Senate and the clerk of the House of Representatives and report their contributions and expenditures. The law also required similar financial disclosures from the groups that lobbyists represented.

1522. Professional staffers on congressional committees were hired after their use was authorized by Congress in the Legislative Reorganization Act of July 1946, following a recommendation by the Joint Committee on the Organization of Congress that committees be allowed to expedite their work by employing professional researchers, aides, and legislative assistants, in addition to clerical staff. Each standing committee was authorized to hire four professional staff members, with the exception of the House and Senate appropriations committees, which were entitled to hire more.

1523. "Daily Digest" of the Congressional Record was published on March 17, 1947. The digest, with brief entries describing each day's activity of the Congress, was intended to make the proceedings more accessible to the public.

1524. Congressional hearings to be nationally televised were the so-called Army-McCarthy Senate hearings of 1954. During the sensational 36-day proceedings, the Army defended itself against charges, brought by Wisconsin Republican Joseph Raymond McCarthy, that it had been infiltrated at the highest levels by communist subversives. Two crucial pieces of evidence were produced by Senator McCarthy: a photo of the Secretary of the Army having a private discussion with the head of the Communist Party of America, and a letter from FBI director J. Edgar Hoover confirming the existence of communist infiltrators in the Army. Both were shown by Army counsel Joseph Welch to be forgeries. Near the end of the hearings, Welch demanded to see the list of supposed subversives, and McCarthy countered by accusing one of Welch's former aides of being a communist. Welch's reply—"Until this moment Senator, I think I never really gauged your cruelty. Have you no sense of decency, sir, at long last? Have you left no sense of decency?"—earned applause from the Senate floor and marked the end of McCarthy's influence. On December 2, 1954, the Senate voted to condemn McCarthy, 67–22, for conduct "contrary to Senate traditions."

1525. Public disclosure of foreign travel expenditures by members of Congress was mandated in 1961, when federal legislators were required to publish in the *Congressional Record* the amount of federal money they had spent on visits to foreign countries. This requirement was lifted in 1973 and reinstated in 1976.

1526. Mandatory congressional 30-day summer recess began on August 6, 1971, when both houses adjourned under the 1970 Legislative Reorganization Act. While previous law provided for Congressional adjournment "not later than July 31 of each year," Congress rarely finished its work before October in election years or before December in off years. The Legislative Reorganization Act was passed to provide legislators with guaranteed vacation time.

1527. Congressional Budget Office as an independent agency was authorized on July 12, 1974, through the Congressional Budget Act of 1974. The CBO provides Congress with basic budget data and with analyses of alternative fiscal, budgetary, and programmatic policy issues. The first director was Georgianna Alice Mitchell Rivlin, who served from February 24, 1975, to January 3, 1979.

CONGRESS—HOUSE

1528. House of Representatives of the United States Congress was elected in 1788 by voters who, it is estimated, numbered between 75,000 and 125,000 (about 3 percent of the total population of free adult male citizens). A total of 65 representatives were elected, of whom 29 were from the Southern states (ten from Virginia, six from Maryland, five each from North and South Carolina, and three from Georgia), 19 from the Middle Atlantic states (eight from Pennsylvania, six from New York, four from New Jersey, and one from Delaware), and 17 from the New England states (eight from Massachusetts, five from Connecticut, three from New Hampshire, and one from Rhode Island). The majority—55 congressmen—belonged to the Federalist Party (then known more generally as the Administration Party); the remainder were Anti-Federalists (the Opposition Party). Virtually all of them had previous political experience, having served either in the Continental Congress, the Constitutional Convention, a state legislature, or more than one of these.

1529. Mace of the House of Representatives was probably similar in form to the current mace, which has a shaft of 13 ebony rods held together by crisscrossed bands of silver, at the head of which is a silver American eagle, with wings outspread, perched atop a silver globe. The original mace was made in New York, NY, in 1789 by an unknown silversmith (possibly Myer Myers, a Jewish craftsman who was the head of the Gold and Silver Smiths' Society). It was destroyed on August 24, 1814, when the Capitol was burned the British. A substitute made of carved pine was used until 1841, when the current mace, 46 inches tall, was ordered from William Adams, a New York silversmith, at a cost of $400. The choice of a mace to represent the authority of the legislature—a tradition inherited from the British colonial legislatures—was made by the first speaker of the House, Frederick Augustus Conrad Muhlenberg of Pennsylvania, who did so in fulfillment of the House resolution of April 14, 1789, requiring him to appoint a Sergeant at Arms and provide him with "a proper symbol of office." When the House is in session, the mace is carried into the House chamber by the Sergeant at Arms and is set upright on a marble pedestal near the Speaker's chair.

1530. Oath of office for members of Congress was the brief statement, "I do solemnly swear [or affirm] that I will support the Constitution of the United States." This oath was written in 1789 by the First Congress, meeting in New York City, in fulfillment of the Constitution's requirement that members of Congress "shall be bound by Oath or Affirmation to support this constitution." It was revised in the early days of the Civil War with the addition of the Ironclad Test Oath, a statement of past, present, and future loyalty that was intended to prevent subversion of the federal government. A perjury prosection awaited any federal civil servant or military officer who was discovered to have sworn falsely, and salaries were withheld from those who declined to swear. Congress made the Test Oath mandatory for its own members in 1864, and the Senate went so far as to require its members to sign a printed copy (as all suppliers of goods or services to the federal government had to do). After the war, Northerners continued to take the full Test Oath, but former Confederates were allowed to dispense with its troublesome first section and swear only to its second section, which read: "I do solemnly swear [or affirm] that I will support and defend the Constitution of the United States against all enemies, foreign and domestic; that I will bear true faith and allegiance to the same; that I take this obligation freely, without any mental reservation or purpose of evasion; and that I will well and faithfully discharge the duties of the office on which I am about to enter: So help me God." This has been the entire oath for all members of Congress since 1884.

1531. Object from the early House of Representatives still in use is a silver inkwell with three wells, which dates from circa 1789. During House sessions, it rests on the Speaker's desk.

CONGRESS—HOUSE—*continued*

1532. Entry in *Journal of the House of Representatives of the United States* was dated March 4, 1789. The *Journal* notes the matters considered by the House and the votes and other actions taken but does not record the actual debates. The first entry records that the House had difficulty gathering in New York City in time for the opening of the first session. "The House tact according to adjournment. Several other members, to wit: from Hew Hampshire, Nicholas Gilman; from Massachusetts, Benjamin Goodhue; from Connecticut, Roger Sherman and Jonathan Sturges: and from Pennsylvania, Henry Wynkoop; appeared and took their seats. But a quorum of the whole number not being present, The House adjourned until tomorrow morning eleven o'clock." Gales & Seaton published the first public edition of the *Journal* under Congressional contract in 1826.

1533. Session of the House of Representatives met in New York City on March 4, 1789. It was attended by four delegates from Massachusetts, three from Connecticut, four from Pennsylvania, one from Virginia, and one from South Carolina. Meetings were constantly called and adjourned for lack of a quorum.

1534. Clerk of the House of Representatives was chosen on April 1, 1789, when the First Congress, following the instructions of the Constitution (Article 1, Section 2), chose and installed two officers, the speaker of the House and the clerk of the House, whose role was modeled on that of the secretary of the Continental Congress. John James Beckley of Virginia was elected to the position of clerk. He served from April 1, 1789, to May 15, 1797, in the First through the Fifth Congresses, and from January 10, 1803, to October 26, 1807, in the Seventh through the Tenth Congresses.

1535. Quorum of the House of Representatives assembled in New York City on April 1, 1789. Thirty representatives were present. The first business transacted was the balloting for the office of speaker of the House (the winner was Frederick Augustus Conrad Muhlenberg of Pennsylvania).

1536. Committee of the House of Representatives was appointed on April 2, 1789, the day after a quorum of representatives had finally assembled at the first session of the House of Representatives in New York City. The committee, consisting of eleven members, was charged with preparing and reporting standing rules and orders of proceeding. Its report was delivered and accepted on April 7. Additional rules were adopted on April 13.

1537. Standing rules adopted by the House of Representatives were drawn up by an eleven-member committee headed by Elias Boudinot of New Jersey and were adopted by the House on April 7, 1789, during its first session, held in New York City. The first standing rule set forth the duties to be carried out by the speaker, the House's presiding officer. The second rule covered matters of decorum, debate, and voting. The third prescribed the procedure to be followed by congressional committees in preparing, reading, and reporting bills. The fourth provided for the operation of the House as the "committee of the whole" in proposing legislation and deliberating on its merits before referring the matter to a select committee for bill preparation, as well as in considering and amending proposed bills. The first amendments to these standing rules were made on June 9, 1789, and January 12, 1791.

1538. Select committee appointed by the House of Representatives was a committee charged with preparing a bill on the regulation of import duties. Its nine members were elected by ballot in New York City on April 11, 1789.

1539. House of Representatives election that was contested was the race between David Ramsay and William Loughton Smith of South Carolina. Smith took his seat on April 13, 1789. On April 15, 1789, Ramsay presented a petition that Smith be declared ineligible, on the ground that he had not been "seven years a citizen of the United States," as he had studied abroad during that period. The dispute was referred to April 18, 1789, to the Committee on Elections, which ruled that Smith was entitled to his seat.

1540. Standing committee of the House of Representatives that is still operating was the Committee of Elections, appointed in New York City on April 13, 1789, to determine the eligibility and rights of admission of those who had been elected. It was composed of seven members, who were elected by ballot.

1541. Chaplain of the House of Representatives was the Reverend William Linn, a Presbyterian minister, who was elected by ballot on May 1, 1789, and served in the First Congress from that day until December 10, 1790.

1542. Response by the House of Representatives to an inaugural address was drafted in 1789 by a committee of five representatives chaired by James Madison of Virginia. The response, which expressed the House's respect and congratulations, was unanimously approved by the House on May 5 and presented to President George Washington by the speaker of the House, Frederick Augustus Conrad Muhlenberg, on May 8. Washington had been inaugurated on April 30.

1543. Sergeant at Arms of the House of Representatives was Joseph Wheaton of Rhode Island, who was elected to the post on May 12, 1789, and continued to serve until October 27, 1807. A House resolution dated April 14, 1789, required the House to appoint an officer "whose duty it shall be to attend the House during its sitting, to execute the commands of the House from time to time, and all such process, issued by authority thereof, as shall be directed to him by the Speaker." Wheaton was a veteran of the Revolutionary War and went on to serve as colonel in the War of 1812.

1544. House Ways and Means Committee was created as a fiscal advisory committee during the first session of Congress. Its members, one from each of the states, were appointed on July 24, 1789. Less than two months later, the House dissolved the committee, preferring to receive its advice from Alexander Hamilton, the secretary of the treasury. The committee was reconstituted as a permanent standing committee in 1795.

1545. Year in which the Federalist Party won control of the House of Representatives was 1790, the first election in which the Federalists and the Democratic-Republicans were formally identified by that name. The Federalists received 37 seats, the Democratic-Republicans 33. The Federalists also won control of the Senate that year.

1546. Response by the House of Representatives to a president's State of the Union message was presented to President George Washington at his New York City residence on January 14, 1790, six days after he had delivered the message to a joint session of Congress. The House came in a body to make the presentation. The reply, which assured the president that the House would give its immediate attention to the issues he had raised, was drafted by a three-member committee.

1547. House of Representatives filibuster to delay legislative action occurred on June 11, 1790, when Elbridge Gerry of Massachusetts and William Loughton Smith of South Carolina made long speeches during consideration of the resolution to change the seat of government.

1548. Instance of congressional "log-rolling" (vote-trading) took place in 1790. Alexander Hamilton, the secretary of the treasury, was anxious to persuade Congress to adopt a proposal allowing the federal government to assume the debts of the individual states. Virginia led the southern states in opposition to this idea, arguing that assumption would produce a burdensome national debt, unduly increase the power of the federal government, and give commercial interests an unfair advantage. Congressmen from Virginia and Pennsylvania worked out a compromise by which the southern states agreed to drop their opposition to the plan if the northern states agreed to allow the seat of government to be located on the Potomac River, rather than in Philadelphia. The House voted on July 10, by a vote of 32 to 29, to accept the Potomac location and to move the federal government from New York City to Philadelphia for ten years while the permanent site was under construction. It passed the Assumption Act by a vote of 34 to 28 on July 26.

1549. Year in which the Democratic-Republican Party won control of the House of Representatives was 1792. It was the second election in which the Democratic-Republicans participated. They won 57 seats, the Federalists 48.

1550. Congressional apportionment of representatives under the Constitution was authorized by act of April 14, 1792, an "act for apportioning representatives among the several states according to the first enumeration." The first apportionment was made in 1793. It was based on the results of the first decennial census, the census of 1790, and provided for 106 representatives, one for every 33,000 of population. The first Congress, which met before this apportionment was made, had consisted of 65 representatives, one for every 30,000.

1551. Brawl in the House of Representatives took place in Philadelphia, PA, on January 30, 1798, when Matthew Lyon of Vermont had an argument with Roger Griswold of Connecticut and spat in Griswold's face. A resolution was introduced to expel Lyon. Lyon acted as his own attorney and defended himself in the proceedings, which lasted from January 30 to Feb-

CONGRESS—HOUSE—_continued_
ruary 12, 1798, and occupied practically all the attention of the House. The resolution was carried by a vote of 52 to 44, but because expulsion requires a two-thirds vote, Lyon was not expelled.

1552. Use of the mace of the House of Representatives to keep order took place on January 30, 1798, at Congress Hall, Philadelphia, PA. A fight broke out on the House floor between two representatives, Roger Griswold of Connecticut and Matthew Lyon of Vermont. The speaker of the House, Frederick Augustus Conrad Muhlenberg, directed Joseph Wheaton, the Sergeant at Arms, to display the mace to the combatants as a sign of his authority and as a warning that the dignity of the House must be restored. It has been used for this purpose numerous times since.

1553. Meeting place of the House of Representatives in Washington, DC, was a room in the north wing, the only part of the Capitol that was completed when the federal government moved from Philadelphia to Washington in 1800, and which it shared with the Senate, the Supreme Court, and the Library of Congress. The congressmen met here for the first time on November 17, 1800, the opening day of the second session of the Sixth Congress. The House moved in December 1802 into a brick building on the future site of the Capitol's south wing. In 1807 it moved to its newly completed chamber in the south wing, but this was destroyed with the rest of the Capitol on August 24, 1814, in the fire set by British troops, and the House had to meet in rented quarters until 1819, when its chamber in the rebuilt south wing was ready for occupancy. The House continued to meet in this chamber (now known as National Statuary Hall) until 1857.

1554. Hall of the House of Representatives in the Capitol was designed by Benjamin Henry Latrobe and constructed between 1803 and 1807. It was gutted in the fire set by the British in 1814. A second Hall, also designed by Latrobe in the Greek Revival style and constructed in the same space, was completed in 1819 and first occupied by the 16th Congress. Now popularly known as the Splendid Hall, it is no longer used for legislative business.

1555. Gerrymander was carried out on February 11, 1812, when Governor Elbridge Gerry of Massachusetts reluctantly signed a bill redrawing the state's congressional districts in a manner that gave most of them a majority of Democratic-Republican voters, squeezing out the Federalists. The practice of rearranging districts for political advantage was afterwards called by his name. A political cartoon by Elkanah Tisdale, "The Gerry-mander," published in the _Boston Gazette_ of March 26, 1812, showed the absurdly shaped map of the Essex County district as a bird of prey, with wings, claws, and a beaked head.

1556. Year in which the Democratic Party won control of the House of Representatives was 1828. Andrew Jackson's victory in the presidential race helped get 139 of his followers elected to the House, compared to 74 of the National Republicans, and gave the Democrats control of the Senate as well. Four years earlier, the Jacksonian faction of the Democratic-Republicans, though not yet known as Democrats, won 119 seats; their rivals in the Administration Party—another faction of the Democratic-Republicans—won 94.

1557. Year in which House seats were won by third parties was 1830, when 14 seats were taken by the Anti-Masonic Party and the Nullifiers. The majority of seats were held by the Democrats, with 141, and the rest by the National Republicans, with 58.

1558. Chaplain of the House of Representatives who was Catholic was Father Charles Constantine Pise, ordained in 1825, who served the 22nd Congress from March 4, 1831, to March 3, 1832.

1559. Gag rule in the House of Representatives was adopted on May 26, 1836, when the House voted 117 to 68 to ban any consideration of the contentious subject of slavery. The resolution read: "Whereas it is extremely important and desirable that the agitation of this subject should be finally arrested, for the purpose of restoring tranquility to the public mind, your committee respectfully recommend the adoption of the following additional resolution: Resolved that all petitions, memorials, resolutions, propositions, or papers, relating in any way, or to any extent whatever, to the subject of slavery, or the abolition of slavery, shall without being either printed or referred, be laid upon the table, and that no further action whatever shall be had thereon."

1560. Year in which the Whig Party won control of the House of Representatives was 1840, when 133 party members were voted into office along with the Whig presidential candidate, William Henry Harrison. The Democrats took 102 seats. The Whigs also received a majority in the Senate.

1561. Presidential commission whose creation was challenged by Congress was a commission appointed by President John Tyler to investigate the operations of the New York Customs House. On February 7, 1842, the House of Representatives passed a resolution requesting the president to explain the purpose of the commission, justify his authority to create it, and identify its source of funding. Tyler's reply, dated February 9, cited the Constitution's mandate to the president "to take care that the laws be faithfully executed."

1562. Congressional committee witness to be jailed for refusing to give testimony was John W. Simonton, who appeared before a House investigating committee in 1857. When he declined to answer questions, he was arrested by the Sergeant at Arms, charged with "contempt of the authority of this House," and ordered to be kept in custody until he changed his mind. He did so after nearly three weeks.

1563. Meeting of the House of Representatives in its present location took place on December 16, 1857, one week into the first session of the 35th Congress. The House moved out of its old quarters in the south part of the Capitol and occupied the chamber that had been built for it in the new south wing, which had been under construction since 1851. The old chamber was eventually renovated and reopened as National Statuary Hall.

1564. Year in which the Republican Party won control of the House of Representatives was 1854, in the elections for the 34th Congress. This was the first year in which the newly founded Republican Party offered candidates to the voters. They won 108 seats. The Democrats won 83, and the Know-Nothings took most of the remaining 46.

1565. Rabbi to open the House of Representatives with prayer was Rabbi Morris Jacob Raphall, rabbi of Congregation B'nai Jeshurun, New York City, who delivered the invocation on February 1, 1860, at the first session of the 36th Congress.

1566. African-American preacher to deliver a sermon in the House of Representatives was the Reverend Dr. Henry Highland Garnet, pastor of the 15th Street Presbyterian Church, Washington, DC. President Abraham Lincoln, with the unanimous consent of his Cabinet and the two congressional chaplains, arranged for the special Sunday morning service. The chaplain of the House, the Reverend William Henry Channing, extended an invitation to Dr. Garnet to preach a sermon commemorating the triumph of the Union Army and the deliverance of the country from chattel slavery. He delivered the sermon on Sunday, February 12, 1865, to a crowded chamber. He was also the first African-American allowed in the House, as previously African-Americans had been forbidden to enter the grounds.

1567. House majority leader was Sereno E. Payne, Republican of New York. The office was formally created in the 56th Congress, which met from March 4, 1899, through March 3, 1911.

1568. House majority whip was James A. Tawney, Republican of Minnesota. The office was formally created in the 56th Congress, which met from March 4, 1899, through March 3, 1911.

1569. House minority leader was James D. Richardson, Democrat of Tennessee. The office was formally created in the 56th Congress, which met from March 4, 1899, through March 3, 1911.

1570. House minority whip was Oscar W. Underwood, Democrat of Alabama, who was elected to that office in 1901.

1571. Political cartoonist elected to Congress was John M. Baer of North Dakota, who served two terms in the House of Representatives. Before his election in 1917, he drew cartoons for the North Dakota Nonpartisan League. One of his cartoons, drawn during his term in office, appeared in the *Washington Times* on January 7, 1918. It shows a huge barrel labeled "National Resources" with its contents pouring out of a hole in its side, unnoticed by an investigator wearing a Sherlock Holmes cap, who is examining the spigot with a magnifying glass. The heading reads "Learned Senators—This Picture is For You."

1572. Congressional standing committee headed by an African-American was the Committee on Expenditures in the Executive Departments, to which William Levi Dawson of Chicago, IL, was appointed on January 18, 1949.

1573. Vote in the House of Representatives to be tallied by machine took place on March 3, 1971, when 391 votes were cast on a motion to pass the Wright Patman amendment to delete an interest rate section in a proposed piece of debt-ceiling legislation. Representatives displayed a green card if they were in favor, a red card if they were against. The name of the voter appeared on each card. There were 180 green cards and 211 red.

CONGRESS—HOUSE—*continued*

1574. Vote in the House of Representatives to be recorded electronically took place on January 23, 1973, when 331 members recorded their presence at a quorum call. Forty-four voting stations were located throughout the House Chamber. Each member placed a personalized plastic identification card in one of the vote stations to vote yea, nay, or present. A large panel on the south wall of the room, above the Speaker's podium, displayed the names of all the representatives and indicated their presence by means of light signals. The recorder, which cost $1.1 million, was designed by Dr. Frank B. Ryan, director of the House Information Systems.

1575. Incumbent president to testify before a committee of Congress was Gerald Rudolph Ford, who succeeded to the presidency on August 9, 1974, following the resignation of Richard Milhous Nixon. Ford's presidential pardon of Nixon on September 9 generated immediate national outrage. He voluntarily appeared before the House Judiciary Committee on October 17, 1974, to affirm that no deal had been struck with Nixon and that he had granted the pardon to spare the nation a potentially long and divisive trial.

1576. Bilingual report of a congressional committee was the 215-page report of a hearing that took place on March 28, 1978, at Miami, FL. It was entitled *Needs of the Hispanic Elderly, hearing before the Select Committee on Aging, House of Representatives, Ninety-Fifth Congress, second session,* and was simultaneously printed in Spanish under the title *Las Necesidades de los Ancianos Hispanos.*

1577. Campaign finance law allowing members of the House to pocket leftover campaign funds was the Federal Election Campaign Act of 1971, as amended in 1979. Under a "grandfathering" clause of the 1979 rules, senior members who had been in the House from January 8, 1980, could take leftover campaign money and gifts with them when they left Congress—even if they later ran for election again. In 1989, a revised rule forced members eligible for the bonus to choose either to leave the House before the beginning of the 103rd Congress or to renounce the money. About $900,000 in cash, gifts, and services was "grandfathered" to departing representatives before the loophole was closed for good in 1993.

1578. Muslim to offer the invocation to the House of Representatives was Imam Siraj Wahhaj, who led the opening prayer for the first session of the House in January 1991.

1579. House of Representatives that included a substantial number of African-American women assembled in January 1993. It included nine African-American women: Maxine Waters of California; Eleanor Holmes Norton, the delegate from the District of Columbia; Carrie Meek of Florida; Eddie Bernice Johnson of Texas; Corrine Brown of Florida; Eva Clayton of North Carolina; Cynthia McKinney of Georgia; Barbara-Rose Collins of Michigan; and Cardiss Collins of Illinois.

1580. "Corrections Day" was July 25, 1995. On that day, the House of Representatives inaugurated a monthly procedure in which lawmakers "corrected" past regulatory "errors." The first such action was a vote to exempt the city of San Diego, CA, from a requirement under the Clean Water Act to purify sewage before releasing it into the Pacific Ocean. "Corrections Day" was given its name by House speaker Newt Gingrich.

1581. Midterm election since World War II in which the president's party gained seats in the House of Representatives was the election of November 3, 1998, during the presidency of William Jefferson Clinton, in which Democrats picked up five House seats, maintained their seats in the Senate, and won the coveted governorship of California. The last time the president's party showed a net gain in a midterm election was in 1934, under Franklin Delano Roosevelt. Typically, the president's party loses seats in Congress in the mid-terms, especially if it is the president's final term in office.

1582. Chaplain of the House of Representatives who was a Catholic priest was the Reverend Daniel Coughlin of Chicago, IL, sworn in on March 23, 2000, in the House chambers by Speaker J. Dennis Hastert, Republican of Illinois. Coughlin had been recommended by the archbishop of Chicago, Francis Cardinal George. The appointment followed months of accusations that the Republicans, who controlled the House, had displayed anti-Catholic bias in originally selecting the Reverend Charles Parker Wright, a Protestant minister, over a Catholic priest, the Reverend Timothy O'Brien, even after O'Brien had received the greatest number of votes from a bipartisan nominating committee.

CONGRESS—HOUSE—REPRESENTATIVES

1583. Congressional representative appointed to a presidential cabinet was James Madison of Virginia, who served in Congress from March 4, 1789, to March 3, 1797, and as Thomas Jefferson's secretary of state from May 2, 1801, to March 3, 1809.

1584. Congressional representative who was Catholic was Thomas FitzSimons of Pennsylvania, who was elected as a Federalist to the first three Congresses. He served from March 4, 1789, to March 3, 1795. Another Catholic, Charles Carroll of Maryland, also served in the First Congress.

1585. Congressional representative to die was Theodoric Bland of Virginia, who died on June 1, 1790, in New York City at the age of 48. He was buried in Trinity Churchyard, New York City. His body was reinterred in the Congregational Cemetery, Washington, DC, on August 31, 1828.

1586. Congressional representative who was Jewish was Israel Jacobs, who was elected by Pennsylvania to sit in the Second Congress. He served from March 4, 1791, to March 3, 1793. The next was Lewis Charles Levin, representative from Pennsylvania, who was elected as a candidate of the American Party and served from March 4, 1845, to March 3, 1851.

1587. Congressional representative to serve before his 25th birthday in contravention of the constitutional requirement was William Charles Coles Claiborne of Tennessee, a Jeffersonian Democrat, who served from March 4, 1797, to March 3, 1801. He was born in Sussex County, VA, in 1775.

1588. Duel between representatives in Congress was held on the famous Bladensburg, MD, dueling field in 1808, when George Washington Campbell of Tennessee shot Barent Gardenier of New York through the body. Gardenier had accused Congress of being under the influence of France, which Campbell denied, at the same time assailing Gardenier with a torrent of personal abuse. Gardenier challenged him to a duel, was wounded, and after his recovery returned to his attacks with more animosity than before. Campbell served in Congress from October 17, 1803, to March 3, 1809; Gardenier served from March 4, 1807, to March 3, 1811.

1589. Latino to serve in Congress was Joseph Marion Hernández, who was born in Florida to a Spanish family that owned a sugar plantation on Cuba. He served in 1822–23 as the Florida Territory's first delegate to the U.S. House of Representatives. He later became the presiding officer of the territorial house of representatives and a brigadier general in the Army in the wars against the Seminole Indians.

1590. Congressional representative to be refused a seat was John Bailey of Canton, MA, an Independent, who was elected in 1823. He was excluded on the ground that he was not a resident of the district he purported to represent. An election was held to fill the resulting vacancy, and Bailey ran and won again. He was seated on December 13, 1824, was reelected three times, and served to March 3, 1831.

1591. Congressman who was a Catholic priest was Father Gabriel Richard, 56, who served as a nonvoting delegate from the Michigan Territory from March 4, 1823, to March 3, 1825. He was ordained a priest in France on October 15, 1790, and served as a missionary in Detroit, MI.

1592. Brothers to serve as representatives in Congress simultaneously were the three Washburn brothers, each of whom represented a different state. Israel Washburn, Jr., of Maine, served two terms as a Whig and three terms as a Republican, from March 4, 1851, to January 1, 1861. Elihu Benjamin Washburne of Illinois, who spelled his name with a final *e,* served as a Whig from March 4, 1853, to March 6, 1869. Cadwallader Colden Washburn of Wisconsin served as a Republican from March 4, 1855, to March 3, 1861. The three brothers served simultaneously as congressmen from March 4, 1855, to January 1, 1861. Another brother, William Drew Washburn of Minnesota, served as a Republican from March 4, 1879, to March 3, 1885.

1593. Child of a president to serve in the House of Representatives (aside from John Quincy Adams, who was himself a president and who served in both the Senate and the House) was his son, Charles Francis Adams, who represented Congress in the House from March 4, 1859, to May 1, 1861.

1594. Congressional representative who was African-American was Joseph Hayne Rainey of Georgetown, SC, a Republican, who was sworn in on December 12, 1870, to fill the vacancy caused by the action of the House of Representatives in declaring the seat of Benjamin Franklin Whittemore vacant. Rainey served 10 years, until March 3, 1879.

CONGRESS— HOUSE— REPRESENTA-TIVES—*continued*

1595. Congressional representative to serve a single day was George Augustus Sheridan of Lake Providence, LA, elected as a Liberal on November 5, 1872, to the 43rd Congress, which ran from March 4, 1873, through March 3, 1875. He finally took his seat on March 3, 1875, the last day of the session, after an unsuccessful challenge by Pinckney Benton Stewart Pinchback.

1596. Congressional representative elected by prohibitionists was Kittel Halvorson, born in Telemarken, Norway, who was elected as the candidate of the Farmers' Alliance and the prohibitionists. He served as a representative from Minnesota from March 4, 1891, to March 3, 1893.

1597. Congressional representative who was a Socialist was Victor Louis Berger of Wisconsin, who served from March 4, 1911, to March 3, 1913, in the 62nd Congress as representative from Milwaukee. He was elected to the 66th and 67th congresses but was not permitted to take his seat. He was subsequently elected to the 68th, 69th, and 70th congresses and served from March 4, 1923, to March 3, 1929.

1598. Congressional representative to attend college after his term of service was George Arthur Bartlett, a Democrat from Nevada, who served from March 4, 1907, to March 3, 1911. On August 18, 1911, he enrolled as a freshman in the University of Nevada, Reno, NV. He had already been graduated from the law department of Georgetown University, Washington, DC.

1599. Woman elected to the House of Representatives was Jeannette Rankin, who was elected as a Republican from Montana and served from March 4, 1917, to March 4, 1919, and from January 3, 1941, to January 3, 1943.

1600. Congresswoman who was a mother was Winnifred Sprague Mason Huck, a Republican from Chicago, IL, who was elected on November 7, 1922, to fill the vacancy caused by the death of her father, William Ernest Mason, on June 16, 1921. She served from November 20, 1922, to March 3, 1923, in the 67th Congress.

1601. Congresswoman elected to serve in the place of her husband was Mae Ella Nolan of the Fifth District of California. A Republican, she filled the vacancy in the House of Representatives caused by the death of her husband, John Ignatius Nolan. She served from January 23, 1923, to March 3, 1925.

1602. Democratic congresswoman was Mary Teresa Hopkins Norton, who was elected to represent the district encompassing Jersey City, NJ, on November 4, 1924. She was also the first female representative of any eastern state. Norton was noted for introducing the first bill for the repeal of the 18th Amendment to the Constitution.

1603. Congresswoman to serve 18 terms was Edith Frances Nourse Rogers, a Republican representing the 5th District of Massachusetts, who served in the 69th through the 86th Congresses, from December 7, 1925, to September 10, 1960. Her husband, John Jacob Rogers, who died on March 28, 1925, served from March 4, 1913, to his death.

1604. Congressman from a northern state who was African-American was Oscar Stanton De Priest of Chicago, IL, a Republican, who served from March 4, 1929, to January 3, 1935. The first from the Democratic Party was Arthur Wergs Mitchell of Illinois, who served from January 3, 1935, to January 3, 1943.

1605. Woman to chair a House committee was Mary Teresa Hopkins Norton, Democrat of Jersey City, NJ, who became chair of the District of Columbia Affairs Committee on December 15, 1931, during her fourth term in office. This committee shared with its counterpart in the Senate the task of governing the city of Washington, DC. Norton served until June 22, 1937, when she became the chair of the House Committee on Labor.

1606. Congresswoman who was not sworn in was Elizabeth ("Bessie") Hawley Gasque, a Democrat, of Florence, SC, who was elected to the 75th Congress to fill the vacancy caused by the death of her husband, Allard Henry Gasque. She served from September 13, 1938, to January 3, 1939. She was not sworn in because Congress was not in session.

1607. Member of Congress to enter active duty in the military during World War II was Lyndon Baines Johnson, representative from Texas in the House of Representatives since April 10, 1937. On June 21, 1940, he was made a special duty officer in naval intelligence in the United States Naval Reserve. In December 1941, after the Japanese strike against Pearl Harbor, Johnson received the permission of the House of Representatives to take a leave of absence in order to enter active duty with the Naval Reserve. He served in the Pacific Theater as a pilot and was decorated for gallantry under fire.

1608. Congressional representative to vote twice against entry into war was Jeannette Rankin, Republican from Montana. She voted on April 6, 1917, against American entry into World War I, and on December 8, 1941, against American entry into World War II.

1609. African-American to head a major congressional committee was William L. Dawson, Democratic representative from Illinois. During his tenure in office (1943–70), he served as chairman of the Government Operations Committee.

1610. Congresswoman to visit a theater of war was Frances Payne Bolton, Republican of Ohio's 22nd Congressional District. In 1944 she traveled in England and France to study the care of American wounded in hospitals. The following year, she visited 20 European countries with a Congressional Foreign Affairs Committee subcommittee.

1611. Congresswoman who had been an actress was Helen Gahagan Douglas, Democrat of California, who served from January 3, 1945, to January 3, 1951.

1612. Congressional representative who received a Medal of Honor and was graduated from the U.S. Naval Academy was Willis Winter Bradley, Jr., who served as a representative from the 18th District of California from January 3, 1947, to January 3, 1949, in the 80th Congress. He was graduated from Annapolis on September 12, 1906, and served as lieutenant on the U.S.S. *Pittsburgh,* rescuing a sailor and extinguishing a fire in the explosives section on July 23, 1917.

1613. Congresswoman to advance to the Senate was Margaret Chase Smith of Skowhegan, ME, a Republican, who was elected on June 3, 1940, to the 76th Congress to fill the vacancy caused by the recent death of her husband, Representative Clyde Harold Smith. She was reelected to the four succeeding congresses, serving from June 3, 1940, to January 3, 1949. She was elected to the Senate for the term beginning January 3, 1949, and served until January 3, 1973. The first congresswoman from the Democratic Party to serve in both houses of Congress was Barbara Ann Mikulski of Baltimore, MD, who was elected to the House of Representatives in November 1976 and to the Senate in November 1986.

1614. Mother and son simultaneously elected to Congress were Ohio Republicans elected on November 4, 1952, to serve in the 83rd Congress. Frances Payne Bolton, 67, represented Ohio's 22nd District, and had served since February 27, 1940, when she was elected to fill the vacancy caused by the death of her husband, Chester Castle Bolton. Her son, Oliver Payne Bolton, 35, represented Ohio's 11th District.

1615. Congressional representative of Asian ancestry was Dalip Singh Saund, who was born to a Sikh family in the village of Chhajalwadi in northern India. On November 6, 1956, he ran in the contest for California's 29th Congressional District, winning 54,989 votes to 51,690 for Republican Jacqueline Cochran Odlum. He was the first democrat elected from the district.

1616. Congressional representative reelected after serving a prison term was Thomas Joseph Lane, a Democrat of Massachusetts, who was elected to the 77th Congress at a special election on December 30, 1941, and served eight terms before being convicted of income tax evasion and sentenced to four months in jail. He served his sentence in the Federal Correctional Institution, Danbury, CT, from May 7, 1956, to September 4, 1956. He was subsequently elected on November 6, 1956, to serve his ninth term.

1617. Congressional representative sworn in before eight o'clock in the morning was James Jarrell ("Jake") Pickle, a Democrat from Texas, elected December 17, 1963, at a special election to fill the vacancy caused by the resignation of Homer Thornberry. The December 24, 1963, session opened in the House of Representatives at 7:00 AM. for the discussion of the foreign aid bill. At 7:15 AM Pickle was sworn in as a member of the 88th Congress.

1618. African-American woman elected to the House of Representatives was Shirley Anita St. Hill Chisholm, a Democrat and an immigrant from Barbados, who was elected on November 5, 1968, from New York City's 12th District, in the Bedford-Stuyvesant section of Brooklyn. She was sworn in on January 3, 1969, and was reelected six times, leaving the House of Representatives in 1982.

1619. Roman Catholic priest to serve as a voting member of Congress was the Rev. Robert F. Drinan, S.J., a civil rights and antiwar activist. Drinan scored an upset win for the seat of the 4th Congressional District of Massachusetts in the midterm elections of November 1970, and was reelected four times. In

CONGRESS— HOUSE— REPRESENTA-TIVES—*continued*

1980, he announced that he would not seek a sixth term, citing Pope John Paul II's reaffirmation of a Church ruling that prohibited Roman Catholic clergymen from seeking public office. The Rev. Gabriel Richard, who represented the territory of Michigan in 1823, was the first nonvoting Catholic clergyman to serve as a delegate to the House.

1620. Congressional representative of Puerto Rican ancestry was Herman Badillo, a Democrat, who was born on August 21, 1929, in Caguas, Puerto Rico. He was elected on November 3, 1970, by the 21st district of New York. He served in the 92nd, 93rd, 94th, and 95th congresses and resigned on December 31, 1977.

1621. Congresswoman who was Jewish was Bella Savitsky Abzug, a Reform Democrat from the 19th Congressional District of New York. In the election of November 3, 1970, Abzug won handily with 47,128 votes to the 38,438 cast for her opponent, Republican-Liberal candidate Barry Farber. Abzug was an aggressive advocate for women's rights, abolition of the draft, and statehood for New York City.

1622. Congressional candidate elected while missing was Thomas Hale Boggs, Democrat of Louisiana and House majority leader, who was elected to his 15th term on November 7, 1972. He had been missing since October 16, when the small plane in which he was a passenger disappeared. He was declared dead, and his wife, Corinne Claiborne "Lindy" Boggs, was elected in his stead on March 20, 1973.

1623. African-American congresswoman from a Southern state was Barbara Charline Jordan, elected as a Democrat from the 18th District of Texas in 1972. She took office on January 3, 1973. Jordan, who held degrees in political science, history, and law, was the first African-American elected to Congress from Texas since Reconstruction. In 1966 she was the first African-American ever elected to the Texas state senate, where she served until her election to the House of Representatives.

1624. Congresswoman to give birth while holding office was Yvonne Braithwaite Burke, 41, Democrat of California, who gave birth to a daughter, Autumn Roxanne Burke, in Los Angeles, CA, on November 23, 1973. She had been elected to the 93rd Congress on November 7, 1972, and reelected to serve in the 94th

and 95th congresses. Previously, she was the first African-American woman to be elected to the General Assembly of California. Burke was also the first representative to be granted maternity leave by the speaker of the House.

1625. Congresswoman who was a grandmother was Millicent Hammond Fenwick, a Republican of New Jersey, who was elected to the 94th Congress on November 5, 1974, and was reelected to two subsequent terms. She was born on February 25, 1910. She had eight grandchildren.

1626. Congressional representatives to marry each other were Martha Elizabeth Keys, Democrat of Kansas, and Andrew Jacobs, Jr., Democrat of Indiana. Both were elected on November 5, 1974, to the 94th Congress. They were married on January 3, 1976, at Topeka, KS. He had first been elected on November 3, 1964, and had served in the 89th, 90th, 91st, and 92nd congresses; he was subsequently elected to the 95th and 96th Congresses. She was reelected to serve in the 95th Congress.

1627. Congressman to acknowledge that he was a homosexual was Barney Frank, elected in 1980 to be the Democratic representative from the 4th Congressional District of Massachusetts. In a May 1987 interview with the *Boston Globe,* Frank admitted that he was a homosexual, also remarking "I don't think my sex life is relevant to my job." Frank was reelected in 1988, 1992, and 1996.

1628. Latina elected to the House of Representatives was Ileana Ros-Lehtinen, Republican of Florida, who took her seat on August 29, 1989, representating the state's 18th District. Ros-Lehtinen was born in Havana, Cuba, and emigrated to the United States when she was seven years old. In 1982 she was elected to the Florida house of representatives, becoming the first woman of Hispanic descent elected to that state's legislature. She was elected to the state senate in 1986. In 1989 she was elected to the U.S. House of Representatives in a special election to fill the vacancy caused by the death of Claude D. Pepper. In the 104th Congress, she became the first Latina appointed to chair a subcommittee, the Africa Subcommittee.

1629. Congresswoman who was a former welfare mother was Lynn C. Woolsey, a Democrat from California elected in November 1992. In 1967, she went on family assistance after a divorce.

1630. African-American congressman to deliver the Republican Party's official response to the State of the Union message was Julius Caesar Watts, Jr., Republican from Oklahoma, who was elected in 1994 to the 104th Congress. On February 4, 1997, Watts gave the national response to President William Jefferson Clinton's State of the Union address. He had the prior distinction of being the first African-American politician to win a statewide election in Oklahoma when he ran successfully in 1990 for a seat on the Oklahoma Corporation Commission, a utilities commission.

CONGRESS—HOUSE—SPEAKERS

1631. Speaker of the House was chosen on April 1, 1789, the first day on which the House of Representatives had a quorum. Following the instructions of the Constitution (Article 1, Section 2), the members chose and installed two officers, the speaker of the House and the clerk of the House. Frederick Augustus Conrad Muhlenberg of Pennsylvania was elected speaker. He served as speaker in the First Congress from April 1, 1789, to October 23, 1791, and in the Third Congress from December 2, 1793, to December 6, 1795.

1632. Speaker of the House who was simultaneously member, parliamentarian, and leader was Henry Clay of Kentucky, who served as speaker at a time when that office was in the process of being redefined and expanded. A Jeffersonian Republican who later became a leader of the Whigs, Clay took his oath of office as a congressional representative on November 4, 1811, and was elected speaker on the same day. He was 34 years old. He continued to be elected speaker during his intermittent years of membership in the House—November 4, 1811, until his resignation on January 18, 1814; December 4, 1815, to October 28, 1820; and December 1, 1823, to March 3, 1825. He once remarked that it was the task of the speaker of the House to "remain cool and unshaken amidst all the storms of debate, carefully guarding the preservation of the permanent laws and rules of the House from being sacrificed to temporary passions, prejudices or interests."

1633. Speaker of the House who became president was James Knox Polk of Tennessee, who served as speaker from December 7, 1835, to March 3, 1839, in the 24th and 25th Congresses. From 1839 to 1841 he served as governor of Tennessee. He was elected president on the Democratic ticket on November 5, 1844, and took office on March 4, 1845.

1634. Speaker of the House to die in the Capitol was John Quincy Adams of Massachusetts, who suffered a stroke in the chamber of the House of Representatives on February 21, 1848, as he was delivering a forceful speech against the Treaty of Guadalupe Hidalgo at the end of the Mexican War. He was moved to the nearby Speaker's Room, where he died on February 23 at the age of 80. His funeral was held five days later at the Capitol, where he had served for five years (1803–08) as a senator and for 17 years (1831–48) as a congressman, and where he had been inaugurated in 1825 as the sixth president of the United States.

1635. Speaker of the House who became vice president was Schuyler Colfax of Indiana, who served as speaker during the 38th, 39th, and 40th Congresses, from December 7, 1863, through March 3, 1869. On March 4, 1869, he took office as vice president, having been elected on November 3, 1868, on the Republican ticket that was headed by Ulysses Simpson Grant.

1636. Speaker of the House of Representatives to serve longer than ten years was Samuel Taliaferro ("Sam") Rayburn of Texas, who became speaker of the House of the 76th Congress on September 16, 1940. Rayburn held that post until the 83rd Congress, which ended on January 3, 1953. His total time served as speaker, not including times when Congress was in recess, was ten years, three months, and 14 days. During the 80th Congress, from January 3 to December 19, 1947, Rayburn was minority leader. The previous record for length of service as speaker, held by Henry Clay, was eight years, four months, and eleven days.

1637. Speaker who was punished by the House was Georgia Republican Newton Leroy "Newt" Gingrich, the combative 50th speaker of the House, chosen on December 5, 1989. On January 21, 1997, the House formally reprimanded him and fined him $300,000 for using tax-exempt funds to promote Republican causes and lying about it to a House ethics committee. In 1989, Gingrich had engineered the downfall of his predecessor, Democratic speaker Jim Wright, after an ethics inquiry found financial irregularities in sales of a book written by Wright. Wright resigned before a verdict was reached.

CONGRESS—HOUSE—SPEAKERS—*continued*

1638. Former speaker of the House to become a television news commentator was Newt Gingrich, Republican of Georgia, who was hired in October 1999 by Fox News to provide political commentary for its news shows and to host programs on a variety of topics. Gingrich resigned as speaker of the House of Representatives in January 1999 after the Republican Party sustained losses in the 1998 congressional elections.

CONGRESS—PAGES

1639. Congressional pages were employed as errand-runners in the House in 1800 and in the Senate in 1829.

1640. Senate page was Grafton Hanson, the nine-year-old grandson of Sergeant at Arms Mountjoy Bayly. He was appointed on December 7, 1829, through the sponsorship of senators Daniel Webster and Henry Clay. Hanson later became Senate postmaster.

1641. School for congressional pages was the Capitol Page School in the Library of Congress, established following the passage of the Legislative Reorganization Act of 1946. It was a public school within the District of Columbia school system. Previously, boys had to arrange for private tutoring if they wished to continue their education while serving as pages.

1642. Senate page who was African-American was Lawrence Wallace Bradford, Jr., age 16, of New York City, who was appointed by Senator Jacob Javits of New York on April 13, 1965.

1643. House page who was African-American was Frank Mitchell, age 15, of Springfield, IL, who was appointed on August 14, 1965, by Representative Paul Findley, Republican of Illinois.

1644. House page who was female was appointed by Representative Carl Albert of Oklahoma in 1973. Thirteen-year-old Gene Cox, the daughter of Representative Edward Eugene Cox of Georgia, served on January 3, 1939, the first day of the 76th Congress, and received a check for $4 for her services.

1645. Senate pages who were female were Paulette Desell, who was sponsored by Democratic senator Jacob Javits of New York, and Ellen McConnell, sponsored by Republican senator Charles Percy of Illinois. Both began their duties on May 14, 1971.

1646. Sex scandals involving congressional pages were made public in 1983, when the House censured Daniel B. Crane, Republican from Illinois, for having sexual relations with a female page in 1980, and Gerry E. Studds, Democrat from Massachusetts, for having sexual relations with a male page in 1973. Both pages were 17 years old. In the wake of these disclosures, Congress established a residence hall for pages, who had previously lived on their own.

CONGRESS—SALARIES

1647. Law setting pay rates for Congress was passed by Congress in 1789. The House version of the bill called for congressmen and senators alike to be paid six dollars per day. Representative Thomas Sedgewick then offered an amendment that would have given representatives five dollars per day and senators six dollars. This was defeated, and the measure was passed to the Senate on August 10, 1789, by 30 votes to 16. The senators then voted themselves a pay raise to eight dollars, to become effective on March 4, 1795. A conference vote resulted in a compromise that allowed the senators to receive seven dollars as of March 4, 1795. The bill became law on September 22, 1789.

1648. Travel expenses for members of Congress were allowed in the appropriations bill of September 22, 1789. This bill included a mileage allowance of six dollars for every 20 miles between the member's home and the Congress (which was then meeting in New York City), to be paid at the beginning and end of each session. William Maclay, the acerbic senator from Pennsylvania, remarked in his journal that a fellow senator who represented Connecticut but resided in New York City nevertheless collected the mileage allowance for travel from his home state.

1649. Annual salary for members of Congress was enacted in 1816. Since 1789, senators and representatives had been paid by the day. The Compensation Act of 1816 set their pay at $1,500 per year, made retroactive for the previous year. This unpopular law resulted in the resignation of nine members and the replacement of many more in the next election, after which it was repealed. The permanent substitution of an annual salary for a per-diem payment was not made until August 18, 1856, when the salary was set at $3,000, made retroactive for the previous session. The law also authorized the secretary of the Senate to dock the pay of senators for unexcused absences, although this provision has never been invoked. The salary was increased to $5,000 in 1866.

1650. Increase in the travel expenses allowed to members of Congress was made in 1818, when the amount was raised from 30 cents per mile (or six dollars for every 20 miles) to 40 cents. It was reduced to 20 cents in 1866.

1651. Bonus paid to members of Congress by themselves was made possible by the last-minute passage of an appropriations bill on March 3, 1873, just before the end of the third and final session of the 42nd Congress. The bill contained a rider authorizing an annual salary of $7,500 for senators and representatives. Since the annual salary had, since 1866, been $5,000, the new salary represented a 50 percent raise, and since this raise retroactively covered the previous two years of the 42nd Congress, each member received a total bonus of $5,000. Public opinion denounced this arrangement as a "salary grab," and at the beginning of the next session it was repealed. About a third of the senators and about a fifth of the representatives returned their bonuses to the United States Treasury, and a few used their bonuses for charitable purposes.

1652. Salary cut for Congress was passed on January 20, 1874, when a pay raise from $5,000 to $7,500 adopted by the 42nd Congress in 1873 was reversed after intense public protest. Congress had to take a pay cut again during the Great Depression, when the Economy Act of June 30, 1932, dropped salaries from $10,000 to $9,000, and then to $8,500 in 1933.

1653. Comprehensive bill appropriating payments to legislative employees and clerks was passed by Congress in 1924. It allocated $200,490 for 120 House committee clerks and $270,100 for 141 Senate committee clerks.

1654. Congress whose members received a salary of $10,000 was the 69th Congress, which convened on March 4, 1925. The Legislative Appropriation Bill passed at the end of the 68th Congress included a rider raising the pay of senators and representatives from $7,500 to $10,000 yearly. Although President Calvin Coolidge had been actively discouraging government officials from receiving pay raises as an economy measure, he signed the bill into law so as not to delay the other appropriations it authorized.

1655. Year in which the salary of members of Congress exceeded $20,000 per year was 1955. The pay of senators and representatives was raised from $15,000 to $22,500 by a compensation bill that was signed into law by President Dwight David Eisenhower on March 2, 1955. The same act raised the annual pay of the vice president and the speaker of the House from $30,000 to $35,000; of the chief justice of the Supreme Court, from $25,500 to $35,000; of associate Supreme Court justices, from $25,000 to $35,000; of higher court judges, from $17,500 to $25,000; of lower court judges, from $15,000 to $22,500; of deputy attorney generals, from $17,500 to $21,000; and of the solicitor general, from $17,500 to $20,500.

1656. Salary review commission for elected officials was the Commission on Executive, Legislative, and Judicial Salaries, created by Congress in 1967 with the support of President Lyndon Baines Johnson. The commission's task was to review the salaries paid to Congress, high-ranking members of the executive branch, and federal judges, and make recommendations for change every four years. Three members of the nine-member commission were apponted by the president, two by the speaker of the House, two by the president of the Senate, and two by the chief justice of the Supreme Court.

CONGRESS—SENATE

1657. Method of electing senators was through voting by state legislatures, as codified in Article I of the Constitution. The delegates to the Constitutional Convention of 1787 also considered four other plans: appointment by the president; direct election by the people; selection by a panel of special electors; and selection by the House of Representatives. The 17th Amendment to the Constitution, proposed on May 16, 1912, and ratified on May 31, 1913, replaced the original method with direct election, whose sole advocate at the Convention had been James Wilson of Pennsylvania.

1658. Proposal that senators should serve for free without compensation of any kind was put forward by Charles Pinckney of South Carolina at the Constitutional Convention of 1787, held in Philadelphia, PA. Pickney declared: "As this branch was meant to represent the wealth of the country, it ought to be composed of persons of wealth; and if no allowance was to be made, the wealthy alone would undertake the service." Benjamin Franklin seconded the motion, but it was voted down by a narrow margin.

1659. Senate of the United States Congress met in New York City in April 1789, the senators having been elected in 1788 by their state legislatures, in accordance with the Constitution. There were 26 senators, two from each of the 13 states. Their average age was 48, the oldest being 62, the youngest 34. Eleven of them had graduated from college and twelve

CONGRESS—SENATE—*continued*

others had had some higher education. The majority were veterans of state legislatures and constitutional conventions. Nineteen had served in the Continental Congress or the Congress of the Confederation, seven had been officers in the Continental Army, and four had signed the Declaration of Independence. The senators were aligned into two general groups, one designated as the Administration Party, the other as the Opposition Party, with 17 senators belonging to the former and nine to the latter.

1660. Deadlocked senatorial election was the first election of senators by the state legislature of New York in the spring of 1789. Because the state senate was controlled by Federalists and the state assembly by their opponents, the parties could not agree on whether the senatorial election should be conducted by a joint ballot of both houses or by the senate alone.

1661. Senate journal was the *Journal of the First Session of the Senate of the United States. Begun and Held at the City of New York, March 4, 1789*, published in 1789 in New York City.

1662. Session of the Senate met in New York City on March 4, 1789. The only members present were Senators John Langdon and Paine Wingate of New Hampshire, William Samuel Johnson and Oliver Ellsworth of Connecticut, William Maclay and Robert Morris of Pennsylvania, Caleb Strong of Massachusetts, and William Few of Georgia. Various sessions were called but had to be adjourned because no quorum was present.

1663. Gavel used in the Senate was a small piece of solid ivory in the shape of an hourglass and without a handle, probably employed by the Senate from its earliest sessions in 1789. Although in deteriorating condition, the gavel remained in use until 1954, when Vice President Richard Nixon cracked it beyond repair while bringing a late-night debate to order. It was replaced by a new ivory gavel, modeled on the old, that was provided as a gift from the Government of India. Sir Sarvepalli Radhakrishnam, vice president (and later president) of India, presented it to Vice President Nixon on November 17, 1954. Both gavels are kept in a box on the presiding officer's desk.

1664. Quorum of the Senate assembled in New York City on April 6, 1789. The first business transacted was the election of a president pro tempore (the winner was John Langdon of New Hampshire).

1665. Senate president pro tempore was John Langdon of New Hampshire, who was elected on April 6, 1789, and who then presided over the counting of the electoral votes for president and vice president in the first presidential election. April 6 was the first occasion on which a Senate quorum assembled. The counting resulted in the election of George Washington as president and the runner-up, John Adams, as vice president. Since the Constitution provides that the vice president shall act as president of the Senate (and the president pro tempore only in his absence), Adams took over from Langdon on April 21, 1789.

1666. Senate doorkeeper was James Mathers, a Revolutionary War veteran who had served as sergeant at arms and doorkeeper to the Continental Congress. The creation of the post of doorkeeper—the first official post to be established by the Senate—and the appointment of Mathers were both made in New York City on April 7, 1789. Since the Senate met behind closed doors during its first six years, the doorkeeper was charged with making sure that only authorized persons were admitted to the chamber during deliberations. Mathers also performed the functions of a sergeant at arms for the Senate, though that post was not formally established until February 5, 1798.

1667. Method of choosing standing committees in the Senate was set forth in the original Rules of the Senate, adopted on April 16, 1789, which called for appointment by ballot, with a plurality of votes required for each appointment. In 1823 the power to appoint committees was given to the presiding officer of the Senate. John Caldwell Calhoun's abuse of this power (he packed committees with senators hostile to the administration of John Quincy Adams) prompted the Senate to rescind it in 1825. Various methods and combinations of methods have been used since then.

1668. Senate rules of procedure were adopted in New York City on April 16, 1789, at the first session of the Senate. A committee to draw up rules of procedure had been formed on April 8. The 20 adopted rules of procedure followed closely those drafted in 1776 by Thomas Jefferson to govern the behavior of members at the Continental Congress. The rules were revised in 1806, 1820, 1828, 1868, 1877, 1884, and 1979.

1669. President of the Senate was John Adams, whose election as vice president in 1789 made him simultaneously, according to the Constitution, the presiding officer of the Senate. On April 21, 1789, he was escorted by two senators to the Senate chamber at Federal Hall,

New York City, where he was greeted by John Langdon, the Senate's president pro tempore. He was not sworn in, however, until June 3, since Congress had not yet enacted a law prescribing the form of the oath to be taken by federal officials.

1670. Chaplain of the Senate was the Reverend Samuel Provoost, Episcopal Bishop of New York, who accepted the appointment on April 27, 1789.

1671. Response of the Senate to an inaugural address was initiated on the afternoon of April 30, 1789, as soon as the senators returned to Federal Hall after attending the inauguration of George Washington and the prayer service that followed. A three-member committee was appointed to compose an answer, which was submitted a week later. This draft was accepted after the removal of a sentence which seemed to imply that the United States had been engulfed in confusion before the president saved it. The final version, which assured the president that the Senate would cooperate with him "in every measure which might strengthen the Union," was read aloud to him at his residence by John Adams, the president of the Senate and the executive vice president, in the presence of the senators.

1672. Bill passed by the Senate was an act providing for the administration of oaths to federal officials, including members of Congress. It was passed on May 5, 1789.

1673. Entry in the *Journal of the Executive Proceedings of the Senate of the United States of America* contained the text of a message sent by President George Washington to the Senate and delivered in person by General Henry Knox, the secretary of war. It concerned treaties with "certain northern and northwestern Indians." The message read: "Gentlemen of the Senate: In pursuance of the order of the late Congress, treaties between the United States and several nations of Indians have been negotiated and signed. These treaties; with sundry papers respecting them, I now lay before you, for your consideration and advice, by the hands of General Knox, under whose official superintendence the business was transacted; and who will be ready to communicate to you any information on such points as may appear to require it. Go. WASHINGTON. New York, May 25th, 1789." The *Journal of the Executive Proceedings of the Senate of the United States of America* records the Senate's executive proceedings with regard to confirming presidential nominees and consenting to the making of treaties. The first public edition was published in 1828.

1674. Treaties reviewed by the Senate were several Native American treaties, delivered to the body on May 25, 1789, by War Secretary Henry Knox. These were accompanied by a message from President George Washington asking the Senate for its "consideration and advice." The treaties were approved on September 8, 1789.

1675. Senate's use of its constitutional power to advise and consent to appointments made by the president occurred on June 16, 1789, when the Senate received a letter from President George Washington nominating William Short of Georgia to become chargé d'affaires at the court of France during the temporary absence of Thomas Jefferson, the official minister to France. Although some members preferred a voice vote to a vote by secret ballot, the Senate opted for the ballot, chiefly out of concern that the nominee and the president would retaliate against senators who were known to have voted in the negative. The Senate passed a resolution to inform the President that "the Senate advise and consent to his appointment of William Short."

1676. Select committee appointed by the Senate was appointed on April 7, 1789, and instructed to "prepare rules for the government of the two Houses in cases of conference and take under consideration the manner of electing chaplains, and to confer thereon with a committee of the House of Representatives." It was later given the additional task of preparing procedural rules for the Senate.

1677. Standing committee of the Senate was an administrative committee, the Joint Standing Committee on Enrolled Bills, created on July 31, 1789, with three members. Eleven ongoing standing committees, each with five members, were created on December 10, 1816. Several of them still exist, including the Finance, Foreign Relations, and Judiciary committees.

1678. Year in which the Federalist Party won control of the Senate was 1790, when they also received a majority in the House. Federalists took 16 Senate seats, to 13 for the Democratic-Republicans.

1679. Birthday visit made to a president by the entire Senate was made on February 22, 1791, to President George Washington on the occasion of his fifty-ninth birthday. The Senate, led by Vice President John Adams, walked to Washington's residence in Philadelphia and paid their respects to the president.

CONGRESS—SENATE—*continued*

1680. Special session of the Senate was held on March 4, 1791, at the Senate Chamber, Philadelphia, PA. It was summoned by President George Washington to transact urgent business: the nomination of district supervisors, of military officers, and of the various officers necessary to put the federal government into operation in the newly admitted state of Vermont.

1681. Senate proceedings that were open to the public took place on February 20, 1794, when the Senate began debating the case of Abraham Alfonse Albert Gallatin, the Swiss-born senator from Pennsylvania, on the charge that he did not qualify for a seat in the Senate because, in contravention of the Constitution, he had not held American citizenship for nine years. (His election was declared void on February 28.) During its first five years, the Senate met in secret and did not publish the records of its proceedings. A motion that was passed on the first day of Gallatin's trial required that the Senate chamber "be provided with galleries which shall be permitted to be open every morning so long as the Senate shall be engaged in their legislative capacity, unless in such cases as may in the opinion of the Senate require secrecy." A gallery that could accommodate some 50 spectators was built within the Senate chamber at Philadelphia's Congress Hall. All Senate legislative sessions were opened to the public beginning in December 1795.

1682. Sergeant at arms of the Senate was James Mathers. A man named William Finnie had petitioned the Senate for appointment as "Serjeant at Arms" on April 22, 1789, but the Senate had declined to establish the position. Mathers had already been named to the post of doorkeeper on April 7. Over the next several years, he also, though unofficially, fulfilled the duties of a sergeant at arms, including keeping order, enforcing the Senate's rules, fetching absent senators to make up a quorum, and taking into custody people charged with contempt of the Senate. He was also required to arrange for firewood to heat the chamber. On February 5, 1798, Mathers's title was formally changed to doorkeeper and sergeant at arms. Unlike his counterpart in the House, he was not provided with a mace or any other symbol of authority.

1683. Use of sergeant at arms of the Senate to make an arrest took place in the spring of 1798, when James Mathers, the Senate's first sergeant at arms, was given a warrant for the arrest of William Blount, the former senator from Tennessee. Blount had been expelled from the Senate the previous December on suspicion of having conspired to help the British acquire parts of Louisiana and Florida. Mathers was instructed to go to Tennessee and escort him back to Philadelphia, PA, the seat of Congress, to face an impeachment trial. Blount's arrest was prevented, however, by the authorities in Tennessee, where he had meantime been elected to the state senate.

1684. Year in which the Democratic-Republican Party won control of the Senate was 1800, when the party's first president, Thomas Jefferson, was elected. The total was 18 for the Democratic-Republicans, 14 for the Federalists, who thus relinquished the control they had had since the Senate's first session (when they were known as the Administration party).

1685. Contempt citation issued by the Senate to a journalist was voted on March 27, 1800, against William Duane, editor of *The Aurora* of Philadelphia, PA. The Senate charged that Duane's paper contained "false, defamatory, scandalous and malicious assertions" about the Senate. The Senate did not enforce its citation, and Duane never retracted his comments.

1686. Meeting place of the Senate in Washington, DC, was the north wing of the Capitol, which was also the location of the House of Representatives, the Supreme Court, and the Library of Congress, since it was the only part of the Capitol that was ready for use when the federal government arrived in Washington, DC, from Philadelphia. The Senate met here for the first time on November 17, 1800, the opening day of the second session of the Sixth Congress. The north wing quickly deteriorated and had to be entirely rebuilt. The Senate occupied its new hall in 1810, but the Capitol was burned by the British on August 14, 1814, and the senators had to meet in rented quarters during its reconstruction. In 1819 they moved into their new chamber in the south wing, where the Senate remained until 1859.

1687. Senate quorum in Washington, DC, was assembled on November 21, 1800, four days after the Senate took up residence in its new quarters in the north wing of the Capitol.

1688. Guide to parliamentary rules of order was Thomas Jefferson's *A Manual of Parliamentary Practice, for the Use of the Senate of the United States,* a 199-page book, printed in 1801 by Samuel Harrison Smith in Washington, DC.

1689. Note-takers in the Senate were allowed on the chamber floor on January 5, 1802. The use of shorthand was introduced in 1848.

1690. Senate filibuster took place February 11–21, 1811, to disrupt the Senate's debate over the Bank of the United States. The filibuster was not continuous, as other business was transacted during the period. The bank's charter had been approved on February 25, 1791.

1691. Edition of the *Journal of the Senate of the United States of America* was published by Gales & Seaton in 1820 by order of the Senate. This official record of the minutes of floor action of the Senate was kept from the first session in New York City on March 4, 1789, in accordance with Article I, Section 5 of the Constitution, which provides that "Each House shall keep a journal of its proceedings, and from time to time publish the same, excepting such parts as may in their judgment require secrecy; and the yeas and nays of the members of either House, on any question, shall, at the desire of one-fifth of those present, be entered on the journal."

1692. President pro tempore of the Senate to appoint committee members was John Gaillard of South Carolina. In 1823, the Senate passed a resolution giving the power to appoint committees to the presiding officer, which, in the absence of the vice president, was the president pro tempore. Since Vice President Daniel Tompkins was almost always absent from the Senate, the opportunity to appoint was usually Gaillard's.

1693. President of the Senate to abdicate his power to keep order was John Caldwell Calhoun of South Carolina, vice president from 1825 to 1832. Unwilling to antagonize senators whose support he might need for a future presidential campaign, Calhoun routinely failed to call senators to order, even when they used abusive or insulting language.

1694. Funeral held at taxpayer expense was held in 1826 at the Congressional Cemetery in Washington, DC, for Senator John Gaillard of South Carolina.

1695. Year in which the Democratic Party won control of the Senate was 1828, in the election that brought Andrew Jackson to the presidency and gave his party a majority in both houses of Congress. The Democrats took 26 seats, to 22 for the National Republicans. In the previous election, the Jacksonian faction of the rapidly self-destructing Democratic-Republican Party had received a majority of 28 seats, the Administration faction 20 seats.

1696. Year in which Senate seats were won by a third party was 1830, when two seats were won by members of South Carolina's Nullification Party. Twenty-five seats were held by the Democrats, 21 by the National Republicans.

1697. Permanent Committee on Roads and Canals was established on January 18, 1830, marking Senate recognition of the rapidly expanding national system of transportation.

1698. Senate committee system empowering the majority party was organized on December 7, 1835. The system assigned the chairmanship of major Senate committees to whichever political party had the highest number of senators. That party was also entitled to control a majority of the seats on the committee. In 1846, the task of making committee assignments, which had previously been accomplished by Senate ballot, was given to the party caucuses.

1699. Year in which the Whig Party won control of the Senate was 1840. Twenty-eight seats were taken by the Whigs and 22 by the Democrats, with two other seats held by neither party. The Whigs also gained control of the House that year, assisted by the presidential victory of William Henry Harrison.

1700. Continuous Senate filibuster extended from February 18, 1841, to March 11, 1841. The topic was the dismissal of the printers of the Senate and the election of a public printer.

1701. Senate press gallery was in the crowded eastern gallery of the old Senate chambers. Official accommodations were first offered to journalists on July 8, 1841.

1702. Use of shorthand in the Senate to keep a record of its proceedings was introduced in 1848.

1703. Journalist arrested by the Senate was *New York Tribune* reporter John Nugent, arrested on March 26, 1848, under allegations that he illegally obtained for the paper the text of the Treaty of Guadalupe Hidalgo, which ended the Mexican-American War. Nugent was confined during the day in a room belonging to the Capitol's Committee on Territories but was allowed to eat and sleep at night at the home of the Senate sergeant at arms. He never revealed how he had received the treaty, and he was released on April 28.

1704. Beating in the Senate chamber took place on May 22, 1856, when Preston Brooks, a Democratic congressman from South Carolina, entered the Senate chamber and beat Masschusetts senator Charles Sumner with a cane. Brooks claimed that this was an act of re-

CONGRESS—SENATE—*continued*

venge for Sumner's verbal attacks on Brooks's relative, South Carolina senator Albert Butler. The question of disciplinary action was taken up in the House, where an investigating committee recommended that Brooks be expelled, but the resolution fell short of a majority vote. Brooks then resigned and was promptly reelected.

1705. Meeting of the Senate in its present location took place on January 4, 1859, one month after the beginning of the second session of the 35th Congress. The Senate moved out of its old quarters in the north part of the Capitol and occupied the chamber that had been built for it in the new north wing, which had been under construction since 1851 under the direction of Thomas Ustick Walter, the Architect of the Capitol. The old chamber was put to use as the home of the Supreme Court.

1706. Senate session in the new Senate Chamber took place on January 4, 1859. After bidding farewell to the old chamber, which was no longer spacious enough to accommodate the Senate, its visitors, and the public galleries, the senators were led by Vice President John Cabell Breckinridge down the hall to the new and much larger chamber that the Senate still occupies today.

1707. Senate committee witness to be jailed for refusing to give testimony was Thaddeus Hyatt, who was called in 1860 to testify before the Senate select committee charged with investigating the raid on the arsenal at Harpers Ferry, VA, by the militant abolitionist John Brown. Hyatt did not appear and the Sergeant at Arms was sent to arrest him. He remained more than three months in the District of Columbia jail, until the committee had been dissolved. Another recusant witness, Frank B. Sanborn, was also arrested, but was freed by the Supreme Court of Massachusetts because the arrest had been made by an unauthorized deputy, rather than by the Sergeant at Arms.

1708. Year in which the Republican Party won control of the Senate was 1860. The Republicans, successors to the Whigs, won 31 seats, the Democrats 10. Most of the 25 remaining seats were vacant because their states had seceded from the Union.

1709. Senator to address the Senate in military uniform was Edward Dickinson Baker, Republican of Oregon. On August 11, 1861, he was drilling his regiment at Meridian Hill when he was summoned to refute Senator John Cabell Breckinridge, Democrat of Kentucky, who was speaking against a proposal to send troops

against the South. Baker did not have time to change into civilian attire but removed his sword prior to delivering his speech. He was killed at the Battle of Balls Bluff, VA, on October 21, 1861, making him the only incumbent member in Senate history to have died in a military engagement.

1710. National procedures for electing senators were enacted into law on July 25, 1866. Previously, each state determined the procedures for electing its senators according to Section 4 of Article 1 of the Constitution: "The Times, Places and Manner of holding Elections for Senators and Representatives, shall be prescribed in each State by the Legislature thereof; but the Congress may at any time by Law make or alter such Regulations, except as to the Places of chusing Senators." Passage of the federal law was motivated by the case of New Jersey Democratic senator John Stockton, who was elected in November 1865 by a plurality rather than a majority of the state legislature. Stockton was eventually unseated.

1711. Senate appropriations committee was created on March 6, 1867, to relieve legislative committees from the task of appropriating as well as authorizing funds.

1712. Senate rules allowing the referral of nominations to appropriate committees were the revised rules of 1868. However, the practice of requiring nominees for high appointive office to appear before the relevant committee was not adopted until the mid-20th century.

1713. Woman to testify as a witness at a Senate hearing was Elizabeth Cady Stanton, who addressed the Senate District Committee on January 20, 1869, in a plea to save the women of the District of Columbia from being debarred from voting.

1714. Senate library independent of the Library of Congress was established on August 1, 1871. The first librarian was George S. Wagner.

1715. Abolition of the Senate franking privilege was enacted under an act of January 31, 1873. Abuse of the franking privilege, originally adopted by the first Congress of 1789 to enable legislators to communicate freely with their constituents, was believed to be widespread, with stories circulating of senators using the frank to send home their dirty laundry. The franking privilege was later restored.

1716. Arrangement of desks according to party began on March 5, 1877. Party members were allowed to move their desks so all could sit together on one side of the center aisle. Previously, desks were arranged so that an equal number was on each side of the aisle.

1717. Telephone in the Senate was installed on January 14, 1881, under an agreement to "cause a telephone to be placed at some convenient point, for the use of the Senate, in connection with the general telephone system of the city of Washington."

1718. Date on which the Senate was equally divided between Republicans and Democrats was September 20, 1881, when Vice President Chester Alan Arthur succeeded to the presidency following the assassination of President James A. Garfield. As presiding officer of the Senate, Arthur, a Republican, had been able to cast tie-breaking votes; his departure from the office left the Senate exactly balanced between the two parties.

1719. Secretarial help for senators at public expense was authorized by Congress in 1885. The act allowed each senator to receive six dollars a day out of the Senate's contingent fund as long as Congress was in session. This amount paid for one clerk per senator.

1720. Annual reading of George Washington's "Farewell Address" in the Senate as a custom began on February 22, 1888, to commemorate the president's birthday. The address was delivered as a letter to Congress but was never actually read by Washington in person. It was first published in David C. Claypoole's paper, the *American Daily Advertiser,* on September 19, 1796.

1721. Committee on Irrigation and Reclamation was established on December 16, 1891, to address the concerns of the western states and territories with regard to water rights, development, and conservation.

1722. Senate investigating committee was formed in May 1894 in response to published charges that senators had taken bribes to support tariffs favorable to the sugar industry. On August 16, 1894, the Senate ordered a comprehensive survey of all previous congressional investigations, later published as "Decisions and Precedents of the Senate and House of Representatives Relating to their Powers and Privileges Respecting their Members and Officers," a 1,000-page compilation.

1723. Fistfight in the Senate took place on February 28, 1902, between two South Carolina senators, Benjamin Tillman and John McLaurin. Tillman accused McLaurin of changing his position on a treaty for political gain. McLaurin called Tillman a liar, and a brawl ensued. The Senate later adopted a rule providing that "No Senator in debate shall, directly or indirectly, by any form of words impute to another Senator or to other Senators any conduct or motive unworthy or unbecoming a Senator."

1724. Senate permanent office building was the Richard B. Russell Senate Office Building in Washington, DC. Congress authorized purchase of land for the structure on April 28, 1904, and the building was opened in March 1909. Previously, the Senate had made use of temporary offices in the Maltby Building, but it was condemned as unsafe for occupation.

1725. Senate majority leader was Shelby M. Cullom, Republican of Illinois. The office was formally created in the 62nd Congress, which met from March 4, 1911, through March 3, 1913.

1726. Senate minority leader was Thomas S. Martin, Democrat of Virginia. The office was formally created in the 62nd Congress, which met from March 4, 1911, through March 3, 1913

1727. Democratic floor leader was John W. Kern, designated on March 5, 1913.

1728. Senate majority whip was James Hamilton Lewis, Democrat of Illinois. The office was formally created in the 63rd Congress, which met from March 4, 1913, through March 3, 1915. Lewis was appointed on May 28, 1913, by the Democratic Party to see that Democrats were present or paired at every roll call.

1729. Smoking ban in the Senate chambers began on March 9, 1914, following a lobbying campaign by Senator Benjamin Tillman of South Carolina. The ailing Tillman claimed that the smell of the smoke sickened him, forcing him to limit his time in the chamber. The Senate unanimously voted to end the practice of smoking in the Senate chamber and meeting rooms.

1730. Senate speech that lasted from sunset to sunrise was made by Reed Smoot of Utah, who spoke continuously for eleven hours and 25 minutes from dark to dawn on January 27–28, 1915, as part of a filibuster against the Ship-Purchase Bill.

CONGRESS—SENATE—continued

1731. Movies in the Senate chambers were taken on October 9, 1915. The footage, which showed the Senate being called to order, the chaplain's prayer, reading of the journal, and the introduction of several bills, was intended for use in a lecture on the workings of the U.S. government.

1732. Senate minority whip was James Wolcott Wadsworth, Jr., Republican of New York, who served for one week, from December 6 to December 13, 1915, and was then replaced by Charles Curtis, Republican of Kansas.

1733. Formal address by a president to the Senate in the Senate chamber took place on January 22, 1917, when President Woodrow Wilson addressed the upper house on his plans for devising a lasting "peace without victory" to end World War I, with the United States serving as the principal peacemaker. On April 6, after German U-boats began attacking U.S. shipping, the U.S. officially entered the war on the side of the Allies.

1734. Senate rule allowing the limitation of debate was the "cloture rule," enacted on March 8, 1917, as a way of countering filibusters. The rule allowed debate on any measure to be closed with a supermajority of two-thirds. Its first successful application took place on November 15, 1919, when, by a vote of 78 to 16, the Senate adopted a motion to place limits on the debate over the ratification of the Treaty of Versailles. This was intended to prevent the five senators who opposed the treaty from continuing the debate until the session expired.

1735. President who came before the Senate to discourage action on a bill was Warren Gamaliel Harding. On July 12, 1921, he addressed the senators on the subject of a piece of legislation that was currently under debate, the Soldiers' Bonus Bill, asking them to delay action on it. The senators did so, but Harding's temerity in presuming to interfere with the legislative branch was widely condemned. The purpose of the bill was to compensate veterans who received lower pay while in the service than did civilians working in war industries. A bonus bill that passed Congress in September 1922 was vetoed by President Harding. Another was passed over President Calvin Coolidge's veto in May 1923.

1736. Republican floor leader was Charles Curtis of Kansas, designated on March 5, 1925.

1737. Senate election in which neither candidate was seated after a recount was the election of November 2, 1926, in Pennsylvania. William Bauchop Wilson, a Democrat, was narrowly defeated by William Scott Vare, a Republican, who presented his credentials as senator-elect for the term beginning March 4, 1927. The Senate, on December 6, 1929, decided by a vote of 58–22 that Vare was not entitled to the seat. Governor John Stuchell Fisher appointed Joseph Ridgway Grundy, a Republican, to the vacant seat. Grundy served from December 11, 1929, to December 1, 1930.

1738. Senate leader to occupy the party floor leader's desk was Democratic leader Joseph T. Robinson of Arkansas. On December 5, 1927, he began the tradition in which the party floor leader occupies the center-aisle, front-row desk in the Senate chamber. The first Republican leader to occupy that seat for his party was Charles McNary of Oregon, in 1937.

1739. Radio broadcast from the Senate chamber in the Capitol building, Washington, DC, was made on March 4, 1929, in connection with the inauguration ceremonies of President Herbert Clark Hoover. The retiring vice president, Charles Gates Dawes, and the incoming vice president, Charles Curtis, were both heard.

1740. President who came before the Senate unannounced was President Herbert Clark Hoover, who appeared in the Senate Chamber on May 31, 1932, to urge the senators to cease procrastinating over what to do about the nation's economic crisis and focus their attention on crafting a relief bill. They took his advice.

1741. Senate parliamentarian was Charles Lee Watkins, who was formally appointed on July 1, 1937, although he had served as parliamentarian and journal clerk since July 1, 1935, and in other capacities in the Senate since July 16, 1914. He resigned on January 1, 1965, and was designated parliamentarian emeritus by Senate Resolution No. 4 on January 4, 1965.

1742. Woman to serve as presiding officer of the Senate was Hattie Ophelia Wyatt Caraway, a Democrat from Jonesboro, AR, who presided over the Senate chamber on October 19, 1943.

1743. Republican and Democratic policy committees in the Senate were funded by a supplemental appropriations act signed on August 8, 1946 by President Harry Truman. The seven-member staff of each committee was required to "assist in study, analysis, and research on problems involved in policy determinations." Fearing a challenge to the authority of his position, Speaker Sam Rayburn rejected provisions that would have created similar policy committees in the House.

1744. Senate solo filibuster to last for more than 24 hours was conducted by Senator James Strom Thurmond, Democrat of South Carolina, who spoke against civil rights legislation for 24 hours and 18 minutes on August 28–29, 1957.

1745. Senate election race in which both candidates were women was held on November 8, 1960, in Maine. Incumbent Margaret Chase Smith, Republican, defeated Lucia Marie Cormier, Democrat, by a vote of 255,890 to 159,809.

1746. Photograph of the Senate in session that was authorized was taken on September 24, 1963, by National Geographic Society photographers for the U.S. Capitol Historical Society, Washington, DC. It showed the Senate during the debate on the nuclear test ban treaty.

1747. Permanent Senate internal disciplinary committee was the Select Committee on Standards and Conduct, established on July 24, 1964, in the wake of the ethics investigation of senate aide Bobby Baker. The Select Committee on Standards and Conduct was superseded on February 11, 1977, by the permanent Select Committee on Ethics.

1748. Filibuster against a Supreme Court appointment was directed against Associate Justice Abe Fortas, a judicial liberal, who was nominated to replace retiring Chief Justice Earl Warren by President Lyndon Baines Johnson. On October 4, 1968, Senate conservatives mounted a filibuster to block approval of his appointment, and Fortas withdrew his name from consideration.

1749. Senate proceeding to be shown on television was the installation ceremony for Nelson Aldrich Rockefeller of New York, who was sworn in as the 41st vice president of the United States on December 19, 1974, in the Senate chamber, Washington, DC, immediately after being confirmed. He was selected by President Gerald Rudolph Ford on August 20, 1974, eleven days after Ford took office following the resignation of President Richard Milhous Nixon.

1750. Limitations on senatorial earnings from honoraria were imposed on January 1, 1975, as part of Congress's revision of the campaign finance laws. Previously, members of congress and other federal officials could earn an unlimited amount from giving speeches, making appearances, or writing articles. The new law limited payments for appearances or speeches to $1,000 each and set total per annum earnings from honoraria at $15,000. Members of the House were required to abide by similar rules starting in 1978.

1751. Senate committee meetings open to the public were held beginning on November 5, 1975. Previously, committee meetings were closed to the public and the media. Under the new rules, Senate meetings could still be closed if committee members voted to do so.

1752. Regular television coverage from the Senate chamber was instituted on June 2, 1986, by the cable channel C-SPAN-2. Electronic signals were fed by closed circuit to monitors outside the chamber and by cable and microwave to networks for national broadcast.

1753. Muslim to offer the invocation to the Senate was Imam Warith Deen Mohammed (the son of Elijah Muhammad and his successor as leader of the Nation of Islam), who led the opening prayer for the first session of the Senate in January 1992.

1754. Senate staff furlough began on November 14, 1995, and lasted six days. Staff were furloughed, a step never taken before, because of a stalemate between Republicans in Congress and President William Jefferson Clinton over approval of the federal budget. The deadlock prevented government employees from receiving their regular paychecks.

CONGRESS—SENATE—SENATORS

1755. Senators elected to office were William Maclay and Robert Morris, both of Pennsylvania, elected on September 30, 1788. Each served a single term, Maclay for two years and Morris for six years. Since no official records of the Senate's proceedings were kept, Maclay's private journal is the only source of day-to-day information about the Senate's early years.

1756. Senator appointed by a governor was John Walker of Virginia, who was appointed on March 31, 1790, by Governor Beverley Randolph. Walker was appointed to the Senate to fill the vacancy caused by the death of William Grayson. He produced his credentials, took his seat on April 26, and served until November 9, when James Monroe was elected to fill the unexpired term ending March 3, 1791.

CONGRESS—SENATE—SENATORS—continued

1757. Senate election that was contested was that of Abraham Alfonse Albert Gallatin of Pennsylvania, who was born in Switzerland and emigrated to the United States in 1780. He was elected to the Senate from Pennsylvania and presented his credentials on February 28, 1793. No action was taken during the Second Congress, which adjourned March 2, but on December 2 a petition was presented alleging that he had not been a citizen of the United States for the nine years required by the Constitution. The trial began on February 20, 1794, and on February 28 the Senate declared his election void. Gallatin was later elected to the House of Representatives, where he served from March 4, 1795, to March 3, 1801. Gallatin's trial was the first occasion on which members of the public were admitted to the Senate.

1758. Senators elected but not seated were William Blount and William Cocke of Tennessee, elected by the Tennessee legislature, who presented their credentials on May 9, 1796. They were refused seats because Tennessee was not admitted to the Union until June 1, 1796. They were elected again on August 2, 1796, and took their seats on December 6, 1796.

1759. Senator to be impeached was William Blount, Tennessee's first senator. He was elected on August 2, 1796, and took office on December 6. On July 8, 1797, he was expelled from the Senate, having been accused of entering into a conspiracy with British officers to divert part of Florida and Louisiana from Spain to Great Britain, "a high misdemeanor, entirely inconsistent with his public trust and duty as a Senator." The trial before the Senate, acting as the High Court of Impeachment, was held from December 17, 1798, to January 14, 1799, when the vice president announced that the charges were dismissed for want of jurisdiction, as Blount was at the time a private citizen and not a federal official. While the case was in progress in Washington, DC, Blount was elected to serve in the Tennessee state senate, and at the opening session in 1798 was chosen to be its speaker.

1760. Senator to take office despite being too young to serve was Henry Clay of Kentucky, who served from November 19, 1806, to March 3, 1807. He was born on April 12, 1777, in Hanover County, VA, and was 29 years 221 days old when he took office, although the Constitution states that "no person shall be a Senator who shall not have attained to the age of thirty years."

1761. Senator to be censured was Timothy Pickering, a Federalist of Massachusetts, and a former postmaster general, secretary of war, and secretary of state. On January 2, 1811, the Senate approved a motion to censure him, by a vote of 20 to 7. The motion stated that Pickering, who "read from his place certain documents confidentially communicated by the President of the United States to the Senate, the injunction of secrecy having been removed, has, in so doing, committed a violation of this body." He served in the Senate from March 4, 1803, to March 3, 1811, and in the House of Representatives from March 4, 1813, to March 3, 1817.

1762. Senator to be appointed as a treaty negotiator by a president, possibly in the hope that he would influence his fellow senators to favor the resulting treaty, was Senator James Asheton Bayard of Delaware. On April 7, 1813, President James Madison appointed Bayard to serve with John Quincy Adams and Albert Gallatin on a commission to negotiate a peace treaty with Great Britain during the War of 1812. Bayard resigned from the Senate after a charge of conflict of interest was raised in the press. The Treaty of Ghent was signed on December 24, 1814.

1763. Senator of Jewish descent was David Levy Yulee (born David Levy), a convert to Christianity. Yulee, a Democrat, served as Florida's territorial delegate to Congress in the early 1840s and was instrumental in persuading Congress to grant statehood to Florida. He was then elected to the Senate, serving from 1845 to 1851 and from 1855 to 1861.

1764. Father and son who were senators at the same session were Henry Dodge of Wisconsin and his son Augustus Caesar Dodge of Iowa, who sat together from December 7, 1848, to February 22, 1855, in the 30th to 33rd Congresses. Previously they had served as delegates to the House of Representatives in the 27th and 28th Congresses, from March 4, 1841, to March 3, 1845, prior to the statehood of their territories. Henry Dodge continued to serve in the Senate until March 3, 1857.

1765. Senator to serve three states was James Shields of Illinois, Minnesota, and Missouri. He was elected as a Democrat to serve Illinois in the 33rd Congress for the term commencing March 4, 1849. His election was declared void because he had not been a citizen for the requisite number of years. He was then reelected for the same term and served from October 27, 1849, to March 3, 1855. In the 35th Congress, he represented Minnesota, serving from May

12, 1858, to March 3, 1859. He was elected by Missouri on January 22, 1879, to fill the vacancy caused by the death of Lewis Vital Bogy, and served in the 44th Congress from January 27, 1879, to March 3, 1879.

1766. Senator who was returned to the Senate after being defeated for the presidency was Henry Clay of Kentucky, who served in the Senate in 1806–07 and 1810–11, spent many years in the House of Representatives and as secretary of state, served again in the Senate from 1831 to 1842, ran unsuccessfully for president as the candidate of the Whig Party in the election of November 5, 1844, and was returned to the Senate on March 4, 1849, serving until 1852.

1767. Senator to threaten another senator with a gun in the Senate chamber was Mississippi senator Henry Foote. On April 17, 1850, during a heated argument over the slavery issue, Missouri senator Thomas Hart Benton advanced threateningly on Foote, who drew a pistol. After a brief standoff, Foote gave up his weapon, and the two men were separated. Both senators received no other disciplinary action but a rebuke from a Senate select committee.

1768. Senator to serve as long-term head of a standing committee was William Allison, Republican of Iowa, who chaired the Appropriations Committee from 1881 to 1893 and again from 1896 to 1908, a total of 24 years

1769. Senator to serve for 30 years was Thomas Hart Benton, a Jacksonian Democrat who represented Missouri in the Senate from 1821 through 1851. He was eventually turned out of office by the state legislature because of his opposition to the idea of allowing slavery in newly organized territories. The voters, however, sent him to the House of Representatives from 1853 to 1855. He was the author of a memoir, *Thirty Years' View of the American Government.*

1770. Senator who was a practicing Jew was Judah Philip Benjamin of New Orleans, LA, who was elected to the Senate in 1852 and reelected in 1856. He resigned his seat in 1861, after Louisiana seceded from the Union, and was appointed attorney general of the Confederacy and then its secretary of war.

1771. Incumbent senator to win a vice presidential nomination was William Rufus de Vane King, an Alabama Democrat. On June 5, 1852, the Democratic National Convention, meeting in Baltimore, MD, selected King, at that time the second longest-serving member in Senate history, as the running mate of Franklin Pierce in the 1952 presidential election. King died shortly after taking the vice presidential oath of office, and never served in his capacity as Senate president.

1772. Senator to face allegations of corrupt election practices was Simon Cameron of Pennsylvania, who served in the Senate from 1845 to 1849, 1857 to 1861, and 1867 to 1877. Members of the state legislature of Pennsylvania complained in 1857 that Cameron had employed "corrupt and unlawful means" in his successful campaign for reelection. The case was referred to the Senate Judiciary Committee, which declined to take action.

1773. Senator removed from a committee chairmanship against his will was Stephen Arnold Douglas of Illinois. On December 9, 1858, allies of President James Buchanan in the Senate Democratic Caucus removed him as chairman of the Committee on Territories, owing to Douglas's persistent disagreements with Buchanan over the organization of the Kansas territory.

1774. Senator killed in a duel during his term in office was David Broderick, Democrat of California. When Broderick intemperately charged California chief justice David Terry with corruption, Terry resigned his office and challenged Broderick to a duel. The two met on September 16, 1859, and faced each other at ten paces. Broderick fired first, discharging his pistol into the ground. Terry, a dead shot, then put a bullet through Broderick's chest.

1775. Senator to draw a gun on the Senate sergeant at arms was Senator Willard Saulsbury of Delaware. On January 27, 1863, Saulsbury caused an uproar when he made a speech calling President Abraham Lincoln a "weak and imbecile man." The presiding Senate official, Vice President Hannibal Hamlin, ordered him to take his seat. Saulsbury refused, and Hamlin instructed the sergeant at arms to arrest him. Saulsbury drew a pistol and replied, "Let him do it at his expense." Saulsbury later apologized for his actions.

1776. African-American senator was Hiram Rhoades Revels, Republican of Natchez, MS, an ordained minister of the African Methodist Episcopal Church and a former Civil War chaplain, who was elected to the Senate on January 20, 1870, by the legislature of Mississippi for

CONGRESS—SENATE—SENATORS—*continued*

the unexpired term beginning March 4, 1865, and ending March 3, 1871. He was sworn in on February 25, 1870. After his Senate service he became president of Alcorn Agriculture and Mechanical College in Lorman, MS.

1777. Senator to resign in a case of a fraudulent election was Alexander Caldwell of Arkansas. An investigation by the Senate Judiciary Committee found evidence that his election in 1872 was tainted. In 1873, while the Senate was debating a resolution to declare his election invalid, he resigned.

1778. African-American senator to serve a full term was Blanche Kelso Bruce, a former Virginia slave who became a wealthy planter and politician in Mississippi after the Civil War. He served in the U.S. Senate from March 4, 1875, to March 3, 1881. After his term, he became the register of the U.S. treasury and recorder of deeds for Washington, DC.

1779. Senator of Native American descent was Charles Curtis of Kansas, who served from January 23, 1907, to March 3, 1913, and from March 4, 1915, to March 3, 1929, when he resigned to assume the vice presidency under President Herbert Clark Hoover. His mother was descended from the Kansa-Kaw chief White Plume, and he lived with the Kaw tribe as a child.

1780. Senator who was the victim of an assassination attempt during a filibuster was probably Robert Marion La Follette of Wisconsin, a man with many political enemies. On May 29, 1908, he was conducting a filibuster against the Aldrich-Vreeland Bill, periodically drinking an eggnog from the Senate restaurant to keep him going. Suddenly he felt deathly ill and exclaimed, "Take it away—it's drugged!" Nonetheless, La Follette kept up the filibuster for 18 hours and 30 minutes, a record. Subsequent analysis showed that someone had poisoned the drink with a lethal dose of ptomaine.

1781. Senator expelled from the Senate for corrupt election practices was William Lorimer of Illinois, who was elected in 1909. Two lengthy investigations by the Committee on Privileges and Elections concluded that his election was valid and in accordance with "existing political conditions in the State of Illinois." However, a resolution declaring his election invalid was put to a vote on July 13, 1912, and passed by a vote of 55 to 28.

1782. Senator elected by popular vote under the 17th Amendment to the Constitution was Augustus Octavius Bacon, Democrat of Georgia, who was elected by popular vote on July 15, 1913, and sworn in on July 28. Before the adoption of the 17th Amendment on May 31, 1913, U.S. senators were elected by the state legislatures (as specified in the Constitution, Section 3, Article 1). The first general election in which senators were elected by popular vote took place on November 4, 1913, and the first senator elected on that day was Blair Lee of Maryland.

1783. Woman to be appointed a senator was Rebecca Latimer Felton, aged 87, a Democrat and a women's rights activist. On October 3, 1922, Governor Thomas William Hardwick of Georgia gave her a temporary appointment to fill the vacancy caused by the death of Thomas Edward Watson. Although Hardwick, an antisuffragist, expected Felton's credentials to be refused by the Senate, she was allowed to take her seat, and occupied it for two days, November 21–22, 1922. She was the oldest person ever to begin serving in the Senate.

1784. Senator unseated after a recount was Smith Wildman Brookhart, Republican of Iowa, the presumed winner of the election of November 4, 1924. He presented his credentials as a senator-elect for the term commencing March 4, 1925, and served until April 12, 1926, when he was ousted by a Senate vote of 45–41. A recount had proved the winner to be Daniel Frederic Steck, the Democrat candidate, who served from April 12, 1926, to March 3, 1931.

1785. Senator barred for spending too much on an election campaign was senator-elect Frank Smith of Illinois. On December 7, 1927, the Senate voted to refuse him his seat because of the unethically large amount he had spent on his campaign—$458,000, considered an astronomical sum at the time. Smith was barred from the Senate chamber on January 17, 1928, and his seat was declared to be vacant.

1786. Latino elected to the Senate was Octaviano Larrazolo, Republican of New Mexico, who served in the 70th Congress from December 7, 1928, to March 3, 1929. Larrazolo was born in 1859 in the Mexican state of Chihuahua and in 1875 emigrated to the United States, where he studied law. He opened a law practice in Las Vegas, NM, in 1895 and later served in a series of local and statewide elective posts. Originally a Democrat, he was elected governor in 1918 as a Republican. He entered the state House of Representatives in 1927. In 1928 he was elected to fill the unexpired term of Democratic senator Andieus A. Jones, who had died in office.

1787. Father-mother-son senatorial dynasty consisted of Louisiana Democratic senator Huey Pierce Long, his wife Rose McConnell Long, and their son Russell B. Long. Huey Long, elected to the Senate in 1932, was assassinated in Baton Rouge, LA, on September 10, 1935. Rose McConnell Long served out the remainder of his term. Russell B. Long was elected to the Senate in November 1948, was sworn in on December 31, 1948, and served until 1987.

1788. Woman elected to the Senate for a full term was Hattie Ophelia Wyatt Caraway, a Democrat from Jonesboro, AR. She first entered the Senate in November 1931 by appointment, to fill the vacancy left by the death of her husband, Senator Thaddeus Horatio Caraway. She was elected to a full term on January 12, 1932, and was reelected in 1938.

1789. Woman to chair a Senate committee was Hattie Ophelia Wyatt Caraway, Democrat of Arkansas. At the opening of the 73rd Congress in 1933, Caraway was elected chair of the Committee on Enrolled Bills and served in that position until she left the Senate in 1945. She also served on the Committee on Commerce and the Committee on Agriculture and Forestry.

1790. Child of a president to serve in the Senate (aside from John Quincy Adams, who was himself a president and who served in both the Senate and the House) was Robert Alphonso Taft, the son of William Howard Taft, who served as senator from Ohio from January 3, 1939, to July 31, 1953.

1791. Veteran of World War II to be elected to the Senate was the conservative isolationist William E. Jenner, Republican of Indiana. Jenner had been majority leader and president pro tem of the Indiana state senate in 1939 and 1941. On June 1, 1942, he enlisted in the Army Air Corps and saw service in Europe, where he was injured. In October 1944 Jenner was discharged with the rank of captain and returned to Indiana politics. He was sworn in on November 14, 1944, to complete the unexpired term of the late senator Frederick Van Nuys, who had died in January. Jenner was noted for opposing all international involvements, including the Marshall Plan and NATO.

1792. Woman elected to the Senate in her own right rather than to fill another senator's unexpired term was Margaret Chase Smith, Republican of Skowhegan, ME, a four-term veteran of the House of Representatives (June 3, 1940, through January 3, 1949). She won election to the Senate on September 13, 1948, and remained there from January 3, 1949, through January 3, 1973. She lost her 1972 bid for reelection after 24 years of continuous service, during which she became the first woman to be elected to the Senate for three terms. The first woman senator from the Democratic Party to be elected in her own right was Barbara Ann Mikulski of Maryland, who was also the first Democratic woman senator to serve in both houses of Congress. She took her seat in the House of Representatives on January 3, 1977, and in the Senate on January 6, 1987.

1793. Senator to win a seat that had been occupied by his father and mother was Russell Long of Louisiana, who was elected on November 2, 1948, and sworn in on December 31, 1948, for the term expiring January 2, 1951. His father, Huey Pierce Long, the boss of the Democratic party machine in Louisiana, was elected on November 4, 1930, and took the oath of office on January 25, 1932. He was assassinated in 1935. Rose McConnell Long, wife of Huey Long and mother of Russell Long, was appointed on January 31, 1936, to fill the seat left vacant by the assassination. She served until January 2, 1937.

1794. Senator who had been a newspaper reporter was Blair Moody, a Democrat, who joined the *Detroit News* in 1923 and served as its Washington correspondent for 18 years (1933–51). On April 23, 1951, Governor Gerhard Mennen Williams of Michigan appointed him to serve the unexpired term of the late Republican senator Arthur H. Vandenberg. He was sworn in on April 25, on which date Vice President Alben William Barkley called upon him to preside over the Senate.

1795. Three brothers from one family to serve in the Senate were the three sons of Joseph Patrick Kennedy and Rose Elizabeth Fitzgerald Kennedy of Boston, MA: John Fitzgerald Kennedy, senator from Massachusetts, who was sworn in on January 3, 1953; Edward Moore Kennedy, also from Massachusetts, who was sworn in on January 9, 1963; and Robert Francis Kennedy, senator from New York, who was sworn in on January 3, 1965.

CONGRESS—SENATE—SENATORS—*continued*

1796. Senator elected by a write-in vote was James Strom Thurmond, Democrat of South Carolina, who was elected on November 2, 1954, for the term ending January 3, 1961. Thurmond received 139,106 votes, defeating Edgar Brown, the official candidate of the Democratic Party, who received 80,956 votes.

1797. Democratic senator from Maine was Edmund Sixtus Muskie of Rumford, ME, liberal and environmentalist governor of the strongly Republican state from 1955 to 1959. Muskie was elected to the Senate in November 1958 and served until May 1980, when he was appointed secretary of state in the last months of the Carter administration. He also made an unsuccessful run for the presidency in 1972.

1798. Senator of Asian ancestry was Hiram Leong Fong, who was elected on July 29, 1959, by the voters of Hawaii, who were preparing for admission to the Union. Hawaii achieved statehood on August 21 and Fong was sworn in on August 24. His parents, emigrants from China, were laborers on sugar plantations.

1799. African-American senator to be elected by popular vote was Edward William Brooke, the attorney general of Massachusetts, who was elected on November 8, 1966, by a plurality of approximately 439,000 votes. He was seated on January 10, 1967. Significantly, Brooke was not only an African American, but was also a Republican and a Protestant; Massachusetts voters are predominantly Catholics of Irish descent and members of the Democratic party.

1800. Senator to act in the movies was Everett McKinley Dirksen of Illinois, who appeared in *The Monitors,* a satire released on October 9, 1969. It was a 91-minute film produced by Bell and Howell Productions in association with Commonwealth United Entertainment. Based on the science-fiction novel by Keith Laumer, the film depicted a pacifistic, nonviolent United States dominated from the White House down by a horde of robot-like young men in bowlers. It featured Ed Begley as the president, Keenan Wynn as the general, and Larry Storch as the colonel.

1801. Republican senator from North Carolina elected in the 20th century was Jesse Helms, who defeated Democrat Nick Galifianakis by capturing 56 percent of the vote in the November 1972 election. Helms was reelected in 1978 and regularly thereafter. An ultra-conservative hardliner, Helms in his first term introduced an amendment requiring prayer in the public schools, voted in favor of the death penalty, and voted against school busing, government abortion subsidies, licensing of handguns, the Panama Canal treaties, and federal loans to New York City.

1802. Senator who had been an astronaut was John Herschel Glenn, Jr., of New Concord, OH, the first astronaut to orbit the earth, who was elected as a Democrat on November 5, 1974. He was the pilot of the Mercury spacecraft *Friendship,* launched on February 20, 1962, by an Atlas booster. He made three orbits in 4 hours 55 minutes and landed east of the Bahamas in the Atlantic Ocean. In October 1998, Glenn, then 77 years old, returned to space aboard the Space Shuttle *Discovery,* the oldest astronaut ever to fly.

1803. Woman elected to the Senate without prior experience in the House of Representatives was Maurine Brown Neuberger, Democrat of Oregon. In 1960 she ran successfully in the general election for the seat left vacant some months earlier by the death of her husband, Richard Lewis Neuberger. She served in the Senate from 1961 until 1967. She had served in the Oregon house of representatives from 1951 to 1955.

1804. Basketball star elected to the Senate was Democrat Bill Bradley, who from 1967 to 1977 played professional basketball for the New York Knickerbockers. In his first bid for public office, he was elected on November 7, 1978, to the U.S. Senate from New Jersey by a margin of more than 220,000 votes, garnering 56 percent of the ballots cast. He was sworn in on January 15, 1979.

1805. Woman elected to the Senate whose political career owed nothing to a male relative was Paula Hawkins, Republican of Florida, who defeated Democrat Bill Gunter, the state insurance commissioner, on November 3, 1980. Most previous woman senators, including Hattie Wyatt Caraway, Margaret Chase Smith, and Maurine Brown Neuberger, were the wives or widows of politicians when they first ran for office. Nancy Landon Kassebaum of Kansas, elected in 1978, had a family connection to national politics through her father, Alf Landon, the former Republican presidential candidate.

1806. American prisoner of war in Vietnam who was elected to Congress was Jeremiah Andrew Denton, Jr., conservative Republican from Alabama and a former Navy combat pilot. Denton was shot down over North Vietnam on July 18, 1965, in his A6 Intruder and spent the next seven years and seven months in a succession of POW camps. In a propaganda videotape sanctioned by the North Vietnamese and aired on Japanese and American television, Denton managed to blink out the Morse code for "torture," alerting American intelligence officials to the brutal conditions in the camps. In February 1973, he led the first group of American prisoners of war released by the North Vietnamese. Denton entered Alabama politics in 1980 and carried the traditionally Democratic state by slightly more than 33,000 votes in the November 4 general election, defeating his Democratic opponent James E. Folsom, Jr., and becoming the first Republican senator from Alabama since Reconstruction.

1807. Senator to fly in space was Jake Garn, Republican senator from Utah. As chairman of a Senate subcommittee that oversees spending by the National Aeronautics and Space Adminstration, Garn, a former Navy pilot, received permission from NASA officials to fly aboard the space shuttle as a congressional observer. Garn joined the crew of Space Shuttle *Discovery* on the flight that lifted off from Cape Canaveral, FL, on April 12, 1985. Another senator, John Herschel Glenn, Jr., of Ohio, was an astronaut in the 1960s, before he entered politics.

1808. State to be represented in the Senate by two women was California. The senators were Dianne Feinstein and Barbara Boxer, both of whom were elected as Democrats in November 1992. Senator Feinstein was the former mayor of San Francisco and director of the Bank of California. Elected to the Senate seat left vacant when Pete Wilson resigned to seek the governorship, she was reelected in 1994. Senator Boxer, a longtime member of the Marin County Board of Supervisors, served in the House of Representatives from 1983 to 1993, when she entered the Senate. She was reelected in 1998. The second state to have two women senators was Maine, which sent Olympia J. Snowe to the Senate in 1994 and Susan M. Collins in 1996. Both were Republicans.

1809. African-American woman to serve as a senator was Carol Moseley Braun, a Democrat from Chicago, IL, who was elected on November 3, 1992. She was also the first African-American and the first woman from Illinois to capture a Senate seat. Running against Richard Williamson in the election, Braun received 55 percent of the vote, including support by 90 percent of African-Americans in the state.

1810. Senator elected posthumously was Mel Carnahan. The Democratic governor of Missouri since 1993, Carnahan campaigned in 2000 for the Senate seat occupied by Republican John Ashcroft. On October 16, a few weeks before the election, Carnahan was killed in a plane crash that also took the lives of his son and an associate. There was not enough time to withdraw his name from the ballot, and his widow, Jean Carnahan, indicated her willingness to be appointed in his place if he were elected. On November 7, the voters gave Carnahan 50 percent of the vote to Ashcroft's 48 percent.

CONGRESS—SESSIONS

1811. Session of Congress under the Constitution took place in New York City from March 4, 1789, to September 29, 1789. The 13 states were represented by 26 senators and 65 representatives. The largest number of representatives from any state was 10, from Virginia. The first quorum of the House of Representatives met on April 1 and the first Senate quorum on April 6. The final meeting in New York City was held on August 12, 1790, after which the capital was moved to Philadelphia, PA, where the First Congress continued to meet until it expired on March 3, 1791. In all, the First Congress enacted 118 acts, comprising 94 public acts, 14 public resolutions, eight private acts, and two private resolutions.

1812. Joint meeting of the Senate and the House of Representatives was held on April 6, 1789, in the Senate Chamber, New York City. The House of Representatives attended the opening of the Senate session and the counting by the Senate of the electoral votes for president and vice president in the country's first presidential election. The electoral votes were cast as follows: George Washington 69, John Adams 34, Samuel Huntingdon 2, John Jay 9, John Hancock 4, Robert H. Harrison 6, George Clinton 3, John Rutledge 6, John Milton 2, James Armstrong 1, Edward Telfair 1, and Benjamin Lincoln 1.

1813. Session of Congress to meet in Philadelphia was the third session of the First Congress, which was held from December 6, 1790, to March 3, 1791. Congress continued to meet in Philadelphia until May 14, 1800, the last day of the first session of the Sixth Congress.

1814. Special session of Congress was held on May 15, 1797, in Philadelphia, PA. President John Adams had issued a proclamation on March 25 for convening the Senate and the House of Representatives to consider the difficulty with France.

CONGRESS—SESSIONS—*continued*

1815. Session of Congress to meet in Washington, DC, was the second session of the Sixth Congress, which convened in Washington on November 17, 1800.

1816. Joint session of Congress to meet in the Capitol took place on November 22, 1800, in the Senate chamber. The legislators were addressed by President John Adams, who said: "I congratulate the people of the United States on the assembling of Congress at the permanent seat of their government, and I congratulate you, gentlemen, on the prospect of a residence not to be changed. . . . In this city may that piety and virtue, that wisdom and magnanimity, that constancy and self-government, which adorned the great character whose name it bears, be forever held in veneration!" This was the last time a president addressed a joint session of Congress until 1913, when Woodrow Wilson did so, shortly after his inauguration.

1817. Radio broadcast of an open session of Congress took place on December 3, 1923, from noon to 12:45 P.M., during the first session of the 68th Congress. The swearing-in ceremony was broadcast by radio station WRC, Washington, DC, from the Senate. Three newly elected senators—Alva Blanchard Adams of Colorado, a Democrat; Magnus Johnson of Minnesota, a member of the Farmer-Labor Party; and Porter Hinman Dale of Vermont, a Republican—were sworn in alphabetically. The session adjourned in memory of the recently deceased senators whose seats they were taking—Samuel Danford Nicholson, Knute Nelson, and William Paul Dillingham, respectively.

1818. Congress in session a full year was the third session of the 76th congress, in session from January 3, 1940, to January 3, 1941, a total of 366 days. The first session of the 77th Congress lasted 365 days, from January 3, 1941, to January 2, 1942.

1819. Congressional opening session to be televised was the joint session of the 80th Congress that met on January 3, 1947. The proceedings were televised by the major networks.

1820. Session of Congress held outside Washington, DC, since 1800 was a ceremonial joint session of 25 senators and more than 175 representatives that was held on July 16, 1987, at Independence Hall, Philadelphia, PA, during the bicentennial of the Constitution. It commemorated the events of July 16, 1787, when the delegates to the Federal Convention agreed to the historic compromise that allowed the formation of two legislative chambers, one (the Senate) in which the states would have equal representation, and the other (the House) in which representation would be proportionate to each state's population. The ceremony was presided over by Representative Lindy Boggs of Louisiana.

CONSTITUTION

1821. Bill of Rights was written by George Mason as part of his draft for the state constitution of Virginia. It was entitled *A Declaration of Rights made by the representative of the good people of Virginia, assembled in full and free convention; which rights do pertain to them and their posterity, as the basis and foundation of government* and was adopted by the states constitutional convention on June 12, 1776. In 16 paragraphs, the Declaration laid out a set of fundamental principles of liberty, beginning with the precepts "that all men are by nature equally free and independent, and have certain inherent rights," and "that all power is vested in, and consequently derived from the people," and continuing with an insistence on separation of the branches of government, free elections, trial by impartial jury, due process of law, no cruel and unusual punishment, no searches without specific warrants, freedom of the press, a citizen militia under civilian control, and free exercise of religion. The lack of a similar Bill of Rights in the national Constitution was decried by Mason and others concerned with protecting individual liberties, including five states whose legislatures were reluctant to ratify the Constitution without one. Of twelve amendments to the Constitution proposed to the states on September 25, 1789, ten were ratified and were incorporated into the Constitution as the Bill of Rights on December 15, 1791. Mason's work was a model not only for these amendments but also for bills of rights that were incorporated into several state constitutions.

1822. Question considered by the Constitutional Convention meeting in New York City in 1787, after the principle of a tripartite national government was established, was whether the national legislature should consist of one branch (following the tradition laid down by the Continental Congress and the Congress of the Confederation) or two (following the practice of ten of the 13 states, as well as of the British Parliament).

1823. Printed copies of the Constitution were printed from plates engraved by Jacob Shallus, assistant clerk of the Pennsylvania Assembly, who received $30 for the work. Sixty proof sheets were printed August 1–3, 1787, and laid before the Constitutional Convention on August 6.

1824. Proposal in the Constitutional Convention for civil liberties was made by Charles Pinckney of South Carolina on August 20, 1787. His proposals for freedom of the press and other rights were turned over to the Committee of Detail, which allowed them to expire.

1825. Constitution of the United States was signed at the conclusion of the Constitutional Convention, which met at Philadelphia, PA, from May 25, 1787, to September 17. Of the original 55 delegates, only 41 remained to the conclusion, and three of them refused to sign. It was agreed that the Constitution would become binding on the 13 former colonies when it was ratified by nine states. This took place on June 21, 1788, when the legislature of New Hampshire approved ratification by a 57–47 vote. The Constitution was declared to be in effect on March 4, 1789.

1826. Newspaper to publish the Constitution was the *Pennsylvania Packet and Daily Advertiser,* Philadelphia, PA, published by John Dunlap and David C. Claypoole. The text of the Constitution was published in the issue dated September 19, 1787.

1827. Public copies of the Constitution were distributed throughout the states beginning on September 19, 1787. It was the public's first look at the new document, which defined a more powerful central government than many had expected.

1828. State to ratify the federal Constitution was Delaware, on December 6, 1787.

1829. Formal announcement that the Constitution was in effect was made on July 2, 1788, by George Washington, the president of Congress, meeting in New York. The Constitution had just been ratified on June 21, 1788, by the required nine states, the last of which was New Hampshire.

1830. Legal treatise analyzing the Constitution was St. George Tucker's *American Blackstone,* published in Philadelphia, PA, in 1803. The five-volume work included a lengthy appendix on the character and interpretation of the new federal Constitution. Much of Tucker's commentary was written as early as 1790 and

was therefore nearly contemporaneous with the writing of the Constitution itself. His views are generally accepted as the definitive source for original intent by the Supreme Court, which has cited Tucker in more than 40 major cases.

1831. Definitive edition of *The Debates in the Several State Conventions on the Adoption of the Federal Constitution* was compiled by Jonathan Elliot and fully published in 1836 under sanction of Congress. This edition is the most comprehensive source for materials on the period between the end of the Constitutional Convention in September 1787 and the first session of Congress in March 1789. The full title is *The Debates in the Several State Conventions, On the Adoption of the Federal Constitution, As Recommended by the General Convention at Philadelphia, in 1787. Together With the Journal of the Federal Convention, Luther Martin's Letter, Yates's Minutes, Congressional Opinions, Virginia and Kentucky Resolutions Of '98—'99, and Other Illustrations of the Constitution.*

1832. Use of the word "male" in the Constitution appeared in the 14th Amendment, which was declared ratified on July 28, 1868. Section 2 of the amendment reads in part: "But when the right to vote at any election for the choice of electors for President and Vice President of the United States, Representatives in Congress, the Executive and Judicial officers of a State, or the members of the Legislature thereof, is denied to any of the male inhabitants of such State . . . the basis of representation therein shall be reduced in the proportion which the number of such male citizens shall bear to the whole number of male citizens twenty-one years of age in such State."

1833. Edition of the complete *Records of the Federal Convention of 1787* was collected by Max Farrand, professor of history at Yale University, New Haven, CT, and published in 1911. The official proceedings of the Constitutional Convention were printed in 1819 under the supervision of the secretary of state, John Quincy Adams, but Farrand's edition includes such essential additional material as James Madison's private notes.

CONSTITUTION—AMENDMENTS

1834. Constitutional amendments to fail the ratification process were the first two of twelve proposed articles of amendment that were adopted by Congress and submitted to the states on September 25, 1789. The remaining ten articles were ratified by the states and enacted into law on December 15, 1791, as the

CONSTITUTION—AMENDMENTS—*continued*

Bill of Rights. Article I, if ratified, would have established a minimum of 200 congressional representatives and a maximum of one for every 50,000 persons. Article II, if ratified, would have prevented Congress from voting midterm pay raises for its own members. Article II was resubmitted to the states nearly two centuries later, was declared ratified on May 7, 1992, and was incorporated into the Constitution as the 27th Amendment. Its text reads: "No law varying the compensation for the services of the Senators and Representatives shall take effect until an election of Representatives shall have intervened."

1835. State to ratify the Bill of Rights was New Jersey, which acted on November 20, 1789.

1836. Constitutional amendment and the first guarantee of free speech to be established anywhere in the world was the First Amendment to the Constitution of the United States, proposed by Congress in September 1789 and ratified by the states on December 15, 1791. The text of the First Amendment reads: "Congress shall make no law respecting an establishment of religion, or prohibiting the free exercise thereof; or abridging the freedom of speech, or of the press; or the right of the people peaceably to assemble, and to petition the Government for a redress of grievances." It was authored by James Madison. Although many other nations have based their constitutions on that of the United States, few have chosen to include such a sweeping guarantee of freedom of speech.

1837. Statement of the principle of due process requiring governments, when taking action against citizens, to do so according to law, giving prior notice and affording a fair hearing, was enunciated in the Fifth Amendment to the U.S. Constitution (declared in force on December 15, 1791), which reads: "Nor [shall any person] be deprived of life, liberty or property without due process of law." The Fifth Amendment applied only to the federal government. The 14th Amendment, ratified in 1867, applied the principle of due process to state governments as well.

1838. State to ratify the Eleventh Amendment to the Constitution after it was submitted to the states by the Third Congress on March 5, 1794, was New York, on March 27, 1794. The amendment, which made it unlawful for states to be sued by citizens of another state or of a foreign country, was prompted by the Supreme Court's 1793 decision in *Chisholm v. Georgia,* which allowed a citizen of South Carolina to recover property confiscated by Georgia from a Loyalist during the American Revolution. It was declared law on January 8, 1798.

1839. Constitutional amendment enacted after the passage of the Bill of Rights was the Eleventh Amendment, which prevented citizens of one state from instituting lawsuits against another state. The proposed amendment was passed by Congress on March 4, 1794, and was submitted to the states for ratification on the following day. It was declared ratified on January 8, 1798, although the total number of votes needed for ratification had been accumulated three years earlier, on January 23, 1795. The difference was due to the failure of the state governments to notify Congress of their votes in a timely manner.

1840. State to ratify the Twelfth Amendment to the Constitution after it was submitted to the states by the Eighth Congress on December 12, 1803, was North Carolina, which ratified it on December 22. It was declared ratified on September 25, 1804. The amendment changed the method of electing presidents that was set forth in the Constitution in the first paragraph of Article II, Section 1.

1841. Constitutional amendment proposal to bear the signature of a president was an amendment that would have prevented Congress from banning or regulating slavery in the states. It was passed by the House on February 28, 1861. The Senate passed it on March 2, 1861, and President Abraham Lincoln, hoping to avert a civil war, signed it that same day. It read: "No amendment shall be made to the Constitution which will authorize or give to Congress, the power to abolish or interfere, within any State, with the domestic institutions thereof, including that of persons held to labor or service by the laws of said State." The proposal was not ratified and was not made law.

1842. State to ratify the 13th Amendment to the Constitution was Illinois, which so voted on February 1, 1865, the same day that the 38th Congress submitted the amendment to the states. The secretary of state declared it ratified on December 18, 1865. The 13th Amendment abolished slavery.

1843. Constitutional amendment that resulted from the Civil War was the 13th Amendment, which was passed by Congress on January 31, 1865, proposed to the states on February 1, and declared ratified on December 18. It prohibited slavery and involuntary servitude, except for convicted criminals. The other amendments that resulted from the Civil War were the 14th Amendment, declared ratified on July 28, 1868, and the 15th, declared ratified on March 30, 1870. The former extended citizenship and the equal protection of the law to former slaves. The latter provided for universal male suffrage.

1844. State to ratify the 14th Amendment to the Constitution was Connecticut, on June 30, 1866. The amendment was proposed to the states by the 39th Congress on June 16, 1866, and was declared ratified on July 28, 1868. The amendment granted citizenship to anyone born in the United States, including former slaves; required the states to grant equal protection under the law to all citizens and to afford them due process of law at all times; required former slaves to be counted in the apportionment of congressional representatives; disqualified certain leaders of the Confederacy from holding public office; and voided debts incurred by rebellious states. States that had seceded from the Union were obliged to ratify the amendment as a condition of their return.

1845. State to ratify the 15th Amendment to the Constitution was Nevada, on March 1, 1869. The amendment, which banned racial discrimination in voting, was proposed to the states by the 40th Congress on February 27, 1869, and was declared ratified on March 30, 1870.

1846. State to ratify the 16th Amendment to the Constitution after its submission to the states by the 61st Congress on July 12, 1909, was Alabama, which did so on August 10. The amendment authorized Congress to levy income taxes. It was declared law on February 25, 1913.

1847. State to ratify the 17th Amendment to the Constitution was Massachusetts, on May 22, 1912. The 17th Amendment, which replaced parts of Article I, Section 3, of the Constitution, changed the method of electing United States senators from election by the state legislature to direct popular election and instituted a method of filling vacancies in the Senate. It was proposed to the states by the 62nd Congress on May 16, 1912, and was declared ratified on May 31, 1913.

1848. Constitutional amendment requiring ratification within seven years was the 18th Amendment, which prohibited the manufacture, sale, or transportation of intoxicating liquors within the United States. The amendment was adopted by Congress and submitted to the states on December 18, 1917. Within two years

it had been ratified by a sufficient number of states—three-fourths of the total, as required by the Constitution—to allow its enactment into law on January 29, 1919. Several later amendments, including the 20th, 21st, and 22nd Amendments, also specified a seven-year deadline. The U.S. Constitution does not specify a time limit for the passage of amendments.

1849. States to ratify the 18th Amendment to the Constitution after its submission to the states by the 65th Congress on December 18, 1917, were Mississippi and Maine, both of which ratified it on January 8, 1918. The amendment established Prohibition, making it illegal to make, sell, or transport intoxicating liquors. It was declared ratified on January 29, 1919, effective as of January 16, 1920, but was repealed by the 21st Amendment in 1933.

1850. States to ratify the 19th Amendment to the Constitution were Illinois, Michigan, and Wisconsin, whose state legislatures voted to ratify the amendment on June 10, 1919. The 19th Amendment gave women the right to vote. It was proposed to the States by the 66th Congress on June 4, 1919, and was declared law on August 26, 1920.

1851. State to ratify the 20th Amendment to the Constitution after its submission to the states by the 72nd Congress on March 2, 1932, was Virginia, on March 4. The 20th Amendment changed the beginning of presidential and vice presidential terms of office from March 20 to January 20, moved the beginning of senatorial and congressional terms and the convening of Congress to January 3, authorized the vice president-elect to replace a deceased or disqualified president-elect, and authorized Congress to make laws providing for the deaths of presidential and vice presidential replacements. It was delcared ratified on February 6, 1933.

1852. State to ratify the 21st Amendment to the Constitution was Michigan, which did so on April 10, 1933. The amendment repealed Prohibition (the 18th Amendment), making it legal once again to manufacture, sell, and transport intoxicating liquors, except in "dry" states whose legislatures had banned these activities. It was submitted to the states by the 72nd Congress on February 20, 1933, and was declared ratified on December 5.

1853. Constitutional amendment ratified by state conventions rather than state legislatures was the 21st Amendment, which repealed Prohibition. Article V of the Constitution states that proposed amendments can be deemed valid "when ratified by the Legislatures of three fourths of the several states, or by Conventions in three fourths thereof, as the one or the other

CONSTITUTION—AMENDMENTS—continued

Mode of Ratification may be proposed by the Congress." The first 20 amendments to the Constitution were ratified by the state legislatures. Section 3 of the proposed 21st Amendment specified that it was to be considered by state conventions. It was offered by Congress to the states on February 20, 1933. By December 5, the amendment had accumulated 36 approvals and was declared ratified.

1854. Constitutional amendment submitted to the states for repeal was the 18th Amendment, also known as the Prohibition Amendment, which prohibited the manufacture, sale, or transportation of intoxicating liquors within the United States. The amendment became law on January 29, 1919, after it was ratified by 36 states. A bill to repeal the amendment, and thereby end Prohibition, was passed in the Senate by a 63–23 vote on February 16, 1933, and in the House by a 289–121 vote on February 20. The 72nd Congress then offered it as a proposal to the states. It was declared ratified on December 5, 1933.

1855. State to ratify the 22nd Amendment to the Constitution after its submission to the states by the 80th Congress on March 24, 1947, was Maine, which ratified it on March 31. The amendment placed a two-term limit on Presidents. It was declared ratified on February 26, 1951.

1856. State to ratify the 23rd Amendment to the Constitution was Hawaii, on June 23, 1960. The proposed amendment had been sent to the states by the 86th Congress on June 16. The Amendment granted to citizens of Washington, DC, the right to vote in presidential elections. It achieved the necessary number of ratifications on March 29, 1961.

1857. State to ratify the 24th Amendment to the Constitution was Illinois, which ratified it on November 14, 1962. The amendment had been submitted to the states by the 87th Congress on August 27, 1962. It banned the use of the poll tax in federal elections. Poll taxes had been instituted in the South as a means of disqualifying poor people, particularly African-Americans, from voting. The 24th Amendment became law on January 23, 1964, when 38 states had ratified it.

1858. State to ratify the 25th Amendment to the Constitution was Nebraska, on July 12, 1965. The amendment had been proposed to the states by Congress on July 6, 1965. It provided for cases in which the president is unable to discharge the powers and duties of his office. On February 10, 1967, it was ratified by the necessary number of states to become law.

1859. State to ratify the 26th Amendment to the Constitution was Minnesota, which ratified it on March 23, 1971, the same day that the 92nd Congress submitted the amendment to the states for consideration. The amendment lowered the voting age in federal elections to 18. It was made law on July 1, 1971.

1860. Constitutional amendment to be ratified two centuries after its proposal was the 27th Amendment, which bars Congress from giving itself midterm pay increases. It was originally submitted to the states by the First Congress on September 25, 1789, as one of twelve proposed amendments to the Constitution. Although ten of them were ratified by the requisite number of states and were adopted in 1791 as the Bill of Rights, this amendment was not among them, having been approved by only six states, starting with Maryland in 1789. In 1873, the citizens of Ohio, angered by the infamous "salary grab" enacted by Congress earlier that year, decided to ratify the long-dormant amendment. It was revived a hundred years later by Wyoming, which ratified it on March 6, 1978. More states followed, and the amendment was declared ratified on May 7, 1992.

D

DISTRICT OF COLUMBIA

1861. Capital to be located at the site of Washington, DC, was that of the Powhatan confederacy of Virginia and Maryland circa 1600, when Wahunsonacock (also known as Powhatan) united a group of Algonkian-speaking tribes under his rule. The junction of the Anacostia and the Potomac rivers was the location of a number of villages that formed a seat of government. The chief's headquarters was at Greenleaf Point, and the tribe's council house stood near what is now Capitol Hill.

1862. European to visit the future site of Washington, DC, of record was the English mariner Henry Fleet, who arrived in 1631 in the bark *Warwick*. It is possible that he was preceded by John Smith, who led an expedition up the Potomac River from the English colony at Jamestown, VA, in 1607.

1863. Proposal for a national capital was advanced in the summer of 1783. On June 20, a group of Revolutionary War veterans who had not received payment for their military service came to Philadelphia seeking redress from Congress, which was meeting in Philadelphia's Old City Hall. Though no violent acts took place, the episode left some congressmen eager to see the establishment of a separate capital where the federal government could function unmolested. The result was the inclusion in the Constitution (Article 1, Section 8) of a provision allowing Congress "to exercise exclusive Legislation in all Cases whatsoever over such District (not exceeding ten Miles square) as may, by Cession of particular States, and the acceptance of Congress, become the Seat of the Government of the United States. . . ."

1864. Congressional vote on a location for the national capital took place in September 1789, when the House of Representatives, meeting in New York, NY, passed, by a vote of 31–19, a resolution to establish the capital on the Susquehanna River. The other proposals included Philadelphia, PA; Germantown, PA; and Havre de Grace, MD. The Senate's choice was Germantown. The session of Congress ended before further action could be taken.

1865. Vote to establish Washington, DC, was held on July 10, 1790, by the House of Representatives. The House chose a ten-square-mile site along the Potomac River in Maryland as the permanent national capital. President George Washington, who had been a surveyor, was requested to choose the exact location.

1866. State to cede land to the federal government was Maryland, which in 1791 ceded 67 square miles of land on the banks of the Potomac River for construction of the newly designated federal city. The modern Washington, DC, at 69 square miles, is only slightly larger.

1867. Use of the name "District of Columbia" and "Washington" for the federal city appears to have originated with Daniel Carroll of Maryland, Thomas Johnson of Maryland, and David Stuart of Virginia, the three commissioners appointed by President George Washington on January 22, 1791, to survey the site he had chosen for the city and to negotiate with landowners concerning the ceding of their property. Although the commissioners were not legally empowered to confer names, the ones they chose were accepted, together with their proposed system of street names. In a letter to Pierre Charles L'Enfant, the chief architect of the city, they wrote: "We have agreed that the Federal district shall be called the 'Territory of Columbia,' and the Federal City the 'City of Washington.' The title of the map will, therefore, be 'A Map of the City of Washington in the Territory of Columbia.'"

1868. Design for Washington, DC, was prepared by Pierre Charles L'Enfant, a French-born engineer and architect who had served as a volunteer on the Continental Army during the Revolutionary War. He was engaged in March 1791 to draw up a plan for the federal city, submitted his first draft in June 1791, and submitted a revised version in August, together with an annotated map. However, he refused to make the map public in the hope of preventing the sale of land lots, which he feared would result in changes to his artistic vision. After he was fired in February 1792, the task of building Washington was given to the city's surveyor, Andrew Ellicott. Among the ideas that were retained from L'Enfant's plan was a network of avenues radiating from two central points, the Capitol Building and the White House, connected by small parks adorned with statuary. Among the ideas that were deleted was a waterfall on Capitol Hill, five grand fountains, a national nondenominational church for state funerals and public prayer, and places of worship for "all religious denominations."

1869. Sale of building lots in Washington, DC, took place in October 1791. Twenty-two lots were sold over the course of a three-day auction. An additional 34 lots were sold in 1792 and 30 more in 1793. So few buyers showed an interest in the lots that the Commissioners, with the approval of President George Washington, sold 3,000 lots to James Greenleaf, a land speculator, who bought them for $80 each and resold them for nearly $300 each. Greenleaf and two partners, the financiers Robert Morris and John Nicholson, then contracted to sell 3,000 more. The enterprise failed, and all three partners ended up in debtors' prison, where Nicholson died.

1870. Authorized plan of the City of Washington, DC, was engraved in Philadelphia, PA, in 1792 from a drawing made by Andrew Ellicott, surveyor of the territory set aside for the nation's capital. Ellicott's plan was a revision of an earlier one made by the architect Pierre Charles L'Enfant, whose final draft, submitted to President George Washington in August 1791, included elements that Washington disliked. After L'Enfant's dismissal for insubordination, Ellicott made the necessary amendations, and the plan was sent to the engravers for reproduction.

DISTRICT OF COLUMBIA—*continued*

1871. College in Washington, DC, was founded in Georgetown, VA, in 1789 by John Carroll, the first Bishop of Baltimore. Originally a seminary, it became Georgetown University in 1815, by which time the village had been encompassed by the District of Columbia. It is the nation's oldest Catholic institution of higher learning.

1872. Building erected in Washington, DC, by the federal government was the White House, originally known as the Executive Mansion. It was modeled after the palace of the Duke of Leinster in Ireland and was designed by James Hoban. The cornerstone was laid on October 13, 1792. The Executive Mansion was first occupied by President John Adams in 1800, and the first New Year's reception there was held on January 1, 1801. The mansion was burned by the British in 1814, during the War of 1812, and only the four walls were left standing. It was restored in 1818. In order to obliterate the marks of fire, the stones were painted white. Since that time, the Executive Mansion has been known as the White House. When Adams first took occupancy, there was only a path through an elder swamp leading from the president's house to the Capitol.

1873. Block of buildings constructed in Washington, DC, was Wheat Row, a block of brick buildings on Fourth Street between N Street and O Street southwest. They were constructed in 1796 by the partnership of Robert Morris and John Nicholson, who (together with their former partner, James Greenleaf) put up numerous private buildings in areas of the future city that they expected to be much sought after. The bricks were made at a local brickyard owned by Daniel Carroll.

1874. Congressional jurisdiction over Washington, DC, began on February 27, 1801, under the act of April 24, 1800, providing for the relocation there of the federal government.

1875. Location in Washington, DC, of the State Department was a brick building on 17th Street, where the department, having relocated with the rest of the federal government from Philadelphia, established itself in May 1801.

1876. Location in Washington, DC, of the Treasury Department was a two-story brick and stone building that burned down in 1833. It was the only administrative building that was ready for use when the federal government moved to the District of Columbia in May 1801.

1877. Circulating library in Washington, DC, was founded by James Lyon, the publisher of the *National Magazine.* It was located on Pennsylvania Avenue and opened on June 1, 1801.

1878. Government of Washington, DC, was established by Congress in 1802. It consisted of a mayor appointed by the president of the United States and a city council whose members were elected by the voters. (The first president to appoint a mayor of Washington, DC, was thus Thomas Jefferson.) Between 1812 and 1820 the mayor was elected by the council. Ultimate authority for enacting legislation affecting Washington, DC, rested with Congress, and the local government had few real powers.

1879. Vice president to be buried at Washington, DC, was Elbridge Gerry of Massachusetts, President James Madison's second vice president, a former member of the Continental Congress, Constitutional Convention, and House of Representatives and the former governor of Massachusetts. He took the oath of office on March 4, 1813, and died in Washington on November 23, 1814. He was buried in the Washington Parish Burial Ground, better known as the Congressional Cemetery.

1880. Public college in Washington, DC, was chartered by Congress in 1821 as a nonsectarian college, the Columbian College in the District of Columbia. With the aid of an endowment from William Wilson Corcoran, the college became a university in 1873. Its name was changed in 1904 to the George Washington University, in honor of the first president, who expressed in his will the hope that an institution of higher learning would be founded in the capital.

1881. Police force in Washington, DC, originated in 1825 as a band of three watchmen who patrolled the Capitol grounds at night under the supervision of a sergeant. They also gave tours of the Capitol by day.

1882. Washington social scandal with an important effect on national politics was the so-called "Petticoat War," which took place during the first term of President Andrew Jackson. On March 9, 1829, Senator John Eaton of Tennessee took office as Jackson's secretary of war. Eaton's wife, Peggy, had a scandalous reputation, and was snubbed by many of the Washington ladies, especially Floride Calhoun, the wife of Jackson's vice president, John Caldwell Calhoun. Jackson took personal exception to the treatment of Peggy Eaton—he had already fought a number of duels over the reputation of his own wife, Rachel—and snubbed Calhoun, chosing secretary of state (and future president) Martin Van Buren as vice president for his second term.

1883. Railroad to run trains to Washington, DC, was the Baltimore and Ohio Railroad. On July 1, 1835, the president, directors, and other officers of the road made a trial run from Baltimore to Washington and back.

1884. Telegraph line to Washington, DC, was installed in 1844 by the businessman Ezra Cornell, an associate of Samuel Finley Breese Morse. It ran from Washington, DC, to Baltimore, MD. Its construction was made possible by a congressional appropriation of $30,000, made in 1843.

1885. Free church in Washington, DC, was an Episcopal church that was built on St. Alban's Mount, on land donated in the 1840s by a descendant of Joseph Nourse, the first registrar of the Treasury after the seat of government moved to Washington. The National Episcopal Cathedral was erected on the same site in 1907.

1886. National art collection was established in 1846, when Congress authorized the newly created Smithsonian Institution to serve as a depository of art. This function was largely ignored until 1903, when Harriet Lane Johnson bequeathed her collection of paintings to the nation and the Smithsonian's mandate was reactivated. In the meantime, banker William Wilson Corcoran donated his collection of American paintings to the public, resulting in the chartering by Congress in 1870 of the Corcoran Gallery of Art. The Smithsonian's National Gallery of Art was opened in 1941.

1887. Smithsonian Institution was founded as the result of a bequest made in 1829 by James Smithson, an English mineralogist and chemist, whose property was given to the United States "to found at Washington, under the name of the Smithsonian Institution, an establishment for the increase and diffusion of knowledge among men." The legacy, then worth about $500,000, was actively pursued by John Quincy Adams against the will of various members of Congress who believed that its acceptance would be unconstitutional. The Smithsonian Institution was established by Congress in 1846 under the directorship of the physicist Joseph Henry, with its headquarters in Washington, DC, and became a center for research in the arts and sciences.

1888. Public university in Washington, DC, was Howard University, chartered by Congress in 1867 to educate African-Americans. Its first president was General Oliver O. Howard, after whom the institution was named.

1889. Modernization of the infrastructure of Washington, DC, began in 1871, when Alexander R. Shepherd became head of the newly created municipal board of public works. Over the course of three years, during which he became governor of the District, he and architect Alexander Mullett oversaw the installation of citywide sewage and water systems, 180 miles of street paving, 200 miles of sidewalk, and 3,000 gaslights, as well as the planting of 25,000 shade trees.

1890. Territorial government of Washington, DC, was established by Congress in 1871, replacing the format of appointed mayor and elected council that had been in place since 1802. The territorial government consisted of a governor, a legislature (composed of a Council of eleven members and a House of Delegates with 22 members), and a board of public works. The residents were entitled to elect one nonvoting delegate to the House; other than that, all government officials were appointed by the president of the United States. The territorial plan lasted only a few years and was then replaced by a commission form of government.

1891. Commission government for Washington, DC, was instituted in 1874 and made permanent on January 11, 1878, replacing the previous and short-lived territorial government, which had included an appointed legislature. In the new system the city was run by three commissioners who were appointed by the president of the United States. All laws for the city were made by Congress. As the residents of the District of Columbia were not entitled to vote in presidential elections, and there were no local elections in which they could vote, they were completely disenfranchised.

1892. Legal recognition of the term "District of Columbia" was made on June 11, 1878, when Congress passed an act declaring "that all the territory which was ceded by the State of Maryland to the Congress of the United States for the permanent seat of the Government of the United States shall continue to be designated as the District of Columbia." The term had been in use since 1791.

DISTRICT OF COLUMBIA—*continued*

1893. Presidential candidate from Washington, DC, was Belva Ann Bennett Lockwood, who was nominated by the Equal Rights Party, also known as the Woman's Rights Party, on September 20, 1884, at its convention in San Francisco, CA. She was renominated by the party in 1888.

1894. Cherry trees planted in Washington, DC, were 80 trees that were planted in West Potomac Park, along the banks of the Potomac River, in 1909. The project was overseen by Helen Herron Taft, wife of President William Howard Taft. She was persuaded to undertake it by the writer and photographer Eliza Ruhama Scidmore, who had seen cherry trees in bloom during a visit to Japan in 1885. The government of the city of Tokyo contributed another 2,000 trees, but they were found to be diseased and could not be planted. Japan's consul in New York then arranged for a gift of 3,020 trees to be sent to Washington. On March 27, 1912, Mrs. Taft and the Viscountess Chinda, wife of Japan's ambassador to the United States, planted the first two of these. Another gift of trees was made by Japan in 1965.

1895. Park planning agency with oversight of the capital city was the National Capital Planning Commission, established by act of June 6, 1924. In 1952, under the National Capital Planning Act, the Commission was designated the central planning agency for the federal and District of Columbia governments, including all land areas within the boundaries of Montgomery and Prince Georges Counties in Maryland and Fairfax, Loudoun, Prince William, and Arlington Counties in Virginia.

1896. Federal government airport for civilian passengers was the Washington National Airport at Washington, DC, operated by the Civil Aeronautics Administration starting on June 16, 1941. The manager was John Groves.

1897. Year when citizens of Washington, DC, could vote in a presidential election was 1964. The residents of Washington, DC, were granted the right to vote in presidential elections by the 23rd Amendment to the Constitution, which was proposed to the states on June 16, 1960, and ratified on March 29, 1961. They went to the polls on November 3, 1964, to choose between Republican Barry Goldwater and Democrat Lyndon Baines Johnson who received 85.6 percent of their votes.

1898. Commissioner and council government of Washington, DC, was established by Congress in 1967 to allow the city's residents a somewhat greater share in managing their own political affairs. In place of the former system of three commissioners, it created a government headed by one commissioner (the equivalent of a mayor) and an assistant commissioner, with a city council exercising some regulatory and legislative powers. The holders of all eleven offices were appointed by the president of the United States, and the federal government continued to fund municipal expenditures through congressional appropriations and to hire municipal employees. Walter Edward Washington, a former housing official, was appointed commissioner by President Lyndon Baines Johnson and was sworn in on September 28, 1967.

1899. Vice presidential candidate from Washington, DC, was Julius Hobson, who was nominated by the People's Party in July 1972 at its convention in St. Louis, MO.

1900. Elected mayor of Washington, DC, in the 20th century was Walter Edward Washington. A Democrat, Washington had served in the National Capital Housing Authority and as chief of the New York City Housing Authority. On September 28, 1967, he was appointed commissioner of Washington, DC, a job equivalent to that of mayor. In December 1972 Congress granted the citizens of the capital city the right to elect their own mayor. Walter Washington was elected in November 1974 and was sworn in by Justice Thurgood Marshall on January 2, 1975.

1901. African-American woman to serve as mayor of Washington, DC, was Sharon Pratt Dixon (later called Sharon Pratt Kelly). A former treasurer of the Democratic National Party, she won handily over her Republican opponent, Maurice Turner, taking 86 percent of the vote in the general election held on November 6, 1990. She remarried in 1991, taking the name Sharon Pratt Kelly.

1902. Vice president born in Washington, DC, was Albert Gore, Jr., who was born there in 1948. His father was a senator from Tennessee. Gore became senator from Tennessee himself in 1984 and in 1993 was inaugurated as vice president under William Jefferson Clinton.

1903. State flag for Washington, DC, was raised on July 4, 1993, in a ceremony attended by Mayor Sharon Pratt Kelly, members of the Washington City Council, and the city's congressional delegation of Jesse Jackson, Eleanor Holmes Norton, Charles Moreland, and

Florence Pendleton. The 51-star flag symbolized the aspirations of the District of Columbia to be admitted to the union as the 51st state. Later that year, statehood votes were taken for the first time in both the Senate and the House.

E

EQUALITY

1904. Federal civil rights agency was the Commission on Civil Rights, created by the Civil Rights Act of 1957, and reestablished by the United States Commission on Civil Rights Act of 1983. The Commission on Civil Rights is charged with collecting and studying information on discrimination or denials of equal protection of the laws due to race, color, religion, sex, age, handicap, national origin, or in the administration of justice in such areas as voting rights, enforcement of Federal civil rights laws, and equal opportunity in education, employment, and housing. The commission has no enforcement authority.

1905. Affirmative action order issued by the federal government was Executive Order 10925, signed by President John Fitzgerald Kennedy on March 6, 1961. The order required all federal contractors to "take affirmative action to ensure that applicants are treated equally without regard to race, color, religion, sex, or national origin." The order created the President's Committee on Equal Employment Opportunity with the mandate "to consider and recommend additional affirmative steps which should be taken by executive departments and agencies to realize more fully the national policy of nondiscrimination within the executive branch of the Government." Executive Order 11246, signed by President Lyndon Baines Johnson in 1965, required federal contractors to take affirmative action in hiring workers from minority populations. Affirmative action for businesses owned by women was mandated by Executive Order 12138, signed by President Jimmy Carter in 1979.

EQUALITY—DISABILITY

1906. Federal law granting equal access to disabled people was the Architectural Barriers Act of 1968, which required the federal government to make its buldings more accessible to people with physical disabilities by providing such design features as ramps for wheelchair users. The responsibility for prescribing standards for these features was assigned to the General Services Administration in consultation with the secretary of health and human services. The law applied to buildings used for offices, recreation, education, and medical services. It was largely ignored until the Rehabilitation Act of 1973 created the Architectural and Transportation Barriers Compliance Act.

1907. Federal civil rights law for people with disabilities was the Rehabilitation Act of 1973, signed into law by President Richard M. Nixon on September 26, 1973. The act prohibited federally funded programs, including education, employment, and social service programs, from discriminating against people with handicaps and provided extensive funding for rehabilitation services. Title V of the act required the executive departments and agencies of the federal government to offer equal employment opportunities to people with disabilities.

1908. Comprehensive civil rights legislation for people with disabilities was the Americans with Disabilities Act, signed into law by President George Herbert Walker Bush on July 26, 1990, at a White House ceremony. The wide-ranging legislation was intended to make American society more accessible to people with disabilities. The ADA is divided into five titles covering employment, public services, public accommodations, telecommunications, and miscellaneous issues. Its protection applies primarily, but not exclusively, to individuals with a physical or mental impairment or a history of disability that substantially limits their major life activities.

EQUALITY—HOMOSEXUAL

1909. State to decriminalize homosexual acts between consenting adults in private was Illinois, which removed the relevant sodomy laws from its books in 1962.

1910. Homosexual civil rights legislation proposed at the federal level was *H.R. 14752,* introduced into the House of Representatives in 1974 by Bella Abzug and Edward Koch, both Democrats of New York. The bill proposed that the categories of "sex, sexual orientation, and marital status" be protected under the 1964 Civil Rights Act.

1911. City to extend domestic partnership benefits to homosexual employees was Berkeley, CA, which did so in 1984.

EQUALITY—HOMOSEXUAL—*continued*

1912. Federal law to include the term "sexual orientation" was the Hate Crimes Statistics Act, signed into law by President George Herbert Walker Bush in 1990. The act authorized the FBI to collect and publish data on hate crimes supplied by local and state agencies. A hate crime was defined as a crime based on race, religion, sexual orientation, ethnicity, nationality, disability, or multiple prejudices.

1913. State law prohibiting specific civil rights protection for homosexuals was the Amendment 2 ballot measure passed by Colorado voters in 1992. A state district court overturned the measure in 1993, ruling that it violated the constitutional guarantee of equal protection, and that decision was upheld by the Supreme Court in 1996.

1914. Federal protection against discrimination on the basis of sexual orientation was contained in a bill passed by the 103rd Congress providing $8.6 billion in relief for victims of the January 17, 1994, Northridge earthquake in Los Angeles, CA. The bill specifically forbade discrimination on the basis of sexual orientation in the distribution of the aid.

1915. Vote on homosexual civil rights in the Senate took place in 1996, when the Senate failed to pass the Employment Non-Discrimination Act by a narrow margin of 50–49. The act was intended to prohibit workplace discrimination based on sexual orientation.

1916. State appeals court decision ordering the extension of insurance benefits to homosexual partners of government employees was made on December 9, 1998, when a three-judge panel of Oregon's State Court of Appeals upheld the 1996 ruling of a trial judge. The case involved three lesbian nurses who were employed by Oregon Health Sciences University, a public corporation that was formerly a state institution. They had applied in 1991 for medical and dental insurance for their domestic partners, but the university turned down the applications because it provided benefits to married spouses only. The court ruled that this denial violated the equal protection clause of the state constitution. Courts in New Jersey and other localities had rejected the equal-protection argument in previous cases.

1917. State to establish civil unions for homosexual couples was Vermont. In December 1999 the state supreme court issued a ruling requiring the state legislature to adopt some form of legal domestic partnership for same-sex couples that would afford them the rights, benefits, and obligations of marriage. The resulting bill

was signed into law by Governor Howard Dean on April 26, 2000, to become effective on July 1. It provided for a statutory definition of marriage as a union between a man and a woman and at the same time set up a parallel legal institution for gay and lesbian couples, giving them the right to receive a license from a town clerk and to have that license certified by a justice of the peace or a member of the clergy. The union could be dissolved through Family Court in the same manner as marriages are dissolved. The new arrangement affected Vermont's adoption and inheritance laws. A 1993 ruling by the supreme court of Hawaii had declared that state's marriage laws discriminatory, but no civil union law for homosexuals was enacted there because a constitutional amendment passed in 1998 empowered the legislature to place limits on the definition of marriage.

EQUALITY—RACIAL

1918. School desegregation lawsuit was filed by Benjamin F. Roberts in 1849 to compel the public schools of Boston, MA, to admit his five-year-old daughter Sarah. His lawyers included Charles Sumner, later to become famous for his antislavery stand in the Senate. The suit was denied. An appeal was heard by the state Supreme Court, which ruled that the government was not obligated to provide integrated schools and other services as long as there was equal provision for both races—the first statement of the principle of "separate but equal."

1919. Successful desegregation of public transportation took place in 1855, when a New York court ruled in favor of an African-American woman who had refused to leave her seat on a segregated horse-drawn streetcar in New York City. (Her lawyers included Chester Alan Arthur, then a young attorney, who went on to become the 21st president of the United States.) A similar case involving the Rev. James W. C. Pennington, author of *Textbook of the Origin and History of the Colored People*, took place the same year, and with the same outcome.

1920. Freedmen's Bureau was created by act of Congress on March 3, 1865, and signed by President Abraham Lincoln. Its object was to establish schools and better the conditions of the formerly enslaved African-Americans. The first commissioner was General Oliver Otis Howard, who took office on May 15, 1865.

1921. Civil rights law enacted by Congress was an "Act to Protect all Persons in the United States in their Civil Rights and Furnish the Means of Their Vindication," enacted on April 9, 1866, during the first session of the 39th Congress. The act provided that "citizens of every race and color, without regard to any previous condition of slavery or involuntary servitude . . . shall have the same right, in every State and Territory in the United States, to make and enforce contracts, to sue, be parties, and give evidence, to inherit, purchase, lease, sell, hold and convey real and personal property and to full and equal benefit of all laws and proceedings for the security of person and property, as is enjoyed by white citizens, and shall be subject to like punishment, pains, and penalties, and to none other, any law, statute, ordinance, regulation or custom, to the contrary notwithstanding."

1922. Federal law granting African-American men the right to vote was the congressional act of January 8, 1867, amending voting practices in Washington, DC. Every male citizen of the city who was 21 years of age or over was given the right to vote, except paupers, those under guardianship, men convicted of infamous crimes, and men who gave voluntary comfort to the rebels during the Civil War. The bill was vetoed by President Andrew Johnson on January 5, 1867. His veto was overridden in the Senate by a vote of 29 to 10 and in the House by a vote of 112 to 38.

1923. African-American to vote under authority of the 15th Amendment to the Constitution was Thomas Peterson-Mundy of Perth Amboy, NJ, who voted in Perth Amboy on March 31, 1870, in a special election for ratification or rejection of a city charter. The charter was adopted and he was appointed to the committee to revise the charter. The 15th Amendment to the Constitution, allowing African-American male citizens to vote, became law on March 30, 1870.

1924. Laws authorizing the use of force against the Ku Klux Klan were the four Force Acts, popularly known as the Ku Klux Klan Acts, passed by Congress between May 31, 1870, and March 1, 1875, with the aim of enduring the constitutional rights guaranteed to African-Americans by the 14th and 15th Amendments. The third Force Act, passed on April 20, 1871, enabled President Ulysses Simpson Grant to put nine South Carolina counties where the Klan was especially active under martial law. It also authorized the president to suspend the writ of habeas corpus, use

federal troops to suppress the Klan's paramilitary attacks on African-American freedmen and their white supporters, and imposed heavy penalties on those convicted. By the early 1880s, the combined weight of the Force Acts drove the Klan so far underground that it did not reemerge for many years. By that time, however, it had achieved its goal of restoring the South to white control.

1925. Jim Crow law intended specifically to discriminate against African-Americans was enacted by the Tennessee legislature in 1875 and was struck down as unconstitutional in 1880 by a federal circuit court. In 1881, Tennessee passed another law that segregated African-American passengers on railroads, establishing a precedent that was quickly imitated by other Southern states. The constitutionality of Jim Crow laws was upheld on May 18, 1896, by the Supreme Court in the case of *Plessy v. Ferguson*. The result was a flurry of state laws that segregated everything from restaurants to drinking fountains. The term "Jim Crow" was borrowed from a character in a minstrel show.

1926. Lynching ban enacted by a state was a statute approved on December 20, 1893, by Georgia, "an act to prevent mob violence in this state, to prescribe a punishment for the same, to provide a means for carrying this act into effect, to punish a failure to comply with its requirements, and for other purposes." Violators were guilty of a felony punishable by imprisonment of up to 20 years. If death resulted, a murder charge could be instituted.

1927. Federal attempt to address racial discrimination in employment was the creation of the Fair Employment Practice Committee, established by Congress on June 25, 1941, to encourage fair treatment of African-Americans by companies involved in war production, as well as by federal government agencies. When President Franklin Delano Roosevelt issued an executive order on May 27, 1943, requiring military contractors to pledge that they would not practice racial discrimination, white mobs in Detroit, MI, protested by rioting and were subdued by federal troops. On three subsequent occasions (1946, 1950, and 1952) the Senate declined to make the committee permanent.

EQUALITY—RACIAL—*continued*

1928. Challenge to school segregation in the South took place in Summerton, SC, where, in 1947, a farmer named Levi Pearson sued the Clarendon County Schools to obtain for African-American children the same free bus service made available to white students at public expense. Eventually, this suit was bundled with others, including *Brown v. Board of Education of Topeka,* when it reached the Supreme Court in 1952.

1929. President to address the National Association for the Advancement of Colored People was Harry S. Truman. On June 20, 1947, he spoke at the closing session of the 38th Annual Convention of the NAACP, which was held at the Lincoln Memorial in Washington, DC. Truman remarked that the nation had "reached a turning point in the long history of our country's efforts to guarantee freedom and equality to all our citizens. . . . We cannot wait another decade or another generation to remedy these evils [of racism]. We must work, as never before, to cure them now. The aftermath of war and the desire to keep faith with our nation's historic principles makes the need a pressing one."

1930. Year in which there were no reported lynchings of African-Americans was 1952. Record-keeping began in 1881.

1931. Use of federal troops to enforce integration took place after Arkansas governor Orval E. Faubus defied a desegregation plan adopted by the city school board of Little Rock and ordered the state militia to prevent nine African-American students from entering Central High School. On September 24, 1957, President Dwight David Eisenhower trumped Faubus in this test of federal versus state power and called out the Arkansas National Guard to enforce racial integration of the city's schools.

1932. Comprehensive civil rights law enacted by Congress was the Civil Rights Act of 1964, introduced in Congress after the March on Washington of August 28, 1963, at which the Reverend Dr. Martin Luther King, Jr., gave his "I Have a Dream" speech before a crowd of 200,000. The act was signed by President Lyndon Baines Johnson on July 2, 1964. It barred racial discrimination in public accomodations, public schools and facilities, and employment, and extended some federal protection to African-American voting rights.

1933. Federal law to effectively protect the voting rights of African-Americans was the Voting Rights Act of 1965, signed into law by President Lyndon Baines Johnson on August 6, 1965. The act prevented states from using literacy tests as a ploy to prevent African-Americans from registering to vote and made states liable to federal court action for the use of another such ploy, the poll tax. It also placed the election operations of seven states under the supervision of the federal attorney general. The law was introduced in Congress after a dramatic march by civil rights activists led by Martin Luther King, Jr., from Selma to Montgomery, AL. The constitutionality of the Voting Rights Act was upheld by the Supreme Court in March 1966 in *South Carolina v. Katzenbach.*

1934. State law to end de facto segregation in schools was "an act providing for the elimination of racial imbalance in the public schools," enacted in Massachusetts on August 18, 1965.

1935. School district to implement court-ordered busing to achieve racial integration was Charlotte, NC, which began busing its students on September 9, 1970. The program was the result of a lawsuit brought against the school board by Vera and Darius Swann, whose six-year-old son James had been denied a place in the school closest to his home because he was African-American and the school was designated for white students. In 1969 the school board was ordered by Federal District Court Judge James McMillan to comply with federal law by desegregating its schools. The school board refused to cooperate and was then ordered by Judge McMillan to implement a plan that involved busing students to different schools so that each building would have a set percentage of black and white students in its population. The case was appealed to the Supreme Court, which upheld the lower court's ruling on April 20, 1971, by a unanimous decision.

1936. Racial bias suit in which one African-American claimed discrimination by another African-American was mounted in 1989 by Tracy L. Morrow of Atlanta, GA, against her ex-boss, Ruby Lewis, and her former employers, the Internal Revenue Service and the Treasury Department. Morrow claimed that in 1986 she was fired from her IRS job as a clerk-typist because Lewis, a dark-skinned African-American, was prejudiced against her as a light-skinned African-American. In July 1990, a federal judge in Atlanta threw out the suit, ruling that Morrow was fired from her job because of her bad attitude and her inability to type.

1937. African-American woman nominated to head the Justice Department's Civil Rights Division was University of Pennsylvania law professor and former NAACP Legal Defense and Education Fund litigator Lani Guinier, offered the post of assistant attorney general for civil rights in May 1993 by attorney general Janet Reno. Her nomination was opposed by Senate conservatives, and the *Wall Street Journal* printed several editorials criticizing her scholarly articles supporting racial weighting in voting. In June, President William Jefferson Clinton withdrew her nomination, declaring that some of her ideas were "antidemocratic."

1938. Compensation paid to victims of mass racial violence was authorized by the legislature of Florida and signed into law on May 4, 1994, to indemnify the survivors of a massacre that had taken place 72 years earlier. In January 1923, the African-American town of Rosewood was burned to the ground by a mob of white people incensed by a rumor that an African-American man had assaulted a white woman. Eight of Rosewood's residents were killed. An investigation beginning in 1991 acknowledged that state officials of the time knew of the potential for violence and did nothing to stop it. The 1994 bill appropriated payments of more than $2 million to nine people who survived the attack and to descendants of the victims.

1939. Federal prosecution of a hate crime on the Internet was the case of Richard Machado of Los Angeles, CA, accused of violating the civil rights of 59 Asian students at the University of California at Irvine by sending them threatening, racist electronic mail. The case was tried in the federal district court at Santa Ana, CA. On November 25, 1997, the jury returned deadlocked and Judge Alicemarie H. Stotler declared a mistrial. Machado was tried a second time, convicted, and sentenced on May 4, 1998, to a year of probation and a $1,000 fine. Machado had already served a year in Federal custody for fleeing to Mexico after his indictment in November 1996.

1940. Federal judge to reduce a sentence as a protest against racial profiling by police departments was Nancy Gertner, judge of the Federal District Court in Boston, MA, who presided over the trial of Alexander Leviner. The defendant, an African-American man with a long record of minor drug offenses and traffic violations, was convicted of being a felon in possession of a gun. The judge set aside the Federal sentencing guidelines, which calculate sentencing based on previous jail terms, because, she said, the defendant's arrests were the result of discriminatory racial profiling by the police and because the calculations did not take into account the severity of the offenses. Instead of the four- to six-year prison term he would have received under the guidelines, she sentenced him on December 3, 1998, to a term of two and a half years.

EQUALITY—RELIGIOUS

1941. Settlement to welcome refugees of all faiths was Providence, RI, founded in June 1636 as a refuge "for such as were destitute for conscience' sake." Both the town and the colony of Rhode Island were established, with the help of the Narragansett Native Americans, by Roger Williams, a minister who had been banished from the Massachusetts Bay Colony the previous year for holding dissident religious and political opinions. Among those who found a haven there were Anne Hutchinson, who was exiled from Massachusetts for theological reasons; some of the first families of Jews to settle in North America; and the Quakers, who were a persecuted sect in Massachusetts.

1942. Document calling for religious toleration in America was "The Bloudy Tenent of Persecution, for cause of Conscience, discussed in a Conference between Truth and Peace . . .," a plea for freedom of conscience composed in 1644 by Roger Williams, the Baptist dissenter and founder of Rhode Island. In it, he wrote: "God requireth not an uniformity of Religion to be inacted and inforced in any civil state; which inforced uniformity (sooner or later) is the greatest occasion of civill Warre, ravishing of conscience, persecution of Christ Jesus in his servants, and of hypocrisy and destruction of millions of souls."

1943. Ban on Jesuits was passed in Puritan Massachusetts on May 26, 1647. It provided that "no Jesuit or eclesiasticl person ordayned by the authoritie of the pope shall henceforth come within our jurisdiction" excepting survivors of shipwrecks and traders who "behave themselves inoffencively during their abode here." A second offense was punishable by death.

EQUALITY—RELIGIOUS—*continued*

1944. Religious toleration law enacted by a colony was the Tolerance Act, enacted by Maryland on April 21, 1649. It ordered toleration for all who professed faith in Jesus Christ and subscribed to the orthodox interpretation of the Trinity, but prescribed the death penalty for Arian heretics, atheists, and Jews. It stated that "whatsoever person or persons within this province and the islands thereunto belonging shall from henceforth blaspheme God or deny our Saviour Jesus Christ to be the Son of God, or shall deny the Holy Trinity, the Father, Son and Holy Ghost, or the Godhead of any of these said persons of the Trinity, or the unity of the Godhead, shall be punished with death and forfeiture of all his or her lands and goods to the Lord Proprietary." The Arians were Christians who did not believe that Jesus was of the same substance as God.

1945. Ban on Quakers was passed by the General Court of the Massachusetts Bay Colony on October 14, 1656, at the urging of Governor John Endecott. The law provided for a fine of £100 for any ship captain who delivered Quakers "or any other blasphemous heretics" to the colony. Possessing Quaker books and coming to the defense of Quakers was also outlawed and punished with fines, whipping, and jailing. Subsequent anti-Quaker laws included the penalties of having the ears cut off and the tongue bored through with a hot iron.

1946. State test of religious qualifications for public office was imposed by New Jersey. Its original constitution of 1776 opened public office to "all persons, professing a belief in the faith of any Protestant sect, who shall demean themselves peaceably under the government," thus setting a barrier to anyone else. Profession of Christian beliefs, or of specifically Protestant beliefs, was required by most of the state constitutions drafted in 1776 and 1777.

1947. State to ban clergymen from serving in the legislature was Virginia, whose constitution of June 12, 1776, rendered "all ministers of the gospel, of every denomination, incapable of being elected members of either House of Assembly, or the Privy Council." The first state to rescind its exclusion of clergymen was Georgia, which did so in 1798.

1948. State law mandating separation of church and state was the Virginia Statute of Religious Liberty, drafted by Thomas Jefferson and enacted on January 16, 1786, with the support of George Mason, James Madison, and other prominent Virginians. It began with the statement that "Almighty God hath created the mind free," and included the requirement "that no man shall be compelled to frequent or support any religious worship, place or ministry whatsoever . . . nor shall otherwise suffer on account of his religious opinions or belief; but that all men shall be free to profess, and by argument to maintain, their opinion in matters of religion, and that the same shall in no wise diminish, enlarge or affect their civil capacities."

1949. Church disincorporated by Congress was the Mormon Church (formally known as the Church of Jesus Christ of Latter-day Saints) in Utah, primarily over the issue of polygamy, which was established as a Mormon religious tenet in 1852. (Strictly speaking, the Mormons practiced polygyny, with one man having multiple wives.) In 1862, Congress sought to break the theocratic power of the Mormon leaders by explicitly prohibiting polygamy in the territory, disincorporating the church, and restricting its property to $50,000. For many years the law was not enforced because the Mormons controlled the courts in Utah. In 1885, as a result of determined federal efforts to enforce the law, 23 Mormons were convicted and sent to jail. Many polygamous Mormons, including church leaders, went underground. In 1887, the Utah legislative assembly, petitioning for statehood and with the support of Mormon leaders, enacted a law prohibiting the practice. Finally, on October 6, 1890, a general conference of Mormons unanimously advised church members to refrain from polygamy in conformance with U.S. civil law. Some breakaway sects continue to practice it nonetheless.

1950. Legal clash between evolutionists and creationists was the famed Scopes "Monkey Trial," which began on July 10, 1925, in the Rhea County Courthouse, Dayton, TN, under Judge John Raulston. On trial was John Thomas Scopes, a high school science teacher accused of violating a new Tennessee law that banned classroom instruction in "any theory that denies the story of the Divine Creation of man as taught in the Bible." Scopes's guilt was never in question: he freely admitted to teaching the theory of evolution to his students, and in fact had conspired to be arrested to produce a test case. Supporting Scopes was the American Civil Liberties Union (ACLU); his attorney was the prominent defense lawyer Clarence Darrow. On the prosecution side was William Jennings Bryan, a three-time Democratic presidential candidate and a devout Christian. The trial quickly developed a carnival atmosphere, with trained monkeys performing right outside the courthouse. Most newspaper accounts portrayed the trial as a momentous clash between old-time religion and modern rationality—a not inaccurate assessment, as the main action of the case turned out to be Darrow's thorough public humiliation of Bryan and his biblical literalism. The jury returned a guilty verdict, and Scopes was fined $100. In 1927, the Tennessee Supreme Court overturned the verdict on a technicality.

EQUALITY—WOMEN AND MEN

1951. Woman whose vote was recorded was the widow of Josiah Taft of Uxbridge, MA, who participated in a town referendum in 1756. She was granted this privilege because her son, Bazaleel, was a minor. She voted in favor of levying a town tax.

1952. State to grant limited voting rights to women was New Jersey. Its new constitution, adopted on July 2, 1776, provided "that all the inhabitants of this Colony of full age who are worth 50 Pounds Proclamation money, with clear estate in the same, and have resided within the county in which they claim a vote for twelve months immediately preceding the election" were entitled to vote at the general election. In 1790 this was interpreted to mean both men and women. It did not, however, apply to married women, but only to spinsters and widows. On November 16, 1807, the General Assembly passed laws providing that only free white male citizens could exercise the franchise.

1953. State law giving property rights to married women was enacted by the state legislature of New York in 1848. It had first been introduced by Thomas Herttel in 1836. The campaign to persuade the legislature to pass the bill was spearheaded by Ernestine Rose, who authored the first petition for such a law in 1840, and by Elizabeth Cady Stanton and Paulina Kellogg Wright Davis.

1954. State constitution to recognize property rights for women was the first constitution of California, which took effect upon statehood on September 9, 1850.

1955. Federal law giving property rights to married women was the Married Women's Property Act, enacted by Congress in 1857. Among other provisions, it allowed married women to inherit and bequeath property; gave wives separated from their husbands the ability to make contracts and participate in lawsuits; and enabled wives deserted by their husbands to retain their own earned income.

1956. African-American women's rights activist who attempted to vote in a presidential election was Sojourner Truth, a former slave. On November 3, 1868, intending to vote for Ulysses S. Grant in the presidential election, she appeared at a polling booth in Grand Rapids, MI, and demanded a ballot but was turned away.

1957. Women to cast unofficial votes in a presidential election were a party of New Jersey suffragists, including four African-American women and the 84-year-old suffragist Margaret Pryer, who attempted to vote in the election of November 19, 1868, as a test of the recently ratified 14th Amendment to the Constitution. Section I of the amendment reads: "All persons born or naturalized in the United States, and subject to the jurisdiction thereof, are citizens of the United States and of the State wherein they reside. No State shall make or enforce any law which shall abridge the privileges or immunities of citizens of the United States." They were not allowed to vote with the men but cast votes in a separate ballot box.

1958. Territory to grant full voting rights to women was Wyoming, which was organized as a territory by Congress on July 25, 1868. In 1869, the upper house of the legislature of the Wyoming Territory passed a bill granting women the right to vote. After much debate, the lower house passed it also, fully expecting Governor John Campbell to veto it. But the governor surprised everyone by signing it into law on December 10, 1869, a day whose anniversary is celebrated annually as Wyoming Day. The women of Wyoming thus became the first in the world to receive the right to vote.

1959. State ban on sex discrimination in employment was passed by Illinois and approved by Governor John McAuley Palmer on March 22, 1872. The act provided that "no person shall be precluded or debarred from any occupation or employment (except military) on account of sex; Provided that this act shall not be construed to affect the eligibility of any person to an elective office. Nothing in this act shall be construed as requiring any female to work on streets or roads, or serve on juries. All laws inconsistent with this act are hereby repealed."

1960. Woman to argue for women's suffrage before a major committee of Congress was Susan B. Anthony, who on March 8, 1884, addressed the Judiciary Committee of the House of Representatives. Her remarks, reprinted in *Congressional Action in the First Session of the 48th Congress* (1884), began: "We appear before you this morning . . . to ask that you will,

EQUALITY—WOMEN AND MEN—*continued*

at your earliest convenience, report to the House in favor of the submission of a Sixteenth Amendment to the Legislatures of the several States, that shall prohibit the disfranchisement of citizens of the United States on account of sex." Anthony and other suffragists had been petitioning Congress for women's right to vote since 1865, and had addressed select committees for many years.

1961. State to grant full voting rights to women was Wyoming. When it became a state on July 10, 1890, Wyoming already had on the books a law granting women the right to vote and hold office. It had been enacted by the territorial legislature on December 10, 1869.

1962. Constitutional amendment proposal to guarantee women the right to vote was submitted in 1868 and at intervals thereafter without success. The woman suffrage amendment that eventually became law was passed by the House of Representatives on May 21, 1919, and by the Senate on June 4. It was ratified by Illinois, Wisconsin, and Michigan on June 10. Tennessee was the 36th state to ratify, on August 18, 1920, completing the necessary three-quarters of the states to put the amendment into effect. On August 26, 1920, the 19th amendment to the Constitution was proclaimed to be in effect.

1963. Proposal for a constitutional amendment mandating equal legal rights for women and men was submitted to Congress in 1923. The author was Alice Paul. The amendment was reintroduced at every subsequent session of Congress without success until March 22, 1972, when the Senate passed the Equal Rights Amendment by a vote of 84N8. The first state to ratify the amendment was Hawaii, which did so later the same day. Ratification by three-fourths of the 50 states, or 38 states, was required for adoption. Although the deadline for ratification of the ERA was extended in 1978 to June 30, 1982, it fell short by three states.

1964. President's Commission on the Status of Women was created on December 14, 1961, by Executive Order 10980, signed by President John Fitzgerald Kennedy. Eleanor Roosevelt was the first commissioner. On October 11, 1963, the commission issued its first report, *American Women.*

1965. Congressional ban on sex discrimination in wages was the Equal Pay Act of 1963, enacted on June 10, 1963, "to prohibit discrimination on account of sex in the payment of wages by employers engaged in commerce or in the production of goods for commerce."

1966. Federal law prohibiting discrimination in employment on the basis of sex was Title VII of the Civil Rights Act of 1964, signed into law on July 2, 1964, by President Lyndon Baines Johnson. A chief sponsor of the title was Democratic congresswoman Martha Griffiths of Michigan.

1967. Ban on sex discrimination in hiring by the federal government was instituted by Executive Order 11246, issued by President Lyndon Baines Johnson on October 13, 1967. It applied also to businesses and organizations under contract to the federal government.

1968. Parental leave law enacted by a state that applied to both mothers and fathers was passed by the Minnesota legislature in 1987. It allowed parents up to six weeks of unpaid leave from work.

1969. Sex discrimination case to establish the rights of fathers of newborn babies under the Federal Family and Medical Leave Act of 1993 was the result of a lawsuit brought by Kevin Knussman, a Maryland state trooper and helicopter paramedic, who was denied an extension of paid parental leave after the premature birth of his daughter and the hospitalization of his wife in December 1994. Although Maryland law allowed state employees with primary responsibility for newborns to take 30 days of sick leave, Knussman was not allowed to do so because he was the father, not the mother. On February 3, 1999, a jury ruled in his favor and awarded him $375,000.

F

FEDERAL COURTS

1970. Creation of federal courts was accomplished through the first Judiciary Act, drafted by William Paterson of New Jersey and Oliver Ellsworth of Connecticut, and enacted on September 24, 1789. It established a federal judicial system consisting of district courts (one for each state), circuit courts (one for each of three regions), a six-member Supreme Court, and the post of attorney general. The Supreme Court judges were required to preside over the circuit courts twice a year, which forced them to adopt a debilitating traveling schedule.

1971. Attorney of the United States was Samuel Sherburne, Jr., of New Hampshire, who was appointed United States attorney in and for the New Hampshire District on September 26, 1789. Twelve other attorneys, one for each state district, were appointed on the same date.

1972. Federal judge to be impeached was John Pickering, judge of the U.S. District Court for the district of New Hampshire, who was removed from office after his conviction by the Senate on March 12, 1804, on charges of drunkenness, profanity, and violence on the bench. The vote was 19–7.

1973. Claims court established by the federal government was established by an act "to establish a court for the investigation of claims against the United States," signed on February 24, 1855, by President Franklin Pierce. It required the appointment by the president, with the consent of the Senate, of three judges with life tenure. President Pierce appointed Isaac Blackford of Indiana and John James Gilchrist of New Hampshire on March 3, 1855, and George P. Scarborough of Virginia on May 8, 1855. The judges received $4,000 annually. The court was organized on May 11, 1855, with Judge Gilchrist as presiding judge. It was reorganized by act of March 3, 1863. Until March 3, 1887, it was the only court in which cases could be prosecuted against the government.

1974. Interracial jury composed of both white and African-American jurors was the grand jury that indicted Jefferson Davis, the president of the Confederacy, on a treason charge on May 8, 1866. The petit jury in this case was the second interracial jury. Davis, his wife, and their four children were captured at Irwinville, GA, on May 10, 1865, by Lieutenant Colonel Benjamin Dudley Pritchard, commanding the 4th Michigan Cavalry. Davis was imprisoned and indicted for treason. In 1867 he was released on bond. The case was finally brought to trial on December 3, 1868, in the Circuit Court of the United States at Richmond, VA, before Judges Salmon Portland Chase and John Curtiss Underwood, but was dismissed because of President Andrew Johnson's general amnesty proclamation, issued on December 25, 1868. The charge was dropped by the district attorney on February 15, 1869.

1975. Pensions for federal judges were authorized by Congress in the Judiciary Act of 1869, which provided that federal judges over the age of 69 who had a record of ten years of service could receive a retirement pension commensurate with the salary earned in the last year of service.

1976. Woman admitted to practice before the Court of Claims was Belva Ann Bennett Lockwood of Washington, DC, who was admitted in 1876 after convincing Congress to pass legislation making women eligible. She then served as sponsor for Samuel L. Lowery, who became, in 1877, the first African-American from the South to be admitted.

1977. Commerce court established by the federal government was established by act of Congress on June 18, 1910. A presiding judge and five associates were appointed by President William Howard Taft for terms that extended from one to five years. The court was organized on February 8, 1911, and opened on February 15 in Washington, DC. Appeal of its decisions could be made only to the Supreme Court. Because of various abuses, the court was abolished on December 31, 1913.

1978. U.S. district attorney who was a woman was Annette Abbott Adams, who served as U.S. district attorney in the Northern California District from July 25, 1918, to June 26, 1920.

1979. Woman justice on the federal bench was Genevieve Rose Cline of the U.S. Customs Court, New York, who was appointed on May 4, 1928, by President Calvin Coolidge

1980. Woman to serve as justice of the Circuit Court of Appeals was Florence Ellinwood Allen, nominated on March 6, 1934, by President Franklin Delano Roosevelt to fill the vacancy brought about by the death of Judge Smith Hickenlooper. She was sworn in on April 9, 1934. She served in the sixth judicial court.

1981. Woman to serve as foreman on a federal grand jury was Julia Isabelle Sims of Newark, NJ, who served on the federal grand jury in the U.S. District Court for the District of New Jersey in session at Newark from April 6, 1937, to October 19, 1937. Judge William Clark presided.

1982. Administrative Office of the United States Courts was created by act of August 7, 1939, and established on November 6, 1939. The body is charged with the nonjudicial, administrative business of the United States Courts, including the maintenance of workload statistics and the disbursement of funds for the maintenance of the judicial system. Its director is appointed by the chief justice of the United States.

1983. African-American judge on the federal bench was Irvin Charles Mollison of Chicago, IL, sworn in and inducted as a judge of the U.S. Customs Court on November 3, 1945, in New York City.

FEDERAL COURTS—*continued*

1984. African-American justice of the Circuit Court of Appeals was William Henry Hastie, former governor of the U.S. Virgin Islands, who was unanimously confirmed by the Senate on July 19, 1950, for a recess appointment to the Third Judicial Circuit (Pennsylvania, New Jersey, Delaware, and the Virgin Islands). He was sworn in by Chief Judge John Biggs, Jr., in Philadelphia, PA.

1985. Television eyewitness allowed to testify in a federal court was Mrs. Sophie Eisenberg of Brooklyn, New York City, who testified in U.S. Federal Court, New York City, on January 29, 1951, before Judge Irving Robert Kaufman. The lawsuit before the court had been brought by Jonas Walvisch of New York City, who had been a spectator at a hockey game between the Montreal Canadiens and the New York Rangers at Madison Square Garden on March 16, 1947. Walvisch accused Emile "Butch" Bouchard, the captain of the Canadiens, of hitting him, and sued him for $75,000. Mrs. Eisenberg testified that she was watching the game on television when she saw Bouchard hit Walvisch. The spectator, however, lost his suit.

1986. U.S. district attorney who was African-American was Cecil Francis Poole, who was sworn in July 6, 1961, at San Francisco, as attorney for the northern district of California. He retired February 3, 1970. Previously, four African-Americans had served as United States attorney in the U.S. Virgin Islands, which are territorial possessions of the United States.

1987. African-American judge to serve on a federal district court was Judge James Benton Parsons, who was sworn in on September 22, 1961, at Chicago, IL, as a U.S. district judge for the Northern District of Illinois. His appointment had been confirmed by the Senate on August 30, 1961.

1988. African-American woman to serve as judge of a federal district court was Constance Baker Motley, who was nominated by President Lyndon Baines Johnson on April 4, 1966, confirmed on August 30 by the Senate Judiciary Committee, and sworn on September 9, 1966, at the U.S. Court House, Foley Square, New York City, as judge for the Southern District of New York. In 1982 she was appointed chief judge. Previously, she had been the first African-American woman elected to the New York State Senate.

1989. Federal Judicial Center was created by act of December 20, 1967, to "further the development and adoption of improved judicial administration in the courts of the United States." It is the judicial branch's agency for policy research and continuing education. The Federal Judicial Center Board is made up of the Chief Justice of the United States, who is the permanent chairman; two judges of the U.S. courts of appeals; three judges of the U.S. district courts; one bankruptcy judge; and one magistrate judge. All are elected for four-year terms by the Judicial Conference of the United States. The director of the administrative office of the United States Courts is also a permanent member of the Board.

1990. African-American woman to serve as judge on the U.S. Court of Appeals was Amalya Lyle Kearse of New York City, who was sworn in on June 27, 1979, by Chief Judge Irving Robert Kaufman at the U.S. Court of Appeals, New York City.

1991. United States Sentencing Commission was established as an independent agency in the judicial branch of the Federal Government by the Sentencing Reform Act of 1984. The commission, which is composed of seven voting and two nonvoting members appointed by the president, develops sentencing policies and practices for the federal courts, including guidelines prescribing the appropriate form and severity of punishment for offenders convicted of federal crimes.

1992. African-American to serve as chief United States magistrate was Joyce London Alexander, who presided for the District of Massachusetts following her appointment in 1996.

FEDERAL GOVERNMENT

1993. Proposals for the organization of the executive branch were advanced by a number of political planners during the early years of the Republic, especially Alexander Hamilton, who held the view (expressed in a private letter of 1780) that "Congress should instantly appoint the following great officers of State, a Secretary for Foreign Affairs, a President of War, a President of Marine, a Financier, a President of Trade. These officers should have nearly the same powers and functions as those in France analogous to them; and each should be chief in his own department; with subordinate boards composed of assistants, clerks, etc., to execute his orders."

1994. Rebellion against the federal government took place in Massachusetts in 1786, when Daniel Shays of Pelham, MA, organized a group of malcontents into an armed force that overthrew courts and committed other acts of violence. They were protesting the depreciation of paper money, the insistence of creditors on being paid in silver money, and the imprisonment of debtors. On December 5, 1786, the rebels seized Worcester, and attempted to capture Springfield on January 25, 1787. By February 1787, however, they were completely routed.

1995. Federal charter was issued for the Bank of the United States by Congress on February 25, 1791. About 350 federal charters were granted between 1791 and 1974 to three types of organization: corporations carrying out some federal governmental or public function; private non-profit corporations with patriotic, civic-improvement, charitable, or educational purposes; and ordinary corporations organized in the District of Columbia.

1996. Federal building erected for public use was the U.S. Mint in Philadelphia, PA, a plain brick edifice built on the east side of Seventh Street. The cornerstone was laid by David Rittenhouse, director of the Mint, on July 31, 1792. The mint was established by the act of April 2, 1792, an "act establishing a mint and regulating the coins of the United States."

1997. Important exercise of an implied power of the government was the purchase of the Louisiana Territory, bought from France on April 30, 1803, for $15 million, and formally handed over to the United States on December 20. The treaty was arranged by Robert R. Livingston, minister at Paris, and James Monroe. No provision of the Constitution empowered President Thomas Jefferson, a strict Constitutionalist, to approve the acquisition of territory, but waiting for the passage of an amendment to validate the purchase would have allowed time for the deal to fall apart. Jefferson therefore approved the purchase on the general basis of Article 2, Section 2 of the Constitution—"[The President] shall have Power, by and with the Advice and Consent of the Senate, to make Treaties, provided two thirds of the Senators present concur"—without explicit Constitutional justification for his specific action, thereby exercising for the first time an implied power of the federal government.

1998. Airplane owned by the United States was purchased on August 2, 1909, from its manufacturers, Orville and Wilbur Wright of Dayton, OH, for $30,000, which included a $5,000 bonus thrown in because the plane was faster than anticipated (its top speed was 44 miles per hour). Dubbed *Miss Columbia,* the plane was a 28-foot biplane with a 25-horsepower motor and a wingspan of 36 feet 4 inches. Its first flight under government ownership was made at College Park, MD, on October 8, 1909, with Wilbur Wright and Lieutenant Frank Purdy Lahm at the controls.

1999. African-American woman to serve as a federal administrator was Mary Jane McLeod Bethune, born in Mayesville, SC, in 1875, the daughter of slaves. On June 24, 1936, she was named director of the Negro Division of the National Youth Administration by President Franklin Delano Roosevelt, thus becoming the first African-American woman to receive a major federal appointment. In 1904, Bethune founded the Daytona Normal and Industrial Institute for Negro Girls, later known as Bethune-Cookman College, located in Daytona Beach, FL. She was also the founder and first president of the National Council of Negro Women. In 1991, her home and offices in Washington, DC, were designated a national historic landmark.

2000. Federal government office to be computerized was the Bureau of the Census. On June 14, 1951, a UNIVAC I (Universal Automatic Computer) was demonstrated and dedicated at the Bureau of the Census in Philadelphia, PA. The world's first fully electronic computer available for civilian use, the UNIVAC was developed by J. Presper Eckert, Jr., and John W. Mauchly in 1951 and was manufactured by the Remington Rand Corporation, Philadelphia, PA. The machine could retain a maximum of 1,000 separate numbers, accept information contained on magnetic tape at the rate of more than 10,000 characters per second, add, subtract, multiply, divide, sort, collate, and take square and cube roots as needed, making it ideal for collating the data just gathered in the 1950 census.

2001. Federal government building built to withstand a nuclear attack was the laboratory for the Armed Forces Institute of Pathology, Walter Reed Army Medical Center, Washington, DC, which was occupied on March 13, 1955, and dedicated by President Dwight David Eisenhower on May 23. The eight-story reinforced concrete bomb-resistant building contained eight floors, five above ground and three

FEDERAL GOVERNMENT—*continued*

underground. It had a gross area of approximately 215,000 square feet and a net usable area of 130,000 square feet. It was constructed by the Cramer-Vollmerhousen Company of Washington, DC.

2002. Woman to serve on a federal government commission was Virginia Mae Brown of Pliny, WV, a Charleston lawyer, who was appointed to the Interstate Commerce Commission on March 4, 1964, by President Lyndon Baines Johnson. She was sworn in on May 25, 1964. She became vice chairman in 1968 and served as chairman from January 1 to December 31, 1969.

2003. Standardized criteria for federal incorporation were the "Standards For the Granting of Federal Charters," jointly developed in 1969 by subcommittees of the House and Senate Judiciary Committees. They mandated that all private organizations seeking a federal charter meet the following five minimum standards: (1) that it is operating under a charter granted by a State or the District of Columbia and that it has so operated for a sufficient length of time to demonstrate its permanence and that its activities are clearly in the public interest; (2) that it is of such unique character that chartering by the Congress as a Federal corporation is the only appropriate form of incorporation; (3) that it is organized and operated solely for charitable, literary, educational, scientific, patriotic, or civic improvement purposes; (4) that it is organized and operated as a nonpartisan and nonprofit organization; and (5) that it is organized and operated for the primary purpose of conducting activities which are of national scope and responsive to a national need, which need cannot be met except upon the issuance of a Federal charter.

2004. E-mail addresses for officials of the federal government were the addresses assigned to the president (president@whitehouse.gov) and the vice president (vice-president@whitehouse.gov) in 1993.

2005. Federal government Web site on the Internet was the World Wide Web site (http://www.whitehouse.gov/) established for the White House in 1993. This was the first Web site established by a national government anywhere in the world.

2006. Attack by domestic terrorists on a federal facility resulting in large loss of life occurred at 9:02 A.M. on April 19, 1995, when a massive truck bomb destroyed the Alfred R. Murrah Federal Building in Oklahoma City, OK. It was the first large-scale attack on a federal facility by domestic terrorists. One hundred sixty-eight people were killed, including 19 children, and an estimated 850 were injured. The rescue effort lasted two weeks and involved more than 12,000 volunteers, one of whom was killed by falling debris. A nationwide manhunt resulted in the arrest of Timothy McVeigh and Terry Nichols, both of whom had connections to the far-right militia movement. On June 2, 1997, McVeigh was convicted on fifteen counts of murder and conspiracy, and on August 14 he was sentenced to die by lethal injection. Nichols was found guilty of conspiracy and involuntary manslaughter and received a life sentence.

FEDERAL GOVERNMENT—AGENCIES

2007. Federal regulatory agency was the Interstate Commerce Commission, created by Congress on February 4, 1887. The ICC was developed to regulate surface transportation among the states by trains, trucks, buses, water carriers, and freight and parcel carriers, following less-than-successful attempts by several states to regulate rail rates, practices and operating rights. The five ICC commissioners were appointed for five-year terms.

2008. National emergency council was authorized on November 17, 1933, under Executive Order No. 6433A "for the purpose of coordinating and making more efficient and productive the work of the numerous field agencies" that were concerned with emergency management and relief. Frank Comerford Walker was appointed the executive director. He was also appointed executive secretary of the executive council of 23 members that was established on July 11, 1933.

2009. Federal codification board was created by congressional act of June 19, 1937. Its purpose was "to supervise and coordinate the form, style, arrangement and indexing of codifications to be prepared by each agency of the administrative branch of the Federal Government which is empowered by Congress to exercise rule-making power." The board consisted of six members. The first chairman was Major Bernard Reilly Kennedy, appointed on June 19, 1937. The first codification was filed on July 1, 1938.

2010. Reorganization of the federal government in the 20th century was accomplished under the Administrative Reorganization Act of 1939, which was passed on April 3. Plans I and II of the program went into effect on July 1. They redistributed the tasks of the multitudinous agencies, commissions, boards, and other entities of the federal government, leaving only 24, and placed these under the supervision of three superagencies that were created for the purpose. These were the Federal Security Agency, which included the Employment Service, the Office of Education, the Public Health Service, the National Youth Administration, the Social Security Board, and the Civilian Conservation Corps; the Federal Works Agency, which included the Public Buildings Administration, the Public Roads Administration, the Public Works Administration, the Works Projects Administration, and the United States Housing Authority; and the Federal Loan Agency. The Executive Office of the President also underwent a reorganization. Three additional plans were implemented in 1940. The act had been stalled for two years by congressmen and senators concerned that the changes would give excessive power to the president.

2011. General Services Administration was established by section 101 of the Federal Property and Administrative Services Act of 1949. It establishes policy for and provides economical and efficient management of government property and records, including construction and operation of buildings; procurement and distribution of supplies; utilization and disposal of real and personal property; transportation, traffic, and communications management; and management of the governmentwide automatic data processing resources program.

2012. Agency overseeing national elections was the Federal Election Commission, an independent agency established by section 309 of the Federal Election Campaign Act of 1971. The six-member commission has exclusive jurisdiction in the administration and civil enforcement of laws regulating the acquisition and expenditure of campaign funds to ensure compliance by participants in the Federal election campaign process.

2013. Agency promoting ethical conduct in government was the Office of Government Ethics, an executive agency established under the Ethics in Government Act of 1978. It provides overall direction of executive branch policies in preventing conflicts of interest on the part of officers and employees of all executive agencies.

2014. Federal agency charged with protecting whistleblowers in the federal government was the Office of Special Counsel, established on January 1, 1979, by Reorganization Plan No. 2 of 1978. Under the Whistleblower Protection Act of 1989, the OSC functions as an independent investigative and prosecutorial agency within the executive branch. Its primary role is to protect federal employees, former employees, and applicants for employment from prohibited personnel practices, especially reprisal for whistleblowing.

2015. Federal agency for national emergency management was the Federal Emergency Management Agency, the central agency within the federal government for emergency planning, preparedness, mitigation, response, and recovery. It was established by Executive Order 12127 of March 31, 1979, which consolidated all federal emergency-related programs. FEMA funds emergency programs, offers technical guidance and training, and deploys federal resources in times of catastrophic disaster.

FEDERAL GOVERNMENT—ARTS

2016. Woman artist to be commissioned by the federal government was Wisconsin-born sculptress Vinnie Ream (1847–1914). At the age of 17, having established herself in the Washington, DC, studio of sculptor Clark Mills, she received permission to make a bust of Abraham Lincoln from life. She was the last artist Lincoln sat for before his death. On July 28, 1866, Congress awarded her a commission to create a life-size statue of Lincoln for the rotunda of the Capitol; it was unveiled on January 25, 1871.

2017. Federal fine arts commission was established by Congress on May 17, 1910. The act authorized the appointment of seven commissioners knowledgeable in the arts to serve four-year terms and appropriated $10,000 for expenditures.

2018. Federal theater project was operated by the Civil Works Administration during the Depression, under the direction of Margaret Smith. Its first production was *The Family Upstairs,* for which $28,000 was authorized on January 12, 1934. The first performance took place on January 30 at the Central School of Business and Arts in New York City. Within three months, the project had staged 17 plays in more than 100 locations.

FEDERAL GOVERNMENT—ARTS—*continued*

2019. Consolidated arts funding agency was the National Foundation on the Arts and the Humanities, created as an independent agency by the National Foundation on the Arts and the Humanities Act of 1965. It consists of the National Endowment for the Arts, the National Endowment for the Humanities, the Federal Council on the Arts and the Humanities, and the Institute of Museum and Library Services.

FEDERAL GOVERNMENT—CIVIL SERVICE

2020. Federal government employees who were women were Sarah Waldrake and Rachael Summers, who were employed in 1795 by the Mint in Philadelphia, PA, as adjusters to weigh gold coins. Their pay was 50 cents a day.

2021. President to introduce the spoils system into the civil service was Thomas Jefferson, albeit on a much smaller scale than Andrew Jackson, who made the spoils system an entrenched and formidable institution. In 1802, President Jefferson directed the postmaster general, Gideon Granger, to fire a large number of postmasters and deputy postmasters appointed by his Federalist predecessors and replace them with people loyal to Jefferson's Democratic-Republican party. Postmasters who also held jobs as newspaper editors or printers—a frequent occurrence—were particularly singled out. Political patronage in postal service jobs continued until 1970, when the Postal Reorganization Act put a stop to it.

2022. Federal law fixing term limits for civil service employees was the Four Years' Law, enacted on May 15, 1820. It prescribed a fixed term of four years for a wide variety of federal officeholders, including customs collectors and district attorneys.

2023. Spoils system of presidential patronage on a large scale was instituted by President Andrew Jackson, who rewarded hundreds of his political supporters by appointing them to federal jobs. Jackson served as president from March 4, 1829, to March 3, 1837.

2024. Use of the phrase "to the victor belong the spoils" was made by William Learned Marcy, a member of the Albany Regency, New York State's first Democratic machine. He used it in a speech he made on the Senate floor in 1831. From this phrase developed the term "spoils system" to describe the awarding of government jobs to friends of the party in power.

2025. African-American to hold a federal civil service job was William Cooper Nell, who was a postal clerk in Boston, MA, from 1861 until his death in 1874. Nell was active in the campaign to make public education in Massachusetts available to African-American children and was the author of *Services of Colored Americans in the Wars of 1776 and 1812* and *Colored Patriots of the American Revolution.*

2026. Federal law to reform the civil service was a rider attached to the Civil Appropriation Bill of March 3, 1871. It gave to the president the power to prescribe rules for admission to the civil service and to "ascertain the fitness of each candidate in respect to age, health, character, knowledge and ability for the branch of the service into which he asks to enter." The Civil Service Commission created through this law lasted only until 1874 and perished for lack of funding from Congress.

2027. Civil Service Commission was appointed by President Ulysses S. Grant pursuant to the Civil Appropriation Bill of 1871, which authorized him to prescribe regulations for admissions of persons into the Civil Service. The commission, consisting of George William Curtis, Alexander Gilmore Cattell, Joseph Medill, D. A. Walker, Ezekiel Brown Elliott, Joseph H. Blackfan, and David C. Cox, became effective on January 1, 1872. Congress refused to make any further appropriations, and despite two direct appeals from President Grant, reform of the civil service was abandoned in 1874. The Pendleton bill reestablishing the commission was approved by President Chester Alan Arthur on January 16, 1883.

2028. Federal civil service reform law that was effective was the Pendleton Law, passed by Congress on January 16, 1883, in reaction to the assassination of President James Abram Garfield by a man who had been turned down for a civil service job. The law, named after its sponsor, George H. Pendleton of Ohio, established a new Civil Service Commission charged with holding competitive examinations for seekers of government jobs and awarding those jobs on the basis of merit rather than as a reward for political loyalty. The first head of the commission was Dorman B. Eaton, who had drafted the law.

2029. Woman appointed to a federal government job through the Civil Service was Mary Francis Hoyt. After passing the Civil Service examination, she was appointed on September 5, 1883, to a $900-a-year clerkship in the Bank Redemption Agency of the Treasury Department. She held the position five years.

2030. Woman employed by the executive branch of the federal government for official duties was Alice B. Sanger of Indianapolis, IN. On January 2, 1890, she began work as a stenographer to President Benjamin Harrison.

2031. Woman to serve as Civil Service commissioner was Helen Hamilton Gardener of Washington, DC, who was appointed by President Woodrow Wilson and sworn in on April 13, 1920. She had earlier been active in the movement for women's suffrage.

2032. Agency for administering federal personnel policies was the Office of Personnel Management, an independent agency established by Reorganization Plan No. 2 of 1978, effective January 1, 1979. Transferred to the OPM were many of the functions of the former United States Civil Service Commission. The OPM ensures compliance with federal personnel laws and regulations and assists agencies in recruiting, examining, and promoting people on the basis of merit.

FEDERAL GOVERNMENT—DEPARTMENTS

2033. Executive department authorized by Congress was the Department of Foreign Affairs, established by Congress in New York, NY, on July 27, 1789. Its first secretary was John Jay of New York, who had served since 1784 as the Continental Congress's secretary for foreign affairs. Jay was succeeded by Thomas Jefferson on March 22, 1790, when the department's name was changed to the State Department; thus Jefferson, rather than Jay, is considered the first secretary of state.

2034. Department of War was established as an executive department at the seat of government by an act approved on August 7, 1789, by Congress meeting in New York, NY. The first secretary of war was Henry Knox of Massachusetts, who took office on September 12, 1790. The Department of War was renamed the Department of the Army in 1947 and was placed under the National Military Establishment, later known as the Department of Defense.

2035. Department of the Treasury was created by act of Congress dated September 2, 1789, to manage the financial affairs of the government. The first secretary of the Treasury was Alexander Hamilton, appointed by President George Washington on September 11, 1789. The modern Department of the Treasury performs four basic functions: formulating and recommending economic, financial, tax, and fiscal policies; serving as financial agent for the U.S. Government; enforcing the law; and man-

ufacturing coins and currency. The position of deputy secretary of the Treasury was established by act of May 18, 1972, to act as the principal advisor to the secretary on all matters of policy and administration within the jurisdiction of the department.

2036. Secretary of a federal executive department to take orders from Congress was Alexander Hamilton, the first secretary of the treasury. On September 17, 1789, the House of Representatives, having disbanded its fiscal advisory committee (known as the Ways and Means Committee), sent an order to Hamilton directing him to provide an estimate of the funding required by the War Department and the civil list. This was in accordance with the statute that created the Treasury Department, which specified that the secretary would provide fiscal information to the Senate and House and act in an advisory capacity. Hamilton worked closely with the House throughout its first session, and indeed was accused of having far too much influence over it. Although the statutes creating the departments of State and War contained no such language, the House directed Secretary of State Thomas Jefferson on January 15, 1790, to draw up plans for a uniform system of measurements, and directed Secretary of War Henry Knox on April 23, 1790, to provide an assessment of the contribution, in men and ordnance, that each state had made toward the Revolutionary War.

2037. Department of the Navy was established by congressional act of April 30, 1798. Its first secretary, appointed on June 18, was Benjamin Stoddert of Maryland. Previously, by act of August 7, 1789, the conduct of naval affairs was under the Secretary of War, though the Continental Navy had ceased to exist in 1785. In 1949, under the National Security Act Amendments, the Department of the Navy became a military department within the Department of Defense.

2038. Department of the Interior was originally called the Home Department. It was created by congressional act of March 3, 1849, and took over bureaus formerly handled by the state, treasury, war, and navy departments, including the Office of the Census, the Office of Indian Affairs, the General Land Office, the Patent Office, and the Bureau of Mines. The first secretary was Thomas Ewing of Ohio.

2039. Department of Agriculture was proposed by President George Washington but was not created by Congress until May 15, 1862. Its first commissioner was Isaac Newton, formerly chief of the Patent Office's agriculture section, which had for many years been handling the

FEDERAL GOVERNMENT—DEPARTMENTS—*continued*

distribution of seeds, livestock, and technical information. The Agriculture Department was raised to cabinet status on February 11, 1889, with Norman Jay Colman of Missouri as its secretary.

2040. Department of Education was created by congressional act of March 2, 1867, an "act to establish a Department of Education," an agency "for the purpose of collecting such statistics and facts as shall show the condition and progress of education in the several states and territories, and of diffusing such information respecting the organization and management of school systems and methods of teaching as shall aid the people of the United States in the establishment and maintenance of efficient school systems and otherwise promote the cause of education." The act of July 28, 1868, effective June 30, 1869, abolished the Department of Education and established the Office of Education in the Department of the Interior. In 1953, education oversight was given to a new department, the Department of Health, Education, and Welfare. When this department was reorganized in 1979, the Department of Education was revived, with cabinet status. Its first secretary was Shirley Mount Hufstedler of California.

2041. Department of Justice was established by Congress on June 22, 1870, and was placed in the charge of the attorney general, a post that had been established in 1789 with cabinet status but that had never before been associated with an executive department. Its first head was Amos Tappan Akerman of Georgia. Previously, government court cases were prosecuted by hired private attorneys.

2042. Lifesaving medal awarded by the Treasury Department as authorized by act of June 20, 1874, was given on June 19, 1876, to Lucian M. Clemons, keeper of the United States Lifesaving Service Station at Marblehead, OH, for saving men from the schooner *Consuelo* on May 1, 1875. The award was estabalished for "persons who should thereafter endanger their own lives in saving or endeavoring to save the lives of others from the perils of the sea within the United States or upon any American vessel."

2043. Department of Commerce and Labor was authorized by congressional act of February 14, 1903. Its first secretary was George Bruce Cortelyou of New York. It included the Bureau of Immigration (taken from the Treasury Department) and the former Department of Labor, an executive department that did not have cabinet status. On March 4, 1913, Congress reorganized the department as the Department of Commerce and created a new Department of Labor.

2044. Department of Commerce was established on March 4, 1913, by act of Congress, which authorized the division of the Department of Commerce and Labor into two departments. The secretary of commerce and labor, William Cox Redfield, became the first secretary of commerce on March 5, 1913, and served until March 5, 1921.

2045. Department of Labor was authorized by act of Congress of June 13, 1888. It was headed by a commissioner and did not have cabinet status. On February 14, 1903, it was incorporated into the new cabinet-level Department of Commerce and Labor, whose first secretary was George Bruce Cortelyou. On March 4, 1913, Congress separated the department's two areas of authority and created a new Department of Labor, with William Bauchop Wilson as its first secretary.

2046. Department of Defense originated on September 18, 1947, as the National Military Establishment, created by the National Security Act of July 26, 1947, to unite the various service arms under a central administration. The same act provided for the appointment of a secretary of defense, of whom the first was James Vincent Forrestal of New York. Amendments to the act, made in 1949, gave the department its current name and made the secretary of defense the sole military representative in the cabinet.

2047. Department of the Air Force was established as part of the National Military Establishment by the National Security Act of 1947, and came into being on September 18, 1947. The Department of the Air Force, which is organized under the secretary of the Air Force, is responsible for defending the United States through control and exploitation of air and space.

2048. Department of Health, Education, and Welfare was established by Congress on April 11, 1953. On that same day, Oveta Culp Hobby of Texas was sworn in as the department's first secretary, with cabinet status. She had previously been the administrator of the Federal Security Agency, whose functions were absorbed into the new department. At the time of its creation, HEW oversaw the activities of 37,500 workers in 550 offices throughout the country.

2049. Department of Housing and Urban Development was established by Congress as a cabinet-level agency on September 9, 1965, taking over the functions of the Housing and Home Finance Agency. The first secretary was Robert Clifton Weaver of New York.

2050. Department of Transportation began functioning on April 1, 1967, having been created by act of Congress of October 15, 1966, to provide for federal regulatory oversight of railroads, highways, and air transportation. Alan Stephenson Boyd of Florida was the first secretary.

2051. Department of Energy was created on August 4, 1977, when President Jimmy Carter signed Public Law 95-91, the Department of Energy Organization Act. James Rodney Schlesinger became the first secretary of energy, with cabinet status. The formal opening took place on October 1, 1977, when approximately 20,000 employees of the Federal Power Commission, the Federal Energy Administration, the Energy Research and Development Administration, and components of other departments and agencies were consolidated in the new department.

2052. Department of Health and Human Services was created on October 17, 1979, when the Department of Health, Education, and Welfare was split into the Department of Education and the Department of Health and Human Services. The first secretary was Patricia Roberts Harris of Washington, DC.

2053. Department of Veterans Affairs was established on March 15, 1989, when the Veterans Administration was elevated to cabinet status. The first secretary was Edward Joseph Derwinski of Illinois.

FEDERAL GOVERNMENT—DOCUMENTS AND RECORDS

2054. Government Printing Office was created as an independent establishment by an act of Congress of June 23, 1860, to provide printing and binding for Congress and the federal departments, bureaus, and independent offices. On February 19, 1861, the amount of $135,000 was appropriated for the purchase of the printing plant of Joseph T. Crowell, Washington, DC. The plant was purchased on March 2 and began to function on March 4. The first superintendent of public printing was John Dougherty Defrees of Indiana, appointed on March 23, 1861, by President Abraham Lincoln. On January 12, 1895, Congress authorized the hiring of a superintendent of documents to take charge of the preparation of official catalogs and indexes of the government and of the distribution and sale of government publications. The first was F. A. Crandall, who served from March 26, 1895, to November 17, 1897. Sales were initially small, but from June 30, 1895, to June 30, 1896, 3,581 publications were sold, yielding a revenue of $889.09.

2055. Catalog of government publications was *A Descriptive Catalogue of the Government Publications of the U.S.—Sept. 5, 1774–March 4, 1881,* compiled by order of Congress. The work was given to printer Benjamin Perley Poore on March 1, 1883, and was finished in 1885. It was arranged chronologically with a general index and was published by the Government Printing Office, Washington, DC.

2056. Federal archiving agency was the National Archives Establishment, which was created in 1934 and subsequently incorporated into the General Services Administration as the National Archives and Records Service in 1949. Its successor, the National Archives and Records Administration, was established as an independent agency by act of October 19, 1984, effective April 1, 1985. NARA establishes policies and procedures for managing U.S. government records and assists federal agencies in documenting their activities, administering records management programs, scheduling records, and retiring noncurrent records. NARA also manages the presidential libraries system and publishes laws, regulations, and other public documents.

2057. Microfilm editions of federal publications and documents were offered as a regular service by University Microfilms, Ann Arbor, MI, in April 1952. The price was $900 for *Hearings, Reports, Committee Prints for the 82nd Congress.*

2058. Freedom of Information Act was approved on July 4, 1966, effective one year later, to clarify and protect the right of the public to information. It amended a preliminary act passed on June 11, 1946.

FEDERAL GOVERNMENT—DOCUMENTS AND RECORDS—*continued*

2059. Ruling requiring retention of all electronic records of the federal government was handed down on April 9, 1998, by Judge Paul L. Friedman of the U.S. District Court for the District of Columbia., who ordered the Archivist of the United States, John W. Carlin, to instruct federal agencies not to destroy electronic records without special approval. The ruling reinforced an earlier decision by Friedman nullifying General Records Schedule 20, a federal regulation allowing the destruction of federal electronic records according to a set schedule as long as paper copies were available.

2060. Government report posted on the internet before its publication on paper was "Referral to the United States House of Representatives Pursuant to United States Code, S 595(c) Submitted by The Office of the Independent Counsel, September 9, 1998," commonly known as the Starr Report. The 445-page report by independent prosecutor Kenneth Starr on the Clinton-Lewinsky affair claimed to contain "substantial and credible information that may constitute grounds for impeachment" of President William Jefferson Clinton.

FEDERAL GOVERNMENT—LIBRARIES

2061. Librarian of Congress was John James Beckley of Virginia, clerk of the House of Representatives, who was appointed on January 29, 1802, and served until his death on April 8, 1807. Until 1815, when George Watterston was appointed, the librarians were the clerks of the House of Representatives.

2062. Library of Congress was established by authority of the act of April 24, 1800, appropriating $5,000 "for the purchase of such books as may be necessary for the use of Congress at the said city of Washington and for fitting up a suitable apartment for containing them and for placing them therein." The books were housed in a room in the Capitol and went up in flames when the British put the building to the torch during the War of 1812. On September 21, 1814, former president Thomas Jefferson wrote to Samuel Harrison Smith, chairman of the Library Committee for the Library of Congress, and offered to donate his private book collection to Congress immediately, rather than wait until his death. He estimated the collection, acquired over the course of half a century, to comprise some nine or ten thousand volumes, adding that "it includes what is chief-ly valuable in science and literature generally [and] extends more particularly to whatever belongs to the American statesman. In the diplomatic and parliamentary branches, it is particularly full." Congress accepted the offer.

2063. Library of the Supreme Court originated as the law collection of the Library of Congress, which was made available to the justices of the Supreme Court in 1812. The 2,011 volumes in this collection were donated to the Court in 1832 on condition that members of Congress could still consult them.

2064. Fireproofing in the Library of Congress was installed in 1852. Congress appropriated the funds for the project after some 36,000 books—two-thirds of the 55,000-volume collection—were lost in a fire in December 1851.

2065. Librarian of the Supreme Court was Henry Deforest Clarke, who served from 1887 to 1900. The Court's book collection, acquired in 1832, was originally put in the charge of clerk of the Court, a post that was then held by William T. Carroll of Maryland. In 1884 it was transferred to John C. Nicolay, the marshal of the Court, who established the post of librarian within his department three years later. Congress made the librarianship a separate office in 1948.

2066. Library of Congress building was constructed on Capitol Hill in Washington, DC, in the late 19th century at the suggestion of Ainsworth Spofford, librarian of Congress, to relieve the overcrowding in the Capitol's Congressional Reading Room, where the collection had been housed. Funds for the project were authorized by Congress in 1886. The building was designed by John L. Smithmeyer and Paul J. Pelz, built under the supervision of Thomas Casey and Bernard Green, and opened to the public on November 1, 1897. It was named for Thomas Jefferson, whose personal library formed the nucleus of the national collection. Two other buildings are now part of the library complex.

2067. Archivist of the United States was Robert Digges Wimberley Connor, appointed on October 10, 1934. The position was created by an act of Congress that established the Archives Bureau. Connor served until September 15, 1941. The archivist has an official seal and is chairman of a national publications committee.

2068. Federal aid to libraries was authorized by the Library Services Act of June 19, 1956, "to promote the further development of public library service in rural areas." It authorized the appropriation for the fiscal year ending June 30, 1957, and for each of the four succeeding fiscal years, of the sum of $7.5 million, to be used for making payments to states.

2069. Library of U.S. foreign-policy papers on Africa and the Caribbean was the Arthur R. Ashe Jr. Foreign Policy Library and Resource Center, located at the headquarters of the TransAfrica lobbying organization in Washington, DC. The library was dedicated in June 1993.

FEDERAL GOVERNMENT—SCIENCE AND TECHNOLOGY

2070. Observatory established by the federal government was established by the Navy on December 6, 1830, in Washington, DC. The first instrument installed was a 30-inch portable transit telescope, which was made by Richard Patten of New York. Lieutenant Louis Malesherbes Goldsborough was appointed the first officer in charge of the observatory and served until 1833.

2071. National scientific advisory body was the National Academy of Sciences, incorporated by act of Congress and approved by President Abraham Lincoln on March 3, 1863, with the stipulation that "the Academy shall, whenever called upon by any department of the Government, investigate, examine, experiment, and report upon any subject of science or art, the actual expense of such investigations, examinations, experiments, and reports to be paid from appropriations which may be made for the purpose, but the Academy shall receive no compensation whatever for any services to the Government of the United States." The Academy's first president was Alexander Dallas Bache.

2072. Science and technology advisory board was authorized on July 31, 1933, under Executive Order No. 6238, to appoint committees to deal with specific scientific and technological problems in the various departments of the federal government. The nine-member board held its first meeting on August 21, 1933. The first president was Dr. Karl Taylor Compton, president of the Massachusetts Institute of Technology.

2073. Radiation experiments on human beings conducted by the federal government were performed between 1944 and 1974 by Atomic Energy Commission researchers on thousands of unsuspecting civilians and military personnel, including children, pregnant women, and prisoners. Several dozen research centers, nuclear weapons facilities, and hospitals were involved. The classified research was believed to have caused the deaths by radiation poisoning or cancer of as many as several hundred Americans. In January 1994, a 14-member panel, the President's Advisory Committee on Human Radiation Experiments, was formed by President William Jefferson Clinton to review federal involvement in secret radiation experiments. The committee's final report was released on October 3, 1995, and included a plan for compensation of the few surviving victims and the families of the deceased.

2074. Federal agency to support civilian scientific research was the National Science Foundation, created by the National Science Foundation Act of 1950. The NSF promotes the progress of science and engineering through the support of research and education programs and advances international cooperation through science and engineering.

2075. Aerospace agency of the federal government was the National Aeronautics and Space Administration (NASA), established by the National Aeronautics and Space Act of 1958. It conducts research for the solution of problems of flight within and outside the Earth's atmosphere; develops, constructs, tests, and operates aeronautical and space vehicles; conducts activities required for the exploration of space with manned and unmanned vehicles; and coordinates aerospace scientific and engineering programs with other nations.

2076. Rules to prevent secret government-sponsored human experimentation were announced on March 28, 1997, by President William Jefferson Clinton in response to a study by the Advisory Committee on Human Radiation Experiments. Experiments were conducted by the Atomic Energy Commission between 1944 and 1972 to test the effects of ionizing radiation and radioactive substances on thousands of unsuspecting Americans.

FINANCE

2077. Treasurer of the United States was Michael Hillegas, the owner of a music business in Philadelphia, PA. He served as treasurer of the new nation from July 29, 1775, until September 11, 1789. His co-treasurer was George Clymer. Hillegas's successor, Samuel

FINANCE—*continued*

Meredith, also of Philadelphia, was the first treasurer to serve under a president; he occupied the post from September 11, 1789, to October 31, 1801, during the administrations of Washington, Adams, and Jefferson.

2078. Foreign loan to the Continental Congress by a central governmental agency was negotiated with France. A resolution of December 23, 1776, authorized the loan of $181,500 (1 million livres), which was used for the purchasing of supplies and construction of cruisers. The length of the loan was indefinite. Bonds were sold at par. The rate of interest was 5 percent, payable annually. The loan was received on June 4, 1777. The final redemption was made on December 31, 1793, when the balance due was merged into the general account of the French debt.

2079. Broker to the Office of Finance of the United States was Haym Salomon, a Jewish immigrant from Poland who was active in the Sons of Liberty before the American Revolution. After the federal department of finance was created in February 1781, its superintendent, Robert Morris, relied on Salomon's Philadelphia brokerage firm to make a profit for the Treasury through the sale of securities and products. Salomon's commission was one quarter of one percent. He outfitted military units with his own funds and loaned large sums at no interest to members of the Continental Congress whose states could not afford to support them. The debts owed to him by the federal government at the time of his death in 1785 were never repaid to his family.

2080. Superintendent of finance under the Continental Congress was Robert Morris, a Philadelphian in the shipping business who had purchased weapons and imported military supplies for the Americans during the Revolution. The Continental Congress, faced with a devastating financial crisis, created a department of finance on February 6, 1781, and appointed Morris on February 20 to serve as its superintendent. He succeeded in establishing the Bank of North America, improving the credit of the United States, strengthening its currency, and reorganizing the financing of the army.

2081. Comptroller of the United States Treasury was Nicholas Eveleigh of South Carolina, who served from September 11, 1789, to April 16, 1791. The office was authorized on September 2, 1789.

2082. Loan to the United States was negotiated by Alexander Hamilton. Between September 13, 1789, and February 17, 1790, he obtained from the Bank of New York and the Bank of North America a total of $191,609. It was known as the Temporary Loan of 1789 and was obtained without authority of law. The money was used to pay salaries of the president, senators, representatives, and officers of the first Congress during the first session under the Constitution. The interest rate was 6 percent. The final redemption of the loan was made on June 8, 1790.

2083. Federal refunding act was approved by Congress on August 4, 1790, in "an act making provision for the [payment of the] debt of the United States," which provided that state, domestic, and foreign debts be consolidated and refinanced by three classes of bonds.

2084. Gold price fixed by Congress was $19.39 an ounce, authorized on April 2, 1792. Except for the period between August 1814 and February 1817, this value remained firm until June 28, 1834, when the value of an ounce of gold was raised to $20.67. This price remained firm until May 29, 1933, except during the panics of 1837 and 1857 and from February 25, 1862, to January 1, 1879.

2085. Economic depression of record took place in 1807, due largely to the total embargo on American exports passed by Congress that year. President Thomas Jefferson proposed the embargo as a way to coerce Britain and France into abandoning their practice of illegally impressing American sailors, but its main effect was to decimate New England industries. Depressions also took place, for varying reasons, in 1837, 1873, 1882, 1893, 1920, 1933, and 1937.

2086. Establishment of a treasury system took place during the Martin Van Buren administration with the passage by Congress of the Independent Treasury System Act of 1840. Under the act, which was inspired by widespread bank failures in the Panic of 1837, the United States withdrew its funds from state-chartered banks and placed them in newly established federal depositories. This had the effect of protecting federal funds from market instabilities, but also seriously weakened the state and private banking sector, which was deprived of its largest depositor. The act was repealed in 1841 under John Tyler, reinstated under James Knox Polk, and finally superseded by the National Bank Act of 1863.

2087. Comptroller of the Currency was Hugh McCulloch, who served from May 9, 1863, to March 8, 1865, when he resigned to accept appointment as secretary of the Treasury. His office was authorized on February 25, 1863. The term was five years, at a salary of $5,000 a year.

2088. Congressional legislation to control government expenditures was the Anti-Deficiency Act of 1870, part of the legislative appropriations bill for that year. At the time, agencies frequently overspent their appropriations and covered the difference through "coercive deficiency" requests to Congress. The Anti-Deficiency Act ended that practice, requiring departments to spend only what they had been appropriated.

2089. Demonetization of silver (abolishing bimetallism and making gold the sole monetary standard) was effected by the act of February 12, 1873, known as "the Crime of '73," which stopped the coinage of the old standard silver dollar of 412½ grains and authorized the coinage of a trade silver dollar of 420 grains for export. The trade dollar, not intended for circulation in the United States, but inadvertently made legal tender up to five dollars by this act, was deprived of its legal tender feature by joint resolution of July 22, 1876, and was dropped from the list of coins on March 3, 1887.

2090. Loan made by the United States to a war ally was a loan of $200 million at 3.5 percent, made to Great Britain on April 25, 1917.

2091. Liberty loans were authorized by Congress on April 24, 1917, through "an act to authorize an issue of bonds to meet expenditure for the national security and defense, and for the purpose of assisting in the prosecution of the war, to extend credit to foreign governments and for other purposes." Between May 2 and June 15, 1917, some 4 million people subscribed for $3,035 million in bonds that yielded 3.5 percent.

2092. Comptroller general of the United States was John Raymond McCarl, appointed by President Warren Gamaliel Harding on June 27, 1921. The term was 15 years, without eligibility for reappointment, and the salary was $10,000 per annum. McCarl served from July 1, 1921, to June 30, 1936. He was, at the same time, the first head of the General Accounting Office, which was created by the Budget and Accounting Act of June 10, 1921.

2093. Reconstruction Finance Corporation was created by the Reconstruction Finance Corporation Act, approved by Congress on January 22, 1932, "to provide emergency financial facilities for financial institutions, to aid in financing agriculture, commerce and industry, and other purposes." The act authorized the corporation to create, in any of the twelve Federal Land Bank Districts, intermediate credit corporations to assist farm stockmen. Interest at 7 percent was charged for the loans, which included all costs of inspection. The original capital of the corporation was set at $500 million. It was authorized to have up to three times its subscribed capital outstanding. The corporation was organized on February 2, 1932, and was managed by the secretary of the treasury and six directors.

2094. Gold hoarding order was issued by President Franklin Delano Roosevelt on April 5, 1933. It forbade the hoarding of gold in anticipation of the abrogation of the gold standard, which took place two months later. On April 20, Roosevelt placed an embargo on gold exports. This was modified on August 28 to permit the exportation of mined gold.

2095. Abrogation of the gold standard was authorized by the House on May 29, 1933, and by the Senate on June 3. The bill was signed by President Franklin Delano Roosevelt on June 5. It provided that all obligations which gave the obligee the right to require payment in gold or any particular kind of currency were against public policy and that payment could be made dollar for dollar in any currency that was legal tender at the time of payment.

2096. Federal gold vault was the U.S. Bullion Depository, a bomb-proof structure with elaborate mechanical security systems built at the military reservation at Fort Knox, KY, in 1936. Most of the nation's gold deposits are held there. The Depository was also used during World War II to safely store the original copies of the U.S. Constitution, the Declaration of Independence, and the Magna Carta, and a draft of the Gettysburg Address.

2097. International Monetary Fund meeting was held on December 27, 1945, in Washington, DC, with delegates from the United States attending. The IMF, now a United Nations agency charged with promoting international monetary cooperation, was founded in July 1944 at the Bretton Woods Conference in New Hampshire. The headquarters of the IMF are in Washington, DC.

FINANCE—*continued*

2098. Woman treasurer of the United States was Georgia Neese Clark, a banker and businesswoman of Kansas, who was appointed to that Federal post by President Harry S. Truman on June 4, 1949. She had been a member of the Democratic National Committee since 1936.

2099. Presidential commission on overhauling the budgetary process was the President's Commission on Budget Concepts, established by executive order of President Lyndon Baines Johnson in 1967. The commission's mandate was to make a thorough study of the federal budget and the manner of its presentation and make recommendations for improvement. The *Report of the President's Commission on Budget Concepts* was issued by the Government Publications Office in October 1967. Among its recommendations was that a unified budget presentation replace the many competing measures of federal financial activity.

2100. Detailed financial statement for the federal government showing all aspects of the government's assets and liabilities was publicly released on March 31, 1998, by the Clinton administration. Previously, the federal government provided to the public a general summary of its financial condition but did not release full details.

2101. Federal payment over the Internet was a $32,000 contract payment issued on June 30, 1998, by the U.S. Treasury's Financial Management Service to a unit of the GTE Corporation. The electronic checking system was developed by the non-profit Financial Services Technology Consortium.

FINANCE—BANKING

2102. Private bank chartered by Congress was the Bank of North America in Philadelphia, PA, which was organized on November 1, 1781. It began business on January 7, 1782, with a total capital of $400,000, of which the government subscribed $250,000. Thomas Willing was elected president and Tench Francis cashier. Later the bank entered the National Banking System.

2103. Bank of the United States was sponsored by the Federalist Party and was chartered in Philadelphia, PA, on February 25, 1791, by "an act to incorporate the subscribers to the Bank of the United States." Although the charter made no specific provision for the deposit of government funds, the secretary of the treasury, Alexander Hamilton, used the bank as a fiscal agent. The charter expired in 1811 and was not renewed by Congress because of the opposition of the Democratic-Republicans. The closing of the bank was partly responsible for the panic of 1814. The second Bank of the United States was authorized on April 10, 1816, and was opened on January 7, 1817. It ceased functioning as a national institution in March 1836.

2104. Location of the Bank of the United States was Carpenters' Hall in Philadelphia, PA, where it began operations in February 1791. In August of that year, it moved into a marble building that had been erected on Third Street. The building, designed by Samuel Blodget, was the first important marble building in the United States.

2105. Bank deposit insurance law enacted by a state was the Safety Fund Banking Law of New York, "an act to create a fund for the benefit of the creditors of certain monied corporations," enacted on April 2, 1829. Banking organizations were assessed one-half of 1 percent of the capital stock, until 3 percent was set aside for a bank fund. Three commissioners, known as Bank Commissioners of the State of New York, were appointed for two-year terms at an annual salary of $1,500. Banks, their officers, and their servants were required to be examined under oath at least once every four months.

2106. State bank to receive federal deposits after President Andrew Jackson required the removal of public funds from the Bank of the United States was the Girard Bank of Philadelphia, PA, in September 1833. These state depositories were known as "pet banks."

2107. State banking commission was created in Massachusetts in 1838, following a failed attempt by the state to regulate banks directly through the legislature.

2108. Banking reform after the Civil War was the Owens-Glass Act, signed by President Woodrow Wilson on December 23, 1913. The act created the Federal Reserve System, a central banking authority with a seven-member (now eight-member) board charged with setting interest rates, regulating the nation's supply of currency and credit, and functioning as the fiscal agent of the federal government. Twelve district banks were set up to serve as regional cash repositories for member banks, which were required to invest a portion of their holdings in the system.

2109. Federal reserve banks were formally opened on November 16, 1914, inauguarating the federal reserve system. The Federal Reserve Act, approved on December 23, 1913, was an "act to provide for the establishment of Federal Reserve Banks, to furnish an elastic currency . . . to establish a more effective supervision of banking in the United States." The twelve regional district banks were under the supervision of a seven-member Board of Governors.

2110. Bank wholly owned and operated by a state was the Bank of North Dakota, Bismarck, ND, established by special referendum election on June 26, 1919, under jurisdiction of the federal Industrial Commission, and opened on July 28. It was the only legal depository of all state funds and those of state institutions.

2111. Federal Home Loan Bank board was created by Congress on July 22, 1932, through the Federal Home Loan Bank Act, for the purpose of establishing and supervising the Federal Home Loan Banks as a permanent credit reserve system for savings and loan associations and similar local thrift and home financing institutions and for savings banks and insurance companies making long-term home mortgage loans. The board consisted of five members—Franklin William Fort, chairman, Dr. John Matthew Gries, William Edward Best, Nathan Adams, and Morton Bodfish—who took the oath of office and held the first meeting on August 9, 1932.

2112. Bank deposit insurance law enacted by Congress was the Glass-Steagall Act, known as the Banking Act of 1933, which was passed by Congress on June 16, 1933, "to provide for the safer and more effective use of the assets of banks, to regulate interbank control, and to prevent the undue diversion of funds into speculative operation." It insured deposits up to $2,500 each in all Federal Reserve banks. Deposits in approved banks were insured on a sliding scale: 100 percent up to $10,000; 75 percent from $10,000 to $50,000; and 50 percent over $50,000. A later law, entitled "an act to provide for the sound, effective and uninterrupted operation of the banking system, and for other purposes," approved on August 23, 1935, limited the insurance to $5,000 for any one depositor.

2113. Federal Deposit Insurance Corporation was created by Congress on June 16, 1933, by the Banking Act of 1933, "to provide for the safer and more effective use of the assets of banks, to regulate interbank control, to prevent the undue diversion of funds into speculative operations." The management of the corporation was vested in a board of three directors,

one of whom was the comptroller of the currency. The first board was composed of chairman Walter Joseph Cummings of Chicago, Elbert Gladstone Bennett of Salt Lake City, and James Francis Thaddeus O'Connor, comptroller of the currency. The first official meeting of the board of directors was held on September 11, 1933. The system went into effect on January 1, 1934.

2114. Savings and loan association established by the federal government was the First Federal Savings and Loan Association of Miami, FL, which was chartered on August 8, 1933. The creation of savings and loan institutions had been authorized by the Home Owners Loan Act of June 13, 1933, to provide a convenient place for the investment of small and large sums and to lend money to local applicants for first mortgages.

2115. Federal insurance program for bank deposits was the Federal Deposit Insurance Corporation (FDIC), established under the Banking Act of 1933 in response to numerous bank failures during the Great Depression. The Corporation began insuring banks on January 1, 1934. Its first payment to depositors of a closed insured bank was $125,000, paid to 1,789 depositors of the Fond du Lac State Bank of East Peoria, IL, which suspended business on May 28, 1934, and went into receivership on June 25, 1935. The first depositor to receive her share of the payment was a widow, Lydia Lobsiger, whose check arrived on July 3, 1934.

2116. World bank was the International Bank for Reconstruction and Development, which entered into force on December 27, 1945, when it was subscribed to by 21 countries, whose subscription amounted to $7,173 million. The United States subscription was $3,175 million. The first loan was made on May 9, 1947, to France—a 30-year loan of $250 million at 3.25 percent and of $150 million at 3 percent.

FINANCE—BONDS

2117. Bonds issued by the federal government were interest-bearing obligations that were authorized by the congressional act of August 4, 1790, for the refunding of the domestic debt and for that part of the state debt which was assumed by the federal government. The total issue amounted to $64,456,963.90, of which $30,088,397.75 drew interest at 6 percent, $19,719,237.39 at 3 percent, and $14,649,328.76 at 6 percent after 1800. Nearly the entire issue was retired by 1836.

FINANCE—BONDS—*continued*

2118. War bond issued by the federal government aside from the refunding of the Revolutionary War debts was authorized on March 14, 1812, for the purchase of weapons and equipment and the enlargement of the Army in preparation for the impending War of 1812 against Britain. The amount authorized was $11 million. Bonds were issued to the amount of $8,134,700 and sold exclusively in the United States.

2119. Treasury notes bearing interest were authorized by an act of Congress of June 30, 1812. The president was authorized to issue treasury notes to an amount not exceeding $5 million. The interest was fixed at "five and two-fifths per centum a year."

2120. Confederate government bond was authorized by act of February 28, 1861, "to raise money for the support of the government and to provide for the defense of the Confederate States of America." The bond issue limit was $15 million. The Confederacy's treasury secretary was Christopher Gustavus Memminger.

FINANCE—CREDIT

2121. Credit union law enacted by a state was sponsored by Pierre Jay, the first bank commissioner of Massachusetts, and was passed by the Massachusetts legislature. It was approved on May 21, 1909, by Governor Eben Sumner Draper.

2122. Credit union act passed by Congress was approved on June 26, 1934, "to establish a Federal Credit Union System, to establish a further market for securities of the United States and to make more available to people of small means credit for provident purposes through a national system of cooperative credit, thereby helping to stabilize the credit structure of the United States."

2123. Federal credit union chartered under the Federal Credit Union Act of 1934 was the Morris Shepard Federal Credit Union in Texarkana, TX, named in honor of the law's sponsor, which held its organizational meeting on October 1, 1934.

2124. Federal agency for administering credit unions was the National Credit Union Administration Board, established by act of March 10, 1970, and reorganized by act of November 10, 1978. NCUAB is responsible for chartering, insuring, supervising, and examining federal and state-chartered credit unions and administering the National Credit Union Share Insurance Fund. It also administers the Community

Development Revolving Loan Fund and manages the Central Liquidity Facility, a mixed-ownership Government corporation whose purpose is to supply emergency loans to member credit unions.

2125. Federal savings and loan bailout took place in 1987 under the Competitive Equality Banking Act, which pumped $10.8 billion into the bankrupt Federal Savings and Loan Insurance Corporation. Losses by thrifts in Texas and elsewhere, due largely to mismanagement and embezzlement, led to the FSLIC's insolvency in 1986. The unprecedented cost of the bailout, plus continued financial instability among thrift institutions, was a primary factor in the Wall Street crash of October 16, 1987. In 1989, Congress passed the Financial Institutions Reform, Recovery, and Enforcement Act, a new bank and thrift regulatory system.

FINANCE—DEBTS AND DEFICITS

2126. Year the public debt of the United States exceeded $100 million was 1815, during the administration of James Madison. Most of the debt was run up in connection with the War of 1812. On January 1, 1816, the debt totaled $127,334,933.74.

2127. Year in which the United States was free from debt was 1835. The total public debt was $77 million in 1790, $83 million in 1800, and $127 million in 1815. The sale of government securities and public lands in the 1820s and 1830s cut the debt to $7 million by 1832 and allowed it to be paid off three years later. The debt was retired on January 8, 1835.

2128. Year the public debt of the United States exceeded $1 billion was 1863, due to expenses connected with the Civil War. On July 1, 1863, the Treasury Department announced the debt to be $1,119,772,138.63.

2129. Year when the United States became a creditor nation rather than a debtor nation was 1914. Until that year, the United States owed more money to other nations than other nations owed to the United States.

2130. Year the public debt of the United States exceeded $10 billion was 1918, owing to expenses connected with America's entry into World War I. On July 1, 1918, the debt was $14,592,161,414.00.

2131. Year the public debt of the United States exceeded $100 billion was 1943, as the United States borrowed heavily to finance a global war on two fronts. On July 30, 1943, the Treasury Department announced the debt to be $136,696,090,329.90.

2132. U.S. balance of trade deficit in the 20th century began in 1968. Previously, the United States was a net exporter. The last time the United States had a trade deficit was in 1893.

2133. Year the public debt of the United States exceeded $500 billion was 1975, the last year of America's involvement in the Vietnam War. On March 1, 1975, the debt was $576,649,000,000.00, rounded to millions, including legal tender notes, gold and silver certificates, and other negotiables and securities.

2134. Year the public debt of the United States exceeded $1 trillion was 1981, following the energy crisis of the 1970s, tax cuts, and the beginning of "Reaganomics." On December 31, 1981, the debt was $1,028,729,000,000.00, rounded to millions.

2135. City to file for bankruptcy was Bridgeport, CT, whose mayor, Mary Moran, declared in June 1991 that the city would seek federal bankruptcy protection after it failed to reduce its $308 million annual budget sufficiently to remain solvent. The move was successfully contested by the state legislature.

2136. County to file for bankruptcy was the wealthy community of Orange County, CA, which on December 6, 1994, filed for Chapter 9 bankruptcy protection and defaulted on its municipal bonds. Beginning in February of 1994, the county's highly leveraged $7.8 billion investment fund had plunged $1.7 billion in value, the result of a risky investment strategy that was blindsided by rising interest rates. County treasurer Robert Citron pled guilty on April 27, 1995, to six felony counts, including misappropriating funds and misleading the county's bond investors. On June 27, 1995, Orange County residents voted to reject a half-cent increase in the sales tax intended to help restore the solvency of county government, choosing instead to rely on a prospective state bailout plan, which was passed by the California legislature on September 17. In 1998, Merrill Lynch, the firm handling Orange County's investment portfolio, agreed to pay $437 million to settle civil suits brought against it.

2137. Year the public debt of the United States exceeded $5 trillion was 1996. On September 30, 1996, the Treasury Department announced that the United States was $5,224,810,939,135.73 in debt.

FINANCE—MARKETS

2138. Closing of the New York Stock Exchange took place on September 20, 1873, when the exchange shut down in the wake of a banking crisis, caused by the financial panic of 1873.

2139. Federal agency to regulate the securities markets was the Securities and Exchange Commission, created under authority of the Securities Exchange Act of 1934, and organized on July 2, 1934. The purpose of the SEC was to administer federal securities laws that seek to provide protection for investors; to ensure that securities markets are fair and honest; and to provide the means to enforce securities laws through sanctions.

2140. Federal regulatory agency for futures trading was the Commodity Futures Trading Commission, established by the Commodity Futures Trading Commission Act of 1974. It began operation in April 1975. The five-member CFTC was intended to promote healthy economic growth, protect the rights of customers, and ensure fairness and integrity in the marketplace through regulation of futures (commodities) trading.

FINANCE—MONEY

2141. Use of bullets as currency took place in 1635, when the Massachusetts Bay Colony allowed musket bullets to be exchanged as legal tender. A maximum of twelve bullets was set for each transaction. Other forms of currency in this era were beaver skins and wampum, a Native American medium of exchange consisting of strings of small white and black shells. Wampum was declared unacceptable for payment of taxes in Massachusetts in 1651.

2142. Monetary regulation act was passed on September 27, 1642, by the General Court of the Massachusetts Bay Colony. The act regulated the value of the Holland "ducatour" (probably the ducatone, a silver coin issued in the Spanish Netherlands beginning in 1618), setting the value of the three-guilder coin at six shillings. A five-shilling value was set for the so-called "rix" dollar and the Spanish American eight-reales coin.

2143. Minting act was passed on May 27, 1652, by the General Court of the Massachusetts Bay Colony, authorizing the minting of local silver shillings and pence. The silver was obtained from melting foreign coins and from silver plate sold to the mint. Previously, an order had allowed the counterstamping of foreign coins with new faces, but this was deemed un-

FINANCE—MONEY—*continued*

successful, since few people wanted to use the poorer quality counterstamped coins when the originals were still legal tender. The text of the mint act provided "that all persons whatsoever have libertie to bring unto the mint howse at Boston all Bullion plate or Spanish Coyne there to be melted & brought to the Allay of Sterling silver by John Hull master of the said mint, & his sworne officers & by him to be Coyned into twelve pence Six pence & three pence peeces which shalbe for forme flatt & square on the sides & Stamped on the one side with N E & on the other side with xiid. vid & iiid according to the value of each peece together with a privie marke which Shalbe appoynted every three monethes by the governor & knowne only to him & the sworne officers of the mint."

2144. Mint was opened in Boston, MA, on June 10, 1652, by mintmaster John Hull and Robert Saunderson. It was authorized by the General Court of the Massachusetts Bay Colony to melt down foreign silver coins and from them mint new local coins. A legislative committee consisting of Richard Bellingham, William Hibbins, Edward Rawson, John Leveritt, and Thomas Clark oversaw the establishment and operation of the mint. The mint's first coin was the Pine Tree Shilling. It displayed a pine tree with the words "In Masathvsets" on the obverse and the words "New England An: Dom" and the year 1652 on the reverse.

2145. Paper money was an issue of bills of credit, offered by the Massachusetts Bay Colony as a way of raising money for its military campaign in Quebec. The bills, worth £40,000 pounds in all, were printed in December 1690.

2146. Continental money was an issue of $3 million, of which $2 million was issued on June 22, 1775, and $1 million on July 25. A second issue of $3 million was authorized on November 29 of that year. The largest share of the original issue, $434,244, was given to Massachusetts, and the next largest share was the $372,208 awarded to Pennsylvania. Only twelve states were granted money. Georgia was not included, as it was not represented in Congress.

2147. Decimal system of money with the dollar as a unit was adopted on July 6, 1785, by the Continental Congress, which established "that the money unit of the United States of America be one dollar; that the smallest coin be of copper, of which two hundred shall pass

for one dollar; that the several pieces shall increase in a decimal ratio." On August 8, 1786, it was voted "that the standard of the United States of America for gold and silver, shall be eleven parts fine and one part alloy."

2148. Coin to use *E pluribus unum* **as a motto** was the cent issued by New Jersey in 1786, the obverse of which showed a horse's head above a plow with the date of coinage and the name of the state in Latin, *Nova Caesarea*. The reverse showed a heart-shaped shield of the United States and the national motto *E pluribus unum* ("from many, one"). The first United States coin bearing the motto was the half eagle, authorized by act of Congress of April 2, 1792, and coined in 1795. The obverse showed the draped bust of Liberty facing right, with long, loose hair, and a liberty cap; above, "Liberty" and 15 stars; below, "1795." The reverse displayed an eagle bearing the shield of the United States on its breast, with arrows in its right claw and an olive branch in its left; in its beak, a scroll inscribed *E pluribus unum*; above its head, 16 stars; beneath it, an arch of clouds. The coin had a reeded edge and weighed 135 grains.

2149. Continental coin was the copper Fugio or Franklin cent, designed by Benjamin Franklin and authorized on July 6, 1787. One side showed 13 circles linked together to form a circle around the edge; a small circle in the middle bore the words "United States" around it, with the words "We are one" in the center. The other side showed a dial with hours on the face and a meridian sun above; on the left was the word *Fugio* ("I fly"), and on the right, "1787"; below the dial were the words "Mind Your Business." A contract for the manufacture of 300 tons of the coins was awarded to James Jarvis, who manufactured them in New Haven, CT. The dies were made by Abel Buell, also of New Haven.

2150. Adoption of the dollar as the standard monetary unit was made by Congress in the Coinage Act of April 2, 1792. It defined the dollar in terms of both gold and silver, with one dollar equal to 371.25 grains of silver or 24.75 grains of gold. It also provided for the minting of coin in a silver-to-gold ratio of 15:1, and allowed citizens to take gold or silver to a federal mint and have the bullion minted into coins free of charge.

2151. Mint of the United States was located at Philadelphia, PA. Robert Morris, as head of the Finance Department of the federal government, laid a plan for American money coinage before Congress on January 15, 1782. Through his efforts and the cooperation of Thomas Jefferson and Alexander Hamilton, an act "establishing a mint and regulating the coins of the United States" was approved by both houses and signed by George Washington on April 2, 1792. The cornerstone was laid on July 31, 1792, and construction was completed on September 7. The first director was David Rittenhouse. The first woman to serve as director was Nellie Tayloe Ross, formerly the governor of Wyoming, who took office on May 3, 1933.

2152. Coins made by the U.S. Mint in Philadelphia, PA, were one-cent and half-cent copper coins, of which there were four designs, the "chain cent," the "wreath cent," the "flowing hair," and the "liberty cap," which were authorized by Congress on April 2, 1792. Six pounds of old copper, the first metal purchased for coinage by the United States government, costing one shilling and three pence per pound, was coined and delivered to the treasurer in 1793. The cent equaled the hundredth part of a dollar and contained eleven pennyweights of copper, while the half cent contained five pennyweights of copper. This issue was discontinued by act of February 21, 1857.

2153. Silver coins issued by the Mint were minted from silver obtained from French coins, which were deposited by the Bank of Maryland on July 18, 1794. The first to be minted were the half dollar, quarter dollar, dime, and half dime, which were authorized under the congressional act of April 2, 1792, along with silver dollars. Under this act, all gold and silver coins struck at the Mint in Philadelphia, PA, were full tender. President George Washington, in his address to Congress of November 6, 1792, reported: "There has been a small beginning in the coinage of silver half dimes; the want of small coins in circulation calling the first attention to them." Silver coins continued in use until February 12, 1873, when Congress passed an act, known by its opponents as "the Crime of '73," that made gold the sole monetary standard.

2154. Gold coins issued by the Mint were minted from gold ingots delivered by Moses Brown, a Boston merchant, on February 12, 1795. The coins were authorized by Congress in the Coinage Act of April 2, 1792, which permitted the Mint to coin eagles ($10), half eagles ($5), and quarter eagles ($2.50). On March 3, 1849, the coinage of double eagles ($20) and one-dollar gold pieces was authorized, and on February 21, 1853, three-dollar gold pieces were authorized. Minting of the one-dollar and three-dollar gold pieces was dis-

continued on September 26, 1890. All gold coins were discontinued by the Gold Reserve Act of January 30, 1934, which stated that "no gold shall hereafter be coined." On April 5, 1933, President Franklin Delano Roosevelt issued an order forbidding the hoarding of gold, and on June 5 he signed a bill making it illegal to require repayment of financial obligations in gold.

2155. Return of coins to the Treasury took place on July 31, 1795. It consisted of 744 gold half eagles. The first return of gold eagles took place on September 22, 1795, and consisted of 400 pieces. The first return of silver coins to the Treasury took place on October 15, 1794.

2156. Private mint authorized by the federal government was the Moffat Assay Office, Mount Ophir, Mariposa County, CA, built in 1850 by John L. Moffat. The mint manufactured $50 hexagonal gold ingots used as legal tender to replace gold dust and nuggets. Beginning on February 20, 1851, the ingots were made under the supervision of the United States Assayer, and on July 3, 1852, Congress passed an "act to establish a branch of the mint of the United States in California." Augustus Humbert of New York was appointed United States Assayer to place the government stamp upon the ingots produced by Moffat and Company. In 1852 the mint became the United States Assay Office.

2157. Confederate coin was a silver half dollar produced at the mint in New Orleans, LA, in 1861. Only four pieces were minted. On the obverse was the Confederate shield with a liberty cap and a wreath of sugar cane and cotton branches. On the reverse side was the regular United States die.

2158. Paper money issued by the federal government was authorized by acts of Congress of July 17 and August 5, 1861, in the amount of $50 million. The notes were first issued on March 10, 1862. The denominations were $5 (Hamilton), $10 (Lincoln), and $20 (Liberty). They were called "demand notes" because they were payable on demand at certain designated subtreasuries. They were not legal tender when first issued but were made so by act of March 17, 1862.

2159. Bureau of Engraving and Printing for the production of paper money was authorized by Congress on February 25, 1862, and began operation on August 28. Signatures were engraved in facsimile and the seal of the Treasury imprinted on the notes after they had been delivered to the engravers. Certain stamps, notes, and bills were printed by individuals under contract.

FINANCE—MONEY—*continued*

2160. Legal tender was authorized by act of Congress of February 25, 1862, "an act to authorize the issue of United States notes and for the redemption or funding thereof, and for funding the floating debt of the United States." This was known as the Legal Tender Act and authorized the issuance of greenbacks up to $150 million.

2161. Bill bearing the likeness of a president was the $10 bill issued on March 10, 1862, which bore a portrait of Abraham Lincoln.

2162. Coin to use the motto "In God We Trust" was the two-cent piece of 1864. Salmon Portland Chase, secretary of the treasury, addressed a letter to the director of the Mint at Philadelphia, PA, stating that American coinage should bear a motto expressing in the fewest words possible that no nation can be strong except in the strength of God. Congress established the motto by act of April 22, 1864, which authorized the director of the Mint to fix the shape, mottoes, and devices to be used. On July 11, 1955, Congress enacted a law to provide that "all United States currency (and coins) shall bear the inscription 'In God We Trust.'" The phrase was made the national motto of the United States on July 30, 1956, when President Dwight David Eisenhower signed a joint resolution of Congress.

2163. Coins minted for a foreign government were produced by the U.S. Mint, Philadelphia, PA, during the fiscal year ending June 30, 1876, when 2 million two-and-a-half-centavo coins and 10 million one-centavo coins were struck for Venezuela. The coins were composed of copper, nickel, and zinc and had a diameter of 23 millimeters and 19 millimeters respectively. A congressional act of January 29, 1874, authorized coinage to be executed for foreign countries at the mints of the United States.

2164. Coin bearing the likeness of a president was the 1909 Lincoln penny, a copper cent, designed by Victor David Brenner and based on a photograph of President Abraham Lincoln taken in 1864 by Mathew B. Brady. The design was adopted in April 1909 and in May 1909 coinage began at the Mint in Philadelphia, PA. The first delivery of the coins was made on June 30, 1909, to the Cashier of the Mint, and distribution began on August 2. The reverse was redesigned in 1959 to show the Lincoln Memorial.

2165. Coin bearing the likeness of a living president was the 1926 Sesquicentennial half dollar, the obverse of which bore the heads of Presidents George Washington and Calvin Coolidge. The reverse depicted the original Liberty Bell. The net coinage was 141,120 pieces, struck at the Mint at Philadelphia, PA.

2166. Currency of the standard size of 6.14 inches by 2.61 inches was printed beginning in July 1929. Previously, U.S. currency was 7.42 inches by 3.13 inches, a size more expensive to print and harder to handle.

2167. Wooden money used in modern times was issued in 1932 by the town of Tenino, WA, when the local bank failed, freezing the town's assets. The scrip, in denominations of 25 cents, 50 cents, and a dollar, was printed on spruce and cedar chips, the most common material available.

2168. Currency note printed with the Great Seal of the United States was the $1 Silver Certificate, Series 1935. The seal has appeared on the reverse (green) side of all $1 notes since then, but does not appear in full on any other note or coin.

2169. Bill to depict both sides of the Great Seal of the United States was the one-dollar silver certificate, series of 1935, issued on December 18, 1935. The steel plates from which the bills were printed did not carry the signature of the Secretary of the Treasury or the Treasurer. The signatures were printed in a blank space on the face of bills at the same time that the bills were numbered and sealed.

2170. One-dollar Federal Reserve notes were issued in November 1963. Previously, nearly all one-dollar bills were silver certificates (a type of paper money authorized by Congress in 1878), which were issued in exchange for silver dollars.

2171. Popular hoarding of a lower-denomination coin took place beginning in 1964, with the issuing of the Kennedy half-dollar. Millions of Americans retained the coin, which was engraved with the likeness of John Fitzgerald Kennedy, as a keepsake of the assassinated president. As it was also the last coin issued by the United States with a substantial content of silver, it remained scarce in general circulation.

2172. Act eliminating silver from most coinage was the Coinage Act of 1965. Responding to a worldwide shortage of silver, Congress authorized the recomposition of dimes, quarters, and half-dollars, which had been 90 percent silver. Silver was eliminated from the dime and the quarter. The half-dollar's silver content was first reduced to 40 percent and then eliminated altogether in 1970.

2173. Coin to bear the depiction of an American woman was the Susan B. Anthony dollar, first issued on July 29, 1979. Anthony was a pioneer in women's rights, and was the first woman arrested (in 1872) for attempting to cast a vote in a presidential election. The coin was a conspicuous failure: it was too close in size and weight to the quarter coin, it was not considered more convenient than a dollar bill, and it was not accepted by many vending machines.

2174. Electronic anti-counterfeiting features in U.S. currency were security threads and microprinting, added in the series 1990 notes. The security thread contained electronic information that identified authentic currency, and microprinting was extremely difficult to reproduce with typical counterfeiting methods. Additional anti-counterfeiting features were incorporated into a series of redesigned notes that first appeared in 1996 with the $100 note. The revamped $50 and $20 notes appeared in 1997 and 1998, respectively.

2175. Alternate printing facility for U.S. currency was opened in Fort Worth, TX, in 1991, under the administration of the Bureau of Engraving and Printing, which still miantained the main paper money printing facilties in Washington, DC. By the year 2000, Fort Worth produced about half the nation's currency.

2176. United States coins depicting state symbols were approved by Congress through the 50 States Quarters Program Act of 1997. The act provided for the redesign of the reverse side of quarters to depict emblems of each of the 50 states, with a separate design for each state. The 50 new designs were to be introduced into general circulation at the rate of five per year, starting in 1999 and ending in 2008. They were issued in the order in which the states signed the Constitution or joined the Union.

H

HOLIDAYS

2177. Maryland Day commemorates the arrival on March 25, 1634, of the first colonists, some 200 in all, who crossed the Atlantic in two ships and landed on St. Clement's Island in the Potomac River. Their leader was Leonard Calvert, brother of the colony's sponsor, Lord Baltimore. The tercentennial of the date of their departure from England on November 22, 1633, was celebrated at Cowes, the port from which they sailed.

2178. Law against the celebration of Christmas was promulgated by the Puritans of the Massachusetts Bay Colony in 1659. The law was repealed in 1681, but not because of popular demand; by then, Puritan leaders were confident that no one wanted to celebrate the holiday.

2179. Tammany Day was celebrated in Philadelphia, PA, on May 1, 1732, by the members of the Schuylkill Fishing Company, who invoked the 17th-century Delaware Indian leader Tammany as the guarantor of Quaker fishing rights on the Schuylkill River. Tammany eventually became a familiar figure in Philadelphia's May Day festivities, particularly after the founding, in 1772, of a political organization, the Sons of King Tammany. The holiday spread to other states as new chapters of the organization were formed.

2180. Georgia Day commemorated the landing of James Edward Oglethorpe and a group of English settlers at Savannah, GA, in February 1733. Though the date is uncertain—it was either the twelfth or the thirteenth of the month—the state holiday is held on February 12.

2181. Saint Patrick's Day parade was held in New York City on March 17, 1762, by the city's Irish population.

2182. Commemoration of the Boston Massacre took place in Boston, MA, on March 5, 1771, one year to the day after the event, in which five Bostonians had been shot dead by a group of seven British soldiers who had been provoked by a hostile crowd into opening fire. The day was observed by a public meeting at which funds were collected for the survivors of the shooting. It was marked annually until 1783, when the city decided to celebrate the Fourth of July instead, but its observance was continued in Philadelphia by the Crispus Attucks Post of the American Legion, named after the first man to fall in the massacre.

HOLIDAYS—*continued*

2183. Halifax Resolutions Day was held to commemorate the adoption of the first declaration of independence issued by a colony. The event took place on April 12, 1776, at North Carolina's old capital, Halifax, where the Provincial Congress voted to instruct its delegates to the Second Continental Congress to declare independence. It is a legal holiday in North Carolina.

2184. Independence Day was celebrated in Philadelphia, PA, on July 4, 1777, one year to the day after the adoption of the Declaration of Independence by the Continental Congress. The idea for the celebration was broached on July 2 and the city had less than two days to prepare. Bonfires were lit in the streets, church bells were rung all day, and warships were dressed in banners. A dinner for political dignitaries was held at three o'clock, to the accompaniment of music played by a band of Hessian prisoners of war. A parade of soldiers followed. In the evening there was a display of fireworks, and the residents of the city illuminated their windows with candles. Those few who declined to do so had their windows broken.

2185. Mummers' play featuring George Washington instead of St. George was performed on New Year's Day, January 1, in Philadelphia, PA, shortly after the end of the Revolutionary War (circa 1785). The mummers' play, a holiday tradition in England and parts of Scandinavia, is a ritual reenactment of death and rebirth derived from pagan religion. In the Christianized English version, which was brought to Philadelphia by English settlers, the players act out the story of St. George killing the dragon. After George Washington became the national hero, it was natural to put him in the place of St. George. The character introduced himself with the lines "Here am I, great Washington! On my shoulders I carry a gun."

2186. Statehood Day (Tennessee) was celebrated on June 1, 1897, as part of the Centennial Exposition, held in Nashville from May through October. Tennessee had been admitted to the Union in 1786. The day was made a legal holiday by the state legislature in 1929.

2187. Constitution Day commemorating the signing of the Constitution on September 17, 1787, was an annual observance at Philadelphia, PA, in whose Independence Hall the event took place. The centennial of the signing was marked by a three-day celebration in Philadelphia that was planned by a national commission and was attended by President Grover Cleveland, the cabinet, the state and territorial governors, and other dignitaries. Adoption of the holiday by other cities and states was the result of advocacy by an anti-radical group, the National Security League, which began in 1914 to promote wider knowledge of the Constitution.

2188. Statehood Day (Kentucky) was the anniversary of June 1, 1792, the day on which Kentucky was admitted to the Union. It was originally part of Virginia and received the legislature's consent to form a separate state in 1789.

2189. Columbus Day was celebrated in New York City on October 12, 1792, by a political club, the Society of St. Tammany (also known as the Columbian Order), which held a ceremonial dinner on the occasion of the 300th anniversary of the first voyage of Christopher Columbus. The first nationwide observance of Columbus Day took place on the 400th anniversary in 1892, which was followed the next year by a world's fair, the Columbian Exposition, held in Chicago, IL. New York State made the day a legal holiday in 1909. Numerous other states followed suit, especially those with large Italian populations for whom Columbus was a national hero.

2190. Jackson Day commemorated the Battle of New Orleans, which ended on January 8, 1815, when the American troops under General Andrew Jackson defeated a British expeditionary force under General Packenham. Neither side knew that the War of 1812 had already been ended by the Treaty of Ghent. Jackson Day—also called Old Hickory Day and Battle of New Orleans Day—became an annual celebration and eventually a legal holiday in Louisiana. Jackson was guest of honor at the celebration in New Orleans in 1828 and used the occasion and its accompanying fanfare to begin his presidential campaign.

2191. Indiana Day was the anniversary of the admission to the Union of the state of Indiana on December 11, 1816. Indiana, together with Michigan and Illinois, was a part of the Indiana Territory, organized in 1800.

2192. Commemoration of the birthday of Benjamin Franklin became a tradition among many institutions in Philadelphia, PA, including the University of Pennsylvania, the Poor Richard Club, and the American Philosophical Association, following his death in 1790. One of the earliest known commemorations was a festive supper held on January 17, 1826, in Boston, MA, by the Franklin Typographical Society, an organization of printers. Franklin, born in Boston in 1706, learned the printing trade as an apprentice to his older brother and eventually set up shop for himself in Philadelphia as the publisher and printer of the *Philadelphia Gazette*.

2193. Commemoration of the birthday of Thomas Jefferson took place at Washington, DC, on April 13, 1830. A dinner in Jefferson's honor was held by the faction of the Democratic-Republican Party that supported Vice President John Caldwell Calhoun, the champion of states' rights and nullification. Several congressmen left the hall after realizing that all the toasts were intended to promote Calhoun's opinions. At the end, President Andrew Jackson offered a toast of his own: "Our Federal Union: It must and shall be preserved." Calhoun countered with the toast, "The Union: next to our liberty the most dear." Calhoun resigned from the vice presidency in 1832 and was replaced by Martin Van Buren. Jefferson's birthday is now a state holiday in Alabama and Oklahoma.

2194. Commemoration of the Mecklenburg declaration of independence as a legal holiday in North Carolina took place on May 20, 1831. The declaration, one of the earliest to be issued by the residents of an English colony, is said to have been signed in Charlotte, Mecklenburg County, by leading citizens of North Carolina. No copy survives.

2195. Texas Independence Day was a legal holiday in Texas, held to commemorate the declaration of independence from Mexico made by some 60 Texans on March 2, 1836, at Washington, TX. The declaration was made during the doomed defense of the Alamo in San Antonio by Texan rebels. Texas was declared an independent republic after the defeat of the Mexican army on April 21.

2196. San Jacinto Day was observed in Houston, TX, on April 21, 1837, one year after the Battle of San Jacinto, at which the Mexican army under General Antonio López de Santa Anna was defeated by an army of Texans under Sam Houston, securing Mexico's recognition of the declaration of independence that had been issued by the Texans on March 2. It was afterward adopted as a state holiday.

2197. Pioneer Day (Utah) was celebrated at Salt Lake City, Utah, on July 24, 1849, the second anniversary of the founding of the city by members of the Church of Jesus Christ of Latter-day Saints, led by its president, Brigham Young. It was marked by a procession and a public banquet. The territorial legislature declared the day a legal holiday in 1882.

2198. Admission Day (California) was held belatedly in San Francisco, CA, on October 26, 1850, to celebrate the admission of California to the Union the previous September 9. Several weeks had been required for the news to arrive from Washington, DC.

2199. West Virginia Day was the anniversary of June 20, 1863, the day on which West Virginia was admitted to the Union. West Virginia declared its independence from Virginia in June 1861, after Virginia's secession from the Union, and adopted a separate constitution on May 3, 1862.

2200. Nevada Day was celebrated on October 31, 1865, the anniversary of Nevada's admission to the Union. It was formed from the Nevada Territory, organized in 1861, when the area was separated from the Utah Territory.

2201. Commemoration of the birthday of Abraham Lincoln took place in Washington, DC, on February 12, 1866, ten months after President Lincoln's assassination. A joint session of Congress assembled at noon at the Capitol in the chamber of the House of Representatives, joined by President Andrew Johnson, most of his cabinet secretaries, the Justices of the Supreme Court, the governors of the various states, military officers, and other dignitaries. Following a brief performance by the Marine Band and a prayer by the House chaplain, the historian and diplomat George Bancroft delivered an address. Lincoln was born in Hardin County, Kentucky, in 1809.

2202. Alaska Day was held in commemoration of Alaska's transfer of ownership from Russia to the United States, which took place on October 18, 1867, pursuant to a treaty signed in Washington the previous March 30. Alaska was organized as a territory in 1912 and achieved statehood in 1959.

2203. Memorial Day as a national holiday was observed on May 30, 1868, by order of John A. Logan, commander in chief of the Grand Army of the Republic. The day, then called Decoration Day, was set aside "for the purpose of strewing with flowers or otherwise decorating the graves of comrades who died in defense of their country during the late rebellion, and whose bodies now lie in almost every city, village, and hamlet churchyard in the land." It was marked by a ceremony at Arlington National Cemetery. Tending the graves of the Civil War dead was a responsibility that had already been taken on in several states by local volunteer organizations, particularly women's memorial associations. The holiday was celebrated on May 30 until 1971, when Congress altered the date to the last Monday in May.

HOLIDAYS—*continued*

2204. Emancipation Day (Texas) was held on June 19, 1869. It commemorated events that took place in Galveston, TX, four years earlier, when Major General Gordon Granger of the Union Army announced that African-American slaves had been freed by the Emancipation Proclamation of 1863. After it ceased to be an official state holiday, it was observed informally by African-American Texans as Juneteenth. The day was designated as Black Heritage Day by Texas in 1979.

2205. Labor Day was inaugurated on December 28, 1869, by the Knights of Labor workers' organization. The first public Labor Day celebration was held in New York City in September 1882. Oregon declared the day a state holiday in February 1887, followed by Colorado in March and New York in May. The annual nationwide observance of Labor Day was sponsored by the American Federation of Labor, which resolved in convention at Chicago, IL, on October 7, 1884, "that the first Monday in September be set aside as a laborer's national holiday." On June 28, 1894, Congress designated the first Monday in September a legal holiday for federal employees and for the District of Columbia.

2206. Confederate Memorial Day was approved as a state holiday in 1874 by the Georgia General Assembly. The date of April 26 was chosen because on that date in 1865, Confederate general Joseph E. Johnston officially surrendered to General William Tecumseh Sherman, marking the end of the war for Georgia. Florida also celebrates April 26 as Confederate Memorial Day, but by 1912 several other southern states had chosen June 3, Jefferson Davis's birthday, as Confederate Memorial Day. Alabama and Mississippi celebrate the fourth Monday in April; North and South Carolina celebrate May 10, when Jefferson Davis was captured by Union troops.

2207. Kansas Day was observed on January 29, 1877, at the instigation of L. G. A. Copley, a Paola teacher.

2208. Flag Day took place on June 14, 1877, when the government requested that the flag be flown from all public buildings in commemoration of the 100th anniversary of the adoption of the American flag by the Continental Congress. The first state to make it a legal holiday was Pennsylvania, which held its first celebration on June 14, 1937. It became a national holiday through congressional joint resolution dated August 3, 1949.

2209. Colorado Day was held on August 1, 1877, to celebrate the anniversary of the admission of Colorado to the Union the previous year.

2210. Labor Day parade was held in New York City on September 5, 1882, under the auspices of the Central Labor Union. It featured musical bands and 10,000 marchers who carried placards reading "Less Work and More Pay," "Less Hours More Pay," "Labor Pays All Taxes," "Labor Creates All Wealth," "To the Workers Should Belong the Wealth," and "The Laborer Must Receive and Enjoy the Full Fruit of His Labor." The idea came from Peter J. McGuire, president of the United Brotherhood of Carpenters and Joiners of America.

2211. Ticker-tape parade took place in lower Manhattan on October 28, 1886, the day that the Statue of Liberty was dedicated. The day had been declared a public holiday in the city, and a parade of 20,000 people headed for the Battery, viewed by a crowd of more than 1 million. The streets were draped with red, white, and blue bunting in the designs of the French and American flags. As the parade came down Wall Street, according to the *New York Times,* workers in the financial houses "from a hundred windows began to unreel the spools of tape that record the fateful messages of the 'ticker.' In a moment the air was white with curling streamers."

2212. Commemoration of the birthday of Robert Edward Lee was made a legal holiday in Georgia in 1889 and in Virginia in 1890. Eight other Southern states also adopted the custom. Lee, the son of a Revolutionary War hero, was born at Stratford Hall, Westmoreland County, Virginia, on January 19, 1807. He graduated from West Point, married into the family of George Washington, and had a distinguished military career before resigning in 1861 to become commander of Virginia's forces and eventually commander of the Confederate armies. He died in 1870. In Virginia, the commemoration of his birthday was held in conjunction with that of Thomas Jonathan "Stonewall" Jackson, another Confederate general, who was born on January 21, 1824, and died in 1863.

2213. National holiday was April 30, 1889, authorized by act of Congress on March 21, 1889, in observance of the centennial of the inauguration of George Washington. The day was "hereby declared to be a national holiday throughout the United States." A committee of five senators and five representatives of the 51st Congress was appointed to arrange an appropriate celebration in Congress on December 11, 1889, at which Chief Justice Melville Weston Fuller was the guest speaker.

2214. Pan-American Day was occasioned by the founding of the International Bureau of American Republics (later renamed the Pan-American Union) at the first International American Conferences, held in Washington, DC, from October 2, 1889, through April 19, 1890. The official anniversary of the founding was celebrated for the first time on April 14, 1931, with ceremonies in the Pan-American Building in Washington, which were attended by the president, the cabinet, and diplomats from the countries of Central and South America.

2215. Kansas Day was celebrated by Republican Party clubs in Topeka, KS, on January 29, 1892, to commemorate the day in 1861 when Kansas was admitted to the Union as the 34th state. The admission followed a violent conflict over whether the territory would become a slave state or a free state. A proposed proslavery constitution was twice rejected by the territory's voters, and a constitution forbidding slavery was adopted on October 4, 1859.

2216. State to declare Lincoln's Birthday a legal holiday was Illinois, the state Lincoln had represented in Congress. Its first observance took place on February 12, 1892.

2217. Commemoration of the birthday of Jefferson Davis was observed as a legal holiday in Florida on June 3, 1892. Legal holidays were also established in Virginia, Texas, South Carolina, Mississippi, Louisiana, Georgia, Arkansas, and Alabama. Davis was born in 1808 in Kentucky, graduated from West Point, served in the United States Army, represented Mississippi as a Democrat in the House and Senate, and served as Secretary of War. The Confederacy elected him its president and commander-in-chief in February 1861.

2218. Patriots' Day was celebrated in Massachusetts on April 19, 1894, the 119th anniversary of the Battle of Lexington and Concord, the first military encounter in the War for Independence. The day had been declared a state holiday at the urging of the Sons of the American Revolution. It is now celebrated on the third Monday in April. It is also a state holiday in Maine, which was part of Massachusetts during the Revolution. Public observances usually include a reenactment of the famous ac-tivities of Paul Revere and William Dawes, who spent the early-morning hours of April 19, 1775, riding through the towns surrounding Boston to warn the inhabitants of the approach of British troops.

2219. Commemoration of the birthday of William McKinley took place on January 29, 1902. President McKinley had died on the previous September 14, a few months into his second term, of gunshot wounds inflicted by an assassin. He had been born in Niles, OH, in 1843. Many of the people who attended the memorial observances on his birthday in 1902 wore carnations, the flower that McKinley had frequently worn in his buttonhole. The following year's anniversary commemoration was officially known as Carnation Day, and in subsequent years it received particular attention in Ohio.

2220. Pioneer Day (Idaho) was observed on June 15, 1910, the fiftieth anniversary of the founding of Franklin, the first pioneer settlement. It was originally called Idaho Day. In 1911 the name was changed and the day was made a legal holiday.

2221. Missouri Day was enacted by the legislature of Missouri on March 2, 1915, as a day set aside for reflection on the state's history and achievements. The holiday was designated for the first Monday in October. It does not commemorate any particular event.

2222. Commemoration of the birthday of the Marquis de Lafayette (Marie-Joseph-Paul-Yves-Roch-Gilbert du Motier de Lafayette) took place informally in various places. Its first formal celebration was held on September 6, 1916, during World War I, as a way of showing solidarity with the French. Ceremonies took place in New York City, New Orleans, St. Louis, Providence, and numerous other cities. Lafayette, who was born in 1757, came to the United States at the age of 19 and volunteered to serve with the Continental Army.

2223. Armistice Day was observed nationally on November 11, 1919, on the anniversary of the day on which World War I was brought to an end. Public meetings, prayers, and parades were held, and two minutes of silence were observed at eleven o'clock, the hour at which hostilities ceased. President Woodrow Wilson in 1920 declared the Sunday nearest to Armistice Day to be Armistice Sunday, an appropriate day for prayer for world peace. The majority of states adopted the day as a legal holiday.

HOLIDAYS—*continued*

2224. Veterans Day observances took place simultaneously in many cities on November 11, 1919, to mark the anniversary of the signing of the armistice that ended World War I. The day, then known as Armistice Day, was designated as an annual day of mourning by President Woodrow Wilson. In Washington, DC, two California redwood trees were planted in Lafayette Square, opposite the White House, in the presence of cabinet officers, General John Joseph Pershing, and other military and federal officials. In 1954, the name was changed to Veterans Day and all American veterans were included in the tribute. It was made a legal holiday on May 13, 1938.

2225. Women's Equality Day has been observed yearly by advocates of women's rights on June 8, the day in 1920 when the proclamation observing the final ratification of the 19th Amendment, which reads in part: "The right of citizens of the United States to vote shall not be denied or abridged by the United States or by any State on account of sex."

2226. Commemoration of the birthday of Woodrow Wilson as a legal holiday took place in South Carolina on December 28, 1928, about five years after his death. He was the only president other than George Washington and Abraham Lincoln whose birthday was designated a state holiday.

2227. Pennsylvania Day was established by the Pennsylvania Legislature in 1931 to commemorate the birth of William Penn, founder of the colony of Pennsylvania. He was born on October 14, 1644, but the adoption of the new calendar altered this date to October 24, the day on which his birthday is now celebrated.

2228. Maritime Day took place on May 22, 1933. It was established by joint resolution of Congress on May 20, 1933. The resolution authorized and requested the president "annually to issue a proclamation calling upon the people of the United States to observe National Maritime Day by displaying the flag." The designated day was the anniversary of the sailing of the steamship *Savannah* from Savannah, GA, on May 22, 1819.

2229. Delaware Day was celebrated as a state holiday on December 7, 1933, the 146th anniversary of the day in 1787 when Delaware became the first state to ratify the Constitution.

2230. National Aviation Day took place on August 19, 1939, the 68th birthday of aviation pioneer Orville Wright. Orville and Wilbur Wright had made the first documented flights by motor-powered aircraft in 1903.

2231. Armed Forces Day was celebrated by presidential proclamation on the third Saturday of May in 1947. It replaced Army Day, formerly observed on April 6; Navy Day, formerly observed on October 27 (the birthday of President Theodore Roosevelt); and Air Force Day, formerly observed on the second Saturday in September.

2232. Federal law creating Monday holidays was Public Law No. 363, enacted by Congress on June 28, 1968, effective on January 1, 1971, and applicable to federal employees and residents of the District of Columbia. It established new days for the observance of Washington's Birthday (the third Monday in February), Memorial Day (the last Monday in May), Labor Day (the first Monday in September), Columbus Day (the second Monday in October), and Veterans Day (the fourth Monday in October). Many states have adopted similar legislation.

2233. Earth Day was held nationwide on April 22, 1970, to increase public awareness of the world's environmental problems. Twenty million Americans participated in marches, educational programs, and rallies, including the students at some 2,000 colleges and 10,000 high schools. The event, organized by environmental activist Denis Hayes, is generally credited with inaugurating the modern environmental movement in the United States.

2234. Martin Luther King Day was officially observed as a national holiday on January 20, 1986. It marked the birthday of the African-American minister and civil rights leader Martin Luther King, Jr., the champion of nonviolent social protest and winner of the 1964 Nobel Peace Prize, who was born on January 15, 1929, in Atlanta, GA. A bill to make his birthday a national holiday was submitted to Congress by Representative John Conyers of Michigan in April 1968, four days after Reverend King was killed by an assassin. The observance was moved to the third Monday in January when the new holiday was created by Congress in November 1983.

2235. Native American Day was celebrated by Native Americans in South Dakota on October 8, 1990. The day was also Columbus Day, and was chosen for that reason.

HOLIDAYS—INDEPENDENCE DAY

2236. Public celebration of national independence took place in Philadelphia, PA, on Monday, July 8, 1776, four days after the Continental Congress adopted a resolution accepting the Declaration of Independence, which had been drafted by a five-member committee that consisted of John Adams, Benjamin Franklin, Robert Livingston, and Roger Sherman, with Thomas Jefferson as the chairman. A large crowd congregated in the State House Yard (now Independence Square) to hear Colonel John Nixon read the Declaration aloud. Church bells and chimes were rung for hours, and soldiers paraded on the common.

2237. Independence Day to be observed as a state holiday was celebrated by Massachusetts on July 4, 1781.

2238. Independence Day after the adoption of the Constitution was celebrated in Philadelphia, PA, on July 4, 1788. Planning had begun on June 21, when New Hampshire became the ninth state to ratify the Constitution, establishing it as the law of the land. By the time the Fourth of July arrived, a tenth state, Virginia, had joined the ratifiers. The day began with pealing bells from the steeple of Christ Church and celebratory cannon fire from a vessel in the harbor, where ships and wharves were decorated with banners. The morning was taken up by a parade of five thousand people stretching over a mile and a half, including numerous floats—one for each state, one for the Union, and many others that were sponsored by groups of tradespeople, who gave demonstrations in motion. (The printers' float, for example, carried a working press, on which the printers were striking off copies of a poem written by Francis Hopkinson, the nation's first composer, who was also a judge and a leader of the procession.) At Union Green the marchers and spectators assembled to hear an address by James Wilson, a signer of the Declaration of Independence and an associate justice of the Supreme Court. Finally, there was a dinner, at which ten toasts were given, each answered by ten artillery rounds. According to Hopkinson's account, they were "The People of the United States; Honor and Immortality to the Members of the Late Federal Convention; General Washington; The King of France; The United Netherlands; The Foreign Powers in Alliance with the United States; The Agriculture, Manufactures and Commerce of the United States; The Heroes who Have Fallen in Defense of Our Liberties; May Reason, and not the Sword, hereafter Decide all National Disputes; The Whole Family of Mankind."

2239. City to forbid the sale of firecrackers for Fourth of July celebrations was Springfield, MA, which banned firecrackers in 1903 to prevent the fires, deaths, and mutilations that had become typical aspects of Independence Day.

HOLIDAYS—THANKSGIVING

2240. Thanksgiving proclamation was dated June 20, 1676, and issued by Governor William Bradford of the Massachusetts Bay Colony. It read in part: "The Holy God having by a long and Continual Series of his Afflictive dispensations in and by the present Warr with the Heathen Natives of this land, written and brought to pass bitter things against his own Covenant people in this wilderness, yet so that we evidently discern that in the midst of his judgements he hath remembered mercy, having remembered his Footstool in the day of his sore displeasure against us for our sins, with many singular Intimations of his Fatherly Compassion, and regard . . . the Council has thought meet to appoint and set apart the 29th day of this instant June, as a day of Solemn Thanksgiving and praise to God for such his Goodness and Favour."

2241. National day of thanksgiving was authorized by the Continental Congress and held on December 18, 1777, to celebrate the surrender of Lieutenant General John Burgoyne on October 17 at Saratoga (now Schuylerville), NY. The first to be designated by presidential proclamation was November 26, 1789, which was appointed by President George Washington as a day of general thanksgiving to God for the adoption of the Constitution, the survival and independence of the nation, the arrival of prosperity and tranquillity, the establishment of civil and religious liberty, and the opportunity to gain and spread knowledge, and as a day of prayer and supplication for divine forgiveness and divine aid.

2242. Thanksgiving Day was held on November 26, 1863, to commemorate the feast of thanksgiving held by the Pilgrims at Plymouth, MA, in 1621. A proclamation by President Abraham Lincoln, dated October 3, 1863, set aside the fourth Thursday in November for an annual nationwide observance. The establishment of Thanksgiving Day was the result of a long campaign by Sarah Josepha Hale, the editor of the popular magazine *Godey's Lady's Book*. The holiday was moved forward to the third Thursday in November in 1939 to accommodate merchants who wanted more time for the pre-Christmas shopping rush but was returned to its traditional spot two years later.

I

INTERNATIONAL RELATIONS

2243. Alliance between the United States and another country was formalized in the treaties of amity and alliance with France, drafted in Paris on February 6, 1778. The only alliance established by the United States until the 20th century, the relationship was negotiated mainly by the French foreign minister, Comte de Vergennes, and the U.S. minister to France, Benjamin Franklin. Not only did France supply sorely needed funds and supplies to the Continental Army, but it also supplied troops; Washington commanded an army almost evenly divided between American and French forces at the siege of Yorktown, the decisive battle of the Revolutionary War, where he defeated the British on October 19, 1781.

2244. Foreign nation to recognize the independence of the United States was France, whose royal council agreed to do so in December 1777. The recognition was formally made in a treaty of military alliance that was signed in Paris on February 6, 1778, along with a treaty of amity. Benjamin Franklin and Silas Deane represented the Americans in the negotiations. The Comte de Vergennes, France's minister of foreign affairs and an antagonist of the British, hastened his country's recognition of the new nation after failing to persuade Spain to join in an anti-British alliance.

2245. Salute fired by Great Britain in honor of an officer of the United States was fired on May 8, 1783, when General George Washington and Governor George Clinton arrived at the British ship *Ceres,* commanded by Sir Guy Carleton, in New York Harbor to arrange for the British evacuation. When they departed, 17 guns were fired in honor of Washington's rank. New York was evacuated by the British on November 25, 1783.

2246. President to dispatch a personal envoy on an overseas mission was George Washington, who informed the Senate on February 14, 1791, that the lawyer and former revolutionary leader Gouverneur Morris had gone to Britain at the president's request to conduct confidential discussions. When the discussions were concluded some months later, the president forwarded to the Senate his envoy's report. He also sent Colonel David Humphreys, his aide, on a similar msision to Spain and Portugal.

2247. British ambassador to the United States was George Hammond. He was appointed on July 5, 1791.

2248. Anti-American satirical medalets were the Paine medalets, also known as the Condor tokens (for their first cataloguer), small medals struck in Great Britain beginning in 1793. They carried messages directed against Thomas Paine, the American revolutionary and author of the anti-Royalist tract *Common Sense,* who was then a Jacobin refugee in France and the subject of British ire. The medals, imported into the United States in some numbers, showed his body hanging from a gallows or his head on a pole, with inscriptions such as "The Wrongs of Man" or "May the Knave of Jacobin Clubs Never Get a Trick."

2249. Neutrality regulation enacted by Congress that governed the actions of citizens was passed by act of Congress on June 5, 1794. The act provided that any citizen who "accepts and exercises a commission to serve a foreign prince, state, colony, district or people, with whom the United States are at peace shall be fined not more than $2,000 and imprisoned not more than three years." The first conviction was that of Isaac Williams of Norwich, CT, who accepted a commission in a French armed vessel and served against Great Britain. He was tried in September 1799 at Hartford, CT, in U.S. Circuit Court, found guilty under two counts, and sentenced on each count to a fine of $1,000 and imprisonment for four months.

2250. American passport was issued on July 8, 1796, by the U.S. State Department.

2251. Isolationist address by a president was George Washington's Farewell Address, published in Philadelphia, PA, on September 19, 1796, in David Claypoole's *American Daily Advertiser.* (Washington never delivered the address in person.) Washington warned the young republic to avoid "foreign alliances, attachments & intriegues" and noted that "The nation which indulges toward another an habitual hatred or an habitual fondness is in some degree a slave." So well were Washington's words heeded that the United States did not enter into a permanent alliance with another nation until the 20th century.

2252. Foreign aid bill was "an act for the relief of the citizens of Venezuela," enacted by Congress on May 8, 1812. An appropriation of $50,000 was made to enable the president to obtain such provisions as he should deem advisable for the relief of the citizens of Venezuela "who have suffered by the late earthquake."

2253. Recognition by the United States of a newly independent nation was accorded on June 19, 1822, when the United States formally recognized the Republic of Colombia. Over the course of the next four years, the United States gave formal recognition to Mexico (December 1822), Chile and Argentina (January 1823), Brazil (May 1824), the United Provinces of Central America (August 1824), and Peru (May 1826). Recognition of the emerging Latin American nations, as they claimed their independence from Spain and Portugal, was urged by Representative Henry Clay beginning in 1818. On May 4, 1821, Congress passed legislation providing for the possibility of recognition and the establishment of diplomatic relations.

2254. Articulation of the Monroe Doctrine was contained in President James Monroe's seventh annual message to Congress, delivered on December 2, 1823. The text was drafted by Monroe's secretary of state, John Quincy Adams. Promulgation of the doctrine was occasioned by fears that Spain and France might attempt to regain control of their recently liberated colonies in Latin America. In the message, Monroe warned the European colonial powers that the United States "should consider any attempt on their part to extend their system to any portion of this hemisphere as dangerous to our peace and safety. With the existing colonies or dependencies of any European power we have not interfered and shall not interfere. But with the Governments who have declared their independence and maintain it, and whose independence we have, on great consideration and on just principles, acknowledged, we could not view any interposition for the purpose of oppressing them, or controlling in any other manner their destiny, by any European power in any other light than as the manifestation of an unfriendly disposition toward the United States."

2255. Conference of American republics was the General Congress of South American States, assembled on March 14, 1826, at Panama. Convoked by Simon Bolivar, who sent invitations in December 1824, it was attended by delegates from Mexico, Colombia, Peru, and Central America. Richard Clough Anderson and John Sargeant were appointed delegates from the United States in July 1825, but their appointment was not confirmed until December 6, 1825, and the conference adjourned before they reached it.

2256. Continent claimed for the United States was Antarctica. On January 19, 1840, an expedition led by Captain Charles Wilkes sighted the eastern coast of Antarctica and claimed it for the United States. The United States never formally annexed land in Antarctica, and on December 1, 1959, signed the Antarctic Treaty, which prohibited the signatories (including Argentina, Australia, Belgium, Chile, France, Japan, New Zealand, Norway, South Africa, the Soviet Union, and the United Kingdom) from claiming sovereignty over any part of the continent.

2257. Use of the term "manifest destiny" appeared in 1845 in the July–August issue of *The United States Magazine and Democratic Review*. The author of an anonymous article (probably the editor, John L. O'Sullivan) wrote that foreign governments opposed to the annexation of Texas by the United States hoped to prevent "the fulfillment of our manifest destiny to overspread the continent allotted by Providence for the free development of our yearly multiplying millions." Robert C. Winthrop of Massachusetts used the term the following January 3 in a speech in the House of Representatives.

2258. Japanese diplomatic delegation to the United States arrived in 1860, six years after the signing of a treaty that opened trade between the two nations. The "nobles of Niphon," as they were called by Walt Whitman in a poem published in the *New York Times,* were honored in New York City on June 26, 1860, with a parade down Broadway.

2259. Passport fee was levied under the Internal Revenue Act of July 1, 1862, "to provide internal revenue to support the government and to pay interest on the public debt." It fixed a fee of $3 for "every passport issued in the office of the Secretary of State." Prior to this time, consuls in foreign countries charged a fee not exceeding $1 for passports they issued, but passports issued in the United States were free.

2260. Recognition by a European nation of the right of its subjects to acquire American citizenship was tendered by Britain in an expatriation treaty signed in 1869. The War of 1812 was fought in part because the British Navy refused to recognize the new citizenship of American sailors who had been born in Britain and routinely seized them as deserters.

2261. Korean embassy was received by President Chester Alan Arthur on September 18, 1883, at the Fifth Avenue Hotel, 23rd Street, New York City. Min Yong Ik, the ambassador, presented his credentials. He was accompanied by Hong Yong Sik, the vice ambassador, and

INTERNATIONAL RELATIONS—*continued*
by his secretary, the foreign secretary, and five attachés. The Koreans were dressed in court robes and dropped upon their knees as they bowed to President Arthur and Secretary of State Frederick Theodore Frelinghuysen.

2262. Conference of American states initiated by the United States was the First International Conference of American States, which opened in Washington, DC on October 2, 1889, at the invitation of Secretary of State James Gillespie Blaine. Ten participating nations signed an arbitration treaty. After 1910 the conference members became known as the Pan-American Union. In 1948, the Ninth International Conference of American States, held in Bogotá, Colombia, established the Organization of American States as the successor to the Pan-American Union.

2263. Pan-American union was the International Bureau of American Republics, established on April 14, 1890, by the First International Conference of American States, which met at Washington, DC, from October 2, 1889, to April 19, 1890, and was presided over by James Gillespie Blaine, secretary of state. The name of the bureau was changed by resolution of August 11, 1910, to the Pan-American Union. The first director of the Bureau was William Eleroy Curtis, who was appointed on August 26, 1890, and who served until May 17, 1893. In 1948, the Ninth International Conference of American States, held in Bogotá, Colombia, established the Organization of American States (OAS) as the successor to the Pan-American Union.

2264. United States case to be arbitrated in the Hague Permanent Court of Arbitration was the Pious Fund Case of the Californias, a dispute between the United States and Mexico. The Pious Fund consisted of money collected by Jesuits in Mexico for missions in California. This money was withheld by Mexico after 1848, when Mexico ceded Upper California to the United States. The issue that was presented to the Court of Arbitration was whether the claim of the United States for indemnity on behalf of two Roman Catholic officials (the archbishop of San Francisco and the bishop of Monterey) was governed by the principle of *res judicata*. The Court unanimously agreed that it was, and ordered Mexico to pay $1,420,682.67 in Mexican currency and $43,059.99 annually, beginning on February 2, 1903.The protocol of agreement was signed on May 22, 1902, and the award of the court was made on October 14, 1902.

2265. Use of the term "dollar diplomacy" took place in a 1910 speech by William Howard Taft, who was then in the middle of his single presidential term. According to Taft, dollar diplomacy was a foreign policy that was based on "active intervention to secure for our merchandise and our capitalists opportunity for profitable investment which shall insure to the benefit of both countries concerned." In his annual message to Congress of December 3, 1912, Taft characterized the policy as "substituting dollars for bullets." During his term, the United States attempted to apply dollar diplomacy in China and Latin America, with limited success.

2266. Arms sales to Russia took place in 1915, during World War I, when the Remington Arms Company of Connecticut shipped 1 million rifles and 100 rounds of ammunition to Czar Nicholas II's Imperial Russian Army. Remington later built a huge munitions factory in Bridgeport, CT, with accomodations for 1,500 Russian arms inspectors. The munitions contract lapsed after the Bolshevik Revolution of 1917.

2267. General association of nations promoted by a president was the League of Nations, founded at the Paris Peace Conference in 1919 at the instigation of President Woodrow Wilson. It was headquartered in Geneva, Switzerland. The League's main purpose was to maintain stable international relations and to prevent another world conflict. In theory, the Covenant of the League of Nations provided for collective security, international arbitration, and a permanent court of justice for its members. In practice, the League lacked any power to discipline member states and failed completely in its mission. The harshest blow to its viability was the fact that Wilson was unable to sell the idea to the American people; the Senate never ratified United States membership. The League of Nations was disbanded in 1946.

2268. American woman to become a member of the British Parliament was Lady Astor, born Nancy Witcher Langhorne in Danville, VA. She succeeded her second husband, Waldorf Astor, in the House of Commons when he moved to the House of Lords in 1919 after becoming Viscount Astor of Hever on the death of his father. She was elected to represent the Plymouth constituency and took her oath of office on December 1, 1919. She was not only the first American-born woman to sit in Parliament, but the first woman of any nationality to do so.

2269. Arms control conference held in the United States was the International Conference on Naval Limitation, held in Washington, DC, from November 12, 1921, to February 6, 1922. Attending were representatives from the United States, Britain, France, Japan, and Italy, who discussed how to forestall a naval arms race in the Pacific region. At the conference, Secretary of State Charles Evans Hughes proposed that the major powers scrap some 1,900,000 tons of existing warships and stop building new large battleships for a period of ten years. Eventually, all the participant nations signed the Five-Power Naval Limitation Treaty, which set strict limits on the numbers and tonnages of capital ships owned by the navies of each signatory. Japan, which had built one of the most formidable navies in the world, was especially resentful that the United States was allowed, under the treaty, to launch five ships for every three built in Japan.

2270. Conference of great powers to be held on American soil and affecting American interests was the Conference on the Limitation of Armaments, which assembled in at Memorial Continental Hall in Washington, DC, from November 12, 1921, to February 6, 1922. Nine nations took part in the conference: the United States, Great Britain, France, Italy, Japan, China, Holland, Belgium, and Portugal. The American delegation was headed by Secretary of State Charles Evans Hughes.

2271. International friendship park was the International Peace Garden, located on the border between North Dakota in the United States and the province of Manitoba, Canada. It was founded in 1932 to mark the lasting friendship between the two countries. About two-fifths of the park's area is in the United States.

2272. Diplomatic relations between the United States and the Soviet Union began on November 16, 1933, during the first administration of Franklin Delano Roosevelt. The first American ambassador to the Soviet Union, William Christian Bullitt, presented his credentials in Moscow on November 21, 1933.

2273. President to negotiate with the Soviet Union was President Franklin Delano Roosevelt, who inaugurated diplomatic recognition of the Union of Soviet Socialist Republics by the United States on November 16, 1933, in an agreement with Maksim Maksimovich Litvinov, the People's Commissar for Foreign Affairs.

2274. Large foreign aid package was authorized by the Lend-Lease Act, passed by Congress at the urging of President Franklin Delano Roosevelt on March 11, 1941. Under the program, the United States shipped large quantities of war supplies to Great Britain, China, the Soviet Union, and other allied or friendly nations. Altogether, some $47.9 billion was lent to 38 countries by August 21, 1945, when the program was terminated.

2275. International oil embargo was imposed by the United States on Japan, in response to the Japanese occupation beginning July 26, 1941, of military bases in southern Indochina (now Vietnam). It was this action, more than any other, which led the Japanese Navy, desperate to secure new supplies of petroleum, to plan the attack on Pearl Harbor on December 7 of that year.

2276. President to visit Asia during his term in office was Franklin Delano Roosevelt. FDR attended the Teheran Conference in Teheran, Iran, from November 27 to December 2, 1943, along with the Soviet premier, Josef Stalin, and the British prime minister, Winston Churchill.

2277. Meeting of an American president and a Soviet leader took place on November 28, 1943, at the Teheran Conference in Iran, where Franklin Delano Roosevelt met with Soviet general secretary Josef Stalin and British prime minister Winston Churchill to plot the Allied strategy for the remainder of World War II. The leaders also discussed the division of Europe after the war, with Stalin pressing with some success for Soviet control over most of Eastern Europe.

2278. Use of children's fiction as propaganda in occupied territory overseas took place in 1945, when General Douglas MacArthur convinced the State Department to have the *Little House* books by Laura Ingalls Wilder translated into German and Japanese and distributed in the defeated Axis nations. The series of eight autobiographical novels portray pioneer life in the American Midwest in the late 19th century.

2279. Woman to head a congressional mission abroad was Frances Payne Bolton, a Republican, who represented Ohio's 22nd Congressional District. In 1947, she toured the Middle East, the Soviet Union and Poland.

2280. U.S. aid program to contain the spread of communism was a package of $400 million given to Turkey and Greece in 1947. Greece was fighting a communist insurrection sponsored by the Soviet Union, and Turkey faced pressure from the Soviet Union to share control of the Dardanelles, the straits between the Ae-

INTERNATIONAL RELATIONS—*continued*
gean and the Sea of Marmara. The aid package was announced in a speech given by President Harry S. Truman to a joint session of Congress on March 12, 1947. This was the same speech in which Truman articulated what came to be known as the Truman Doctrine: "to put the world on notice that it would be our policy to support the cause of freedom wherever it was threatened." The aid package was approved by Congress in May.

2281. Policy of containment of world communism was articulated by George Frost Kennan in "The Sources of Soviet Conduct," an article in the July 1947 issue of *Foreign Affairs*. As a member of the Foreign Service, Kennan had lived in the Soviet Union and traveled widely in Eastern Europe. In the article (which Kennan wrote under the pseudonym "X"), he argued that American counterforce, not appeasement or conciliation, was the most effective way to contain efforts by the Soviet Union to expand its political and economic influence. The policy of containment became the de facto U.S. policy toward the U.S.S.R. during most of the Cold War.

2282. Agency for disseminating information about the United States to foreign countries was the United States Information Agency, created under the United States Information and Educational Exchange Act of 1948, with an expanded mandate derived from the Mutual Educational and Cultural Exchange Act of 1961. The mission of the USIA is to inform and influence foreign communities in promotion of the national interest. The Agency is known as the U.S. Information Service overseas. With certain exceptions, dissemination within the United States of materials produced by the agency for distribution overseas is prohibited. The agency's first African-American inspector general was Washington lawyer Marian C. Bennett, appointed in late 1993.

2283. Economic Cooperation Administration was authorized on April 3, 1948, "to promote world peace and the general welfare, national interest, and foreign policy of the United States through economic, financial and other measures necessary to the maintenance of conditions abroad in which free institutions may survive and consistent with the maintenance of the strength and stability of the United States." The first administrator was Paul Gray Hoffman, who was sworn in on April 9, 1948, at $20,000 a year. On April 19, 1949, $1.15 billion was authorized for the April–June 1949 period and $4.28 billion for the fiscal year commencing July 1, 1949. The first European Recovery Program relief purchases totaled $21 million for Italy, France, Greece, Austria, and the Netherlands.

2284. Peacetime alliance of European and North American nations was the North Atlantic Treaty Organization, formed in response to the military threat posed by the Soviet Union. It was established on August 24, 1949, following the signing of the North Atlantic Treaty in Washington, DC, on April 4, 1949, by Belgium, Canada, Denmark, France, Iceland, Italy, Luxembourg, the Netherlands, Norway, Portugal, the United Kingdom, and the United States. Greece and Turkey joined NATO in 1952, West Germany (now Germany) in 1955, and Spain in 1982. The main headquarters of NATO's military command, the Supreme Headquarters Allied Powers in Europe (SHAPE), is located in Brussels, Belgium. In December 1950, the American general Dwight David Eisenhower was appointed NATO's first Supreme Allied Commander, Europe. In Article 5 of the North Atlantic Treaty, the members "agree that an armed attack against one or more of them in Europe or North America shall be considered an attack against them all; and consequently they agree that, if such an armed attack occurs, each of them, in exercise of the right of individual or collective self-defense recognized by Article 51 of the Charter of the United Nations, will assist the Party or Parties so attacked by taking forthwith, individually and in concert with the other Parties, such action as it deems necessary, including the use of armed force, to restore and maintain the security of the North Atlantic area."

2285. Congresswoman to represent the United States in the United Nations was Frances Payne Bolton, born Frances Payne Bingham, who was elected in March 1940 to represent Ohio's 22nd Congressional District. In 1953, on the recommendation of the House Foreign Affairs Committee, President Dwight David Eisenhower named her a U.S. delegate to the United Nations General Assembly.

2286. Moratorium on nuclear testing was informally observed from November 1958 to September 1961 by the United States, the Soviet Union, and Great Britain. The Soviet Union ended the moratorium by performing a test on September 1, 1961, and the United States resumed its nuclear testing program on September 15.

2287. Captive Nations Week was observed in 1959 by President Dwight David Eisenhower, in accordance with a joint resolution of Congress passed on July 17, 1959, authorizing and requesting the president of the United States to issue such a proclamation each year in the third week of July. Initially a public relations move aimed at the Soviet Empire, Captive Nations Week still has value, as President William Jefferson Clinton observed when proclaiming it in 1996, as "a national expression of solidarity and support for all those around the globe who suffer the harshness of oppressive rule."

2288. Peace Corps was established by the Peace Corps Act of 1961 and was made an independent federal agency by Title VI of the International Security and Development Cooperation Act of 1981. The purpose of the Peace Corps was to promote world peace and friendship, to help other countries in meeting their needs for trained men and women, and to promote understanding between the American people and other peoples. By 1999, the Peace Corps operated eleven area offices and maintained overseas operations in more than 80 countries. The first director was R. Sargent Shriver, the brother-in-law of President John Fitzgerald Kennedy. The first woman to serve as director was Dr. Carolyn Robertson Payton, in 1977.

2289. Break between the United States and a member of the Organization of American States took place in January 1961, when the United States ended formal diplomatic relations with Cuba after its leader, Fidel Castro, installed a radical Marxist-Leninist regime favorable to the Soviet Union. On January 31, 1962, at the urging of the United States, the OAS suspended Cuba's membership indefinitely. Cuba had been a member of the OAS since its formation in 1948.

2290. Telephone hot line between nations was instituted on June 20, 1963, by the United States and the Soviet Union. It was intended to provide an emergency communications link between the leaders of the two superpowers. The hot line was never actually used.

2291. Federal agency for the support of economic development in Latin America and the Caribbean was the Inter-American Foundation, an independent federal agency created in 1969 as an experimental U.S. foreign assistance program. It awards grants directly to private, indigenous organizations throughout the region that carry out self-help projects benefiting poor people. By mid-1999, the IAF had made 3,996 grants totaling $448 million.

2292. Shuttle diplomacy as a standard tool of foreign policy was instituted by Henry Alfred Kissinger, secretary of state in the Nixon and Ford administrations. The term was first used in connection with Kissinger's personal back-and-forth trips to arrange a ceasefire between Israel and the Arab states in the Yom Kippur War of October 1973.

2293. Oil embargo in peacetime was the temporary embargo on crude oil shipments to the United States and the Netherlands in December 1973 by the Arab members of the Organization of Oil Exporting Countries, meeting in Teheran, Iran, following the October 1973 Yom Kippur War between the Arab states and Israel. OPEC members, including Iraq, Kuwait, Saudi Arabia, the United Arab Emirates, and Libya, hoped to use the embargo to pressure western nations to withdraw their support for the Jewish state.

2294. Radiation attacks against an American embassy were confirmed by American officials on February 10, 1976, when it was revealed that Soviet KGB agents had been bombarding the U.S. embassy in Moscow with non-ionizing microwave radiation since the mid-1950s. The radiation was blamed for the deaths of at least two U.S. ambassadors and for an unusually high level of cancers among embassy personnel. The CIA learned of the attacks circa 1962, but for security reasons, American diplomatic staff were not informed of the danger. After the attacks, Soviet officials reluctantly admitted to the practice, claiming that the microwaves were only employed to damage American surveillance devices.

2295. Diplomatic relations between the United States and the People's Republic of China were established on January 1, 1979, during the administration of President Jimmy Carter. This was the culmination of a process that began seven years earlier, when President Richard Milhous Nixon arrived in Beijing on February 21, 1972, for talks with Chairman Mao Zedong and Premier Zhou Enlai.

2296. Large-scale hostage crisis in which a large number of American citizens were held prisoner by representatives of a foreign government in peacetime began on November 4, 1979, when the U.S. embassy in Teheran, Iran, was occupied by Islamic revolutionary troops who took 52 Americans hostage. The occupiers, acting on behalf of Iran's religious dictator, Ayatollah Ruhollah Khomeini, demanded the forced return of the Shah of Iran, Mohammed Reza Pahlavi, whose regime had been overthrown in January. Pahlavi was in the United

INTERNATIONAL RELATIONS—*continued*
States undergoing treatment for cancer. President Jimmy Carter imposed economic sanctions on Iran and ordered a military rescue effort that failed. The hostages were released on January 21, 1981.

2297. Full diplomatic relations between the Vatican and the United States in the 20th century were established on January 10, 1984. A full diplomatic relationship had not been in existence since 1868.

2298. Post–Cold War summit of North American and European nations was the Conference on Security and Cooperation in Europe, held in Paris, France, on November 19–21, 1990. The summit resulted in a treaty by which the United States and the Soviet Union agreed to reduce the number of troops, tanks, personnel carriers, and conventional weapons deployed in Europe. Other participants were Canada and 31 nations of Europe.

2299. Alliance between the United States and the Soviet Union in an international crisis since World War II occurred during the Gulf War, when the Soviet Union's delegation to the United Nations Security Council agreed to support a plan for military action against Iraq by a coalition of nations led by the United States and Britain. The Security Council resolved on November 29, 1990, that force could be used unless Iraq withdrew its troops from Kuwait, which it had invaded the previous August. The war began on January 16, 1991, one day after the expiration of the United Nations deadline, and ended on February 28.

2300. African–African-American Summit was held in April 1991 in West Africa by African and American government officials, diplomats, businesspeople, and religious leaders.

2301. Post–Cold War summit between the United States and the Soviet Union took place on July 30–31, 1991, in Moscow, where Soviet president Mikhail S. Gorbachev met with President George Herbert Walker Bush. The two leaders signed the Strategic Arms Reduction Treaty, committing their nations to reductions in short-range nuclear weapons. Their first summit meeting had taken place on a ship off the Mediterranean island of Malta on December 3, 1989.

2302. Payment by the United States to a foreign nation for destroying nuclear weapons was arranged between the United States and Ukraine. The deal was made public on January 10, 1994, while President William Jefferson Clinton was visiting Kiev. Clinton announced that Ukraine would receive cash from the United States in return for dismantling its nuclear arsenal, the third largest in the world.

2303. Cold war enemy of the United States to join NATO was Romania, the former Warsaw Pact member. It was accepted into the North Atlantic Treaty Organization on January 26, 1994.

2304. Summit of the Americas was held in Miami, FL, in December 1994, and was attended by 34 democratically elected leaders of the American nations, including the United States. The only American nation that did not send a representative was Cuba. President William Jefferson Clinton addressed the summit on December 9, 1994. The summit's Declaration of Principles committed signatories to support "open markets, hemispheric integration, and sustainable development" and to "preserve and strengthen our democratic systems for the benefit of all people of the Hemisphere." New international initiatives were launched in the areas of democratic reform, mutual security, trade, drug trafficking, and corruption.

2305. Protest against the government of a black African country by African-Americans was mounted in 1995 by TransAfrica, a Washington-based African-American lobby on African and Caribbean affairs, against the rule of General Sani Abacha, military dictator of Nigeria. TransAfrica's executive director was Randall Robinson.

2306. American citizen to become a Russian official was Steve R. Smirnoff, a public relations professional and special assistant to the mayor of Anchorage, AK. On March 14, 1997, Smirnoff became an honorary consul to the Russian Federation, serving as liaison and translator for Russian visitors to the city.

2307. Secretary of state to visit Vietnam was Madeline Korbel Albright. On June 24, 1997, she arrived in Hanoi on an official visit, a little less than two months after Ambassador Peter Peterson, the first ambassador to Vietnam after the end of the Vietnam War, took up his new post. Relations were officially normalized with Vietnam on July 11, 1995.

130

2308. Non-NATO ally of the United States in the Western Hemisphere was Argentina, who gained that distinction in October 1997. The title gave Argentina preferential access to surplus American military equipment. Other non-NATO allies of the United States were Israel, Egypt, Jordan, Japan, South Korea, and Australia.

INTERNATIONAL RELATIONS—FOREIGN SERVICE

2309. Foreign service committee was formed on November 29, 1775, when the Continental Congress voted "that a committee of five be appointed for the sole purpose of corresponding with our friends in Great Britain, Ireland and other parts of the world." The members of this secret Committee of Correspondence were William Samuel Johnson of Connecticut, John Jay of New York, John Dickinson of Pennsylvania, Benjamin Harrison of Virginia, and Benjamin Franklin of Pennsylvania, who was the chairman.

2310. U.S. consular post was established in Bordeaux, France, in March 1778. It was not closed until 1996, making it the building used longest as a diplomatic post.

2311. Representative of a foreign country to the United States was Conrad Alexandre Gérard of France, who arrived at Philadelphia, PA, on July 14, 1778. He was styled minister plenipotentiary and also bore a commission as consul general. On August 6 he was formally admitted to the meeting room of the Continental Congress and presented his letter of appointment from the King of France.

2312. Minister plenipotentiary was Benjamin Franklin of Philadelphia, PA, who was elected by the Continental Congress on September 14, 1778, to represent the United States in the court of France.

2313. Consul to die in service was Colonel William Palfrey, paymaster general of the Continental Armies, who was elected consul to Paris, France, on November 4, 1780, by the Continental Congress at a salary of $1,500 a year. He received his commission on November 9, 1780, and sailed for his post in France on the *Shillala,* an armed ship of 16 guns. The ship stopped en route at the port of Wilmington, DE, on December 23, 1780, and was lost at sea after it passed the Delaware capes.

2314. Location of the national Department of Foreign Affairs when it was established by the Continental Congress in 1781 was Peter Du Ponceau's house at 13 South Sixth Street in Philadelphia, PA. In New York City, where the government moved in 1785, the department was located for some years in Fraunces Tavern on Pearl Street and afterwards in various houses on Broadway, by which time it had been reconstituted as the Department of State.

2315. Secretary of foreign affairs was Robert R. Livingston, a delegate from New York to the Continental Congress, who took office on October 20, 1781, and served until June 4, 1783. Later, as minister to France, Livingston negotiated the Louisiana Purchase.

2316. Minister plenipotentiary appointed after the Revolutionary War was Thomas Jefferson, who was appointed on March 10, 1785, and served in Paris, France, until October 1789.

2317. Minister to Great Britain was John Adams of Quincy, MA, who on June 1, 1785, was introduced by the Marquis of Carmarthen to the King of Great Britain as ambassador extraordinary from the United States of America to the Court of London. The first minister plenipotentiary to Great Britain was Thomas Pinckney of South Carolina, who was appointed on January 12, 1792.

2318. Consul to take office under the Constitution was Major Samuel Shaw of Massachusetts, who was appointed consul to Canton, China, on January 1, 1786, prior to the ratification of the Constitution, and confirmed on February 10, 1790, after its ratification.

2319. Diplomatic Service of the United States was authorized by Article II, Section 2, of the Constitution, which empowered the president to appoint "Ambassadors, other public Ministers, and Consuls." This was the basis for the creation in 1789 of the Diplomatic Service, which staffed U.S. legations and embassies.

2320. Consuls appointed after the adoption of the Constitution were Joseph Fenwick of Maryland; Nathaniel Barrett, Sylvanus Bourne, Burrell Carnes, and William Knox of Massachusetts; John Marsden Pintard of New York; and James Maury and Fulwar Skipwith of Virginia, all of whom were appointed on June 7, 1790.

2321. Minister plenipotentiary to Great Britain was Thomas Pinckney of South Carolina, who was appointed on January 12, 1792.

INTERNATIONAL RELATIONS—FOREIGN SERVICE—*continued*

2322. Consular Service of the United States was created by an act of Congress of April 14, 1792, providing for U.S. consuls abroad. The Consular Service was primarily responsible for promoting American commerce overseas and assisting American sailors. U.S. consuls, who did not have to be American citizens, received no salary (except for the consuls appointed to the Barbary States of North Africa, who enjoyed quasi-diplomatic status), and were expected to support themselves from private trade or fees charged for official services.

2323. Jewish diplomat was Mordecai Manuel Noah, who served from 1813 to 1816 as consul to Tunis, where he negotiated the release of American sailors held prisoner by Barbary pirates.

2324. Father and son to serve as U.S. ministers were John Adams and his son John Quincy Adams, both of Massachusetts. John Adams, the first U.S. minister to Great Britain, presented his credentials to the court of King George III on June 1, 1785. John Quincy Adams was the first U.S. minister to Great Britain after the War of 1812. He was appointed on February 28, 1815, and served until May 14, 1817. John Quincy Adams's grandson Charles Francis Adams served in the same post from 1861 to 1868.

2325. Pan-American delegates from the United States were Caesar Augustus Rodney, Theodore Bland, and John Graham, who were appointed in July 1817 by President James Monroe "to obtain information of the actual condition and political prospects of the Spanish provinces which were contending for independence." They served at Buenos Aires, Argentina, from February 1818 to April 30, 1818.

2326. Diplomatic property owned by the United States was the U.S. Legation building in Tangier, Morocco. The Sultan of Morocco made a gift of the building in 1821. Retired from official service in 1956, the historic building is now a museum and study center.

2327. Consul to California was Thomas Oliver Larkin, who was appointed consul to Monterey, CA, on May 1, 1843, and special agent on October 17, 1845.

2328. African-American vice consul was William A. Leidesdorff, appointed vice consul at Yerba Buena (now San Francisco, CA) on October 29, 1845, by Thomas Oliver Larkin, U.S. consul in Monterey. At that time, northern California was part of Mexico. Leidesdorff, born in the Danish West Indies (now the U.S. Virgin Islands), became a naturalized U.S. citizen in 1834. He served as vice consul until the U.S. occupation of northern California in July 1846.

2329. Consul to Japan was Townsend Harris, a New York-born trader based in East Asia, who obtained the appointment in August 1855. Harris negotiated the first comprehensive diplomatic and commercial between the United States and Japan on July 29, 1858. The Harris Treaty, building upon the foundation established with the Treaty of Kanagawa (1854), opened new ports to U.S. trade and granted special privileges to U.S. citizens in these ports.

2330. Salaries for consuls were provided for by an act of Congress of August 18, 1856. This established two schedules of consular posts. Schedule B posts were paid between $1,000 and $2,500 per year but could not engage in trade. Schedule C appointees earned less—between $500 and $1,000 per year—but could engage in personal trade.

2331. Published records of American diplomacy were the diplomatic dispatches of Secretary of State William Henry Seward, published beginning in 1861. These formed the nucleus of *Foreign Relations of the United States,* the official record of American diplomacy (and the first regular publication of its kind undertaken by any nation). The series now includes "all documents needed to give a comprehensive record of the major foreign policy decisions within the range of the Department of State's responsibilities, together with the appropriate materials concerning the facts which contributed to the formulation of policies."

2332. African-American consul was Ebenezer Don Carlos Bassett, consul general to Haiti, where he served from April 16, 1869, to November 27, 1877.

2333. African-American minister was John Mercer Langston, the former dean of Howard University, who served as minister to Haiti and chargé d'affaires to Santo Domingo from 1877 to 1885. In 1890 he became the first African-American to represent Virginia in the House of Representatives.

2334. Naval attaché was Lieutenant Commander French Ensor Chadwick. He was sent to London on November 15, 1882, and remained there until April 3, 1889.

2335. Jewish minister and envoy was Oscar Solomon Straus of New York City, who was appointed envoy extraordinary and minister plenipotentiary to Turkey on March 24, 1887, and served again during crises in 1890, 1897, and 1909.

2336. Ambassador of the United States was Thomas F. Bayard, appointed ambassador to Great Britain on March 30, 1893. This was the first year that the rank of ambassador was used by the United States. Prior to this date, the highest-ranking U.S. diplomats were ministers.

2337. Standardized foreign service examinations were instituted by President Grover Cleveland. On September 20, 1895, Cleveland issued an executive order requiring appointees to consular positions with salaries between $1,000 and $2,500 to be either qualified officers of the State Department or to pass a written and oral examination in which the candidate had to demonstrate knowledge of consular regulation and proficiency in a foreign language. The examination requirement was extended by President Theodore Roosevelt on November 10, 1905, to the lower grades of the Consular Service and for secretaries in the Diplomatic Service.

2338. Foreign service school in a college was the School of Comparative Jurisprudence and Diplomacy of George Washington University, Washington, DC, which opened on November 15, 1898. It was discontinued as a separate school in 1913, though courses continued to be given by Columbian College. In September 1928 training in foreign service and governmental theory and administration was reestablished as a separate branch under the School of Government.

2339. Foreign Service of the United States was created on July 1, 1924, by the Rogers bill, approved by Congress on May 24, 1924. The act merged the nation's diplomatic and consular services under the Department of State.

2340. Woman vice consul in the American Foreign Service was Pattie Hockaday Field of Denver, CO. She was appointed Foreign Service officer unclassified on March 20, 1925, and as American vice consul. She was assigned to Amsterdam, Holland, on September 2, 1925. She resigned on June 27, 1929.

2341. Woman to serve as legation secretary was Lucille Atcherson of Columbus, OH. She was appointed on December 4, 1922, and was recommissioned as Foreign Service Officer of Class 8 on July 1, 1924, serving thereafter as third secretary of legation at Bern, Switzerland (beginning April 11, 1925) and later as a legation secretary in Panama. On May 24, 1924, the diplomatic and consular services were amalgamated under the Rogers Act into the American Foreign Service.

2342. Chief executive-elect of a foreign country to serve in a diplomatic position in Washington was Dr. Enrique Olaya Hererra, who arrived on April 20, 1930. He was sworn in on August 7, 1930, as president of Colombia. Previously he had served as Colombian ambassador to the United States.

2343. Woman to take charge of an American legation was Frances Elizabeth Willis, third secretary of the American Legation at Stockholm, Sweden, who was placed in charge while Minister John Motley Morehead was on furlough. She became the ex-officio American chargé d'affaires ad interim on October 12, 1932. Edwin S. Crocker, 2d, second secretary of the legation, who had also been absent from Stockholm, returned on October 29 and succeeded Willis as chargé d'affaires ad interim.

2344. Woman diplomat to hold the rank of minister was Ruth Bryan Owen, who was appointed by President Franklin Delano Roosevelt on April 12, 1933, as envoy extraordinary and minister plenipotentiary to Denmark and Iceland. Her nomination was confirmed by the Senate on the same day, without even the customary formality of reference to a committee. She was the eldest daughter of William Jennings Bryan.

2345. Ambassador to the Soviet Union was William Christian Bullitt, who served from November 21, 1933, until August 25, 1936.

2346. Soviet representative to the United States was Alexander Antonovich Troyanovsky, who was accredited as the Soviet ambassador from January 8, 1934, to June 22, 1938.

2347. Ambassador to Canada was Ray Atherton, who was nominated as ambassador extraordinary and plenipotentiary on November 18, 1943. He held this office until his resignation and mandatory retirement on August 31, 1948. Previously, on July 7, 1943, he had been confirmed as envoy extraordinary and minister plenipotentiary of the United States to Canada and to Denmark.

INTERNATIONAL RELATIONS—FOR-
EIGN SERVICE—*continued*

2348. Ambassador to India was Henry F.
Grady, who arrived in Delhi in May 1947 and
took up his post on August 15, the same day
that India achieved independence from Great
Britain.

2349. Ambassador to Israel was James Grover
McDonald, who served from July 2, 1948, to
January 14, 1951, as ambassador extraordinary
and plenipotentiary to Israel.

**2350. Woman to serve as ambassador to the
United States** was Her Excellency Shrimati
Vijaya Lakshmi Pandit, ambassador of India,
who presented her letter of credence to President Harry S. Truman on May 12, 1949.

**2351. Woman to hold the rank of ambassa-
dor** was Eugenie Moore Anderson of Red
Wing, MN, who was sworn in on October 28,
1949, in Washington, DC, as ambassador to
Denmark. She remained in the post until 1953.
In 1962, she was appointed ambassador to Bulgaria.

**2352. Woman to serve as ambassador to a
major nation** was Clare Boothe Luce, who
was sworn in on March 3, 1953, in Washington, DC, as ambassador to Italy by Frederick
Moore Vinson, chief justice of the United
States. Luce had served in the House of Representatives from 1943 to 1947 as a member
from Connecticut, and worked actively in the
Republican presidential campaigns of 1940,
1944, and 1952. She resigned her ambassadorial post on November 19, 1956.

**2353. Woman career diplomat to advance to
the rank of ambassador** was Frances Elizabeth Willis, appointed ambassador to Switzerland on July 20, 1953, and sworn in at the
State Department, Washington, DC, on August
10. She presented her credentials on October 9.
Willis served until May 5, 1957, and later held
ambassadorial posts in Norway and Ceylon
(now Sri Lanka).

**2354. African-American with the rank of
ambassador** was Jessie D. Locker. He was appointed ambassador to Liberia on July 22,
1953, and presented his credentials on October
16.

**2355. African-American to become chief of a
diplomatic mission** was Clifton R. Wharton,
who joined the Foreign Service in 1925. He
was appointed minister to Romania on February
5, 1958, and served in this post until October
21, 1960, after which he was appointed ambassador to Norway.

2356. Ambassador to Nepal was Henry Endicott Stebbins of Milton, MA, appointed on August 29, 1959. The nomination was approved
on September 9. Previously, the United States
ambassador to India had served as envoy to
Nepal.

**2357. Member of the Foreign Service to hold
the three top diplomatic posts in Europe** was
David Kirkpatrick Este Bruce, one of the ad-
ministrators of the Marshall Plan following
World War II. Bruce served as ambassador to
France from 1949 to 1952; as ambassador to
West Germany from 1957 to 1959, and as am-
bassador to Great Britain from 1961 to 1969.
He was also ambassador to NATO from 1974
to 1976.

**2358. Woman ambassador to a Communist-
bloc nation** was Helen Eugenie Moore Anderson of Red Wing, MN, who presented her credentials on August 3, 1962, to Dimiter Ganev,
Bulgarian chief of state, at Sofia, Bulgaria.

**2359. Announcement that a U.S. embassy
was bugged** came on May 19, 1964, when the
State Department announced that the U.S. embassy in Moscow, Soviet Union, was wired
with at least 40 KGB microphones embedded
in the building's walls.

**2360. African-American woman to serve as a
United States ambassador** was Patricia Roberts Harris, who was sworn in on July 9, 1965,
in Washington, DC, as ambassador to Luxembourg. She presented her credentials on September 7, 1965, and served until September 22,
1967.

2361. Ambassadors in service to wed were
Ellsworth Bunker, ambassador-at-large, and
Carol Clendening Laise, ambassador to Nepal,
who married at Katmandu, Nepal, on January
3, 1967. The ceremony was performed by Rev.
H. Norman Gibley of North Eastham, MA.
Bunker was ambassador to Vietnam from 1967
to 1973.

**2362. African-American to become chief of a
State Department bureau** was Barbara M.
Watson, appointed administrator of the Bureau
of Security and Consular Affairs on July 31,
1968. She served until December 31, 1974, and
was reappointed on April 7, 1977.

2363. Ambassador assassinated in office was
John Gordon Mein, ambassador to Guatemala,
who was attacked and killed in his automobile
on August 27, 1968, about 10 blocks away
from the American embassy in the downtown
section of Guatemala City, Guatemala.

2364. Ambassador killed by a terrorist attack was John Gordon Mein, ambassador to Guatemala. On August 28, 1968, he was assassinated by Marxist guerillas on his way to the U.S. embassy in Guatemala City. The murder was probably in retaliation for clandestine CIA support of the Guatemalan military's brutal counterinsurgency campaign.

2365. Woman to become an assistant secretary of state was Carol Clendening Laise, the former ambassador to Nepal. She was appointed assistant secretary of state for public affairs on September 20, 1973. Laise later served as director general of the Foreign Service from April 11, 1975 to December 26, 1977.

2366. Woman to serve as ambassador to the Court of St. James was Anne Legendre Armstrong, who was nominated on January 14, 1976, confirmed on January 28, and sworn in on February 19. She presented her credentials to Queen Elizabeth II on March 17, 1976.

2367. Woman to serve as under secretary of state was Lucy Wilson Benson. On March 23, 1977, she was appointed under secretary of state for security assistance, science, and technology, making her the highest-ranking woman in the State Department at that time. She served until January 5, 1980.

2368. U.S. embassy to be destroyed by a suicide bombing was the embassy in Beirut, Lebanon, which in 1983 was in the midst of a civil war between Palestinian and leftist Muslim guerrillas and militias of the Christian Phalange Party and other Christian groups. The building was nearly leveled on April 18 by a car-bomb explosion that killed 63 people. The bomber himself was killed along with 17 American citizens.

2369. Woman to head a regional bureau of the State Department was Rozanne L. Ridgway. She was appointed assistant secretary of state for European and Canadian affairs on July 18, 1985, and served until June 30, 1989. Previsouly, she had been the first woman to serve as counselor of the Department of State, beginning on March 18, 1980, and continuing until February 24, 1981.

2370. African-American ambassador to the Republic of South Africa was Edward Joseph Perkins, who served in that post from 1986 to 1989. From 1985 to 1986, Perkins was ambassador to the Republic of Liberia.

2371. African-American to become director general of the Foreign Service was Edward Joseph Perkins, a former Marine and long-time career diplomat. He was sworn in by Secretary of State James Baker in October 1989 and served as director general and director of personnel for the Department of State until 1992.

2372. Ambassador to Vietnam after the end of the Vietnam War was Peter Peterson, who presented his portfolio in Hanoi on May 9, 1997. Peterson, a former Air Force captain, had been held as a prisoner of war in Vietnam for more than six years after his bomber was shot down near Hanoi in 1966. He was released in March 1973. The United States had not maintained formal diplomatic relations with Vietnam since its previous ambassador, Graham Martin, left Saigon by helicopter in 1975 as the city fell to North Vietnamese forces.

INTERNATIONAL RELATIONS—HEADS OF STATE

2373. Native American envoys received as guests of the British crown were four Mohawks who had an audience with Queen Anne on April 19, 1710, at Buckingham Palace. An interpreter translated into English an address by the leader of the delegation, Tee Yee Neen Ho Ga Prow (Tiyanoga), known to the British as Hendrick, concerning the eagerness of the Mohawks to assist the British in pushing back their colonial rivals, the French. The other envoys were Sa Ga Yean Qua Prah Ton, called Brant; Elow Oh Kaom, called Nicholas; and Oh Nee Yeath Ton No Prow, called John. The four spent two weeks traveling in and around London, during which time they watched a performance of *Macbeth* and were guests at numerous banquets and receptions.

2374. President of the Republic of Texas was Sam Houston, who was elected on September 5, 1836, and took the oath of office in Columbia, TX, on October 22. He served until December 10, 1838, was succeeded by Mirabeau Buonaparte Lamar, and was then reelected, serving from December 14, 1841, to December 9, 1844. After the admission of Texas as the 28th state on December 29, 1845, Houston was elected as a Democrat to the Senate, where he served from February 21, 1846, to March 3, 1859.

INTERNATIONAL RELATIONS—HEADS
OF STATE—*continued*

**2375. American to become president of an
African republic** was Joseph Jenkins Roberts
of Virginia. At the age of 20, Roberts emigrated to the African-American colony of Liberia
and entered the colonial administration, becoming governor in 1842. He proclaimed the colony an independent republic in 1847 and the following year was elected to the office of president, in which he served until 1856.

**2376. President of a Central American coun-
try born in the United States** was the adven-
turer William Walker. In 1856, Walker was invited by a revolutionary faction to seize power
in Nicaragua, which he did with the help of
Cornelius K. Garrison and Charles Morgan, officials of Cornelius Vanderbilt's Accessory
Transit Company. Walker was president of Nicaragua from July 12, 1856, to May 1, 1857,
when he surrendered to the U.S. Navy and fled
the country. He was executed by a firing squad
in Honduras in 1860 after a failed coup attempt
in that country.

**2377. Prince of Wales to visit the United
States** was Albert Edward, Prince of Wales
(later King Edward VII), who left Plymouth,
England, on July 10, 1860, and arrived in Detroit, MI, on September 20 from Hamilton, Ontario, Canada. He was received by Moses
Wisner, governor of Michigan, and Mayor
Christian Buhl of Detroit, and lived for a time
as a guest in the White House. After touring
the United States, he sailed from Portland, ME,
on October 20. He used the name Baron Ren-
frew during his travels.

**2378. First Lady of Mexico to reside in the
United States** was Margarita Maza de Juárez
of Oaxaca, who married Benito Juárez in 1843
and became the first lady of Mexico when he
was elected president in 1857. During the
French invasion of Mexico (1862–1867), she
and her children lived in exile on the east coast
of the United States, spending time in the New
York City area and making a diplomatic visit
to Washington, DC. She returned to Mexico in
1867.

2379. Queen to visit the United States was
Queen Emma, widow of King Kamehameha IV
of the Sandwich Islands (Hawaii), who arrived
in New York City from England on August 8,
1866, on the Cunard liner *Java*. She was received on August 14 by President Andrew
Johnson and was introduced to his family.

2380. Reigning king to visit the United States
was David Kalakaua, who was elected king of
the Sandwich Islands (Hawaii) on February 12,
1874, by a vote of 39–6. He embarked on the
U.S.S. *Benicia* on November 17, 1874, and was
received at the White House by President Ulysses Simpson Grant on December 15. Congress
tendered him a reception on December 18. He
arranged for a treaty of reciprocity, which was
concluded on January 30, 1875, and returned to
his country on February 15 on the U.S.S. *Pensacola*.

**2381. Coronation on territory that would lat-
er become part of the United States** took
place on February 12, 1883, when King
Kalakaua and Queen Kapiolani were crowned
king and queen of the Hawaiian Islands at
Iolani Palace, Honolulu.

**2382. Queen to visit the United States during
her reign** was Queen Marie of Rumania, who
arrived in New York City on October 18, 1926,
on the *Leviathan* and received a 21-gun salute
from the fort at Governors Island. She was accompanied by Prince Nicholas and Princess
Ileana. They departed for home on November
24 on the *Berengaria*.

2383. King born in the United States was
Bhumibol Adulyadej (Phumiphon Auldet),
king of Thailand, who was born on December
5, 1927, at Mount Auburn Hospital, Cambridge,
MA. He was the son of Prince Mahidol. He
was crowned on May 5, 1950, as King Rama
IX.

**2384. Absolute monarch to visit the United
States** was King Prajadhipok of Siam, who
crossed from Canada to Portal, ND, on April
29, 1931, accompanied by his wife, Queen
Rambai Barni, and the royal entourage. They
were received on the same day by President
Herbert Clark Hoover. The king had visited the
United States in 1924, when he was a prince.

**2385. Pope to visit the United States before
his election** was Eugenio Pacelli, the future
Pope Pius XII, who visited America from October 8 to November 7, 1936, while serving as
papal secretary of state. His headquarters were
at Inisfada, the Long Island mansion of the Papal Duchess Genevieve Garvan Brady.

2386. Woman of American ancestry to become a queen was Countess Geraldine Apponyi of Hungary, who married King Zog of Albania on April 27, 1938, at the Royal Palace, Tirana, Albania. The marriage was proclaimed by Heqmet Delvina, vice president of the Albanian Parliament. The countess was the daughter of Count Julius Apponyi, a Hungarian nobleman, and Virginia Gladys Stewart, his American-born wife.

2387. British monarchs to visit the United States were King George VI and Queen Elizabeth, who crossed the international border from Canada at 10:39 P.M. on June 7, 1939, at the Suspension Bridge Station, Niagara Falls, NY. They visited New York City and Washington, DC, and recrossed the border at 5:22 A.M. on June 12. They sailed from Halifax, Nova Scotia, on June 15.

2388. Prime minister of Great Britain to address Congress in person was Winston Churchill. On December 26, 1941, a joint session of Congress gathered in the Senate chamber (chosen for its superior acoustics over the larger House chamber) to hear an address by Churchill on the Anglo-American accords that he, with President Franklin Delano Roosevelt, were forging at the Arcadia Conference.

2389. President of a black African country to visit the United States was President Edwin James Barclay of the Republic of Liberia, who addressed the Senate on May 27, 1943, the day following his arrival. He was accompanied by the vice president, William Vacanarat Shadrach Tubman, who was also the president-elect. They were welcomed by President Franklin Delano Roosevelt.

2390. Pope to visit the United States was Pope Paul VI, who arrived at Kennedy International Airport, New York City, on October 4, 1965, at 9:27 A.M. He went to Saint Patrick's Cathedral and Cardinal Spellman's residence at 11:44 A.M., conferred with President Lyndon Baines Johnson at the Waldorf-Astoria Hotel at 1:40 P.M., addressed the General Assembly of the United Nations in French at 3:30 P.M., attended a public Mass at Yankee Stadium at 8:20 P.M., visited the Vatican Pavilion at the New York World's Fair at 10:25 P.M., and returned to Rome the same day at 11 P.M. on an Alitalia jet liner. He was seen by about 1 million persons and by 100 million on television.

2391. Emperor of Japan to visit the United States was Emperor Hirohito, who landed at Patrick Henry Airport, Williamsburg, VA, on September 30, 1975, accompanied by his wife. He paid a visit to the White House on October 2. In 1971, he had stopped briefly at Alaska on his way to Europe. Hirohito was emperor of Japan during World War II.

2392. Pope to visit the White House in Washington, DC, was Pope John Paul II, who flew across the Atlantic in the *Shepherd 1,* landing in Boston, MA, on October 1, 1979. In six days, he visited Boston, New York, Philadelphia, Urbandale, IA, Chicago, and Washington. He returned to Rome from Andrews Air Force Base, near Washington, on October 6.

2393. British monarch to address Congress was Queen Elizabeth II, who spoke before a joint session of Congress on May 16, 1991.

2394. Son of a Soviet premier to become an American citizen was Sergei Khrushchev, son of the late Soviet Communist Party chairman Nikita Khrushchev. On June 23, 1999, at the U.S. Immigration and Naturalization Service office in Providence, RI, Sergei Khrushchev passed the standard U.S. citizenship written exam, correctly answering 19 out of 20 questions. He took the oath of U.S. citizenship on July 12, 1999.

INTERNATIONAL RELATIONS—TREATIES

2395. Treaty between English settlers and a Native American tribe was the Pilgrim-Wampanoag Peace Treaty, signed on April 1, 1621, at Plymouth, MA, by the leaders of the Plymouth colonists and by the Wampanoag chief Massasoit. Acting as translator was Tisquantum, also known as Squanto, a member of the Patuxet people who had spent time in England. The two sides agreed not to "doe hurt" to each other and to extradite wrongdoers who broke the law. The agreement lasted some 40 years, until the death of Massasoit.

2396. Treaties entered into by the federal government were A Treaty of Amity and Commerce and a Treaty of Alliance, signed by the United States and France in Paris on February 6, 1778. Benjamin Franklin, Silas Deane, and Arthur Lee represented the United States, and Conrad Alexandre Gérard, first secretary to France's foreign minister, signed for France. These pacts were the first treaties made by the federal government with a foreign power. The treaty was ratified by the Second Continental Congress at York, PA, on May 4, 1778, and by France on July 16, 1778. Ratifications were ex-

INTERNATIONAL RELATIONS—TREA-
TIES—*continued*

changed in Paris on July 17, 1778, and the treaty was declared in force. The treaty was abrogated on July 7, 1798, when Congress passed an act "to declare the treaties heretofore concluded with France no longer obligatory on the United States."

2397. Treaty between the federal government and a nation with which it had been at war was the armistice with Great Britain that ended the Revolutionary War. Preliminary articles of peace were signed on November 30, 1782, in Paris. Hostilities ceased on January 20, 1783. The treaty was proclaimed by the Continental Congress on April 11, 1783. The definite treaty of peace was signed in Paris on September 3, 1783, by David Hartley, plenipotentiary of Great Britain, and Benjamin Franklin and John Adams of the United States. The treaty was ratified and proclaimed on January 14, 1784. It set the borders of the United States as Canada in the north, Spanish Florida in the south, and the Mississippi River in the west. It also granted the Americans fishing rights off the Newfoundland coast.

2398. Treaty entered into by the federal government after independence was concluded with Prussia and signed at the Hague on September 10, 1785, by Benjamin Franklin, John Adams, and Thomas Jefferson, representing the United States. The treaty was ratified by Congress on May 17, 1786, and the ratifications were exchanged in October 1786.

2399. Treaty with a non-European nation was a Treaty of Friendship and Amity signed with Morocco on June 23, 1786. It was negotiated by Thomas Barclay, the U.S. consul general in Paris. The treaty was renewed in 1837.

2400. Treaty for which a president sought the Senate's advice and consent in person was a treaty with the Cherokee nation. President George Washington and his secretary of war, Henry Knox, arrived at the Senate chamber on August 22, 1789, to answer questions concerning the treaty's provisions but were rebuffed by the senators, some of whom believed that an attempt was being made to intimidate them. The president returned two days later, at which time the Senate agreed to appropriate the requested $20,000 needed to conclude the treaty.

2401. Treaty approved by the Senate that was held up for lack of funding was an agreement for the release of Americans held for ransom by the Dey of Algiers, who sought by this means to ensure the annual payment of tribute by the United States. The Senate, in 1791, gave President George Washington its consent to proceed with the treaty but set a limit of $40,000 on the sum that could be attached to it. However, the Senate was unwilling to submit the treaty to the House of Representatives for an appropriation, preferring that the president take the money directly from the Treasury and keep the amount a secret. President Washington and Secretary of State Thomas Jefferson felt otherwise, and the appropriation was passed by the House during the Second Congress.

2402. Treaty rejected by the Senate was an agreement with the tribal leaders of the Wabash and Illinois nations that was signed on September 27, 1792. The Senate, in 1794, refused to confirm it.

2403. Extradition treaty with a foreign country was the Treaty of Amity, Commerce and Navigation, popularly known as the Jay Treaty, between the United States and Great Britain, which was signed in London on November 19, 1794. Article XXVII provided for the apprehension and delivery of persons charged with certain crimes. The signatory for the United States was John Jay, and for Great Britain, William Wyndham Grenville, Baron Grenville of Wotton, one of His Majesty's Privy Council and His Majesty's Principal Secretary of State for Foreign Affairs. The treaty was ratified by the Senate on June 24, 1795, amid acrimonious argument between the Federalists, who supported the treaty, and the Jeffersonian Democrats, who opposed it. It was signed by President George Washington on October 28, 1795. The ratification was proclaimed on February 29, 1796.

2404. Treaty terminated by a joint resolution of Congress rather than by the executive branch was a treaty of mutual defense between the United States and France, which had been in effect since 1778. On July 7, 1798, Congress repealed the treaty in anticipation of war with France over the XYZ Affair, in which French government agents tried to extort a bribe from a commission of American diplomats (Charles Cotesworth Pinckney, John Marshall, and Elbridge Gerry) in exchange for a Franco-American treaty of commerce and amity. The joint resolution of Congress declared the United States to be "freed and exonerated" from its obligation. An undeclared naval war ensued while a second commission negotiated with France over new terms, resulting in the Treaty of Morfontaine (also known as the Convention of 1800).

2405. Standing Senate rule for the consideration of treaties was enacted in January 1801. It established that the Senate would give each treaty three readings: an introductory first reading; a second reading, on a different day, to be followed by debate by the senators in their character as the Committee of the Whole, with a two-thirds vote required for amendment; and a third reading, on yet another day, in which each proposed amendment and the complete treaty would undergo further debate and voting, two-thirds again being required for passage.

2406. Withholding of a signed treaty by a president took place in March 1807, when President Thomas Jefferson received a treaty with Great Britain that had been negotiated by two envoys, James Monroe and William Pinkney. Jefferson, angered by the failure of the envoys to come to an acceptable agreement on a critical subject (the British Navy's policy of impressing sailors out of American vessels), refused to forward the treaty to the Senate.

2407. Treaties establishing the United States as a transcontinental power were negotiated primarily by Secretary of State John Quincy Adams under President James Monroe. Quincy helped draft the Adams-Onís Treaty (also called the Transcontinental Treaty) of 1819, which purchased the Florida territory from Spain and extended the U.S.–Spanish border to the Pacific Ocean along a line from Louisiana west to the Pacific. Adams also concluded the 1818 treaty with Great Britain that set the boundary between the United States and Canada along the line of 49 degrees north latitude as far as the Rocky Mountains.

2408. Treaty between the federal government and a South American nation was the General Convention of Peace, Amity, Navigation and Commerce between the United States and the Republic of Colombia, which was signed at Bogotá, Colombia, on October 3, 1824. Its main provision was to guarantee the United States access to Colombian ports, and vice versa. The Republic of Colombia then included Venezuela and Ecuador. The treaty was submitted to the Senate on February 22, 1825, ratified on March 7, ratified by Colombia on March 26, and proclaimed on May 31. The plenipotentia-

ries who signed the treaty were Richard Clough Anderson, minister plenipotentiary of the United States to the Republic of Colombia, and Pedro Gual, secretary of state and foreign relations of Colombia.

2409. International treaty rejected by the Senate was a pact with Colombia for suppressing the African slave trade, which was rejected on March 9, 1825, by a vote of 0–40.

2410. Treaty between the federal government and a foreign nation to provide for mutual reduction of import duties was the Convention with France, Regarding Claims and Regarding Duties on Wines and Cottons, signed in Paris on July 4, 1831. The ratifications were exchanged on February 2, 1832, and the treaty was proclaimed on July 13.

2411. Treaty between the federal government and an Asian nation was the Treaty of Amity and Commerce with Siam (now called Thailand), concluded on March 20, 1833, the last day of the fourth month of the Siamese year 1194, called Pi-Marông-chat-tava-sôk, or the Year of the Dragon. One copy of the treaty was in Siamese and one in English, with a Portuguese and a Chinese translation annexed. Edmund Roberts was the envoy of the United States. Ratifications were exchanged on April 14, 1836, in the royal city of Bangkok, and the treaty was proclaimed on June 24, 1837, by President Martin Van Buren.

2412. Treaty between the United States and China was the Treaty of Wangxia (or Wanghia), negotiated by Caleb Cushing of Massachusetts in 1844 at the direction of President John Tyler. The treaty, under which the United States was granted "most-favored nation" status in relations with China, extended extraterritoriality rights to U.S. diplomats and favorable trading rights to U.S. merchants similar to those secured by the British after China's defeat in the first Opium War (1840–43).

2413. Treaty with Mexico was the Treaty of Guadalupe Hidalgo, signed in Mexico City on February 2, 1848. It formally ended the Mexican War, ceded more than 525,000 square miles of former Mexican territory to the United States—for the first time extending the boundaries of the United States to the Pacific Ocean—and established a permanent border between the two countries. Present-day Arizona, California, western Colorado, Nevada, New Mexico, Texas, and Utah were created from territory won by this treaty. In return, the United States paid Mexico $15 million and took on some $3 million in claims made by American citizens against Mexico.

INTERNATIONAL RELATIONS—TREATIES—*continued*

2414. Treaty between the United States and Japan was the Treaty of Kanagawa, also called the Perry Convention, concluded in Edo (now Tokyo) on March 31, 1854, by Commodore Matthew C. Perry and representatives of Japan's Tokugawa shogunate. It was Japan's first treaty with a western power in more than two centuries, and led directly to the establishment of a constitutional monarchy there in 1868. The treaty guaranteed protection for shipwrecked sailors, opened the ports of Shimoda and Hakodate for trade and as sources of coal for American vessels, and accepted a permanent U.S. consulate.

2415. Treaties withdrawn by a president after they were submitted to the Senate were three treaties that were sent to the Senate by President Chester Alan Arthur. They were still under consideration by the senators when his term expired. Arthur's successor, Grover Cleveland, found fault with them and withdrew them in March 1885, shortly after he took office.

2416. Treaty between the United States and Germany was signed on August 25, 1921, ending the state of war between the two nations that had pertained since 1917.

2417. Federal treaty signed by a woman was the Charter of the United Nations, signed on June 26, 1945, at San Francisco, CA, by Virginia Crocheron Gildersleeve, a delegate to the United Nations Conference on International Organization.

2418. Mutual-defense pact for the Western Hemisphere was the Inter-American Treaty of Reciprocal Assistance, signed in 1947 by all the hemisphere's independent nations including the United States. It was superseded by provisions of the charter of the Organization of American States, signed on April 30, 1948, in Bogotá, Colombia.

2419. Regional cooperative in Oceania was the South Pacific Commission (SPC), formed in 1947 and now including Australia, France, the United Kingdom, New Zealand, and the United States—nations with dependencies in the South Pacific—and 21 island states and territories. The SPC was intended to promote health, social, and economic development in the region.

2420. Regional agreement for collective defense under the U.N. Charter signed by the United States was the Inter-American Treaty of Reciprocal Assistance (Rio Treaty), devised by the United States in September 1947 and eventually signed by all 21 American republics. The aim of the agreement was to protect the Western Hemisphere against Communist intrusion by serving notice that armed aggression against one signatory would be considered an attack upon all.

2421. Nuclear arms-control treaty was the Nuclear Test Ban Treaty, formally the Treaty Banning Nuclear Weapons Tests in the Atmosphere, in Outer Space and Under Water. It was signed in Moscow on August 5, 1963, by the United States, the Soviet Union, and the United Kingdom. The treaty banned tests of nuclear weapons above ground, in the ocean, and in outer space, but did allow testing underground. It made no allowance for verification of compliance. More than 100 nations ratified the treaty. Two nations that did not were France and the People's Republic of China, both of which continued to conduct aboveground tests.

2422. Space treaty signed by the United States was the Treaty on Principles Governing the Activities of States in the Exploration and Use of Outer Space, Including the Moon and Other Celestial Bodies, endorsed by the United Nations General Assembly on December 19, 1966. The treaty was signed by the United States, the Soviet Union, the United Kingdom, and other countries beginning on January 27, 1967. Signatories were prohibited from placing weapons of mass destruction into space, and agreed not to claim sovereignty over other celestial bodies.

2423. Nonproliferation treaty for weapons of mass destruction in the world was the Treaty on the Non-proliferation of Nuclear Weapons, agreed to on July 1, 1968, by representatives of the United Kingdom, the United States, the Soviet Union, and 59 other nations. It went into force on March 5, 1970. France and China ratified the treaty in 1992. The signatories agreed not to sell or give nuclear weapons to nonnuclear states or to assist them in developing such weapons. The treaty was renewed on May 11, 1995, by 178 nations.

2424. Strategic Arms Limitation Treaty (also called SALT 1) between the United States and the Soviet Union was signed in Moscow by President Richard Milhous Nixon and General Secretary Leonid Brezhnev on May 26, 1972, culminating negotations that began in November 1969. SALT 1 and its successors were designed to slow the arms race in strategic nuclear weapons.

2425. Middle East peace treaty brokered by an American president was the Camp David Accords between Israel and Egypt, signed on September 18, 1978, by Israeli prime minister Menachem Begin and Egyptian president Anwar Sadat at Camp David, near Thurmont, MD. President Jimmy Carter was credited with bringing the two former antagonists together.

2426. Nuclear arms limitation treaty not approved by the Senate was the Strategic Arms Limitation Talks II (SALT II) Treaty signed on June 18, 1979, in Vienna, Austria, by President Jimmy Carter and Soviet leader Leonid Brezhnev. The treaty was presented to the Senate for ratification, but on December 26 of that year, the Soviet Union invaded Afghanistan, and Carter withdrew the SALT II Treaty from consideration in January 1980. The two superpowers informally observed the limitations of SALT II until November 26, 1986, when the United States deployed one more air-launched ballistic missile platform than provided for in the treaty.

2427. Treaty to reduce the number of nuclear missiles in the United States and the Soviet Union was signed by President Ronald Wilson Reagan and Mikhail S. Gorbachev, secretary general of the Soviet Union, on December 8, 1987, in Washington, DC. The agreement, known as the Intermediate-Range Nuclear Forces Treaty, required the two nations to destroy 2,611 short-range and medium-range missiles based in Europe and to allow inspection and verification of the destruction.

2428. Chemical arms control treaty was signed on June 1, 1990, at a summit meeting in Washington, DC, by President George Herbert Walker Bush and Soviet leader Mikhail Gorbachev. The treaty called for an 80-percent reduction of each country's chemical weapon arsenal and provided for on-site inspectors to observe the destruction of weapons stockpiles.

2429. Treaty ending the Cold War was the Treaty on Conventional Forces in Europe, signed in Paris, France, on November 19, 1990, by the Warsaw Pact nations and members of the North Atlantic Treaty Organization, including the United States. The treaty drastically slashed the size of conventional forces maintained on European soil, limiting the two sides to 20,000 battle tanks, 20,000 artillery tubes, 6,800 combat aircraft, 30,000 other armored vehicles, and 2,000 attack helicopters. The Charter of Paris for a New Europe, also signed at that time, declared an end to the military and economic blocs that had divided Europe since the end of World War II.

INTERNATIONAL RELATIONS—UNITED NATIONS

2430. Meeting to establish the United Nations took place at the Dumbarton Oaks mansion in Washington, DC, from August 21 to October 7, 1944. Representatives of China, Great Britain, the Soviet Union, and the United States met to discuss the establishment of an international organization for maintaining peace and security. On October 9, the participants made public their "Proposals for the Establishment of a General International Organization," which eventually formed the basis for the United Nations Charter.

2431. United Nations conference was the United Nations Conference on International Organization, often called the San Francisco Conference, which took place in San Francisco, CA, beginning on April 25, 1945. Delegates from 50 nations finalized the structure and mission of the organization and drafted the text of the Charter of the United Nations, which was approved on June 25 and signed on June 26. The negotiations were nearly scuttled by a disagreement between the Soviet Union and the United States over the extent of the veto powers assigned to the Big Five (the Soviet Union, the United States, France, Great Britain, and China), but resumed when Soviet dictator Josef Stalin assented to a compromise.

2432. United States representative to the United Nations was Edward Reilly Stettinius, Jr., an American industrialist and the last secretary of state under President Franklin Delano Roosevelt. Stettinius was named to the post by President Harry S. Truman and served from December 1945 to June 1946. The present U.S. mission to the United Nations was created by the United Nations Participation Act of 1947.

2433. United Nations General Assembly meeting took place in Flushing Meadow, NY, on October 23, 1946. The United Nations Charter, which had been signed on June 26, 1945, entered into force the following day. The General Assembly is comprised of representatives of all members of the United Nations. It is convened yearly or by special session.

INTERNATIONAL RELATIONS—UNITED NATIONS—*continued*

2434. United States delegation to the United Nations was formally designated the United States Mission to the United Nations by Executive Order 9844, dated April 28, 1947, and signed by President Harry S. Truman under authority of the United Nations Participation Act of 1945.

2435. African-American delegate to the United nations was Edith Spurlock Sampson, who was appointed alternate delegate to the fifth General Assembly on August 24, 1950. Her first assignment, on September 28, 1950, was to the Social, Humanitarian and Cultural Committee.

2436. United States representative to the United Nations Educational, Scientific and Cultural Organization was South African-born physicist, oceanographer, and inventor Frederick Athelstan Spilhaus, a former consultant to the Armed Forces Special Weapons Project (a nuclear weapons program under the Department of Defense). Spilhaus was appointed to UNESCO in 1954 by President Dwight David Eisenhower.

2437. United Nations permanent ambassador who was a woman was Marietta Peabody Tree, who was sworn in on October 28, 1964, to the Trusteeship Council of the United Nations. She had served since 1961 as a United Nations delegate.

2438. United Nations Security Council resolution vetoed by the United States was a resolution to condemn Great Britain for not using force to overthrow the white minority government of Rhodesia. The veto was cast on March 17, 1970, by Ambassador Charles Woodruff Yost. Great Britain also rejected the resolution. The Security Council met at the United Nations headquarters in New York City.

2439. Woman to serve as the United States representative to the United Nations was political scientist Jeane Duane Jordan Kirkpatrick of Georgetown University in Washington, DC. She was nominated by President Ronald Wilson Reagan and was sworn in on January 29, 1981. She returned to the Georgetown faculty in 1985.

2440. Vice president to chair the United Nations Security Council was Albert Gore, Jr., the vice president of William Jefferson Clinton. For some 40 minutes on January 10, 2000, Gore presided over a Security Council session on the AIDS epidemic. He promised that the United States would contribute an additional $150 million to fight AIDS worldwide, with a focus on bringing treatments to African nations ravaged by the disease.

L

LABOR

2441. Labor bureau established by a state was the Massachusetts Bureau of Statistics of Labor, established by legislation approved on June 23, 1869, by Governor William Claflin. The duties of the bureau, under a chief and deputy, were "to collect, assort, systematize and present in annual reports to the legislature . . . statistical details relating to all departments of labor in the Commonwealth." Henry Kemble Oliver was appointed chief on July 31, 1869, at a salary of $2,500 a year.

2442. Labor bureau of the federal government was authorized by congressional act of June 27, 1884. The first chief of the bureau, established in the Department of Interior, was Carroll Davidson Wright, whose title was commissioner of labor. He was appointed on January 31, 1885, by President Chester Alan Arthur and served until January 31, 1905.

2443. Women's Bureau of the Labor Department was permanently organized by act of Congress on June 5, 1920. Its purpose was to formulate standards and policies to promote the welfare of wage-earning women, improve their working conditions, increase their efficiency, and advance their opportunities for profitable employment. The first director was Mary Anderson.

2444. Secretary of labor who was not a member of the American Federation of Labor was William Nuckles Doak, who was appointed by President Herbert Hoover and sworn in December 9, 1930.

2445. Labor advisory board of the federal government was authorized on June 16, 1933, under the National Industrial Recovery Act. It was organized on June 20 and was composed of nine members. The first chairman was Leo Wolman.

2446. Federal agency regulating labor relations was the National Labor Board, an independent agency authorized on August 5, 1933, under the National Industrial Recovery Act. The first chairman was Senator Robert Ferdinand Wagner of New York. In 1935 it was replaced by the National Labor Relations Board. As amended by acts of 1947 (the Taft-Hartley Act), 1959 (the Landrum-Griffin Act), and 1974 (the Health Care Amendments), the NLRB affirms the right of employees to self-organization and collective bargaining through representatives of their own choosing, to engage in other protected, concerted activities, or to refrain from such activities. The first woman to chair the board was Betty Southard Murphy of Virginia, who was appointed by President Gerald Rudolph Ford and was sworn in on February 18, 1975. The first African-American chair was Stanford University law professor William Benjamin Gould IV, nominated by President William Jefferson Clinton and confirmed in March 1994.

2447. Collective bargaining agency for the federal government was the Federal Mediation and Conciliation Service, which assists federal sector labor and management in resolving disputes in collective bargaining contract negotiation through voluntary mediation and arbitration services. It was created by the Labor Management Relations Act of 1947.

2448. Consolidated labor relations agency was the Federal Labor Relations Authority, which oversees labor-management relations for the federal government. It was created as an independent establishment by Reorganization Plan No. 2 of 1978, effective January 1, 1979, pursuant to Executive Order 12107 of December 28, 1978, to consolidate the central policymaking functions in Federal labor-management relations. FLRA administers the law that protects the right of federal employees to organize, bargain collectively, and participate through labor organizations of their own choosing in decisions affecting them.

2449. City to ban products made in sweatshops was North Olmsted, OH, a blue-collar suburb of Cleveland. In February 1997 the city passed an ordnance banning all municipal purchases of products made in sweatshops, whether in the United States or overseas.

LABOR—ARBITRATION

2450. State arbitration board for labor disputes was the New York Board of Mediation and Arbitration, organized on June 1, 1886, under authority of an act of May 18, 1886. On June 2, 1886, Massachusetts authorized a state arbitration board "for the settlement of differences between employers and their employees."

2451. Federal arbitration board for labor disputes was the United States Board of Mediation and Conciliation, authorized by congressional act of March 4, 1913, which gave the secretary of labor "power to act as mediator and to appoint commissioners of conciliation in labor disputes whenever in his judgment the interests of industrial peace may require it."

2452. Effective state arbitration law under which an agreement to arbitrate controversies arising from a contract was recognized as valid and enforceable was an "act in relation to arbitration constituting chapter seventy-two of the consolidated laws," Chapter 275 of the Laws of 1920, New York, which became effective on April 19, 1920, the date when it was signed by Governor Alfred Emanuel Smith. Many laws were passed between 1886 and 1920 by several states, but they were not effective.

2453. National Mediation Board was created by a congressional act of June 21, 1934, that amended the Railway Labor Act. The new board replaced the U.S. Board of Mediation. It was organized "to avoid any interruption to commerce or to the operation of any carrier engaged therein, . . . to provide for the prompt and orderly settlement of all disputes concerning rates of pay, rules or working conditions." Dr. William Morris Leiserson was the first chairman.

LABOR—CHILD

2454. Child labor law enacted by a state that included an education requirement was passed by Massachusetts on April 16, 1836. It required all children to attend school at least three months of the year until they reached the age of 15. Manufacturers were not allowed to hire children to work in their mills for more than nine months a year, but the children were conveniently transferred from mill to mill so that this legislation was not effective. Child labor in mills and factories had been used since at least 1793, when Samuel Slater, owner of the cotton mill of Almy, Brown, and Slater in Pawtucket, RI, hired children because their small hands could do finer work.

LABOR—CHILD—*continued*

2455. Child labor law enacted by a state that regulated hours of employment was approved by Massachusetts Governor John Davis on March 3, 1842. Massachusetts prohibited children under twelve years of age from working more than ten hours a day. Connecticut enacted a similar law, which prohibited children under 14 years of age from working more than ten hours a day.

2456. Child labor law enacted by a state that restricted the age of the worker was approved on March 28, 1848, by Governor Francis Rawn Shunk of Pennsylvania. The law prohibited children under twelve years of age from engaging in commercial labor. In 1849 the age limit was raised to 13 years. Similar legislation was enacted in 1853 by Rhode Island, in 1855 by Connecticut, and in 1866 by Massachusetts, with age limits of twelve, nine, and ten years, respectively.

2457. Federal child labor law was "an act to prevent interstate commerce in the products of child labor," passed on September 1, 1916. The provisions of the law were to be administered by the Children's Bureau. Since the government did not have the constitutional power to regulate labor directly, this law represented an attempt to deal with the problem of child labor through the government's constitutional power to regulate interstate commerce. The act became effective on September 1, 1917, but on June 3, 1918, it was declared unconstitutional by the Supreme Court as an invasion of states' rights.

LABOR—DISCRIMINATION

2458. Ban enacted by a state on the employment of women in an occupation was "an act providing for the health and safety of persons employed in coal mines," passed and approved by Illinois on May 28, 1879. It prohibited the employment of women in mines in Illinois.

2459. State agency for enforcing equal treatment in employment was the New York State Commission Against Discrimination, appointed on July 1, 1945, "to formulate policies to eliminate and prevent discrimination in employment because of race, creed, color or national origin, either by employers, labor organizations, employment agencies or other persons." It consisted of five commissioners at $10,000 a year whose terms ranged from one to five years. The first chairman was Henry C. Turner.

2460. Federal law mandating equal pay for women was the Equal Pay Act, which was enacted on June 10, 1963. The bill required equal pay for equal work for women involved in interstate commerce. The House of Representatives had passed the measure as early as July 1962, but a version acceptable to the Senate was not approved until May 17, 1963.

2461. Federal law requiring fair employment practices was Title VII of the Civil Rights Act of 1964, which prohibited discrimination based on race, color, religion, sex, national origin, disability, or age in hiring, promoting, firing, setting wages, testing, training, apprenticeship, and all other terms and conditions of employment. Enforcement of the law was given to a federal Equal Opportunity Commission, which became operational on July 2, 1965. Its first chairman was Franklin D. Roosevelt, Jr., the son of FDR and a former congressman from New York.

LABOR—EMPLOYMENT

2462. State employment service was created on April 28, 1890, by Ohio. Authorization was given to establish public employment offices in cities of the first and second class, including Cincinnati, Cleveland, Columbus, Dayton, and Toledo. The first office was opened on June 4, 1890, in Toledo, with Charles W. Murphy as superintendent. The Commissioner of Labor Statistics, under whom the system of five offices was set up during the year 1890, was John McBride.

2463. City employment office was authorized by Seattle, WA, on March 5, 1894, by a vote of 2,058 to 523. John Lamb, the city's first labor commissioner, opened an office on April 1, 1894, in a rough board shanty containing one small room. The following year, the office moved to larger quarters in City Hall.

2464. Federal employment service as a distinct and separate unit of the Department of Labor was inaugurated under an order promulgated on January 3, 1918, by the secretary of labor pursuant to an act approved on October 6, 1917. Previously, the employment service had functioned under authority of an act to establish a Division of Information in the Bureau of Immigration and by the provisions of the organic act creating the Department of Labor (March 4, 1913).

2465. State unemployment insurance was established by Wisconsin on January 28, 1932. The act was signed by Governor Philip La Follette. Every employer of ten or more people was required to put 2 percent of the payroll aside until a fund accrued equaling $75 per eligible worker. An employee who lost his or her job could draw on the fund at the rate of $10 a week for a maximum of ten weeks. The first payment was made on August 17, 1936. The chairman of the Industrial Commission, which regulated the department, was Voyta Wrabetz.

2466. Federal Emergency Relief Administration was created by the Federal Emergency Relief Act of 1933, approved on May 12, 1933, "to provide for cooperation by the federal government with the several states and territories, and the District of Columbia in relieving the hardships and suffering caused by unemployment." The Federal Emergency Relief Administration became operative ten days after approval of the act. Its first administrator was Harry Lloyd Hopkins, who took office on May 22, 1933.

2467. National employment system was the United States Employment Service, created on June 6, 1933, "to provide for the establishment of a national employment system and for cooperation with the states in the promotion of such a system." The first director was William Frank Persons, who received $8,500 annually. Within ten weeks, 3,220 local offices opened, which registered 9 million people. It was successively under the Department of Labor, the Social Security Board, and the War Manpower Commission.

2468. Large-scale federal jobs-creation programs were authorized by Congress during the Great Depression as part of President Franklin Delano Roosevelt's New Deal. The Public Works Administration, established on June 16, 1933, as part of the National Industrial Recovery Act, provided for the hiring of unemployed laborers to work on road and building construction; its first chief was Harold L. Ickes. The Civil Works Administration, a similar relief program, operated from November 1933 to March 1934 under Harry Lloyd Hopkins, who also headed the Works Progress Administration, enacted by Congress on April 8, 1935, under the Emergency Relief Appropriation Act. The WPA (renamed the Work Projects Administration in 1939) was disbanded in 1943, after the war effort eliminated unemployment, by which time it had employed some 8.5 million people on 1.4 million public projects at a cost of approximately $11 billion.

2469. National guestworker program was the so-called "bracero" program, begun in 1942 to allow Mexican nationals to work temporarily in the United States. The program, which was intended to maintain the nation's farm production while much of the native-born work force was fighting World War II, brought in several hundred thousand agricultural guestworkers, mostly from Mexico, until it was ended in 1964. Generally, *braceros* were better paid than resident Mexican-American or Filipino laborers.

LABOR—PENSIONS

2470. Pension law enacted by Congress was passed by the Continental Congress on August 26, 1776. It provided "that every commissioned officer, non-commissioned officer, and private soldier who shall have lost a limb in any engagement, or be so disabled in the service of the United States of America as to render him incapable afterwards of getting a livelihood, shall receive, during his life or the continuance of such disability, one half of his monthly pay from and after the time that his pay as an officer or soldier ceases." As the resources of the Continental Congress were meager, the states were asked to furnish the payments.

2471. Pensions paid by the federal government were those paid under the act of September 29, 1789, which took up the obligation of paying the pensions granted by the Continental Congress and appropriated money for payments to invalids who were wounded and disabled in the Revolutionary War for one year from March 4, 1789. The act of July 16, 1790, continued the payment of pensions for another year. The act of April 30, 1790, provided for pensions to those wounded or disabled in the line of duty, and the act of March 23, 1792, provided for pensions of those suffering wounds or disabilities known to be of service origin.

2472. Pension fund for teachers was set up in New York City under a state law passed on April 14, 1894, which provided for a retirement fund for public school teachers. Contributions to the fund were not drawn from teachers' regular salaries, but from deductions to their salaries on days when they were absent from work.

2473. Pension plan sponsored by a company was offered to some 20,000 employees of the American Telephone and Telegraph Company and put into effect on January 1, 1913. The plan included coverage of employees 60 years of age with more than 20 years of employment, accident and disability benefits with full pay for 13 weeks or half-pay up to six years, sickness disability (for those employed more than ten years) paying full pay for 13 weeks or half-pay for 39 years, and a life insurance policy with a maximum value of $5,000.

LABOR—PENSIONS—*continued*

2474. Jurisdiction to provide for old-age pensions was Alaska, in 1915.

2475. State pension laws were enacted on March 5, 1923, by Montana and Nevada, whose respective governors signed their pension measures at the same hour on the same day. Montana instituted the first statewide mandatory system. It granted pensions of $25 a month to people who were over 70 years of age and who had been citizens and residents of the state for the previous 15 years. The funds were derived from the counties.

2476. Pensions paid by the federal government to workers in private industry were inaugurated on July 13, 1936, when checks totaling $901.56 were mailed to 18 retired railroad employees. This was done in accordance with the Railroad Retirement Act of August 29, 1935, which appropriated $46.7 million "to establish a retirement system for employees of carriers subject to the Interstate Commerce Act, and for other purposes."

LABOR—STRIKES

2477. Strike in which a militia was called out occurred in Paterson, NJ, on July 21, 1828, when the Godwin Guards of the national militia were ordered to keep peace during a strike brought about by the changing of the factory lunch hour from noon to one o'clock. The strikers were defeated, but the noon lunch hour was afterwards restored.

2478. Use of federal troops to suppress a strike took place on January 29, 1834, near Williamsport, MD, where a strike was under way by Irish-born construction crews building the Chesapeake and Ohio Canal between Washington, DC, and Cumberland, MD. The War Department, acting under instructions from President Andrew Jackson, sent troops to stop the unrest.

2479. Strike suppressed by federal troops in peacetime was an action by railroad employees that began on July 16, 1877. In response to requests for aid from the governors of West Virginia, Maryland, Pennsylvania, and other states, President Rutherford Birchard Hayes called out federal troops.

2480. Strike settlement mediated by the federal Labor Department was a dispute by the railway clerks of the New York, New Haven and Hartford Railroad. Commissioners of conciliation had not yet been appointed by the board, but the secretary of labor assigned the dispute to Glossbrenner Wallace William Hanger, chief statistician of the Bureau of Labor Statistics, who entered the case on May 24, 1913, and effected a settlement on June 2.

2481. Sit-down strike occurred in the packing plant of George A. Hormel and Company, Austin, MN, on November 13, 1933, when striking employees seized control of the plant. The Industrial Commission of Minnesota, of which Niels Henriksen Debel was chairman, held mediation hearings on November 16–18, 1933, and rendered a decision on December 8 affecting the specific issues involved. Various forms of stay-in strikes, slowdown strikes, and refusal-to-work strikes had been attempted previously in a variety of industries.

2482. State to outlaw sit-down strikes was Vermont, which banned them on April 9, 1937. The act prohibited "the conspiring of three or more persons unlawfully to occupy, hold and possess certain buildings against the will and without the consent of the lessee thereof." It was introduced by Ernest Walter Dunklee, state senator from Windham, and provided for penalties of not more than two years' imprisonment or a $1,000 fine.

2483. Labor dispute in which the Taft-Hartley Act was invoked took place in 1948 between the American Federation of Labor Atomic Trades and Labor Council and the Oak Ridge National Laboratory, Oak Ridge, TN. The Taft-Hartley Act, also known as the Labor-Management Relations Act of 1947, gave the president power to seek an 80-day injunction against strikes in cases of national emergency. On March 19, 1948, at Knoxville, TN, federal judge George Caldwell Taylor, responding to a request from President Harry S. Truman, issued an injunction to the Justice Department that restrained 900 members of the union from leaving their jobs on a walkout for an 80-day period, thus averting a strike by seven hours.

2484. Strike of postal employees was a wildcat strike of locals of the National Association of Letter Carriers that began in New York City on March 18, 1970, and spread to parts of New York, New Jersey, and Connecticut. On March 23 President Richard Milhous Nixon declared a state of national emergency and called out 30,000 troops to move the mail. The troops in-

146

cluded 15,000 army, navy, and marine reservists from the New York City area; 12,000 members of the Army and Air National Guard in New York; and 2,500 men on active duty in New York. The strike ended on March 24.

LABOR—UNIONS

2485. Labor union to nominate its own political candidates was the Mechanics Union, which nominated candidates for the New York State Assembly in 1784.

2486. Labor union whose candidates won an election was the New York Working Men's Party, whose candidate, Ebenezer Ford, president of the Carpenter's Union, was elected to the New York State Assembly on the Mechanic and Working Men's Ticket on November 7, 1829. Ford polled 6,166 votes.

2487. Labor cooperatives to be authorized by a state were authorized in Michigan on March 20, 1865. The act allowed the incorporation of "any ten or more persons, who shall be desirous of uniting as mechanics and laboring men, in any cooperative association."

2488. State to legalize labor unions was New Jersey, in "an act relative to persons combining and encouraging other persons to combine," approved on February 14, 1883. The law provided that combinations organized to persuade workers to enter or leave employment were not unlawful.

2489. State law on union discrimination prohibiting employers from discriminating in matters of employment against members of trade unions was "an act in relation to the employment of labor by corporations," approved on May 15, 1894, by New Jersey. Violation was subject to a fine not to exceed $500 or three months' imprisonment.

2490. Labor union chartered by the federal government was the National Education Association, which was founded as the National Teachers' Association in Philadelphia, PA, on August 26, 1867, not as a union but as a professional and charitable association. It received its charter on June 30, 1906, under the section of the congressional chartering provisions that covers private non-profit corporations existing "for patriotic, civic-improvement, charitable, or educational purposes." Since 1962 the NEA's main activity has been organizing and operating teacher unions, and it was defined as a 501(c)(5) labor union by the Internal Revenue Service in 1978.

2491. National union for public employees was the American Federation of State, County, and Municipal Employees. AFSCME was founded in Madison, WI, in 1932 as the Wisconsin State Administrative, Clerical, Fiscal and Technical Employees Association (later the Wisconsin State Employees Association), led by A. E. Garey, director of the state civil service system. Under Arnold Zander, a state personnel examiner, the union changed its name to the American Federation of State, County, and Municipal Employees and went national. In September 1936 Zander was chosen as AFSCME's first international president. By the end of 1936, AFSCME had 10,000 members drawn from other state employees' associations. In 2000, membership was over 1.3 million, making it the second largest union in the country.

2492. Capitol Hill employees to unionize were the United States Capitol police force, which joined a police union in 1997 under the Congressional Accountability Act. The act allowed all Capitol Hill employees to organize for the first time beginning on October 1, 1996.

LABOR—WAGES AND HOURS

2493. State law mandating a ten-hour workday was enacted by New Hampshire on July 9, 1847. It stated that "in all contracts relating to labor, ten hours actual labor shall be taken to be a day's work unless otherwise agreed by the parties." As a result of the bargaining provision, the law was ineffective.

2494. State law regulating women's work hours was enacted by Ohio on March 29, 1852. This law fixed ten hours per day as the maximum number of working hours for manual labor by children under 18 and women. It was repealed in 1887, when a new code was adopted.

2495. Federal law mandating an eight-hour workday was passed on June 25, 1868, and signed by President Andrew Johnson. It provided, among other things, that "eight hours shall constitute a day's work for all laborers, workmen, and mechanics who may be employed by or on behalf of the Government of the United States."

2496. Minimum wage law enacted by a state was enacted by Massachusetts on June 4, 1912. It established a three-member Minimum Wage Commission to be appointed by the governor with the advice of the Council. The act did not go into effect until July 1, 1913. Oregon, in advance of all other states, set up an administrative body to carry out the provisions of an act

LABOR—WAGES AND HOURS—*continued*
of February 17, 1913, which provided for the appointment, within 30 days, of a Welfare Commission to consist of three members, one representing the employer, one the employee, and one the public.

2497. Federal law mandating a 40-hour work week was the Public Contract Act of 1936 "to provide conditions for the purchase of supplies and the making of contracts by the United States," approved on June 30, 1936. Workers on government contracts over $10,000 were required to receive overtime compensation at the rate of not less than time and a half for hours worked in excess of 40 a week or eight hours in any one day (if such compensation yielded a greater amount than on the weekly 40-hour basis). Workers were not to be paid less than the prevailing minimum wage of industry and locality. The act was known as the Walsh-Healy Act.

2498. Minimum wage law enacted by Congress was one of the provisions of the Fair Labor Standards Act of 1938, "an act to provide for the establishment of fair labor standards in employment in and affecting interstate commerce," enacted on June 25, 1938.

2499. Minimum hourly wage of one dollar was set by the federal government on August 12, 1955. Since then, the minimum hourly wage has undergone a series of raises. It was set at $3.10 effective January 1, 1980, and at $4.25 effective April 1991.

2500. Minimum wage law established by a city for public contract work was the City Contracts Minimum Wage law, approved by Mayor Robert Ferdinand Wagner of New York City on December 29, 1961. It applied to "every contract for or on behalf of the city for the manufacture, furnishing or purchase of supplies, material or equipment, or for the furnishing of work, labor or services, and entered into by public letting founded in sealed bids."

LABOR—WORKERS' COMPENSATION

2501. Workers' compensation agreement was made on January 26, 1695, by Captain William Kidd of New York City, commander of the *Adventure Galley* of 787 tons burden. He promised to distribute to the crew one-fourth of all booty captured on privateering expeditions. According to the agreement, "If any man should Loose a Leg or Arm in the said service, he should have six hundred pieces of Eight, or six able slaves; if any man should loose a joynt on the said service, he should have a hundred pieces of eight."

2502. Workers' compensation insurance law enacted by a state was enacted by Maryland in 1902, followed by Montana in 1909 and New York in 1910, but all three were declared unconstitutional. The first law to remain on the books was approved by Washington on March 14, 1911, but it did not go into effect until October 1. Meantime, Wisconsin passed a law on May 3, 1911, that went into effect the same day. New Jersey's law was approved on April 4, 1911, and went into effect on July 4.

2503. Workers' compensation insurance law enacted by Congress was approved on May 30, 1908. It was applicable to the following classes of federal employees: artisans or laborers in any manufacturing establishment, arsenal, or navy yard; employees in the construction of river and harbor fortifications; employees in hazardous employment on construction work in the reclamation of arid lands; and employees in hazardous employment under the Isthmian Canal Commission in Panama.

LAW—COPYRIGHT

2504. Colonial copyright law securing benefit of copyright was passed on May 15, 1672, by the General Court of Massachusetts assembled in Boston, MA, which granted John Usher, a bookseller, the privilege of publishing on his own account a revised edition of *The General Laws and Liberties of the Massachusetts Colony*. It was ordered "that for at least seven years, unless he shall have sold them all before that time, there shall be no other or further impression made by any person thereof in this jurisdiction." The penalty for violation of the copyright was treble the whole charges of printing and paper.

2505. State copyright law was "an act for the encouragement of literature and genius," passed during the session of the General Court of Assembly of the Governor and Company of the State of Connecticut, held in Hartford, CT, from January 8 to February 7, 1783. The law gave authors sole right of publication for 14 years with power of renewal. Massachusetts passed a copyright law on March 17, 1783, for a 21-year period. Both laws extended rights only to other states having reciprocal legislation.

2506. Copyright law enacted by Congress was an act "for the encouragement of learning by securing the copies of maps, charts and books to the authors and proprietors of such copies during the times therein mentioned." The bill was signed by the speaker and the president of the Senate on May 25, 1790, laid before President George Washington on May 27, and signed on May 31. Rights were granted only to citizens of the United States, a policy which continued until 1891. Protection was extended over a 14-year period, renewal rights being granted only if the author was still alive.

2507. Copyright law on photographs enacted by Congress was enacted on March 2, 1861, and signed the next day by President James Buchanan.

2508. International copyright agreement was the Platt-Simonds Copyright Act, passed on March 4, 1891. The act enabled citizens of Switzerland, France, Belgium, and Great Britain to obtain copyright protection in the United States. The United States had been represented by Boyd Winchester at the Bern International Copyright Convention in 1886 but had not become a signatory to the convention.

2509. Copyrights registrar of the United States was Thorvald Solberg, who served from July 1, 1897, to April 22, 1930. The first woman to fill the post was Barbara Alice Ringer, who was appointed on November 19, 1973.

LAW—DOCUMENTS

2510. Law book of colonial laws was *The Book of the General Lawes and Libertyes concerning the inhabitants of the Massachusets, collected out of the records of the General Court for the several years wherein they were made and established and now revised by the same Court and disposed into an Alphabetical order and published by the same Authoritie in the General Court held at Boston the fourteenth of the first month Anno 1647.* The work was published in Cambridge, MA, in 1648 and sold by Hezekiah Usher in Boston, MA.

2511. State to abolish the laws of entail and primogeniture was Georgia, whose constitution of February 5, 1777, abrogated those two bulwarks of legal tradition. Entail is a means of willing property to a specified and unchangeable hierarchy of inheritors. Primogeniture is the right of the eldest child in a family, usually the eldest son, to inherit his parent's entire estate.

2512. Insurance law treatise was a reprint of an English book, *A System of the Law of Marine Insurances; with three chapters on bottomry, on insurance on lives and on insurances against fire,* by Sir James Alan Park, published in Philadelphia, PA, in 1789.

2513. Law report was Ephraim Kirby's *Reports of Cases Adjudged in the Superior Court of the State of Connecticut from the year 1785 to May 1788 with some determinations in the Supreme Court of Errors,* published in 1789 by Collier and Adam, Litchfield, CT. It consisted of 456 pages of text, twelve pages of index, and a five-page list of subscribers. Volume 1 of Harris and McHenry's *Maryland Reports,* published in 1809, reported cases from as far back as 1658.

2514. Law book containing laws enacted by more than one session of Congress without regard to whether or not they had been subsequently repealed prior to publication was *The Laws of the United States of America. Vol 1. Containing the Federal Constitution; the Acts of the Three Sessions of the First Congress; The Treaties Existing Between the United States and the Foreign Nations, and the Several Indian Tribes. Also the Declaration of Independence and Sundry Resolves and Ordinances of Congress Under the Confederation. The whole collated with and corrected by the original rolls in the Office of the Secretary of State, agreeably to a resolve of Congress, passed February 18, 1791. To which is added a complete index,* 592 pages, printed in 1791 and sold by Francis Childs and John Swaine, New York City.

2515. Law book of federal laws was *Acts passed at a Congress of the United States of America, begun and held at the City of New York, on Wednesday the fourth of March 1789, being the acts passed at the first session of the First Congress of the United States, to wit, New Hampshire, Massachusetts, Connecticut, New York, New Jersey, Pennsylvania, Delaware, Maryland, Virginia, South Carolina and Georgia, which eleven states ratified the Constitution of Government for the United States.* The book contained 486 pages and was published in Hartford, CT, in 1791 by Barzillai Hudson and George Goodwin.

2516. Law text published in the United States was *An Enquiry into the Law-Merchant of the United States; or Lex Mercatoria Americana; on Several Heads of Commercial Importance,* a 648-page book by George Caines, published in 1802 by Abraham and Arthur Stansbury, New York City.

2517. Digest of American law was *An Abridgement of the Laws of the United States or a complete digest of all such acts of Congress as concern the United States at large, to which is added an appendix containing all existing treaties, the Declaration of Independence,*

LAW—DOCUMENTS—*continued*

the Articles of Confederation, the rules and articles for the government of the army and the ordinance for the government of the territory north-west of Ohio. It was edited by William Graydon and published in Harrisburg, PA, in 1803. It contained 650 pages.

2518. Treatise on common law written for the American legal profession was St. George Tucker's *American Blackstone,* an annotated edition of *Blackstone's Commentaries on the Laws of England.* The treatise, published in Philadelphia, PA, in 1803, consisted of Blackstone's four original volumes, annotated by Tucker, plus numerous appendices on American law and the Constitution. Tucker's *American Blackstone* was considered the standard work on American common law for a generation and was used as a legal textbook through the mid-19th century.

2519. Law code adopted by a state was *A System of Penal Law, Divided into Code of Crimes and Punishments, Code of Procedure, Code of Evidence, Code of Reform and Prison Discipline, Beside a Book of Definitions,* written by L. Moreau Lislet, Edward Livingston, and Pierre Derbigny, who had been appointed by the legislature of Louisiana to remodel the colonial code of 1808. The code was approved on April 12, 1824, and promulgated on June 13, 1825. Louisiana is the only state whose justice system is based on a civil code of laws, an inheritance from its years as a French colony. (The remaining states rely on common law and statutory law.)

2520. Dictionary of American law was John Bouvier's *A Law Dictionary Adapted to the Constitution and Laws of the United States of America and of the Several States of the American Union With References to the Civil and Other Systems of Foreign Law.* It was published in two volumes in Philadelphia, PA, in 1839.

2521. Edition of the *United States Statutes at Large* was published in 1845 by Little, Brown and Company, Boston, MA, under authority granted by a joint resolution of Congress. The *United States Statutes at Large* is the official source for all the laws and resolutions passed by Congress. It also includes the texts of treaties passed before 1948, and of presidential proclamations and constitutional amendments.

2522. Law book of federal laws then in force was *The Public Statutes at Large of the United States of America, from the organization of the government in 1789 to March 3, 1845, arranged in chronological order with references to the matter of each act and to the subsequent acts on the same subject, and copious notes of the decisions of the Courts of the United States construing those acts and upon the subjects of the laws with an index to the contents of each volume.* The first volume, containing 777 pages, was published in 1845 in Boston, MA, by Charles C. Little and James Brown. It was edited by Richard Peters. Publication was authorized by act of March 3, 1845, "a resolution to authorize the Attorney General to contract for copies of a proposed edition of the laws and treaties of the United States."

LAW—EDUCATION

2523. Law instruction at a college was offered by King's College (now Columbia University), New York City, in 1755. The fourth year of study was described as containing, among other things, "the Chief Principles of Law and Government together with History, Sacred and Profane."

2524. Law school at a college was established in 1779 at the College of William and Mary, Williamsburg, VA. Professors did not receive a stipulated amount from the college but were paid by the students attending the course. The first professor was George Wythe, who was appointed professor of law on December 4, 1779. One of his students was John Marshall, the future chief justice of the Supreme Court, whose entire legal education consisted of Wythe's six-week course.

2525. College law school to be permanently organized was the Harvard College School of Law, Cambridge, MA, which was opened in 1817.

2526. Civil rights chair at a college was established at Lafayette College, Easton, PA, through the gift of Fred Morgan Kirby. The first lectures were given in February 1921 by Professor Herbert Adams Gibbons.

LAW ENFORCEMENT

2527. Interstate anticrime pact was effected between New York and New Jersey and signed on September 16, 1833, in New York City by Benjamin Franklin Butler, Peter Augustus Jay, Henry Seymour, Theodore Frelinghuysen, James Parker, and Lucius Quintius Cincinnatus Elmer. The pact was ratified by act of Congress of June 28, 1834.

2528. Sentence of branding by a federal court was imposed at Pensacola, FL, in 1844. Jonathan Walker, a ship captain, was convicted of stealing seven slaves, whom he carried into his 30-foot schooner. He set sail on June 23, 1844, intending to go to Nassau, but was captured by the U.S. steamer *General Taylor* and taken to Pensacola on July 20. He was imprisoned, tried in the District Court, and placed in the pillory on the public highway to be pelted with rotten eggs. He was sentenced to one year in jail for each of the seven slaves and was fined $600 for each slave plus all the costs of the trial. The initials SS, for "slave stealer," were branded on the palm of his right hand.

2529. State police were the Texas Rangers. The force was created in 1835 by the General Council of the Provisional Government of Texas, which authorized the organization of three companies of Rangers. The Rangers became the state police force in 1845, when Texas was admitted to the Union. The first African-American officer was Lee Roy Young, who joined the force in 1988.

2530. Fingerprinting in federal penitentiaries was undertaken on November 2, 1904, by the Bureau of Criminal Identification at the United States Penitentiary at Leavenworth, KS. This work was carried on until October 1, 1924, when it was taken over by the Federal Bureau of Investigation.

2531. International exchange of fingerprints between the United States and Europe was made on July 6, 1905, when the St. Louis Metropolitan Police Department, St. Louis, MO, obtained the fingerprints of John Walker, alias Captain John Pearson, a frequent offender, from New Scotland Yard, London. The prints were later forwarded to New Orleans, LA, and introduced as part of his criminal record.

2532. Federal Bureau of Investigation was originally known as the Bureau of Investigation. It was founded in July 1908 by Attorney General Charles J. Bonaparte to serve as the fact-gathering branch of the Department of Justice. The first director was Alexander Bruce Bialaski, a Polish immigrant of Lithuanian extraction, who served from 1912 to 1919. The current name was adopted in 1935.

2533. Woman bailiff was Eva Rider. A district judge, faced with the need to seat an all-woman jury for a trial in El Dorado, KS, appointed her to the post in 1912.

2534. National file on suspected political radicals was assembled by J. Edgar Hoover, a former librarian, who between 1919 and 1921, as special assistant to Attorney General Alexander Mitchell Palmer, amassed a card file with some 450,000 entries on every known political radical, group, and publication. This card file made possible the mass "Red Scare" arrests carried out under Palmer's authority in 1920 and formed the basis of an expanded national database developed by the Justice Department's Bureau of Investigation (the Federal Bureau of Investigation from 1935) after Hoover became its director on May 10, 1924.

2535. Woman sheriff was Mabel Chase of Haviland, KS. In 1926 she was elected sheriff of Kiowa County. Her husband had been elected sheriff in 1922 and 1924. The first sheriff who was an African-American woman was Michelle B. Mitchell, elected sheriff in Richmond, VA, in November 1993. Mitchell ran unopposed for the post following a primary election in which she received 59 percent of the vote.

2536. Police bureau of criminal alien investigation was started by the New York Police Department, New York City, on December 23, 1930. The purpose was to bring to the attention of federal immigration authorities undesirable aliens who were subject to deportation under the Immigration Law, because of either their criminal records or their illegal entry into the United States.

2537. Community to fingerprint its citizens was Oskaloosa, IA, which acted upon the suggestion made by Police Chief Howard Ray Allgood on May 21, 1934. Although registration was not compulsory, a Personal Identification Bureau was established through which most of the town's residents had their fingerprints recorded.

2538. Public Enemy Number 1 so labeled by the Federal Bureau of Investigation was Indiana-born bank robber John Dillinger, the most notorious criminal of the 1930s. In 1933–34, the charismatic, nattily dressed Dillinger held up banks throughout the Midwest and made spectacular escapes from prisons in Indiana and Ohio. He was finally shot and killed by federal agents on July 22, 1934, as he emerged from the Biograph Movie Theater in Chicago, IL.

2539. National conference on crime was held on October 11–12, 1935, in Trenton, NJ, with a roster of delegates from 41 states and from the federal government. Its purpose was to curb crime throughout the country by developing reciprocal legislation and interstate cooperation agreements.

LAW ENFORCEMENT—*continued*

2540. Sky marshals were appointed in accordance with President Richard Milhous Nixon's presidential directive of October 28, 1970, to deal with the proliferation of hijackings of commercial airplanes. The Treasury Law Enforcement Officers Training School graduated 46 marshals on December 23, 1970, and 81 marshals, including four women, on April 9, 1971.

2541. Women to serve as federal marshals were Jacqueline P. Balley, of Washington, DC, and Joanne Neely, of Oxon Hill, MD, sworn in on November 21, 1973, at Washington, DC.

2542. Senate investigation of the FBI and the CIA began on January 27, 1975, when a bipartisan Senate committee led by Senator Frank Church of Idaho began looking into allegations that both the FBI and the CIA had conducted illegal surveillance of thousands of U.S. citizens. The committee's report, released on November 20, 1975, also alleged that the CIA was involved in illegal efforts to assassinate foreign leaders (notably Salvador Allende, the Marxist former president of Chile, overthrown by a military coup on September 11, 1973) and that the CIA kept secret stockpiles of poisons despite a presidential order to destroy them.

2543. State ban on cheap handguns was enacted in Maryland on May 23, 1988, effective January 1, 1990. The law banned the manufacture and sale of pistols that were unsafe or easy to conceal.

2544. Mercenaries arrested for planning terrorist acts on behalf of a foreign government were members of the El Rukns street gang of Chicago, IL, who received funds from the government of Libya during the mid-1980s to commit terrorist acts in the United States. As part of the conspiracy, El Rukns leader Melvin Edward Mays purchased an anti-tank weapon from an undercover FBI agent. Mays eluded authorities during an attempted arrest in 1986 and was placed on the FBI's Top Ten Most Wanted List on February 7, 1989. He was apprehended by members of the FBI's Chicago Joint Terrorism Task Force on March 9, 1995, and charged with more than 40 federal counts of conspiracy to conduct terrorist activities.

2545. Woman to serve as the police chief of a major city was Elizabeth M. Watson, who headed the police force of Houston, TX, from January 19, 1990. She was a 17-year veteran of the department who began in the juvenile division. She was also the first police chief to give birth while on active duty.

2546. Municipal education program for men convicted of patronizing prostitutes was the First Offender Prostitution Program, started in San Francisco, CA, in 1995 by Norma Hotaling, a former prostitute, and the city's police department. First offenders who enrolled in the program had the arrest cleared from their records. The daylong course, given at the San Francisco Hall of Justice, included talks by prostitutes who described their diseases, drug addictions, and violent hatred of men; health educators who displayed slides showing the effects of venereal diseases; prosecutors and police officers who explained the workings of the sex industry and the personal consequences of arrest and conviction; and local residents who described the effects of prostitution on their neighborhoods. Some of the fees charged for the class went to an organization that assists prostitutes to find alternative sources of income.

2547. National DNA database was brought online on October 13, 1998, by the Federal Bureau of Investigation. The database, a network of 50 state databases coordinated by FBI software, was maintained at computers in a secret location. The system made it possible for the first time to compare an identifying DNA sample from a crime in one state with all other DNA samples in the United States.

2548. Bounty of $5 million for an enemy of the United States was posted on November 5, 1998, for information leading to the arrest and conviction of the Saudi Arabian national Osama Bin Laden. Bin Laden was charged in a Manhattan court with a 238-count indictment for masterminding the bombings on August 7 of American embassies in Nairobi, Kenya, and Dar es Salaam, Tanzania. The $5 million reward was the largest ever offered by the State Department.

2549. State police department to be monitored for racial profiling was the New Jersey State Police, an organization with 2,700 officers. Following complaints made by the Black Ministers' Conference of New Jersey and other groups, the federal Justice Department charged the state police with violating the civil rights laws by targeting African-American and Hispanic drivers for traffic stops. To avoid a lawsuit, the state attorney general, Peter G. Verniero, negotiated a settlement in April 1999 committing the police to following a set of protocols intended to prevent discrimination. In December 1999 the Justice Department decided to place the police under the supervision of an outside monitor who would report directly to a federal judge. The Justice Department was authorized by the Federal Crime Bill of 1994 to file civil suits against police departments that demonstrate "patterns of misconduct."

LAW ENFORCEMENT—DEATH PENALTY

2550. Execution in America was that of John Billington, one of the signers of the Mayflower Compact, who was hanged in Plymouth, MA, on September 30, 1630. He was "arraigned, and both by grand and petie jurie found guilty of willful murder, by plaine and notorious evidence, and was for the same accordingly executed. This, as it was the first execution amongst them, so was it a matter of great sadness unto them. He way-laid a young man, one John Newcomin (about a former quarele), and shote him with a gune, whereof he dyed."

2551. Law authorizing the penalty of death for blasphemy was passed in 1644 by the Bay Colony, Boston, MA. Aimed at cynical unbelievers and Native Americans, it claimed that "common reason requireth every state & society of men to be more carefull of preventing the dishonor & contempt of ye Most High God . . . then of any mortall princes & magistrates." Any resident, "whether Xtian or pagan," could be put to death for "willfull or obstinate denying ye true God, or reproach of ye holy religion of God, as if it were but a politicke devise to keepe ignorant men in awe." As far as is known, no one was actually executed under this statute.

2552. Colonist hanged for treason was Jacob Leisler, who led an insurrection against Governor Francis Nicholson of New York in 1689 "for the preservation of the Protestant religion" and in behalf of the sovereigns William and Mary. Through trickery, the aristocratic party regained power and in a manifestly unfair trial convicted Leisler of treason. He was hanged on May 16, 1691, from a scaffold erected in City Hall Park.

2553. Execution by the Army occurred on June 27, 1776. A guard, Thomas Hickey, plotted with others to capture George Washington and deliver him to Sir William Howe. Hickey was tried, convicted, and hanged in New York City. The execution took place at a field near Bowery Lane in the presence of 20,000 persons, including an armed assembly of all the off-duty officers and men of four brigades.

2554. State to ban the death penalty was Pennsylvania, on April 22, 1794. The law abolished all executions except in cases of murder in the first degree. Michigan enacted a general ban on the death penalty on May 4, 1846, except in cases of treason against the state.

2555. Death penalty in a tax riot was given to John Fries, a Pennsylvania auctioneer. In February 1799, mobs of German settlers in the eastern counties of Pennsylvania, outraged by Congress's imposition of a direct federal property tax, assaulted the tax assessors who were attempting to collect it. Federal troops were called out by President John Adams to suppress the uprising, and Fries, at the head of an armed band, freed a number of rebels from the courthouse where they were being held. He was arrested in Bethlehem, PA, after resisting a federal marshal. He was convicted of treason and sentenced to death by Supreme Court justice Samuel Chase in a manifestly unfair trial, with Chase forcing Fries to defend himself without counsel. Adams pardoned Fries in 1800.

2556. Execution for slave trading carried out by the federal government was the hanging of Nathaniel Gordon at the Tombs prison, New York City, on February 21, 1862. He had been tried and convicted of piracy under the law of May 15, 1820, which defined slave trading as piracy. Gordon, a native of Portland, ME, was the captain of the *Erie*. His ship was stopped by the U.S.S. *Mohican* about 50 miles off the African coast and was found to be carrying 890 Africans, including 600 children, to a slave market. The captives were released in Liberia and Gordon's ship was brought to New York City, where his trial was held.

2557. American citizen hanged for treason was William Bruce Mumford, a retired gambler. During the Civil War, Captain Theodorus Bailey was sent by Admiral David Glasgow Farragut to New Orleans, LA, where he hoisted the American flag over the mint on April 28, 1862. After the troops left, Mumford tore down the flag. On May 1, General Benjamin Franklin Butler arrived in New Orleans with 2,000 troops and took possession of the St. Charles Hotel. A crowd gathered in front of it, among them Mumford, who boasted of his exploit in humbling the "old rag of the United States." Mumford was arrested, tried under the direction of the provost marshal of the district of New Orleans, convicted, and hanged on June 7, 1862.

LAW ENFORCEMENT—DEATH PENAL-
TY—*continued*

2558. Federal execution of a woman ended the life of Mary Eugenia Surratt, the proprietor of a boardinghouse in Washington, DC. Her son was a friend of the actor John Wilkes Booth and met with him and other plotters in the boardinghouse to plan the assassination of President Abraham Lincoln. The assassination was carried out on April 14, 1865. Mrs. Surratt was arrested and tried for conspiracy by a military commission of nine army officers headed by Major General David Hunter. Although serious proof of her involvement was never produced, it was generally held that she "kept the nest that hatched the egg" and was therefore in some measure part of the plot. She was convicted on June 30, 1865, of "treasonable conspiracy" and was hanged on July 7 in the yard of Washington's Old Penitentiary along with three other convicted conspirators, Lewis Powell (alias Lewis Payne), David Herold, and George Atzerodt. Her guilt is still a subject of controversy. Her son was brought to trial, but the government failed to obtain an indictment and he was released.

2559. Labor activists to be executed were four men accused of participating in the Haymarket Riot that occurred on May 4, 1886, in Chicago, IL. A labor rally had been called in Haymarket Square to protest the shooting of several strikers by Chicago police the previous day. Anarchist and communist speakers were addressing a crowd of several hundred mostly German-born workers when a squad of 180 police officers arrived to break up the rally. A bomb, thrown by a person who was never positively identified, fatally injured 7 officers and wounded 70. Police fired into the crowd, killing one worker and injuring more than a dozen. A grand jury indicted 31 suspected labor radicals in connection with the bombing. Eight men were tried for murder; seven were convicted. On November 11, 1887, four men—August Spies, Samuel Fielden, Adolph Fischer, and Albert Parsons—were executed by hanging. The other three were pardoned in 1893 by Illinois governor John Peter Altgeld.

2560. State to allow execution by electrocution was New York State. The electric chair, which employed a system of high-voltage alternating current, was invented by Dr. Alphonse David Rockwell. At first, it was thought to be such a brutal form of execution that it would lead to a ban on the death penalty, but this did not occur. The first convict to be executed in the electric chair was William Kemmler, alias John Hart, a fruit peddler from Buffalo, NY, who died on August 6, 1890, at Auburn Prison, Auburn, NY, for the murder of Matilda Ziegler. The first woman to be executed by electrocution was Martha M. Place of Brooklyn, NY, who was electrocuted at Sing Sing Prison, Ossining, NY, on March 20, 1899, for the murder of her stepdaughter.

2561. Death penalty imposed by a woman judge was imposed by Florence Ellinwood Allen, a judge of the Court of Common Pleas of the County of Cuyahoga, Cleveland, OH. She gave a sentence of death by electrocution to Frank Motto, who had been convicted by a jury on a charge of first-degree murder on May 14, 1921. The sentence was carried out on August 20, 1921.

2562. State to allow execution by lethal gas was Nevada, which adopted it on March 28, 1921. The first execution under the law took place on February 8, 1924, in Carson City, NV. The executed man was a Chinese gang member, Gee Jon, who had been convicted of killing a rival tong man.

2563. American executions to excite worldwide protest were those of Nicola Sacco and Bartolomeo Vanzetti, two Italian immigrants who were sentenced to death on August 9, 1921, for the double murder of a paymaster and a guard in South Braintree, MA. Although the evidence against them was questionable, a series of pleas for a retrial was denied, even after another man, Celestino Madeiros, confessed on November 18, 1925, that he had taken part in the crime. On August 3, 1927, Governor Alvan T. Fuller of Massachusetts refused to grant them clemency, an act that sparked worldwide protests from leftists who believed that Sacco and Vanzetti were being persecuted for their radical political beliefs. Protesters also set off bombs in New York City and Philadelphia. Sacco and Vanzetti were electrocuted at Charlestown Prison in Massachusetts on August 23, 1927.

2564. Death penalty authorized by federal law made the killing of a federal officer a mandatory capital offense. The law was enacted on May 18, 1934. The first man executed under the law was George W. Barrett, for the murder of federal agent Nelson Bernard Klein in College Corner, IN, on August 16, 1935. He was tried before U.S. District Judge Robert C. Baltzell, convicted on December 14, 1935, and hanged on March 24, 1936, at the Marion County Jail, Indianapolis, IN.

2565. Federal execution of an organized crime boss was that of Louis Buchalter, better known as Louis Lepke, the head of Murder Incorporated, a gang of mob assassins based in New York City. Lepke surrendered to FBI chief J. Edgar Hoover on August 24, 1939, to face a charge of union racketeering. Under a secret agreement, he pleaded guilty to a lesser charge and was sentenced to a 14-year term in the federal penitentiary at Fort Leavenworth, KS. After New York State authorities found out from a mob informer about Lepke's career of murder, he was tried again and sentenced to death. On March 4, 1944, Lepke went to the electric chair at Sing Sing Prison in Ossining, NY.

2566. Peacetime death sentence for espionage was imposed on April 5, 1951, by Judge Irving Robert Kaufman of the U.S. District Court, Southern District, who sentenced Ethel and Julius Rosenberg to death for passing secret information about nuclear weapons to the Soviet Union. The trial began on March 6, 1951, and the jury rendered its verdict of guilty on March 29. The chief witness was Ethel Rosenberg's brother David Greenglass, an army sergeant who admitted that he had given them the information. The Rosenbergs were electrocuted on June 19, 1953, at Sing Sing Prison, Ossining, NY. They were the first native-born Americans executed for espionage by order of a civilian court, and also the only married couple ever executed together in the United States.

2567. Federal execution for the killing of an FBI agent took place at Sing Sing Prison, Ossining, NY, on August 12, 1954, when Gerhard Puff was electrocuted. He had been convicted of killing Joseph Brock, an agent of the Federal Bureau of Investigation, in a gun battle in New York City on July 26, 1952. Brock had been attempting to arrest Puff for participating in the robbery of $62,650 from the Johnson County National Bank and Trust Company of Prairie Village, KS. He was confined for 15 months in the death house and his execution was postponed five times pending various appeals.

2568. State to allow execution by lethal injection was Oklahoma, which authorized it on May 10, 1977. The law provided that "the punishment of death must be inflicted by continuous, intravenous administration of a lethal quantity of an ultrashort-acting barbiturate in combination with a chemical paralytic agent until death is pronounced by a licensed physician according to accepted standards of medical practice." The first execution by lethal injection

took place on December 7, 1983, in the state penitentiary at Huntsville, TX. Charles Brooks, Jr., who had been convicted of murdering an auto mechanic, received an intravenous injection of sodium pentathol, a barbiturate.

2569. State to enact a moratorium on executions was Illinois. On January 31, 2000, Governor George Ryan, a Republican, announced that the state would stop executing criminals on Death Row while a special panel conducted an investigation into the death penalty system. Since Illinois restored capital punishment in 1977, 13 men on death row had been proven innocent and released, sometimes only a few days before their executions were scheduled. Nationwide, 85 people convicted of capital crimes since 1973 were exonerated before their executions. The Nebraska legislature enacted a moratorium in 1999, but it was vetoed by the governor.

LAW ENFORCEMENT—PRISONS

2570. Prison was constructed in 1676 in Nantucket, MA. The court hired William Bunker on November 16, 1676, to keep the prison for one year and agreed to pay him "foeur pounds, halfe in wheat, the other in other graine."

2571. Federal law exempting debtors from prison on processes issuing from a United States court amounting to less than $30 was "an act for the relief of persons imprisoned for debt," passed on May 28, 1796. On February 28, 1839, an act of Congress prohibited imprisonment for debt by a United States court in states where such imprisonment had been abolished.

2572. State law to abolish imprisonment for debt was passed by Kentucky on December 17, 1821.

2573. State reformatory for boys was the reformatory school at Westborough, MA, later known as the Lyman School for Boys. It was authorized on April 9, 1847.

2574. State reformatory for women was the Reformatory Prison for Women, Sherborn, MA, opened November 7, 1877. The first superintendent was Eudora Clark Atkinson and the first resident physician was Dr. Eliza Maria Mosher. The part of Sherborn in which the reformatory was located was annexed to the town of Framingham, MA, in 1925.

2575. Probation system for offenders was legally established as a judicial policy by the city of Boston, MA, in 1878 and by the state of Massachusetts in 1880. This was the first such system in the world.

LAW ENFORCEMENT—PRISONS—*continued*

2576. Federal penitentiary was the Federal Penitentiary at Atlanta, GA, which was authorized in 1899 and completed in January 1902. The Federal Penitentiary at Leavenworth, KS, was authorized earlier, on March 3, 1891, but was not completed until February 1, 1906.

2577. Federal prison for women was the Federal Industrial Institution for Women, Alderson, WV, established by act of Congress in 1926 and opened the same year. The first superintendent was Dr. Mary Belle Harris, sworn in on March 12, 1925. The compound contained 17 two-story brick dormitories, each designed to accommodate 30 persons, and built on the college plan. They cost over $2 million and occupied 500 acres of land. There were no prison walls or guards.

2578. Woman to serve as director of a state bureau of corrections was Ward E. Murphy, who became director of the Bureau of Corrections under the Department of Mental Health and Corrections at Augusta, ME, in July 1970. She had been superintendent of the Women's Correctional Center at Skowhegan, ME, from 1961 to 1970.

LAW ENFORCEMENT—SECRET SERVICE

2579. Secret service established in a colony was the Headquarters Secret Service, organized by Aaron Burr and Major Benjamin Tallmadge in June 1778. On July 4, 1778, General George Washington issued a special order making Burr head of the Department for Detecting and Defeating Conspiracies and ordered him "to proceed to Elizabeth Town to procure information of movements of the enemy's shipping about New York." This was the first official intelligence-gathering government service in the united colonies. Previously, information about the activities of the British had been gathered secretly by individuals and informal groups.

2580. Secret service established by the federal government was created by act of June 23, 1860, under the Treasury Department to suppress the counterfeiting of U.S. coins, and, by later legislation, of paper money and securities. The first chief was William P. Wood, sworn in by Secretary of the Treasury Hugh McCulloch on July 5, 1865, in Washington, DC. After the assassination of President Abraham Lincoln, the Secret Service was given the duty of guarding the president. Subsequent legislation extended permanent protection to the president, his immediate family, the president-elect, the vice president, the vice president-elect, former presidents and their wives, the widows of former presidents unless they remarry, minor children of former presidents until they reach 16, major presidential and vice presidential candidates and candidate hopefuls, visiting heads of foreign governments, and official government representatives performing special missions abroad.

2581. Secret Service agent killed in the line of duty was operative Joseph A. Walker, murdered on November 3, 1907, while working on a case involving the western land frauds of the period. The first woman agent killed in the line of duty was Julie Yvonne Cross, who was involved in surveillance of a counterfeiting operation when she was fatally wounded on June 4, 1980, in Los Angeles, CA.

2582. Women to become Secret Service agents were Laurie B. Anderson, Sue A. Baker, Kathryn I. Clark, Holly A. Hufschmidt, and Phyllis Frances Shantz, who were sworn in as special agents on December 15, 1971, in Washington, DC. All were former agents of the Executive Protective Service, a uniformed security force operated by the Secret Service to guard the White House, the president, his wife and family, and diplomatic missions in Washington.

LAW—LAWYERS

2583. State lawyers' society was the New York Bar Association, New York City, which operated from 1747 to 1770. Its purpose was to develop collective opinion on the economic issues prior to the Revolutionary War and to control admission to practice.

2584. Lawyers admitted to practice before the Supreme Court were Elias Boudinot of New Jersey, Thomas Hartly of Pennsylvania, and Richard Harrison of New York, who were admitted on February 5, 1790. The requirements for admittance were "membership for three years past in the Supreme Court of the State in which they respectively belong, and that their private and professional character shall appear to be fair."

2585. African-American lawyer formally admitted to the bar was Macon B. Allen, who passed his legal examination in Worcester, MA, and was admitted on May 3, 1845. He had practiced for two years previously in Maine, where no license was required.

2586. African-American lawyer admitted to practice before the Supreme Court was John S. Rock, who was admitted on February 1, 1865. His admittance was moved by Senator Charles Sumner of Massachusetts. Chief Justice Salmon Portland Chase presided

2587. Woman to practice law was Arabella Aurelia Babb Mansfield of Mount Pleasant, IA. A graduate of Iowa Wesleyan University, she studied law privately and passed the state bar exam in 1866 along with her husband, but was not granted admission to the bar because the Iowa Code of 1851 specified that it was open to qualified white males. Mrs. Mansfield, appearing as her own counsel, persuaded Judge Francis Springer to remove the impediment and was admitted to practice in June 1869. On March 8, 1870, the state legislature deleted the words "white male" from the statute.

2588. African-American woman to practice law was Charlotte E. Ray, who received an LL.B. degree from the School of Law, Howard University, Washington, DC, on February 27, 1872. On April 23, 1872, she was admitted to the Supreme Court of the District of Columbia, the first African-American woman to be admitted to the Washington bar.

2589. National lawyers' society was the American Bar Association, organized on August 21, 1878, at an informal meeting in Saratoga, NY, at the suggestion of Judge Simeon Eben Baldwin. At the close of the meeting, the membership consisted of 291 lawyers from 29 states. The first president was James Overton Broadhead of St. Louis, MO. The first woman to serve as its president was Roberta Cooper Ramo of Albuquerque, NM, who was elected on August 9, 1995.

2590. Woman lawyer admitted to practice before the Supreme Court was Belva Ann Bennett Lockwood, who was admitted on March 3, 1879. The bill admitting women passed the House of Representatives on February 21, 1878, and the Senate on February 7, 1879. It was titled an "act to relieve certain legal disabilities of women" and was signed on February 15, 1879, by President Rutherford Birchard Hayes. It provided that any female member of the bar of good moral character who had practiced for three years before a state supreme court was eligible for admittance to practice before the Supreme Court of the United States.

2591. National arbitration organization devoted exclusively to advancing principle and practice in this field was the Arbitration Society of America, formed in New York City on May 15, 1922. On January 29, 1926, this group merged with two others to form the American Arbitration Association, whose first president was Anson W. Burchard.

2592. African-American woman lawyer admitted to practice before the Supreme Court was Violette Neatly Anderson of Chicago, IL, who was admitted on January 29, 1926.

2593. Woman elected president of a state lawyers' association was Marie M. Lambert, who served from June 30, 1974, to June 30, 1976, as president of the New York State Trial Lawyers Association.

2594. Modern proposal to ban lawyers from serving in state or local government was made in Missouri in 1991, when a constitutional amendment that would have instituted such a ban was submitted to the voters. They turned it down. Massachusetts banned lawyers from government service in the 17th century.

LAW—PATENTS

2595. Patent granted by a colony was awarded to Samuel Winslow in 1641 by Massachusetts for a new method of extracting salt: "Whereas Samuel Winslow hath made a proposition to this Court to furnish the contrey with salt at more easy rates then otherwise can bee had, & to make it by a meanes & way which hitherto hath not bene discovered, it is therefore ordered, that if the said Samuel shall, within the space of one yeare, set upon the said worke, hee shall enjoy the same, to him & his associates, for the space of ten yeares, so as it shall not bee lawfull to any other pson to make salt after the same way during the said yeares; pvided, nevthelesse, that it shall bee lawfull for any pson to bring in any salt, or to make salt after any othrway, dureing the said tearme."

2596. English patent granted to a resident of America was issued on November 25, 1715, to "Thomas Masters, Planter of Pennsylvania, for an invention found out by Sibylla his wife for cleaning and curing the Indian Corn growing in several colonies in America."

2597. Patent law passed by Congress was an "act to promote the progress of useful arts," approved on April 10, 1790. The board in charge of granting patents styled itself the Patent Board, the Patent Commission, or the Commissioners for the Promotion of Useful Arts. Its first members were Thomas Jefferson, the secretary of state; Henry Knox, the secretary of war; and Edmund Randolph, the attorney general. The responsibility for administering the patent laws was given to the Department of State. The name was changed to the Patent and Trademark Office on January 2, 1975, by act of Congress.

LAW—PATENTS—continued

2598. Patent granted by the federal government was issued to Samuel Hopkins of Vermont on July 31, 1790, for a process of making potash and pearl ashes. The document bore the signatures of George Washington, president; Thomas Jefferson, secretary of state; and Edmund Randolph, attorney general. Under an act approved on April 10, 1790, "to promote the progress of useful arts," the holders of these three offices constituted a patent commission empowered to issue patents. Only three patents were issued that first year.

2599. Federal patent office was organized in May 1802 with Dr. William Thornton, the architect of the Capitol, as superintendent. In 1833, after 9,000 patents had been issued, the head of the Patent Office announced that he would resign because "everything seems to have been done" and he did not expect many more patents to be needed.

2600. Patent commissioner was Henry Leavitt Ellsworth, who was appointed on June 15, 1835, by President Andrew Jackson. Prior to that time the Patent Office had been directed by the superintendent of patents. Ellsworth resigned on April 30, 1845, to act as land agent in Lafayette, IN, for the purchase and settlement of public lands.

2601. Numbering system for patents was introduced on July 13, 1836. Prior to that time, 9,957 unnumbered patents had been issued. Patent No. 1 under the consecutive numbering system was issued on July 13, 1836, to John Ruggles of Thomaston, ME, for "traction wheels for locomotive steam-engine for rail and other roads." Ruggles was chairman of the Senate Committee on Patents.

2602. Patent issued by the Confederate States of America was issued on August 1, 1861, to James J. Van Houten of Savannah, GA, on a breech-loading gun.

2603. Woman to serve as a patent examiner was Anna R. G. Nichols of Melrose, MA, a clerk in the Patent Office, who took office on July 1, 1873, as an assistant examiner. On August 24, 1971, Brereton Sturtevant of Wilmington, DE, became the first woman to hold the position of examiner-in-chief of the Patent Office.

M

MILITARY

2604. Arsenal of the federal government was the Springfield Armory, Springfield, MA, founded in April 1778 as a laboratory for the preparation of all kinds of ammunition and established on April 2, 1794, as a national armory for the manufacture of small arms. The first superintendent was David Ames and the master armorer was Robert Orr. It took a month to complete the first 20 muskets. Two hundred and forty-five muskets were made the first year.

2605. Military department of the federal government was the Department of the Navy, established by act of Congress approved on April 30, 1798. The conduct of naval affairs had previously been overseen by the secretary for the Department of War, under act of Congress approved on April 7, 1789.

2606. Consolidated headquarters for the Department of Defense was the Pentagon, designed by George Edwin Bergstrom and completed on January 15, 1943, on a large site in Arlington, VA. The huge, pentagonal building, made of steel-reinforced concrete with limestone facing, houses the central command and administration of all the armed services. It consists of five rings of buildings connected by 10 radial corridors. Long the world's largest office building, it covers some 34 acres. As many as 25,000 workers can be accommodated in its 3,700,000 square feet of office space.

2607. Continental air defense alliance was the North American Air Defense Command, created on August 1, 1957, by the United States and Canada. The command and control facilities of NORAD (now called the North American Aerospace Defense Command) are located in the hollowed-out interior of Cheyenne Mountain, near Colorado Springs, CO.

2608. Use of the term "military-industrial complex" was made by President Dwight David Eisenhower in his Farewell Address, delivered on January 17, 1961, from the White House and broadcast on television and radio. In Part IV of the speech, which was written for him by Malcolm Moos, Eisenhower made mention of the necessity for military readiness, requiring a permanent arms-manufacturing industry. He continued: "This conjunction of an immense military establishment and a large arms industry is new in the American experience. The total influence—economic, political, even spiritual—is felt in every city, every statehouse, every office of the federal government. We recognize the imperative need for this development. Yet we must not fail to comprehend its grave implications. Our toil, resources, and livelihood are all involved; so is the very structure of our society. In the councils of government, we must guard against the acquisition of unwanted influence, whether sought or unsought, by the military-industrial complex. The potential for the disastrous rise of misplaced power exists and will persist. We must never let the weight of this combination endanger our liberties or democratic processes. We should take nothing for granted. Only an alert and knowledgeable citizenry can compel the proper meshing of the huge industrial and military machinery of defense with our peaceful methods and goals, so that security and liberty may prosper together."

2609. Independent disarmament agency was the United States Arms Control and Disarmament Agency, created by act of September 26, 1961, to centralize arms control and disarmament responsibilities in one agency of the government. The United States Arms Control and Disarmament Agency formulates and implements arms control nonproliferation and disarmament policies that promote the national security of the United States and its relations with other countries.

2610. Federal agency with safety oversight of defense nuclear facilities was the Defense Nuclear Facilities Safety Board, established as an independent agency on September 29, 1988, under an amendment to the Atomic Energy Act of 1954. The five-member board reviews and evaluates the content and implementation of standards relating to the design, construction, operation, and decommissioning of defense nuclear facilities of the Department of Energy.

2611. Woman to head a branch of the United States military was Sheila E. Widnall, who was sworn in on August 6, 1993, as secretary of the Air Force. She oversaw an annual budget of $62 billion, a force of 380,000 men and women on active duty, the 251,000 members of the Air National Guard and the Air Reserve, and 184,000 civilian employees. Previously, Widnall spent nearly three decades as a professor of aeronautics and astronautics at the Massachusetts Institute of Technology, Cambridge, MA.

2612. Public information about the United States chemical arsenal was released by the Department of Defense on January 22, 1996, when it was announced that the nation's entire stockpile of 3.6 million chemical weapons would be destroyed by 2004.

MILITARY—ACADEMIES

2613. Military academy established by the federal government was "a military school for young gentlemen previous to their being appointed to marching regiments," founded by congressional resolution of June 20, 1777, at the urging of General Henry Knox. It was run at Philadelphia, PA, by the Corps of Invalids, a regiment of disabled veterans, and was moved in 1781 to the military post at West Point, NY. In 1793 it was replaced with a school run by a Corps of Artillerists and Engineers, which in turn was replaced by the United States Military Academy, established at West Point by act of Congress of March 16, 1802, with Major Jonathan Williams as its first superintendent. The academy opened on July 4 with five faculty members and ten cadets (five from Massachusetts and one each from Connecticut, Maryland, Missouri, New York, and Virginia). Two cadets completed the course and were graduated on October 12: Joseph Gardner Swift of Massachusetts, who went on to became head of the academy in 1816, and Simon Magruder Levy of Maryland.

2614. Military academy for naval officers was a small training school for midshipmen that opened on December 10, 1815, at the navy yard at Charlestown, MA, under the guidance of Commodore William Bainbridge. Similar schools were started at the navy yards in New York City and Norfolk, VA, and at the Naval Asylum in Philadelphia, PA, where Professor William Chauvenet instituted a formal one-year course in 1842. Under Secretary of the Navy George Bancroft, Chauvenet's school was transferred to a former Army fort at Annapolis, MD, and reopened on October 10, 1845, as the United States Naval School, with a faculty of seven and a class of 50 midshipmen. The first superintendent was Commander Franklin Buchanan. A full four-year course was adopted in 1850, when the school was renamed the United States Naval Academy. The first war in which academy-trained naval officers fought was the Mexican War, in 1850. The establishment of a naval academy had been proposed as early as 1783 by the celebrated Revolutionary War captain John Paul Jones, who is buried in the crypt at Annapolis.

MILITARY—ACADEMIES—*continued*

2615. Naval war college was established at Coaster's Harbor Island, Newport, RI, on October 6, 1884, by order of the Secretary of the Navy. Commander Stephen Bleecker Luce was the first superintendent. The college opened on September 3, 1885. It offered naval officers an eleven-month course in military science, the art of naval warfare, and marine international law. On January 11, 1889, the college was consolidated with the Torpedo Station on Goat Island in Newport harbor.

2616. Army war college was authorized by the War Department on November 27, 1901, to furnish advanced military instruction to regularly commissioned army officers, using $20,000 that had been authorized by Congress on May 26, 1900. The first president was Major General Samuel Baldwin Marks Young. The first class of 16 officers was convened on November 1, 1904, and ended on May 31, 1905. Classes were held in rented quarters until June 20, 1907, when a permanent building was opened in Washington, DC.

2617. Military academy for Air Force officers was the United States Air Force Academy, founded by act of Congress on April 1, 1954. Temporary headquarters were established on July 11, 1955, at Lowry Air Force Base, Denver, CO, where 306 candidates were sworn in. The first commandant was Lieutenant General Hubert Reilly Harmon. A $135 million academy was built at Colorado Springs, CO, and received its first cadets on August 29, 1958. The first graduating class of 207 cadets was commissioned on June 3, 1959.

MILITARY—AIR FORCE

2618. Air force in the world was a tiny unit established on July 1, 1907, under the Office of the Chief Signal Officer of the U.S. Army. The Aeronautical Division was commanded by Captain Charles de Forest Chandler and consisted of one noncommissioned officer, one enlisted man, and, eventually, one aircraft, the Wright military flyer of 1909.

2619. Air force branch of the military was the Army Air Corps, established by congressional act of July 2, 1926, which authorized a Chief of the Air Corps (major general), 3 assistants (brigadier generals), 1,514 officers (from second lieutenants to colonels), and 16,000 enlisted men.

2620. Air defense military organization was the Air Defense Command, created on February 26, 1940, with headquarters at Mitchel Field, Long Island, NY, pursuant to War Department Orders dated February 26, 1940, for defense against air attack through the practical application of the coordinated effort of aviation, antiaircraft artillery, and aircraft warning agencies, including fixed military and civilian installations. It was charged with the development of a system for unified air defense of an area and the determination of tasks within the capabilities of the various combinations of tactical units that might be assembled for the air defense of cities, continental bases, manufacturing and industrial areas, or of armies in the field. The first commander was Brigadier General James Eugene Chaney.

MILITARY—ARMY

2621. Army of the United States was the American Continental Army, now called the United States Army, which was established by the Continental Congress meeting in Philadelphia, PA, on June 14, 1775, more than a year before the Declaration of Independence.

2622. General of the Continental Army was George Washington, who was appointed commander of all continental armies on June 15, 1775, by the Second Continental Congress assembled at the State House, Philadelphia, PA. Congress resolved "that five hundred dollars per month be allowed for the pay and expenses of the general." Washington took command the following month at Cambridge, MA, and led the American forces for six years during the Revolutionary War. After forcing Britain's Lord Cornwallis to surrender in October 1781, he served until December 23, 1783, when he resigned his commission.

2623. Army organization under the Constitution was enacted on April 30, 1789. It provided for one regiment of infantry to consist of three battalions of four companies each, one battalion of artillery with four companies, and a total strength not to exceed 1,216 noncommissioned officers, privates, and musicians. The monthly authorized pay was $60 for the lieutenant colonel commandant, majors $40, captains $30, lieutenants $22, corporals $4, privates $3, and musicians $3.

2624. Commander-in-chief of the United States Army was Josiah Harmar, who served from September 29, 1789, to March 4, 1791, with the rating of lieutenant colonel of infantry. He had been brevetted brigadier general in 1787. He was succeeded by Arthur St. Clair, Anthony Wayne, James Wilkinson, and George Washington, the fifth commander-in-chief, who served from July 3, 1798, to December 14, 1799, as lieutenant general and general.

2625. General of the U.S. Army was Ulysses Simpson Grant, commander of the Union forces during the Civil War, who was appointed on July 25, 1866. He served until March 4, 1869, when he was inaugurated as president of the United States.

2626. General of the Armies of the United States was General John Joseph Pershing, commander in chief of the American Expeditionary Forces during World War I, whose appointment was unanimously confirmed by the Senate on September 4, 1919.

2627. U.S. Army Band was created in 1923 by order of General of the Armies John J. Pershing. Based in Washington, DC, it is the official band for most diplomatic and state functions in the nation's capital and performs musical honors for the arrival in Washington of foreign heads of state, diplomats, and high-ranking military officers. Its first director was Captain William J. Stannard, who served in the post from 1923 to 1935.

2628. Army officer to occupy the nation's highest military post and its highest nonelective civilian post was General George Catlett Marshall of Pennsylvania. He was the Army's chief of staff with rank of major general from September 1, 1939, to November 20, 1945; secretary of state from January 21, 1947, to January 20, 1949; and secretary of defense from September 21, 1950, to September 12, 1951.

2629. Central administration for all branches of the military was the National Military Establishment, created by the National Security Act of July 26, 1947. The Department of War, renamed the Department of the Army, came under its aegis, together with the Department of the Navy and the Department of the Air Force. The National Military Establishment was reorganized in 1949 as the Department of Defense.

MILITARY—DRAFT

2630. Draft law enacted by a colony was enacted on April 18, 1637, in Boston, MA, by the Massachusetts Bay Colony legislature, which provided "there shalbee 160 men pvided to be chosen out of the severall townes according to the portion underwritten," to serve in the conflict known as the Pequot War. The conscription call was as follows: Boston 26, Salem 18, Ipswich 17, Saugus 16, Watertown 14, Dorchester 13, Charlestown twelve, Roxbury ten, Cambridge nine, Newbury eight, Hingham six, Weymouth five, Medford three, and Marblehead three.

2631. Conscientious objectors who refused for religious reasons to participate in war were the Shakers, members of a pacifist Christian sect that had originated in England. The group's formal title was "The United Society of Believers in Christ's Second Appearing." A group of Shakers, led by their founder, Ann Lee, had emigrated from England in 1774 and settled in Watervliet, NY. They refused to aid the colonies in the Revolutionary War, with the result that they were accused of treason and imprisoned without trial in the old fort in Albany, NY. On December 20, 1780, they were all released from prison with the exception of Ann Lee, who was transferred to the jail at Poughkeepsie, NY. She was released soon thereafter.

2632. Draft of civilians by Congress was authorized by the Militia Act of May 8, 1792, "effectually to provide for the National Defense by establishing a uniform militia throughout the United States." It was prompted by the defeat of American forces by the Ohio Indians in the Northwest Territory the previous November. Every free able-bodied white male citizen between the ages of 18 and 45 was required to be enrolled in the militia of the United States and to supply himself with a gun and no fewer than 24 cartridges suited to the bore of his musket. There was no penalty for noncompliance. This law left the militia under the command of the states.

2633. Draft law enacted by the Confederacy was the Confederate Conscription Act, passed by the Confederate Congress in Richmond, VA, on April 16, 1862, after the pace of enlistments had slowed. The act required all white men between the ages of 18 and 35 to serve in the armed forces for a three-year term, with exemptions for men working in specified occupations or wealthy enough to pay for a substitute.

2634. Draft law enacted by Congress during wartime was passed on March 3, 1863, "an act for enrolling and calling out the national forces, and for other purposes." It required men 20 to 45 years of age to be enrolled on April 1, 1863, by provost marshals. Exemptions could be bought for $300. The first draft call was

MILITARY—DRAFT—*continued*

made on July 7, 1863. Earlier draft bills had been passed separately by the House and Senate during the War of 1812, but the need to produce a compromise bill ended with the signing of a peace treaty on December 24, 1814.

2635. Draft riots took place in New York City on July 13–16, 1863, to protest inequalities in the Union's draft laws. According to the Union Enrollment Act, in effect from March 3, 1863, all able-bodied men aged 20 to 45 were liable for the draft unless they could pay $300 or find someone willing to take their place. In effect, this limited the draft to those who could not afford to buy their way out. The riots were led mainly by Irish laborers. Most of the dead, who numbered about 1,200, were African-Americans.

2636. Draft law enacted by Congress during peacetime was passed on September 14, 1940, by a vote of 47–35 in the Senate and 232–124 in the House. It called for a total of 900,000 men to be trained in any given year. Registration was required of all men who had attained the age of 21 and who had not reached the age of 36 on October 16, 1940. Each registrant was assigned a number, so that quotas of soldiers could be filled by lottery.

2637. Draft number drawing was made on October 29, 1940, in Washington, DC. The first number to come up, No. 158, was drawn by Secretary of War Henry Lewis Stimson from a glass bowl full of numbered lots. As a blindfold, the secretary wore a strip of upholstery taken from a chair in Philadelphia's Independence Hall. On November 15, the government issued a call for 75,000 men. The director of the draft was Dr. Clarence Addison Dykstra.

MILITARY—FOREIGN WARS

2638. Proclamation of U.S. neutrality in time of war was the Proclamation of Neutrality issued on April 22, 1793, by President George Washington. It ran in part: " Whereas it appears that a state of war exists between Austria, Prussia, Sardinia, Great Britain, and the United Netherlands, of the one part, and France on the other; and the duty and interest of the United States require, that they should with sincerity and good faith adopt and pursue a conduct friendly and impartial toward the belligerent Powers; I have therefore thought fit by these presents to declare the disposition of the United States to observe the conduct aforesaid towards those Powers respectfully; and to exhort and warn the citizens of the United States carefully to avoid all acts and proceedings whatsoever, which may in any manner tend to contravene such disposition."

2639. Undeclared war involving the United States and a foreign country was the Quasi-War of 1798–1800, which resulted from the "XYZ Affair" of 1798. Finding that the treaty of mutual defense with France, then at war with Britain, was an embarrassment to the United States, President John Adams sent three commissioners—Charles Cotesworth Pinckney, John Marshall, and Elbridge Gerry—to Paris to renegotiate its terms. Before it would open negotiations, the French revolutionary government demanded a bribe through three intermediaries, a Swiss banker named Hottenguer ("X"), a Hamburg merchant named Bellamy ("Y"), and a Monsieur Hauteval ("Z"). On July 7, 1798, Congress repealed the treaty, and an undeclared naval war between America and France ensued. In 1800, the conflict ended with the signing of a new treaty of amity, the Treaty of Morfontaine (also known as the Convention of 1800).

2640. African polity to declare war on the United States was the piratical Barbary state of Tripolitania (part of modern Libya), whose pasha declared war on American shipping on May 14, 1801, in an effort to extort increased tribute from the U.S. government. President Thomas Jefferson rejected the pasha's demands and appropriated special "Mediterranean" funds to rebuild the U.S. Navy, which had been reduced to a single ship of the line and 13 frigates, seven of which were in drydock. In a series of stunning American victories in 1804–05, the Tripolitan navy was subdued, the city was bombarded into submission, and the pasha was forced to sign a peace treaty favorable to the United States.

2641. President to sign a declaration of war against a European power was President James Madison, who on June 18, 1812, signed a declaration of war against Great Britain, thus initiating the War of 1812. Madison had asked for war in an address to Congress of June 1, 1812 (it was read by a clerk before a closed session of the combined House and Senate), arguing that the conduct of Great Britain presented "a series of acts hostile to the united States as an independent and neutral nation."

2642. Presidential call for volunteer troops to fight in the Spanish-American War was made by William McKinley on April 23, 1898, two months after the explosion of the battleship U.S.S. *Maine* in the harbor of Havana, Cuba, which was thought to have been done by Spain. The President asked for 125,000 volunteers to enlist for two-year terms. On April 25 the United States declared war against Spain.

2643. Federal propaganda bureau was the Committee on Public Information, established on April 14, 1917, by President Woodrow Wilson to oversee a public relations campaign aimed at encouraging support for American involvement in World War I. It was headed by Denver journalist George Creel. The CPI sponsored a News Division, which sent out press releases, and an Advertising Division, which designed and distributed patriotic posters. Movies, pamphlets, and lectures were also part of its campaign. On occasion, the committee functioned as a censor, asking newspaper editors to withhold certain news items from publication.

2644. Declaration of U.S. alliance in World War II was the Atlantic Charter, signed on August 14, 1941, by President Franklin Delano Roosevelt and British prime minister Winston Churchill aboard warships in the North Atlantic. The signatories enumerated the following principles: "First, their countries seek no aggrandizement, territorial or other; Second, they desire to see no territorial changes that do not accord with the freely expressed wishes of the peoples concerned; Third, they respect the right of all peoples to choose the form of government under which they will live; and they wish to see sovereign rights and self government restored to those who have been forcibly deprived of them; Fourth, they will endeavor, with due respect for their existing obligations, to further the enjoyment by all States, great or small, victor or vanquished, of access, on equal terms, to the trade and to the raw materials of the world which are needed for their economic prosperity; Fifth, they desire to bring about the fullest collaboration between all nations in the economic field with the object of securing, for all, improved labor standards, economic advancement and social security; Sixth, after the final destruction of the Nazi tyranny, they hope to see established a peace which will afford to all nations the means of dwelling in safety within their own boundaries, and which will afford assurance that all the men in all lands may live out their lives in freedom from fear and want; Seventh, such a peace should enable all men to traverse the high seas and oceans without hindrance; Eighth, they believe that all of the nations of the world, for realistic as well as spiritual reasons must come to the abandonment of the use of force. Since no future peace can be maintained if land, sea or air armaments continue to be employed by nations which threaten, or may threaten, aggression outside of their frontiers, they believe, pending the establishment of a wider and permanent system of general security, that the disarmament of such nations is essential. They will likewise aid and encourage all other practicable measure which will lighten for peace-loving peoples the crushing burden of armaments."

2645. State to declare war on a foreign power before the U.S. government was Vermont. On September 11, 1941, the Vermont legislature passed a resolution defining "armed conflict" and declared war on Germany, two months before the U.S. declaration of December 11, 1941.

2646. Wartime population relocation order was Executive Order 9066, signed on February 19, 1942, by President Franklin Delano Roosevelt at the urging of U.S. Army general John DeWitt, who was in charge of West Coast security. It authorized the War Department "to prescribe military areas in such places and of such extent as he or the appropriate Military Commanders may determine, from which any or all persons may be excluded, and with such respect to which, the right of any person to enter, remain in, or leave shall be subject to whatever restrictions the Secretary of War or the appropriate Military Commander may impose in his discretion." Under Executive Order 9066, some 110,000 Americans of Japanese descent were relocated from their homes in California, Arizona, Oregon, and Washington to rural internment camps, without compelling evidence that they posed any security risk to the United States. The displaced people were not allowed to leave the camps until January 2, 1945. No mainland citizen of Japanese descent was ever convicted of espionage or treason against the United States during or after World War II.

2647. Doctrine of unconditional surrender by a foreign enemy of the United States was first proposed by President Franklin Delano Roosevelt on January 24, 1943, at the World War II Allied conference in Casablanca, Morocco. The Casablanca conference was also attended by British prime minister Winston Churchill and the Free French leader Charles de

MILITARY—FOREIGN WARS—*continued*

Gaulle. As the conference ended, FDR announced (without prior discussion with Churchill) that the Allies would require the "total military and political capitulation" of the Axis powers.

2648. Technical advisors sent to Vietnam were 425 helicopter crewmen dispatched by President John Fitzgerald Kennedy on December 11, 1961, to provide support and training for South Vietnamese forces. The first American ground troops did not arrive until March 8, 1965, when 3,500 Marines landed at the port of Da Nang in South Vietnam to guard the air base there. The first troop withdrawals from Vietnam began on July 8, 1969, the same day that they were announced by President Richard Milhous Nixon at a meeting on Midway Island with South Vietnamese President Nguyen Van Thieu.

2649. Nuclear war confrontation was the Cuban Missile Crisis of October 1962. At the request of Cuban communist leader Fidel Castro, Soviet premier Nikita Khrushchev shipped Soviet nuclear missiles to Cuba that were capable of reaching U.S. targets along the eastern seaboard. Between August 29 and October 14, U.S. spy planes uncovered evidence of the construction of launching sites, and on October 22, President John Fitzgerald Kennedy ordered a naval blockade of Cuba to prevent further missile shipments. After a tense week in which nuclear war seemed imminent, on October 28 Khrushchev backed down and ordered the missiles withdrawn. In return, Kennedy secretly promised not to invade Cuba, and also to withdraw U.S. nuclear missiles based in Turkey.

2650. American military massacre of political importance took place on March 16, 1968, at My Lai 4, a village in Vietnam, where unarmed civilians were massacred by troops belonging to Charlie Company of Task Force Barker, a U.S. Army infantry unit. The area was known to be a Vietcong stronghold. American troops on a search-and-destroy mission under the command of Captain Ernest L. Medina and Lieutenant William L. Calley, Jr., fired for four hours on the village, killing 504 people. The victims were mainly women, children, and old men. A similar operation by another infantry unit, Bravo Company, took place simultaneously at the nearby hamlet of My Khe 4. Some of the Americans refused to take part in the massacre. Ronald Ridenhour, a Vietnam veteran and journalist who had heard about the My Lai action, reported the incident to the Office of the Inspector General of the Army. The first news reports about My Lai were published on November 19, 1969. This spurred the Army to mount its own investigation, which was overseen by Lieutenant General William R. Peers. A total of 25 soldiers and officers were charged for taking part in the killings or in a subsequent cover-up. On March 29, 1971, Lieutenant Calley was convicted by court-martial of the murders of 22 Vietnamese civilians and received a life sentence. Widely seen as a scapegoat who had been carrying out the orders of his superiors, Calley served only three days before President Richard Milhous Nixon ordered his release to house arrest. He was paroled three years later and began a successful civilian career as a jeweler. No other participant was convicted of any crime. More than any other single event, the My Lai massacre turned American public opinion against the Vietnam War.

2651. U.S. peacekeeping forces killed by suicide bombing were a contingent of U.S. Marines killed in Beirut, Lebanon, on October 23, 1983, by a car bomb. A Marine peacekeeping force of approximately 1,600 was sent to preserve order after Christian Phalangists massacred several hundred Palestinians at a refugee camp. The Marines were ordered to occupy an exposed position near the Beirut airport, but for political reasons the Marine commander was not allowed to establish a completely secure perimeter. A Muslim terrorist driving a truck packed with 2,000 pounds of explosives was able to drive right into the barracks, killing 241 U.S. military personnel, many of whom were asleep at the time. Simultaneously, a similar attack was aimed at the headquarters of the French peacekeeping force, killing 50.

2652. Compensation paid to Japanese-Americans interned during World War II was authorized by Congress and signed into law on August 10, 1988. The bill provided for a payment of $20,000 to each surviving internee and a formal apology from the federal government. More than 110,000 men, women, and children of Japanese descent, including both American citizens and aliens, were rounded up from their homes in California, Arizona, Oregon, and Washington in the spring of 1942 and confined in rural internment camps until the end of the war, on suspicion that they might collaborate with Japan. The evacuation was carried out by executive order of President Franklin D. Roosevelt.

2653. United States officials to die in the conflict in Bosnia were Deputy Assistant Secretary of State Robert C. Frasure, Deputy Assistant Secretary of Defense Joseph J. Kruzel, and Colonel Samuel Nelson Drew of the National Security Council in Fort Myer, VA. They were killed on August 19, 1995, when a mountain road gave way and plunged their vehicle—a French armored personnel carrier—into a ravine. The three were en route to Sarajevo for a peace conference with Serbian President Slobodan Milosevic.

MILITARY—LAWS

2654. United States code of military justice for governing foreign territory was developed during the Mexican War of 1846–48, the first war in which a significant number of American troops occupied foreign soil. Forced to maintain order among volunteer and unenlisted soldiers who often resisted regular military discipline, General Winfield Scott, commander of troops in Mexico's central region, set up strict military tribunals to try all offenses. Scott's orders became the basis for the U.S Army code of justice in occupied territories.

2655. National code of the laws of war in the world was *The Lieber Code, Instructions for the Government of Armies of the United States in the Field by Order of the Secretary of War, General Orders No. 100,* drafted by the German-born American political philosopher and jurist Francis Lieber in Washington, DC, on April 24, 1863. Intended for the use of the United States armed forces during the American Civil War, the Lieber Code formed the basis for all important international formulations of the rules of war, including the Hague Conventions.

2656. Federal law giving African-American soldiers pay and benefits equal to those of white soldiers was the Army Appropriations Bill, passed by Congress in June 1864. The law provided for equal pay, retroactive to January 1, 1864, for African-American soldiers who had been freemen at the beginning of the Civil War. It also mandated equality in medical services, weapons, and equipment.

2657. State law prohibiting discrimination against soldiers was passed on May 5, 1908, by Rhode Island. The bill, sponsored by Theodore Francis Green, imposed a penalty for excluding soldiers in uniform from public places.

2658. Order integrating the armed forces was issued by President Harry S. Truman on July 26, 1948. However, the U.S. Army began desegregating its training camp facilities exactly four years earlier, on July 26, 1944.

2659. Uniform Code of Military Justice was passed by Congress in 1950. Applicable to all U.S. military personnel worldwide, it was enacted to standardize the practice of military justice following abuses that had occurred during World War II. Previously, U.S. military law was modeled on earlier British articles of war.

MILITARY—MARINES

2660. United States Marines were established by the Continental Congress, meeting in Philadelphia, PA, on November 10, 1775, when it passed a resolution, sponsored by John Adams, requiring that "two Battalions of Marines be raised" for service with the Navy. The two battalions were called the 1st and 2nd Battalions of American Marines and were commanded by a colonel, two lieutenant colonels, and two majors. The Marines were under the jurisdiction of the War Department until April 30, 1798, when Congress created the Navy Department. The present Marine Corps was created by act of July 11, 1798, which authorized a major, four captains, 16 first lieutenants, 12 second lieutenants, 48 sergeants, 48 corporals, 32 drums and fifes, and 720 privates, including enlisted men.

2661. Commandant of marines was Samuel Nicholas, a Philadelphia Quaker, who was commissioned a captain on November 28, 1775. His pay was $32 a month. He set up the corps's first recruitment office at the Tun Tavern in Philadelphia, PA, and recruited the proprietor.

MILITARY—MILITIAS

2662. Militia was established by the Court of Assistants of the Massachusetts Bay Colony, Boston, MA, which ordered on April 12, 1631, "that there shall be a watch of 4 kept [every] night att Dorchester and another of 4 att Waterton, the watches to begin att sunset."

2663. Military organization established by a colony was the Ancient and Honorable Artillery Company, chartered in Boston, MA, on March 13, 1638. At the first elections, in June 1638, Captain Robert Keayne was elected commander; Daniel Haugh (Howe), lieutenant; and Joseph Weld, ensign.

2664. Use of the term "national guard" to refer to a militia unit took place on August 16, 1824, when the term was applied to the 7th New York Regiment.

2665. Naval militia established by a state was the Massachusetts Naval Battalion, organized under executive order of March 18, 1890, authorizing the formation of four companies. The companies were formed on March 25, 1890, with Thomas A. DeBlois, William M. Paul,

MILITARY—MILITIAS—*continued*

William M. Wood, and John W. Weeks, all of Boston, commanding companies A, B, C, and D, respectively. On May 7, 1890, John Codman Soley, a graduate of the U.S. Naval Academy, was commissioned lieutenant commander of the naval battalion.

MILITARY—NATIONAL CEMETERIES

2666. National cemetery was established in Washington, DC, in a section of Christ Church known as the Washington Parish Burial Ground. Records show that burials were made in 1804, but the date of the deed is recorded as March 31, 1812. In 1816 the federal government, seeking a burial place "for the interment of members of Congress, any heads of General Government and members of their familes," accepted the cemetery from the vestry of Christ Church. Located at 18th and E streets, SE, it is more familiarly known as the Congressional Cemetery and occupies 30 acres alongside the Anacostia River.

2667. National cemeteries act was authorized by Congress on July 17, 1862. Prior to this act a number of cemeteries had been established for the burial of military dead, although it was not until later that they were designated "national cemeteries." Among these are the following: Mexico City National Cemetery, Mexico, 1851; Fort Leavenworth National Cemetery, Kansas, 1861; Loudon Park National Cemetery, Baltimore, MD, 1861; Lexington National Cemetery, Kentucky, 1861; Soldiers' Home National Cemetery, Washington, DC, 1861; and Cypress Hills National Cemetery, Brooklyn, NY, 1862.

2668. Soldier buried at Arlington National Cemetery in Arlington, VA, was a member of the Confederate Army who died at a local hospital as a Union prisoner of war. He was buried on May 13, 1864, on the grounds of Arlington House, the estate of Confederate general Robert E. Lee, which had been taken over by the Union Army for use as a military headquarters. The house had symbolic significance, having been built in 1802 by George Washington's step-grandson, whose daughter, Mary Ann Randolph Custis, had married Lee. A military cemetery was established on the grounds in 1864. Veterans of all American wars, from the Revolutionary War to the present, are buried there. Compensation of $150,000 was eventually paid to the Lee family for the estate, and Arlington House, also known as the Custis-Lee Mansion, was restored as a memorial to Lee in the 1920s.

2669. Federal cemetery containing the remains of both Union and Confederate soldiers was opened in Springfield, MO, by act of Congress dated March 3, 1911. Part of it was formerly a Confederate cemetery maintained by the state of Missouri, which deeded it to the federal government on June 21, 1911. A stone wall separates the graves of the Confederate troops from those of the Union soldiers. The cemetery contains over 3,100 graves.

2670. Burial at the Tomb of the Unknown Soldier in the National Cemetery at Arlington, VA, took place on November 11, 1921. President Warren Gamaliel Harding, accompanied by practically every prominent government official, attended the services and the unveiling of the national shrine, which was built to honor the large number of American soldiers who lost their lives in World War I but whose bodies were never identified.

MILITARY—NATIONAL SECURITY

2671. Independent intelligence organization was the Office of the Coordinator of Information, created by executive order of President Franklin Delano Roosevelt on July 11, 1941. The OCI was later reorganized and renamed the Office of Strategic Services by a military order of June 13, 1942. The first and only director of Strategic Services was Major General William J. Donovan. The OSS, which coordinated U.S. intelligence gathering and counterintelligence during World War II, was the forerunner of the CIA, created in 1947.

2672. Defense Department think tank was the RAND Corporation, founded on October 1, 1946, at Hamilton Field, San Francisco, CA, by a group of scientists and researchers associated with the Army Air Force under the direction of General Henry Harley "Hap" Arnold. Arnold appropriated $10 million from leftover wartime research funds to establish a semi-independent organization devoted to the scientific study of national security issues. The acronym RAND stood for "research and development." Frank Collbohm was RAND's first president. In May 1948 RAND became an independent nonprofit enterprise.

2673. National Security Council was established by the National Security Act of July 26, 1947, to advise the president with respect to the integration of domestic, foreign, and military policies relating to the national security. Its statutory members, in addition to the president, are the vice president and the secretaries of state and defense. The chairman of the Joint Chiefs of Staff is the statutory military advisor to the Council, and the director of Central Intelligence is its intelligence advisor.

2674. Federal agency for the gathering of foreign intelligence was the Central Intelligence Agency, established on September 18, 1947, by the National Security Act of July 26, 1947, under the National Security Council. The CIA's mission is to gather intelligence and perform counterintelligence activities on foreign soil only; an early NCS directive ordered the CIA to "counteract Soviet and Soviet-inspired activites which constitute a threat to world peace and security or are designed to discredit and defeat the aims and activities of the United States." The first CIA director was Rear Admiral Roscoe H. Hillenkoetter.

2675. Civil Defense director was Paul J. Larsen, who assumed office on March 1, 1950, as director of the Office of Civilian Mobilization of the National Security Resources Board.

2676. Cryptologic agency of the federal government was the National Security Agency, headquartered at Ft. Meade, MD. The NSA was established by presidential directive in 1952 to provide signals intelligence and communications security activities of the government. Later the NSA's mandate was enlarged to include the development of electronic cryptologic technology and signals intelligence training for other departments. While not a military organization, NSA is one of several elements of the national intelligence community administered by the Department of Defense.

2677. Overthrow of a democratic foreign government arranged by the Central Intelligence Agency was the Guatemalan coup of June 1954, which ousted leftist Jacobo Arbenz Guzmán, the democratically elected president of Guatemala. Arbenz Guzmán enjoyed the support of Guatemalan Communists and was attempting to raise export taxes and expropriate lands claimed by the United Fruit Company, a U.S. agribusiness and the largest landowner in Guatemala. Fearing that Arbenz Guzmán was preparing to establish the first communist regime in the Americas, presidents Harry S. Truman and Dwight David Eisenhower approved secret plans to destabilize his government by "psychological warfare and political action" and "subversion" and replace him with a more compliant leader. The CIA organized an insurgent guerrilla army of exiles under Colonel Carlos Castillo Armas and embarked on a disinformation campaign to dishearten the Gua-

temalan military. Arbenz Guzmán fled the country on June 27, 1954. Armas assumed control and dismantled Arbenz Guzmán's reform program. From this action sprang the CIA's long history of counterrevolutionary activities in Latin America, which continued into the 1990s. From 1954 to 1990, Guatemalan military regimes are believed to have killed more than 100,000 civilians. In 1997, the CIA declassified some 1,400 pages of secret archives detailing the Guatemalan destabilization program and the agency's role in the 1954 coup.

2678. Civil defense test held nationwide was held on June 14, 1954, in the continental United States, Alaska, Hawaii, Puerto Rico, and the Virgin Islands, as well as ten provinces of Canada, from 10:00 to 10:10 A.M., when the all-clear signal was given.

2679. Spy satellites in space were the Corona satellites, launched by the United States beginning in early 1959. In twelve years of highly classified operation, 145 Corona satellites were placed in low polar orbits by rockets launched from California. Each contained high-resolution cameras designed to photograph Soviet territory and eject film canisters to the earth.

2680. Signal intelligence satellite in space was the *SolRad* satellite, launched by the United States into orbit in 1960 atop a Navy Transit-2A navigation satellite. Ostensibly designed to monitor solar radiation, *SolRad* in fact contained a secret signal intelligence payload developed by the U.S. Naval Research Laboratory to discover the nature and location of Soviet air defense radars.

2681. Assassination planned by the U.S. government in peacetime was intended to kill Fidel Castro, the Communist dictator of Cuba. After a CIA-sponsored invasion of the island by Cuban exiles in April 1961 failed disastrously, the Department of Defense, with the support of Attorney General Robert Francis Kennedy and the knowledge of a special Senate committee, prepared a series of proposals to embarrass Castro, provoke his removal from power, or assassinate him. These were presented to President John Fitzgerald Kennedy under the code name "Operation Mongoose." Papers describing the schemes were declassified and made public in 1997 by the Assassination Records Review Board. As far as is known, none of the schemes was actually put into operation.

MILITARY—NATIONAL SECURITY—
continued

2682. Government official convicted of espionage for leaking secrets to the press was Samuel Loring Morison, a former Navy intelligence analyst who received a two-year sentence under the 1917 Espionage Act for leaking KH-11 spy satellite photos of a Soviet nuclear-powered aircraft carrier to the British publication *Jane's Fighting Ships.* In October 1988 the Supreme Court refused to review an appellate court's decision to let the conviction stand.

2683. Doomsday plan was the "Continuity in Government" plan, devised by the United States to regroup the federal government and organize a last-ditch military reprisal in the event of a nuclear attack against the nation. Elements of the secret plan were developed in the 1950s and early '60s and finalized during the 1980s. In 1989 COG was under investigation by the Pentagon, the Justice Department, and the House Armed Services Committee for waste and mismanagement.

2684. Espionage budget made public was disclosed by the Central Intelligence Agency on October 15, 1997, the first time in the agency's 50 year-history. According to the CIA, the United States spent an average of $26.6 billion per year for intelligence services and operations. The Constitution requires the government to publish a "regular statement and account" of its spending, but the nation's spymasters had long argued that publicizing the intelligence budget would endanger the national security.

MILITARY—NAVY

2685. National naval force was a small squadron of armed merchant schooners manned by volunteers and known as Washington's Navy, as they were commissioned by General George Washington. The first of these warships was the *Hannah,* a schooner commanded by Captain Nicholas Broughton of Marblehead, MA, and commissioned on September 5, 1775. Two days later, the *Hannah* became the first American ship to make a capture when it took a British ship, the *Unity.* The squadron, headed by Captain John Manley, also of Marblehead, succeeded in capturing 55 British vessels, 38 of which were declared lawful prizes, and seizing their cargoes, which included ammunition, weapons, and food.

2686. Navy of the United States was the Continental Navy, which was created by the Continental Congress on October 13, 1775, in Philadelphia, PA. (A makeshift navy of armed fishing vessels had been put together some weeks earlier by Colonel John Glover of Massachu-

setts at the request of General George Washington.) It went out of existence in 1785, when the *Alliance,* its last remaining vessel, was sold. The United States did not establish another navy until 1794, but Congress nonetheless passed legislation on August 7, 1789, giving the secretary of war responsibility for the conduct of naval affairs.

2687. Ship commissioned by the Continental Navy was the 30-gun *Alfred,* a converted merchant ship that was commissioned on December 3, 1775. The Navy's first squadron also included the 28-gun ship *Columbus,* the 16-gun brig *Andrea Doria,* the twelve-gun sloop *Providence,* the 14-gun brig *Cabot,* the ten-gun sloop *Hornet,* the eight-gun schooner *Wasp,* and the six-gun schooner *Fly.* The Continental Navy had been established on October 30, 1775.

2688. Commander-in-chief of the Continental Navy was Esek Hopkins of Rhode Island, who served from December 22, 1775, to January 2, 1778. The Navy, when he took office, consisted of one squadron of eight vessels.

2689. Coast guard service was the Revenue Cutter Service, organized by an act of Congress of August 4, 1790, "an act to provide more effectually for the collection of the duties imposed by law on goods, wares and merchandise imported into the United States and on the tonnage of ships and vessels." The Life Saving Service was authorized by an act of June 18, 1878. The two services were combined on January 28, 1915, into the Coast Guard. The motto of the Coast Guard is *Semper paratus (Always Ready).* The first commandant was Alexander V. Fraser.

2690. Ship constructed by the federal government was the *Chesapeake,* built at the Navy Yard, Gosport, VA, under an act of Congress of March 27, 1794, "to provide a naval armament." The president was authorized to obtain six ships by purchase or otherwise and to equip and employ four ships of 44 guns each and two ships of 36 guns each to protect commerce. Virginia loaned the marine yard to the federal government for this purpose. The *Chesapeake* was launched on December 2, 1799. In June 1807 it became the subject of an international dispute when the British frigate *Leopard,* searching for deserters from the British Navy, fired on the *Chesapeake,* killing three men and wounding 18. The ship was captured by the British during the War of 1812.

2691. United States Navy was created by act of Congress of March 27, 1794, in response to piratical actions by Algiers, whose cruisers were preying on American merchant vessels in the Mediterranean. The act authorized the building of six frigates, of which three were actually constructed. The Navy was part of the War Department from August 7, 1789, until April 30, 1798, when a separate Department of the Navy was established by Congress. The first secretary was Benjamin Stoddert, named on June 18, 1798. In 1949, under the National Security Act Amendments, the Department of the Navy became a military department within the Department of Defense.

2692. Ship launched by the United States Navy was the *United States,* a 44-gun ship launched on May 10, 1797. It was one of six frigates whose construction was authorized by Congress on March 27, 1794, when it created the United States Navy in anticipation of war with Algiers. Only two others were built, the 36-gun *Constellation* and the 44-gun *Constitution.* During the War of 1812, the 44-gun ships distinguished themselves in actions against British frigates: the *Constitution* under Captain Isaac Hull defeated the *Guerriére* on August 19, 1812; the *United States* under Commodore Stephen Decatur defeated the *Macedonian* on October 25; and the *Constitution* under Commodore William Bainbridge defeated the *Java* on December 29.

2693. Navy regulation barring African-Americans was an order by Benjamin Stoddert, the Secretary of the Navy, dated August 8, 1798, which prohibited African-Americans from serving on warships.

2694. Shipbuilding law enacted by Congress was the shipbuilding act of February 25, 1799, which authorized the president to direct a sum "not exceeding $200,000 to be laid out in the purchase of growing or other timber, or of lands on which timber was growing, suitable for the navy." On December 19, 1799, a tract of 350 acres on Grover's Island, GA, was purchased for $7,500.

2695. United States warship assigned to capture slave ships was the corvette *Cyane,* which captured nine slavers in 1820 as it cruised on patrol along the western coast of Africa. Participation in the slave trade had been condemned as an act of piracy by Congress the year before. Patrols by American warships continued until 1824 and were renewed between 1842 and 1861.

2696. Admiral of the Navy was Admiral George Dewey, who served from March 3, 1899, until his death on January 16, 1917. The rank was conferred by act of Congress, passed on March 2, 1899.

MILITARY—VETERANS

2697. Colonial law to aid disabled veterans was enacted by the Plymouth Colony in 1636. The legislation provided that "if any [man] shalbee sent forth as a souldier and shall returne maimed, hee shalbee maintained competently by the Collonie of New Plymouth during his life." The act applied particularly to the soldiers engaged in the Pequot Indian War, which concluded on November 20, 1637.

2698. Military pension awarded to a woman was awarded to Margaret Corbin of Pennsylvania, known as Captain Molly. During the Revolutionary War, she volunteered to serve as a nurse in the Army regiment of her husband, John Corbin. She was present on November 16, 1776, in New York, NY, when the regiment made a doomed defense of Fort Washington, at the northern tip of Manhattan Island. During the battle, the Corbins manned a cannon together, Margaret loading and sponging while John fired. After he was shot dead, she continued firing alone until she was wounded in the chest, jaw, and arm by grapeshot. Permanently disabled, she was allowed by Congress to enroll in the Invalid Regiment that operated at West Point, NY, from July 1777 through 1783. The Supreme Council of Pennsylvania awarded her a military pension of $30 in July 1779, and the Continental Congress approved a lifetime pension amounting to half the disability pay of a regular soldier. She died in 1800 and was buried at the United States Military Academy Cemetery at West Point.

2699. Revolutionary War national veterans' organization was the Society of the Cincinnati, founded on May 13, 1783, at the Verplanck house, near Fishkill, NY. The first general meeting was held on May 7, 1784, in Philadelphia. Membership was limited to officers who had served three years in the Continental army or who had been honorably discharged for disability. George Washington was elected the first president general in 1783; he remained in office until his death and was succeeded by Major General Alexander Hamilton. The first state branches were established in New York and Massachusetts on June 9, 1783. The French branch was organized on January 7, 1784, in Paris. The name was derived from Lucius Quinctius Cincinnatus, the distinguished Roman who, called from the plow, "left all to save the republic."

MILITARY—VETERANS—*continued*

2700. Soldiers' homes established by Congress for disabled veterans were authorized by act of Congress of March 21, 1866, an "act to incorporate a national military and naval asylum for the relief of the totally disabled officers and men of the volunteer forces of the United States." The first homes, which began operating in 1867, were the Eastern Home, Togus, ME; the Central Home, Dayton, OH; and the Northwestern Home, Milwaukee, WI.

2701. Veterans of Foreign Wars of the United States was founded on August 18–20, 1913, in Denver, CO. It was composed of Army, Navy, and Marine Corps veterans who served in time of war in theaters of operation. Rice W. Means was the first commander in chief. The VFW was an amalgamation of three separate groups: the American Veterans of Foreign Service, organized in September 1899; the Army of the Philippines, organized in December 1899; and the American Veterans of Foreign Service, organized on September 10–12, 1903, which was itself a combination of the Philippine War Veterans, organized in October 1901, and the American Veterans of the Philippines and China Wars, organized in July 1902.

2702. American Legion was founded in Paris, France on March 15–17, 1919, at a meeting attended by delegations from various units of the American Expeditionary Force. The Legion's first convention was held later that year in St. Louis, MO, and Congress granted it a national charter on September 16, 1919. National headquarters were established in Indianapolis, IN. Originally formed as a patriotic organization to promote the welfare and interests of veterans of World War I, the Legion now represents veterans of World War II, Korea, Vietnam, and the Gulf War.

2703. Consolidated federal agency for veterans' affairs was the Veterans Administration, established as an independent agency under the president by Executive Order 5398 of July 21, 1930, in accordance with the act of July 3, 1930. This act authorized the president to consolidate and coordinate the U.S. Veterans Bureau, the Bureau of Pensions, and the National Home for Volunteer Soldiers. The first administrator was Brigadier General Frank T. Hines, who served until 1945. The Veterans Administration was later superseded by the Department of Veterans Affairs, which oversees the Veterans Health Administration, the Veterans Bene-

fits Administration, and the National Cemetery System. The health care system, which consisted of 54 hospitals in 1930, now comprises more than 170 hospitals and more than 350 clinics, as well as nursing homes.

2704. Federal law providing for the education of veterans was the Servicemen's Readjustment Act, better known as the G.I. Bill, signed by President Franklin Delano Roosevelt on June 22, 1944. The G.I. Bill entitled anyone who had 90 days' military service to one year of higher education, with further benefits for additional service. About 2.25 million veterans took advantage of the program to gain a college education by the expiration of the original G.I. Bill in 1952.

MONUMENTS

2705. Design for the Washington Monument was to be a huge statue of the first president in Roman dress, on horseback, with a laurel wreath on his head and a truncheon in his hand, following the tradition that linked George Washington with the Roman farmer-warrior Cincinnatus. The design, submitted as part of Pierre Charles L'Enfant's plan for the capital city in June 1791, was deemed too expensive by Washington himself, although Federalists attempted to revive it after his death. The private Washington Monument Society, formed in 1833, finally approved a design by Robert Mills that called for a 600-foot obelisk of Egyptian influence. Mills also planned a statue of Washington driving a chariot for the base, but this was also considered too expensive.

2706. Proposal for a national monument to George Washington was made by the architect Pierre Charles L'Enfant in his 1791 design for the capital city. He planned to build a mile-long avenue bordered by gardens, public buildings, and the residences of diplomats and important officials. At the end of this avenue, on a rise, he proposed placing an equestrian statue of President Washington. The avenue was constructed as The Mall, now an open greensward lined with museums. Near the spot intended for the equestrian monument, the obelisk known as the Washington Monument was erected in 1884.

2707. Statue cast by the federal government was a bronze statue of Admiral David Glasgow Farragut. On January 28, 1875, George Maxwell Robeson, secretary of the Navy, awarded a $20,000 contract to the sculptor Vinnie Ream. It was cast at the Washington Navy Yard, Washington, DC, and the mechanical work was performed by artisans employed by the government. It was accepted on April 25, 1881, by President James Abram Garfield. The base of the monument is formed of three tiers of uncut granite, the lower tier measuring 20 feet. The figure is of heroic size, standing in an easy position with one foot resting upon a pulley block around which a cable is coiled. In the hands is a telescope. The statue is located at Farragut Square, Washington, DC.

2708. Monument to George Washington authorized by the federal government was the Washington Monument in Washington, DC, a white marble obelisk 555 feet in height and 55 feet square at the base. The cornerstone was laid on July 4, 1848. The capstone with the aluminum tip was set in place on December 6, 1884. The monument was dedicated on February 21, 1885, by George Winthrop, who had delivered the formal address at the cornerstone ceremonies 37 years earlier. The public was admitted to the monument on October 9, 1888.

2709. Monument to a traitor was erected in 1887 in Saratoga, NY, to mark Benedict Arnold's brilliant action commanding advance battalions at the Battle of Saratoga in 1777. Shaped in the form of a military boot and epaulets, it was inscribed "In memory of the most brilliant soldier in the Continental Army who was desperately wounded on this spot—7th October, 1777—winning for his countrymen the decisive battle of the American Revolution." However, the monument, out of embarassment over Arnold's later treachery, does not actually mention his name.

2710. Monument to a president's mother that was paid for by women was erected for Mary Ball Washington, mother of George Washington, at her gravesite in Fredericksburg, VA, on May 10, 1894. Mary Ball Washington died on August 25, 1789, at the age of 81. The monument is a smaller version of the Washington Monument in Washington, DC.

2711. Plymouth Rock monument that was permanent was constructed in 1920 at Plymouth, MA. It consisted of a Greek-style temple erected at the water's edge over Plymouth Rock, where the Pilgrim Separatists landed in 1620. Plymouth Rock itself was much diminished from its original size. Patriots had dug it up after the Revolutionary War and carried to the town square, where, over the years, most of it was chipped off and carried away by souvenir hunters.

2712. National monument to Abraham Lincoln was the Lincoln Memorial in Potomac Park, Washington, DC, dedicated on Memorial Day, May 30, 1922. The idea originated in the celebrations that were held in February 1909 to mark the centenary of his birth. A bill to create a national memorial, introduced by Senator Shelby M. Cullom of Illinois, was passed in 1911. The building's architect, Henry Bacon, designed it to resemble the Parthenon in Athens, Greece; its 36 marble columns symbolize the states of the Union during Lincoln's presidency. The marble statue of Lincoln within is by the sculptor Daniel Chester French. Lincoln's Gettysburg Address is inscribed on the south wall, and the Second Inaugural Address on the north wall.

2713. Monument to the American flag was dedicated at Schenley Park, Pittsburgh, PA, on June 14, 1927, on the 150th anniversary of the adoption of the Stars and Stripes as the national banner. It was designed by Harvey A. Schwab, dedicated by William T. Kerr, founder of the American Flag Day Association, and unveiled by Florence Bent of Pittsburgh's Bellefield High School.

2714. Monument to four presidents was the sculpture of George Washington, Thomas Jefferson, Theodore Roosevelt, and Abraham Lincoln carved and blasted into the southeastern face of Mount Rushmore, SD, by sculptor Gutzon Borglum. Borglum began drilling into the 5,700-foot-high mountain in 1927, following dedication ceremonies led by President Calvin Coolidge. The work took 14 years, of which only 6.5 were spent actual carving the heads. The eventual cost was $1 million, including $836,000 of federal money. The Washington head was completed in 1930, the Jefferson head in 1936, Lincoln in 1937, and Roosevelt in 1939. Work formally ended on the site in 1941.

2715. National monument to Thomas Jefferson was the Thomas Jefferson Memorial in East Potomac Park in Washington, DC. Designed by John R. Pope, Otto R. Eggers, and Daniel P. Higgins in the domed classical style favored by Jefferson in his own architectural works, the monument was dedicated on April 13, 1943, for the 200th anniversary of Jefferson's birth. Under the central dome is a monumental bronze statue of Jefferson by sculptor Rudolph Evans.

MONUMENTS—*continued*

2716. National monument dedicated to an African-American was the George Washington Carver National Monument, authorized on July 14, 1943, officially established on June 14, 1951, and dedicated on July 14, 1953. It consists of 210 acres about 2.5 miles southwest of Diamond in Newton County, MO. It is administered by the National Park Service.

2717. Statue of an American woman in uniform was "Molly Marine," a monument to women who served in the U.S. Marines, dedicated in New Orleans, LA, on November 10, 1943.

2718. Monument to a Native American was carved out of a granite mountain north of Custer, SD. The world's largest sculpture, it was a 563-foot-high, 600-foot-long monument to Crazy Horse, the Lakota chief who led the victory over Custer's forces at the Little Big Horn in 1876. In 1939, sculptor Korczak Ziolkowski, an assistant on the construction of the Mount Rushmore presidential monument, was asked by Lakota chief Henry Standing Bear to "caress a mountain so that the white man will know that the red man had heroes, too." Ziolkowski started work in 1948 and removed some 7 million tons of granite. He died in 1982, leaving the monument unfinished.

2719. National monument to Vietnam veterans was the Vietnam Veterans Memorial, dedicated in November 1982 in Washington, DC. Designed by Maya Lin, an architecture student at Yale University, the monument consists of two polished black granite walls in the form of a "V," engraved with the names of the more than 58,000 Americans killed or missing-in-action in the war. A realistic bronze sculpture of three soldiers by Frederick Hart was placed facing the wall to mollify those who felt that Lin's design was too minimal.

N

NATIVE AMERICANS

2720. Armed conflict between Europeans and Native Americans on American soil occurred in May 1539 in Clarke County, AL, when Hernando de Soto's Spanish forces killed several thousand Native Americans, members of a war party under Chief Tuscaloosa, in nine hours of fighting at the Battle of Mauvilla. The Spanish loss was 70 killed and 900 wounded, including de Soto.

2721. Confederation in what is now the United States was the league of the Haudenosaunee, also called the Iroquois Confederacy, a union of Native American tribes located in what is now New York State and the surrounding area. According to tradition, the Confederacy was formed sometime between 1000 and 1550 by Haionhwat'ha (Hiawatha) and his mentor, Deganawidah. It included the Cayuga, Mohawk, and Oneida tribes, which were later joined by the Seneca and the Onondaga. The Tuscarora joined in a nonvoting capacity in 1715. The league was formed on cooperative principles, with each tribe represented at a policy-making council. The earliest account of it by a European writer was the journal of a Dutch traveler, Harmen Meyndertsz van den Bogaert, which appeared in 1635. Confederations were also formed by many other Native American groups, including the Creek, Choctaw, Cherokee, Powhatan, and Miami.

2722. Law code compiled in North America that is known in any detail was the *Kaiainerekowa,* or Great Law of Peace, developed by the Haudenosaunee (Iroquois) in New York State sometime before 1550 and recorded graphically in belts of wampum shells. Among its notable provisions was payment of compensation to the relatives of a murdered person, introduced as an alternative to the blood feud. It also set forth a federal system in which each of the member nations (Onondaga, Oneida, Mohawk, Seneca, and Cayuga) was governed by a council of sachems nominated by (and subject to removal by) the clan mothers, with the leaders of all five nations meeting frequently at a grand council.

2723. Colonial law banning "Indianizing" was enacted in Jamestown, VA, in 1612. Any Virginian who tried to "runne away from the Colonie" to join the community of Powhatan "or any Weroance else whatsoever" was liable for the death penalty.

2724. Reservation for Native Americans was established in 1638 by the colony of Connecticut, which designated an area of 1,200 acres for the Quinnipiac tribe, of whom 47 were still alive. Thirteen additional reservations were set aside by Connecticut over the next three decades.

2725. Law forbidding Native American religious rituals was passed by the Massachusetts Bay Colony in November 1646. The law forbade any Native American to "pawwow or performe outward worship to their falce gods or to the deuill upon any land or ground which is proper to the English." The penalty was a fine of £10.

2726. Colonial badges issued to friendly Native Americans were authorized in Virginia by the Act of 1661, which authorized "silver and plated placques to be worn by the Indians when visiting the settlements." One of these has a crude representation of a tobacco plant and scrolls, above which is "The King Of" on the obverse, while on the reverse is a similarly engraved plant and the word "Patomeck" with the *e* overlined. The surface edges were engraved to represent scrolls and foldings, while the medal was holed for suspension. On December 2, 1662, an act "prohibiting the entertainment of Indians without badges" was passed by the Assembly at James City, VA.

2727. Reservation for Native Americans established by a state was set aside on August 29, 1758, when the New Jersey Legislature appropriated 1,600 acres of a tract of 3,044 acres in the township of Evesham, Burlington County, NJ, to be used as a reservation for the Native Americans of New Jersey. Governor Francis Bernard named the tract Brotherton. About 200 Native Americans, probably Lenapes and Unamis, were settled on it. In 1801 the land was sold and the Native Americans moved to the Lake Oneida Reservation.

2728. Restriction by a European colonial power on settlements in Native American territory was imposed by the Proclamation of 1763, formulated by the Earl of Hillsborough and signed by King George III on October 7, 1763, with the intention of fostering better relations between Britain and the Native American tribes. The proclamation dealt with the territory ceded to Britain by France in the Peace of Paris, which ended the French and Indian War. The part of this territory west of the Allegheny Mountains was assigned to the Native Americans, and British settlers were prohibited from surveying and purchasing land there. The Treaty of Lochaber, made with the Cherokee in 1770, moved the line farther west, and the onset of the American Revolution voided the arrangement.

2729. Map of the British colonies showing Native American lands was a hand-colored map printed for the map and print dealer Carington Bowles in London, England, in 1771, with this title: *A general map of the middle British colonies in America, viz. Virginia, Maryland, Delaware, Pensilvania, New-Jersey, New York, Connecticut & Rhode-Island: Of Aquanishuonigy the country of the confederate Indians comprehending Aquanishuonigy proper, their places of residence, Ohio & Thuchsochruntie their deer hunting countries,* *Couchsachrage & Skaniadarade their beaver hunting countries, of the Lakes Erie, Ontario and Champlain. Wherein is also shewn the antient & present seats of the Indian nations.* The map was printed on a scale of 1:2,250,000.

2730. Congressional agency to conduct negotiations with Native Americans was established by the Continental Congress at Philadelphia, PA, in 1775. It was run by eleven commissioners and consisted of three regional departments (north, central, and south). When the newly independent United States was organized under the Articles of Confederation in 1781, the management of relations with the Native Americans was given to the individual states. Under the Constitution, adopted in 1787, the right "to regulate Commerce . . . with the Indian tribes" was reserved to Congress, which made Indian affairs one of the responsibilities of the War Department in 1789.

2731. Native American delegation to the Continental Congress was a group of 21 Iroquois chiefs who came to Philadelphia, PA, in May 1776 to confer with revolutionary leaders and were spectators at meetings of the Congress. On June 11 they attended as official guests. John Hancock, president of the Congress, received from one of the envoys the ceremonial name Karanduawn, meaning "great tree." Another delegation of Iroquois and Ohio chiefs visited Congress in the fall of that year.

2732. Proposal to form a Native American state within the Union was made in the the Articles of Agreement and Confederation signed at Fort Pitt (Pittsburgh), PA, on September 17, 1778, by two United States commissioners and four chiefs of the Delaware Nation. The treaty created a military alliance between the parties. One provision gave the Delaware the right to create an association of Native American tribes "and form a state whereof the Delaware Nation shall be the head and have a representative in Congress."

2733. Treaty between the United States and a Native American nation was the Articles of Agreement and Confederation signed on September 17, 1778, at Fort Pitt, PA (now Pittsburgh), with delegates of the Delaware nation. Commissioners Andrew and Thomas Lewis signed for the United States and chiefs White Eyes, John Kill Buck, Junior, and Pipe made their marks on behalf of the Delaware. The treaty specified "That a perpetual peace and friendship shall from henceforth take place, and subsist between the contracting: parties aforesaid, through all succeeding generations: and if either of the parties are engaged in a just and

NATIVE AMERICANS—*continued*

necessary war with any other nation or nations, that then each shall assist the other in due proportion to their abilities, till their enemies are brought to reasonable terms of accommodation: and that if either of them shall discover any hostile designs forming against the other, they shall give the earliest notice thereof that timeous measures may be taken to prevent their ill effect."

2734. Reservation for Native Americans established by the federal government was set aside in 1786. The first official notice of the removal of Native Americans residing east of the Mississippi River to reservations west of the river was contained in the congressional act of March 26, 1804. Reservations established by executive order without an act of Congress were not held to be permanent before the general allotment act of February 8, 1887, an "act to provide for the allotment of lands . . . severally to Indians on the various reservations, and to extend the protection of the laws of the United States and the territories over the Indians."

2735. Federal law regulating commerce with Native Americans was the Trade and Intercourse Act of July 22, 1790, the first of a series of similar acts of Congress enacted through 1834. They made the federal government the sole authorized purchaser of Native American lands, excluding both states and private individuals, and required settlers engaged in trade with Native Americans to obtain a government license.

2736. Battle fought by federal troops after the formation of the Union was the Miami Expedition. On October 19, 1790, Colonel John Hardin, under Brigadier General Josiah Harmar, led 400 troops against 150 Miami in the Great Lakes region northwest of Ohio, but because of poor leadership, insufficient training, and unworkable guns, the attack ended in a retreat.

2737. Congressional protection of Native American hunting grounds was included in an act approved on May 19, 1796, "to regulate the trade and intercourse with the Native American tribes and to preserve peace on the frontiers." The penalty for crossing the line to hunt or destroy game within Native American territory was a fine of $100 and six months in jail. A later treaty with the Native Americans signed in 1832 is generally regarded as the first national hunting law.

2738. Battle in the "Frontier War" between the United States and the Native Americans is considered to have been the Battle of Tippecanoe, which took place on November 7–8, 1811, at Tippecanoe Creek in the Indiana Territory. The region was inhabited by the Shawnees, whose chief, Tecumseh (or Tecumtha), was in the process of organizing a defensive alliance of Native American tribes, with the support of the British. A Shawnee army under Tecumseh's brother, the mystic leader Tenskwatawa, attacked an American army under General William Henry Harrison, who had come to enforce a corrupt treaty that had opened the area to white settlement. The Shawnees were defeated and their village, Prophet's Town, destroyed.

2739. Native American government modeled on that of the United States was established in a constitutional convention held in 1828 at New Echota, GA, by the Cherokees. It was a tripartite system, with an elected executive, a bicameral legislative council, and a judiciary. The first president was John Ross.

2740. Native American newspaper was the *Cherokee Phoenix,* a bilingual English–Cherokee paper that was published weekly in New Echota, GA, between February 21, 1828, and October 1835 under the management of a Cherokee editor, Elias Boudinot. Cherokee was the first of the Native American languages to acquire a written form, invented by Sikwayi (Sequoyah), a silversmith, painter, and soldier.

2741. Claims by Native Americans for compensation for confiscated land were made possible in 1855, when the United States Court of Claims was established by Congress to hear claims against the federal government. The Indian Claims Commission was established by Congress in 1946 to settle all remaining claims. It heard 850 claims for restitution in its first six years, awarding more than $800 million, with compensation calculated according to the market value of the land when it was acquired. It was terminated in 1988.

2742. Native Americans to become United States citizens were the Wyandot tribe, whose members became American citizens in 1855, followed by the Potawatomi and Kickapoos. Individuals acquired citizenship under the terms of the Dawes Allotment Act of 1887. The Citizenship Act of October 1901 gave American citizenship to the Five Civilized Tribes living in Indian Territory (now Oklahoma). The Indian Citizenship Act, also known as the Snyder Act, enacted by Congress on June 2, 1924, declared all Native Americans to be citizens, without the loss of citizenship in their respective tribes.

2743. School for Native American children run by the Bureau of Indian Affairs was opened in 1860 in the state of Washington, on the Yakima Indian Reservation, five years after the end of the Yakima War. Federal involvement in educating Native Americans began in 1775 with an appropriation of $500 by the Continental Congress to enable Native Americans to attend Dartmouth College, Dartmouth, NH. The first treaty to obligate the United States to provide educational services was concluded with the Oneida, Tuscarora, and Stockbridge tribes in 1794.

2744. Native American general may have been Tecumseh (or Tecumtha), leader of the Shawnee, who helped the British to defend the Detroit area in the War of 1812 and is said to have been commissioned a brigadier general; he was killed in battle in 1813. The first Native American general of record was Stand Watie, born Degataga Uwetie or Oowatie, who was named a brigadier general by the Confederate Army in 1864. He had been a prominent member of the Cherokee Nation and was one of the signers in 1835 of the Treaty of New Echota, which bound the Cherokee to move from Georgia to Indian Territory (now Oklahoma) against the will of the majority. In 1861 he raised a regiment, the Cherokee Mounted Rifles, to serve in the Confederate Army. He surrendered on June 23, 1865, the last Confederate general to do so.

2745. Native American to win territorial concessions from the federal government was Red Cloud, a chief of the Oglala Sioux. After years of leading successful assaults against U.S. forts in the Powder River area of Montana, Red Cloud signed a treaty at Fort Laramie on November 6, 1868. The treaty provided for the abandonment of Forts Reno, Kearney, and C.F. Smith.

2746. Indian Affairs commissioner who was Native American was Brigadier General Ely Samuel Parker (Donehogawa), a prominent civil engineer and chief of the Tonawanda Seneca who had served as military secretary to General Ulysses S. Grant during the Civil War. As president, Grant appointed Parker to the post of commissioner of Indian affairs on April 21, 1869. He served until December 1871. The first Native American superintendent of an agency of the Bureau of Indian Affairs was Shirley Plume, an Oglala Sioux, who was designated as acting superintendent of the Standing Rock Agency at Fort Yates, ND, on August 20, 1973. She was appointed superintendent on January 24, 1974.

2747. Federal law withdrawing recognition of Native American tribal autonomy was the Indian Appropriations Act, passed by Congress on March 3, 1871. It provided that "no Indian nation or tribe within the territory of the United States shall be acknowledged or recognized as an independent nation, tribe, or power with whom the Unted States may contract by treaty." The law left intact all treaties lawfully made prior to that date.

2748. Major defeat inflicted by Native Americans on regular U.S. Army troops was the Battle of the Little Bighorn in southeastern Montana, fought on June 25, 1876. More than 200 men of the 7th Cavalry Regiment, commanded by Lieutenant Colonel George Armstrong Custer, were killed in an attack by Dakota Sioux and Northern Cheyenne under Chief Sitting Bull (Tatanka Iyotake) and the Oglala war leader Crazy Horse (Ta-Sunko-Witko). The battle was brought on when Custer's troops, charged with subduing any Sioux who did not return to their reservations as ordered by the U.S. government, stumbled upon Sitting Bull's camp on the banks of the Little Bighorn River. Custer ordered an immediate attack but was far outnumbered by the Sioux, who killed him and all of his men. The greatest defeat inflicted in the Indian Wars on the U.S. Army, it was also the last important military victory by Native Americans. The Little Bighorn Battlefield National Monument commemorates the battle.

2749. Federal law dissolving Native American tribes as legal entities and converting their communally held lands to private property owned by individuals was the Land in Severalty Act, better known as the Dawes Allotment Act after its main sponsor, Senator Henry Dawes. It was passed by Congress on February 8, 1887, and was intended to break down tribal cohesion and assimilate Native Americans into the general population. It allowed reservation land that was formerly held by tribes to be divided up among individuals as farms, with heads of households receiving 160 acres; single adults over the age of 17, 80 acres; and other people, 40 acres. Each grant of land was held in trust by the federal government for 25 years, after which the individual acquired full ownership and United States citizenship. Land still remaining after allotment could be bought and resold to homesteaders by the federal government. Allotment was undertaken on 118 reservations, resulting in the loss of 82 million acres of Native American land. The policy was reversed by the Indian Reorganization Act of June 18, 1934.

NATIVE AMERICANS—*continued*

2750. Formal appeal for recognition of Native Americans as United States citizens was made on September 28, 1915, by Sherman Coolidge, the president of the Society of American Indians. In his invitation to the nation to observe the second Saturday in May as American Indian Day, he asked Americans to join with the society in honoring "our early philosophy, our love of freedom, our social institutions and our history," and to consider "our present and our future as a part of the American people . . . consistent with American citizenship."

2751. American Indian Day began as a Boy Scout observance in 1912. The idea was suggested to them by Arthur C. Parker, director of the Museum of Arts and Sciences in Rochester, NY. In 1914 a Blackfoot Indian, Red Fox James of Montana, made a 4,000-mile trip by pony to petition state governments to adopt the idea, collecting endorsements from 24 governors, which he delivered to the White House. The first state to observe American Indian Day as a state holiday was New York, on the second Saturday in May, 1916.

2752. Law by which Native Americans became American citizens was the Indian Citizenship Act, passed by Congress on June 2, 1924. It granted citizenship to all Native Americans born in the United States. Previously, the granted of citizenship was a patchwork affair, based on military service, marriage, or racial makeup.

2753. Native American tribal constitution under the Indian Reorganization Act of June 18, 1934, was signed October 28, 1935, in the office of the secretary of the interior, Harold Le Claire Ickes, in Washington, DC. The signatories of the constitution affecting the Flathead Reservation at Dixon, MT, were Roy E. Courville, chairman of the election board; Joseph R. Blodgett, president of the Tribal Council; Luman W. Shotwell, superintendent and ex-officio secretary of the Tribal Council; Martin Charlo of the Confederated Salish Tribe; and Paul Koos-ta-ta, chief of the Kootenai Tribe.

2754. National organization of Native Americans was the National Congress of American Indians, founded in Denver, CO, on November 15, 1944, to protect tribal rights and resources. The group eventually comprised 160 member tribes.

2755. Occupation of federal territory by Native American protesters in the modern era lasted for four hours on March 9, 1964, when five Sioux led by Richard McKenzie took over Alcatraz Island in San Francisco Bay, off San Francisco, CA, demanding the establishment of a cultural center and university on the island. On November 20, 1969, these demands were raised again by Richard Oakes and a group of about 100 Native Americans, mostly college students, who began an organized occupation of Alcatraz that lasted 19 months.

2756. Militant Native American civil rights organization of national importance was the American Indian Movement, founded in 1968 in Minneapolis, MN, by Dennis Banks, Clyde Bellecourt, Eddie Benton Banai, and George Mitchell, with the goal of promoting Native American claims against the U.S. government. The group participated in the occupations of Alcatraz Island in San Francisco Bay in 1969, the office of the Bureau of Indian Affairs in Washington, DC, in 1972, and of Wounded Knee, SD, in 1973. Some 24 members died in shootouts with federal officials. The group had largely disbanded by the mid-1980s.

2757. Restoration of land to a Native American tribe was ordered by Congress on December 15, 1970. The act returned to the Taos Pueblo Indians of New Mexico 48,000 acres of sacred land that had been appropriated by the United States Forest Service in 1906.

2758. Armed occupation by Native American protesters in the modern era began on February 27, 1973, when 200 members of the American Indian Movement, led by Russell Means and Dennis Banks, occupied Wounded Knee, SD, a town on the Pine Ridge Indian Reservation and the site of an 1890 massacre of Oglala Sioux by the U.S. Seventh Cavalry. The protesters set up what they called an "Independent Oglala Sioux Nation" and issued a number of demands, including a review of treaties between the federal government and indigenous peoples, a Senate investigation into the treatment of Native Americans, and free elections of tribal leaders. The occupation ended on May 8 when the group surrendered to federal marshals. Gunfights during the siege killed one marshal and two protesters.

2759. Native American tribe restored to federally recognized status after termination was the Menominee tribe of Wisconsin, restored by Congress in Public Law 93-197 on December 22, 1973. The policy of terminating federal supervision of tribes, which also entailed the cessation of "all disabilities and limitations specially applicable to Indians," was started on June 9, 1953, through House Concurrent Resolution 108 and was repealed in 1988. Native American groups are now classified as federally recognized (more than 500), state-recognized, terminated, and unrecognized (more than 200).

2760. Federal law returning autonomy to Native American tribes was the Indian Self-Determination and Educational Assistance Act, passed by Congress on January 4, 1975. The law gave the tribes control over the management of federal assistance programs on their reservations.

P

POLITICAL CAMPAIGNS

2761. Campaign committee appointed by a political party was set up in February 1804 by the Democratic-Republicans at their caucus in Washington, DC, to drum up support for their presidential candidate, Thomas Jefferson. The committee consisted of 13 senators and congressmen, all from different states.

2762. Opinion poll for political purposes was taken during the presidential election of 1824. The results appeared on July 24, 1824, in the *Harrisburg Pennsylvanian*. The four candidates were Andrew Jackson of Tennessee, John Quincy Adams of Massachusetts, William Harris Crawford of Georgia, and Henry Clay of Kentucky. The poll put Jackson in first place. In the election, Jackson received a majority of the popular vote (which was held in 18 of the 24 states), but since none of the candidates received a majority of the electoral vote, the election was decided in the House of Representatives, and Adams won. This was not a scientific poll, but the first of what were to be called "straw polls," in which the opinions of unselected groups of voters are solicited and used, like a straw held up in the breeze, to gauge which way the political wind is blowing.

2763. Presidential campaign of the modern type was conducted by General Andrew Jackson, the first presidential candidate to make a direct appeal to the emotions and prejudices of voters. To launch his bid for election in 1828, he appeared as the guest of honor at a four-day celebration of the Battle of New Orleans (held in that city on the anniversary of Jackson's victory over the British on January 8, 1815). Banquets, torchlight parades, and flag-waving rallies were organized on his behalf, and local Democratic clubs erected giant hickory poles, meant to remind voters of "Old Hickory." Personal vituperation between the candidates and fights among their supporters were also features of this campaign.

2764. Campaign song used as an integral part of a presidential campaign was sung by the supporters of William Henry Harrison, the general known as the hero of Tippecanoe, and his running mate, John Tyler, who were running for office in 1840 on the Whig Party ticket against Martin Van Buren and Richard Mentor Johnson on the Democratic. The song, which was sung over and over by people marching in procession with symbols of Harrison (log cabins, coonskin caps, and cider barrels), went: "What has caused this great commotion-motion-motion-motion, / Our country through? / It is the ball a-rolling on / For Tippecanoe and Tyler too. / And with them we will beat little Van. / Van, Van is a used-up man."

2765. Presidential candidate to make a campaign speech was Whig candidate William Henry Harrison, who spoke on June 6, 1840, from the steps of the National Hotel in Columbus, OH. Before that time, candidates gave no speeches themselves, but let others in the party speak on their behalf. Harrison gave 23 stump speeches in all, mostly at rallies held in his home state of Ohio.

2766. Presidential candidate to campaign throughout the country was James Baird Weaver of Iowa, the 1880 candidate of the Greenback Labor Party, who is estimated to have traveled some 20,000 miles during the campaign and to have brought the Greenback message of monetary and commerce reform to half a million listeners in the course of making 100 speeches. He won 308,578 votes, mainly from the West, in the election of November 2.

2767. Presidential candidate to make campaign speeches in a foreign language was James Abram Garfield of Ohio, who made several political speeches in German. He was elected in November 1880.

2768. Election board game was probably "Presidential Election," invented by George Parker, Jr., and produced by the Massachusetts firm of Parker Brothers circa 1892. Players competed to be the first to move the wooden tokens denoting their candidates into the White House; moves were determined by cards marked with electoral and popular votes.

POLITICAL CAMPAIGNS—*continued*

2769. Presidential candidate to run his campaign by telephone was Republican candidate William McKinley. He called 38 of his campaign managers in as many states from Canton, OH, in 1896 during the presidential campaign that resulted in his election.

2770. Corrupt election practices law enacted by Congress was passed on January 26, 1907. It prohibited corporations from contributing to candidates' campaign funds in presidential and congressional races. An act passed on March 4, 1909, further prohibited national banks and corporations from making financial contributions to campaign funds in connection with any election to any political office.

2771. Election campaign using radio was undertaken by Senator Harry Stewart New, Republican of Indiana, who waged an unsuccessful campaign for reelection in 1922. He made a number of radio speeches during the campaign and hired several halls in which the speeches could be heard over loudspeakers. He was defeated by Samuel Moffett Ralston, the Democratic candidate.

2772. Negative election campaign run by media specialists took place during the California governor's race of 1934. The Democratic candidate was the writer and social reformer Upton Beall Sinclair, a Socialist, whose platform was called EPIC ("End Poverty in California"). The Republican Party, for the first time in any major American election, hired outside political consultants and advertising specialists to conduct a wholly negative campaign. It included attack ads on radio and film, thousands of negative cartoons and leaflets comparing Sinclair to Hitler and Stalin, and a secret dirty tricks squad that tapped his phones. The Republican candidate, Frank Merriam, won by more than 250,000 votes.

2773. Scientific public opinion polls were used to predict the outcome of the 1936 presidential election. Polling firms formed by the three leaders in the field—George Gallup, Elmo Roper, and Archibald Crossley—employed a statistical method called quota sampling that was originally developed by businesses for market research. In quota sampling, the polled sample was chosen according to factors such as sex, age, race, and income in ratios that supposedly matched those of the general population. Each polling firm correctly picked the winner: the incumbent, Franklin Delano Roosevelt.

2774. Presidential campaign manager who was a woman was Ruth Hanna McCormick Simms, daughter of Republican senator Mark Hanna, who was named one of two managers of Thomas Edmund Dewey's campaign on December 2, 1939. The other manager was J. Russel Sprague, Republican leader of Nassau County, NY. The first woman to manage the presidential campaign of a Democratic candidate was Harvard law professor Susan R. Estrich, who did so for Michael Dukakis in the election of 1988. In 1976, as a law student, Estrich had been the first woman to serve as president of the *Harvard Law Review*.

2775. Political campaign based on talkathons was the 1952 Arkansas gubernatorial campaign mounted by Francis A. Cherry. Cherry employed 21 marathon radio broadcasts to get his message out to the Arkansas voters, sometimes talking for more than 24 hours at a stretch while taking telephoned and written questions from his listeners. Cherry defeated former governor Sidney S. McMath for the Democratic nomination, and was elected governor on November 4, 1952.

2776. Televised debate among competitors for a party's presidential nomination took place on January 5, 1980, in Des Moines, IA, where six Republican competitors faced each other in a two-hour debate. The six were John Anderson of Illinois, Howard Baker, Jr., of Tennessee, George Herbert Walker Bush of Texas, John Connally of Texas, Philip Crane of Illinois, and Robert Dole of Kansas. Ronald Wilson Reagan was absent. The confrontation was sponsored by the *Des Moines Register and Tribune*.

POLITICAL CAMPAIGNS—ADS

2777. Television ad saturation campaign was the "Eisenhower Answers America" campaign, created by advertising executive Rosser Reeves for Dwight David Eisenhower's presidential bid in 1952. Reeves proposed a series of short spots showing Eisenhower answering questions from supposedly ordinary citizens (all questions were actually prewritten and delivered by actors). The spots were broadcast so frequently just before Election Day on November 4, 1952, that they "saturated" the airwaves and thereby obscured the message of Eisenhower's opponent, Adlai Ewing Stevenson.

2778. Political ad raising fears of nuclear war was the so-called "Daisy" ad, created by advertising agency Doyle, Dane, Bernbach (DDB) for President Lyndon Baines Johnson's 1964 election campaign. The spot begins with a little girl counting flower petals; then a voice starts a countdown that ends with an atomic blast. "Daisy" was aired only once, but it was extensively discussed and rebroadcast by the media. It effectively capitalized on fears that Johnson's hard-right opponent, Republican Barry Goldwater, would be quick to start a nuclear war, and was perhaps the crucial element in Goldwater's defeat in November.

2779. Soft-sell nostalgia ads became popular in the 1984 presidential campaign. Best known of these was the "Morning in America" television spot, the centerpiece of President Ronald Wilson Reagan's reelection campaign, which aired nationally in the summer and fall of 1984. Created by the Reagan/Bush "Tuesday Team" of political and media advisors, and paid for by the Republican National Committee, the ad said nothing at all about Reagan or campaign issues. It did show hopeful, unchallenging images of sunrises, flags, churches, farms, and mountains and asked, in a folksy voiceover, whether viewers were better off than just "four short years ago"—a reference to the unpopular presidency of Jimmy Carter and a fatal blow against Reagan's opponent, Walter Mondale, who had been Carter's vice president.

POLITICAL CAMPAIGNS—FINANCE

2780. Campaign expenditure of record was dispensed by George Washington in support of his campaign for the Virginia House of Burgesses in 1757. Washington handed out 28 gallons of rum, 50 gallons of rum punch, 34 gallons of wine, 46 gallons of beer, and two gallons of cider royal, all consumed by the 391 voters in his district.

2781. Campaign assessments on government workers were levied circa 1830 on New York City customs workers by the Democratic Party. The assessment was made whether or not workers were members of the party. The practice of mandatory party assessments expanded until after the Civil War, when the first federal laws were passed against it.

2782. Federal law regulating campaign finances was the Naval Appropriations Act of March 2, 1867. Among its clauses was one that read: "Be it further enacted: That no officer or employee of the government shall require or request any working man in any navy yard to contribute or pay any money for political purposes . . . and any officer or employee of the government who shall offend against the provisions of this section shall be dismissed from the service of the United States."

2783. Campaign finance reform proposal was made by Theodore Roosevelt in his annual message to Congress on December 5, 1905. Roosevelt, who had been accused of taking large contributions from several corporations during his 1904 presidential campaign, declared: "All contributions by corporations to any political committee or for any political purpose should be forbidden by law." He reiterated this message in his subsequent annual addresses. The first Congressional campaign finance law was passed in 1907.

2784. Federal act regulating corporate contributions to election campaigns was the Tillman Act, passed by Congress in 1907 under the sponsorship of Senator Benjamin Ryan Tillman of South Carolina. It barred corporations and national banks from making "a money contribution in connection with any election" of federal candidates.

2785. Federal act requiring congressional campaigns to disclose their finances was the Federal Corrupt Practices Act of 1910, which applied solely to elections for the House of Representatives. Political committees and lobbyists active in two or more states were required to file a full financial disclosure of their campaign expenditures and contributions with the clerk of the House within 30 days of each election. Similar legislation was passed for the Senate in 1911.

2786. Federal act limiting campaign expenditures by candidates for Congress was the 1911 extension of the Federal Corrupt Practices Act of 1910. Senators running for office were allowed to spend no more than $10,000 or the maximum allowed by their state, whichever was less; candidates for the House could spend no more than $5,000. It also, for the first time, required the reporting of expenditures related to party primaries.

POLITICAL CAMPAIGNS—FINANCE—
continued

2787. Federal act regulating the receipt of gifts by candidates for Congress was the Federal Corrupt Practices Act of 1925. It barred federal employees and certain other groups from contributing "a gift, subscription, loan, advance, or deposit of money, or anything of value" to candidates for federal office, and required candidates receiving nonmoney contributions from political party organizations operating in two or more states to report them. In practice, the limitations were easily evaded and served mainly to expand the variety of means by which campaigns were financed.

2788. Federal act regulating contributions by labor unions to congressional campaigns was the War Labor Disputes Act, also called the Smith-Connally Act, passed by Congress in 1943. It barred labor unions from making political contributions to the campaign of any candidate for federal office. The prohibition was reinforced in 1947 by provisions of the Labor-Management Relations Act, also known as the Taft-Hartley Act.

2789. Campaign finance law that set limits on media spending was the Federal Election Campaign Act of 1971, which was signed into law by President Richard Milhous Nixon and went into effect on April 7, 1972. It set a ceiling on the amount any candidate for federal office could spend on newspaper, radio, television, and other forms of advertising for primaries and general elections. A candidate for the House could spend the greater of $50,000 or ten cents for each voter in his or her district. Senatorial candidates were limited to the greater of $50,000 or ten cents for each voter in the state. Presidential candidates could spend no more than ten cents for each voter in the country. Moreover, the amount spent directly on electronic media advertising (television and radio) could not exceed 60 percent of total media expenditures. The media limits were repealed by Congress in 1974.

2790. Independent government agency to oversee political campaign contributions was the Federal Election Commission, an the independent regulatory agency charged with administering and enforcing the Federal Election Campaign Act of 1971. The FEC, established in 1974, has jurisdiction over the financing of campaigns for the House, the Senate, the presidency and the vice presidency. It began operation in 1975 and administered the first publicly funded presidential election in 1976.

2791. Campaign funding organization for political candidates who support legal abortion was EMILY's List, founded Washington, DC, in 1985, by Ellen Malcolm, a former press liaison in the Carter administration, and other politically active women. The name is an acronym for "Early Money is Like Yeast." The mission of EMILY's List was to increase the number of Democratic woman officeholders with "pro-choice" positions on abortion by helping them get funding early in their campaigns. By the year 2000, EMILY's List had assisted in the election of six women to the Senate and 44 to the House, as well as three governors.

POLITICAL CAMPAIGNS—PARAPHER-
NALIA

2792. Political buttons were actual brass or copper buttons created for the inauguration of President George Washington on April 30, 1789, in New York City. A typical example was marked with the letters "GW" surrounded by the inscription "Long Live the President." Washington is said to have worn a set on his coat at the inauguration ceremony.

2793. Campaign medalets were large copper and pewter pieces commemorative pieces issued for the election of John Adams in 1796. Medalets—small medals with engraved images of a candidate or a party message—first came into wide popularity with supporters of Andrew Jackson in 1824.

2794. Political snuffboxes date from the Andrew Jackson campaign of 1824, and were decorated with a bust of the candidate. The snuffboxes were made of lacquered papier-mâché.

2795. Campaign biography was "The life of Andrew Jackson, major-general in the service of the United States: comprising a history of the war in the South, from the commencement of the Creek campaign, to the termination of hostilities before New Orleans." Written by Senator John Henry Eaton and John Reid in 1817 and published by M. Carey, Philadelphia, PA, it was reissued in 1827 by the Cincinnati publishing house of Hatch & Nichols in time for Jackson's 1828 election campaign.

2796. Campaign torch mass-produced for use at night-time political rallies and parades was patented in 1837. Political torchlight parades had long been a popular element of campaigns; the mass-produced torches, which used liquid fuel, were purchased for parades in urban areas where the usual materials—straw and pitch—might not be available in sufficient quantities. Later they evolved into campaign promotional items in their own right, with designs of eagles or other symbols and pictures of the candidates.

2797. Campaign banners were created beginning in the early 19th century, but few, if any, surviving examples predate the William Henry Harrison presidential campaign of 1840. Most early banners were one-of-a-kind items hand-painted on silk or broadcloth, such as a "log cabin" banner of 1840 inscribed with the initials "W.H.H./O.K.," the first known political use of the term "O.K."

2798. Campaign hat was the coonskin cap, worn by the supporters of Whig presidential candidate Henry Clay in 1844. The raccoon was a party symbol, and such caps identified the wearer as a loyal Whig. Fifty years earlier, supporters of the presidential bids of John Adams and Thomas Jefferson wore cockades attached to their own hats. Adams supporters opted for brown and black cockades while Jefferson's partisans preferred cockades of red, white, and blue.

2799. Campaign biography by a prominent author was *Life of Franklin Pierce,* written for the future president by his Bowdoin College friend and classmate Nathaniel Hawthorne in 1852. It is probably the Hawthorne work of least literary merit.

2800. Campaign poster showing the candidate and his wife was probably a poster created for the 1856 election showing the Republican presidential nominee John Charles Frémont of California cavorting on horseback with his wife Jessica, the daughter of Missouri senator Thomas Hart Benton. Although labeled "Fremont and Jessie," the figures bore no likeness whatsoever to the real individuals.

2801. Uniformed political marching group was the Republican Wide-Awakes of Hartford, who first performed in honor of a visit by presidential candidate Abraham Lincoln to Hartford, CT, in March 1860. Dressed in suits, capes, and kepi hats, they staged a torchlight parade with military precision. So successful was the demonstration that Wide-Awake groups quickly formed in other cities, and Lincoln gave them credit for helping him win the election.

2802. Political figurals were glass bottles made in the likenesses of Civil War notables, including General George Brinton McClellan, the Democratic candidate in the 1864 presidential election, and General Winfield Scott, Whig candidate in 1852 and commander of the Union Army in defense of Washington, DC. The blown-glass figurals, colored black or purple, were six inches high and were made for a tonic manufacturer.

2803. Celluloid campaign buttons date from at least 1876, when solid celluloid buttons were produced for the Rutherford Birchard Hayes campaign. They showed a bust of the candidate. Celluloid buttons were crafted from solid celluloid, an early form of plastic, or a shell of celluloid over a photograph on a metal backing, and had a stick pin or clasp on the back. The celluloid button-making process was patented in 1893 by Whitehead and Hoag of Newark, NJ.

2804. Lithographed buttons appeared for the 1920 presidential campaign. A large number of designs were printed on a sheet of metal by the lithographic process, then punched out, curled at the edge, and mounted with a pin. The process was cheap and amenable to mass production, making "lithos" the first truly widespread political buttons.

2805. Campaign bumper stickers with political slogans and/or images of the candidates were introduced for the 1928 campaign. Automotive window stickers, the first variety of automotive political paraphernalia, had been introduced for the Warren Gamaliel Harding and Calvin Coolidge campaign of 1924. Political license plate attachments were introduced at about the same time; these were made in a variety of widths and shapes, and were attached by screws or metal clamps.

2806. Campaign hosiery was novelty nylons distributed for the 1952 presidential campaign. These were printed with such slogans as "I Like Ike" and "Madly for Adlai."

2807. Plastic skimmer campaign hats were introduced for the 1952 campaigns of both major parties. Plastic "straw" campaign hats, with an embossed or molded straw texture, came into use in the 1970s, and, despite their poor fit, were ubiquitous by the 1990s.

POLITICAL MOVEMENTS AND ADVOCACY GROUPS

2808. Prison reform society was the Philadelphia Society for Alleviating the Miseries of Public Prisons, formed on May 8, 1787, in the German School House on Cherry Street, Philadelphia, PA, by Philadelphia Quakers. The first president was William White. A similar organi-

POLITICAL MOVEMENTS AND ADVOCACY GROUPS—*continued*

zation for war prisoners was the Philadelphia Society for Relieving Distressed Prisoners Owing to the War of Independence, organized on February 7, 1776, which ceased operations in September 1777.

2809. Pacifist tract written by an author who was not a Quaker was *The Mediator's Kingdom Not of This World but Spiritual, Heavenly and Divine*, published anonymously in 1809. The author was David Low Dodge of New York City, a devout Calvinist who was convinced that the tenets of Christianity, as expressed in the Bible and particularly in the Sermon on the Mount, required the renunciation of violence and war in all forms, including self-defense. The first edition sold a thousand copies in two weeks. Dodge's second tract, *War Inconsistent with the Religion of Jesus Christ*, was published in 1815, after the close of the War of 1812. Dodge was the founder in 1815 of the West's first pacifist society, the New York Peace Society.

2810. Pacifist society was the New York Peace Society, which was founded on August 16, 1815, with a New York businessman, David Low Dodge, as its first president. The Massachusetts Peace Society was founded by Noah Worcester in the same year. On May 8, 1828, the New York Peace Society became a member of a national organization called the American Peace Society, which held its first annual meeting on May 13, 1829, in New York City, and of which Dodge was a founder and life director.

2811. Anarchist was Josiah Warren, who was known as the "father of anarchy." He was of the intellectual type of anarchist and was not an advocate of violence. He was a veteran of the short-lived utopian colony in New Harmony, IN, whose failure convinced him that communistic social arrangements suppress individual initiative and responsibility. In May 1827 he opened his Equity Store in Cincinnati, OH, to vindicate his theory of "labor for labor," in which all labor is held to be equally valuable. The store sold merchandise at cost, plus seven percent for handling and the clerk's hire. Instead of money, the store also accepted "labor notes," in which the customer agreed to provide a specified amount of time and labor (for example, washing or carpentry) in exchange for merchandise. Warren also advocated the transference of government activities to private persons.

2812. Radical student leader was Theodore Welt, a student at the Lane Theological Seminary in Cincinnati, OH. In 1833, Welt organized the sons of slave holders attending the seminary to speak out in favor of abolition. Expelled from Lane, they enrolled at Oberlin College and continued their activities.

2813. Statement of the principles of the Greenback movement were explained in *Labor and Other Capital: The Rights of Each Secured and the Wrongs of Both Eradicated*, published in 1849 and redistributed in an abridged version as *A New Monetary System* in 1861. The author was Edward Kellogg, a New York drygoods merchant who advocated a system of freely circulating money, distributed by the government to all sectors of society, rather than controlled by banking interests.

2814. Ku Klux Klan was organized in 1865 in Pulaski, TN. It was originally founded as a social organization, but quickly became a secret terrorist group that tried to enforce white supremacy by means of intimidation and violence. The first leader, with the title of Grand Wizard, was the brilliant Confederate general Nathan Bedford Forrest of Tennessee, elected at a convention in Nashville, TN, in the summer of 1867. At that meeting, the KKK first called itself the "Invisible Empire of the South," and was organized into a hierarchy of grand dragons, grand titans, and grand cyclopses. The first national congress was held in Washington, DC, on August 8, 1925, when an estimated 40,000 Klan members marched through the capital.

2815. National organization to advocate universal voting rights was the American Equal Rights Association, organized in 1866 to advocate the extension of the voting rights to all citizens, regardless of race, color, or sex. Lucretia Mott was president and Susan Brownell Anthony secretary. In 1869 the association split over the question of whether to place priority on securing voting rights for women or for African-Americans. The result was the formation of two new organizations, the American Woman Suffrage Association, led by Lucy Stone and Julia Ward Howe, and the National Woman Suffrage Association, led by Elizabeth Cady Stanton and Susan B. Anthony. Some 20 years later, the two were reunited to form the National American Woman Suffrage Association.

2816. National political organization of farmers was the National Grange of the Patrons of Husbandry, organized in Washington, DC, on December 4, 1867, with William Saunders of the Department of Agriculture as master and Oliver Hudson Kelley as secretary. Its goal was to promote regulatory solutions to the problems of farmers in the depressed economy of the post-Civil War era. There were also numerous local granges which met to improve the cultural life of rural communities and to push for state reforms through their political wings, the Independent Parties. The granges were secret or semi-secret societies.

2817. National firearms lobby was the National Rifle Association of America, founded in 1871 by Union veterans Colonel William C. Church and General George Wingate. The goal of the association was to "promote and encourage rifle shooting on a scientific basis." The NRA was granted a charter by the state of New York on November 17, 1871, and elected as its first president General Ambrose Burnside, who was also the former governor of Rhode Island and a U.S. senator. The NRA formed a Legislative Affairs Division in 1934 to promote Second Amendment issues to its members but did not lobby Congress or state legislatures directly until 1975, when it established the Institute for Legislative Action. The first woman to head the NRA was Marion P. Hammer of Florida, elected in 1995. The NRA's headquarters are in Fairfax, VA.

2818. Development of the "Wisconsin Idea" of progressivism took place at the University of Wisconsin at Madison. Beginning in 1874, a number of influential social scientists, including John Bascom, Richard T. Ely, and Frederick Jackson Turner, taught a theory of government that envisioned an alliance of educational, business, and government institutions working together to improve conditions for everyone. Their students included a number of young political leaders, among them the future state governor and U.S. senator Robert M. La Follette and the future state supreme court justice Robert G. Siebecker.

2819. Proponent of the Single Tax principle was Henry George, a California journalist and self-taught economist who developed the idea that the source of all government revenue should be a tax on land, leaving labor and commerce free of any tax burden. He explained his theory in *Progress and Poverty,* published in January 1880. The book became a bestseller—during the years of its top popularity, it was outsold only by the Bible—and propelled George into an unsuccessful political career in which he was allied with the trade union movement.

2820. Single-tax proponent was the economic reformer Henry George of San Francisco, CA, who advocated the elimination of all government taxes except for the tax on land in order to free industry of restrictive tax burdens and equalize opportunities for individuals. His influential book, *Poverty and Progress,* was published in January 1880.

2821. Single Tax League national conference assembled on September 1, 1890, in New York City and adopted a platform on September 3. Five hundred delegates from 30 states formed a national organization, the Single Tax League of the United States, with a national committee composed of one member from each state and an executive committee of which William T. Croasdale was the chairman.

2822. Daughters of the American Revolution was founded on October 11, 1890, to promote patriotic endeavor, historic preservation, and education in American history and values. The organization, formally known as the National Society of the Daughters of the American Revolution, was incorporated by act of Congress on December 2, 1895. Its first president general was Caroline Scott Harrison, the wife of President Benjamin Harrison. Members were, and are, required to be direct descendants of someone who supported the American cause in the Revolutionary War. By 2000 the DAR had nearly 3,000 chapters in all 50 states, plus the District of Columbia (where its headquarters are located), Australia, Canada, France, Mexico, Great Britain, and Japan. The meeting of the group's Continental Congress takes place annually during the week of April 19, the anniversary of the Battle of Lexington.

2823. National environmental organization was the Sierra Club, co-founded by Scottish-born naturalist John Muir in California in 1892 to protect the mountain regions of the Pacific Coast. Muir served as president until 1914, steering the Sierra Club to become a politically active group with public education programs and lobbyists in the state legislature. By the end of the century it was the largest conservationist group in the United States, with a membership of more than 600,000. The organization campaigned successfully for the establishment of protected national parks and forests.

2824. Protest march on Washington was mounted in March 1894 by "Coxey's Army," a group of unemployed farmers and others led by a retired Army general named Jacob S. Coxey. The "commonwealers," as they called themselves, demanded that the goverment give work to the unemployed, reduce the workday, elimi-

POLITICAL MOVEMENTS AND ADVOCACY GROUPS—*continued*

nate child labor, and improve the highways. Most of "Coxey's Army" was arrested by police, and Coxey himself was jailed for trespass on the White House lawn. Later, he used "Keep Off the Grass" as a political slogan.

2825. National anti-imperialist organization was the Anti-Imperialist League, formed on November 19, 1898, to protest the American annexation of Cuba, Puerto Rico, Guam, and the Philippines in the wake of the Spanish-American War. The League grew out of an anti-imperialist committee of correspondence founded by Boston reformer Gamaliel Bradford in June 1898. Its first action was to circulate a petition in the Senate opposing the ratification of the Treaty of Paris, in which Spain agreed to surrender its Caribbean and Pacific colonies to the United States.

2826. National student socialist organization was the Intercollegiate Socialist Society, founded in 1905 by Upton Sinclair and Jack London, and later including Walter P. Reuther, Sidney Hook, and Walter Lippman. The ISS was reorganized as the Student League for Industrial Democracy after World War I.

2827. National civil liberties advocacy group was the National Civil Liberties Bureau, founded in New York City in 1917 by Norman Thomas and Roger Nash Baldwin, who became its first director. Baldwin, a Boston-born pacifist and reformer, was jailed the following year for refusing to be drafted. In 1920, he and Thomas joined with Jane Addams, Helen Keller, Morris Hillquit, Albert DiSiver, Walter Nelles, Clarence Darrow, Morris Ernst, Felix Frankfurter, and John Dewey to found the American Civil Liberties Union, with Baldwin serving as executive director from 1920 to 1950 and as national chairman from 1950 to 1955. The ACLU's mandate is to provide legal counsel and advocacy in cases involving constitutionally based civil liberties, in such areas as freedom of speech, right to privacy, and separation of church and state.

2828. Red scare took place immediately after World War I, as the Bolshevik government tightened its grip on Russia. In the United States, a national hunt for alleged Communist radicals was led in 1919 and 1920 by Alexander Mitchell Palmer, U.S. attorney general in the last years of the Wilson administration. The so-called Palmer Raids culminated in an order on January 2, 1920, for the roundup of suspected subversives in 30 cities across the country.

About 6,000 people were arrested, nearly half of whom were not formally charged with any crime. Nearly all were released by May 5, when the government ruled that membership in a communist or radical party was not in itself a crime.

2829. Bonus Army assembled in Washington, DC, beginning on May 29, 1932, in an effort to convince the federal government to address the grievances of American veterans of World War I who found themselves impoverished by the Great Depression. They wanted Congress to authorize the immediate payment, in cash, of an early pension-fund disbursement that had been authorized by Congress in 1924, but that was not scheduled to take effect until 1945. Tens of thousands of veterans and their families camped on the flats near the Anacostia River, waiting for an answer. On June 17 the bill they supported was defeated in the Senate. Some 2,000 angry men continued the protest after the rest had left the camp. At the request of the city government, whose police had tried in vain to evict them, President Herbert Clark Hoover ordered them removed by the Army, which routed them on July 28 with tanks, cavalry, and tear gas. Another Bonus Army gathered in Washington the following spring and received a welcome from the new First Lady, Eleanor Roosevelt. Payment of veterans' benefits was authorized by Congress in 1936.

2830. Organized civil rights protest by people with disabilities took place in New York City in 1935, when a group called the League for the Physically Handicapped, made up of 300 persons with polio, cerebral palsy, and other disabilities, occupied the offices of the Home Relief Bureau of New York City for nine days. LPH members had discovered that the Home Relief Bureau was stamping all their job requests with a special code that signalled the Works Progress Administration to deny them federal jobs.

2831. National advocacy organization for people with physical disabilities of all kinds was the American Federation of the Physically Handicapped, founded in Washington, DC, in 1940 by Paul A. Strachan, special assistant to the secretary of labor. The organization was chartered on August 20, 1942. It successfully lobbied Congress to encourage employment of people with disabilities (1945), to expand funding for rehabilitation services (1954), and to establish the Social Security Disability Insurance Program (1956).

2832. Political action committee (PAC) was the Congress of Industrial Organizations Political Action Committee, organized by CIO leader Sidney Hillman in 1944 to assist the reelection campaign of President Franklin Delano Roosevelt. The committee effectively marshalled the support of organized labor on behalf of the Democrats, paid for advertisements and publications about the labor movement, conducted a door-to-door voter registration drive, had a hand in the drafting of the party platform, and was influential in the choice of Harry S. Truman as the vice-presidential nominee at the Democratic National Convention, held in July 1944 in Chicago, IL.

2833. Ban-the-bomb demonstrations took place in Times Square, New York City, in July 1946, a few days after the United States conducted its first underground nuclear weapons test at Bikini, an atoll of the Marshall Islands in the central Pacific.

2834. National lobbying group for retirees was the American Association of Retired Persons (AARP), founded in 1957 by Ethel Andrus, who became its first president. Andrus had founded the National Retired Teachers Association in 1947.

2835. John Birch Society was founded on December 8–9, 1958, by Robert H. W. Welch, Jr., a retired candy manufacturer from Boston, MA. In a two-day lecture, Welch outlined the society's fiercely conservative and anti-communist beliefs, principles, and plan of action. The earliest *John Birch Society Bulletin,* which appeared in 1959, urged Congress to end all foreign aid, especially aid to communist countries, and attacked Cuba's Fidel Castro as a secret communist. (Castro had not yet openly declared his alliance with the Soviet Union.) Welch also led campaigns against the United Nations, the Communist Party USA, and left-wing media figures. The society was named after John Birch, an American intelligence officer killed by Chinese Communists on August 25, 1945.

2836. Shutdown of a college campus by student protesters took place at the University of California, Berkeley, in September 1964, when demonstrators belonging to the Free Speech Movement occupied the administration building, and then additional buildings, to protest a ban on campus political activities. After more than 800 demonstrators were arrested by order of Governor Edmund G. Brown, graduate students and faculty members began a general strike that shut down the university. The ban was rescinded.

2837. Common Cause was founded in 1970 by John W. Gardner, former U.S. secretary of health, education, and welfare, as "a nonprofit, nonpartisan citizen's lobbying organization promoting open, honest and accountable government." Common Cause's first major action took place in 1971, when it sued both the Democratic and the Republican national committees, alleging that the parties violated campaign fundraising and spending limits.

2838. Law allowing corporations to form political action committees was the Federal Election Campaign Act of 1971, which lifted prohibition against using corporate and trade association money to create political action committees, or PACs (private organizations established to support political candidates), thereby creating a new and extremely wealthy lobbying sector.

2839. Eagle Forum was organized in 1972 by lawyer and activist Phyllis Schlafly to press for conservative, pro-family public policies. It is headquartered in Alton, IL. The group was instrumental in organizing opposition to the Equal Rights Amendment to the Constitution, which was proposed to the states by Congress on March 22, 1972, but failed to attain a sufficient number of ratifications.

2840. National Right to Life Committee was founded in Detroit, MI, in June 1973, six months after the Supreme Court imposed a liberal abortion policy on the states in its ruling in *Roe v. Wade.* The organization was founded as a nonsectarian and nonpartisan effort to restore the protection of law to children before birth. It now has 3,000 chapters nationwide.

2841. Christian Coalition was founded in 1989 by a Southern Baptist minister, Pat Robertson, with the aim of giving politically conservative Christians an increased voice in government. In 2000 the Christian Coalition, which is headquartered in Chesapeake, VA, had more than 2 million members and supporters, maintained a permanent lobbying staff in Washington, DC, had affiliates in every state, and supported more than 2000 local chapters.

2842. International Conservative Congress was held in Washington, DC, in September 1997. It was attended by some 90 notable political conservatives from four continents who discussed the international aspects of conservatism. The event was sponsored by the American conservative magazine *National Review,* as well as several American institutions and foundations.

POLITICAL MOVEMENTS AND ADVO-CACY GROUPS—*continued*

2843. Internet march on Washington was the Billion Byte March, which took place on January 20, 1999. It was sponsored by Third Millennium and Economic Security 2000, two organizations concerned with rescuing the Social Security system. Participants sent the following e-mail message to the White House and Congress from the Web site of Economic Security 2000: "With 76 million Baby Boomers retiring, Social Security is in trouble. Save the safety net for all seniors, survivors and the disabled. Add individual accounts to open meaningful savings to all Americans. Fix Social Security this year." According to the organizers, tens of thousands of messages were sent.

POLITICAL MOVEMENTS AND ADVO-CACY GROUPS—AFRICAN-AMERICAN

2844. Black nationalist movement was organized by Paul Cuffe (also spelled Cuffee), a Quaker merchant and shipowner from Westport, CT, of African-American and Wampanoag Indian descent. From 1808, Cuffe encouraged free blacks to emigrate to Sierra Leone, on the West African coast. He sailed there in his brig *Traveler* in 1810 and began efforts to form a sugar-trading cooperative between the United States, England, and small West African nations. He also became the first African-American to sponsor an emigration effort, financing a colony of 38 former slaves with his own funds in 1815.

2845. National convention of African-Americans was held at the Bethel African Methodist Episcopal Church in Philadelphia, PA, on September 20–24, 1830. The organizer was the businessman and abolitionist James Forten. Bishop Richard Allen of Philadelphia presided. The formal title of the convention was "The American Society of Free Persons of Colour, for Improving their Condition in the United States; for Purchasing Lands; and for the Establishment of a Settlement in Upper Canada." The convention founded the Free Produce Society, whose members agreed to never to purchase goods produced by slave labor.

2846. National political organization for African-American women was the National Association of Colored Women, founded in 1896 in Washington, DC, by Mary Church Terrell, Ida B. Wells-Barnett, Margaret Murray Washington, Fanny Jackson Coppin, Frances Ellen Watkins Harper, Charlotte Forten Grimké, and Harriet Tubman. Its first president was

Terrell, a schoolteacher who was the daughter of former slaves. She was one of the first African-American women to earn a college degree (she received her bachelor's degree in 1884 and her master's degree in 1888, both from Oberlin College, Oberlin, OH) and the first to serve on the school board of Washington, DC, where her husband, Robert Terrell, was a judge.

2847. National Association for the Advancement of Colored People was founded in 1909, following a call issued in New York City on February 12, the centennial of Abraham Lincoln's birthday, to form an association that would aggressively promote social justice for African-Americans. Among the founders were the progressives Ida Wells Burnett and Henry Moscowitz and the Fabian Socialists Mary White Ovington, Oswald Garrison Villard, and William English Walling. The resulting organization was incorporated as the NAACP in 1911. Its first director of publications and research was W. E. B. Du Bois, founder of the earlier Niagara Movement, which provided a template for the activities and positions of the NAACP. Du Bois was also editor of the monthly magazine *Crisis: A Record of the Darker Races,* the NAACP's first regular publication.

2848. Summer of national race riots was the summer of 1919. Alabama, Arkansas, Florida, Georgia, Mississippi, and the cities of Washington, DC, and Chicago, IL, all saw riots, with the Chicago riot lasting 13 days and costing 36 lives. Many of the rioters were African-American soldiers back from World War I and protesting racism at home.

2849. Mass boycott by civil rights protesters took place in Montgomery, AL, over a period of 381 days in 1955–56, when the African-American residents of the city refused to ride the municipal buses. The boycott was organized to protest the arrest on December 1, 1955, of an African-American seamstress, Rosa Parks, for refusing to give up her seat to a white passenger, as required by law. The protest was led by a young minister, the Reverend Dr. Martin Luther King, Jr. Eventually the city agreed to treat all riders equally and to hire African-Americans as bus drivers.

2850. Civil rights sit-in occurred on February 1, 1960, when four African-American freshmen from the Agricultural and Technical College in Greensboro, NC—Joseph McNeil, Izell Blair, Franklin McCain, and David Richmond—sat down at the lunch counter of the Woolworth's in Charlotte, NC. They were protesting the store's policy of refusing to allow African-American customers to sit down. The students were denied service but sat at the counter until closing time. Within weeks, similar "sit-in" protests were held in other Southern cities.

2851. Black Power advocate was Stokely Carmichael, chairman of the Student Nonviolent Coordinating Committee (SNCC), based in Atlanta, GA. In June 1966, during the civil rights "March Against Fear" from Memphis, TN, to Jackson, MS, he issued a call urging African-Americans to reject integration as a goal of the civil rights movement and to adopt militant action instead of the pacifist methods of Martin Luther King, Jr.

2852. All-male march on Washington was the "Million Man March," convened by Louis Farrakhan, the controversial leader of the Nation of Islam. On October 16, 1995, several hundred thousand African-American men converged on Washington, DC, for a "day of atonement" and speechmaking, mostly by Farrakhan. No women or whites were allowed to attend.

POLITICAL MOVEMENTS AND ADVOCACY GROUPS—ALCOHOL

2853. Liquor reform movement was undertaken by the Dutch Reformed Church on Manhattan Island in 1623. It maintained a strong position against liquor, particularly with regard to excessive use.

2854. Temperance movement dates from 1789, when 200 farmers meeting at Litchfield, CT, agreed that they would refrain from drinking any distilled liquor while doing farm work. The first organized society to promote temperance was founded at Moreau, NY, in 1808.

2855. Temperance address by a future president was Abraham Lincoln's temperance address of February 22, 1842, before the Washington Temperance Society in Springfield, IL. The address, executed in the florid oratorical style of the time, began: "Although the temperance cause has been in progress for near twenty years, it is apparent to all that it is just now being crowned with a degree of success hitherto unparalleled. The list of its friends is daily swelled by the additions of fifties, of hundreds, and of thousands. The cause itself seems suddenly transformed from a cold abstract theory to a living, breathing, active, and powerful chieftain, going forth 'conquering and to conquer.' The citadels of his great adversary are daily being stormed and dismantled; his temple and his altars, where the rites of his idolatrous worship have long been performed, and where human sacrifices have long been wont to be

made, are daily desecrated and deserted. The triumph of the conqueror's fame is sounding from hill to hill, from sea to sea, and from land to land, and calling millions to his standard at a blast."

2856. State temperance society of women was the New York Women's State Temperance Society, founded on April 20, 1852, at a convention held in Rochester, NY, principally through the efforts of Susan B. Anthony. Approximately 500 women attended.

2857. National temperance society of women was the National Woman's Christian Temperance Union, organized in the Second Presbyterian Church, Cleveland, OH, on November 18–20, 1874. The first president was Mrs. Annie T. Wittenmyer of Philadelphia, PA. The World Woman's Christian Temperance Union, an outgrowth of the national group, was organized at a convention held from October 31 to November 3, 1883, in Detroit, MI.

2858. National anti-saloon league was the Anti-Saloon League of America, formed December 17–18, 1895, at the Calvary Baptist Sunday School, Washington, DC, by a coalition of the Anti-Saloon League of the District of Columbia, the Anti-Saloon League of Ohio, and 45 other local temperance organizations. The first president was Hiram Price.

POLITICAL MOVEMENTS AND ADVOCACY GROUPS—ANTIWAR

2859. Demonstration in Washington against the Vietnam War took place in April 1965, when 20,000 protesters organized by the radical group Students for a Democratic Society picketed the White House and marched from the Washington Monument to the steps of the Capitol building. The first campus teach-in was also held that month, at the University of Michigan at Ann Arbor.

2860. Roman Catholic clergyman sentenced to jail in the United States for political crimes was Philip Berrigan, a former priest and political protester who served a total of three years and two months in prison for destroying Selective Service records. He led raids on draft-board offices in Baltimore, MD, on October 27, 1967, and in the Baltimore suburb of Catonsville on May 17, 1968, both in protest of American military involvement in Vietnam. As one of the celebrated "Catonsville Nine," he was tried in United States District Court in Baltimore and found guilty of conspiracy and destruction of government property. The sentence—three and a half years—was handed down on November 8, 1968, and was to be

POLITICAL MOVEMENTS AND ADVOCACY GROUPS—ANTIWAR—*continued*

served concurrently with a six-year sentence for the 1967 raid in Baltimore. After the trial, Berrigan went underground, but he was apprehended by FBI agents in a New York City church on April 21, 1970. He served his time in the Federal Penitentiary in Lewisburg, PA.

2861. Vietnam War Moratorium Day demonstration took place on October 15, 1969. Millions of antiwar protesters wearing black armbands marched in major cities across the country. The largest protest was in Washington, DC, where 250,000 demonstrators gathered and were led in a candlelight march past the White House by Coretta Scott King, the widow of Martin Luther King, Jr.

2862. Nationwide campus rioting occurred on May 6, 1970, in response to the shootings at Kent State University in Ohio on May 4, when four students were killed by National Guardsmen. Rioting students forced more than 100 colleges across the country to shut down, some for several days.

2863. Mass return of military decorations by war veterans took place on April 23, 1971, during an antiwar protest on the Capitol steps in Washington, DC, when about 100 veterans of the Vietnam War returned their medals to the government.

POLITICAL MOVEMENTS AND ADVOCACY GROUPS—CHICANO

2864. Chicano civil rights organization was the Orden Hijos de América (Order of the Sons of America), founded in San Antonio, TX, in 1921.

2865. Statewide Chicano civil rights organization was the League of United Latin American Citizens, established in 1929 in Corpus Christi, TX. LULAC focused mainly on residential and school desegregation cases.

2866. Chicano radical nationalist movement was the Alianza Federal de Mercedes (Federal Alliance of Land Grants), founded in New Mexico in 1963 by Reies López Tijerina, a charismatic Texas preacher and land-grant activist. This organization was dedicated to reclaiming historic lands granted to Mexican Americans under the 1848 Treaty of Guadalupe Hidalgo. On October 15, 1966, Tijerina and a group of 350 supporters attempted to establish a Chicano state they called Pueblo de San Joaquin de Chama in part of Kit Carson National Forest, NM. On June 5, 1967, Tijerina led an armed raid on New Mexico's Tierra Amarilla County Courthouse to arrest District Attorney Alfonso Sanchez, whom he held responsible for withholding the lands. Two court officials were wounded, and Tijerina briefly went underground. In 1968, Tijerina ran for governor of New Mexico on the People's Constitutional Party ticket.

2867. National Chicano civil rights organization was the Mexican American Legal Defense and Educational Fund, incorporated in San Antonio, TX, in 1967. MALDEF was formed to protext the civil rights of Mexican-Americans through community education and class action litigation.

POLITICAL MOVEMENTS AND ADVOCACY GROUPS—HOMOSEXUAL

2868. Homosexual rights demonstration in the United States took place on September 19, 1963, at the Whitehall Induction Center in New York City, where gay men mounted a protest against discrimination in the U.S. military.

2869. Radical homosexual organization was the Gay Liberation Front, formed in New York City in 1969. The GLF sought to make common cause with liberationist coalitions of women, African-Americans, Hispanics, and student radicals.

2870. Homosexual rights protest took place on June 27, 1969, outside the Stonewall Inn in New York City's Greenwich Village neighborhood. Gay patrons and local residents rioted after a raid on the bar by Manhattan police.

2871. Gay pride march took place on June 28, 1970, in New York City, in commemoration of the anniversary of the Stonewall Rebellion (the riot in lower Manhattan that marked the beginning of the gay liberation movement in the United States). The march started in Greenwich Village and ended in Central Park. About 2,000 people participated. Gay pride marches were also held in three other cities, including Los Angeles, CA, where 1,200 took part.

2872. National homosexual rights organization was the National Gay Task Force (later called the National Gay and Lesbian Task Force), formed in New York City in 1973 with the goal of bringing "gay liberation into the mainstream of American civil rights."

2873. Homosexual rights protest of large scale took place in Washington, DC, on April 25, 1993. The march and rally drew an estimated 300,000 to 1 million demonstrators demanding a federal gay rights bill and more federal money to fight AIDS.

POLITICAL MOVEMENTS AND ADVOCACY GROUPS—LABOR

2874. Labor organization in a colony was an association of the "shoomakers of Boston," which was given official recognition by the General Court of the Massachusetts Bay Colony on October 18, 1648.

2875. Strike of African-American laborers took place in Charleston, SC, in October 1763, when a group of chimney sweeps demanded higher wages.

2876. Strike benefit by a union was authorized on May 31, 1786, at the home of Henry Myers, Philadelphia, PA, when 26 members of the Typographical Society met to plan a protest against a reduction in wages. They agreed "that we will support such of our brethren as shall be thrown out of employment on account of their refusing to work for less than $6 per week." They won their demands.

2877. Strike in which women participated took place in the textile mills in Pawtucket, RI, in 1824, when 202 female weavers went on strike along with the male workers. Their pay had been cut and their workday extended at the same time. The first all-woman strike took place circa 1825 in New York City, when the United Tailoresses struck in the hope of winning a wage increase. The first all-woman strike by operatives in textile mills took place at the Dover Manufacturing Company, Dover, NH, in 1828, when some 400 women went on strike, unsuccessfully, to protest a wage cut, a ban on talking, and compulsory attendance at church.

2878. Woman to become a union organizer is believed to have been Sarah George Bagley, a textile mill worker at the Hamilton Company in Lowell, MA, who became active in the movement for a ten-hour day circa 1840. In 1844 she became the cofounder and first president of the Female Labor Reform Association, the country's first women's union to operate on a regional basis, with chapters throughout New England. She became the editor of the weekly newspaper *Voice of Industry* in 1845. The following year she became the first woman to qualify as a telegraph operator.

2879. National labor congress was the First Industrial Congress of the United States, which convened in New York City on October 12, 1845. William E. Wait of Illinois was elected president. Annual meetings were held regularly until 1856.

2880. National labor organization was the National Labor Union, founded in Baltimore, MD, on August 20, 1866, by 77 delegates from 13 states, most of them representatives of local trade unions. Its initial goal was to press for an eight-hour working day, an idea that had first been proposed in 1860. It was also an early supporter of paper currency, or "greenbacks." The Labor Reform Party was an outgrowth of the NLU.

2881. National labor organization for African-American workers was the National Labor Union, Colored (known as the CNLU), which was founded circa 1868 by African-American trade union delegates who had been refused admittance to a convention of the original National Labor Union. The first president was Isaac Meyers of Baltimore, MD, who was followed in 1871 by Frederick Douglass.

2882. National labor organization of importance was the American Federation of Labor, which was organized in Pittsburgh, PA, in 1881 as the Federation of Organized Trades and Labor Unions. It adopted the new title on December 8, 1886, in Columbus, OH, at a meeting attended by 25 officers of national craft unions representing over 300,000 members. Samuel Gompers, head of the Cigarmakers Union, led the AFL from its founding until 1924. The first woman to serve as a delegate to a national AFL convention was Mary Burke, who represented the Retail Clerks' Union of Findlay, OH, at the convention held in Detroit, MI, December 8–13, 1890.

2883. Bellamy Nationalist Club was founded in Boston, MA, in 1888 to promote the ideas of social reform expressed by Edward Bellamy in his bestselling novel *Looking Backward,* published earlier that year. The novel described a utopian communist society completely free of inequality, one in which the government runs all industries, as well as all social services, and in which all individuals, in exchange for their labor, receive an equal share of the national product. The movement became allied with the Populist Party in 1891, but died out within a few years.

2884. National labor organization to establish a women's division was the Knights of Labor, which created a Department of Women's Work at its national convention in 1888. The department's first general investigator was Leonora Barry of New York, who produced the first compilation of statistics on working women nationwide. The Knights of Labor had admitted

POLITICAL MOVEMENTS AND ADVOCACY GROUPS—LABOR—*continued*

their first woman member, Elizabeth Flynn Rodgers, in 1847. Rodgers, the mother of twelve children, was a housewife, an occupation that received formal recognition by the organization.

2885. Industrial Workers of the World (Wobblies) convention was held in Chicago, IL, in June 1905. The labor activist William Dudley "Big Bill" Haywood of the Western Federation of Miners was chairman; among the attendees were Mother Jones, the socialist Eugene V. Debs, Father Thomas J. Hagerty, Lucy Parsons, and Daniel De Leon of the Socialist Labor Party. Under Haywood's leadership, the Wobblies, as they were known, developed into a revolutionary labor organization. By 1925, federal and local prosecution of IWW officials had left the organization with little political clout, and membership declined. Haywood skipped bail and fled to the Soviet Union in 1928, where he lived the remainder of his life as a minor Communist Party functionary.

2886. Massacre of strikebreakers by union members began on June 21, 1922, at the Southern Illinois Coal Company's strip mine near Herrin, IL. During a nationwide strike by the United Mine Workers, a group of recruited strikebreakers arrived at the mine. Fighting broke out, and one striker and two strikebreakers were killed. The mine was quickly surrounded by armed UMW members. On June 22, approximately 60 strikebreakers inside the mine surrendered to union members, who marched them to a barbed wire fence and gunned them down. A few who managed to escape were hunted down and slain in a nearby cemetery. Twenty-one strikebreakers and one mine official were killed, and most of the rest were severely wounded.

2887. African-American labor union of importance was the Brotherhood of Sleeping Car Porters, organized in 1925 by employees of the Pullman Company, operator of railway sleeping cars. At the time, more African-Americans worked for the Pullman Company than for any other single employer. In 1935, after a long legal struggle, the union was recognized by the company and entered into collective bargaining, resulting two years later in a contract that raised wages for the porters and reduced their work schedule from 400 to 240 hours a month. The founder and leader of the union was Asa Philip Randolph, editor of the radical socialist newspaper *The Messenger* in New York, NY, who went on to become the first African-American vice president of the AFL-CIO and a leader in the effort to end racial discrimination in the armed forces and the defense industry.

2888. Chicano labor convention was El Congreso del Pueblo de Habla Española (Spanish-Speaking Peoples Congress), held on December 4, 1938, in Los Angeles, CA. Organized by Luisa Moreno and Josefina Fierro de Bright, the congress brought together Chicano labor and left-wing political figures to promote a unified Mexican-American labor movement.

2889. Strike to last longer than a year started on December 26, 1945, when Local 180 of the United Automobile Workers of America struck the J.I. Case Manufacturing Company, Racine, WI, a manufacturer of farm implements. On March 9, 1947, the workers voted 927–448 in favor of accepting the company offer of an increase in wages from 25 cents to 26 cents an hour.

2890. National Chicano labor organization was the Asociación Nacional México-Americana, founded in 1949 in Phoenix, AZ. The first president was Alfred Montoya. The ANMA, a left-wing organization focused on supporting Chicano labor struggles, was targeted by the FBI in 1952 under the Internal Security Act of 1950, and Montoya was investigated by the House Un-American Activities Committee and the Senate Subversive Activities board.

2891. Nationwide consumer boycott in support of workers was the grape boycott begun in September 1965 by César Estrada Chávez and the National Farm Workers Association. The principle targets were Schenley Industries, the Di Giorgio Corporation, S & W Fine Foods, and TreeSweet, all California growers accused by the NFWA of maltreating and underpaying migrant grape pickers. The five-year-long strike and boycott was the first product boycott to attract support from liberals nationwide. Chávez founded the NFWA in Delano, CA, in 1962. In 1966, it merged with an AFL-CIO group, and in 1971 became the United Farm Workers of America.

POLITICAL MOVEMENTS AND ADVOCACY GROUPS—WOMEN

2892. Woman to appeal for the right to vote was Margaret Brent, a niece of Lord Baltimore, the founder of the colony of Maryland. She came to America from England in January 1638 and was the first woman in Maryland to own property in her own name. She became one of the colony's principal landowners and a person of influence, raising a troop of soldiers in 1644. After the death of Governor Leonard Calvert in 1646, she became his executor, as well as attorney for the absent Lord Baltimore, in which capacity she averted a fiscal crisis that nearly destroyed the colony. On June 24, 1647, she appealed for the right to vote in the colonial assembly, asking for a "place and voyce," but was refused because "it would set a bad example to the wives of the colony." She moved to Virginia in 1650.

2893. Book advocating voting rights for women was a reprint of *A Vindication of the Rights of Women, with Strictures on Political and Moral Subjects,* by Mary Wollstonecraft Godwin, 276 pages, printed in 1792 in Philadelphia, PA, by William Gibbons. Another edition, of 340 pages, was published in Boston, MA, by Peter Edes with a slight subtitle variation. The book was originally published in England in 1790.

2894. Women's rights convention was held in the Wesleyan Chapel, Seneca Falls, NY, on July 19–20, 1848. The convention, attended by about 100 women and men, was assembled through the initiative of the reformers Lucretia Mott, Elizabeth Cady Stanton, Martha C. Wright, and Mary McClintock. A Declaration of Sentiments was adopted, calling for women to be granted voting rights, property rights, and familial rights. The document opened with a paraphrase of the Declaration of Independence, stating "We hold these truths to be self-evident: that all men and women are created equal," and continued: "The history of mankind is a history of repeated injuries and usurpations on the part of man toward woman, having in direct object the establishment of an absolute tyranny over her. . . . Now in view of this entire disfranchisement of one-half the people of this country, their social and religious degradation—in view of the unjust laws above mentioned, and because women do feel themselves aggrieved, oppressed and fraudulently deprived of their most sacred rights, we insist that they have immediate admission to all the rights and privileges which belong to them as citizens of the United States."

2895. National convention for women's rights was the National Woman's Rights Convention, held at Brinley Hall in Worcester, MA, on October 23–24, 1850, "to consider the question of woman's rights, duties and relations." The organizers were Lucy Stone and Lucretia Mott. The convention continued to meet annually until 1860.

2896. Periodical of the women's rights movement was the *Una,* published by Paulina Kellogg Wright Davis in Providence, RI, from February 1853 through 1855. Davis was an early feminist and one of the founders, in 1868, of the New England Woman Suffrage Association.

2897. National anti-women's suffrage organization of importance was the National Association Opposed to Woman Suffrage, organized in 1911 by Mrs. Arthur Dodge and other wealthy women, along with some Catholic clergymen. The NAOWS worked to prevent the passage by Congress of the 19th Amendment.

2898. League of Women Voters was founded in 1920 by suffragist Carrie Chapman Catt during a convention of the National American Woman Suffrage Association, the New York–based women's rights organization founded by Elizabeth Cady Stanton and Susan B. Anthony in 1869. The League of Women Voters is a nonpartisan political organization created to encourage the informed and active participation of citizens in government. The League's first president was Maud Wood Park.

2899. National Organization for Women was founded on June 30, 1966, in Washington, DC, by 28 women attending the Third National Conference of the Commission on the Status of Women. NOW's official priorities are securing economic and legal equality for women and homosexuals and promoting legal abortion, women's health issues, and an end to violence against women. The organization's first president was Betty Friedan, author of the influential feminist tract *The Feminine Mystique* (1963).

2900. National Women's Political Caucus was founded on July 10, 1971, to promote political participation among women, including running for office.

POLITICAL PARTIES

2901. Local political machine was organized in Boston, MA, where caucus clubs held secret meetings as early as 1763 (the year when the activities of one such club were described by John Adams in his diary). The members—usually propertied men and merchants—gathered before elections to identify the candidates most likely to benefit their interests and encouraged the intended outcome by exerting influence over other voters and distributing ballots selectively. Similar groups were active in other New England and Middle Atlantic towns.

POLITICAL PARTIES—*continued*

2902. Tammany political club was the Sons of King Tammany, founded in Philadelphia, PA, on May 1, 1772, to replace the city's original revolutionary organization, the Sons of Liberty. The adoption of the 17th-century Delaware chief Tammany as the group's figurehead was intended to unite, under a strictly American symbol, Philadelphians from various parts of the British Isles. The group changed its name the following year to the Sons of Saint Tammany. Chapters were formed in other states, all of them celebrating May 1 as St. Tammany's Day. The New York City chapter, founded in 1787, eventually grew into the infamously corrupt Tammany Hall, the city's Democratic Party machine.

2903. Political parties originated during the national public debate over the adoption of the Constitution, after that document, drafted in Philadelphia during the summer of 1787, was presented to the states for ratification. The idea of a strong central government to oversee fiscal policy and foreign relations appealed to the country's merchants and exporters but not to its farmers and frontiersmen, who viewed it as a threat to local autonomy. These groups coalesced, respectively, into the Federalists and the Anti-Federalists—not political parties in the formal sense, but alliances of people united by common concerns. After the ratification of the Constitution in 1788 and the launching of the federal government, the Federalists began to function as a quasi-party in Congress, while the Anti-Federalists reinvented themselves as the Democratic-Republicans and developed the nation's first real party organization.

2904. Federalist Party consisted of believers in a federal government more powerful than its constituent states and a national economic policy that favored commercial interests. Among their number were most of the men who led the federal government during its formative years, including George Washington and John Adams, who were responsible for the first three presidential administrations (1789–1801); Andrew Hamilton, Washington's secretary of the treasury; John Jay, the first chief justice of the Supreme Court; and John Marshall, its chief justice from 1801 to 1835. As suffrage was extended, bringing more farmers, laborers, and artisans into the political process, the Federalists lost their influence and in 1816 became extinct. A major factor in their downfall was popular resistance to their tax policy.

2905. Coalition between Northern and Southern politicians was achieved by Thomas Jefferson, who along with his fellow Virginian, James Madison, made alliance with George Clinton, the governor of New York, in forming the Democratic-Republican party in 1792.

2906. Democratic-Republican Party existed in 1792 as a faction within Congress whose adherents sought to check the power of the federal government, preserve the sovereign identities of the states, and emphasize agricultural over commercial interests. It was viewed by its supporters as a democratizing force, opposed to the aristocratic methods of the Federalists, and by its critics as a promoter of mob rule. The Democratic-Republicans developed a formal party structure during George Washington's second presidential term and succeeded in 1800 in electing Thomas Jefferson to the White House and winning majorities in both houses of Congress—the beginning of their 24-year reign in Washington, which ended when they separated into irreconcilable factions. In their day they called themselves Republicans, the word "democrat" then being something of an insult; the term "Democratic-Republicans" is a modern usage coined by historians to distinguish them from the modern Republican Party.

2907. Presidential warning against party politics was sounded by George Washington in his Farewell Address, never delivered in person but published in Philadelphia's *American Daily Advertiser* on September 19, 1796. He wrote: "Let me . . . warn you in the most solemn manner against the baneful effects of the spirit of party generally. This spirit, unfortunately, is inseparable from our nature, having its root in the strongest passions of the human mind. . . . It serves always to distract the public councils and enfeeble the public administration. It agitates the community with ill-founded jealousies and false alarms; kindles the animosity of one part against another; foments occasionally riot and insurrection. It opens the door to foreign influence and corruption, which find a facilitated access to the government itself through channels of party passion."

2908. Party to continue in power in the White House for more than 20 years was the Democratic-Republican party, which entered the White House on November 4, 1800, with the election of Thomas Jefferson and remained in power for 28 years, through the administrations of James Madison, James Monroe, and John Quincy Adams. The next run of more than 20 years was made by the Republicans, beginning in 1860 with the election of Abraham Lincoln and continuing for 24 years through the administrations of Andrew Johnson, Ulysses Simpson Grant, Rutherford Birchard Hayes, James Abram Garfield, and Chester Alan Arthur, until the election of a Democrat, Grover Cleveland, in 1884.

2909. Quids political faction was organized during the administration of President Thomas Jefferson. Its members took an extreme position in favor of states' rights and were opposed to Jefferson's attempts to acquire West Florida. They were led from 1804 to 1808 by John Randolph of Roanoke, VA. In 1808 they ran James Monroe as a presidential candidate against James Madison. The name is derived from the Latin *tertium quid* ("a third thing"), indicating separation from both existing political parties, or from both administration and opposition forces.

2910. Era of one-party rule lasted from 1816, when the Federalist Party expired, to 1828, when the reigning Democratic-Republican Party splintered into factions. By 1832 one of these factions had evolved into the Democratic Party, the other into the National Republicans, precursors of the Whigs.

2911. State political machine that was well organized was the Albany Regency, made up of a group of Democrats who, from 1820 to 1854, exercised a controlling influence over the politics of New York State. Their headquarters were in Albany, NY, but their power extended into national politics. Prominent among them were Martin Van Buren, William Learned Marcy, Silas Wright, and John Adams Dix. The group was supported by a partisan newspaper, the *Argus*.

2912. Anti-Masonic Party was formed in 1827 in western New York as a populist organization of farmers and laborers who were suspicious of the Masons and their influence on politics. Many Anti-Masons were also prominent in the early antislavery and temperance movements. They held the country's first national nominating convention in Baltimore, MD, in September 1831, and won two statehouses and 53 seats in the House of Representatives in the election of 1832. Most of their members affiliated with the new Whig Party after 1836.

2913. Independent labor party was the Workingmen's Party, branches of which were organized in New York City and Philadelphia, PA, in 1828. They were founded and controlled chiefly by supporters of the socialist utopian reformer Robert Owen. The party held its first convention on August 25, 1828, but dissolved within a few years.

2914. Democratic Party originated in the 1820s as a faction of the Democratic-Republicans, the party that had held power continuously since 1800. This faction was led by Andrew Jackson, a self-made man who had been born into poverty in backwoods South Carolina and had risen to become a popular war hero and the symbol of energetic, anti-elitist democracy. By 1832 the Democratic-Republicans had splintered apart and the Jacksonian group had emerged as the Democratic Party, holding their first national convention that year to nominate Jackson for his second presidential term. Except for brief periods when the Whig Party held power, the Democrats continued to control the federal government until the emergence of the Republican Party during the crisis that led to the civil war.

2915. Symbol of the Democratic Party was the donkey, which appeared soon after the party emerged under Andrew Jackson in 1832. The symbol has varied from time to time, however, appearing sometimes as a rooster (especially in the South), a fox (in cartoons by Thomas Nast), and an eagle.

2916. Whig Party took shape in 1834 as a party of opposition to President Andrew Jackson. The coalition included businessmen from the National Republican party who were angry over Jackson's fiscal policies, Southerners angry at his denial of the principle of nullification, and members of the Anti-Masonic Party angry over his autocratic ways. The name "Whig" was adopted from the 18th-century Whigs of Britain, who sought to limit the authority of the monarch. The Whigs ran their first presidential campaign in 1836, won the presidency in 1844 and 1848, and split apart in 1856 over the slavery issue.

2917. Use of the term "Loco-Focos" to describe the radical anti-monopoly faction of the Democratic Party took place on October 29, 1835, when the Democrats of New York City held a primary meeting at the party's headquarters, Tammany Hall, to choose a congressional candidate. The mainstream Democrats nominated their man and shut off the gaslights to prevent further action by the insurgents, who relit the lamps using "loco-focos"—self-igniting friction matches, a recent invention. Early the following year, evolving into the Equal Rights Party, they announced a platform opposing paper money, chartered banks, and monopolies supported by legislation, stating their Jeffersonian view "that the true foundation of republican government is the equal rights of every citizen in his person and property and in their management."

POLITICAL PARTIES—*continued*

2918. Single-issue political party on the national level was the Liberty Party, also known as the Abolition Party, founded in 1839. Local antislavery societies, some of which sponsored candidates for local office, were already functioning in Massachusetts, Pennsylvania, New York, New Jersey, New Hampshire, Ohio, and Michigan. The unwillingness of the major congressional parties—the Democrats and Whigs—to take action on the issue of slavery, and the imposition in 1836 of the gag rule in the House of Representatives (which excluded all petitions on the subject), prompted members of the American Antislavery Society to organize a political party of their own. After an unsuccessful attempt in July 1839, they gathered 500 delegates on November 13, 1839, at Warsaw, NY, and formed the Liberty Party, with James Gillespie Birney as their candidate for president. Although the party fared poorly in the presidential elections of 1840 and 1844, it was, for a short time, a major player in Massachusetts politics.

2919. Use of the terms "Hunkers" and "Barnburners" originated in 1843 in New York State, where the Democratic Party split into two factions. The militants, who were adamantly opposed to the extension of slavery into United States territories and the annexation of Texas as a slave state, compared to the Dutch farmer of legend who got rid of the rats in his barn by burning it down. Their opponents were mocked as "hunkers," whose hankering for power and public office led them to compromise their principles. The Barnburners quit the party in 1848 to join the Free Soil Party and eventually wound up with the newly minted Republicans.

2920. Third party with an appeal broader than a single issue was the Free Soil Party, formed in 1848. It had a diverse membership, taking in people from the antislavery factions of the two main parties, the Democrats and the Whigs, as well as former members of the Liberty Party, an exclusively abolitionist party that had fared badly at the polls. The chief goal of the Free Soilers was a ban on the extension of slavery, but its leaders, seeking to attract a wider range of voters, expanded the party's platform to include free homesteading, low-cost postage, tariff reform, a reduction in federal spending, and internal improvement. The party's presidential candidate in 1848 was former president Martin Van Buren, who took fewer than 300,000 votes, most of them from New England and New York. The party disappeared in 1852, after most of its members had been absorbed back into the major parties.

2921. Know-Nothing Party originated in 1854 as an anti-immigrant movement made up of secret clubs. Members were required to be American-born and wholly unconnected with the Roman Catholic Church, and those who ran for office were obligated to vote in accordance with the instructions of the society. In the two years before the movement declared itself to be a political party, it succeeded in electing five senators, 43 congressmen, and the governors of seven states (California, Connecticut, Delaware, Kentucky, Massachusetts, New Hampshire, and Rhode Island). It ran a presidential campaign in 1856, finishing third with 21.5 percent of the popular vote, but its adherents were divided on the issue of slavery, and the party fell apart soon afterwards. Its formal name was the American Party.

2922. Founding of the Republican Party took place at Ripon, WI, on February 28, 1854. The participants included former members of the Whig, Democratic, and Free Soil parties who were outraged by the possibility that Congress might pass the Kansas–Nebraska Act, repealing the Missouri Compromise and allowing territories to enter the Union as slave states. The act was passed on May 30. On July 6 Michigan residents opposed to slavery met at Jackson, MI, and formed a new state party, to be known as the Republican Party. State Republican organizations were formed in Ohio, Wisconsin, Indiana, and Vermont soon thereafter, and in all the states of the North by the year's end, by which time they had succeeded in electing to Congress eleven senators and many more representatives.

2923. Symbol of the Republican Party was a raccoon, which appeared often on Republican campaign paraphernalia from 1854, the year of the party's founding, to as late as 1884, in the unsuccessful presidential campaign of James Gillespie Blaine. The raccoon appeared on Whig campaign material as early as 1844, to support Henry Clay's bid for the presidency, and was adopted along with other aspects of Whig symbology as the party's antislavery wing evolved into the Republican Party. Typically, the animal was depicted as thumbing its nose at the candidate's opponents. The use of the elephant to symbolize the GOP originated with the political cartoonist Thomas Nast in 1874. The Republican National Committee held a contest in 1966 to find a name for its elephant and chose "Republic Ann."

2924. Constitutional Union Party was formed in 1859 by former Know-Nothings and Whigs who hoped to find a way to reconcile the regional differences that were leading the country toward civil war. Their presidential candidate in the 1860 election received about half a million votes and finished fourth in a field of four. The onset of the Civil War put an end to the party.

2925. Southern Democratic Party was put together in Richmond, VA, in June 1860 by southerners who had seceded from the Democratic party in search of a stronger proslavery platform. They met in convention on June 28, 1860, at Market Hall in Baltimore, MD. A similar group, which called itself the National (or Independent) Democratic Party, had met at Maryland Institute Hall in Baltimore five days earlier. Both groups nominated John Cabell Breckinridge of Kentucky. Breckinridge and the mainstream Democratic candidate, Stephen A. Douglas, split the Democratic vote on election day, resulting in the election of the Republican candidate, Abraham Lincoln.

2926. Labor Reform Party was the National Labor Union, founded in Baltimore, MD, on August 20, 1866, by 77 delegates from 13 states, most of them representatives of local trade unions. Its initial goal was to press for an eight-hour working day, an idea that had first been proposed in 1860. It was also an early supporter of paper currency, or "greenbacks." The Labor Reform Party, organized in 1872, was an outgrowth of the NLU.

2927. Prohibition Party had its roots in state temperance parties that appeared in Maine, New York, and Pennsylvania in the 1850s. Many of their members were also active in the abolition movement and were freed to concentrate on the alcohol issue after the Civil War. In September 1869 some 500 delegates from 19 states met in Chicago, IL, and organized the Prohibition Party, which ran its first presidential campaign in 1872, collecting 5,608 votes, and its strongest presidential campaign in 1872, when it won 271,000 votes. The organ of the party was *The Voice,* a magazine published in Chicago, the first issue of which appeared on September 25, 1884. The Prohibition Party survived the repeal of the 18th Amendment to the Constitution and is now the nation's oldest extant third party. In the elections of 1984, 1988, 1992, 1996, and 2000, it ran Earl F. Dodge of Colorado as its presidential candidate.

2928. Liberal Republican Party originated in St. Louis, MO, as a movement to restore the vote to former Confederate sympathizers. In 1870 the group succeeded in electing its leader, Benjamin Gratz Brown, to the statehouse. By 1872 it had built a national following with its call for a general amnesty, reform of the corrupt civil service, and a revenue tariff. Withdrawing from the mainstream Republican Party after its renomination of incumbent president Ulysses Simpson Grant, these dissidents convened in May in Cincinnati, OH, and nominated their own candidate, New York newspaper publisher Horace Greeley, who subsequently won the endorsement of the Democrats. Grant won the election and the party disappeared.

2929. National labor party was the Labor Reform Party, which was organized by members the National Labor Union. The first state candidates were fielded in 1870 in New Hampshire and Massachusetts, where the Labor Reformers and Prohibitionists ran Wendell Phillips for governor. The party held its first national convention at Columbus, OH, on February 22, 1872.

2930. Anti-Monopoly Party originated in 1873 in Illinois, where farmers disturbed by the high rates charged by the railroads successfully petitioned the state legislature to regulate them. They then organized to elect farmer-friendly candidates to district judgeships and county offices, and the following year ran a campaign for state offices. Similar groups were formed in other midwestern and western states, sometimes under different names (Reform, Independent Reform, People's). By 1884 the party had become a nationwide organization.

2931. Socialist Labor Party was founded in New York City on July 4, 1874, by members of the Socialist International. The party's name, originally the Social Democratic Workmen's Party of North America, was changed in December 1877. Its first leader was Daniel De Leon, a former Columbia University law professor whose belief in the necessity of a socialist revolution and contempt for the American labor movement kept the party out of politics for decades. The SLP ran its first presidential campaign in 1892. It fielded presidential nominees in every election thereafter until 1976, then concentrated on fielding local candidates in its home region of New York and New Jersey.

POLITICAL PARTIES—*continued*

2932. Use of the term "mugwump" took place in 1884, when Charles Dana, editor of the *New York Sun,* applied it to Republicans who disliked James G. Blaine, the Republican presidential candidate, and switched sides in the election to vote for the Democrat, Grover Cleveland. Prominent Republican bolters of 1884 included the journalists E. L. Godkin and George William Curtis and the reformer and politician Carl Schurz. The word was derived from *mugwomp,* the Natick Indian word for captain. Harold Willis Dodds, president of Princeton University, defined a mugwump as "a fellow with his mug on one side of the fence and his wump on the other."

2933. Farmers' Alliance Party held its first convention at St. Louis, MO, in December 1889, when, it voted to confederate with the Knights of Labor and to exchange friendly greetings with the Greenback Party and the Single Tax Party. A meeting of this confederation took place at Ocala, FL, in December 1890, but no candidates were chosen. The party's main concern was to protect farmers and to advocate reform of the national monetary system, including the free coinage of silver.

2934. Populist Party was founded (as the People's Party) in May 1891 in Cincinnati, OH, by members of western and midwestern farm cooperative associations, many of whom had belonged to the Greenback Party. Their main concern was to alleviate the plight of the nation's farmers by expanding the currency supply through the free coinage of silver and nationalizing the railroads. In the 1892 elections the Populists gained more than 1 million votes in their first presidential campaign, coming in third. By 1895 they had succeeded in electing six candidates to the Senate and seven to the House of Representatives. The Democrats took over the issue of free silver the following year and the Populists went out of business in 1908.

2935. Sound Money Democratic Party (also known as the National Democratic Party) was founded in 1896 by conservatives who had bolted from the Democratic Party when it decided to champion free coinage of silver. Meeting at Indianapolis, IN, on September 2–3, 1896, they adopted a platform favoring the gold standard and nominated their own candidates, who received the support of former Democratic president Grover Cleveland. The currency issue was eclipsed by other developments after the election and the party was reabsorbed by the Democrats.

2936. Social Democracy of America Party was formed by the Brotherhood of the Cooperative Commonwealth, organized by Julius Augustus Wayland and members of the American Railway Union. Its first national convention was held on June 7, 1898, in Chicago, IL.

2937. Socialist Party was formally established in July 1901 in Indianapolis, IN, when a group of moderates from the Socialist Labor Party, led by Morris Hillquit, joined with the Social Democratic Party of America, led by Eugene Victor Debs and Victor Louis Berger. They had been participants in an unofficial alliance since the previous year, when they agreed to support Debs's first presidential campaign. At their first national nominating convention, held in Indianapolis on May 1, 1904, the Socialists nominated Debs again, and continued to do so until 1920, making their best showing in 1912, when they received more than 900,000 votes (6 percent).

2938. Year that a substantial number of Socialists were elected to public office was 1911, when 73 Socialist mayors and 1,200 Socialist city officials were elected in 340 municipalities across the nation.

2939. Progressive Party (Bull Moose) was organized in Chicago, IL, on June 19, 1912, at the Republican national convention, after a challenge to the renomination of incumbent president William Howard Taft by former president Theodore Roosevelt was rebuffed. Roosevelt's supporters in the progressive movement convened in Chicago on August 5–7 and nominated him as their candidate. The election was won by the Democrats, and the party reunited with the mainstream Republicans in 1916.

2940. Communist Labor Party of America was formed on August 31, 1919, in Chicago, IL, to advance the principles laid down by the Third Internationale in Moscow. Its first convention was held the following day, attended by 140 delegates representing 58,000 party members. They adopted as the party's emblem a hammer and sickle surrounded by a wreath of wheat and the motto "Workers of the world unite." Alfred Wagenknecht was made executive secretary.

2941. Communist Party of America held its first convention on September 2, 1919, in Chicago, IL. Members of the party adopted as an emblem the figure of earth with a red flag across the face bearing the inscription "All power to the workers." Their program was the seizure of political power, the overthrow of capitalism, and the destruction of the bourgeois state.

2942. American political party funded and operated by a foreign nation was the Communist Party USA, founded in 1924. Secret Politburo documents made public by Russian authorities after the fall of the Soviet Union in 1991 revealed that the CPUSA illegally received millions of dollars from the Communist Party of the Soviet Union and other Soviet organizations, and that the party was directly operated by the Kremlin as the primary vehicle for disseminating Soviet propaganda in the United States. Many individual members of the CPUSA were employed as spies by OGPU, the NKVD, and the KGB. The CPUSA reached the peak of its political influence in the elections of November 1932, in which presidential nominee William Zebulon Foster won 102,000 votes, taking fourth place. After 1991 outside support disappeared and the party declined rapidly.

2943. Progressive Party (of 1924) was launched in 1924 by the Conference for Progressive Political Action, a coalition that included former members of Theodore Roosevelt's Progressive Party (the Bull Moosers), members of the Socialist Party, and railway union leaders with a reform and antimonopoly agenda. Its first and only presidential campaign took place that year. The candidate, Wisconsin senator Robert Marion La Follette, came in third. He died the following year, and the party never recovered.

2944. National Union for Social Justice was founded in November 1934 in Royal Oak, MI. At its first national convention, held on August 14, 1936, at the Public Auditorium, Cleveland, OH, the delegates voted 8,153–1 to support William Lemke and Thomas Charles O'Brien as candidates for president and vice president of the United States.

2945. Union Party was organized on June 18, 1936, by a group of activists led by Father Charles E. Coughlin, head of the National Union for Social Justice, who sought a more radical redistribution of wealth than what was possible under the New Deal. The party's presidential campaign of that year was a failure, and within three years the group was defunct.

2946. Socialist Workers Party was organized in Chicago, IL, on December 31, 1937, by former members of the Communist Party who had been expelled by order of the Soviet dictator Josef Stalin for adhering to the teachings of the Bolshevik leader Leon Trotsky. (Trotsky was murdered by an agent of Stalin three years later.) The party ran its first presidential campaign in 1948.

2947. Progressive Party (of 1948) was founded in 1948 by Henry Agard Wallace, the former secretary of agriculture and vice president under President Franklin Delano Roosevelt whose positive stance toward the Soviet Union had cost him his job as secretary of commerce under President Harry S. Truman. His presidential campaign of that year stressed his philosophy of "progressive capitalism" and called for the United States and the Soviet Union to end the Cold War through negotiation. Wallace himself withdrew from the party in 1950 when it voted to oppose the Korean War, and it ceased to function after a poor showing at the polls in 1952.

2948. States' Rights Democratic Party was founded at Birmingham, AL, on July 17, 1948, by the Dixiecrats, a faction of the Democratic Party opposed to racial integration whose leaders sought to prevent the reelection of President Harry S. Truman by drawing off the votes of southern Democrats. It went out of existence as soon as Truman won the election.

2949. Workers World Party was organized in 1959 by hardline American communists who bolted from the Socialist Workers Party. The WWP was pro-Soviet down the line, fully supporting the Soviet invasions of Hungary in 1956 and Czechoslovakia in 1968. It fielded its first candidate for president in 1980. In the 1990s the WWP moved to a platform espousing Cuban and Chinese communism.

2950. American Nazi Party was founded in Arlington, VA, in March 1959 by George Lincoln Rockwell, a naval officer and graphic artist who had been converted to Nazi beliefs after reading Adolf Hitler's *Mein Kampf* in 1951. He gave his first soapbox-style public address on the Mall in Washington, on April 3, 1960, and ran as the party's first presidential candidate in 1964. Rockwell was assassinated by a disgruntled former ANP member on August 25, 1967.

2951. Black Panther Party was founded in 1966 by Robert "Bobby" Seale and Huey Newton in Oakland, CA, as the Black Panther Party for Self-Defense. The group was a Marxist revolutionary organization with a violent racialist agenda. After several bloody shootouts with police in the late 1960s, the Panthers publicly renounced violence in 1971. Riven by internal dissention, with many of its original members dead or in prison for murder and other crimes, the Black Panthers disbanded in 1982.

POLITICAL PARTIES—*continued*

2952. American Independent Party was started in 1968 by George Corley Wallace, the former (and future) governor of Alabama. Wallace had sought the Democratic Party presidential nomination in 1964 as an opponent of the African-American civil rights movement and had done well in three northern primaries. His 1968 third-party campaign appealed to conservative blue-collar whites who had been antagonized by inner-city riots and by the antiwar movement. Wallace returned to the Democratic Party after the election, in which he won 46 electoral votes, but the party continued to exist, eventually splitting into two parties, one still called the American Independent Party, the other called the American Party.

2953. Right to Life Party was founded in 1970 by a group of women from Merrick, NY, who started out as a book-discussion society and evolved into a political organization after the legalization of abortion by the state legislature. They entered New York State politics in November 1970, when they ran Vincent Carey in the race for the fifth congressional district and won 5,000 votes. In 1978 RTLP candidate Mary Jane Tobin received 130,193 votes in New York's gubernatorial election. The party's first presidential campaign took place in 1980. Most party leaders are Catholics and former members of the Democratic Party.

2954. People's Party was founded in Dallas, TX, in November 1971, with pediatrician and peace activist Dr. Benjamin Spock and author and gay activist Gore Vidal as co-chairmen. The party advocated the transfer of federal funds from the defense establishment to social programs and a grassroots, anti-elitist approach to government. Its first presidential campaign took place in 1972.

2955. Libertarian Party was founded on December 11, 1971, to promote a laissez-faire political philosophy that insists on minimal government interference in the lives of individuals and the activities of corporations. It thus opposed a wide range of domestic government programs and mandates, including compulsory education, Social Security, gun control laws, antipoverty programs, labor regulations, and price controls, and favored the repeal of laws against drug use and pornography. Its foreign policy called for disengagement of the United States from international affairs. The Libertarians ran their first presidential campaign in 1972

and elected their first state legislator, Dick Randolph of Alaska, in 1978. The first state in which the party achieved permanent ballot status was California, where more than 80,000 voters registered as Libertarians in 1979.

2956. U.S. Labor Party was founded in 1973 as the political wing of the National Caucus of Labor Committees, a Marxist organization, and ran its first presidential campaign in 1976.

2957. Citizens Party was organized in 1979 as an alternative party for liberals sympathetic to the anti-nuclear and environmentalist movements. Its message, including a call for restrictions on multinational corporations and public control of energy production, was popularized in the election campaign of 1980, in which the party fielded candidates for the presidency, the Senate, and the House.

2958. Green Party was organized in 1984 as the U.S. Green Party, a loosely organized affiliate of the left-wing environmentalist European Green movement. The name was later changed to the Green Party USA. The party achieved ballot status in Alaska in 1990 and California in 1992. The Greens ran their first presidential campaign in 1996. The first state legislator from the Green Party was Audie Bock, a film distributor and ethnic-studies instructor from Piedmont, CA, who was elected to the California state assembly for the 16th District on March 30, 1999, after narrowly defeating her Democratic opponent in a runoff election.

2959. Labor Party was founded in June 1996 and held its first national convention held in Pittsburgh, PA, beginning on November 13, 1998. Attending were delegates from six international unions and 233 local unions. The Labor Party, not to be confused with various labor-oriented parties formed in the 19th and early 20th centuries, is a liberal political group created by unions, including the United Mine Workers, the Longshoremen, the American Federation of Government Employees, and the California Nurses Association. It endorsed its first state and federal candidates in 1998 in Wyoming under the "Green/Labor Alliance" banner.

2960. African-American elected to a national leadership post in the Republican Party was Julius Caesar Watts, Jr., congressional representative from the 4th District in southwestern Oklahoma. On November 18, 1998, he was elected chairman of the Republican Conference for the 106th Congress. In 1990 Watts had become the first African-American to win statewide elective office in Oklahoma when he won a seat on the Oklahoma Corporation Commission.

POLITICAL PARTIES—COMMITTEE LEADERSHIP

2961. Political party run by a national committee was the Democratic Party. At its national convention of 1848, held in Baltimore in May, the delegates chose a national committee, consisting of one member from each state, to oversee the business of the party for the next four years.

2962. National committee of a major political party to admit women as members was the Democratic National Committeee, whose executive committee did so on September 27, 1919. The 19th amendment to the Constitution, giving women nationwide the right to vote, had been proposed to the states the previous June, and was ratified the following August.

2963. Woman to head the state committee of a major political party was Mary Teresa Hopkins Norton, who was elected chairman of the Democratic State Committee of New Jersey at the state convention held in Trenton on May 22, 1934. Norton was a member of the House of Representatives from Jersey City, New Jersey.

2964. Woman to serve as secretary of a major political party was Dorothy McElroy Vredenburgh of Alabama, who on February 29, 1944, began serving in that post for the Democratic National Committee.

2965. Latino caucus of a major political party was the Democratic National Committee Hispanic Caucus, founded in 1957 by ranking Latino officials in the Democratic party. The caucus was active in developing policies for the DNC and other issues affecting Hispanic voters.

2966. Woman to serve as chairman of a major political party was Frances Jean Miles Westwood of West Jordan, UT, elected chairman on July 14, 1972, at the Democratic National Committee meeting, Miami Beach, FL, which was attended by 303 members from 50 states.

2967. Woman to serve as chairman of the Republican Party was Mary Louise Smith of Iowa, elected chairman of the party's national committee on September 16, 1974, at Washington, DC. She was named by President Gerald R. Ford to succeed outgoing chairman George Herbert Walker Bush, who had recommended her for the post. Anne Legendre Armstrong served as co-chair of the Committee in 1971.

2968. Professional political consultant to head a major political party was Harvey Leroy "Lee" Atwater, the combative Georgia-born Republican who is credited with perfecting the "negative campaign" of the 1980s. Atwater orchestrated the successful presidential campaigns of Ronald Wilson Reagan in 1984 and of George Herbert Walker Bush in 1988. For the latter campaign, he crafted one of the most damaging and controversial television ads in history, the "Willie Horton" spot, an attack on Bush's Democratic opponent, Governor Michael Dukakis of Massachusetts. The ad, which was paid for not by the Bush campaign but by a political action committee, featured a convicted murderer named Willie Horton who, while on a weekend furlough from a Massachusetts state prison, had raped a woman in another state. Bush won the election, and Atwater was named chairman of the Republican National Committee on November 17, 1988.

2969. African-American to serve as the chairman of a major political party was Ronald H. Brown, who was elected chairman of the Democratic Party National Committee on February 10, 1989. Brown later served as secretary of commerce in the cabinet of President William Jefferson Clinton.

POLITICAL PARTIES—CONVENTIONS

2970. Party endorsement of a presidential candidate took place in October 1792, when a group of Democratic-Republican leaders meeting in Philadelphia, PA, gave their formal support to George Clinton, the governor of New York. He stood no real chance of being elected president, since George Washington was certain to be unanimously chosen for a second term, but the Democratic-Republicans hoped to place him in the vice presidency in place of John Adams. Their hopes were defeated by a vote of 77 to 50.

2971. Political party to hold a secret presidential nominating caucus was the Federalist Party. In May 1796 the Federalists in Congress gathered in Philadelphia, PA, and decided to give their support to John Adams, the incumbent vice president, and Thomas Pinckney, the U.S. minister to Britain. The Democratic-Republicans held a similar conference to choose a running mate for their standard-bearer, Thomas Jefferson, but were unable to reach an agreement.

POLITICAL PARTIES—CONVENTIONS—
continued

2972. Presidential election in which both parties nominated candidates in secret caucus was the election of 1800. The Federalist caucus was held in the Senate chamber in Philadelphia, PA, where the participants agreed to nominate incumbent president John Adams for a second term, together with General Charles Cotesworth Pinckney of South Carolina. The Democratic-Republicans convened at a Philadelphia boardinghouse and Aaron Burr as the running mate of Thomas Jefferson.

2973. Political party to hold an open presidential nominating caucus was the Democratic-Republican Party, whose caucus of 108 senators and representatives was held in Washington, DC, on February 25, 1804, with Vermont senator Stephen R. Bradley as chairman. They renominated Thomas Jefferson by acclamation. Since the Twelfth Amendment to the Constitution had gone into effect, mandating separate candidates for president and vice president, the delegates chose Governor of George Clinton of New York to be Jefferson's running mate, using a written ballot rather than a voice vote "to avoid unpleasant discussions."

2974. Convention call was issued by Stephen R. Bradley of Vermont, who formally summoned his fellow Democratic-Republicans to a congressional caucus at Washington, DC, in January 1808 for the purpose of nominating candidates for the presidency and vice presidency. Some 90 of the party's 146 senators and congressmen attended, nominating James Madison for president and George Clinton for vice president.

2975. Presidential election in which both candidates were nominated at open congressional caucuses was the election of 1812. The Democratic-Republicans convened in New York City on September 15–16, 1812, and nominated President James Madison for a second term. Elbridge Gerry of Massachusetts was nominated for the vice presidency, the latter office being vacant as a result of the death of George Clinton of New York. The Federalists also convened in New York City and nominated De Witt Clinton of New York and Jared Ingersoll of Pennsylvania. In the election, Madison received 128 electoral votes against 89 for Clinton and was elected president. Gerry received 131 electoral votes against 86 for Ingersoll. The votes were counted on February 10, 1813.

2976. Year in which the congressional nominating caucus began to decline was 1816, when public protests against the caucus system took place and some Democratic-Republicans in Congress declined to attend their own. The last nominating caucus took place in February 1824, when a group of Democratic-Republicans from four states nominated William H. Crawford, the secretary of the treasury. He was opposed in the election by three other Democratic-Republicans—Andrew Jackson, Henry Clay, and John Quincy Adams—who were all nominated by state legislatures and who mocked Crawford as "King Caucus."

2977. Year in which there was no mechanism for nominating presidential candidates was 1828, after the congressional caucus was repudiated as undemocratic. Since no other system had arisen to replace it, the state legislature of Tennessee stepped forward to nominate Andrew Jackson in October 1825, a full three years before the election. He accepted John C. Calhoun as his running mate in 1827. Their opponents, incumbent president John Quincy Adams and running mate Richard Rush, were nominated by a Pennsylvania state convention. Other politicians communicated their agreement with these choices through endorsements by other state legislatures and conventions.

2978. Convention city was Baltimore, MD. The city's proximity to Washington—close, but not too close—made it popular with party conventioneers before the Civil War. Baltimore hosted the first nominating convention of the Anti-Masonic Party on September 26, 1831, as well as the first six Democratic conventions (May 21–23, 1832; May 20–22, 1835; May 5–6, 1840; May 27–29, 1844; and June 1–5, 1852), two Whig conventions, and one National Republican convention.

2979. National nominating convention held by a political party took place on September 26, 1831, when 116 Anti-Masonic Party delegates from 13 states met at the Athenaeum in Baltimore, MD, to cast their votes. They used an open ballot box, and the ballots were counted by two tellers. According to the rules adopted by the convention, potential candidates needed to garner 84 votes to gain the nomination. The winner was William Wirt of Maryland, who received 108 votes out of 111 cast.

2980. National nominating convention held by a political party of importance met at the Athenaeum in Baltimore, MD, on December 12–15, 1831, where the delegates nominated Henry Clay of Kentucky for president and John Sergeant of Pennsylvania as his running mate. Although this was not the first national convention held by a political party, it was the first held by a party of consequence. The National Republicans brought together many politicians who had been in the Federalist camp and quickly evolved into the Whig Party. The National Republicans bore no relationship to the modern Republican Party, which was formed in the 1850s.

2981. Convention to renominate a sitting president was the Democratic-Republican convention held at Baltimore, MD, in May 1832, which chose President Andrew Jackson as its nominee. Jackson handily won the election on November 6, 1832.

2982. Democratic Party national convention was held on May 21–23, 1832, in Baltimore, MD, under the name Republican Delegates from the Several States. Delegates from 21 states and the District of Columbia nominated Andrew Jackson for president and Martin Van Buren for vice president. The Democratic party received 687,502 votes in the election of November 6, 1832, and the National Republicans 530,189 votes. The use of the name "Republican" had come down from the time of Jefferson, and the party was popularly known as the Democratic-Republican party. In the party's early national conventions, the names "Democrat" and "Republican" were often used interchangeably. In 1840 the word "Republican" was dropped entirely and the official title of the convention became the Democratic National Convention, although even then speakers employed the name "Republican" when referring to what is now the Democratic party.

2983. National political convention to adopt the two-thirds rule was the Democratic-Republican convention, held May 21–22, 1832, at the Athenaeum, Baltimore, MD. The rule requires a candidate for nomination to receive two-thirds of the votes of the delegates. Robert Lucas of Ohio was chairman of the convention, which nominated Andrew Jackson for president and Martin Van Buren for vice president.

2984. Politician to control a national convention was President Andrew Jackson, when he sought reelection to a second term in 1832. Jackson was then the undisputed head of the Democratic Party (then known officially as the Republican Party, and informally as the Democratic-Republicans), and his own renomination was assured. To guarantee that Martin Van Buren of New York would be nominated as his running mate, despite Van Buren's unpopularity in the party, he arranged for the Democrats to hold their first convention, used his influence to secure the election of delegates willing to take

orders from him, and let it be known to the rest that he would look unfavorably at those who opposed him. The party met at Baltimore, MD, on May 21–23. On the first ballot, Van Buren received 208 votes to 49 for Philip Pendleton Barbour of Virginia and 26 for Richard Mentor Johnson of Kentucky.

2985. Presidential candidate nominated in a church was Martin Van Buren, who was nominated by the Democrats on May 20, 1835, at the First Presbyterian Church in Baltimore, MD, where the party's convention was held. Van Buren went on to win the election. In 1839, William Henry Harrison was nominated by the Whig Party at a Lutheran church in Harrisburg, PA.

2986. National political convention to adopt the unit rule was the Whig convention of 1840, held at Harrisburg, PA. The results of the balloting for the presidential nomination were 148 votes for William Henry Harrison of Ohio, 90 votes for Henry Clay, and 16 votes for Winfield Scott. John Tyler of Virginia was nominated for vice president. The unit rule had been adopted on December 4, 1839, when the party instructed each state to select a committee of three delegates who together formed a Committee of the Whole. The state delegates, meeting separately, gave instructions to the members of their committee, who later voted as a unit in the Committee of the Whole.

2987. Politician to receive and decline a nomination by telegraph was Silas Wright, then a senator from New York. Wright was present at the Capitol in Washington, DC, on May 29, 1844, when he received a telegraph message from the Democratic Party convention then meeting at Baltimore, MD, informing him that he had been nominated as the party's candidate for vice president as the running mate of James Knox Polk. Wright's nearly unanimous nomination was intended to appease New York delegates who had unsuccessfully supported Martin Van Buren to be the party's candidate. Wright, however, was himself a backer of Van Buren, and telegraphed back his refusal to accept. The following year, he became governor of New York.

2988. Use of the telegraph in politics took place on May 29, 1844, during the Democratic national convention, which was meeting at Baltimore, MD7. Telegraph wires ran from the experimental Baltimore station to the east wing of the Capitol in Washington, DC, so that Congress could receive immediate news of the outcome. Dispatches came in at half-hour intervals, bringing word of the impasse that was

POLITICAL PARTIES—CONVENTIONS—
continued
keeping any of the various candidates from attaining the necessary two-thirds of the vote. The bulletins were posted on the walls of the Capitol rotunda. When James Knox Polk was finally nominated on the ninth ballot, the Democrats in Congress telegraphed a message of congratulations.

2989. Credentials fight at a Democratic Party convention of importance took place in 1848, at the convention held in Baltimore, MD, on May 22–25. Rival New York state factions called the Barnburners and the Hunkers sent competing delegations. Challenges to the credentials of each faction were resolved, to no one's satisfaction, by splitting the New York vote between them. Eventually, the Barnburners left the convention before voting, and the Hunkers refused to vote.

2990. National convention of a major party that failed to nominate a presidential candidate was the Democratic Party convention that was held at the Hall of the South Carolina Institute in Charleston, SC, starting on April 23, 1860. Fifty-seven ballots were taken over the course of ten days, but no candidate received the 202 votes necessary to win the nomination. Stephen Arnold Douglas of Illinois came closest with 151.5 ballots. The Democrats reconvened on June 18 at the Front Street Theatre in Baltimore, MD, where they unanimously nominated Douglas on the second ballot. A breakaway faction calling itself the National (or Independent) Democratic Party met separately in Baltimore on June 23 and nominated John Cabell Breckinridge for president. Breckinridge was also nominated in Baltimore on June 28 by the Southern Democratic Party. The election was won by Abraham Lincoln, the Republican candidate.

2991. National party convention to which the general public was admitted was the convention of the Republican Party that met at the Wigwam in Chicago, IL, from May 16 through 18, 1860. Some 10,000 people were crowded into the hall. The spectators, who far outnumbered the delegates, sat in the balcony. While the supporters of William Henry Seward, several thousand strong, were parading outdoors to the accompaniment of a brass band, the supporters of his rival, Abraham Lincoln, packed most of the balcony seats. Nonetheless, there were enough spectators from each camp to mount long displays of cheering, yelling, stamping, and screaming. The convention was thus the first to be interrupted by orchestrated pandemonium.

2992. Hall built to house a national party convention was the Wigwam, designed by architect William Boyington and built on Lake Street in Chicago, IL, for the Republican Party convention of May 16–18, 1860. It was also the first convention hall in which telegraph equipment was installed.

2993. Republican Party credentials dispute took place at the national convention held at Chicago, IL, on May 16–18, 1860. At issue was whether to seat delegates from slave states, and how to determine the voting strength of delegates from states where the Republican Party had few members.

2994. Candidate to withdraw from the presidential race after the adjournment of his party's national convention was Benjamin Fitzpatrick, chosen as Stephen Arnold Douglas's running mate by Democrats meeting at Baltimore, MD, on June 18, 1860. Fitzpatrick withdrew for personal reasons shortly after the convention ended, and he was replaced on June 25 by Herschel Vespasian Johnson, the selection of the national committee.

2995. Presidential election in which both candidates came from the same state was the election of November 6, 1860, in which Abraham Lincoln of Springfield, IL, the Republican candidate, competed against Stephen Arnold Douglas of Jacksonville, IL, the Democratic candidate. Lincoln had been born in Kentucky, Douglas in Vermont.

2996. Delegate to a national political convention who was African-American was Frederick Douglass of Rochester, NY, who attended the National Loyalists' Loyal Union Convention at Philadelphia, PA, on September 6, 1866.

2997. Year in which both major parties nominated incumbent governors for the presidency was 1876. The Democrats, meeting at St. Louis, MO, from June 27 to 29, nominated Samuel Jones Tilden, governor of New York. The Republicans, meeting at Cincinnati, OH, from June 14 to 16, chose Rutherford Birchard Hayes, governor of Ohio.

2998. Woman to address a national political convention was Sara Andrews Spencer, who addressed the Republican National Convention in Cincinnati, OH, on June 15, 1876. She spoke against the disfranchisement of women and presented a memorial of the National Woman Suffrage Association stating "that the right to use the ballot inheres in the citizens of the United States."

2999. African-American to receive nominating votes for the vice presidency at the convention of a major party was Blanche Kelso Bruce, Republican senator from Mississippi, who had been born into slavery. In June 1880, during the Republican convention at Chicago, IL, Bruce received the votes of eleven delegates during the balloting for the vice presidency.

3000. Credentials fight at a Republican Party convention that determined the selection of the candidate took place at the convention held on June 2–8, 1880, in Chicago, IL. The dispute turned on the credentials of the Illinois delegation, whose votes were crucial for the nomination of Ulysses Simpson Grant, the former president. Anti-Grant forces eventually won all challenges to the legitimacy of the Illinois delegates, thus making possible the nomination of a dark horse candidate, James Abram Garfield, after a record 36 ballots.

3001. African-American to preside over the national political convention of a major party was John Roy Lynch, three-term congressman from Mississippi, who presided over the convention of the Republican Party that met in the Exposition Building, Chicago, IL, on June 3, 1884. He was nominated for temporary chairman of the Republican Party by Henry Cabot Lodge. The nomination was supported by Theodore Roosevelt and George William Curtis and was carried by a vote of 424 for Lynch to 384 for Powell Clayton. John Brooks Henderson was the permanent chairman. The convention nominated James Gillespie Blaine for president and General John Alexander Logan for vice president.

3002. African-American to receive nominating votes for the presidency at the convention of a major party was Frederick Douglass of Rochester, NY, who received one vote on June 23, 1888, on the fourth ballot of the Republican national convention. On June 25, on the eighth ballot, the convention nominated Benjamin Harrison, who was elected as the 23rd president. Douglass was later appointed U.S. minister to Haiti.

3003. Women to attend a national political convention as delegates were alternates Therese A. Jenkins of Cheyenne, WY, and Cora G. Carleton of Hilliard, WY, who attended the 10th Republican Party convention at Minneapolis, MN, on June 7–10, 1892.

3004. Woman to make a seconding speech at a national political convention was Elizabeth Cohn, delegate from Utah. On July 5, 1900, she seconded the nomination of William Jennings Bryan at the Democratic National Convention held at Kansas City, MO.

3005. Year the Republican party renominated its entire ticket from the previous election was 1912, when the delegates, meeting at Chicago, IL, on June 18–22, chose William Howard Taft and James S. Sherman, who were also the nominees when the party met in Chicago in 1908.

3006. Change in the method of allocating convention delegates among the various states took place in 1916. The traditional method, used by both major parties, was a proportional allocation based on the number of each state's total Electoral College votes, without regard to party allegiance. Since most of the voters in the southern states were Democrats, the Republican convention delegates from the South were able to wield power far beyond their actual numbers. In the convention of 1912, their influence resulted in the nomination of William Howard Taft over Theodore Roosevelt, which led to the creation of the breakaway Bull Moose Party and the split in the Republican vote that gave the victory to the Democrats. Four years later the Republican leadership broke with tradition and reduced the number of delegates allocated to the southern states.

3007. Year in which the Democratic party renominated its entire ticket from the previous election was 1916, when the delegates, meeting at St. Louis, MO, on June 14–18, chose Woodrow Wilson and Thomas R. Marshall, who were also the nominees when the party met in Baltimore, MD, in 1912.

3008. Bonus voting system was instituted by the Republican Party at its national convention held in Cleveland, OH, on June 10–12, 1924. Under the system, states were awarded three extra votes for supporting the Republican presidential candidate in the previous election. The Democratic Party adopted a bonus system in 1944.

3009. Political convention to be broadcast on radio took place on June 10, 1924, when the Republican Convention assembled at Cleveland, OH, to nominate Calvin Coolidge of Massachusetts and Charles Gates Dawes of Illinois for president and vice president. Graham McNamee was the announcer for the program, which was carried by 15 stations of the National Broadcasting Company from Boston, MA, to Kansas City, MO.

POLITICAL PARTIES—CONVENTIONS—
continued

3010. Nominating convention that required more than 100 ballots was the Democratic Party convention that met at Madison Square Garden in New York City from June 24 through July 9, 1924. The names of 60 candidates were placed in contention, and 731 votes were necessary to secure the nomination. On the 103rd ballot, John William Davis of West Virginia won the nomination with 844 votes. Charles Wayland Bryan of Nebraska was nominated as his running mate. The election was won by the Republican incumbent, Calvin Coolidge.

3011. Woman delegates to a Democratic convention attended the convention held at Madison Square Garden in New York City on July 9, 1924, the party's first national convention after women received the right to vote in presidential elections. There were 182 with 292 alternates. At the convention, Lena Jones Springs of South Carolina became the first Democratic woman to be nominated for the vice presidency. She received 18 votes.

3012. Woman to receive nominating votes for the vice presidency at the convention of a major party was Lena Jones Springs, South Carolina's delegate-at-large at the Democratic Party's convention that met in New York City in the summer of 1924. Mrs. Springs was also the national Democratic committeewoman for South Carolina. On July 9, she received 18 votes from her state's delegation. This was the first election in which women were allowed to participate as delegates.

3013. Presidential nomination ceremony broadcast on radio was the ceremony held at Leland Stanford Junior University Stadium, Palo Alto, CA, on August 11, 1928, when Herbert Hoover was formally notified of his nomination for the presidency by the Republican Party and accepted. The broadcast was carried by more than 107 stations.

3014. Presidential candidate to accept his party's nomination in person was Franklin Delano Roosevelt, who flew from Albany, NY, to Chicago, IL, on July 2, 1932, to address the Democratic National Convention. He delivered the first acceptance speech by a nominee at a convention.

3015. Presidential candidate to fly to a political convention to make an acceptance speech was Franklin Delano Roosevelt, then governor of New York, who chartered a ten-passenger trimotor plane for himself and his party on July 2, 1932, and flew from Albany, NY, to Chicago, IL, where he addressed the Democratic Convention.

3016. Political party to nominate the same candidate six times was the Socialist Party, which nominated Norman Mattoon Thomas of New York in 1928, 1932, 1936, 1940, 1944, and 1948. In the election of November 8, 1932, he received his maximum number of votes, 884,782. Thomas was a co-founder of the American Civil Liberties Union and co-director of the League for Industrial Democracy.

3017. National political convention to abrogate the two-thirds rule was the Democratic National Convention held at Philadelphia, PA, in 1936. On June 25 the Committee on Rules and Order of Business declared that "all questions, including the question of nomination of candidates for President of the United States and Vice President of the United States, shall be determined by a majority vote of the delegates to the convention, and the rule heretofore existing in Democratic conventions requiring a two-thirds vote in such cases is hereby abrogated."

3018. Nominating convention of a major party in which the delegates nominated a candidate without taking a ballot took place on June 23–27, 1936, at Convention Hall in Philadelphia, PA, where the Democratic Party nominated, by acclamation, incumbent president Franklin Delano Roosevelt. Roosevelt took 98.49 percent of the electoral vote on November 3.

3019. Political convention to be televised was the 22nd Republican Convention, held on June 24–29, 1940, in Philadelphia, PA, at which Wendell Lewis Willkie of New York and Charles Linza McNary of Oregon were nominated for president and vice president. The telecast was made by station W2XBS of the National Broadcasting Company, New York City.

3020. Republican presidential candidate to give his acceptance speech at the national convention was Thomas E. Dewey, who addressed the Republican delegates on June 26–28, 1944, in Chicago, IL.

3021. Woman to serve as secretary of the Republican National Convention was Mrs. Dudley C. Hay, born Regina Deem Hay, of Michigan. She was designated temporary secretary of the Republican National Convention at the party gathering in Philadelphia, PA, in June 1948. On June 21, she read the roll call of the convention delegates, becoming the first woman to do so at a Republican convention.

3022. Political party convention at which spectators were charged an admission fee was the Progressive Party Convention, which met from July 23 to 25, 1948, in Philadelphia, PA. This policy gained the party about $15,000 for its campaign war chest. The convention nominated Henry Agard Wallace as its candidate for president.

3023. National conventions to receive gavel-to-gavel television coverage were the Republican and Democratic Party conventions of 1952, both of which took place in Chicago, IL, in July. They were televised by CBS News, which had recently been started and was then under the direction of Sig Mickelson. The chief newscaster for the conventions was Walter Cronkite, a television reporter from Washington, DC, who thus became the first television news anchor.

3024. National convention to require a pledge of party loyalty from its delegates was the 1952 convention of the Democratic Party, held in Chicago, IL, on July 21–26. In the previous convention, in 1948, a Southern faction, the Dixiecrats, had bolted from the party's convention to protest the adoption of a civil rights plank and had held its own convention, nominating James Strom Thurmond, whose name appeared on the ballot in some Southern states in place of the Democratic candidate, Harry S. Truman. To prevent another such occurrence, Senator Blair Moody of Michigan introduced a resolution requiring delegates to promise that they would support the national party ticket. It was approved by voice vote.

3025. Woman to receive nominating votes for the presidency at the convention of a major party was Margaret Chase Smith of Maine, who was nominated by Senator George David Aiken of Vermont on July 15, 1964, at the Republican National Convention at San Francisco, CA. She was one of eight contenders for the nomination. Barry Morris Goldwater of Arizona was chosen on the first ballot, with 883 votes from a total of 1308. Smith received 27.

3026. Choice of an island city for a convention was made by the Republican Party, which held its national gathering in Miami Beach, FL, on August 5–8, 1968. It was thought that the location, with limited access by foot, would be an advantage in reducing the possibility of mass protests such as those that occurred outside the Democratic convention in Chicago, IL, later that month.

3027. Political convention to be televised in color was the 29th Republican Convention, held on August 5–7, 1968, at Miami Beach, FL. The proceedings were broadcast by both the National Broadcasting Company and the Columbia Broadcasting System.

3028. National political convention to propose African-Americans for the offices of president and vice president was the 35th Democratic convention, held on August 26–29, 1968, at Chicago, IL. On August 28, 1968, the Reverend Channing Emery Phillips of Washington, DC, received 67.5 of the 2,622 votes cast for the presidential nomination. On August 29, Julian Bond of Atlanta, GA, was nominated but declined, as he did not fulfill the necessary age requirement.

3029. Woman to receive nominating votes for the presidency at a Democratic Party convention was Shirley Anita St. Hill Chisholm, congressional representative from New York City. She received 101.45 votes at the Democratic Convention that met at Convention Hall in Miami Beach, FL, on July 10–13, 1972. The winner, on the first ballot, was George Stanley McGovern of South Dakota, who received 1,864.95 votes. Chisholm came in fourth in a field of twelve.

3030. Democratic Party convention between presidential elections was held in Kansas City, MO, on December 6–8, 1974. The party gathered to ratify its first major charter, which required affirmative action in all party affairs, with representation for women and minorities according to their proportion in the American electorate.

3031. Woman to deliver the keynote speech at a Democratic National Convention was Barbara Charline Jordan, Democrat from the 18th District of Texas, who delivered the keynote address on July 12, 1976, at the Democratic Convention in New York City. She was also the first African-American to do so.

POLITICAL PARTIES—CONVENTIONS— *continued*

3032. Presidential nomination acceptance speech to mention homosexuals was delivered by Arkansas governor William Jefferson Clinton at the Democratic Party Convention held in New York City on July 13–16, 1992. Remarking on his political philosophy, Clinton said: "Old or young, healthy as a horse or a person with a disability that hasn't kept you down, man or woman, Native American, native-born, immigrant, straight or gay—whatever the test ought to be: I believe in the Constitution, the Bill of Rights and the Declaration of Independence. I believe in religious liberty, I believe in freedom of speech, and I believe in working hard and playing by the rules."

3033. African-American to actively campaign for the presidential candidacy of the Republican Party was Alan L. Keyes of Maryland, a radio talk-show host and former official of the Reagan administration. Keyes ran unsuccessfully for the 1996 and 2000 Republican nominations. He was twice the Republican nominee to the U.S. Senate for the state of Maryland, and in 1992 was the featured speaker at the Republican National Convention in Houston, TX.

POLITICAL PARTIES—PLATFORMS

3034. Whig Party resolutions were adopted at the state convention in Albany, NY, on February 3, 1836, in lieu of an official party platform. They pledged Whig support for William Henry Harrison and enmity for his opponent, Martin Van Buren, who, it was claimed, "by intriguing with the Executive to obtain his influence to elect him to the Presidency, has set an example dangerous to our freedom and corrupting to our free institutions." Van Buren was Andrew Jackson's vice president and had been groomed by Jackson to be his successor.

3035. Liberty Party platform was adopted at the founding party convention held in Warsaw, NY, on November 13, 1839. It read: "Resolved: That in our judgement, every consideration of duty and expediency which ought to control the action of Christian freemen requires of the Abolitionists of the United States to organize a distinct and independent political party, embracing all the necessary means for nominating candidates for office and sustaining them by public suffrage." The platform called on Congress to put an end to the interstate slave trade and to outlaw slavery in Washington, DC, which was within its constitutional power to accomplish. A full platform was adopted at the party's 1843 convention.

3036. Political party platform was adopted in May 1840 at the Democratic Party's national convention in Baltimore, MD, at which Martin Van Buren was nominated, unsuccessfully, for reelection. It was a document of fewer than 1,000 words, drafted by a committee that was charged with setting forth the principles of the party. The platform called for a strict interpretation of the Constitution with respect to the powers of the federal government, rejecting any claim that it was empowered to assume state debts, charter a national bank, raise surplus revenue, interfere with slavery, or undertake internal improvements, and spoke in favor of giving asylum to "the oppressed of every nation" and extending to them the rights of citizenship. These principles were explained at more length in an address to the people that was drafted by a different committee.

3037. Free Soil Party platform was adopted at the national party convention held in Buffalo, NY, on August 9–10, 1848. The 16-point platform concerned itself primarily with attacking the institution of slavery and its extension into new territories of the United States, and also called for cheap postage, a free grant of land to pioneers, internal improvments, and reduction of the national debt.

3038. Know-Nothing Party platform was drafted at the party convention at Philadelphia, PA, on February 22–25, 1856. Among its resolutions were several aimed at restricting immigration, reserving public office for native-born Americans, strengthening states' rights, and preventing the federal government from interfering with slavery. The party's official name was the American Party.

3039. Republican Party platform was adopted at the party's first convention, held at Philadelphia, PA, on June 17, 1856. The platform condemned "those twin relics of barbarism, polygamy and slavery," and insisted that Congress was empowered by the Constitution to prohibit both of them in the territories. It also called for the federal government to undertake river and harbor improvement projects (which the Democrats claimed was unconstitutional); called for the construction of a transcontinental railroad (with which the Democrats agreed); and denounced the Ostend Manifesto, in which an American diplomat recommended that the United States either purchase Cuba from Spain or take it by force.

3040. Constitutional Union Party platform was adopted at the party's first and only convention, held in Baltimore, MD, on May 9, 1860. In its platform, the Constitutional Union Party pledged only to "recognize no political principles other than the Constitution of the Country, the Union of the States, and the Enforcement of the Laws," claiming that "experience has demonstrated that platforms adopted by the partisan conventions of the country have had the effect to mislead and deceive the people." The Constitutional Union Party was formerly known as the American (or Know-Nothing) Party.

3041. Southern Democratic Party platform was issued in Baltimore, MD, on June 28, 1860. It reiterated standard policies of the mainstream Democrats, including acquisition of Cuba and construction of a transcontinental railroad. It also contained a plank calling on the federal government to allow and protect slaveowning in the territories. The defeat of this plank at the earlier Democratic convention was the cause of the walkout by southerners that resulted in the formation of the party.

3042. Platform of the Independent Republicans was adopted on May 31, 1864, at the party's only convention, held in Cleveland, OH. Like the platform of the Republican Party, it called for the preservation of the Union and condemned slavery, but it also advocated the establishment of a one-term presidency. The Independent Republicans were also known as the Radical Republicans.

3043. Labor Reform Party platform was drafted at its first national convention at Columbus, OH, on February 22, 1872. Delegates were mainly trade unionists, and the party platform called for the government "to establish a just standard of distribution of capital and labor" by issuing legal tender (greenbacks) directly to the people without the intermediary of banking corporations. It also inveighed against the importation of Chinese laborers and the system of contract labor in prisons.

3044. Prohibition Party platform was put forward at the national convention that met in Columbus, OH, on February 22, 1872. The platform demanded prohibition, declaring that the "traffic in intoxicating beverages is a dishonor to Christian civilization, a political wrong of unequalled enormity, subversive of ordinary objects of government, not being capable of being regulated or restrained by any system of license whatever." It also advocated women's suffrage, a direct popular presidential vote, a sound currency, the encouragement of immigration, and a reduction of transportation rates.

3045. Liberal Republican Party platform was drafted at the convention held in Cincinnati, OH, on May 1, 1872, at which meeting the party was formed. The platform called for an end to Radical Reconstruction, insisted on the creation of a one-term presidency, and vowed to end the patronage system, which the party claimed was "a mere instrument of partisan tyranny and personal ambition, and an object of selfish greed."

3046. Straight-out Democratic Party platform was adopted in Louisville, KY, on September 3, 1872, by liberal Democrats who felt betrayed by the Democratic Party's nomination of the same candidates as the Liberal Republicans. It was the one of the first party platforms to speak of "class legislation" and of labor in opposition to capital. One clause resolved that "the interests of labor and capital should not be permitted to conflict . . . [and] when such a conflict continues, labor, which is the parent of wealth, is entitled to paramount consideration."

3047. American National Party platform was adopted at the party convention at Pittsburgh, PA, on June 9, 1875. Its platform began "We hold that ours is a Christian, and not a heathen, nation, and that the God of the Christian Scriptures is the author of civil government." The platform advocated national prohibition, the elimination of "secret lodges" chartered by federal and state legislatures, "justice to Indians," and the abolition of the electoral college.

3048. Greenback Party platform was adopted at the party convention in Indianapolis, IN, on May 16–18, 1876. The platform advocated the payment of the national debt of the government in greenbacks—that is, legal tender issued directly by the United States government and not through a banking system. The Greenbacks also called for an end to the sale of gold-backed government bonds to foreign investors.

3049. Anti-Monopoly Party platform was published at the party convention held in Chicago, IL, on May 14, 1884. Its first two declarations read: "1. That labor and capital should be allies; and we demand justice for both, by protecting the rights of all against privileges for the few. 2. That organizations, the creatures of law, should be controlled by law." The platform went on to decry the development of giant transportation monopolies and demand that the government institute regulations curbing them, including an interstate commerce bill. "The Anti-Monopoly Organization of the United States," as it was formally named, was later absorbed into the People's Party.

POLITICAL PARTIES—PLATFORMS—
continued

3050. Equal Rights Party platform was adopted on September 20, 1884, at the party convention in San Francisco, CA. It began: "We pledge ourselves, if elected to power, so far as in us lies to do equal and exact justice to every class of our citizens, without distinction of color, sex, or nationality. We shall recommend that the laws of the several states be so amended that women will be recognized as voters, and their property rights made equal with that of the male population, to the end that they may become self-supporting rather than a dependent class." The Equal Rights Party was also known as the Woman's Rights Party.

3051. Union Labor Party platform was published at the party convention that took place on May 15–17, 1888, in Cincinnati, OH. Beginning with the assertion that "General discontent prevails on the part of the wealth-producers," the platform called for an end to land-monopolies and speculation, nationalization of the transportation industries, establishment of a national monetary system based on gold and silver, improvement in labor conditions, and institution of a graduated income tax.

3052. American Party platform was promulgated on August 14, 1888, at the party convention in Washington, DC. The platform's main concern was to limit immigration. Decrying "the degrading competition with and contamination by imported foreigners," as well as the arrival of "paupers, criminals, communists, and anarchists," it demanded that any prospective immigrant obtain a passport from the American consul at the port of embarkation and at the same time pay $100 into the U.S. treasury.

3053. Farmers' Alliance Party platform was the Ocala Platform, adopted at Ocala, FL, in December 1890. It demanded the abolition of national banks, direct issuance of legal tender by the government to the people, free coinage of silver, elimination of land speculation, prohibition of foreign ownership of U.S. land, and no tax breaks for the rich.

3054. Populist Party platform was drafted at the party's first national convention, held on July 2–5, 1892, in Omaha, NE (when it was formally called the People's Party). Asserting that the nation was at "the verge of moral, political, and material ruin," the lengthy platform called for a national union of labor; free and unlimited coinage of silver and gold at a ratio

of 16 to 1; a graduated income tax; nationalization of the railroads; low taxes; disbanding of the Pinkerton detective organization, which had been used to suppress labor protests; and a one-term presidency.

3055. Socialist Labor Party platform was drafted at the party convention held in New York City on July 6, 1896. The platform, declaring "the obvious fact that our despotic system of economics is the direct opposite of our democratic system of politics," went on to call for an "immediate improvement in the condition of labor" and nationalization of all industries affecting the public sector.

3056. National Silver Party platform was drafted by delegates at the Exposition Building in St. Louis, MO, on July 23–25, 1896. The party was also known as the Bi-Metallic League. The party declared itself "unalterably opposed to the single gold standard," and demanded "the immediate return to the constitutional standard of gold and silver, by the restoration of this government, independently of any foreign power, of the unrestricted coinage of both gold and silver into standard money at the ratio of 16 to 1."

3057. Sound Money Democratic Party platform was adopted at the convention held in Indianapolis, IN, on September 2–3, 1896. The party, also known as the National Democratic Party, was composed of Democrats who refused to accept the Democratic platform adopted at the party convention in Chicago, IL, on July 7. The platform denounced the dangers of protectionism while advocating a regulated bi-metallic currency based on the gold standard.

3058. Social Democratic Party of the United States platform was adopted at the party convention held in Rochester, NY, on January 27, 1900. The party's platform "affirmed its allegiance to the revolutionary principles of international socialism" and declared that "the supreme issue in America to-day to be the contest between the working class and the capitalist class for the possession of the powers of government."

3059. Social Democratic Party of America platform was written by party co-founder Eugene Victor Debs and others and was adopted at the party convention held in Indianapolis, IN, on March 6, 1900. It affirmed the party's object as "the organization of the working class into a political party to conquer the public powers now controlled by the capitalist class."

3060. Silver Republican Party platform was drafted at the party's national convention, held at the Auditorium in Kansas City, MO, on July 5–6, 1900. The platform advocated bimetallism, as well as a graduated income tax, direct election of senators, and dismantling of the trusts. It also expressed sympathy for the Boers, who had just lost a war with Britain.

3061. Union Reform Party platform was passed at the party convention on September 3, 1900, in Baltimore, MD. The platform called for direct legislation by the people under the initiative and referendum.

POLITICS—EDUCATION

3062. Political economy course at a college was given at the College of William and Mary of Williamsburg, VA, in 1784.

3063. Political economy chair at a college was established at Harvard University, Cambridge, MA, in 1871. The first professor was Charles Franklin Dunbar. An earlier chair in moral philosophy and political economy was established in 1818 at Columbia College, New York City, with Professor John McVickar the first occupant.

3064. Oratory course was established in December 1892 at the University of Michigan, Ann Arbor, MI, with Thomas Clarkson Trueblood as professor of elocution and oratory. Similar courses had been given in 1887, but without departmental status.

3065. Citizenship and public affairs school at a college was opened on October 3, 1924, by Syracuse University, Syracuse, NY, through the generosity of George Holmes Maxwell. The first dean was William Eugene Mosher.

3066. Propaganda course at a college was given by Professor Harold Dwight Lasswell of the Department of Political Science, University of Chicago, Chicago, IL, in 1927. It was entitled "Political Opinion and Propaganda."

3067. Industrial and labor relations school at a college was the New York State School of Industrial and Labor Relations, Cornell University, Ithaca, NY, opened for registration on November 2, 1945. Irving McNeil Ives was the first dean.

POLITICS—POLITICAL PHILOSOPHY

3068. Document claiming a special spiritual mission for America was "A Modell of Christian Charity," a lay sermon written on board the ship *Arbella* in 1630 by John Winthrop. Winthrop was leading the first large party of Puritans to settle in the Massachusetts Bay Colony. In concluding, Winthrop wrote: "Wee

shall finde that the God of Israell is among us, when ten of us shall be able to resist a thousand of our enemies; when hee shall make us a prayse and glory that men shall say of succeeding plantations, 'the Lord make it like that of New England.' For wee must consider wee shall be as a Citty upon a Hill, the eies of all people are uppon us."

3069. Treatise on politics and government was *Arbitrary Government Described: and the Government of the Massachusetts Vindicated from that Aspersion,* written by the Puritan leader John Winthrop, the longtime governor of the Massachusetts Bay Colony, and published in 1644. He identified a "power of Authority" inherent in the governor, deputy governor, and assistants (magistrates), and a "power of Liberty" invested by the colony's charter in its freemen, which gave them the right to be consulted in matters of laws, taxes, and decrees. The treatise met with a rebuttal from the House of Deputies (the lower legislative house), which declared, "Concerninge the distinction therein made of the bodye Politick, & the members thereof, in attributing Authorytye to the one, & onely Liberty to the other: we finde not any suche distinction in the Patent. . . . We conceive it a takinge awaye of the power & priviledges of the ffreemen."

3070. Document expressing American democratic ideals was *A Vindication of the Government of New-England Churches,* written in 1717 by John Wise, a Congregational clergyman of Ipswich, MA. In this short book, Wise expressed the liberal democratic ideas later incorporated into the Declaration of Independence (1776). He observed a "natural equality of men amongst men"; listed their fundamental rights to "life, liberty, estate"; and claimed that government, "the produce of mans reason, of human and rational combinations," should operate "under due restrictions," and that human rights are to "be cherished in all wise Governments; or otherwise a man in making himself a subject, he alters himself from a freeman, into a slave, which to do is repugnant to the law of nature." Wise, who led a tax rebellion in his home town for which he was briefly imprisoned, also excoriated "the prince who strives to subvert the fundamental laws of the society."

3071. Issue of the *Federalist* papers was published in a New York City newspaper, the *Independent Journal,* on October 27, 1787, during the vigorous public debate over whether to adopt the Constitution in place of the Articles of Confederation. The author proposed to write a series of articles in which he would discuss

POLITICS—POLITICAL PHILOSOPHY—
continued

"—The utility of the UNION to your political prosperity—The insufficiency of the present Confederation to preserve that Union—The necessity of a government at least equally energetic with the one proposed, to the attainment of this object—The conformity of the proposed Constitution to the true principles of republican government—Its analogy to your own State constitution—and lastly, The additional security which its adoption will afford to the preservation of that species of government, to liberty, and to property." The author was a young lawyer, Alexander Hamilton. A total of 76 articles, written by Hamilton, James Madison, and John Jay, appeared in New York newspapers at intervals through April 2, 1788, all signed with the pen name "Publius" and addressed "To the People of the State of New York."

3072. Publication of *Democracy in America* in the United States took place in 1838, three years after the appearance of the first volume in France. The complete four-volume work, *De la démocratie en Amérique (Democracy in America)*, brought out in 1840 by the French political philosopher Alexis Charles-Henri-Maurice Clerel de Tocqueville, was the first comprehensive study of the American democratic and social system by a sympathetic outsider and remains a classic of liberal political thought.

3073. National political science society was the American Political Science Association, founded in New Orleans, LA, on December 30, 1903, for the encouragement of the scientific study of politics, public law, administration, and diplomacy. The first president was Professor Frank Johnson Goodnow.

3074. National creed was "The American's Creed," penned in 1917 by William Tyler Page, clerk of the House of Representatives, and accepted by the House "on behalf of the American people" on April 3, 1918. It declared: "I believe in the United States of America as a government of the people, by the people, for the people, whose just powers are derived from the consent of the governed; a democracy in a republic; a sovereign Nation of many sovereign States; a perfect union, one and inseparable; established upon those principles of freedom, equality, justice, and humanity for which American patriots sacrificed their lives and fortunes. I therefore believe it is my duty to my country to love it, to support the Constitution, to obey its laws, to respect its flag, and to defend it against all enemies."

3075. Use of the term "New Deal" was in the speech given by Franklin Delano Roosevelt to the Democratic National Convention held in Chicago, IL, on July 2, 1932. In closing, Roosevelt said: "I pledge you, I pledge myself, to a new deal for the American people. Let us all here assembled constitute ourselves prophets of a new order of competence and of courage. This is more than a political campaign: it is a call to arms. Give me your help, not to win votes alone, but to win in this crusade to restore American to its own people." The phrase was borrowed from Mark Twain's *A Connecticut Yankee in King Arthur's Court.*

3076. Motto of the United States was "In God We Trust," authorized by congressional act of July 30, 1956, a joint resolution "to establish a national motto of the United States." It was signed into law by President Dwight David Eisenhower.

3077. Theory of fair division was published by political scientist Steven Brams of New York University, New York City, and mathematician Alan Taylor of Union College, Schenectady, NY, in the January 1995 issue of *American Mathematical Monthly*. Their technique made it possible to fairly divide anything—from cakes to war reparations—even among parties that strongly disagree.

POPULATION

3078. States with populations of more than 1 million were New York, with 1,372,812; Virginia, with 1,065,366; and Pennsylvania, with 1,049,456, according to the census of 1820.

3079. City with a population of more than 1 million was New York City, whose population according to the census of 1880 was 1,206,299. This number was for Manhattan alone. Brooklyn was then an independent city. Brooklyn and three other areas (the Bronx, Queens, and Staten Island) were combined with Manhattan in 1898 to form the five boroughs of New York City. The population of the city in 1920 was 5,620,048, making it the first city with a population exceeding 5 million.

3080. State with a population of more than 5 million was New York, which reached 5,082,871 in the census of 1880.

3081. State with a population of more than 10 million was New York. It reached that mark in the 1920 census, when the state had a population of 10,385,227.

3082. Year when the urban population of the United States exceeded the rural population was 1920, according to census data released for that year. The total U.S. population reported in the 1920 census was 117.8 million, of whom 54 million were listed as urban and 51.5 million as rural.

3083. Year in which suburbanites outnumbered city and rural dwellers conbined was 1990, according to that year's census. The United States was the first nation in history to be composed primarily of citizens living in suburbs.

POPULATION—CENSUS

3084. Census of the population of the United States was conducted in 1790, following the passage by Congress on March 1 of the Census Act, in accordance with Article 1, Section 2, of the Constitution. The census was completed on August 1. It found a total population of 3,929,625 persons in the states and western territories. African-Americans accounted for 19 percent (697,624 enslaved and 59,557 free). Native Americans were not counted.

3085. Census in which the national population exceeded 10 million was the fifth census, the census of 1830, which showed a population of 12,866,620.

3086. Census that included deaf, mute, and blind people was taken in 1830. Previously, people with these disabilities were not enumerated at all.

3087. Census in which no slaves were counted was the census of 1870. Slavery had been abolished in the United States since the ratification of the 13th Amendment to the Constitution on February 18, 1865. The census of 1860 counted 4,441,830 African-American slaves—about 14 percent of the population of the United States—and 488,070 free African-Americans. In two states, African-Americans were in the majority: South Carolina, where they represented 58.6 percent of the population, and Mississippi, where they represented 55.3 percent. In ten others—Maryland, Virginia, North Carolina, Georgia, Florida, Tennessee, Alabama, Arkansas, Louisiana, and Texas—African-Americans constituted between one quarter and one half of the population.

3088. Census in which the national population exceeded 50 million was the tenth census, the census of 1880, which listed the population as 50,155,783.

3089. Census compiled by machines was the 1890 census, which recorded a population of 62,979,766 on June 1, 1890.

3090. Census of Puerto Rico administrated by the U.S. government was taken in 1899. The island's population count was then 953,000.

3091. Census Bureau permanent organization was established by congressional act of March 6, 1902, which authorized the appointment of a census director at $6,000 a year to superintend and direct the taking of the 13th Census (1910). On February 14, 1902, the Census Bureau was transferred from the Department of the Interior to the Department of Commerce and Labor. The bureau at that time had 70,286 employees.

3092. Census in which the national population exceeded 100 million was the census of 1920, which showed a population of 105,710,620.

3093. Central statistical board was created by Executive Order No. 6225, dated July 27, 1933, under authority vested in the president by the National Industrial Recovery Act "to formulate standards for and to effect coordination of the statistical services of the Federal Government incident to the purposes . . . of the National Industrial Recovery Act." It was organized on August 9, 1933, and was originally composed of eight members. The first chairman was Winfield William Riefler.

3094. Census in which the national population exceeded 150 million was that of 1950, which showed a population of 150,697,361.

3095. Census in which the national population exceeded 200 million was that of 1970, which showed a population of 203,302,031. According to federal statisticians, the 200 million mark was passed on November 20, 1967. A public ceremony celebrating the event was held on that day at the Department of Commerce, Washington, DC.

3096. Census compiled in part from statistics obtained by mail was the 19th decennial census, mailed on April 1, 1970.

3097. Census to count the homeless was the census of 1990. The Census Bureau collected data for various components of the homeless population at different stages. "Shelter and Street Night" (S-Night) was a special census operation to count the population in four types of locations where homeless people are found. On the evening of March 20, 1990, and during the early morning hours of March 21, enumerators counted persons in the following pre-identified locations: (1) emergency shelters for the homeless population (public and private;

POPULATION—CENSUS—_continued_

permanent and temporary); (2) shelters with temporary lodging for runaway youths; (3) shelters for abused women and their children; and (4) open locations in streets or other places not intended for habitation.

3098. Multiracial census category was included in the 2000 census, according to rules issued by the Office of Management and Budget for listing racial and ethnic makeup on federal forms. Respondents were allowed to identify themselves as members of more than one race. Previously, respondents had to choose a single racial category or select "other."

3099. Person to be counted in the 2000 census was Stanton Katchatag, an 82-year-old resident of Unalakleet, AK. He was interviewed on January 20, 2000, by Kenneth Prewitt, director of the Census Bureau, who arrived in the village by dogsled. Unalakleet lies 450 miles northwest of Anchorage and has 800 residents, most of them Inuit Native Americans.

POPULATION—IMMIGRATION AND CITIZENSHIP

3100. Colonial naturalization law allowing aliens to become citizens was enacted by the Maryland assembly in 1666. Maryland's first settlements, other than trading posts, had been founded in 1634.

3101. Naturalization act enacted by Congress was passed on March 26, 1790. It authorized courts of record to "entertain the applications" of alien free white persons who had resided in the United States for two years or more, one year of which should be in a particular state, on proof of good character and on their taking an oath or affirmation to support the Constitution.

3102. Deportation of aliens authorized by Congress was authorized in the early summer of 1798, when the nation was anticipating a war with France. To counter the influence on American politics of the many French refugees who had come to the United States during the French Revolution, Congress passed the Naturalization Act (June 18), extending the period of residence before citizenship from five to 14 years; the Alien Act (June 25), authorizing the deportation of aliens suspected of engaging in treason or subversive activities; and the Alien Alien Enemies Act (July 6), provided that, during wartime, aliens above the age of 14 who were subjects of enemy nations and who were "not actually naturalized shall be liable to be apprehended, restrained, rescued and removed as alien enemies."

3103. Federal immigration law requiring the collection of information on aliens was the Alien Act of June 25, 1798, which required the master or commander of a vessel to make a written report to the customs officer in charge of the port of entry, giving the names of all arriving aliens and other prescribed data pertaining to them.

3104. Year in which more than 10,000 immigrants arrived in the United States was 1825. According to records kept by the U.S. Bureau of the Census, the number of alien passengers who arrived in the United States that year was 10,199.

3105. Year in which more than 100,000 immigrants arrived in the United States was 1842. According to records kept by the U.S. Bureau of the Census, the number of alien passengers who arrived in the United States that year was 104,565. The numbers dropped below 100,000 in 1843 and 1844 and again in 1861 and 1862.

3106. Immigration of Chinese nationals to the U.S. mainland began in 1852, when the California Gold Rush lured about 20,000 Chinese to San Francisco, CA. However, Hawaii has the oldest Chinese community in the United States; Chinese merchants and sugar growers settled there in the early 19th century.

3107. Tax to limit immigration was the Foreign Miner's License Tax, passed in 1852 by the California legislature. The state collected $3 a month from every foreign-born miner, including those who were prohibited by law from becoming citizens. The intention was to discourage Chinese from immigrating to California and competing with American gold miners.

3108. Immigration receiving station anywhere in the world was Castle Garden (originally called Castle Clinton), a circular stone fortress built on an island in New York Harbor. In 1855 the New York State Immigration Commission, charged with protecting newly arrived immigrants from being cheated by merchants and boarding-house operators, built a causeway from the island to the mainland and put the building to use as a receiving station where newcomers could speak with social workers, change money, and prepare for entry into the city. After a series of investigative hearings into official corruption at Castle Garden, it was replaced in 1892 by a much larger processing station run by the federal government on nearby Ellis Island.

3109. National definition of citizenship was enunciated in 1868 in the 14th Amendment to the Constitution, which declared that "all persons born or naturalized in the United States, and subject to the jurisdiction thereof, are citizens of the United States and of the State wherein they reside." Although the original Constitution made reference to citizens, it gave no definition of the term, leaving open the possibility that a class of persons, such as those of African descent, could be refused the status of citizens. It also made no provision for a process by which citizenship could be acquired. The Supreme Court ruled in 1898 that children born in the United States are citizens regardless of the status of their parents.

3110. Year in which more than 500,000 immigrants arrived in the United States was 1881. According to records kept by the U.S. Bureau of the Census, the number of alien passengers who arrived in the United States that year was 669,431.

3111. Restrictions by Congress on immigration of Chinese laborers were passed on May 6, 1882, suspending Chinese immigration for a 10-year period and forbidding naturalization. According to the provisions of a treaty between China and the United States, signed on May 9, 1881, by President Chester Alan Arthur and proclaimed on October 5, it was agreed that the United States could "regulate, limit or suspend" the immigration of Chinese labor, but not prohibit it altogether. The Chinese exclusion acts were repealed on December 17, 1943.

3112. Immigration ban enacted by Congress was passed on August 3, 1882. The law denied entry to convicts, paupers, and people with physical or mental defects and required each immigrant to pay a tax of 50 cents. In 1903 the fee went up to two dollars; in 1907, to four dollars; and in 1918, to eight dollars.

3113. Immigration bureau superintendent was William D. Owen, whose appointment on June 15, 1891, was confirmed by the Senate on December 16. The office of immigration superintendent was created by Congress on March 3, 1891, under the Treasury Department. Owen resigned on March 20, 1893.

3114. Federal immigration station was constructed on Ellis Island in New York Harbor, off New York, NY. The island was formerly a place of execution for pirates and the site of a small military outpost. The immigration station consisted of the main processing hall, four hospital buildings, a kitchen building, a disinfection house, a records office, and four other buildings. The complex burned to the ground on June 14, 1897, with no loss of life, and was rebuilt. More than 12 million immigrants came through Ellis Island between January 1892 and November 1954. (The first was Annie Moore, a 15-year-old girl from Ireland, who arrived on January 1, 1892.) Their descendants are estimated to number more than 100 million.

3115. Year in which more than 1 million immigrants arrived in the United States was 1905. According to records kept by the U.S. Bureau of the Census, the number of immigrant aliens admitted to the United States that year was 1,026,499.

3116. Immigration quotas enacted by Congress were authorized on May 19, 1921, when Congress limited immigration to 3 percent of the number of foreign-born persons of any given nationality in the United States as shown in the 1910 census. Not more than 20 percent of any country's quota was permitted to arrive in one month. The act also set 357,000 as the total number of people who could be admitted— a figure that was cut in half by the Immigration Act of May 26, 1924, which also changed the quota calculation to a percentage based on the number of persons of a particular nationality living in the United States in 1890 (later changed to 1920). The quotas, which did not apply to immigrants from Canada and Latin America, were intended to limit immigration from countries in southern and eastern Europe and encourage immigration from countries in northern and western Europe. Quotas based on national origin were abolished in 1968 under the Immigration and Naturalization Act of 1965.

3117. State law establishing English as an official language was the Illinois law enacted on June 19, 1923, which stated that "the official language of the State of Illinois shall be known hereafter as the 'American' language."

3118. Large-scale repatriation program was undertaken in 1930 by the U.S. Immigration and Naturalization Service. Under the five-year program, between 300,000 and 500,000 people of Mexican descent, including some U.S. citizens, were repatriated to Mexico. Between 1953 and 1958 a larger INS effort, popularly known as "Operation Wetback," deported nearly 4 million Mexicans.

3119. Registration of aliens by the federal government was authorized by Congress under the Alien Registration Act of 1940, approved on June 28, 1940, "to amend certain provisions of law with respect to the admission and deportation of aliens; to require the fingerprinting and registration of aliens." The registration was

POPULATION—IMMIGRATION AND CITIZENSHIP—*continued*

conducted by the Alien Registration Division of the Immigration and Naturalization Service. Earl Grant Harrison was the director in charge of registration. During the period from August 27 to December 26, 1940, the number of noncitizens who registered was 4,741,971.

3120. Citizenship granted on foreign soil was conferred on December 4, 1942, in the Panama Canal Zone by Thomas Buckman Shoemaker, assistant commissioner of the Immigration and Naturalization Service, on Private James Alexander Finnell Hoey, who had been born in Ireland. The Second War Powers Act of March 27, 1942, authorized the commissioner of Immigration and Naturalization to designate a representative who shall have power to naturalize "any person entitled to naturalization, who while serving honorably in the military or naval forces of the United States is not within the jurisdiction of any court authorized to naturalize aliens."

3121. Honorary citizenship authorized by Congress was conferred on Sir Winston Churchill, the former prime minister of Great Britain, by proclamation of April 9, 1963, by President John Fitzgerald Kennedy.

3122. Immigration quota applied to Mexico was established under the Immigration and Naturalization Act of 1965. Although there had been several mass deportations of Mexican immigrants, notably in 1930 and the mid-1950s, this was the first time that immigration from Mexico to the United States was legally limited. The total number of immigrants from Western Hemisphere countries was set at 120,000 per year.

3123. Naturalization ceremony in the White House was held on November 23, 1968, when 54 immigrants from 26 nations became citizens. The youngest was an eight-year-old Filipino girl and the oldest was a 72-year-old Chinese laundry worker.

3124. Boatlift of Cuban refugees began on April 21, 1980, when the Carter Administration agreed to accept into the United States a large number of refugees seeking political asylum from Cuba's communist regime. Most of the 125,262 immigrants traveled in small boats to Key West, FL, from the Cuban port of Mariel. The boatlift lasted until September 26, when Mariel was closed by Cuban authorities.

3125. Migration study jointly conducted by the United States and Mexico was the Binational Study on Migration, released on August 30, 1997. It contained the first authoritative estimate of the net annual flow of illegal Mexican workers into the United States, which the report placed at approximately 105,000 per year during the 1990s.

POSTAL SERVICE

3126. Transatlantic mail service began in the early 1600s between Britain and its American colonies. An open sack was set up at dockside coffeehouses and taverns and collect outgoing mail, which was carried by merchant ships bound for the other side. The ship captain received one penny per letter, paid sometimes by the sender, sometimes by the recipient. Warships carried official government correspondence.

3127. Colonial post office established by law was a tavern in Boston, MA, run by Richard Fairbanks. On November 5, 1639, the General Court of Massachusetts designated the tavern as the colony's official postal station, declaring it to be "the place appointed for all letters, which are brought from beyond the seas, or are to be sent thither." Fairbanks was charged "to take care, that they bee delivered, or sent according to their directions, and hee is allowed for every such letter 1d. and must answer all miscarriages through his owne neglect." Individuals remained free to deposit mail directly with ship captains or at other taverns. This law dealt with foreign mail only.

3128. Colonial law regulating domestic transmission of official mail was passed by the Virginia Assembly in 1661. It directed that "all letters superscribed for the service of his Majesty or publique shall be immediately conveyed from plantation to plantation to the place and person they are directed to and a penalty of 350 pounds of tobacco to each defaulter."

3129. Colonial law providing a fixed compensation for mail carriers was passed by Massachusetts in January 1673. It directed that messengers carrying mail should receive 3d. for each mile traveled, "as full satisfaction for the expense of horse and man." The same statute fixed 2d. per bushel of oats and 4d. for hay as the maximum amount that any innkeeper could charge a public mail carrier. A similar law was passed in Connecticut the following year.

3130. Overland mail service between colonies to be run by a colonial government was a monthly trip between Boston, MA, and New York, NY, which was operated under the sponsorship of New York's governor, Francis Lovelace. The first rider left New York on horseback on January 22, 1673, and arrived in Boston three weeks later. The messengers carried, in sealed bags, both official correspondence and private mail from individuals. The service lasted only until August 1673, when New York was recaptured by the Dutch. Though the British reacquired New York by treaty the following year, the route was not reestablished for some 15 years.

3131. Colonial postmaster was John Hayward, known as "the Scrivener," who was appointed on December 27, 1677, by the General Court of Massachusetts "to take and convey letters according to direction" and to "sett the prices on letters." He was reappointed in 1680. Another John Hayward, probably his son, took over the job in 1687.

3132. Intercolonial postal system was set up by Thomas Neale under a patent granted on February 17, 1691, by the English sovereigns William and Mary, who conferred "full power and authority to erect, settle and establish within the chief parts of their Majesties' colonies and plantations in America, an office or offices for the receiving and dispatching of letters and pacquets, and to receive, send and deliver the same under such rates and sums of money as the planters shall agree to give, and to hold and enjoy the same for the term of 21 years." Neale, who served as the royal Master of the Mint, did not go to America himself but sent in his stead Andrew Hamilton, whom he appointed postmaster general. The first colony to join the system was New York, on November 11, 1692, followed by Pennsylvania, New Hampshire, Massaachusetts, and Connecticut. Mail service between colonies began on May 1, 1693, between Portsmouth, NH, and Philadelphia, PA.

3133. Postmaster general of the English colonies was Andrew Hamilton, who was appointed to the post by Thomas Neale, recipient of a patent from the British crown that permitted him to set up a postal system in its American colonies. The appointment was confirmed by the English postmaster general on April 4, 1692.

3134. Postmarked mail was required by the colony of Massachusetts. On June 9, 1693, the legislature voted to join the intercolonial postal system that had been founded the previous year by Thomas Neale under a royal British patent. Among the conditions set by the legislature was the requirement that the receiving post office mark the day, month, and year of receipt on each letter "with a print."

3135. Postmaster general of the British colonies was John Hamilton. His father, Andrew Hamilton, had been administrator of Thomas Neale's intercolonial postal system with the title of Deputy Postmaster in the Colonies. After the British government acquired ownership of Neale's system in 1707, John Hamilton was named Postmaster General for America. The title was changed to deputy postmaster general in 1711, when the Postmaster General of England took charge of the system.

3136. Woman to serve as a postmaster was Anne Catherine Hoof Green, the widow of Jonas Green, who was appointed circa 1768 to fill her husband's post as printer and postmaster of Maryland. She was the publisher of the *Maryland Gazette*. She was followed by Mary Katherine Goddard, postmaster at Baltimore, MD, from 1775 to 1789. Sarah De Crow, appointed postmaster at Hertford, NC, on September 27, 1792, was the first woman postmaster appointed after the adoption of the Constitution. Of 195 postmasters appointed, she was the only woman.

3137. Independent postal service during the Revolution was set up in May 1775, when the separate colonies from Massachusetts to Virginia established post offices and routes to rival those of the British. A committee to oversee mail service, headed by Benjamin Franklin, was appointed by the Continental Congress on May 29. Its recommendations were delivered and enacted into law on July 26 at Philadelphia, PA. Franklin was unanimously elected postmaster general.

3138. Postmaster general under the Continental Congress was Benjamin Franklin of Pennsylvania, who was appointed on July 26, 1775, by the Second Continental Congress at a salary of $1,000 a year and who served until November 7, 1776. He had served the crown as deputy postmaster at Philadelphia, PA, from 1737 to 1753, and as deputy postmaster general for the colonies from 1753 to 1774.

POSTAL SERVICE—*continued*

3139. Mail franking privilege allowing free use of the mail was granted to members of Congress and private soldiers in service on November 8, 1775. Regulations of January 9, 1776, provided that soldiers' mail was to be franked by the officer in charge. On April 3, 1800, Congress granted Martha Washington free franking of mail during her natural life.

3140. Postal rates after the Revolution were continued from the rates that had been in force under the British and were codified under the Ordinance of 1782. A letter consisting of a single sheet of paper cost eight cents for transportation up to 60 miles, twelve cents between 60 and 100 miles, and 16 cents between 100 and 200 miles. A surcharge of four cents was applied for each additional 100 miles. Higher rates were charged for heavier letters consisting of multiple sheets and for letters enclosed in packets.

3141. Federal monopoly on postal services was established in 1787, when Congress enacted a law declaring that "the United States in Congress assembled are invested with the sole exclusive right of establishing and regulating post offices from one state to another throughout the United States and exacting such postage on the papers passing on the same as may be requisite to defray the expense of said office."

3142. Post office west of the eastern seaboard was established in Pittsburgh, PA. On July 3, 1788, Congress established mail delivery from Philadelphia to Pittsburgh along a route that went through Lancaster, Yorktown, Carlisle, Chamberstown, and Bedford. The mail reached Chamberstown once a week and was brought to Pittsburgh every other week. The route was extended to Wheeling, in the western part of Virginia, in 1794.

3143. Post Office Department was temporarily established by act of Congress on September 22, 1789, which also created the office of postmaster general. The congressional act of February 20, 1792, was the first to provide in detail for the Post Office Department and the postal service generally. Originally the responsibility of the Treasury Department, the Post Office became a separate institution in 1829 and was made an executive department by act of June 8, 1872. The change of status was made during the term of Postmaster General John Angel James Creswell of Maryland, who served from March 5, 1869, to March 17, 1873.

3144. Postmaster general of the United States was Samuel Osgood of Massachusetts, who was appointed by President George Washington and who served from September 26, 1789, to August 19, 1791. His office was authorized by act of Congress of September 22, 1789, which gave the general supervision of the post office to a postmaster general under the direction of the president. The salary was $1,500 a year. Osgood and his immediate successors were considered informal members of the President's cabinet. In 1829 the job of postmaster general was officially raised to a cabinet-level appointment. It was demoted from that status in 1971.

3145. Foreign mail service of the United States Post Office was established in 1792 by Postmaster General Timothy Pickering, who set up a system of mail exchange between Burlington, VT, and Montreal, Canada.

3146. Postal service law enacted by Congress was signed by President George Washington on February 20, 1792. This act set the rates at 6 cents for letters to be carried not more than 30 miles, 8 cents between 30 and 60 miles, 10 cents between 60 and 100 miles, and 12.5 cents between 100 and 150 miles.

3147. Year in which gross revenue from postage exceeded $100,000 was 1793, when the gross revenue amounted to $104,747. The figure for the previous year was $67,444. The increase was the result of a change in postal rates, enacted in 1792, that made it cheaper to send letters long distances and thus encouraged a higher volume of mail. For single-sheet letters, the lowest rate was six cents (for transportation up to 30 miles) and the highest was 25 cents (for transportation farther than 450 miles).

3148. Year in which the number of letters carried by the Post Office Department exceeded 1 million was 1795, when a total of 1,124,340 letters were transmitted. The number of miles of post roads totaled 13,207 that year, up from 1,875 in 1790, and the number of post offices was 453, up from 75. Most of the mail was transported in stagecoaches.

3149. Ban on African-American slaves as mail carriers was effected by Congress in the post office law of 1802, which stipulated that only free whites could carry the mail. African-American slaves had been serving as post riders in the South for some time, but white Southerners, fearful of a slave uprising, complained that such a job gave them too much access to information.

3150. Treaties for postal routes through Native American territory were concluded in 1805 in land that had been acquired by the United States through the Louisiana Purchase. The Cherokee Nation agreed to allow the federal government to run two roads through an area that is now in Tennessee and Alabama. The Creek Nation agreed to clear a path through its territory, lay log bridges across streams, maintain boats for river crossings, and give lodging to the mail riders.

3151. Use of the Post Office to generate revenue in wartime was made during the War of 1812. On December 23, 1814, Congress raised postage rates 50 percent. (The current rates had been in force since 1799.) They remained at the higher rates until February 1816. The gross revenue thus generated amounted to $1,043,000—an increase of about $313,000 over the previous year's tally.

3152. Year in which gross revenue from postage exceeded $1,000,000 was 1815, when it reached $1,043,000. That year's revenue, however, had been artificially inflated by special rates imposed during the War of 1812. Beginning in 1817, gross revenue from postage always exceeded $1,000,000, even though the rates were returned to their prewar levels.

3153. Express mail was a network of horse-and-rider relays that carried letters on direct routes between leading commercial cities. It was instituted by Postmaster General John McLean in 1825. The postage for express service was three times the normal rate. The system reduced the delivery time between New York City and New Orleans, LA, to one week.

3154. Year in which the number of letters carried by the Post Office Department exceeded 10 million was 1825. A total of 10,016,488 letters were carried that year, transmitted through 5,677 post offices and along 94,052 miles of post road.

3155. Federal post office built for the purpose was authorized on May 24, 1828, by Congress, which received title to a site in Newport, RI, on November 12, 1828. The building, known as the Custom House and Post Office, was occupied in 1830.

3156. Postmaster general to become a member of the president cabinet was William Taylor Barry, appointed by President Andrew Jackson, who served from April 6, 1829, to April 30, 1835. Barry resigned under congressional charges of inefficiency and corruption.

3157. Post office building built for that purpose was the Custom House and Post Office in Newport, RI, built in 1829 and occupied in 1830. An act of Congress approved on May 24, 1828, authorized the erection of the building. The title to the site was vested in the government on November 12, 1828.

3158. Post office west of the Mississippi River was established in Dubuque, IA, in 1836.

3159. Extension of mail service to the West Coast took place in 1858, when the Butterfield Overland Mail began deliveries to California from St. Louis, MO, and Memphis, TN.

3160. Postmaster general of the Confederate States of America was John H. Reagan of Texas, who was appointed in March 1861. Mail service to the post offices of the rebellious states was prohibited in June 1861 by the federal government, whose naval blockade also hampered the transmittal of the Confederacy's overseas mail.

3161. Free mail delivery in cities was authorized by congressional act of March 3, 1863. City delivery service was placed in operation on July 1, 1863, in 49 major cities, using 440 carriers at an annual cost of $300,000. On January 3, 1887, free delivery service was extended to cities with populations of 50,000 or more and was permitted in places having a population of at least 10,000 and postal receipts of $10,000.

3162. Mail fraud law enacted by Congress was enacted on June 8, 1872. It outlawed any "fraudulent lottery, gift enterprise, or scheme for the distribution of money, or of any real or personal property, by lot, chance, or drawing of any kind, or in conducting any other scheme or device for obtaining money through the mails by means of false or fraudulent pretenses, representations, or promises." The postmaster general was authorized to stamp mail, registered mail, and money orders "fraudulent" and return them to the sender instead of making the delivery to the addressee.

3163. Rural free mail delivery was established on October 1, 1896, when three routes were designated in West Virginia: one from Charles Town, one from Uvilla, and one from Halltown.

POSTAL SERVICE—STAMPS

3164. Postage stamp depicting a president was authorized by act of Congress of March 3, 1847. The issue consisted of two stamps: a five-cent red-brown stamp depicting Benjamin Franklin, of which 3,712,200 were printed, and a ten-cent black stamp bearing the likeness of

POSTAL SERVICE—STAMPS—*continued*

President George Washington, of which 891,000 were printed. Both stamps were printed in New York City by Rawdon, Wright, Hatch, and Edson and were placed on sale there on July 1, 1847. They were withdrawn from use on June 30, 1851.

3165. Postage stamps issued by the Confederacy were five-cent stamps printed in London, England, by Thomas De La Rue & Company and sold in Southern post offices beginning in April 1862. Stamps in denominations of two, ten, and twenty cents were printed in Richmond, VA, by Archer & Daly in the spring of 1863.

3166. Postage stamp honoring a dead president was the 15-cent black postage stamp depicting Abraham Lincoln that was issued on June 17, 1866. Black postage stamps showing portraits of George Washington had been issued on July 1, 1847, and July 1, 1851, but these were not mourning stamps.

3167. Postage stamp issue depicting all the presidents who had served until that time was the ordinary postage stamp issue of 1938, which showed likenesses of the 29 presidents from George Washington to Calvin Coolidge. They were issued over the course of nine months, beginning on April 25 with Washington, who was depicted on a one-cent green stamp, and ending on December 8 with Theodore Roosevelt, depicted on a 30-cent blue stamp, and William Howard Taft, depicted on a 50-cent lavender stamp.

3168. Commemorative postage stamp depicting a First Lady was the five-cent light purple stamp issued on October 11, 1963, at Washington, DC, on the anniversary of the birthday of Eleanor Roosevelt, the wife of Franklin Delano Roosevelt.

PRESIDENTIAL ELECTIONS

3169. Method of electing the president was outlined in Article II, Section 1, of the Constitution, ratified in 1788. According to this article, the president was to be chosen by electors from each state, appointed "in such Manner as the Legislature thereof may direct." The number of electors was the same as the state's total number of senators and congressional representatives. Sealed certificates showing the electors' choices were transmitted to the capital to be counted by the president of the Senate, who declared the person with the highest number of votes to be president and the runner-up to be vice president. Senators, congressmen, and fed-

eral officials were not eligible to become electors, who were expected to be impartial in their decision-making and to judge potential presidents on the basis of merit only. This nonpartisan system was compromised as early as 1796, when electors came under pressure to select candidates chosen by party caucuses. The first formal change to the Constitution's system was made in 1804 by the Twelfth Amendment, which allowed for separate votes for president and vice president.

3170. Presidential election was authorized on September 13, 1788, by the Constitutional Convention, which "resolved that the first Wednesday in January next be the day for appointing electors in the several states, which, before the said day, shall have ratified the said Constitution; that the first Wednesday in February next be the day for the electors to assemble in their respective states, and vote for a President; and that the first Wednesday in March next be the time, and the present seat of Congress the place for commencing the proceedings under the said Constitution." Congress was then located in New York City. The presidential election authorized in this resolution took place on February 4, 1789. The ballots were counted on April 6.

3171. President to receive the unanimous vote of the presidential electors was George Washington, who received all of the 69 votes cast by the electors from the ten states that voted on February 4, 1789. A nearly unanimous vote took place in November 1816, when James Monroe received 231 of the 232 votes cast by the electors from 24 states. The dissenting vote was cast by William Plumer of New Hampshire.

3172. Presidential election won by the Federalist Party was the election of 1789, in which George Washington of Virginia was unanimously elected by 69 electors from ten states. The balloting took place at Federal Hall, New York, NY, on April 6, 1789. John Adams of Massachusetts, who was elected as vice president, was also a Federalist. The party advocated a political philosophy that required the various states to surrender the greater part of their powers to a strong, unifying central government. In all, it participated in eight elections, winning the first three and losing the last five (1800–16).

3173. Presidential election in which a candidate was endorsed by a political party was the election of 1792. Though it was a foregone conclusion that George Washington would be reelected to a second term, the choice of vice president remained open to contest. In October of that year, a group of Democratic-Republican leaders met in Philadelphia, PA, and gave their endorsement to one of their own, George Clinton, the governor of New York. However, the election was won by incumbent John Adams, who received 77 electoral votes to Clinton's 50.

3174. Electoral vote cast contrary to instructions was cast by Samuel Miles, a Pennsylvania Federalist, in the presidential election of 1796. Instead of voting for John Adams, the Federalist candidate, Miles voted for Thomas Jefferson, a Democratic-Republican. The electors were pledged, but not legally bound, to support a candidate belonging to their party.

3175. Presidential election in which the Democratic-Republican Party participated was the election of 1796, which was won by John Adams of Massachusetts, a Federalist. During the campaign, a group of congressmen who favored strong state governments over a strong central government gathered in caucus and agreed to support two candidates for the presidency, Aaron Burr of New York and Thomas Jefferson of Virginia, who received enough electoral votes to be named vice president. This group, originally called the Republican Party, was better known as the Democratic-Republican Party, the predecessor of the Democratic Party.

3176. Presidential election in which more than one candidate declared for the presidency was the election of 1796, in which 13 candidates received electoral votes: John Adams of Massachusetts received 71, Thomas Jefferson of Virginia 68, Thomas Pinckney of South Carolina 59, Aaron Burr of New York 30, Samuel Adams of Massachusetts 15, Oliver Ellsworth of Connecticut eleven, George Clinton of New York seven, John Jay of New York five, James Iredell of North Carolina three, John Henry of Maryland two, Samuel Johnston of North Carolina two, George Washington of Virginia two (although he had already declined a third term), and Charles Cotesworth Pinckney of South Carolina one. The winner became president and the runner-up vice president. In the elections of 1789 and 1792, George Washington was the only avowed presidential candidate.

3177. Presidential election that produced a change in the party in power was the election of November 4, 1800. The first two presidents, George Washington and John Adams, were Federalist in philosophy. The election of 1800 brought to power the Democratic-Republicans under Thomas Jefferson. The next change of presidential parties did not occur until 1828, when Andrew Jackson, the first of the Democrats, was elected.

3178. Presidential election won by the Democratic-Republican Party was the election of November 4, 1800. The electors cast 276 votes for five candidates, including two who were supported by the Democratic-Republican group in Congress—Jefferson and Aaron Burr—and three who were supported by the Federalists: incumbent president John Adams, Charles Cotesworth Pinckney, and John Jay. Jefferson and Burr topped the field with 73 votes each, guaranteeing that the offices of president and vice president would both be held by Democratic-Republicans. A tie-breaking vote was taken in the House of Representatives, which eventually gave the presidency to Jefferson.

3179. President elected by decision of the House of Representatives was Thomas Jefferson. After the election of November 4, 1800, the electoral vote stood as follows: Thomas Jefferson 73, Aaron Burr 73, John Adams 65, Charles Cotesworth Pinckney 64, and John Jay one. The House of Representatives assembled on February 11, 1801, and on the 36th ballot elected Jefferson. Delaware and South Carolina cast blank ballots, with the result that the vote was ten states for Jefferson and four for Burr.

3180. Presidential election in which candidates were separately nominated for the vice presidency was held on November 6, 1804. Prior to the adoption of the Twelfth Amendment to the Constitution on September 25, 1804, the candidate for president receiving the highest number of votes became president, and the candidate receiving the second highest number became vice president. George Clinton was the vice presidential candidate of the Democratic-Republican Party, which won the election, and Rufus King was the candidate of the Federalist Party.

3181. Presidential election in which the candidates of a single party ran unopposed was the election of 1820. The Federalist Party, which had always been less of a party than an alliance, went out of existence in 1816, leaving the field to the Democratic-Republicans. All 232 presidential electors voted for James Mon-

PRESIDENTIAL ELECTIONS—*continued*

roe that year except for William Plumer of New Hampshire, who cast his vote for John Quincy Adams to preserve for George Washington the honor of being the sole president elected unanimously.

3182. Vice presidential candidate to run with three presidential candidates simultaneously was John C. Calhoun of South Carolina. Calhoun was one of five Democratic-Republicans to declare their interest in running for the presidency in 1824. When William H. Crawford won the party's nomination in February at a caucus held by a minority of congressional party members, three of his opponents—Henry Clay, John Quincy Adams, and Andrew Jackson—arranged to have themselves nominated by state legislatures. Calhoun withdrew from the race and agreed to run as the vice presidential candidate of all three. Adams was the winner.

3183. Popular vote in a presidential election had its origins in 1788, when five states decided to entrust the selection of presidential electors to the voters, rather than to the state legislatures. By 1824, 18 of the 24 states were choosing their electors by popular vote. In that year's four-way presidential race (held November 2), Andrew Jackson received 153,544 popular and 99 electoral votes, while John Quincy Adams received 108,740 popular and 84 electoral votes, though none of the four candidates appeared on the ballot in all states and the popular vote did not represent a true assessment of the will of the people (despite Jackson's claim that it did). The contest was decided by the House of Representatives, which gave the decision to Adams. By the year 2000, a total of 14 presidents had been elected with less than a majority of the popular vote.

3184. Presidential election in which all candidates were from the same political party took place on November 2, 1824. The four candidates represented four different factions of the Democratic-Republican Party, which was the only party in existence, the Federalist Party having collapsed in 1816. Andrew Jackson received 99 electoral votes, John Quincy Adams 84, William Harris Crawford 42, and Henry Clay 37. Since no candidate had a majority of the electoral votes, the House of Representatives was called on to exercise its constitutional responsibility to choose from the highest three. In the meantime, Crawford was eliminated after becoming ill, and Clay agreed to use his influ-

ence to have Adams elected, provided that Adams promised to appoint him secretary of state. The balloting in the House of Representatives was four for Crawford, seven for Jackson, and thirteen for Adams, who thus became president.

3185. Presidential election won by the Democratic Party was the election of November 4, 1828, which was also the first presidential election in which the Democratic Party participated. The Democratic-Republicans, who had controlled the White House and both houses of Congress since 1800, had split into factions, and in 1828 gave way entirely. The faction supporting Andrew Jackson, now called the Democrats, defeated the faction supporting John Quincy Adams, known variously as the Federalists or National Republicans, with Jackson taking 68.2 percent of the electoral vote to Adams's 31.8.

3186. Presidential election in which all the candidates were nominated at party conventions was the election of November 6, 1832. The winner, Andrew Jackson, was nominated by the Democrats at Baltimore, MD, in May 1832, at the party's first national convention. The runner-up, Henry Clay of Kentucky, was nominated by the National Republican Party (later known as the Whigs) at their first convention, which took place in Baltimore in December 1831. John Floyd of Virginia was nominated by a group of pro-nullification Democrats calling themselves the Independent Party, who met in convention at Charleston, SC, in November 1831. William Wirt of Maryland, the first candidate ever to be nominated at a convention of party delegates, was nominated by the Anti-Masonic Party at Baltimore in September 1831.

3187. Presidential election in which the Whig Party participated was the election of November 6, 1832, which was won by the Democratic-Republican candidate, Andrew Jackson. His opponent was Henry Clay of Kentucky, who ran on the ticket of the National Republicans, a loose coalition of people opposed for various reasons to the policies of President Jackson. This coalition, originally a faction of the Democratic-Republicans, was reorganized in 1834 under the Whig name.

3188. Presidential election won by the Whig Party was the election of November 3, 1840, which was won by William Henry Harrison of Ohio. Zachary Taylor, elected in 1848, was also a Whig.

3189. Third party to participate in a presidential election was the Liberty Party, founded in New York State in 1839 by antislavery activists impatient with the footdragging tactics of the two major parties, the Whigs and the Democrats. They nominated James Gillespie Birney as their presidential candidate in the election of 1840, but Birney did not campaign, visiting England instead, and the party won only 7,000 votes on Election Day, November 3. Most of the nation's antislavery votes went to the Whig candidate, William Henry Harrison, whose early death left Vice President John Tyler, himself a slaveowner, in the White House. The Liberty Party ran Birney again in 1844 and received 62,000 votes.

3190. Election day for presidential voting held nationwide was authorized by act of Congress of January 23, 1845, "an act to establish a uniform time for holding elections for electors of President and Vice President in all the states of the Union." The day selected for voting was "the Tuesday next after the first Monday in the month of November of the year in which they are to be appointed." The first election under the act was held on November 7, 1848.

3191. Presidential election in which the Republican Party participated took place on November 4, 1856, when the Republican candidates, John Charles Frémont of California and William Lewis Dayton of New Jersey, lost by about half a million popular votes and 60 electoral votes to James Buchanan of Pennsylvania and John Cabell Breckinridge of Kentucky, the Democratic candidates. (A third party, the American Party, or Know-Nothings, took nearly 875,000 popular votes.) The Republican Party had originated in 1854 to oppose the extension of slavery into the new western territories.

3192. Third party to make a substantial showing in a presidential election was the American Party, also known as the Know-Nothing Party. In the election of November 4, 1856, the party's candidates, Millard Fillmore of New York and Andrew Jackson Donelson of Tennessee, received eight electoral votes out of 296 cast, carrying one state, Maryland. They won 874,534 popular votes, which represented 21.5 percent of the total. Fillmore, originally a member of the Whig Party, had already served as the nation's 13th president, taking office in July 1850 after the death of Zachary Taylor.

3193. Presidential election in which more than 80 percent of eligible voters cast ballots was the election of November 6, 1860, when ballots were cast by 81.2 percent of eligible voters. There were galvanizing issues that year: the future of slavery and the continued existence of the Union. Abraham Lincoln, the Republican candidate, polled 1,866,452 popular votes and 59.41 percent of the electoral vote; Stephen Arnold Douglas, the Democratic candidate, polled 1,375,157 popular votes and 3.96 percent of the electoral vote; John Cabell Breckinridge, the Southern Democratic candidate, polled 847,953 popular votes and 23.76 percent of the electoral vote; and John Bell, the Constitutional Union candidate, polled 590,631 popular votes and 12.87 percent of the electoral vote.

3194. Presidential election won by the Republican Party was the election of November 6, 1860, when Abraham Lincoln of Illinois and his running mate, Hannibal Hamlin of Maine, defeated their Democratic opponents, Stephen Arnold Douglas of Illinois and Herschel Vespasian Johnson of Georgia, by some half a million popular votes (1,866,452 to 1,375,157) and 168 electoral votes (180 to 12). They also defeated two third parties, the Southern Democrats and the Constitutional Union Party.

3195. Third party to win more than 10 percent of the electoral vote in a presidential election was the Constitutional Union Party, formerly known as the American (or Know-Nothing) Party. Its candidates, John Bell of Tennessee and Edward Everett of Massachusetts, received 39 of 303 electoral votes cast, or 12.87 percent, in the election of November 6, 1860. They were from Kentucky, Tennessee, and Virginia.

3196. Year in which two presidents were elected was 1861, after the formation of the Confederacy as a rival government. Both presidents were from Kentucky. Abraham Lincoln, born on February 12, 1809, in Hardin County, KY, became president of the United States on March 4, 1861. Jefferson Davis, born in Todd County, KY, on June 3, 1808, was chosen president of the Confederacy by the provisional congress on February 18, 1861. He was inaugurated at Richmond, VA, on February 22, 1862, after he was elected by popular vote.

PRESIDENTIAL ELECTIONS—*continued*

3197. Vice president to declare the election of the candidate who had opposed him for the presidency was John Cabell Breckinridge, vice president from 1857 to 1861 under James Buchanan. Breckinridge ran for the presidency in 1860 as the candidate of two proslavery parties, the National Democratic Party, also called the Independent Democratic Party, and the Southern Democratic Party. On February 13, 1861, Vice President Breckinridge presided over a joint session of Congress at which the electoral votes were counted. It then fell to Breckinridge to announce that the winner was Abraham Lincoln, his Republican opponent, who had received 180 votes to Breckinridge's 72. John Bell of the Constitutional Union Party had received 39 and the Democratic candidate, Stephen Arnold Douglas, twelve.

3198. Presidential election in which a bloc of states did not participate was the election of November 8, 1864, during the Civil War. No votes were collected from the citizens of the eleven states that had seceded from the Union, and the electoral vote was reduced by a total of 80 votes, to 233. These states were Alabama, with eight electoral votes; Arkansas, with five; Florida, three; Georgia, nine; Louisiana, seven; Mississippi, seven; North Carolina, nine; South Carolina, six; Tennessee, ten; Texas, six; and Virginia, ten.

3199. Presidential election in which soldiers in the field were allowed to vote was the election of 1864. Thirteen states—California, Iowa, Kansas, Kentucky, Maine, Maryland, Michigan, Minnesota, New Hampshire, Ohio, Pennsylvania, Vermont, and Wisconsin—made arrangements to enable their soldiers to cast ballots, but those from Kansas and Minnesota arrived too late to be counted. Of a total of 150,635 votes cast by the soldiers on November 8, 116,887 were for Abraham Lincoln, Republican, and 33,748 for George Brinton McClellan, Democrat.

3200. Presidential election in which neither candidate received a majority of the electoral vote was the election of November 7, 1876, in which Rutherford Birchard Hayes of Ohio, the Republican candidate, faced Samuel Jones Tilden of New York, the Democratic candidate. Tilden won a majority of the popular vote, taking 4,300,590 votes to Hayes's 4,036,298, but neither candidate succeeded in winning enough electoral votes to be declared the winner. (Tilden had 184, one short of the necessary number, and Hayes had 165.) The counting of the electoral vote was delayed by an argument con-

cerning 20 disputed votes from three Southern states. A 15-man bipartisan commission was set up to decide the election, but the one independent member was replaced by a Republican. With the parties unequally represented, the final electoral decision was 185 for Hayes, 184 for Tilden. Reportedly, the outcome involved a deal in which the Democrats agreed to accept Hayes's election as president in exchange for the removal of all Republican-controlled Reconstruction governments in the Southern states.

3201. Presidential election with a margin of difference of less than 1 percent of the popular vote was the election of November 2, 1880, in which the Republican candidate, James Abram Garfield of Ohio, received 4,454,416 votes and his Democratic opponent, Winfield Scott Hancock of Pennsylvania, received 4,444,952 votes. The difference was about one tenth of 1 percent of the total number of votes. However, Garfield won 57.99 percent of the electoral votes, compared to Hancock's 42.01.

3202. Presidential election in which a socialist party participated was the election of November 8, 1892, in which the Socialist Labor Party fielded candidates for the presidency and vice presidency (they were Simon Wing of Massachusetts and Charles Horatio Matchett of New York). They received 21,512 popular votes and no electoral votes, coming in fifth behind the Democrats, Republicans, Populists, and Prohibitionists.

3203. Presidential primary was held by Florida in 1904, when the state's Democrats elected their national convention delegates under the first law allowing a general party primary. Twelve other states followed suit in the next eight years.

3204. New Hampshire presidential primary was instituted in 1910. Originally, the primary was open to voters from any or no party. On May 21, 1913, a Democratic majority in the state legislature passed an "Act to Provide for the Election of Delegates to National Conventions by Direct Vote of the People." This allowed any candidate capable of paying $10 or producing two petitions with 100 signatures to put his name on the ballot. On April 11, 1915, the date of the primary was set for the second Tuesday in March. This was changed to the first Tuesday in March in 1971, then, in 1975, to the first Tuesday immediately before the primary of any other New England state. The confusion this caused led the legislature to fix the primary date at the Tuesday a week before all other primaries in the country, thus ensuring that New Hampshire would always have the first primary of every presidential election.

3205. Presidential election in which two former presidents were defeated was the election of November 5, 1912, which was won by Woodrow Wilson, the Democratic candidate, who received 6,293,454 popular votes and 435 electoral votes. Theodore Roosevelt, the former Republican president who was running on the Progressive Party (Bull Moose) ticket, received 4,119,538 popular votes and 88 electoral votes. The incumbent president, Republican William Howard Taft, came in third with 3,484,980 popular votes and eight electoral votes. Wilson was a career academic who had entered politics only two years before, when he ran successfully for the governorship of New Jersey.

3206. Third party to win more than 25 percent of the popular vote in a presidential election was the Progressive Party, also known as the Bull Moose Party. Its candidates, Theodore Roosevelt of New York and Hiram Warren Johnson of California, took 27.4 percent of the popular vote in the election of November 5, 1912. Their total of 4,119,538 votes was less than that of the Democrats (6,293,454 for Woodrow Wilson) but more than that of the Republicans (3,484,980 for the incumbent, William Howard Taft). The Progressives also received 16.57 percent of the electoral vote, compared to 81.92 percent for the Democrats and 1.51 for the Republicans.

3207. President to advocate the creation of a national presidential primary was Woodrow Wilson. In his first annual message to Congress, delivered on December 2, 1913, he urged "the prompt enactment of legislation which will provide for primary elections throughout the country at which voters of the several parties may choose their nominees for the presidency without the intervention of nominating conventions."

3208. Election in which returns were broadcast on radio was the presidential election of November 7, 1916. The De Forest Radio Laboratory in the Highbridge section of the Bronx, New York City, an experimental station run by radio pioneer Lee De Forest, broadcast bulletins from the *New York American* on the results of the presidential race for approximately six hours. The broadcasters signed off about 11 P.M. with the announcement that Charles Evans

Hughes had been elected. In fact, Woodrow Wilson was the winner. On November 2, 1920, Leo H. Rosenberg of station KDKA in Pittsburgh, PA, broadcast the correct results of the Harding–Cox presidential election.

3209. Presidential election in which the wrong candidate was declared the winner by early newspaper editions was the election of November 7, 1916, in which the candidates of the major parties were Woodrow Wilson of New Jersey, the Democratic incumbent, and Charles Evans Hughes of New York, the Republican challenger. The race was one of the closest in history, and the early results appeared to favor Hughes. The news of his victory was reported by many newspapers and by the one radio station that was broadcasting election results, but the final tally showed that Wilson had won California by a mere 4,000 votes, giving him the advantage. Wilson received 52.17 percent of the electoral vote (30 states) and 9,129,606 popular votes. Hughes received 47.83 percent of the electoral vote (18 states) and 8,538,221 popular votes. A more famous case of mistaken early results was that of Harry S. Truman and Thomas Edmund Dewey in 1948.

3210. Presidential election in which the candidates of both major parties were newspaper publishers was the election of November 2, 1920. The Democratic candidate, James Middleton Cox, was the publisher of the *Daily News* in Dayton, OH. The Republican candidate, Warren Gamaliel Harding, was the publisher and editor of the *Star* in Marion, OH. The winner was Harding.

3211. Presidential election in which women voted was the election of November 2, 1920, in which the Republican candidate, Warren Gamaliel Harding, defeated the Democratic candidate, James Middleton Cox. Harding received 16,152,200 votes and Cox received 9,147,353. Five smaller parties—Socialist, Farmer Labor, Prohibition, Socialist Labor, and Single Tax—also participated. Women were granted the right to vote by the 19th Amendment to the Constitution, which was declared ratified on August 26, 1920.

3212. Presidential election in which a communist party participated was the election of November 4, 1924, in which the incumbent president, Calvin Coolidge, was reelected. The Workers Party (Communist Party) met at St. Paul, MN, on July 11, 1924, and nominated William Zebulon Foster of Illinois for president and Benjamin Gitlow of New York as his running mate. They received 36,386 popular votes and no electoral votes.

PRESIDENTIAL ELECTIONS—*continued*

3213. Electoral college members invited to a presidential inauguration were the 531 electors who participated in the election of 1932. All but 59 of them were Democrats. The winner, Franklin Delano Roosevelt, officially invited them to attend the inauguration, which took place on March 4, 1933.

3214. Presidential election in which a computer was used to predict the outcome was the 1952 presidential race between Dwight David Eisenhower and Adlai Ewing Stevenson. The CBS television network employed the UNIVAC to choose the winner. Only an hour after the polls had closed on November 4, 1952, when less than 10 percent of the votes had been counted, the computer correctly projected Eisenhower's landslide victory, trumping human experts who had predicted a close race.

3215. Presidential election debates shown on television were the debates between Richard Milhous Nixon, the Republican candidate, and John Fitzgerald Kennedy, the Democratic candidate, that took place during the 1960 presidential campaign. The first of four debates was held on September 26 in a Chicago studio; the second on October 7 in a Washington, DC, studio; the third on October 13, with Kennedy in New York City and Nixon in Hollywood, CA; and the fourth on October 21 in a New York City studio.

3216. Presidential election in which the Republican Party earned a significant number of votes in the South was the presidential election of 1964, in which Barry M. Goldwater, senator from Arizona, ran against the Democratic incumbent, Lyndon Baines Johnson. Johnson crushed the ultra-conservative Goldwater in the November 3, 1964, election, in which Goldwater polled only 38.7 percent of the vote to Johnson's 61.3 percent. Many of the votes Goldwater did receive were from the South and West, marking the first time the Republican Party received significant support in those regions.

3217. Presidential election in which the state of Vermont was carried by a Democrat was the election of November 3, 1964. The Democratic candidate, Lyndon Baines Johnson, received 66.3 percent of the vote, which gave him Vermont's three electoral votes. The Republican candidate, Barry Morris Goldwater, received 33.6 percent.

3218. Presidential election in which votes were tallied electronically was the election of November 3, 1964, when Coleman Vote Tally Systems were used in Hamilton County (Cincinnati), OH; Orange County (Santa Ana-Anaheim), CA; and Contra Costa (Martinez), CA. They counted 600 ballots a minute. Data from each machine and counting center were automatically transmitted by wire to a central computer in the Registrar of Voters office, where countywide returns were made available as fast as the votes were counted.

3219. State to mandate the votes of its presidential electors was Maine. On March 25, 1969, the state legislature of Maine enacted a law requiring presidential electors to cast their ballots for the presidential and vice presidential candidates of the political party for which they were chosen.

3220. Electoral vote cast for a woman presidential candidate was cast by Roger Lea MacBride of Charlottesville, VA, whose vote for Theodora "Tonie" Nathan of Oregon, vice presidential candidate of the Libertarian Party, was counted on January 6, 1973.

3221. Year in which abortion was mentioned in the national platforms of the major parties was 1976, three years after the Supreme Court legalized abortion nationwide in *Roe v. Wade*. The Democratic platform stated, "We fully recognize the religious and ethical nature of the concerns which many Americans have on the subject of abortion. We feel, however, that it is undesirable to attempt to amend the U.S. Constitution to overturn the Supreme Court decision in this area." The Republican platform stated, "The Republican Party favors a continuance of the public dialogue on abortion and supports the efforts of those who seek enactment of a constitutional amendment to restore protection of the right to life for unborn children."

3222. Televised presidential election debate between an incumbent president and a challenger was held on September 23, 1976, when three networks pooled their efforts to telecast a debate between President Gerald Rudolph Ford, a Republican, and Jimmy Carter, the Democratic candidate, at the Walnut Street Theatre, Philadelphia, PA. The debate, limited to domestic issues, was sponsored by the League of Women Voters. A second debate took place on October 6, 1976, from the Palace of Fine Arts Theatre, San Francisco, CA. A third debate took place on October 22, 1976, from the stage of Phi Beta Kappa Hall on the campus of the College of William and Mary, Williamsburg, VA. Each confrontation was 90 minutes long.

3223. Presidential election in which a Democratic winner failed to carry Texas was the election of November 3, 1992, which was won by William Jefferson Clinton of Arkansas. The 32 electoral votes from the state of Texas went to the Republican candidate, the incumbent President George Herbert Walker Bush, who had represented Texas in the House of Representatives from 1967 through 1971.

3224. National urban presidential primary was CityVote, a nonbinding presidential preference primary held on November 7, 1995, in 17 cities across the United States. The goal of CityVote was to to give urban voters more of a voice in the selection of presidential nominees and to focus attention on urban issue such as gun control and homelessness. Participating cities included Tucson, AZ; Pasadena, CA; Boston, MA; Baltimore, MD; Minneapolis–St. Paul, MN; Fayette, MO; and Burlington, VT. Other than Boston, no major metropolis took part. The voting closely mirrored the national trend, with President William Jefferson Clinton taking first place on every CityVote ballot.

3225. Presidential election in which all candidates and significant political parties operated sites on the Internet was the election of 2000. This was also the first presidential election in which major polling organizations took polls on the Internet and in which every candidate made significant efforts to solicit Web-based donations.

PRESIDENTIAL ELECTIONS—CANDIDATES

3226. Brothers who were candidates for the presidency simultaneously were Charles Cotesworth Pinckney, the governor of South Carolina, and diplomat Thomas Pinckney, who had served as minister to Great Britain from 1792 to 1796 and envoy extraordinary to Spain in 1794–95. In the presidential election of 1796, the members of the electoral college cast 276 ballots for thirteen candidates, including the Pinckneys. Thomas Pinckney received 59 votes and his brother received one. The winners were John Adams, who received 71 votes, and Thomas Jefferson, the runner-up with 68 votes, who thus became president and vice president, respectively.

3227. Vice presidential candidate to decline the nomination was John Langdon of New Hampshire, who was nominated in Washington, DC, on May 12, 1812, by the congressional caucus of the Republican Party, which gave him 64 votes to James Madison's 82. Langdon declined to run, and a second caucus was held at which Elbridge Gerry was nominated.

3228. Presidential candidate nominated by a state legislature instead of a congressional caucus was Andrew Jackson, who was nominated by the legislature of his home state, Tennessee, in October 1825. He spent three years campaigning before he won the election of 1828.

3229. Presidential candidate to be nominated in an open party convention instead of a secret caucus was William Wirt of Maryland, who was nominated on the first ballot at the national convention of the Anti-Masonic Party, held in Baltimore, MD, on September 26, 1831. Wirt lost to Andrew Jackson in the election of 1832.

3230. Presidential candidate of a major party to be nominated at a national convention was incumbent President Andrew Jackson of Tennessee, who was nominated by the Democrats at their national convention in Baltimore, MD, which met on May 21–23, 1832. Martin Van Buren of New York was nominated as the Democratic candidate for vice president.

3231. Presidential candidate to be nominated on the first ballot at a national party convention was Andrew Jackson, who received the unanimous vote of the Democratic Party delegates at Baltimore, MD, in May 1832.

3232. Presidential candidate unanimously nominated by a national party convention was Andrew Jackson, who was nominated for his second term by the delegates of the Democratic Party at Baltimore, MD, in May 1832. The Anti-Masonic Party, which met in convention in September 1831, eight months earlier, declared William Wirt its unanimous candidate, but he had actually received 108 votes out of 111 cast.

3233. Presidential "dark horse" candidate was James Knox Polk. At the Democratic convention on May 29, 1844, in Baltimore, MD, the delegates found themselves split between former president Martin Van Buren and Lewis Cass over the issue of the annexation of Texas. Polk's name was added on the eighth ballot and received 44 votes to Van Buren's 104 and Cass's 114. On the ninth ballot, amid great confusion, the convention stampeded for him, and the vote was declared unanimous. Polk, a former Tennessee congressman and governor, was not present at the convention and received the news by letter. He replied: "It has been well observed that the office of President of the United States should neither be sought nor declined. I have never sought it, nor should I feel

PRESIDENTIAL ELECTIONS—CANDIDATES—continued

at liberty to decline it, if conferred upon me by the voluntary suffrages of my fellow citizens." He ran against Republican candidate Henry Clay and was elected president on November 5, 1844.

3234. Vice presidential nominee from a major party to decline the nomination after he had already been chosen was Silas Wright, who was nominated on May 29, 1844, at the Democratic Party's fourth convention, which was meeting in Baltimore, MD. The supporters of Martin Van Buren, Lewis Cass, and other potential presidential candidates had put themselves in a deadlock, with no candidate receiving the necessary two-thirds of the vote in eight ballots. After finally nominating a dark-horse candidate, James Knox Polk, on the ninth, they chose Wright, a close associate of Van Buren, to be Polk's running mate. Wright, then a senator from New York, received the news by telegraph at the Capitol in Washington, DC, and telegraphed back his refusal—the first time that telegraphy was used for such a purpose. The convention then nominated George Mifflin Dallas of Pennsylvania.

3235. Presidential candidate to be assassinated was Joseph Smith, founder and leader of the Church of Jesus Christ of Latter-day Saints (Mormon Church), a rapidly growing religious community that had established a major settlement at Nauvoo, IL. The idea of a presidential candidacy for Smith was put forward in January 1844 by the church's Council of Twelve. The National Reform Party confirmed the nomination in a state convention at Nauvoo on May 17, naming Sidney Rigdon of Pennsylvania as his running mate. However, a charge of treason was brought against Smith after conflicts within his church erupted into violence, and he and his brother Hyrum were jailed at Carthage, IL, to await trial. A mob broke into the jail on June 27 and shot both of them to death.

3236. Presidential candidate whose opponent had been his military commander was Franklin Pierce, the candidate of the Democratic Party in 1852. A lawyer and former U.S. senator from New Hampshire, Pierce enlisted in the United States Army when the Mexican War broke out in 1847 and was commissioned a brigadier general of volunteers. His commander was General Winfield Scott. Scott was nominated in 1852 as the candidate of the Whig Party and on November 2 was defeated by his former subordinate, who took 85.81 percent of the electoral vote to Scott's 14.19 percent.

3237. Republican Party candidate to be nominated on the first ballot was John Charles Frémont of California, who was the first Republican presidential candidate ever nominated. At the party's first national convention, held in Philadelphia, PA, in June 1856, the delegates gave Frémont 359 of 553 votes cast on the first informal ballot and 520 of 558 votes cast on the first official ballot. Frémont went on to lose the election to the Democrat, James Buchanan.

3238. Republican presidential candidate to win an election was Abraham Lincoln, nominated at the party's second national convention, which met at the Wigwam in Chicago, IL, in May 1860. Lincoln was nominated on the third ballot, with Hannibal Hamlin of Maine as his running mate. His chief opponents in the election were Stephen A. Douglas of the (Northern) Democratic Party and John Cabell Breckinridge of the (Southern) Democratic Party.

3239. Republican presidential candidate chosen unanimously on the first ballot was Ulysses Simpson Grant, selected immediately by the delegates at the national convention held at Chicago, IL, on May 20–21, 1868.

3240. African-American vice presidential candidate was Frederick Douglass, who was nominated on May 10, 1872, by the National Woman Suffrage Association convention, assembled at Apollo Hall, New York City, under the name of the National Radical Reformers. About 500 delegates attended from 26 states and 4 territories. The presidential nominee was Victoria Claflin Woodhull.

3241. Woman to run as a presidential candidate was Victoria Claflin Woodhull, who was nominated by the Equal Rights Party at a convention held on May 10, 1872, at Apollo Hall, New York City, after the group seceded from the National Woman Suffrage Assocation. She was nominated by Judge Carter of Cincinnati, OH. Frederick Douglass was the vice presidential nominee.

3242. Presidential candidate who was Catholic was Charles O'Conor of New York, who was nominated at Louisville, KY, on September 3, 1872, by the Straight-out Democratic Party, a group of Democrats who refused to accept the nomination of Horace Greeley that had already been made at the Democratic Convention in July. O'Conor declined the nomination, but his name nevertheless was listed and he received approximately 30,000 votes from 23 states.

3243. Presidential candidate to die during the election was Horace Greeley of New York, who ran for the presidency on the Liberal Republican and Democratic tickets in 1872. On Election Day, November 5, he received 2,834,079 popular votes, carrying six states—Georgia, Kentucky, Maryland, Missouri, Tennessee, and Texas—and gaining 66 electors. The electoral college had not yet assembled when Greeley died on November 29. His electors were released to vote for whomever they pleased, but the House of Representatives declined to count their votes. The election was won by Ulysses S. Grant, who had received 3,597,132 popular votes and 286 electoral votes.

3244. Presidential candidate who was present at the convention that nominated him was James Abram Garfield, who attended the Republican national convention of 1880, held on June 2–5 and 7–8 in Exposition Hall, Chicago, IL. Garfield was nominated on the 36th ballot with 399 votes out of a total of 755. The number of votes needed for nomination was 378.

3245. Brothers nominated for the presidency at the same convention were John Sherman, senator from Ohio, and William Tecumseh Sherman of Missouri, retired general and commander of the US Army. They were nominated at the eighth Republican Party convention in Chicago, IL, June 3–6, 1884. On the first ballot, Senator Sherman received 30 votes out of 818 cast and General Sherman received two. On the fourth ballot, the nomination was won by James G. Blaine, and neither brother received any votes. Blaine eventually lost the election to Grover Cleveland.

3246. Woman vice presidential candidate was Marietta Lizzie Bell Stow of California, who was nominated by the Equal Rights Party on September 20, 1884, at San Francisco, CA. Her running mate was Belva Ann Bennett Lockwood of Washington, DC.

3247. Presidential candidate from the Democratic Party to be elected after the Civil War was Grover Cleveland, elected on November 4, 1884. All the Presidents from Abraham Lincoln through Chester Alan Arthur were Republicans, with the exception of Andrew Johnson, a Tennessee Democrat who sided with the Union during the secession crisis, was given the second spot on the Republican ticket in 1864, and succeeded to the presidency after Lincoln's murder.

3248. Candidate of a major party to be nominated for the presidency three times was Grover Cleveland, who was nominated by the Democrats in July 1884 at Chicago, IL, June 1888 at St. Louis, MO, and June 1892 at Chicago. He won the first election, lost the second, and won the third.

3249. Defeated presidential candidate to be renominated by a major party was Grover Cleveland. After completing one term in the White House (1885–1889), he lost the election of November 6, 1888, to the Republican candidate, Benjamin Harrison, but was renominated by the Democrats at Chicago, IL, on June 23, 1892, and was reelected for another term on November 8. The first Republican presidential candidate to win renomination after losing an election was Thomas E. Dewey, who was nominated in 1944 and again in 1948, but who was defeated both times.

3250. Presidential candidate to ride in a car was William Jennings Bryan, who was given a ride in 1896 at Decatur, IL, in an automobile made by the Mueller Manufacturing Company, accompanied by his wife. There were only ten cars in the United States at that time.

3251. Presidential candidate who had served a prison term was the union organizer and socialist reformer Eugene Victor Debs of Indiana. Debs was jailed for six months in Illinois for interfering with interstate commerce during the Pullman Sleeping Car Company strike of 1894. He received the presidential nomination of the Socialist Party of America in 1900, 1904, 1908, 1912. He ran his last presidential race in 1920, while he was serving a ten-year term in a federal penitentiary for violating the Espionage Act by making a speech.

3252. Presidential candidate to appear in movie footage was William Jennings Bryan, who was filmed receiving congratulations at his residence at Fairview, NE, after his nomination as the Democratic Party presidential candidate on July 10, 1908. The film was developed on the train that transported it to New York City and was shown on July 12 at Hammerstein's Roof, 42nd Street and Broadway.

3253. Presidential candidate wounded in an assassination attempt was Theodore Roosevelt, during his unsuccessful campaign in 1912 as the candidate of the Progressive Party. On October 12 he was in Milwaukee, WI, to deliver a speech. He was leaving his hotel when a saloon keeper, John Nepomuk Schrank, shot him in the chest. Roosevelt insisted on de-

PRESIDENTIAL ELECTIONS—CANDI-
DATES—*continued*

livering the speech before going to the hospital, where surgeons extracted a bullet that had broken a rib and lodged near his right lung. Schrank was committed for life to a hospital for the insane.

3254. Presidential candidate who had been divorced was James Middleton Cox, the governor of Ohio, who had been divorced and remarried when he ran as the Democratic candidate for president in the election of 1920. He was defeated by Warren G. Harding.

3255. Presidential candidate to run for office while in prison was the union organizer and socialist reformer Eugene Victor Debs of Indiana, who was convicted in 1918 of violating the Espionage Act after he made a speech denouncing the entry of the United States into World War I. He was sentenced to a term of ten years, which he began serving in April 1919. He was nominated as the Socialist Party candidate for president—his fifth nomination— on May 13, 1920, and ran his campaign from the federal penitentiary in Atlanta, GA. On Election Day he received more than 917,000 votes. President Warren Gamaliel Harding, who won the election, pardoned Debs on December 25, 1921. (A Nevada man, Martin R. Preston, was nominated for the presidency by the Socialist Labor Party in 1908 while he was serving a 25-year prison sentence for murder, but he was ineligible to run and was replaced on the ticket.)

3256. Woman vice presidential candidate in the 20th century was Marie Caroline Brehm of California, who was nominated by the Prohibition Party on June 6, 1924, at Columbus, OH. Brehm and her running mate, Herman Preston Faris of Missouri, received 57,520 votes on November 4.

3257. Presidential candidate killed in a rescue attempt was Frank T. Johns of Oregon, who ran for president on the Socialist Labor ticket in 1924 and 1928. On May 21, 1928, he delivered a speech at Bend, OR, near the Deschutes River. While he was speaking, a boy swimming in the river was pulled out into the current and called for help. Johns jumped in, grabbed him, and struggled to the shore, but collapsed before he reached it. Both were drowned. Johns was 39 years old and the boy, Charles Rhodes, was eleven.

3258. Presidential candidate from a major party who was Catholic was the governor of New York, Alfred Emanuel Smith, nominated on June 28, 1928, at the Democratic convention held in Houston, TX. Smith won on the first ballot, and formally accepted the nomination on August 22. Despite running a vigorous and colorful campaign, Smith was too closely identified with the urban Northeast to appeal to Southern and rural Democratic voters, and that, plus his religion, lost him the election to the Republican candidate, Herbert Clark Hoover.

3259. Television broadcast of a presidential candidate accepting his nomination was made on August 22, 1928, from the chamber of the New York State Assembly in Albany, NY, where Alfred Emanuel Smith, the governor of New York, formally accepted the presidential nomination of the Democratic Party. Radio station WGY, located in the nearby city of Schenectady, picked up television images of the event and transmitted them to the General Electric Company, which relayed them by short wave over radio stations 2XAF and 2XAD. This was the first televised news broadcast in the world and the first remote television pick-up.

3260. African-American vice presidential candidate in the 20th century was James William Ford of New York, who was nominated by the Communist Party convention held at the People's Auditorium in Chicago, IL, on May 28, 1932. Ford and his running mate, William Zebulon Foster of Illinois, garnered 102,785 popular votes. He was renominated by the Communists in 1936 and 1940, both times as the running mate of Earl Russell Browder of Kansas.

3261. Defeated presidential and vice presidential candidates to die during the term they had sought were Wendell Lewis Willkie of New York and Charles Linza McNary of Oregon, who ran together on the Republican Party ticket in 1940. The election was won by Franklin Delano Roosevelt and Henry Agard Wallace. Willkie died on October 8, 1944, and McNary on February 25, 1944. The term of office they had sought ended on January 19, 1945.

3262. Presidential candidate who was renominated after a defeat was Thomas Edmund Dewey of New York, who was defeated in the election of November 7, 1944, by the incumbent president, Franklin Delano Roosevelt, and went on to be nominated by the Republican national convention at Philadelphia, PA, on June 24, 1948. He was defeated in the 1948 election by Harry S. Truman.

3263. African-American woman to run for vice president was Charlotta A. Bass, who ran for election in 1952. She was nominated on July 5 by the Progressive Party at its convention in the International Amphitheatre, Chicago, IL, and on August 28 by the American Labor Party at its convention in the City Center Casino in New York City. Her running mate on both tickets was Vincent William Hallinan. The Progressive Party received 135,007 votes on Election Day.

3264. Televised speech that confirmed a candidate's place on the vice presidential ticket was the infamous "Checkers Speech" delivered by Senator Richard Milhous Nixon in September 1952. Nixon's nomination for the Republican vice presidential spot under Dwight David Eisenhower was threatened by the revelation that he had amassed a secret $18,000 slush fund. Democratic charges that Nixon was using the money for personal purposes were so damaging that Eisenhower considered dropping him from the ticket. To restore his credibility, Nixon bought network television time in the slot after the popular "Milton Berle Show." In a maudlin but effective performance, Nixon recounted his personal history and struggles, He then gave an accounting of his finances, referring to his wife's "respectable Republican cloth coat" as proof of his thrift and honesty, and denied accepting any gifts except for a cocker spaniel named Checkers, which he gave to his daughters, and in the crowning touch, added "I want to say right now that regardless of what they say, we're going to keep it." The speech was a public relations triumph for Nixon and secured his place on the ticket.

3265. Presidential candidate to run for office after suffering a heart attack was Dwight David Eisenhower, who ran for reelection in the campaign of 1956 and was elected on November 6. He had suffered a heart attack on September 24, 1955, towards the end of his first term in office, and recuperated in the Fitzsimons Army Hospital in Denver, CO.

3266. African-American presidential candidate was Clennon King, who was nominated by the Independent Afro-American Party in 1960. His running mate was Reginald Carter. Both candidates were from Georgia. The party received 1,485 votes on Election Day.

3267. Politician to be assassinated while campaigning for his party's presidential nomination was Senator Robert Francis Kennedy of New York, a leading contender to win the nomination of the Democratic Party in 1968. On June 6, he was assassinated by Sirhan Bishara Sirhan at the Biltmore Hotel, Los Angeles, CA. The nomination went to Hubert Horatio Humphrey, who lost the election to Richard Milhous Nixon.

3268. African-American woman to run for president was Charlene Mitchell of California, who was nominated by the Communist Party USA during its convention at the Diplomat Hotel in New York, NY, July 3–7, 1968. Her running mate was Michael Zagarell of New York. They won 415 votes in Minnesota and 23 in Ohio.

3269. Secret Service protection for major presidential and vice presidential candidates and nominees was authorized by Congress on October 21, 1968, following the assassination of Robert F. Kennedy during his primary campaign for the nomination of the Democratic Party.

3270. Women to run as presidential candidates in the 20th century ran in 1968. They were Ventura Chavez of New Mexico, who was nominated by the People's Constitutional Party, and Charlene Mitchell of California, who was nominated by the Communist Party USA. On November 5, Chavez won 1,519 votes in New Mexico, and Mitchell won 415 votes in Minnesota and 23 in Ohio.

3271. Vice presidential candidate of a major political party to resign before the election was Senator Thomas Francis Eagleton of Missouri, who was nominated as George Stanley McGovern's vice president on July 13, 1972, at the Democratic National Convention at Miami Beach, FL. Following the convention, Eagelton was forced to admit to the press that he had been hospitalized for "nervous exhaustion" three times over the previous twelve years, and that his treatment had included electric shock therapy. Eagleton submitted his resignation on July 31, 1972. The National Democratic Committee nominated Robert Sargent Shriver of Maryland in his stead. Benjamin Fitzpatrick, chosen as Stephen Arnold Douglas's running mate by Democrats meeting at Baltimore, MD, on June 18, 1860, withdrew shortly after the convention of his own choice, and not due to pressure from the party or press.

PRESIDENTIAL ELECTIONS—CANDI-
DATES—*continued*

3272. Presidential candidate who had been an astronaut was Ohio senator John Herschel Glenn, Jr., the first American to orbit the earth, who sought the Democratic nomination in 1984. Glenn entered the race on April 21, 1983, with a speech in his hometown of New Concord, OH, but failed to generate widespread interest in his campaign, despite the release in 1984 of a Hollywood film, *The Right Stuff,* celebrating his status as an American hero. He tried again, also without success, in 1988.

3273. Woman to run for vice president as the candidate of a major political party was Geraldine Ferraro, congressional representative from New York State. She was chosen by Democratic presidential nominee Walter F. Mondale as his running mate on July 12, 1984, at the Democratic National Convention.

3274. Presidential candidate in the 20th century to come within two percentage points of winning the entire electoral vote was Franklin Delano Roosevelt, the Democratic candidate in 1936. In the November 3 election, he and his running mate, John Nance Garner, received 98.4 percent of the electoral vote, representing 523 votes from 46 states. Their Republican opponents, Alfred Mossman Landon and Frank Knox, received 1.51 percent of the electoral vote, carrying two states, Maine and Vermont. The next closest election was that of November 6, 1984, when the Republican candidates, Ronald Wilson Reagan and George Herbert Walker Bush, received 97.58 percent of the electoral vote, representing 525 votes from 49 states, while their Democratic opponents, Walter Frederick Mondale and Geraldine Anne Ferraro, received 2.42 percent of the electoral vote, carrying one state—Mondale's home state of Minnesota—and the District of Columbia.

3275. Presidential candidate to receive more than 50 million popular votes was Ronald Wilson Reagan, who received 54,451,521 popular votes in the election of November 6, 1984. His Democratic opponent, Walter Frederick Mondale, received 37,565,334.

3276. Woman presidential candidate and African-American presidential candidate to get on the ballot in all 50 states was Lenora B. Fulani of New York, who was nominated for president by the New Alliance Party, a Marxist-Leninist group, at its convention in New York City on August 20–21, 1988. Her running mate was Joyce Dattner of New York. They polled 217,200 votes in the election of November 8. Fulani ran again on the same party's ticket in 1992 and polled 73,248 votes.

3277. Presidential candidate convicted in a federal criminal case was Lyndon LaRouche, who first ran for president in 1976 on the U.S. Labor Party ticket and continued to do the same in subsequent elections. On December 16, 1988, he was convicted of mail fraud and tax evasion. He was sentenced to 15 years in federal prison, of which he served five years before his release on parole in 1994.

3278. Candidate for vice president who had been a prisoner of war in Vietnam was Vice Admiral James Bond Stockdale, who graduated from the U.S. Naval Academy, Annapolis, MD, on June 5, 1946. While serving during the Vietnam War, he parachuted from his stricken A-4 jet over North Vietnam and was captured. He endured 2,714 days of imprisonment, during which he was kept in solitary confinement for three years, suffering torture on numerous occasions. He was released on February 12, 1973, and on October 13, 1977, was promoted to the rank of vice admiral. In the presidential election of 1992, he was the running mate of the Texas businessman Ross Perot.

3279. Vice presidential candidate who was Jewish was Joseph Isadore Lieberman, senator from Connecticut. On August 8, 2000, he was selected to be the running mate of Vice President Albert Gore, Jr., the Democratic Party candidate, in the presidential election of November 2000. Lieberman, elected to the Senate in 1988, was the first Orthodox Jew to serve there.

PRESIDENTIAL ELECTIONS—CANDI-
DATES—PARTIES

3280. Democratic-Republican presidential candidate was Thomas Jefferson, who was promoted for office by the Democratic-Republicans in the election of 1796 but was defeated by John Adams. (In the first two presidential elections, of 1789 and 1792, George Washington was the unanimous choice of the electors, and the only contest was for the vice presidency.)

3281. Federalist Party presidential candidate might be considered to have been George Washington, who was the first Federalist president, except for the fact that he was not a true candidate; he was asked to fill the office as the only leader who could unite the people of the new nation, and he left a comfortable retirement to do so. The first Federalist candidate to take part in a contested presidential election was Washington's vice president and successor, John Adams, in 1796.

3282. Anti-Masonic Party presidential candidate was nominated at Baltimore, MD, on September 26, 1831. The convention was attended by 113 delegates from 13 states. William Wirt of Maryland was nominated for president and Amos Ellmaker of Pennsylvania for vice president. In the 1832 elections Wirt received seven electoral votes, compared with 219 cast for the Democratic nominee, Andrew Jackson.

3283. Independent Party presidential candidate was nominated in 1831–32. The party was a pro-nullification faction of the Democratic-Republicans. At its convention, held on November 20, 1831, at Charleston, SC, the delegates nominated John Floyd of Virginia for the presidency and Henry Lee of Massachusetts as his running mate. They carried the state of South Carolina in the election of November 6, 1832, and received its eleven electoral votes.

3284. Democratic Party presidential candidate was Andrew Jackson, who was nominated during the party's national convention at Baltimore, MD, in May 1832. The party was officially called the Republican Party and was informally known as the Democratic-Republicans. The name was changed to the Democratic Party in 1840.

3285. Whig Party presidential candidate was William Henry Harrison of Ohio, unanimously nominated for president in Albany, NY, on February 3, 1836, with Francis Granger of New York as his running mate. This was a state convention attended by delegates from 32 of the 52 counties. In the election of November 8, Harrison received 73 electoral votes, compared with 170 cast for the winner, the Democratic candidate Martin Van Buren. In 1832 the National Republican party, a faction of the Democratic-Republican Party and the predecessor of the Whig Party, ran Henry Clay of Kentucky as its candidate.

3286. Liberty Party presidential candidate was nominated at the party's founding convention in Warsaw, NY, on November 13, 1839. James Gillespie Birney of Kentucky, a repentant slaveowner, was nominated for the presidency and Francis Julius LeMoyne of Pennsylvania for the vice presidency. In the Harrison–Van Buren election of 1840, they polled 7,069 votes. The Liberty Party, also known as the Abolition Party, was the nation's first antislavery party and its first single-issue party, and was organized by activists from the American Antislavery Society. After its collapse in 1845, its members split between the Free Soil Party and the Liberty League.

3287. National Democratic Tyler Party presidential candidate was John Tyler of Virginia, the incumbent president, chosen at Calvert Hall in Baltimore, MD, on May 27–28, 1844, by Democrats who preferred him to their party's own candidate, James Knox Polk. Tyler was a Whig, but the Whigs had nominated Henry Clay on the first ballot. Nothing came of the Tyler Party's efforts, and it disappeared.

3288. Liberty League presidential candidate was the abolitionist and social reformer Gerrit Smith of New York, nominated on June 14–15, 1848, at Buffalo, NY. Charles C. Foote of Michigan was nominated as vice president. They garnered 2,733 popular votes in the election of November 7, 1848. The Liberty League was formed from a faction of the antislavery Liberty Party.

3289. Free Soil Party presidential candidate was Martin Van Buren of New York. He and his running mate, Charles Francis Adams of Massachusetts, were nominated at the party's convention in Buffalo, NY, on August 9–10, 1848. Van Buren received 291,263 popular votes in the election, compared with 1,360,099 cast for Zachary Taylor, the Whig candidate. The Free Soil Party was formed by the antislavery faction of the New York Democratic Party and received support from likeminded Whigs and from members of the defunct Liberty Party. Its slogan was "Free Soil, Free Speech, Free Labor, Free Men." It was the only party to endorse the Wilmot Proviso of 1848, which banned the spread of slavery into any territory acquired by treaty from Mexico.

3290. Know-Nothing Party presidential candidate was nominated at a convention held on February 18, 1856, in Philadelphia, PA. The party, formally known as the American Party, had been founded in 1854 as a secret anti-immigrant organization. The 1856 convention abolished the secret character of the organization and nominated former president Millard Fillmore of New York for president and Andrew Jackson Donelson of Tennessee for vice president. Fillmore received only eight electoral votes.

3291. North American Party presidential candidate was nominated on June 12, 1856, in New York City. The ticket consisted of Nathaniel Prentice Banks of Massachusetts and William Freame Johnson of Pennsylvania. Both candidates declined to run, and the party instead supported the candidates of the newly

PRESIDENTIAL ELECTIONS—CANDI-
DATES—PARTIES—continued

created Republican Party, John Charles Frémont and William Lewis Dayton, who were defeated in the election of November 4. The party was made up of dissidents from the American Party, better known as the Know-Nothings.

3292. Republican Party presidential candidate was John Charles Frémont of California, who was nominated on June 17, 1856, at the Music Fund Hall in Philadelphia, PA. William Lewis Dayton was his running mate. The election was won by the Democratic candidate, James Buchanan. The Republican Party had been organized two years earlier, in February 1854, by antislavery factions among the Free Democrats and the Whigs.

3293. Constitutional Union Party presidential candidate was nominated at the party's convention on May 9, 1860, in Baltimore, MD, the occasion on which the party may be said to have been definitely organized. This was the party's first and only convention. The delegates nominated John Bell of Tennessee for president and Edward Everett of Massachusetts for vice president. They received twelve electoral votes in the election of November 6, 1860. Abraham Lincoln, the Republican candidate, received 180.

3294. Southern Democratic Party presidential candidate was John Cabell Breckinridge of Kentucky, the incumbent vice president. He was nominated in Baltimore, MD, on June 28, 1860, by a breakaway group of Democrats from the southern states. Senator Joseph Lane of Oregon was given second place on the ticket. In the election of November 6, Breckinridge received 847,953 popular votes and Stephen Douglas Arnold, the mainstream Democratic candidate, received 1,375,157, giving Abraham Lincoln the majority with 1,866,452. In the electoral college, Breckinridge took eleven states and Douglas one and a half, to the Republicans' 18.

3295. Independent Republican Party presidential candidate was John Charles Frémont of California, nominated on May 31, 1864, at Cleveland OH, with running mate John Cochrane of New York. The group, better known as the Radical Republicans, was a faction of the Republican Party and gave its support to the Republican candidate, Abraham Lincoln, after its own candidates withdrew.

3296. Labor Reform Party presidential candidate was David Davis of Illinois, nominated at the party's convention at Columbus, OH, on February 22, 1872. Joel Parker of New Jersey was the vice presidential candidate. Both candidates declined to run but received popular votes nevertheless. Davis received a single electoral vote.

3297. Prohibition Party presidential candidate was James Black of Pennsylvania, nominated at the party's national convention in Columbus, OH, on February 22, 1872. John Russell of Michigan was nominated for vice president. They received 5,608 votes in the 1872 election. The party had been organized in Chicago, IL, on September 12, 1869.

3298. Liberal Republican Party presidential candidate was nominated at the party's organization meeting in Cincinnati, OH, on May 1, 1872. Horace Greeley of New York was the presidential candidate and Benjamin Gratz Brown of Missouri the vice presidential candidate. They were also the candidates of the Democratic Party.

3299. National Working Men's Convention assembled in New York City on May 23, 1872, where delegates from 31 states nominated incumbent President Ulysses Simpson Grant and Henry Wilson—the same ticket fielded by the Republicans.

3300. Straight-out Democratic Party presidential candidate was Charles O'Conor of New York, the first Roman Catholic presidential candidate. He was chosen in Louisville, KY, on September 3, 1872, by Democrats protesting the Democratic Party's nomination of the same candidates as the Liberal Republicans (Horace Greeley and Benjamin Gratz Brown). Charles Francis Adams of Massachusetts was his running mate. O'Conor and Adams received 29,489 popular votes and no electoral votes on November 5.

3301. Liberal Republican Convention of Colored Men met at Weissiger Hall in Louisville, KY, on September 25, 1872, where the delegates nominated Horace Greeley of New York and Benjamin Gratz Brown of Missouri, the ticket already nominated by the Liberal Republican Party on May 1 and the Democratic Party on July 10. Greeley was defeated by the incumbent Republican President, Ulysses Simpson Grant, on November 5.

3302. Independent Liberal Republican Party presidential candidate was nominated at the Fifth Avenue Hotel in New York, NY, on June 21, 1872, by Liberal Republicans who were unhappy with their own party's nomination of Horace Greeley and Benjamin Gratz Brown. Their preferred candidates, William Slocum Groesbeck of Ohio and Frederick Law Olmsted of New York, received one of Missouri's 15 electoral votes on November 5, Election Day. The party was also known as the Opposition Party.

3303. American National Party presidential candidate was James B. Walker of Illinois. He and Donald Kirkpatrick of New York were nominated on June 9, 1875, at Pittsburgh, PA. The candidates received 2,636 votes in the election of November 7.

3304. Greenback Party presidential candidate was Peter Cooper of New York, nominated in Indianapolis, IN, on May 16–18, 1876. His running mate was Samuel Fenton Cary of Ohio. They received 81,737 votes in the 1876 election. In 1880 the party combined with the Labor Reform party to produce the Greenback Labor Party, which nominated James Baird Weaver of Iowa for the presidency on June 9–11, 1880, in Chicago, IL, with Benjamin J. Chambers of Texas as his running mate. They received 308,578 votes on Election Day, November 2—the best third-party showing since the Civil War.

3305. American Party presidential candidate was John Wolcott Phelps of Vermont, who ran on an anti-Masonic platform with Samuel Clarke Pomeroy of Kansas in 1880. They garnered 700 popular votes on Election Day, November 2. Another party of the same name was founded on August 14, 1919, in Texas, and nominated former Texas governor James Edward Ferguson for president in 1920.

3306. Anti-Monopoly Party presidential candidate was nominated in Chicago, IL, on May 14, 1884. The party was officially formed earlier that same day. General Benjamin Franklin Butler of Massachusetts was nominated for the presidency and General Absolom Madden West of Mississippi for the vice presidency; both were also the candidates of the Greenback Labor Party. In the 1884 election, Butler received 175,370 votes, as compared with 4,874,986 cast for Grover Cleveland of New York, the Democratic candidate. The existence of "The Anti-Monopoly Organization of the United States," as it was formally named, was of short duration, and its members joined the People's Party.

3307. American Prohibition Party presidential candidate was Samuel Clarke Pomeroy of Kansas, nominated on June 19, 1884, at Chicago, IL, with John A. Conant of Connecticut. Their results in the election of November 4 were negligible, though the better-established Prohibition Party won more than 150,000 votes.

3308. Equal Rights Party presidential candidate was nominated in San Francisco, CA, on September 20, 1884, at a convention of the Woman's Rights Party or Female Suffragettes. Belva Ann Bennett Lockwood of the District of Columbia was nominated as the presidential candidate and Marietta Lizzie Bell Stow of California as the vice presidential candidate. The party was formed on May 10, 1872, when 500 delegates from 26 states and four territories seceded from the National Woman Suffrage Association convention in New York City and nominated Victoria Claflin Woodhull of New York for president and Frederick Douglass for vice president under the People's Party ticket.

3309. Industrial Reform Party presidential candidate was Albert E. Redstone of California. He and John Colvin of Kansas were nominated on February 22–23, 1888, in Washington, DC.

3310. Union Labor Party presidential candidate was nominated on May 15–17, 1888, in Cincinnati, OH, when 274 delegates from 25 states nominated Alson Jenness Streeter of Illinois for president and Samuel Evans of Texas for vice president. Evans refused the nomination and Charles E. Cunningham of Arkansas was selected instead. They received 146,935 votes in the election of November 6, 1888, which was won by Benjamin Harrison of Indiana, the Republican candidate. The party was formed on February 22, 1887, when 300 delegates, including 10 women, attended the Industrial Labor Conference in Cincinnati. A platform was adopted the following day.

3311. United Labor Party presidential candidate was nominated on May 15–17, 1888, at the Grand Opera House, Cincinnati, OH. Robert Hall Cowdrey of Illinois was nominated for president and William H.T. Wakefield of Kansas for vice president. In the popular election of November 6, 1888, in which Benjamin Harrison, the Republican candidate, was elected president, Cowdrey received 2,818 votes. The party was formed at Clarendon Hall, New York City, on January 6, 1887, by secessionists from the Union Labor Party.

PRESIDENTIAL ELECTIONS—CANDI-
DATES—PARTIES—*continued*

3312. Populist Party presidential candidate was James Baird Weaver of Iowa, nominated on July 2–5, 1892, in Omaha, NE, with James Gaven Field of Virginia as his running mate. They came in third in the election of November 8, receiving 1,041,028 popular votes and 22 electoral votes from four western and midwestern states. The People's Party was founded in 1886 by members of the Farmers' Alliance and the Knights of Labor, and later developed into the Populist Party.

3313. Socialist Labor Party presidential candidate was nominated at the party's convention in New York City on August 28, 1892. Simon Wing of Massachusetts was nominated for president and Charles Horatio Matchett of New York for vice president. They received 21,512 votes in six states on November 8. The party had been founded on July 4, 1874, as the Social Democratic Workmen's Party of North America; its name was changed in 1877.

3314. National Party presidential candidate was Charles Eugene Bentley of Nebraska, nominated at Pittsburgh, PA, on May 28, 1896, on a platform advocating silver coinage on an unlimited basis. James Haywood Southgate of North Carolina was his running mate. The party received 13,969 votes on Election Day, November 3.

3315. Silverite presidential candidate was nominated at the party's first national convention in St. Louis, MO, on July 22, 1896. The delegates, who favored silver as a monetary standard, endorsed the Democratic candidates, William Jennings Bryan and Arthur Sewall. The temporary chairman of the convention was Francis Griffith Newlands of Nevada, and the permanent chairman was William Pope St. John of New York.

3316. National Silver Party convention took place at the Exposition Building in St. Louis, MO, on July 23–25. The party was also known as the Bi-Metallic League. The delegates endorsed the Democratic candidates, William Jennings Bryan of Nebraska and Arthur Sewall of Maine, who were beaten by Republican candidate William McKinley on November 3.

3317. Sound Money Democratic Party presidential candidate and his running mate were nominated in Indianapolis, IN, on September 2–3, 1896. They were Senator John McAuley Palmer of Illinois and General Simon Bolivar Buckner, the former governor of Kentucky. The party, also known as the National Democratic Party, received 133,148 popular votes on November 3.

3318. Social Democratic Party of the United States presidential candidate were nominated in Rochester, NY, on January 27, 1900. The delegates nominated Job Harriman for president and Max S. Hayes for vice president.

3319. Social Democratic Party of America presidential candidate was nominated in Indianapolis, IN, on March 6, 1900. The ticket consisted of Eugene Victor Debs for president and Job Harriman for vice president. In the election of November 1900, the party received a popular vote of less than 100,000, compared with 7.2 million cast for the Republican candidate, William McKinley. The party was formed in 1898 by Debs, Victor Louis Berger, and Seymour Stedman, dissenters from the Social Democracy of America Party.

3320. United Christian Party presidential candidate were nominated on May 2, 1900, at which time Silas Comfort Swallow of Pennsylvania was nominated for president and John Granville Woolley of Illinois for vice president. The candidates withdrew and were replaced by Jonah Fitz Randolph Leonard of Iowa for president and David H. Martin of Pennsylvania for vice president. The party's popular vote in the election of November 6, 1900, was 1,060, compared with 7.2 million cast for William McKinley, the Republican candidate. The party was organized in Rock Island, IL, and was devoted to the inculcation of religious and moral ideas as controlling forces in politics.

3321. Silver Republican Party presidential candidate was nominated at the Auditorium in Kansas City, MO, on July 5–6. In addition to silver coinage, the Silver Republicans advocated a graduated income tax and direct election of senators. The party's first choice as a presidential candidate, Charles Arnette Towne, declined the nomination and was replaced by the Silverite leader William Jennings Bryan, together with Adlai Ewing Stevenson as his running mate, both of whom appeared on the Democratic ticket.

3322. Union Reform Party presidential candidate was nominated in Baltimore, MD, on September 3, 1900. Seth Hockett Ellis of Ohio was nominated for president and Samuel T. Nicholson of Pennsylvania for vice president. They received fewer than 6,000 votes, compared with 7.2 million cast for William McKinley of Ohio, the Republican candidate, in the election of November 6, 1900. The platform had been adopted on March 1, 1899, in Cincinnati, OH.

3323. Socialist Party presidential candidate was Eugene Victor Debs, former president of the American Railway Union, who had been a founder of the party in 1900. He was nominated at Indianapolis, IN, on May 1, 1904. Debs was the party nominee for president five times between 1900 and 1920, making his best showing in 1912, when he received more than 900,000 votes (6 percent).

3324. Continental Party presidential candidate was Austin Holcomb of Georgia. He and his running mate, A. King of Missouri, were nominated at Chicago, IL, on August 31, 1904. On Election Day, November 8, they garnered 1,000 votes.

3325. Independence Party presidential candidate was Thomas Louis Hisgen of Massachusetts and his running mate, John Temple Graves of Georgia, who were nominated on July 29, 1908, at Chicago, IL. On Election Day, November 3, they received 82,872 votes.

3326. Progressive Party (Bull Moose) presidential candidate was Theodore Roosevelt of New York, nominated on August 6–7, 1912, at the Coliseum, Chicago, IL, by 1,800 delegates who had seceded from the Republican Party. Hiram Warren Johnson of California was nominated for vice president. Roosevelt received 4,126,000 popular and 88 electoral votes; William Howard Taft, the Republican candidate, 3,487,922 popular and 8 electoral votes; and Woodrow Wilson, the Democratic candidate, 6,297,099 popular and 435 electoral votes.

3327. Farmer Labor Party presidential candidate was Parley Parker Christensen of Utah. He and his running mate, Maximilian Sebastian Hayes of Ohio, were nominated on June 13, 1920, in Carmen's Hall, Chicago, IL. They received approximately 265,000 votes. The party was an outgrowth of the National Labor Party, which was formed in 1919. The party merged with the Democratic Party in 1944.

3328. Single Tax Party presidential candidate was Robert Colvin Macauley of Pennsylvania, nominated on July 12–14, 1920, at Chicago, IL. Macauley and his running mate, R. G. Barnum of Ohio, received 5,837 votes on November 2.

3329. Commonwealth Land Party presidential candidate was William J. Wallace of New Jersey, who was nominated on February 29, 1924, together with John Cromwell Lincoln of Ohio. The convention took place at the Engineering Society Building, New York City. On Election Day, November 4, they received 1,582 votes.

3330. Progressive Party (1924) presidential candidate was Republican senator Robert Marion La Follette of Wisconsin, a longtime leader in the progressive movement. He was nominated at Cleveland, OH, on July 4, 1924, with Burton Kendall Wheeler, the Democratic governor of Montana, as his running mate. Because they had the support of the Socialist Party, they were hurt in the polls by charges of radicalism, but nevertheless succeeded in reaching third place on Election Day, November 4, with 4,822,856 votes.

3331. Jobless Party presidential candidate was James Renshaw Cox of Pennsylvania. He was nominated on August 17, 1932, at the Crevecoeur Speedway, St. Louis, MO. V. C. Tisdal of Oklahoma was nominated for vice president.

3332. Liberty Party (modern) presidential candidate was nominated on August 17, 1932, at St. Louis, MO. William Hope Harvey of Arkansas and his running mate, Frank B. Hemenway of Washington, received 53,425 votes on Election Day, November 8.

3333. National Greenback Party presidential candidate was John Zahnd of Indiana, nominated at Indianapolis, IN, on April 6, 1936. Florence Garvin of Rhode Island was nominated for the vice presidency. The party had been known as the National Independent Party until 1934.

3334. Union Party presidential candidate was William Lemke of North Dakota, nominated on August 15, 1936, in Cleveland, OH, with Thomas Charles O'Brien of Massachusetts as his running mate. The ticket was supported by Father Charles E. Coughlin's National Union of Social Justice and by Dr. Francis Everett Townsend, the social security insurance advocate. It received 892,793 votes on November 3.

PRESIDENTIAL ELECTIONS—CANDI-
DATES—PARTIES—*continued*

3335. America First Party presidential candidate was nominated at the party's convention in Detroit, MI, on August 30, 1944. The ticket consisted of Gerald Lyman Kenneth Smith of Michigan and Henry A. Romer of Ohio. The same candidates were renominated in August 1948 by the Christian Nationalist Party.

3336. Socialist Workers Party presidential candidate was nominated at Irving Plaza Hall in New York City on July 2–3, 1948. The candidates, Farrell Dobbs of New York and Grace Carlson of Minnesota, received 13,613 votes on November 2.

3337. Vegetarian Party presidential candidate ran for office in 1948. The group convened at the Hotel Commodore in New York City on July 7, 1948, and nominated John Maxwell of Illinois for president and Symon Gould of New York for vice president. The party was later known as the American Vegetarian Party.

3338. States' Rights Democratic Party presidential candidate was James Strom Thurmond, governor of South Carolina, whose running mate was Fielding Lewis Wright, governor of Mississippi. The convention met on July 17, 1948, in Birmingham, AL. The party, also known as the Dixiecrats, came in third on Election Day, November 2, with 1,169,021 popular votes and 7.35 percent of the electoral vote (39 votes from Alabama, Louisiana, Mississippi, and Tennessee).

3339. Progressive Party (1948) presidential candidate was chosen on July 23–25, 1948, at Convention Hall in Philadelphia, PA. This was a leftist party, not the same as the one that nominated Theodore Roosevelt for president in 1912. Its candidates, Henry Agard Wallace of Iowa and Glen Hearst Taylor of Idaho, came in fourth in the popular vote with 1,156,103 votes on November 2, 1948. Wallace was the former secretary of agriculture and secretary of commerce and had served as vice president in Franklin Delano Roosevelt's third term.

3340. Poor Man's Party presidential candidate was Henry B. Krajewski, a chicken farmer. He and his running mate, Frank Jenkins, both of New Jersey, received 4,203 votes in the election of November 4. Krajewski ran for president again in 1956 as the candidate of the American Third Party, with Ann Marie Yezo of New Jersey as his running mate, and received 1,829 votes.

3341. Church of God Party presidential candidate was nominated during the 46th annual general assembly of the Church of God, which met on July 2–8, 1952, at Moses Tabernacle in Nashville, TN. Homer Aubrey Tomlinson of New York was nominated for president and Willie Isaac Bass of North Carolina for vice president. Tomlinson was nominated again on May 21, 1960, as the presidential candidate of the Theocratic Party, which was organized at the Church of God in Fulton, MO, in March 1960. His running mate was Raymond L. Teague of Alaska.

3342. American Labor Party convention met at the City Center Casino in New York City on August 28 and nominated the slate of candidates already chosen by the Progressive Party, Vincent William Hallinan of California and Charlotta A. Bass of New York, the first African-American woman to be a candidate for the vice presidency. They received 135,007 popular votes on November 4.

3343. Constitution Party presidential candidate was General Douglas MacArthur of Wisconsin, nominated on August 31, 1952, in Philadelphia, PA. Harry Flood Byrd of Virginia received the nomination for vice president. The same slate of candidates was nominated by the America First Party. On Election Day, November 4, the Constitution Party received 3,089 popular votes and the America First Party received 233. Byrd was nominated for president by the States' Rights Party of Kentucky and the South Carolinians for Independent Electors in 1956.

3344. Pioneer Party presidential candidate was nominated in Milwaukee, WI, on November 26–27, 1955. The ticket consisted of William Langer of North Dakota and Burr McCloskey of Illinois.

3345. Liberal Party convention took place on September 11, 1956, at New York City's Manhattan Center. The party endorsed the candidates of the Democratic Party, Adlai Ewing Stevenson and Estes Kefauver. The Liberal ticket received 292,557 popular votes on November 6.

3346. States' Rights Party presidential candidate was nominated on October 15 at the Mosque Auditorium in Richmond, VA. Thomas Coleman Andrews of Virginia and Thomas Harold Werdel of California were nominated for the presidency and the vice presidency. They received 109,961 votes on November 6, 1956. Both were renominated in 1964 by the Independent States' Rights Party.

3347. Texas Constitution Party presidential candidate was William Ezra Jenner of Indiana. He and Joseph Bracken Lee of Utah ran for president and vice president on November 6, 1956. Jenner was also nominated for vice president by the States' Rights Party of Kentucky. Lee was the presidential candidate of the Conservative Party of New Jersey in 1960 and received 8,708 votes, together with his running mate, Kent H. Courtney of Louisiana.

3348. National States' Rights Party presidential candidate was Orval Eugene Faubus, the governor of Arkansas, who was nominated at the party's convention on March 19–20, 1960, in Dayton, OH, over his objections. His running mate was John Geraerdt Crommelin of Alabama. They received 214,195 popular votes on November 8.

3349. Conservative Party of Virginia presidential candidate was C. Benton Coiner. He and his running mate, Edward M. Silverman, both of Virginia, won 4,204 votes in the election of November 8, 1960.

3350. Independent Afro-American Party presidential candidate was Clennon King of Georgia. Another Georgian, Reginald Carter, ran for vice president. They received 1,485 votes on Election Day, November 8. King was the first African-American presidential candidate.

3351. Tax Cut Party presidential candidate was Lar Daly of Illinois. He and running mate Merritt Barton Curtis of Washington, DC, received 539 votes in the presidential election of November 8, 1960. The Tax Cut Party, based in Michigan, had its antecedents in the American Party and the America First Party. Curtis also ran as the candidate of two other parties in 1960: He was the presidential candidate, with running mate B. N. Miller, of the Constitution Party (Washington), which received 1,401 votes, and the vice presidential candidate, together with presidential candidate Charles Loten Sullivan of Mississippi, of the Constitution Party (Texas), which received 18,169 votes.

3352. Peace and Freedom Party presidential candidate was Eldridge Cleaver, the Black Panther leader and convicted felon. He and his running mate, Judith Mage of New York, were nominated on August 18, 1968, in Ann Arbor, MI. They received some 74,014 votes on Election Day. The PFP, based in California, was an extreme left-wing party comprised of Marxist-Leninst, Trotskyite, and other radical factions.

3353. American Independent Party presidential candidate was Alabama governor and one-time Democrat George C. Wallace, who founded the AIP in 1968 to support his right-wing, anti-government, segregationist platform. He named Samuel Marvin Griffin of Georgia as his running mate, but Griffin withdrew and was replaced by Curtis Emerson LeMay of Ohio. In New York State, the pair ran as the candidates of the Courage Party, rather than the AIP. In the November 1968 elections, Wallace won five Southern states and garnered nearly 9,901,151 votes (13.5 percent) nationwide, one of the best third-party showings in history. Wallace abandoned the party in 1970. By the end of the century the AIP had become a local affiliate of the Constitution Party.

3354. Freedom and Peace Party presidential candidate was Richard Claxton Gregory of Illinois, better known as the comedian Dick Gregory, who ran in the election of November 5, 1968.

3355. People's Constitutional Party presidential candidate was Ventura Chavez, the first woman to run for the presidency in the 20th century. She and running mate Adelicio Moya received 1,519 votes in New Mexico on November 5, 1968.

3356. Libertarian Party presidential candidate was nominated at the party's first convention, held in Denver, CO, in June 1972. He was John Hospers, a philosophy professor at the University of Southern California. His running mate was Theodora "Tonie" Nathan of Oregon, the first woman in U.S. history to receive an electoral vote. They were on the ballot in Colorado and Washington and received 3,907 votes on Election Day. The party's first nationwide presidential campaign was mounted in 1980 by Edward E. Clark, who appeared on the ballot in all 50 states, the District of Columbia, and Guam. Clark received almost 1 million votes in the November 3 election, the best showing for any Libertarian candidate up to that time.

3357. People's Party presidential candidate was Dr. Benjamin Spock, pediatrician and author, who had helped to found the party in 1971. He was nominated in July 1972 at the party's convention in St. Louis, MO. Black activist Julius Hobson was nominated as his running mate. In the election of November 7, they received 78,751 votes, mostly from California voters.

PRESIDENTIAL ELECTIONS—CANDIDATES—PARTIES—*continued*

3358. U.S. Labor Party presidential candidate was Lyndon LaRouche, a self-taught economist from New Hampshire, who was nominated in 1976. His running mate was steelworker R. Wayne Evans of Detroit. They appeared on the ballot in 23 states and the District of Columbia and polled 40,043 votes. LaRouche, a former Trotskyist who later embraced a rightist ideology, was convicted of mail fraud and tax evasion in 1988 and spent five years in a federal penitentiary.

3359. Citizens Party presidential candidate was Barry Commoner of New York, a prominent environmentalist, who was nominated at the party's convention in Cleveland, OH, on April 10–13, 1980. LaDonna Harris of New Mexico was nominated for vice president. They received 234,279 popular votes in the election of November 4.

3360. Right to Life Party presidential candidate was Ellen McCormack, a homemaker from Merrick, NY, who helped to found the party in 1970. In the Democratic Party's primary elections for the 1976 presidential election, she received 238,000 votes from 18 states. Four years later the party nominated McCormack as its own candidate, with Carroll Driscoll of New Jersey as her running mate. They qualified to appear on the ballot in New York, New Jersey, and Kentucky, under the name Right to Life Party or Respect for Life Party, and received 32,327 votes in the election of November 4.

3361. Workers World Party presidential candidate was Deirdre Griswold of New Jersey. She had her running mate, Larry Holmes of New York, received 13,300 popular votes in the election of November 4, 1980.

3362. New Alliance Party presidential candidate was nominated on August 20–21, 1988, at the party's convention in New York City. The ticket consisted of Lenora B. Fulani and Joyce Dattner, both of New York. They polled 217,200 votes in the election of November 8. Fulani ran again on the same party's ticket in 1992 and polled 73,248 votes. The New Alliance Party was a Marxist-Leninist organization.

3363. Consumer Party presidential candidate was former Senator Eugene Joseph McCarthy of Minnesota, who ran with Susan Gardner of Illinois in 1988. They polled 30,903 popular votes on November 8.

3364. U.S. Taxpayers Party presidential candidate was Howard Phillips, a former Nixon administration official, who founded the party in 1992 from elements of the American Independent Party and other small extreme right-wing parties. It was originally intended to provide a vehicle for the presidential aspirations of ultraconservative speechwriter and commentator Patrick Buchanan, but Buchanan declined to bolt the Republican Party in the 1992 or 1996 elections, so Phillips was the U.S. Taxpayers Party candidate in both years. In 1999 Buchanan joined the Reform Party, and the U.S. Taxpayers Party was renamed the Constitution Party. Phillips was the Constitution Party candidate in 2000.

3365. Grassroots Party presidential candidate was Jack Herer, who garnered 1,949 votes in the election of November 1992. The Grassroots party is a liberal party, based in Minnesota and Vermont, that promotes marijuana legalization and the adoption of a universal health-care system. It first achieved permanent ballot status in Vermont.

3366. Natural Law Party presidential candidate was John Hagelin, who ran on November 3, 1992. He received 37,137 popular votes.

3367. Reform Party presidential candidate was billionaire Texas businessman Ross Perot, who founded the party in Dallas, TX, in 1995 as a vehicle for his presidential aspirations. Perot's run in 1996, with Vice Admiral James Bond Stockdale as his running mate, garnered him 8,085,000 votes, or 8 percent of the vote, a respectable showing for a newly minted third party. The party's political platform was generally a mix of social libertarianism, conservative fiscal policies, and protectionist/isolationist international views.

3368. Green Party presidential candidate was consumer advocate Ralph Nader, who was nominated in August 1996 at the party's national convention in Los Angeles, CA. His running mate was Winona LaDuke, a Native American activist based in Minnesota. Nader refused to campaign and spent no more than $5,000 during the race but qualified for the ballot in 22 states and as a write-in candidate in 23 more. The Green ticket won more than 700,000 votes to take fourth place after Ross Perot in the November election. The Nader/LaDuke vote in Oregon was more than 4 percent.

3369. Family Values Party presidential candidate was Tom Wells, founder of the party. Wells claimed that God instructed him on December 25, 1994, to create a religious party that would urge people to protest the public funding of abortions by withholding their taxes. Wells ran for Congress in Florida in 1998 and for president in 2000.

PRESIDENTS

3370. President of the United States under the Articles of Confederation was Thomas McKean of Delaware. After the adoption of the Articles of Confederation on March 1, 1781, the presidents of the sessions of the Continental Congress, beginning with McKean, signed themselves "President of the United States in Congress Assembled." McKean later served as chief justice of the supreme court of Pennsylvania (1777–99) and governor of Pennsylvania (1799–1808).

3371. President of the United States elected under the Constitution was George Washington of Mount Vernon, VA, the former general and commander-in-chief of the Army of the United Colonies, who was chosen by the unanimous vote of the electors on February 4, 1879, and was inaugurated in New York, NY, on April 30, 1789. He was reelected unanimously for a second term on December 5, 1792, and was inaugurated in Philadelphia, PA, on March 4, 1793. He declined to serve a third term.

3372. Title formally proposed for the chief executive of the United States was "His Highness, the President of the United States of America, and Protector of their Liberties." This was the title submitted in May 1789 by a Senate committee, the title "His Excellency" having already been voted down in debate. However, since the House of Representatives was opposed to the use of a title, and had already established a precedent by addressing a message to "the President of the United States,", the Senate agreed to continue the use of this simple form of address.

3373. Presidential proclamation concerned the surveying of the future site of the nation's capital and was made in New York City on January 24, 1791, by George Washington. The proclamation directed surveyors "to survey and limit a part of the territory of ten miles square on both sides of the river Potomac, so as to comprehend Georgetown, in Maryland, and extend to the Eastern Branch."

3374. President to govern more than the original 13 states was George Washington. The 14th state, Vermont, joined the Union on March 4, 1791, during his first term in office.

3375. Statement of the principle of executive privilege was formulated in 1792 by Thomas Jefferson, who was then George Washington's secretary of state. In response to a request by the House of Representatives for military documents held by President Washington, Jefferson advised: "The executive ought to communicate such papers as the public good would permit, and ought to refuse those the disclosure of which would injure the public."

3376. Law establishing presidential succession was passed by Congress on March 1, 1792. It read: "In case of the removal, death, resignation, or disability of both the President and Vice-President of the United States, the President of the Senate, pro tempore, and in case there shall be no President of the Senate, then the speaker of the House of Representatives for the time being shall act as President of the United States until such disability be removed or until a President be elected." This plan was altered by Congress in 1886, 1947, and 1955, when the presidential succession was fixed as follows: vice president, speaker of the House, president pro tempore of the Senate, secretary of state, secretary of the treasury, secretary of defense, attorney general, postmaster general, secretary of the interior, secretary of agriculture, secretary of commerce, and secretary of labor.

3377. President to be reelected was George Washington. When the electoral ballots were opened on November 6, 1792, Washington received 132 of the 264 votes, making him president for another term. John Adams received the next highest number, 77, making him again the vice president. Both were Federalists. The three Democratic-Republican candidates were George Clinton, who received 50 votes; Thomas Jefferson, who received four; and Aaron Burr, who received one. Since each of the 132 electors cast two votes, Washington's reelection was unanimous; the Democratic-Republicans, who opposed his policies, were unable to field a candidate strong enough to rival him.

3378. Presidential amnesty issued to rebellious citizens was issued by President George Washington on July 10, 1795, when he extended a full pardon to participants in the Whiskey Rebellion who were willing to sign an oath of allegiance to the United States.

PRESIDENTS—*continued*

3379. Incumbent president to decline to run for reelection was George Washington, who declined to run for a third term when his second term expired in March 1797. He announced his decision in his "Farewell Address," dated September 17, 1796. The Constitution originally allowed presidents to be reelected indefinitely. The 22nd Amendment, ratified on February 26, 1951, restricted future presidents to a maximum of two terms.

3380. President to serve two full terms was George Washington of Virginia, who was elected on April 6, 1789, by the unanimous vote of 69 electors and was reelected on November 6, 1792, by the unanimous vote of 132 electors. He served as president from April 30, 1789, to March 3, 1797.

3381. President who had served as vice president was John Adams. He was sworn into office as the nation's first vice president on April 21, 1789. He took the oath of office as the nation's second president on March 4, 1797. Both ceremonies took place in Philadelphia, PA.

3382. President who was older than 60 when he took office was John Adams, who was 61 years and 125 days old when he was inaugurated as the second president on March 4, 1797. George Washington was 57 years and 67 days old when he took office on April 30, 1789.

3383. Incumbent president who ran for reelection and was defeated was John Adams of Massachusetts, the second president. In the election of 1796, he received 71 electoral votes to Thomas Jefferson's 68. When he ran for reelection in 1800, he received 65 electoral votes, fewer than both Thomas Jefferson and Aaron Burr, who received 73 each.

3384. President who was defeated for reelection by his own vice president was John Adams, whose vice president, Thomas Jefferson, was declared the winner of the election of 1800.

3385. Presidential team from Virginia and New York was the Democratic-Republican ticket consisting of Thomas Jefferson, the former governor of Virginia, and Aaron Burr, the former senator from New York, who were elected in 1800. The party's successful Virginia–New York combination continued in 1804, when Jefferson and George Clinton were elected; 1808, when James Madison was paired with Clinton; 1816, when James Monroe was paired with Daniel D. Tompkins; and 1820, when the same team was reelected.

3386. President to reside in Washington, DC, was John Adams. On June 3, 1800, he took up residence at the Union Tavern, Georgetown, DC (now part of Washington, DC). In November 1800, he moved into the President's House, the Executive Mansion. George Washington was the only president who did not live in Washington, DC, as the Executive Mansion was not completed during his administration. In 1798 he did purchase two lots near the Capitol for $963, on the condition than he build two brick houses there. The houses were never built.

3387. Defeated presidential candidate to run again successfully was Thomas Jefferson of Virginia. Jefferson was one of 13 candidates for the presidency in 1796, after George Washington declined to run for a third term. He came in second to John Adams. Under the election laws then in place, he became vice president and Adams became president. Jefferson was elected president himself in the election of November 4, 1800.

3388. President to review the nation's military forces at his residence was Thomas Jefferson. On July 4, 1801, he reviewed the Marines, led by the Marine Band, on the White House grounds.

3389. President to have two vice presidents was Thomas Jefferson. In the election of November 4, 1800, the two top vote-getters were Jefferson and Aaron Burr, each of whom received 73 electoral votes from a total of 276. A vote in the House of Representatives gave Jefferson the presidency and Burr the vice presidency. Both were Democratic-Republicans. In the election of 1804—the first in which separate electoral votes were cast for the two executive offices—the party declined to renew its support for Burr as vice president and instead supported George Clinton, the longtime governor of New York. Jefferson and Clinton were both elected and were inaugurated on March 4, 1805.

3390. President who was younger than his vice president was Thomas Jefferson, during his second term in office. At their inauguration on March 4, 1805, President Jefferson was a few weeks short of his 62nd birthday, and his vice president, George Clinton, was 65. His first vice president, Aaron Burr, was younger than Jefferson by twelve years. Jefferson himself was eight years younger than John Adams, whose vice president he had been, and Adams was four years younger than George Washington, whose vice president he had been. Clinton continued to serve as vice president under Jefferson's successor, James Madison, who was younger than Clinton by twelve years.

3391. President to invoke executive privilege was Thomas Jefferson, during the 1807 treason trial in Richmond, VA, of former vice president Aaron Burr. Official documents in Jefferson's possession were requested by Burr's defense counsel. Chief Justice John Marshall ruled that a general subpoena could be issued to the president under the Constitution, and Jefferson was duly subpoenaed to appear at the trial with the documents. This was the first subpoena issued to a sitting president. Initially, Jefferson refused to appear or to yield up the documents. In a letter dated June 20, 1807, to the prosecutor, George W. Hay, he wrote: "The leading principle of our constitution is the independence of the Legislature, Executive and Judiciary of each other, and none are more jealous of this than the Judiciary. But would the Executive be independent of the Judiciary if he were subject to the commands of the latter and to imprisonment for disobedience; if the several courts could bandy him from pillar to post, keep him constantly trudging from North to South and East to West, and withdraw him entirely from his constitutional duties? The intention of the constitution that each branch should be independent of the others is further manifested by the means it has furnished to each to protect itself from enterprises of force attempted on them by the others, and to none has it given more effectual or diversified means than to the Executive." Jefferson eventually sent the documents to Hay "to avoid conflicts of authority between the high branches of government which would discredit it equally at home and abroad," but he did not appear at the trial.

3392. President whose administration lost two vice presidents to death was James Madison. His first vice president, George Clinton (who had also served as vice president to Madison's predecessor, Thomas Jefferson), served three years and 47 days and died on April 20, 1812, at the age of 72. His second vice president, Elbridge Gerry, took office on March 4, 1813, at the start of President Madison's second term, but died one year and 264 days later, on November 23, 1814.

3393. President elected from a state west of the Mississippi River was Zachary Taylor, a native of Virginia who made his home in Baton Rouge, LA, after 1840. He took office in 1849.

3394. Democratic presidential and vice presidential team to lose a bid for reelection consisted of President Martin Van Buren and Vice President Richard Mentor Johnson, who were elected on November 1, 1836. They were both renominated by the Democrats, but lost the election of November 3, 1840, to the Whig candidates, William Henry Harrison and John Tyler.

3395. Year in which three presidents held office was 1841. Martin Van Buren, a Democrat, left office on March 3, 1841, after one term, having lost the election of 1840 to the Whig candidate, William Henry Harrison. Harrison took office the following day and died on April 4 of pneumonia he contracted at his inauguration. He was succeeded on April 6 by his vice president, John Tyler. The second year in which three Presidents held office was 1881, which began with Rutherford Birchard Hayes in office, continued with the inauguration of James Abram Garfield in March, and closed with Chester Alan Arthur in the White House, Garfield having died in September of a gunshot wound inflicted by an assassin.

3396. President to serve without a vice president was John Tyler, who was elevated from the vice presidency to the presidency on April 6, 1841, after the death of William Henry Harrison. The office went vacant until the election on November 5, 1844, of George Mifflin Dallas of Pennsylvania, the running mate of James Knox Polk.

3397. Vice president to succeed to the presidency after the death of a president was John Tyler, the tenth president. The election of November 3, 1840, was won by the Whig candidates, William Henry Harrison and Tyler, his running mate. Harrison died of pneumonia on April 4, 1841, a few weeks after his inauguration. A messenger from the secretary of state conveyed the news to Tyler at his home in Williamsburg, VA. He arrived in Washington, DC, before daybreak on April 6, and took the oath of office at the Indian Queen Hotel from William Cranch, chief justice of the U.S. Circuit Court of the District of Columbia. He held his first cabinet meeting later that day.

3398. Incumbent president whose party refused to renominate him was John Tyler of Virginia. Tyler was elected to the vice presidency in 1840 on the Whig Party ticket as the running mate of William Henry Harrison, took office on March 4, 1841, and succeeded to the presidency a month later when Harrison died. At the Whig Party convention in Baltimore, MD, on May 1, 1844, the party gave the nomi-

PRESIDENTS—*continued*

nation to Henry Clay of Kentucky, who was nominated by acclamation on the first ballot. An impromptu third party, the National Democratic Tyler Party, met in Baltimore at the end of May to nominate Tyler for the presidency. The election was won by the Democratic candidate, James Knox Polk, with Tyler receiving a negligible number of popular votes and no electoral votes.

3399. President to announce before his election that he would not run for reelection was James Knox Polk of Tennessee, the 11th president, who made the announcement after his surprise nomination at the Democratic convention in Baltimore, MD, on May 29, 1844. One of the hardest-working and most diligent presidents, Polk died of exhaustion a mere three months after leaving office in 1849.

3400. Senator to serve as unofficial president between two presidential terms may have been David Rice Atchison, senator from Missouri, although this is a matter of debate. There was a hiatus of one day between the end of James Knox Polk's term and the beginning of Zachary Taylor's. Polk's term in office ended at noon on March 4, 1849, as did the term in office of his vice president, George Mifflin Dallas. Because March 4 fell on a Sunday, the Christian Sabbath, Taylor and his vice president, Millard Fillmore, postponed taking their oaths of office until the following day. For 24 hours, therefore, the office of president and vice president were not filled. Senator Atchison, who had been elected president of the Senate pro tempore on March 2, is considered by some historians to have been the senior federal officer, and thus the "acting president." His gravestone reads: "President of the U.S. one day."

3401. President who was younger than 50 when he took office was Franklin Pierce, who was 49 years and 122 days old when he was inaugurated on March 4, 1853.

3402. Former president to run for reelection on a different party's ticket was Millard Fillmore of New York. Fillmore was elected to the vice presidency in 1848 on the Whig Party ticket as the running mate of Zachary Taylor, took office in March 1849, and succeeded to the presidency in July 1850, after Taylor's death. He sought renomination by the Whigs for the election of 1852, but at the party's convention, held in June 1852, the delegates chose General Winfield Scott on the 53rd ballot, giving him 159 votes to Fillmore's 112. Scott

eventually lost to Democrat Franklin Pierce. Four years later, the delegates of the recently formed American Party (the Know-Nothings) nominated Fillmore as their candidate when they met in convention on February 22, 1856, at Philadelphia, PA. Fillmore also received the nomination of the Whig Party, but it had ceased to be an important political group, most of its members having split between the Democrats and the newly organized Republicans. In the election, Fillmore took 21.5 percent of the popular vote and 2.7 percent of the electoral vote.

3403. Elected incumbent president whose party refused to renominate him was Franklin Pierce of New Hampshire. Pierce was nominated by the Democratic Party in June 1852 in Baltimore, MD, during a contentious convention in which 49 ballots were taken because the delegates could not agree on a candidate. His name was not even offered for consideration until the 35th ballot, but on the 49th, he received 283 of 289 votes cast. Four years later, when the Democrats convened in Cincinnati, OH, in June 1856 to prepare for the next presidential election, President Pierce received 122.5 votes on the first ballot to James Buchanan's 135.5. Sixteen ballots later, Buchanan received 296 votes and Pierce received none.

3404. Presidential estate to be opened to the public was Mount Vernon, VA, the home of George and Martha Dandridge Custis Washington. The property, about 16 miles below Washington, DC, on the Potomac River, had been in the family since the days of the President's great-grandfather in the 17th century. The mansion was built in the 1730s. Washington inherited the estate in 1751 and operated it as a plantation. After his death in 1799, it passed to his widow, his nephew, and eventually to his descendant John Augustine Washington, Jr., who offered it to the nation in 1850. Congress declined to purchase it and the estate was put on the market. The mansion and a portion of the property were bought in 1859 by the Mount Vernon Ladies' Association, founded and headed by Ann Pamela Cunningham of South Carolina, which collected $200,000 in charitable donations for the purpose. The restored house was made available to the public.

3405. President to function as an effective commander in chief was Abraham Lincoln, who was inaugurated on March 4, 1861, a week after seven Southern states seceded from the Union. Lincoln was in the unique position of having to prosecute a war on American soil almost from the moment he took office, and in the unenviable position of commanding a roster of second-rate or timid generals who often ignored the instructions he sent them. Moreover, Lincoln had no military training. By his own admission, his service in the Blackhawk War of 1832 mainly consisted of "a good many bloody struggles with the mosquitoes." Nonetheless, over the course of the war, Lincoln developed a large-scale, coordinated offensive plan—the first continent-wide strategy of war—and patiently searched for a staff capable of carrying it out. In March 1864 he found his general in Ulysses Simpson Grant, to whom Lincoln gave command of all the federal armies. Lincoln also developed what is considered the first modern unified high command, consisting of secretary of war Edwin M. Stanton, military advisor General Henry W. Halleck, Grant as general of the armies, and Lincoln as grand strategist.

3406. Presidential executive order to be numbered was issued by President Abraham Lincoln on October 20, 1862. It read: "I do hereby constitute a provisional court, which shall be a court of record, for the State of Louisiana, and I do hereby appoint Charles A. Peabody of New York to be a provisional judge to hold said court." Lincoln's order was not the first executive order issued by a president, but it is the first one in the files of the Department of State.

3407. Presidential amnesty granted during the Civil War was issued by President Abraham Lincoln on December 8, 1863. He issued another on March 26, 1864. President Andrew Johnson issued supplementary proclamations on May 29, 1865; September 7, 1867; July 4, 1868; and December 25, 1868.

3408. Vice president to succeed to the presidency after the assassination of a president was Andrew Johnson, who took the oath of office at ten o'clock in the morning on Saturday, April 15, 1865, in his suite of rooms at the Kirkwood House in Washington, DC. The oath was administered by Chief Justice Salmon Portland Chase. President Abraham Lincoln had died earlier that morning, at 7:21 A.M., after being shot by John Wilkes Booth the previous night.

3409. President elected after the Civil War who had not served in it was Grover Cleveland. He was a lawyer in Buffalo, NY, when the war broke out. In 1862–63 he served as a ward supervisor, and from 1863 to 1865 as Erie County assistant district attorney. He went on to become county sheriff, mayor of Buffalo, and governor of New York State, and was elected president on November 4, 1884.

3410. President elected for two nonconsecutive terms was Grover Cleveland, who served as the 22nd president (1885–89) and the 24th president (1893–97).

3411. President during whose term more than five states were admitted to the Union was Benjamin Harrison, during whose term in office six states were admitted. Four of these were admitted during the first two weeks of November 1889: North and South Dakota on November 2, Montana on November 8, and Washington on November 11. Two others were admitted in July 1890: Idaho on July 3, and Wyoming on July 19. Prior to Harrison, the president holding the record for the largest number of states admitted during his term was James Monroe (Mississippi on December 19, 1818; Illinois on December 3, 1818; Alabama on December 14, 1819; Maine on March 15, 1820; and Missouri on August 10, 1821).

3412. President whose predecessor and successor were the same man was Benjamin Harrison of Indiana, a Republican. He defeated the incumbent Democratic president, Grover Cleveland of New York, in the election of November 6, 1888—a close election in which Cleveland won a majority of the popular vote, with 5,540,309 votes to Harrison's 5,444,337, but Harrison won a majority of the electoral vote, with 233 votes to Cleveland's 168. In the election of November 8, 1892, Harrison was the incumbent and Cleveland the challenger. Cleveland won, taking 5,556,918 popular votes and 277 electoral votes to Harrison's 5,176,108 popular votes and 145 electoral votes.

3413. President protected by the Secret Service was Grover Cleveland, who received informal part-time protection in 1894. The Secret Service had been founded in 1860 in the Treasury Department as an anti-counterfeiting agency. Its role in protecting the president was expanded after the assassination of President William McKinley in 1901; McKinley's successor, Theodore Roosevelt, was the first to receive protection full-time, and two operatives were permanently assigned to the White House detail in 1902. After the unsuccessful attack by Puerto Rican extremists on President Harry S. Truman in November 1950, Congress enacted legislation that permanently authorized Secret Service protection of the president, his immediate family, the president-elect, and the vice president.

PRESIDENTS—*continued*

3414. President whose government included all 48 contiguous states was William Howard Taft, who served from 1909 to 1913. On February 14, 1912, the last remaining territory in what is now the main body of the United States was admitted to the Union as the state of Arizona.

3415. Democratic presidential and vice presidential team to be reelected was that of President Woodrow Wilson and Vice President Thomas Riley Marshall, who were elected on November 5, 1912, and reelected on November 7, 1916.

3416. Woman to act as unofficial president of the United States was Edith Bolling Galt Wilson, who was in charge of the presidency from the fall of 1919 to at least April 1920 during the illness of her husband, Woodrow Wilson, who had suffered a paralyzing stroke on September 26, 1919. Edith Wilson controlled all access to the president and kept him sequestered. She signed documents with his name and acted as the sole spokesperson for the presidency. The extend of her assumed powers was not generally known, and even today it is not clear whether the president was aware of her actions.

3417. President who had been defeated in a earlier campaign for the vice presidency was Franklin Delano Roosevelt, who was nominated for the vice presidency in July 1920 at the Democratic Party convention in San Francisco, CA. Heading the ticket was James Middleton Cox of Ohio. On Election Day, November 2, Cox and Roosevelt received 9,147,353 popular votes and 23.92 percent of the electoral vote. The Republican winners, Warren Gamaliel Harding and Calvin Coolidge, received 16,152,200 popular votes and 76.08 percent of the electoral vote. Roosevelt returned to his law practice in New York City and was elected governor of New York in 1928. On November 8, 1932, he was elected to the first of his four terms as president.

3418. Republican presidential and vice presidential team to lose a bid for reelection was that of President Herbert Clark Hoover and Vice President Charles Curtis, who were elected on November 6, 1928. They were both renominated by the Republicans but lost the election of November 8, 1932, to the Democratic candidates, Franklin Delano Roosevelt and John Nance Garner.

3419. President to invite the president-elect to confer with him concerning issues of government was Herbert Clark Hoover. On November 12, 1932, Hoover invited president-elect Franklin Delano Roosevelt to confer with him regarding the request made by Great Britain for suspension of payments of its war debt. An installment of $95 million was due on December 15, 1932. Roosevelt, then governor of New York, called on President Hoover on November 22, 1932.

3420. President with a serious physical disability was Franklin Delano Roosevelt, elected to the first of four terms in 1933. He was stricken with polio in 1921, when he was 39, and suffered paralysis in his legs. Though a rehabilitation program restored some of his mobility, he continued to rely on crutches and wheelchairs for the rest of his life, a fact that he was at pains to conceal from the public out of concern that voters would not accept a leader with a physical infirmity. He helped to found the March of Dimes, an organization that raised funds for polio research and rehabilitation, and in his first annual message as governor of New York he called on the state "to give the same care to removing the physical handicaps of its citizens as it now gives to their mental development."

3421. President elected for third and fourth terms was Franklin Delano Roosevelt. In the election of November 1940, when he was running for a third term, he received 27,241,939 popular votes, against Wendell Lewis Willkie's 22,304,755. In November 1944 he received 25,603,152 votes against Thomas Edmund Dewey's 22,006,616. He served only a few months of his fourth term, from January 20, 1945, until his death on April 12, 1945, when he was succeeded by his vice president, Harry S. Truman. The ratification of the 22nd Amendment to the Constitution on February 26, 1951, limited future presidents to two terms in office.

3422. Presidential library was the Franklin Delano Roosevelt Presidential Library. Roosevelt had announced on December 10, 1938, that he would donate his papers to a library that would be open to the public. Previously, presidential papers had remained the private property of each chief executive's estate. Construction began on November 19, 1939, at the Roosevelt family estate in Hyde Park, NY. Roosevelt donated the land, but public donations funded the library building. The library was dedicated on June 30, 1941.

3423. President to have three vice presidents was Franklin Delano Roosevelt, the nation's only four-term president. During his first and second terms (1933–1941), his vice president was James Nance Garner of Texas, who retired after eight years in office. The vice president during his third term (1941–45) was Henry Agard Wallace of Iowa, the former secretary of agriculture. Wallace was not renominated by the Democrats in 1944, but he did serve in 1945–46 as secretary of commerce under the man who replaced him as Roosevelt's running mate, Harry S. Truman of Missouri, who took office on January 20, 1945, and was elevated to the presidency three months later after Roosevelt's sudden death.

3424. President to watch the swearing-in ceremony of a Supreme Court justice he appointed was Harry S. Truman, who was present in the Supreme Court Chamber on October 1, 1945, when Harold Hitz Burton took the oath of office. He had been nominated by President Truman on September 18, 1945, and confirmed by voice vote in the Senate the following day.

3425. President barred under the 22nd Amendment from running for a third term was Dwight David Eisenhower. The 22nd Amendment to the Constitution, declared ratified on February 26, 1951, provided that "no person shall be elected to the office of the President more than twice, and no person who has held the office of President, or acted as President, for more than two years of a term to which some other person was elected President shall be elected to the office of the President more than once." The amendment specifically excluded from coverage the person who was president at the time of its proposal by Congress. The proposal took place on March 26, 1947, during the first administration of President Harry S. Truman, who was therefore eligible to run for a third term in 1952 but declined. Eisenhower won that election and took office on January 20, 1953.

3426. Republican president to win reelection in the 20th century was Dwight David Eisenhower, who was elected on November 4, 1952, and reelected on November 6, 1956. Of the previous Republican presidents elected in the 20th century, Theodore Roosevelt did not run for reelection in 1908, William Howard Taft was defeated by Woodrow Wilson in 1912, Warren Gamaliel Harding died in office, Calvin Coolidge declined to run again in 1928, and Herbert Clark Hoover was defeated by Franklin Delano Roosevelt in 1932.

3427. Republican presidential and vice presidential team to be reelected was the team of President Dwight David Eisenhower and Vice President Richard Milhous Nixon, elected on November 4, 1952, and reelected on November 6, 1956.

3428. President of all 50 states was Dwight David Eisenhower. There were 48 states when his second administration began on January 20, 1957. Alaska was admitted to the Union on January 3, 1959, and Hawaii on August 20, 1959.

3429. President from a Southern state since the Civil War was Lyndon Baines Johnson, who succeeded to the presidency on November 22, 1963, and was elected on November 3, 1964. He was born, raised, and educated in Texas and represented Texas in the House of Representatives (1937–1948) and the Senate (1948–1961). He was the first Southerner in the White House since Andrew Johnson of Tennessee, who succeeded to the presidency in 1865 after the assassination of Abraham Lincoln, but who was not subsequently elected to a second term. The last Southerner elected to the White House before Lyndon Baines Johnson was Zachary Taylor, a native of Virginia and a resident of Louisiana, who was elected in 1848. Of the twelve Presidents from Washington to Taylor, nine were Southerners.

3430. Secret Service protection for former presidents and their families was authorized by Congress on September 15, 1965. Former presidents were granted protection for the remainder of their lives. Former First Ladies received protection as long as their husbands were alive. A president's widow and minor children were authorized to receive protection "for a period of four years after he leaves or dies in office, unless such protection is declined." A law enacted on October 21, 1968, allowed widowed a First Lady to receive protection until she died or remarried, and continued Secret Service protection for an ex-president's minor children until they reached 16.

3431. President to meet with a pope in the United States was Lyndon Baines Johnson, president from 1963 to 1969. On October 4, 1965, he came to New York City to call upon Pope Paul VI in his suite at the Waldorf-Astoria Hotel. The pope was in New York to deliver an address to the United Nations.

PRESIDENTS—*continued*

3432. President to tape all his conversations in the White House was Richard Milhous Nixon, who ordered the installation of secret recording devices in the Oval Office, the president's office in the Executive Office Building, and the cabinet room in 1971. The first two of these devices were automatically activated by the sound of a voice, and the third was activated manually. Recording devices were also installed in telephones used by the president in the Oval Office, the Executive Office Building, and the Lincoln sitting room, as well as in his personal telephone at the Camp David retreat in Maryland. The existence of these devices was revealed by Alexander P. Butterfield, the former appointments secretary to the president, on July 16, 1973, during testimony before the Senate select committee investigating the Watergate burglary. Some of the president's tapes were eventually subpoenaed by U.S. District Court Judge John J. Sirica and by congressional committees, but the president refused to surrender them until ordered to do so by the Supreme Court on July 24, 1974. He resigned from office on August 9, after the release of transcripts that proved his complicity in the cover-up of the Watergate incident.

3433. President to resign was Richard Milhous Nixon, who submitted his resignation to Secretary of State Henry Alfred Kissinger on August 8, 1974, and announced at 9:04 P.M., via radio and television, his intention to resign at noon on August 9, an intention that he carried out. He had been named an unindicted co-conspirator in the Watergate corruption case and was at risk of being impeached.

3434. President and vice president elected together to resign their offices were President Richard Milhous Nixon and Vice President Spiro Theodore Agnew. They were elected on November 5, 1968, and reelected on November 7, 1972, taking their oaths of office for the second time on January 20, 1973. Agnew resigned on October 10, 1973, to face federal charges of income tax evasion, to which he pleaded no contest; he was given a fine and probation. President Nixon resigned on August 9, 1974, after he was named as an unindicted co-conspirator in the Watergate scandal and was threatened with impeachment proceedings. He accepted a pardon from his successor, Gerald Rudolph Ford, on September 8, 1974.

3435. President who came to the office through appointment rather than election was Gerald Rudolph Ford. Ford had been a longtime member of the House of Representatives when he was appointed by President Richard Milhous Nixon on October 12, 1973, to succeed Spiro T. Agnew, the vice president, who had resigned after he was charged with taking bribes. The president himself resigned effective August 9, 1974, after he was named as an unindicted co-conspirator in the Watergate political burglary case. He was succeeded by Ford, who took the oath of office at noon on August 9 in the Oval Office of the White House, Washington, DC, as the 38th president. Ford was thus the first person to hold the offices of both the president and the vice president without having been elected to either.

3436. Vice president to succeed to the presidency after the resignation of the president was Gerald Rudolph Ford, who took the oath of office on August 9, 1974, at 12:03 P.M., three minutes after the resignation of President Richard Milhous Nixon took effect. He was sworn in by Chief Justice Warren Earl Burger in the East Room of the White House.

3437. President and vice president to hold office together without either having been elected was the team of President Gerald Rudolph Ford and Vice President Nelson Aldrich Rockefeller. Ford was appointed to the vice presidency by President Richard Milhous Nixon on October 12, 1973, after the resignation of Spiro Theodore Agnew; was confirmed by the Senate and sworn in on December 6, 1973; and succeeded to the presidency on August 9, 1974, after Nixon's own resignation. On August 20, 1974, President Ford appointed Rockefeller to fill the vacant vice presidency. He was confirmed by the Senate on December 19, 1974, and sworn in immediately. Appointments to the vice presidency in time of vacancy were made possible by the 25th Amendment to the Constitution, ratified on February 10, 1967.

3438. President to donate his papers to the federal government during his term in office was Gerald Rudolph Ford, whose term ran from August 9, 1974, to January 20, 1977. His collection of papers and documents from his political career, which began with his election to Congress in 1948, was given to the University of Michigan, his alma mater, which built the Gerald R. Ford Library at its Ann Arbor campus to house them. Although he was entitled by law to take a tax exemption for the donation, he declined to do so.

3439. President to make human rights a cornerstone of his foreign policy was Jimmy Carter, who announced his focus on human rights in his inaugural address on January 20, 1977, and repeated it on March 17 in an address to the General Assembly of the United Nations. During his term, he denounced regimes that practiced human-rights violations on a large scale, particularly those of the Soviet Union and Czechoslovakia, and cut American aid programs to violators in South and Central America and in Africa.

3440. President to formally transfer the presidency to an acting president was Ronald Wilson Reagan, on July 13, 1985. Before he entered the Bethesda Naval Center in Bethesda, MD, for colon surgery, President Reagan sent letters to the speaker of the House, Thomas P. O'Neill, and the president pro tempore of the Senate, James Strom Thurmond, transferring presidential powers and duties to Vice President George Herbert Walker Bush for the duration of the operation. He did so "mindful of the provisions of Section 3 of the 25th Amendment," which covers cases in which the president is incapacitated, although he expressed his doubt "that the drafters of this Amendment intended its application to situations such as the instant one" and stated his unwillingness "to set a precedent binding anyone privileged to hold this Office in the future." The operation lasted two hours and 53 minutes, but President Reagan did not regain consciousness for several hours. At the end of seven hours and 54 minutes, he signed letters to Speaker O'Neill and Senator Thurmond declaring his resumption of the presidency. The 25th Amendment was ratified on February 10, 1967.

3441. Incumbent vice president to be elected president in the 20th century was George Herbert Walker Bush, who served as vice president under Ronald Reagan from January 20, 1981, to January 20, 1989. On November 8, 1988, he was elected president. The last incumbent vice president to be elected president was Martin Van Buren, vice president under Andrew Jackson from 1833 to 1837, who was elected president on November 1, 1836.

3442. President and vice president in the 20th century who were both Southerners were William Jefferson Clinton, the former governor of Arkansas, and Albert Gore, Jr., former representative and senator from Tennessee. They were elected on the Democratic ticket on November 3, 1992. The last election in which the successful running mates were both from the South was the election of November 4, 1828, which was won by the Democratic-Republican candidates, Andrew Jackson of Tennessee and John Caldwell Calhoun of South Carolina.

3443. Outgoing president to order military action in the last week of his term was George Herbert Walker Bush, who took office on January 20, 1989, and lost his bid for re-election on November 3, 1992. On January 13, 1993, with one week to go before the inauguration of his successor on January 20, President Bush ordered the resumption of bombing raids on installations in Iraq as a warning to its leader, Saddam Hussein, to stop violating the terms of the ceasefire that had ended the Gulf War of 1991.

PRESIDENTS—ASSASSINATIONS

3444. President who was the target of an assassination attempt while in office was Andrew Jackson. On January 30, 1835, Richard Lawrence fired two pistols at President Jackson as he attended the funeral of Representative Warren Ransom Davis of South Carolina at the Capitol in Washington, DC. Both weapons misfired. The president counterattacked with his cane, and, with the help of a Navy lieutenant, disarmed his attacker. Lawrence was later found to be insane and was sent to a prison for the mentally disturbed.

3445. Assassination attempt on Abraham Lincoln took place in February 1861. Lincoln, who was then the president-elect, had boarded a special train in Springfield, IL, on February 11, bound for his inauguration in Washington, DC. On February 22, his guard, the detective Allan Pinkerton, uncovered a conspiracy by assassins who intended to kill Lincoln when the train arrived at Baltimore's Calvert Street Station. Lincoln quietly switched trains in Harrisburg, PA, and arrived safely in Washington the next morning.

3446. President to be assassinated was Abraham Lincoln. On April 14, 1865, a few days after the Civil War came to an end with the surrender of Confederate General Robert E. Lee, Lincoln attended a performance of *Our American Cousin* at Ford's Theatre, Washington, DC, where he was shot by the actor and Confederate sympathizer John Wilkes Booth. He died the following day, April 15, 1865.

PRESIDENTS—ASSASSINATIONS—*continued*

3447. Presidential funeral cortege that included a caparisoned horse was that of Abraham Lincoln. When Lincoln's body was taken from the White House on April 18, 1865, to lie in state in the Capitol rotunda, the casket was followed by the president's horse with its master's boots backwards in the stirrups. Inclusion of the caparisoned horse is an honor accorded to officers in the Army or Marine Corps of the rank of colonel or above, and to the president of the United States as the commander-in-chief of the armed forces.

3448. Rewards offered by the federal government for suspects in the assassination of a president were announced on May 2, 1865, by President Andrew Johnson in a proclamation. A reward of $100,000 was offered for Jefferson Davis, the president of the Confederacy. Rewards of $25,000 each were offered for Clement C. Clay, Jacob Thompson, George N. Sanders, and Beverley Tucker, and a reward of $10,000 was offered for William C. Cleary. All were suspected of complicity in the assassination of President Abraham Lincoln by John Wilkes Booth and the attempted assassination of Secretary of State William Henry Seward, who had been attacked at his home by Lewis Powell at the same time.

3449. President-elect who was the target of an assassination attempt was Franklin Delano Roosevelt, who was elected to the presidency on November 8, 1932. On February 15, 1933, with his inauguration still three weeks away, Roosevelt was visiting Miami, FL, with an entourage that included Anton Joseph Cermak, the mayor of Chicago. As they rode in an open touring car, six shots were fired at them by Giuseppe Zangara, a bricklayer. Roosevelt escaped injury, but five others were hit, including Cermak, who died on March 6, two days after Roosevelt's inauguration. Zangara was executed on March 20.

3450. Federal law against threatening the president was enacted by Congress on June 25, 1948. The law provided for a fine of $1,000 or a prison term of up to five years, or both, for sending a threat through the mail. The same protection was extended to the vice president and the president-elect on June 1, 1955.

3451. Assassination of a president captured on film was the murder of President John Fitzgerald Kennedy in Dallas, TX, on November 22, 1963. Among the people in the crowd watching the presidential motorcade pass by was Abraham Zapruder, a dress manufacturer, who was taking pictures with an 8-millimeter home movie camera. His 26-second footage showed a clear view of President Kennedy at the moment he was shot by sniper Lee Harvey Oswald. The film was purchased by the U.S. government for safekeeping in the National Archives. An arbitration panel agreed on August 3, 1999, to pay Zapruder's heirs $16 million for it, the highest price ever paid for a historical American artifact.

3452. Vice president who was present at the assassination of the president he succeeded was Lyndon Baines Johnson. On November 23, 1963, President John Fitzgerald Kennedy and Vice President Johnson, in separate cars, were traveling in a motorcade through the streets of Dallas, TX, accompanied by their wives and other dignitaries. Two people in the president's car were hit by sniper fire: the governor of Texas, John Bowden Connally, Jr., and Kennedy, who died of his wounds at Parkland Memorial Hospital. After the first shot, Johnson was protected by Secret Service agent Rufus Youngblood, who shielded him with his own body.

3453. Commission appointed to investigate the assassination of a president was the President's Commission on the Assassination of President John F. Kennedy, usually called the Warren Commission, appointed on November 29, 1963, by President Lyndon Baines Johnson. The commission was charged with investigating the assassination of Kennedy on November 22, 1963, and the murder two days later of Kennedy's suspected killer, Lee Harvey Oswald, by nightclub owner Jack Ruby. It was headed by Supreme Court chief justice Earl Warren; the other members were Senator Richard B. Russell of Georgia, Senator John Sherman Cooper of Kentucky, U.S. Representative Hale Boggs of Louisiana, Representative Gerald R. Ford of Michigan, former CIA director Allen W. Dulles, and John J. McCloy, who had been one of Kennedy's closest advisors. The *Report of the President's Commission on the Assassination of President John F. Kennedy,* often called the *Warren Report,* was published in September 1964; it found that Oswald was the lone assassin.

3454. Federal law specifying penalties for the kidnappers and assassins of presidents was enacted by Congress on August 28, 1965, and covered vice presidents and presidents-elect in addition to presidents. It provided for imprisonment "for any term of years or for life" for someone convicted of kidnapping one of these officials, and the same possible prison sentence or the death penalty for someone convicted of murdering one of them. Congress further authorized the attorney general to pay a reward of up to $100,000 to individuals who provided information or services in this regard.

3455. President to survive two assassination attempts in one month was Gerald Rudolph Ford, who succeeded to the presidency on August 9, 1974. On September 5, 1975, in Sacramento, CA, Lynette Alice "Squeaky" Fromme tried to fire a pistol at President Ford, but was stopped by a Secret Service agent, Larry Beundorf. On September 22, 1975, in San Francisco, CA, Sara Jane Moore fired a revolver at President Ford. The bullet missed him and wounded a taxi driver. Ford was not harmed in either incident. Fromme, a follower of the mass-murderer Charles Manson, and Moore, a Berkeley radical and former FBI informant, were both sentenced to life imprisonment.

3456. President to be wounded in an unsuccessful assassination attempt while in office was Ronald Wilson Reagan. On March 30, 1981, President Reagan was shot in the chest by a lone gunman, John Warnock Hinckley, Jr., as he was walking to his limousine from the Washington Hilton Hotel in Washington, DC. The president was rushed to nearby George Washington University Hospital, where a bullet was removed from his left lung. Three other people were wounded in the attack: Secret Service agent Timothy J. McCarthy, city police officer Thomas K. Delehanty, and President Reagan's press secretary, James Brady, who was left paralyzed from the waist down. Hinckley was tried for attempted murder, found not guilty by reason of insanity, and confined to a psychiatric hospital.

3457. Internet camera showing the site of a presidential assassination went live on June 24, 1999, with a 24-hour-a-day Webcast of the view from the window perch occupied by Lee Harvey Oswald when he shot President John Fitzgerald Kennedy on November 22, 1963. The Webcast was a joint project of Internet company Earthcam.com and the Sixth Floor Museum in the former Texas Book Depository on Dealey Plaza in Dallas, TX.

PRESIDENTS—BIRTHS

3458. President from the working class was Andrew Jackson, the seventh president, who took office on March 4, 1829. Of the six previous presidents, four—Washington, Jefferson, Madison, and Monroe—came from well-to-do Virginia families, and the two Adamses came from an eminent Boston clan; all but Washing-ton had college educations. Jackson was born on March 15, 1767, in a log cabin in Waxhaw, SC. His parents had emigrated from Ireland, where his father had been a linen weaver. He received little or no formal education and was orphaned during the British invasion of the Carolinas in the Revolutionary War. However, the war proved to be his ticket out of poverty: He volunteered for the Continental Army at the age of 13, served with distinction, and was afterwards offered an opportunity to study law. Jackson was also the first president born west of the Allegheny Mountains.

3459. President born an American citizen was Martin Van Buren. He was born in Kinderhook, NY, on December 5, 1782. All previous presidents were born before the American Revolution and were British subjects at the time of their births.

3460. President whose ancestry was not British was Martin Van Buren, born on December 5, 1782. His parents, Maria Goes Hoes Van Alen Van Buren and Abraham Van Buren, came from Dutch families. George Washington, John Adams, James Madison, and John Quincy Adams were all of English descent; Thomas Jefferson had an English mother and a Welsh father; James Monroe came from a Scottish family; and Andrew Jackson's parents were Scotch-Irish.

3461. President born during the administration of another president was John Tyler, who was born in Greenway, VA, on March 29, 1790, about a year after the inauguration of George Washington as the first president.

3462. President who did not reside in the state of his birth was Andrew Jackson, a native of South Carolina. He studied law in North Carolina, was admitted to that state's bar, and in 1788 became solicitor of North Carolina's western district, from which the state of Tennessee was formed in 1796. In 1804 Jackson became a planter at the Hermitage, an estate near Nashville, which remained his home for the rest of his life, though he spent the greater part of his time away on military campaigns or in politics.

3463. President born in the 19th century was Franklin Pierce, who was born in Hillsborough (now Hillsboro), NH, on November 23, 1804.

3464. President born beyond the boundaries of the original 13 states was Abraham Lincoln. He was born near Hodgenville, KY, on February 12, 1809.

PRESIDENTS—BIRTHS—*continued*

3465. President and vice president to be born in the same county were William Henry Harrison and John Tyler, who were elected on November 3, 1840, on the Whig Party ticket. Both were born in Charles City County, VA. Harrison was born in the town of Berkeley on February 9, 1773, and Tyler in the town of Greenway on March 29, 1790.

3466. President born west of the Mississippi River was Herbert Hoover, who was born in West Branch, IA, on August 10, 1874.

3467. President who was born in the 20th century was John Fitzgerald Kennedy. He was born on May 29, 1917, in Brookline, MA.

3468. President who was born in a hospital was Jimmy Carter, born on October 1, 1924, in Wise Sanitarium in the town of Plains, GA.

3469. President who was born after World War II was William Jefferson Clinton, born in Hope, AR, on August 19, 1946, a year after the end of the war.

PRESIDENTS—CAREERS

3470. President who had been a schoolteacher was John Adams, who taught school in Worcester, MA, in 1755, when he was 20. Millard Fillmore taught school in Scott, NY, in 1818. James Abram Garfield taught a term of school in Solon, OH, in 1849.

3471. President who was admitted to the bar was John Adams, who practiced law in Boston, MA, after he was admitted to the bar in 1758.

3472. President who had served in Congress was George Washington. The Virginia Provincial Congress elected him as a delegate to the First Continental Congress on August 5, 1774. He attended its first session, in Philadelphia, PA, beginning on September 5. He was elected as a delegate to the Second Continental Congress on March 5, 1775. On June 15, 1775, the Congress elected him general and commander-in-chief of the Army of the United Colonies. Other presidents who served in the Continental Congress were John Adams (1774–78), Thomas Jefferson (1775–76 and 1783–85), James Madison (1780–83 and 1786–88), and James Monroe (1783–86).

3473. President to have written a book was John Adams of Massachusetts. Before he took office in 1797, Adams had published three books: *Thoughts on Government* (1776), *History of the Dispute with America from Its Origin in 1754* (1784), and *Defence of the Constitutions of Government of the United States of America* (3 vols., 1787–88). After leaving office in 1801, he published *Discourses on Davila* (1805).

3474. President who had been governor of a state was Thomas Jefferson, who was elected governor of Virginia on June 1, 1779, and was reelected on June 2, 1780. He resigned on June 3, 1781. He was elected president in 1800.

3475. President who had served as minister to a foreign country was John Adams of Massachusetts, who became the United States minister to the Netherlands beginning on December 29, 1780, and to Great Britain on May 14, 1785, serving until 1788.

3476. President who had been a cabinet member was Thomas Jefferson, who took office as George Washington's secretary of state on February 14, 1790.

3477. President who had been a medical student was William Henry Harrison, who was enrolled in the Medical Department of the University of Pennsylvania in 1791. The course lasted 32 weeks, but Harrison quit halfway through to join the army, receiving his ensign's commission from General George Washington on August 16. He eventually rose to become a major general and entered politics on the strength of his reputation as a scourge of Native Americans.

3478. President who had served as secretary of state was Thomas Jefferson, secretary of state under President George Washington from February 14, 1790, through December 31, 1793. He took office as the third president on March 4, 1801.

3479. President who had been a college professor was John Quincy Adams, who was appointed professor of rhetoric and belles lettres at Harvard College, Cambridge, MA, in 1805.

3480. President who had served in the House of Representatives was James Madison, who was a representative from Virginia in the 1st through the 4th Congresses, from March 4, 1789, to March 3, 1797.

3481. President who had served in the Senate was James Monroe, who served as senator from Virginia from November 9, 1790, to May 27, 1794, filling the vacancy caused by the death of William Grayson on March 12, 1790.

3482. Former president to head a university was Thomas Jefferson, who was installed as rector of the University of Virginia on March 29, 1819, ten years after leaving the White House. James Madison was named to the same post in 1826.

3483. President who had been governor of a territory was Andrew Jackson, who served as territorial governor of Florida from March 10 to July 18, 1821.

3484. President whose name was changed was Ulysses Simpson Grant. He was born on April 27, 1822, at Point Pleasant, OH, and was given the name Hiram Ulysses Grant. During his childhood he rearranged it to Ulysses Hiram Grant. The congressman who sponsored his application to West Point in 1839 mistakenly used the name Ulysses Simpson Grant, probably because his mother's name was Hannah Simpson Grant. (President Grant's second vice president, Henry Wilson, changed his name from Jeremiah Jones Colbaith when he was 21.) Other presidents who changed their names were Grover Cleveland, who was born Stephen Grover Cleveland; Woodrow Wilson, who was born Thomas Woodrow Wilson; Calvin Coolidge, who was born John Calvin Coolidge; Dwight David Eisenhower, who was born David Dwight Eisenhower; Gerald Rudolph Ford, who was born Leslie Lynch King, Jr.; and William Jefferson Clinton, who was born William Jefferson Blythe 4th. Both Ford and Clinton took the surnames—in Ford's case, the entire name—of their adoptive stepfathers.

3485. Manuscript by Abraham Lincoln known to historians is a page of Lincoln's student sum book, which dates to circa 1824–26. Because arithmetic texts were scarce in the Indiana backwoods of Lincoln's youth, he apparently stitched together his own small mathematical notebook. This was given to Lincoln's law partner and biographer William H. Herndon by the president's stepmother, Sarah Bush Johnston Lincoln, and was later acquired by the Library of Congress. One of the extant pages is inscribed with a characteristic verse in Lincoln's hand: "Abraham Lincoln / his hand and pen / he will be good but / — knows When."

3486. Former president who was elected to the House of Representatives was John Quincy Adams. After his 1828 bid for reelection was defeated by Andrew Jackson, Adams went into retirement, but his friends in Massachusetts politics persuaded him to run as a candidate on the Whig ticket for the Plymouth district's congressional seat. An entry in his diary, written after his victory, reads: "My election as

President of the United States was not half so gratifying to my inmost soul. No election or appointment conferred upon me ever gave me so much pleasure." Known as a powerful orator—his nickname was "Old Man Eloquent"—Adams served in the House for 17 years, from March 4, 1831, to February 23, 1848, when he died of a stroke that occurred during a House debate.

3487. President who had served in both the House of Representatives and the Senate before taking office was Andrew Jackson, who represented Tennessee in the House from December 5, 1796, to March 3, 1797, and in the Senate from September 26, 1797, through April 1798, and again from March 4, 1823, to October 14, 1825, when he resigned to concentrate on running for president.

3488. President who had served as mayor of a city at the start of his political career was Andrew Johnson, who was mayor of Greeneville, TN, from 1830 to 1834.

3489. President with no congressional experience was Zachary Taylor, who joined the United States Army as a young man and spent nearly all his adult life in military campaigns, rising to become major general, until he retired at the age of 64 to enter the White House (March 4, 1849). All eleven of his predecessors served either in the Continental Congress or the United States Congress.

3490. President who had received a patent was Abraham Lincoln. On March 10, 1849, in Springfield, IL, he applied for a patent on a device for "buoying vessels over shoals" by means of inflated cylinders. His application was granted on May 22, 1849.

3491. President to publish a book of poetry was John Quincy Adams of Massachusetts, whose *Poems of Religion and Society* was published in 1854.

3492. Former president to serve as an official of an enemy government was John Tyler of Virginia, president of the United States from 1841 to 1845. On August 1, 1861, he became a delegate to the provisional Congress of the Confederate States. He was elected a member of the House of Representatives of the permanent Confederate Congress on November 7, 1861, but died on January 18, 1862, before taking his seat.

PRESIDENTS—CAREERS—*continued*

3493. President who had neither military nor legal experience when he entered the White House was Andrew Johnson, who succeeded to the presidency on April 15, 1865. He was apprenticed to a tailor at the age of 13 and two years later began running his own shop. He had no education and was taught to read and write by the woman who became his wife. He entered politics as a young man, organizing a local party of workingmen, and by the time he was 25 had been elected alderman and then mayor of Greeneville, TN. He moved on to the state assembly, the state senate, the House of Representatives, the governorship of Tennessee, and the Senate (in which he was the only Southern senator to adhere to the Union). From March 4, 1862, to March 3, 1865, he served as the military governor of Tennessee with the rank of brigadier general of volunteers, but this was an administrative, not a combat, post.

3494. President who had been an executioner was Grover Cleveland, elected president in 1884 and 1892. Early in his political career, as sheriff of the Erie County jail in Buffalo, NY, he carried out death sentences that had been passed on two murderers. On September 6, 1872, he hanged a man who had been convicted of stabbing his mother. On February 14, 1873, he hanged a gambler who had shot a man during a card game.

3495. President to serve as a senator both before and after his term in office was Andrew Johnson. He served as a senator from Tennessee from October 8, 1857, through March 4, 1862, when he was appointed military governor of his state. His term in the White House lasted from April 15, 1865, through March 3, 1869. He ran unsuccessfully for a Senate seat in 1869 and for a seat in the House of Representatives in 1872. Two years later he won election to the Senate, where he served from March 4, 1875, until his death on July 31, 1875.

3496. President who had been a newspaper publisher was Warren Gamaliel Harding. In 1884, after teaching school and trying to make a start in the insurance business, he joined with two partners to buy the *Star,* a weekly newspaper in Marion, OH. Harding became the editor. Some years later, he reorganized it as a daily.

3497. President who held a doctorate in a field other than law was Woodrow Wilson, who received a doctorate in political science from the Johns Hopkins University, Baltimore, MD, in June 1886. His dissertation, *Congressional Government, a Study in American Politics,* was published by the Houghton Mifflin

Company. He had earned his bachelor's degree in 1879 from Princeton University, where he had majored in history and government (the first future president to do so), and took his law degree from the University of Virginia in 1881.

3498. President who had been an engineer was Herbert Clark Hoover, who graduated in 1895 from Leland Stanford University in Stanford, CA, with an engineering degree. Until 1913, when he was named to chair the first of a series of overseas relief projects, he worked as an international mining engineer. His book *Principles of Mining* was published in 1909. A translation by Hoover and his wife, Lou Henry Hoover, of the classic Latin work *De re metallica,* by the 16th-century German mineralogist Georgius Agricola, was published in 1912. In 1964 Hoover was named one of the greatest engineers in U.S. history by the School of Engineering and Applied Science of Columbia University.

3499. President who had been president of a university was Woodrow Wilson. On October 25, 1902, Wilson was installed as president of Princeton University, Princeton, NJ, having been unanimously elected by the faculty. He had taught jurisprudence and political economy at Princeton since 1890. He went on to serve as the Democratic governor of New Jersey (1911–13) before his election to the White House in 1912.

3500. President since the Civil War who was a former cabinet member was William Howard Taft, who served as secretary of war in the cabinet of Theodore Roosevelt from February 1, 1904, through June 1908. He succeeded Roosevelt as president. He was also the first president to have served in a presidential cabinet in a capacity other than as secretary of state.

3501. Incumbent senator to be elected president was Ohio Republican Warren Gamaliel Harding. He won the party nomination on June 12, 1920, and went on to win the election on November 2, 1920.

3502. Former president to become chief justice of the Supreme Court was William Howard Taft. He joined the law faculty of Yale University in 1913 at the end of his term in the White House. He was appointed chief justice on June 30, 1921, and resigned on February 3, 1930, a few weeks before his death.

3503. President who had been president of a union was Ronald Wilson Reagan, who was an actor before he entered politics. From 1946 to 1952 he served on the board of directors of the Screen Actors Guild. He was elected president of the Guild on November 17, 1947, and was reelected for five consecutive terms, ending in June 1960.

3504. President who had served as Senate majority leader was Lyndon Baines Johnson, Democrat of Texas. Johnson was elected to the Senate on November 2, 1948. He was elected the majority leader on January 3, 1955, and served until January 3, 1961, when he took the oath of office as vice president of the United States. He succeeded to the presidency on November 22, 1963, after the assassination of President John Fitzgerald Kennedy.

3505. President who had college experience as a Senate staff member was William Jefferson Clinton, who served on the staff of Senator J. William Fulbright of Arkansas in 1967 while he was an undergraduate at Georgetown University, Washington, DC. Clinton graduated in June 1969 with a degree in international affairs.

3506. President who had served as ambassador to the United Nations was George Herbert Walker Bush, who was appointed to that post on December 11, 1970, by President Richard Milhous Nixon. He was confirmed by the Senate and served in 1971–72.

3507. President who had served as chairman of his political party was George Herbert Walker Bush, who served as chairman of the Republican National Committee in 1973–74. Bush began moving up in the ranks of the Republican Party in 1962, when he was elected chairman of the Republican organization of Harris County in Texas.

3508. President who had served as director of the Central Intelligence Agency was George Herbert Walker Bush. On November 2, 1975, when Bush was serving as liaison officer in Beijing, People's Republic of China, he was named by President Gerald Rudolph Ford to replace CIA director William E. Colby. Colby had been dismissed after a congressional inquiry turned up evidence of abuses by the CIA, including espionage work against politically restive American citizens and illegal schemes to assassinate foreign leaders. In February 1976 Bush was also appointed to chair a newly created coordinating committee for intelligence operations.

3509. President who had been a professional actor was Ronald Wilson Reagan. Reagan began his performing career as a radio sportscaster in Iowa and played a crusading radio announcer in his first Hollywood picture, *Love Is On the Air* (1937). His best-known movie roles were George Gipp, the doomed Notre Dame University football player in *Knute Rockne—All American* (1940), and Drake McHugh, whose legs are amputated in *Kings Row* (1941). In the latter picture, Reagan uttered the famous line "Where's the rest of me?" which he later used as the title of his 1965 autobiography. Reagan was president of the Screen Actors' Guild (SAG) from 1947 to 1952 and again in 1959 and 1960.

PRESIDENTS—CONGRESS

3510. President to visit the Senate while it was in session was President George Washington, who came to the Senate chamber in Federal Hall, New York City, on August 22, 1789, accompanied by Secretary of War Henry Knox, to receive the senators' advice on and consent for a treaty with the Cherokee. Some of the senators, unwilling to give their consent without further investigation but uncomfortable at the thought of debating the issues in his presence, moved to have the documents referred to a committee, which caused Washington to remark angrily, "This defeats every purpose of my coming here!" He returned two days later and listened quietly while the language of the treaty was debated, the Senate eventually voting to advise and consent to an appropriation of $20,000 to conclude the treaty. From then on, Washington conducted treaty business with the Senate in writing.

3511. President to be censured by Congress was Andrew Jackson, who displeased the Senate by opposing the recharter of the Bank of the United States. On December 11 the Senate directed Jackson to produce a bank document that he had read to his cabinet, but he refused, retorting that Constitution did not empower the Senate to require of a president "an account of any communication, either verbally or in writing, made to the heads of departments acting as a cabinet council." On March 28, 1834, by a vote of 26–20, the Senate passed a resolution declaring that Jackson "in the last executive proceedings in relation to the public revenue, has assumed upon himself authority and power not conferred by the constitution and laws, but in derogation of both." A motion expunging the censure resolution was passed by the Senate on March 16, 1837.

PRESIDENTS—CONGRESS—continued

3512. Presidential protest to Congress was signed on April 15, 1834, by President Andrew Jackson, who sent it to the Senate with the request that its text be entered in the journal of the Senate's daily proceedings. The message was a formal protest against the Senate resolution of March 28, in which the senators censured him for his refusal to supply them with a document that he wished to keep confidential. The Senate refused to allow it into the journal.

3513. President-elect who was simultaneously a senator-elect and a member of the House was James Abram Garfield, who was elected to the presidency on November 2, 1880. He was already a congressman from Ohio, having been elected in 1862 while serving in the Union Army as brigadier general of volunteers and reelected continuously thereafter. He was also senator-elect from Ohio, having been chosen by the state legislature on January 13, 1880, to serve in the Senate in the term beginning March 4, 1881. Six days after his election as president, he resigned his prospective Senate seat.

3514. President since Washington to submit a treaty to the Senate in person was Woodrow Wilson, who came to the Senate chamber on July 10, 1919, to present the Treaty of Versailles, which had been signed by Germany on June 28.

PRESIDENTS—CRIMES AND MISDEMEANORS

3515. President to run afoul of the law was George Washington. A Boston newspaper, the *Columbian Centinel,* reported in December 1789 that the president, en route from a town in Connecticut to one in New York State one Sunday, was ordered to stop by a Connecticut tithingman because he was breaking the state's Sabbath law, which limited excessive walking or riding on the Christian Sabbath. The president was allowed to continue because he was on his way to church.

3516. President summoned to court as a witness in a trial was Thomas Jefferson, who was served on June 10, 1807, with a subpoena requiring him to appear at the trial of Aaron Burr for high treason. Although the Constitution does not prevent a sitting president from being summoned as a witness, Jefferson refused to obey on the ground that the president's duties and responsibilities were more important to the country than his appearance at the trial of an individual, and that the constitutional separation of powers protected the chief executive from a summons by the judiciary branch.

3517. Convictions in the Watergate case were handed down on January 20, 1973, by a jury in U.S. District Court, Washington, DC, against G. Gordon Liddy and James W. McCord, Jr., two associates of President Richard Milhous Nixon. The presiding judge was John J. Sirica. Liddy had served as the finance counsel for the Committee for the Re-election of the President (CREEP) and McCord had been the group's security director. Both were convicted of four felony counts of conspiracy, burglary, illegal wiretapping, and eavesdropping in connection with the break-in on June 17, 1972, at the Democratic National Committee headquarters in the Watergate complex. McCord was also convicted of two counts of possessing illegal bugging equipment. Liddy and McCord had been indicted on September 15, 1972, along with the five men who had been arrested in the burglary (E. Howard Hunt, Bernard Barker, Virgilio Gonzalez, Eugenio Martinez, and Frank Sturgis), all of whom pleaded guilty.

3518. President to receive a presidential pardon was Richard Milhous Nixon, who accepted a pardon from his successor, Gerald Rudolph Ford, on September 8, 1974, exactly a month after Nixon resigned from the presidency in the wake of the Watergate scandal. Ford unconditionally pardoned Nixon for all federal offenses that the former president "committed or may have committed or taken part in" while in office.

3519. Sexual harassment lawsuit against a president was lodged on May 6, 1994, against President William Jefferson Clinton by Paula Corbin Jones, a former employee of the Arkansas Industrial Development Commission. In 1991, when Clinton was governor of Arkansas, she was employed as a hostess for the Arkansas Quality Management Governors' Conference at Little Rock's Excelsior Hotel. Jones claimed that on May 8, 1991, Clinton had a state trooper summon her to his hotel room, where he made unwanted sexual advances toward her, and that he later took steps to destroy her career. Clinton categorically denied the charges. The lawsuit blossomed into a major scandal for the Clinton administration, ultimately leading to his impeachment. Jones's $700,000 civil case was resolved on January 12, 1999, when Clinton sent her a check for $850,000 (an amount that included additional lawyers' fees). The money was raised from personal accounts and from an insurance policy.

3520. President to have a legal defense fund during his term in office was William Jefferson Clinton, president from 1993 through 2001, who came under investigation for real estate fraud, sexual harassment, and campaign finance irregularities, culminating in his impeachment trial in the Senate in 1999 in the Monica Lewinsky case. The fund was established in June 1994 and took in some $1.3 million to pay legal bills. It was dissolved in December 1997 amid charges that it had accepted unlawful donations and was replaced by a second fund, the Clinton Legal Expense Trust. By the end of his second term, President Clinton and First Lady Hillary Rodham Clinton owed nearly $9 million to private lawyers.

3521. Convictions in the Whitewater case were handed down on May 28, 1996, by a jury in Little Rock, AR, against James McDougal, his wife Susan McDougal (both of the Madison Guaranty Savings and Loan Association of Augusta, AR), and Jim Guy Tucker, the governor of Arkansas. All three were convicted of various counts of fraud and conspiracy for irregular financial dealings between 1985 and 1987 in connection with the Whitewater Development Company, a real estate investment firm. President William Jefferson Clinton and his wife Hillary Rodham Clinton also invested in Whitewater and were implicated in the fraud, but the prosecutor in the case, independent counsel Kenneth W. Starr, never produced evidence that they had committed a crime.

3522. President to give testimony before a grand jury during his term in office was William Jefferson Clinton, who on August 17, 1998, submitted to four-and-a-half hours of questioning before a grand jury convened in Washington, DC, by special prosecutor Kenneth Starr. Starr was investigating whether Clinton lied under oath in earlier testimony given in connection with a sexual harassment lawsuit brought against the president by Paula Corbin Jones. In the grand jury session, Clinton admitted that he had had "inappropriate intimate physical contact" with White House intern Monica Lewinsky, a fact he had denied both in the Jones testimony and in public. However, Clinton maintained that he had not committed perjury because the "contact" did not fit the definition of sex used by the Jones lawyers.

PRESIDENTS—DEATHS

3523. Congressional eulogy for a president was delivered by Representative Henry Lee of Virginia on December 26, 1799, before both houses of Congress, in honor of George Washington. This was the speech in which Washington was called "first in war, first in peace and first in the hearts of his countrymen."

3524. Mourning ribbons to mark the death of a president were silk ribbons issued following the deaths of Thomas Jefferson and John Adams on July 4, 1826. The best known shows the two former presidents on a pedestal, with an eagle and a weeping willow above them. The ribbon is inscribed "Together they laboured for our Country, together they have gone to meet their reward."

3525. President who became a nonagenarian was John Adams, who died in Quincy, MA, on July 4, 1826, at the age of 90.

3526. President to die in office was William Henry Harrison, who died in the White House on April 4, 1841. He had caught pneumonia a month earlier at his inauguration on March 4, 1841, having stood in the cold with neither coat nor hat for nearly two hours while he made his inaugural address. He was also the first president to die in the White House. Nine years later, Zachary Taylor died in the White House after a sudden illness, after serving a little more than one year.

3527. President who narrowly escaped a fatal accident while in office was John Tyler. On February 28, 1844, the president took a trip down the Potomac River on the U.S.S. *Princeton,* the first propeller-driven warship. He was accompanied by his cabinet and by numerous senators, representatives, diplomats, and dignitaries, together with their families—some 400 people in all. The ship was about 15 miles below Washington on the return trip when the captain ordered his men to fire a salute from its biggest gun, the 15-foot "Peacemaker," with a 25-pound cannonball. The gun exploded, killing six people, including Secretary of State Abel Parker Upshur and Secretary of the Navy Thomas Walker Gilmer. The president happened to be below decks at the time.

3528. President who was survived by his mother was James Knox Polk, who died in Nashville, TN, on June 15, 1849, at the age of 53. His mother, Jane Knox Polk, died on January 11, 1852, at the age of 75.

PRESIDENTS—DEATHS—*continued*

3529. Former president whose death was officially ignored was John Tyler of Virginia, who was president from April 6, 1841, through March 3, 1845, having succeeded to the presidency from the vice presidency after the death of William Henry Harrison. In February 1861, as the conflict between the slave states and the free states was reaching its height, the former president presided over a secret conference of delegates from 22 states that met at Washington, DC, in the unsuccessful hope of finding a peaceful resolution. When Virginia seceded from the Union, Tyler, the state's former governor and senator, lent it his support, serving as a delegate to the Provisional Congress of the Confederate States in August 1861. His death on January 18, 1862, at Richmond, VA, prevented him from taking the seat in the Confederate Congress to which he had been elected. The federal government, contrary to its usual practice, made no announcement of his death and held no ceremony in his memory. More than half a century later, Congress appropriated funds for the erection of a public monument to Tyler at Richmond's Hollywood Cemetery.

3530. President whose grave was opened by thieves was Abraham Lincoln, who had been laid to rest in a tomb at the Oak Ridge Cemetery in Springfield, IL, on May 4, 1865. The tomb was broken into on November 7, 1876, by thieves who intended to hide the casket in Indiana and ransom it for a payment of $200,000 and the freedom of a colleague of theirs who was in prison for counterfeiting. They had already begun pulling Lincoln's casket from the tomb when they were interrupted by the arrival of Secret Service agents, who had been alerted by a Pinkerton detective whose help they had sought. Because there was no law against stealing the bodies of the dead, the thieves were sentenced to a year in prison for the break-in. In 1901, Lincoln's body was placed in a new tomb made of concrete.

3531. President and First Lady to die during the term for which he had been elected were Warren Gamaliel Harding, who died on August 2, 1923, in San Francisco, CA, and Florence Kling De Wolfe Harding, who died on November 21, 1924, in Marion, OH. The term for which Harding had been elected was March 4, 1921–March 3, 1925.

3532. President buried in Washington, DC, was Woodrow Wilson. He was buried on February 5, 1924, in the National Cathedral, the Protestant Episcopal Cathedral of Sts. Peter and Paul, in Washington, DC.

3533. President buried in the National Cemetery at Arlington, VA, was William Howard Taft. He was buried on March 11, 1930.

3534. President whose father and mother both survived him was John Fitzgerald Kennedy, who took office on January 20, 1961, and was assassinated on November 22, 1963. His father, Joseph Patrick Kennedy, died on November 18, 1969, at the age of 81. His mother, Rose Elizabeth Fitzgerald Kennedy, died on January 22, 1995, at the age of 104.

3535. President whose body was exhumed was Zachary Taylor, who died suddenly of acute gastrointestinal illness on July 9, 1850, during his second year in the White House. Some historians suggested that he might have been poisoned. To test this theory, on June 17, 1991, his remains were exhumed from a cemetery in Louisville, KY. A coroner's report dated June 26 found no evidence of foul play.

PRESIDENTS—DEPICTIONS

3536. Presidential portrait of importance was the full-length portrait of George Washington painted in New York City by Gilbert Stuart in the spring of 1796. Washington agreed to sit for the artist beginning on April 12. The portrait shows Washington as he appeared before Congress in Philadelphia, and depicts various objects symbolic of the new republic. Several replicas exist, including the most famous, the one rescued by Dolley Madison from the White House before it was sacked by the British in 1814. This work now hangs in the East Room of the White House. The paintings are collectively known as the Lansdowne portraits because one of them was given by Mrs. William Bingham, the wife of Senator William Bingham, who commissioned them, to William Petty, second Earl of Shelburne and first Marquis of Lansdowne. Lansdowne was a British supporter of the American cause during the Revolutionary War.

3537. Artist to paint five presidents was Gilbert Stuart, who was commissioned by Colonel George Gibbs of Rhode Island to paint portraits of George Washington, John Adams, Thomas Jefferson, James Madison, and James Monroe. The set of five portraits were completed in Boston, MA, in 1821. Now known as the Gibbs-Coolidge Set of the First Five Presidents, they are in the collection of the National Gallery of Art in Washington, DC.

3538. Photograph of a former president was taken by the Southworth and Hawes Studio, Tremont Street, Boston, MA. It was a photograph of John Quincy Adams taken in 1843 at his home in the town of Braintree (now Quincy), MA. In 1845, Mathew B. Brady photographed Andrew Jackson at the Hermitage, Nashville, TN.

3539. Photograph of a president in office was a picture of President James Knox Polk, made on February 14, 1849, in New York City by Mathew B. Brady.

3540. Portrait of Abraham Lincoln known to historians and accepted as authentic was painted in 1856 by Philip O. Jenkins, an itinerant physician and artist, before Lincoln became a national figure. It was discovered hanging in the Illinois home of one of Jenkins's descendants in 1988. The earliest known photograph of Lincoln is thought to be a daguerrotype taken in 1843.

3541. Photographic pictorial biography of a president was *Lincoln: His Life in Photographs,* a biography of Abraham Lincoln published in 1941 by the Hungarian-born journalist Stefan Lorant.

PRESIDENTS—FAMILY

3542. President who was orphaned in childhood was Andrew Jackson, who was born in South Carolina on March 15, 1767, a few days after the death of his father, who was also called Andrew Jackson. (He was thus the first president whose father died before his own birth.) His mother, Elizabeth Hutchinson Jackson, died during the British invasion of the Carolinas in 1781, when Jackson was 14. Herbert Hoover lost his father when he was six years old and his mother when he was nine.

3543. President whose father was a state governor was William Henry Harrison. His father, Benjamin Harrison, was governor of Virginia from November 30, 1781, to November 30, 1784. John Tyler (Harrison's successor as president) and Franklin Pierce were the sons of governors of Virginia and New Hampshire respectively.

3544. President who was a widower when he took office was Thomas Jefferson. He was married on January 1, 1772, to Martha Wayles Skelton, the 23-year-old widow of Bathurst Skelton. They were married for ten years, during which time Martha gave birth to six children, only two of whom survived to adulthood (her child by her first husband had also died at

a young age). She was 33 years old when she died on September 6, 1782, at their home in Monticello, VA. Jefferson, who took office as president on March 4, 1801, outlived her by 43 years.

3545. President to have children was John Adams of Massachusetts. He and his wife, Abigail Smith Adams, had two daughters and three sons. Four of their children were still living when Adams entered the White House in 1797. Two were still living when Adams died on July 4, 1826, at the age of 90. Adams's predecessor, George Washington of Virginia, had no children of his own, though he did have two stepchildren by his wife, Martha Custis Washington, and helped to raise two step-grandchildren who had been orphaned.

3546. President whose son became president was John Adams, the second president, who was inaugurated on March 4, 1797. He was the father of John Quincy Adams, the sixth president, inaugurated on March 4, 1825.

3547. President who was married overseas was John Quincy Adams, who was married on July 26, 1797, to Louisa Catherine Johnson, the daughter of the American consul in London. The wedding took place at the Church of the Parish of All Hallows, Barking. Adams was on his way to Prussia to serve as minister plenipotentiary.

3548. Child of a president to die during his father's term in office was Charles Adams, the fourth of the five children of John Adams and Abigail Smith Adams. John Adams was president from March 4, 1797, to March 3, 1801. Charles Adams died on November 30, 1800, at the age of 30. Other children of presidents to die during their terms were Mary Jefferson, the daughter of Thomas Jefferson, who died in 1804 at the age of 26; William Wallace Lincoln, the son of Abraham Lincoln, who died in 1862 at the age of eleven; Calvin Coolidge, Jr., who died in 1924 at the age of 16; and Patrick Bouvier Kennedy, the son of John Fitzgerald Kennedy, who died in 1963, two days after he was born.

3549. Child of a president to be born in a foreign country was George Washington Adams, the first child of Louisa Catherine Johnson Adams and John Quincy Adams, who was born on April 13, 1801, in Berlin, Germany. His father was then serving as United States minister to Prussia. The family's fourth child, Louisa Catherine Adams, was born in 1811 in St. Petersburg, during her father's assignment as United States minister to Russia; she died in

PRESIDENTS—FAMILY—*continued*

1812. John Quincy Adams was elected president on November 2, 1824. On April 30, 1829, a few weeks after his father left office, George Washington Adams was lost at sea in Long Island Sound.

3550. President who was a descendant of a signer of the Declaration of Independence was John Quincy Adams. His father, John Adams, was a member of the committee of the Continental Congress that drafted the Declaration in Philadelphia, PA, in 1776. Benjamin Harrison, the father of William Henry Harrison, was also a signer of the Declaration.

3551. President whose father was alive when he was inaugurated was John Quincy Adams, inaugurated on March 4, 1825. His father, former president John Adams of Massachusetts, died on July 4, 1826, at the age of 90. The president's mother, Abigail Smith Adams, had died on October 28, 1818, at the age of 73.

3552. President who was a former state governor and the son of a state governor was John Tyler. His father, a lawyer and judge who was also named John Tyler, was the Democratic-Republican governor of Virginia from 1808 to 1811. The younger John Tyler served as the Democratic-Republican governor of Virginia from December 1, 1825, to 1827. He was elected vice president on the Whig ticket in 1840 and succeeded to the presidency on April 6, 1841, after the death of President William Henry Harrison (whose father had been governor of Virginia from 1781 to 1784).

3553. Child of a president to attend West Point was Abraham Van Buren, son of Martin Van Buren. He was graduated from the United States Military Academy at West Point, NY, in 1827. Frederick Dent Grant, the son of Ulysses S. Grant, was graduated from West Point on June 12, 1871, and John Sheldon Doud Eisenhower, the son of Dwight David Eisenhower, was graduated from West Point on June 6, 1944.

3554. President who had a stepmother was Millard Fillmore, who became the 13th president on July 10, 1850. His parents, who had nine children, were Nathaniel and Phoebe Millard Fillmore. His mother died in 1831, when he was 31, and three years later his father married Eunice Love. Millard Fillmore's own first wife, Abigail Powers Fillmore, died when she was 55, leaving two grown children, and some years later he married Caroline Carmichael McIntosh.

3555. Presidents who were related by marriage were Zachary Taylor, the twelfth president of the United States, and Jefferson Davis, the first and only president of the Confederate States of America. Taylor's daughter, Sarah Knox Taylor, the second of his six children, married Davis on June 17, 1835, near Lexington, KY. She died in Louisiana the following September. Davis married a second time, to Varina Howell Davis, in 1845.

3556. President whose grandson became president was William Henry Harrison, the ninth president (1841). His grandson, Benjamin Harrison, was the 23rd president (1888–93).

3557. President to marry while in office was John Tyler. He married Julia Gardiner, daughter of a New York State senator, on June 25, 1844, at the Church of the Ascension, New York City. His first wife, Letitia Christian Tyler, whom he had married on March 29, 1813, had died on September 10, 1842, in the White House.

3558. Presidents who were cousins were James Madison, who took office in 1809, and Zachary Taylor, who took office in 1849. They were second cousins. Theodore Roosevelt and Franklin Delano Roosevelt were fifth cousins, and the latter was married to the former's niece, Eleanor Roosevelt.

3559. Marriage of two descendants of the same president took place on June 30, 1853, when Mary Louise Adams, a descendant of Presidents John Adams and John Quincy Adams, married William Clarkson Johnson, a descendant of John Adams.

3560. Child of a president to decline a nomination for the presidency was John Scott Harrison, the fifth of the ten children of Anna Tuthill Symmes Harrison and William Henry Harrison, the ninth president (elected on the Whig ticket in 1840, died shortly after taking office in 1841). The Whig Party offered the younger Harrison the nomination in 1856, but he declined, and the party instead nominated former president Millard Fillmore. The election was won by the Democratic candidate, James Buchanan. In 1888, John Scott Harrison's son, Benjamin Harrison, was elected president on the Republican ticket.

3561. President whose mother lived at the White House was James Abram Garfield, who was elected in November 1880. His mother, Elizabeth Ballou Garfield, lived in the Executive Mansion with her son. Garfield died from an assassin's bullet in September 1881.

3562. President who was the son of a minister was Chester Alan Arthur, who succeeded to the presidency on September 20, 1881. His father, William Arthur of New York, born in Ireland in 1796, was a Baptist minister. Grover Cleveland was also the son of a Baptist minister. Woodrow Wilson's father was a Congregational minister.

3563. Child of a president to serve in the armed forces was James Webb Cook Hayes, the son of Rutherford Birchard Hayes, who served in the Philippines during the Spanish-American War. He won the Medal of Honor on December 4, 1899.

3564. President who was the child of divorced parents was Gerald Rudolph Ford, who was born in Omaha, NB, to Dorothy Ayer Gardner King and Leslie Lynch King on July 14, 1913. His parents divorced in 1915, when he was still a baby. The following year, his mother married Gerald Rudolff Ford, a Michigan businessman, who adopted him and changed his name from Leslie Lynch King, Jr., to Gerald Rudolff Ford. (The spelling of "Rudolff" was later altered to "Rudolph.") His father also remarried, to Margaret Atwood of Arizona. Ford entered the White House on August 9, 1974, after the resignation of Richard M. Nixon.

3565. Child of a president to die in combat was Quentin Roosevelt, the son of Theodore Roosevelt, who served as a pilot during World War I. He was shot down over France on July 14, 1918. His brother, Theodore Roosevelt, Jr., survived World War I, became a general in the Army, and died of a heart attack on July 12, 1944, during the Allied invasion of Normandy, France.

3566. President whose father outlived him was Warren Gamaliel Harding, who died at the age of 55 on August 2, 1923, during his term in office. His father, George Tryon Harding, died on November 19, 1928, at the age of 84. He had been a physician.

3567. President whose mother was eligible to vote for him was Franklin Delano Roosevelt, who first ran for the presidency in 1932. Suffrage for women was made the law of the land on August 26, 1920, with the ratification of the 19th Amendment. The first president elected after that date was Warren Gamaliel Harding, in 1920, but his mother, Phoebe Elizabeth Dickerson Harding, had died in 1910. Calvin Coolidge was elected in 1924; his mother, Victoria Josephine Moor Coolidge, had died in 1885. Herbert Clark Hoover was elected in 1928; his mother, Hulda Randall Minthorn Hoover, had died in 1884. Sara Delano Roosevelt, the mother of Franklin Delano Roosevelt, was 78 years old on November 8, 1932, when her son was elected.

3568. President to become a godfather to a member of the British royal family was Franklin Delano Roosevelt. On August 4, 1942, the Duke of Kent, youngest brother of King George VI, served as proxy for President Roosevelt at the christening of his son, Michael George Charles Franklin, Prince George of Kent, who was born on July 4, 1942.

3569. Presidential pet to star in a movie was Fala, the black Scottie owned by President Franklin Delano Roosevelt. In 1943, the Metro-Goldwyn-Mayer movie studio made a short film about Fala's typical day at the White House, starting with the dog's morning biscuit, delivered to him on the presidential breakfast tray.

3570. President with a brother in the Senate was John Fitzgerald Kennedy, whose brother Edward Moore Kennedy was elected on November 6, 1962, to fill his unexpired term as senator from Massachusetts after he was elected president.

3571. Marriage of two descendants of different presidents took place on November 16, 1962, when Jane Harrison Walker, great-granddaughter of President Benjamin Harrison, married Newell Garfield, the great-grandson of President James Abram Garfield. Julie Nixon, the daughter of President Richard Nixon, married David Eisenhower, the gradnson of President Dwight David Eisenhower, on December 22, 1968.

3572. President's mother to serve on a diplomatic mission was Lillian Gordy Carter, the mother of President Jimmy Carter. When Fakhruddin Ali Ahmed, the president of India, died in 1977, President Carter asked his mother to represent the United States at the funeral, which was held in New Delhi on February 11. Mrs. Carter had served in India from 1966 to 1968, when she was in her late 60s, as a Peace Corps nurse. She was accompanied by President Carter's son, Chip Carter.

PRESIDENTS—FIRST LADIES

3573. First Lady was Martha Dandridge Custis Washington, who was often known as Lady Washington. Her marriage to George Washington took place on January 6, 1759. She was 27 years old, the widow of a Virginia planter, Daniel Parke Custis, and the mother of four children, two of whom had died in infancy. Washington was then 26 years old, a plantation owner in Mount Vernon, VA, and the former commander-in-chief of Virginia's army.

3574. First Lady who was the mother of a president was Abigail Smith Adams, wife of John Adams, the second president, and the mother of John Quincy Adams, the sixth president. She gave birth to John Quincy Adams on July 11, 1767, in Braintree (now Quincy), MA.

3575. First Lady who was educated at a school was Anna Tuthill Symmes Harrison, the wife of William Henry Harrison, president for the first four months of 1841. Born in 1775, she was educated at the Clinton Academy in Easthampton, Long Island, NY, and at Mrs. Isabella Graham's Boarding School for Young Ladies, located at 1 Broadway, New York City.

3576. First Lady who was not born in the United States was Louisa Catherine Johnson, who married John Quincy Adams. She was born on February 12, 1775, in London. Her father was Joshua Johnson of Maryland, the first American consul in London. The wedding took place on July 26, 1797, at the Church of the Parish of All Hallows, Barking, England. At the time, Adams was serving as U.S. minister to Prussia.

3577. Warship named for a First Lady was the *Lady Washington,* a small wooden river gunboat built in 1776 by New York State to defend the Hudson River. It was named in honor of Martha Washington.

3578. President's wife to die before he took office was Martha Wayles Skelton Jefferson, who married Thomas Jefferson on January 1, 1772, when she was 23 and he was 28. She died at their estate in Monticello, VA, on September 6, 1782, at the age of 33. She was the mother of six children, three of whom died in infancy and another of whom died a few years later. Jefferson did not remarry. He became president on March 4, 1801.

3579. President's wife to die before he was elected to office was Martha Wayles Skelton Jefferson of Virginia, the wife of Thomas Jefferson. She died at Monticello, VA, on September 6, 1782, of complications resulting from childbirth. Jefferson, who never remarried, was inaugurated as the third president of the United States on March 4, 1801.

3580. First Lady who was born an American citizen was Hannah Hoes Van Buren, childhood sweetheart of Martin Van Buren and his wife from February 21, 1807, to her death on February 5, 1819. She was born on March 8, 1783, in Kinderhook, NY. All first ladies before her were British subjects.

3581. First Lady who had previously been divorced was Rachel Donelson Jackson, whose first husband was Lewis Robards of Nashville, TN. Although Robards sued for divorce, the marriage, as it turned out, had not yet been entirely dissolved when Donelson married Andrew Jackson in Natchez, MS, in August 1791, and charges of bigamy were raised. The Jacksons held a second wedding in Nashville, TN, on January 17, 1794. Rachel Donelson Jackson was also the first president's wife to die after he was elected but before he took office.

3582. First Lady who was the daughter of a minister was Abigail Smith Adams. Her father, William Smith, was a Congregational minister, ordained in Connecticut on November 4, 1729. He presided over her wedding at Weymouth, MA, in 1764 to John Adams, who became president on March 4, 1797. Abigail Powers Fillmore was the daughter of a Baptist minister, Jane Means Appleton Pierce of a Congregational minister, Caroline Scott Harrison of a Presbyterian minister, and Ellen Louise Axson Wilson of a Presbyterian minister.

3583. First Lady to receive free mail franking privileges was Martha Dandridge Custis Washington of Mount Vernon, VA. On April 3, 1800, an "act to extend the privilege of franking letters and packages to Martha Washington" was passed. This privilege was granted her "for and during her life."

3584. First Lady to attend her husband's inauguration was Dolley Todd Madison, wife of James Madison, the fourth president. Madison was inaugurated on March 4, 1809, in Washington, DC; Dolley Madison hosted the inaugural ball held that evening at Long's Hotel, on Capitol Hill, at 7 P.M.

3585. First Lady to redecorate the White House was Elizabeth Kortwright Monroe, wife of James Monroe, who was inaugurated on March 4, 1817. An accomplished hostess who spent years in France and Great Britain with her husband when he was an ambassador, she oversaw the refurbishment of the White House after it was burned by the British during the War of 1812.

3586. President who was a bachelor was James Buchanan. Although he never married, in his youth Buchanan had been engaged to Ann Caroline Coleman of Lancaster, PA. She died of an overdose of laudanum on December 9, 1819.

3587. First Lady to write an autobiography was Louisa Catherine Adams, born Louisa Catherine Johnson, the wife of John Quincy Adams. Her autobiography, titled *Adventures of a Nobody,* was published in 1825.

3588. First Lady who had an occupation other than homemaking was Abigail Powers Fillmore, who taught school before and after her marriage to young New York lawyer Millard Fillmore in 1826, when she was 27 years old. Fillmore succeeded to the presidency on July 10, 1850.

3589. First Lady born west of the Mississippi was Julia Boggs Dent Grant, the wife of President Ulysses Simpson Grant, who held office from 1869 to 1877. The daughter of a judge, she was born in St. Louis, MO, on January 26, 1826.

3590. First Lady who died after her husband's election but before his inauguration was Rachel Donelson Robards Jackson, who had married Andrew Jackson in August 1791, when both were 24 years old. She died in Nashville, TN, on December 22, 1828, at the age of 61, a few weeks after Jackson's election to the presidency on November 4, 1828. At his inauguration, which took place on March 4, 1829, Jackson was in mourning for her, and the ceremonies were kept to a minimum, although a large and rowdy crowd showed up at the White House that evening for a public reception.

3591. First Lady who was the grandmother of a president was Anna Tuthill Symmes Harrison. She was the wife of William Henry Harrison, whose presidency lasted a single month, March–April 1841. The Harrisons were the parents of ten children. The fifth child, John Scott Harrison, born in 1804 in Vincennes, IN, had three children by his first wife, Lucretia Knapp Johnson Harrison, and ten by his second, Eliza-beth Ramsey Irwin Harrison. The second child of the second marriage was Benjamin Harrison, born on August 20, 1833, who became the 23rd president on March 4, 1889. Anna Harrison was alive when Benjamin Harrison was born. She died on February 25, 1864, at the age of 88.

3592. First Lady who was widowed while her husband was in office was Anna Tuthill Symmes Harrison, the wife of William Henry Harrison, the ninth president. William Henry Harrison died on April 4, 1841, a month after taking office. Anna Symmes Harrison never saw or lived in the White House, because her husband died before she could join him in Washington.

3593. Pension granted to the widow of a president was authorized by Congress on June 30, 1841, in "an act for the relief of Mrs. Harrison, widow of the late President of the United States." The law provided a grant of $25,000 to Anna Tuthill Symmes Harrison, the widow of William Henry Harrison, who had died in April 1841 after only four months in office. The amount was equal to one year of his salary.

3594. First Lady who died while her husband was in office was Letitia Christian Tyler, the wife of John Tyler. She died at Washington, DC, on September 10, 1842, at the age of 51, during Tyler's single term.

3595. Former First Lady to be granted a seat in the House of Representatives was Dolley Madison, the widow of President James Madison, who had died in 1836. On January 9, 1844, she paid a visit to the House and took a seat in the spectators' gallery. A resolution offering her a lifetime seat within the House was introduced by Romulus Saunders of North Carolina and passed unanimously.

3596. First Lady to graduate from college was Lucy Ware Webb Hayes, the wife of Rutherford Birchard Hayes, president from 1877 to 1881. She graduated in 1850 from Ohio Wesleyan University in Delaware, OH, and married Hayes two years later.

3597. African-American woman to become a First Lady's confidante was Elizabeth Hobbs Keckley, a Virginia slave who won her freedom and went into business as a dressmaker in Washington, DC. After Abraham Lincoln moved his family into the White House in 1861, Mary Todd Lincoln engaged Keckley as her seamstress, and found in her a sympathetic

PRESIDENTS—FIRST LADIES—*continued*

friend to whom she could tell her troubles. Keckley's memoir, *Behind the Scenes, or Thirty Years a Slave and Four Years in the White House,* was published in 1868, three years after Lincoln's assassination.

3598. Pension granted to the widow of an assassinated president was authorized by an "act granting a pension to Mary Lincoln," approved by Congress on July 14, 1870. She received $3,000 a year. A congressional act of February 2, 1882, increased the annual pensions to $5,000 for the three widows then living and made a special grant of $15,000 to Mary Lincoln.

3599. First Lady active in charitable causes was Lucy Ware Webb Hayes, the wife of Rutherford Birchard Hayes, who took office on March 3, 1877. She was active in the temperance movement and paid official visits to prisons and asylums.

3600. First Lady to ban liquor in the White House was Lucy Ware Webb Hayes, the wife of Rutherford Birchard Hayes, the 19th president, sworn in on March 3, 1877. Known as "Lemonade Lucy" for her habit of serving soft drinks instead of liquor at White House functions, Lucy Hayes was a complete abstainer (as was her husband). She was a prominent member of the Women's Christian Temperance Union.

3601. Use of the term "First Lady" to refer to the president's wife was applied to Lucy Ware Webb Hayes, wife of President Rutherford Birchard Hayes, who was thus described by journalist Mary Clemmer Ames in her newspaper account of the President's inauguration on March 5, 1877. The term was popularized by Charles Nirdlinger's musical comedy about Dolley Madison, *The First Lady in the Land,* which premiered at the Gaiety Theatre in New York, NY, on December 4, 1911.

3602. President and First Lady to celebrate their silver wedding anniversary in the White House were Rutherford Birchard Hayes and Lucy Ware Webb Hayes. On December 31, 1877, they renewed their vows in a reenactment of their original marriage on December 30, 1852. Reverend Dr. Lorenzo Dow McCabe of Ohio Wesleyan University performed both ceremonies. The second couple whose silver wedding anniversary took place at the White House was William Howard Taft and Helen Herron Taft, who celebrated with a garden party on the night of June 19, 1911. Among the gifts was a solid silver service presented by the House of Representatives.

3603. First Lady to give birth during her husband's term in office was Frances Folsom Cleveland, the wife of Grover Cleveland. They were married on June 2, 1886, during Cleveland's first term in office, which ended in 1889 after Cleveland lost his bid for reelection. Their first child, Ruth, was born on October 3, 1891, in New York City. She was known as "Baby Ruth," and her nickname was applied to a popular candy bar. Cleveland was reelected in 1892 and the family moved back to the White House, where Mrs. Cleveland gave birth to another daughter, Esther, on September 9, 1893. A third daughter, Marion, was born on July 7, 1896. After the end of President Cleveland's second term, two sons were added to the family: Richard Folsom, born on October 28, 1897, and Francis Grover, born on July 18, 1903.

3604. First Lady to sit next to her husband at state dinners was Ida Saxton McKinley, wife of William McKinley, who was inaugurated on March 4, 1897. She suffered from epilepsy, and this break with protocol allowed him to give her immediate help if she had a seizure (which she did at McKinley's second inaugural ball on March 4, 1901).

3605. First Lady to attend all her husband's cabinet meetings was Helen Herron Taft, the wife of William Howard Taft, the 27th president, who was inaugurated on March 4, 1909. A suffragist who claimed that she "always had the satisfaction of knowing almost as much as he [President Taft] about the politics and intricacies of any situation," Helen Taft also attended many other political and official conferences.

3606. First Lady to remarry after the death of her husband was Frances Folsom Cleveland, the widow of President Grover Cleveland. They were married in the White House on June 2, 1886, during Cleveland's first term, when he was 49 years old and she was 22. He died on June 24, 1908. Mrs. Cleveland married Thomas Jex Preston, Jr., professor of architecture at Princeton University, on February 10, 1913.

3607. First Lady to write a book published by a commercial publisher was Helen Herron Taft, the wife of William Howard Taft. Her book *Recollections of Full Years* appeared in 1914, soon after her husband left office. The publisher was the New York firm of Dodd, Mead & Company.

3608. First Lady to undertake a career of public service was Eleanor Roosevelt of New York, the wife of President Franklin Delano Roosevelt. She was already an experienced social-welfare and Democratic party activist by the time her husband entered the White House in March 1933. During his long stay in office, as a speechmaker, columnist, and private lobbyist, she shaped public opinion and public policy on a wide range of issues, including civil rights, economic reform, the labor movement, and veterans' aid. She served as assistant director of the Office of Civilian Defense during World War II. After the death of President Roosevelt in 1945, she was prominent in Democratic political campaigns and served several terms as a delegate to the United Nations General Assembly, helping to draft the Universal Declaration of Human Rights, which was passed in 1948.

3609. First Lady to hold a White House press conference was Eleanor Roosevelt, the wife of Franklin Delano Roosevelt, who spoke to 35 reporters, all women, in the Red Room on March 6, 1933.

3610. First Lady to travel in an airplane to a foreign country was Eleanor Roosevelt, who left Miami, FL, in a commercial airplane on March 6, 1934, and visited Puerto Rico, the Virgin Islands, Port au Prince in Haiti, and Nuevitas in Cuba in the course of a trip of 2,836 air miles. She returned to the United States on March 16.

3611. First Lady buried in Arlington National Cemetery in Arlington, VA, was Helen Herron Taft, the wife of William Howard Taft, the 27th president. She died on May 22, 1943, in Washington, DC, outliving her husband by 13 years.

3612. First Lady appointed to a federal post after the death of her husband was Eleanor Roosevelt, whose husband, Franklin Delano Roosevelt, died in April 1945. On December 19, 1945, President Harry S. Truman named her to serve in the United States delegation to the United Nations General Assembly. She was elected chief of the United Nations Human Rights Commission on January 27, 1947.

3613. President who had been divorced was Ronald Wilson Reagan, who was elected in November 1980. He had married his first wife, actress Jane Wyman, on January 24, 1940, when Reagan was a successful movie actor. They were divorced on July 19, 1949. They had two children, Maureen and Michael. Reagan married his second wife, Nancy Davis, on March 4, 1952. They had two children, Patricia Ann and Ronald Prescott.

3614. First Lady to be received by the pope was Bess Wallace Truman, the wife of Harry S. Truman, president from 1945 to 1953. Mrs. Truman was received by Pope Pius XII on May 20, 1951. Julia Boggs Dent Grant, a former First Lady, had been received by Pope Leo XIII in March 1878, during the world tour made by the Grants following the end of President Ulysses Simpson Grant's term in office.

3615. First Lady to have a private audience with the pope was Jacqueline Lee Bouvier Kennedy, the wife of John Fitzgerald Kennedy (served 1960–1963) and the first Roman Catholic First Lady. She was received by Pope John XXIII on March 11, 1962.

3616. First Lady who was president of the student government at college was Hillary Rodham Clinton, who was elected the student president at Wellesley College, Wellesley, MA, in 1968–69. In the spring of 1969 she became the first student to give a commencement address at Wellesley.

3617. First Lady to earn a professional degree was Hillary Rodham Clinton, the wife of Bill Clinton, who was elected president in 1992 and again in 1996. She received a law degree from Yale Law School, New Haven, CT, in 1973. Bill Clinton, whom she married in 1975, was her classmate.

3618. First Lady to pilot an airship was Rosalynn Smith Carter, who was a passenger on the Goodyear airship *America* on her 51st birthday, August 18, 1978. The airship left Dulles Airport, Washington, DC, under the command of Captain Larry Chambers, who invited Mrs. Carter to pilot the ship as it cruised over northern Virginia.

3619. First Lady to deliver a major speech at a national political convention was Barbara Pierce Bush, the wife of George Herbert Walker Bush, president from 1988 to 1993. She addressed the Republican national convention that met in Houston, TX, in August 1992 to nominate her husband for reelection.

3620. First Lady to be given an office in the West Wing of the White House was Hillary Rodham Clinton, whose husband, William Jefferson Clinton, was inaugurated on January 20, 1993. The West Wing, added in 1902, contains office space for the president and his aides.

PRESIDENTS—FIRST LADIES—*continued*

3621. First Lady who was also a federal official was Hillary Rodham Clinton, wife of President William Jefferson Clinton. On June 22, 1993, the U.S. Appeals Court in Washington, DC, ruled that Mrs. Clinton was a "de facto" federal official. The issue arose in the wake of controversy surrounding her chairmanship of a closed-door task force to revise the national health care system.

3622. First Lady to be depicted on a monument to a president was Eleanor Roosevelt, the wife of Franklin Delano Roosevelt. The Franklin Delano Roosevelt Monument in Washington, DC, was dedicated on May 2, 1997. Eleanor Roosevelt was depicted in a sculpture in the fourth room of the monument, with the symbol of the United Nations in the background. The statue was sculpted by Neil Estern. The memorial was designed by Lawrence Halprin and occupied 7.5 acres between the Tidal Basin and the Potomac River.

3623. First Lady elected to public office was Hillary Rodham Clinton, the wife of President William Jefferson Clinton. On February 6, 2000, after many months of testing the waters for her candidacy, she declared herself in the race for the seat being vacated by the retiring U.S. senator from New York, Daniel Patrick Moynihan. The Clintons purchased a home in Chappaqua, NY, to enable Mrs. Clinton, who was born in Chicago and lived most of her life in Arkansas or Washington, to qualify as a resident of the state. Her Republican opponent, Rudolph Giuliani, the mayor of New York City, dropped out of the race after he was diagnosed with cancer and was replaced by Congressman Rick Lazio of Long Island. On November 7, Mrs. Clinton won the election with 55 percent of the vote. This was the first time that any First Lady had ever run for public office and the first time a woman was elected to the Senate from New York.

PRESIDENTS—HONORS

3624. Honorary degree awarded to a president was conferred on George Washington, who received the degree of LL.D. from Washington College, Chestertown, MD, in 1789 and from Brown University, Providence, RI, in 1790. Before he became president, Washington had already received honorary degrees from Harvard College in 1776, Yale College in 1781, and the University of Pennsylvania in 1783.

3625. Tribute accorded by the populace to a president-elect was given to George Washington in April 1789 during his journey from Mount Vernon, his estate in Virginia, to New York City, where he was to be inaugurated. Leaving Mount Vernon on the morning of April 16, he was greeted at Alexandria by a group of his neighbors, who held a public banquet in his honor. At each leg of his journey—from Alexandria to Georgetown, and thence to Baltimore, Wilmington, Philadelphia, Trenton, Elizabethtown, and New York—a collection of local people accompanied him to the next stop. Each city also welcomed him with parades, banquets, military escorts, illuminated houses, and similar displays of respect. Crossing New York Harbor in a barge, he received a salute from the guns at the Battery and cheers from the immense crowd. Governor George Clinton then walked with him to his future residence at Cherry Street, at the head of a procession that included state dignitaries, congressmen, clergymen, and ordinary people.

3626. President to receive the Nobel Peace Prize was President Theodore Roosevelt, who was given the award in 1906 for acting as mediator between Russia and Japan in the negotiations that brought about an end to the Russo-Japanese War of 1904–05. The peace treaty, concluded in Portsmouth, NH, on September 5, 1905, adjudicated territorial claims made by both countries in Korea, the Chinese province of Manchuria, and Sakhalin Island. President Woodrow Wilson received the Nobel Peace Prize in 1919. The Nobel Prizes, established by the Swedish inventor Alfred Nobel, are awarded annually in six fields to individuals or institutions whose accomplishments have been of great benefit to humanity. Roosevelt's was the first Nobel Prize given to an American.

3627. President in whose honor an asteroid was named was Herbert Clark Hoover, president from 1929 to 1933. In March 1920, astronomer Johann Palisan of the University of Vienna in Austria discovered a new asteroid, which he named Hooveria in honor of the American commissioner responsible for bringing food to thousands of Europeans during and after World War I.

3628. President who had been awarded the Distinguished Flying Cross was George Herbert Walker Bush, the 41st president, awarded the medal for his service during World War II. Bush served for three years with the Third and Fifth Fleets in the Pacific and, while attached to the light aircraft carrier U.S.S. *San Jacinto,* was shot down near Chichi Jima in the Bonin Islands. He received his decoration, plus three Air Medals, in 1944.

3629. President and First Lady to receive honorary degrees at the same time were Lyndon Baines Johnson and Lady Bird Johnson (Claudia Alta Taylor Johnson), who were awarded honorary degrees from the University of Texas at Austin on May 30, 1964. The president received the degree of Doctor of Laws and the First Lady the degree of Doctor of Letters. Johnson was president from November 22, 1963, to January 20, 1969.

PRESIDENTS—IMPEACHMENT

3630. Attempt to bring impeachment proceedings against a president was made on January 10, 1843, in the House of Representatives. Congressman John Minor Botts of Virginia introduced a resolution charging "John Tyler, Vice President acting as President," of corruption, malconduct in office, and high crimes and misdemeanors. The nine charges were rejected and the resolution was not accepted by a vote of 83 ayes, 127 nays.

3631. President to be impeached was Andrew Johnson, who succeeded to the presidency after the assassination of Abraham Lincoln in 1865. On February 24, 1868, the House of Representatives voted to impeach him because he had dismissed Edwin McMasters Stanton, the secretary of war, and had declared several laws unconstitutional. The charges were usurpation of the law, corrupt use of the veto power, interference at elections, and misdemeanors. The trial was held in the Senate from March 13 to May 16, 1868, with Chief Justice Salmon Portland Chase presiding. Fifty-four senators took oaths as jurors. The vote was 35–19 against Johnson, but since this was one vote short of the two-thirds necessary for a conviction, he was acquitted.

3632. Elected president to be impeached was William Jefferson Clinton. At 1:22 P.M. on December 19, 1998, the House of Representatives approved by a vote of 228 to 206 the first of four articles of impeachment brought against him by the House Judiciary Committee, chaired by Henry J. Hyde of Illinois, on recommendation of independent prosecutor Kenneth Starr.

The article accused Clinton of committing perjury while testifying before a Federal grand jury on August 17, 1998, about his relationship with White House intern Monica S. Lewinsky. In the Republican-dominated House, five Republicans voted against impeachment and five Democrats voted for it. A second article of impeachment charging Clinton with obstruction of justice was approved by 221 to 212, with twelve Republicans voting against impeachment. Two other articles were defeated.

PRESIDENTS—INAUGURATIONS

3633. Inaugural address was delivered by George Washington in the Senate Chamber of Federal Hall, New York, NY, on April 30, 1789. It was addressed to "Fellow-citizens of the Senate and of the House of Representatives." The president spoke in a low, somber, almost sad voice. He spoke of his anxiety over the great task facing him and of the sense of public responsibility that compelled him to leave his longed-for retirement; apologized for his deficiencies; expressed deep gratitude to God for having guided the creation and the progress of the United States; paid tribute to the men who had devised the Constitution; reminded his listeners that the happiness of the country and the success of its experiment in republican government would depend on the moral character of its people, since "the propitious smiles of Heaven can never be expected on a nation that disregards the eternal rules of order and right which Heaven itself has ordained"; and declined to accept a salary for his service as chief executive.

3634. Inaugural chintzes were produced for George Washington's inaugural in 1789. Typical examples showed Washington receiving laurels from Columbia, or heralded by trumpeting angels, or displaying the scroll of the Constitution. Chintzes, usually made of cotton printed in one or more colors, were popular as commemoratives until the mid-19th century, and were also used as campaign items.

3635. Inaugural tankards were created for the inauguration of George Washington in 1789. Most of these were of the white ceramic known as Washington Liverpoolware. Typically, they were decorated with a portrait of Washington, often flanked by the figures of Liberty and Justice, with a verse on the opposite side, such as: "Deafness to the Ear that will patiently hear / & Dumbness to the Tongue that will utter /A Calumny against the immortal Washington / Long Live the president of the United States."

PRESIDENTS—INAUGURATIONS—*continued*

3636. President inaugurated in New York City was George Washington. He was sworn in by Robert R. Livingston, Chancellor of New York State, at Federal Hall on Wall Street, in Manhattan, on April 30, 1789.

3637. President to be inaugurated after his vice president was George Washington, who took the oath of office on April 30, 1789, in New York City. His vice president, John Adams, had been sworn in nine days earlier, on April 21.

3638. President whose mother was alive when he was inaugurated was George Washington, who was sworn in on April 30, 1789. His mother, Mary Ball Washington of Virginia, died the following August 25 at the age of 81. His father, Augustine Washington, had died on April 12, 1743, aged about 49.

3639. Presidential inauguration took place on Thursday, April 30, 1789, in New York City, on the balcony of the Senate Chamber at Federal Hall, at the corner of Wall and Nassau streets. Robert R. Livingston, Chancellor of New York State, administered the oath of office to George Washington, whose right hand rested on a Bible borrowed from St. John's Lodge, Free and Accepted Masons. The Bible was opened to the first verse of Psalm 127. Washington, who wore a suit of homespun cloth, then delivered his inaugural address in the Senate Chamber.

3640. Religious service held as part of a presidential inauguration took place on April 30, 1789, in New York City, when George Washington took the oath of office at Federal Hall, on Wall Street. After the inaugural address had been delivered, President Washington and his audience, accompanied by a military escort that included a company of bagpipers, walked to nearby St. Paul's Chapel, where they attended a service conducted by the Bishop of New York.

3641. Inaugural ball was held on May 7, 1789, at the Assembly Rooms, on the east side of Broadway, a little way north of Wall Street, New York City. A medallion portrait of President George Washington in profile on a fan was presented as a souvenir to the ladies. The guests included Vice President John Adams, Henry Knox, John Jay, Alexander Hamilton, Robert R. Livingston, senators, congressmen, and foreign diplomats.

3642. President inaugurated in Philadelphia was George Washington, whose second inauguration took place in the Senate Chamber at Congress Hall, at the corner of Sixth and Chestnut streets, on Monday, March 4, 1793. The temporary seat of government had been moved from New York City to Philadelphia in 1790. John Adams, who succeeded Washington in 1797, was also sworn in at Congress Hall.

3643. President who was sworn in by the chief justice of the Supreme Court was John Adams, who took the oath of office on March 4, 1797, at Philadelphia, PA. The oath was administered by Chief Justice Oliver Ellsworth.

3644. President inaugurated in Washington, DC, was Thomas Jefferson, who was inaugurated on March 4, 1801. Jefferson, wearing his everyday clothes, walked from his boarding house to the unfinished Capitol building, escorted by a Virginia artillery company and a group of dignitaries that included a number of congressmen and two cabinet secretaries. He was greeted by his vice president, Aaron Burr, and took the oath of office in the Senate chamber from Chief Justice John Marshall. He then delivered his first inaugural address, in a voice so quiet that few in the audience could hear him.

3645. President who declined to attend the inauguration of his successor was John Adams, who bitterly opposed the political views of his successor, Thomas Jefferson. When Jefferson arrived at the unfinished Capitol building on March 4, 1801, to take the oath of office, Adams was no longer in the city of Washington. He had left at dawn for his home in Massachusetts.

3646. Presidential inauguration at which the Marine Band played music was the inauguration of Thomas Jefferson on March 4, 1801, beginning a long tradition. The Marine Band, which Jefferson called "The President's Own," had been created on July 11, 1798, by Congress, which authorized the appointment of 32 drummers and fifers under a drum major and a fife major.

3647. Inaugural ball held at Washington, DC took place at Long's Hotel, on Capitol Hill, at 7 P.M. on March 4, 1809. James Madison had been inaugurated earlier that day. This was the first inaugural ball to be held since 1789, when George Washington's inauguration as the first president was celebrated with a ball a week after the event. There was no inaugural ball after his second inauguration, and none for the inaugurations of John Adams and Thomas Jefferson.

3648. President inaugurated in the Chamber of the House of Representatives was James Madison of Virginia, who was sworn in by Chief Justice John Marshall on March 4, 1809, while a crowd of ten thousand waited outside. Madison was a veteran of the House, having served in the first four Congresses. His second inauguration, on March 4, 1813, likewise took place in the House chamber, with Chief Justice Marshall officiating.

3649. President to be inaugurated in a suit of clothes entirely American-made was James Madison, at his first inauguration, on March 4, 1809. His jacket was made of oxford cloth loomed in Hartford, CT, and his breeches and waistcoat of merino wool from the New York State farm of Chancellor Robert R. Livingston. A Massachusetts silk mill made his stockings. Massachusetts was also the source of his shoes.

3650. Presidential inauguration held outdoors in Washington, DC was the first inauguration of James Monroe, which took place on Tuesday, March 4, 1817, outside the Brick Capitol. This was a building that Congress had leased from private individuals in order to have a place to meet while the Capitol, wrecked by the British in 1814, was being rebuilt. (It was located on Capitol Hill, on the present site of the U.S. Supreme Court building.) In order to avoid a clash between the House and the Senate over whose chairs to use at the inauguration, Monroe took the oath of office out of doors, on a temporary wooden platform. The oath was administered by Chief Justice John Marshall. George Washington's first inauguration, which took place in New York City, was also held out of doors.

3651. Presidential inauguration to be postponed from Sunday to Monday was the inauguration of James Monroe, who took the oath of office in Washington, DC, on March 5, 1821.

3652. President to wear long pants at his inauguration was John Quincy Adams, who took office on March 4, 1825, wearing a black suit of American-made cloth that included a pair of trousers. His predecessors had worn knee breeches, the style that was current in the Revolutionary era.

3653. Mob scene at the White House took place on March 4, 1829, during Andrew Jackson's first inauguration. Jackson took the oath of office at the Capitol before several thousand of his supporters, many of whom had come long distances to be present. The crowd was so enthusiastic that a ship's cable had to be stretched across the Capitol steps to keep people back. President Jackson then proceeded to the White House on horseback. The crowd followed him on foot and rushed in as soon as the doors were opened, trampling furniture and knocking over barrels full of orange punch. The president was pinned against a wall and had to be protected by a circle of men who linked arms.

3654. President inaugurated in Washington in a ceremony open to the public was Andrew Jackson, who took the oath of office on March 4, 1829, on the east front steps of the Capitol. Previous presidents inaugurated in Washington had taken the oath of office inside the building, in the presence of guests who were there by invitation only. However, the ceremony was curtailed because President Jackson was in mourning for his wife, who had died less than three months earlier. At a public reception held that evening at the White House, some 20,000 people crowded inside and wrecked the furnishings.

3655. Presidential inauguration at which both the president and the chief justice had suffered earlier rejections by the Senate was the inauguration of Martin Van Buren on March 4, 1837. Chief Justice Roger Brooke Taney, who administered the oath of office, had been rejected in 1834, when the Senate refused to confirm his nomination by President Andrew Jackson to the post of Secretary of the Treasury, and again in 1835, when it refused to act on his nomination as associate justice of the Supreme Court. (His nomination as Chief Justice had been confirmed later in 1835.) Van Buren had been appointed by Jackson as minister to Great Britain on June 25, 1831; the nomination was turned down by the Senate on January 25, 1832, when he was already overseas.

3656. President to travel to his inauguration by train was William Henry Harrison of Ohio, the winner of the election of November 3, 1840. He boarded a passenger train at Baltimore, MD, on February 9, 1841, for the last leg of his trip to Washington, DC, where he was inaugurated on March 4.

3657. Presidential inauguration reported by telegraph was that of James Knox Polk, who took the oath of office on March 4, 1845, on the east portico of the Capitol. Present on the platform was Samuel Finley Breese Morse, the telegraph pioneer, who wired reports of the events to Baltimore, MD.

PRESIDENTS—INAUGURATIONS—*continued*

3658. President to deliver his inaugural address from memory was Franklin Pierce, who took the oath of office on March 4, 1853, on the east portico of the Capitol. He had been trained in oration at Bowdoin College and did not require the use of notes to deliver his address, which comprised 3,319 words.

3659. President whose oath of office did not include the word "swear" was Franklin Pierce, who was inaugurated on March 4, 1853. Pierce had religious objections to the swearing of oaths. In accordance with the Constitution, which allows a choice of two words in this matter, he began his oath: "I do solemnly affirm that I will faithfully execute the Office of President of the United States . . . "

3660. Inauguration of a rival president took place on February 18, 1861, at Montgomery, AL, where Jefferson Davis was sworn in as the President of the Confederacy. He had been chosen nine days earlier by the Confederacy's provisional government. On February 22, 1862, after a formal election, he was inaugurated at Richmond, VA, for a six-year term, but the Confederacy failed after three.

3661. President-elect to require military protection at his inauguration was Abraham Lincoln, who arrived secretly by train in Washington, DC, at 6:30 A.M. on February 23, 1861, and was spirited away to Willard's Hotel in a hired cab. He had already been the target of an assassination attempt during the journey. On March 4, the day of his inauguration, Lincoln rode from the hotel to the Capitol in a carriage, together with President James Buchanan and members of the Senate Committee on Arrangements. The carriage was surrounded by a squadron of mounted soldiers. It was guarded from above by riflemen who had been stationed in upper floors and on rooftops to watch for snipers. More soldiers and a battery of artillery were deployed at the Capitol, and the inauguration platform was protected by a fence. The preparations were carried out under the personal direction of General Winfield Scott.

3662. Presidential inauguration in which African-Americans formally participated was the second inauguration of Abraham Lincoln, which took place on March 4, 1865. The military escort included four companies from the 54th United States Colored Troops, and members of African-American civic organizations marched in the procession to the Capitol.

3663. Inaugural ball in the Treasury Building was held following the inauguration of Ulysses Simpson Grant on March 4, 1869, by arrangement of the First Lady, Julia Dent Grant. A newly completed section of the building was used. Confusion in the coat room resulted in long delays for attendees recovering their possessions, and reportedly thousands of dollars in jewels were lost or stolen.

3664. President whose parents were both alive at the time of his inauguration was Ulysses Simpson Grant, who was inaugurated on March 4, 1869. His father, Jesse Root Grant, died in 1873 at the age of 79. His mother, Hannah Simpson Grant, died in 1883 at the age of 84.

3665. President to take the oath of office twice in one year was Rutherford Birchard Hayes, who was inaugurated at Washington, DC, in 1877. The results of the election of November 7, 1876, had been in doubt for months because of a partisan dispute over the validity of 20 electoral votes. The final count, completed on March 2, 1877, gave the election to Hayes, who took the oath of office privately the following day. His public inauguration, during which he took the oath of office again, was held on March 5.

3666. President to view his inaugural parade from a platform outside the White House was James Abram Garfield, who was inaugurated on March 4, 1881. Some 15,000 people marched past the reviewing stand through a heavy snowfall over the course of two and a half hours.

3667. President's mother to attend her son's inauguration was Mrs. Elizabeth Ballou Garfield, the mother of James Abram Garfield. Kissing her was Garfield's first act after his inauguration on March 4, 1881.

3668. President to deliver his inaugural address bareheaded was Theodore Roosevelt, on March 4, 1905.

3669. President whose inaugural address did not include the word "I" was Theodore Roosevelt. Except for the word "my" in the opening phrase "My fellow citizens," his speech, delivered on March 4, 1905, contained no reference to himself or to his personal agenda as president. Instead, it was couched entirely in the second person plural—"we," "us," and "our"—and described in 985 words the responsibilities that faced the American people collectively and their duty to preserve, enlarge, and pass on the heritage of free self-government that was built by the Americans of previous generations. The speech was written with the assistance of Senator Henry Cabot Lodge.

3670. First Lady to accompany her husband on the post-inauguration ride from the Capitol to the White House was Helen Herron Taft, who rode with William Howard Taft after his inauguration on March 4, 1909.

3671. Inaugural address broadcast to a crowd with loudspeakers was that of Warren Gamaliel Harding, delivered on March 4, 1921. Harding declaimed most of the lengthy, platitudinous speech from memory, standing with one hand in his coat pocket in the oratorical pose made famous by Senator Henry Clay.

3672. President who rode to his inauguration in a car was Warren Gamaliel Harding. On March 4, 1921, an automobile took both Harding and outgoing President Woodrow Wilson to the Capitol, where Harding was sworn in by Chief Justice Edward Douglass White.

3673. Presidential inauguration broadcast over a public address system for the benefit of the crowds gathered at the Capitol was the inauguration of Warren Gamaliel Harding on March 4, 1921.

3674. Presidential inauguration speech read on radio at the same time that it was delivered in Washington was President Warren Gamaliel Harding's 41-minute inaugural address, delivered on March 4, 1921. At the same time that Harding was reading the speech in Washington, DC, radio listeners heard Harold W. Arlin of station KDKA, Pittsburgh, PA, read a copy of the speech. Arlin's reading was carried by 24 stations and heard by an audience estimated at 22.8 million.

3675. President who was sworn in by his father was Calvin Coolidge. He had been elected to the vice presidency on the Republican ticket with Warren Gamaliel Harding on November 2, 1920, and succeeded to the presidency on August 3, 1923, after Harding's sudden death. Coolidge received the news at his parents' home in Plymouth, VT. At 2:47 A.M., he was sworn in as president by his father, John Calvin Coolidge, a storekeeper who was also a justice of the peace and a notary public. After Coolidge returned to Washington, DC, the oath was administered to him a second time by Adolph August Hoehling, justice of the Supreme Court of the District of Columbia, at the Willard Hotel.

3676. President who was sworn in by a former president was Calvin Coolidge, whose second term began on March 4, 1925, with an inauguration ceremony that was held at the east portico of the Capitol. The oath of office was administered by Chief Justice William Howard Taft, who had been president himself from 1909 to 1913. Taft also administered the oath of office to Herbert Clark Hoover in 1929.

3677. Presidential inauguration to be broadcast on radio took place on March 4, 1925, when 24 stations broadcast the ceremony in which Calvin Coolidge and his vice president, Charles Gates Dawes, took the oath of office in Washington, DC.

3678. President inaugurated on January 20 in accordance with the 20th Amendment to the Constitution was Franklin Delano Roosevelt. The amendment was ratified on February 6, 1933, and President Roosevelt was inaugurated for his second term on January 20, 1937, in Washington, DC. Previously, presidents had been inaugurated in March.

3679. President whose second inauguration was attended by his mother was Franklin Delano Roosevelt, who was inaugurated on January 20, 1937, in the presence of his mother, Sara Delano Roosevelt.

3680. President whose third inauguration was attended by his mother was Franklin Delano Roosevelt, who was inaugurated on January 20, 1941. His mother, Sara Delano Roosevelt, died the following September at the age of 86.

3681. President inaugurated at the White House was Franklin Delano Roosevelt. His fourth swearing-in ceremony, on January 20, 1945, was held at the south portico of the White House.

3682. Presidential inauguration in which a rabbi participated was the inauguration of Harry S. Truman on January 20, 1949. During the ceremony, a prayer was offered by Samuel Thurman, rabbi of the United Hebrew Temple of St. Louis, MO. President Truman and Rabbi Thurman had both been officers of Missouri's Grand Lodge of Masons, Truman as Grand Master, Thurman as Grand Chaplain.

3683. Presidential inauguration to be televised was the inauguration of President Harry S. Truman on January 20, 1949. An estimated 10 million viewers watched the inauguration ceremonies and the three-hour inaugural parade on television. Another 100 million listened to radio broadcasts of the events. Some 44,000 people witnessed the inauguration in person.

PRESIDENTS—INAUGURATIONS—continued

3684. Presidential inauguration to be televised in color was the inauguration of John Fitzgerald Kennedy on January 20, 1961.

3685. Woman to administer the presidential oath of office was Sarah Tilghman Hughes, district judge of the North District of Texas, who gave the oath to Vice President Lyndon Baines Johnson on November 22, 1963, aboard Air Force One, the presidential jet, at Love Field, Dallas, TX. President John Fitzgerald Kennedy had been assassinated in Dallas earlier that day. Jacqueline Lee Bouvier Kennedy and Lady Bird Johnson were both present, along with 25 other witnesses. This was the first time that a president took the oath of office aboard an airplane.

3686. First Lady to hold the Bible at her husband's inauguration was Lady Bird Johnson (Claudia Alta Taylor Johnson). On January 20, 1965, she held the Bible on which her husband, Lyndon Baines Johnson, took the oath of office. The Bible had been a gift from President Johnson's mother, Rebekah Baines Johnson.

3687. President-elect to ride in an armored car at his inauguration was Lyndon Baines Johnson, who took the oath of office on January 20, 1965. He rode to the inauguration in an armored automobile, delivered his 22-minute inaugural address from within a three-sided enclosure made of bullet-proof glass, and reentered the armored car for the motorcade that took him from the Capitol to the White House.

3688. President to view his inaugural parade from a heated reviewing stand was Lyndon Baines Johnson, who was sworn in on January 20, 1965. He and his family watched the inaugural parade from a reviewing stand set up at the White House. It was equipped with heat, although the temperature that afternoon rose to 45 degrees. The parade included 15,000 marchers and 52 bands and took two and a half hours to pass.

3689. President to take the oath of office using a nickname was Jimmy Carter, who was sworn into office in Washington, DC, on January 20, 1977, by Chief Justice Warren E. Burger. Instead of his formal name, James Earl Carter, Jr., he used his nickname, Jimmy.

3690. President inaugurated on the west front of the Capitol was Ronald Wilson Reagan, who took the oath of office in January 20, 1981. The west front was chosen because it faced toward the midwest, where the president had grown up, and California, where he had served two terms as governor.

3691. Inaugural parade cancelled in the 20th century was the parade that had been planned for the second inauguration of Ronald Wilson Reagan, which took place on January 20, 1985. Cold winds brought the temperature below zero, and all outdoor events were cancelled. The swearing-in ceremony was moved indoors to the grand foyer of the White House. Since January 20 was a Sunday, a second swearing-in ceremony was held the next day, in the rotunda of the Capitol, where President Reagan delivered his inaugural address.

3692. President inaugurated in the Capitol rotunda was Ronald Wilson Reagan, whose second swearing-in ceremony was held there on Monday, January 21, 1985. He had already taken the oath of office the previous day in a semi-private ceremony.

PRESIDENTS—MILITARY SERVICE

3693. President who had been wounded in action during a war was James Monroe, who was an officer in the 3rd Virginia Regiment during the Revolutionary War. On September 16, 1776, he was wounded at the Battle of Harlem Heights in what is now New York City. He was wounded in the shoulder on December 26, 1776, at Trenton, NJ, and received a promotion to the rank of captain from General George Washington for demonstrating bravery under fire.

3694. President who served in more than one war was Andrew Jackson, whose victories on the battlefield prepared the way for his presidential campaigns. His conquest of the Creek Indians, culminating in the Battle of Horseshoe Bend on March 27, 1814, secured to the United States a large area that eventually became part of Georgia and Alabama. He invaded the Spanish territory of Florida during the War of 1812 and drove the British out of Louisiana in the Battle of New Orleans on January 8, 1815. In 1818, during the Seminole War, he invaded and occupied Florida. His first encounter with war came in 1780–81, when, as a young teenager, he was imprisoned by the British during their invasion of the western Carolinas.

3695. President to face enemy gunfire while in office and the first president actively to use his authority as commander-in-chief was James Madison. On August 25, 1814, he assumed command of Commodore Joshua Barney's battery, stationed a half mile north of Bladensburg, MD.

3696. President to attend West Point was Ulysses Simpson Grant, who occupied the White House from March 4, 1869, to March 1877. Grant attended the United States Military Academy at West Point, NY, from 1839 to 1843. He was an average student, ranking 21st in a class of 39, but showed exceptional ability in mathematics and horsemanship. Also at West Point during Grant's years were the Confederate generals Simon Bolivar Buckner and James Longstreet and the Union generals George Brinton McClellan and William Tecumseh Sherman.

3697. Battle in which two future American presidents were combatants was the Battle of Buena Vista in the Mexican-American War, which took place on February 22–23, 1847, at the Angostura Pass near Monterrey, Mexico. An American force of about 5,000 under General Zachary Taylor was defending the pass against 14,000 Mexican troops led by General Antonio López de Santa Anna. On the morning of the 23rd, two divisions of Mexicans attacked the American flanks; one was driven back with heavy casualties by American artillery, and the other was halted by First Mississippi riflemen under Colonel Jefferson Davis. Taylor was elected president of the United States in 1848; Davis became president of the Confederate States of America in 1861. Santa Anna was president of Mexico for several periods between 1833 and 1845.

3698. General to become president was George Washington, who was appointed commander of all continental armies on June 15, 1775. Washington was unanimously chosen as President of the United States by the electors on February 4, 1789. Other professional soldiers who were elected president included Andrew Jackson, William Henry Harrison, Zachary Taylor, Ulysses Simpson Grant, and Dwight David Eisenhower.

3699. President who had served in the U.S. Navy was John Fitzgerald Kennedy, who enlisted in the Navy in September 1941, during World War II, and was commissioned a lieutenant, junior grade.

3700. President who had been a military pilot was Lyndon Baines Johnson (president from 1963 to 1969), who entered active duty in the United States Naval Reserve in December 1941 and was commissioned a lieutenant commander. He was awarded a Silver Star for gallantry under fire in July 1942 after the patrol bomber he was flying came under enemy attack.

3701. President who had served as a Navy pilot was George Herbert Walker Bush, who enlisted in the Navy on June 12, 1942, his 18th birthday, and was commissioned as a pilot. In 1943 he became the pilot of a torpedo bomber based on the aircraft carrier *San Jacinto* in the Pacific. In all, he flew 58 combat missions and was awarded three air medals. He received the Distinguished Flying Cross for his actions on September 2, 1944, when he succeeded in carrying out his bombing mission even after his plane was hit by Japanese fire, bailing out before the plane crashed. Bush was elected president in 1988.

3702. President in the 20th century to receive a medal for heroism was John Fitzgerald Kennedy, who served during World War II as commander of a torpedo boat, PT-109. On August 1, 1943, the Japanese destroyer *Amagiri* rammed the boat while it was traveling near the Solomon Islands in the Pacific. It broke apart and sank. The Navy and Marine Corps Medal was awarded to Kennedy in 1945 for his actions that night. According to the citation, "Lieutenant Kennedy, captain of the boat, directed the rescue of the crew and personally rescued three men, one of whom was seriously injured. During the following six days, he succeeded in getting his crew ashore, and after swimming many hours attempting to secure aid and food, finally effected the rescue of the men."

3703. President who was a graduate of the United States Naval Academy was Jimmy Carter. After studying at Georga Southwestern University, Americus, in 1941–42, and in 1942–43 at the Georgia Institute of Technology, Atlanta, where he served in the naval Reserve Officers' Training Corps, he entered the U.S. Naval Academy at Annapolis, MD, in 1943, graduating on June 4, 1946, with a B.S. degree. He spent seven years as a career naval officer, rising to the rank of lieutenant commander.

PRESIDENTS—MILITARY SERVICE—
continued

3704. Postwar President who had never served in the armed forces was William Jefferson Clinton, who took office on January 20, 1993. All eight of the previous Presidents who served since the end of World War II in 1945 served in the military, though not all saw combat. During World War II, Dwight David Eisenhower was supreme commander of the Allied Expeditionary Forces and General of the Army; John Fitzgerald Kennedy commanded a torpedo boat in the U.S. Navy; Lyndon Baines Johnson was a bomber pilot in the U.S. Naval Reserve; Richard Milhous Nixon was a company commander of the 10th Armored Division (and also served in the Korean War); Gerald Rudolph Ford served aboard an aircraft carrier in the U.S. Naval Reserve; Ronald Wilson Reagan made training films for the Army; and George Herbert Walker Bush was a Navy bomber pilot. Jimmy Carter spent eight years on battleships and submarines as a career officer in the Navy.

PRESIDENTS—POLITICAL PARTIES

3705. President from the Federalist Party was George Washington of Virginia, elected in 1789 by the unanimous vote of the electors. John Adams of Massachusetts, the second president, was also a Federalist.

3706. President whose party was in the minority in the House of Representatives was George Washington, a Federalist, who was President from April 30, 1789, through March 3, 1797. Throughout his two terms, the Federalists maintained a small majority in the Senate. In the House, however, the Democratic-Republicans outnumbered the Federalists 38 to 37 in the 2nd Congress (1791–93) and 57 to 45 in the 3rd Congress (1793–95).

3707. President whose political party was not the same as the vice president's was John Adams of Massachusetts, the second president, elected in 1796. Adams had served as vice president under George Washington. Both were Federalists, favoring a strong central government. When Washington declined to run for a third term, the members of the electoral college found themselves voting for a slate of thirteen candidates who represented a variety of political views. Adams received the greatest number of votes, 71, and was named president-elect. The runner-up, with 68 votes, was Thomas Jefferson of Virginia, who was named Adams's vice president. Jefferson belonged to the Democratic-Republicans, who sought a weak federation of strong state governments.

3708. President from the Democratic-Republican Party was Thomas Jefferson of Virginia. In the election of 1800, Jefferson and Aaron Burr of New York, both members of the Democratic-Republican party (the forerunner of the Democrats), tied for first place in a field of five candidates (the other three belonged to the Federalist Party). The final outcome was decided in the House of Representatives. Jefferson took office on March 4, 1801.

3709. President from the Democratic Party was Andrew Jackson, elected on November 4, 1828. The Democratic Party evolved from the Democratic-Republicans, who had first come to power under Thomas Jefferson in 1801, but who had since undergone a schism, with Jackson's supporters calling themselves Democrats and John Quincy Adam's supporters merging with the Federalists to form the National Republicans.

3710. President from the Whig Party was William Henry Harrison of Ohio, who received the nomination of the Whig Party at its convention in Harrisburg, PA, during December 1839. On November 3, 1840, he defeated incumbent president Martin Van Buren, who was running for reelection as the Democratic-Republican candidate.

3711. President without a party was John Tyler, the vice president who succeeded William Henry Harrison after his sudden death in 1841. At the Whig convention of 1840, Tyler had been given second place on the ticket to placate the supporters of Henry Clay, a fellow Southerner, who had not received the presidential nomination as anticipated. Tyler, however, was a former Democrat who was out of sympathy with most of the Whig agenda, and during his three years in the White House, he vetoed numerous Whig-supported bills, accepted the resignations of nearly all the members of his cabinet, and was the target of an impeachment attempt. The Whigs repudiated him and refused to renominate him in 1844.

3712. Democratic president whose party was in the minority in the House of Representatives was third president from the Democratic Party, James Knox Polk, in office from March 4, 1845, through March 3, 1849. In the 30th Congress, elected in November 1846, the Democrats held 108 House seats and the Whigs 115, with nine others held by other parties, including two by the Independent Democrats and one by the Know-Nothings.

3713. President whose party was in the minority in both houses of Congress was Zachary Taylor, a Whig, who was in office from March 5, 1849, until his death on July 9, 1850. In the 31st Congress, elected in November 1848, the Whigs were outnumbered in the Senate, where they held 25 seats to the Democrats' 35 (with two other seats belonging to the Free Soil Party), and also in the House, where they held 109 seats to the Democrats' 112 (with eleven other seats, including nine belonging to the Free Soil Party). This was also the first time that the party of the president was ever in the minority in the Senate. The situation worsened under Taylor's successor and former vice president, Millard Fillmore, for the House of the 32nd Congress, elected in November 1850, had 140 Democrat seats, 88 Whig seats, and four seats held by the Free Soil Party, and one other.

3714. President from the Republican Party was Abraham Lincoln of Illinois. On November 6, 1860, the Republicans defeated three other parties—the Northern Democrats, the Southern Democrats, and the Constitutional Union Party—to win the presidency. He took office on March 4, 1861. One week later, the seceding Southern states formally adopted the Constitution of the Confederate States of America.

3715. Republican president whose party was in the minority in the House of Representatives was Ulysses Simpson Grant, the second president from the Republican Party, whose two terms in the White House lasted from March 4, 1869, to March 3, 1877. The House of the 44th Congress, elected in November 1874, consisted of 169 Democrats, 109 Republicans, and 15 seats held mainly by Democratic sympathizers from other parties.

3716. Republican president whose party was in the minority in both houses of Congress was Rutherford Birchard Hayes, the third president from the Republican Party, who served as president from March 3, 1877, to March 3, 1881. In the 46th Congress, elected in November 1878, there was a Democratic majority in the Senate (42 seats, compared to 33 for the Republicans and one seat not held by either) and in the House (149 seats, compared to 130 for the Republicans, plus 13 held by the Greenback Party and one other). This was also the first time that the Republican Party had a minority in the Senate during the administration of a Republican president.

3717. Democratic president whose party was in the minority in the Senate was Grover Cleveland, the sixth president from the Democratic Party, during his first term in office, which lasted from March 4, 1885, through March 3, 1889. In the 49th Congress, elected in November 1884, the Democrats held 34 Senate seats and the Republicans 42. In the 50th Congress, elected in November 1886, the Democrats held 37 seats to the Republicans' 39.

3718. Democratic president whose party was in the minority in both houses of Congress was Grover Cleveland, during his second term (March 4, 1893, to March 3, 1897), when he was the seventh president from the Democratic Party. In the 54th Congress, elected in November 1894, the Senate had a Republican majority, with 44 seats to the Democrats' 40, plus four for the People's Party and two for the Silver Party. The Republican majority in the House had 244 seats to the Democrats' 105, with an additional eight held by other parties, mostly the People's Party.

3719. President whose party was in the minority in both houses of Congress during three congresses was Dwight David Eisenhower, a Republican, who was elected in 1952. When he entered the White House on January 20, 1953, there was a Republican majority in both houses of the 83rd Congress: 48 Senate seats, as opposed to 47 for the Democrats and one held by an independent, and 221 of the 435 House seats, as opposed to 211 for the Democrats. The 84th Congress (1955–57) had a Democratic majority in both the Senate (48 seats, versus 47 for the Republicans) and the House (232 seats, versus 203 for the Republicans). In the 85th Congress (1957–59), the Democrats raised their Senate majority to 49 and their House majority to 233 (the Republicans held 47 and 203 seats, respectively). The Democratic majorities grew substantially in 86th Congress (1959–61): in the Senate, the ratio of Democratic to Republican seats was 64 to 34, and in the House, 283 to 153 seats.

3720. President to switch parties in the 20th century was Ronald Wilson Reagan, who was a Democrat until 1962, when he joined the Republican Party. He campaigned for the Democratic presidential candidate, Harry S. Truman, in 1948 and for the Republican candidate, Barry Morris Goldwater, in 1964. After switching parties, he was twice elected to the governorship of California, in 1966 and 1970, and twice failed to win the Republican presidential nomination (in 1968 and 1976) before succeeding in 1980. He was elected president on November 4, 1980.

PRESIDENTS—POLITICAL PARTIES—
continued

3721. Postwar Democrat to win a second term as president was William Jefferson Clinton of Arkansas, who was reelected president of the United States on November 5, 1996. Clinton won decisively in the popular vote and achieved a landslide in the Electoral College, defeating Republican candidate Robert Dole.

PRESIDENTS—PRESS AND MEDIA

3722. President to be stung by press criticism was George Washington. In 1792, three years into his first administration, he was made the target of editorial attacks in Philip Morin Freneau's *National Gazette,* the organ of the Jeffersonian Democrats. In his diary Thomas Jefferson recounted the president's reaction: Washington raged "that he had never repented but once the having slipped the moment of resigning his office, and that was every moment since; that *by God* he had rather be in his grave than in his present situation; that he had rather be on his farm than to be made *Emperor of the World;* and yet they were charging him with wanting to be a King. That that *rascal Freneau* sent him three of his papers every day, as if he thought he would become the distributor of his papers; that he could see in this nothing but an impudent design to insult him."

3723. Newspaper reporter accredited to the White House was Emily Edson Briggs, correspondent for the *Philadelphia Press* of Philadelphia, PA, who wrote a series of letters that were published between January 1866 and January 1882, during the administrations of Presidents Johnson, Grant, Hayes, and Garfield. She wrote under the pseudonym "Olivia."

3724. President whose private life was harassed by reporters was Grover Cleveland. Although his predecessor, Chester Alan Arthur, had complained during his term that the press intruded on his family life, he was spared the full-scale media siege that accompanied Cleveland's marriage to Frances Folsom on June 2, 1886. Newspaper reporters surrounded the White House during the wedding, then tracked the couple to their private retreat in Deer Park, MD, during their honeymoon and set up a press camp nearby. Some 400,000 words on the subject of the president's wedding appeared in print. Cleveland protested vigorously, but the *New York World* replied, "Is it not true that the president first drove journalism to the keyhole by shutting the door of information rudely in his face?"

3725. President to hold regular press conferences was Woodrow Wilson, who held his first one in the Oval Office on March 15, 1913, before an audience of 125 reporters, and who continued to hold press conferences twice a week, on Monday and Thursday mornings, for many months. However, though Wilson had declared his belief in open communication between the government and the press when he was governor of New Jersey, he had a cold and uncongenial manner with journalists, whom he plainly did not trust. In December 1914 the press conferences were reduced to once a week, and in May 1915 they were discontinued.

3726. White House Correspondents Association was founded on February 25, 1914, by members of the White House press corps to determine attendance at presidential press conferences and to deal with journalists' grievances. The White House press secretary at the time (though he did not carry that title) was Joseph Patrick Tumulty, secretary to President Woodrow Wilson.

3727. White House press secretary was George Edward Akerson, a former newpaper correspondent appointed to the newly created post by President Herbert Hoover in 1929. Akerson had previously been Hoover's public relations assistant when Hoover served as secretary of commerce under Calvin Coolidge. Akerson instituted the practice of providing regular press briefings by a member of the White House staff. He resigned in 1931 to take a job in the motion picture industry.

3728. Presidential press conference recorded on tape was held on January 25, 1951, at the White House, Washington, DC. Portions were released by consent of President Harry S. Truman. It was recorded for the White House archives by the Army Signal Corps unit that handled White House communications.

3729. Presidential news conference filmed for television and newsreels was held on January 19, 1955, in the treaty room of the State Department building, Washington, DC, where President Dwight David Eisenhower held a 33-minute conference at which he answered questions about relations with China and matters of national security. The film was cut to 28 minutes 25 seconds, plus introductory and closing remarks. The television film was recorded by the National Broadcasting Company and Fox Movietone News on a pooled basis with the Columbia Broadcasting System, the American Broadcasting System, and the DuMont Network. The cost was prorated.

3730. Presidential news conference to be televised live was held on January 25, 1961, in the auditorium of the State Department building, Washington, DC. President John Fitzgerald Kennedy answered 31 questions in 38 minutes. The conference was also broadcast on radio.

3731. Large-scale presidential media event was the trip by Richard Milhous Nixon to the People's Republic of China in February–March of 1972. The White House carefully orchestrated the visit, the first by any president to the world's most populous nation. Nixon was accompanied by some 70 tons of transmitting equipment and an army of journalists who generated round-the-clock television, radio, and print coverage. Events were scheduled to begin and end within U.S. network prime-time hours for maximum domestic political impact.

3732. Radio broadcast in which citizens telephoned the president was the "Ask President Carter" show, in which President Jimmy Carter, sitting in the Oval Office in the White House, Washington, DC, replied to 42 listeners from 26 states who phoned in questions on the nationwide radio broadcast. The program was presented on March 5, 1977, on the CBS network. Walter Cronkite served as the moderator.

3733. President to participate in a live chat over the Internet was President William Jefferson Clinton. On November 8, 1999, he appeared on what was billed as a "virtual town meeting" on the Web site Excite@Home, answering questions that were sent to him by e-mail. While he sat on a stage at George Washington University in Washington, DC, a laptop computer streamed his image to the computer screens of the 50,000 participants, who also received a scrolling text of his remarks, transmitted by means of voice-recognition software. Participants from state and local governments included Jeanne Shaheen, governor of New Hampshire; Kathleen Kennedy Townsend, lieutenant governor of Maryland; Don Cunningham, mayor of Bethlehem, PA; Ron Gonzales, mayor of San Jose, CA; Antonio Riley, state assemblyman from Wisconsin; and the moderator, Al From, president of the Democratic Leadership Council, which sponsored the event.

PRESIDENTS—RELIGION

3734. President to conduct religious services as commander-in-chief of the Navy was Franklin Delano Roosevelt, who read from the *Book of Common Prayer* of the Episcopal Church on Easter Sunday, April 1, 1934, while on the quarterdeck of Vincent Astor's yacht *Nourmahal* east of Key West, FL. The services were attended by the crew of the *Nourmahal* and the U.S.S. *Ellis,* a destroyer.

3735. President-elect to attend a religious service along with his staff was Dwight David Eisenhower, who was elected to the presidency on November 4, 1952. On the morning of January 20, 1953, before his inauguration at noon, Eisenhower attended a service at the National Presbyterian Church in Washington, DC, together with the members of his staff. The service was conducted by the Reverend Edward L. R. Elson.

3736. President to become a full communicant of a church during his term in office was Dwight David Eisenhower. On February 1, 1953, a few weeks after his first inauguration, he was baptized at the National Presbyterian Church in Washington, DC, made a confession of faith, and participated as a church member in the communion service. The pastor of the church was Edward L. R. Elson.

3737. President who was Catholic was John Fitzgerald Kennedy, the descendant of Irish Catholic immigrants, who was inaugurated on January 20, 1961, in Washington, DC, as the 35th president.

PRESIDENTS—SALARY AND EXPENSES

3738. Salary established for the president was $25,000, paid quarterly. A bill establishing this amount for the president's salary was passed by Congress on September 24, 1789. Article II, Section 1, of the Constitution directs that the president should receive compensation for his services.

3739. Salary established for the vice president was $5,000. This amount was set by Congress in an act dated September 24, 1789.

3740. Presidential secretary to receive a governmental salary was James Buchanan Henry, who served as private secretary to President James Buchanan from 1857 to 1859. He was appointed to the job after Congress authorized payment of a salary of $2,500 on March 3, 1857. Until that time, presidents used their own money to pay their secretaries' salaries.

PRESIDENTS—SALARY AND EXPENSES—*continued*

3741. Salary raise for the vice president was authorized by Congress on March 3, 1873, when the vice president's yearly compensation was raised from $5,000 to $10,000.

3742. President to receive a salary raise was Ulysses Simpson Grant. In his first term, which began on March 4, 1869, he earned $25,000 a year, the salary set by the 1st Congress in 1789. In his second term, which began on March 4, 1873, he earned $50,000 a year. The amount was raised by Congress on March 3, 1873, one day before Grant's second inauguration.

3743. Travel expenses for the president were authorized by Congress on June 23, 1906. The expense account was capped at $25,000. At the time, the president's salary was $50,000 a year.

3744. President to receive an annual salary of $75,000 was William Howard Taft, who took office on March 4, 1909. Congress voted to raise the president's salary to $75,000 on the day of Taft's inauguration.

3745. President to receive an annual salary of $100,000 was Harry S. Truman, whose second inauguration took place on January 20, 1949, one day after Congress voted to raise the president's salary. Congress also authorized an expense account of $50,000, which carried no tax liability. The president's expense allowance was made subject to federal income tax in 1951.

3746. Vice president to receive a salary of $30,000 was Alben William Barkley, Harry S. Truman's vice president. On January 19, 1949, the day before Barkley took his second oath of office, Congress voted to raise the vice president's salary to $30,000 and to provide him with an expense allowance of $10,000.

3747. Pension for presidents and their widows was enacted by Congress on August 25, 1958. The act provided an annual pension of $25,000 for former presidents and $10,000 to their widows. Former presidents were also granted office help, to a maximum of $50,000 a year; free office space; and free mailing privileges.

3748. President to receive an annual salary of $200,000 was Richard Milhous Nixon. An act of Congress of January 17, 1969, which took effect on January 20, the day of Nixon's inauguration, provided for an annual salary of $200,000, a taxable expense allowance of $50,000, a tax-exempt travel allowance of $100,000, and a tax-exempt entertainment allowance of $12,000.

PRESIDENTS—SPEECHES AND ADDRESSES

3749. Annual message was delivered to Congress by President George Washington in New York City on January 8, 1790. Rather than a vigorous statement of policies and plans, it was a brief series of cautious recommendations; Washington preferred to leave the detailed formulation of policy to his cabinet, especially to Thomas Jefferson and Alexander Hamilton. The address concluded: "The welfare of our country is the great object to which our cares and efforts ought to be directed, and I shall derive great satisfaction from a cooperation with you in the pleasing though arduous task of insuring to our fellow citizens the blessings which they have a right to expect from a free, efficient, and equal government."

3750. Address to a president by a Jewish congregation was presented to President George Washington on August 17, 1790, by the Hebrew Congregation of Newport, RI. It was drafted by Moses Seixas, and read in part: "Deprived as we heretofore have been of the invaluable rights of free citizens, we now (with a deep sense of gratitude to the Almighty disposer of all events) behold a government erected by the Majesty of the People—a Government which to bigotry gives no sanction, to persecution no assistance, but generously affording to All liberty of conscience and immunities of Citizenship, deeming every one, of whatever Nation, tongue, or language, equal parts of the great governmental machine." In his reply, Washington remarked: "It is now no more that toleration is spoken of as if it was the indulgence of one class of people that another enjoyed the exercise of their inherent natural rights. For happily, the government of the United States, which gives to bigotry no sanction, to persecution no assistance, requires only that they who live under its protection should demean themselves as good citizens, in giving it on all occasions their effectual support."

3751. Farewell address by a president was written by George Washington with the aid of James Madison, Alexander Hamilton, and John Jay, and published in Philadelphia, PA, on September 19, 1796, in David Claypoole's *American Daily Advertiser*. Washington never delivered the address in person. In it, the president announced his retirement from public life and warned the nation against party rivalries and "foreign alliances, attachments & intriegues." The Farewell Address is read in Congress every year on Washington's birthday.

3752. Annual message submitted by a president to Congress in writing rather than read aloud in person at a joint session of both Houses was the first annual message prepared by Thomas Jefferson. On December 8, 1801, reversing the precedent set by George Washington and John Adams, he instructed an aide to deliver copies of his message to the presiding officers of the House and Senate, citing the inconvenience and waste of time that would be incurred by speechmaking. Also, Jefferson, though a brilliant author, was uncomfortable as an orator. His practice of sending annual messages to Congress in writing was continued by his successors. It was reversed once again by Woodrow Wilson in 1913.

3753. President who did not deliver an annual message to Congress was William Henry Harrison, who never had the opportunity to prepare one, since he died on April 4, 1841, after only 32 days in office.

3754. Annual message delivered by a president in person since the 18th century was Woodrow Wilson's first annual message, which he read before a joint session of Congress on December 2, 1913. The last president to deliver an annual address to Congress had been John Adams, on November 22, 1800. His successor, Thomas Jefferson, was a diffident speechmaker and sent an aide to deliver his annual messages instead. That practice was followed by subsequent presidents until Wilson reversed it.

3755. President to make a radio broadcast was Warren Gamaliel Harding. His speech at the dedication of the Francis Scott Key Memorial at Fort McHenry, Baltimore, MD, on June 14, 1922, was broadcast by WEAR, Baltimore, MD. His voice was carried over telephone lines to the studio and broadcast from there. On November 5, 1921, a message from President Harding had been broadcast from Washington, DC, to 28 countries. It was sent in code over the 25,000-volt RCA station at Rocky Point (near Port Jefferson), NY.

3756. Presidential message to Congress that was broadcast on radio was heard on December 6, 1923, when President Calvin Coolidge delivered his message to a joint session of Congress held in the House of Representatives, Washington, DC. It was broadcast by KSD, St. Louis, MO; WCAP, Washington, DC; WDAF, Kansas City, MO; WEAF, New York City; WFAA, Dallas, TX; and WJAR, Providence, RI. His voice was transmitted over telephone wires.

3757. President to make a radio broadcast from the White House was Calvin Coolidge, who delivered a speech from his study in the White House, Washington, DC, on February 22, 1924, on the occasion of George Washington's birthday. The speech was heard on 42 stations from coast to coast.

3758. Presidential voice to become nationally familiar was that of Calvin Coolidge, the taciturn Vermonter who took the oath of office on March 4, 1925. Coolidge, whose plain style of speaking and nasal Yankee drawl fit the new medium of radio, had campaigned over the airwaves in 1924. After his inauguration, he made radio speeches to the public every few weeks.

3759. Presidential fireside chat was broadcast from the White House on March 12, 1933, by President Franklin Delano Roosevelt, on the subject of the reopening of the banks after a week-long bank holiday enacted by presidential order. The speech, couched as an informal talk between the president and his listeners, began: "I want to talk for a few minutes with the people of the United States about banking—with the comparatively few who understand the mechanics of banking but more particularly with the overwhelming majority who use banks for the making of deposits and the drawing of checks. I want to tell you what has been done in the last few days, why it was done, and what the next steps are going to be. I recognize that the many proclamations from State capitols and from Washington, the legislation, the Treasury regulations, etc., couched for the most part in banking and legal terms, should be explained for the benefit of the average citizen. I owe this in particular because of the fortitude and good temper with which everybody has accepted the inconvenience and hardships of the banking holiday. I know that when you understand what we in Washington have been about I shall continue to have your cooperation as fully as I have had your sympathy and help during the past week." The term "fireside chat" was coined by journalist Robert Trout and was meant t invoke a down-to-earth image of the president entering into the audience's homes (via radio) and speaking personally with them about his policies. Roosevelt had introduced radio talks during his first term as governor of New York State.

3760. President to make a radio broadcast from a foreign country was Franklin Delano Roosevelt, whose speech at Cartagena, Colombia, on July 10, 1934, was relayed to New York and transmitted over the combined WEAF, WJZ, and WABC networks.

PRESIDENTS—SPEECHES AND AD-
DRESSES—*continued*

**3761. President to read a veto message to
Congress** was Franklin Delano Roosevelt, who
appeared before a joint session of Congress at
Washington, DC, on May 22, 1935, to read his
veto of the Patman Bonus Bill. The bill, introduced by Representative Wright Patman of
Texas, was intended to relieve the financial distress suffered by many veterans of World War
I. It authorized the government to distribute
cash to the veterans by redeeming the certificates that had been issued to them as compensation for their military service. These certificates, similar to savings bonds, were not due to
reach maturity until 1945, but Patman's bill
called for their immediate redemption at full
value. President Roosevelt refused to sign it
into law on the grounds that it was economically unsound and would increase monetary infla-
tion and the nation's deficit. Within an hour after the veto, the House voted to override it by
a vote of 322–98 (the original vote on the measure had been 318–90). The following day, the
Senate voted 54–40 to override the veto (the
original vote had been 55–33).

**3762. President to deliver an address on tele-
vision** was Franklin Delano Roosevelt, who
spoke at the Federal Building on the exposition
grounds overlooking the Court of Peace at the
opening session of the New York World's Fair,
Flushing, Queens, New York City, on April 30,
1939. His address was transmitted by WNBC-
TV, the station of the National Broadcasting
Company. Two NBC mobile vans were used,
one containing a transmitter and the other handling the pickup. Burke Crotty was the produc-
er of the show, which lasted 3.5 hours. It began
with a view of the World's Fair Trylon and the
Perisphere.

**3763. President to make a radio broadcast in
a foreign language** was Franklin Delano
Roosevelt. He addressed the French people on
November 7, 1942, from Washington, DC, at
the same time that the American army was taking part in the invasion of French territorial
possessions in Africa.

3764. State of the Union address was the
presidential message to the 80th Congress, delivered by President Harry S. Truman in January 1947. Previously, the messages were known
simply as "Annual Messages."

**3765. Presidential address televised from the
White House** was a speech by President Harry
S. Truman about food conservation and the
world food crisis, delivered on October 5,
1947. The telecast was relayed from Washington, DC, to New York City, Philadelphia, and
Schenectady. The president proposed meatless
Tuesdays and eggless and poultryless Thurs-
days.

3766. President to appear on color television
was Dwight David Eisenhower, who was photographed on color film on June 6, 1955, when
he spoke at the United States Military Academy
at West Point, NY, at the 40th reunion of the
Class of 1915. The film was broadcast the following day on the National Broadcasting Company's "Home Show."

**3767. Former president to address the Sen-
ate** was Harry S. Truman, who had served as
a senator from Missouri (1935–45) and as the
33rd president (1945–53). On May 8, 1964, his
80th birthday, he was present in the Senate
chamber in Washington, DC. His presence was
formally acknowledged, and he responded with
a 68-word speech. On October 1, 1963, the
Senate had adopted a resolution stating that
"former Presidents of the United States shall be
entitled to address the Senate upon giving appropriate notice of their intentions to the Presiding Officer."

**3768. President to address Soviet citizens on
Soviet television** was President Richard Milhous Nixon, who gave a short televised speech
on May 28, 1972, during his visit to Moscow.

PRESIDENTS—STAFF AND OFFICES

3769. Presidential appointment was made by
President George Washington on June 15,
1789, when he nominated William Short of
Georgia to become chargé d'affaires in Paris
during the temporary absence of the United
States minister to France, Thomas Jefferson.
The Senate received the letter of nomination on
June 16 and confirmed the appointment after
polling its members by secret ballot.

3770. Presidential appointment to be rejected
was that of Benjamin Fishbourn, nominated by
President George Washington to be naval officer of the port of Savannah, GA. On August 5,
1789, Congress refused to accept the nomination because Washington, ignoring the concept
of "senatorial courtesy," had failed to consult
with Georgia's senators on the matter. On August 7 the president expressed his irritation:
"Permit me to submit to your consideration
whether on occasions where the propriety of
Nominations appear questionable to you, it

would not be expedient to communicate that circumstance to me, and thereby avail yourselves of the information which led me to make them, and which I would with pleasure lay before you."

3771. Presidential commission was appointed by President George Washington to deal with the Whiskey Rebellion of 1794, in which the farmers of Washington and Allegheny counties, PA, attacked federal officers who were trying to collect an excise tax on whiskey. In his sixth annual address, delivered on November 19, 1794, he declared: "The report of the commissioners marks their firmness and abilities, and must unite all virtuous men, by shewing that the means of conciliation have been exhausted." The rebellion was then put down by an army of 13,000 militiamen.

3772. President to make extensive use of his constitutional power to remove officeholders was Andrew Jackson, who exercised the presidential power of removal from office 252 times during his two terms in office (from 1829 to 1837). The combined total of all six of his predecessors was 193. The officeholders he dismissed were replaced by men to whom Jackson owed political favors, rather than by those whom Jackson considered most qualified.

3773. Executive Office of the President was created under authority of the Reorganization Act of 1939, by which various agencies were transferred to the Executive Office of the President effective July 1, 1939. Executive Order 8248 of September 8, 1939, established the divisions of the Executive Office and defined their functions, although these divisions have been later modified to suit the needs of each president. The original divisions were the White House Office, the Office of Management and Budget, the National Resources Planning Board, the Liaison Office for Personnel Management, the Office of Government Reports, and the Office for Emergency Management.

3774. White House budget office was the Office of Management and Budget, established on July 1, 1939, through the Administrative Reorganization Act. It was created out of the former Bureau of the Budget, which was transferred from the Treasury Department. The Office of Management and Budget evaluates, formulates, and coordinates management procedures and program objectives within and among Federal departments and agencies, and also controls the administration of the Federal budget. The first African-American to head this office was Franklin Delano Raines, former chairman of the Federal National Mortgage Association, who was appointed in 1996.

3775. Council of Economic Advisers in the Executive Office of the President was established by the Employment Act of February 20, 1946. The Council consists of three members, appointed by the president, who analyze the national economy and its various segments, advise the president on economic developments, assess the economic programs and policies of the Federal Government, recommend policies for economic growth and stability, and help prepare the president's annual economic report to Congress.

3776. Woman to serve as a president's personal physician was Dr. Janet Graeme Travell of New York City, whose appointment was announced on January 25, 1961, by President John Fitzgerald Kennedy. Earlier presidents had received treatment from female medical practitioners. One of these was Dr. Susan Ann Edson, a graduate of the Cleveland Homeopathic Medical College in Cleveland, OH, who treated President James Abram Garfield from July 2, 1881, the day he was shot by an assassin, to September 19, 1881, when he died.

3777. Council on Environmental Quality was established within the Executive Office of the President by the National Environmental Policy Act of 1969. The Environmental Quality Improvement Act of 1970 established the Office of Environmental Quality, which is administratively within the Council. The CEQ formulates and recommends national policies to promote the improvement of the environment and oversees Federal agency and department implementation of NEPA.

3778. Office of Science and Technology Policy was established within the Executive Office of the President by the National Science and Technology Policy, Organization, and Priorities Act of 1976. The office provides the president with policy advice related to science, technology, and engineering and coordinates national funding for fundamental science, scientific education, applied research, and international scientific cooperation.

3779. Office of Administration was established within the Executive Office of the President by Reorganization Plan No. 1 of 1977, and was activated effective December 4, 1977. The Office of Administration provides administrative support services to the Executive Office of the President, including information processing, library services, records maintenance, and general office operations.

PRESIDENTS—STAFF AND OFFICES—
continued

3780. White House Office for Women's Initiatives and Outreach was created in June 1995 to serve as a liaison between the White House and women's organizations and to advocate issues that are important to women. The first director was Lauren Supina.

3781. White House Office of National AIDS Policy was created within the Executive Office of the President by President William Jefferson Clinton and Vice President Albert Gore, Jr., to provide policy guidance and leadership on the government's response to the AIDS epidemic. ONAP's first director, Sandra L. Thurman, was appointed on April 7, 1997.

3782. Woman appointed as chief White House counsel was Beth Nolan, a native of Irvington, NY. She was named chief counsel of the White House on August 19, 1999, succeeding Charles F.C. Ruff. Nolan had been deputy attorney general of the United States since 1996 and was a former White House associate counsel.

PRESIDENTS—TRAVELS

3783. President who had made a transatlantic crossing was John Adams, who sailed to Paris in February 1778 to serve with Benjamin Franklin as commissioner to France. He was accompanied by his eldest son, John Quincy Adams, himself a future president, who was then eleven years old. They returned within the year. In 1780 Adams went back to Europe to begin a long sojourn, first as minister to the Netherlands, then as a member (with Franklin and John Jay) of the team that negotiated peace terms with the British, and finally as minister to Great Britain. He took the presidential oath of office on March 4, 1797. When John Quincy Adams did the same on March 4, 1825, he had already made a multitude of transatlantic trips, including several during his childhood and numerous others during his career as a diplomat (he served during the 1790s as minister to the Netherlands and Prussia and from 1809 to 1817 as minister to Russia and Britain).

3784. President to tour the country was George Washington, who traveled through the New England states from October 15 to November 13, 1789. He traveled in a hired coach accompanied by Major William Jackson, his aide-de-camp, and Tobias Lear, his private secretary, along with six servants, nine horses, and a luggage wagon. He went as far north as Kittery, ME (then part of Massachusetts). As Rhode Island and Vermont had not yet joined the new government, he did not visit those states. Washington's first tour of the southern states was made from April 7 to June 12, 1791, during which time he made a 1,887-mile trip from his estate in Mount Vernon, VA, through Philadelphia, south through Virginia and the Carolinas into Georgia, and back to Mount Vernon.

3785. President to ride on a steamboat while in office was James Monroe. On May 11, 1819, during his first term, President Monroe left Savannah, GA, on an excursion to Tybee Light, along with a group of officials that included the secretary of war, John Caldwell Calhoun, and a number of generals. The president rode on the steamboat *Savannah*, which was accompanied by another steamboat, the *Alatamaha*, and two barges

3786. President to ride on a railroad train while in office was Andrew Jackson, who on June 6, 1833, took the stagecoach to Ellicott's Mills, where he boarded the Baltimore and Ohio train for Baltimore, MD, on a pleasure trip. John Quincy Adams had made a trip on the same line a few months earlier, after he had left the presidency.

3787. President to visit the West Coast of the United States while in office was Rutherford Birchard Hayes, who arrived at San Francisco, CA, on September 8, 1880, and returned to his home in Ohio on November 1. He was accompanied by his wife, two of his sons, General William Tecumseh Sherman, and a number of other people. Former president Ulysses Simpson Grant had visited San Francisco a year earlier, towards the end of the round-the-world trip that he undertook after he left office. Both Hayes and Grant stayed in the same suite at the Palace Hotel.

3788. Presidential yacht was the USS *Mayflower*, a 275-foot gunboat that had been part of the United States fleet in the Spanish-American War. It was reassigned in 1902 for use as a yacht by President Theodore Roosevelt and continued in use until 1929, when President Herbert Hoover ordered it laid up as an economy measure.

3789. President to ride in a car was Theodore Roosevelt, who rode in a purple-lined Columbia Electric Victoria on August 22, 1902, at Hartford, CT. He was accompanied by Colonel Jacob Lyman Greene. Twenty carriages followed the presidential car during the tour of the city.

3790. President to go underwater in a submarine was Theodore Roosevelt, who was a passenger on the *Plunger* on August 25, 1905, when it submerged to a depth of 20 feet in Long Island Sound, off Oyster Bay, NY, the location of Roosevelt's estate. The submarine remained submerged and stationary for about 45 minutes. Navy Lieutenant Charles Preston Nelson, who was in command, allowed the president to operate the controls himself. The *Plunger,* the Navy's first submarine built for the purpose, had been commissioned on September 19, 1903.

3791. President to visit a foreign country while in office was Theodore Roosevelt, who went to Panama in 1906 to see for himself the progress of the Panama Canal, then under construction, which he called "the biggest thing that's ever been done." He sailed from Norfolk, VA, on November 9 aboard the battleship U.S.S. *Louisiana,* intentionally arriving during the worst part of the rainy season so that he could experience the greatest hardship. On the return trip, he visite Puerto Rico.

3792. Former president to fly in an airplane was Theodore Roosevelt. He was a passenger in a Wright biplane piloted by Archibald Hoxsey at the St. Louis Aviation Field, St. Louis, MO, on October 11, 1910, more than a year after he had left office. The flight lasted four minutes. Roosevelt was the first of the presidents, in or out of office, to fly in an airplane.

3793. President to receive a passport while in office was Woodrow Wilson, whose passport was made out on November 27, 1918. He left the United States on December 5, 1918, on the transport *George Washington* and arrived at Brest, France, on December 13.

3794. President to visit Europe while in office was Woodrow Wilson, who went to Europe at the end of World War I to attend a preliminary meeting of the Paris Peace Conference and press for enactment of his 14-point plan for world peace. On December 4, 1918, Wilson traveled from the White House to Hoboken, NJ, where he embarked on the S.S. *George Washington* for Brest, France. He arrived there on December 13. His return trip was made between Brest and Boston, MA, between February 15, 1919, and February 24. At the beginning of March he returned to France, returning to Hoboken in July.

3795. President to visit Alaska while in office was Warren Gamaliel Harding, who visited Metlakahtla, AK, on July 8, 1923, and Vancouver, British Columbia, Canada, on July 26, 1923. He sailed on the U.S. naval transport *Henderson.* Alaska was then a territory of the United States.

3796. President to visit Canada during his term in office was Warren Gamaliel Harding. On July 26, 1923, Harding attended an official reception in Vancouver, Canada, on his return from a trip to the Alaskan Territory.

3797. President to visit South America while in office was Franklin Delano Roosevelt. He stopped off at Cartagena, Colombia, on July 10, 1934, to return the visit of President Enrique Olaya Herrera of Colombia, who had paid a formal visit to Roosevelt on board the cruiser U.S.S. *Houston.*

3798. President to go through the Panama Canal while in office was Franklin Delano Roosevelt. He passed through the canal on July 11, 1934, on the U.S.S. *Houston* on his way to Hawaii. He was greeted at Balboa, Panama, by President Harmodio Arias of Panama.

3799. President to visit Hawaii while in office was Franklin Delano Roosevelt, who landed on July 25, 1934, at Hilo, HI. He was officially welcomed by Governor Joseph Poindexter on board the cruiser U.S.S. *Houston.* Hawaii was then a territory of the United States.

3800. Day on which the president and the vice president were both out of the country was October 16, 1936, when President Franklin Delano Roosevelt was on vacation aboard a naval cruiser, the U.S.S. *Houston,* and Vice President John Nance Garner was en route to Japan on board the *President Grant.* The secretary of state, Cordell Hull, served as acting president, as prescribed by Congress in the succession act of 1886.

3801. President to ride on a diesel train was President Franklin Delano Roosevelt, whose trip home from Washington, DC, to Hyde Park, NY, on October 23, 1937, included a stretch on a Baltimore and Ohio Railroad Diesel train between Washington and New York City.

3802. President to hold an airplane pilot's license was Dwight David Eisenhower. While serving as a lieutenant colonel under General Douglas MacArthur in the Philippines, Eisenhower was issued a private pilot's license by Manila's Bureau of Aeronautics in July 1939. He also received pilot's license No.

PRESIDENTS—TRAVELS—*continued*

93,258 on November 30, 1939, from the Civil Aeronautics Administration. Eisenhower was the first chief executive to be a pilot, the first modern president to ride in a light plane, and the first to ride in a jet aircraft.

3803. Presidential railroad car was U.S. Car No. 1, formerly known as the *Ferdinand Magellan,* built in 1942 by the Association of American Railroads. It was purchased for a nominal fee by the government and assigned to the White House. It weighed 285,000 pounds, was built on extra heavy trucks, and was sheathed throughout with armor plate 0.625 inches thick. It had bulletproof glass three inches thick in all of the windows and doors. The car had a lounge-observation compartment, a dining room seating twelve persons, a kitchen, and four bedrooms. It carried no identification marks other than the presidential seal on the brass-railed rear platform. A private railroad car had been built for Abraham Lincoln, but it was never accepted by him or assigned to the White House. It was used to bear his remains from Washington, DC, to Springfield, IL.

3804. President to fly in an airplane while in office was Franklin Delano Roosevelt, who in January 1943 flew 5,000 miles in a four-engine Boeing Flying Boat from Miami, FL, to the west coast of French Morocco to participate in the Casablanca Conference with British Prime Minister Winston Churchill.

3805. President to visit a foreign country in wartime was Franklin Delano Roosevelt, who flew from Miami, FL, to Trinidad, British West Indies, on January 10, 1943. From Trinidad, he continued on to Belém, Brazil; Bathurst, Gambia; and Casablanca, Morocco, where he arrived on January 14. He returned to Miami by plane via South Africa and Trinidad, and arrived in Washington, DC, by train on January 31.

3806. President to visit Africa during his term in office was Franklin Delano Roosevelt. On January 14–25, 1943, he attended the Casablanca Conference with British prime minister Winston Churchill and Free French generals Charles de Gaulle and Henri Giraud at Casablanca, Morocco.

3807. Presidential airplane was the *Sacred Cow,* a four-engine Skymaster C-54 built at the Douglas Aircraft Company's plant in Santa Monica, CA, and delivered on June 1944 to the Air Transport Command. Its first mission outside the United States was to fly Henry Lewis Stimson, the secretary of war, from Washington, DC, to Naples, Italy, a distance of 4,200 miles, in 24 hours.

3808. President who had parachuted from an airplane was George Herbert Walker Bush, the 41st president, who was inaugurated on January 3, 1989. On September 2, 1944, Bush was piloting a TBM *Avenger* torpedo bomber over the island of Chichi-Jima when his plane was hit by Japanese anti-aircraft fire. Bush bailed out and landed in the Pacific. He drifted on a raft until he was picked up by an American submarine, the U.S.S. *Finback.* In March 1997, at the age of 75, ex-president Bush made his second jump at Yuma, AZ.

3809. President to travel underwater in a submarine was Harry S. Truman. On November 21, 1946, he embarked at Key West, FL, in the *U-2513,* a captured German submarine. At sea off Key West, the vessel engaged in exercises during which it submerged.

3810. President to pay a state visit to Canada was Harry S. Truman, who visited Ottawa, Canada, from June 10 through 12, 1947, as the guest of the governor general, Harold Alexander, Viscount Alexander of Tunis.

3811. President to fly in a helicopter was Dwight David Eisenhower. On July 12, 1957, he flew in a three-seat Bell Ranger H-47J piloted by Major Joseph E. Barrett from the White House to an undisclosed site chosen for relocation of the White House during an atomic attack drill. He had previously flown in a helicopter while he was supreme Allied commander of the North Atlantic Treaty Organization.

3812. President to go underwater in an atomic-powered submarine was Dwight David Eisenhower, who was a passenger on the *Seawolf* on September 26, 1957, when it submerged to a depth of 60 feet in the Atlantic Ocean, five miles southwest of Brentons Reef, off Newport, RI. The submarine remained submerged and stationary for about 15 minutes. The first atomic submarine the *Nautilus,* had been launched in 1954. In the 1920s, when he was stationed in the Panama Canal Zone, Eisenhower had twice submerged in submarines.

3813. President to visit a nation not recognized by the U.S. government was Richard Milhous Nixon, who visited the People's Republic of China in 1972. This was also the first trip to China, the world's most populous nation, by any American president. Accompanied by a small army of journalists, Nixon left the United States on February 17, 1972. He arrived in Beijing on February 21 for talks with Chairman Mao Zedong and Premier Zhou Enlai.

3814. President to visit the Soviet Union was Richard Milhous Nixon, who arrived in Moscow on May 22, 1972, for a summit meeting with Soviet leaders. Among the agreements that were reached during the visit was the Strategic Arms Limitation Treaty, signed by President Nixon and the Soviet leader Leonid I. Brezhnev on May 26, which limited both nations to 200 antiballistic missiles each, divided between two defensive systems.

3815. President to spend holidays with United States troops overseas was George Herbert Walker Bush. In November 1990 he spent Thanksgiving in the Persian Gulf, paying visits by helicopter to American troops stationed in Saudia Arabia and on offshore vessels and sharing holiday dinners with them. The troops had been ordered to the area to prepare for the multinational offensive against Iraq's occupation of Kuwait. On January 1, 1993, President Bush spent the New Year holiday with United States peacekeeping troops in Somalia.

3816. Visit by an American president to a country on the U.S. list of terrorist states took place on October 27, 1994, when President William Jefferson Clinton visited Damascus, Syria, to meet with that country's president, Hafez al-Assad. Clinton made the visit to urge Assad, a longtime foe of Israel, to take part in the Middle East peace process between the Jewish state and neighboring Arab states.

3817. President to visit Bulgaria was President William Jefferson Clinton. He arrived in Sofia, the capital, on November 21, 1999, to thank Bulgarians for allowing NATO warplanes to use their airspace in missions to Kosovo in the spring of 1999. On November 22, Clinton addressed a crowd of 10,000 in the Cathedral of St. Alexander Nevsky, the scene, a decade earlier, of the rallies that led to the downfall of Communist rule.

PRESIDENTS—VARIOUS

3818. President who was a Mason was George Washington, who was inducted into the Fredericksburg Lodge No. 4 at Fredericksburg, VA, on August 4, 1753, with the rank of Master Mason.

3819. President who received a college education was John Adams, who was graduated from Harvard College, Cambridge, MA, on July 16, 1755, with the degree of bachelor of arts.

3820. President who was fluent in a foreign language was John Quincy Adams. During his boyhood, he accompanied his father, John Adams, on diplomatic trips to Europe, studying in Paris at a private school in 1778–79. He acquired so strong a command of French that in 1781, when he was 14 years old, he served as the interpreter for Francis Dana, the United States minister to Russia (where French was the language of diplomacy).

3821. President who had been elected to Phi Beta Kappa in recognition of outstanding scholarship was John Quincy Adams, who was elected in 1787 as a member in course from Harvard College, Cambridge, MA. The first president elected as an alumnus, in recognition of scholarly accomplishment after graduation, was Franklin Pierce, who was elected from Bowdoin College, Brunswick, ME, in 1825, the year after he graduated. The first to receive honorary election was Martin Van Buren, who never attended college—he studied law privately—but was elected by Union College in 1830, after he had already been New York's senator and governor.

3822. President who owned slaves was George Washington, whose plantation at Mount Vernon, VA, relied on the labor of several hundred African-American slaves. Washington, who took office on April 30, 1789, was acutely conscious of the contradiction between the principles of freedom for which he had fought and his own reliance on slave labor, but he could find no alternative that would not result in financial disaster for the farm. His fellow Virginian, Thomas Jefferson, was in much the same situation.

3823. Biography of a president was *A History of the Life and Death, Virtues and Exploits, of General George Washington* by Mason Locke Weems, a Maryland-born Anglican pastor who earned his living as a publisher's agent and a hack writer of popular biographies. The first edition was published in 1800 with remarkable success, and the book has been through more than 80 editions altogether, despite the fact that it was recognized early on to be mainly a fabrication rather than a work of scholarship. To Weems we owe some of the best-known fictions about Washington, such as the story of the hatchet and the cherry tree, which was added to the fifth (1806) edition.

PRESIDENTS—VARIOUS—*continued*

3824. President to request a handshake from visitors instead of a bow was President Thomas Jefferson, who introduced the new custom on July 4, 1801, at a White House reception.

3825. President who had killed a man in a duel was Andrew Jackson. On May 30, 1806, when he was 39 years old, Jackson shot and killed Charles Dickinson at Harrison's Mills on the Red River in Logan County, KY. The combatants stood 24 feet apart. Dickinson fired first. The shot broke a couple of Jackson's ribs and grazed his breastbone. Despite the injury, Jackson fired and killed Dickinson. It was one of a hundred duels and brawls in which Jackson is said to have participated.

3826. President who learned reading and writing from his wife was Andrew Johnson, who married Eliza McCardle on May 17, 1827, in Greeneville, TN. Johnson was 18 years old, the son of a handyman and a washerwoman, and had had no schooling at all. Eliza Johnson was 16, the daughter of a shoemaker. Before their marriage, she helped him improve his rudimentary reading skills and taught him how to write.

3827. President to be arrested was Franklin Pierce, in 1853. Pierce was arrested in Washington, DC, by Constable Stanley Edelin, after the carriage he was driving ran down an elderly lady, Mrs. Nathan Lewis. He was cleared and the case was dropped.

3828. President to wear a beard was Abraham Lincoln. He was clean-shaven before his election in 1860. During the campaign, he received a letter from an eleven-year-old girl, Grace Bedell of Westfield, NY, who suggested that his thin face would look better with a beard. "All the ladies like whiskers," she wrote, "and they would tease their husbands to vote for you and then you would be President." Lincoln wrote back, asking whether people wouldn't call it "a silly affection," but after he was elected on November 6, he began growing a beard, which he wore without a mustache. Beards were also worn by Ulysses Simpson Grant, Rutherford Birchard Hayes, James Abram Garfield, and Benjamin Harrison. Mustaches without beards were worn by Chester Alan Arthur, Grover Cleveland, Theodore Roosevelt, and William Howard Taft.

3829. President to use a telephone was James Abram Garfield, who first used a telephone while he was a member of Congress in 1878.

3830. President who advocated physical fitness was Theodore Roosevelt, who succeeded to the presidency in 1901 and won the election of 1904 as the Republican Party candidate. As a child, Roosevelt suffered from severe asthma, but he transformed himself through unremitting exercise into a prodigious athlete. As president, he religiously performed his own daily regimen of exercise and recommended a similar program to anyone who would listen. He often preached what his biographer Henry Pringle called "the gospel of strenuosity," in which physical conditioning and strenuous endeavor was equated with national greatness. Notably, in his inaugural address of March 4, 1905, Roosevelt claimed that American life called for "vigor and effort without which the manlier and hardier virtues wither away."

3831. President to pitch a ball to open the baseball season was William Howard Taft. On April 14, 1910, he threw the baseball that opened the American League's Washington–Philadelphia game, in which the Washington Senators beat the Philadelphia Athletics by a score of 3–0. The crowd, which included 12,226 paying spectators, broke all previous baseball attendance records.

3832. President to use a radio was Warren Gamaliel Harding, who had a vacuum-tube detector and two-stage amplifier receiving set installed in a bookcase in his study on the second floor of the White House, Washington, DC, on February 8, 1922.

3833. President who had been a Boy Scout was John Fitzgerald Kennedy. In 1929, when he was twelve years old, he belonged to Troop 2 of Bronxville, NY. The first president who achieved the rank of Eagle Scout in his youth was Gerald Rudolph Ford.

3834. President to have a telephone on his desk in the White House was Herbert Clark Hoover. The telephone was installed in the Oval Office on March 27, 1929. Previously, there had been a telephone booth in an adjoining room and another in the president's study on the second floor.

3835. President to use Camp David as a retreat was Franklin Delano Roosevelt, who originally called it "Shangri-La." The retreat was built by the National Park Service atop the Catoctin Mountains near Thurmont, MD. Construction was begun on May 11, 1942, and FDR made his first official visit on July 5, 1942. In May 1943, British prime minister Winston Churchill was the first foreign leader to visit the retreat. President Dwight David

Eisenhower later renamed "Camp David" after his grandson, David Eisenhower. During Eisenhower's presidency, the camp became the exclusive retreat of the president and his family.

3836. President to attain the rank of 33rd-degree Mason was Harry S. Truman, who was accorded the rank of 33rd degree of the Supreme Council of the Scottish Rite for the Southern jurisdiction at the House of the Temple, Washington, DC, on October 19, 1945, six months after he succeeded to the presidency. President Warren Gamaliel Harding had been scheduled to receive the rank in 1923 but was prevented by his sudden death.

3837. Presidential hot line was installed on August 30, 1962, between the White House, Washington, DC, and the Kremlin, Moscow, during the administration of President John Fitzgerald Kennedy.

3838. President to witness the firing of a Polaris missile was John Fitzgerald Kennedy. On November 16, 1963, while aboard the U.S.S. *Observation Island* 32 miles off Cape Canaveral, FL, Kennedy watched the submerged nuclear submarine U.S.S. *Andrew Jackson* fire a Polaris A-2 missile, which broke through the surface of the water and headed on a 1,500-mile flight into the Caribbean.

3839. President who was a Rhodes Scholar was William Jefferson Clinton, who attended University College, Oxford University, in Oxford, England, from 1968 to 1970 on a Rhodes Scholarship. He studied politics. The scholarship program, founded by bequest of the British colonial administrator and financier Cecil Rhodes, allows outstanding students from the British colonies, the United States, and Germany to study at Oxford. Oxford awarded Clinton an honorary doctorate in civil law in 1994, during his first term in the White House.

3840. President to attend the launching of a manned space flight was Richard Milhous Nixon, who viewed the launching of *Apollo 12* at 11:22 A.M. on November 14, 1969, from Pad A at Cape Canaveral, FL.

3841. President to make public the results of a routine medical examination was Gerald Rudolph Ford, who spent four hours at the Naval Medical Center in Bethesda, MD, on January 25, 1975, receiving a complete checkup. The White House physician, Rear Admiral William Matthew Lukash, announced that the results of all the tests were normal.

3842. President to attend a hockey game during his term in office was William Jefferson Clinton. On May 25, 1998, he attended a National Hockey League playoff game between the Buffalo Sabres and the Washington Capitals at the MCI Center in Washington, DC. Also at the game were Vice President Albert Gore, Senator Daniel Patrick Moynihan of New York, and the NHL commissioner, Gary Bettman. Washington won the game 3–2 in overtime.

PRESIDENTS—VETOES

3843. Presidential veto of a congressional bill was exercised by President George Washington on April 5, 1792, when he vetoed a bill for the apportionment of representation on the grounds that it contradicted the Constitution. The House of Representatives sustained the veto on April 6, 1792, by a vote of 33 to 22. A two-thirds vote of both houses is necessary to override a veto. Washington exercised the veto a second time on February 28, 1797, when he rejected a bill to reduce the size of the army's cavalry.

3844. Presidential veto to be overridden by Congress concerned "an act relating to revenue cutters and steamers," which provided that no revenue cutter could be built without prior appropriation. President John Tyler vetoed the bill on February 20, 1845, arguing that contracts for two revenue cutters had already been arranged, one with a firm in Richmond, VA, and another with a contractor in Pittsburgh, PA. The bill was reconsidered by the Senate and House on March 3, 1845. The Senate overrode the veto without debate by a vote of 41–1, and the House by a vote of 127–30.

3845. President to veto more than 100 bills in a single term was Grover Cleveland, who vetoed a total of 414 bills, including 304 regular vetoes and 110 pocket vetoes, during his first term in office, from March 4, 1885, through March 3, 1889. Two of these vetoes were overridden by Congress and 412 were sustained. In his second term, from March 4, 1893, to March 3, 1897, Cleveland vetoed 170 bills, including 42 regular vetoes and 128 pocket vetoes, of which five were overridden and 165 were sustained. Prior to Cleveland, the only president who came close to 100 vetoes was Ulysses Simpson Grant, who made 92; the next closest was Andrew Johnson, who made 28.

3846. President to use the line-item veto was William Jefferson Clinton, who used it on August 11, 1997, to eliminate three provisions from legislation that had been passed by Congress. One provision, deleted from a bipartisan bill to balance the federal budget, would have

PRESIDENTS—VETOES—*continued*

allowed the state of New York to tax Medicaid funding received by health-care providers. Two other provisions, deleted from a tax-cutting measure, would have allowed special tax deferrals for food-processing plants and financial service companies. The line-item veto, a power sought by presidents since Ulysses S. Grant, enables presidents to strike particular items from newly enacted federal laws without having to veto the entire bill. Congress passed the line-item veto in 1996, but it was declared unconstitutional by the Supreme Court on June 25, 1998.

PRESS AND MEDIA

3847. Political censorship of the press occurred during colonial times. On September 25, 1690, the first number of the early American newspaper *Publick Occurrences Both Foreign and Domestick* was published in Boston, MA. It was printed by Richard Pierce and edited by Benjamin Harris. British authorities suppressed the paper after only one issue, as it represented an independent source of political information not controlled by the government, and barred future publications of any kind that were published without "licence first obtained from those appointed by the Government to grant the same."

3848. Trial of a printer for sedition took place in Philadelphia in March 1693. The defendant was William Bradford, an English Quaker who had emigrated, by invitation, to the Quaker colony of Pennsylvania in 1685 to set up a printing press. In September 1692 he was jailed for printing several tracts by George Keith, a dissident who wished to impose more church structure and biblical authority on the Society of Friends. At his trial Bradford declared that the material he had published was "not Seditious, but wholly relating to a Religious Difference," and persuaded the chief judge to allow the jury to decide whether such publication was, in fact, illegal. The trial ended with a hung jury, with the nine Quaker members voting to convict and the three others voting to acquit. After his release, Bradford successfully petitioned for the return of his confiscated press and took it to New York, where he became the official government printer and converted to Anglicanism. His son Andrew returned to Pennsylvania in 1712 and set up his own printing business, eventually starting Philadelphia's first newspaper, the *American Weekly Mercury*.

3849. Political crusade by a newspaper was launched by the *New-England Courant,* published in Boston, MA, by James Franklin, the older brother of Benjamin Franklin. Beginning with the first issue, published on August 7, 1721, the newspaper threw itself into the public debate over smallpox prevention that had erupted at the end of June, when Dr. Zabdiel Boylston made experimental inoculations on his own child and two of his servants. The people of Boston, dying of smallpox that summer at the rate of 50 a day, were suspicious of the new treatment but were encouraged to put aside their fears by the Puritan minister Cotton Mather, one of the most influential people in the city. The *Courant* built up its circulation by publishing scathing attacks on inoculation, on Mather himself, and on Boston's Puritan leadership in general.

3850. Legal precedent for freedom of the press was established on August 4, 1735, when John Peter Zenger, editor of the *New-York Weekly Journal,* was found innocent of a charge of seditious libel. Zenger had published a report asserting that William Cosby, the governor of New York, had attempted to rig an election. Cosby ordered him arrested and held him in prison for nine months, during which time his wife, Anna, continued to publish the paper. At his trial in New York City, Zenger was defended by lawyer Andrew Hamilton of Philadelphia, who convinced the jury that printing the truth does not constitute libel, since "nature and the laws of our country have given us . . . the liberty of both exposing and opposing arbitrary power by speaking and writing truth." Zenger's refusal to name the writer of the report also established a precedent regarding the confidentiality of a journalist's sources.

3851. Persecution of a newspaper editor by American revolutionaries took place in Boston, MA, a hotbed of revolutionary sentiment where Loyalist opinions were unwelcome. John Mein, the editor of the *Boston Chronicle,* was hanged in effigy in 1768 for disagreeing with the policy of nonimportation of British goods and with other Patriot activities. He was repeatedly assaulted and had to flee the country after he wounded one of his attackers. Once the Revolution was under way, vigilantes among the Sons of Liberty in Philadelphia, New York, and other cities wrecked printing presses and intimidated newspaper editors with pro-British opinions.

3852. Political newspaper to carry partisanship to extremes was the *Aurora* (originally called the *General Advertiser and Political, Commercial, Agricultural and Literary Journal*), founded in Philadelphia, PA, on October 1, 1790. The editor was Benjamin Franklin Bache, the grandson of Benjamin Franklin, who had himself been a printer and newspaper publisher. Bache, nicknamed "Lightning Rod Junior," was a rabid opponent of President George Washington and lampooned him mercilessly in comments and cartoons, for which he was assaulted by supporters of Washington on several occasions. On December 23, 1796, as the president was preparing to leave office, Bache wrote, "If ever a nation has been debauched by a man, the American nation has been debauched by Washington. If ever a nation has suffered from the improper influence of a man, the American nation has suffered from the influence of Washington. If ever a nation was deceived by a man, the American nation has been deceived by Washington. Let his conduct then be an example to future ages. Let it serve to be a warning that no man may be an idol."

3853. Federal law intended to intimidate the press was the Sedition Act, enacted on July 14, 1798, during the escalating conflict with France. Leading the movement in favor of a declaration of war was the Federalist faction headed by Alexander Hamilton. Opposing them were the editors of the influential Democratic-Republican newspapers, many of whom were immigrants (or refugees) from France, England, and Ireland. The Sedition Act threatened them with a fine of up to $2,000 and imprisonment up to two years if found guilty of publishing "any false, scandalous and malicious writing" against the government. Of the 25 people arrested under the act, ten were convicted. They were pardoned by Thomas Jefferson when he became president in 1801, after the law had expired.

3854. Prosecution under the Sedition Act took place in October 1798. The defendant was Congressman Matthew Lyon of Vermont, a fervent opponent of the Federalists. Because his local newspaper refused to publish his opinions, Lyons founded his own outlet, *The Scourge of Aristocracy and Repository of Important Political Truths.* He was indicted four days later and charged with sedition for ridiculing President John Adams. The trial judge, Supreme Court Justice William Paterson (presiding here as part of his circuit-riding duties), refused to allow the jury to decide the question of whether the Sedition Act was constitutional. Lyon was convicted and sentenced to a four-month jail term and

a $1,000 fine. While he was in prison, he was overwhelmingly reelected to his seat in Congress, and as soon as he was released he went directly from the jail to Congress Hall, Philadelphia, with crowds of supporters cheering him along the way.

3855. News agency to cover foreign politics was established in Boston, MA, in 1814, when Samuel Topliff became the owner of the Merchant's Reading Room (formerly Gilbert's Coffee House and Marine Diary), one of several Boston coffeehouses where customers read local weekly newspapers and discussed current news. Topliff maintained a correspondence with associates in foreign countries who supplied him with news. He kept a record of their reports for his own patrons and also distributed their reports to the newspapers for publication.

3856. Press censorship by military authorities occurred shortly after the beginning of the Civil War. Worried that press accounts of activities in Washington, DC, might prove helpful to the enemy, Winfield Scott, general in chief of the Union army, announced on July 8, 1861, that the Washington telegraph office would no longer carry "dispatches concerning the operations of the Army not permitted by the commanding general."

3857. Transcontinental telegram of a political nature was sent on October 24, 1861, when Stephen Johnson Field, chief justice of California, sent a message to President Abraham Lincoln. The telegram traveled from from San Francisco, CA, to Washington, DC. The following day, telegrams were exchanged between Mayor Fernando Wood of New York City and Mayor H. F. Teschemacher of San Francisco, CA.

3858. Gridiron Club was founded in 1885 at a gathering of journalists that took place at Welcker's, a Washington restaurant, where Ben Perley Poore, editor of the *Providence Journal,* was elected president. The club held dinners featuring speeches and entertainment, mainly on political themes. Members were required to be journalists, but were also required to adhere to a rule prohibiting newspaper accounts of club events. Guests at the dinners often included statesmen, politicians, and military leaders.

3859. Use of the term "muckraker" occurred in remarks made at Washington's Gridiron Club in May 1906 by President Theodore Roosevelt. Borrowing the term from the filth-obsessed Man With the Muck Rake in John Bunyan's *Pilgrim's Progress,* Roosevelt applied it somewhat derogatorily to crusading journal-

PRESS AND MEDIA—*continued*

ists who indiscriminately publish sensational exposés of public figures. Roosevelt elaborated on the idea in a well-known speech of April 14, 1906, at the ceremony for the laying of the cornerstone for the Congressional Office Building.

3860. Movie censorship board established by a state was the State Board of Censors, created in Pennsylvania by act of June 19, 1911. No appropriation was made until April 4, 1913, when $7,500 was provided. Censors were appointed on February 1, 1914. Ohio approved an act on May 3, 1913, providing for a three-member censorship board. Kansas approved an act on March 13, 1913, but no provisions to enforce it were made until 1915. The Supreme Court in February 1915 held the Ohio and Kansas censorship laws unconstitutional.

3861. Movie censorship law enacted by Congress was the act of July 31, 1912, "to prohibit the importation and the interstate transportation of films or other pictorial representations of prize fights." The penalty for violation was not more than $1,000, or one year at hard labor, or both.

3862. Presidential press conference was held at the White House on March 15, 1913, by Woodrow Wilson, who had taken office less than a week before. Some 125 journalists were present.

3863. Newsreels showing presidential candidates were filmed on August 11, 1924, by Theodore W. Case and Lee De Forest. They showed the Republican incumbent, President Calvin Coolidge, on the grounds of the White House in Washington, DC, and his Progressive opponent, Senator Robert Marion La Follette, on the steps of the Capitol. The Democratic candidate, John William Davis, was photographed at Locust Valley, NY. The newsreel was shown in various theaters in September 1924.

3864. Federal sedition law passed in peacetime since the Sedition Act of 1798 was the Smith Act, formally known as the Alien Registration Act, enacted on June 28, 1940. The law made it a crime to advocate violent revolution against any United States government. Eleven leaders of the American Communist Party who were convicted of conspiracy under the Smith Act challenged the law in the Supreme Court, which upheld its constitutionality in 1951 by a vote of 6 to 2 (in *Dennis v. United States*).

3865. Book censorship board established by a state was appointed by Georgia in March 1953 under authority of an act approved on February 19, 1953, with the power to make recommendations for prosecution. The first chairman of the three-member committee was James Wesberry. Newspapers were not subject to review or censorship.

3866. Presidential press conference that was entirely "on the record" took place on December 16, 1953, at the White House, where an audience of 161 reporters heard remarks by President Dwight David Eisenhower. For the first time, they were allowed to make direct quotations in their accounts of the proceedings, rather than resort to paraphrase. The press conference was also broadcast, and a tape recording was made for use on radio and television.

3867. Courtroom verdict to be televised was delivered on March 14, 1964, at the 3rd Criminal District Court of Dallas County, Dallas, TX. The telecast took place from 12:37 to 2 P.M. Judge Joseph Brantley Brown sentenced Jack Ruby (Jacob L. Rubenstein) to die in the electric chair for the murder with malice of Lee Harvey Oswald, the alleged assassin of President John Fitzgerald Kennedy, on November 24, 1963. The broadcast was pooled by the Columbia Broadcasting System, sent to New York City, and shared with the NBC and ABC networks.

3868. Prior restraint of the press by order of the federal government came about in the matter of the Pentagon Papers, a series of classified reports, commissioned in 1967 by Secretary of Defense Robert S. McNamara, that detailed the secret history of America's military involvement in Southeast Asia. The papers were leaked to the *New York Times* by Daniel Ellsberg, a senior researcher at the Massachusetts Institute of Technology's Center for International Studies. In a move highly embarrassing to the government, the *Times* began publishing the reports on June 13, 1971. On June 15, the Justice Department obtained a court order barring the *Times* and other newspapers from publishing further excerpts from the reports. This was the first time that the government applied prior restraint to prevent publication of material it deemed objectionable. On June 30, 1971, the court order was overturned by the U.S. Supreme Court, which, by a vote of 6 to 3, held that the government had not produced sufficient proof of "immediate and irreparable harm" to justify contravening the First Amendment.

3869. Censorship of the Internet was attempted under the Communications Decency Act, signed into law by President William Jefferson Clinton on February 8, 1996.

3870. Trial broadcast by the court over the Internet was the murder trial of Shirley Egan, age 68, a wheelchair-bound invalid, for the shooting death of her daughter, Georgette Smith, 42. The daughter had survived the shooting with paralysis from the neck down and had received court permission to have her life-support system turned off. After Smith died, Egan went on trial on August 16, 1999, in Orlando, FL, at the Orange County Courthouse. The courtroom was equipped with fiber-optics, audio and video output, and an Internet server, and proceedings of the trial were available daily on a special Web site. Previous trials had been broadcast over the Internet by private companies; this was the first broadcast by the judicial system.

PRESS AND MEDIA—ELECTRONIC

3871. Political news item transmitted by telegraph was sent on May 25, 1844, from Washington, DC, to the offices of the *Baltimore Patriot* newspaper. The message read: "One o'clock. There has just been made a motion in the House to go into committee of the whole on the Oregon question. Rejected. Ayes 79—Nays 86." This was the first news item of any kind to be telegraphed.

3872. Political news broadcast by radio was a prediction that Republican nominee Charles Evans Hughes would win the presidential election of 1916. It was broadcast from New York by the radio pioneer Lee De Forest. Hughes was narrowly defeated on November 7, 1916, by Democrat Woodrow Wilson.

3873. National Radio Conference convened in Washington, DC, on February 27, 1922. It was called by Secretary of Commerce Herbert Clark Hoover to discuss regulations necessary for the industry and was attended by government officials, radio representatives, and radio amateurs.

3874. Radio Commission of the United States was created on February 23, 1927, and consisted of Henry Adams Bellows, Admiral William Hannum Grubb Bullard, Orestes Hampton Caldwell, John Forrest Dillon, and Eugene Octave Sykes. They were granted authority to license broadcasting stations for one year, to determine to whom licenses should be granted, and to fix wavelengths and hours of operation. The organizational meeting was held on March 15, 1927. On March 15, 1928, this authority was placed under the secretary of commerce, the commission becoming an appellate body.

3875. Federal agency to regulate broadcast media and use of the electromagnetic spectrum was the Federal Board of Radio Control, appointed on March 1, 1927, by President Calvin Coolidge.

3876. Federal Communications Commission was created by a congressional act approved on June 19, 1934, to provide for the regulation of interstate and foreign commerce by wire or radio and to centralize these duties and responsibilities with a view to more effective supervision of communication. A committee of seven was appointed on July 11, 1934. The first chairman was Eugene Octave Sykes, who served until March 11, 1935. Successors to the original committee were to be appointed for seven years, unless appointed to fill an unexpired term.

3877. Full-time Spanish-language television station owned and operated by a Mexican-American was KCOR in San Antonio, TX, which began Hispanic programming in 1946.

3878. Live atomic bomb explosion shown on television took place on February 1, 1951, at Frenchman Flat, NV. It was the third blast set off by the Atomic Energy Commission. A telescopic camera on Mount Wilson, CA, 300 miles away, telecast the explosion for station KTLA, Los Angeles, CA. It was shown on Channel 4 of the NBC network, and kinescopes of the explosion footage were later broadcast widely. This was the first look most Americans had at a nuclear blast.

3879. Political editorial broadcast on radio and television was an editorial by Dr. Frank Stanton, president of the Columbia Broadcasting System, protesting the Senate's decision to bar television and radio journalists from covering its hearings into the conduct of Senator Joseph Raymond McCarthy, Republican of Wisconsin. McCarthy had been conducting hearings into the infiltration of communists into American industries and institutions. The editorial was broadcast over the CBS network on August 26, 1954, between 8 P.M. and 8:15 P.M.

3880. Television newswoman to report from Capitol Hill was Nancy Dickerson, born Nancy Hanschman, a correspondent for the CBS and NBC networks. In 1960, working for CBS, she became the first woman television reporter to cover a national political convention. In 1963 she joined the Washington bureau of NBC; her first major story was the 1963 March on Washington. She was active as a reporter and commentator until 1996.

PRESS AND MEDIA—ELECTRONIC—
continued

3881. Political interview aired on a television newsmagazine was an interview with Ramsey Clark, attorney general under President Lyndon Baines Johnson. It was the first interview shown on *60 Minutes*, which premiered on September 24, 1968, with hosts Mike Wallace and Harry Reasoner. The show was produced for the CBS television network by Don Hewitt.

3882. Televised Watergate hearings were the proceedings of the Select Committee on Presidential Campaign Activities, a special Senate investigatory committee established in February 1973 under the direction of Senator Samuel James Ervin of North Carolina. Broadcasts on all three major networks began on May 17, 1973.

3883. All-news television network in the world was Cable News Network, headquartered in Atlanta, GA. It was founded in June 1980 by Robert Edward Turner III, better known as Ted Turner, head of the Turner Broadcasting System. CNN used satellite feeds to provide live coverage of global events, supplied by a network of news bureaus in cities worldwide. The network broadcast 24 hours a day.

3884. Talk-radio host to seek the presidential candidacy of a major party was the conservative commentator and orator Alan L. Keyes of Maryland, a former official of the Reagan administration and head of the Ronald Reagan Alumni Association. Keyes ran in primary elections for the GOP presidential nomination in 1996 and 2000, but he was better known as the host of the nationally syndicated radio talk show *The Alan Keyes Show: America's Wake Up Call*. Keyes's program was also simulcast on the America's Voice/Political News Talk satellite and cable TV network.

PRESS AND MEDIA—JOURNALISTS

3885. Conflict-of-interest case involving a journalist erupted in Philadelphia, PA, in 1791, when Thomas Jefferson, the secretary of state, gave Philip Morin Freneau a job as a translating clerk in the State Department so that he could support himself while editing the *National Gazette*, a pro-Jefferson newspaper. Jefferson's ideological opponent, Alexander Hamilton, charged (anonymously) that the situation was "indelicate, unfit, and inconsistent with republican purity," prompting an affidavit by Freneau stating that his newspaper received no material or editorial support from Jefferson.

3886. Reporters at sessions of the Senate were granted access to the Senate Chamber in 1801, four years after the newspapers had requested permission to send reporters to the impeachment trial of William Blount, senator from Tennessee.

3887. Washington news correspondent of importance was James Gordon Bennett (the elder), whose articles first appeared on January 2, 1828, in the *New York Enquirer,* later known as the *Courier and Enquirer.*

3888. Political photographer of importance was Mathew B. Brady, best known for his photographs of the Civil War. Brady was taught the art of the daguerreotype by Samuel F.B. Morse, and in 1845 he began a series documenting famous Americans of his day, especially politicians. Brady managed to photograph or copy the photographs of every president from John Quincy Adams to William McKinley, starting with Andrew Jackson, whom he photographed in 1845 at the Hermitage, Nashville, TN. Many of the photos appeared in Brady's book *A Gallery of Illustrious Americans* (1850), the first such book of its type.

3889. Woman reporter to cover a political convention was Mary Ashton Rice Livermore, one of the editors of the *New Covenant,* who covered the Republican National Convention, May 12–18, 1860, at the Wigwam, Chicago, IL, which nominated Abraham Lincoln.

3890. Muckraking journalist was Henry Demarest Lloyd, chief editorial writer of the *Chicago Tribune,* who had become familiar with the practices of railroad tycoons and financial speculators in his earlier days as the paper's financial editor. In March 1881, the *Atlantic Monthly* magazine published, under the title "The Story of a Great Monopoly," the text of a lecture Lloyd had delivered to the Chicago Literary Club on the activities of John D. Rockefeller, founder of Standard Oil. His book *Wealth against Commonwealth*, an attack on Standard Oil and similar giant corporations, was published in 1894. Lloyd ran unsuccessfully for Congress as a Populist and allied himself with the trade union movement and the Socialist Party.

3891. Muckraking journalist who was a woman was Ida Minerva Tarbell, a writer from the oil-production region of Pennsylvania who was hired by Samuel Sidney McClure, the New York publisher of *McClure's Magazine*, to do an investigative report on Standard Oil. Her book *The History of the Standard Oil Company,* a devastating critique that was published in

1904, ran as a series in *McClure's* from November 1901 through October 1904, concurrently with *The Shame of the Cities* by Lincoln Steffens and *The Right to Work* by Ray Stannard Baker. The Supreme Court dismantled Standard Oil in 1911. Tarbell went on to write *The Tariff in Our Time* and several books on American women.

3892. Muckraking novel of importance was *The Jungle*, by Upton Sinclair, serialized in the socialist magazines *Appeal to Reason* and *One Hoss Philosophy* in 1905 and published in book form in February 1906. The novel vividly depicted the life of a Chicago slaughterhouse worker and called attention to the filthy and dangerous conditions in which the country's meat supply was produced. A mere four months after the book's appearance, Congress, pushed into action by the public revulsion it aroused, passed a law requiring federal inspection of meat-packing plants.

3893. African-American newspaper reporter accredited to the White House was Harry McAlpin, who attended his first White House press conference on February 8, 1944, as the correspondent of the *Daily World* of Atlanta, GA, and the press service of the Negro Newspaper Publishers Association.

3894. African-American newspaper reporter accredited to the congressional press gallery was Percival L. Prattis, representative of *Our World*, New York City, who was accredited on February 3, 1947.

PRESS AND MEDIA—MAGAZINES AND JOURNALS

3895. Political magazine and the first magazine of any kind published in America was *The American Magazine, or a Monthly View of the Political State of the British Colonies*, published in Philadelphia, PA, by Andrew Bradford. Three issues appeared, in February, March, and April 1741. The editor was John Webbe. Its first appearance preceded by three days that of Benjamin Franklin's *General Magazine and Historical Chronicle for All the British Plantations in America*, which was also published in Philadelphia.

3896. Satirical political magazine was *The Wasp*, edited by Robert Rusticoat, Esq., and printed by Harry Crosswell, Hudson, NY. The first issue, dated July 7, 1802, consisted of four pages and lampooned politics and politicans.

3897. Law magazine was the *American Law Journal*, which was published in Baltimore, MD, from 1808 to 1817. It was edited by John Elihu Hall.

3898. Political magazine published quarterly was *The American Review of History and Politics and General Repository of Literature and State Papers*, which was published in Philadelphia, PA, from January 1811 to October 1812. The eidtor was Robert Walsh.

3899. Factory workers' magazine was *The Lowell Offering*, "a repository of original articles on various subjects, wholly written, edited and published by female operatives employed in the mills." It was published bimonthly and cost six and a quarter cents a copy. It had already been in existence for some time when Sarah George Bagley, a mill worker who went on to become the first woman union organizer, began contributing to it in 1841.

3900. Muckraking journal of importance was *McClure's Magazine*, founded in New York City in 1893 by Samuel Sidney McClure. *McClure's* published the exposés of such notable crusading journalists as Ida M. Tarbell, Ray Stannard Baker, and Lincoln Steffens, and was the leading muckraking journal of the Progressive Era, along with *Collier's, Everybody's, Cosmopolitan,* and the *Arena*. It ceased publication in 1933.

3901. Weekly newsmagazine was *Time*. The first issue was published by Henry Luce and Briton Hadden in New York on March 3, 1923.

3902. Magazine of the federal government was the daily *Federal Register*, first issued on March 14, 1936. The masthead was decorated with the eagle shield and the Latin motto *Littera scripta manet* ("the written word endures"). It was published in Washington, DC, by the National Archives under the Federal Register Act approved on July 26, 1935, and contained 16 two-column pages containing federal laws, orders, and reports.

PRESS AND MEDIA—NEWSPAPERS

3903. Newspaper suppressed by the government was the first newspaper ever published in the British colonies in America, *Publick Occurrences, Both Foreign and Domestic*, which was printed by R. Pierce in Boston, MA, for publisher Benjamin Harris. The first and only issue was distributed from Boston's London Coffee House on September 25, 1690. Although Harris had planned to publish the newspaper once a month, "or if any Glut of Occurrences happen, oftener," he was prevented from doing so by Governor Simon Bradstreet and the members of the Council, who disliked some of the contents. The paper had included a critical comment about the colony's employment of Mohawk Indians in a military raid against Quebec and a scurrilous reference to the King of France.

PRESS AND MEDIA—NEWSPAPERS—
continued

3904. Newspaper published with government approval was the *Boston News-Letter,* the first American newspaper to be published regularly, which appeared for the first time on April 24, 1704. It was edited by John Campbell, bookseller and postmaster of Boston, MA, and printed by Bartholomew Green in a back room of his home. The masthead bore the legend "Published by Authority," which testified to its contents having been vetted in advance by the governor of Massachusetts or his secretary. Both domestic and foreign news was included, though the foreign news was often well out of date. In its early years, the *News-Letter* was kept going with the help of an occasional subsidy from the public treasury, making it the first American newspaper to receive government assistance.

3905. Editorial retraction of false political news appeared in the Philadelphia, PA, *American Weekly Mercury* of April 20, 1721. It stated: "N.B. In our last week's *Mercury* No. 70, there is an account inserted from a private Letter sent to Boston, dated the 20th of September last, That the Government of Pennsilvania is Surrendered to the Crown, etc. These are to give Notice that we have now Letters from London, of a later Date, by which we find that the said Report concerning the Province of Pennsilvania is false and groundless and therefore was both by them and us too rashly inserted."

3906. Political newspaper was the *New York Weekly Journal,* established on November 5, 1733, by John Peter Zenger as a political organ to expose Governor William Cosby's corruption. Zenger was arrested on November 17, 1734, and charged with seditious libel. His acquittal on August 4, 1735, was seen as a vindication of the right of free speech.

3907. Regulation allowing newspapers to be sent through the mails was established in 1758 by Benjamin Franklin of Philadelphia, PA, co-postmaster general for the colonies (the other was William Hunter of Virginia). Postage was set at 9d. for newspapers carried less than 50 miles, 1s. 6d. for newspapers carried up to 100 miles, and so on. Previously, newspaper publishers contracted privately with mail carriers to deliver their own newspapers and exclude all rivals—a situation made possible by the fact that many newspaper publishers were also postmasters.

3908. Political newspaper of national importance was the *Gazette of the United States,* the political organ of Alexander Hamilton and the Federalists, edited by John Fenno, formerly a Boston schoolteacher. The first issue appeared in New York City on April 15, 1789, with the announcement that future issues would be published every Wednesday and Saturday, that annual subscriptions would cost three dollars plus postage, and that the contents would include "1. Early and authentic accounts of the proceedings of Congress. 2. Impartial sketches of the debates in Congress. 3. Essays on the great subject of government in general, and the Federal Legislature in particular. . . . " The newspaper moved to Philadelphia when the government moved its headquarters there in 1790.

3909. Newspapers provided to senators and representatives at public expense were authorized on December 9, 1790, when Congress made arrangements to provide each member with his choice of three local newspapers.

3910. Democratic-Republican (Jeffersonian) political newspaper was the *National Gazette,* a semiweekly news journal that was published in Philadelphia, PA, from October 31, 1791, through 1793. It was founded at the instigation of Thomas Jefferson and James Madison for the purpose of counteracting the influence of the *Gazette of the United States,* Alexander Hamilton's Federalist organ. As editor, they brought in a college friend of Madison's, Philip Morin Freneau, to whom Jefferson gave a part-time job in the State Department. Hamilton denounced it as "an incendiary and pernicious publication," but Jefferson said that the *Gazette* "has saved our constitution which was galloping fast into monarchy."

3911. Free newspaper exchange between publishers was a tradition in the colonies and was officially provided for by Congress in 1792. Newspaper publishers were given the right to send copies of their newspapers through the mail to one another without charge. Attempts to limit this right during the 1820s, when the increase in the number of newspapers made this practice very costly to the government, were denounced as attacks on freedom of the press.

3912. Political newspaper published in Washington, DC was the *National Intelligencer,* founded on October 31, 1800, by Samuel Harrison Smith at the invitation of Thomas Jefferson, who was expecting to be elected president and wanted an official newspaper for his administration. Until the *Register of Debates* began publication in 1824, the *Intelligencer* was the only source of information in the country about congressional activities. Except for an interruption during the War of 1812, when its premises were destroyed by the invading British, the paper continued to publish through the Civil War, successively taking Jeffersonian, Whig, and secessionist positions.

3913. Political newspaper using the word "Democratic" in its title was the *Democratic Press,* published in Philadelphia, PA, three times a week from March 27 through June 29, 1807. It then became a daily, *The Democratic Press for the Country.* The editor was John Binns.

3914. Abolition newspaper was the *Philanthropist,* published and edited by Charles Osborn, which appeared in Mount Pleasant, OH, on August 29, 1817. It published "An Appeal to Philanthropists" by Benjamin Lundy, which is said by some to be the most powerful abolition appeal ever made.

3915. Washington news bureau was opened in 1822 by Elias Kingman, who compiled accounts of government activities and distributed them to editors of out-of-town newspapers. It continued in operation until the Civil War.

3916. Official Jacksonian newspaper was the *United States Telegraph,* founded in Washington, DC, in 1826. The editor was Duff Green, a friend of Andrew Jackson's. After Jackson's election to the presidency in 1828, he rewarded the paper for its partisanship by naming it the official organ of his administration, but Green allied himself with the vice president, John Caldwell Calhoun, and quickly lost his favored position to Francis P. Blair's *Washington Globe.*

3917. Political newspaper published by African-Americans was the weekly *Freedom's Journal,* whose first issue appeared in New York, NY, on March 16, 1827. It was founded by John Brown Russwurm, one of the first African-Americans to earn a college degree (he had graduated from Bowdoin College the previous year), and Samuel E. Cornish. The name was changed to *The Rights of All* in 1829.

3918. Campaign newspapers were a feature of the election of 1828. They were published by partisans of incumbent president Andrew Jackson and of his rival, former president John Quincy Adams, and specialized in smearing the opponent's personal morality, character traits, White House record, and so forth. A typical Adams paper was called the "Anti-Jackson Expositor," and a typical pro-Jackson example was entitled "We the People."

3919. Labor newspaper was *The Working Man's Advocate,* first published in New York City on February 18, 1834, by George Henry Evans. He advocated free homesteads, equal rights for women, and abolition of all laws governing collection of debts and imprisonment for debt. An earlier newspaper, the *Daily Sentinel,* first published on February 15, 1830, in New York City, was sympathetic to labor.

3920. Campaign newspaper of importance was *The Log Cabin,* a four-page paper published in 1840 to promote the presidential campaign of William Henry Harrison. The masthead displayed a large image of a log cabin in which, according to propaganda put forth by Harrison's campaign, the candidate was supposedly born.

3921. Official Whig administration newspaper was the venerable Washington newspaper *National Intelligencer,* selected by William Henry Harrison after his election to the presidency in 1840. He died a month into his term, however, and was succeeded by John Tyler, who established his own newspaper, the *Madisonian.*

3922. Edition of *The New York Tribune* was published by founding editor Horace Greeley in 1841. Greeley was first a Whig and later a Republican in political orientation, and his paper, considered the most influential and best-written of its time, was an important champion for various reforms and causes, including emancipation, temperance, universal free public-school education, and labor rights.

3923. Issue of the *New York Times* was published in New York City on September 18, 1851, by the paper's founder, Henry Jarvis Raymond. Raymond's intent was to publish an inexpensive daily that would objectively report the news without sensationalism.

3924. Edition of the *Wall Street Journal* was published in New York City on July 8, 1889, by Charles Dow, Edward Jones, and Charles Bergstresser, founders of Dow Jones & Company. The *Wall Street Journal* evolved from Dow's earlier two-page daily, the *Customer's Afternoon Letter,* the first paper to publish consolidated stock tables as well as accurate financial information for public companies. The internet version of the *Wall Street Journal* was first published on April 29, 1996.

3925. Mexican-American political newspaper still extant is *La Opinión,* founded by Ignacio Lozano in Los Angeles, CA, in 1926.

PRESS AND MEDIA—NEWSPAPERS—
continued

3926. Important Muslim American weekly was *Muhammad Speaks,* launched in 1962 by the Nation of Islam. It later became the one of the largest minority weekly publications in the country and attained a peak circulation of 800,000 readers. The paper was also published as *Bilalian News,* the *A.M. Journal,* and the *Muslim Journal.*

PRESS AND MEDIA—POLITICAL CARTOONS

3927. Political cartoon was "The Waggoner and Hercules," an illustration that appeared in *Plain Truth,* a pamphlet written and published by Benjamin Franklin in Philadelphia, PA, in 1747. The cartoon shows a wagon driver on his knees, praying that Hercules, who is seen enthroned in the clouds, will haul his wagon out of the mud. The caption reads *"Non Votis, &c,"* which is the beginning of the Latin proverb whose English equivalent is "God helps those who help themselves." The pamphlet was intended to rouse the citizens of Pennsylvania to make preparations for their own defense, despite their annoyance at the pacifist Quakers in their midst who refused to assist them.

3928. Political cartoon published in an American newspaper was "Join, or Die," drawn by Benjamin Franklin and published in Philadelphia, PA, on May 9, 1754, in the *Pennsylvania Gazette.* It was printed in the first column of the second page. The drawing, based on the folk belief that the pieces of a cut-up snake could rejoin and come alive, depicted a snake divided into eight segments, representing (beginning with the tail) South Carolina, North Carolina, Virginia, Maryland, Pennsylvania, New Jersey, New York, and New England. Franklin drew it to publicize his proposal for a federation of the British colonies. The cartoon was reprinted in newspapers throughout the colonies, and the image of the divided snake continued in use until the Revolution. A segment for Georgia was added in 1774.

3929. Public figure lampooned in political cartoons was Benjamin Franklin, whose activities as a political philosopher, diplomat, scientist, educator, and inventor kept him in the public eye after he retired from his Philadelphia printing and publishing business in 1748. One surviving cartoon, "The Counter-Medly," from 1764, shows the Devil murmuring to Franklin, "Thee Shall be Agent BEN For all my Realms."

3930. Political cartoon to interfere with a trial was the famous engraving of the Boston Massacre of March 5, 1770, engraved by Paul Revere from an uncredited drawing by Henry Pelham. It was not an accurate picture of the massacre, since it showed the British soldiers apparently firing on a crowd of innocent bystanders, when in fact they had been menaced. At the trial of the soldiers in October, their lawyers, John Adams and Josiah Quincy, Jr., reminded the jurors to preserve their impartiality despite the message conveyed by the cartoon.

3931. Political cartoon lampooning President George Washington appeared in New York City immediately after his inauguration in April 1789. Entitled "The Entry," it showed David Humphreys, the president's assistant, leading a donkey with President Washington on its back. The caption read: "The glorious time has come to pass / When David shall conduct an ass."

3932. Political cartoon produced by lithography appeared in 1829. It showed an alligator squatting on the western half of the United States and a tortoise crawling on the eastern half. The alligator symbolized Andrew Jackson, the winner of the presidential election of 1828, and the tortoise symbolized the loser, incumbent president John Quincy Adams. Lithography, a method of printing from a limestone slab, allowed publishers to mass-produce drawings and sell them directly to the public. The New York firm of Henry R. Robinson specialized in publishing lithographed political cartoons. They were also made by the more famous firm of Currier & Ives.

3933. Political cartoon featuring Uncle Sam appeared in 1834 and was entitled "Uncle Sam in Danger." It showed President Andrew Jackson, Vice President Martin Van Buren, Senator Thomas Hart Benton, and Amos Kendall, a Jackson aide soon to be named postmaster general, in the guise of ignorant doctors bleeding a sick man sitting in a chair. Uncle Sam appears as a cleanshaven man with dark hair, a cap on his head and a striped robe, something like the American flag, surrounding him. In early cartoons, he was often dressed like Benjamin Franklin. By the 1840s he was portrayed with striped trousers, a top hat, and a long coat, but he was still cleanshaven. It was many decades before he took on his current image as an elderly but vigorous man with a long white beard.

3934. Political cartoon showing the Democratic Party as a donkey was "The Modern Balaam and His Ass," published in 1837. It shows Andrew Jackson as the biblical Balaam, riding a donkey and beating it with his hickory stick because it refuses to go forward. In the donkey's path is an angel labeled "Bankruptcy of 1837," "The Regency," "Deposit Banks," and other references to contentious issues of the day. The great cartoonist Thomas Nast used the donkey to represent northern Democrats who sympathized with the South. His first cartoon to do so was "A Live Jackass Kicking a Dead Lion," a wood engraving that appeared in *Harper's Weekly* on January 15, 1870. The jackass was tagged "Copperhead papers" and the dead lion represented Edwin McMasters Stanton, the former secretary of war, who had clashed with President Andrew Johnson over his refusal to enforce tougher measures in the South.

3935. Political cartoon with mass popularity was "Why Don't You Take It?," drawn by Frank Beard in 1861. It showed an enormous bulldog in epaulets and a Napoleonic officer's hat, identified on its collar as "Old General U.S.," guarding a pile of supplies and weapons from a cowering greyhound in a Southern planter's hat, with the name "Jeff" on its collar. The greyhound represented Jefferson Davis, whose Confederate Army was preparing to attack Washington, DC, and the bulldog represented General Winfield Scott, who, as commander of the Union army, was preparing to defend it. More than 100,000 copies of this cartoon were sold throughout the North.

3936. Crusading political cartoonist was Thomas Nast, the German-born artist who joined the staff of the magazine *Harper's Weekly* in 1862 as a battlefield illustrator during the Civil War and emerged as a cartoonist of rare power. He was most famous for his attack on William Marcy "Boss" Tweed, the corrupt head of New York City's Democratic party organization, Tammany Hall, who had plundered millions of dollars from the city's treasury. Tweed and his associates were brought down by investigative reporting in the *New York Times* and Nast's devastating cartoons in *Harper's Weekly,* which whipped up public opinion and forced prosecutors and reformers to take action. The most famous of these was "The Tammany Tiger Loose," which appeared on November 11, 1871. It showed Tweed as a Roman emperor, sitting in a crowded arena under an ensign marked "Tammany Spoils" and smiling as a tiger mutilates human figures representing the American republic and the rule of law. Tweed went to jail and died there in 1878.

3937. Political cartoon showing the Republican Party as an elephant was drawn by Thomas Nast and appeared in *Harper's Weekly,* New York City, on November 7, 1874. It was entitled "The Third-Term Panic" and referred to the possibility that President Ulysses S. Grant might seek a third term. It depicts an ass labeled "N.Y. Herald" in a lion's skin labeled "Caesarism," frightening numerous timid animals labeled "N.Y. Times," "N.Y. Trib.," etc., while a berserk elephant, labeled "Republican vote," about to fall into an abyss labeled "Southern Claims Chaos," tosses platform planks to right and left. The Democratic Party appears in the form of a fox. The quotation accompanying the title read: "An Ass having put on the Lion's skin, roamed about the Forest, and amused himself by frightening all the foolish Animals he met with in his wanderings."

3938. Political cartoons in color were developed by Joseph Keppler, an Austrian-born artist and actor who came to the United States in 1868 and the following year began drawing political caricatures. He began tinting his lithographs in 1878. Keppler also abandoned the use of speech balloons in his cartoons, instead using entirely visual details, including full backgrounds, to make his point.

3939. Political cartoon to decisively influence a presidential election was "The Royal Feast of Belshazzar Blaine and the Money Kings," which showed the Republican candidate, James Gillespie Blaine, sitting at a banquet with captains of industry and financiers and partaking of dishes labeled "lobby pudding," "monopoly soup," and "patronage cake." The drawing, by Walt McDougall, was printed in the *New York World* on October 30, 1884, just before the election. The Democratic Party had the cartoon blown up into billboards and plastered New York State with them. This, plus Blaine's blunder in countenancing a public insult to Catholic Democrats by one of his supporters, cost him New York's 36 electoral votes, which would have given him the presidency. The winner was Republican candidate Grover Cleveland.

3940. State law outlawing political caricatures was passed by California in 1899. The statute provided criminal penalties for anyone who published a portrait without the subject's permission. Insulting caricatures were also banned.

3941. Cartoon unit run by a government was the Bureau of Cartoons, founded by George J. Hecht in December 1917 in Washington, DC, as an independent organization of the National Committee of Patriotic Societies and subsumed into the federal government in June 1918. Its

PRESS AND MEDIA—POLITICAL CARTOONS—*continued*

purpose was to shape public opinion in favor of the war effort, encouraging enlistment in the armed forces, purchase of Liberty Bonds, and similar activities. Ideas were suggested to artists each week in the bureau's *Bulletin for Cartoonists.*

PUBLIC WELFARE—ALCOHOL

3942. Alcohol temperance law enacted by a colony was signed on March 5, 1623, by Governor Sir Francis Wyatt of Virginia and 32 others. It provided that "the proclamations for swearing and drunkenness set out by the Governor and Counsell are confirmed by this assembly, and it is further ordered that the churchwardens shall be sworne to present them to the commanders of every plantation and that the forfeitures shall be collected by them to be for publique uses."

3943. Alcohol prohibition law enacted by a state was passed by Tennessee on January 26, 1838. The bill, an "act to repeal all laws licensing tippling houses," provided that "all persons convicted of the offense of retailing spirituous liquors shall be fined at the discretion of the court" and that the fines and forfeitures be used for the support of common schools.

3944. Federally mandated alcohol abuse programs in schools were established under a law enacted in 1882. The law, the first in the world, required "temperance education" to be included in the standard course of studies in public schools. Temperance education became mandatory in Washington, DC, in 1886. By 1900, similiar laws had been enacted by all the states.

3945. Alcohol prohibition vote taken in Congress that showed the House of Representatives with a dry majority was taken on December 22, 1914. The representatives voted 197–189 in favor of a resolution to provide a constitutional amendment banning the manufacture and sale of intoxicating beverages. The resolution, offered by Representative Richmond Pearson Hobson of Alabama, failed to win the necessary two-thirds majority.

3946. Alcohol prohibition law enacted by Congress forbidding the sale of intoxicating liquors except for export was the Wartime Prohibition Act, passed on November 21, 1918.

3947. Federal Alcohol Control Administration was authorized on December 4, 1933, by executive order No. 6,474, issued by President Franklin Delano Roosevelt. Joseph Hodges Choate, Jr., was appointed director.

PUBLIC WELFARE—BIRTH, MARRIAGE, AND DEATH

3948. Legal divorce in the American colonies was granted on January 5, 1643, by the Quarter Court of Boston, MA, to Anne Clarke of the Massachusetts Bay Colony, who ended her marriage to Denis Clarke on the grounds of adultery. Clarke admitted by affidavit to having deserted Anne and her two children for another woman, and he refused to return to her.

3949. State birth registration law was passed by Georgia on December 19, 1823. It required the "clerks of the court of ordinary, in each county respectively to enter and register in a book" the dates of births of all persons upon due proof made by affidavit or oath. The clerk was entitled to charge 25 cents for each registration.

3950. Polygamy ban enacted by Congress was enacted on July 1, 1862, "an act to punish and prevent the practice of polygamy in the territories of the United States and other places, and disapproving and annulling certain acts of the legislative assembly of the territory of Utah." Most of the settlers in Utah belonged to the Mormon Church (Church of Jesus Christ of Latter-day Saints), which encouraged men to marry multiple wives. Little effort was made to enforce this law. The first anti-polygamy law with teeth was the act of March 22, 1882, known as the Edmunds law, which defined simultaneous marriages as bigamy and prescribed loss of citizenship as a penalty. It legitimized children born in polygamy before January 1, 1883. The territorial assembly prohibited polygamy in 1887 and the state constitution did so in 1895.

3951. State-run crematory was built by Dr. Miles Lewis Davis at Swinburne Island in New York City. The construction was funded by $20,000 appropriated by New York State on May 21, 1888. The following year, the crematory was used to burn bodies disinterred from the Quarantine cemetery at Sequine's Point.

3952. Sterilization of humans by a state government as a matter of public policy was approved by Indiana on March 9, 1907. The law, which allowed sterilization for eugenic, punitive, and therapeutic reasons, was entitled "an act to prevent the procreation of criminals, idiots, imbeciles and rapists." One hundred and twenty operations were performed under the law. The constitutionality of the law was challenged, and on May 11, 1921, the Supreme Court of Indiana, in the case of *Williams v.*

Smith, held it unconstitutional because it denied the appellee due process of law. A sterilization bill had been passed by the Pennsylvania legislature on March 21, 1905, but was vetoed by Governor Samuel Whitaker Pennypacker.

3953. State to require blood tests for marriage licenses was New York, which mandated them in the Demond-Breitbart Law, signed on April 12, 1938, by Governor Herbert Henry Lehman. The blood tests, along with other medical tests, were intended to prevent the spread of syphilis.

3954. Birth registration uniform numbering system was adopted on March 18, 1948, by the American Association of Registration Executives and was approved on August 30 by the Council on Vital Records and Vital Statistics. The system was inaugurated on January 1, 1949. It required each birth certificate to be assigned a three-part number. The first number identified the state—101 for Alabama, 102 for Arizona, 103 for Arkansas, and so on. The second number referred to the year, and the third number to the order of the birth in the state's record. The lowest number in the classification was given to Leonard Blake Gunnells of Prattville, AL, whose name was the first on the roll of the first county in Alabama's alphabetical county list. His number was 101-49-000001.

3955. State law legalizing abortion for medical reasons was an act signed on April 25, 1967, by Governor John Arthur Love of Colorado. It permitted therapeutic abortions in cases where pregnancy resulted from rape or incest, endangered a woman's physical or mental health, or was likely to result in the birth of a child with severe mental or physical defects. Abortions could be performed only with the unanimous approval of a three-doctor board of an accredited hospital licensed by the Colorado State Department of Health.

3956. No-fault divorce law enacted by a state was enacted by California on July 6, 1970. It allowed divorces in cases of incurable insanity and irreconcilable differences.

3957. State voluntary sterilization regulation was enacted on April 10, 1976, by the state of Virginia. It barred physicians from performing a vasectomy, salpingectomy, or other surgical sterilization procedure upon any person under the age of 21, or over 21 and legally incompetent.

3958. Right-to-die law enacted by a state was the Natural Death Act of California, enacted on September 30, 1976, which allowed physicians of terminally ill patients to withhold life-sustaining procedures under certain conditions.

3959. Ban on surrogate motherhood enacted by a state was signed into law on June 27, 1988, by Governor James J. Blanchard of Michigan. The act made it illegal for women to enter into contracts that require them to bear other people's children in exchange for money.

3960. Law permitting doctor-assisted suicide was passed in Oregon in 1994.

3961. Judicial decision allowing physicians to terminate the life of terminally ill patients at their request was issued on May 3, 1994, by federal judge Barbara Rothstein of Seattle, WA. In her decision, Rothstein held that the privacy of a terminally ill person is constitutionally protected, and that, as the law permits such people to refuse treatments aimed at prolonging life, it also permits them access to methods of hastening death.

PUBLIC WELFARE—EDUCATION

3962. Compulsory education law in a colony was passed by Massachusetts on June 14, 1642. It stated: "This Court, taking into consideration the great neglect of many parents and masters in training up their children in learning and labor and other imployments which may be profitable to the common wealth, so hereupon order and decree, that in every towne the chosen men appointed for managing the prudentiall affayers of the same shall henceforth stand charged with the care of the redresse of this evil . . . and for this end . . . they shall have power to take account from time to time of all parents and masters, and of their children, concerning their calling and imployment of their children."

3963. Colonial law requiring towns to hire teachers and construct schools was passed on November 11, 1647, by Massachusetts. It "ordered that every township in this jurisdiction, after the Lord hath increased them to the number of fifty householders, shall then forthwith appoint one within their town to teach all such children as shall resort to him to write and read, whose wages shall be paid either by the parents or masters of such children, or by the inhabitants in general." Towns of 100 families were required to "set up a grammar school, the master thereof being able to instruct youths so far as they may be fitted for the university."

3964. College named after George Washington was Washington College in Washington College, TN, founded in 1780 by the Reverend Dr. Samuel Doak, who became its first president. On April 24, 1783, it was chartered as Martin Academy by North Carolina, of which Tennessee was then a part. A second charter

PUBLIC WELFARE—EDUCATION—*continued*

was received on March 31, 1785, from the state of Franklin, which was never officially recognized. A third charter, received on July 8, 1795, changed the name to Washington College. The name was proposed to the legislature of the "Territory of the United States South of the River Ohio" by General John Sevier.

3965. Land set-aside for schools authorized by the Continental Congress was authorized by an ordinance of May 20, 1785: "There shall be reserved the lot No. 16 of every township for the maintenance of public schools within said township." This applied to the Western Reserve (now Ohio) and other unsurveyed lands to the west. A new system of surveying was established, with the land laid out in townships six miles square, subdivided into 36 numbered sections, each a mile square. Section No. 16 was popularly known as the "school section."

3966. State university was the University of North Carolina at Chapel Hill, chartered in 1789. Construction on its first building, a dormitory known as Old East, began on October 12, 1793—now commemorated as University Day, a state holiday—and the first students arrived in 1795.

3967. Land-grant university was Ohio University, Athens, OH, which was chartered on February 18, 1804, and opened with three students on June 1, 1808. According to the terms of a federal contract signed on October 27, 1787, the Ohio Company of Associates agreed that rental fees derived from land belonging to Ohio's townships should be set aside for the support of a university.

3968. State superintendent of schools was Gideon Hawley, who took office on January 14, 1813, as New York State's superintendent of common schools. An act was passed on April 15, 1814, making him secretary of the New York State Board of Regents at a salary of $400 a year. He was removed in 1821 for political reasons.

3969. State tax enacted to support public schools was "an act providing for the establishment of free schools," enacted on January 15, 1825, by Illinois. It provided for a common school in each county, open to every class of white citizens between the ages of 5 and 21 years and supported by a tax of $2 of every $100 and five-sixths of the interest from the school fund.

3970. Superintendent of schools hired by a city was Roswell Willson Haskins, who was appointed "city superintendent of common schools" in 1836 by Buffalo, NY. He resigned before the end of the year, claiming that the law was imperfect and that restrictions hampered his work.

3971. State board of education was established by Massachusetts on April 30, 1837. The first secretary of the board, later designated as commissioner, was the educational reformer Horace Mann. He was appointed on June 29, 1837, and received $1,000 a year.

3972. State compulsory education law was approved on May 18, 1852, by Governor George Sewall Boutwell of Massachusetts. It prescribed that children must attend school "between the ages of eight and fourteen years" for twelve weeks in the year, six of which must be consecutive.

3973. National teachers' organization was the National Teachers Association, which was organized on August 26, 1867, at a national convention attended by representatives of state teachers' associations, who met in the Hall of the Controllers of the Public Schools in Philadelphia, PA. The organization was intended "to elevate the character and advance the interest of the profession of teaching and to promote the cause of popular education in the United States." John L. Enos was the first chairman. The first women members were admitted in 1866. In 1870 the NTA merged with the National Association of School Superintendents and the American Normal School Association to form the National Education Association. The NEA began its conversion from professional society and charitable organization to labor union in 1962. It was defined as a 501(c)(5) labor union by the Internal Revenue Service in 1978.

3974. Land-grant college founded under the Morrill Act was Iowa Agricultural College (later Iowa State University). The Morrill Act, enacted by Congress on July 2, 1862, made federal lands available to endow colleges in states loyal to the Union. Iowa was the first state to accept the terms of the act.

3975. Commissioner of education of the United States was Henry Barnard, appointed on March 14, 1867, by President Andrew Johnson. He served until March 17, 1870. Barnard, who was born in Connecticut, was a leader of the movement to establish American public school systems

3976. State university supported by a direct property tax was the University of Michigan, Ann Arbor, MI. An act of the state legislature approved on March 15, 1867, assessed all taxable property one twentieth of a mill on each dollar of value, to be used for the use, aid, and maintenance of the university. The funds paid to the university in 1867 totalled $15,398.

3977. National parent-teacher association was the National Congress of Mothers, organized on February 17, 1897, in Washington, DC, by Alice McLellan Birney and Phoebe Apperson Hearst at a meeting attended by 2,000 persons. At the annual meeting of March 9, 1908, the name was changed to the National Congress of Mothers and Parent-Teacher Associations. On May 9, 1924, the name was changed to the National Congress of Parents and Teachers.

3978. State system of vocational, technical, and adult education was instituted in 1911 in Wisconsin by the state legislature.

3979. State-run adult education program was the Racine Continuation School, Racine, WI, which opened on November 3, 1911. It provided night classes for adults, as well for teenagers between 14 to 16 years of age who had work permits.

3980. Federal education grants to the children of deceased veterans were authorized by Congress on June 29, 1956, which voted "to establish an educational assistance program for children of servicemen who died as a result of a disability or disease incurred in line of duty during World War One, World War Two, or the Korean conflict." It authorized the Veterans Administration to pay a subsistence grant of up to $110 a month not in excess of 36 months to a son or daughter between the ages of 18 and 23. The first grant under the law was awarded to George A. Turner, 19, of Brooklyn, New York City, the son of William G. Turner, who died in 1954 at the age of 43 from a disability incurred during the Normandy invasion in World War II.

3981. Office of Economic Opportunity was authorized by the Economic Opportunity Act of 1964, enacted on August 20, 1964, "to mobilize the human and financial resources of the Nation to combat poverty in the United States," as well as to prepare residents for the responsibilities of citizenship and to increase the employability of men and women age 16 through 21. Robert Sargent Shriver, Jr. was sworn in on October 16, 1964, as director.

3982. Federal aid program for primary and secondary schools was the Elementary and Secondary School Act, signed into law by President Lyndon Baines Johnson on April 11, 1965. The act allocated $1.3 billion for school districts according to the number of needy children they contained, and included funds for parochial and private schools.

3983. Urban land-grant college was Federal City College, founded in Washington, DC, in 1968. It was granted accreditation in 1974.

3984. State teacher-testing requirement was enacted by Arkansas, which passed a law in 1983 requiring all teachers in public skills to pass an examination of basic teaching skills. Teachers who failed the exam lost their state teaching licenses. Ninety percent of Arkansas teachers passed the first administration of tests in 1985.

3985. Summit conference on education by the nation's governors was held on September 27–28, 1989, in Washington, DC. The governors identified eight goals to be met by the year 2000: school readiness for all young children; more parental involvement in schools; school environments free of drugs and violence; student competence in core subjects, to be demonstrated in grades four, eight, and twelve; a high school graduation rate of 90 percent; availability of professional development assistance for teachers; attainment by the United States of first place, internatonally, in math and science; and universal adult literacy. The National Education Goals Panel, an 18-member panel established by Congress to monitor progress by the states, marked the tenth anniversary of the conference in December 1999 by renewing its commitment to the same eight goals without setting deadlines for their achievement.

3986. Community service requirement for high school graduation was passed into law on July 29, 1992, by the Maryland legislature. The plan require public high school students to perform a minimum of hours of local community service before they could receive their diplomas.

3987. Federal legislation recommending academic standards was the Goals 2000: Educate America Act, passed by Congress on March 26, 1994, and signed by President William Jefferson Clinton in April 1994. The first federal blueprint for education, it recommended academic standards for students in the fourth, eighth, and eleventh grades. Goals 2000 created a framework for establishing eight voluntary

PUBLIC WELFARE—EDUCATION—continued

national education goals by the turn of the century. The controversial program touched off a debate between educators seeking uniform national standards and advocates of local control of education.

3988. State to enact a school voucher plan was Florida, which approved it on April 30, 1999. The program, which was initiated by Governor Jeb Bush, passed the state senate by a vote of 25 to 15 and the lower house by a vote of 70 to 48. It offered vouchers worth $3,000 and upwards to all students attending the state's worst public schools, enabling their families to enroll them in private schools that charge tuition. The program was declared unconstitutional by a state court in March 2000, but the state appealed the decision.

3989. Statewide school voucher program paid for with tax revenues was passed by the Florida legislature on June 21, 1999. The plan issued vouchers to students attending public schools if the schools failed to meet state criteria on standardized test scores two years in a row. The vouchers, funded by state tax revenue, could be used to pay tuition at private or parochial schools of the student's choice. On March 14, 2000, a state judge ruled that the program violated Florida's constitution, but Governor Jeb Bush announced his intention to appeal the ruling.

PUBLIC WELFARE—FAMILIES AND CHILDREN

3990. Case of child abuse brought to court was that of Mary Ellen Wilson McCormack of New York. At age four, she was stolen from an orphanage by Francis and Mary Connolly. Mary Connolly beat and whipped her, forced her to work, locked her in closets, never let her outside, and showed her no affection. A Methodist caseworker named Etta Wheeler learned of her plight, visited the Connolly home, and saw evidence of abuse. At the time, however, state law provided no means for any public agency or private society to intervene in the home to protect a child. Wheeler finally asked Henry Bergh, the founder of the American Society for the Prevention of Cruelty to Animals, to lodge a complaint that the Connollys were breaking animal welfare laws. Bergh's lawyer, Elbridge T. Gerry, cited the little-used New York law on April 9, 1874, when McCormack, then nine years old, was brought into the New York courtroom of Judge Abraham Lawrence. Within a year, the New York State Legislature

enacted laws permitting the chartering of Societies for the Protection of Children. Mary Ellen McCormack was transferred to the care of Etta Wheeler's niece. She later married and raised six children.

3991. Child delinquency law enacted by a state was passed on April 28, 1909, by Colorado. The law made it illegal to "encourage, cause or contribute to the dependency, neglect or delinquency of a child."

3992. State welfare payments to mothers with dependent children were authorized by the Illinois legislature in 1911.

3993. Children's Bureau was established by Congress on April 9, 1912, "to investigate and report . . . upon all matters pertaining to welfare of children and child life among all classes of our people." The bureau was put in the charge of the Department of Commerce and Labor. Its first chief, Julia Clifford Lathrop, was appointed on June 4, 1912, by President Woodrow Wilson and was confirmed by the Senate at a salary of $5,000 a year.

3994. Birth control clinic was opened on October 16, 1916, in the Brownsville section of Brooklyn, New York City, by Fania Mindell, Ethel Byrne, and Margaret Sanger. The handbill announcing its opening was printed in English, Yiddish, and Italian. Sanger was jailed for operating the clinic; she had recently spent time in jail for writing *Family Limitations,* the first American book on birth control The first birth-control clinic staffed entirely by doctors opened in 1923.

3995. Birth control clinic run by a state government was opened on March 15, 1937, in Raleigh, NC, when the North Carolina State Board of Health officially introduced a program setting up contraceptive clinics for poor married women in local maternity and child health services. The first director was Dr. George Marion Cooper of the Division of Preventive Medicine. Roberta Pratt, a Raleigh nurse, was hired to work with the health officers.

3996. Smart-card welfare payments were instituted by Ramsey County, MN, in 1988. The electronic benefits transfer system replaced the traditional grant program, Aid to Families with Dependent Children, with electronically coded cards that could be used at bank ATM machines to withdraw benefits. While expensive, the EBT system was more efficient to administer, reduced the number of stolen AFDC checks, and enabled AFDC recipients to obtain cash without paying high fees at check-cashing stores.

PUBLIC WELFARE—GAMBLING

3997. Gambling law for ministers enacted by a colony was passed in 1624 by the Virginia Assembly. It specified that "mynisters shall not give themselves to excesse in drinking or yette spend their tyme idelie by day or by night, playing at dice, cards or any unlawful game."

3998. Colonial gambling law for residents was passed on March 22, 1630, in Boston, MA: "It is . . . ordered that all persons whatsoever that have cards, dice or tables in their houses, shall make away with them before the next court under pain of punishment."

3999. Horse racing ban was enacted on June 4, 1674, by Massachusetts. It provided "that whatsoever p'son shall run a race with any horse in any street or Comon road shall forfeite five shillings in Mony forthwith to be levied by the Constable or set in the stockes one hour if it be not payed."

4000. Federal law hostile to lotteries was the act of Congress of March 2, 1827, which provided "that no postmaster or assistant postmaster shall act as agent for lottery offices or under any color of purchase, or otherwise, send lottery tickets; nor shall any postmaster receive free of postage or frank lottery schemes, circulars or tickets."

4001. State to legalize casino gambling was Nevada. In 1910, Nevada's legislature passed an anti-gambling law so strict that it forbade customers even to flip a coin for the price of a drink. Nonetheless, illegal gambling flourished and was unofficially tolerated. On March 17, 1931, at the height of the Great Depression, the Nevada legislature legalized casino gambling in the hope of reversing the state's severe economic decline. A few months later, quick divorces were also made legal. By the end of the century, gaming accounted for some 40 percent of state tax revenues.

4002. Pinball ban enacted by a city was approved on June 19, 1939, by Atlanta, GA, and was signed by Mayor William Berry Hartsfield. The act provided that any person convicted of a violation of this ordinance be subject to a fine not to exceed $20 and a sentence to the public works of the city for a period of 30 days, at the discretion of the recorder.

4003. Gambling permit stamp issued by the federal government was authorized on October 20, 1951, by the Revenue Act of 1951. The ungummed stamps measured 6.5 by 4 inches and cost $50 per year. In the first six months of issue, 22,401 stamps were purchased, mostly in Nevada.

4004. State lottery in modern times was instituted by New Hampshire in 1964. The state lacked a sales tax or a state income tax, and came to depend heavily on the lottery to help defray its expenses.

4005. State to allow publicly traded corporations to obtain gambling licenses was Nevada, which authorized them in 1967. The law greatly expanded the range of gambling businesses and helped end the era of organized-crime control of the Nevada gambling industry.

PUBLIC WELFARE—HEALTH AND SAFETY

4006. Medical regulations enacted by a colony were passed by Virginia on October 21, 1639, in an "act to compel physicians and surgeons to declare on oath the value of their medicines." Another law, enacted on May 3, 1649, in Massachusetts, was directed to "physicians, chirurgians, midwives or others" and forbade them "to exercise or put forth any act contrary to the known rules of art, nor exercise any force, violence, or cruelty upon or towards the bodies of any, whether young or old." The act was "not intended to discourage the lawful use of their skill but to encourage and direct them in the right use thereof and to inhibit and restrain the presumptious arrogance of such as . . . exercise violence upon . . . bodies."

4007. Government assistance to the family of an insane person was extended in 1676 by the Upland Court of Delaware County, PA, which declared: "Jan Cornelissen of Amesland, Complayning to the Court that his son Erick is bereft of his naturall Senses and is turned quyt madd and that; he being a poore man is not able to maintaine him; Ordered: that three or four persons bee hired to build a little blockhouse at Amesland for to put in the said madman, and at the next Court, order will be taken that; a small Levy be Laid for to pay for the building of the house and the maintaining of the said madman according to the laws of the Government."

4008. Medical licensing law enacted by a city that was actually enforced was an "act to regulate the practice of Physick and Surgery in the City of New York," passed on June 10, 1760. It provided that "no person whatsoever shall practice as a physician or surgeon . . . before he shall first have been examined in physick or surgery and approved of and admitted by one of His Majesty's Council, the Judges of the Supreme Court, the King's Attorney General and

301

PUBLIC WELFARE—HEALTH AND SAFETY—*continued*

the Mayor of the City of New York for the time being or by any three or more of them." Violators were subject to a penalty of £5, half of which went to the informer and the remainder to the funds for the poor.

4009. Medical licensing law enacted by a colony was New Jersey's law of September 26, 1772. The act was effective for a five-year period. It authorized a licensing board consisting of two judges of the Supreme Court of New Jersey and a third individual appointed by them, and forbade the practice of medicine without a license. Very severe fines were imposed upon violators, but the law did not apply to those who drew teeth, bled patients, or gave medical assistance for which they received no fee or compensation.

4010. Health service established by the federal government was the Marine Hospital Service, established by congressional act of July 16, 1798. The law provided that the master of every American merchant ship arriving from a foreign port should pay to the collector of customs the sum of 20 cents a month for each seaman, which he was authorized to deduct from the seamen's wages. The money was spent for health services in the district in which it was collected. The service was reorganized as a national hospital system, the Public Health Service, on June 29, 1870.

4011. Quarantine law enacted by Congress was passed on February 25, 1799. It required federal officers to aid and assist the enforcement of state and municipal regulations.

4012. State ban on dueling was an "act to prevent the evil practice of duelling," passed by the Fourth General Assembly held at Knoxville, TN, and signed on November 10, 1801, by Governor Archibald Roane.

4013. State vaccination law was "an act to diffuse the benefits of inoculation for the Cow-Pox," enacted on March 6, 1810, by Massachusetts, which required every town, district, and plantation to guard against smallpox by choosing "three or more suitable persons, whose duty it shall be to superintend the inoculation of the inhabitants . . . with the cowpox."

4014. Vaccination law enacted by Congress was the act of February 27, 1813, to encourage vaccination against smallpox. It authorized the president to appoint a vaccine agent to furnish vaccine through the Post Office to any citizen of the United States who might apply for it. The act was repealed on May 4, 1822.

4015. Vaccination program by the federal government to protect Native Americans against smallpox was authorized by congressional act of May 5, 1832, "an act to provide the means of extending the benefits of vaccination, as a preventive of the smallpox, to the Native American tribes, and thereby, as far as possible, to save them from the destructive ravages of that disease." An appropriation of $12,000 was made. Physicians were paid $6 a day for their services.

4016. Pure food and drug law established by Congress to prevent the importation of adulterated drugs was the Drug Importation Act, passed on June 26, 1848. It was enforced by the Treasury Department through the Customs Service.

4017. City to build a comprehensive sewer system was Chicago, IL, whose sewer plan was initiated in 1855. Over the next half century, sewer systems were built in all U.S. cities with more than 4,000 inhabitants.

4018. State board of health was the Massachusetts State Board of Health and Vital Statistics, established on June 21, 1869. The first chairman was Henry Ingersoll Bowditch.

4019. Surgeon general was John Maynard Woodworth, appointed Supervising Surgeon of the Marine Hospital Service in April 1871. In 1870, Congress reorganized the MHS, previously a loose network of local hospitals, into a centrally controlled national health agency based in Washington, DC, under the administration of the Treasury Department. Woodworth, formerly the sanitary inspector for the Chicago Board of Health, had distinguished himself during the Civil War as army physician in charge of the ambulance train during General William Tecumseh Sherman's march through Georgia. Woodworth served in the new post until his death in March 1879. The title was changed to supervising surgeon general in 1875 and to surgeon general in 1902.

4020. Federal lifesaving service was the Life Saving Service, created by Congress as part of the Treasury Department on June 18, 1878, to rescue people from shipwrecks. This service and the Revenue Cutter Service were merged on January 28, 1915, to form the Coast Guard.

4021. State pure food and drug law was "an act to prevent the adulteration of food or drugs," passed on May 28, 1881, by New York. Violators were guilty of a misdemeanor, subject to a fine up to $50 for the first offense and not exceeding $100 for each subsequent offense. Laws prohibiting the adulteration of specific products had been passed earlier.

4022. Health laboratory established by a city was established on January 1, 1888, in Providence, RI. Dr. Charles Value Chapin was in charge. Dr. Gardner Taber Swarts was the medical inspector.

4023. Meat inspection law enacted by Congress was approved on August 30, 1890. It provided for the inspection of salted pork and bacon intended for export, as well as the inspection of export swine, cattle, sheep, and other ruminants.

4024. Dog licensing ordinance was passed in New York City on March 8, 1894. Purchase of a $2 annual dog license was required for every dog; unlicensed dogs were destroyed if not claimed within two days.

4025. Municipal milk station was opened in 1897 in Rochester, NY, through the efforts of Dr. George Washington Goler. Its purpose was to ensure the availability of clean, raw, tuberculin-tested milk for children during July and August, when infected milk was common, and to raise the standard of the milk supply

4026. State licensing law for nurses was enacted by North Carolina on March 3, 1903. It provided for voluntary registration with the county clerk of the Superior Court of any licensed trained nurse and for an examining and licensing board composed of two physicians and three registered nurses.

4027. State licensing law for pharmacists was enacted on May 3, 1904, by New York. It required pharmacists to have two years of training and four years of practical experience.

4028. Federal law on product safety was the Federal Food and Drug Act, passed by Congress on June 30, 1906, and signed into law by President Theodore Roosevelt. The law prohibited interstate commerce of misbranded and adulterated foods, drinks, and drugs, allowed for the seizure of adulterated or misbranded products, and provided for criminal penalties if the law was broken. The Meat Inspection Act was passed the same day. Both laws were inspired by the public outrage stirred up by Upton Sinclair's novel *The Jungle*, which dramatized the filthy conditions in the meatpacking industry.

4029. State law regulating chiropractic was passed on March 18, 1913, by Kansas. It regulated the practice of chiropractic, provided for licensing and examination of chiropractors, and created a three-member board for examination and regulation. Applicants were required to be graduates of a chartered chiropractic school or college having a course of three years, with actual attendance of more than six months each year.

4030. Commissioner of Food and Drugs under the Food, Drug, and Cosmetic Act of 1938 was Walter G. Campbell. He assumed the post in 1940, when authority for food and drug regulation was transferred from the Department of Agriculture to the Federal Security Agency (later renamed the Department of Health, Education, and Welfare).

4031. Fluoridation program for a city water supply was adopted by Grand Rapids, MI. Fluoride, which reduces tooth decay, was added to the city's water beginning on January 25, 1945.

4032. Published federal guidelines for food toxicity was *Guidance to Industry: Procedures for the Appraisal of the Toxicity of Chemicals in Food,* issued in 1949 by the U.S. Food and Drug Administration. The "black book" of the food additive industry, it listed minimum toxicity levels for hundreds of foods and food additives. In 1982, it was superseded by *Toxicological Principles for the Safety Assessment of Direct Food*

4033. Crop recalled by order of the Food and Drug Administration was the cranberry crop of fall 1959, affecting growers in the Northeast and North Central states. The crop was withdrawn three weeks before Thanksgiving so that the FDA could test it for aminotriazole, a weedkiller found to cause cancer in laboratory animals. Cleared berries were allowed a label stating that they had been tested and had passed FDA inspection, the only such endorsement ever allowed by the FDA on a food product.

4034. Federal laws requiring drug manufacturers to prove the effectiveness of their products were the 1962 Kefauver-Harris amendments to the Food, Drug, and Cosmetic Act of 1938. These were passed by Congress in the wake of the Thalidomide scandal, in which a sleeping pill widely prescribed in Europe was found to cause serious birth defects. Drug manufacturers were required to prove the effectiveness of their products to the FDA before marketing them. The amendments exempted animal drugs and animal feed additives shown to induce cancer but which leave no detectable levels of residue in the human food supply.

PUBLIC WELFARE—HEALTH AND SAFETY—*continued*

4035. State to ration health care was Oregon, whose legislature passed the main components of the Oregon Health Plan in 1989. The purpose of the plan was to ensure widespread insurance coverage for a range of basic medical services by eliminating coverage for certain treatments that were deemed less important. The task of ranking medical treatments in priority order was given to an eleven-member Health Services Commission, which evaluated each service based on its cost, the duration of its benefit, its effectiveness (as determined by physicians), and citizen opinion (ascertained through telephone polls and community meetings). The number of covered treatments was adjusted by the legislature during its biennial sessions in accordance with the state's fluctuating financial situation.

4036. Statewide registration of assault weapons was mandated under the Assault Weapons Control Act passed by California in 1989. Drafted by California Democratic state senator David A. Roberti, the law required all assault weapons to be registered with the state by January 1, 1991. By the deadline, only about 6 percent of the state's estimated 300,000 assault weapons had been registered, mainly because of resistance by individual owners but also because the state made little effort to enforce the law. A recall effort mounted by Californians Against Corruption, an anti-gun-control political group funded by the National Rifle Association, unsuccessfully attempted to unseat Roberti in April 1994.

4037. Nationwide nutritional labeling standards were detailed in the Nutrition Labeling and Education Act of 1990. The regulations were made public on December 28, 1992, and published in the *Federal Register* on January 6, 1993. The act required all packaged foods to bear nutrition labeling and all health claims for foods to be consistent with terms defined by the secretary of health and human services. The law preempted state requirements about food standards, nutrition labeling, and health claims and, for the first time, authorized some health claims for foods. The food ingredient panel, serving sizes, and terms such as "low fat" and "light" were standardized.

4038. Federal AIDS policy coordinator was Kristine M. Gebbie, former chair of the committee on HIV infection of the Centers for Disease Control and Prevention, appointed in August 1993 by President William Jefferson Clinton. She was responsible for coordinating the development of a unified strategy for fighting AIDS (acquired immune deficiency syndrome) on the federal level and for ensuring that the strategy was followed by government agencies. Gebbie resigned on July 8, 1994, and was replaced on November 10, 1994, by Patricia S. Fleming, an African-American AIDS activist.

PUBLIC WELFARE—HEALTH AND SAFETY—SURGEON GENERAL

4039. Woman to serve as surgeon general was Dr. Antonia C. Novello, appointed by President George Herbert Walker Bush in October 1989. A native of Fajardo, PR, she was also the first Latina to hold the post of surgeon general. Novello was previously a professor of pediatrics at Georgetown University Medical Center in Washington, DC, and deputy director of the National Institute of Child Health and Human Development.

4040. Surgeon general who was African-American was Dr. Joycelyn Elders, born in 1933 in Schaal, AR. Elders, the former health director of the state of Arkansas, was confirmed by a Senate vote of 65 to 34 on September 7, 1993.

PUBLIC WELFARE—HOUSING

4041. Federal law prohibiting racial discrimination in housing was the Civil Rights Act of 1866, the nation's first civil rights act, passed on April 8, 1866. It specified that "citizens of every race and color" were entitled to "purchase, lease, sell, hold, and convey real and personal property" on an equal basis with all other citizens. The law was widely ignored for the next hundred years. It was the basis for the Supreme Court's 1968 decision in *Jones v. Alfred H. Mayer,* which affirmed that the law applied to both individuals and governments.

4042. City housing code was passed in New York City in 1867. It specified the size of backyard spaces between rows of buildings and required that all rooms for habitation be equipped with windows.

4043. Theater safety codes were adopted in many municipalities across the United States following the disastrous fire of December 30, 1903, at the Iroquois Theatre in Chicago, IL, which killed 588 people.

4044. State-run old age home for pioneers was the Home for Aged and Infirm Arizona Pioneers in Prescott, AZ, authorized by the legislative assembly of the Territory of Arizona on March 10, 1909. Applicants for admission were required to be residents of Arizona not less than 35 years or over 60 years of age who were citizens of the United States for at least 5 years prior to the date of application, who were active in the development in Arizona, and who were unable to provide themselves with the necessities and comforts of life because of adverse circumstances or failing health. The home was opened for guests on February 6, 1911. The first superintendent was Major A. J. Doran.

4045. Home owners' loan corporation was authorized by the Home Owners' Loan Act of 1933, approved by President Franklin Delano Roosevelt on June 13, 1933, "to grant long term mortgage loans at low interest rates to those in urgent need of funds for the protection, preservation or recovery of their homes who were unable to procure the needed financing through normal channels." The Home Owners' Loan Corporation was a temporary emergency corporation loaning directly to home owners who were threatened with foreclosure and were unable to obtain the money for refinancing.

4046. Emergency housing corporation was authorized by Congress on October 28, 1933, through the powers delegated to the administrator of the Public Works Administration under the act of June 16, 1933. The corporation, which developed emergency housing construction and financing programs, was organized on November 18, 1933, under Delaware laws and was composed of five officers and five directors. The president of the corporation was Harold Le Claire Ickes, administrator of Public Works. The Federal Housing Administration took over this function in mid-1934.

4047. Federal Housing Administration was created by the National Housing Act, approved by Congress on June 27, 1934, "to encourage improvement in housing standards and conditions, to provide a system of mutual mortgage insurance." Its first administrator was James Andrew Moffett, appointed for the four-year term at an annual salary of $10,000.

4048. Initiative guaranteeing homeless people overnight shelter was approved by the city of Washington, DC, in 1984.

PUBLIC WELFARE—INSURANCE

4049. Insurance regulation enacted by a state was enacted by Massachusetts on February 13, 1799, pursuant to a law establishing the Massachusetts Fire Insurance Company." It required that the company "shall, when and as often required by the legislature of the Commonwealth, lay before them such a statement of their affairs as the said legislature may deem it expedient to require, and submit to an examination hereon under oath."

4050. Insurance board established by a state government was the New Hampshire Insurance Department, established on July 1, 1851, which authorized the governor to appoint three suitable residents of the state to examine personally each year the affairs of all insurance companies and report to the legislature. Each member was appointed to a one-year term. The first board consisted of Albert S. Scott, Jacob E. Ela, and Timo Hoskins.

4051. Insurance department of a state charged with the execution of the laws relating to insurance was the New York Insurance Department, which was approved on April 15, 1859, and became effective on January 1, 1860. The first superintendent was William Barnes, appointed on January 11, 1860.

4052. Employer's Liability Act enacted by Congress was passed on June 11, 1906, but was declared unconstitutional by the Supreme Court in the *Employer's Liability Cases* (1908) because its provisions extended to include the employees of interstate carriers even when such employees were not themselves engaged in any of the processes of interstate commerce. A revised act was passed on April 22, 1908.

4053. War Risk Insurance Bureau was established by act of Congress on September 2, 1914, to insure American vessels against war risks. The act was amended on June 12 and October 6, 1917, to provide yearly renewable term insurance against total disability and death to those in active military or naval service. The bureau was under the general direction of the secretary of the Treasury and directly supervised by William C. De Lanoy. Policy No. 1 was issued on October 17, 1917, to Cope Flannagan, who received a $10,000 policy payable, in case of death or permanent disability, in monthly installments of $57.50.

PUBLIC WELFARE—INSURANCE—*continued*

4054. Car insurance law enacted by a state was "an act requiring owners of certain motor vehicles and trailers to furnish security for their civil liability on account of personal injury caused by their motor vehicles and trailers," approved on May 1, 1925, by Massachusetts. Automobiles were required to carry $5,000 to $10,000 liability.

4055. Health insurance law enacted by a state was the Rhode Island Cash Sickness Compensation act, approved on April 29, 1942. It required employers to collect 1 percent from employees after June 1, 1942, on salaries up to $3,000 paid in any calendar year, and granted benefits ranging from $6.75 to $18 a week.

4056. Government-funded health care program for the poor was Medicaid, first proposed in 1958 by Democratic Congressman Aime Forand of Rhode Island. It was enacted in 1965 as an amendment (Title XIX) to the Social Security Act and became effective in 1966. Medicaid was one of the most controversial of the Johnson Administration's Great Society programs. By 1972 the program had become so expensive that the first of a series of cost-containment measures were passed, resulting in reimbursements to medical providers that were much lower than the actual cost of care, which prompted many doctors and hospitals to turn poor patients away.

4057. Health insurance plan enacted by Congress was Medicare, enacted on July 30, 1965, as an amendment (Title XVIII) to the Social Security Act. The program, which had been discussed as early as the Truman Administration, was intended to help pay the cost of medical care for people aged 65 and over. It was financed by mandatory contributions from employers, employees, and the self-employed, as well as contributions from the general revenue of the federal government. The first payments to medical providers were made on July 1, 1966. The first payments for skilled nursing facilities, made under the extended care benefit provision of the statute, were made on January 2, 1967. The first system of standard Medicare payments for the care of specific medical diagnoses was instituted in 1983. Like its companion program, Medicaid, it quickly became more expensive than anticipated.

4058. Medicare identification cards were presented to former President Harry S. Truman and his wife, Bess Wallace Truman, by President Lyndon Baines Johnson at the Truman Library, Independence, MO, on January 20, 1966.

4059. No-fault car insurance law enacted by a state was enacted by Massachusetts, "an act providing for compulsory personal injury protection for all registered motor vehicles, defining such protection, restricting the right to claim damages for pain and suffering in certain actions of tort, regulating further the premium charges for compulsory automobile insurance and amending certain laws relating thereto." The act was approved by Governor Francis Williams Sargent on August 13, 1970. It permitted policyholders to collect up to $2,000 for medical expenses and out-of-pocket costs including wages, to be paid directly by the insurance company, irrespective of fault. A similar law had been enacted previously by Puerto Rico.

4060. Year in which Medicare spending declined was fiscal year 1999, which ended on September 30, 1999. The Treasury Department reported that spending for Medicare by the federal government declined by 1 percent during that period, decreasing from $213.6 billion in fiscal year 1998 to $212 billion, $19 billion less than was predicted by the Congressional Budget Office. The Medicare program, which was founded in 1965 to provide health-care benefits to elderly and disabled people, reached an annual increase rate of 10 percent during the 1990s.

PUBLIC WELFARE—NARCOTICS

4061. Narcotics tariff enacted by Congress was enacted by the Tariff Act of August 30, 1842, which placed a levy of 75 cents a pound on opium. Prior to this act, opium was exempted from duty by the act of July 14, 1832, and the act of March 2, 1833. The McKinley Tariff Act of October 1, 1890, provided for an internal revenue tax of $10 a pound upon all opium manufactured in the United States for smoking purposes, and limited the manufacture to United States citizens.

4062. Narcotics ban enacted by Congress was enacted on February 9, 1909. The act made it illegal to import opium and opium derivatives into the United States, except for medicinal purposes.

4063. Drug control law enacted by Congress was the Harrison Narcotics Act of 1914, sponsored by Representative Francis Burton Harrison of New York. It required sellers of narcotic drugs to register with the Internal Revenue Service.

4064. Marijuana ban enacted by Congress was the Marijuana Traffic Act of 1937, which banned the possession, cultivation, and sale of the marijuana plant and its products. It was signed into law by President Franklin Delano Roosevelt on August 2, 1937.

4065. State narcotics ban was enacted by Nevada on March 19, 1965. It stated that "the possession of dangerous drugs without a prescription is punishable as a gross misdemeanor upon first and second conviction and is punishable as a felony upon third conviction, and exempting physicians, dentists, chiropodists, veterinarians, pharmacists, manufacturers, wholesalers, jobbers and laboratories, and exempting ranchers under certain conditions."

4066. Office of National Drug Control Policy was established by the National Narcotics Leadership Act of 1988, effective January 29, 1989, as amended by the Violent Crime Control and Law Enforcement Act of 1994, to coordinate federal, state, and local antidrug efforts. The director of National Drug Control Policy is appointed by the president with the advice and consent of the Senate.

4067. Federal drug control chief was William J. Bennett, the former secretary of education, who was named to the newly created post of director of national drug control policy by President George Bush in 1989. The press quickly gave Bennett the informal title of "drug czar." At the time, an estimated 14.5 million Americans were using illegal drugs at least once a month. Bennett's plan, announced on September 5, 1989, included new policing efforts funded by the federal government.

PUBLIC WELFARE—PRIVACY

4068. National identification scheme for American citizens was the Social Security number, made possible under the Social Security Act approved by President Franklin Delano Roosevelt on August 14, 1935. The act authorized some form of record-keeping scheme for participants in the program. A number scheme was formalized under Treasury Decision 4704 of 1936, which required the issuance of an account number to each employee covered by Social Security. Approximately 30 million applications for SSNs were processed between November 1936 and June 30, 1937. Although the federal government has resisted calling the Social Security Number a "national identifier," the SSN has functioned unofficially in that capacity since 1943, when Executive Order 9397, the first federal order mandating the use of SSNs as an employee identifier, required all federal agencies and organizations to use the SSN exclusively whenever it was advisable to set up a new identification system for individuals. In 1962 the Internal Revenue Service adopted the SSN as its official taxpayer identification number; in 1967, the Department of Defense adopted the SSN in lieu of the military service number for identifying Armed Forces personnel; and the Social Security Amendments of 1972 authorized the enumeration of children when they first enter school.

4069. Law limiting the use of Social Security numbers was the Privacy Act of 1974, enacted by Congress effective September 27, 1975, to limit governmental use of the SSN. It provided that "no state or local government agency may withhold a benefit from a person simply because the individual refuses to furnish his or her SSN." This act was the first mention of the use of Social Security numbers by local governments.

4070. Law making misuse of Social Security numbers a federal crime was the Tax Reform Act of 1976, which included the following amendments to the Social Security Act: "To make misuse of the SSN for any purpose a violation of the Social Security Act; To make, under federal law, unlawful disclosure or compelling disclosure of the SSN of any person a felony, punishable by fine and/or imprisonment." The Social Security Benefits Act of 1981 made it a federal crime to alter or forge a Social Security card.

4071. Law making identity theft a federal crime was the Identity Theft and Assumption Deterrence Act of 1998, which made transferring or using another person's means of identification a crime subject to federal penalties. Means of identification was defined as including name, Social Security number, date of birth, official state or federal driver's license or identification number, alien registration number, government passport number, and employer or taxpayer identification number.

4072. State criminal prosecution for the sale of confidential personal information took place on June 25, 1999, when private detective James J. Rapp and his wife, Regana L. Rapp, both of Aurora, CO, were indicted by a grand jury on two counts each of racketeering. They were believed to have sold personal information, including credit card records, confidential phone numbers, and bank account registers, to anyone willing to pay the price, including crim-

PUBLIC WELFARE—PRIVACY—*continued*

inals. While it is not a federal crime to impersonate anyone except a law officer or government official, it is against the law in the state of Colorado to impersonate someone else for gain.

PUBLIC WELFARE—SOCIAL SECURITY

4073. Federal social security system was established by the Social Security Act of August 14, 1935. It authorized the appointment of a three-member board to administer a federal system of old-age insurance benefits, approve state unemployment compensation laws, and administer grants-in-aid to the states to help the needy aged, the blind, and dependent children. These programs, and others added later, were funded by mandatory contributions by workers, employers, and the self-employed, and provided coverage to people with a documented history of employment. Several groups of unemployment insurance cards were issued simultaneously, so that the recipient of the first social security card is not known. The first monthly payment was made to Ida May Fuller of Ludlow, VT, who received check No. 00-000-001 for $22.54, dated January 31, 1940. By 1975, when she died at the age of 100, she had received more than $20,000 in benefits.

4074. Independent agency for administering Social Security was the Social Security Administration, established by Reorganization Plan No. 2 of 1946, effective July 16, 1946. The SSA was made an independent agency by the Social Security Independence and Program Improvements Act of 1994, effective March 31, 1995. The original Social Security Act was approved by President Franklin Delano Roosevelt on August 14, 1935. The SSA manages the nation's social insurance program, consisting of retirement, survivors, and disability insurance programs.

PUBLIC WELFARE—TOBACCO

4075. Tobacco tax enacted by a colony was authorized on October 3, 1632, by the Massachusetts Court of Assistants and General Court, which ruled in Boston "that no person shall take any tobacco publicly, under pain of punishment; also that everyone shall pay 1d. for every time he is convicted of taking tobacco in any place, and that any Assistant shall have power to receive evidence and give order for the levying of it, as also to give order for the levying of the officer's charge. This order to begin the tenth of November next."

4076. Smoking ban enacted by a colony was the work of Willem Kieft, the third governor of New Netherlands (later New York City). In 1637, he introduced an ordinance to outlaw tobacco use and trade everywhere in the colony.

4077. Tobacco tax enacted by Congress was levied in 1794, but after two years it was abandoned. A similar attempt was made in 1812 and repealed in 1816.

4078. Tobacco tax enacted by the federal government for internal revenue purposes was levied by an act of Congress of July 1, 1862.

4079. Federal cigarette tax was levied by the United States under an act of Congress of June 30, 1864. The system of placing stamps on each package to indicate payment of tax was inaugurated in 1868.

4080. State cigarette tax was established on April 11, 1921, when Iowa enacted a tax applicable to cigarettes, cigarette papers, and cigarette tubes. The tax on cigarettes was one mill on each cigarette ($1 per 1,000). This act repealed an existing law prohibiting the sale of cigarettes in Iowa.

4081. Federal regulations restricting tobacco sales to minors were implemented on February 28, 1997, by the Food and Drug Administration, which required retailers to check the ages of all customers younger than 27 in order to prevent persons under 18 years of age from buying tobacco. Store owners caught selling cigarettes and other tobacco products to minors faced federal fines of $250 per violation. All states already had laws banning the sale of tobacco to persons under 18.

PUBLIC WELFARE—TRANSPORTATION

4082. Traffic law enacted by a colony was passed on June 27, 1652, by New Amsterdam (the future New York City): "The Director General and Council of New Netherland in order to prevent accidents do hereby ordain that no Wagons, Carts or Sleighs shall be run, rode or driven at a gallop within this city of New Amsterdam, that the drivers and conductors of all Wagons, Carts and Sleighs within this city (the Broad Highway alone excepted) shall walk by the Wagons, Carts or Sleighs and so take and lead the horses, on the penalty of two pounds Flemish for the first time, and for the second time double, and for the third time to be arbitrarily corrected therefor and in addition to be responsible for all damages which may arise therefrom."

4083. State toll bridge was built over the Newbury River at Rowley, MA, in 1654 by authority of the General Court of Massachusetts. The builder and toll collector was Richard Thurley, who charged two shillings a head for cows, oxen, and horses, and a half shilling for sheep, hogs, and goats.

4084. Federal highway was the Cumberland Road, also called the National Road. In April 1802 Congress appropriated funds for the construction of a toll-free paved road from the mid-Atlantic region to Ohio and the Northwest Territory. Completed in 1837, it followed the route of the present U.S. Route 40, from Cumberland, MD, to Vandalia, IL. In 1833, financing was turned over to the states, which began charging tolls.

4085. State aid to railroads was granted by Illinois, which was empowered by Congress on March 2, 1833, to sell land it had acquired from the federal government and to use the proceeds to aid in the construction of railroads. This grant did not become effective and was not used by the state.

4086. Steamboat inspection authorized by Congress was authorized on July 7, 1838, for the "better security of the lives of passengers on board of vessels propelled in whole or in part by steam." Inspectors were appointed by federal district judges and received $5 for each inspection. They gave the owners a certificate stating the age of the boat and the soundness of the vessel. An annual inspection was required.

4087. Land-grant railroad was the Illinois Central Railroad, chartered in 1851 under congressional act of September 20, 1850. More than 2.5 million acres of public land were granted to the railroad's developers, who sold most of the acreage to raise money with which to build the line. It was finished in 1856 and linked Chicago with Galena and Cairo.

4088. State railroad safety law was passed by Georgia on March 5, 1856. The law, which made railroad companies liable for injuries to employees and passengers caused by negligence, was "an act to define the liability of the several railroad companies of this state for injuries to persons or property, to prescribe in what counties they may be sued, and how served with process."

4089. Transcontinental railroad was completed on May 10, 1869, when Senator Leland Stanford drove a golden spike into the Union Pacific's rails at Promontory, UT, completing a rail network that stretched across the country and that was made up of numerous railroad companies. The stretch completed last was begun in 1866 by the Union Pacific in Sacramento, CA, and the Central Pacific in Omaha, NE.

4090. Roads improvement aid bill enacted by a state was "an act to provide for the more permanent improvement of the public roads of this state," passed on April 14, 1891, by New Jersey and signed by Governor Leon Abbett. It placed the administration of state aid under the direction of the president of the State Board of Agriculture, who served without fee or reward for two and a half years. On March 29, 1892, the act was amended to provide for the appointment of a commissioner of public roads. The first commissioner was Edward Burroughs, appointed on May 17, 1894.

4091. Railroad safety law enacted by Congress was the Safety Appliance Act, passed on March 2, 1893, "an act to promote the safety of employees and travelers upon railroads by compelling common carriers engaged in interstate commerce to equip their cars with automatic couplers and continuous brakes and their locomotives with driving wheel brakes, and for other purposes."

4092. Federal road agency was the Office of Road Inquiry, established in the Department of Agriculture by statute approved on March 3, 1893, "to make inquiries in regard to the systems of road management throughout the United States, to make investigations in regard to the best method of road making, to prepare publications on this subject suitable for distribution." General Roy Stone was appointed head of the new organization as special agent and engineer for Road Inquiry.

4093. License plates for vehicles were required by New York State under a law that took effect on April 25, 1901. Owners of automobiles were obliged to register their names and addresses and a description of their machines with the office of the secretary of state. Each owner received a small license plate, at least three inches high, which bore the owner's initials. The registration fee was one dollar. In 1901 fees totaling $954 were received, and in 1902, $1,082. Modern-style license plates were issued by Connecticut and became effective on March 1, 1937. The plates, of plain aluminum, had black letters. A changeable colored insert designated the year.

PUBLIC WELFARE—TRANSPORTA-
TION—*continued*

4094. Speeding driver law enacted by a state was passed by the General Assembly of Connecticut on May 21, 1901. The bill, which was introduced by State Representative Robert Woodruff of Orange, CT, provided that the speed of all motor vehicles should not exceed 12 miles per hour on country highways and eight miles per hour on highways within city limits.

4095. Railroad operated by the federal government was the Alaska Railroad, acquired under the Alaska Railroad Enabling Act of March 12, 1914, from various private railroad companies. The golden spike marking the completion of the rail network was driven by President Warren Gamaliel Harding at Nenana, AK, on July 15, 1923. The railroad, which operated 478 miles of track, was under the control of the Federal Railroad Administration within the Department of Transportation.

4096. Federal advisory committee on aeronautics was established by act of Congress, approved on March 3, 1915. The membership, appointed by the president, consisted of two representatives each from the aviation sections of the War and Navy departments, one each from the Smithsonian Institution, the Weather Bureau, and the Bureau of Standards, and eight others "acquainted with the needs of aeronautical science, either civil or military, or skilled in aeronautical engineering or its allied sciences." The first chairman was Brigadier General George Percival Scriven. Naval Constructor Holden Chester Richardson was secretary. The committee was appointed on April 2, 1915, and the organizational meeting was held on April 23, 1915.

4097. Government operation of railroads began on January 1, 1918, during World War I. A proclamation was made by President Woodrow Wilson on December 26, 1917, and William Gibbs McAdoo, secretary of the treasury, was appointed director general of the nationalized rail system. The railroads were returned to private ownership on March 1, 1920.

4098. Nationwide highway planning surveys authorized by Congress were included in the Hayden-Cartwright Act, approved on June 18, 1934. The surveys were designed to obtain traffic volume, load weight, and other information needed for the rational planning of a nationwide system of interstate highways. They were made by the Bureau of Public Roads of the Department of Agriculture, in cooperation with state highway departments.

4099. Mediation agency for railroads and commercial aviation was the National Mediation Board, created on June 21, 1934, by amendment of the Railway Labor Act. It assists in maintaining a free flow of commerce in the railroad and airline industries by resolving disputes that could disrupt travel or imperil the economy. The board also handles railroad and airline employee representation disputes, and provides administrative and financial support in adjusting minor grievances in the railroad industry.

4100. Federal motor carrier legislation was the act of August 9, 1935, to amend the Interstate Commerce Act "by providing for the regulation of the transportation of passengers and property by motor carriers operating in interstate or foreign commerce."

4101. Civil Aeronautics Authority was created by act of Congress passed on June 23, 1938, "to create a Civil Aeronautics Authority and to promote the development and safety and to provide for the regulation of civil aeronautics." It was established as an independent agency composed of a five-member board, an administrator, and a three-member Air Safety Board.

4102. Seat belt law enacted by a state was enacted by Illinois on June 27, 1955, and signed by Governor William Grant Stratton on July 6, 1955. The law provided that on or after July 1, 1956, no new motor vehicle could be registered unless equipped with seat belt attachments conforming to the specifications of the Society of Automotive Engineers.

4103. Statewide automotive emissions standards were instituted in 1959 by the California legislature, which passed a statute requiring all cars sold in the state to be outfitted with a $7 "blow-by" valve to recycle crankcase emissions.

4104. National railroad was the National Railroad Passenger Corporation, commonly known as Amtrak, established in 1970 under the Rail Passenger Service Act to provide a balanced national transportation system by developing, operating, and improving U.S. intercity rail passenger service. By the late 1990s, Amtrak operated an average of 212 trains per day, serving more than 540 stations in 45 states, and maintained a track system of approximately 24,500 route miles.

4105. Speed limit for highway traffic established by Congress was enacted in 1974 in an effort to conserve fuel during the energy crisis of the 1970s. The speed limit was set at 55 miles per hour. The law was repealed on November 28, 1995, after which most states proceeded to raise their speed limits to 65 miles per hour or higher, despite ample evidence that the lower speed limit resulted in fewer deaths in traffic accidents.

4106. Federal agency promoting safe transportation was the National Transportation Safety Board, which seeks to ensure that all types of transportation in the United States are conducted safely. Established as an independent agency on April 1, 1975, by the Independent Safety Board Act of 1974, the NTSB investigates accidents, conducts studies, and makes recommendations to government agencies and the transportation industry on safety measures and practices.

4107. Air bag requirement by the federal government took effect on September 1, 1989, when all newly manufactured cars were required to have air bags installed on the driver's side.

R

RESOURCE MANAGEMENT—AGRICULTURE

4108. Colony to order surplus crops destroyed was Virginia, whose General Assembly voted on January 6, 1639, to require the burning of excess tobacco in order to bolster the price. The decree said: "Tobacco by reason of excessive quantities made, being so low that the planters could not subsist by it or be enabled to raise more staple commodities or pay their debts, enacted that the tobacco of that year be viewed by sworn viewers and the rotten and unmerchantable, and half the good to be burned, so the whole quantity made would come to 1,500,000 pounds without stripping and smoothing."

4109. State agricultural board was provided for in New York State by a law passed April 7, 1819, but was not actually organized until January 20, 1820. It was made up wholly of agricultural society delegates and was a quasi-public organization.

4110. Agricultural appropriation by a state for carrying out extension training work along agricultural lines was made by New York on May 12, 1894, when Governor Roswell Pettibone Flower signed the act "to amend the agricultural law in relation to agricultural experiment stations within this state, and to make an appropriation therefor." The appropriation was $16,000.

4111. Federal horse farm was the United States Morgan Horse Farm, established in 1907 in Middlebury, VT. The development of a utility horse suitable for American needs had been a project of the federal government since 1904.

4112. Federal Office of Agricultural Markets was created on May 16, 1913, by the secretary of agriculture. The sum of $50,000 was appropriated for its operation. The first chief was Charles John Brand, who served from May 16, 1913, to June 30, 1919. In the appropriation act of June 30, 1914, a similar paragraph was headed "Office of Markets" and the amount increased to $200,000. The Office of Markets and the Office of Rural Organization were combined on July 1, 1914, and the resulting unit was called the Office of Markets and Rural Organization. It was changed to the Bureau of Markets by the act of March 4, 1917.

4113. Federal farm loan board was created in the Department of the Treasury to administer the Federal Farm Loan Act, approved by Congress on July 17, 1916. The first federal land bank was chartered on March 1, 1917, and the first national farm loan association on March 27, 1917. The first farm loan commissioner was George William Norris, who took the oath of office on August 7, 1916. Executive Order No. 6084 of March 27, 1933, effective May 27, 1933, transferred its functions to the Farm Credit Administration.

4114. Federal farm board met on July 15, 1929. It consisted of eight members appointed by the president and confirmed by the Senate, in addition to the secretary of agriculture, who was an ex-officio member. The board was organized "to protect, control and stabilize the currents of interstate and foreign commerce" by minimizing speculation, by preventing inefficient and wasteful distribution, by encouraging farmers' organizations, and by preventing surpluses through orderly production. The Agricultural Marketing Act, passed by Congress on June 15, 1929, authorized $500 million to be used by the board as a revolving fund. The board was later designated as the Farm Credit Administration.

RESOURCE MANAGEMENT—AGRICULTURE—continued

4115. Grain stabilization corporation was authorized on February 10, 1930, under an act of Congress approved on June 15, 1929. It was composed of 28 members. The first president was George Sparks Milnor.

4116. Farm credit administration was authorized on March 27, 1933, by executive order of President Franklin Delano Roosevelt under power granted by the 73rd Congress's special session "Economy Act." The administration was "to provide a complete and coordinated credit system for agriculture by making available to farmers long-term and short-term credit" Henry Morgenthau, Jr., was the first administrator.

4117. Federal regulatory agency for agricultural lending was the Farm Credit Administration, established by Executive Order 6084 of March 27, 1933. The FCA was responsible for ensuring the safe and sound operation of the banks, associations, affiliated service organizations, and other entities of the Farm Credit System, and for protecting the interests of the public and those who borrow from Farm Credit institutions or invest in Farm Credit securities.

4118. Agricultural Adjustment Administration was authorized by act of Congress "to relieve the existing national economic emergency by increasing purchasing power." The act, approved May 12, 1933, was known as the Agricultural Adjustment Act. The first administrator was George Nelson Peek of Moline, IL, named May 4, 1933, who served under Henry Agard Wallace, secretary of agriculture, until December 15, 1933, when he was appointed President Franklin Delano Roosevelt's special advisor on commercial policy.

4119. Federal Crop Insurance Corporation was established by the Federal Crop Insurance Act, part of the Agricultural Adjustment Act of 1938, approved on February 16, 1938, to provide for insuring wheat yields against natural hazards such as drought, flood, hail, winterkill, lightning, insect infestation and plant diseases. The directors were Milburn Lincoln Wilson, Jesse Washington Tapp, and Rudolph Martin Evans. The first insurance payment, in the sum of $129.32, was made on April 14, 1939, to John F. Biggs, Floydada, Floyd County, TX, to compensate him for the total loss of his share in a 52-acre wheat crop.

RESOURCE MANAGEMENT—CONSERVATION AND ENVIRONMENT

4120. Political speech on conservation was delivered on September 30, 1847, by Vermont congressman George Perkins Marsh to the Agricultural Society of Rutland County. He called attention to the destructive impact of deforestation and advocated the careful management of forested lands. Marsh's speech was published in 1848.

4121. Conservationist document submitted to Congress was the two-volume *Report of the Commissioner of Patents, for the Year 1849* (House of Representatives Executive Document No. 20), compiled by Thomas Ewbank, the United States commissioner of patents. Ewbank noted that "the waste of valuable timber in the United States, to say nothing of firewood, will hardly begin to be appreciated until our population reaches fifty millions. Then the folly and shortsightedness of this age will meet with a degree of censure and reproach not pleasant to contemplate." Ewbank also forecast the destruction of the great bison herds of the Great Plains, due to "the ceaseless war carried on against them," and urged Congress to protect them.

4122. State environmental protection law enacted in connection with advertising was passed by New York on March 28, 1865, amending an 1853 law entitled "an act for the more effectual prevention of wanton and malicious mischief and to prevent the defacement of natural scenery." The amendment declared that painting and printing upon stones, rocks, or trees and the defacement of natural scenery in certain localities constituted a misdemeanor punishable by a fine not exceeding $250, or six months' imprisonment, or both.

4123. President with an environmental agenda was Theodore Roosevelt, who took office in 1901, at a time when the country's natural resources were being exploited by business interests, including power companies, livestock ranchers, and timber and mining companies. Roosevelt took the novel position, now commonly accepted, that the federal government has an obligation to preserve and control these resources for the benefit of the nation as a whole. During his administration, he established programs to reclaim arid land and protect forest reserves; created four volunteer commissions to oversee the regulation of inland waterways and other resources; and added 194 million acres to the lands under federal protection, five times the combined amount set aside by Benjamin Harrison, Grover Cleveland, and William McKinley.

4124. Environmental meeting for state governors was the Governors' Conference on the Conservation of Natural Resources, held on May 13–15, 1908, at the White House. It was organized and financed by National Forest Service chief Gifford Pinchot. Proceedings of the conference were published in 1909.

4125. National Conservation Commission was appointed in June 1908 by President Theodore Roosevelt to compile a national inventory of natural resources and present conservation policy recommendations to Congress. The commission's chairman was Gifford Pinchot, director of the recently created Forest Service. A three-volume report was submitted to Congress in early 1909.

4126. International conservation conference in which the United States participated was the North American Conservation Conference, held in Washington, DC, in early 1909 at the instigation of President Theodore Roosevelt. It was also attended by representatives from Canada and Mexico.

4127. Youth conservation corps was the Civilian Conservation Corps, authorized by Congress on March 31, 1933. Intended to provide work for unemployed men, it was operated jointly by the federal departments of War, Interior, Agriculture, and Labor. The first director was Robert Fechner of Boston. Young people enrolled in the CCC lived in camps and worked on flood control, road construction, reforestation, and similar projects. The first work camp, Camp Roosevelt, opened near Luray, VA, on April 17.

4128. Federal Superfund for cleaning up toxic wastes was established by Congress on December 11, 1980. The law set aside $1.6 billion, supplied mainly from fees generated by the affected industries, to pay for the cleanup of hazardous chemicals. It was prompted by the discovery some years earlier that people living in the Love Canal neighborhood of Niagara Falls, NY, were being poisoned by toxic chemicals buried in the ground under their homes.

RESOURCE MANAGEMENT—ENERGY

4129. State gas commission was the Department of Public Utilities, established by the Massachusetts legislature on June 11, 1885, to regulate the industry, supervise the issue of capital stock, hear consumer complaints, and work for price reducations. Gas companies were required to file annual returns with the commission.

4130. Federal hydroelectric plant was the Minidoka Dam on the Snake River in Idaho, constructed by the Bureau of Reclamation, Department of the Interior. The first unit of the power plant was started on May 1, 1909, and had a capacity of 1,400 kilovolt amperes.

4131. County hydroelectric plant was built on the Flint River in Crisp County, GA, and went into service on August 1, 1930. Emmet Stephen Killebrew was the chief engineer. It had a capacity of 14,000 horsepower and produced 47 million kilowatt-hours per year.

4132. Electric power contract between a city and the federal government was signed by J. P. Nanney, mayor of Tupelo, MS, and Arthur Ernest Morgan, chairman of the Tennessee Valley Authority, on November 11, 1933. It went into effect on February 7, 1934. The 20-year contract required the city to purchase electricity from TVA and sell it to its customers at rates agreed upon with the Authority. The electricity cost the city of Tupelo about 5.5 mills per kilowatt hour.

4133. State in which all electricity came from public power plants was Nebraska. In 1945, the creation of the Omaha Public Power District consolidated all private electricity generation into a public authority.

4134. Regulating agency of the nuclear industry was the Atomic Energy Commission, established by the Atomic Energy Act of 1946, which was signed into law by President Harry S. Truman on August 1, 1946. It took over the research and other programs of the Manhattan Engineer District of the U.S. Army Corps of Engineers, which had developed the atomic bomb. The AEC's function was to control the development of military and civilian uses of nuclear energy. The AEC's licensing, oversight, and related regulatory functions were transferred to the Nuclear Regulatory Commission (NRC) under the provisions of the Energy Reorganization Act of 1974, effective January 19, 1975.

4135. Commercial-scale synthetic fuels plant owned by the federal government was a plant constructed at Beulah, ND, beginning in 1980. It was designed to convert lignite into natural gas, as part of an effort to increase the nation's domestic capacity to produce petrofuels. In 1985, with the default of $1.5 billion in federally guaranteed loans and a slump in foreign oil prices, the plant passed into the hands of the U.S. Department of Energy, which vainly sought a buyer.

RESOURCE MANAGEMENT—FORESTRY

4136. Colonial forestry law was the act of March 29, 1626, passed by the Plymouth Colony, which required the approval of the governor and the council to sell or transport lumber out of the colony.

4137. State forestry inquiry commission was appointed by Wisconsin under act of March 23, 1867. The state agricultural society and the state horticultural society were each authorized to appoint one person, these two to appoint a third, to constitute a committee "to inquire and make report in detail" on "increasing the growth and preservation of forest and other trees." The first commissioners were Increase Allen Lapham, Joseph Gillett Knapp, and Hans Crocker. Their findings were issued in 1867 in *Report on the Disastrous Effects of the Destruction of Forest Trees.*

4138. Federal law encouraging settlers to grow trees was the "Act to encourage the Growth of Timber on Western Prairies," better known as the Timber Culture Act, passed by Congress in 1873. Under the law, settlers were granted 160-acre plots of federal land if they cultivated trees on 40 acres of the land for ten years. It was repealed in 1891 by the Forest Reserve Act, which laid the foundation for the national forest system.

4139. Forestry association of national importance was the American Forestry Association, organized on September 10, 1875, in Chicago, IL. The first president was Robert Douglas and the first secretary was Henry H. McAfee, professor of Horticulture and Forestry at Iowa State College. Douglas immediately resigned and Dr. John Aston Warder was elected in his place. The American Forestry Congress (organized in Cincinnati, OH, on April 25, 1882) merged with the American Forestry Association at a meeting held on June 29, 1882, in Rochester, NY. It was incorporated on January 25, 1897.

4140. State forestry association was the Minnesota Forestry Association, organized on January 12, 1876, in St. Paul, MN, to promote the planting of forest trees. E. F. Drake was president and Leonard B. Hodges secretary. On March 2, 1876, the state appropriated $2,500 to carry on the work.

4141. Forestry supervision by the federal government was begun on August 15, 1876, after an appropriation for this purpose was provided by an amendment to the appropriations act for the year ending June 30, 1877. The total appropriation for the Division of Forestry for the fiscal year 1877 was $10,000, including $2,000 for salaries and $8,000 for the "purpose of enabling the Commissioner of Agriculture to experiment and to continue an investigation and report upon the subject of forestry and the collection and distribution of valuable economic forest-tree seeds and plants." Franklin Benjamin Hough was placed in charge of the survey on August 30, 1876.

4142. State forest commission was the Board of Forestry of California, authorized by the legislature on March 3, 1885. The first meeting was held on April 1, 1885, in San Francisco, CA. James V. Coleman was elected chairman.

4143. Forest service of the United States was organized as the Division of Forestry and received permanent statutory recognition by the act of June 30, 1886. Dr. Bernhard Eduard Fernow was the first chief and served until 1898. By the act of March 2, 1901, the Division of Forestry became the Bureau of Forestry. The congressional act of February 1, 1905, signed by President Theodore Roosevelt, provided for the transfer of Forest Reserves from the Department of the Interior to the Department of Agriculture, opened natural resources of the forests to legitimate use, and stabilized principles of reserving for public purposes the federally owned forest lands. The Appropriation Act of March 3, 1905, designated the old Bureau of Forestry as the Forest Service.

4144. Federal foresting project was undertaken in the sand hills of Nebraska, four miles west of Swan, NE, to stop sand erosion. The land was acquired under authority of the act of March 3, 1891, "an act to repeal timber culture laws, and for other purposes." Jack and Norway pines were planted.

4145. Forest and fish reserve was the Afognak Forest and Fish-Culture Reserve, a protected tract of land in Alaska created in 1892 by proclamation of President Benjamin Harrison. This was the first national wildlife refuge, although it was not formally known as such.

RESOURCE MANAGEMENT—PARKS

4146. National reservation was Hot Springs National Park in Arkansas, consisting of 911 acres with 46 hot springs. It was established as a reservation by an act of Congress on April 20, 1832, and was designated as a national park on March 4, 1921.

4147. State park was the Yosemite Valley park in California, an area embracing the valley itself and the Mariposa Grove of Big Trees some miles south of it. It was granted to the state of California by act of Congress of June 30, 1864, but actual control of the area and its development were delayed some 10 years by the adverse claims of settlers in the area. The Yosemite National Park was created in 1890, and in 1905 the California State Legislature passed an act of retrocession by which the valley and grove were returned to the federal government to be included in the national park.

4148. National park was the Yellowstone National Park in Wyoming, authorized on March 1, 1872, by "an act to set aside a certain tract of land (2,142,720 acres) lying near the headwaters of the Yellowstone River as a public park." The first superintendent was Nathaniel Pitt Langford. The first ranger, hired in 1880, was Harry Yount, a Civil War veteran. Additional grants of land to Yellowstone Park were later made in Wyoming, Montana, and Idaho.

4149. Federal law forbidding hunting on national park land was the "Act to Protect the Birds and Animals in Yellowstone National Park," better known as the National Park Protective Act, enacted in 1894 by Congress.

4150. National monument designated by the federal government was the Devils Tower, a massive fluted column of volcanic rock 865 feet tall in the Black Hills at Belle Fourche River, WY. The base of this gray igneous rock is 1,700 feet in diameter. President Theodore Roosevelt signed a bill on September 24, 1906, establishing 1,153 acres as a national monument.

4151. National Parks Conference was convened in 1911 at Yellowstone National Park to discuss the formation of a National Park Service. Attending were members of the Interior Department and Forest Service, a group of park resort owners, and railroad officials. Additional conferences were held in 1912, 1915, and 1917.

4152. National Park Service was created by act of August 25, 1916, to promote and regulate the use of the federal areas known as national parks, monuments and reservations. The secretary of the Treasury appointed Stephen Tyng Mather director and Horace Marden Albright as assistant director.

4153. National Parks Association was founded in 1919 in Washington, DC, by Robert Sterling Yard, a retiring Park Service official. The privately staffed and funded organization, organized to build, protect, and educate about the national park system, was renamed the National Parks and Conservation Association in 1970.

4154. Wilderness area to be formally named was the Gila Wilderness Area, a rugged 500,000-acre tract of mountains, canyons, and hidden meadows on the continental divide. It was established in 1924 as part of the Gila National Forest in New Mexico after a long effort by Forest Service conservationists Arthur Carhart and Aldo Leopold. Leopold first published an argument for a permanent wilderness area within the Gila National Forest in the November 1925 issue of *Outdoor Life* magazine.

4155. National seashore was Cape Hatteras National Seashore, an area of 30,319 acres along the coast of North Carolina. Set aside by Congress in 1937, it was one of the longest stretches of undeveloped shoreline on the Atlantic seaboard.

4156. Conservation park dedicated to Theodore Roosevelt was the Theodore Roosevelt National Memorial Park, which was dedicated on June 4, 1949, at Medora, ND. It was created in recognition of Roosevelt's concern for the conservation of natural resources and wildlife.

4157. Federal undersea park was the Key Largo Coral Reef Preserve, an area 21 miles long and 3.5 miles wide in the Atlantic Ocean off Key Largo, FL, which was established on March 15, 1960, by presidential proclamation of President Dwight David Eisenhower. This wildlife refuge contains 40 of the 52 known coral species. Previously, it had been the John Pennekamp Coral Reef State Park, the title to which had been obtained on December 3, 1959, by the Florida Board of Parks and Historic Monuments.

4158. Federal network of protected wilderness was the National Wilderness Preservation System, created by the Wilderness Act of September 3, 1964, an act "to secure for the American people of present and future generations the benefits of an enduring resource of wilderness." In the first year of the program, 54 areas of federally owned wilderness, totaling some 9.1 million acres, were protected.

RESOURCE MANAGEMENT—PARKS—
continued

4159. African-American history trail was the Black History Trail, dedicated in Washington, DC, in 1988. The seven-and-a-half-mile trail visited important sites in African-American history. It was the brainchild of Willard Andre Hutt, who came up with the idea in 1978, when he was a 17-year-old Boy Scout.

RESOURCE MANAGEMENT—POLLUTION AND WASTE

4160. Survey of urban air pollution was undertaken in 1926 in Salt Lake City, UT.

4161. Smoke control ordinance was adopted by the city of St. Louis, MO, in 1941. The law was prompted by serious smog episodes that took place in 1939, caused mainly by the burning of soft coal for heating and power generation. Residents were encouraged to switch to hard coal and fuel oil.

4162. Air pollution control bureau was the Los Angeles, CA, Air Pollution Control District, formed in 1947.

4163. Water pollution law enacted by Congress was the Water Pollution Control Act, which took effect on June 30, 1948. It provided funds for sewage treatment systems and pollution research and empowered the Justice Department to file suit against polluters.

4164. City to discontinue garbage collection because of the installation of waste disposing units was Jasper, IN, which discontinued service on August 1, 1950. The reduction of taxes by a corresponding amount helped homeowners amortize the cost of their disposal units.

4165. Large area of the United States contaminated by nuclear radiation was a 250-square-mile area of Nevada desert, contaminated by plutonium-237 from numerous above-ground nuclear tests conducted from the 1950s through the early '60s. People picnicked outside the test range to watch the first blast, which took place in 1951. The Atomic Energy Commission officially revealed the contamination problem in 1971.

4166. Air pollution law of importance enacted by Congress was the Clean Air Act of 1963, signed into law on December 17, 1963. It authorized $93 million in matching grants for state-funded air pollution prevention and control programs. The Clean Air Act of 1970, signed into law on December 31, 1970, was the first to set national standards for air polluting emissions from motor vehicles.

4167. State bottle bill was passed by Oregon on July 2, 1971. The law, favored by environmentalists as a way of reducing litter, prohibited the use of nonrefundable beverage bottles and cans.

4168. State litter law affecting containers of soft drinks and beer was enacted by Oregon on July 2, 1971. The bill outlawed pull-tab cans and nonreturnable bottles.

4169. Noise-control law enacted by a state was New Jersey's Noise Control Act of 1971, signed on January 24, 1972, by Governor William Thomas Cahill. The act empowered the state Department of Environmental Protection to promulgate codes, rules, and regulations to lessen noise pollution, created a Noise Control Council, and made a $100,000 appropriation.

4170. Deep underground nuclear waste storage site was the Waste Isolation Pilot Plant, located in salt beds 2,150 feet (655 meters) under the desert near Carlsbad, NM. The site, created to store hundreds of thousands of barrels of radioactive wastes from nuclear weapons production, was licensed for plutonium storage by the U.S. government on May 13, 1998. Selecting a site for long-term plutonium storage had been a matter of intense disagreement among the western states, none of which wanted the facility within their boundaries, and the federal government.

4171. Billion-dollar settlement in an environmental lawsuit was reached on October 22, 1998, between the Environmental Protection Agency and the Justice Department and seven diesel truck engine manufacturers—Caterpillar Inc., Cummins Engine Co. Inc., Navistar International Corp., the Detroit Diesel Corp., Mack Trucks, Renault SA, and Volvo—charged with violating clean air laws. The manufacturers were alleged to have sold as many as 1.3 million engines designed to evade motor vehicle pollution standards.

RESOURCE MANAGEMENT—PUBLIC LANDS

4172. Surveyed line separating North from South was the Mason-Dixon line, completed in 1767 by Charles Mason and Jeremiah Dixon to set the boundary lines between Maryland and Pennsylvania. Their work was based on the map of Virginia prepared by explorer John Smith in 1608. In the 19th century, the Mason-Dixon line, extended to the west, was held to mark the division between the free states of the North and the slaveholding states of the South.

4173. Expressions of official U.S. policy toward lands outside the 13 colonies were the Northwest Ordinances, also known as the Ordinances of 1784, 1785, and 1787, enacted by Congress to encourage the settlement and political incorporation of the Northwest Territory (the land west of Pennsylvania, north of the Ohio River, east of the Mississippi River, and south of the Great Lakes). The Ordinance of 1784, drafted by Thomas Jefferson, divided the territory into self-governing districts, each of which was allowed to send a representative to Congress when its population reached 20,000. A district was eligible for statehood when its population equaled that of the least populous existing state. The later ordinances, especially the Ordinance of 1787, expanded upon and refined this basic framework.

4174. Sale of federal land was authorized by the Continental Congress on May 20, 1785, under the Land Ordinance of 1785. The minimum size of a lot was set at 640 acres, and the minimum price per acre was set at one dollar. The price was raised to two dollars in 1796.

4175. Survey of public lands was authorized by the Land Ordinance of 1785, which was passed by the Continental Congress on May 20, 1785. The first surveys were made in the Seven Ranges in the Western Reserve (Ohio). The Ordinance of 1785 provided for the division of all public lands into townships six miles square, numbered east and west from primary meridians and north and south from base lines, containing 36 lots of 640 acres each. This rectangular system of surveying prevails throughout the United States except in the original 13 states and in Maine, Vermont, Kentucky, Tennessee, and West Virginia.

4176. Sale of federal land to an individual was authorized by act of Congress of May 17, 1796, "an act providing for the sale of the lands of the United States in the territory northwest of the River Ohio, and above the mouth of the Kentucky River." Congress granted Ebenezer Zane three tracts of land in Ohio, each one mile square, for the purpose of operating ferries: one on the Muskingum River, one on the Sciota, and one on the Hockhocking. These grants were confirmed and patented to Zane on February 14, 1800, in return for his activities in opening Zane's "trail" or "trace" in 1797. The trail, about 200 miles long, led from Wheeling, WV, through Ohio to Limestone (now Maysville), KY.

4177. Federal district land office opened on July 2, 1800, in Steubenville, OH, with David Hoge as the first registrar. It was established under the congressional act of May 10, 1800, known as the Land Act of 1800 or the Harrison Land Act, which also authorized district land offices in Cincinnati, Chillicothe, and Marietta, OH. Land was sold for two dollars an acre with a minimum purchase of 320 acres. Purchasers were given four years to complete the payment and received a discount of 8 percent if they paid the full amount in cash. Some 398,466 acres had been sold by November 1, 1801.

4178. Land preemption act passed by Congress was enacted on March 3, 1801, giving the right of preemption to certain persons who had contracted with John Cleves Symmes, or his associates, for lands lying along the Miami River in what is now Ohio. These persons were living upon the lands once within the Symmes tract but were not included in the patent for the reduced area, which he finally obtained. Settlers received preference over persons desiring to purchase and hold for investment or speculation.

4179. Land subsidy by Congress for road improvements was authorized on April 30, 1802, by "an act to enable the people of the eastern division of the territory northwest of the river Ohio to form a constitution and state government, and for the admission of such state into the union on an equal footing with the original states." It authorized Ohio to appropriate a twentieth of the net proceeds of the funds received from the sale of public lands to the laying out and construction of public roads.

4180. Grant of federal land to a foreigner was enacted by Congress on March 3, 1803. The act authorized the secretary of war to issue land warrants to the Marquis de Lafayette (Major General Marie-Joseph-Paul-Yves-Roch-Gilbert du Motier) for 11,520 acres, which at his option were to be located, surveyed, and patented in conformity with the provisions of the act regulating the grants of land appropriated for military services.

4181. Large-scale free land distribution by the federal government was the Homestead Act, "an act to secure homesteads to actual settlers on the public domain," passed by both houses of Congress on May 19, 1862, and approved on May 20, 1862, by President Abraham Lincoln. Under this law, "any person who is the head of a family, or who has arrived at the age of twenty-one years, and is a citizen of the United States, or who shall have filed his

RESOURCE MANAGEMENT—PUBLIC LANDS—*continued*

declaration of intention to become such" could secure title to 160 acres of public land by living on it for five years, making certain improvements, and paying fees of approximately $18.

4182. Homestead grant under the Homestead Act was taken by Daniel Freeman, a Union soldier, on January 1, 1863, near Beatrice, NE. The Homestead National Monument of America is now located on this site.

4183. Homestead act for desert lands owned by the federal government was enacted on March 3, 1875, "to sell the desert land in Lassen County, California, at $1.25 an acre." This act differed from the Homestead Act of May 20, 1862, in that the owner was not required to reside on the land and that he could purchase four times the quantity of land permitted under the first Homestead Act.

4184. Public Lands Commission was appointed by Congress in 1879. Among its members were John Wesley Powell, Clarence Dutton, and Clarence King. After assessing the use of federal lands in the West, the commission submitted a report to Congress in late 1879.

4185. United States Geological Survey was established by Congress on March 3, 1879, as part of an appropriations bill. The Survey was designated as a bureau of the Interior Department and was given the task of classifying the public lands and examining their geological structure, mineral resources, and products. Its first director was Clarence King, nominated on March 21, 1879, and sworn in on May 24.

4186. Federal ban on fencing public lands was enacted by Congress on February 25, 1885, at the prompting of Land Commissioner William Andrew Jackson Sparks, to stop ranchers and railroad companies from gaining further control over lands in the West.

4187. Land trust was the Trustees of Public Reservations, established in 1891 by the Massachusetts legislature at the urging of Charles William Eliot, the president of Harvard University. The privately-funded, tax-exempt association was charged with protecting and preserving the state's natural and historical treasures.

4188. Rights of way on federal reserves were authorized for utilities and services in 1901 under the Right of Way Act. It allowed electrical power, telecommunication, and irrigation and water supply rights of way in national forests and parks.

4189. Bureau of Mines was established in the Department of the Interior by act of Congress approved on May 16, 1910, effective July 1. The first director was Dr. Joseph Austin Holmes. On July 1, 1925, the bureau was transferred to the Department of Commerce.

4190. Grant-in-aid enacted by Congress to help the states build roads was the Federal Aid Road Act, "to provide that the United States shall aid the states in the construction of rural post roads, and for other purposes," passed on July 11, 1916. For the fiscal year ending June 30, 1917, $5 million was appropriated, an amount that was increased by $5 million every year until 1921, when the appropriation was $25 million. The first project was in Contra Costa County, CA, for 2.55 miles between the Alameda-Contra Costa boundary and the city limits of Richmond, CA. The contract was awarded on July 10, 1916. The work cost $53,938, of which $24,247 came from the federal appropriation.

4191. Federal flood control legislation was the Flood Control Act, passed by Congress on May 15, 1928, in the wake of severe Mississippi River flooding the previous year. The Flood Control Act authorized the expenditure of $325 million over a ten-year period to pay for dams and other flood control projects to be constructed by the U.S. Army Corps of Engineers.

4192. Statewide land-use program was adopted in 1961 by Hawaii, which faced serious environmental and land-use challenges as its economy developed following the proclamation of statehood in 1959.

RESOURCE MANAGEMENT—WATER

4193. Waterpower development grant to a colonist was part of a charter obtained from the English crown in 1620 by the English mariner Sir Ferdinando Gorges, who planned to start new fiefdoms and noble estates in New England. The charter gave him the right to develop the territory lying between the 40th and 48th parallels, north latitude, from sea to sea, and required him to develop waterpower. Gorges constructed a log dam at the future site of South Berwick, ME, on that part of the Piscataqua River known as the Newwichawanick River. He erected a grist mill and sent some of the meal to England as proof that he was conforming to the agreement. The establishment of the colonies of Plymouth and Massachusetts ruined his plans, though he retained his claim to Maine.

4194. Irrigation law enacted by Congress was the act of July 26, 1866, which ruled that control of waterways was a matter of state control subject to "local customs, laws and decisions of the court."

4195. Federal law encouraging settlers to irrigate desert lands was the Desert Land Act, formally "An act to provide for the sale of desert lands in certain States and Territories," enacted by Congress in 1877. Under the law, settlers were granted up to 640 acres of arid Southwestern land at a bargain price if they agreed to irrigate it.

4196. Large-scale federal irrigation legislation was the Newlands Reclamation Act, an act "appropriating the receipts from the sale and disposal of public lands in certain States and Territories to the construction of irrigation works for the reclamation of arid lands," passed by Congress in 1902 under the sponsorship of Senator Francis G. Newlands. The act directed that proceeds from the sale of federal lands in 16 western states be deposited into a revolving fund for regional irrigation projects.

4197. Reclamation service of the federal government was the United States Reclamation Service, a bureau of the Interior Department, created by act of Congress of June 17, 1902, for reclamation of arid and semiarid lands. It was an outgrowth of the United States Geological Survey, authorized on March 30, 1888.

4198. Irrigation project authorized by the federal government was the Tonto Basin Dam, now the Theodore Roosevelt Dam, in the Tonto Basin in Arizona. It was approved by President Roosevelt in 1903 and completed in 1911. The dam is located 76 miles northeast of Phoenix at the confluence of the Salt River and Tonto Creek where it is operated and maintained by the Salt River Project. The dam created the Theodore Roosevelt Lake, now a major water recreational area in the state, and provided a stable source of water for agricultural use.

4199. American Heritage Rivers were 14 rivers and watersheds designated in 1998 by the federal government for protection. They included the New River in North Carolina, the oldest extant river in the United States; the Willamette River in Oregon; the Blackstone and Woonasquatucket Rivers in Massachusetts and Rhode Island; the Cuyahoga River in Ohio; the Detroit River in Michigan; the Hanalei River in Hawaii; the Hudson River in New York; the Rio Grande in Texas; the Potomac River in the District of Columbia, Maryland, Pennsylvania, Virginia, and West Virginia; the St. Johns River in Florida; the Upper Mississippi River in Iowa, Illinois, Minnesota, Missouri, and Wisconsin; the Lower Mississippi River in Louisiana and Tennessee; and the Upper Susquehanna and Lackawanna Rivers in Pennsylvania.

RESOURCE MANAGEMENT—WILDLIFE

4200. Hunting law enacted by a colony was passed on March 24, 1629, by Virginia and provided that "no . . . hides or skins whatever be sent or carried out of this colony upon forfeiture of thrice the value, whereof the half to the informer and the other half to public use."

4201. Fish protection law enacted by a city was an act for "preserving fish in fresh water ponds," enacted on May 28, 1734, by New York City. Fishing by hoop-net, draw-net, purse-net, catching-net, cod-net, bley-net, or with any other engine, machine, arts, or ways and means whatsoever, other than by angling with angle-rod, hook, and line, was subject to a fine of 20 shillings.

4202. State fish commission was authorized by Massachusetts on May 16, 1856, "to ascertain, and report to the next General Court, such facts respecting the artificial propagation of fish, as may tend to show the practicability and expediency of introducing the same into this Commonwealth, under the protection of law." The commission consisted of R. A. Chapman as chairman, Henry Wheatland, and N. E. Atwood.

4203. Federal law to protect fur seals was "An Act to prevent the Extermination of Fur-Bearing Animals in Alaska," passed by Congress in 1870. Seal fur was still an economically important product in the Northwest and it was feared that unregulated hunting would result in the animals' extinction.

4204. Federal office to protect U.S. fisheries was authorized by Congress on February 9, 1871. The act empowered President Ulysses Simpson Grant to appoint "from among the civil officers or employees of the Government, one person of proved scientific and practical acquaintance with the fishes of the coast to be Commissioner of Fish and Fisheries to serve without additional salary." An appropriation of $5,000 was made on March 3, 1871, for expense in "prosecuting the inquiry authorized by law into the cause of the decrease of the food fishes of the coast and lakes." The first commissioner was Spencer Fullerton Baird, who served without pay from March 8, 1871, to August 17, 1887. The first full-time salaried commissioner was Marshall McDonald, who served from February 18, 1888, to September 1, 1895.

RESOURCE MANAGEMENT—WILD-LIFE—*continued*

The office was known as the United States Fish Commission until 1903, when it was made the Bureau of Fisheries in the Department of Commerce and Labor. In 1913, when the departments were separated, the Bureau of Fisheries was placed under the jurisdiction of the Department of Commerce.

4205. Federal fish hatchery was established in Maine to increase the population of Atlantic salmon. The facility, which was run by Charles Grandison Atkins, was a joint venture of the federal government and the states of Connecticut, Massachusetts, and Maine. It opened in 1872 at Bucksport and was later moved to East Orland.

4206. Bird refuge established by a state was established at Lake Merritt, Oakland, CA, by authority of a law enacted on February 14, 1872.

4207. Federal bird protection agency was begun on July 1, 1885, as a section of Economic Ornithology, Division of Entomology, Department of Agriculture. It became the Bureau of Biological Survey on July 1, 1905, was transferred to the Department of Interior on July 1, 1939, and was consolidated with the Bureau of Fisheries on June 30, 1940, to form the present Fish and Wildlife Service.

4208. Federal act to protect salmon fisheries was "An act to provide for the protection of the salmon fisheries of Alaska," enacted by Congress in 1889.

4209. Audobon society for the protection of birds, and more generally of the natural environment, was the Massachusetts Audubon Society, founded in Boston, MA, in 1896 by Harriet Lawrence Hemenway and others. This was the start of the national Audubon movement, which spread to most states by the end of the century. The National Association of Audubon Societies for the Protection of Wild Birds and Animals was organized in New York in 1905. In 1940, the organization's name was changed to the National Audubon Society.

4210. Comprehensive federal legislation to protect wildlife was the Lacey Act, passed by Congress in 1900. It banned interstate shipping of wild animals or birds killed in violation of state laws.

4211. Federal bird reservation was established on March 14, 1903, at Pelican Island, situated in the Indian River near Sebastian, FL, by executive order of President Theodore Roosevelt. Its goal was to protect a nesting colony of pelicans and herons. This wildlife refuge was enlarged in 1909 to include adjacent mangrove islands and swamps.

4212. Federal wildlife refuge was established by executive order of President Theodore Roosevelt on March 14, 1903, at Pelican Island, situated in the Indian River near Sebastian, FL. Its goal was to protect a nesting colony of pelicans and herons. This wildlife refuge was enlarged in 1909 to include adjacent mangrove islands and swamps.

4213. Bird protection international treaty was the Migratory Bird Treaty for the protection of migratory birds in the United States and Canada, signed on August 16, 1916, by the United States and Great Britain at Washington, DC. It was signed by President Woodrow Wilson on September 1, 1916, ratified by Great Britain on October 20, and proclaimed on December 8.

4214. Game preserve appropriation by the federal government to assist state wildlife restoration projects was passed on September 2, 1937. A million dollars was appropriated on June 16, 1938. The federal government paid 75 percent of the costs of such projects and the state 25 percent. The first project was the Utah Fish and Game Commission's plan to stabilize the water levels on some 2,000 acres of land bordering Great Salt Lake, approved on July 23, 1938, by the Fish and Wildlife Service.

4215. Comprehensive wilderness law was the Wilderness Act of 1964, which led to the creation of a system of wilderness preserves. The act was the culmination of the work of several government conservationists, including Arthur Carhart, Aldo Leopold, and Robert Marshall of the Forest Service, and Howard Zahniser of the Bureau of Biological Survey.

4216. Federal endangered species list was issued by the Department of the Interior in 1966. It listed 78 species of rare and endangered plants, reptiles, birds, and mammals.

4217. State ban on the capture and display of whales and dolphins was passed by South Carolina in 1992. Sponsored by state representative Alex Harvin, the Humane Society of Columbia, and the South Carolina Association for Marine Mammal Protection, the law was intended to block the construction of a marine mammal theme park in Myrtle Beach.

S

SLAVERY

4218. Escape of slaves from a colony in what is now United States territory took place at San Miguel de Guadalupe, the first Spanish (and first European) settlement in the continental United States, which was probably located at Winyah Bay in South Carolina, at the mouth of the Pee Dee River. Among the 500 settlers who arrived in July 1526 from Hispaniola with the founder, Lucas Vazquez de Ayllón, were a number of African slaves. In November, after the death of Ayllón, some of them escaped from the settlement, presumably to live with local Native Americans. The remaining Spanish colonists returned to Hispaniola.

4219. African slaves in America arrived in 1581 at the Spanish colony of St. Augustine, FL. They belonged to King Philip II of Spain. They were not, however, the first slaves of any kind in America, since forms of slavery were practiced among Native American peoples from ancient times.

4220. Africans in the English colonies were brought to Jamestown, VA, on August 20, 1619, by a Dutch man-of-war whose captain sold 20 kidnapped Africans to the planter colonists. They were treated as indentured servants, since slavery was not legalized in Virginia for several decades. The vast majority of indentured servants in Virginia were white.

4221. African-American who was free was Anthony Johnson, who was recorded as a free citizen of Old Accomack, VA, in 1622. He had arrived in Jamestown, VA, some time earlier and, in accordance with common practice of the time, had been released after a fixed term of indentured labor. He was married to Mary Johnson, a white woman. An individual named Anthony Johnson—perhaps the same man—began importing European and African indentured servants to Virginia in 1651.

4222. Colony to legalize slavery was Massachusetts, whose law code of 1641, the *Body of Liberties,* recognized as lawful the enslavement of Native Americans and Africans as long as "unjust violence" was not employed. Slavery was given legal recognition in Virginia in 1661, in Maryland in 1663, and in New York and New Jersey in 1664.

4223. Colony to pass a slavery emancipation law was Rhode Island. The law was one of several "Acts and Orders made at the General Court of Election held at Warwick, RI, this 18th day of May, anno 1652." It contained the following provision: "No blacke mankind or white . . . [may be] forced by covenant bond or otherwise to serve any man or his assignes longer than ten years, or until they come to be 24 years of age, if they be taken in under 14, from the time of their coming within the Liberties of the Collonie, and at the end or terme of ten years . . . [are to be set] free, as is the manner with the English servants. And that man that will not let them goe free, or shall sell them away elsewhere, to that end that they may be enslaved to others for a long time, he or they shall forfeit to the Collonie forty pounds."

4224. Colonial laws making slavery lifelong and hereditary were enacted in Virginia. A law enacted in 1661 prescribed lifelong servitude, rather than a temporary period of indentured servitude, for slaves of African descent and their children. The following year, Virginia passed a law that made the status of a child dependent on the status of his or her mother, making a slave of any child whose mother was an African slave and whose father was an English colonist. This was a reversal of English law, which recognized the condition of freedom or servitude as passing through the father.

4225. Colonial law prohibiting slavery was enacted in the western part of New Jersey in 1676.

4226. Protest against slavery made by a religious group in the New World was made by the Mennonites, a pacifist Protestant sect that had emigrated in 1683 from Germany to the Quaker colony of Pennsylvania, settling at Germantown (now a neighborhood of Philadelphia). Finding that slaveowning was practiced by Quakers, they drew up a protest denouncing slavery as a form of theft, forbidden to Christians, and presented it to the local Quaker meeting on February 18, 1688. It said in part: "Pray, what thing in the world can be done worse towards us, than if men should rob or steal us away, and sell us for slaves to strange countries; separating husbands from their wives and children. Being now that this is not done in the manner we would be done at therefore we contradict and are against this traffic of men-body. And we who profess that it is not lawful to steal, must, likewise, avoid to purchase such things as are stolen, but rather help to stop this robbing and stealing if possible."

SLAVERY—*continued*

The protest was signed by Francis Daniel Pastorius, the Mennonite leader, and by Garret Henderich, Derick up den Graeff, and Abraham up den Graeff. The Quakers referred the question to the quarterly meeting, which referred it to the annual meeting, which declined to act on it, but in later years they became active abolitionists, founding the first antislavery organization.

4227. Essay calling for the abolition of slavery to be published in the British colonies was *The Selling of Joseph,* a three-page pamphlet by Samuel Sewall, justice of the superior court of Massachusetts. The pamphlet was printed in 1700 and distributed by Sewall on the streets of Boston. Comparing enslaved Africans to Joseph, the Jew who was sold into Egyptian slavery by his brothers, he wrote: "Joseph was rightfully, no more a Slave to his brethren, than they were to him, and they had not more Authority to Sell him than they had to Slay him." Sewall also wrote an essay calling for humane treatment of the Kennebeck Indians and was part of an abolitionist group, the Boston Committee of 1700, that proposed to discourage slavery by enacting a punitive tax on the importation of slaves. He had presided in 1692 over the Salem witch trials, at which he had condemned 19 defendants to death, but made a public act of repentance in 1697.

4228. Rebellion of African-American slaves in a British colony of record occurred in 1708, when seven white people were killed in New York, NY. The uprising resulted in the execution of four African-American slaves, three men and a woman. Another uprising in New York took place on April 6, 1712, and was quelled after the militia was called out.

4229. Law barring the importation of slaves into a British colony was passed on June 7, 1712, by the Pennsylvania Assembly, acting on a petition brought by William Sotheby. The law imposed a ban on the importation of both African and Native American slaves. Restrictions on the importation of slaves had already been enacted in 1708 at the request of mechanics in the building trades who wanted to avoid competition by African-American workers, but these restrictions were invalidated by the British crown, as was a 1711 law banning the slave trade.

4230. Antislavery book is likely to have been *A Brief Examination of the Practice of the Times, by the Foregoing and the Present Dispensation,* by Ralph Sandyford, a Philadelphia Quaker. It was printed in Philadelphia in 1729 by Benjamin Franklin.

4231. Abolition organization was the Society for the Relief of Free Negroes Unlawfully Held in Bondage, formed on April 14, 1775, in Philadelphia, PA. Among the founders were John Baldwin and Benjamin Rush. The society was incorporated in 1789 as the Pennsylvania Society for Promoting the Abolition of Slavery and for the Relief of Free Negroes Unlawfully Held in Bondage and for Improving the Condition of the African Race.

4232. State constitution to provide for emancipation from slavery was Vermont. The state constitution of July 2, 1777, provided that "no male person born in this country or brought from over sea, ought to be holden by law, to serve any person as a servant, slave or apprentice, after he arrives to the age of twenty-one years, nor female, in like manner, after she arrives to the age of eighteen years, unless they are bound by their own consent, after they arrive to such age, or bound by law, for the payment of debts, damages, fines, costs or the like."

4233. State to abolish slavery by a decision of the judiciary was Massachusetts, whose Supreme Judicial Court ruled in 1783 that the state's Declaration of Rights was incompatible with the institution of slavery. The decision was rendered in a suit brought by a slave named Quork Walker. It was largely the work of the chief justice, William Cushing, who was appointed an associate justice of the United States Supreme Court in 1789.

4234. Underground Railroad activities began as early as 1786, although the name did not come into use until 1830, by which time there were participants in 14 Northern states. The "conductors" were free African-Americans and antislavery whites who, in defiance of federal law, provided shelter, food, and transportation to refugees from slavery who were making their way north, often with slavehunters in pursuit. Scholars have identified more than 3,000 people who helped to run escape routes, of whom the best known are Levi Coffin, a Quaker abolitionist active in Indiana and Ohio; William Still, chairman of Philadelphia's secret network and the author of *Underground Railroad* (1872); and Harriet Tubman, an escaped slave from Maryland who succeeded in bringing out hundreds of slaves on repeated forays into the South.

4235. Suggestion that slaves be counted as full members of the population was considered by James Madison in July 1787, when he was a delegate at the Constitutional Convention in Philadelphia, PA. In the course of the debate over equal versus proportional representation, Madison developed a plan for a bicameral legislature in which representation for one chamber would be based on the free population and for the other chamber on the entire population, including slaves. He did not make a formal suggestion to the Convention. The Constitution compromised on the issue by counting each slave as three-fifths of a free person.

4236. Territory of the United States in which slavery was banned was the Northwest Territory, a region east of the Mississippi River, north of the Ohio River, south and west of the Great Lakes, and west of Pennsylvania. The Continental Congress, meeting in New York City on July 13, 1787, approved a statute prepared by Nathan Dane of Massachusetts that prohibited slavery forever within the territory's borders.

4237. Regional compromise over the issue of slavery was worked out in July, August, and September of 1787, when the delegates to the Constitution Convention in Philadelphia, PA, were negotiating some of the most delicate and contentious issues facing the federated states. Since there was no prospect of finding common ground on the problem of slavery between the views generally prevailing in the North and South, the drafters of the Constitution agreed to postpone for 20 years, until 1808, any attempt by Congress to stop the importation of slaves, and to count three-fifths of each state's African-American population when apportioning representation in the federal House of Representatives. The draft was approved by the Continental Congress on September 17, 1787.

4238. Fugitive slave law enacted by Congress was passed on February 12, 1793. It required the forcible return of slaves who had escaped. The law stated: "No person held to service or labor in one state, under the laws thereof, escaping into another, shall, in consequence of any law or regulation therein, be discharged from such service or labor, but shall be delivered up on claim of the party to whom such service or labor may be due."

4239. Petition to Congress by African-Americans was submitted in 1797 by four North Carolinians who had been freed by their owners in accordance with the owners' Quaker beliefs. The petitioners asked Congress to protect them from a state law that voided their emancipation and returned them to slavery, and to grant liberty to all the enslaved. The petition was denied.

4240. State in which slavery was illegal from the time it was admitted to the Union was Ohio, which was admitted on March 1, 1803. The following year, however, it became the first of the northern states to pass statutes impairing the civil rights of African-Americans, including restricting their freedom of movement and banning them from testifying in court.

4241. Federal ban on the importation of African slaves was enacted by Congress on March 2, 1807, effective January 1, 1808. The bill made it unlawful to import African slaves and to fit out vessels for transporting them, though it did not outlaw the owning of slaves. Congress had been prevented by the Constitution (Article I, Section 9) from legislating an end to the African slave trade before the year 1808. President Thomas Jefferson, in his Sixth Annual Message, delivered in December 1806, drew the attention of Congress to the opportunity that would soon be presented, writing: "I congratulate you, fellow-citizens, on the approach of the period at which you may interpose your authority constitutionally to withdraw the citizens of the United States from all further participation in those violations of human rights which have been so long continued on the unoffending inhabitants of Africa."

4242. Organized emigration of freed slaves to Africa commenced on February 6, 1820, when a party of former slaves took ship from New York Harbor to Freetown, Sierra Leone, then under British control. The operation was funded by the American Colonization Society, headed by Robert Finley, and by Congress, which in 1819 approved funding to repatriate Africans illegally brought to the United States after the African slave trade was abolished in 1808.

4243. Antislavery magazine was *The Emancipator*, issued monthly from April 30 to October 31, 1820. It was edited and published by Elihu Embree and cost $1 a year.

SLAVERY—*continued*

4244. Antislavery pamphlet by an African-American writer was *Walker's Appeal in 4 articles, together with a Preamble to the Colored Citizens of the World, but in Particular and very expressly to those of the U.S.A.,* published in Boston, MA, in 1829 by David Walker, a Boston businessman.

4245. Major antislavery periodical was the *Liberator,* published by William Lloyd Garrison in Boston, MA. The first issue appeared on January 1, 1831. Among antislavery activists, Garrison was a militant who demanded the immediate emancipation of all slaves, denounced the Constitution for giving slavery sanction, and spurned the Liberty (Abolition) Party, the nation's first antislavery party, because of his conviction that political action would result in moral compromise. He was also an early advocate of pacifism and women's rights.

4246. Slave rebellion after the Revolution on a large scale took place beginning August 21, 1831, in Southampton County, VA. It was led by Nat Turner, an African-American slave and religious visionary who believed that he was divinely chosen to lead his fellow slaves to freedom. With seven accomplices, Turner killed his owner, Joseph Travis, and the Travis family in their sleep, then led more than 70 followers in a two-day revolt in which 55 to 60 whites were killed. State militiamen and armed whites confronted the rebels near Jerusalem, VA, and killed as many as 100 slaves, a number of whom had not taken part in the rebellion. Turner escaped but was caught six weeks later and was hanged on November 11.

4247. African-American to give antislavery lectures was Charles Lenox Remond, who began speaking publicly in favor of abolition in 1838. He was the son of a prosperous merchant family from Salem, MA, and was an organizer of the Massachusetts Anti-Slavery Society. The first African-American woman to make speeches against slavery was Sojourner Truth, who began lecturing in 1846, speaking also on behalf of voting rights for women after 1850. Sojourner Truth had had 30 years of personal experience of slavery in New York State, until her freedom was bought for $20 by friends.

4248. Antislavery political organization was the Liberty Party, also called the Abolitionist Party, which was organized in 1839 by members of the American Antislavery Society. It advocated as much legal suppression of slavery as possible, including abolishing the interstate slave trade, outlawing slavery in the District of Columbia, rejecting the application of Texas to be annexed to the Union as a slave state, and appealing to England to buy its raw cotton from India rather than from the American South. The party's founding convention took place in Warsaw, NY, on November 13, 1839. Its presidential nominee in 1840 and 1844 was James Gillespie Birney, a former slaveowner from Kentucky who had had a change of heart.

4249. President to bring slaves with him to Washington, DC, was John Tyler, who moved his household, including the slaves, to the White House from his home in Virginia when he succeeded to the presidency in April 1841.

4250. Senator elected on an antislavery ticket was John Parker Hale of New Hampshire, who was elected on June 9, 1846, for the six-year term that began on March 4, 1847. Previously, he had served as a Democrat in the House of Representatives from March 4, 1843, to March 3, 1845.

4251. African-American captured under the Fugitive Slave Law of 1850 was James Hamlet of New York City, who was ransomed by his fellow New Yorkers in October 1850 after having been misidentified as a runaway slave the previous month. The law, passed by Congress on September 18 as part of the Compromise of 1850, expanded the power of slavehunters to arrest people identified as fugitive slaves and established penalties (a fine of $1,000 and six months' imprisonment) for anyone who failed to assist them.

4252. Speech by Abraham Lincoln denouncing slavery was delivered in Springfield, IL, on October 4, 1854, and repeated at Peoria, IL, on October 16. Lincoln was then a Springfield lawyer who had served one term in the state General Assembly and another in the U.S. House of Representatives. His address was a rejection of the Kansas-Nebraska Act, which had been passed by Congress the previous May and which allowed slavery in newly organized territories of the United States. He was nonetheless respectful of the Southern point of view and supported gradual, rather than abrupt, emancipation of African-American slaves. The address is known as Lincoln's Peoria Speech.

4253. Intervention of federal troops in a territorial conflict over slavery took place on April 22, 1856, during the violent debate over the future status of Kansas as a slave or a free state. President Franklin Pierce ordered the army into the town of Lawrence, an antislavery settlement founded by New England abolitionists, to keep the peace. In the course of 1856–57, federal troops were repeatedly ordered into Lawrence, Topeka, Lecompton, and other Kansas towns.

4254. American national constitution to expressly legitimize slavery was the Constitution of the Confederate States of America, adopted in Montgomery, AL, on March 11, 1861. While based closely on the United States Constitution, it included several clauses regarding the importation and sale of slaves. Article IV, Section 3, reads: "No slave or other person held to service or labor in any State or Territory of the Confederate States, under the laws thereof, escaping or unlawfully carried into another, shall, in consequence of any law or regulation therein, be discharged from such service or labor, but shall be delivered up on claim of the party to whom the slave belongs, or to whom such service or labor may be due."

4255. Emancipation proclamation made by President Abraham Lincoln was the Preliminary Emancipation Proclamation, issued on September 22, 1862, to take effect on January 1, 1863. It declared that "all Persons held as Slaves" in all the Confederate states, excepting a number of counties under federal control, were to be considered "forever Free." It also enjoined members of the federal armed forces from returning fugitive slaves to their owners. The Emancipation Proclamation in its final form was signed on January 1, 1863.

4256. Model community for freed slaves founded by the federal government was Freedman's Village, dedicated on December 4, 1863. It was located in the District of Columbia near the current Memorial Amphitheater. More than 1,100 freed slaves were given land by the government, where they farmed and lived during and after the Civil War. The villagers were dispossessed in 1890 when the estate was repurposed as a military installation.

STATES

4257. Treaty between states after the Declaration of Independence was concluded between Georgia and South Carolina on May 20, 1777, at Dewitt's Corner, SC. Under its provisions, the Cherokees were forced to retire behind a line running southwest through Georgia from the straight part of Pickens County on the North to a point just below the mouth of the Tallulah at the western tip the state.

4258. State seal was the seal of Massachusetts, commissioned in 1780 and engraved by Paul Revere. It showed a Native American man holding a longbow and an arrow, with a star over his right shoulder symbolizing Massachusetts, and the state motto *Ense petit placidam sub libertate quietem* ("by the sword we seek peace under liberty").

4259. States-righters were the so-called Anti-Federalists, the forerunners of the Jeffersonians or Democratic-Republicans (afterwards known as the Democrats). These were opponents of the strong national government and federal system laid out in 1787 in the Constitution. Chief among them was Patrick Henry of Virginia. The states-righters, who gained power with the election of Thomas Jefferson in 1780, also opposed an effective centralized financial system and were strict constitutional constructionists.

4260. State to elect senators to the United States Senate was Pennsylvania. On September 30, 1788, the state legislature elected William Maclay and Robert Morris. Maclay served a two-year term; Morris served for a single six-year term.

4261. Contact between the Congress and state governments took place in May 1789, when two such contacts occurred: first, the state legislatures of New York and Virginia wrote to Congress proposing that a convention should be held for the purpose of amending the Constitution by the addition of articles guaranteeing specific rights; second, the state legislatures of Virginia and Maryland each offered to cede ten square miles of territory, to serve as the location of a federal city.

4262. Statement of the doctrine of nullification in which a state claimed the right to nullify any federal law it deemed unconstitutional appeared in the Kentucky Resolutions of 1798, adopted to oppose the Alien and Sedition Acts passed by Congress on June 25, 1798. The issue of how matters of constitutionality were to be decided was as yet unresolved by the courts. The Alien and Sedition Acts were considered by Jeffersonians as an illegitimate exercise of

STATES—*continued*

central authority, and therefore unconstitutional. The Resolutions held that "whensoever the general government assumes undelegated powers, its acts are unauthoritative, void, and of no force" and therefore each state has "an equal right to judge for itself, as well of infractions as of the mode and measure of redress." Thomas Jefferson, who was then vice president under John Adams, secretly drafted the Resolutions on November 16, 1798; they were introduced in the Kentucky legislature by John Breckinridge and approved by Governor James Garrard. James Madison drafted a similar though less radical set of resolutions for Virginia, which were adopted on December 24, 1798. The issue of whether state or federal courts determine the constitutionality of a law was settled by the Supreme Court in 1821 in the case of *Cohens v. Virginia.*

4263. Secession idea to be mentioned in Congress was mentioned in the House of Representatives on June 4, 1811, during a debate on the proposal to create a state from the Orleans Territory, which entered the Union as Louisiana on April 30, 1812. The debate concerned the extension of slavery to the proposed state. Representative Josiah Quincy of Massachusetts declared: "It will be the right of all and the duty of some [of the states] definitely to prepare for a separation; amicably, if they can; violently, if they must." Representative Poindexter of Mississippi called Quincy to order, as did the speaker of the House. On appeal, the speaker's decision was reversed, and Quincy was sustained by a vote of 53 ayes to 56 nays on the point of order.

4264. Threat of secession by a regional group of states came from New England during the War of 1812, when its inhabitants were troubled by the possibility of invasion, the economic consequences of embargoes, the unequal distribution of federal defense money, the accession of naturalized foreigners to public office, and similar issues. These and a variety of reforms of the Constitution were discussed at the Hartford Convention, a secret assembly of 26 Federalist delegates from Connecticut, Massachusetts, New Hampshire, Rhode Island, and Vermont who met at Hartford, CT, from December 15, 1814, to January 5, 1815, with George Cabot of Massachusetts as president. The war ended before the idea of secession became popular.

4265. Federal treasury surplus to be returned to the states was authorized by congressional act of June 23, 1836. Twenty-six states received a total of $28,101,645, which was distributed in proportion to their respective representation in the Senate and House and delivered in three installments. This money was supposed to remain on deposit until Congress directed otherwise, but no request for its return was ever made.

4266. State to be governed by two rival elected administrations was Rhode Island. When it entered the Union in 1790, Rhode Island retained as its constitution the royal charter that had been granted to it in 1663. This charter made voting rights contingent on land ownership and required all plaintiffs in court cases to get a landowner's support before filing suit. In 1841, after several attempts at reform came to nothing, a People's Party was founded by Thomas Wilson Dorr, a Providence lawyer and state legislator. This party held a convention, drafted a constitution that called for universal white male suffrage, won overwhelming approval for it at the polls, set up its own state government, called for the General Assembly to dissolve itself as illegitimate, and elected Dorr governor. The statehouse was already occupied by Samuel Ward King, elected on the Whig and Antimasonic tickets in 1839. He declared martial law, and Dorr, after a futile attempt to seize the Providence arsenal on May 18, 1842, was arrested, tried for treason, and given a life sentence of solitary confinement and hard labor, though he was freed the following year.

4267. State to repudiate a debt was Mississippi, in 1842. The sovereign state of Mississippi sold $5 million worth of bonds in June 1838 to pay for 50,000 shares in the Union Bank of Mississippi. The bank became hopelessly insolvent in 1840, and in 1842 the legislature denied that the state was under legal or moral obligation to pay the bonds in question.

4268. State constitutional reform movement began after the Panic of 1837, which bankrupted many of the nation's 26 state governments. A reform movement in New York State, led by upstate politician Michael Hoffman, led to the New York Constitution of 1846, which put new fiscal controls on state government. New York's example was followed by most other states, creating the first constitutional revolution since the time of the Founders.

4269. State constitution telegraphed in its entirety was that of Nevada. Anxious to admit Nevada as a state in 1864 so that its senators could add to the Republican majority in Congress, President Abraham Lincoln asked to see the prospective state's constitution as soon as possible. It was completed in September and was telegraphed to him from Carson City at a cost of $4,303.27, the longest and most expensive telegram ever sent.

4270. State constitution to ban bribery was Maryland's constitution of 1867, which set penalties both for holders of public office who were found guilty of accepting or demanding bribes and for anyone who offered a bribe to a government official.

4271. Major sale of land in the continental United States to a foreign consortium took place in 1870, when the Maxwell Land grant, a holding of 1,714,765 acres in Colfax County, NM—the largest tract of land held by a single owner in U.S. history—was sold by its private owner, Lucien Maxwell, to the Dutch East Indies Company for $1,350,000.

4272. State named for a person born in America was Washington, the 42nd state, admitted into the Union on November 11, 1889. The first governor was Elisha Peyre Ferry, a Republican, who served from 1889 to 1893. Washington was also the first state named for a president.

4273. State seal designed by a woman was the Seal of Idaho, designed by Emma Sarah Edwards. The seal was officially adopted on March 14, 1891.

4274. American provincial government in Hawaii took power on January 17, 1893, after a cabal of American sugar planters, with the help of the U.S. Marines and the tacit support of the U.S. state department, overthrew the government of Liliuokalani, the first and only Hawaiian queen. Sugar magnate Sanford Ballard Dole, who was also the leader of a reform movement that drafted the Hawaiian constitution of 1887, was installed as president of the new provisional government. The bloodless coup was organized after Liliuokalani promulgated a new Hawaiian constitution in 1891 that increased the power of the monarchy, a move seen as disadvantageous to U.S. interests. On February 1, 1893, the U.S. minister to Hawaii, John Stevens, proclaimed Hawaii to be a U.S. protectorate. Initially, President Grover Cleveland refused to recognize the new government and demanded Liliuokalani's restoration to the throne. Dole retaliated by declaring a Republic

of Hawaii while seeking political support in America for annexation. Hawaii's strategic importance became clear with the outbreak of the Spanish-American War in 1898, and it was made a U.S. territory in 1900, with Dole as the first territorial governor.

4275. Bonding law enacted by a state for the bonding of all officers, deputies, and state employees was enacted by North Dakota on March 1, 1913, but was declared unconstitutional in 1914. Another law was approved on March 5, 1919. The premiums were 25 cents a year for each $100 of the required bond. A state bonding fund was created which in the first year showed a net income of $63,172. The first claim was filed on August 4, 1919, by Riggin Township, Benson County, for $1,000 for misappropriations of funds. It was paid on February 4, 1920.

4276. Transcontinental highway was the Lincoln Highway, a 3,300-mile highway stretching from New York City to San Francisco, CA. It opened for traffic on September 10, 1913. The route was originally proposed by Carl Graham Fisher, president of the Indiana-based Prest-O-Lite carbide headlight manufacturing company and founder of the Indianapolis 500, and Henry Joy, president of the Packard Motor Car Company. The highway, built with about $10 million in state and private funds, traversed 13 states: New York, New Jersey, Pennsylvania, Ohio, Indiana, Illinois, Iowa, Nebraska, Colorado, Wyoming, Utah, Nevada, and California.

4277. State aviation department was the Connecticut Department of Aviation, established by the state legislature on May 10, 1927. It was headquartered at Brainard Field in Hartford.

4278. State-run liquor stores were opened on January 2, 1934, at 90 locations throughout the state of Pennsylvania. The legislature had authorized them at a special session on November 29, 1933.

4279. State to have a state sport was Maryland, which established jousting as the official state sport in 1962.

4280. State ombudsman as an official position in state government was instituted by Hawaii in 1967.

4281. State building located outside a state was the Florida House, Washington, DC, a three-story remodeled building originally erected in 1887, purchased by voluntary contributions in 1972, and opened October 26, 1973. It is maintained by tax-deductible contributions as a hospitality house for Floridians.

STATES—*continued*

4282. State plain-language law was enacted on May 31, 1978, by the state of New York, effective the following November 2. It was "an act to amend the general obligations law, in relation to plain language requirements for certain agreements involving consumer transactions or to which a consumer is a party for the lease of space to be occupied for residential purposes (for personal family or household purposes)."

4283. State to declare sovereignty over a large tract of federal land was Nevada, which passed Nevada assembly bill 413, signed June 2, 1979, by Republican governor Robert List, declaring state sovereignty over 49 million acres administered by the Bureau of Land Management. All but 13 percent of Nevada is owned and administered by the federal government. The action, the culmination of a long-running protest against federal management of most of the state, had no legal standing and was ignored by Washington.

4284. State to adopt a containership as its official ship was Washington, which in 1983 proclaimed the *President Washington* as the official state ship. The 860-foot seagoing vessel was one of the largest container ships ever built in the U.S. and was powered by a 43,000-horsepower diesel engine.

4285. State to have women serving simultaneously in the statehouse, House of Representatives, and Senate was Kansas. In 1991, Joan Finney was the governor, Jan Meyers represented Kansas in the House of Representatives, and Nancy Landon Kassebaum was the state's senior senator.

4286. Statewide vote paid for by a single individual was a June 17, 1997, special election on public financing of a football stadium in Seattle, WA. The entire $4.2 million cost was borne by billionaire Paul Allen, the co-founder of Microsoft, Inc. The bill in question approved public financing for a new $425 million home for the Seattle Seahawks football team, which Allen planned to purchase if the bill was passed.

4287. Court decision preventing the enactment of term limits for state legislators was issued by a three-judge panel of the U.S. Court of Appeals for the Ninth Circuit on October 7, 1997. The ruling, written by Judge Stephen Reinhardt, declared unconstitutional California's Proposition 140 initiative on term limits. Proposition 140, passed in 1990, set lifetime limits of three terms, or six years, in the state assembly and two terms, or eight years, in the state senate.

4288. State government to completely privatize its computer services was Connecticut. In January 1999 the state awarded a $1 billion contract to Electronic Data Systems Corporation of Plano, TX, to handle all of its information technology services. The seven-year contract was expected to save some $400 million on computer systems and related services.

4289. State in which all of the top elected offices were held by women was Arizona. On January 4, 1999, at a ceremony at the state capitol in Phoenix, Republican Jane Dee Hull was sworn in as governor. Also taking office that day were Betsey Bayless, secretary of state; Carol Springer, treasurer; Lisa Graham Keegan, superintendent of public instruction; and Janet Napolitano, attorney general. (Arizona has no lieutenant governor.) All but Napolitano were Republicans. Administering the oath was Supreme Court Justice Sandra Day O'Connor, a resident of Arizona.

STATES—ADMISSION

4290. State denied admission into the Union was Franklin, founded on August 23, 1784, on land ceded to the United States by North Carolina. It was formed by three counties between the Bald Mountains and the Holston River, an area that is now in eastern Tennessee. Its citizens established a senate and a house of commons at Jonesboro and elected John Sevier as governor for a four-year term with an annual salary of £200 or 1,000 deerskins. North Carolina refused to recognize this new entity and Sevier was arrested in 1788 on charges of high treason. After his release, he was elected to the House of Representatives. He served as the first governor of Tennessee after it was admitted to the Union in place of Franklin in 1796.

4291. State admitted to the Union after the ratification of the Constitution was Vermont, which joined the Union on March 4, 1791. The residents of Vermont had declared their region an independent republic in 1777, rejecting claims on their territory by the three bordering states (New York, New Hampshire, and Massachusetts). These claims were withdrawn by 1790, and Congress authorized the admission of Vermont to the Union as the 14th state on February 18, 1791.

4292. State of the Union that was formerly an independent republic was Vermont, which became the 14th state on March 4, 1791. Vermont was formed from the New Hampshire Grants, a region that was claimed by Massachusetts, New York, and New Hampshire. In 1777 it declared itself an independent commonwealth, the Republic of Vermont, and elected Thomas Chittenden as the first governor. All claims by other states were withdrawn by 1790. Chittenden went on to become the first state governor, serving to 1797.

4293. State founded within the borders of an existing state was Kentucky, which was originally part of Virginia. Residents of Kentucky petitioned the Virginia state legislature for permission to separate, as required by the Constitution, and received that consent in 1786. At a convention held on July 26, 1790, the Kentuckians decided to go forward with the separation, and having secured the agreement of Congress in February 1791, they drafted a state constitution at a second convention in April 1792 and put it into effect on June 1, when Kentucky became the 15th state. The second state to be founded within the borders of an existing state was Maine, which received the consent of Massachusetts to separate in 1819 and was admitted to the Union on March 15, 1820.

4294. State created from the Northwest Territory was Ohio, admitted as the 17th state in 1803 in recognition of its rapid population growth. The Northwest Territory, created by Congress in 1787, eventually was divided into five states, Ohio, Indiana, Illinois, Michigan, and Wisconsin, with an additional tract of land becoming part of Minnesota.

4295. State admitted into the Union without a resolution of Congress was Ohio, which became the 17th state on March 1, 1803. It was the first state to be formed entirely from public lands, but Congress never bothered to vote on a resolution actually admitting Ohio into the Union. Ohio did not officially become a state until 1953, when Congress tardily passed a law approving Ohio's constitution.

4296. State admitted to the Union with a population of less than 60,000 was Illinois, which became a state 1818 despite the fact that it had less than the minimum number of residents required.

4297. State west of the Mississippi River to be admitted to the Union was Missouri, which joined on August 10, 1821. Louisiana, admitted on April 30, 1812, is both east and west of the Mississippi.

4298. Annexation of territory by joint resolution of Congress after failure to accomplish the same object by treaty occurred in 1845, when Texas was annexed to the United States. A treaty of annexation was submitted to the Senate on April 22, 1844, but was opposed by abolitionists from the Northern states because it would have added another slaveholding territory and because it would have resulted in war with Mexico. It was rejected by the Senate on June 8 by a vote of 35 to 16. A joint resolution approving annexation passed the House on January 25, 1845, by a vote of 120 to 98 and eventually passed the Senate by a vote of 27 to 25. Three months later, after the voters of Texas had agreed to annexation, a joint resolution conferring statehood on Texas was passed by both Houses and signed into law by President John Tyler. Texas became a state on December 29, 1845.

4299. Independent nation annexed by the United States was Texas, which voted to join the Union on June 23, 1845, after nine years as an independent republic. Texas declared its independence from Mexico in March 1836 and won it on the battlefield in April. At that time, Texans voted to become part of the United States, but disagreement about whether it would be admitted as a slave state or a free state held up approval in the U.S. Congress. A compromise reached in 1844 under the guidance of secretary of state John Caldwell Calhoun allowed Texas to join the United States as a slave territory, and on December 29, 1845, Texas became the 28th state.

4300. State in the West to be denied admission to the Union was Deseret, founded on March 12, 1849, by the Mormon settlers who had come to Utah and founded Salt Lake City two years earlier. Brigham Young, president of the Mormon Church (the Church of Jesus Christ of Latter-day Saints), was elected governor. The boundaries of the state would have encompassed present-day Utah, Nevada, Arizona, and parts of Colorado, New Mexico, California, Idaho, Wyoming, and Oregon. Congress refused to recognize the new state and instead established the Utah Territory, including Utah and parts of Colorado, Wyoming, and Nevada, in 1850. Utah was admitted as a state in 1896.

4301. State on the Pacific coast to be admitted to the Union was California, which joined on September 9, 1850. The first state governor was Peter Hardeman Burnett, a Democrat, who served from 1849 to 1851.

4302. State founded within the borders of a seceded state was West Virginia, which was originally part of Virginia, one of the 13 colonies that formed the United States in 1776. The region of Virginia to the west of the Allegheny Mountains was different geographically and ecologically from the eastern region, and its economy did not depend on slavery. In fact, the British had intended, before the Revolution, to make that area a separate colony, to be called

STATES—ADMISSION—*continued*

Vandalia. When Virginia voted in May 1861 to secede from the Union, the westerners moved to secede from Virginia, calling for the creation of another state, to be called Kanawha. On April 20, 1863, President Abraham Lincoln issued a proclamation stating that West Virginia would be admitted to the Union after a 60-day period. The admittance took effect on June 20. The immediate gain to the Lincoln administration included the addition of two Republican senators from the new state.

4303. States admitted to the Union simultaneously were North and South Dakota, which were formed from the Dakota Territory. The act of admission was signed on February 22, 1889, by President Grover Cleveland. Each state held a constitutional convention beginning on July 4, 1889, and both held the ratifying election on October 1, 1889. President Benjamin Harrison signed the proclamations of admission on November 2, 1889, without knowing which was which. The first governors of both states were Republicans: John Miller, in North Dakota; Arthur Calvin Mellette, in South Dakota. Washington and Montana were admitted by the same enabling act, but the proclamations were not signed until a few days later.

4304. Native American state denied admission to the Union was Sequoyah, which applied for admission in 1904. It was organized in Indian Territory by the Five Civilized Tribes (the Cherokee, Muscogee, Choctaw, Chickasaw, and Seminole), whose members had been forced to relocate there from the southeastern United States in the previous century. They drafted a constitution in 1905. The request for admission was denied by Congress, which instead voted to combine the Indian Territory and the Oklahoma Territory into the state of Oklahoma, admitted to the Union in 1907. In the mid-19th century, Congress had made tentative plans to create within Oklahoma a state for Native Americans to be called Neosho, but these plans were shelved after the tribes allied themselves with the Confederacy during the Civil War.

4305. State admitted to the Union that had no border with another state was Alaska, which was admitted as the 49th state on January 3, 1959, by proclamation of President Dwight David Eisenhower. Alaska had become a territory on August 24, 1912. A constitution was approved by popular vote on April 24, 1956, and was ratified by Congress on July 7, 1958. Voters approved statehood on August 26, 1958, and the first state election was held on November 25.

4306. State admitted to the Union that was separated by a substantial body of water from the contiguous United States was Hawaii, 2,090 miles across the Pacific from San Francisco, CA. It was voted into the Union by Congress on March 12, 1959, by a vote of 323–89. Hawaii was admitted as the 50th state by proclamation of President Dwight David Eisenhower on August 21, 1959.

STATES—CAPITALS

4307. Statehouse was a building on Duke of Gloucester Street, Williamsburg, VA, in which the General Assembly met. The building was erected in 1698 by Governor Francis Nicholson, who was the first person to apply the term "capitol" to a government building.

4308. Delaware state capital was New Castle, which served briefly as the first state capital from September 21, 1776, when it was the site of the Lower Counties-on-Delaware, to 1777, when the capital was moved to its present location at Dover. Delaware's formal admission to the Union took place on December 7, 1787.

4309. Pennsylvania state capital was Philadelphia, the major metropolis in the state from the city's founding under William Penn's charter in 1681. It was the capital of Pennsylvania from December 12, 1787, when the state was admitted to the Union, to 1812, when Harrisburg, located on the Susquehanna River in south central Pennsylvania, was made the capital.

4310. New Jersey state capital was Princeton, settled in 1696 by Quakers, who called the site Stony Brook. It was renamed Princeton in 1724 in honor of William III, Prince of Orange-Nassau, and became the state capital upon statehood on December 18, 1787. The present capital, Trenton, located on the Delaware River in west central New Jersey, was founded by an English Quaker family in 1679. It became the state capital in 1790.

4311. Georgia state capital was Savannah, the colonial government seat, which became the capital of the state in 1776. Georgia's formal admission to the Union took place on January 2, 1788. Milledgeville, in Baldwin County, was the capital of Georgia from 1807 to 1867. Atlanta, the present capital, was founded as railroad terminus in 1836 on land ceded by the Creek Indians in 1821. It became the temporary state capital in 1868 and the permanent capital in 1887.

4312. Connecticut state capital was Hartford, from the time that Connecticut was admitted to the Union on January 9, 1788. Hartford and New Haven both served as seats of colonial government from 1701 to 1784. Hartford was incorporated as a town and city in 1784.

4313. Massachusetts state capital was Boston, whose Indian name was Shawmut. When the Puritans arrived in 1630 they originally called the settlement Trimountain because at the time there were three peaks on Beacon Hill. The name "Boston," from a town in England that bred many Puritans, was adopted later. Boston became the capital of the colony in 1632 and the state capital on February 6, 1788.

4314. Maryland state capital was Annapolis, the colonial capital since 1694. Founded by Virginia colonists in 1649 as Providence, it was renamed Annapolis in honor of Princess Anne of England, and became the state capitol on April 28, 1788. The State House in Annapolis, completed in 1772, served briefly as the capitol of the United States when Congress ratified the Treaty of Paris there on January 14, 1784. The first colonial capital was St. Mary's City, located near the mouth of the Potomac River at the site of the Indian village of Yaocomico, which was purchased by English Catholic settlers under Leonard Calvert in 1634.

4315. South Carolina state capital was Charleston, named the state capital by the South Carolina legislature in 1776. South Carolina's official date of admission to the Union was May 23, 1788. In 1790, the seat of government was moved from Charleston to its present location at Columbia as a compromise site acceptable to both the aristocratic Low country and the poorer, industrial Up country.

4316. New Hampshire state capital was Exeter, founded in 1638 by the Reverend John Wheelwright and other exiles from the Massachusetts Bay Colony. Portsmouth was the meeting place for the provincial assembly until 1774, when the royal governor, John Wentworth, dissolved the assembly to prevent the election of delegates to a continental congress. A series of provincial congresses began to convene at the Exeter town house later that year. In July 1775 the provincial records were taken from royal officials and brought to Exeter, which continued as the capital when New Hampshire joined the Union on June 21, 1788. The permanent state capital was established in 1808 at Concord, on the Merrimack River in south central New Hampshire. Originally known as Penacook Plantation, it was settled in 1727 and incorporated as Rumford, MA, in 1733. After years of litigation by New Hampshire, it was reincorporated there as Concord in 1765.

4317. Virginia state capital was Williamsburg, first settled in 1633 and declared the capital in 1776. The official date of statehood is June 25, 1788. The state capital was moved to Richmond in 1779.

4318. New York state capital was New York City, so designated when New York officially became a state on July 26, 1788. The seat of government was permanently moved to Albany in 1796. New York City also served as the capital of the United States from 1785 to 1790.

4319. North Carolina state capital was Halifax, founded on the south bank of the Roanoke River in 1760. It became the state capital on April 12, 1776. North Carolina officially joined the Union on November 21, 1789. The present capital, Raleigh, named after Sir Walter Raleigh, was chosen for settlement in 1788. It became the state capital in 1792.

4320. Rhode Island state capitals were Providence, founded by the Baptist dissenter Roger Williams in 1636, and Newport, founded in 1639 by religious refugees from Massachusetts under William Coddington. Following the admission of Rhode Island into the Union on May 29, 1790, each city alternated as the seat of the General Assembly. Providence became the sole state capital in 1900.

4321. Vermont state capital was Arlington, where Vermont's first elected governor, Thomas Chittenden, established the seat of state government in 1778 in a house in the center of town. The view from this house is depicted in the seal of Vermont. Statehood became official on March 4, 1791. Since 1805 the state capital has been Montpelier, located on the Winooski River in north central Vermont.

4322. Kentucky state capital was Frankfort, located on the Kentucky River in north central Kentucky. The seat of Franklin County, it was founded in 1786 by General James Wilkinson and became the capital when Kentucky was admitted to statehood on June 1, 1792, despite fierce competition from Louisville and Lexington.

STATES—CAPITALS—*continued*

4323. Tennessee state capital was Knoxville, named for George Washington's secretary of war, Henry Knox. On June 1, 1796, when the territory of the United States south of the Ohio River became the state of Tennessee, Knoxville became the first capital. Nashville, the present capital, was founded in 1779 as Fort Nashborough, renamed in 1784, and made the state capital in 1843.

4324. Ohio state capital was Chillicothe, which served as the capital from statehood on March 1, 1803, to 1810 and again from 1812 to 1816, following a two-year period when the capital was in Zanesville. Columbus, on the Scioto and Olentangy rivers, became the permanent capital in 1816.

4325. Louisiana state capital was New Orleans, which succeeded Biloxi (now the capital of Mississippi) as the territorial capital and became the state capital when Louisiana was admitted to the Union on April 30, 1812. The present capital, Baton Rouge, was incorporated as a town in 1817. It served as the state capital from 1849 to 1861 and again from 1882.

4326. Indiana state capital was Corydon, the capital when Indiana achieved statehood on December 11, 1816. In 1825 the capital was moved permanently to Indianapolis. Vincennes, the oldest town in Indiana, was designated capital of the Indiana Territory in 1800. The capital was transferred to Corydon in 1813.

4327. Mississippi state capital from December 10, 1817, when statehood was granted, was Washington, a town near the former territorial capital of Natchez. In 1821 the legislature decided to move the capital to Le Fleur's Bluff, a trading post settled in 1792 by Louis Le Fleur, a French-Canadian trader. It was renamed Jackson in honor of President Andrew Jackson in 1822, and was laid out in April of that year according to a checkboard plan designed by Thomas Jefferson. The state legislature met there for the first time on December 23, 1822.

4328. Illinois state capital was Kaskaskia, which functioned as the capital from statehood on December 3, 1818, until 1820. The capital was then moved to nearby Vandalia, the western terminus of the Cumberland Road, located on the Kaskaskia River in south-central Illinois. In 1839, at the urging of state representative Abraham Lincoln, the capital was moved to its present location at Springfield.

4329. Alabama state capital was Huntsville, AL, originally Twickenham, founded in 1805 in Madison county. It was renamed Huntsville (for John Hunt of Virginia, the earliest English settler in the area) in 1811, the year it received the state's first town charter, and served as the capital when statehood was achieved on December 4, 1819. The seat of government was successively installed at Cahaba and Tuscaloosa before Montgomery became the permanent capital in 1847.

4330. Maine state capital was Portland, Maine's largest city, which served as the capital beginning on March 14, 1820, when the state was admitted to the Union. In 1832 the capital was transferred to Augusta, on the Kennebec River in southwest Maine.

4331. Missouri state capital was Jefferson City, located on the Missouri River in central Missouri. The city, laid out by Daniel M. Boone, the son of the frontiersman Daniel Boone, was built on a site selected for the future capital in 1821, the year in which Missouri achieved statehood (on August 10). The land was donated under a Congressional act stipulating that the state capital be within 40 miles of the mouth of the Osage River. Jefferson City was incorporated as a town in 1825 and as a city in 1839, and served as the capital from 1826.

4332. Arkansas state capitol was Little Rock, made the territorial capital in 1821 when the seat of government was transferred from Arkansas Post. Little Rock became the state capital on June 15, 1836. The state's first capitol building, where the legislature met from 1821 to 1836, is part of the modern Territorial Capitol Restoration.

4333. Michigan state capital was Detroit, the capital of the Territory of Michigan from January 11, 1805. It became the state capital on January 26, 1837. The seat of government was moved to its present location at Lansing in 1847.

4334. Florida state capital was Tallahassee, located in the northwestern part of Florida. The site of seven missions to the Native American inhabitants during the Spanish colonial era, Tallahassee was founded in 1823 as the capital of the territory of Florida. It was incorporated in 1825 and became the state capital on March 3, 1845, when Flordia was admitted to the Union.

4335. Texas state capital was Austin. Founded as Waterloo in 1835, it was renamed in honor of Stephen F. Austin in 1839, when it was selected to be the capital of the Republic of Texas. The government was temporarily moved to Houston during the war with Mexico, 1842–45, but Austin was restored as the permanent capital with the granting of statehood on December 29, 1845.

4336. Iowa state capital was Iowa City, where the cornerstone of the territorial capital was laid on July 4, 1840. Iowa City became the capital of the state of Iowa on December 28, 1846, when Iowa was admitted to the Union. In 1857 the capital was permanently moved to Des Moines.

4337. Wisconsin state capital was Madison, where the territorial legislature held its first session in 1838. It was incorporated as a village in 1846 and became the state capital on May 29, 1848. The first territorial capital was the village of Belmont, in Lafayette County, selected in 1836 by Henry Dodge, a land speculator and the first territorial governor. That same year, Dodge's political rival, James Duane Doty, bribed the legislature into moving the capital to Madison, which was then an uninhabited stretch of swampy woods in the Four Lakes region.

4338. California state capital was San Jose, founded by José Joaquin Moraga in 1777 under the name Pueblo de San José de Guadalupe. San Jose was selected as the first capital when California achieved statehood on September 9, 1850; in December 1849 it was the site of the first state legislative assembly. The capital was moved to Vallejo in 1852, to Benicia in 1853, and permanently to Sacramento in 1854.

4339. Minnesota state capital was St. Paul, located on the Mississippi River in eastern Minnesota. It was founded in 1838 and until 1841 was called Pig's Eye, after its first settler, Pierre "Pig's Eye" Parrant. Incorporated in 1854, St. Paul became the territorial capital in 1849 and the state capital on May 11, 1858, when Minnesota was granted statehood.

4340. Oregon state capital was Salem, which replaced Oregon City as the seat of territorial government in 1852. The legislature met at Corvallis for a brief period in 1855. When Oregon was admitted to the Union on February 14, 1859, Salem begame the state capital.

4341. Kansas state capital was Topeka, located on the Kansas River in northeast Kansas. It was founded in 1854 by settlers opposed to the introduction of slavery into new territories and was chosen as the state capital on December 5, 1861, the year Kansas was admitted to statehood.

4342. West Virginia state capital was Wheeling, in the northern panhandle of the state. Wheeling was twice the state capital, at the achievement of statehood on June 20, 1863, to 1870, and again from 1875 to 1885. The present capital, Charleston, located at the junction of the Elk and Kanawha rivers in western West Virginia, was founded as Charles Town in 1788. On February 10, 1869, it was named the state capital "on and after April 1, 1870." The seat of government was permanently moved there in 1885.

4343. Nevada state capital was Carson City, named for the explorer Kit Carson. It was originally the site of a frontier station. Founded in 1858, it became the territorial capital in 1861 and the state capital on October 31, 1864. It was incorporated as a city in 1869.

4344. Nebraska state capital was Omaha, where the Nebraska territorial legislature first met on January 16, 1855. The site was chosen by promoters from Council Bluffs, IA, just across the Missouri River, who hoped that the eastern terminus of the first transcontinental railroad would be located nearby, as it indeed was during the Lincoln administration. The capital of Nebraska was moved to Lancaster, renamed Lincoln, soon after statehood on March 1, 1867. Lincoln is the only capital of a Plains state that is not a river port.

4345. Colorado state capital was Denver, the largest city in the state, founded in 1860 through the combination of two previous settlements, Auraria and St. Charles. It became the territorial capital in 1876 and was made the state capital upon Colorado's admission to the Union on August 1, 1876.

4346. North Dakota state capital was Bismarck, located on the Missouri River in south central North Dakota. It was founded in 1872 as a military post called Camp Greeley (later Camp Hancock) and was renamed the following year. The capital of the Dakota Territory was transferred from Yankton (now in South Dakota) to Bismarck in 1883 after Bismarck offered the best bid for the honor—$100,000 and 160 acres of land. It became the capital when North Dakota was admitted to the Union on November 2, 1889.

STATES—CAPITALS—*continued*

4347. South Dakota state capital was Pierre, located on the Missouri River in central South Dakota. The site was the capital of the Arikara Indian nation prior to 1800, when a settlement was founded as the western terminus of the Chicago and North Western Railway. Pierre became the temporary state capital on November 2, 1889, and the permanent capital in 1890.

4348. Montana state capital was Helena, founded as Last Chance Gulch in 1864, three months after gold was discovered at the site. It was the territorial capital from 1875 to 1889, replacing Virginia City (1865–75), and became the state capital on November 8, 1889.

4349. Washington state capital was Olympia, located on Puget Sound in northwestern Washington. Settled in 1845 and laid out as Smithfield in 1851, it became the territorial capital in 1853 and was chartered as a city six years later. Olympia became the state capital when Washington was admitted into the Union on November 11, 1889.

4350. Idaho state capital was Boise, the largest city in the state, located on the Boise River in southwestern Idaho. Originally an army camp, it was founded as a settlement in 1863 and was incorporated as a city the following year, when it also became the territorial capital. Boise became the state capital on July 3, 1890, when Idaho entered the Union.

4351. Wyoming state capital was Cheyenne, the largest city in the state, located on Crow Creek in southeast Wyoming. Founded by squatters on railroad land in 1867, it made the territorial capital in 1868 and the state capital on statehood, July 10, 1890. The first territorial legislature convened there on October 12, 1869.

4352. Utah state capital was Salt Lake City, the largest city in the state, located on the Great Salt Lake in north central Utah. It was founded by Mormon pioneers in 1847 and named Great Salt Lake City (the name was changed in 1868). In 1849–50 it was the capital of the provisional state of Deseret; it served as the territorial capital of Utah in 1850, in 1857, and from 1859 to 1896, when it became the state capital on January 4, the date Utah was admitted as the 45th state.

4353. Statehouse with an all-marble dome was the Rhode Island State House in Providence, RI, occupied by the General Assembly and other state officers beginning on January 1, 1901. Ground was broken on September 16, 1895, and the cornerstone was laid on October 15, 1896. The architects were McKim, Mead and White, and the builders were Norcross Brothers, Worcester, MA. The dome was made of 327,000 cubic feet of white Georgia marble, and was 94 feet high. The diameter of the dome below the top of the gallery was 70 feet; the diameter above the top of the gallery, 56 feet; and the diameter of the dome proper, 50 feet.

4354. Oklahoma state capital was Guthrie, founded on April 22, 1889, the first day of the Oklahoma Land Rush, when native American lands were opened to white settlement. Incorporated in 1890, it was the capital of the Oklahoma Territory. It became the state capital on November 16, 1907. The present capital, Oklahoma City, was also founded by homesteaders in 1889 on the first day of legal settlement. The state capital was moved from Guthrie to Oklahoma City in 1910.

4355. New Mexico state capital was Santa Fe, NM. Originally named Villa Real de la Santa Fé de San Francisco de Asis (Royal City of the Holy Faith of St. Francis of Assisi), it was founded in 1610 by the Spanish governor, Don Pedro de Peralta. This was 14 years before Dutch settlers came to Albany, NY, and 20 years before the English settlement of Boston, MA. Santa Fe became the capital of the Territory of New Mexico in 1851 and the state capital on January 6, 1912.

4356. Arizona state capital was Phoenix, which was made the state capital on February 14, 1912. Fort Whipple, near Prescott, was the first territorial capital, designated in 1864. The capital was moved to the nearby town of Prescott as soon as construction had been completed. After several further moves, the capital finally was moved permanently to Phoenix in 1889.

4357. Alaska state capital was Juneau, which had been the seat of government since 1900 and became the state capital on January 3, 1959. The first territorial capital was Sitka, founded in July 1799 by Aleksandr Baranov, the first Russian governor of Alaska, and refounded as Novo Arkhangelsk (New Archangel) in 1804. Sitka was the territorial capital from October 18, 1867, when the Russians handed over Alaska to the United States.

4358. State capital that was the capital of a sovereign kingdom was Honolulu, HI, located in the southeast part of Oahu Island. It was settled, according to Hawaiian legend, approximately in the year 1100, and after flourishing as a trade center in the early 19th century, was made the capital of the kingdom of Hawaii on August 31, 1850, by King Kamehameha III. It continued as the capital when Hawaiian statehood was proclaimed on August 20, 1959.

STATES—CONSTITUTIONS

4359. Massachusetts constitution in colonial times was the royal charter that was granted by King Charles I to the Massachusetts Bay Company on March 4, 1629. On May 16, 1775, following the outbreak of hostilies in the American Revolution, a temporary constitution was adopted by the provincial congress. A state constitution was drafted in 1777 by a committee of the legislature, but when it was submitted to the voters for ratification, they turned it down because they had had no say in its composition. Instead, they elected delegates to a convention that assembled at Cambridge on September 1, 1779. The constitution they adopted was written by John Adams, submitted to and approved by the voters, and put into effect on October 25, 1780. It has never been superseded, though it was revised in 1917–19 and is now the world's oldest written constitution still in force.

4360. South Carolina constitution was adopted at Charleston on March 26, 1776, by the provincial congress. A revised constitution, adopted by the legislature on March 19, 1778, and put into effect the following November, terminated the established status of the Anglican Church. Successive constitutions were adopted in June 1790; in April 1861, following the state's secession from the Union; in September 1865, preparatory to its restoration to the Union; in April 1868, to meet the standards imposed by the Reconstruction Acts of Congress; and on January 1, 1896, when the present constitution, drafted in Columbia between September and December 1895, went into effect. Like several of South Carolina's earlier constitutions, the present one was not submitted to the voters.

4361. Virginia constitution was the work of George Mason, who included in it a guarantee of specific liberties to the people of the state. This, the world's first bill of rights, was entitled *A Declaration of Rights made by the representative of the good people of Virginia, assembled in full and free convention; which rights do pertain to them and their posterity, as the basis and foundation of government.* Mason's draft was adopted on June 12, 1776, by the state's constitutional convention. (Mason was later instrumental in the addition to the Constitution of the federal Bill of Rights, which incorporated many of his ideas; he also endeavored, in vain, to replace the system of slave labor with a program of emancipation and education.) Requests from the western counties of Virginia for political reforms, including fairer legislative apportionment and extension of voting rights, led to the adoption of a second constitution in 1830 and a third in 1851. A constitution that was drawn up after Virginia joined the Confederacy was defeated by the voters in 1861; another, drafted in 1864, was never put to a vote; and a post–Civil War constitution, approved in 1869, was replaced in 1902. The present constitution took effect on July 1, 1971.

4362. New Jersey constitution in the colonial era was a declaration of royal government issued by Britain's Queen Anne in 1702. In 1776, while British and American forces fought in New Jersey, a temporary charter of government was drafted at Princeton over the course of five days by a committee of the revolutionary provincial congress. It was promulgated on July 2, 1776. Despite its provisional character, it continued to serve as the state constitution for nearly seven decades, surviving a court challenge in 1828. A revised constitution was drafted at Trenton in 1844. The present constitution was drafted between June and September 1947 in New Brunswick and has been in effect since January 1, 1948.

4363. Delaware constitution in the colonial era was the Frame of Government issued by William Penn in 1682 to Pennsylvania, to which the Delaware counties of New Castle, Kent, and Sussex had been added. A separate Charter of Privileges was issued to these counties by Penn in 1701. Delaware declared itself a separate state in 1776 under a constitution that was drafted by a convention in New Castle and adopted on September 21. Subsequent constitutions, all drafted by conventions meeting in Dover, were put in effect in 1792, 1831, and 1897, the last of which is still in force. Alone among the states, Delaware does not require its constitutions and their amendments to be submitted to the voters for approval.

4364. Pennsylvania constitution in colonial times was the document known as the Frame of Government of Pennsylvania, issued by the colony's founder, William Penn, in 1682. Pennsylvania continued to operate under Penn's charters and declarations of rights until 1775, when

STATES—CONSTITUTIONS—*continued*

the revolutionary Committee of Public Safety drew up a provisional state constitution. A permanent one was drafted by a constitutional convention that assembled at Philadelphia on July 15, 1776, under the leadership of Benjamin Franklin. This document was adopted, without electoral ratification, on September 28, 1776. A new constitution was adopted in September 1790, another in January 1839, and still another in January 1874. The present constitution was ratified by the electorate on April 23, 1968.

4365. Maryland constitution was adopted on November 9, 1776, having been drafted by a constitutional convention that assembled in Annapolis on August 14. It was replaced by a second constitution on July 4, 1851. A pro-Union constitution, produced during the Civil War, went into effect on November 1, 1864, after surviving a court challenge, but within three years it had been superseded by another constitution that received the support of former Confederate sympathizers. This document, drafted in a convention at Annapolis and approved at the polls, has been in effect since October 5, 1867.

4366. North Carolina constitution was drafted in Halifax in the closing months of 1776 by the provincial congress, which approved it on December 18. An amendment providing for secession from the Union was adopted in 1861 and repealed in 1865. Three years later, a second constitution providing for universal male suffrage was drafted at Raleigh to satisfy the requirements of the Reconstruction Acts. It was superseded on July 1, 1971, by the present constitution, which was not written by the members of a constitutional convention, but by a team of legal and political experts hired by the legislature.

4367. New Hampshire constitution was framed at Exeter and adopted on January 5, 1776, making New Hampshire the first state to act on the suggestion of the Continental Congress (December 21, 1775) that the newly independent colonies develop governmental frameworks for themselves. The Exeter constitution established a bicameral legislature but made no provision for a chief executive. This problem was remedied in the constitution of June 2, 1784, which remains in force. The present constitution was created by a constitutional convention that assembled in Concord in June 1778; it produced two proposed constitutional

revisions, in 1779 and 1781, before the third was accepted by the voters. This convention was formed as an independent body, rather than as a legislative committee, and was the first of its kind in the nation and in the world.

4368. Georgia constitution in colonial times was the charter granted by King George II in 1732. On April 15, 1776, Georgia's provincial congress adopted a frame of government known as the Rules and Regulations, but as this took place before Georgia proclaimed statehood, most historians consider its first state constitution to be the document that was adopted on February 5, 1777, in Savannah, GA. New constitutions were adopted in 1789 and 1798. The secession constitution of 1861 was followed in 1865 by a constitution that was disallowed by Congress, in 1868 by a Reconstructionist constitution, and in 1877 by a counter-Reconstructionist constitution. During the 20th century, four new constitutions have been drafted in Georgia: the first was adopted in 1945, the second was invalidated by a federal court in 1966, the third took effect in 1977, and the fourth has been the supreme state law since July 1, 1983.

4369. New York State constitution in colonial times was a charter adopted by the legislative assembly in 1683 with the permission of the Duke of York, who had captured the area from the Dutch. The first state constitution was adopted on April 3, 1777, by a convention of framers that had assembled at Kingston the previous July. Subsequent constitutions were adopted in 1822, 1847, and 1895. The current constitution has been in place since January 1, 1939.

4370. Vermont constitution was written at what is now called the Old Constitution House, in Windsor, and was adopted on July 2, 1777, though it was not recognize by the governments of the neighboring states of Massachusetts, New York, and New Hampshire, which maintained claims to its territory. The document included a clause banning slavery and involuntary servitude for men over the age of 21 and women over the age of 18, except in cases where they were sentenced to servitude by a court of law. This was the first state law limiting slavery. The 1777 constitution also established an elected council of 13 censors who were charged with reviewing the state's laws to ensure their constitutionality. On the recommendation of this council, the state adopted a second constitution, framed in convention at Manchester in 1786. A third, framed in Windsor and adopted on July 9, 1793 (though without provision for the council of censors), is still in place. At a little more than 8,000 words, it is the shortest of the state constitutions. It was adopted two years after Vermont's admission as the 14th state of the Union on March 4, 1791.

4371. Constitutional convention of a popular character anywhere in the world took place in Concord, NH, in June 1778. The early constitutions of the former British colonies were written (or adapted from colonial charters) by committees of revolutionary leaders or by delegates appointed by the legislature. In this case the decision to call a convention for the purpose of crafting a revision to the state's original constitution of 1776 was made by the voters of New Hampshire, to whom the question was submitted by the state assembly. The voters were also required to approve the work of the convention by a two-thirds majority. They rejected two drafts, in 1779 and 1781, before approving the current constitution in 1784.

4372. State constitution to be submitted to the people for ratification was a proposed constitution that was drafted by a convention in Concord, NH, in 1779. The document did not win the approval of the necessary two-thirds majority of the voters and did not become law. The first state constitution to win ratification by the electorate was the present constitution of Massachusetts, which was drafted at Cambridge and submitted to the people for their approval in 1780. It received the assent of two-thirds of the voters and became law on October 25, 1780.

4373. Connecticut constitution in colonial days was the Fundamental Orders of Connecticut, a covenant made on January 14, 1639, by the freemen of the towns of Hartford, Windsor, and Wethersfield. The government instituted by this agreement was the first in the world to be created by a written constitution. Starting on October 9, 1662, Connecticut operated under a royal charter granted by King Charles II of England. In 1776, after independence from Britain had been declared, Connecticut adopted the charter as the state constitution, and continued to consider this document binding after the state's formal entry into the Union on January 9, 1788. In 1818 another constitution, containing a declaration of rights and disestablishing the Anglican Church, was drafted at a convention in Hartford and ratified by the electorate. In 1965 the legislature initiated a convention at Hartford for the purpose of making specific revisions to the text, but the delegates undertook to write an entirely new constitution, which became law on December 30 after ratification by the voters. It remains in force.

4374. Rhode Island constitution was the Munificent Charter, the royal charter of self-government issued by King Charles II in 1663 to the colony under Roger Williams, and effective from July 8, 1663. So solidly was it conceived that it served as the state constitution as well from May 29, 1790, when Rhode Island entered the Union as the 13th state, until May 3, 1843, when the current constitution went into effect. The adoption of the present constitution was the consequence of Dorr's Rebellion, a voting-rights movement led by state legislator Thomas Wilson Dorr and made up of disenfranchised farmers, who produced their own constitution in 1841 and elected Dorr govenor. The state government responded by drafting two reform constitutions, of which the first was defeated at the polls and the second was approved in November 1842. The current constitution was modernized during a constitutional convention held in 1986.

4375. Kentucky constitution was drafted by a convention that met at Danville in April 1792 and became law when Kentucky entered the Union as the 15th state on June 1, 1792. Subsequent constitutions were adopted in 1800, 1850, and 1891. This fourth document, still in effect, was drafted in Frankfort over the course of seven months beginning in September 1890. After its ratification by the voters, it was reviewed by the Frankfort convention, whose members decided to change some of its provisions before it was declared in force on September 28, 1891. Despite this irregularity, the state courts allowed the constitution to stand.

4376. Tennessee constitution was drafted by a constitutional convention that assembled on January 11, 1796, at Knoxville, capital of the Territory of the United States South of the River Ohio. After a petition to outlaw slavery was defeated, the constitution was adopted on February 6 without being submitted to the voters. It became valid on June 1, 1796, when Tennessee joined the Union as the 16th state. A revised convention that created an independent judiciary branch was approved by the voters in 1835. This document was amended by a pro-Union convention towards the end of the Civil War, but many of the changes were reversed by another convention that met in Nashville five years later. This third constitution has been in effect since May 5, 1870.

STATES—CONSTITUTIONS—_continued_

4377. Ohio constitution was framed in Chillicothe by a constitutional convention that met in the fall of 1802. It was adopted by the convention on November 29 and went into effect when Ohio was granted statehood as the 17th state on March 1, 1803. The present constitution was drafted at Columbus and put in place on September 1, 1851, after its ratification by the voters.

4378. Louisiana constitution was composed in New Orleans, where a constitutional convention formed in November 1811. Although it specified that English would be the state's official language, the document was written in French, with an English translation. It became law on April 30, 1812, when Louisiana became the 18th state of the Union. Since then, Louisiana has been governed under a series of constitutions that took effect, successively, in 1845 (Jacksonian), 1852 (Whig), 1861 (secessionist), 1864 and 1868 (Reconstructionist), 1879 (counter-Reconstructionist), 1898 and 1913 (anti-Populist), and 1921 (reform). The current constitution was drafted at Baton Rouge, ratified at the polls, and put in force on December 31, 1974.

4379. Indiana constitution became operative on December 11, 1816, when Indiana was admitted to the Union as the 19th state. It was drafted in Corydon by a convention that assembled on June 10, 1816, following the passage by Congress of an enabling act for statehood. The present constitution, drafted at Indianapolis, was approved by the voters in August 1851 and went into effect the following November 1.

4380. Mississippi constitution was produced by a constitutional convention at Natchez in July–August 1817 and went into effect on December 10, when Mississippi became the 20th state of the Union. It was replaced in 1832 by another whose provisions were more democratic, and which remained in place until 1869, though its merits and problems were aired in a constitutional convention in 1851. A secession amendment was passed in 1861 and repealed in 1865. Mississippi was readmitted to the Union on February 18, 1869, with a Reconstructionist constitution. The present constitution, though it was not submitted to the voters for ratification, has been in force since November 1890.

4381. Illinois constitution was drafted at Kaskaskia by a constitutional convention that assembled in August 1818. It took effect on December 3, when Illinois entered the Union as the 21st state. It was replaced by a revised constitution in April 1847. A constitution that favored the Confederacy was submitted to the voters in 1862 but was rejected. A third constitution, giving African-American men the right to vote, took effect in August 1869. The current constitution was written over the course of a year in 1969–70, received ratification on December 15, 1970, and has been in force since July 1, 1971. The state's voters defeated a 1988 call for a new constitutional convention.

4382. Alabama constitution was drafted between July 5 and August 2, 1819, by the constitutional convention that met in Huntsville, and went into effect on December 14, when Alabama was admitted to the Union as the 22nd state. A secession constitution was instituted in 1861 and another, based on the maintenance of white supremacy, in 1865. It was replaced in 1868 by a Reconstructionist document that gave the vote to African-American men. The constitution of 1875 returned suffrage to former Confederate leaders. The current constitution, drafted at a convention in Montgomery, was ratified by the voters and has been in place since November 28, 1901. Some of its provisions, including the poll tax, were later disqualified by federal courts because they were intended to obstruct the voting rights of African-American citizens.

4383. Maine constitution went into effect on March 25, 1820, when Maine was admitted to the Union as the 23rd state. The area that is now Maine had been a province of Massachusetts since the mid-17th century. After a movement for separation was approved by referendum, a convention assembled in Portland and drew up a constitution that was passed by the voters on December 6, 1819. It has not been superseded.

4384. Missouri constitution took effect on August 10, 1821, when Missouri entered the Union as the 24th state. Its original version, drafted in a convention that met at St. Louis in June 1820, included a slavery provision. The congressional debate over this provision resulted in the Missouri Compromise, which allowed the admission of an equal number of slave and free states. Missouri was admitted as a slave state on condition that free African-Americans be allowed to settle there, despite a clause to the contrary in the constitution. An attempt to revise the constitution in 1845 was defeated at the polls. A Reconstruction constitution was adopted in 1865 and was superseded by a third constitution in 1875. The present constitution was written at Jefferson City during the convention of 1943–44 and took effect on March 30, 1945, after ratification by the voters.

4385. Arkansas constitution was written by delegates who gathered at Little Rock on January 4, 1836, at a convention called by the territorial legislature. It took effect on June 15, when Arkansas was admitted as the 25th state. A second constitution, reflecting Arkansas' secession from the Union, was adopted in 1861. This was superseded in 1864 by a pro-Union constitution drafted under the aegis of the occupying military government and in 1868 by a Reconstructionist constitution that was mandated as a condition of rejoining the Union, which took place despite an attempt by President Andrew Johnson to veto it. The current constitution was drafted at a convention in Little Rock, ratified at the polls, and put in effect on October 30, 1874. None of the three constitutional conventions held since then has resulted in a new document.

4386. Michigan constitution was drafted in Detroit by a constitutional convention that met in May and June 1835. It was ratified by the voters and submitted to Congress with a petition for statehood but was rejected because the boundary between Michigan and Ohio was in dispute. The boundary claim was resolved in December 1836 and statehood was granted to Michigan (the 26th state) on January 26, 1837, when the constitution took effect. A more democratic constitution was put in place in 1850; a third constitution, embodying principles of the progressive movement, replaced it in 1908. The current constitution has been in force since January 1, 1964. It was drafted at Lansing and was approved by the voters in April 1963.

4387. Florida constitution was drafted at St. Joseph in 1838 by a territorial convention and became the state constitution on March 3, 1845, when Florida joined the Union as the 27th state. At the outbreak of the Civil War, in 1861, Florida joined the Confederacy and adopted a new constitution. A constitution abolishing slavery was prepared in 1865 but did not take effect because the state was placed under martial law. This was followed by a Reconstructionist constitution in 1868 and a counter-Reconstructionist constitution in 1887. The present constitution was approved by the electorate in November 1968 and has been in effect since January 7, 1969.

4388. Texas constitution establishing Texas as an independent unitary republic was adopted in March 1836 by a convention of American settlers who met at Washington, on the Brazos River, shortly after their declaration of independence from Mexico. Texas was annexed by the United States on March 1, 1845, and became the 28th state on December 29, at which time the first state constitution, ratified by the voters on October 13, went into effect. It was replaced in 1861 after Texas seceded from the Union. A third state constitution, allowing Texas to rejoin the Union, was approved at the polls in June 1866, and a fourth, mandated by Congress under Reconstruction, in December 1869. The present constitution was drafted at Austin in 1875 and went into effect on February 15, 1876.

4389. Iowa constitution was a local constitution, the Constitution of the Citizens of the North Fork of the Maquoketa, that was adopted in February 1838, while Iowa was part of the Wisconsin Territory. Similar frames of government were adopted by settlers in other localities. A constitution for the future state of Iowa was drawn up in a convention at Iowa City in 1844, was amended after it was rejected by the voters, and was eventually ratified on August 3, 1846, becoming law on December 28, when Iowa became the 29th state. The present constitution, drafted in Iowa City, has been in effect since September 3, 1857.

4390. Wisconsin constitution was drafted in 1846 at a constitutional convention that assembled soon after the passage by Congress of an enabling act for Wisconsin statehood. This draft was found unacceptable, in part because it gave married women the right to own property. A convention of 69 framers, held in Madison from December 1847 to February 1848, produced another draft, which was accepted by the voters on March 13. It went into effect on May 29, when Wisconsin became the 30th state, and continues in force.

4391. California constitution was drawn up in both English and Spanish by a constitutional convention that met at Monterey in September–October 1849, some months after the announcement of the discovery of gold at Sutter's Mill brought tens of thousands of settlers into the territory. It prohibited slavery and granted property rights to women. It was submitted to the voters and ratified in November 1849. California became the 31st state on September 9, 1850. Its present constitution was drafted in Sacramento in 1879, took effect on January 1, 1880, and underwent a major revision in 1966.

4392. Minnesota constitution was drafted in July–August 1857 by a constitutional convention that met in St. Paul. The convention produced two documents, one supported by the Republicans, the other by the Democrats. Both versions were submitted to the voters on Octo-

STATES—CONSTITUTIONS—*continued*

ber 13, received their approval, and went into effect jointly on May 11, 1858, when Minnesota joined the Union as the 32nd state. They were resolved in 1974 into a single constitution, which remains in place.

4393. Oregon constitution was drawn up in August and September of 1857 at Salem, the capital of the Oregon territory. It was approved by the voters on November 9 and became effective on February 14, 1859, when Oregon joined the Union as the 33rd state. It has not been superseded.

4394. Kansas constitution was the outcome of the struggle over slavery that consumed Kansas in the years prior to statehood. The first group to draft a constitution was the Free State Party, which convened at Topeka in October 1855. Their constitution, adopted on December 15, served as the basis for the formation of an anti-slavery territorial government, complete with legislature and governor, that rivalled the pro-slavery government already in existence. The proslavery legislature sent delegates to a constitutional convention at Lecompton in the fall of 1857, but the document that they produced was rejected by the voters. A third constitution, similar to the Topeka Constitution, was not accepted by Congress. Kansas was finally admitted to the Union as the 34th state, and as a free state, on January 29, 1861, under the Wyandotte Constitution, which was drafted in a convention at Wyandotte (now Kansas City) and approved by the voters on October 4, 1859. This constitution remains in effect.

4395. West Virginia constitution was drafted by a constitutional convention that assembled at Wheeling on November 26, 1861, representing the voters of 39 counties in the western part of Virginia. Virginia had seceded from the Union six months earlier, prompting the voters in its trans-Allegheny region to call for the creation of a separate, pro-Union state. This constitution, revised to incorporate provisions for the emancipation of slaves, was approved by the voters on March 12, 1863, and went into effect when West Virginia became the 35th state on June 20. It was replaced on August 22, 1872, by the present constitution, which included provisions that were intended to end discrimination against Confederate veterans and sympathizers, who had been barred under Reconstruction policies from voting and holding public office.

4396. Nevada constitution took effect on October 31, 1864, when Nevada was admitted to the Union as the 36th state. It was drafted by a convention that assembled at Carson City in July 1864 and was ratified by the voters the following September. An earlier proposal for a constitution had been rejected by the voters in 1863 because it allowed the federal government to tax Nevada's silver mines. The original constitution is still in effect.

4397. Nebraska constitution was composed by the legislature in 1866, following two failed attempts, in 1860 and 1864, to call a constitutional convention. It went into effect on March 1, 1867, when Nebraska joined the Union as the 37th state. The first attempt to revise this constitution, in 1871, was rejected by the voters. The second, drafted at Lincoln in May and June 1875, received the electorate's approval and was made law on November 1 of that year. It remains in effect.

4398. Colorado constitution was the Constitution of Jefferson Territory, a frame of government composed by miners working for the West Denver Company. It formed the basis for a territorial legislature in 1859, although Congress did not recognize its validity. Congress created the Colorado Territory two years later and passed an enabling act for statehood in 1864. The first state constitution to be drafted was rejected by the voters to whom it was submitted for ratification. The second was rejected by President Andrew Johnson. The third, drafted in Denver between December 1875 and March 1876, was accepted by the voters, the president, and Congress, and has been in effect since August 1, 1876, when Colorado joined the Union as the 38th state.

4399. North Dakota constitution was drafted by a convention held at Bismarck, the capital of Dakota Territory, between July 4 and August 17, 1889, and received the approval of the voters on October 1. It has been in effect since November 2, 1889, when North Dakota was admitted to the Union as the 39th state.

4400. South Dakota constitution was drafted on July 4, 1889, by a constitutional convention that met in Sioux Falls. The act enabling South Dakota to pursue statehood had been passed by Congress the previous February 22. The constitution was ratified by the electorate on October 1, 1889, and has been in effect since November 2, 1889, when South Dakota became the 40th state.

4401. Montana constitution was drafted by a constitutional convention in 1866 but was discarded because the population of the Montana Territory was too low for statehood. A second proposal was turned down by Congress in 1884. Congress passed an enabling act for Montana statehood in February 1889, and the following summer still another constitution was drafted, at a convention in Helena. It was ratified on October 1 by the voters and took effect on November 8, 1889, when Montana became the 41st state. The current constitution, also drafted by a convention meeting in Helena, has been in effect since July 1, 1973.

4402. Washington State constitution was drafted in July–August 1889 at the constitutional convention that met in Olympia. It was ratified by the electorate on October 1 with the exception of two provisions, one that would have prohibited alcoholic beverages and another that would have extended voting rights to women. The constitution, which is still in force, went into effect on November 11, 1889, when Washington was admitted as the 42nd state. An earlier constitution was drafted in 1872 but was premature, since Congress did not pass an enabling act for Washington's statehood until February 1889.

4403. Idaho constitution has been in force since July 3, 1890, when Idaho was admitted to the Union as the 43rd state. It was drafted in Boise at a convention that met from July 4 to August 6, 1889, and approved at the polls on November 5. The voters considered proposals for new constitution in 1902 and 1970 but rejected them both.

4404. Wyoming constitution was drafted over the course of 25 days in September 1889 at a convention that met in Cheyenne. It received the approval of the voters on November 5 and went into effect on July 10, 1890, when Wyoming became the 44th state. This was the first state constitution to establish voting rights for women. (Women residents of Wyoming had been granted suffrage by the territorial legislature in 1869, making them the first women in the world to be granted the permanent right to vote.) The 1890 constitution has not been superseded.

4405. Utah constitution was rejected by Congress in 1860, as was a second constitution drafted in 1872. The western part of what is now the state of Utah was then a colony of the Church of Jesus Christ of Latter-day Saints (the Mormon Church). Known as Deseret, it had had a government and a constitution since 1849, and had been included since 1850 in the

Utah Territory, but was subjected to punitive actions by Congress after the Mormons declared the practice of polygamy to be official church doctrine. Plural marriage was abolished by the church in 1890, and Congress agreed in 1894 to accept proposals for statehood. A constitutional convention met in Salt Lake City from March 4 to May 8, 1895, and produced a document that guaranteed the separation of church and state and declared polygamous marriage "forever prohibited." It was approved by the voters on November 5 and went into effect on January 4, 1896, when Utah became the 45th state. It remains in effect.

4406. Oklahoma constitution was drafted at Guthrie by at a constitutional convention that met from November 20, 1906, to July 16, 1907. It was ratified at the polls on September 17, 1907, and became law on November 16, when Oklahoma joined the Union as the 46th state. It is still in use.

4407. New Mexico constitution was the present one, drafted by a constitutional convention in Santa Fe between October 3 and November 21, 1910, and ratified by the voters on January 21, 1911. Two of its provisions—for the popular recall of judges and for the adoption of future constitutional amendments—had to be altered to meet the objections of Congress and of President William Howard Taft. The voters accepted the new version in November 1911, and the constitution went into effect on January 6, 1912, when New Mexico became the 47th state. Two earlier constitutions, written during the movement for statehood, were rejected, the first by Congress in 1850, the second by the voters in 1890.

4408. Arizona constitution was a provisional document adopted by its settlers in 1860, when Arizona was part of the territory of New Mexico. During the Civil War, Arizona was designated a territory of the Confederacy and was then placed under martial law and organized as a territory of the United States. A constitution was drafted in 1891 at Phoenix and was ratified by the voters, but the enabling act passed by Congress in 1910 mandated the calling of a second constitutional convention, which produced a document that was ratified on February 9, 1911. Arizona was granted statehood as the 48th state on February 14, 1912, after its voters agreed to remove from their constitution a provision allowing the popular recall of judges. The 1912 constitution is still in use.

STATES—CONSTITUTIONS—*continued*

4409. Alaska constitution was the present one. It was drafted at the University of Alaska, Juneau, at a convention that continued from November 8, 1955, through February 5, 1956, and drew on the three organic laws—the Civil Government of Alaska Act (1884), the Carter Act (1900), and the Alaska Home Rule Act (1912)—under which the area had been governed since it was brought under the formal jurisdiction of the United States in 1884. The voters of Alaska ratified the constitution in April 1956; two years later, they gave approval to a set of amendments required by the federal government to protect its own interests. The constitution has been in force since January 3, 1959, when Alaska became the 49th state.

4410. Hawaii constitution during its years as an independent monarchy was promulgated by King Kamehameha III on October 8, 1840, and created a lower house of legislators elected by the people. A Declaration of Rights, based on the American Declaration of Independence, and an Edict of Toleration had been instituted in June 1839. Additional constitutions followed in 1852, 1864, and 1887. A republican constitution was issued on July 4, 1894, after the monarchy was overthrown in a coup by American planters. Hawaii was annexed to the United States in 1898. On November 7, 1950, its residents approved a proposed constitution that had been drafted by a convention. After modifications by Congress, the document took effect on August 21, 1959, when Hawaii became the 50th state. It remains in force.

STATES—COURTS

4411. State to allow election of lower court judges instead of appointment was Georgia, which did so in 1812.

4412. State constitution to provide for election of judges was the first constitution of Iowa, which went into effect upon statehood on December 28, 1846.

4413. African-American justice of a state supreme court was Jonathan Jasper Wright of Beaufort, SC, who served as one of the three members of the court from February 2, 1870, to December 1, 1877.

4414. State court of small claims was authorized on March 15, 1913, by Kansas, to deal with cases of debt involving not more than twenty dollars. Plaintiffs and defendants appeared without legal representation. Judges served without fee, pay, or award and were not required to be lawyers. Appeals could be taken to the district court. The first court met at Topeka, KS, with W. H. Kemper as judge.

4415. Woman to serve as a judge in a general court was Florence Ellinwood Allen of Ohio, who was elected in 1920 to the office of judge of the Court of Common Appeals.

4416. Woman to serve as a justice of a state supreme court was Florence Ellinwood Allen of Cleveland, OH, who was elected on December 16, 1922, to the Ohio Supreme Court.

4417. State supreme court in which all the judges were women was the Special Supreme Court of Texas, appointed by Governor Pat Morris Neff on January 8, 1925. When an application for writ of error in the case of *W.T. Johnson, et al. v. J.M. Darr, et al.*, from El Paso County (a Woodmen of the World case), reached the Supreme Court of Texas, all three judges found themselves disqualified to consider it and immediately certified their disqualifications to the governor as required by law. The governor appointed Hortense Ward of Houston as special chief justice and Hattie L. Henenberg of Dallas and Ruth Brazzil of Galveston as special associate justices. The case was decided on May 23, 1925, affirming the judgment of the Court of Civil Appeals.

4418. Woman to serve as chief justice of a state supreme court was Lorna Elizabeth Lockwood of Douglas, AZ, who was elected as chief justice of the Arizona Supreme Court by unanimous vote of the other justices on January 8, 1965, as chief justice of the Arizona Supreme Court. She served as chief justice from 1965 to 1975. She had been elected an associate justice of the court in 1961.

4419. Public defender hired by a state was Peter Murray, appointed director of the Office of State Public Defender by Governor Richard Joseph Hughes of New Jersey on June 20, 1967, for a five-year term. A deputy public defender was appointed for each of New Jersey's 21 counties.

4420. African-American to serve as chief justice of a state supreme court was James Benton Parsons, who became chief justice of the Illinois Supreme Court on April 18, 1975.

4421. Federal agency to promote the development of judicial administration in state courts was the State Justice Institute, created by the State Justice Institute Act of 1984 as a private, nonprofit corporation to further the development and improvement of judicial administration in the states. The institute directs a national program of assistance to ensure that all citizens have ready access to a fair and effective judicial system; fosters coordination and cooperation with the federal judiciary; serves as a clearinghouse and information center for state judicial systems; and encourages education for state judges and support personnel.

4422. Full TV coverage of a state supreme court began in 1995 in the state of Washington, when Washington Public Affairs Network (or TVW), a free, 24-hour cable channel, began broadcasting full coverage of arguments before the state Supreme Court on the TVW channel. Washington Public Affairs Network was the brainchild of former state legislator Denny L. Heck.

STATES—ELECTIONS

4423. State to grant universal voting rights to freemen without restriction as to property or wealth was Vermont. The state constitution adopted at a general convention held on July 28, 1777, at Windsor, VT, permitted all freemen who were natural-born citizens over 21 years of age to elect officers and to be elected to office.

4424. State to remove property ownership as a qualification for voting rights was South Carolina, which abolished the requirement in 1778.

4425. Printed ballot was authorized by the "act to regulate the general elections within this commonwealth," enacted on February 15, 1799, by Pennsylvania. The law provided that "every elector may deliver written or printed tickets." The ballots were prepared by political parties and were known as "vest pocket tickets." They contained only the names of the issuing party's candidates.

4426. Voting registration law enacted by a state was enacted by Massachusetts and signed on March 7, 1801, by Governor Caleb Strong.

4427. State nominating convention assembled at Utica, NY, in August 1824 for the purpose of nominating candidates for governor and lieutenant governor. The number of delegates corresponded to the number of representatives in the assembly. De Witt Clinton was nominated by the Democratic-Republican Party and was elected on November 3, 1824. He served as governor from January 1, 1825, to his death on February 11, 1828. He had previously served as governor from January 1, 1818, to December 31, 1822.

4428. Literacy qualification for voting was required by Massachusetts. An amendment was passed on May 1, 1857, by a vote of 23,833 for and 13,746 against, providing that "no person shall have the right to vote, or to be eligible to office under the constitution of this commonwealth, who shall not be able to read the constitution in the English language, and write his name," excepting those unable to qualify because of physical disability or those over 60 years of age.

4429. Corrupt election practices law enacted by a state was passed by the legislature of California and signed by Governor Frederick Low on March 26, 1866.

4430. State law requiring candidates to file itemized accounts of campaign expenditures under penalty of imprisonment and loss of office was passed by New York State and signed by Governor Theodore Roosevelt on April 4, 1890.

4431. Absentee voting law enacted by a state was enacted by Vermont on November 24, 1896. According to its provisions, a voter could obtain a certificate declaring that he was qualified to vote in the state. He could then vote for state officers at any election booth in the state.

4432. State to adopt the use of the initiative and referendum was South Dakota, whose Joint Resolution No. 101, calling for a constitutional amendment permitting their use, was passed on January 27, 1897, by the state House and on February 27, 1897, by its Senate. The amendment was submitted to the voters on November 8, 1898, and passed with 23,816 votes in favor and 16,483 against. On June 2, 1902, Oregon adopted an amendment to the state constitution authorizing both initiative and referendum on legislation, by popular vote. The Supreme Court declared the initiative and referendum constitutionally valid on February 19, 1912.

4433. Voting machines in congressional elections were approved by Congress in a bill signed by President William McKinley on February 14, 1899. It provided that "all votes for representatives in Congress must be by written or printed ballot, or voting machines, the use of which has been duly authorized by the state."

STATES—ELECTIONS—*continued*

4434. Primary election law enacted by a state was passed by Minnesota on April 20, 1899. It applied to candidates for city and county offices, judges, and elective members of school, library, and park boards in counties having a population of 200,000 or more. Hennepin County was the only one that had the required population when the law went into effect.

4435. State to establish statewide primary elections was Wisconsin, in 1903.

4436. Election law lowering the voting age in a state to 18 was enacted on March 3, 1943, as an amendment to the Georgia state constitution. Georgians heeded the "fight at eighteen, vote at eighteen" slogan by ratifying the constitutional amendment on August 4, 1943, by a 3–1 majority. The first election held under this law took place on November 7, 1944. The national voting age was lowered to 18 in 1971, when the 26th Amendment to the Constitution was ratified by the required number of states. It became law on July 5, 1971.

4437. Trial by a panel of judges to determine the winner of a state election was held in March 1963 to decide the winner of the Minnesota gubernatorial election of November 6, 1962. In the longest gubernatorial recount in United States history up to that time, Karl F. Rolvaag, the Democratic lieutenant governor, was declared the victor over incumbent Republican Governor Elmer L. Andersen four and a half months after the election. The returns in the November election were so close that both Rolvaag and Andersen claimed victory. On March 21, 1963, a panel of three district judges declared Rolvaag the winner by 91 out of a total of 1,239,593 valid ballots—less than 0.001 percent, probably the smallest margin in any U.S. gubernatorial election. Andersen continued to serve as governor during the interim between the election and March 25, 1963, when Rolvaag was sworn into office. Rolvaag's term would normally have begun on January 9.

4438. Politician who was openly homosexual to win a state election was Elaine Noble, a Democrat, who was elected on November 5, 1974, to the Massachusetts State Legislature from the 6th Suffolk district, the Fenway–Back Bay district of Boston, MA. She received 1,730 of the 2,931 votes cast.

4439. State to have a gubernatorial runoff election was Arizona, which passed a constitutional amendment in 1989 requiring a successful gubernatorial candidate to win at least 51 percent of the vote. The impetus for this law was the impeachment of former Arizona governor Evan Mecham, who had been elected in a three-way race in 1986 with only 40 percent of the vote. No candidate emerged from the November 1990 election with a 51 percent majority. A runoff election between the two leaders, Democrat Terry Goddard and Republican J. Fife Symington III, was held on February 26, 1991. Symington won the runoff, but he too was convicted of crimes during his second term and was forced out of office.

4440. Ku Klux Klan leader to mount a credible campaign for state governor was Republican David Duke, a Louisiana state legislator and a former grand wizard of the Ku Klux Klan. Duke beat incumbent governor Buddy Roemer in Louisiana's open-to-both-parties gubernatorial primary but lost in the election on November 5, 1991, to Democrat Edwin W. Edwards. Edwards, a former three-term governor, won by a landslide margin of 61 percent to 39 percent, largely driven by an unprecedented African-American voter turnout estimated at 80 percent.

4441. State law banning corporate contributions to ballot question campaigns was passed by the Montana legislature in 1996. The Montana Public Interest Research Group was the main lobbying organization pressing for this legislation.

4442. Voting rights in space were authorized by the Texas legislature in July 1997. The law was enacted after astronaut John Blaha, a registered voter in Houston, TX, requested the opportunity to vote in the election of November 1996 while he was millions of miles from home aboard the Russian space station *Mir*. Absentee ballots were not available when his mission began, and existing communications technology did not permit him to cast a secret ballot, as required by law. On August 25, 1997, Texas secretary of state Tony Garza announced a new computer program that would allow NASA to collect coded votes from astronauts in space by e-mail. Soviet cosmonauts had already participated in elections while in space, but their votes were not secret.

4443. Reform Party candidate to win a governorship was former wrestler Jesse "The Body" Ventura, elected governor of Minnesota on November 3, 1998. Ventura used his surprise victory over favored candidate Hubert Humphrey, Jr., to wrest control of the Reform Party organization from its founder, Ross Perot, and position himself for a presidential bid in 2000.

STATES—GOVERNORS

4444. New Hampshire state governor was Josiah Bartlett, a signer of the Declaration of Independence. Beginning in 1775, New Hampshire was governed by state presidents, of whom the first was council president Matthew Thornton (1775–76). The last president was Bartlett, who took office in 1790, after eight years of service as associate justice and then chief justice of the superior court of New Hampshire. He became the state's first governor in 1792, serving until 1794. He also had the distinction of being the first man to sign the Articles of Confederation.

4445. Connecticut state governor was Jonathan Trumbull, Sr., who occupied the office from 1776 to 1784. Since 1769, Trumbull had been the colonial governor of Connecticut.

4446. Georgia state governor was Archibald Bulloch, who served from 1776 to 1777.

4447. New Jersey state governor was William Livingston, a Federalist. He was inaugurated at Nassau Hall, Princeton, in 1776, and served until 1790.

4448. North Carolina state governor was Richard Caswell, a longtime member of the colonial assembly and a delegate to the Continental Congress. He led the North Carolina militia at the Battle of Moore's Creek Bridge (February 27, 1776). That action, against a force of loyalists and regular British troops under General Donald McDonald, resulted in a crushing defeat for the loyalists. Caswell was elected governor later that year by the Fifth Provincial Congress and served six one-year terms.

4449. Virginia state governor was Patrick Henry, radical revolutionary and former member of the Continental Congress, who was elected on May 6, 1776, by the delegates of the Fifth Virginia Convention in session at Williamsburg. He served until 1779 and again from 1784 to 1786.

4450. Maryland state governor was Thomas Johnson, former member of the Continental Congress and the man who nominated George Washington to be commander in chief of the Continental Army. He was elected in 1777 and served for two years, later becoming an associate justice of the Supreme Court.

4451. New York state governor was George Clinton, who occupied that office from 1777 to 1795, and later served an additional term from 1801 to 1804. Clinton, who had been a member of the Continental Congress, ran as Thomas Jefferson's vice president in the 1804 election, serving from 1805 to 1809, and was James Madison's vice president from 1809 to 1812.

4452. Vermont state governor was Thomas Chittenden, a popular local farmer who had served from 1778 to 1789 as the first president of the independent republic of Vermont. Chittenden was returned to office in 1790. The following year, Vermont joined the Union and he became its governor. He continued in office until 1797.

4453. South Carolina state governor was John Rutledge, who had previously served as president of the state from 1776 to 1778. His term as governor lasted from 1779 to 1782.

4454. Massachusetts state governor was John Hancock of Braintree (now Quincy), MA, the prominent merchant, Revolutionary leader, and signer of the Declaration of Independence. He was elected under the state's first permanent constitution in 1780. Hancock served as governor for nine terms between 1780 and 1793, except for 1785–86, the period of Shays's Rebellion, when he temporarily resigned from the governorship to serve in Congress under the Articles of Confederation.

4455. Rhode Island state governor was John Collins, elected in 1786 for a four-year term.

4456. Pennsylvania state governor was Thomas Mifflin, former Continental Army general and member of the Constitutional Convention. Beginning in 1777 with Thomas Wharton, Jr., the state of Pennsylvania was governed by the presidents of the Supreme Executive Council. Mifflin, a Federalist, was the last of these (succeeding Benjamin Franklin), and after the adoption of Pennsylvania's second constitution in 1790, he became the state governor. He continued to serve until 1799.

STATES—GOVERNORS—*continued*

4457. Kentucky state governor was Isaac Shelby, a Democratic-Republican who had served in the Revolutionary War. He was elected in 1791, the year before Kentucky, originally part of Virginia, was admitted to the Union as a separate state. Shelby occupied the office until 1796 and again from 1812 to 1816. He afterwards was a member of the North Carolina legislature.

4458. Delaware state governor was Joshua Clayton, a Federalist and the state's former treasurer. In June 1789 he was chosen by the General Assembly to be the last of Delaware's state presidents. He was elected governor in October 1792 and served until 1796. He was subsequently elected to the U.S. Senate.

4459. Tennessee state governor was the frontiersman John Sevier, who served six terms— 1796–1801 and 1803–09—after Tennessee was admitted to the Union as the 16th state in 1796. Sevier was also notable for being the only governor of the unrecognized state of Franklin (1784–1788), formed in the area (originally part of North Carolina) that later became the state of Tennessee.

4460. Ohio state governor was Edward Tiffin, an immigrant from England and a physician by training. A member of the Democratic-Republicans, he served in the territorial legislature before his election as governor in 1803, when Ohio entered the Union. He was reelected in 1805, but resigned two years later to enter the Senate. He later served in the state house of representatives and as commissioner of the General Land Office and surveyor general.

4461. Louisiana state governor was William Charles Coles Claiborne, a Jeffersonian Democrat and former congressman from Tennessee who had served as governor of the Mississippi Territory from 1801 to 1803 and as governor the Territory of Orleans, part of the Louisiana Territory, from 1804 to 1812. When Louisiana was admitted to the Union on April 30, 1812, as the 18th state, Claiborne became its governor, serving until 1816. In 1817, the year of his death, he represented Louisiana in the Senate.

4462. State governor who had previously been governor of a territory was William Charles Coles Claiborne, the first governor of Louisiana (1812–16). He had served as the territorial governor Louisiana from 1804 to 1812 and of Mississippi from 1801 to 1803.

4463. Indiana state governor was Jonathan Jennings, a Democratic-Republican. A New Jersey-born lawyer, he served as territorial delegate to Congress in 1809, 1811, 1812, and 1814. He was governor from 1816 to 1822, when he was elected to Congress.

4464. Mississippi state governor was David Holmes, a Democratic-Republican who had served previously for eight years as the last of Mississippi's territorial governors. He was elected in 1817 and served until 1820. He was briefly returned to office in 1826.

4465. Illinois state governor was Shadrach Bond, a Democrat-Republican, who occupied the statehouse from 1818 to 1822.

4466. Alabama state governor was William W. Bibb, a Democratic-Republican, who was the territorial governor from 1817 to 1819 and became the state governor when Alabama entered the Union on December 14, 1819, as the 22nd state.

4467. Maine state governor was Democratic-Republican William King, who took office in 1820 and served until 1821. Maine was a part of Massachusetts until 1819, when it voted to separate and adopted a constitution.

4468. Missouri state governor was Alexander McNair, a Democratic-Republican elected in 1820. He served a single four-year term. Missouri entered the Union on August 10, 1821.

4469. Brothers to serve simultaneously as governors of their respective states were Governor Levi Lincoln, Jr., who served as governor of the Commonwealth of Massachusetts from May 27, 1825, until January 21, 1834, and Governor Enoch Lincoln, who served as governor of Maine from January 4, 1827, until his death on October 8, 1829. Both were Whigs.

4470. Governor who was Catholic was Edward Douglass White, who served as governor of Louisiana from 1835 to 1839. Before and after his term, he served in the U.S. House of Representatives.

4471. Michigan state governor was Stevens T. Mason, a Democrat who had been the last of Michigan's territorial governors (1834–35). In 1835, when Michigan entered the Union, he was elected state governor at the age of 23. He served until 1840.

4472. Arkansas state governor was Democrat James S. Conway, who served from 1836 to 1840.

4473. Florida state governor was William Dunn Moseley, a Democrat, who defeated former territorial governor Richard Keith Call to win election in 1845. He served one term, until 1849, afterwards becoming a citrus grower.

4474. Iowa state governor was Ansel Briggs, a native of Vermont. He was a Democratic member of the Iowa territorial House of Representatives from 1842 to 1846 before his election to the governor's office in 1846. He served until 1850.

4475. Texas state governor was J. Pinckney Henderson, a Democrat from San Augustine. The first elections for statewide office were held on December 15, 1845. Henderson was inaugurated on February 19, 1846, at the capital, Austin, and served until 1847. Albert Clinton Horton, the first lieutenant governor, took the oath of office on May 2, 1846.

4476. Wisconsin state governor was Nelson Dewey, a Democrat, who served in the statehouse from 1848 to 1852.

4477. California state governor was Peter H. Burnett, a Democrat, who took office on December 20, 1849. California's first constitutional convention had nominated W. Scott Sherwood as the first governor of the state, but in the election Burnett garnered 6,783 votes to Sherwood's 3,220. The pro-slavery Burnett resigned on January 8, 1851, to protest California's entrance into the Union as a free state. Burnett later served as a justice of the State Supreme Court.

4478. State governor to be removed from office by a state supreme court was William Augustus Barstow, Democrat of Wisconsin, who served a full term from January 2, 1854, to January 7, 1856. He was installed for a second term on January 7, 1856. On March 20, 1856, the supreme court held that Coles Bashford, a Republican, was entitled to the office because of irregularities in the election. On March 21 Barstow resigned and the lieutenant governor, Arthur MacArthur, was sworn in. The state assembly recognized Bashford on March 27, 1856.

4479. Minnesota state governor was a Democrat, Henry Hastings Sibley, who arrived in the territory in 1834 to head the American Fur Company Post near Fort Snelling. He later served as territorial representative to Congress. He was elected governor when Minnesota was admitted to the Union in 1858 and served until 1860.

4480. Governor of two different states was Sam Houston. Born in Virginia, he moved with his family to Tennessee, eventually becoming a lawyer and serving for four years as Tennessee's representative in Congress. In 1827 he took office as the state governor. Two years later he resigned during a marital crisis and went to live with the Cherokee Indians. Settling in Texas, Houston became a leader in the movement for independence from Mexico and led the Texan Army in its victory at the Battle of San Jacinto in April 1836. He served as president of the Republic of Texas from 1836 to 1838 and again from 1841 to 1844, was elected to the Senate after Texas joined the Union in 1845, and was elected governor of Texas in 1859. After Texas seceded from the Union in March 1861, Houston was asked to sign a statement of allegiance to the Confederacy. He refused and was removed from office.

4481. Oregon state governor was "Honest John" Whiteaker, elected the Democratic governor of the state of Oregon in June 1858, though Oregon did not receive statehood until February 14, 1859. Whiteaker was officially sworn in on March 3.

4482. State governor to be impeached and acquitted was Charles Robinson, the first governor of Kansas (1861–63) and a leader of the Free State antislavery party, who was indicted for treason and conspiracy on a charge brought by the proslavery party. He was acquitted in 1862 by a federal grand jury and completed his term as governor.

4483. Kansas state governor was Charles Robinson, a Republican antislavery activist, who served from 1861 to 1863. Kansas entered the Union on January 29, 1861, under the Wyandotte Constitution, which made it a free state. The first Kansas native to become governor was Republican Arthur Capper, who took office on January 11, 1915.

4484. West Virginia state governor was Republican Arthur I. Boreman, elected to three two-year terms from 1863 to 1869. West Virginia was formed by residents of the western region of Virginia who objected to their state's secession in 1861. The new state was admitted on April 20, 1863.

4485. Nevada state governor was Henry G. Blasdel, a Republican, who served from 1864 to 1871. His salary was $4,700 a year, making him the highest-paid official in the state.

4486. Nebraska state governor was David Butler, a Republican, who took office in 1867. In 1871, he was impeached and removed from office for misappropriating state funds.

STATES—GOVERNORS—*continued*

4487. State governor who had previously been governor of a territory in which his state was not included was John White Geary, who served as governor of the Kansas Territory from September 9, 1856, to March 4, 1857. He served as governor of Pennsylvania from January 15, 1867, to January 21, 1873.

4488. State governor to be impeached and convicted was William Woods Holden, the 39th governor of North Carolina. On December 20, 1870, impeachment proceedings were brought against him in which he was charged with "high crimes and misdemeanors." The trial was conducted by Chief Justice Richmond Mumford Pearson. On March 22, 1871, he was ordered to be removed from office, two-thirds of the state senate having found him guilty of six of the eight charges brought against him.

4489. State governor who was African-American was Pinckney Benton Stewart Pinchback, the lieutenant governor of Louisiana, who served as the state's governor from December 11, 1872, to January 14, 1873, during the impeachment of Governor Henry Clay Warmoth.

4490. Colorado state governor was John Routt, a Republican, who took office in 1875 as the last of Colorado's territorial governors and went on to serve from 1876 to 1879 as its first state governor.

4491. Gubernatorial election in which two brothers were the opposing candidates was held on November 2, 1886, in Tennessee. Robert Love Taylor, the Democratic candidate, received 125,151 votes, defeating his brother, Alfred Alexander Taylor, the Republican candidate, who received 109,837 votes. Robert Love Taylor served as governor from January 17, 1887, to January 19, 1891, and from January 21, 1897, to January 16, 1899. Alfred Alexander Taylor defeated Albert Houston Roberts in the election of November 2, 1920, and served as governor of Tennessee from January 15, 1921, to January 16, 1923.

4492. Montana state governor was a Democrat, Joseph K. Toole, who served from 1889 to 1893.

4493. South Dakota state governor was a Republican, Arthur C. Mellette, who had been the last of the Dakota territorial governors. Mellette served in the statehouse at Pierre from 1889 to 1893.

4494. Washington state governor was Elisha P. Ferry, Republican, who occupied the statehouse from 1889 to 1893.

4495. North Dakota state governor was John Miller, a Republican and a native of New York state, who was inaugurated on November 20, 1889, three weeks after North Dakota was admitted to the Union on November 2. Miller had been a major landholder in the Dakota Territory, owning a 17,000-acre ranch in the Red River Valley.

4496. Idaho state governor was Republican George L. Shoup, elected in 1890. Shoup had been appointed the previous year as Idaho's last territorial governor.

4497. Wyoming state governor was Massachusetts-born businessman Francis E. Warren, a Republican who had won the Congressional Medal of Honor for his service in the Civil War. He served as the territorial governor from In 1885–86 and again in 1889–90. Warren was elected state governor on September 11, 1890, but was elected in November as the second U.S. senator for Wyoming and resigned his office. His term was finished by Amos W. Barber.

4498. Utah state governor was Heber M. Wells, who served from 1896 to 1905.

4499. Oklahoma state governor was Charles N. Haskell, a Democrat, who was elected in 1907 and served until 1911.

4500. New Mexico state governor was William C. McDonald, elected as a Democrat in 1912. He served until 1917.

4501. Arizona state governor was George W. P. Hunt, elected as a Democrat in 1911 and inaugurated on February 14, 1912, the day on which Arizona was admitted to statehood. A noted prison reformer, Hunt served for a total of seven two-year terms (1912–19, 1923–29, and 1931–33).

4502. State governor who was Jewish was Moses Alexander of Idaho, a Democrat, who served from January 4, 1915, to January 6, 1919. A previous governor of Jewish descent was David Emanuel of Georgia, a convert to Christianity, who served from March 3, 1801, to November 7, 1801, after the resignation of Governor James Jackson. It is not clear whether he became governor by virtue of the fact that he was president of the senate when Governor Jackson resigned, or whether he was regularly elected.

4503. Governor of Utah who was not a Mormon was the railroad tycoon Simon Bamberger, a Democrat of Jewish descent who served from 1917 to 1920. As governor, Bamberger establishment a state public service commission to regulate utilities and transportation companies and signed legislation establishing vocational education.

4504. New Mexico state governor of Latino ancestry was Ezequiel Cabeza de Baca, the state's second governor, who entered the state house in 1917 but died shortly thereafter. DeBaca County is named for him. The fourth governor, Octaviano Larrazolo, who served from 1919 to 1921, afterwards became the nation's first Latino senator.

4505. Woman to serve as a state governor was Nellie Tayloe Ross, who was elected governor of Wyoming on November 4, 1924, to fill the unexpired term of her late husband, William Bradford Ross. Texas elected its first woman governor, Miriam "Ma" Amanda Wallace Ferguson, on the same day, but Ross was sworn in first. From 1933 to 1935 Ross served as director of the Mint, the first woman to do so.

4506. Quack who almost became a state governor was Dr. John Brinkley, who made his fortune transplanting goat glands into men to restore their sexual potency. He would have won the 1930 Kansas gubernatorial election if the Kansas attorney general had not disqualified the majority of write-in votes.

4507. State governor to be granted almost dictatorial power was Paul Vories McNutt of Indiana. The Democrat-controlled legislature empowered him in February 1933 to organize the state government, which at that time was spread among 168 boards and commissions, into nine departments: Executive, State, Audit, Treasury, Law, Education, Public Works, Commerce, and Industry. He was authorized to hire and fire all state employees and to raise or lower salaries as he saw fit. His power was limited by legislative appropriations and by the authority of the courts to review and void his decisions.

4508. State governor to appoint two United States senators in one year for interim terms was Governor Robert Crosby of Nebraska, who appointed Eve Bowring to replace Senator Dwight Palmer Griswold (deceased April 12, 1954) and Samuel Williams Reynolds to replace Senator Hugh Alfred Butler (deceased July 1, 1954). Bowring was sworn in on April 26, 1954, and Reynolds on July 7. Hazel Hempel Abel was elected to fill out the remaining time in Griswold's term and Roman Lee Hruska was elected to fill out the remaining time in Butler's term.

4509. Alaska state governor was William A. Egan, a Democrat, who occupied the statehouse in Juneau from 1959 to 1966 and again from 1970 to 1974.

4510. Hawaii state governor was William F. Quinn, who had been the last territorial governor. Quinn, a Republican, was elected in 1959 and served until 1962.

4511. Democratic governor of Vermont since the Civil War was Philip H. Hoff, a lawyer, who became the first Democratic governor of Vermont since 1854 by narrowly defeating the incumbent Republican, F. Ray Keyser, Jr., on November 6, 1962. The election was upheld after a recount by the Vermont legislature, and Hoff took office for a two-year term on January 17, 1963.

4512. Republican governor of Oklahoma was Henry Bellmon, a farmer, former member of the Oklahoma House of Representatives, and chairman of the Republican state committee from 1960 to 1962. He was elected on November 6, 1962, to a four-year term. Since the state was admitted to the Union in 1907, all its governors had been Democrats.

4513. Republican governor of Arkansas since Reconstruction was Winthrop Rockefeller, second youngest of the five sons of John D. Rockefeller, Jr. He was elected in 1966, succeeding six-term Democrat Orval Faubus, and served until 1971. Among his accomplishments was passage of the state's first minimum-wage law. The last Republican governor left office in 1874.

4514. Republican governor of Florida since Reconstruction was Claude Roy Kirk, Jr., elected on November 8, 1966, with 821,190 votes, against 668,233 votes for his Democratic opponent. All state governors since 1877 had been Democrats.

4515. Woman governor of Alabama was Lurleen B. Wallace, elected in November 1966 to succeed her husband and political mentor, George Corley Wallace. She was inaugurated on January 16, 1967. Her brief administration, which lasted until she died in office in 1968, was viewed by many as a puppet administration that allowed her husband to continue his political control of the state.

STATES—GOVERNORS—*continued*

4516. Republican governor of Virginia since Reconstruction was Linwood Holton, a Roanoke lawyer. He was elected on November 4, 1969, with more than 52 percent of the vote, becoming the first Republican governor of the state in 84 years.

4517. State governor of Asian ancestry was George Ryoichi Ariyoshi, Democrat of Hawaii. Ariyoshi, whose parents were both born in Japan, was serving as lieutenant governor in October 1973 when he took over as acting governor after his predecessor fell ill. He defeated Republican Randolph A. Crossley, CEO of Hawaii Corporation, in the November 1973 general election with 55 percent of the vote.

4518. Woman governor elected in her own right was Ella Grasso, a Democrat, elected on November 5, 1974, as the 83rd governor of Connecticut. She was reelected in November 1978 for a second term, which, because of illness, she did not complete. She resigned on December 31, 1980, and died on February 5, 1981.

4519. Woman governor of Washington was Dixy Lee Ray, elected in 1976. Ray, a Democrat and an anti-environmentalist, was also the first chairwoman of the Atomic Energy Commission.

4520. Republican governor of Texas since Reconstruction was William P. Clements, Jr., elected in 1978. Clements served two nonconsecutive terms, 1979–1983 and 1987–1991. The last Republican in the Texas statehouse, Edmund J. Davis, was elected in 1870.

4521. Woman governor of Kentucky was Martha Layne Collins, a Democrat, who served a single term from 1984 to 1987. She decisively defeated Republican candidate Jim Bunning on November 6, 1983, taking 55 percent of the vote to his 44 percent. A former high-school teacher, Collins presented an educational reform package to the state legislature as one of the first acts of her administration.

4522. Hawaii state governor of Hawaiian ancestry was John Waihee, elected in 1986.

4523. Woman governor of Nebraska was Kay Orr, a Republican, elected governor in 1986. She had been the state's first woman chief-of-staff (to governor Charles Thone) and the first woman to win statewide office in Nebraska (she was state treasurer in 1982). She was also the first woman Republican governor of any state.

4524. African-American state governor elected in his own right was L. Douglas Wilder, a Democrat, who was elected governor of Virginia on November 7, 1989.

4525. State to elect two woman governors was Texas. On November 4, 1924, the state elected Miriam "Ma" Amanda Wallace Ferguson, a Democrat, who served two terms, from 1925 to 1927 and from 1933 to 1935. In November 1990, Democratic state treasurer Ann Richards became Texas's second woman governor, defeating Republican Clayton Williams, Jr. Richards served a single term.

4526. Woman governor of Kansas was Democrat Joan Finney, the former state treasurer, elected in November 1990. A right-to-life candidate, she defeated incumbent Mike Hayden, a pro-choice Republican.

4527. Woman governor of Oregon was Barbara Roberts, a Democrat and the former secretary of state, who served as Oregon's 34th governor from January 14, 1991, to January 8, 1995. In 1981, she was elected to the Oregon House of Representatives, where, during her second term, she became Oregon's first woman House majority leader.

4528. Woman governor of New Jersey was Christine Todd Whitman, a Republican. She was elected on November 2, 1993, defeating incumbent governor Jim Florio by a narrow margin of 50 percent to 49 percent.

4529. Woman governor of New Hampshire was Jeanne Shaheen. In November 1996, she defeated her Republican opponent, conservative Ovide LaMontagne, with 57 percent of the vote. Shaheen had served three terms in the state senate.

4530. State in which two consecutive governors were forced to resign from office was Arizona. Republican governor Evan Mecham was found guilty by a state senate court of impeachment of obstructing justice and misusing public funds and was removed from office on April 4, 1988. On September 3, 1997, a federal jury meeting in a court in Phoenix, AZ, convicted his successor, Republican J. Fife Symington III, of seven felony counts of defrauding his lenders as a commercial real estate developer. Symington immediately resigned. He was later sentenced to two and a half years in prison plus five years' probation.

4531. Woman governor of Arizona was Jane Dee Hull, born Jane Dee Bowersock, a Republican, who was sworn in at Phoenix, AZ, as the 20th governor of the state on September 5, 1997. She succeeded J. Fife Symington III, who had just been convicted of real-estate fraud. Hull previously served in the Arizona House of Representatives, representing District 18 in north central Phoenix, and, from 1994, as Symington's secretary of state.

4532. State governor who had been a professional wrestler was Jesse "The Body" Ventura, who was elected governor of Minnesota on November 3, 1998, on the Reform Party ticket. A former Navy Seal, wrestler on the World Wrestling Federation Circuit, and action-film actor, Ventura defeated Democrat candidate Hubert Humphrey, son of the former vice president.

4533. Woman governor of Ohio was Nancy P. Hollister, the state's lieutenant governor, who succeeded George V. Voinovich on December 31, 1998, after he resigned to enter the Senate. She served until January 11, 1999, when Robert Taft was sworn in as the newly elected governor.

4534. Woman governor of Delaware was Ruth Ann Minner, a Democrat, formerly the state's lieutenant governor. On November 7, 2000, she defeated Republican candidate John Burris, taking 59 percent of the vote.

4535. Woman governor of Montana was Judy Martz, a Republican, elected on November 7, 2000. She had been Montana's lieutenant governor. She took 51 percent of the vote, beating her Democratic opponent, state auditor Mark O'Keefe.

STATES—LEGISLATURES

4536. State to enact a conflict-of-interest law concerning its legislature was Maryland, whose constitution of 1776 barred from the General Assembly and the Council any contractor or merchant who stood to make a profit from selling military supplies to the state, as did North Carolina's a month later. Maryland also required its governor and legislators to take an oath renouncing any such profits.

4537. State to give its legislature sole power to determine the eligibility of legislators was New Jersey, which did so in its constitution of 1776. Seven decades earlier, in 1707, the colonial governor of New Jersey, Lord Cornbury, had disqualified three deputies in the hope of replacing them with others more congenial to him. The Assembly responded in 1709 by enacting a law providing that its deputies "are and shall be judges of the qualifications of their own members."

4538. State with a unicameral legislature was Pennsylvania, under the original state constitution adopted in 1776. Its second constitution, adopted in 1790, provided for a bicameral General Assembly consisting of a Senate and a House of Representatives. The 1777 constitutions of Georgia and Vermont also provided for unicameral legislatures, both of which were later changed to bicameral.

4539. State legislature with a lower house known as the House of Representatives was New Hampshire, which used the term in its constitution of January 5, 1776, with "Assembly" as an alternative. The first state to use the term exclusively was Pennsylvania, also in 1776. Lower houses were variously known as the House of Burgesses, the House of Delegates, the House of Commons, the Assembly, the House of Assembly, and the General Assembly.

4540. State to set an age qualification for state senators was South Carolina, whose constitution of March 26, 1776, established that members of the state legislature's upper house had to be at least 30 years old. The 1776 constitutions of Virginia and Maryland set the age requirement at 25. The word "senator" is derived from the Latin word for "mature."

4541. State legislature with an upper house known as the Senate was Virginia, whose first state constitution, adopted on June 12, 1776, provided for a bicameral legislature in which the lower house would elect the upper house. Following a suggestion by Thomas Jefferson, the upper house was designated by the term "Senate." In the colonies, upper houses were referred to by a variety of terms, including Council, Provincial Council, Legislative Council, and House of Deputies.

4542. State to fix a time limit on legislative sessions was Louisiana, whose constitution of 1845 gave its legislators a limit of 60 days in which to accomplish the business of the state.

4543. Community leader in the United States to exercise the authority of king and high priest was James J. Strang, an expelled Mormon elder who organized a dissident sect of 5,000 Mormons. In 1847 the group settled on Big Beaver Island, MI, where Strang crowned himself King James I in 1850. He was elected to the Michigan legislature in 1852. Strang was assassinated by two of his followers on June 16, 1856.

STATES—LEGISLATURES—*continued*

4544. African-American state legislators were Edwin Garrison Walker and Charles Lewis Mitchell of Boston, MA, who in 1866 were elected to the Massachusetts House of Representatives.

4545. State legislator who was African-American to represent a constituency with a white majority was Bishop Benjamin William Arnett of the African Methodist Episcopal Church, Greene County, OH, who served in the lower house of the Ohio State Legislature from 1885 to 1887. He served in the 66th session, which convened on January 6, 1885, and adjourned on May 4, 1885, and the 67th, which convened on January 4, 1886, and adjourned on May 19, 1886.

4546. Women elected to a state legislature were elected to the Colorado General Assembly on November 6, 1894. They were Clara Cressingham and Frances Klock, both elected from Arapahoe County, and Carrie Holly, elected from Pueblo County.

4547. Woman to serve as a state senator was Martha Hughes Cannon, elected to the second session of the Utah senate on November 3, 1896, and reelected to the third. She was a Democrat and represented the 6th Senatorial District, comprising Salt Lake County.

4548. State legislature to use an electric vote recorder was that of Wisconsin. The machine was installed on January 11, 1917, in the Wisconsin Assembly Chamber in Madison. It displayed green and white signal lights opposite the name of each legislator to show how he or she voted. A roll call could be recorded in eleven seconds, at a savings of more than 99 percent of the time previously consumed in roll calls. The acquisition of the vote recorder was approved on July 29, 1915.

4549. Woman to serve in a state legislature as speaker of the House was Minnie Davenport Craig of Esmond, ND, a Republican, who was elected speaker on January 3, 1933. She served for one session, until March 31, 1933.

4550. Interstate legislative conference assembled in Washington, DC, on February 3, 1933, under the auspices of the American Legislators' Association. The conference was attended by 100 state legislators and tax experts from 32 states who discussed double taxation, overlapping and conflicting of federal and state taxes, and similar matters. Only the legislators were entitled to vote.

4551. State legislature with a single chamber in the post-Revolutionary era was Nebraska, which adopted a unicameral system by constitutional amendment on November 6, 1934. A single body of 43 members replaced a House of 100 members and a Senate of 33. The first bill, passed on January 21, 1937, appropriated $10,000 for mileage, postage, and incidental expenses for the members. All of the original states adopted bicameral systems at the formation of the United States, except Pennsylvania, Georgia, and Vermont, which changed to a bicameral system after four, twelve, and 58 years, respectively.

4552. African-American woman to serve as a state legislator was Crystal Bird Fauset of Philadelphia, PA, elected on November 8, 1938, to the Pennsylvania House of Representatives. Her term of office began on December 1, 1938, and she was sworn in and assumed her seat on January 3, 1939.

4553. Husband and wife to be elected simultaneously to both chambers of a state legislature were Richard Lewis Neuberger and Maurine Brown Neuberger, both Democrats, who were elected to the Oregon legislature on November 7, 1950—he to the state senate, and she to the house of representatives. He had already served one term in the state senate, having been elected on November 2, 1948, to represent the 13th district. The couple co-authored "Adventures in Politics: We Go to the Legislature, published in 1954.

4554. State legislative hearing to be shown on television was a hearing by the New Jersey senate's Committee on Federal and Interstate Relations that took place on April 11, 1954, and was aired from 7:30 to 8 P.M. on WATV, Newark, NJ. The subject was a proposal by Senator Malcolm Forbes to stop all new projects by the Port of New York Authority (later known as the Port Authority of New York and New Jersey). The proposal was defeated.

4555. Mexican-American elected to the Texas state senate in the 20th century was Henry B. Gonzalez, elected in 1956. A Mexican-American had last been state senator in 1846.

4556. African-American to serve as chief sergeant-at-arms of a state legislature was Charles E. Bell, who was appointed to that post by the California legislature in 1983 and served until 1996.

4557. Father and daughter to serve simultaneously in the same house of representatives were James Edward "Billy" McKinney and his daughter, Cynthia Ann McKinney. They served together in the Georgia house of representatives from 1989 to 1992.

4558. State in which women constituted more than 40 percent of the legislature was Washington State. The election of November 1998 produced a state legislature that was 40.8 percent female and 59.2 percent male. The legislature of Nevada was 36.5 percent female; of Arizona, 35.6 percent; of Colorado, 33 percent; and of Kansas, 32.7 percent. The state with the lowest percentage of women in its legislature was Alabama, with 7.9. Nationwide, the average percentage was 22.3.

STATES—PRESIDENTIAL CANDIDATES

4559. Presidential candidate from Connecticut was Samuel Huntington, the governor of Connecticut. He was one of twelve candidates whose names were submitted to the electors in 1789. He received two of 69 votes cast.

4560. Presidential candidate from Maryland was Robert Hanson Harrison. He was one of twelve candidates whose names were submitted to the electors in 1789. He received six of 69 votes cast, the fourth highest number (a tie with John Rutledge of South Carolina).

4561. Presidential candidate from Pennsylvania was Congressman James Armstrong, later a senator, minister to France, and secretary of war. He was one of twelve candidates whose names were submitted to the electors in 1789. He received one vote out of 69 cast.

4562. Presidential candidate from South Carolina was John Rutledge, former governor of South Carolina, later an associate justice of the Supreme Court. He was one of twelve candidates whose names were submitted to the electors in 1789. He received six votes out of 69 cast, the fourth highest number (a tie with Robert Hanson Harrison of Maryland).

4563. Presidential candidates from Georgia were John Milton and Edward Telfair, former and future governor of Georgia. They were among the twelve candidates whose names were submitted to the electors in 1789. Milton received two of 69 votes cast and Telfair received one.

4564. Presidential candidates from Massachusetts were John Adams, the former minister to Great Britain; John Hancock, the governor of Massachusetts; and Benjamin Lincoln, general in the Continental Army and former secretary of war. They were among the twelve candidates whose names were submitted to the electors in 1789. Adams received 34 of 69 votes cast, the second highest number, making him the vice president under George Washington, who finished first. Hancock received four votes and Lincoln received one.

4565. Presidential candidates from New York State were John Jay, the U.S. secretary of foreign affairs, later the chief justice of the Supreme Court, and George Clinton, the governor of New York, later the vice president in Thomas Jefferson's second administration and James Madison's first. Jay and Clinton were among the twelve candidates whose names were submitted to the electors in 1789. Jay received nine of 69 votes cast, the third highest number. Clinton received three. Both were presidential candidates again in 1796 and 1800.

4566. Presidential candidate from Virginia was George Washington, who stood for election on March 4, 1789, at Federal Hall in New York, NY, along with eleven other candidates. He was chosen president by unanimous vote of the 69 electors.

4567. Presidential candidates from North Carolina were Samuel Johnston, the governor of North Carolina, and James Iredell, associate justice of the Supreme Court, later governor of North Carolina. They were among the 13 candidates whose names were submitted to the electors in 1796. Iredell received three of 276 votes cast and Johnston received two.

4568. Presidential candidate from Tennessee was Andrew Jackson, army general and Democratic-Republican senator, and one of four candidates who stood for office in 1824. None received a majority of the electoral vote, and the House of Representatives chose John Quincy Adams, the runner-up, over Jackson. In the next election, in 1828, Jackson defeated Adams. He was reelected in 1832.

4569. Presidential candidate from Kentucky was Henry Clay, the Democratic-Republican congressman, later senator. He was one of four men who were candidates for president on November 2, 1824. Each had the support of a congressional caucus or at least one state legislature. None received a majority of the electoral vote. Clay came in fourth, placing him out of contention, and his supporters switched their

STATES—PRESIDENTIAL CANDI-
DATES—*continued*

votes to John Quincy Adams, who was named the winner by the House of Representatives, although he had originally come in second to Andrew Jackson. Clay ran again for president in 1832, on the National Republican ticket, and in 1844, on the ticket of the Whig Party, successor to the National Republicans.

4570. Presidential candidate from Ohio was William Henry Harrison, who was nominated by a faction of the Whig Party on December 14, 1835, at a state convention held in Harrisburg, PA. He lost the 1836 election to the Democratic-Republican candidate, Martin Van Buren, but was renominated by the Whigs in 1840 and defeated Van Buren in his bid for reelection.

4571. Presidential candidate from Michigan was Lewis Cass, who was nominated on the fourth ballot by the Democratic Party in May 1848 at its convention in Baltimore, MD.

4572. Presidential candidate from Louisiana was Zachary Taylor, who was nominated on the fourth ballot by the Whig Party in June 1848 at its convention in Philadelphia, PA. He won the election on November 7, 1848. Taylor was born in Virginia and spent most of his adulthood as an army officer but had special ties to Louisiana, where he had been stationed in the 1820s.

4573. Presidential candidate from New Hampshire was John Parker Hale, who was nominated on October 20, 1848, by the a faction of the Free Soil Party at its convention in Buffalo, NY. He was renominated by the entire Free Soil Party in 1852.

4574. Presidential candidate from New Jersey was General Winfield Scott, who was nominated on the 53rd ballot by the Whig Party in June 1852 at its convention in Baltimore, MD.

4575. Presidential candidate from California was John Charles Frémont, who was nominated by the Republican Party in June 1856 at its convention in Philadelphia, PA. This was the first time the Republican Party fielded a candidate for the presidency. Frémont was also nominated in 1864 by a Republican faction, the Independent Republican Party, but gave his support to the Republican candidate, Abraham Lincoln, before the election.

4576. Presidential candidates from Illinois were Abraham Lincoln and Stephen Arnold Douglas, both of whom ran for president in 1860. Lincoln was nominated on the third ballot by the Republican Party in May 1860 at its convention in Chicago, IL. Douglas was nomi-

nated on the second ballot by the Democratic Party in June 1860 at its convention in Baltimore, MD. The election, on November 6, was won by the Republicans. Lincoln was reelected in 1864.

4577. Presidential candidate from Vermont was John Wolcott Phelps, who was nominated by the American Party in 1880.

4578. Presidential candidate from Iowa was James Baird Weaver, who was nominated on the first ballot by the Greenback Labor Party at its convention in Chicago, IL, in June 1880. Weaver ran again on the People's Party ticket in 1892.

4579. Presidential candidate from Texas was Benjamin J. Chambers, who was nominated on the first ballot by the Greenback Labor Party in June 1880 at its convention in Chicago, IL.

4580. Presidential candidate from Maine was Neal Dow, who was nominated by the Prohibition Party (the National Prohibition Reform Party) on June 17, 1880, at its convention in Cleveland, OH.

4581. Presidential candidate from Kansas was Samuel Clarke Pomeroy, who was nominated by the American Prohibition Party at its convention in Chicago, IL, on June 19, 1884.

4582. Presidential candidate from Indiana was Benjamin Harrison, who was nominated by the Republican Party in June 1888 at its convention in Chicago, IL. He was elected on November 6, 1888. He ran for reelection in 1892 but was defeated by Grover Cleveland.

4583. Presidential candidate from Nebraska was William Jennings Bryan, who was nominated on the fifth ballot by the Democratic Party in July 1896 at its convention in Chicago, IL. He was also nominated by the Middle-of-the-Road branch of the Populist Party (People's Party) and by the National Silver Party (Bi-Metallic League). Bryan ran for president again in 1900 as the Democratic, People's, and Silver Republican candidate, and for a third time in 1908 as the Democratic candidate.

4584. Presidential candidate from Missouri was William Wesley Cox, who was nominated by the Socialist Labor Party in May 1920 at its convention in New York, NY.

4585. Presidential candidate from Utah was Parley Parker Christensen, who was nominated by the Farmer Labor Party in June 1920 at its convention in Chicago, IL.

4586. Presidential candidate from Oregon was Frank T. Johns, who was nominated by the Socialist Labor Party in May 1924 at its convention in New York, NY. He was renominated by the party in May 1928 but was killed two weeks later when he tried to rescue a drowning child.

4587. Presidential candidate from West Virginia was John William Davis, former congressman, solicitor general, and ambassador, who was nominated on the 103rd ballot by the Democratic Party in July 1924 at its convention in New York, NY.

4588. Presidential candidate from Wisconsin was Robert Marion La Follette, senator from Wisconsin and former governor, who was nominated by the Progressive Party and the Socialist Party in July 1924. Both parties met in convention in Cleveland, OH.

4589. Presidential candidate from Arkansas was William Hope Harvey, who was nominated by the Liberty Party on August 17, 1932, at its convention in St. Louis, MO.

4590. Presidential candidate from North Dakota was William Lemke, who was nominated by the Union Party on June 19, 1936.

4591. Presidential candidate from Washington State was Frederick C. Proehl, who was nominated by the Greenback Party in 1952. He was renominated in 1956. Anna Milburn received the nomination of the Greenback party in 1940 but declined it.

4592. Presidential candidate from Mississippi was Charles Loten Sullivan, who was nominated by the Constitution Party of Texas in 1960.

4593. Presidential candidate from Alaska was Raymond L. Teague, who was nominated by the Theocratic Party on May 21, 1960, at Fulton, MO, where the party had been organized two months earlier.

4594. Presidential candidate from Arizona was Barry Morris Goldwater, who was nominated on the first ballot at the Republican Party's convention in San Francisco, CA, in July 1964. In 1960 he had received the nomination of the Conservative Party of New Jersey but declined it and was replaced on the ticket by Joseph Bracken Lee of Utah.

4595. Presidential candidate from Minnesota was Hubert Horatio Humphrey, who was nominated by the Democratic Party in August 1968 at its convention in Chicago, IL. Humphrey was then the vice president, having been elected in 1964 as the running mate of Lyndon Baines Johnson.

4596. Presidential candidate from South Dakota was George Stanley McGovern, senator from South Dakota, who was nominated by the Democratic Party in July 1972 at its convention in Miami Beach, FL.

4597. Presidential candidate from Colorado was Earl F. Dodge, who was nominated by the National Statesman Party in 1984. He had been nominated for vice president by the Prohibition Party in 1976 and by the National Statesman Party in 1980.

STATES—PRESIDENTS

4598. President from Virginia was George Washington, president from 1789 through 1793, who was born at Pope's Creek in Westmoreland County, VA, in 1732 and was a resident of Virginia for most of his life. Seven other presidents (Jefferson, Madison, Monroe, William Henry Harrison, Taylor, Tyler, and Wilson) were natives of Virginia and were residents of the state when they entered the White House.

4599. President from Massachusetts was John Adams, born in 1735 at Braintree (now Quincy), MA, where he made his home for most of his life. He entered the White House in 1797. Three other presidents were born in Massachusetts: John Quincy Adams, John Fitzgerald Kennedy, and George Herbert Walker Bush. Calvin Coolidge, though born in Vermont, lived most of his life in Massachusetts, where he was elected governor in 1919.

4600. President born in South Carolina was Andrew Jackson, who was born in Waxhaw, SC, in 1767. He came to Tennessee as a young lawyer and served as congressman, senator, and judge of the state supreme court before making his name as a soldier. He entered the White House in 1829.

4601. President from Tennessee was Andrew Jackson, who was born in South Carolina and came to Tennessee as a young lawyer, representing the state in the House and Senate and serving as judge of the state supreme court. From 1812 to 1821 he was a general in the U.S. Army. He was president from 1829 to 1837. The two other presidents from Tennessee, Polk and Andrew Johnson, were both born in North Carolina.

4602. President from New York State was Martin Van Buren, who was born in Kinderhook, NY, in 1782 and was active in New York politics as state senator, state attorney general, United States senator, and governor before becoming secretary of state in 1829,

STATES—PRESIDENTS—*continued*

vice president in 1833, and president in 1837. Three other presidents (Millard Fillmore, Theodore Roosevelt, and Franklin Delano Roosevelt) were born in New York, and four more (Chester Alan Arthur, Grover Cleveland, Dwight David Eisenhower, and Richard Milhous Nixon) were residents of New York when they entered the White House.

4603. President from Ohio was William Henry Harrison, who represented Ohio in Congress before he entered the White House in 1841. He was, however, born in Charles City County, VA. The first president born in Ohio was Rutherford Birchard Hayes, who was born in Delaware, OH, in 1822, served twice as governor of Ohio, and was elected president in 1876. Six other presidents (James Abram Garfield, Ulysses Simpson Grant, Benjamin Harrison, William McKinley, William Howard Taft, and Warren Gamaliel Harding) were born in Ohio, and all were residents of the state when they entered the White House.

4604. President born in North Carolina was James Knox Polk, who was born near Pineville in 1795. From the age of eleven he lived in Tennessee, returning to North Carolina to attend the state university. He entered the White House in 1845, having served as congressman from and governor of Tennessee. Andrew Johnson was born in Raleigh, NC, in 1808 and moved to Tennessee in his 20s.

4605. President from Louisiana was Zachary Taylor. He was born in Virginia and spent most of his adult life as an army officer, commanding troops from Mississippi to Minnesota. When the Whig Party nominated him as its presidential candidate in 1848, he received notice of his nomination at his headquarters in Baton Rouge, LA.

4606. President from New Hampshire was Franklin Pierce, a native of Hillsborough (now Hillsboro), NH. He was elected to the state legislature, then represented New Hampshire in the House of Representatives and the Senate. After serving as an army officer during the Mexican War, he was elected to the White House in 1852.

4607. President from Pennsylvania was James Buchanan, a resident of the state for most of his life. He was born in Cove Gap, PA, and became a lawyer in Lancaster, where he eventually bought a 22-acre estate. He served as a state legislator, congressional representative, senator, secretary of state, and diplomat before entering the White House in 1857.

4608. President from Illinois was Abraham Lincoln, who was 21 when he moved there with his family from Indiana. He had been born in Kentucky. He represented Illinois in the House from 1847 to 1849 and was elected president in 1860. Ulysses Simpson Grant was also a resident of Illinois but was born in Ohio. The only president to have been born in Illinois was Ronald Wilson Reagan, but he entered the White House as a resident of California, where he was a movie and television actor and eventually governor.

4609. President born in Kentucky was Abraham Lincoln, who was born in 1809 in Hodgenville. The family moved to Indiana and then to Illinois, where Lincoln was a storekeeper, postmaster, state legislator, lawyer, and congressman before he was elected president in 1860.

4610. President born in Vermont was Chester Alan Arthur, who was born in Fairfield in 1829. He taught school in Vermont before moving to New York State, where he was practiced law and eventually became collector of the Port of New York. He was elected vice president in 1881 and succeeded to the presidency six months later after the assassination of James Abram Garfield. Calvin Coolidge was born in Plymouth, VT, but spent most of his life in Massachusetts, of which he became governor in 1919.

4611. President from Indiana was Benjamin Harrison, who was born in Ohio and moved to Indiana when he was 21. He was a lawyer, soldier, and senator before entering the White House in 1889.

4612. President born in New Jersey was Grover Cleveland, born in Caldwell, NJ, in 1837. He moved at a young age to New York State, where he eventually became governor. He entered the White House in 1885. Woodrow Wilson, born in Virginia, was president of Princeton University, Princeton, NJ, and served as governor of New Jersey before his election to the presidency in 1912.

4613. President born in Iowa was Herbert Clark Hoover, who was born in West Branch in 1874. He moved to Oregon at the age of 10 and went to California in 1891 to attend college. He lived much of his adult life abroad, first as a mining engineer, then as chairman of American relief efforts during and after World War I. He was elected president in 1928 after seven years as secretary of commerce.

4614. President from California was Herbert Clark Hoover, who was born in Iowa but came to California as a young man to attend Leland Stanford University. His term as president began in 1929. Two other presidents, Nixon and Reagan, were residents of California when they entered the White House, but only Nixon was born there; Reagan was born in Illinois.

4615. President from Missouri was Harry S. Truman, who was born in Lamar, MO, and attended public school in Independence. He represented Missouri in the Senate from January 1935 through January 1945, when he was inaugurated as vice president. He entered the White House three months later, after the death of President Franklin Delano Roosevelt.

4616. President born in Texas was Dwight David Eisenhower, whose birthplace was Denison, TX. He graduated from high school in Abilene, KS, became a career army officer, and during World War II was supreme commander of the Allied Expeditionary Force. When he was elected to the presidency in 1952, he was a resident of New York, NY, where he had been president of Columbia University. President Lyndon Baines Johnson was a lifelong resident of the state. George Herbert Walker Bush was born in Massachusetts but came to Texas to work in the petroleum industry.

4617. President born in Nebraska was Gerald Rudolph Ford, who was born in Omaha in 1913. He moved with his mother to Michigan when he was two years old. He succeeded to the White House after President Richard Milhous Nixon's resignation in 1974.

4618. President from Michigan was Gerald Rudolph Ford. A native of Omaha, NB, he grew up in Grand Rapids, MI. He was representing Michigan in the House of Representatives in 1973 when he was nominated to replace former Vice President Spiro Theodore Agnew, who had resigned. The following year, he was elevated to the presidency after the resignation of President Richard Milhous Nixon.

4619. President from Georgia was Jimmy Carter, who was born in the town of Plains in 1924. After serving in the Navy, he returned to Plains to run his family's peanut farm and warehouse business, then went into politics and was elected governor of Georgia. He became president in 1977.

4620. President from Arkansas was William Jefferson Clinton, who was born in Hope in 1946. He returned to Arkansas after law school and became state attorney general in 1976. He was elected governor in 1978 and again in 1982, 1984, and 1988. He entered the White House in 1992.

STATES—VICE PRESIDENTIAL CANDIDATES

4621. Vice presidential candidate from New York State was George Clinton, the governor of New York, who was nominated by the Democratic-Republicans as a replacement for Vice President Aaron Burr when Thomas Jefferson ran for a second term in 1804. Jefferson and Clinton were elected on November 6, 1804. (The election of 1804 was the first in which the candidates for president and vice president received separate votes. In previous years, there was a single field of candidates for whom the electors could vote, the winner becoming president and the runner-up becoming vice president.) Clinton was reelected vice president in 1808 with 113 votes out of 175 cast, and also received three votes for the presidency, which was won by James Madison.

4622. Vice presidential candidate from New Hampshire was John Langdon, the governor of New Hampshire, who was one of five candidates—one from the Federalist Party, the other four supported by the Democratic-Republicans—whose names were submitted to the electors in 1808. Langdon received nine of 175 votes cast.

4623. Vice presidential candidates from Virginia were James Madison, the secretary of state, and James Monroe, former senator and governor of Virginia and minister to England and France. Both were supported by the Democratic-Republicans. They were part of a field of five candidates, including two other Democratic-Republican candidates and a Federalist, whose names were submitted to the electors in 1808. Each received three of 175 votes cast. Madison also ran for president in 1808 and was elected. He was reelected in 1812. James Monroe was elected president in 1816 and 1820. Thomas Jefferson, the first vice president from Virginia, was never a candidate for that office.

4624. Vice presidential candidate from Pennsylvania was Jared Ingersoll, who was nominated by the Federalist Party in 1812. He received 86 votes out of 217 cast.

STATES—VICE PRESIDENTIAL CANDI-DATES—*continued*

4625. Vice presidential candidate from Massachusetts was Elbridge Gerry, who was nominated by the Democratic-Republican Party on September 16, 1812, to replace the late George Clinton as James Madison's running mate. The election was won by the Democratic-Republicans. Gerry received 131 of 217 electoral votes cast, three more than Madison received. John Adams was the first vice president from Masschusetts, but he was never nominated for that office.

4626. Vice presidential candidates from Maryland were John Eager Howard and Robert Goodloe Harper, who were among the five candidates whose names were submitted to the electors in 1816. Howard, Harper, and two others were supported by the Federalists; the winner was Daniel D. Tompkins, the candidate supported by the Democratic-Republicans. Howard received 22 of 217 votes cast and Harper received three. Harper ran for the vice presidency again as a Whig candidate in 1820 and received one of 235 votes cast.

4627. Vice presidential candidate from Delaware was Daniel Rodney, who was one of five candidates whose names were submitted to the electors in 1820. He received four of 218 votes cast.

4628. Vice presidential candidate from New Jersey was Richard Stockton, who was one of five candidates whose names were submitted to the electors in 1820. He received eight of 218 votes cast.

4629. Vice presidential candidate from North Carolina was Nathaniel Macon, senator from North Carolina, who was one of six candidates whose names were submitted to the electors in 1824. Macon, who had the support of a faction of the Whig Party, received 24 votes out of 260 cast.

4630. Vice presidential candidate from South Carolina was John Caldwell Calhoun, the secretary of war, who was one of six candidates whose names were submitted to the electors in 1824. Calhoun, a Democratic-Republican, received 182 votes out of 260 cast and was declared the winner, although John Quincy Adams, the man who won the presidency, was a Federalist. He was reelected in 1828 to serve under Andrew Jackson. An earlier statesman from South Carolina, Charles Cotesworth Pinckney, was a Federalist candidate for president in 1796, 1800, 1804, and 1808. In the elections of 1796 and 1800, there was no separate contest for the vice presidency, but a single field of candidates in which the winner was declared the president and the runner-up the vice president; hence Pinckney could possibly be considered the first vice presidential candidate from South Carolina.

4631. Vice presidential candidate from Tennessee was Andrew Jackson, army general and Democratic-Republican senator. In 1824, when Jackson ran a losing race for the presidency, he also received 13 electoral votes out of 260 cast for vice president. He was elected president in 1828 and 1832.

4632. Vice presidential candidate from Kentucky was Henry Clay, in 1824, when he was a candidate for both the presidency and the vice presidency. In the presidential race, he came in fourth in a field of four. In the vice presidential race, he came in sixth in a field of six. The election was held on November 2, 1824.

4633. Vice presidential candidate from Ohio was Thomas Morris, who was nominated by the Liberal Party on August 30, 1843, at its convention in Buffalo, NY.

4634. Vice presidential candidate from Michigan was Charles C. Foote, who was nominated by the National Liberty Party in June 1848 at its convention in Buffalo, NY.

4635. Vice presidential candidate from Indiana was George Washington Julian, who was nominated by the Free Soil Party on August 11, 1852, at its convention in Pittsburgh, PA.

4636. Vice presidential candidate from Maine was Hannibal Hamlin, who was nominated by the Republican Party in May 1860 at its convention in Chicago, IL, as Abraham Lincoln's running mate. They were elected on November 6, 1860. Hamlin was replaced by Andrew Johnson in Lincoln's second term. He afterwards became a senator from Maine and minister to Spain.

4637. Vice presidential candidate from Georgia was Herschel Vespasian Johnson, who was nominated by the Democratic Party in June 1860 at its convention in Baltimore, MD.

4638. Vice presidential candidate from Oregon was Joseph Lane, who was nominated on June 23, 1860, by the National Democratic Party (also known as the Independent Democrats) and on June 28, 1860, by the Southern Democratic Party (the Southern, or Breckinridge, Democrats). Both parties met in convention in Baltimore, MD.

4639. Vice presidential candidate from Missouri was Francis Preston Blair, Jr., who was nominated by the Democratic Party in July 1868 at its convention in New York, NY.

4640. Vice presidential candidate from Kansas was Samuel Clarke Pomeroy, who was nominated by the American Party, an anti-Masonic party, in 1880.

4641. Vice presidential candidate from Mississippi was Absolom Madden West, who was nominated by both the Anti-Monopoly Party and the Greenback Party in May 1884.

4642. Vice presidential candidate from Illinois was John Alexander Logan, who was nominated by the Republican Party in June 1884 at its convention in Chicago, IL.

4643. Vice presidential candidate from Connecticut was John A. Conant, who was nominated by the American Prohibition Party on June 19, 1884, at its convention in Chicago, IL.

4644. Vice presidential candidate from California was Marietta Lizzie Bell Stow, who was nominated by the Equal Rights Party on September 20, 1884, at its convention in San Francisco, CA. Stow was the first woman ever to run for the office of vice president.

4645. Vice presidential candidate from Arkansas was Charles E. Cunningham, who was nominated by the Union Labor Party in May 1888 at its convention in Cincinnati, OH. The party had been organized in Cincinnati in February 1887.

4646. Vice presidential candidate from Texas was James Britton Cranfill, who was nominated by the Prohibition Party in June 1892 at its convention in Cincinnati, OH. Samuel Evans had been nominated in 1888 by the Union Labor Party but declined the nomination.

4647. Vice presidential candidate from Minnesota was Ignatius Donnelly, who was nominated by the Anti-Fusionist faction of the Populist Party, known as the Middle-of-the-Road Populists, or People's Party, in May 1900 at its convention in Cincinnati, OH.

4648. Vice presidential candidate from Rhode Island was Henry Brewer Metcalf, who was nominated by the Prohibition Party in June 1900 at its convention in Chicago, IL.

4649. Vice presidential candidate from West Virginia was Henry Gassaway Davis, who was nominated by the Democratic Party in July 1904 at its convention in St. Louis, MO.

4650. Vice presidential candidate from Nebraska was Thomas Henry Tibbles, who was nominated by the People's Party, also known as the Populists, on July 4, 1904, at its convention in Springfield, IL.

4651. Vice presidential candidate from Iowa was Lorenzo S. Coffin, who was nominated by the United Christian Party at its convention in Rock Island, IL, on May 1, 1908.

4652. Vice presidential candidate from Nevada was Martin R. Preston, who was nominated unanimously by the Socialist Labor Party in July 1908 at its convention in New York, NY. He was ineligible to run for the presidency because he was under the constitutional age and because he was serving a 25-year term in a Nevada penitentiary for murder.

4653. Vice presidential candidate from Wisconsin was Emil Seidel, who was nominated by the Socialist Party in May 1912 at its convention in Indianapolis, IN.

4654. Vice presidential candidate from Louisiana was John Milliken Parker, who was nominated by the Progressive Party in June 1916 at its convention in Chicago, IL. The party ceased to exist before the election, which was held on November 7. The first vice presidential candidate from Louisiana to participate in an election was Kent H. Courtney, who was nominated by the Conservative Party of New Jersey in 1960.

4655. Vice presidential candidate from Montana was Burton Kendall Wheeler, who was nominated by the Socialist Party in May 1924 and by the Progressive Party in July 1924. Both conventions were held in Cleveland, OH.

4656. Vice presidential candidate from Oklahoma was V. C. Tisdal, who was nominated by the Jobless Party on August 17, 1932, at its convention in St. Louis, MO.

4657. Vice presidential candidate from Washington State was Frank B. Hemenway, who was nominated by the Liberty Party on August 17, 1932, at its convention in St. Louis, MO. William Bouck had been nominated by the Farmer Labor Party in 1924, but withdrew and gave his support to the candidates of the Communist Party.

4658. Vice presidential candidate from Arizona was James Elmer Yates, who was nominated by the Greenback Party on July 4, 1940, at its convention in Indianapolis, IN.

4659. Vice presidential candidate from Idaho was Glen Hearst Taylor, who was nominated by the Progressive Party in July 1948 at its convention in Philadelphia, PA.

STATES—VICE PRESIDENTIAL CANDIDATES—continued

4660. Vice presidential candidate from Utah was Joseph Bracken Lee, who was nominated by the Texas Constitution Party in 1956. The Conservative Party of New Jersey nominated him for president in 1960.

4661. Vice presidential candidate from Florida was Christopher Gian-Cursio, who was nominated by the Vegetarian Party in 1960.

4662. Vice presidential candidate from Colorado was Theodore C. Billings, who was nominated by the Constitution Party in July 1964 at its convention in Houston, TX.

4663. Vice presidential candidate from New Mexico was LaDonna Harris, who was nominated by the Citizens Party in April 1980 at its convention in Cleveland, OH.

STATES—VICE PRESIDENTS

4664. Vice president from Massachusetts was John Adams, born in 1735 in Braintree, MA (now Quincy, MA), who was President George Washington's vice president from 1789 to 1797, when he entered the White House himself as president. Elbridge Gerry, like Adams, was born in the state and resided there. Henry Wilson and Calvin Coolidge, though residents of Massachusetts when they took office, were born in New Hampshire and Vermont, respectively. George Herbert Walker Bush, vice president under Ronald Reagan, was born in Massachusetts, but moved to Texas.

4665. Vice president from Virginia was Thomas Jefferson, born in 1743 at Shadwell in what is now Albemarle County, who took office as vice president under John Adams in 1797. John Tyler was also both a native and a resident of Virginia.

4666. Vice president from New York was Aaron Burr, a native of New Jersey. After distinguishing himself in the Continental Army during the Revolutionary War, Burr moved in 1792 to New York State, which sent him to the Senate from 1791 to 1797. From 1801 to 1805 he was vice president in Thomas Jefferson's first term. His successor, George Clinton, was the first vice president to have been born in New York State. He was its governor from 1777 to 1795 and again from 1801 to 1804. He served as vice president under Thomas Jefferson from 1805 to 1908 and then under James Madison from 1809 to 1812. Ten other vice presidents (Daniel D. Tompkins, Martin Van Buren, Millard Fillmore, Schuyler Schuyler,

William Almon Wheeler, Chester Alan Arthur, Levi Parsons Morton, Theodore Roosevelt, James Schoolcraft Sherman, and Nelson Aldrich Rockefeller) were residents of New York when they took office; all were natives of New York except Morton, who was born in Vermont, and Rockefeller, who was born in Maine. Schuyler Colfax was born in New York but was a resident of Indiana when he took office.

4667. Vice president from South Carolina was John Caldwell Calhoun, born in Abbeville District, SC, in 1782. He entered the vice presidency in 1825, under President John Quincy Adams, after serving as congressman and secretary of war. He was elected again in 1828 to serve under President Andrew Jackson but resigned in 1832 to run for a seat in the Senate and was replaced by Martin Van Buren.

4668. Vice president from Kentucky was Richard Mentor Johnson, vice president from 1837 to 1841 under Martin Van Buren. Johnson was born in Floyd's Station, KY, in 1780, and represented the state in the House and Senate until his election as vice president in 1836. Three other vice presidents were born in Kentucky: John Cabell Breckinridge, Alben William Barkley, and Adlai Ewing Stevenson (who eventually moved to Illinois).

4669. Vice president from Pennsylvania was George Mifflin Dallas, President James Knox Polk's vice president. He was born in Philadelphia, where he became mayor. Eventually, he served as US senator and minister to Russia. He was inaugurated as vice president in 1845.

4670. Vice president born in North Carolina was William Rufus de Vane King, who, as a resident of Alabama, took office as vice president in 1853 under Franklin Pierce. He was born in Sampson County, NC, in 1786, and had the distinction of serving in the House of Representatives from North Carolina and later in the Senate from Alabama. He died only a few weeks into his term. Andrew Johnson was born in Raleigh, NC, but carried on his political career in Tennessee.

4671. Vice president from Alabama was William Rufus de Vane King, Franklin Pierce's vice president. King was born and educated in North Carolina and represented North Carolina in the House; he eventually moved to Alabama and represented Alabama in the Senate for many years. He was inaugurated as vice president in March 1853 and died a few weeks later.

4672. Vice president from Maine was Hannibal Hamlin, born in Paris, ME, in 1809. Hamlin was senator from and governor of Maine before he took office in 1861 as vice president during the first term of Abraham Lincoln. Nelson Aldrich Rockefeller was born in Maine but resided in New York, where he served for many years as governor.

4673. Vice president from Tennessee was Andrew Johnson, who was the former governor of Tennessee and senator from Tennessee when he took office in 1865 as vice president in Abraham Lincoln's second term. He was born in Raleigh, NC. Albert Gore, Jr., was serving as senator from Tennessee when he was picked to join the Democratic ticket headed by William Jefferson Clinton in 1992. He was born in Washington, DC.

4674. Vice president from Indiana was Schuyler Colfax, vice president from 1869 to 1873 during the first term of Ulysses Simpson Grant. Colfax was born in New York City in 1823 and moved to Indiana in 1836. Thomas Andrews Hendricks and Charles Warren Fairbanks were both Ohio natives who became residents of Indiana before they took office. The first vice president born in Indiana was Thomas Riley Marshall, who served as governor of Indiana from 1909 to 1913 and as vice president under Woodrow Wilson from 1913 to 1921.

4675. Vice president born in New Hampshire was Henry Wilson, born in Farmington, NH, in 1812. His name at birth was Jeremiah Jones Colbaith; he adopted the name Henry Wilson when he was 21. At that time he moved to Massachusetts, where he started his political career. He was inaugurated as vice president in 1873 for Ulysses Simpson Grant's second term.

4676. Vice president born in Vermont was Chester Alan Arthur, who took office in 1881 and succeeded to the presidency six months later, after the death of President James Abram Garfield. Arthur was born in Fairfield, VT, in 1829, but was a resident of New York State when he became vice president. Levi Parsons Morton, vice president under Benjamin Harrison, was also born in Vermont and a resident of New York. Calvin Coolidge, vice president under Warren Gamaliel Harding, was born in Vermont and a resident of Massachusetts.

4677. Vice president born in Ohio was Thomas Andrew Hendricks, who was born in Muskingum County, OH, in 1819. He attended college in Indiana, was admitted to the bar there, and entered politics, becoming governor in 1873. He was sworn in as Grover Cleveland's

vice president in 1885 but died eight months later. Charles Warren Fairbanks, vice president under Theodore Roosevelt, and Charles Gates Dawes, vice president under Calvin Coolidge, were both born in Ohio but represented Indiana and Illinois, respectively.

4678. Vice president from Illinois was Adlai Ewing Stevenson, vice president during the second administration of Grover Cleveland (1893–1897). Stevenson was born in Kentucky and moved to Illinois in his teens. Charles Gates Dawes also came from Illinois, though he was born in Ohio.

4679. Vice president from New Jersey was Garret Augustus Hobart, who was born in Long Branch, NJ, in 1844 and spent many years as a state assemblyman and state senator. He served in President William McKinley's first administration, from 1897 to 1899. He was replaced for McKinley's second term by Theodore Roosevelt, who became president after McKinley was assassinated. Aaron Burr was also born in New Jersey, and attended college there, but entered politics in New York before becoming Thomas Jefferson's vice president in 1801.

4680. Vice president from Kansas was Charles Curtis, longtime senator from Kansas. He was born in Topeka in 1860. He was inaugurated as Herbert Clark Hoover's vice president in 1929.

4681. Vice president from Texas was John Nance Garner, born near Detroit in Red River County, TX, who served 30 years as congressional representative from Texas before his election to the vice presidency in 1932 under Franklin Delano Roosevelt. Lyndon Baines Johnson was, like Garner, both a native of Texas and a longtime veteran of its political life. George Herbert Walker Bush was a resident of Texas but a native of Massachusetts.

4682. Vice president from Iowa was Henry Agard Wallace, vice president during the third term of Franklin Delano Roosevelt. Wallace, a native of Adair County, IA, served as secretary of agriculture before he took office as vice president in 1941. He served afterwards as secretary of commerce.

4683. Vice president from Missouri was Harry S. Truman, born in 1884 in Lamar, MO. He was serving his tenth year as senator from Missouri when he was elected vice president for the fourth term of President Franklin Delano Roosevelt. He was inaugurated in 1945 and became president less than three months later, after Roosevelt's death.

STATES—VICE PRESIDENTS—*continued*

4684. Vice president from California was Richard Milhous Nixon, who was born in Yorba Linda, CA, in 1913. He represented California in the House and Senate before his election as Dwight David Eisenhower's vice president in 1952.

4685. Vice president born in South Dakota was Hubert Horatio Humphrey, who was born in Wallace, SD, in 1911. He went to college in Minnesota and entered politics there. He was inaugurated as Lyndon Baines Johnson's vice president in 1965.

4686. Vice president from Minnesota was Hubert Horatio Humphrey, who was born and grew up in South Dakota, attended college in Minnesota, became a civil servant there, and eventually represented the state in the Senate. He took office as vice president under Lyndon Baines Johnson in 1965. The first vice president born in Minnesota was Walter Mondale, who was born in Ceylon, MN, in 1928.

4687. Vice president from Maryland was Spiro Theodore Agnew, born in Baltimore in 1918. He left the governership of Maryland to take office as vice president under Richard Milhous Nixon in 1969. He resigned in 1973, a few months into his second term, to face charges of income tax evasion.

4688. Vice president born in Nebraska was Gerald Rudolph Ford, who was born in Omaha in 1913. His name at birth was Leslie Lynch King, Jr. He was serving as representative of Michigan in Congress when he was appointed to the vice presidency in 1973 after the resignation of Spiro Theodore Agnew. Half a year later, he succeeded to the presidency after the resignation of Richard Milhous Nixon.

4689. Vice president from Michigan was Gerald Rudolph Ford, who was a Michigan congressman when he was picked to replace Vice President Spiro Theodore Agnew in 1973. Ford was born in Nebraska.

SUPREME COURT

4690. Salary of Supreme Court justices was established by the Federal Judiciary Act of September 24, 1789, which set the annual salary for the chief justice at $4,000 and for the associate justices at $3,500. The first raise in salary was authorized by Congress in 1819, bringing the chief justice's pay to $5,000 and that of the associate justices to $4,500.

4691. Supreme Court of the United States consisted of Chief Justice John Jay of New York (1789–95), and associate justices John Rutledge of South Carolina (1790–91), William Cushing of Massachusetts (1790–1810), James Wilson of Pennsylvania (1789–98), John Blair of Virginia (1790–96), and James Iredell of North Carolina (1790–99). Except for Iredell, the appointments were made by President George Washington on September 24 and were confirmed by the Senate on September 26. (Iredell replaced Robert Hanson Harrison of Maryland, who was both appointed and confirmed but fell seriously ill en route to New York and died without taking his seat.) The Judiciary Act of 1789, which implemented the clause in the Constitution providing for the Supreme Court, was passed on September 24. It provided for six justices, four of whom constituted a quorum.

4692. Publication of Supreme Court decisions was made by a Philadelphia lawyer and journalist, Alexander James Dallas, in his compilations of Pennsylvania state court rulings, to which he began adding Supreme Court rulings in 1790. He eventually published four volumes, covering the first ten years of the Court's activity. Dallas later became secretary of the treasury.

4693. Meeting place of the Supreme Court was the Royal Exchange Building, a large edifice on Broad Street in New York City, where the first session of the Supreme Court began on February 1, 1790. The following year, the Supreme Court moved to Philadelphia, where it met in Independence Hall and (from late 1791 to 1800) in the Old City Hall. During those years, epidemics of yellow fever forced the cancellation of three of the August sessions.

4694. Session of the Supreme Court began on February 1, 1790, at the Royal Exchange Building in New York City. A quorum consisting of four of the six justices assembled on the following day, and the session continued for nine days. The justices wore black and scarlet robes. In deference to the advice of Thomas Jefferson, they did not wear "the monstrous wig which makes the English judges look like rats peeping through bunches of oakum." The Court's first formal act was to establish the office of clerk.

4695. Clerk of the Supreme Court was John Tucker of Boston, MA, appointed on February 3, 1790. His responsibilities included keeping track of documents, managing the Court's personnel, and locating places for the justices to lodge. It was required "that he reside and keep his office at the seat of the national government, and that he do not practice, either as an attorney or a counsellor in this court, while he shall continue to be clerk of the same." Though no salary was provided until 1799, when the clerk's pay was set at ten dollars a day plus varying fees, the office-holder received substantial compensation from the collection of filing fees.

4696. Appeal from the justices of the Supreme Court to end circuit riding was addressed to President George Washington in 1792. The justices traveled thousands of miles a year to preside over regional courts, in addition to their duties at the national capital, and many suffered ill health from the effects of bad weather, bad lodgings, bad roads, and bad food. Washington forwarded their letter to Congress, which refused to make a change. Except for a temporary suspension in 1801–02, circuit riding continued until 1869, though some of the justices' circuit-court responsibilities remained in place until 1891. Circuit riding was formally abolished by Congress in 1911.

4697. Supreme Court dissent was read by Justice Thomas Johnson on August 11, 1792, in the case of *Georgia v. Brailsford*. The constitutional issue in that case was whether a state could be sued by a resident of another state. Johnson, the most junior justice, read his opinion first (as was the custom until the Marshall Court). He dissented from the majority opinion, which granted the state of Georgia a temporary injunction barring Brailsford, a Loyalist, from recovering property seized by the state after the Revolutionary War. Justice William Cushing also dissented.

4698. Residence in Washington, DC, of the justices of the Supreme Court beginning in 1801 was a boarding house not far from the Capitol. The proprietor was a Mrs. Dunn. The Justices roomed there together and took their meals there. This practice of collegial living continued into the 1840s.

4699. Meeting place of the Supreme Court in Washington, DC, was located in the north wing of the unfinished Capitol building, in a room in the basement, where the Court convened for the first time in February 1801 under its new chief justice, John Marshall. By 1808 the room was too dilapidated for use, and the Court set up new quarters within the Capitol in the former library of the House of Representatives, only to find that space unbearably cold during the winter. The next winter session was held at Long's Tavern on Capitol Hill. A permanent courtroom in the Capitol, constructed in the lower half of the former Senate chamber,

became available in February 1810 and was used by the Court until December 1860 (with the exception of the four terms held elsewhere after the burning of the Capitol by the British in 1814). Now called the Old Supreme Court Chamber, it was restored in 1975 for the Bicentennial. From 1860 through 1935 the Court met in the Old Senate Chamber, the Senate having moved into the Capitol's new north wing.

4700. Reporter of Supreme Court decisions to be formally appointed by the Court was Henry Wheaton, who was named to the post in 1816 with a yearly salary of $1,000. He served until 1827, during which time he continued to support himself as a lawyer, sometimes appearing before the Court in his capacity as attorney. The first two reporters, Alexander James Dallas and William Cranch, served unofficially and were not paid.

4701. Marshal of the Supreme Court was Richard C. Parsons, who was appointed in 1867 and served until 1872. The chief duties of the marshal were to keep order in the courtroom, including making formal announcement in the morning of the arrival of the justices, and to keep track of time during the presentation of oral arguments.

4702. Solicitor general was Benjamin Helm Bristow of Kentucky, who was appointed to the newly created post by President Ulysses S. Grant on October 4, 1870. He took office on October 11 and served until November 15, 1872. The solicitor general represents the Justice Department of the executive branch at the Supreme Court.

4703. Criminal trial before the Supreme Court took place in 1906, when the Court tried Joseph F. Shipp, the sheriff of Chattanooga, TN, in connection with the lynching of an African-American man, Ed Johnson. Johnson had been convicted of raping a white woman and sentenced to death, but his lawyers had appealed to the Supreme Court on the grounds that he had not received a fair trial. On March 19, 1906, the day after the Court granted a stay of execution, a mob took Johnson from the city jail, hanged him, and shot him. The sheriff, who bore the responsibility for the prisoner's security, was charged with contempt of court for allowing the Court's order to be disobeyed and was found guilty, along with a number of city police officers and residents. The opinion was written by Justice Oliver Wendell Holmes. Johnson's conviction was formally set aside by a Chattanooga judge on February 25, 2000.

SUPREME COURT—*continued*

4704. Session of the Supreme Court held in its own building began on October 7, 1935. The need for a separate Supreme Court building was articulated by Chief Justice William Howard Taft beginning in 1912. Congress appropriated $9.74 million for the project in 1929. The building was designed by Cass Gilbert in a majestic classical style and was constructed not far from the Capitol on Capitol Hill.

4705. African-American attorney to serve as solicitor general was Thurgood Marshall of Maryland, appointed by Lyndon Baines Johnson on July 13, 1965. He took office on August 11, 1965, and tried his first case before the Supreme Court on October 13. He served until August 30, 1967, when his appointment to the Court as an associate justice was confirmed by the Senate.

4706. Curator of the Supreme Court was Catherine Hetos Skefos, appointed in 1973, although the position was not formally established until the following year. The curator was given the duties of overseeing the Court's historical collections, documenting its activities, and developing educational programs and materials, including lectures, exhibits, and films.

4707. Year in which the salary of a Supreme Court justice topped $100,000 was 1982, when the annual pay of the chief justice was raised from $96,800 to $100,700 in a cost-of-living adjustment. It was raised to $104,700 in 1984, while the annual pay of the associate justices increased from $96,700 to $100,600. Congress raised the salary of the chief justice above $150,000—to $155,000—in 1991, and did likewise for the associate justices in 1992, when their pay reached $159,000.

4708. Recordings of Supreme Court proceedings released without the Court's approval were contained in a publishing project called *May It Please the Court: The Most Significant Oral Arguments Made Before the Supreme Court Since 1955,* compiled in 1993 by Peter Irons, a political science professor at the University of California at San Diego. It contained sometimes heavily edited tape recordings and transcripts of hearings on 23 historic cases, all obtained from the National Archives, and sold for $75 a set. The Supreme Court, which previously had maintained tight control over publication of its proceeds, declared that Irons had violated an agreement stating that he would not use the material for commercial distribution. On November 1, 1993, the Court announced that it would publish its own audiotaped proceeds.

SUPREME COURT—DECISIONS

4709. Supreme Court decision to be recorded was *Georgia v. Brailsford,* argued during the August term in 1792. Brailsford, the defendant, was a British subject who had formerly lived in Georgia and whose property had been confiscated after the Revolution because he had sided with Britain. He sued the state in court and won his case. Georgia, seeking to avoid the return of his property, argued before the Supreme Court that the verdict should be set aside because Brailsford had no right to sue. On August 11, by a 4–2 vote, the Court granted Georgia a temporary injunction. A special jury was convened by the Court in 1794 and found in Brailsford's favor, since the question of whether a state could be sued by a resident of another state had been settled the previous year in the case of *Chisholm v. Georgia.*

4710. Supreme Court decision to be overridden by an amendment to the Constitution was its ruling in *Chisholm v. Georgia* in 1793. A lawsuit had been brought against the state of Georgia by a South Carolina resident to recover $170,000 that Georgia owed to the estate of a certain Tory merchant. Article III of the Constitution gave the federal judiciary the power to adjudicate matters "between a state and citizens of another state." Georgia claimed sovereign immunity from all such lawsuits and refused to appear in court, but this view was rejected by four of the five Justices. The decision left the states open to suits by Tories whose property had been confiscated during the Revolution, a development that would have forced the states to raise taxes considerably. On March 5, 1794, at the urging of the state governments, Congress submitted to the states the Eleventh Amendment, which rendered the states invulnerable to lawsuits filed in federal court by citizens of other states or of foreign countries. It was ratified on January 8, 1789. The abolition of slavery by the 13th Amendment and the authorization of income taxes by the 16th Amendment were also enacted in contravention of Supreme Court rulings.

4711. Supreme Court case challenging the validity of an act of Congress was *Hylton v. United States,* decided on March 8, 1796. At issue was the congressional act of June 5, 1794, in which Congress placed a tax on carriages, snuff, sugar refining, liquor sales, and auctions. The tax on carriages was contested as a direct tax, which the Constitution forbids unless it is levied proportionately throughout the nation. The Court, by a vote of 3–0, identified this tax as an excise tax, rather than a direct tax, and hence not subject to proportionate distribution nor forbidden by the Constitution. Opinions were written by Justices Samuel Chase, William Paterson, and James Iredell.

4712. Supreme Court decision declaring an act of Congress unconstitutional was *Marbury v. Madison,* decided on February 24, 1803. Led by Chief Justice John Marshall, the Court invalidated Section 13 of the Judiciary Act of September 24, 1789, in which Congress authorized the justices to issue writs of mandamus (extraordinary writs compelling actions by government officials in matters outside constitutional law). The plaintiff was William Marbury of Washington, DC, who had been appointed justice of the peace by President John Adams just before he left office, but whose commission had been held back by Secretary of State James Madison for political reasons. By a vote of 5 to 0, the Court ruled that Marbury was entitled to receive his commission, but that it could not order Madison to give it to him, because the power of issuing writs of mandamus was not enumerated in the Constitution. Chief Justice Marshall's opinion further declared unconstitutional Congress's attempt to enlarge the powers of the Court beyond those specified in the Constitution. *Marbury v. Madison* firmly established the doctrine of judicial review, the power of the Supreme Court to rule on the constitutional validity of all legislation. However, no other act of Congress was ruled unconstitutional until the Dred Scott case of 1857.

4713. Supreme Court decision on state recognition of federal court rulings was made on February 20, 1809, when Chief Justice John Marshall, in *United States v. Judge Peters,* rendered an opinion sustaining the federal power and ordered a writ of mandamus issued to carry a previous decree into effect. Judge Richard Peters of the U.S. District Court of Pennsylvania had decreed that a certain sum of prize money be paid to a Mr. Olmstead of Connecticut for his capture of a British sloop during the Revolutionary War. The state of Pennsylvania refused to recognize Olmstead's claim, and the state militia was called out to stop a federal marshal from serving the judge's order. The Supreme Court decided that a state legislature cannot annul the judgment or determine the jurisdiction of a federal court.

4714. Supreme Court decision declaring a state law unconstitutional was handed down on March 16, 1810, in the case of *Fletcher v. Peck.* The case involved an attempt by the state legislature of Georgia to rescind a land sale that had been enacted in a previous session by members who had been bribed by land speculators. The Court ruled that Georgia's rescinding act violated the contract clause of Article 1, Section 10, of the Constitution, and was therefore void. This marked the first time that the contract clause was used by the Supreme Court to give private property protection against the state. Chief Justice John Marshall, writing for a 4–1 majority, said in his opinion that "the Union has a constitution, the supremacy of which all acknowledge, and which imposes limits to the legislation of the several states, which none claim a right to pass."

4715. Supreme Court decision upholding its authority to review state court decisions on appeal was rendered in 1816 in the case of *Martin v. Hunter's Lessee.* The case grew out of an earlier case, *Fairfax's Devisee v. Hunter's Lessee,* in which the Supreme Court ruled that the state of Virginia had to obey the terms of federal treaties. Virginia's Court of Appeals defied the Supreme Court and refused to enforce the decision, rejecting as unconstitutional Section 25 of the Judiciary Act of 1789, which authorized the Supreme Court to review the rulings of lower courts in cases involving Constitution and federal laws and treaties. On March 20, 1816, the Supreme Court unanimously sustained the validity of the clause in question. The opinion was written by Justice Joseph Story.

4716. Supreme Court decision on the power of states to tax federal assets was handed down on March 7, 1819, in the case of *McCulloch v. Maryland.* This involved an attempt by the state of Maryland to tax the Bank of the United States, a branch of which was located in Baltimore, MD. A cashier named James McCulloch was arrested for refusing to pay the tax. In reversing McCulloch's conviction, Chief Justice John Marshall spoke for the Court in holding that a state could not limit a federal statute under the supremacy clause of Article VI of the Constitution. *McCulloch v. Maryland* was also important in establishing the legality of the doctrine of "implied powers" of the federal government. While the power to create a national bank was not specifically mentioned in the Constitution, the court held that it could be reasonably inferred from the powers allocated to Congress in Article I, Section 8.

SUPREME COURT—DECISIONS—*continued*

4717. Supreme Court decision establishing its authority over state courts in matters of federal law was *Cohens v. Virginia,* decided on March 18, 1821. The case involved a conflict between the federal government and the state of Virginia. Congress in 1802 had instituted a national lottery to pay for improvements to Washington, DC. Two brothers, P.J. and M.J. Cohen, sold the lottery tickets in Norfolk, VA. They were arrested and convicted of breaking Virginia's ban on lotteries. The Cohens appealed to the Supreme Court, arguing that the federal law took precedence over the state law. Virginia argued that they could not appeal because the Supreme Court lacked jurisdiction in the matter. Chief Justice John Marshall, writing for a unanimous Court, upheld the conviction but invalidated Virginia's argument, citing Article III of the U.S. Constitution, which says that "the supreme Court shall have original Jurisdiction" and shall prevail over state courts in all cases "in which a State shall be Party." Justice Marshall offered further justification for the Supreme Court's jurisdiction, noting that "In many states, the judges are dependent for office and for salary on the will of the legislature . . . We are the less inclined to suppose that it [the Constitution] can have intended to leave these constitutional questions to tribunals where this independence [of the judiciary] may not exist, in all cases where a state shall prosecute an individual who claims the protection of an act of Congress."

4718. Supreme Court decision establishing the power of the federal government to regulate commerce was *Gibbons v. Ogden,* decided on March 2, 1824, by a vote of 6 to 0. The plaintiff was Thomas Gibbons, who had a federal license to operate steamboats but who had been prevented from doing so in New York State waters because the state had granted a monopoly to Robert Fulton. The Court, ruling that the federal license superseded the state-authorized monopoly, found for Gibbons. The opinion, by Chief Justice John Marshall, set forth a definition of interstate commerce that was broad in scope and included transportation between states and "every species of commercial intercourse."

4719. Supreme Court decision on the status of Native American tribes was *Cherokee Nation v. Georgia,* decided on March 18, 1831, by a vote of four to two. The case concerned the authority of the state of Georgia to try a Cherokee man for a murder committed on Cherokee territory. More broadly, it concerned the question of whether or not the Cherokee tribe constituted a sovereign state. The Cherokees were represented by William Wirt. Despite the fact that colonial and federal governments had concluded treaties with the Cherokees as with any sovereign nation, Chief Justice John Marshall, realizing that such a conclusion would touch off a dangerous confrontation with President Andrew Jackson, ruled that the Cherokee Nation had the status of a domestic dependent nation. The Cherokees responded by bringing a test case, *Worcester v. Georgia,* to challenge the right of a state government to violate treaties made by the federal government. Marshall and a five-to-one majority ruled on March 3, 1832, that states were required to treat Native American tribes as autonomous entities. President Jackson refused to compel Georgia to comply with this ruling, and Georgia, with the assistance of the United States Army, forcibly removed the Cherokees to Oklahoma along the Trail of Tears in 1838.

4720. Supreme Court decision setting limitations on the use of military force against American civilians was *Ex parte Milligan,* decided by the Supreme Court on April 3, 1866. The case concerned a civilian, Lambdin P. Milligan, who had been arrested by the Union commander of Indiana during the Civil War and sentenced to death by a military court for providing "aid and comfort to the rebels." In invalidating the conviction, the Court held that Milligan should have been tried by the Circuit Court of Indiana, not a military court; that he had failed to receive a trial by jury as guaranteed by the Sixth Amendment; and that he had been denied a writ of habeas corpus. Milligan was freed after spending 18 months in prison. As a result of this decision, no civilian can be tried by a military court if a functioning civil court is available.

4721. Supreme Court decision on criminal jurisdiction on Native American reservations was *Ex parte Crow Dog,* decided on December 17, 1883. The case involved a Lakota (Sioux) man who had killed a Lakota chief on the tribe's reservation and had been tried by a federal court in the Dakota Territory. By a unanimous vote, the Court overturned his murder conviction, agreeing with the plaintiff that he should have been tried by the Lakotas. However, the right of the federal government to establish criminal jurisdiction over particular felonies, as Congress did in its Major Crimes Act of 1885, was upheld by the Supreme Court in *U.S. v. Kagama* (1886), which defined the tribes as wards for whom the United States, through its treaty obligations, had acquired the responsibility of guardianship.

4722. Supreme Court decision invalidating a state economic regulation on grounds of substantive due process was made on March 24, 1890, in the case of *Chicago, Milwaukee and St. Paul R.R. Co. v. Minnesota.* The ruling struck down a Minnesota law that would have allowed a state commission to impose rates on railroad companies without giving them the right of judicial review, which, the Court said, was guaranteed them by the Due Process Clause of the 14th Amendment.

4723. Supreme Court decision invalidating a federal tax was *Pollock v. Farmers' Loan & Trust Co.,* decided by the Fuller Court on April 8, 1895, and then redecided after a rehearing on May 20, 1895. Charles Pollock of Massachusetts challenged the constitutionality of the Wilson-Gorman Tariff Act of 1894, which passed a 2 percent tax on income from rents, interest, dividends, salaries, and profits over $4,000. Chief Justice Melville Fuller delivered the three-part decision of the Court, which overturned the act on three grounds: that taxes on real estate and personal property were direct taxes of the kind reserved to the states by Article I, Section 9, of the Constitution; that the $4,000 exemption meant that the tax was not applied uniformly throughout the United States; and that the principle of intergovernmental tax immunity was violated by the tax on state and municipal bonds. This decision led directly to the passage of the 16th Amendment, which authorized Congress to levy a general income tax.

4724. Supreme Court decision validating the doctrine of "separate but equal" provisions for African-Americans was *Plessy v. Ferguson,* delivered on May 18, 1896. The case concerned a Louisiana law requiring railroads to provide "equal but separate accommodations for the white and colored races." The law was challenged by Homer Adolph Plessy, an African-American member of the Louisiana-based Citizen's Committee to Test the Constitutionality of the Separate Car Act. Plessy purchased a ticket to ride in-state, then refused to take a seat in the "colored" car. His conviction by a lower court was upheld by the Supreme Court, thus indicating that the Lousiana law did not violate the 13th or 14th Amendments. In his dissent, Justice John Marshall Harlan asserted that "our Constitution is color-blind, and neither knows nor tolerates classes among citizens." The "separate but equal doctrine" was struck down in 1954 in the school segregation cases of *Brown v. Board of Education of Topeka* and *Bolling v. Sharpe.*

4725. Supreme Court decision concerning food additives was *United States v. Lexington Mill and Elevator Company,* decided in 1914 by the Court under Chief Justice Edward Douglass White. The Lexington Mill sold bleached flour with nitrite residues; at issue was whether this was illegal under the Federal Food and Drug Act, passed by Congress on June 30, 1906. The Court ruled that in order for the flour to be banned from foods, the government must show a relationship between the chemical additive and the harm it allegedly caused in humans. The court also noted that the mere presence of such an ingredient was not sufficient to render the food illegal.

4726. Supreme Court decision barring racial segregation in housing was handed down on November 5, 1917, in *Buchanan v. Warley.* The case involved a system of residential segregation enforced by the city of Louisville, KY, that was used to deny the sale to an African-American of a piece of property in a white neighborhood. The Louisville law was titled "An ordinance to prevent conflict and ill-feeling between the white and colored races in the city of Louisville, and to preserve the public peace and promote the general welfare by making reasonable provisions requiring, as far as practicable, the use of separate blocks, for residences, places of abode, and places of assembly by white and colored people respectively." The Court unanimously reversed a lower court ruling. The opinion, delivered by Justice William Rufus Day, read: "This attempt to prevent the alienation of the property in question to a person of color was not a legitimate exercise of the police power of the state, and is in direct violation of the fundamental law enacted in the 14th Amendment of the Constitution preventing state interference with property rights except by due process of law."

4727. Supreme Court decision invalidating a state law on First Amendment grounds was *Stromberg v. California,* issued on May 18, 1931, in which the Justices, by a vote of 7 to 2, struck down a California law that imposed criminal penalties on anyone who displayed a red flag (the symbol of communism) to make a political statement. Shortly afterward, a 5-to-4 majority invalidated a Minnesota law that gave state prosecutors the power to shut down newspapers and magazines for publishing libelous material. The case, *Near v. Minnesota,* concerned an anti-Semitic weekly in Minneapolis.

SUPREME COURT—DECISIONS—*continued*

4728. Supreme Court decision striking down a major piece of New Deal legislation was *Panama Refining Company v. Ryan,* in which the Court invalidated a section of the National Industry Recovery Act of June 16, 1933, that allowed the President the power to impose fair trade codes on industries. The decision, an 8-to-1 vote, was issued on January 7, 1935. On May 6, 1935, the Railroad Retirement Act was struck down, followed on May 27 by three other New Deal laws, including all the remaining sections of the National Industry Recovery Act (in *Schecter Poultry Corp. v. United States*).

4729. Supreme Court decision banning coerced confessions was *Brown v. Mississippi,* in which the Justices ruled unanimously that such confessions were invalid and a denial of due process of law. The decision, handed down on February 17, 1936, stemmed from a Mississippi case in which five African-American suspects confessed to murder after being hanged and whipped by sheriff's deputies.

4730. Supreme Court decision affirming the right of Congress to set a time limit for the ratification of a constitutional amendment was *Coleman v. Miller,* decided on June 5, 1939, in which the Hughes Court held that the timing of ratification was wholly a political question to be determined by Congress alone. The U.S. Constitution, in Article V, specifies that amendments shall become law "when ratified by the Legislatures of three fourths of the several States, or by Conventions in three fourths thereof, as the one or the other Mode of Ratification may be proposed by the Congress," but says nothing about the timing of such ratifications.

4731. Supreme Court decision extending the protection of the Bill of Rights to defendants in state courts was *Mapp v. Ohio,* decided on June 19, 1961, by the Warren Court. Police officers in Cleveland, OH, had searched the house of Dollree Mapp without a search warrant (although they claimed to have one), and found pornographic material unconnected with the crime they were investigating. The Court, led by Hugo L. Black, reversed Mapp's conviction for breaking a state law banning possession of obscene materials, holding that the Fourth Amendment's prohibition against illegal search and seizure was incorporated within the 14th Amendment. The 14th Amendment states that no state shall "deprive any person of life, liberty, or property, without due process of law; nor deny to any person within its jurisdiction the equal protection of the laws."

4732. Supreme Court decision on legislative apportionment was *Baker v. Carr,* decided by the Warren Court on March 26, 1962. By a vote of 6 to 2, the Court required the legislature of Tennessee to redraw the boundaries of its own electoral districts, using data from the 1960 census. These districts had remained unchanged since 1901. Rural districts had been traditionally overrepresented in the state legislature, but the court held that this was a violation of equal protection under the law as provided for in the 14th Amendment.

4733. Supreme Court decision on school prayer was the case of *Engel v. Vitale,* in which the Court struck down a classroom prayer requirement established by the New York State Board of Regents, which also wrote the prayer. A suit was brought by a parent, Steven Engel, claiming that the prayer violated the First Amendment's prohibition on the establishment of religion. On June 25, 1962, the Warren Court held that government sponsorship of school prayer and Bible reading in public schools was indeed unconstitutional, ruling that "neither the fact that the prayer may be denominationally neutral nor the fact that its observance . . . is voluntary can serve to free it from the limitations of the Establishment Clause." A supporting decision was rendered in *Abington School District v. Schempp* in 1963.

4734. Supreme Court decision giving protection to criticism of public officials was *New York Times Company v. Sullivan,* decided on March 6, 1964. In the case, L. B. Sullivan, the city commissioner of Montgomery, AL, sued the *New York Times* and members of a civil rights group called the Committee to Defend Martin Luther King and the Struggle for the South, claiming he was libeled in an ad run by the group in the *Times.* Overturning the defendants' conviction in lower courts, Justice William J. Brennan, Jr., delivered the Court's opinion that the First Amendment protects all forms of potentially libelous speech when applied to public figures, except those that result from "actual malice" in which the speaker knows them to be false.

4735. Supreme Court decision postulating a constitutional right to privacy took place on June 7, 1965, in *Griswold v. Connecticut.* Citing provisions of the First, Third, Fifth, Ninth, and 14th Amendments, Justice William O. Douglas, delivering the opinion of the Court, declared unconstitutional an 1879 Connecticut statute outlawing the use of contraceptives and barring medical practitioners from discussing them with patients. The statute was held to violate a patient's right to privacy—a right the justices declared to be implicit in the Constitution, though nowhere enumerated.

4736. Supreme Court decision upholding the power of Congress to outlaw racial discrimination in employment was *Griggs v. Duke Power Co.*, issued on March 8, 1971. A unanimous ruling by the Justices barred companies from hiring and promoting employees on the basis of tests that did not directly measure job performance, such as IQ tests, when the result was disproportionately disadvantageous to members of racial minorities. The ruling was based on Title VII of the 1964 Civil Rights Act.

4737. Supreme Court decision invalidating a state law on the grounds of gender discrimination was *Reed v. Reed*, issued on November 22, 1971. The unanimous ruling struck down an Idaho law that favored men over women in the appointment of estate administrators in probate cases.

4738. Supreme Court decision barring the death penalty was the case of *Furman v. Georgia*. On June 29, 1972, the Supreme Court decided by a vote of 5 to 4 that the death penalty constitutes "cruel and unusual punishment," forbidden by the Eighth Amendment. The majority opinion noted that juries tend to impose the death sentence in "arbitrary and capricious ways," notably by sending a higher proportion of African-Americans to death row. However, on July 2, 1976, the Court reversed itself, ruling in *Gregg v. Georgia* that a death penalty imposed under a modified two-stage capital trial system was not discriminatory and was therefore constitutional. The first criminal to be executed after this decision was handed down was convicted murderer Gary Gilmore, executed by firing squad in Utah on January 17, 1977.

4739. Supreme Court decision on the legality of abortion was handed down in the cases of *Roe v. Wade*, which contested a Texas statute making it a crime to destroy an unborn child except on "medical advice for the purpose of saving the mother's life," and *Doe v. Bolton*, which contested a similar Georgia law that restricted abortions except in cases where the woman's life was endangered, when the child would be born with a severe defect, or when the pregnancy was the result of rape. On January 22, 1973, the Court decided by a vote of 7 to 2 that state laws prohibiting abortions in the first six months of pregnancy are unconstitu-

tional under the Ninth and 14th Amendments. The majority opinion was written by Justice Harry Andrew Blackmun, whose legal reasoning was widely criticized for relying on a right to privacy not stated in the Constitution.

4740. Supreme Court decision giving equal legal status to men and women in the armed forces was *Frontiero v. Richardson*, decided on May 14, 1973. In an 8–1 decision, the Court struck down a federal law that distributed supplementary benefits in an unequal way to married men and married women serving in the armed forces. Married men received the benefits with no conditions; married women had to meet eligibility requirements based on their financial contribution to their households. The challenge was brought by Lieutenant Sharron Frontiero of the Air Force.

4741. Supreme Court ruling in a criminal case in which a United States president was named as a conspirator came in *United States v. Nixon*, one of the cases, collectively known as Watergate, that resulted from the burglary at the Democratic National Committee headquarters in 1972. The break-in was carried out by agents of the Committee to Re-Elect the President (CREEP). On March 1, 1974, indictments were brought against seven former aides of President Richard Nixon, charging that they had conspired to obstruct a federal investigation of the break-in. In a sealed report to the House Judiciary Committee, President Nixon was named as a co-conspirator, though he was not indicted. The discovery that the president possessed audiotapes of his White House conversations led to the subpoena of those tapes by congressional committees, by the special Watergate prosecutor, and by Chief Justice John J. Sirica of the U.S. District Court. Asked to rule on President Nixon's claim that executive privilege protected him from such a subpoena, the Supreme Court voted 8–0 that the need for confidentiality in presidential discussions did not give the president the right to withhold evidence in a criminal case, as this would "gravely impair the role of the courts under Article III" of the Constitution. The ruling, written by Chief Justice Warren Burger in consultation with his colleagues, was handed down on July 24, 1974. President Nixon turned over the tapes on July 30 and resigned from office on August 9.

SUPREME COURT—DECISIONS—*continued*

4742. Supreme Court decision upholding the right to parody public figures was in the case of *Hustler Magazine v. Falwell,* decided on February 24, 1988, by the Rehnquist Court. At issue was the right of *Hustler,* a pornographic magazine published by Larry Flynt, to publish a scabrously satirical piece about the Reverend Jerry Falwell, a conservative religious leader and founder of the Moral Majority political party. Falwell claimed emotional distress resulting from the publication of the article and won a libel suit against *Hustler* in a lower court. Flynt appealed to the Supreme Court, which unanimously held that the *Hustler* piece, although tasteless and offensive, was protected by the First Amendment, and that public figures such as Falwell may not recover damages for the tort of intentional infliction of emotional distress without showing that the offending caricature contained a false statement of fact made with actual malice. According to Justice William O. Rehnquist, "the State's interest in protecting public figures from emotional distress is not sufficient to deny First Amendment protection to speech that is patently offensive and is intended to inflict emotional injury when that speech could not reasonably have been interpreted as stating actual facts about the public figure involved."

4743. Supreme Court decision on the right of a citizen to burn the American flag was made by the Supreme Court on June 21, 1989, when it overturned, on First Amendment grounds, a Texas law forbidding desecration of the flag. The case, decided by a 5–4 vote, is known as *Texas v. Johnson.* The plaintiff was Gregory Lee Johnson, an avowed communist, who was jailed in 1984 after he set fire to an American flag in front of the Dallas city hall during the Republican national convention. According to the Court's majority opinion, written by Justice William J. Brennan, "the government may not prohibit the expression of an idea simply because society finds the idea itself offensive or disagreeable." The Senate, by a vote of 97–3, passed a resolution expressing disappointment with the ruling, and joined with the House in enacting legislation to ban flag burning and mutilation. That law was also overturned by the Supreme Court, on June 11, 1990.

4744. Supreme Court decision on the constitutionality of public religious displays was the case of *County of Allegheny, Chabad and City of Pittsburgh v. American Civil Liberties Union et al.,* in which the Supreme Court ruled on July 3, 1989, on the constitutionality of two government religious holiday displays in Pittsburgh, PA. One display, in front of the Allegheny County courthouse, contained a Nativity scene, while the other, in front of the City-County Building, included a Christmas tree, a menorah erected by Chabad (an organization of Chassidic Jews), and a sign declaring the city's "salute to liberty." By a 6–3 vote, the Court ruled that the tree-menorah display was constitutional under the First Amendment's establishment clause because it did not promote one religion over another, while the Nativity display was ruled unconstitutional because it appeared to endorse a single religion.

4745. Supreme Court decisions invalidating three federal laws in three days were handed down during the week of June 23, 1997. On June 25, in the case of *City of Boerne, Texas, v. Flores,* the Rehnquist Court voted 6–3 to strike down the Religious Freedom Restoration Act, ruling that any statute that assumes that Congress can define what does and does not count as protected religious exercise is a threat to the Constitution and religious freedom. On June 26, the justices overturned the Communications Decency Act, which was intended to protect children from Internet pornography, ruling that the law was too broad and too vague. And on June 27, in *Printz v. United States,* the Court rejected a rule included in the Brady Gun Control Act that required state and local law-enforcement officials to do background checks on handgun buyers.

4746. Supreme Court decision on inclusion of candidates in televised political debates was *Arkansas Educational Television Commission v. Forbes,* decided on May 19, 1998. The case concerned a candidates' debate that was sponsored by a state-owned public television station during the congressional election campaign of 1992. The station did not permit an independent candidate, Ralph Forbes, to participate in the debate along with the candidates of the major parties, although he had qualified to appear on the ballot. The Rehnquist Court, by a vote of 6 to 3, agreed with a lower court that the First Amendment allowed the station to give selective access to candidates as long as it did not target specific political views for discrimination.

SUPREME COURT—JUSTICES

4747. Chief justice of the Supreme Court was John Jay of New York, who was appointed by President George Washington on September 24, 1789. He was confirmed by the Senate on September 26, 1789, and took the oath of office on October 19. His most important opinion was written for *Glass v. The Sloop Betsy*, decided on February 18, 1794, in which the justices ruled unanimously that foreign powers do not have the right to establish courts in the United States. The case involved a Swedish merchant vessel that was captured as a prize by a French warship and taken into Baltimore for adjudication by the French consul.

4748. Supreme Court justice who had served in the executive branch was John Jay of New York, the first chief justice, who had served as secretary for foreign affairs from 1784 to 1789, when the nation was still operating under the Articles of Confederation. The first justice to have served in the executive branch under the Constitution was Chief Justice John Marshall (1801–35), who had been sent to France as a special envoy by President John Adams in 1797.

4749. Supreme Court justices born outside the United States were James Wilson, born in 1742 in Caskardy, Fifeshire, Scotland, and James Iredell, born in 1751 in Lewes, England. Both were members of the original Supreme Court that convened in 1790. They were joined in 1793 by William Paterson, who was born in County Antrim, Ireland, in 1745.

4750. Supreme Court nominee to die before taking office was Robert Hanson Harrison, the former chief judge of the General Court of Maryland, who was nominated to the Supreme Court by President George Washington on September 24, 1789, along with the five other members of the first Supreme Court, and was confirmed by the Senate on September 26. Harrison, who was infirm, declined to serve but was persuaded by the president to change his mind. On his way to New York City to take his seat, he became seriously ill, and he died soon thereafter. His place was taken by James Iredell of North Carolina. The next Supreme Court nominee to die before taking office was Edwin McMasters Stanton, who was appointed by President Ulysses Simpson Grant on December 20, 1869, and confirmed the same day by a vote of 46 to 11, but who died four days later.

4751. Supreme Court justice to resign was John Rutledge of South Carolina, who was appointed to the Court by President George Washington. He took the oath of office on February 15, 1790, but he did not attend a single session of the Supreme Court, probably because he was disappointed in not having been named chief justice. He did, however, perform the circuit-riding duties of a Supreme Court justice, riding the Southern Circuit. He resigned on March 15, 1791, to become chief justice of the South Carolina Court of Common Pleas. On July 1, 1795, President Washington nominated him to replace John Jay as the chief justice of the Supreme Court, making him the first Supreme Court justice to be renominated after resignation.

4752. Nominee for associate justice of the Supreme Court to be rejected by the Senate was William Paterson of New Jersey, who was nominated on February 20, 1793, by President George Washington. His name was sent to the Senate for approval on February 27, but he was rejected on a technicality (he had been serving as senator from New Jersey when the office of associate justice was created). On March 4, 1793, after Paterson's Senate term had expired, Washington renominated him under a recess appointment. He was confirmed and served from March 14, 1793, to September 9, 1806.

4753. Supreme Court justice who had been a state governor was William Paterson of New Jersey, who succeeded William Livingston as governor in 1790, serving simultaneously as state chancellor. He took office as associate justice on March 11, 1793.

4754. Supreme Court justice who had served in the Senate was William Paterson of New Jersey, who was a U.S. Senator from 1789 to 1790. He took office as associate justice on March 11, 1793.

4755. Supreme Court chief justice to resign was John Jay, the Court's first chief justice, who took the oath of office in October 1789. In 1794, while still on the Court, he was sent to London by President George Washington to negotiate a treaty of commerce. He returned the following year to find that in his absence he had been elected governor of New York. He resigned on June 29, 1795, and went on to serve two three-year terms as governor. President John Adams renominated him to be chief justice in 1800, after the resignation of Oliver Ellsworth, but Jay declined, though he had already been confirmed by the Senate.

SUPREME COURT—JUSTICES—*continued*

4756. Nominee for chief justice of the Supreme Court to be rejected by the Senate was former associate justice John Rutledge of South Carolina. Rutledge, a Federalist, had been named one of the original associate justices of the Supreme Court in 1789, though he had refused to attend its sessions and had resigned in 1791 to head his state's Court of Common Pleas. President George Washington nominated him in July 1795, during the adjournment of Congress, to succeed John Jay as chief justice. He was sworn in on August 12, 1795, and presided over the Court's August session in Philadelphia, PA. However, his vehement opposition to the Jay Treaty cost him support in Congress, and on December 15, 1795, the Senate refused to confirm him by a vote of 14 to 10.

4757. Associate Supreme Court justice to refuse elevation to the post of chief justice was William Cushing of Massachusetts, associate justice of the Supreme Court since February 1790. The vacancy left by the resignation of Chief Justice John Jay on June 29, 1795, was initially filled by former associate justice John Rutledge, but Rutledge failed to win confirmation from the Senate. Cushing was nominated by President George Washington on January 26, 1796, and was confirmed by the Senate on the following day, but declined the appointment. Jay was replaced on March 8 by Oliver Ellsworth.

4758. Chief justice of the Supreme Court to administer the oath of office to a president was Oliver Ellsworth of Connecticut, chief justice from March 8, 1796, through December 15, 1800. On March 4, 1797, he administered the oath of office to John Adams in Philadelphia, PA. At the two previous inaugurations—those of George Washington—the oath was administered by Robert R. Livingston, Chancellor of New York State (1789), and William Cushing, associate justice of the Supreme Court (1793).

4759. Supreme Court justice who had served in the House of Representatives was John Marshall of Virginia, chief justice from Febuary 4, 1801, to July 6, 1835, who had served in the House of Representatives from March 4, 1799, to June 7, 1800. The first associate justice with experience in the House of Representatives was Gabriel Duvall of Maryland, a member of the Court from February 3, 1812, to January 15, 1835, who had served in the House of Representatives from November 11, 1794, to March 28, 1796.

4760. Former chief justice of the Supreme Court to refuse renomination was John Jay, who served as the Court's first chief justice from October 19, 1789, until June 29, 1795, when he resigned. His replacement was Oliver Ellsworth, who himself resigned in September 1800. Jay, who was then serving his second term as governor of New York, was nominated by President John Adams on December 18 and was confirmed by the Senate next day. However, Jay, who had not been consulted regarding his renomination, declined to accept on the ground that the Court was too weak an institution. Ellsworth was replaced on February 4, 1801, by John Marshall.

4761. Supreme Court justice who had served in a presidential cabinet was John Marshall, secretary of state in 1800–01 under President John Adams, who appointed him chief justice on January 20, 1801.

4762. Supreme Court chief justice who had served in a presidential cabinet was John Marshall of Virginia, who was chief justice from February 4, 1801, to July 6, 1835. For the first month, until March 4, 1801, he continued to serve as President John Adams's secretary of state, the job he had held since June 1800.

4763. Chief justice of the Supreme Court to administer the oath of office to more than one president was John Marshall, chief justice from February 4, 1801, to July 6, 1835, when he died. He gave the oath of office to Thomas Jefferson on March 4, 1801, and March 4, 1805; to James Madison on March 4, 1809, and March 4, 1813; to James Monroe on March 4, 1817, and March 5, 1821; to John Quincy Adams on March 4, 1825; and to Andrew Jackson on March 4, 1829, and March 4, 1833.

4764. Supreme Court justice to be impeached was Samuel Chase, against whom charges were brought on March 12, 1804, by the House of Representatives. The accusation consisted of eight articles, of which the majority had to do with high-handed conduct displayed by Chase in two treason and sedition trials. There were also political reasons for the impeachment, which was encouraged by President Thomas Jefferson. The trial began on January 30, 1805. Chase was acquitted and served until his death on June 19, 1811, at the age of 70.

4765. Supreme Court justice who had served as a federal judge was Robert Trimble, who sat as judge of the United States District Court for the District of Kentucky from 1817 to 1826, when he was appointed as associate justice of the Supreme Court. He took office on June 16, 1828.

4766. Chief Justice to wear long pants at his inauguration was Roger Brooke Taney, who took the oath of office on March 28, 1836, wearing trousers rather than knee breeches.

4767. Supreme Court chief justice who was Catholic was Roger Brooke Taney of Frederick, MD, who was appointed by President Andrew Jackson to succeed John Marshall. He served from March 28, 1836, until his death on October 12, 1864.

4768. Supreme Court justice who had served as attorney general was Roger Brooke Taney, attorney general from 1831 to 1833 under President Andrew Jackson. He replaced John Marshall as chief justice on March 28, 1836.

4769. Supreme Court justice with a university law degree was Benjamin Robbins Curtis, appointed by President Millard Fillmore in 1851. Curtis was a native of Watertown, MA, who received his undergraduate degree from Harvard College in 1829 and his law degree from Harvard Law School in 1832. Two previous justices, John Rutledge and John Blair, both members of the first Court of 1790, had received their legal education in London, at the Middle Temple of the Inns of Court. Most aspiring lawyers in the early decades of the United States studied privately under a practicing lawyer.

4770. Supreme Court justice with no judicial or political experience was George Shiras, Jr., a lawyer who practiced in Dubuque, IA, and Pittsburgh, PA, from 1855 until October 10, 1892, when he took the oath of office as associate justice. He had been offered a Senate nomination by the Pennsylvania state legislature in 1881 but turned it down. He was appointed to the Supreme Court by President Benjamin Harrison and was confirmed despite the objections of his state's U.S. senators, who considered him too independent.

4771. Supreme Court justice to be appointed and confirmed as chief justice was Edward Douglass White, who was appointed associate justice on March 12, 1894, and chief justice on December 12, 1910. He took his seat on December 19 and served until May 2, 1921, a week before his death. John Rutledge was appointed chief justice in 1795 after having served 13 months as associate justice (1790–91), but the Senate refused to confirm him.

4772. Supreme Court justice who was Jewish was Louis Dembitz Brandeis of Boston, MA, who was appointed on January 28, 1916, by President Woodrow Wilson. The nomination was confirmed by the Senate on June 1, 1916, and Brandeis was sworn in on June 3. He served until 1939.

4773. Chief justice of the Supreme Court who had served as president of the United States was William Howard Taft, who was appointed chief justice by President Warren Gamaliel Harding. His appointment was immediately confirmed by the Senate, and he took the oath of office on June 30, 1921. He had entered the White House on March 4, 1909, and left it on March 3, 1913, after losing a bid for reelection. Between the end of his presidency and the beginning of his term on the Court, he taught law at Yale University.

4774. Supreme Court nominee to testify before the Senate Judiciary Committee with regard to his confirmation was Harlan Fiske Stone of New York. Stone, the United States attorney general, was nominated as associate justice by President Calvin Coolidge on January 5, 1925. At his own initiative, Stone appeared in person before the Judiciary Committee to answer allegations about his personal and political ties to big business. His appointment was confirmed on February 5, 1925, by a vote of 61 to 6. The appearance of Supreme Court nominees before the Judiciary Committee did not become a standard part of the confirmation process until the mid-1950s.

4775. Supreme Court justice to be appointed, confirmed, and inaugurated twice was Charles Evans Hughes of New York, who was the governor of New York in 1910 when he was appointed an associate justice of the Supreme Court by President William Howard Taft. He resigned from the Court in 1916 to run for president on the Republican ticket, but was defeated by the incumbent president, Woodrow Wilson. After serving as secretary of state under Presidents Warren Gamaliel Harding and Calvin Coolidge, Hughes was appointed chief justice of the Supreme Court on February 13, 1930, by President Herbert Hoover. He retired in 1941. John Jay, the first chief justice (1790–95), was reappointed and reconfirmed in 1800, but declined to serve; John Rutledge, associate justice in 1790–91, was reappointed as chief justice in 1795, but was not confirmed.

SUPREME COURT—JUSTICES—*continued*

4776. Supreme Court nominee to be rejected by the Senate in the 20th century was John J. Parker of North Carolina, chief judge of the Fourth Circuit Court, who was nominated by Herbert Clark Hoover. On May 7, 1930, the Senate narrowly rejected his nomination after his judicial record was criticized as unfair by the American Federation of Labor and the National Association for the Advancement of Colored People.

4777. Woman to clerk for a Supreme Court justice was Lucille Loman, who was hired by Justice William O. Douglas in 1944. She also served as his personal assistant. No other woman was employed as a clerk until 1966, when Justice Harry Blackmun hired Margaret Corcoran.

4778. Year in which all the justices of the Supreme Court were graduates of a law school was 1957, four years into the tenure of Chief Justice Earl Warren. Warren received his J.D. degree from the University of California in 1914. The associate justices that year were Hugo Lafayette Black (University of Alabama Law School, 1906), Felix Frankfurter (Harvard Law School, 1906), Harold Hitz Burton (Harvard Law School, 1912), Tom Campbell Clark (University of Texas, 1922), Charles Evans Whittaker (University of Kansas City Law School, 1924), William Orville Douglas (Columbia University Law School, 1925), John Marshall Harlan (New York Law School, 1925), and William Joseph Brennan (Harvard Law School, 1931).

4779. Supreme Court justice who was African-American was Thurgood Marshall of Maryland, appointed on June 13, 1967, by President Lyndon Baines Johnson. He was confirmed by the Senate by a vote of 69–11 on August 30, 1967, and sworn in on September 1 in a private ceremony. He was publicly sworn in at the opening ceremony of the new term on October 2, 1967. He was the 96th justice.

4780. Supreme Court justice to participate in a television program was Hugo LaFayette Black, who was interviewed in his home at Alexandria, VA, on December 3, 1968, for CBS News by Eric Sevareid and Martin Agronsky.

4781. Woman to become a Supreme Court justice was Sandra Day O'Connor of Arizona, nominated as an associate justice by President Ronald Reagan on July 7, 1981. The Senate approved her appointment by a vote of 99–0 on September 21. O'Connor took her seat on September 25 after taking the oath of office administered by Chief Justice Warren E. Burger.

4782. Supreme Court nominee accused of sexual harassment was Clarence Thomas, the 106th justice. After Thomas's nomination in 1991, media sources leaked charges of sexual harassment that had been made against him by University of Oklahoma law professor Anita F. Hill, who a decade earlier had worked for Thomas at the Department of Education and the Equal Opportunity Commission. The charges were publicly read by Hill on October 11, 1991, before televised Senate Judiciary Committee hearings watched by some 30 million American households. Thomas vigorously denied Hill's accusations; convincing evidence was not produced to corroborate either side's account. After an unprecedented 107 days of hearings, Thomas was confirmed on October 15, 1991, by a Senate vote of 52 to 48, the closest in a century. The hearings sparked a national debate about sexism and sexual harassment in American society.

4783. Jewish woman to serve as a Supreme Court justice was Ruth Bader Ginsburg of the U.S. Appeals Court for the District of Columbia, nominated by President William Jefferson Clinton on June 14, 1993. She filled the seat vacated by Justice Byron White. She was the second woman to serve on the Supreme Court and the first Jewish justice since the resignation of Abe Fortas in 1969.

4784. Woman to preside over the Supreme Court was associate justice Sandra Day O'Connor of Arizona. On April 3, 1995, she sat in for the chief justice, William H. Rehnquist, when he was out of town.

T

TAXATION—COLONIAL

4785. Property tax levied by a colony was passed on May 14, 1634, and signed by Governor William Bradford of the Plymouth colony in Massachusetts: "It is further ordered that in all rates and public charges, the towns shall have respect to levy each man according to his estate, and with consideration of all other his abilities, whatsoever, and not according to the number of persons."

4786. Statement of the principle of taxation with consent was established in 1636 by the Plymouth Colony, which gave the colony's freemen the right to consider proposals for new taxes at a public assembly and prevented taxes from being levied without their approval. The idea was articulated anew in 1764 by James Otis of Boston, MA, who was followed by Daniel Dulany of Maryland, Patrick Henry of Virginia, and other political leaders.

4787. Property tax established by a colony to support public schools was established by vote of Dorchester, MA, on May 20, 1639: "It is ordered the 20th of May 1639, that there shall be a rent of twenty pounds a year for ever imposed upon Tomsons Island to be paid by every person that hath property in the said island according to the proportion that any such person shall from time to time enjoy and possess there."

4788. Income tax levied by a colony was levied on the colonists of New Plymouth, MA, in 1643, "according to their estates or faculties, that is, according to goods lands improoved faculties and personall abilities." This "faculty tax," as it is known, made a distinction between property and faculty, or the assumed capacity of an individual to produce income.

4789. Poll tax was levied by the colony of Massachusetts in 1646. Each male over the age of 16 was required to pay a tax of 2s. 6d.

4790. Tax on Britain's American colonists imposed without their consent was levied in 1672, when the British Parliament passed a law imposing a duty on sugar, tobacco, ginger, coconuts, indigo, logwood fustic, wool, and cotton.

4791. Revenue-collecting administration in the British colonies was established under Parliament's Revenue Act of 1673, which imposed a "plantation duty" on American exports, such as tobacco, that were shipped to European markets. A staff of customs officials was created to collect the plantation tax.

4792. Inheritance tax levied by a colony was levied by Virginia in 1687, when the Colony of Virginia provided that the governor of the colony should collect a fee of a cask and 200 pounds of tobacco for impressing documents with the public seal, without which they were invalid. These documents included probates, letters testamentary, and letters of administration.

4793. Tax revolt took place in Ipswich, MA, in 1687. Led by the Congregational clergyman John Wise, the Ipswich town meeting refused to authorize collection of a tax that had been levied without its consent by the colonial governor, Sir Edmund Andros. Wise was arrested, tried, and temporarily deprived of his ministry. To commemorate the event, the official seal of the town of Ipswich is inscribed with the words "The Birthplace of American Independence, 1687."

4794. Stamp tax was imposed by the colonial legislature of Massachusetts in 1755, followed by that of New York in 1757. The purpose in both cases was to raise money to pay for military campaigns. Newspaper publishers were required to pay a tax of half a penny per paper and to stamp their copies with a small impression of the King's arms in red ink.

TAXATION—FEDERAL

4795. Congressional resolution on taxation to finance a war was passed on January 13, 1779, during the Revolutionary War, when Congress was meeting in New York City. It read: "Resolved, That these United States be called on to pay in their respective quotas of fifteen millions of dollars in the year 1779, and of six millions of dollars annually for 18 years from and after the year 1779, as a fund for sinking the emissions and loans of these United States to the 31st day of December, 1778, inclusive."

4796. Tax passed by Congress was an 8.5 percent protective tax on various commercial items, passed on July 4, 1789. Goods arriving on foreign ships were taxed at a higher rate than those shipped on American vessels.

4797. Internal revenue tax levied by Congress was imposed on March 3, 1791, as part of the first Excise Act, which was enacted by Congress at the urging of Treasury Secretary Alexander Hamilton to pay for the federal government's assumption of state debts. The law established 14 revenue districts, one for each state, and levied a tax on distilled spirits, both domestic and imported, of eleven to 30 cents a gallon, depending on alcoholic content prior to removal from the distillery. Carriages were also taxed. Subsequent early modifications of the act of 1791 imposed taxes on retail dealers in distilled spirits, as well as on refined sugar, snuff, property sold at auction, legal instruments, and bonds. Receipts for the fiscal year 1792 from internal revenue netted the government $208,943.

TAXATION—FEDERAL—continued

4798. Federal revenue commissioner was Tench Coxe of Pennsylvania, who was assistant to the secretary of the treasury in charge of internal revenue from September 11, 1789, to May 8, 1792. He was designated commissioner on May 8, 1792.

4799. Tax rebellion against the federal government was the Whiskey Rebellion, a popular uprising against the Excise Act of 1791, which placed a tax on spirits distilled from grain. Among the farmers of the frontier (the western regions of Pennsylvania, Maryland, Virginia, and North Carolina), whiskey was used as a medium of exchange in place of money; hence, the excise tax was seen as a punitive Federalist attack on their way of life and a renewal of the hated British excise from the colonial era. The farmers set up Liberty poles and assaulted tax collectors, as they had done in Revolutionary days. President George Washington led federal troops against them in the fall of 1794. Two of their leaders were convicted of treason and sentenced to death by hanging but were pardoned by Washington. The end result was an increase in popular support for Hamilton's enemies, the Democratic-Republican Party.

4800. Direct tax levied by Congress was a direct pro rata tax upon the 16 states, authorized by act of July 14, 1798. It was levied on dwellings, land, and slaves between the ages of twelve and 50. The amount to be collected was $2 million, which was apportioned to the states in direct ratio to the population, as required by the Constitution. The revenue needs of the federal government doubled between 1796, when they amounted to about $5.8 million, and 1800, when they reached $10.8 million, chiefly because of the military conflict with France.

4801. Income tax levied by Congress was imposed during the Civil War by act of August 5, 1861, effective January 1, 1862, which imposed a 3 percent tax on incomes exceeding $800 and a 1.5 percent tax on income derived from government securities. The income tax lists were open to public inspection by "all persons who may apply to inspect the same." This was interpreted in such a way as to eliminate idle curiosity seekers. The law was not enforced and was replaced the following year by another. It was rescinded in 1872 along with other Civil War taxes.

4802. Tax levied by the Confederacy was enacted on August 19, 1861, at Montgomery, AL, by the provisional Confederate Congress, at the urging of Treasury Secretary Christopher Gustavus Memminger. The act imposed a direct war tax of one-half of 1 percent on all property, including real estate, personal property, merchandise, and slaves, and realized about $20 million in revenues. A comprehensive tax statute was enacted on April 24, 1863.

4803. Bureau of Internal Revenue was created within the Treasury Department by act of Congress on July 1, 1862, through the Internal Revenue Act. The first commissioner was George Sewall Boutwell of Massachusetts, who served from July 17, 1862, to March 4, 1863.

4804. Inheritance tax levied by Congress was a part of the Internal Revenue Act of July 1, 1862, which assessed a tax on legacies and distributive shares of personal property. It was repealed after the Civil War. It had a precursor in the Stamp Act of July 6, 1797, which obligated the purchase of stamps for legal documents, including probates of wills and receipts for inheritances. The federal government's first permanent inheritance tax was enacted as part of the "Preparedness" Revenue Act of 1916.

4805. Revenue stamps issued by the federal government were issued in 1862 under authority of the Internal Revenue Act of July 1, 1862, "to provide Internal Revenue to support the government and to pay interest on the public debt." At first, specific taxes were identified on the stamps, such as bill of lading, foreign exchange, probate of will, warehouse receipt, and so on, but after December 25, 1862, they were used indiscriminately. Revenue stamps were issued in various sizes, in valuations from one cent to $200.

4806. Customs fee stamps were issued by the New York Custom House, New York City, in 1887. There were eight denominations, ranging from 20 cents to 90 cents. All were decorated with a distinctive background and a likeness of Silas Wright, New York State's former senator and governor. Their use was discontinued on February 28, 1918.

4807. Income tax levied by Congress in peacetime was passed on August 27, 1894, as part of the tariff act, with the intention of overcoming the effects on the Treasury of a deep economic depression. The law, which affected only a tiny minority of the populace, provided for a tax of 2 percent on personal incomes above $4,000 per year. It was declared unconstitutional by the Supreme Court on May 20,

1895, in the case of *Pollock v. Farmers' Loan & Trust Co.* The 16th Amendment to the Constitution, which was declared ratified on February 25, 1913, gave Congress the power to lay and collect income taxes. It was upheld by the Supreme Court in 1916.

4808. Corporation tax levied by Congress was passed on August 5, 1909. The act taxed all corporations with an income over $5,000. The law was passed prior to the adoption of the U.S. income tax amendment.

4809. Filing date for 1040 tax forms was March 1, 1914. The 16th Amendment to the Constitution, which was declared ratified on February 25, 1913, gave Congress the right to impose and collect income taxes. The new income tax, drafted by Tennessee representative Cordell Hull, affected only the small percentage of American families who made more than $4,000 per year.

4810. Federal tax on war profits was enacted on September 8, 1916. It assessed a tax of 12.5 percent on the net profits of businesses engaged in producing munitions for World War I, including guns, ammunition, shells, and submarines.

4811. Tax act to require publication of national tax statistics was the Revenue Act of 1916, enacted by Congress on September 8, 1916. The act provided for "the preparation and publication of statistics reasonably available with respect to the operation of the income tax law and containing classifications of taxpayers and of income . . . and any other facts deemed pertinent and valuable." Reports were to be made annually by the commissioner of internal revenue with the approval of the secretary of the treasury. The Statistical Division of the Income Tax Unit of the Bureau of Revenue was created in 1917, and its first chief, Dr. Edward White, was appointed the following year.

4812. Year in which federal revenues from income taxes exceeded those from customs duties was 1917. The power to levy income taxes was given to Congress in 1913 by the ratification of the 16th Amendment to the Constitution and upheld by the Supreme Court in 1916.

4813. Federal tax on excess corporate profits was enacted as part of the Revenue Act of March 3, 1917, for the purpose of relieving an anticipated revenue shortage during World War I. The law, modeled on one already adopted by Canada, assessed a tax of 8 percent on the net incomes (above $5,000) of corporations and partnerships and on their actual invested capital.

4814. State of Income report released by the federal government was made public in June 1918 by the Statistical Division of the Bureau of Revenue's Income Tax Unit. It provided information about personal and corporate income tax returns filed for 1916.

4815. Woman to serve as a federal internal revenue collector was Mabel Gilmore Reinecke, who served from June 1, 1923, to March 31, 1929, as collector of Internal Revenue for the 1st District of Illinois. She was appointed by President Warren Gamaliel Harding.

4816. Gasoline tax levied by Congress was the Revenue Act of 1932, enacted on June 6, 1932, which placed a tax of one cent per gallon on gasoline and other motor fuel.

4817. Revenue stamp printed by the Post Office Department was the "Federal duck stamp," a $1 stamp required of all waterfowl hunters over 16 years of age, to be attached to game licenses as required by the Migratory Bird Conservation Act of March 16, 1934. The stamp went on sale on August 14, 1934. It depicted a male and female mallard coming to rest on a marshland and was drawn by Jay Norwood "Ding" Darling, chief of the Bureau of Biological Survey of the Department of Agriculture. Stamps of this class, as well as all other revenue stamps, had previously been issued by the Treasury Department. Although sold through the Post Office Department, the proceeds went to the Department of Agriculture, where 10 percent was used for the expense of printing and selling the stamps and the balance to lease or purchase marsh areas for waterfowl sanctuaries.

4818. Internal Revenue Code was drawn up by the Joint Committee on Internal Revenue Taxation, and Treasury Department, and the Justice Department, for the purpose of simplifying the multiplicity of laws. It was enacted on February 10, 1939.

4819. Internal Revenue Service was established as part of the reorganization of the Bureau of Internal Revenue under Treasury Order 150-06, with the mission to collect federal taxes "according to the law, free of political or corrupt influence." The order was signed on July 9, 1953, by the secretary of the treasury, G. K. Humphrey.

4820. IRS area service center was opened in Kansas City, MO, in 1955 to handle administrative processing of individual income tax returns. This was later followed by centers in Lawrence, MA, and Ogden, UT.

TAXATION—FEDERAL—*continued*

4821. Taxpayer usage study was undertaken in 1956 by the IRS's Statistical Division. A small sample of tax returns was selected early in administrative processing to provide the IRS with a quick glimpse of the reporting practices of taxpayers during the filing season. Early intermittent studies covered several different types of tax returns. Annual taxpayer usage studies of individual income tax returns were conducted beginning in 1969.

4822. IRS Computing Center was the IRS Data Center in Detroit, MI (now the Detroit Computing Center), which became operational in 1965. Much of the IRS's computer work was gradually transferred to the Data Center in succeeding years.

4823. Income-tax checkoff to provide for the financing of presidential general election campaigns and national party conventions was authorized by Congress in 1971 as part of the Federal Election Campaign Act. The checkboxes appeared on tax returns due April 15, 1972. Amendments to the Internal Revenue Code in 1974 established a matching fund program for Presidential primary campaigns.

4824. IRS commissioner who was not an accountant or a lawyer was Charles Rossotti, a former computer company executive, who assumed his duties as the 45th commissioner of internal revenue on November 13, 1997. Rossotti previously served as chairman of American Management Systems of Fairfax, VA.

TAXATION—MUNICIPAL

4825. Single tax adopted by a city for local revenue purposes was adopted by Hyattsville, MD, which operated under this system from July 1892 to March 1893, under laws that were declared unconstitutional. The single tax system eliminates all government taxes except the tax on land.

4826. Municipal aviation tax was enacted in August 1908 by the town of Kissimmee City, FL. The law imposed a tax of $100 on airplanes, $150 on helicopters, $200 on ornithopters, and $300 on all other types of flying machines, plus a tax on their carrying capacity, and authorized the purchase of an "aeroplane of approved modern type" for the marshal to enforce the provisions of the ordinance. No attempt was made to enforce the law.

TAXATION—STATE

4827. State income tax was levied in 1777 by Massachusetts, which assessed its residents "on the amount of their income from any profession, faculty, handicraft, trade, or employment." The same law laid a tax "on the amount of all incomes and profits gained by trading by sea and on shore, and by means of advantages arising from the war and the necessities of the community," making it the first state tax on war profits. Maryland and South Carolina also passed income taxes, then called faculty taxes, in 1777, and Vermont did so the following year.

4828. Bachelor tax enacted by a state was levied by Missouri, which on December 20, 1820, placed a $1 tax "on every unmarried free white male, above the age of 21 years and under 50 years."

4829. Inheritance tax enacted by a state was passed by Pennsylvania on April 7, 1826, and signed by Governor John Andrew Shulze. It established a 2.5 percent collateral inheritance tax. The surviving spouse, the parents, and the descendants of the decedent were exempted.

4830. Gasoline tax levied by a state was enacted on February 25, 1919, when Oregon placed a tax of one cent per gallon on all motor fuel. The funds collected were used for road construction and maintenance.

4831. Sales tax enacted by a state was approved on May 3, 1921, by West Virginia, and became effective on July 1. The funds collected were used largely in place of funds from a tax on corporate net income. The rate was one-fifth of 1 percent on the gross income of banks, street railroads, telephones, telegraph, express, and electric light and power retailers, and two-fifths of 1 percent on timber, oil, coal, natural gas, and other minerals. Payments could be made to the state quarterly or annually.

4832. State tax on chain stores was levied by Indiana. This statute, commonly referred to as the Indiana Chain Store Tax Law, was signed on March 16, 1929, by Governor Harry Leslie. Under the statute, owners were required to pay an annual license fee of $3 to operate a store in Indiana. For two to five stores under the same management, supervision, or ownership, the tax was $10 for each additional store; for stores in excess of five but not in excess of ten, $15 for each additional store; for stores in excess of ten but not in excess of 20, $20 for each additional store; for all stores in excess of 20, $25 plus a 50-cent filing fee for each additional store. An amendment to this act was signed on March 11, 1933, by Governor Paul Vories McNutt, requiring owners of stores in excess of 20 to pay $150 for each additional store.

4833. Income tax enacted by a state was enacted by the legislature of Minnesota in May 1933 and signed by Governor Floyd B. Olson. The law provided for a graduated tax, ranging from 1 percent to 5 percent.

4834. State taxation of religious goods was allowed under a unanimous Supreme Court ruling of January 1990. The ruling in *Jimmy Swaggart Ministries v. Board of Equalization of California* held that state levies on religious goods do not violate the First Amendment provision against undue government interference with religion. The ruling meant that the Louisiana-based Jimmy Swaggart Ministries had to pay taxes on evangelistic crusades and mail order activities conducted in California.

TERRITORIES

4835. Territory owned by the federal government was the Northwest Territory (officially called the Territory Northwest of the River Ohio and also known as the Old Northwest), an area of land about 248,000 square miles around the Great Lakes and the Mississippi River. It was acquired by the United States in the Treaty of Paris of 1783, which ended the Revolutionary War. Pieces of the territory claimed by New York, Virginia, Massachusetts, Connecticut, and other states were ceded to the federal government between 1781 and 1802. Arthur St. Clair was appointed the first governor of the Northwest Territory in October 1787; the first territorial legislature assembled on September 24, 1799; and Ohio, in 1803, became the first state to be admitted from within its boundaries. Beginning in 1800, with the establishment of the Indiana Territory, Congress formed a series of organized territories from its lands, eventually resulting in the creation of the states of Indiana, Illinois, Michigan, Wisconsin, and Minnesota.

4836. Territory annexed by the federal government was the Louisiana Purchase, a tract of land bought from France on April 30, 1803, for $15 million. It covered 1,171,931 square miles and included the entire Mississippi Valley from the Mississippi River to the Rocky Mountains and from the Gulf of Mexico to Canada. This territory included the present states of Louisiana, Arkansas, Missouri, Iowa, North and South Dakota, Nebraska, Kansas, and Oklahoma, part of Colorado and Wyoming, and most of Mon-

tana and Minnesota. The treaty was arranged by Robert R. Livingston, minister at Paris, and James Monroe, who had been sent by President Thomas Jefferson as a special envoy to assist Livingston. The tract was also claimed by Spain, which ceded it to France on November 30, 1803. On December 20, France formally delivered the colony to the American representatives.

4837. Government-sponsored overland expedition to the Pacific Coast was the Lewis and Clark Expedition, organized by President Thomas Jefferson in 1803 to gather information about the lands transferred to the United States by France in the Louisiana Purchase and to initiate friendly relations with their Native American inhabitants. The expedition was financed by federal money appropriated by Congress. Led by two Army officers, Meriwether Lewis and William Clark, the group left St. Louis, MO, on May 14, 1804, and returned there on September 23, 1806, after a long trip that brought them across the Rocky Mountains and within sight of the Pacific Ocean in what is now Oregon.

4838. Territorial government to borrow money from a city was the government of the Louisiana Territory, which in 1805 borrowed money for operating expenses from the city of New Orleans. A letter from Governor William Charles Coles Claiborne to New Orleans mayor James Pitot asked him "to address the Municipality on the subject; and to ask whether any, and what sum they could conveniently Loan the Territory and upon what Terms. . . . Permit me to add, that 1500 or 2000 Dollars would for the present answer the calls of the Government, and I persuade myself that the Municipality will be enabled, without injury to the City, to loan that amount for a few months." This was considered even then to be a rather unusual financial measure.

4839. Vote of record in which participants of different races and both sexes were given an equal voice was taken on November 24, 1805, during the crossing of the American Northwest by the Corps of Discovery, which had been sent out by President Thomas Jefferson. In addition to its two leaders, Meriwether Lewis and William Clark, the group included 23 soldiers and York, Lewis's African-American slave. It also included two translators: Toussaint Charbonneau, a French fur trapper, and his Shoshone wife, Sacagawea, who carried her baby son on the way. After the expedition had succeeded in crossing the Bitterroot Mountains

TERRITORIES—*continued*

amid much hardship and had reached the mouth of the Columbia River, the members took a vote on where to spend the winter, with each one's vote counting equally. Their winter quarters were set up at Fort Clatsop, OR.

4840. Land acquired by the United States from Spain was the Florida peninsula, acquired on February 22, 1819, with the signing of the Florida Purchase Treaty by Spanish minister Luis de Onís and U.S. secretary of state John Quincy Adams. There was no purchase price, but the United States took on $5 million in claims by Americans against Spain. General Andrew Jackson was appointed the area's first military governor in 1821, and Florida was made a territory of the United States in 1822.

4841. American republic on the West Coast was the so-called Bear Flag Republic, which lasted for a brief period in the summer of 1846. At the time, northern California was still under Mexican rule, but the impending Mexican-American war emboldened a small group of American traders and trappers under William B. Ide to capture Sonoma, CA, on June 14, 1846. The rebels declared an independent "Republic of California." It was more popularly known as the Bear Flag Republic, after its flag, which was emblazoned with a grizzly bear facing a red star on a white ground. On June 25, the explorer and Army officer John Charles Frémont, the military governor of California, agreed to become the republic's first president. Northern California was occupied by an American naval force on July 7, and the Bear Flag Republic came to an end on July 9. Frémont lost his command and was dismissed from the U.S. Army.

4842. Overseas territory acquired by the United States was Johnston Atoll, a coral atoll in the Pacific Ocean about 700 miles southwest of the Hawaiian Islands, containing Johnston and Sand Islands. The entire atoll is about half a square mile in area. It was discovered in 1807 by an Englishman, Captain C.J. Johnston. Because the islands were used by migrating birds as a resting place, they were covered with guano, a valuable fertilizer, and were consequently claimed in 1858 by the United States (a rival claim was made by the Kingdom of Hawaii). The atoll remains an unincorporated territory of the United States. It was designated by Congress as the site of a bird sanctuary in 1926 and as a Navy outpost in 1934.

4843. Territory annexed by the federal government that was noncontinguous was Alaska, which was purchased from Russia on June 20, 1867, for $7.2 million. General Lovell Harrison Rousseau, the first military governor of the territory, took formal possession of Alaska in October 1867.

4844. Territory annexed by the federal government beyond the nation's continental limits was Midway Island in the North Pacific Ocean, claimed on August 28, 1867, by Captain William Reynolds of the Navy for the United States.

4845. Island territory annexed by the federal government was the Hawaiian Islands, which were formally annexed on August 12, 1898. The treaty was signed on June 16, 1897, by John Sherman, secretary of state. A joint congressional resolution to provide for the annexation was passed on July 7, 1898.

4846. Civilian government in the Panama Canal Zone was established on January 27, 1914, by executive order of President Woodrow Wilson. The first American governor was George W. Goethals, confirmed by the Senate on February 4. Control of the Canal Zone was ceded to the United States by the newly established state of Panama in 1903 under the Hay-Bunau-Varilla Treaty, and was returned to Panama on January 1, 2000, under the Panama Canal Treaty of 1977.

4847. Territory of the United States to win independence was the Philippines, ceded to the United States by Spain through the Treaty of Paris in 1898 at the end of the Spanish-American War. An armed revolt by Filipinos seeking independence was put down by American military action in 1901–02 and led to the constitution of the Philippines as an unorganized territory with substantial self-government, including a popular assembly, whose first elections were held in 1907. The Jones Act of 1916 increased self-government and provided for American recognition of Philippine independence at a later date. In December 1932 Congress passed the Hawes-Cutting Act, which set independence for 1944, primarily to satisfy American farmers seeking to end protected competition from Filipino oil and sugar producers. The act was vetoed by the Philippine senate because it contained a clause guaranteeing a continued U.S. military presence on the islands. A modified version, the Tydings-McDuffie Act of 1934, also known as the Philippine Commonwealth Independence Act, was accepted by the Philippine senate on May 1, 1934. It provided for full Philippine independence as of July 4, 1946.

4848. Polynesian territory of the United States to adopt a constitution was American Samoa, comprising the eastern islands of the Samoa archipelago in the South Pacific Ocean (the western islands form the independent nation of Western Samoa). Congress accepted these islands as a United States territory on February 20, 1929, under the administration of the Navy (until 1951) and then of the Interior Department. A territorial constitution was adopted in 1960. The current constitution dates from 1967. Since 1977, American Samoa has had an elected house of representatives and an elected governor.

4849. Micronesian territory of the United States to adopt a constitution was the Northern Mariana Islands in the North Pacific Ocean. Along with the other islands in the Mariana archipelago, it was placed under the military administration of the United States by the United Nations in 1947 and was transferred to civilian administration in 1951. By popular vote, the inhabitants of the Northern Mariana Islands agreed in 1975 to become a commonwealth of the United States. A constitution took effect on January 9, 1978, allowing for self-government under an elected governor and legislature, together with an elected representative to the United States.

TERRITORIES—GOVERNORS

4850. Governor of the Northwest Territory was Arthur St. Clair, a former British officer who emigrated to Pennsylvania and served as a general in the Continental Army during the Revolutionary War, losing Fort Ticonderoga to the British in 1777. Appointed in 1787 to be governor of the huge Northwest Territory (officially called the Territory Northwest of the River Ohio), which included what is now Ohio, Indiana, Illinois, Michigan, Wisconsin, and part of Minnesota, he mishandled negotiations with the Native Americans of the area, resulting in an escalation of violence. Federal troops and militiamen under his command were defeated by a much smaller Native American army near present-day Fort Wayne, IN, in 1791. Although he survived a congressional investigation into the defeat, St. Clair's continuing opposition to the Constitution led to his removal from office by President Thomas Jefferson in 1802.

4851. Governor of the Southwest Territory (Tennessee) was William Blount of North Carolina, former member of the Continental Congress and the Constitutional Convention. In 1784–87, settlers in the western part of North Carolina had attempted to form a separate state, Franklin, which failed to gain recognition. On

May 26, 1790, the same area was designated as the Territory South of the River Ohio. Blount, one of the chief organizers, was named its governor and served until 1796, when the territory entered the Union as the state of Tennessee. Blount was elected to the Senate but was impeached the following year for his suspected involvement in a treasonous intrigue with Britain; he was thereupon elected to the state senate.

4852. Mississippi territorial governor was Winthrop Sargent, a Massachusetts Federalist and the former secretary of the Northwest Territory, who served from 1798 to 1801. He was also a scholar of history and of the natural sciences and belonged to the American Philosophical Society and the American Academy of Arts and Sciences. Mississippi, a French colony that was ceded to Britain in 1763 and to Spain in 1779, became a territory of the United States on April 7, 1798. The territory included parts of the modern states of Mississippi and Alabama.

4853. Indiana territorial governor was John Gibson, appointed the first acting territorial governor in 1800. The Indiana Territory was created on May 7, 1800, on land that had been part of the Northwest Territory, and included the present states of Indiana, Illinois, and Wisconsin, as well as eastern Minnesota and most of Michigan. Its capital was Vincennes, IN. Future president William Henry Harrison governed the territory from 1801 to 1812.

4854. Orleans territorial governor was William Charles Coles Claiborne of Tennessee, the former governor of the Mississippi Territory. The Louisiana Purchase, acquired from France in 1803, was divided in two by Congress on March 26, 1804, and Claiborne became governor of the section called the Territory of Orleans, serving in that post until the state of Louisiana was formed from it in 1812. Claiborne served from 1812 to 1816 as the first state governor.

4855. Louisiana territorial governor was General James Wilkinson, appointed in 1805. The Louisiana Purchase, acquired from France in 1803, was divided by Congress the following year, with one area designated as the Orleans Territory (the future state of Louisiana) and the remainder designated as the Louisiana Territory. From 1803 to 1805 the Louisiana Territory was administered by an acting governor general, William Charles Coles Claiborne; a civil commandant, Amos Stoddard; and a district governor, William Henry Harrison. Wilkinson served from 1805 to 1807, when he was ac-

TERRITORIES—GOVERNORS—*continued*

cused of conspiring with Aaron Burr to create a western empire. He was acquitted. His replacement as governor was Meriwether Lewis, one of the leaders of the Lewis and Clark expedition of 1804–06.

4856. Michigan territorial governor was William Hull, who served from 1805 to 1813. The territory was created by Congress on January 11, 1805, from lands had been part of the Missouri Territory. Its capital was Detroit. Michigan entered the Union in 1837.

4857. Illinois territorial governor was Ninian Edwards, whose tenure in office lasted from 1809, when the territory was organized (February 3), to 1818, when Illinois entered the Union as the 21st state. A member of the Democratic-Republicans, he served as the state's third governor from 1826 to 1830. The Illinois Territory, formerly part of the Indiana Territory, comprised what is now Illinois, Wisconsin, and part of Minnesota and Michigan. The capital was Kaskaskia, IL.

4858. Missouri territorial governor after it was split off from the Louisiana Territory in 1812 was Frederick Bates, acting governor (1812–13), who was succeeded by William Clark (1813–20), the soldier and explorer who had traversed the Louisiana Purchase with Meriwether Lewis in 1804–06.

4859. Alabama territorial governor was William C. Bibb. Alabama was originally part of the Mississippi Territory and was under its governors from 1709 until 1817. On March 3, 1817, Congress separated Alabama and organized it as a territory, with Bibb as governor. He was elected the state governor after Alabama was admitted to the Union in 1819.

4860. Arkansas territorial governor was James Miller, who served from 1819 to 1825. The Arkansas Territory, created on March 2, 1819, included lands that were formerly part of the Missouri Territory, and comprised the present state of Arkansas, admitted to the Union in 1836, and most of Oklahoma.

4861. Florida territorial governor was Andrew Jackson, appointed military governor in 1821, several years after he led an invasion and occupation of Spanish Florida that resulted in its purchase by the United States. Jackson went on to become president in 1828.

4862. Wisconsin territorial governor was Henry Dodge, who served from 1836 to 1841 and again from 1845 to 1848. The territory was organized in 1836 with Madison as its capital. It included what is now Wisconsin, Minnesota, Iowa, and parts of the Dakotas, and was composed of lands from the former Michigan Territory.

4863. Iowa territorial governor was Robert Lucas, governor from 1838 to 1841. The territory, formerly part of the Wisconsin Territory, was created on June 12, 1838, taking in the current area of Iowa and parts of Minnesota and the Dakotas.

4864. California territorial governor was General Bennet Riley, who was put in charge of California after it was surrendered to the United States by Mexico in the Treaty of Guadalupe Hidalgo, May 30, 1848. California became a state in 1850.

4865. Minnesota territorial governor was Alexander Ramsey, who took office in 1849 and served until 1853. The Minnesota Territory included the eastern parts of North and South Dakota as well as the current state of Minnesota.

4866. Oregon territorial governor was Joseph Lane, who served in 1849–50 and again in 1853. Oregon Country had been ceded by Britain in 1846 and was administered by a provisional government, headed by an executive committee (1843–45) and then by George Abernethy (1845–49), in the years prior to the creation of the territory on August 14, 1848. Oregon Territory included the present states of Oregon, Idaho, and Washington, as well as parts of Montana and Wyoming.

4867. Utah territorial governor was Brigham Young, leader of the Church of Jesus Christ of Latter-day Saints (the Mormon Church), whose adherents had followed him to Utah in 1847 to escape religious persecution. President Millard Fillmore appointed him in 1850 as the first governor of the newly formed Utah Territory, created from lands ceded by Mexico in 1848, including Utah and parts of Nevada, Colorado, and Wyoming. Polygamy was declared an official tenet of the church in 1852, and Young, a polygamist with more than 20 wives and 47 children, resisted the imposition of federal laws concerning marriage. He was removed from office in 1857 by President James Buchanan and troops were sent to Utah to solidify federal authority.

4868. New Mexico territorial governor was James S. Calhoun, who served from 1851 to 1852. The territory of New Mexico was created by Congress on May 25, 1850, and included the present states of New Mexico and Arizona.

4869. Washington territorial governor was Isaac Ingals Stevens, appointed by Congress in 1853. Washington Territory was created by Congress on March 2, 1853, from lands that had been part of Oregon Territory, including what is now the state of Washington and parts of Idaho and Montana. The capital was Olympia.

4870. Nebraska territorial governor was Francis Burt, a Democrat, who served in 1854. The territory was created by Congress on May 30, 1854, through the Kansas-Nebraska Act, from lands that had formerly been part of the Missouri Territory. The territorial legislature convened for the first time at Omaha on January 16, 1855.

4871. Kansas territory governor was Andrew H. Reeder, appointed in June 1854. The controversial Kansas-Nebraska Act, which established the territory on May 30, 1854, allowed new territories to be admitted either as slave states or as free states. Activists on both sides of the issue poured into Kansas for a confrontation. Reeder was removed from office on July 31 to prevent his interfering with the proslavery territorial legislature and was replaced by Wilson Shannon.

4872. Nevada territorial governor was James W. Nye, appointed in 1861, when the territory was created. He served until 1864, when Nevada was admitted to statehood. Carson City was the territorial capital. The Nevada Territory had formerly been part of the Utah Territory and was part of the area ceded by Mexico in 1848.

4873. Colorado territorial governor was William Gilpin, who served in 1861–62. The territory was created by Congress on February 28, 1861, from lands acquired from France and Mexico that had subsequently been part of a variety of organized territories.

4874. Dakota territorial governor was A. William Jayne, a native of Illinois. A Republican, he had been Abraham Lincoln's personal physician and campaign manager. He was inaugurated as the first governor of the Dakota Territory on May 27, 1861. The territory, most of which had been part of the 1803 Louisiana Purchase, was organized on March 2, 1861, with its capital at Yankton, and included parts of Wyoming and Montana as well as the future North and South Dakotas.

4875. Arizona territorial governor was John N. Goodwin, a Republican, appointed by President Abraham Lincoln in 1863, when Arizona was split off from the New Mexico Territory and given its own territorial organization.

4876. Idaho territorial governor was William H. Wallace, a Republican appointed in 1863 and succeeded shortly afterwards by William B. Daniels. Idaho Territory, including the present states of Idaho, Montana, and Wyoming, was created by Congress on March 4, 1863.

4877. Montana territorial governor was Sidney Edgerton, a Republican, who served from 1846 to 1866. Montana Territory was created by Congress on May 26, 1864, from lands acquired in the Louisiana Purchase. Virginia City was the capital until 1875, when it was transferred to Helena.

4878. Wyoming territorial governor was John A. Campbell, who served from 1869 to 1875. Congress created the Wyoming Territory on July 25, 1868, from lands acquired from France, Texas, Britain, and Mexico. The territorial legislature convened on October 12, 1869, at Cheyenne.

4879. Oklahoma territorial governor was George W. Steele, a Republican, who served in 1890–91. The Oklahoma Territory, the last territory to be organized in the continental United States, was created by Congress on May 2, 1890. It took the place of the Indian Territory, which had been promised by treaty to Native Americans relocated from their homelands in the eastern United States, but which had been opened to settlement by non-Indians in 1889. The land had been acquired from France in 1803 through the Louisiana Purchase.

4880. New Mexico territorial governor who was of Mexican ancestry was Miguel Antonio Otero II, the territory's leading businessman, who had been born in Missouri. He served as governor from 1897 to 1906 and as treasurer from 1909 to 1911, and was a member of the Democratic National Committee. Otero County, NM, is named for him.

4881. Hawaiian territorial governor was sugar magnate, jurist, and reformer Sanford Ballard Dole, who was appointed territorial governor when the United States annexed the Hawaiian Islands in 1900. He held the office until 1903. Dole was the leader of the coup that overthrew the Hawaiian monarchy in 1893 and installed a western-style government led by Americans.

TERRITORIES—GOVERNORS—*continued*

4882. Governor of territorial Alaska was John F. Strong, who served from 1913 to 1918. Alaska was organized as a territory of the United States on August 24, 1912. By a treaty signed on March 30, 1867, the United States had acquired Alaska from Russia for the sum of $7.2 million. Administration of the area was successively under the control of the Army, the Treasury Department, and the Navy. In 1884 civil government was established under federally appointed governors, of whom the first was John H. Kinkead. The capital was Sitka.

4883. African-American territorial governor appointed by the president was William Henry Hastie, appointed by President Harry S. Truman as governor of the U.S. Virgin Islands and confirmed by the Senate on May 1, 1946. He was inaugurated on May 7 at Charlotte Amalie, VI.

4884. Hawaiian territorial governor who was of Hawaiian ancestry was Samuel Wilder King, nominated by President Dwight D. Eisenhower on February 16, 1953, and approved unanimously by the Senate Interior Committee on February 19. King was descended on his mother's side from Mahi, the daughter of a high chief of the island of Oahu in the time of King Kamehameha I.

TERRITORIES—PUERTO RICO

4885. Capital of Puerto Rico was San Juan, the largest city in the commonwealth, located on the Atlantic coast in northeastern Puerto Rico. Founded on August 12, 1508, at the settlement of Caparra by Juan Ponce de Léon, it was named Ciudad de Puerto Rico ("rich port"). At that time, the island was known as San Juan Bautista, the name given it by Christopher Columbus. After 1521 the names were exchanged: Puerto Rico was now the island, and San Juan its capital. San Juan is the oldest city in any territory or state of the United States.

4886. European colonial settlement on Puerto Rico began on August 12, 1508, when Spanish explorers led by Juan Ponce de Léon founded the city of Caparra. In 1521 they abandoned Caparra and established another on an island nearby. Both sites are now part of the capital city, San Juan. Puerto Rico was called Borinquén by its original inhabitants, the Taino Indians.

4887. Political parties in Puerto Rico were the Partido Liberal Reformista (Liberal Reform Party) and the Partido Liberal Conservador (Liberal Conservative Party), both founded in November 1870 to press for a republican form of government and independence from Spain. The Partido Liberal Reformista was headed by Román Baldorioty de Castro, José Julián Acosta, and Pedro Gerónimo Goico.

4888. Charter of autonomy for Puerto Rico was granted by Spain on November 25, 1897, giving the island the status of a Spanish dominion. It allowed the island to retain its representation in the Spanish Cortes, and provided for a bicameral legislature: a Council of Administration with eight elected and seven appointed members, and a Chamber of Representatives with one member for every 25,000 inhabitants. The new government was inaugurated at San Juan on February 9, 1898, under General Manuel Macías.

4889. American flag raised over Puerto Rico was hoisted by American troops on October 18, 1898. Puerto Rico was ceded to the United States by Spain under the Treaty of Paris in December 1898. Intially called "Porto Rico" by Americans, the island's name officially reverted to the Spanish spelling on May 17, 1932, by act of Congress.

4890. Unincorporated territory of the United States was Puerto Rico, where civilian American government was established on April 12, 1900, under the Foraker Law (also known as the Organic Act of 1900). Puerto Rico was conceded to the United States by Spain at the end of the Spanish-American War.

4891. Civil governor of Puerto Rico under the Foraker Act that established an American-led government on the island was Charles H. Allen, who was inaugurated on May 1, 1900, in San Juan. On June 5, President William McKinley named an executive cabinet including five Puerto Rican members (José Celso Barbosa, Rosendo Matienzo Cintrón, José de Diego, Manuel Camuñas and Andrés Crosas) and six U.S. members (William H. Hunt, J. H. Hollander, J. R. Garrison, W. B. Eliot, James A. Harlan, and Dr. M. G. Brumbaugh).

4892. Resident commissioner from Puerto Rico under the Hollander Law, which gave Puerto Rico a commissioner to the federal government, was Federico Degetau, who took up the post on March 4, 1901, in Washington, DC.

4893. Bill calling for independence for Puerto Rico was introduced into the Senate on April 2, 1943, by Senator Millard Tydings of Maryland. Tydings also co-sponsored the bill that led to independence for the Philippines.

4894. Woman mayor of San Juan, PR, was Felisa Rincon de Gautier, who served from 1946 to 1968.

4895. Governor of Puerto Rico to be elected was Luis Muñoz Marín, journalist and founder of Puerto Rico's Partido Popular Democratico, the island's ruling party from 1970 to 1977. Muñoz Marín was elected governor in San Juan, PR, in 1948, having previously served as president of the senate since 1942, and won re-election in 1952, 1956, and 1960. Among his most successful initiatives was "Operation Bootstrap," a plan to improve the Puerto Rican economy through federal tax exemptions, low labor costs, and other pro-business policies. He was instrumental in securing commonwealth status for Puerto Rico in 1952.

4896. Flag of the Commonwealth of Puerto Rico was adopted on March 3, 1952. Based partly on a flag designed in 1895 and partly on the Stars and Stripes, it has five stripes, three red and two white, and a blue triangle with a single five-pointed star.

4897. Commonwealth of the United States was Puerto Rico, which ratified its status as a commonwealth in a constitution that was drafted in a convention, approved by the voters, and adopted on July 25, 1952. Residents of Puerto Rico possess all the rights of U.S. citizens except that of voting in federal elections.

4898. Plebiscite on the political status of Puerto Rico was held on the island on July 23, 1967. The continuation of commonwealth status was affirmed by 60 percent of the voters; 39 percent voted for statehood, and 1 percent chose independence.

4899. Woman governor of Puerto Rico was Sila Maria Calderon, the head of the Popular Democratic Party, who ran on a platform calling for clean government and opposing Puerto Rican statehood. On November 7, 2000, she defeated Carlos Pesquera, the candidate of the pro-statehood New Progressive Party, taking 48.5 percent of the vote to his 45.7 percent.

TERRITORIES—VIRGIN ISLANDS

4900. Governor of the U.S. Virgin Islands who was elected, not appointed, was Melvin H. Evans, who took office on January 4, 1971.

4901. Run-off election in the U.S. Virgin Islands was held in November 1994. Victor O. Frazer defeated Eileen Peterson to become the first African-American Congressional delegate from the Virgin Islands in 20 years.

TRADE AND COMMERCE

4902. Navigation Act affecting the seaboard of the future United States was an "act for the encouraging and increasing of shipping and navigation," passed by the British colonial authorities in 1660. Consolidating and systematizing various acts passed piecemeal over the previous 15 years, the First Navigation Act restricted the marine trade entirely to British citizens and barred trade with any other nation.

4903. Chamber of Commerce was incorporated on March 13, 1770, under a royal charter from King George III. Its motto was *Non nobis nate solum* ("not born for ourselves alone"). The Chamber of Commerce of the United States was founded in 1912 by approximately 500 representatives of commercial organizations, trade associations, and individual establishments, who were invited to participate in a series of discussions by President William Howard Taft and Secretary of Commerce and Labor Charles Nagel. The headquarters of the Chamber of Commerce of the United States was dedicated on May 20, 1925.

4904. Embargo act of the Continental Congress was the nonimportation act enacted on October 14, 1774. It stated: "After the first day of December next, there be no importation into British America, from Great Britian or Ireland, of any goods, wares or merchandize whatsoever, or from any other place of any such goods, wares or merchandize."

4905. Drawback legislation enacted by Congress was Sections 3 and 4 of the Tariff Act of July 4, 1789. It provided that dutiable merchandise imported into the United States that was reexported within a year was entitled to a refund of 99 percent of the duty paid. In lieu of a drawback of the duties imposed on the importation of salt employed and expended in the fish industry, an allowance of five cents was granted on the exportation of every quintal of dried fish and on every barrel of pickled fish or salted provision. From August 1, 1789, to December 31, 1790, drawback to the amount of $10,582 was allowed on dried and pickled fish.

4906. Corporate body chartered by a special act of Congress was the President, Directors and Company of the Bank of the United States, chartered on February 25, 1791, by the First Congress, in session in New York City.

TRADE AND COMMERCE—*continued*

4907. Federal report on exports covered the fiscal year ending September 30, 1791. The exports for the year amounted to $19 million, of which $18.5 million was for domestic merchandise and $512,041 for foreign goods. The imports for the same period amounted to $29.2 million, an excess of imports over exports of more than $10 million.

4908. Industrial report to Congress was *Report on Manufactures to the U.S. Congress,* written by Alexander Hamilton, the secretary of the treasury, and delivered on December 5, 1791. Hamilton's report, the first to give a comprehensive overview of the American manufacturing sector, advocated a policy of low tariffs to maintain a large volume of trade (shipping revenues helped to offset the U.S. trade deficit) and to ensure a market for American-made goods.

4909. Bankruptcy act was the act of Congress of April 4, 1800, "to establish a uniform system of bankruptcy in the United States." It contained 64 sections and applied to "any merchant or other person residing within the United States, actually using the trade of merchandise, by buying and selling in gross, or by retail, or dealing in exchange as a banker, broker, factor, underwriter or marine insurer." The law allowed the release from debtor's prison of Robert Morris, the financier of the American Revolution, who had lost his fortune in land speculation. It was repealed in December 1803.

4910. Embargo by the federal government was established through the Embargo Act, which was signed into law by President Thomas Jefferson on December 22, 1807. The bill was intended to bring pressure on two belligerent powers, the British and the French, by banning all American trade with foreign ports. Supplementary acts were enacted on January 9 and March 12, 1808, along with penalties intended to discourage smugglers. Angry protests were launched by legislatures and governors in New York and New England, where the constitutionality of the embargo was challenged, unsuccessfully, in U.S. district court.

4911. Factory standardization to federal specification was inaugurated as a government practice April 16, 1813, when a contract specifying interchangeable parts was drawn up in Middletown, CT, between Callender Irvine, commissary general of the United States, and Colonel Simeon North of Berlin, CT, owner of a pistol factory in Staddle Hill, a suburb of Middletown. The contract was for 20,000 pistols at $7 each to be produced within five years. It stipulated that "component parts of the pistols are to correspond so exactly that any limb or part of one pistol may be fitted to any other pistol of the 20,000."

4912. Piracy law enacted by Congress was "an act to protect the commerce of the United States and punish the crime of piracy," enacted on March 3, 1819. Offenders convicted by a circuit court could be punished by death.

4913. Warehouse legislation enacted by Congress was passed by Congress on August 6, 1846. This act permitted duty-free storage of imported merchandise in warehouses owned or leased by the federal government, the duty to be paid upon withdrawal of the merchandise within a specified time of not more than one year. Another act, passed on March 28, 1854, extended bonded storage privileges to private warehouses approved by the secretary of the treasury. These warehouses were required to have proper customs officers in charge or to have joint custody with customs officers of all merchandise.

4914. Chamber of commerce established by a state was the New York Chamber of Commerce, formed on April 5, 1868, by 20 merchants at a meeting at Fraunces Tavern, Pearl Street, New York City, for "promoting and encouraging commerce, supporting industry, adjusting disputes relative to trade and navigation, and procuring such laws and regulations as may be found necessary for the benefit of trade in general." John Cruger was the first president.

4915. Holding companies authorized by a state were authorized by New Jersey in a law passed on April 4, 1888. It provided that it was "lawful for any corporation of this state, or of any other state, doing business in this state and authorized by law to own and hold shares of stocks and bonds of corporations of other states, to own and hold and dispose thereof in the same manner and with all the rights, powers and privileges of individual owners of shares of the capital stock and bonds or other evidences of indebtedness of corporations of this state."

4916. Vending machine law enacted by a city was approved by Omaha, NE, on May 10, 1898, by Mayor Frank Edward Moores. The law made all vending machines subject to a $5 permit fee.

4917. Holding company worth a billion dollars was the United States Steel Corporation, which was founded in 1901 by two financiers, Elbert Henry Gary of Chicago, IL, and John Pierpont Morgan of New York, NY, with capital of $1.4 billion.

4918. Boycott law enacted by a state was passed on September 26, 1903, by Alabama, "to prohibit boycotting, unfair lists, picketting, or other interference with the lawful business or occupation of others, and to provide a penalty therefor." The law declared it a misdemeanor for two or more persons to conspire to prevent persons from carrying on a lawful business, to print or circulate stickers, cards, etc., and to use threats. The penalty was a fine of not less than $50 nor more than $500, or imprisonment of not more than 60 days at hard labor.

4919. Interstate Commerce Commission Medal of Honor was a bronze medal awarded on December 5, 1905, to George H. Poell of Grand Island, NE. On June 26, 1905, while a fireman on the St. Joseph and Grand Island Railway, he climbed out on the pilot of his engine and rescued a child on the tracks. Poell was seriously injured and one foot had to be amputated. The medal was authorized by act of Congress of February 23, 1905, for presentation to those "who shall hereafter, by extreme daring, endanger their own lives in saving, or endeavoring to save lives from any wreck, disaster or grave accident, or in preventing or endeavoring to prevent" accidents. Four degrees were established: chief commander, commander, officer, and legionnaire.

4920. Consumer protection law enacted by Congress was "an act forbidding the importation, exportation or carriage in interstate commerce of falsely or spuriously stamped articles of merchandise made of gold or silver or their alloys." It was enacted on June 13, 1906.

4921. Foreign and Domestic Commerce Bureau of the federal government was created by the act of August 23, 1912, which provided that all duties of the Bureau of Manufactures and the Bureau of Statistics should be exercised by the Bureau of Foreign and Domestic Commerce.

4922. Federal Trade Commission came into existence on September 26, 1914, by act of Congress The commission was granted expanded powers to regulate commerce and prohibit unlawful means of obtaining trade. On March 16, 1915, five commissioners—George Rublee, Edward Nash Hurley, Will H. Parry, Joseph Edward Davies, and William Julius Harris—were appointed, each at an annual salary of $10,000.

4923. United States International Trade Commission was created by act of September 8, 1916, and originally named the United States Tariff Commission. The name was changed to the United States International Trade Commission by section 171 of the Trade Act of 1974. The commission furnishes studies, reports, and recommendations involving international trade and tariffs to the president, the U.S. trade representative, and Congress.

4924. Federal Trade Commission trade practice conference was held on October 3, 1919, in Omaha, NE, for the creamery industry. Representatives from six states met with Commissioner William Byron Colver to discuss unfair practice complaints in the industry.

4925. Resale price maintenance law enacted by a state was California's Fair Trade Act, approved on May 8, 1931, which provided "that the buyer will not resell [a] commodity except at the price stipulated by the vendor." The title of the act is "an act to protect trade-mark owners, distributors and the public against injurious and uneconomic practices in the distribution of articles of standard quality under a distinguished trade-mark, brand or name."

4926. Industrial Recovery Act was passed by Congress on June 16, 1933, and signed by President Franklin Delano Roosevelt. Its purpose was "to encourage national industrial recovery, to foster fair competition, and to provide for the construction of certain useful public works, and for other purposes." General Hugh Samuel Johnson was appointed its first administrator on June 17, 1933, and a compliance board was established on October 26. On May 27, 1935, the Supreme Court of the United States declared the act unconstitutional, holding that the code-making provisions of the act constituted an invalid delegation by Congress of its legislative authority to persons wholly unconnected with the legislative functions of the government.

4927. Consumers' advisory board of the federal government was authorized on June 16, 1933, under the National Industrial Recovery Act, and was organized on June 26. The first chairman was Mrs. Charles Cary Rumsey.

4928. Federal industrial advisory board was authorized by President Franklin Delano Roosevelt on June 16, 1933, under the National Industrial Recovery Act. He stated that "it will be responsible that every affected industrial group is fully and adequately represented in an advisory capacity and any interested industrial

TRADE AND COMMERCE—*continued*

group will be entitled to be heard through representatives of its own choosing." The board was organized on June 26, 1933, and was at first composed of seven members. The first chairman was Walter Clark Teagle.

4929. Commodity credit corporation was created by Executive Order No. 6340 dated October 16, 1933, in order to carry out the provisions of the emergency legislation passed by Congress during 1932 and 1933. The Board of Directors consisted of eight members, with Lynn Porter Talley as president. The corporation was given authority to buy, sell, and deal in agricultural and other commodities and to loan and borrow thereon; to assist in crop reduction and marketing programs; and to store, handle, and process commodities of all kinds in connection with relief plans.

4930. Federal trade policy executive committee was organized on November 21, 1933. It was composed of representatives of the various departments, agencies, and commissions of the government concerned with trade relations with other countries. George Nelson Peek, agricultural adjustment administrator, was designated head of this committee as special assistant to the president on American trade policy.

4931. Federal corporation to encourage the purchase of electric appliances was the Electric Home and Farm Authority, authorized by Executive Order No. 6,514 on December 19, 1933. It was incorporated on January 17, 1934, under the laws of the State of Delaware with a capital of $1 million "to encourage the fullest possible utilization of the present productive capacity of industries" and "to avoid undue restriction of production." The directors of the corporation named in the executive order were Dr. Arthur Ernest Morgan as chairman, Dr. Harcourt Alexander Morgan, and David Eli Lilienthal. The first sale of electric ranges, refrigerators, and water heaters financed by the Electric Home and Farm Authority was held at Tupelo, MS, on May 21, 1934. The corporation was dissolved and a new one incorporated on August 1, 1935, under the laws of the District of Columbia.

4932. Gas regulation legislation passed by Congress was the Natural Gas Act, effective on June 21, 1938, "to regulate the transportation and sale of natural gas in interstate commerce."

4933. Price regulation law passed by Congress was the Emergency Price Control Act of 1942, approved on January 30, 1942, which created the Office of Price Administration as an independent agency under the direction of the price administrator. The Office of Price Administration and Civilian Supply was created by Executive Order No. 8,734 on April 11, 1941. Its name was shortened to Office of Price Administration by Executive Order No. 8,875 on August 28, 1941.

4934. Government agency promoting small business was the Small Business Administration, created by the Small Business Act of 1953. It was formed to promote and protect the interests of small business, ensure that small businesss receive a fair proportion of federal contracts, and make loans to small business concerns.

4935. Consolidated federal agency to regulate maritime commerce was the Federal Maritime Commission, established by Reorganization Plan No. 7 of 1961, effective August 12, 1961. It is an independent agency that regulates shipping under the various federal shipping statutes. The FMC regulates the waterborne foreign commerce of the United States, ensures that U.S. international trade is open to all nations on fair and equitable terms, and protects against unauthorized, concerted activity in the waterborne commerce of the United States.

4936. Skyjacking law enacted by Congress was "an act to amend the Federal Aviation Act of 1958 to provide for the application of federal criminal law to certain events occurring on board aircraft in air commerce," enacted on September 5, 1961, and signed by President John Fitzgerald Kennedy. It made hijacking punishable by death or not less than 20 years imprisonment. Carrying a concealed or dangerous weapon was subject to a fine of $1,000 or imprisonment of not more than one year, or both.

4937. Office of the Special Representative for Trade Negotiations was created by Executive Order 11075 of January 15, 1963, signed by President John Fitzgerald Kennedy. Later renamed the Office of the United States Trade Representative, it is responsible for directing all trade negotiations of and formulating trade policy for the United States. The United States Trade Representative is the chief representative of the United States for various trade functions, agreements, and treaties, and holds the rank of Ambassador.

4938. Federal agency to oversee consumer safety was the Consumer Product Safety Commission (CPSC), established in 1972 by Congress with the mandate to protect the public against unreasonable risks of injury from consumer products; assist consumers in evaluating the comparative safety of consumer products; develop uniform safety standards for consumer products and minimizes conflicting state and local regulations; and promote research and investigation into the causes and prevention of product-related deaths, illnesses, and injuries.

4939. Federal bailout of an auto manufacturer was arranged for the Chrysler Corporation of Highland Park, MI, in 1979–1980, after the carmaker made a series of ill-advised business deals and introduced a line of passenger cars that sold poorly in the United States. Under the leadership of Lee A. Iacocca, the near-bankrupt company secured government loans totaling $1.5 billion, by far the largest and most politically controversial corporate bailout undertaken up to that time. Payment of the first installment was received by Chrysler on June 24, 1980. The company's fortunes revived after labor contracts were renegotiated and a new line of cars introduced, and the loans were entirely repaid by the end of 1983.

4940. Trade and Development Agency was established on July 1, 1980, as a component organization of the International Development Cooperation Agency. The organization was renamed and made an independent agency within the executive branch on October 28, 1992, by the Jobs Through Exports Act of 1992. The TDA's mission is to promote economic development in, and simultaneously export U.S. goods and services to, developing and middle-income nations in less-developed areas of the world.

4941. Easing of trade limits on North Korea was put into effect on January 20, 1995, as an enticement to North Korea to freeze its nuclear arms program. For the first time, direct telephone calls could be made between North Korea and the United States, and U.S. travelers were allowed to use their credit cards there. A strict trade embargo was imposed on North Korea by the United States in 1950.

4942. Federal conviction for Internet piracy under federal law was Jeffrey Gerard Levy, 22, a senior at the University of Oregon in Eugene, OR. On August 20, 1999, Levy was found in violation of the No Electronic Theft Act of 1997 for illegally posting computer software programs, musical recordings, entertainment software programs, and digitally recorded movies on his Internet website, and allowing the general public to download and copy the copyrighted material.

TRADE AND COMMERCE—ARBITRATION

4943. Arbitration law enacted by a colony was "an act for the more easy and effectually finishing of controversies by arbitration," passed at the legislative session held from October 11 to November 2, 1753, in New Haven, CT. Three arbitrators were appointed, one by each side and one by the court. The court was granted power to levy and collect the awards.

4944. Arbitration law enacted by a state was passed on December 15, 1778, by the General Assembly of Maryland, in Annapolis, which ruled that "it shall be lawful to and for such court to give judgment upon the award of the person or persons to whom such submission and reference shall be made."

4945. Arbitration law enacted by Congress was "an act to make valid and enforceable written provisions or agreements for arbitration of disputes arising out of contracts, maritime transactions or commerce among the States or Territories or with foreign nations," approved on February 12, 1925.

TRADE AND COMMERCE—TARIFFS

4946. Free trade policy by the federal government was in effect from 1775 to 1780, but imports were taxed by the various states. Trade was free in Massachusetts from 1774 to 1781, in South Carolina from 1776 to 1783, in Maryland and Connecticut from 1776 to 1780. Although there were no federal restrictions, the situation was extremely complicated, and taxes were different in practically every state.

4947. Tariff legislation enacted by Congress after the adoption of the Constitution was the Tariff Act of July 4, 1789, an "act for laying a duty on goods, wares and merchandises imported into the United States." The main purpose was the collection of revenue, but protection was also extended to certain industries that the government wished to encourage, such as glass and earthenware. The act was signed by President George Washington and was to con-

TRADE AND COMMERCE—TARIFFS—
continued

tinue in force until July 1796. It laid specific duties on some articles and ad valorem duties on others, equivalent to an 8.5 percent ad valorem rate, with drawback, up to 1 percent of the duties on all articles exported within twelve months, except distilled spirits other than brandy and geneva.

4948. Tariff passed by Congress for protection rather than primarily for revenue was the "act to regulate the duties on imports and tonnage," passed on April 27, 1816.

4949. Tariff enacted by Congress to prevent the importation of obscene literature and pictures was the Tariff Act of August 30, 1842, an "act to provide revenue from imports." Section 28 stated: "The importation of all indecent and obscene prints, paintings, lithographs, engravings and transparencies is hereby prohibited . . . and all invoices and packages whereof any such article shall compose a part are . . . liable . . . to be seized and forfeited . . . and the said articles shall be forthwith destroyed."

4950. Tariff commission established by Congress was authorized on June 7, 1882. Nine tariff commissioners at $10 a day and expenses were appointed from civil life to investigate tariff questions relating to agriculture, commerce, manufacturing, mining, and mercantile and industrial interests. The first chairman was John Lord.

TRADE AND COMMERCE—TRUSTS AND MONOPOLIES

4951. Price regulation law enacted by a colony was enacted by Rhode Island at Providence on December 31, 1776. It was "an act to prevent monopolies and oppression by excessive and unreasonable prices for many of the necessaries and conveniencies of life, and for preventing engrossers, and for the better supply of our troops in the army with such necessaries as may be wanted." The law regulated prices on farm labor, beef, hides, shoes, cotton, sugar, salt, coffee, cheese, butter, beans, peas, potatoes, pork, wool, flannel, towcloths, flax, tallow, rum, molasses, oats, stockings, wheat, rye, maize, salted pork, and similar commodites. Lawbreakers were assessed fines equivalent to the value of the merchandise. The fines were distributed equally to the state and to informers.

4952. Antitrust law enacted by a state was an act "to prevent monopolies in the transportation of freight, and to secure free and fair competition in the same," approved on February 23, 1883, by Alabama. The first general law was passed on March 9, 1889, by Kansas, "to declare unlawful trusts and combinations in restraint of trade and products, and to provide penalties therefor."

4953. Antitrust law enacted by Congress was an "act to protect trade and commerce against unlawful restraints and monopolies," passed by Congress on July 2, 1890. It provided that "every contract combination in the form of trust or otherwise, or conspiracy, in restraint of trade or commerce among the several states, or with foreign nations, is hereby declared to be illegal." The act is popularly known as the Sherman Antitrust Act, after its chief sponsor, Senator John Sherman.

4954. Judicial test of the Sherman Antitrust Act was *United States v. E. C. Knight*. The defendant, a sugar-refining company, was charged by the federal government with establishing a near-monopoly on the industry. By a vote of 8 to 1, the Supreme Court ruled on January 21, 1895, that intrastate manufacturing combinations like the one established by E. C. Knight were intended for private gain and were not subject to the Sherman Act, which the Court interpreted as applying only to commerce. This decision severely limited the scope of the Sherman Act until the mid-1930s, when a broader interpretation was applied. Chief Justice Melville W. Fuller wrote the decision for the majority.

4955. Antitrust Division in the Department of Justice was created in 1903, during the first administration of Theodore Roosevelt. It was charged with applying the Sherman Antitrust Act, enacted on July 2, 1890, to combat monopolies and restraint of trade.

4956. Price regulation law enacted by a state was enacted by Louisiana and approved on July 2, 1908, by Governor Jared Young Sanders. It prohibited "unfair commercial discrimination between different sections, communities, cities, or localities in the State of Louisiana or unfair competition therein."

V

VICE PRESIDENTS

4957. Vice president who had served in the Continental Congress was John Adams of Massachusetts, a member of the Continental Congress in Philadelphia and other cities in Pennsylvania from 1774 to 1778. He took office as vice president on April 21, 1789.

4958. Vice president who had been governor of a state was Thomas Jefferson, vice president under John Adams from 1797 to 1801. He was elected governor of Virginia on June 1, 1779, and was reelected on June 2, 1780. He resigned office on June 3, 1781.

4959. Vice president who had served as minister to a foreign country was John Adams of Massachusetts, vice president under George Washington from 1789 through 1797. He had served as the United States minister to the Netherlands beginning on December 29, 1780, and to Great Britain on May 14, 1785, serving until 1788.

4960. Vice president who had served in the House of Representatives was Elbridge Gerry of Massachusetts, who served as a representative from March 4, 1789, to March 3, 1793, and as vice president from March 4, 1813, to November 23, 1814, when he died.

4961. Vice president to break a tie vote in the Senate was John Adams. On July 16, 1789, during debates over the establishment of the Department of Foreign Affairs, the senators voted on the question of whether the Senate had the right to place restrictions on the President's power to remove executive officers. The vote was evenly split, ten to ten. Adams cast his vote in the negative, and the motion was defeated.

4962. Vice president who had served in a presidential cabinet was Thomas Jefferson, inaugurated as George Washington's secretary of state on February 14, 1790. He became vice president under John Adams in 1797.

4963. Vice president who had served in the Senate was Aaron Burr, who represented New York in the Senate from March 4, 1791, through March 3, 1797. He was elected to the vice presidency on November 4, 1800.

4964. Vice president to be reelected was John Adams, who took second place in the balloting on November 6, 1792, and thus became vice president for a second term. All 132 electors cast one vote for George Washington, making his reelection as president unanimous. Their additional votes, one per elector, were divided as follows: 77 for Adams, 50 for George Clinton, four for Thomas Jefferson, and one for Aaron Burr.

4965. Vice president to announce his own election as president was John Adams, vice president under George Washington. On February 8, 1797, Adams presided over a joint session of the Senate and the House of Representatives, where he announced the results of the election of 1796, saying: "In obedience to the Constitution and Law of the United States and to the commands of both Houses of Congress . . ., I declare that John Adams is elected President of the United States for four years, to commence with the fourth day of March next; and that Thomas Jefferson is elected Vice President of the United States, to commence with the fourth of March next. And may the Sovereign of the Universe, the ordainer of civil government on earth, for the preservation of liberty, justice, and peace, among men, enable both to discharge the duties of these offices conformably with the Constitution of the United States with conscientious diligence, punctuality and perseverance."

4966. Vice president who was nominated specifically for that office was George Clinton, Governor of New York, who ran with Thomas Jefferson in the 1804 election. He served under Jefferson from 1805 to 1809, and again under James Madison from 1809 to 1812. Prior to the ratification of the Twelfth Amendment to the Constitution on September 24, 1804, the presidential candidate receiving the second highest number of votes became vice president.

4967. Vice president to be indicted while in office was Aaron Burr, vice president during the first term of Thomas Jefferson (1801–05). He was indicted by a grand jury in Bergen County, New Jersey, for the murder of his political rival, former secretary of the treasury Alexander Hamilton, whom he killed in a duel at Weehawken, NJ, on July 11, 1804. On March 2, 1805, Burr gave his farewell address to the Senate while under indictment. His legal troubles over the duel, however, were eclipsed by his subsequent involvement in a conspiracy to invade Mexico and set up an independent empire in its lands. He was betrayed, captured,

VICE PRESIDENTS—*continued*

tried for treason, and acquitted (because the betrayal had prevented him from carrying out his scheme). After a four-year sojourn in Europe, he spent his last 24 years as a lawyer in New York.

4968. Former vice president to be arrested was Aaron Burr, who served under Thomas Jefferson from 1801 to 1805. In 1807, he was accused of organizing an expedition to invade Mexico and set up a separate republic in the Southwest. He was arrested on February 19, 1807, in Wakefield, AL, by Captain Edmund P. Gaines and taken to Richmond, VA, where he was brought before Chief Justice John Marshall of the U.S. Circuit Court on March 30. On June 24, he was indicted for treason, the first high U.S. official to be so accused. The trial began on August 3 and ended in an acquittal on September 1.

4969. Vice president to serve under two presidents was George Clinton, elected for the first time on November 6, 1804, to serve in the second administration of Thomas Jefferson and reelected in November 1808 to serve under James Madison. He died in office on April 20, 1812, with one year left in his term. John Caldwell Calhoun also served under two Presidents, John Quincy Adams and Andrew Jackson, and, like Clinton, he did not complete his second term, resigning with 82 days left in his term in order to take a seat in the Senate.

4970. Vice president to die in office was George Clinton, who served under President Thomas Jefferson from March 4, 1805, to March 4, 1809, and under President James Madison from March 4, 1809, to April 20, 1812, when he died in Washington, DC. William Harris Crawford acted as president pro tempore of the Senate for the unexpired portion of Clinton's term.

4971. Vice president who had served in both the House and the Senate was Richard Mentor Johnson, who represented Kentucky in the House of Representatives from March 4, 1807, through March 3, 1819, and in the Senate from December 10, 1819, through March 3, 1829. He took office as vice president on March 4, 1837.

4972. Vice president who was born an American citizen was John Caldwell Calhoun, who took office along with John Quincy Adams on March 4, 1825, was reelected in 1828 to serve as vice president under Andrew Jackson, and resigned his office in 1832. Calhoun was born on March 18, 1782, in the Abbeville District of South Carolina, near Calhoun Mills. His predecessors were all British subjects at birth.

4973. Vice president to resign before the expiration of his term of office was John Caldwell Calhoun, who served as vice president under President John Quincy Adams from March 4, 1825, to March 4, 1829, and under President Andrew Jackson from March 4, 1829 to December 28, 1832. He resigned to fill the vacancy in the Senate caused by the resignation of Robert Young Hayne, senator from South Carolina. Calhoun was elected to fill the vacancy on December 12, 1832.

4974. Former vice president to serve in the Senate was John Caldwell Calhoun, vice president under John Quincy Adams from 1825 to 1829 and Andrew Jackson from 1829 to 1832. On December 28, 1832, with three months remaining in his term, he resigned from the vice presidency to enter the Senate, having been elected on December 12 by the state legislature of South Carolina to fill the vacancy left by the departure of Robert Young Hayne, who became governor. Calhoun was sworn in as a senator on December 29, 1832, and continued to serve until March 3, 1843, when he resigned. From March 6, 1844, to March 6, 1845, he was secretary of state. He reentered the Senate on November 26, 1845, and served until his death on March 31, 1850. Before his inauguration as vice president, Calhoun had served in the House of Representatives (1811–1817).

4975. Vice presidential candidate named Johnson was Richard Mentor Johnson of Kentucky, who was twice Martin Van Buren's running mate on the Democratic ticket. They were elected on November 1, 1836, and defeated for reelection on November 3, 1840. William Freame Johnson ran on behalf of the North American Party in 1856. Herschel Vespasian Johnson of Georgia ran on the Democratic ticket in 1860 but lost the contest to Andrew Johnson of Tennessee, the Republican vice presidential candidate. The Prohibition Party nominated Hale Johnson in 1896 and Andrew Johnson, from Kentucky, in 1944. Hiram Warren Johnson was the unsuccessful candidate of the

Progressive Party in 1912. Lyndon Baines Johnson of Texas, a Democrat, was elected in 1960. Other surnames have belonged to multiple candidates, but none to so many as "Johnson."

4976. Vice president elected by the Senate was Richard Mentor Johnson, who was chosen by the Senate on February 8, 1837, because no candidate had received a majority of the electoral votes. He served from March 4, 1837, to March 4, 1841, under President Martin Van Buren.

4977. Vice president who served in both houses of Congress from different states was William Rufus de Vane King, elected vice president on November 2, 1852, with President Franklin Pierce. King, a Democrat, was born in North Carolina, where he studied law. From March 4, 1811, through November 4, 1816, he represented North Carolina in the House. After serving in Italy and Russia as secretary of the American legations there, he returned to the United States and moved to Alabama. He was a senator from Alabama from December 14, 1819, to April 15, 1844, and again, after a stint as minister to France, from July 1, 1848, to December 20, 1852.

4978. Vice president sworn in on foreign soil was William Rufus de Vane King, a Democrat, the running mate of Franklin Pierce in the 1852 election. King took the oath of office on March 4, 1853, in Havana, Cuba, where he had gone for his health. The oath was administered by William L. Sharkey, the American consul in Havana. The privilege was extended to King by a special act of Congress.

4979. Vice president to take the oath of office but never serve in office was William Rufus de Vane King, who was ill when he took the oath of office on March 4, 1853, and died a few weeks later, on April 18, in Cahaba, AL. He never served as president of the Senate, which did not assemble until December 5, nor carry out any other function of his office. Since there was no provision in the Constitution for replacing a vice president until the 20th Amendment was ratified in 1933, the office went unfilled during the term of President Franklin Pierce.

4980. Vice president who was younger than 40 was John Cabell Breckinridge, who was 36 years old when he was sworn in as vice president on March 4, 1857.

4981. Former vice president to serve as an official of an enemy government was John Cabell Breckinridge, who was elected vice president on the Democratic ticket with James Buchanan on November 4, 1856. He ran for president on the National Democratic and Southern Democratic tickets in 1860, losing to Abraham Lincoln. After his term ended on March 3, 1861, he entered the Senate, but resigned within the year to become an officer in the Confederate Army, rising to major general. From January to April 1865 he served as Secretary of War in the Confederate cabinet, escaping to Europe when the Confederacy collapsed. He afterwards resumed his law practice in Lexington, KY.

4982. Former vice president who became a state governor was Levi Parsons Morton, who served as vice president from March 4, 1889, to March 3, 1893, under Benjamin Harrison. He served as governor of New York from 1895 to 1897.

4983. Vice president who succeeded to the presidency after a president's death and was then elected to a full term was Theodore Roosevelt, who was elected vice president on November 6, 1900, for the second term of William McKinley and became president on September 14, 1901, after McKinley was assassinated. He was the candidate of the Republican Party in 1904, won the election on November 8, and was inaugurated on March 4, 1905.

4984. Vice president to preside over a cabinet meeting was Thomas Riley Marshall, vice president under Woodrow Wilson from 1913 to 1921. Before President Wilson went to France to participate in the peace negotiations at the close of World War I, his cabinet members agreed that in his absence the vice president would preside over their meetings. At the first such meeting, on December 10, 1918, Marshall read a statement declaring that he was "not undertaking to exercise any official duty or function," but was presiding on a strictly informal basis.

4985. Vice president to regularly attend cabinet meetings was Calvin Coolidge, who was invited to do so by President Warren Gamaliel Harding. Even before their inauguration, which took place on March 4, 1921, Harding declared his intention of giving the vice president the responsibilities of an "assistant president."

VICE PRESIDENTS—*continued*

4986. Vice president to receive the Nobel Peace Prize was Charles Gates Dawes of Ohio, vice president from 1925 to 1929 under President Calvin Coolidge. He was awarded the prize in 1925 for his work in setting up the Dawes Plan, which helped Germany to finance the reparations it was required to pay for its actions in World War I. The prize was jointly awarded to Dawes and to Sir Austen Chamberlain of Britain, who had negotiated the Locarno Treaties to stabilize national borders within Europe.

4987. Vice president's widow to receive a pension was Lois I. Kimsey Marshall, widow of Thomas Riley Marshall, who died on June 1, 1925. A congressional act of January 25, 1929, awarded her an annual allowance of $3,000 and instructed the secretary of the interior to place her name on the pension roll.

4988. Vice president who had served as Senate majority leader was Charles Curtis of Indiana, who took the oath of office as vice president on March 4, 1929, having been elected on November 6, 1928, on the Republican ticket headed by Herbert Clark Hoover. He had served as the Senate majority leader during the 68th, 69th, and 70th Congresses, from November 28, 1924, through March 3, 1929.

4989. Vice president who was of Native American ancestry was Charles Curtis of Kansas, who served under President Herbert Clark Hoover from March 4, 1929, to March 4, 1933. He was born and reared among the Kaw tribe and was descended on his mother's side from White Plume, a Kansa-Kaw chief.

4990. Vice president known as "the Veep" was Alben William Barkley, vice president from January 20, 1949, to January 20, 1953, under Harry S. Truman. The nickname was derived from the initials "V.P."

4991. Vice president to marry during his term in office was Alben William Barkley, vice president from January 20, 1949, to January 20, 1953, under Harry S. Truman. On November 18, 1949, he married Elizabeth Jane Rucker Hadley in St. Louis, MO.

4992. Vice president to be sworn in by the speaker of the House was Lyndon Baines Johnson, who took the oath of office on January 20, 1961. The oath was administered by Speaker of the House Samuel Taliaferro ("Sam") Rayburn, a fellow Texan, member of the House from 1913 to 1961 and speaker from 1940 to 1946, 1949 to 1953, and 1955 until his death on November 19, 1961.

4993. Official residence for the vice president was authorized by Congress on April 9, 1966. The bill provided for the construction, furnishing, and maintenance of an official residence on the site of the United States Naval Observatory in Washington, DC. Congress failed to appropriate the necessary funds, and the plan fell through. An existing house on the observatory grounds, the Admiral's House, was designated as the vice president's residence on July 12, 1974. The first vice president to live there was Walter Frederick Mondale, vice president under Jimmy Carter, who took occupancy of the residence on Inauguration Day, January 20, 1977.

4994. Vice president to become president after a hiatus was Richard Milhous Nixon, who served as vice president for two terms under Dwight David Eisenhower, from 1953 to 1961. He ran for president in 1960 and was defeated by John Fitzgerald Kennedy. After leaving office, Nixon practiced law in California and New York, ran unsuccessfully for the governorship of California, and published a book of political analysis, *Six Crises*. He was nominated for the presidency in August 1968 at the Republican convention in Miami Beach, FL, was elected on November 5, and was inaugurated on January 20, 1969. All previous vice presidents who were elevated to the presidency were either elected president in the final months of their service as vice president (John Adams was the first) or succeeded to the presidency upon the death of the president (John Tyler was the first).

4995. Vice president to resign as a result of a criminal investigation was Spiro Theodore Agnew, vice president under Richard Milhous Nixon. Though he and President Nixon had been reelected in 1972, Agnew resigned on October 10, 1973, after the Internal Revenue Service charged him with violating income tax laws. He pleaded no contest in U.S. District Court and was ordered to pay a fine of $10,000 and undergo three years of unsupervised probation. Charges of bribery, extortion, and conspiracy were dismissed. He then changed careers and became a novelist. On January 4, 1983, he paid the State of Maryland $270,000 after he lost an appeal of an earlier judgment in a civil suit brought against him by state taxpayers. The payment constituted compensation for bribes and kickbacks he allegedly took during his two years as governor (1967–69).

4996. Vice president appointed under the 25th Amendment to the Constitution was Gerald Rudolph Ford, sworn into office as President Richard Milhous Nixon's vice president on December 6, 1973. The 25th Amendment, ratified on February 10, 1967, enables the president to appoint a vice president in the event that the office becomes vacant. On October 10, 1973, Vice President Spiro T. Agnew resigned to face charges of income tax evasion, leaving the vice presidency open for the first time since the passage of the amendment. Ford himself appointed a vice president under the 25th Amendment: Nelson Aldrich Rockefeller, who was sworn in on December 19, 1974.

4997. Vice president to serve as acting president under the 25th Amendment was George Herbert Walker Bush, vice president from January 20, 1981, through January 20, 1989. On July 13, 1985, he served for seven hours and 54 minutes as acting president while Ronald Wilson Reagan underwent surgery at the Bethesda Naval Center in Bethesda, MD, to remove a cancerous polyp in his colon. In accordance with Section 3 of the 25th Amendment, President Reagan formally transferred the powers of the presidency to Vice President Bush on a temporary basis, "commencing with the administration of anesthesia to me," and formally resumed those powers when he regained consciousness. The 25th Amendment, which was ratified on February 10, 1967, provides for cases of vacancy, disability, or incapacity in the presidency and of vacancy in the vice presidency.

VICE PRESIDENTS—POLITICAL PARTIES

4998. Vice president from the Federalist Party was John Adams of Massachusetts, elected in 1789 to serve under George Washington. He received 69 of 138 electoral votes.

4999. Vice president from the Democratic-Republican Party was Thomas Jefferson of Virginia, elected in 1796. Because he came in second to the Federalist Party's John Adams when the electoral vote was counted, Adams became president and Jefferson vice president.

5000. Vice president from the Democratic Party was John Caldwell Calhoun. In 1824, when Calhoun was elected vice president under John Quincy Adams, the contest for the White House was a four-way race among candidates representing different factions of the Democratic-Republican Party. (The other three presidential hopefuls were Andrew Jackson, William Harris Crawford, and Henry Clay.) By 1828, these factions had coalesced into two new parties, the Democrats and the National Republicans. Calhoun ran as a Democrat with Andrew Jackson and won reelection on November 4, 1828. Both men were from Southern states—Jackson from Tennessee and Calhoun from South Carolina, which was also Jackson's birthplace.

5001. Vice president from the Whig Party was John Tyler of Virginia, who was elected as William Henry Harrison's running mate on November 3, 1840. He became president himself on April 6 after Harrison died, but repudiated the Whigs' agenda.

5002. Vice president from the Republican Party was Hannibal Hamlin of Maine, elected on November 6, 1860, to serve under Abraham Lincoln. When Lincoln ran for reelection in 1864, his running mate was Andrew Johnson of Tennessee, a Democrat. The Republican ticket that year was known as the National Union ticket.

W

WHITE HOUSE

5003. Presidential mansion was No. 1 Cherry Street, the Franklin House, at the corner of Pearl and Cherry streets (now Franklin Square), New York City. The house, owned by Samuel Osgood, the first commissioner of the treasury and later the first postmaster general, was torn down in 1856. It was occupied by President George Washington from April 23, 1789, to February 23, 1790, when he and his wife moved to another residence on Broadway. When the capital was transferred to Philadelphia later that year, the Washingtons lived in a house owned by Robert Morris, the Revolution's financier.

5004. Designs for the building of the White House were submitted in 1792 to the Commissioners of the District of Columbia, in response to an advertisement dated March 14 announcing a competition for the best design. The $500 prize went to James Hoban, an Irish-born architect trained in Dublin, whose entry beat one by Thomas Jefferson (submitted anonymously) and several others. Hoban supervised the construction effort from 1793 to 1801 and was recalled to undertake the mansion's reconstruction after it was burned by the British on August 24, 1814.

WHITE HOUSE—*continued*

5005. Ceremony at the White House took place on October 13, 1792, when the cornerstone of the future presidential mansion was laid by George Washington.

5006. Object to be continuously the property of the White House since 1800 is Gilbert Stuart's full-length portrait of George Washington, a replica of an earlier portrait by Stuart (known as the "Lansdowne" portrait) that had been commissioned by Senator William Bingham in 1796. It has left the White House only once, during the War of 1812, when Dolley Madison, the First Lady, made up her mind to rescue it from the invading British troops who were preparing to sack Washington. On August 24, 1814, she delayed her own departure from the White House long enough to have the canvas removed from its frame and given to "two gentleman of New York" for protection. The British burned the White House later that day, and most of its furnishings and decorations were wrecked. The portrait was returned to the White House after it was rebuilt and now hangs in the East Room, a state reception room.

5007. Letter written in the White House by a president was written on November 2, 1800, by John Adams, to inform his wife, Abigail Smith Adams, that he had arrived in Washington the previous day. She had remained at home, making preparations for the move, and did not arrive for another two weeks. The letter is headed "President's House, Washington City," and is addressed to "My dearest friend." It includes these lines: "Before I end my letter, I pray heaven to bestow the best of blessings on this house, and on all that shall hereafter inhabit it. May none but honest and wise men ever rule under this roof!"

5008. Reception held at the White House was held on New Year's Day in 1801. It was hosted by President John Adams and his wife, Abigail Smith Adams.

5009. Child born in the White House was James Madison Randolph, born on January 17, 1806 in Washington, DC. He was the son of Thomas Mann Randolph and Martha (Jefferson) Randolph, the daughter of President Thomas Jefferson.

5010. Additions to the White House were two low pavilions for office and household space, designed by Thomas Jefferson and constructed by his surveyor of public buildings, Benjamin Henry Latrobe, in 1807. The pavilion on the east side of the White House, whose colonnade contained a fireproof vault used by the Trea-sury, was torn down in 1869; another was built on the same site in 1902. The west pavilion was also removed, leaving its foundation, which was incorporated into a greenhouse. This foundation was uncovered during the 1902 renovations and restored as part of a new pavilion.

5011. Sanitary facilities in the White House were installed during the administration of President Thomas Jefferson (1801–09). The water was supplied from a cistern in the attic.

5012. Wedding in the White House took place on March 29, 1812, when Lucy Payne Washington was married to Thomas Todd, associate justice of the Supreme Court. Mrs. Washington was the widow of George Steptoe Washington, a nephew of George Washington. Her sister was Dolley Madison, the wife of James Madison, who was president at the time of the wedding.

5013. Use of the term "White House" took place after the house was burned by the British on August 24, 1814, during the War of 1812. White paint was applied to the sandstone exterior to cover some of the damage. Before that time, the house was referred to as the Executive Mansion.

5014. Renovation of the White House that required the president to relocate was the reconstruction project that began in 1815, following the burning of the White House by the British on August 24, 1814. Until September 1817, James and Dolley Madison lived in borrowed houses in Washington (the first of which was Octagon House, the residence of Colonel John Tayloe). President Harry S. Truman and his family lived in nearby Blair House from early 1949 through March 27, 1952, while the White House, which was near collapse, was rebuilt on new foundations, the interior having been completely removed.

5015. Wedding of a president's daughter in the White House took place in the East Room on March 9, 1820, when Maria Hester Monroe, the youngest daughter of President James Monroe, was married to Samuel Lawrence Gouverneur, the President's nephew and private secretary.

5016. Distinguished foreign personage to stay at the White House as a houseguest was the Marquis de Lafayette, Marie-Joseph-Paul-Yves-Roch-Gilbert du Motier de Lafayette, one of the heroes of the American Revolution and a statesman of France. Late in 1824 he came to the United States as an honored guest, staying at the White House for several months and witnessing the transition of power from President James Monroe to President John Quincy Adams on March 4, 1825.

5017. Wedding of a president's son in the White House took place on February 25, 1828, when John Adams, the son of John Quincy Adams, was married to Mary Catherine Hellen, his mother's niece.

5018. Use of the East Room in the White House was as a laundry room. The mansion was still unfinished when the family of President John Adams moved into the White House in November 1800. First Lady Abigail Smith Adams wrote to her daughter, "We have not the least fence, yard, or other convenience, without, and the great unfinished audience room I make a drying-room of, to hang up the clothes in." Since the windows were not yet fitted with glass, there would have been plenty of fresh air for the purpose. In President Thomas Jefferson's day the hall appears to have been used for washing dishes and for storage, and it was still barely furnished when President John Quincy Adams began using it for New Year's Day receptions. The purchase and installation of elegant furniture, carpeting, and light fixtures was finally done in 1829 by President Andrew Jackson, who spent $9,000 on them.

5019. Running water in the White House was installed during the administration of President Andrew Jackson (1825–37), when the mansion was hooked up to the municipal water-supply system.

5020. Girl born in the White House was Letitia Christian Tyler, born in 1842 to Elizabeth Priscilla Cooper Tyler and Robert Tyler, the son of President John Tyler. She was named after her paternal grandmother, who had had a stroke shortly before Tyler's inauguration in April 1841 and who died in September 1842.

5021. Icebox in the White House was purchased in 1845, during the administration of James Knox Polk, at a cost of $25.

5022. Gaslight illumination in the White House was turned on on December 29, 1848, during the administration of President James Knox Polk.

5023. Library in the White House was founded by Abigail Powers Fillmore, the wife of Millard Fillmore, who set aside a room on the second floor to house a collection of books. On March 3, 1851, Congress appropriated $250 to buy books for it.

5024. Greenhouses at the White House were built circa 1857 and over the next 40 years expanded to take up much of the grounds. They were torn down in 1902 to make way for the expansion of the White House.

5025. Royal personage to stay at the White House as a houseguest was Albert Edward, Prince of Wales (later King Edward VII), while he was visiting the United States from September 20 to October 20, 1860. He was received in the White House by President James Buchanan. The bedroom in which he stayed was long referred to as "the Prince of Wales room," but which bedroom it was is unknown.

5026. Easter Egg roll at the White House was started as an Easter Day tradition by First Lady Lucy Ware Webb Hayes, who invited local children to participate in the event beginning in 1878. Previously, an egg roll was held at the Capitol Building.

5027. Wedding of a president in the White House was Grover Cleveland's marriage to his ward, Frances Folsom, on June 2, 1886, during the first of his two administrations.

5028. Collection of White House china was started in 1889 by Caroline Scott Harrison, the wife of President Benjamin Harrison. Most of the china dishes that had previously been used in the White House had been destroyed, sold, or passed down to descendants of the presidential families. The present collection is displayed in the White House's China Room, which was set aside for the purpose by First Lady Grace Coolidge in 1917.

5029. Plan to enlarge the White House was prepared by architect Fred D. Owen for Caroline Scott Harrison, the wife of President Benjamin Harrison, in 1890. Alternative plans were proposed in 1896, during the second administration of Grover Cleveland, and 1900, during the administration of William McKinley. All these designs called for large wings to be built on either side of the original mansion. None was constructed.

5030. Child born in the White House to a president was Esther Cleveland, born on September 9, 1893, in Washington, DC. She was the second child of President Grover Cleveland and Frances Folsom Cleveland, and was the first child born to a president during his term in office.

WHITE HOUSE—*continued*

5031. African-American to receive a White House dinner invitation was Booker Taliaferro Washington, principal of the Tuskegee Normal and Industrial Institute in Tuskegee, AL, and a leading proponent of racial advancement through industrial and vocational training. At the invitation of Theodore Roosevelt, he came to dinner at the White House on October 16, 1901. Among white Southerners, public opinion concerning this event was so vehemently negative that no president dared to issue another such invitation for some 25 years.

5032. Expansion and comprehensive renovation of the White House was undertaken by the architectural firm of Charles F. McKim, William R. Mead, and Stanford White beginning in June 1902, after Congress appropriated funds for the project at the request of President Theodore Roosevelt. The entire infrastructure of the mansion was in a state of disrepair and had to be replaced, including the flooring, the electrical wiring, and the plumbing (rainwater was still drained from the roof by an ancient network of wooden conduits inside the walls). The architects dug a new basement to house a modern heating system and restored the interior within a matter of months. New pavilions were raised on the east and west sides and office space was provided in a new West Wing.

5033. Airplane to land on the White House lawn was the *Moth,* piloted by Harry Nelson Atwood, who landed on July 14, 1911, about 3 P.M., and was presented by President William Howard Taft with the gold medal of the Aero Club of Washington. Atwood circled the Capitol and the Library of Congress and flew down Pennsylvania Avenue and over the Washington Monument and the Executive Mansion.

5034. Rose garden planted at the White House was planted in 1913 by Ellen Axson Wilson, the first wife of President Woodrow Wilson. The Rose Garden was redesigned in 1962.

5035. White House china service that was made in the United States was made by Walter Scott Lenox of Lenox Incorporated, Trenton, NJ, by order of President Woodrow Wilson. The plates showed the presidential seal in gold on a white background, with concentric borders of gold, dark blue, and gold. The 1,700-piece set was delivered to the White House on July 31, 1918.

5036. White House Police Force was created on October 1, 1922, at the request of President Warren Gamaliel Harding. In 1920 the force was placed under the supervision of the Secret Service. The first White House Police Force officer killed in the line of duty was Leslie Coffelt, shot and killed by Puerto Rican nationalists while protecting President Harry S. Truman at the Blair House on November 1, 1950. In 1970, the Secret Service established the Executive Protective Service, a uniformed security force charged with protecting the White House, the president and members of his immediate family, and diplomatic missions in the metropolitan area of Washington, DC.

5037. Swimming pool in the White House was built by popular subscription. It was located in the west terrace of the mansion and was 50 feet long and 15 feet wide, with a depth ranging from 4 to 8 feet. The pool was lined with aquamarine terra-cotta and a six-foot wainscot of pale green terra-cotta. The water was both filtered and sterilized. The pool was built under the direction of Lieutenant Colonel Ulysses Simpson Grant III, director of public buildings, and was formally accepted by President Franklin Delano Roosevelt on June 2, 1933.

5038. Fireproofing in the White House was installed during the rebuilding of the White House from 1948 through 1952, during the administration of President Harry S. Truman. A fire-detection system was added in 1965.

5039. White House official who was an African-American was Everett Frederic Morrow. Having served as an administrative aide and advisor to President Dwight David Eisenhower on his campaign train in 1952, he joined the White House staff in 1953 as an administrative officer for the Special Projects group.

5040. Outdoor wedding held at the White House was the wedding of Tricia Nixon, daughter of President Richard Milhous Nixon, to Edward Cox on June 12, 1971. The wedding was held in the Rose Garden on the White House grounds.

5041. State dinner televised from the White House took place at the Rose Garden of the White House, Washington, DC, on July 7, 1976. The dinner was held in honor of Queen Elizabeth II of England and Prince Philip and was attended by 224 guests.

Subject Index

The Subject Index is an alphabetical listing of all the subjects mentioned in the entries (excluding most proper names of people and places, which are covered in the Names and Geographical indexes). To find an entry in the main body of the text, please search for the italicized indexing number.

A

abolition and abolitionists
African-American to give antislavery lectures, *4247*
antislavery book, *4230*
antislavery magazine, *4243*
antislavery pamphlet by an African-American writer, *4244*
antislavery political organization, *4248*
essay calling for, to be published in British colonies, *4227*
Liberty Bell and, *1111*
major antislavery periodical, *4245*
newspaper, *3914*
organization, *4231*
radical student leader, *2812*
senator elected on antislavery ticket, *4250*
state to abolish slavery by decision of judiciary, *4233*

Abolition Party
single-issue party, *2918*

abortion
campaign funding organization for political candidates who support legal abortion, *2791*
National Right to Life Committee, *2840*
state law legalizing, for medical reasons, *3955*
Supreme Court decision on legality of, *4739*
year in which it was mentioned in national platforms of the major parties, *3221*

Administration, Office of, *3779*

Administrative Reorganization Act (1939), *2010*

Admission Day (California), *2198*

adult education programs
state-run, *3979*
state system of vocational, technical, and adult education, *3978*

aeronautics and aviation
Civil Aeronautics Authority, *4101*
federal advisory committee on, *4096*
mediation agency for railroads and commercial aviation, *4099*

state department, *4277*

affirmative action
order issued by federal government, *1905*

Africa
library of U.S. foreign-policy papers on Africa and the Caribbean, *2069*
president to visit, during his term in office, *3806*

African-Americans
African–African-American Summit, *2300*
allowed to enter grounds of Congress, *1507*
attorney to serve as solicitor general, *4705*
ban on, as mail carriers, *3149*
black nationalist movement, *2844*
Black Power advocate, *2851*
civil rights sit-in, *2850*
colonial court to hear testimony from, *1440*
compensation to victims of mass racial violence, *1938*
congressional representative who was, *1594*
congressional standing committee headed by, *1572*
congressman from Northern state, *1604*
congressman to deliver its official response to State of Union message, *1630*
congresswoman from Southern state, *1623*
consul, *2332*
delegate to national political convention, *2996*
delegate to U.N., *2435*
elected to a national leadership post in Republican Party, *2960*
federal law giving soldiers pay and benefits equal to those of white soldiers, *2656*
history trail, *4159*
House of Representatives that included a substantial number of women who were, *1579*
House page who was, *1643*
judge on federal bench, *1983*
judge to serve on federal district court, *1987*
justice of Circuit of Appeals, *1984*
justice of state supreme court, *4413*
labor union, *2887*
lawyers
admitted to practice before Supreme Court, *2586*

African-Americans—*Continued*

> formally admitted to the bar, *2585*
> woman admitted to practice before Supreme Court, *2592*
> woman to practice law, *2588*

Liberal Republican Convention of Colored Men, *3301*

mass boycott by civil rights protesters, *2849*

mayoral election in major city in which both candidates were, *1356*

mayors

> Atlanta, *1337*
> Baltimore (Md.), *1348*
> Chicago, *1345*
> chief executive of Washington, DC, *1332*
> Dallas, *1360*
> Denver, *1355*
> Detroit, *1338*
> Fayette (Miss.), *1334*
> Houston, *1364*
> incumbent, of major city to lose to white candidate, *1349*
> Jackson (Miss.), *1363*
> Kansas City, *1354*
> Los Angeles, *1339*
> major city to elect, *1333*
> militant to be elected, of major American city, *1341*
> New York City, *1351*
> Newark (N.J.), *1335*
> Philadelphia, *1347*
> Savannah (Ga.), *1361*
> Seattle, *1350*
> St. Louis, *1358*

military service by, to be authorized by Congress, *1385*

minister (international relations), *2333*

National Association for the Advancement of Colored People, *2847*

national convention of, *2845*

national convention to propose, for offices of president and vice president, *3028*

national monument dedicated to, *2716*

national organization for workers who were, *2881*

Navy regulation barring, *2693*

newspaper reporter accredited to the congressional press gallery, *3894*

newspaper reporter accredited to White House, *3893*

political newspaper published by, *3917*

preacher to deliver sermon in House of Representatives, *1566*

presidential inauguration in which African-Americans formally participated, *3662*

protest against government of black African country by, *2305*

Senate page who was, *1642*

senator, *1776*

senator to be elected by popular vote, *1799*

senator to serve full term, *1778*

state governor elected in his own right, *4524*

state governor who was, *4489*

state law prohibiting discrimination against soldiers, *2657*

state legislators, *4544*

> to represent constituency with a white majority, *4545*

strike of laborers, *2875*

summer of national race riots, *2848*

Supreme Court decision barring racial segregation in housing, *4726*

Supreme Court decision validating doctrine of "separate but equal" provisions for, *4724*

Supreme Court justice who was, *4779*

surgeon general who was, *4040*

to actively campaign for presidential candidacy of Republican Party, *3033*

to become chief of a State Department bureau, *2362*

to become chief of diplomatic mission, *2355*

to become director general of Foreign Service, *2371*

to enlist in U.S. armed forces during Civil War, *1383*

to head major congressional committee, *1609*

to hold elective office, *1279*

to preside over national convention of major party, *3001*

to receive a White House dinner invitation, *5031*

to receive nominating votes for presidency at convention of major party, *3002*

to receive nominating votes for vice presidency at convention of major party, *2999*

to serve as chairman of major political party, *2969*

to serve as chief justice of state supreme court, *4420*

to serve as chief sergeant-at-arms of state legislature, *4556*

to serve as chief U.S. magistrate, *1992*

to serve as secretary of agriculture, *1210*

to serve as secretary of labor, *1214*

to serve in a presidential cabinet, *1191*

town built by free, *1255*

town founded by, after Civil War, *1260*

town in continuous existence west of Mississippi, *1262*

U.S. district attorney who was, *1986*

unit organized during Civil War, *1384*

unit to fight in Civil War, *1386*

vice consul, *2328*

vice presidential candidate, *3240*

vice presidential candidate in 20th century, *3260*

White House official who was, *5039*

automobiles
  air bag requirement by federal government, *4107*
  license plates for vehicles, *4093*
  president to ride in, *3789*
  seat belt law enacted by a state, *4102*
  speed limit for highway traffic established by Congress, *4105*
  speeding driver law enacted by a state, *4094*
  statewide automotive emissions standards, *4103*

B

bachelor tax
  enacted by a state, *4828*
balance of trade, U.S.
  deficit in 20th century, *2132*
bald eagle
  Native American symbols adopted for political purposes by colonial Americans, *1130*
ballot, printed, *4425*
Baltimore and Ohio Railroad
  railroad to run trains to Washington, DC, *1883*
ban-the-bomb demonstrations, *2833*
bank deposit insurance laws
  enacted by a state, *2105*
  enacted by Congress, *2112*
  Federal Deposit Insurance Corporation, *2113*
    program for bank deposits, *2115*
Bank of North America, *2102*
Bank of North Dakota (Bismarck, N.D.), *2110*
Bank of the United States, *2103*
  difference of opinion among members of cabinet, *1142*
  federal charter, *1995*
  location, *2104*
Banking Act of 1933, *2112*
  Federal Deposit Insurance Corporation, *2113, 2115*
banking and finance
  abrogation of gold standard, *2095*
  bank deposit insurance law enacted by a state, *2105*
  bank deposit insurance law enacted by Congress, *2112*
  Bank of the United States, *2103*
    location, *2104*
  bank wholly owned and operated by a state, *2110*
  bonds
    Confederate government, *2120*
    issued by federal government, *2117*
    Treasury notes bearing interest, *2119*

war bond issued by federal government, *2118*
broker to Office of Finance of U.S., *2079*
Comptroller general of U.S., *2092*
Comptroller of the Currency, *2087*
Comptroller of U.S. Treasury, *2081*
congressional legislation to control government expenditures, *2088*
credit unions
  act passed by Congress, *2122*
  federal, *2123*
  federal agency for administering, *2124*
  law enacted by a state, *2121*
debts and deficits
  city to file for bankruptcy, *2135*
  county to file for bankruptcy, *2136*
  U.S. balance of trade deficit in 20th century, *2132*
  year in which U.S. was free from debt, *2127*
  year public debt of U.S. exceeded $1 billion, *2128*
  year public debt of U.S. exceeded $1 trillion, *2134*
  year public debt of U.S. exceeded $10 billion, *2130*
  year public debt of U.S. exceeded $100 billion, *2131*
  year public debt of U.S. exceeded $100 million, *2126*
  year public debt of U.S. exceeded $5 trillion, *2137*
  year public debt of U.S. exceeded $500 billion, *2133*
  year when U.S. became a creditor nation, *2129*
demonetization of silver, *2089*
detailed financial statement for federal government, *2100*
economic depression, *2085*
establishment of treasury system, *2086*
federal charter, *1995*
Federal Deposit Insurance Corporation, *2113*
  program for bank deposits, *2115*
federal gold vault, *2096*
Federal Home Loan Bank board, *2111*
federal payment over Internet, *2101*
federal refunding act, *2083*
federal reserve banks, *2109*
federal savings and loan bailout, *2125*
foreign loan to Continental Congress, *2078*
gold hoarding order, *2094*
gold price fixed by Congress, *2084*
International Monetary Fund meeting, *2097*
liberty loans, *2091*
loan made by U.S. to war ally, *2090*
loan to U.S., *2082*
presidential commission on overhauling budgetary process, *2099*
private bank chartered by Congress, *2102*

banking and finance—*Continued*

Reconstruction Finance Corporation, *2093*

reform act after the Civil War, *2108*

savings and loan association established by federal government, *2114*

state bank to receive federal deposits, *2106*

state banking commission, *2107*

superintendent of finance under Continental Congress, *2080*

Treasurer of U.S., *2077*

woman treasurer of U.S., *2098*

world bank, *2116*

    See also

      money and coinage

      stocks and bonds

bankruptcy

city to file for, *2135*

county to file for, *2136*

bankruptcy act, *4909*

banners

campaign, *2797*

"Barnburners"

use of term, *2919*

baseball

president to pitch a ball to open the season, *3831*

Basketball

star elected to Senate, *1804*

Beirut (Lebanon)

U.S. embassy to be destroyed by suicide bombing, *2368*

U.S. peacekeeping forces killed by suicide bombing, *2651*

Bellamy Nationalist Club, *2883*

Bethune-Cookman College (Daytona Beach, Fla.), *1999*

bicameral legislature

colony to change from, to unicameral legislature, *1478*

colony with, *1473*

Bill of Rights, *1821*

constitutional amendment enacted after passage of, *1839*

state to ratify, *1835*

Supreme Court decision extending protection of, to defendants in state courts, *4731*

bimetallism

demonetization of silver, *2089*

biographies

campaign, *2795*

    written by prominent author, *2799*

biographies and autobiographies

First Lady to write, *3587*

of a president, *3823*

birds

Audubon Society, *4209*

federal reservation, *4211*

protection international treaty, *4213*

refuge established by a state, *4206*

birth control clinics, *3994*

run by state government, *3995*

births and deaths

ban on surrogate motherhood enacted by a state, *3959*

birth registration uniform numbering system, *3954*

law permitting doctor-assisted suicide, *3960*

right-to-die law enacted by a state, *3958*

state birth registration law, *3949*

state-run crematory, *3951*

state voluntary sterilization regulation, *3957*

sterilization of humans by state government as a matter of public policy, *3952*

    See also

      abortion

black nationalist movement, *2844*

Black Panther Party, *2951*

Black Power movement

advocate, *2851*

blasphemy

law authorizing penalty of death for, *2551*

blood tests

state to require, for marriage licenses, *3953*

boards of health

state, *4018*

Body of Liberties (1641)

statement of legislative independence by a colony, *1415*

bombings

attack by domestic terrorists on federal facility resulting in large loss of life, *2006*

bonds

    See

      stocks and bonds

Bonus Army, *2829*

bonus voting system, *3008*

books

antislavery, *4230*

censorship board established by a state, *3865*

describing government of British colony in America, *1070*

    See also

      political satire and history

Bosnia

U.S. officials to die in conflict in, *2653*

Boston Massacre, *1009*

commemoration, *2182*

Boston Tea Party, *1011*

bottles

nonrefundable, state bill prohibiting use of, *4167*

boycott law

enacted by a state, *4918*

boycotts

colonial, of British goods, *1003*

Constitution, U.S.—*Continued*
27th Amendment
amendment to be ratified two centuries after its proposal, *1860*
5th Amendment
statement of principle of due process, *1837*
African-American to vote under 15th Amendment of, *1923*
amendment proposal to bear signature of a president, *1841*
amendments to fail ratification process, *1834*
Bill of Rights, *1821*
state to ratify, *1835*
definitive edition of *The Debates on the Several State Conventions on the Adoption of the Federal Constitution*, *1831*
formal announcement that it was in effect, *1829*
Independence Day celebration after adoption of, *2238*
legal treatise analyzing, *1830*
newspaper to publish, *1826*
president barred under 22nd Amendment from running for third term, *3425*
president of the United States elected under, *3371*
printed copies, *1823*
public copies, *1827*
session of Congress under, *1811*
state admitted to Union after ratification of, *4291*
state to ratify, *1828*
Supreme Court decision to be overridden by amendment to, *4710*
Constitution Day, *2187*
Constitution Party
presidential candidate, *3343*
Constitutional Convention (1787)
edition of complete *Records of the Federal Convention of 1787*, *1833*
proposal in, for civil liberties, *1824*
question considered by, *1822*
Constitutional Union Party, *2924*
political platform, *3040*
presidential candidates, *3293*
constitutions, state
See
state constitutions
Consular Service of U.S., *2322*
Consumer Party
presidential candidate, *3363*
consumer protection law
enacted by Congress, *4920*
consumer safety
federal agency to oversee, *4938*
continental air defense alliance, *2607*
Continental Army, American
Army of the United States, *2621*

general of, *2622*
Continental Association, *1012*
Continental coin, *2149*
Continental Congress
adopts title "The United States in Congress Assembled", *1048*
broker to Office of Finance of U.S., *2079*
call for congress of American colonies, *1037*
chaplain of, *1041*
colonial government to instruct its delegates to proclaim independence, *1054*
complete edition of *Journals of the Continental Congress*, *1049*
congressional agency to conduct negotiations with Native Americans, *2730*
decimal system of money, *2147*
embargo act Olympic Games, *4904*
foreign loan to, *2078*
land set-aside for schools authorized by, *3965*
lottery held by, *1046*
major action taken by, *1044*
medals awarded by
to foreigner, *1047*
to George Washington, *1045*
Native American delegation to, *2731*
objection to opening session with prayer, *1042*
pension law enacted by, *2470*
pensions paid by federal government, *2471*
postmaster general under, *3138*
prayer offered at session of, *1043*
president of, *1038*
seat of, *1039*
Second
proclamation of unification of colonies, *1052*
session of, *1040*
superintendent of finance under, *2080*
vice president who had served in, *4957*
Continental Flag, *1076*
Continental money, *2146*
Continental Navy
commander-in-chief of, *2688*
Navy of the United States, *2686*
ship commissioned by, *2687*
ship constructed by federal government, *2690*
shipbuilding law enacted by Congress, *2694*
"Continuity in Government" plan
doomsday plan, *2683*
Conventional Forces in Europe, Treaty on
treaty ending Cold War, *2429*
coonskin cap
campaign hat, *2798*
copyright laws
colonial, *2504*
copyrights registrar of U.S., *2509*

federal, *2506*
    on photographs, *2507*
    international agreement, *2508*
    state, *2505*
Corona satellites, *2679*
corporation taxes
    federal tax on profits, *4813*
    levied by Congress, *4808*
"Corrections Day", *1580*
counties
    created by federal law, *1263*
    public defender, *1275*
Court of Appeals, U.S. (New York City)
    African-American woman to serve as judge on, *1990*
courtroom verdicts
    to be televised, *3867*
Courts, U.S.
    See
    federal courts
Coxey's Army
    protest march on Washington, *2824*
Crazy Horse
    monument to, *2718*
creationists
    legal clash between evolutionists and, *1950*
credit unions
    act passed by Congress, *2122*
    federal, *2123*
    federal agency for administering, *2124*
    law enacted by a state, *2121*
crime
    See
    law enforcement
Cuban Missile Crisis
    nuclear war confrontation, *2649*
Cuban refugees
    boatlift of, *3124*
currency
    See
    money and coinage
custom fees stamps, *4806*
Customs Court, U.S. (New York)
    woman justice on federal bench, *1979*
Cyane
    U.S. warship assigned to capture slave ships, *2695*

D

Daughters of the American Revolution, *2822*
Dawes Allotment Act of 1887
    federal law dissolving Native American tribes as legal entities, *2749*
    Native Americans to become U.S. citizens, *2742*

death penalty
    American citizen hanged for treason, *2557*
    American executions to excite worldwide protest, *2563*
    authorized by federal law, *2564, 2564*
    colonist hanged for treason, *2552*
    execution by the Army, *2553*
    execution for slave trading carried out by federal government, *2556*
    execution in America, *2550*
    federal execution for killing FBI agent, *2567*
    federal execution of a woman, *2558*
    federal execution of organized crime boss, *2565*
    imposed by woman judge, *2561*
    in tax riot, *2555*
    labor activists to be executed, *2559*
    law authorizing, for blasphemy, *2551*
    peacetime death sentence for espionage, *2566*
    state to allow execution
        by lethal gas, *2562*
        by lethal injection, *2568*
    state to allow execution by electrocution, *2560*
    state to ban, *2554*
    state to enact moratorium on executions, *2569*
    Supreme Court decision barring, *4738*
Debates and Proceedings in the Congress of the United States
    volume of, *1499*
Debates on the Several State Conventions on the Adoption of the Federal Constitution, The
    definitive edition, *1831*
debt, U.S.
    balance of trade deficit in 20th century, *2132*
    year in which U.S. was free from debt, *2127*
    year it exceeded $1 billion, *2128*
    year it exceeded $1 trillion, *2134*
    year it exceeded $10 billion, *2130*
    year it exceeded $100 billion, *2131*
    year it exceeded $100 million, *2126*
    year it exceeded $5 trillion, *2137*
    year it exceeded $500 billion, *2133*
    year when U.S. became creditor nation, *2129*
decimal system of money, *2147*
Declaration of Independence
    congressional vote on, *1056*
    newspaper to publish, *1059*
    president who was descendant of a signer of, *3550*
    printing of, *1058*
    public reading, *1060*
    publication in another language, *1061*
    signer, *1057*

national convention to adopt two-thirds rule, *2983*

national convention to adopt unit rule, *2986*

party endorsement of a presidential candidate, *2970*

party to continue in power in White House for more than 20 years, *2908*

political newspaper, *3910*

political party to hold open presidential nominating caucus, *2973*

president from, *3708*

presidential candidate, *3280*

presidential election in which it participated, *3175*

presidential election won by, *3178*

vice president from, *4999*

year in which it controlled both houses of Congress, *1492*

year in which it won control of Senate, *1684*

year in which it won control of the House of Representatives, *1549*

depression, economic, *2085*

Depression, The
 federal insurance program for bank deposits, *2115*
 federal theater project, *2018*

desegregation
 See
 public transportation, desegregation
 school desegregation

diplomacy
 full relations between Vatican and U.S. in 20th century, *2297*
 relations between U.S. and People's Republic of China, *2295*
 relations between U.S. and Soviet Union, *2272*
 shuttle, *2292*
 See also
 international relations

Diplomatic Service of the United States, *2319*

disabled persons
 comprehensive civil rights legislation for, *1908*
 federal civil rights law for, *1907*
 federal law granting equal access to, *1906*
 national advocacy organization for people with physical disabilities of all kinds, *2831*
 organized civil rights protest by, *2830*

disabled veterans
 colonial law to aid, *2697*
 soldiers' homes established by Congress, *2700*

disarmament
 independent agency, *2609*

Distinguished Flying Cross
 president who had been awarded, *3628*

district attorneys, U.S.
 who was a woman, *1978*
 who was African-American, *1986*

District of Columbia
 See
 Washington, D.C.

Dixicrats
 States' Rights Democratic Party, *2948*

"Dixie" (song), *1119*

DNA
 national database, *2547*

doctor-assisted suicide
 law permitting, *3960*

dog licensing ordinance, *4024*

dollar, as standard monetary unit, *2150*

"dollar diplomacy"
 use of term, *2265*

doomsday plan, *2683*

draft
 See
 military draft

drama
 about Civil War, *1393*

drawback legislation
 enacted by Congress, *4905*

drugs and narcotics
 ban enacted by Congress, *4062*
 control law enacted by Congress, *4063*
 federal drug control chief, *4067*
 federal laws requiring manufacturers to prove effectiveness of their products, *4034*
 marijuana ban enacted by Congress, *4064*
 narcotics tariff enacted by Congress, *4061*
 Office of National Drug Control Policy, *4066*
 state ban, *4065*

ducatone (coin)
 monetary regulation act, *2142*

due process
 statement of principle of, *1837*

dueling
 state ban, *4012*

Dumbarton Oaks
 meeting to establish U.N., *2430*

E

e-mail addresses
 for officials of federal government, *2004*

E pluribus unum
 coin to use, as motto, *2148*

Eagle Forum, *2839*

Earth Day, *2233*

Easter Egg roll
 at White House, *5026*

F

Farmer Labor Party
presidential candidate, *3327*
farmers
national political organization of, *2816*
Farmers' Alliance Party, *2933*
political platform, *3053*
See also
agriculture
federal agencies
aerospace, *2075*
codification board, *2009*
consolidated arts funding, *2019*
cryptologic agency, *2676*
for administering credit unions, *2124*
for administering personnel policies, *2032*
for agricultural lending, *4117*
for economic development in Latin American and Caribbean, *2291*
for gathering of foreign intelligence, *2674*
for veterans' affairs, *2703*
General Services Administration, *2011*
national emergency council, *2008*
overseeing national elections, *2012*
promoting safe transportation, *4106*
regulatory
Interstate Commerce Commission, *2007*
regulatory, for futures trading, *2140*
reorganization of federal government in 20th century, *2010*
to regulate broadcast media, *3875*
to regulate securities markets, *2139*
to support civilian scientific research, *2074*
with safety oversight of defense nuclear facilities, *2610*
federal aid
to libraries, *2068*
Federal Alcohol Control Administration, *3947*
federal budget
presidential commission on overhauling budgetary process, *2099*
federal buildings
attack by domestic terrorists on, resulting in large loss of life, *2006*
built to withstand nuclear attack, *2001*
consolidated headquarters for Department of Defense, *2606*
erected for public use, *1996*
Library of Congress, *2066*
See also
Capitol (Washington, DC)
Federal Bureau of Investigation (FBI), *2532*
national DNA database, *2547*
Public Enemy Number 1, *2538*
Senate investigation of CIA and, *2542*
federal charters
Bank of the United States, *1995*
standardized criteria for incorporation, *2003*
Federal Communications Commission, *3876*

Federal Corrupt Practices Act (1910)
federal act requiring congressional campaigns to disclose their finances, *2786*
Federal Corrupt Practices Act (1925)
federal act regulating receipt of gifts by candidates for Congress, *2787*
federal courts
Administrative Office of U.S. Courts, *1982*
African-American to serve as chief U.S. magistrate, *1992*
African-American woman to serve as judge on U.S. Court of Appeals, *1990*
Attorney of the U.S., *1971*
claims court, *1973*
commerce court, *1977*
creation, *1970*
Federal Judicial Center, *1989*
interracial jury, *1974*
television eyewitness allowed to testify in, *1985*
U.S. district attorney who was a woman, *1978*
U.S. district attorney who was African-American, *1986*
U.S. Sentencing Commission, *1991*
woman admitted to practice before Court of Claims, *1976*
woman to serve as foreman on grand jury, *1981*
Federal Credit Union Act (1934), *2123*
Federal Credit Union System
credit union act passed by Congress, *2122*
federal credit unions, *2123*
Federal Crop Insurance Corporation, *4119*
Federal Deposit Insurance Corporation, *2113*
federal documents and records
archiving agency, *2056*
catalog of government publications, *2055*
Freedom of Information Act, *2058*
Government Printing Office, *2054*
government report posted on Internet before publication on paper, *2060*
microfilm editions, *2057*
ruling requiring retention of all electronic records, *2059*
Federal Election Campaign Act (1971)
campaign finance law that set limits on media spending, *2789*
law allowing corporations to form PACs, *2838*
law allowing members to pocket leftover campaign funds, *1577*
Federal Election Commission (FEC), *2012*
independent government agency to oversee political campaign contributions, *2790*
federal elections
agency overseeing, *2012*
Federal Emergency Relief Administration, *2466*

H

heads of state—*Continued*
Prince of Wales to visit U.S., *2377*
queens
    to visit U.S., *2379*
    to visit U.S. during her reign, *2382*
son of Soviet premier to become American citizen, *2394*
women
    First Lady of Mexico to reside in U.S., *2378*
    of American ancestry to become a queen, *2386*
    See also
    presidents
Health, Education, and Welfare, Department of, *2048*
Health and Human Services, U.S. Department of, *2052*
health insurance
government-funded health care program for the poor, *4056*
law enacted by a state, *4055*
Medicare
    identification cards, *4058*
    year in which spending declined, *4060*
plan enacted by Congress, *4057*
state to ration health care, *4035*
health laboratory
established by a city, *4022*
health services
city to build comprehensive sewer system, *4017*
Commissioner of Food and Drugs, *4030*
crop recalled by order of Food and Drug Administration, *4033*
dog licensing ordinance, *4024*
established by federal government, *4010*
federal AIDS policy coordinator, *4038*
federal law on product safety, *4028*
federal laws requiring drug manufacturers to prove effectiveness of their products, *4034*
federal lifesaving service, *4020*
fluoridation program for city water supply, *4031*
government assistance to family of insane person, *4007*
meat inspection law enacted by Congress, *4023*
municipal milk station, *4025*
nationwide nutritional labeling standards, *4037*
published federal guidelines for food toxicity, *4032*
pure food and drug laws
    established by Congress, *4016*
    state law, *4021*
quarantine law enacted by Congress, *4011*
state board of health, *4018*
state law regulating chiropractic, *4029*
state licensing law for nurses, *4026*

state licensing law for pharmacists, *4027*
surgeon general, *4019*
    who was African-American, *4040*
    woman to serve as, *4039*
vaccination
    law enacted by Congress, *4014*
    program by federal government to protect Native Americans against smallpox, *4015*
    state law, *4013*
heart attack
presidential candidate to run for office after having, *3265*
Held by the Enemy
drama about Civil War, *1393*
hijacking, of airplanes
sky marshals, *2540*
Hill's Political History of the United States . . ., 1075
hoarding
of gold, presidential order about, *2094*
of Kennedy half-dollar, *2171*
holding companies
authorized by a state, *4915*
worth a billion dollars, *4917*
holidays
Admission Day (California), *2198*
Alaska Day, *2202*
Armed Forces Day, *2231*
Armistice Day, *2223*
birthdays
    Abraham Lincoln, *2201, 2216*
    Benjamin Franklin, *2192*
    Jefferson Davis, *2217*
    Marquis de Lafayette, *2222*
    Robert E. Lee, *2212*
    Thomas Jefferson, *2193*
    William McKinley, *2219*
    Woodrow Wilson, *2226*
Boston Massacre, commemoration of, *2182*
Christmas
    law against celebration, *2178*
Colorado Day, *2209*
Columbus Day, *2189*
Confederate Memorial Day, *2206*
Constitution Day, *2187*
Delaware Day, *2229*
Earth Day, *2233*
Emancipation Day (Texas), *2204*
federal law creating Monday, *2232*
Flag Day, *2208*
Georgia Day, *2180*
Halifax Resolutions Day, *2183*
Indiana Day, *2191*
Jackson Day, *2190*
Kansas Day, *2207, 2215*
Labor Day, *2205*
    parade, *2210*
Maritime Day, *2228*
Martin Luther King Day, *2234*

House of Representatives, U.S.—*Continued*

congressional candidate elected while missing, *1622*

congressional representative of Asian ancestry, *1615*

congressional representative of Puerto Rican ancestry, *1620*

congressional representative reelected after serving a prison term, *1616*

congressional representative sworn in before eight o'clock in the morning, *1617*

congressional representative to attend college after his term of service, *1598*

congressional representative to vote twice against entry into war, *1608*

congressional representative who received Medal of Honor and was graduated from U.S. Naval Academy, *1612*

congressional representatives to marry each other, *1626*

congressman from Northern state who was African-American, *1604*

congressman to acknowledge that he was a homosexual, *1627*

congressman who was a Catholic priest, *1591*

congresswoman elected to serve in place of her husband, *1601*

congresswoman to advance to Senate, *1613*

congresswoman to give birth while holding office, *1624*

congresswoman to serve 18 terms, *1603*

congresswoman who was a grandmother, *1625*

congresswoman who was a mother, *1600*

congresswoman who was former welfare mother, *1629*

congresswoman who was Jewish, *1621*

congresswoman who was not sworn in, *1606*

"Corrections Day", *1580*

Democratic congresswoman, *1602*

early object still in use, *1531*

election that was contested, *1539*

entry in *Journal of the House of Representatives of the United States, 1532*

federal law compelling testimony of witnesses before, *1503*

filibuster, *1547*

former First Lady to be granted a seat in, *3595*

former president who was elected to, *3486*

gag rule in, *1559*

gerrymander, *1555*

Hall of, in the Capitol, *1554*

incumbent president to testify before committee of, *1575*

instance of congressional "log-rolling", *1548*

joint committee of House and Senate, *1481*

joint rule of both houses of Congress, *1482*

joint session of House and, *1812*

Latina elected to, *1628*

Latino to serve in, *1493*

mace of, *1529*

majority leader, *1567*

majority whip, *1568*

meeting place in Washington, DC, *1553*

member of Congress to enter active duty in military during World War II, *1607*

member to lie in state in Capitol rotunda, *1237*

midterm election since World War II in which the president's party gained seats in, *1581*

minority leader, *1569*

minority whip, *1570*

mother and son simultaneously elected to, *1614*

Muslim to offer invocation to, *1578*

pages, *1639*

who was African-American, *1643*

political cartoonist elected to, *1571*

president elected by decision of, *3179*

president who had served in, *3480*

president who had served in both, and Senate, *3487*

presidential commission whose creation was challenged by, *1561*

quorum, *1535*

rabbi to open, with prayer, *1565*

representative elected by prohibitionists, *1596*

representative to be refused a seat, *1590*

representative to serve a single day, *1595*

representative who was a Socialist, *1597*

representative who was African-American, *1594*

response by, to inaugural address, *1542*

response by, to president's State of the Union message, *1546*

Roman Catholic priest to serve as voting member of, *1619*

secretarial help for representatives, *1513*

select committee appointed by, *1538*

Sergeant at Arms, *1543*

session, *1533*

Speakers, *1631*

former Speaker to become television news commentator, *1638*

to die in the Capitol, *1634*

to serve longer than ten years, *1636*

who became president, *1633*

who became vice president, *1635*

who was punished by the House, *1637*

who was simultaneously member, parliamentarian, and leader, *1632*

standing committee headed by African-American, *1572*

standing committee still operating, *1540*

standing rules adopted by, *1537*

Supreme Court justice who had served in House of Representatives, *4759*

that included substantial number of African-American women, *1579*

use of the mace in, to keep order, *1552*

vice president who had served in, *4960*

vote in, to be recorded electronically, *1574*

vote in, to be tallied by machine, *1573*

vote to establish Washington, DC, *1865*

Ways and Means Committee, *1544*

woman elected to, *1599*

woman to argue women's suffrage before major committee of Congress, *1960*

woman to chair committee, *1605*

year in which Democratic Party won control, *1556*

year in which Democratic-Republican Party won control, *1549*

year in which Federalist Party won control, *1545*

year in which seats were won by third parties, *1557*

year in which Whig Party won control, *1560*
See also
Congress, U.S.

housing

city code, *4042*

emergency housing corporation, *4046*

Federal Housing Administration, *4047*

federal law prohibiting racial discrimination in, *4041*

home owners' loan corporation, *4045*

initiative guaranteeing homeless people overnight shelter, *4048*

state-run old age home for pioneers, *4044*

theater safety codes, *4043*

Housing and Urban Development, U.S. Department of, *2049*

Howard University

public university in Washington, DC, *1888*

Huguenots

French colonial settlement, *1395*

human rights

president to make, a cornerstone of his foreign policy, *3439*

"Hunkers"

use of term, *2919*

hunting laws

enacted by a colony, *4200*

hydroelectric power

county plant, *4131*

federal plant, *4130*

I

icebox

in White House, *5021*

identification scheme

national, for American citizens, *4068*

identity theft

law making, a federal crime, *4071*

immigration and citizenship

boatlift of Cuban refugees, *3124*

citizenship granted on foreign soil, *3120*

colonial naturalization law, *3100*

deportation of aliens authorized by Congress, *3102*

federal immigration law requiring collection of information on aliens, *3103*

federal immigration station, *3114*

honorary citizenship authorized by Congress, *3121*

immigration ban enacted by Congress, *3112*

immigration bureau superintendent, *3113*

immigration of Chinese nationals, *3106*

immigration quota applied to Mexico, *3122*

immigration receiving station, *3108*

large-scale repatriation program, *3118*

migration study jointly conducted by U.S. and Mexico, *3125*

national definition of citizenship, *3109*

naturalization act enacted by Congress, *3101*

naturalization ceremony in the White House, *3123*

quotas enacted by Congress, *3116*

registration of aliens by federal government, *3119*

restrictions by Congress on immigration of Chinese laborers, *3111*

school at a college, *3065*

state law establishing English as official language, *3117*

tax to limit immigration, *3107*

year in which more than 1 million immigrants arrived in U.S., *3115*

year in which more than 10,000 immigrants arrived in U.S., *3104*

year in which more than 100,000 immigrants arrived in U.S., *3105*

year in which more than 500,000 immigrants arrived in U.S., *3110*

impeachments

attempt to bring proceedings against a president, *3630*

cabinet officer, by the House of Representatives, *1163*

elected president to be impeached, *3632*

federal judge, *1972*

judge, *1445*

president to be impeached, *3631*

senator, *1759*

state governor to be impeached and acquitted, *4482*

state governor to be impeached and convicted, *4488*

Supreme Court justice to be impeached, *4764*

import duties
treaty between federal government and foreign nation to provide for mutual reduction of import duties, *2410*

"In God We Trust"
coin to use motto, *2162*

inaugural addresses
broadcast to a crowd with loudspeakers, *3671*
inaugural address, *3633*
president to deliver his address bareheaded, *3668*
president whose address did not include word "I", *3669*
response by House of Representatives to, *1542*
response of Senate to, *1671*

income taxes
enacted by a state, *4833*
levied by a colony, *4788*
levied by Congress, *4801*
levied by Congress in peace time, *4807*
state, *4827*
State of Income report released by federal government, *4814*
state to ratify 16th Amendment to Constitution, *1846*
year in which federal revenues from, exceeded those from customs duties, *4812*

Independence Day, *2184*
celebration after adoption of Constitution, *2238*
city to forbid sale of firecrackers for celebration of, *2239*
public celebration of national independence, *2236*
to be celebrated as state holiday, *2237*

Independence Party
presidential candidate, *3325*

Independent Afro-American Party
presidential candidate, *3350*

Independent Liberal Republican Party
presidential candidate, *3302*

Independent Party
presidential candidate, *3283*

Independent Republican Party
presidential candidate, *3295*

Independent Republicans
political platform, *3042*

Independent Treasury System Act (1840), *2086*

India
ambassador to, *2348*

Indian Affairs, Bureau of
commissioner who was Native American, *2746*
school for Native American children run by, *2743*

Indian Appropriations Act (1871)
federal law withdrawing recognition of Native American tribal autonomy, *2747*

Indian Citizenship Act (1924)
law by which Native Americans became American citizens, *2752*

Indian Claims Commission
claims by Native Americans for compensation for confiscated land, *2741*

Indian Reorganization Act (1934)
Native American tribal constitution, *2753*

Indian Self-Determination and Educational Assistance Act (1975)
federal law returning autonomy to Native American tribes, *2760*

Indiana Day, *2191*

indictments
cabinet member while in office, *1205*

industrial and labor relations
school at a college, *3067*

Industrial Congress of the United States, First
national labor congress, *2879*

Industrial Reform Party
presidential candidate, *3309*

industrial report
to Congress, *4908*

Industrial Workers of the World (Wobblies)
convention, *2885*

information access
Freedom of Information Act, *2058*

inheritance tax
enacted by a state, *4829*
levied by a colony, *4792*
levied by Congress, *4804*

initiative and referendum
state to adopt use of, *4432*

insurance
board established by a state government, *4050*
department of a state, *4051*
Employer's Liability Act enacted by Congress, *4052*
Federal Crop Insurance Corporation, *4119*
federal social security system, *4073*
law treatise, *2512*
regulation enacted by a state, *4049*
Social Security
independent agency for administering, *4074*
law limiting use of the numbers, *4069*
law making misuse of the numbers a federal crime, *4070*
War Risk Insurance Bureau, *4053*
See also
automobile insurance
health insurance

integration
order for, of armed forces, *2658*

J

Jesuits
ban on, *1943*

Jews
broker to Office of Finance of U.S., *2079*
cabinet member who was, *1169*
congresswoman who was, *1621*
diplomat who was, *2323*
elected to public office in New World, *1427*
minister and envoy who was, *2335*
models of republican liberty, *1024*
rabbi to open House of Representatives with prayer, *1565*
senator of Jewish descent, *1763*
senator who was a practicing, *1770*
settlement to welcome refugees of all faiths, *1941*
state governor who was, *4502*
Supreme Court justice who was, *4772*
vice presidential candidate who was, *3279*
woman to serve as Supreme Court justice, *4783*

Jobless Party
presidential candidate, *3331*

John Birch Society, *2835*

John Q. Public (character), *1132*

Journal of the Executive Proceedings of the Senate of the United States of America
entry in, *1673*

Journal of the House of Representatives of the United States
entry in, *1532*

Journal of the Senate of the United States of America
edition, *1691*

journalists
African-American newspaper reporter accredited to congressional press gallery, *3894*
African-American newspaper reporter accredited to White House, *3893*
arrested by Senate, *1703*
conflict-of-interest case involving a, *3885*
Gridiron Club, *3858*
muckraking, *3890*
woman who was, *3891*
newspaper reporter accredited to White House, *3723*
political photographer, *3888*
reporters at sessions of the Senate, *3886*
Senate press gallery, *1701*
senator who had been newspaper reporter, *1794*
woman reporter to cover a political convention, *3889*

Judiciary Act (1789)
creation of federal courts, *1970*

Judiciary Act (1869)
pensions for federal judges, *1975*

Juneau (Alaska)
city occupying more than 1,000 square miles, *1269*

"Juneteenth"
Emancipation Day (Texas), *2204*

juries
composed of women, *1443*
interracial, *1974*
woman to serve as foreman on federal grand jury, *1981*
See also
grand juries

Justice, Department of, *2041*
African-American woman nominated to head its Civil Rights Division, *1937*
attorney general to head, *1162*

justices of the peace
woman to serve as, *1271*

juvenile court, *1272*

K

Kanagawa, Treaty of
treaty between U.S. and Japan, *2414*

Kansas Colored Volunteer Infantry, 1st, *1386*

Kansas Day, *2207, 2215*

Kellogg-Briand Pact, *1176*

Kennedy family
three brothers from one family to serve in Senate, *1795*

Kennedy half-dollar, *2171*

Kent State University
nationwide campus rioting, *2862*

"kitchen cabinet" of Andrew Jackson, *1152*

Knights of Labor
national labor organization to establish a women's division, *2884*

Knights of Labor workers' organization
Labor Day, *2205*

Know-Nothing Party, *2921*
political platform, *3038*
presidential candidate, *3290*

Korean embassy, *2261*

Ku Klux Klan, *2814*
leader to mount credible campaign for state governor, *4440*

Ku Klux Klan Acts
laws authorizing use of force against Ku Klux Klan, *1924*

L

Labor, U.S. Department of, *2043, 2045*
  federal employment service, *2464*
  strike settlement mediated by, *2480*
  Women's Bureau of, *2443*

Labor bureaus
  established by a state, *2441*
  of federal government, *2442*

Labor Day, *2205*
  parade, *2210*

labor discrimination
  ban enacted by a state on employment of women in an occupation, *2458*
  federal law requiring fair employment practices, *2461*
  state agency for enforcing equal treatment in employment, *2459*

labor newspaper, *3919*

Labor Party, U.S., *2956, 2959*
  presidential candidate, *3358*

Labor Reform Party, *2926*
  political platform, *3043*
  presidential candidate, *3296*

labor relations
  arbitration
    effective state law, *2452*
    federal board, *2451*
    National Mediation Board, *2453*
    state board, *2450*
  consolidated labor relations agency, *2448*
  federal agency regulating, *2446*

labor secretaries
  who was not a member of American Federation of Labor, *2444*

labor strikes
  in which a militia was called out, *2477*
  in which Taft-Hartley Act was invoked, *2483*
  in which women participated, *2877*
  massacre of strikebreakers by union members, *2886*
  nationwide consumer boycott in support of workers, *2891*
  of African-American laborers, *2875*
  of postal employees, *2484*
  settlement mediated by federal Labor Department, *2480*
  sit-down, *2481*
    state to outlaw, *2482*
  suppressed by federal troops in peacetime, *2479*
  to last longer than a year, *2889*
  use of federal troops to suppress, *2478*

labor unions
  Capitol Hill employees to unionize, *2492*
  chartered by federal government, *2490*
  cooperatives to be authorized by a state, *2487*
  federal act regulating contributions by labor unions to congressional campaigns, *2788*
  national, for public employees, *2491*
  state law prohibiting employers from discriminating against members of, *2489*
  state to legalize, *2488*
  to nominate its own political candidates, *2485*
  whose candidates won an election, *2486*

labor unions and organizations
  African-American, *2887*
  Bellamy Nationalist Club, *2883*
  Chicano convention, *2888*
  in a colony, *2874*
  Industrial Workers of the World (Wobblies) convention, *2885*
  national Chicano organization, *2890*
  national labor congress, *2879*
  national labor organizations, *2880*
    of importance, *2882*
    to establish a women's division, *2884*
  national organization for African-American workers, *2881*
  strike benefit of, *2876*
  woman to become union organizer, *2878*

Lafayette College (Easton, Penn.)
  civil rights chair at, *2526*

land-grant railroad, *4087*

land trust, *4187*

land-use program, statewide, *4193*

Latin America
  articulation of Monroe Doctrine, *2254*
  conference of American republics, *2255*
  non-NATO ally of U.S. in Western Hemisphere, *2308*
  recognition by U.S. of newly independent nation, *2253*
  Summit of the Americas, *2304*

Latinos
  caucus of major political party, *2965*
  Latina elected to House of Representatives, *1628*
  mayor of city without large Latino population, *1346*
  New Mexico state governor who was, *4504*
  to serve in House of Representatives, *1493*

law enforcement
  bounty of $5 million for enemy of U.S., *2548*
  community to fingerprint its citizens, *2537*
  Federal Bureau of Investigation, *2532*
  fingerprinting in federal penitentiaries, *2530*
  international exchange of fingerprints, *2531*
  interstate anticrime pact, *2527*
  mercenaries arrested for planning terrorist acts on behalf of a foreign government, *2544*

municipal education program for men convicted of patronizing prostitutes, *2546*
national conference on crime, *2539*
national DNA database, *2547*
national file on suspected political radicals, *2534*
police bureau of criminal alien investigation, *2536*
probation system for offenders, *2575*
Public Enemy Number I, *2538*
secret service
    established by federal government, *2580*
    established in a colony, *2579*
Secret Service, U.S.
    agent killed in line of duty, *2581*
    women to become agents, *2582*
Senate investigation of FBI and CIA, *2542*
sentence of branding by federal court, *2528*
sky marshals, *2540*
state ban on cheap handguns, *2543*
state police, *2529*
state police department to be monitored for racial profiling, *2549*
women
    bailiff, *2533*
    sheriff, *2535*
    to serve as federal marshals, *2541*
    to serve as police chief of major city, *2545*
    See also
    death penalty
law magazine, *3897*
laws and legislation
air pollution law of importance enacted by Congress, *4166*
annual salary for members of Congress, *1649*
bill passed by Congress, *1672*
books and document
    insurance law treatise, *2512*
books and documents
    code adopted by a state, *2519*
    colonial laws, *2510*
    containing laws enacted by more than one session of Congress, *2514*
    dictionary of American law, *2520*
    digest of American law, *2517*
    edition of *United States Statutes at Large*, *2521*
    federal laws, *2515*
    of federal laws then in force, *2522*
    report, *2513*
    text published in U.S., *2516*
    treatise on common law written for American legal profession, *2518*
campaign finance law allowing members to pocket leftover campaign funds, *1577*
car insurance law enacted by a state, *4054*
code of an American colony, *1471*
colonial

mandating Sabbath observance, *1406*
colonial, to control corrupt election practices, *1451*
colonial law providing a fixed compensation for mail carriers, *3129*
colonial law regulating domestic transmission of official mail, *3128*
colonial law to aid disabled veterans, *2697*
colonial naturalization law, *3100*
compelling testimony of witnesses before House and Senate, *1503*
comprehensive federal, to protect wildlife, *4210*
comprehensive wilderness law, *4215*
dog licensing ordinance, *4024*
drug control law enacted by Congress, *4063*
education
    civil rights chair at a college, *2526*
    law instruction at a college, *2523*
    law school at a college, *2524*
    law school to be permanently organized, *2525*
encouraging settlers to irrigate desert lands, *4195*
entail and primogeniture
    state to abolish, *2511*
establishing presidential succession, *3376*
federal flood control legislation, *4191*
federal motor carrier legislation, *4100*
federal statute printed on paper, *1515*
forbidding Native American religious rituals, *2725*
forestry
    colonial law, *4136*
    federal law encouraging settlers to grow trees, *4138*
gambling
    colonial, for residents, *3998*
    for ministers enacted by a colony, *3997*
health insurance
    law enacted by a state, *4055*
irrigation law enacted by Congress, *4194*
judicial decision allowing physicians to terminate life of terminally ill patients at their request, *3961*
large-scale federal irrigation legislation, *4196*
limitations on earnings from senatorial honoraria, *1750*
mandatory congressional 30-day summer recess, *1526*
meat inspection law enacted by Congress, *4023*
medical licensing laws
    enacted by a city, *4008*
    enacted by a colony, *4009*
movie censorship law enacted by Congress, *3861*
naturalization act enacted by Congress, *3101*

laws and legislation—*Continued*

postal service law enacted by Congress, *3146*

pure food and drug laws
established by Congress, *4016*

quarantine law enacted by Congress, *4011*

religious toleration law enacted by a colony, *1944*

Sabbath laws published by a colony, *1412*

setting pay rates for Congress, *1647*

shipbuilding law enacted by Congress, *2694*

Social Security
law limiting use of the numbers, *4069*
law making misuse of the numbers a federal crime, *4070*

statement of legislative independence by a colony, *1415*

traffic law enacted by a colony, *4082*

vaccination
law enacted by Congress, *4014*

wildlife conservation
fish protection law enacted by a city, *4201*
hunting law enacted by a colony, *4200*
to protect fur seals, *4203*
See also
arbitration law
civil rights legislation
copyright laws
federal laws
military laws
slavery, laws
state laws

lawyers

admitted to practice before Supreme Court, *2584*

African-Americans
admitted to practice before Supreme Court, *2586*
formally admitted to the bar, *2585*
woman admitted to practice before Supreme Court, *2592*
woman to practice law, *2588*

ban on, in colonial legislature, *1475*

modern proposal to ban, from serving in state or local government, *2594*

national arbitration organization, *2591*

national society, *2589*

state society, *2583*

women
admitted to practice before Supreme Court, *2590*
elected president of state lawyers' association, *2593*
to practice law, *2587*

League of Women Voters, *2898*

legal tender, *2160*

Legislative Reorganization Act (1970)

mandatory congressional 30-day summer recess, *1526*

Lend-Lease Act (1941), *2274*

lethal gas

state to allow execution by, *2562*

lethal injection

state to allow execution by, *2568*

Lexington and Concord, battles of, *1015*

Patriots' Day, *2218*

tolling of Liberty Bell to announce, *1110*

war hero, *1016*

Liberal Party convention, *3345*

Liberal Republican Convention of Colored Men

presidential candidate, *3301*

Liberal Republican Party, *2928*

political platform, *3046*

presidential candidate, *3298*

Liberia

American to become president of African republic, *2375*

president of black African country to visit U.S., *2389*

Libertarian Party, *2955*

city council composed entirely of members of, *1293*

presidential candidate, *3356*

Liberty Bell

casting of, *1108*

cracking, *1112*

public reading of Declaration of Independence and, *1060*

tolling of
for event of political importance, *1109*
to announce a battle, *1110*

use of name, *1111*

Liberty League

presidential candidate, *3288*

liberty loans, *2091*

Liberty Party

political platform, *3035*

presidential candidate, *3286*

single-issue party, *2918*

Liberty Party (modern)

presidential candidate, *3332*

"Liberty Song, The", *1114*

liberty trees or poles

Native American symbols adopted for political purposes by colonial Americans, *1130*

libraries

circulating, in Washington, DC, *1877*

in White House, *5023*

Senate, *1714*

Library of Congress, *2062*

building, *2066*

Capitol Page School, *1641*

fireproofing, *2064*

librarian, *2061*

Library Services Act (1956)

federal aid to libraries, *2068*

license plates
for vehicles, *4093*

lifesaving service
federal, *4020*

Lighthouse Board
organization in charge of Statue of Liberty, *1126*

Lincoln Memorial
national monument to Abraham Lincoln, *2712*

Lincoln penny, *2164*

Lindbergh Day, *1100*

line-item veto
president to use, *3846*

liquor reform movement, *2853*

liquor stores
state-run, *4278*

lithographed campaign buttons, *2804*

litter law
state, *4168*

Little Big Horn, Battle of the
major defeat inflicted by Native Americans on regular U.S. Army troops, *2748*

loans
liberty, *2091*
made by U.S. to war ally, *2090*
to U.S., *2082*
See also
foreign loans

lobbyists
congressional, who was a woman, *1501*
use of term, *1497*

"Loco-Focos"
use of term, *2917*

"log-rolling"
instance of congressional, *1548*

London Company, *1433*

Long Island, Battle of, *1026*

lotteries
colony financed by, *1404*
federal law hostile to, *4000*
held by Continental Congress, *1046*
state, in modern times, *4004*

Louisiana Purchase
important exercise of implied power of government, *1997*

Louisiana Territory
French governor, *1420*

lynchings
ban enacted by a state, *1926*
year in which there were no reported, of African-Americans, *1930*

M

mace
as symbol of royal authority, *1421*
colonial legislature to use, as symbol of authority, *1477*
colonial legislature's, still extant, *1479*
of House of Representatives, *1529*
use of, in House of Representatives, *1552*

magazines and newspapers
abolition newspaper, *3914*
antislavery magazine, *4243*
campaign newspapers, *3918*
of importance, *3920*
Democratic-Republican (Jeffersonian) political newspaper, *3910*
edition of *The New York Tribune*, *3922*
edition of the *Wall Street Journal*, *3924*
editorial retraction of false political news, *3905*
factory workers' magazine, *3899*
free newspaper exchange between publishers, *3911*
important Muslim American weekly, *3926*
issue of the *New York Times*, *3923*
labor newspaper, *3919*
law magazine, *3897*
major antislavery periodical, *4245*
Mexican-American political newspaper, *3925*
newspaper published with government approval, *3904*
newspaper suppressed by government, *3903*
newspapers provided to senators and representatives, *3909*
of federal government, *3902*
official Jacksonian newspaper, *3916*
official Whig administration newspaper, *3921*
political magazines
muckraking journal of importance, *3900*
political magazine, *3895*
published quarterly, *3898*
satirical, *3896*
political newspaper, *3906*
political newspaper of national importance, *3908*
political newspaper published by African-Americans, *3917*
political newspaper published in Washington, DC, *3912*
political newspaper using word "Democratic" in its title, *3913*
regulation allowing newspapers to be sent through the mails, *3907*
weekly newsmagazine, *3901*

mail
See
Postal Service, U.S.

Manassas
> *See*
> Bull Run, Battles of

"manifest destiny"
> use of term, *2257*

maps
> of United States, *1065*
> to show American flag, *1083*
> use of "America" as geographical designation, *1062*

maps of British colonies showing Native American lands, *2729*

Marbury v. Madison
> Congressional act declared unconstitutional by Supreme Court, *1488*

Margaretta **(schooner)**
> naval battle of Revolutionary War, *1019*

Marie of Rumania, Queen
> to visit U.S., *2382*

marijuana
> ban enacted by Congress, *4064*

Marines, U.S., *2660*
> American flag flown over fortress of Old World, *1086*
> commandant of, *2661*
> statue of American woman in uniform, *2717*

maritime commerce
> consolidated federal agency to regulate, *4935*

Maritime Day, *2228*

marriage and divorce
> legal divorce in American colonies, *3948*
> no-fault divorce law enacted by a state, *3956*
> polygamy ban enacted by Congress, *3950*
> state to require blood tests for marriage licenses, *3953*

Married Women's Property Act (1857), *1955*

Martin Luther King Day, *2234*

Maryland Day, *2177*

Masons
> known to hold high office in colonies, *1422*
> president to attain rank of 33rd-degree, *3836*
> president who was, *3818*

Massachusetts Bay Colony
> ban on Jesuits, *1943*
> ban on lawyers in legislature, *1475*
> ban on Quakers, *1945*
> bicameral legislature, *1473*
> board of selectmen, *1409*
> contested election, *1450*
> election held in a colony, *1447*
> governor, *1455*
> law against celebration of Christmas, *2178*
> law authorizing penalty of death for blasphemy, *2551*
> law forbidding Native American religious rituals, *2725*

> militia, *2662*
> mint, *2144*
> minting act, *2143*
> monetary regulation act, *2142*
> paper ballots, *1448*
> paper money, *2145*
> pay for colonial legislators, *1472*
> smoking ban in legislature, *1474*
> statement of legislative independence, *1415*
> statute establishing religious qualifications for public office, *1416*
> Thanksgiving proclamation, *2240*
> town meeting, *1408*
> use of bullets as currency, *2141*
> voting requirements, *1446*

Massachusetts Colony
> copyright law, *2504*

Massachusetts Naval Battalion
> naval militia established by a state, *2665*

mayors
> Abilene (Tex.), *1322*
> African-American
> > Atlanta, *1337*
> > Baltimore (Md.), *1348*
> > Chicago, *1345*
> > chief executive of Washington, DC, *1332*
> > Dallas, *1360*
> > Denver, *1355*
> > Detroit, *1338*
> > election in major city in which both candidates were, *1356*
> > Fayette (Miss.), *1334*
> > Houston, *1364*
> > incumbent, of major city to lose to white candidate, *1349*
> > Jackson (Miss.), *1363*
> > Kansas City, *1354*
> > Los Angeles, *1339*
> > major city to elect, *1333*
> > militant to be elected, of major American city, *1341*
> > New York City, *1351*
> > Newark (N.J.), *1335*
> > Philadelphia, *1347*
> > Savannah (Ga.), *1361*
> > Seattle, *1350*
> > St. Louis, *1358*
> Augusta (Ga.), *1299*
> Austin (Tex.), *1308*
> Boston, *1302*
> Buffalo, *1305*
> Chicago, *1307*
> city commissioner of Salt Lake City, *1327*
> Cleveland, *1301*
> Corpus Christi (Tex.), *1316*
> elected, of Washington, DC, in 20th century, *1900*
> elected by popular vote, *1306*
> Fairbanks (Alaska), *1325*

statue cast by federal government, *2707*
statue of American woman in uniform, *2717*
to a Native American, *2718*
to a president's mother, *2710*
to a traitor, *2709*
to American flag, *2713*
to four presidents, *2714*
to George Washington authorized by federal government, *2708*

Mormons
church disincorporated by Congress, *1949*
Pioneer Day (Utah), *2197*

Morocco
treaty with non-European nation, *2399*

Morris Shepard Federal Credit Union (Texarkana, Tex.)
federal credit union, *2123*

Mothers' Tree, *1220*

Motto of the United States, *3076*

mourning ribbons
to mark death of a president, *3524*

movies
senator to act in, *1800*
taken in Senate chambers, *1731*

"muckraker"
use of term, *3859*

muckraking
journal of importance, *3900*
journalists, *3890*
　woman who was, *3891*
novel of importance, *3892*

"mugwump"
use of term, *2932*

Mummers' play
featuring George Washington instead of St. George, *2185*

municipal courts
African-American women
　to be appointed judge, *1276*
　to be elected to judgeship, *1277*
judge who had served time in prison, *1278*
juvenile court, *1272*
night court, *1273*
small claims court, *1274*
woman to serve as justice of the peace, *1271*
women to serve as jurors, *1270*

municipal elections
African-American to hold elective office, *1279*
openly homosexual individual to run for public office, *1285*
openly homosexual politician to win, *1286*
results to be announced on radio, *1284*
secret ballot, *1280*
using preferential ballot system, *1282*
using proportional representation, *1283*
voting machines used in, *1281*

municipal government
city council composed entirely of Libertarian Party members, *1293*
city council with majority of Green Party members, *1294*
nationwide reform organization, *1292*
run by city manager, *1289*
use of word "caucus", *1287*
using commission plan, *1288*
using manager plan, *1290*
zoning ordinance, *1291*

municipal milk station, *4025*

municipal taxes
aviation tax, *4826*
single tax adopted by a city for local revenue purposes, *4825*

museums
devoted solely to American political memorabilia, *1069*

Muslim Americans
important weekly, *3926*

Muslims
mayor of American city, *1353*
to offer invocation to House of Representatives, *1578*
to offer invocation to Senate, *1753*

My Lai massacre
American military massacre of political importance, *2650*

N

National Academy of Sciences, *2071*

National Aeronautics and Space Administration (NASA), *2075*

National Archives and Records Administration
federal archiving agency, *2056*

National Archives Establishment
federal archiving agency, *2056*

National Association for the Advancement of Colored People (NAACP), *2847*

National Aviation Day, *2230*

National Banking System
Bank of North America, *2102*

national capital
See
Washington, D.C.

National Capital Planning Commission
park planning agency with oversight of capital city, *1895*

national cemeteries
act, *2667*
Arlington National Cemetery
　burial at Tomb of Unknown Soldier, *2670*

battle fought by federal troops after formation of the Union, *2736*

battle in "Frontier War", *2738*

capital to be located at Washington, DC, *1861*

character personifying United States, *1129*

claims by, for compensation for confiscated land, *2741*

colonial badges issued to friendly, *2726*

colonial law against "Indianizing", *2723*

confederation in what is now the U.S., *2721*

congressional agency to conduct negotiations with, *2730*

congressional protection of hunting grounds of, *2737*

court martial in a colony, *1444*

delegation to Continental Congress, *2731*

envoys received as guests of British crown, *2373*

federal law dissolving tribes as legal entities, *2749*

federal law regulating commerce with, *2735*

federal law returning autonomy to tribes, *2760*

federal law withdrawing recognition of tribal autonomy of, *2747*

formal appeal for recognition of, as U.S. citizens, *2750*

general, *2744*

government modeled on that of U.S., *2739*

Indian Affairs commissioner who was, *2746*

law by which, became American citizens, *2752*

law code compiled in North America, *2722*

law forbidding religious rituals of, *2725*

major defeat inflicted by, on regular U.S. Army troops, *2748*

map of British colonies showing lands of, *2729*

militant civil rights organization, *2756*

models of republican liberty, *1024*

monument to, *2718*

national organization of, *2754*

newspaper, *2740*

objects used as medium of exchange, *2141*

occupation of federal territory by, in modern era, *2755*

proposal to form state within the Union for, *2732*

reservation for, *2724*

reservation for, established by a state, *2727*

reservation for, established by federal government, *2734*

restoration of land to a tribe, *2757*

restriction by European colonial power on settlements in territory of, *2728*

school for children run by Bureau of Indian Affairs, *2743*

senator who was, *1779*

state denied admission to Union, *4304*

Supreme Court decision on criminal jurisdiction on reservations, *4721*

Supreme Court decision on status of tribes, *4719*

symbols adopted for political purposes by colonial Americans, *1130*

to become U.S. citizens, *2742*

to win territorial concessions from federal government, *2745*

treaties for postal routes through territory of, *3150*

treaties reviewed by Senate, *1674*

treaty between English settlers and, *2395*

treaty between U.S. and nation of, *2733*

treaty for which a president sought Senate's advice and consent in person, *2400*

treaty rejected by Senate, *2402*

tribal constitution, *2753*

tribe restored to federally recognized status after termination, *2759*

vaccination program by federal government to protect, against smallpox, *4015*

vice president who was, *4989*

Natural Law Party
presidential candidate, *3366*

naturalization law
colonial, *3100*
naturalization act enacted by Congress, *3101*

Naval Academy, U.S.
congressional representative who received Medal of Honor and was graduated from, *1612*

Naval Appropriations Act (1867)
federal law regulating campaign finances, *2782*

naval attaché, *2334*

Navigation Act, *4902*

Navy, department of, *2037*

Navy, U.S., *2691*
Admiral of, *2696*
military academy for naval officers, *2614*
national naval force, *2685*
naval war college, *2615*
president to conduct religious services as commander-in-chief of, *3734*
regulation barring African-Americans, *2693*
ship launched by, *2692*

Nepal
ambassador to, *2356*

neutrality
proclamation of U.S., in time of war, *2638*
regulation enacted by Congress that governed actions of citizens, *2249*

Nevada Day, *2200*

New Alliance Party
presidential candidate, *3362*

New Deal
Supreme Court decision striking down major piece of legislation of, *4728*

New Deal—*Continued*
use of term, *3075*

New Hampshire primary, *3204*

New Haven Colony
colonial governor of Connecticut, *1459*
Sabbath laws published by a colony, *1412*

New Jersey State Police
department to be monitored for racial profiling, *2549*

New Orleans, Battle of
Jackson Day, *2190*

New York Bar Association
state lawyers' society, *2583*

New York Board of Mediation and Arbitration, *2450*

New York Peace Society
pacifist society, *2810*

New York Police Department
bureau of criminal alien investigation, *2536*

New York State Commission Against Discrimination
state agency for enforcing equal treatment in employment, *2459*

New York State Trial Lawyers Association
woman elected president of state lawyers' association, *2593*

New York Stock Exchange
closing, *2138*

New York Times
issue of, *3923*

New York Tribune, The
edition of, *3922*

New York Women's State Temperance Society
state temperance society of women, *2856*

newspaper publishers
presidential elections in which candidates of both major parties were, *3210*

newspapers
See
magazines and newspapers; press, the
to publish Constitution, *1826*
to publish Declaration of Independence, *1059*

newspapers and periodicals
Native American, *2740*

Nicaragua
president of Central American country born in U.S., *2376*

Nigeria
protest against government of black African country by African-Americans, *2305*

night court, *1273*

no-fault car insurance
enacted by a state, *4059*

no-fault divorce law
enacted by a state, *3956*

Nobel Peace Prize
president to receive, *3626*
Secretary of State to receive, *1176*

"nobles of Niphon"
Japanese diplomatic delegation to U.S., *2258*

noise-control law
enacted by a state, *4169*

North American Air Defense Command (NORAD)
continental air defense alliance, *2607*

North American Party
presidential candidate, *3291*

North Atlantic Treaty Organization (NATO)
Cold War enemy of the U.S. to join, *2303*
peacetime alliance of European and North American nations, *2284*

nuclear arms limitation treaties
Intermediate-Range Nuclear Forces Treaty, *2427*
nonproliferation treaty for weapons of mass destruction, *2423*
not approved by Senate, *2426*
Nuclear Test Ban Treaty, *2421*

nuclear attack
federal government building to withstand, *2001*

nuclear energy
regulating agency of the industry, *4134*

nuclear testing
moratorium on, *2286*

nuclear war
confrontation, *2649*
political ad raising fear of, *2778*

nuclear waste
deep underground waste storage site, *4170*
large area of U.S. contaminated by radiation, *4165*

nuclear weapons
ban-the-bomb demonstrations, *2833*
live atomic bomb explosion shown on television, *3878*
payment by U.S. to foreign nation for destroying, *2302*

nullification, doctrine of
statement of, *4262*

Nullification Party
year in which Senate seats were won by third party, *1696*

Nullifiers
year in which House seats were won by third parties, *1557*

nurses
state licensing law for, *4026*

nutritional labeling
nationwide standards, *4037*

O

P

political radicals
national file on suspected, *2534*

political satire and history, *1072*
American woman, *1071*
comic, *1073*
reference book, *1075*
scholarly, *1074*

political science
national society, *3073*

politics and government
treatise on, *3069*

poll tax, *4789*
state to ratify 24th Amendment to Constitution, *1857*

pollution and waste
air pollution
control bureau, *4162*
law of importance enacted by Congress, *4166*
smoke control ordinance, *4161*
urban, survey of, *4160*
city to discontinue garbage collection, *4164*
deep underground nuclear waste storage site, *4170*
federal Superfund for cleaning up toxic wastes, *4128*
large area of U.S. contaminated by nuclear radiation, *4165*
noise-control law enacted by a state, *4169*
state bottle bill, *4167*
state litter law, *4168*
water pollution
law enacted by Congress, *4163*

polygamy
ban enacted by Congress, *3950*
church disincorporated by Congress, *1949*

Polynesian territory
of U.S. to adopt a constitution, *4848*

Poor Man's Party
presidential candidate, *3340*

popes
First Lady to be received by, *3614*
First Lady to have a private audience with, *3615*
president to meet with, in U.S., *3431*
to visit U.S., *2390*
to visit U.S. before his election, *2385*
to visit White House, *2392*

population
city with population of more than 1 million, *3079*
state with a population of more than 10 million, *3081*
state with a population of more than 5 million, *3080*
states with populations of more than 1 million, *3078*
year in which suburbanites outnumbered city and rural dwellers combined, *3083*

year when urban population of U.S. exceeded rural population, *3082*

population censuses
central statistical board, *3093*
compiled by machines, *3089*
compiled in part from statistics obtained by mail, *3096*
in which national population exceeded 10 million, *3085*
in which national population exceeded 150 million, *3094*
in which national population exceeded 200 million, *3095*
in which national population exceeded 50 million, *3088*
in which no slaves were counted, *3087*
in which the national population exceeded 100 million, *3092*
multiracial census category, *3098*
of Puerto Rico, *3090*
of U.S., *3084*
person to be counted in 2000 census, *3099*
that included deaf, mute, and blind people, *3086*
to count the homeless, *3097*

Populist Party, *2934*
political platform, *3054*
presidential candidate, *3312*

postage stamps
commemorative, depicting a First Lady, *3168*
depicting a president, *3164*
honoring a dead president, *3166*
issue depicting all the presidents, *3167*
issued by the Confederacy, *3165*

postal service
ban on African-Americans as mail carriers, *3149*
colonial law providing a fixed compensation for mail carriers, *3129*
colonial law regulating domestic transmission of official mail, *3128*
colonial post office established by law, *3127*
colonial postmaster, *3131*
Department, *3143*
express mail, *3153*
extension of mail service to West Coast, *3159*
federal monopoly on postal services, *3141*
federal post office built for the purpose, *3155*
foreign mail service of, *3145*
free mail delivery in cities, *3161*
independent postal service during the Revolution, *3137*
intercolonial postal system, *3132*
law enacted by Congress, *3146*
mail franking privilege, *3139*
mail fraud law enacted by Congress, *3162*

overland mail service between colonies, *3130*

post office building, *3157*

post office west of eastern seaboard, *3142*

post office west of Mississippi River, *3158*

postal rates after Revolution, *3140*

postmarked mail, *3134*

postmaster general of British colonies, *3135*

postmaster general of Confederate States of America, *3160*

postmaster general of English colonies, *3133*

postmaster general of U.S., *3144*

postmaster general to become member of presidential cabinet, *3156*

postmaster general under Continental Congress, *3138*

president to introduce spoils system into civil service, *2021*

revenue stamp printed by Post Office Department, *4817*

rural free mail delivery, *3163*

strike of, *2484*

transatlantic mail service, *3126*

treaties for postal routes through Native American territory, *3150*

use of, to generate revenue in wartime, *3151*

woman to serve as postmaster, *3136*

year in which gross revenue from postage exceeded $1,000,000, *3152*

year in which gross revenue from postage exceeded $100,000, *3147*

year in which number of letters carried by Post Office Department exceeded 1 million, *3148*

year in which number of letters carried by Post Office Department exceeded 10 million, *3154*

posters

campaign, showing candidate and his wife, *2800*

Powhatan confederacy

capital to be located at Washington, DC, *1861*

prayer

and meditation room of the Capitol, *1248*

Muslim to offer invocation to House of Representatives, *1578*

objection to opening congressional session with, *1042*

offered at session of colonial legislature, *1468*

offered at session of Continental Congress, *1043*

rabbi to open House of Representatives with, *1565*

preferential ballot system

election using, *1282*

presidency

important exercise of implied power of government, *1997*

state to ratify 20th Amendment to Constitution, *1851*

state to ratify 22nd Amendment to Constitution, *1855*

state to ratify 25th Amendment to Constitution, *1858*

test of presidential authority over cabinet secretaries, *1147*

presidency, U.S.

postage stamp depicting all the presidents, *3167*

postage stamp honoring a dead president, *3166*

presidential airplane, *3807*

presidential appointments

presidential appointment, *3769*

to be rejected, *3770*

woman appointed as chief White House counsel, *3782*

presidential campaigns

campaign medalets, *2793*

candidate to campaign throughout country, *2766*

candidate to make campaign speech, *2765*

candidate to make campaign speeches in foreign language, *2767*

candidate to run campaign by telephone, *2769*

income-tax checkoff to provide for financing of, *4823*

of modern type, *2763*

party endorsement of a presidential candidate, *2970*

political ad raising fear of nuclear war, *2778*

political buttons, *2792*

political snuffboxes, *2794*

scientific public opinion polls, *2773*

soft-sell nostalgia ads, *2779*

television ad saturation campaign, *2777*

presidential candidates

African-Americans, *3266*

vice presidential candidate, *3240*

vice presidential candidate in 20th century, *3260*

woman to run for president, *3268*

woman to run for vice president, *3263*

America First Party, *3335*

American Independent Party, *3353*

American Labor Party convention, *3342*

American National Party, *3303*

American Party, *3305*

American Prohibition Party, *3307*

Anti-Masonic Party, *3282*

Anti-Monopoly Party, *3306*

brothers nominated for the presidency at same convention, *3245*

brothers who were, simultaneously, *3226*

candidate for vice president who had been prisoner of war in Vietnam, *3278*

Church of God Party, *3341*

presents—*Continued*

born during administration of another president, *3461*

born in 19th century, *3463*

born in Iowa, *4613*

born in Kentucky, *4609*

born in Nebraska, *4617*

born in New Jersey, *4612*

born in North Carolina, *4604*

born in South Carolina, *4600*

born in Texas, *4616*

born in Vermont, *4610*

born west of Mississippi River, *3466*

buried in National Cemetery, *3533*

buried in Washington, DC, *3532*

candidate from Washington, DC, *1893*

capture of American president by enemy troops, *1390*

chief justice of Supreme Court to administer oath of office to, *4758*

chief justice of the Supreme Court who had served as, *4773*

child born in the White House to, *5030*

child of a president to serve in Senate, *1790*

children of

    to attend West Point, *3553*

    to be born in a foreign country, *3549*

    to decline nomination for the presidency, *3560*

    to die during his father's term in office, *3548*

    to die in combat, *3565*

    to serve in the armed forces, *3563*

coin bearing likeness of, *2164*

coin bearing likeness of living president, *2165*

congressional eulogy for, *3523*

convictions in Watergate case, *3517*

convictions in Whitewater case, *3521*

day on which, and vice president were both out of the country, *3800*

Democratic, whose party was in minority in both houses of Congress, *3718*

Democratic, whose party was in minority in House of Representatives, *3712*

Democratic, whose party was in minority in Senate, *3717*

Democratic presidential and vice presidential team to be reelected, *3415*

Democratic presidential and vice presidential team to lose bid for reelection, *3394*

during whose term more than five states were admitted to the Union, *3411*

elected after Civil War who had not served in it, *3409*

elected for third and fourth terms, *3421*

elected for two nonconsecutive terms, *3410*

elected from state west of Mississippi River, *3393*

estate to be opened to the public, *3404*

executive order to be numbered, *3406*

executive privilege

    president to invoke, *3391*

    statement of principle of, *3375*

former, to become chief justice of the Supreme Court, *3502*

former, to fly in airplane, *3792*

former, to head a university, *3482*

former, to run for reelection on different party's ticket, *3402*

former, to serve as official of an enemy government, *3492*

former, who was elected to House of Representatives, *3486*

former, whose death was officially ignored, *3529*

from Arkansas, *4620*

from California, *4614*

from Democratic Party, *3709*

from Democratic-Republican Party, *3708*

from Federalist Party, *3705*

from Georgia, *4619*

from Illinois, *4608*

from Indiana, *4611*

from Louisiana, *4605*

from Massachusetts, *4599*

from Michigan, *4618*

from Missouri, *4615*

from New Hampshire, *4606*

from New York State, *4602*

from Ohio, *4603*

from Pennsylvania, *4607*

from Republican Party, *3714*

from Southern state since the Civil War, *3429*

from Tennessee, *4601*

from Virginia, *4598*

from Whig Party, *3710*

from working class, *3458*

general to become, *3698*

honorary degree awarded to, *3624*

impeachments

    attempt to bring proceedings against a president, *3630*

    elected president to be impeached, *3632*

    president to be impeached, *3631*

in 20th century to receive medal for heroism, *3702*

in whose honor an asteroid was named, *3627*

inaugural addresses

    broadcast to a crowd with loudspeakers, *3671*

    inaugural address, *3633*

    president to deliver his address bareheaded, *3668*

    president whose address did not include word "I", *3669*

inaugural balls

    held at Washington, DC, *3647*

to visit West Coast of U.S. while in office, *3787*

to watch swearing-in ceremony of Supreme Court justice he appointed, *3424*

to wear a beard, *3828*

to witness firing of Polaris missile, *3838*

travel expenses for, *3743*

treaties withdrawn by a, after they were submitted to Senate, *2415*

tribute accorded by populace to a president-elect, *3625*

vice president to succeed to presidency after assassination of, *3408*

vice president to succeed to presidency after death of a president, *3397*

vice president to succeed to presidency after resignation of, *3436*

visit by, to country on U.S. list of terrorist states, *3816*

wedding of, in White House, *5027*

wedding of his daughter in the White House, *5015*

wedding of his son in White House, *5017*

who advocated physical fitness, *3830*

who became a nonagenarian, *3525*

who came to office through appointment rather than election, *3435*

who did not reside in state of his birth, *3462*

who had a stepmother, *3554*

who had been a Boy Scout, *3833*

who had been a cabinet member, *3476*

who had been a college professor, *3479*

who had been a medical student, *3477*

who had been a military pilot, *3700*

who had been a newspaper publisher, *3496*

who had been a schoolteacher, *3470*

who had been an engineer, *3498*

who had been an executioner, *3494*

who had been awarded Distinguished Flying Cross, *3628*

who had been defeated in earlier campaign for vice presidency, *3417*

who had been divorced, *3613*

who had been elected to Phi Beta Kappa, *3821*

who had been governor of a state, *3474*

who had been governor of a territory, *3483*

who had been president of union, *3503*

who had been president of university, *3499*

who had been professional actor, *3509*

who had been wounded in action during a war, *3693*

who had college experience as Senate staff member, *3505*

who had killed a man in a duel, *3825*

who had made transatlantic crossing, *3783*

who had neither military nor legal experience, *3493*

who had parachuted from airplane, *3808*

who had received patent, *3490*

who had served as a Navy pilot, *3701*

who had served as ambassador to United Nations, *3506*

who had served as chairman of his political party, *3507*

who had served as director of Central Intelligence Agency, *3508*

who had served as mayor of city, *3488*

who had served as minister to a foreign country, *3475*

who had served as secretary of state, *3478*

who had served as Senate majority leader, *3504*

who had served as vice president, *3381*

who had served in both House of Representatives and Senate, *3487*

who had served in Congress, *3472*

who had served in House of Representatives, *3480*

who had served in the Senate, *3481*

who had served in U.S. Navy, *3699*

who held a doctorate in a field other than law, *3497*

who learned reading and writing from his wife, *3826*

who narrowly escaped a fatal accident while in office, *3527*

who owned slaves, *3822*

who received a college education, *3819*

who served in more than one war, *3694*

who was a bachelor, *3586*

who was a former state governor and son of a state governor, *3552*

who was a Mason, *3818*

who was a widower when he took office, *3544*

who was admitted to the bar, *3471*

who was born after World War II, *3469*

who was born in 20th century, *3467*

who was born in a hospital, *3468*

who was defeated for reelection by his own vice president, *3384*

who was descendant of a signer of Declaration of Independence, *3550*

who was fluent in a foreign language, *3820*

who was graduate of United States Naval Academy, *3703*

who was married overseas, *3547*

who was older than 60 when he took office, *3382*

who was orphaned in childhood, *3542*

who was Rhodes Scholar, *3839*

who was son of a minister, *3562*

who was survived by his mother, *3528*

who was the child of divorced parents, *3564*

who was younger than 50 when he took office, *3401*

who was younger than his vice president, *3390*

who were cousins, *3558*

public defender
county, *1275*

Public Enemy Number 1, *2538*

public lands
Bureau of Mines, *4189*
expressions of official U.S. policy toward lands outside 13 colonies, *4173*
federal ban on fencing, *4186*
federal district land office, *4177*
grant-in-aid enacted by Congress to help states build roads, *4190*
grant of federal land to a foreigner, *4180*
homestead act for desert lands owned by federal government, *4183*
homestead grant under Homestead Act, *4182*
land preemption act passed by Congress, *4178*
land subsidy by Congress for road improvements, *4179*
land trust, *4187*
large-scale free land distribution by federal government, *4181*
Public Lands Commission, *4184*
rights of way on federal reserves, *4188*
sale of federal land, *4174*
sale of federal land to an individual, *4176*
state to declare sovereignty over large tract of federal land, *4283*
statewide land-use program, *4192*
survey of, *4175*
surveyed line separating North from South, *4172*
United States Geological Survey, *4185*

Public Lands Commission, *4184*

public libraries
established after Revolution, *1259*
federal aid to, *2068*
in American city, *1254*

public office
state test of religious qualifications for public office, *1946*

public opinion polls
opinion poll, *2762*
scientific, *2773*

public policy
sterilization of humans by state government as a matter of, *3952*

public religious displays
Supreme Court decision on constitutionality of, *4744*

public schools
property tax established by a colony to support, *4787*

public transportation
desegregation, *1919*

Public Works Administration
large-scale federal jobs-creation programs, *2468*

Puerto Ricans
congressional representative who was, *1620*

Puerto Rico
census of, *3090*

pure food and drug laws
established by Congress, *4016*
state law, *4021*

Puritans
ban on Jesuits, *1943*
law against celebration of Christmas, *2178*

Q

Quakers
ban on, *1945*
settlement to welcome refugees of all faiths, *1941*

Quanpen (Native American sachem)
court martial in a colony, *1444*

quarantine law
enacted by Congress, *4011*

quarters
U.S. coins depicting state symbols, *2176*

Quids political faction, *2909*

Quinnipiac Nation
reservation for Native Americans, *2724*

R

race riots
national, summer of, *2848*

racial discrimination
bias suit in which one African-American claimed, by another African-American, *1936*
federal law prohibiting, in housing, *4041*
in employment, federal attempt to address, *1927*
Jim Crow law, *1925*
state law prohibiting, against soldiers, *2657*
state to ratify 15th Amendment to Constitution, *1845*
Supreme Court decision barring racial segregation in housing, *4726*
Supreme Court decision upholding power of Congress to outlaw, in employment, *4736*

racial equality
affirmative action order issued by federal government, *1905*
federal civil rights agency, *1904*
Freedman's Bureau, *1920*
school desegregation lawsuit, *1918*
successful desegregation of public transportation, *1919*

year in which there were no reported lynchings of African-Americans, *1930*
   See also
   civil rights
   civil rights legislation

racial profiling
federal judge to reduce sentence as protest against, *1940*
state police department to be monitored for, *2549*

racial violence
compensation to victims of mass, *1938*

radiation
attacks against American embassy, *2294*

radiation experiments
on humans by federal government, *2073*
rules to prevent secret government-sponsored human experimentation, *2076*

radio
   See
   television and radio

Radio Commission of the United States, *3874*

Railroad Retirement Act (1935)
pension paid by federal government, *2471*

railroads
government operation of, *4097*
land-grant, *4087*
mediation agency for, and commercial aviation, *4099*
national, *4104*
operated by federal government, *4095*
safety law enacted by Congress, *4091*
state aid to, *4085*
state safety law, *4088*
to run trains to Washington, DC, *1883*
transcontinental, *4089*

RAND Corporation
Defense Department think tank, *2673*

Reconstruction Finance Corporation, *2093*

Records of the Federal Convention of 1787
edition of complete, *1833*

Red Cloud
Native American to win territorial concessions from federal government, *2745*

Red scare, *2828*

Reform Party
candidate to win a governorship, *4443*
presidential candidate, *3367*

reformatories
   See
   prisons and penitentiaries

Register of Debates in Congress
issue of, *1494*

Rehabilitation Act (1973)
civil rights law for disabled persons, *1907*

religion
presidents and

president-elect to attend religious service along with his staff, *3735*
president to become a full communicant of a church during his term in office, *3736*
president to conduct religious services as commander-in-chief of the Navy, *3734*
president who was Catholic, *3737*

religious displays
public, Supreme Court decision on constitutionality of, *4744*

religious freedom
toleration, *1418*
ban on Jesuits, *1943*
ban on Quakers, *1945*
church disincorporated by Congress, *1949*
document calling for religious toleration in America, *1942*
legal clash between evolutionists and creationists, *1950*
settlement to welcome refugees of all faiths, *1941*
state law mandating separation of church and state, *1948*
state test of religious qualifications for public office, *1946*
state to ban clergymen from serving in legislature, *1947*
toleration
   colonial charters, *1436, 1437*
toleration law enacted by a colony, *1944*

religious goods
state taxation of, *4834*

religious qualifications for public office
statute establishing, *1416*

Religious Toleration, Act of, *1436*

Republican Party
African-American congressman to deliver its official response to State of Union message, *1630*
African-American elected to national leadership post in, *2960*
African-American to actively campaign for presidential candidacy of, *3033*
credentials dispute, *2993*
credentials fight at convention that determined selection of candidate, *3000*
date on which the Senate was equally divided between Republicans and Democrats, *1718*
Democratic and Republican policy committees, *1743*
floor leader of Senate, *1736*
founding of, *2922*
governor of Arkansas since Reconstruction, *4513*
governor of Florida since Reconstruction, *4514*
governor of Oklahoma, *4512*

Republican Party—*Continued*

governor of Texas since Reconstruction, *4520*

governor of Virginia since Reconstruction, *4516*

national party convention to which general public was admitted, *2991*

negative election campaign run by media specialists, *2772*

political platform, *3039*

president from, *3714*

president to win reelection in 20th century, *3426*

president whose party was in minority in both houses of Congress, *3716*

president whose party was in minority in House of Representatives, *3715*

presidential and vice presidential team to be reelected, *3427*

presidential and vice presidential team to lose bid for reelection, *3418*

presidential candidate, *3292*

presidential candidate chosen unanimously on first ballot, *3239*

presidential candidate to be nominated on the first ballot, *3237*

presidential candidate to give his acceptance speech at national convention, *3020*

presidential candidate to win an election, *3238*

presidential election in which, earned significant number of votes in the South, *3216*

presidential election in which it participated, *3191*

presidential election won by, *3194*

professional political consultant to head major political party, *2968*

senator from North Carolina elected in 20th century, *1801*

showing, as an elephant, *3937*

symbol of, *2923*

televised debate among competitors for a party's presidential nomination, *2776*

vice president from, *5002*

Wide-Awakes of Hartford, *2801*

woman to serve as chairman of, *2967*

woman to serve as secretary of Republican National Convention, *3021*

year in which both major parties nominated incumbent governors for presidency, *2997*

year in which it controlled both houses of Congress, *1505*

year in which it won control of Senate, *1708*

year it renominated its entire ticket, *3005*

reservations

See

parks and reservations

retirees

national lobbying group for, *2834*

right-to-die laws

enacted by a state, *3958*

judicial decision allowing physicians to terminate life of terminally ill patients at their request, *3961*

permitting doctor-assisted suicide, *3960*

Right to Life Party, *2953*

presidential candidate, *3360*

Rio Treaty

regional agreement for collective defense under U.N. Charter signed by U.S., *2420*

roads and highways

federal agency, *4092*

federal highway, *4084*

grant-in-aid enacted by Congress to help states build, *4190*

land subsidy by Congress for improvement of, *4179*

nationwide planning surveys authorized by Congress, *4098*

road improvement aid bill enacted by a state, *4090*

speed limit for highway traffic established by Congress, *4105*

transcontinental highway, *4276*

Roanoke Island

English colonial settlement, *1397*

Roman Catholics

president who was, *3737*

presidential candidate from a major party who was, *3258*

presidential candidate who was, *3242*

state governor who was, *4470*

Supreme Court chief justice who was, *4767*

Romania

Cold War enemy of U.S. to join NATO, *2303*

rose garden

planted at White House, *5034*

Rumiantzof, Fort

Russian colonial settlement, *1429*

rural population

year in which suburbanites outnumbered city and rural dwellers conbined, *3083*

year when urban population of U.S. exceeded, *3082*

Rushmore, Mt.

monument to four presidents, *2714*

Russell Senate Office Building, *1241*

Russia

American citizen to become Russian official, *2306*

arms sales to, *2266*

S

Sabbath
    colonial law mandating observance of, *1406*
    laws published by a colony, *1412*
Saint Patrick's Day parade, *2181*
salaries
    of Congress
        annual, *1649*
        bonus paid to members of, by themselves, *1651*
        cut in, *1652*
        review committee for elected officials, *1656*
        setting pay rates for, *1647*
        year in which, exceeded $20,000 per year, *1655*
    of president
        president to receive annual salary of $100,000, *3745*
        president to receive annual salary of $200,000, *3748*
        president to receive annual salary of $75,000, *3744*
        raise in, *3742*
        salary established for president, *3738*
    of Supreme Court justices, *4690*
    of vice president
        raise in, *3741*
        salary established for vice president, *3739*
        vice president to receive salary of $30,000, *3746*
    presidential secretary to receive governmental, *3740*
    year in which salary of a Supreme Court justice topped $100,000, *4707*
salaries, wages, and hours
    federal law mandating 40-hour week, *2497*
    federal law mandating eight-hour workday, *2495*
    for consuls, *2330*
    minimum hourly wage of one dollar, *2499*
    minimum wage laws
        enacted by a state, *2496*
        enacted by Congress, *2498*
        established by city for public contract work, *2500*
    state law mandating a ten-hour workday, *2493*
sales taxes
    enacted by a state, *4831*
salmon fisheries
    federal act to protect, *4208*
San Francisco Conference
    United Nations conference, *2431*
San Jacinto Day, *2196*
Saratoga, Battle of, *1031*

savings and loan associations
    established by federal government, *2114*
    bailout, *2125*
school desegregation
    lawsuit, *1918*
    state law to end de facto segregation in schools, *1934*
school integration
    use of federal troops to enforce, *1931*
school prayer
    Supreme Court decision on, *4733*
school vouchers
    state to enact a plan, *3988*
    statewide program paid for with tax revenues, *3989*
science and technology
    aerospace agency of federal government, *2075*
    federal advisory board, *2072*
    federal agency to support civilian scientific research, *2074*
    national scientific advisory body, *2071*
    observatory established by federal government, *2070*
    radiation experiments on humans conducted by federal government, *2073*
    rules to prevent secret government-sponsored human experimentation, *2076*
Science and Technology Policy, Office of, *3778*
Scopes "Monkey Trial"
    legal clash between evolutionists and creationists, *1950*
seashore, national, *4155*
seat belts
    law enacted by a state, *4102*
secret ballot, *1280*
secret service
    established by federal government, *2580*
    established in a colony, *2579*
Secret Service, U.S.
    agent killed in line of duty, *2581*
    president protected by, *3413*
    protection for former presidents and their families, *3430*
    protection for major presidential and vice presidential candidates and nominees, *3269*
    women to become agents, *2582*
Secretary of Agriculture, U.S., *1165*
    African-American to serve as, *1210*
Secretary of Commerce, U.S., *1171*
    woman to serve as, *1199*
Secretary of Commerce and Labor, *1167*
Secretary of Defense, U.S., *1182*
Secretary of Education, *1203*
Secretary of Energy, U.S., *1201*
    woman to serve as, *1211*

Senate, U.S.—*Continued*

standing committee, *1677*

state to elect senators to, *4260*

Supreme Court justice who had served in, *4754*

telephone in, *1717*

treaties reviewed by, *1674*

unseated after recount, *1784*

use of its constitutional power to advise and consent, *1675*

use of shorthand in, *1702*

vice president to break tie vote in, *4961*

vice president who had served in, *4963*

vote on homosexual civil rights in, *1915*

who had served in both House of Representatives and, *3487*

woman to serve as presiding officer, *1742*

woman to testify as witness at a hearing, *1713*

year in which Democratic Party won control of Senate, *1695*

year in which Democratic-Republican Party won control, *1684*

year in which Federalist Party won control, *1678*

year in which Republican Party won control, *1708*

year in which seats were won by third party, *1696*

year in which Whig Party won control, *1699*

See also

Congress, U.S.

Sentencing Commission, U.S., *1991*

Sentencing Reform Act (1984), *1991*

"separate but equal"

school desegregation lawsuit, *1918*

Supreme Court decision validating provisions for African-Americans, *4724*

"separation of church and state"

state law mandating, *1948*

Sergeants at Arms

House of Representatives, *1543*

Senate, *1682*

use of, to make arrest, *1683*

senator to draw a gun on Senate, *1775*

Sesquicentennial half dollar (1926), *2165*

sewer system

city to build comprehensive, *4017*

sex discrimination

ban on, in hiring by federal government, *1967*

case to establish rights of fathers of newborns, *1969*

Congressional ban on, in wages, *1965*

federal law prohibiting, in employment, *1966*

state ban on, in employment, *1959*

sex scandals

involving congressional pages, *1646*

sexual harassment

lawsuit against a president, *3519*

Supreme Court nominee accused of, *4782*

Shawnee Nation

battle in "Frontier War", *2738*

Native American general, *2744*

Shays' Rebellion, *1994*

sheriff

woman, *2535*

shorthand

use of, in Senate, *1702*

shuttle diplomacy, *2292*

Siam

absolute monarch to visit U.S., *2384*

Sierra Club

national environmental organization, *2823*

signs and symbols

character symbolizing American people, *1132*

mace

colonial legislature to use, as symbol of authority, *1477*

colonial legislature's, still extant, *1479*

maces as, of royal authority, *1421*

Native American, adopted for political purposes by colonial Americans, *1130*

of Democratic Party, *2915*

of Republican Party, *2923*

public service symbol of federal government, *1135*

U.S. coins depicting state, *2176*

Uncle Sam

portrait to become famous, *1134*

use of term as reference to United States, *1131*

silver

demonetization, *2089*

mint, *2144*

minting act, *2143*

silver coins

act eliminating silver from most coinage, *2172*

issued by U.S. Mint, *2153*

Silver Republican Party

political platform, *3060*

presidential candidate, *3321*

silver standard

decimal system of money, *2147*

Silverite party

presidential candidate, *3315*

Single Tax League

national conference, *2821*

Single Tax Party

presidential candidate, *3328*

Single Tax principle

proponent of, *2819, 2820*

state constitutions—*Continued*

state courts

State Department, U.S.

state dinner

state education

state elections

status of Native American tribes, *4719*
upholding its authority to review state court decisions on appeal, *4715*
upholding power of Congress to outlaw racial discrimination in employment, *4736*
upholding right to parody public figures, *4742*
dissent, *4697*
filibuster against appointment to, by Senate, *1748*
former president to become chief justice of, *3502*
justices, *4696*
    born outside U.S., *4749*
    Jewish woman to serve as, *4783*
    nominee to be rejected by the Senate, *4752*
    residence in Washington, DC, *4698*
    salary of, *4690*
    to be appointed, confirmed, and inaugurated twice, *4775*
    to be appointed and confirmed as chief justice, *4771*
    to be impeached, *4764*
    to participate in a television program, *4780*
    to refuse elevation to post of chief justice, *4757*
    to resign, *4751*
    who had been a state governor, *4753*
    who had served as a federal judge, *4765*
    who had served as attorney general, *4768*
    who had served in executive branch, *4748*
    who had served in House of Representatives, *4759*
    who had served in presidential cabinet, *4761*
    who had served in Senate, *4754*
    who was African-American, *4779*
    who was Jewish, *4772*
    with no judicial or political experience, *4770*
    with university law degree, *4769*
    woman to become, *4781*
    woman to clerk for, *4777*
    year in which all were graduates of a law school, *4778*
lawyers admitted to practice, *2584*
Library of, *2063*
    librarian, *2065*
Marshal of, *4701*
meeting place of, *4693*
    in Washington, DC, *4699*
nominee accused of sexual harassment, *4782*
nominee to be rejected by Senate in the 20th century, *4776*
nominee to die before taking office, *4750*

nominee to testify before the Senate Judiciary Committee, *4774*
president to watch swearing-in ceremony of justice he appointed, *3424*
publication of, *4692*
recordings of proceedings released without the Court's approval, *4708*
reporter of decisions of, *4700*
ruling in a criminal case in which a U.S. president was named as a conspirator, *4741*
session of, *4694*
    held in its own building, *4704*
solicitor general, *4702*
    African-American attorney to serve as, *4705*
woman lawyer to practice before, *2590*
woman to preside over, *4784*
year in which salary of a justice topped $100,000, *4707*
Supreme Court justices
Cardozo, Benjamin Nathan, *1178*
chief justices
    to lie in state in the Capitol, *1246*
surgeon general, *4019*
who was African-American, *4040*
woman to serve as, *4039*
surrogate motherhood
ban on, enacted by a state, *3959*
Susan B. Anthony dollar, *2173*
sweatshops
city to ban, *2449*
swimming pool
in White House, *5037*
symbols
    See
    signs and symbols
synthetic fuels
commercial-scale plant owned by federal government, *4135*

T

Taft-Hartley Act
labor dispute in which, was invoked, *2483*
talkathons
political campaigns based on, *2775*
Tammany Day, *2179*
Tammany political club, *2902*
Taos Pueblo Indians
restoration of land to Native American tribe, *2757*
tariffs
commission established by Congress, *4950*
enacted by Congress to prevent importation of obscene literature and pictures, *4949*

U

use of name, instead of "United Colonies", *1064*

United States Board of Mediation and Conciliation, *2451*

United States Capitol police force
employees to unionize, *2492*

United States Employment Service
national employment system, *2467*

United States Mission to the United Nations, *2434*

United States Statutes at Large
edition of, *2521*

Unity **(sloop)**
naval battle of Revolutionary War, *1019*

UNIVAC
federal government office to be computerized, *2000*

University Microfilms (Ann Arbor, Mich.)
editions of federal publications and documents, *2057*

University of California at Berkeley
shutdown of college campus by student protesters, *2836*

unknown soldier
to lie in state in Capitol rotunda, *1244*

urban population
year when urban population of U.S. exceeded rural population, *3082*

urban renewal programs
Boston (Mass.), *1267*

Utah
church disincorporated by Congress, *1949*
Pioneer Day, *2197*

V

vaccination
law enacted by Congress, *4014*
program by federal government to protect Native Americans against smallpox, *4015*
state law, *4013*

Vatican
full diplomatic relations between U.S. and, in 20th century, *2297*

Vegetarian Party
presidential candidate, *3337*

vending machines
law enacted by a city, *4916*

Venezuela
coins minted for foreign government, *2163*

veterans
Bonus Army, *2829*
federal education grants to children of deceased, *3980*
national monument to, of Vietnam War, *2719*

veterans (military)
American Legion, *2702*
colonial law to aid disabled, *2697*
consolidated federal agency for veterans' affairs, *2703*
federal law providing for education of, *2704*
mass return of military decorations by, *2863*
military pension awarded to, *2698*
Revolutionary War national veterans' organization, *2699*
soldiers' homes established by Congress, *2700*
Veterans of Foreign Wars of the United States, *2701*

Veterans Administration
consolidated federal agency for veterans' affairs, *2703*
secretary of veterans affairs, *1208*

Veterans Affairs, U.S. Department of, *2053*

Veterans Day, *2224*

Veterans of Foreign Wars of the United States, *2701*

veto
See
presidential veto

vice presidential candidates
African-American candidate, *3240*
African-American candidate in 20th century, *3260*
African-American woman to run for, *3263*
candidate of major political party to resign before election, *3271*
candidate to decline the nomination, *3227*
from Arizona, *4658*
from Arkansas, *4645*
from California, *4644*
from Colorado, *4662*
from Connecticut, *4643*
from Delaware, *4627*
from Florida, *4661*
from Georgia, *4637*
from Idaho, *4659*
from Illinois, *4642*
from Indiana, *4635*
from Iowa, *4651*
from Kansas, *4640*
from Kentucky, *4632*
from Louisiana, *4654*
from Maine, *4636*
from Maryland, *4626*
from Massachusetts, *4625*
from Michigan, *4634*
from Minnesota, *4647*
from Mississippi, *4641*
from Missouri, *4639*
from Montana, *4655*
from Nebraska, *4650*
from Nevada, *4652*
from New Hampshire, *4622*
from New Jersey, *4628*

W

X

Y

Z

Index by Year

Following is a chronological listing of entries, arranged by year. To find an entry in the main body of the text, please search for the italicized indexing number.

1507

Use of "America" as a geographical designation, *1062*

1508

Capital of Puerto Rico, *4885*
European colonial settlement on Puerto Rico, *4886*

1521

Spanish colonial settlement, *1394*

1526

Escape of slaves from a colony in what is now United States territory, *4218*

1539

Armed conflict between Europeans and Native Americans on American soil, *2720*

1550

Confederation in what is now the United States, *2721*
Law code compiled in North America, *2722*

1562

French colonial settlement, *1395*

1565

Permanent Spanish colonial settlement, *1396*

1581

African slaves in America, *4219*

1585

English colonial settlement, *1397*
Letters written by an English colonial governor in America, *1398*

1598

Spanish governor-general of New Mexico, *1399*

1600

Capital to be located at the site of Washington, DC, *1861*

1606

English colonial charter, *1433*

1607

Colonial council, *1400*
Permanent English settlement, *1401*
Rebellion in a British colony, *1402*
Virginia colonial governor, *1452*

1608

Book describing the government of a British colony in America, *1070*

1610

Governor of the colony of Virginia, *1453*
Public building in the United States that has been continuously occupied, *1403*

1612

Colonial law banning "Indianizing", *2723*
Colony financed by a lottery, *1404*

1614

Dutch colonial settlement, *1405*

1619

Africans in the English colonies, *4220*
Colonial law mandating Sabbath observance, *1406*
Fines levied on colonial legislators for lateness or absence, *1467*
Prayer offered at a session of a colonial legislature, *1468*
Representative assembly in colonial America, *1469*

1620

Waterpower development grant to a colonist, *4193*

1621

Permanent Dutch colony, *1407*
Treaty between English settlers and a Native American tribe, *2395*

1622

African-American who was free, *4221*

495

1623

Alcohol temperance law enacted by a colony, *3942*

Colony to give its legislators immunity from arrest, *1470*

Liquor reform movement, *2853*

1624

Colonial court to hear testimony from an African-American, *1440*

Gambling law for ministers enacted by a colony, *3997*

New York colonial governor, *1454*

1625

Transatlantic mail service, *3126*

1626

Colonial forestry law, *4136*

1629

Hunting law enacted by a colony, *4200*

1630

Colonial gambling law for residents, *3998*

Document claiming a special spiritual mission for America, *3068*

Execution in America, *2550*

1631

Election held in a colony, *1447*

European to visit the future site of Washington, DC, *1862*

Governor of the Massachusetts Bay Colony, *1455*

Militia, *2662*

Voting requirements, *1446*

1632

British colony whose charter guaranteed representative government, *1434*

Maryland colonial governor, *1456*

Tobacco tax enacted by a colony, *4075*

1633

Town meeting, *1408*

1634

Board of selectmen, *1409*

Colonial ban on clergymen in the legislature, *1410*

Colonial treason trial, *1411*

Maryland Day, *2177*

Property tax levied by a colony, *4785*

1635

Grand jury, *1441*

Paper ballots, *1448*

Use of bullets as currency, *2141*

1636

Colonial law to aid disabled veterans, *2697*

Law code of an American colony, *1471*

Settlement to welcome refugees of all faiths, *1941*

Statement of the principle of taxation with consent, *4786*

1637

Draft law enacted by a colony, *2630*

Smoking ban enacted by a colony, *4076*

1638

Delaware colonial governor, *1457*

Military organization established by a colony, *2663*

Pay for colonial legislators, *1472*

Pennsylvania colonial governor, *1458*

Reservation for Native Americans, *2724*

Sabbath laws published by a colony, *1412*

1639

Colonial constitution, *1435*

Colonial governor of Connecticut, *1459*

Colonial post office established by law, *3127*

Colony to order surplus crops destroyed, *4108*

Medical regulations enacted by a colony, *4006*

Political document printed in America, *1063*

Property tax established by a colony to support public schools, *4787*

1640

Colonial election held in defiance of the Royal Courts, *1449*

Colonial trial for slander against the government, *1442*

1641

Chartered city in the United States, *1252*

Colony to legalize slavery, *4222*

Patent granted by a colony, *2595*

1642

City incorporated in the British colonies, *1253*

Colonial ban on convicts holding public office, *1413*

Compulsory education law in a colony, *3962*

Monetary regulation act, *2142*

1643

Confederation of English colonies, *1414*

Income tax levied by a colony, *4788*

Legal divorce in the American colonies, *3948*

1644

Colony with a bicameral legislature, *1473*

Contested election in a colonial legislature, *1450*
Document calling for religious toleration in America, *1942*
Law authorizing the penalty of death for blasphemy, *2551*
Treatise on politics and government, *3069*

1646

Law forbidding Native American religious rituals, *2725*
Poll tax, *4789*
Smoking ban in a colonial legislature, *1474*
Statement of legislative independence by a colony, *1415*

1647

Ban on Jesuits, *1943*
Colonial law requiring towns to hire teachers and construct schools, *3963*
Woman to appeal for the right to vote, *2892*

1648

Labor organization in a colony, *2874*
Law book of colonial laws, *2510*

1649

Colonial charter of religious freedom for Christians, *1436*
Colonial law to control corrupt election practices, *1451*
Religious toleration law enacted by a colony, *1944*

1652

Colony to pass a slavery emancipation law, *4223*
Mint, *2144*
Minting act, *2143*
Traffic law enacted by a colony, *4082*

1654

Colonial statute establishing religious qualifications for public office, *1416*
State toll bridge, *4083*

1656

Ban on Quakers, *1945*
Jury composed of women, *1443*

1657

Rhode Island colonial governor, *1460*

1659

Law against the celebration of Christmas, *2178*

1660

Navigation Act, *4902*

1661

Colonial badges issued to friendly Native Americans, *2726*
Colonial law regulating domestic transmission of official mail, *3128*
Colonial laws making slavery lifelong and hereditary, *4224*

1663

Colonial ban on lawyers in the legislature, *1475*
Colonial charter of religious freedom for all faiths, *1437*

1664

North Carolina colonial governor, *1461*

1665

Mayor of New York, NY, *1295*

1666

Colonial naturalization law, *3100*

1669

Rebellion by colonists against an English governor, *1417*
South Carolina colonial governor, *1462*

1672

Colonial copyright law, *2504*
Tax on Britain's American colonists imposed without their consent, *4790*

1673

Colonial governor who was born in America, *1463*
Colonial law providing a fixed compensation for mail carriers, *3129*
Overland mail service between colonies, *3130*
Revenue-collecting administration in the British colonies, *4791*

1674

Horse racing ban, *3999*

1676

Colonial law prohibiting slavery, *4225*
Court martial in a colony, *1444*
Government assistance to the family of an insane person, *4007*
Prison, *2570*
Thanksgiving proclamation, *2240*

1677

Colonial postmaster, *3131*

1680

New Jersey colonial governor, *1464*

1681

Colonial statute establishing religious toleration in public office, *1418*

1682

Colonial legislature whose upper and lower houses had terms of differing lengths, *1476*
Colony requiring rotation in public office, *1419*

1685

Judge to be impeached, *1445*

1687

Concealment of a colonial charter to prevent its revocation, *1438*
Inheritance tax levied by a colony, *4792*
Tax revolt, *4793*

1688

Protest against slavery made by a religious group in the New World, *4226*

1690

Newspaper suppressed by the government, *3903*
Paper money, *2145*
Political censorship of the press, *3847*

1691

Colonist hanged for treason, *2552*
Mayor of Philadelphia, PA, *1296*

1692

Intercolonial postal system, *3132*
Postmaster general of the English colonies, *3133*

1693

Postmarked mail, *3134*
Trial of a printer for sedition, *3848*

1695

Workers' compensation agreement, *2501*

1698

Colonial legislature to use a mace as a symbol of authority, *1477*
Statehouse, *4307*

1699

French governor of the Louisiana Territory, *1420*

1700

Essay calling for the abolition of slavery to be published in the British colonies, *4227*

Public library in an American city, *1254*

1701

Colony to change from a bicameral to a unicameral legislature, *1478*

1704

Newspaper published with government approval, *3904*

1707

Postmaster general of the British colonies, *3135*

1708

Rebellion of African-American slaves in a British colony, *4228*

1710

Native American envoys received as guests of the British crown, *2373*

1712

Law barring the importation of slaves into a British colony, *4229*

1715

English patent granted to a resident of America, *2596*

1717

Document expressing American democratic ideals, *3070*

1721

Editorial retraction of false political news, *3905*
Political crusade by a newspaper, *3849*

1725

Maces as symbols of royal authority, *1421*

1729

Antislavery book, *4230*

1730

Mason known to hold high government office in the colonies, *1422*

1732

Tammany Day, *2179*

1733

Colonial governor of Georgia, *1465*
Georgia Day, *2180*

Political newspaper, *3906*

1734

Fish protection law enacted by a city, *4201*

1735

Legal precedent for freedom of the press, *3850*

1736

Mayor of Norfolk, VA, *1297*

1738

Town built by free African-Americans, *1255*

1741

Political magazine, *3895*

1747

Political cartoon, *3927*
State lawyers' society, *2583*

1751

Casting of the Liberty Bell, *1108*

1753

Arbitration law enacted by a colony, *4943*
President who was a Mason, *3818*

1754

Colonial congress, *1423*
Plan for the union of the British colonies, *1001*
Political cartoon published in an American newspaper, *3928*

1755

Law instruction at a college, *2523*
Patriotic song to achieve popularity during the Revolution, *1113*
President who had been a schoolteacher, *3470*
President who received a college education, *3819*
Stamp tax, *4794*

1756

Colonial legislature's mace still extant, *1479*
Woman whose vote was recorded, *1951*

1757

Campaign expenditure of record, *2780*
Tolling of the Liberty Bell for an event of political importance, *1109*

1758

President who was admitted to the bar, *3471*

Regulation allowing newspapers to be sent through the mails, *3907*
Reservation for Native Americans established by a state, *2727*

1759

First Lady, *3573*

1760

Medical licensing law enacted by a city, *4008*

1762

Saint Patrick's Day parade, *2181*

1763

Local political machine, *2901*
Restriction by a European colonial power on settlements in Native American territory, *2728*
Strike of African-American laborers, *2875*
Use of the word "caucus", *1287*

1764

Colonial boycott of British goods, *1003*
Committee of correspondence formed in a British colony in America, *1002*
Public figure lampooned in political cartoons, *3929*

1765

Direct tax on Britain's American colonists without their consent, *1005*
Local government to refuse to obey the Stamp Act, *1006*
Orator of the Revolution, *1004*

1766

Spanish governor of the Louisiana Territory, *1424*

1767

First Lady who was the mother of a president, *3574*
President from the working class, *3458*
Spanish governor of California, *1425*
Surveyed line separating North from South, *4172*

1768

City to be occupied by the British before the Revolution, *1007*
Independent civil government in America, *1426*
Patriotic song by an American, *1114*
Persecution of a newspaper editor by American revolutionaries, *3851*

1770

Americans killed by British soldiers in the Revolution, *1009*

1770—*continued*

Attack on British soldiers by civilians in the Revolution, *1008*

Chamber of Commerce, *4903*

Political cartoon to interfere with a trial, *3930*

1771

Commemoration of the Boston Massacre, *2182*

Map of the British colonies showing Native American lands, *2729*

Town named for George Washington, *1256*

1772

Medical licensing law enacted by a colony, *4009*

Tammany political club, *2902*

Written constitution adopted by a community of American-born freemen, *1439*

1773

American woman to write political satire and history, *1071*

Destruction of British tea shipments, *1011*

Protest against British taxation of tea shipments, *1010*

1774

Association of British colonies in America, *1012*

Attack against the British by a state militia, *1013*

Call for a congress of the American colonies, *1037*

Chaplain of the Continental Congress, *1041*

Character personifying the United States, *1129*

Declaration of independence by citizens of an American colony, *1050*

Declaration of rights, *1051*

Embargo act of the Continental Congress, *4904*

Major action taken by the Continental Congress, *1044*

Objection to opening a congressional session with prayer, *1042*

Political satire, *1072*

Prayer offered at a session of Congress, *1043*

President of the Continental Congress, *1038*

President who had served in Congress, *3472*

Seat of the Continental Congress, *1039*

Session of the Continental Congress, *1040*

Vice president who had served in the Continental Congress, *4957*

1775

Abolition organization, *4231*

Army of the United States, *2621*

Call for troops to fight in the Revolutionary War, *1018*

Clash of arms in the Revolutionary War, *1015*

Commandant of marines, *2661*

Commander-in-chief of the Continental Navy, *2688*

Congressional agency to conduct negotiations with Native Americans, *2730*

Continental money, *2146*

First Lady who was educated at a school, *3575*

First Lady who was not born in the United States, *3576*

Foreign service committee, *2309*

Free trade policy by the federal government, *4946*

General of the Continental Army, *2622*

Independent postal service during the Revolution, *3137*

Jewish person elected to a public office in the New World, *1427*

Mail franking privilege, *3139*

Major battle of the Revolutionary War, *1020*

Massachusetts constitution, *4359*

Mobilization of American troops in the Revolutionary War, *1017*

National naval force, *2685*

Native American symbols adopted for political purposes by colonial Americans, *1130*

Naval battle in the Revolutionary War, *1019*

New Hampshire constitution, *4367*

New Hampshire state governor, *4444*

Postmaster general under the Continental Congress, *3138*

Proclamation of the unification of the colonies, *1052*

Reconciliation plan to end the rebellion of the British colonies in America, *1014*

Royal proclamation declaring Britain's colonies in America to be in open rebellion, *1021*

Ship commissioned by the Continental Navy, *2687*

Tolling of the Liberty Bell to announce a battle, *1110*

Treasurer of the United States, *2077*

United States Marines, *2660*

War hero, *1016*

Woman to serve as a postmaster, *3136*

1776

American executed as a spy, *1028*

American flag saluted by a foreigner, *1077*

American prisoners of war, *1022*

Artist's design for the Great Seal of the United States, *1105*

Bill of Rights, *1821*

Colonial government to instruct its delegates to the Continental Congress to proclaim independence, *1054*

Colony to declare its independence, *1023*

Congressional vote on a declaration of independence, *1056*

Connecticut state governor, *4445*

Declaration of independence by a British colony, *1053*
Delaware constitution, *4363*
Execution by the Army, *2553*
Flag flown by the Continental Army under Commander-in-Chief George Washington, *1076*
Foreign loan to the Continental Congress, *2078*
Georgia state governor, *4446*
Halifax Resolutions Day, *2183*
Independent government in an American colony, *1428*
Major battle lost by American forces, *1026*
Maryland constitution, *4365*
Medal awarded by the Continental Congress, *1045*
Military pension awarded to a woman, *2698*
Models of republican liberty, *1024*
Native American delegation to the Continental Congress, *2731*
New Hampshire constitution, *4367*
New Jersey constitution, *4362*
New Jersey state governor, *4447*
Newspaper to publish the Declaration of Independence, *1059*
North Carolina constitution, *4366*
North Carolina state governor, *4448*
Peace conference during the American Revolution, *1027*
Pennsylvania constitution, *4364*
Pension law enacted by Congress, *2470*
President to have written a book, *3473*
President who had been wounded in action during a war, *3693*
Price regulation law enacted by a colony, *4951*
Printing of the Declaration of Independence, *1058*
Proposals for the design of the Great Seal of the United States, *1104*
Public call for independence to be published, *1025*
Public celebration of national independence, *2236*
Public reading of the Declaration of Independence, *1060*
Publication of the Declaration of Independence in another language, *1061*
Signer of the Declaration of Independence, *1057*
South Carolina constitution, *4360*
State legislature with a lower house known as the House of Representatives, *4539*
State legislature with an upper house known as the Senate, *4541*
State test of religious qualifications for public office, *1946*
State to ban clergymen from serving in the legislature, *1947*
State to enact a conflict-of-interest law concerning its legislature, *4536*

State to give its legislature sole power to determine the eligibility of legislators, *4537*
State to grant limited voting rights to women, *1952*
State to set an age qualification for state senators, *4540*
State with a unicameral legislature, *4538*
Statement of the principle of inalienable rights, *1055*
Traitor to the American cause during the Revolutionary War, *1029*
Use of the name "United States" instead of "United Colonies", *1064*
Virginia constitution, *4361*
Virginia state governor, *4449*
Warship named for a First Lady, *3577*

1777

American flag displayed on a warship, *1079*
American flag flown in battle, *1080*
American flag flown on the high seas, *1081*
American flag saluted by a foreign nation, *1082*
Foreign officers recruited to the cause of the American Revolution, *1030*
Framework for a national government, *1032*
Georgia constitution, *4368*
Independence Day, *2184*
Lottery held by the Continental Congress, *1046*
Major American victory in the Revolutionary War, *1031*
Maryland state governor, *4450*
Military academy established by the federal government, *2613*
National day of thanksgiving, *2241*
National flag to represent the United States, *1078*
New York State constitution, *4369*
New York state governor, *4451*
State constitution to provide for emancipation from slavery, *4232*
State income tax, *4827*
State to abolish the laws of entail and primogeniture, *2511*
State to grant universal voting rights to freemen, *4423*
Treaty between states after the Declaration of Independence, *4257*
Vermont constitution, *4370*

1778

Alliance between the United States and another country, *2243*
Arbitration law enacted by a state, *4944*
Constitutional convention of a popular character, *4371*
Foreign nation to recognize the independence of the United States, *2244*
Governor of the republic of Vermont, *1466*
Minister plenipotentiary, *2312*
Patriotic war song by an American, *1115*

1778—*continued*

President who had made a transatlantic crossing, *3783*

Proposal to form a Native American state within the Union, *2732*

Representative of a foreign country to the United States, *2311*

Secret service established in a colony, *2579*

State to ratify the Articles of Confederation, *1033*

State to remove property ownership as a qualification for voting rights, *4424*

Treaties entered into by the federal government, *2396*

Treaty between the United States and a Native American nation, *2733*

U.S. consular post, *2310*

Vermont state governor, *4452*

1779

American general to engage in treason, *1034*

Congressional resolution on taxation to finance a war, *4795*

Law school at a college, *2524*

Medal awarded by the Continental Congress to a foreigner, *1047*

Naval hero, *1035*

President who had been governor of a state, *3474*

South Carolina state governor, *4453*

State constitution to be submitted to the people for ratification, *4372*

Vice president who had been governor of a state, *4958*

1780

Conscientious objectors, *2631*

Consul to die in service, *2313*

Massachusetts state governor, *4454*

President who had served as minister to a foreign country, *3475*

Proposal for a presidential cabinet, *1136*

Proposals for the organization of the executive branch, *1993*

State seal, *4258*

Town to be incorporated under the name of Washington, *1257*

Vice president who had served as minister to a foreign country, *4959*

1781

Broker to the Office of Finance of the United States, *2079*

Congress to call itself "The United States in Congress Assembled", *1048*

Independence Day to be observed as a state holiday, *2237*

Location of the national Department of Foreign Affairs, *2314*

President of the United States under the Articles of Confederation, *3370*

President who was fluent in a foreign language, *3820*

President who was orphaned in childhood, *3542*

President whose father was a state governor, *3543*

Private bank chartered by Congress, *2102*

Secretary of foreign affairs, *2315*

Superintendent of finance under the Continental Congress, *2080*

1782

Design for the Great Seal of the United States that was accepted, *1106*

Impression made by the Great Seal of the United States, *1107*

Postal rates after the Revolution, *3140*

President born an American citizen, *3459*

President who was a widower when he took office, *3544*

President whose ancestry was not British, *3460*

President's wife to die before he took office, *3578*

President's wife to die before he was elected to office, *3579*

1783

College named after George Washington, *3964*

First Lady who was born an American citizen, *3580*

Map of the United States, *1065*

Proposal for a national capital, *1863*

Revolutionary War national veterans' organization, *2699*

Salute fired by Great Britain in honor of an officer of the United States, *2245*

State copyright law, *2505*

State to abolish slavery by a decision of the judiciary, *4233*

Territory owned by the federal government, *4835*

Treaty between the federal government and a nation with which it had been at war, *2397*

1784

Expressions of official U.S. policy toward lands outside the 13 colonies, *4173*

Labor union to nominate its own political candidates, *2485*

Map to show the American flag, *1083*

Political economy course at a college, *3062*

Russian colonial settlement, *1429*

State denied admission into the Union, *4290*

1785

Decimal system of money, *2147*

Land set-aside for schools authorized by the Continental Congress, *3965*

1789—*continued*

Diplomatic Service of the United States, *2319*

Drawback legislation enacted by Congress, *4905*

Entry in *Journal of the House of Representatives of the United States*, *1532*

Entry in the *Journal of the Executive Proceedings of the Senate of the United States of America*, *1673*

Executive department authorized by Congress, *2033*

Federalist Party, *2904*

Form of the enacting clause used in congressional bills, *1485*

Gavel used in the Senate, *1663*

Honorary degree awarded to a president, *3624*

House of Representatives election that was contested, *1539*

House Ways and Means Committee, *1544*

Inaugural address, *3633*

Inaugural ball, *3641*

Inaugural chintzes, *3634*

Inaugural tankards, *3635*

Insurance law treatise, *2512*

Joint committee of the House and Senate, *1481*

Joint meeting of the Senate and the House of Representatives, *1812*

Joint rule of both houses of Congress, *1482*

Law report, *2513*

Law setting pay rates for Congress, *1647*

Loan to the United States, *2082*

Mace of the House of Representatives, *1529*

Meeting place of Congress, *1480*

Method of choosing standing committees in the Senate, *1667*

North Carolina state capital, *4319*

Oath of office for members of Congress, *1530*

Object from the early House of Representatives still in use, *1531*

Party tactics in Congress, *1487*

Pensions paid by the federal government, *2471*

Political buttons, *2792*

Political cartoon lampooning President George Washington, *3931*

Political newspaper of national importance, *3908*

Post Office Department, *3143*

Postmaster general of the United States, *3144*

President from the Federalist Party, *3705*

President from Virginia, *4598*

President inaugurated in New York City, *3636*

President of the Senate, *1669*

President of the United States elected under the Constitution, *3371*

President to be inaugurated after his vice president, *3637*

President to receive the unanimous vote of the presidential electors, *3171*

President to run afoul of the law, *3515*

President to tour the country, *3784*

President to visit the Senate while it was in session, *3510*

President who owned slaves, *3822*

President whose mother was alive when he was inaugurated, *3638*

Presidential appointment, *3769*

Presidential appointment to be rejected, *3770*

Presidential candidate from Connecticut, *4559*

Presidential candidate from Maryland, *4560*

Presidential candidate from Pennsylvania, *4561*

Presidential candidate from South Carolina, *4562*

Presidential candidate from Virginia, *4566*

Presidential candidates from Georgia, *4563*

Presidential candidates from Massachusetts, *4564*

Presidential candidates from New York State, *4565*

Presidential election won by the Federalist Party, *3172*

Presidential inauguration, *3639*

Presidential mansion, *5003*

Quorum of the House of Representatives, *1535*

Quorum of the Senate, *1664*

Religious service held as part of a presidential inauguration, *3640*

Response by the House of Representatives to an inaugural address, *1542*

Response of the Senate to an inaugural address, *1671*

Salary established for the president, *3738*

Salary established for the vice president, *3739*

Salary of Supreme Court justices, *4690*

Secretary of a federal executive department to take orders from Congress, *2036*

Secretary of the treasury, *1138*

Select committee appointed by the House of Representatives, *1538*

Select committee appointed by the Senate, *1676*

Senate doorkeeper, *1666*

Senate journal, *1661*

Senate president pro tempore, *1665*

Senate rules of procedure, *1668*

Senate's use of its constitutional power to advise and consent, *1675*

Sergeant at Arms of the House of Representatives, *1543*

Session of Congress under the Constitution, *1811*

Session of the House of Representatives, *1533*

Session of the Senate, *1662*

Speaker of the House, *1631*

Standing committee of the House of Representatives that is still operating, *1540*

Standing committee of the Senate, *1677*

Standing rules adopted by the House of Representatives, *1537*

State to ratify the Bill of Rights, *1835*

State university, *3966*

Supreme Court justice who had served in the executive branch, *4748*
Supreme Court of the United States, *4691*
Tariff legislation enacted by Congress, *4947*
Tax passed by Congress, *4796*
Temperance movement, *2854*
Title formally proposed for the chief executive of the United States, *3372*
Travel expenses for members of Congress, *1648*
Treaties reviewed by the Senate, *1674*
Treaty for which a president sought the Senate's advice and consent in person, *2400*
Tribute accorded by the populace to a president-elect, *3625*
Vice president from Massachusetts, *4664*
Vice president from the Federalist Party, *4998*
Vice president to break a tie vote in the Senate, *4961*
Vice president who had served in the House of Representatives, *4960*

1790

Address to a president by a Jewish congregation, *3750*
Annual message, *3749*
Attorney general, *1139*
Battle fought by federal troops after the formation of the Union, *2736*
Bonds issued by the federal government, *2117*
Census of the population of the United States, *3084*
Clerk of the Supreme Court, *4695*
Coast guard service, *2689*
Congressional representative to die, *1585*
Consuls appointed after the adoption of the Constitution, *2320*
Copyright law enacted by Congress, *2506*
Federal law regulating commerce with Native Americans, *2735*
Federal refunding act, *2083*
Governor of the Southwest Territory (Tennessee), *4851*
House of Representatives filibuster, *1547*
Instance of congressional "log-rolling" (vote-trading), *1548*
Lawyers admitted to practice before the Supreme Court, *2584*
Meeting place of Congress that is still in existence, *1490*
Meeting place of the Supreme Court, *4693*
Naturalization act enacted by Congress, *3101*
Newspapers provided to senators and representatives, *3909*
Patent granted by the federal government, *2598*
Patent law passed by Congress, *2597*
Pennsylvania state governor, *4456*
Political newspaper to carry partisanship to extremes, *3852*

President born during the administration of another president, *3461*
President who had been a cabinet member, *3476*
Publication of Supreme Court decisions, *4692*
Response by the House of Representatives to a president's State of the Union message, *1546*
Rhode Island constitution, *4374*
Rhode Island state capitals, *4320*
Secretary of state, *1140*
Secretary of war, *1141*
Senator appointed by a governor, *1756*
Session of Congress to meet in Philadelphia, *1813*
Session of the Supreme Court, *4694*
Supreme Court justices born outside the United States, *4749*
Supreme Court nominee to die before taking office, *4750*
Vice president who had served in a presidential cabinet, *4962*
Vote to establish Washington, DC, *1865*
Year in which the Federalist Party won control of both houses of Congress, *1489*
Year in which the Federalist Party won control of the House of Representatives, *1545*
Year in which the Federalist Party won control of the Senate, *1678*

1791

Bank of the United States, *2103*
Birthday visit made to a president by the entire Senate, *1679*
British ambassador to the United States, *2247*
Cabinet meeting, *1143*
Conflict-of-interest case involving a journalist, *3885*
Congressional representative who was Jewish, *1586*
Constitutional amendment, *1836*
Corporate body chartered by a special act of Congress, *4906*
Democratic-Republican (Jeffersonian) political newspaper, *3910*
Design for the Washington Monument, *2705*
Design for Washington, DC, *1868*
Difference of opinion among members of the cabinet, *1142*
Federal charter, *1995*
Federal report on exports, *4907*
First Lady who had previously been divorced, *3581*
Industrial report to Congress, *4908*
Internal revenue tax levied by Congress, *4797*
Kentucky state governor, *4457*
Law book containing laws enacted by more than one session of Congress, *2514*
Law book of federal laws, *2515*
Location of the Bank of the United States, *2104*

1791—*continued*

President to dispatch a personal envoy on an overseas mission, *2246*

President to govern more than the original 13 states, *3374*

President who had been a medical student, *3477*

President whose party was in the minority in the House of Representatives, *3706*

Presidential proclamation, *3373*

Proposal for a national monument to George Washington, *2706*

Sale of building lots in Washington, DC, *1869*

Special session of the Senate, *1680*

State admitted to the Union after the ratification of the Constitution, *4291*

State of the Union that was formerly an independent republic, *4292*

State to cede land to the federal government, *1866*

Statement of the principle of due process, *1837*

Supreme Court justice to resign, *4751*

Treaty approved by the Senate that was held up for lack of funding, *2401*

Use of the name "District of Columbia" and "Washington" for the federal city, *1867*

Vermont state capital, *4321*

Vice president who had served in the Senate, *4963*

1792

Adoption of the dollar as the standard monetary unit, *2150*

Appeal from the justices of the Supreme Court to end circuit riding, *4696*

Authorized plan of the City of Washington, DC, *1870*

Book advocating voting rights for women, *2893*

Building erected in Washington, DC, by the federal government, *1872*

Ceremony at the White House, *5005*

Coalition between Northern and Southern politicians, *2905*

College in Washington, DC, *1871*

Columbus Day, *2189*

Congressional apportionment of representatives, *1550*

Congressional investigation, *1491*

Consular Service of the United States, *2322*

Delaware state governor, *4458*

Democratic-Republican Party, *2906*

Designs for the building of the Capitol, *1215*

Designs for the building of the White House, *5004*

Draft of civilians by Congress, *2632*

Federal building erected for public use, *1996*

Federal revenue commissioner, *4798*

Foreign mail service of the United States Post Office, *3145*

Free newspaper exchange between publishers, *3911*

Gold price fixed by Congress, *2084*

Kentucky constitution, *4375*

Kentucky state capital, *4322*

Law establishing presidential succession, *3376*

Minister plenipotentiary to Great Britain, *2321*

Mint of the United States, *2151*

Party endorsement of a presidential candidate, *2970*

Postal service law enacted by Congress, *3146*

President to be reelected, *3377*

President to be stung by press criticism, *3722*

Presidential election in which a candidate was endorsed by a political party, *3173*

Presidential veto of a congressional bill, *3843*

State founded within the borders of an existing state, *4293*

Statehood Day (Kentucky), *2188*

Statement of the principle of executive privilege, *3375*

Supreme Court decision to be recorded, *4709*

Supreme Court dissent, *4697*

Vice president to be reelected, *4964*

Year in which the Democratic-Republican Party won control of the House of Representatives, *1549*

1793

Anti-American satirical medalets, *2248*

Architect of the Capitol, *1216*

Ceremony at the Capitol, *1219*

Coins made by the U.S. Mint, *2152*

Dome on the Capitol, *1217*

Fugitive slave law enacted by Congress, *4238*

Nominee for associate justice of the Supreme Court to be rejected by the Senate, *4752*

President inaugurated in Philadelphia, *3642*

Proclamation of U.S. neutrality in time of war, *2638*

Regular cabinet meetings, *1145*

Senate election that was contested, *1757*

Superintendent of construction of the Capitol, *1218*

Supreme Court decision to be overridden by an amendment to the Constitution, *4710*

Supreme Court justice who had been a state governor, *4753*

Supreme Court justice who had served in the Senate, *4754*

Use of the term "cabinet", *1144*

Year in which gross revenue from postage exceeded $100,000, *3147*

1794

Arsenal of the federal government, *2604*

Changes in the American flag to be authorized by Congress, *1085*

Extradition treaty with a foreign country, *2403*

Neutrality regulation enacted by Congress that governed the actions of citizens, 2249

Presidential commission, 3771

Ship constructed by the federal government, 2690

Silver coins issued by the Mint, 2153

State to ban the death penalty, 2554

State to ratify the Eleventh Amendment to the Constitution, 1838

Tax rebellion against the federal government, 4799

Tobacco tax enacted by Congress, 4077

Treaty rejected by the Senate, 2402

United States Navy, 2691

1795

Cabinet member to serve in two or more cabinet posts, 1146

Federal government employees who were women, 2020

Gold coins issued by the Mint, 2154

Nominee for chief justice of the Supreme Court to be rejected by the Senate, 4756

Presidential amnesty issued to rebellious citizens, 3378

Return of coins to the Treasury, 2155

Senate proceedings that were open to the public, 1681

Supreme Court chief justice to resign, 4755

Year in which the number of letters carried by the Post Office Department exceeded 1 million, 3148

1796

American passport, 2250

Associate Supreme Court justice to refuse elevation to the post of chief justice, 4757

Block of buildings constructed in Washington, DC, 1873

Brothers who were candidates for the presidency simultaneously, 3226

Campaign medalets, 2793

Congressional protection of Native American hunting grounds, 2737

Democratic-Republican presidential candidate, 3280

Electoral vote cast contrary to instructions, 3174

Farewell address by a president, 3751

Federal law exempting debtors from prison, 2571

Federalist Party presidential candidate, 3281

Incumbent president to decline to run for re-election, 3379

Isolationist address by a president, 2251

Political party to hold a secret presidential nominating caucus, 2971

President whose political party was not the same as the vice president's, 3707

Presidential candidates from North Carolina, 4567

Presidential election in which more than one candidate declared for the presidency, 3176

Presidential election in which the Democratic-Republican Party participated, 3175

Presidential portrait of importance, 3536

Presidential warning against party politics, 2907

Sale of federal land to an individual, 4176

Senators elected but not seated, 1758

Supreme Court case challenging the validity of an act of Congress, 4711

Tennessee constitution, 4376

Tennessee state capital, 4323

Tennessee state governor, 4459

Vice president from the Democratic-Republican Party, 4999

1797

Chief justice of the Supreme Court to administer the oath of office to a president, 4758

Congressional representative to serve before his 25th birthday, 1587

First Lady who was the daughter of a minister, 3582

Petition to Congress by African-Americans, 4239

President from Massachusetts, 4599

President to have children, 3545

President to serve two full terms, 3380

President who had served as vice president, 3381

President who was married overseas, 3547

President who was older than 60 when he took office, 3382

President who was sworn in by the chief justice of the Supreme Court, 3643

President whose son became president, 3546

Ship launched by the United States Navy, 2692

Special session of Congress, 1814

Test of presidential authority over the cabinet secretaries, 1147

Vice president from Virginia, 4665

Vice president to announce his own election as president, 4965

1798

Brawl in the House of Representatives, 1551

Constitutional amendment enacted after the passage of the Bill of Rights, 1839

Department of the Navy, 2037

Deportation of aliens authorized by Congress, 3102

Direct tax levied by Congress, 4800

Federal immigration law requiring the collection of information on aliens, 3103

Federal law intended to intimidate the press, 3853

Health service established by the federal government, 4010

1798—*continued*

Mayor of Augusta, GA, *1299*

Mayor of Schenectady, NY, *1298*

Military department of the federal government, *2605*

Mississippi territorial governor, *4852*

Navy regulation barring African-Americans, *2693*

Patriotic song to achieve national popularity, *1116*

Prosecution under the Sedition Act, *3854*

Secretary of the navy, *1148*

Sergeant at arms of the Senate, *1682*

Statement of the doctrine of nullification, *4262*

Treaty terminated by a joint resolution of Congress, *2404*

Undeclared war, *2639*

Use of sergeant at arms of the Senate to make an arrest, *1683*

Use of the mace of the House of Representatives to keep order, *1552*

1799

Congressional eulogy for a president, *3523*

Death penalty in a tax riot, *2555*

Insurance regulation enacted by a state, *4049*

Printed ballot, *4425*

Quarantine law enacted by Congress, *4011*

Russian colonial governor of Alaska, *1430*

Senator to be impeached, *1759*

Shipbuilding law enacted by Congress, *2694*

Supreme Court justice who had served in the House of Representatives, *4759*

1800

Bankruptcy act, *4909*

Biography of a president, *3823*

Cabinet secretaries to be fired, *1149*

Child of a president to die during his father's term in office, *3548*

Commemorative tree planted on the Capitol grounds, *1220*

Congressional pages, *1639*

Contempt citation issued by the Senate to a journalist, *1685*

Defeated presidential candidate to run again successfully, *3387*

Federal district land office, *4177*

First Lady to receive free mail franking privileges, *3583*

Former chief justice of the Supreme Court to refuse renomination, *4760*

Incumbent president who ran for reelection and was defeated, *3383*

Indiana territorial governor, *4853*

Joint session of Congress to meet in the Capitol, *1816*

Letter written in the White House by a president, *5007*

Meeting place of the House of Representatives in Washington, DC, *1553*

Meeting place of the Senate in Washington, DC, *1686*

Object to be continuously the property of the White House since 1800, *5006*

Party to continue in power in the White House for more than 20 years, *2908*

President to reside in Washington, DC, *3386*

President who was defeated for reelection by his own vice president, *3384*

Presidential election in which both parties nominated candidates in secret caucus, *2972*

Presidential election that produced a change in the party in power, *3177*

Presidential election won by the Democratic-Republican Party, *3178*

Presidential team from Virginia and New York, *3385*

Section of the Capitol to be completed, *1221*

Senate quorum in Washington, DC, *1687*

Session of Congress to meet in Washington, DC, *1815*

Year in which the Democratic-Republican Party controlled both houses of Congress, *1492*

Year in which the Democratic-Republican Party won control of the Senate, *1684*

1801

African polity to declare war on the United States, *2640*

Annual message submitted by a president to Congress in writing, *3752*

Chief justice of the Supreme Court to administer the oath of office to more than one president, *4763*

Child of a president to be born in a foreign country, *3549*

Circulating library in Washington, DC, *1877*

Congressional jurisdiction over Washington, DC, *1874*

Guide to parliamentary rules of order, *1688*

Land preemption act passed by Congress, *4178*

Location in Washington, DC, of the State Department, *1875*

Location in Washington, DC, of the Treasury Department, *1876*

Meeting place of the Supreme Court in Washington, DC, *4699*

Political newspaper published in Washington, DC, *3912*

President elected by decision of the House of Representatives, *3179*

President from the Democratic-Republican Party, *3708*

President inaugurated in Washington, DC, *3644*

President to request a handshake from visitors instead of a bow, *3824*

President to review the nation's military forces, *3388*

1807—continued

Political newspaper using the word "Democratic" in its title, *3913*

President summoned to court as a witness in a trial, *3516*

President to invoke executive privilege, *3391*

Withholding of a signed treaty by a president, *2406*

1808

Convention call, *2974*

Duel between representatives in Congress, *1588*

Land-grant university, *3967*

Law magazine, *3897*

Vice president to serve under two presidents, *4969*

Vice presidential candidate from New Hampshire, *4622*

Vice presidential candidates from Virginia, *4623*

1809

First Lady to attend her husband's inauguration, *3584*

Illinois territorial governor, *4857*

Inaugural ball held at Washington, DC, *3647*

Pacifist tract written by an author who was not a Quaker, *2809*

President born beyond the boundaries of the original 13 states, *3464*

President inaugurated in the Chamber of the House of Representatives, *3648*

President to be inaugurated in a suit of clothes entirely American-made, *3649*

President who had served in the House of Representatives, *3480*

Sanitary facilities in the White House, *5011*

Supreme Court decision on state recognition of federal court rulings, *4713*

1810

Black nationalist movement, *2844*

State vaccination law, *4013*

Supreme Court decision declaring a state law unconstitutional, *4714*

1811

Battle in the "Frontier War", *2738*

Political magazine published quarterly, *3898*

Secession idea to be mentioned in Congress, *4263*

Senate filibuster, *1690*

Senator to be censured, *1761*

Speaker of the House who was simultaneously member, parliamentarian, and leader, *1632*

1812

American flag flown over a schoolhouse, *1087*

Comic political history of the United States, *1073*

Foreign aid bill, *2252*

Gerrymander, *1555*

Louisiana constitution, *4378*

Louisiana state capital, *4325*

Louisiana state governor, *4461*

Missouri territorial governor, *4858*

Performance of "Hail to the Chief", *1117*

President to sign a declaration of war against a European power, *2641*

Presidential election in which both candidates were nominated at open congressional caucuses, *2975*

State governor who had previously been governor of a territory, *4462*

State to allow election of lower court judges, *4411*

Treasury notes bearing interest, *2119*

Vice president to die in office, *4970*

Vice presidential candidate from Massachusetts, *4625*

Vice presidential candidate from Pennsylvania, *4624*

Vice presidential candidate to decline the nomination, *3227*

War bond issued by the federal government, *2118*

Wedding in the White House, *5012*

1813

Factory standardization to federal specification, *4911*

Jewish diplomat, *2323*

Senator to be appointed as a treaty negotiator, *1762*

State superintendent of schools, *3968*

Use of the term "Uncle Sam" as a reference to the United States, *1131*

Vaccination law enacted by Congress, *4014*

1814

Library of Congress, *2062*

News agency to cover foreign politics, *3855*

President to face enemy gunfire while in office, *3695*

President who served in more than one war, *3694*

President whose administration lost two vice presidents to death, *3392*

Star-Spangled Banner, *1088*

Threat of secession by a regional group of states, *4264*

Use of the Post Office to generate revenue in wartime, *3151*

Use of the term "White House", *5013*

Vice president to be buried at Washington, DC, *1879*

1815

Cabinet appointee to be rejected by the Senate, *1150*
Father and son to serve as U.S. ministers, *2324*
Jackson Day, *2190*
Mayor of Cleveland, OH, *1301*
Military academy for naval officers, *2614*
Pacifist society, *2810*
Renovation of the White House that required the president to relocate, *5014*
Year in which gross revenue from postage exceeded $1,000,000, *3152*

1816

Annual salary for members of Congress, *1649*
Era of one-party rule, *2910*
Indiana constitution, *4379*
Indiana Day, *2191*
Indiana state capital, *4326*
Indiana state governor, *4463*
National cemetery, *2666*
Reporter of Supreme Court decisions, *4700*
Supreme Court decision upholding its authority to review state court decisions on appeal, *4715*
Tariff passed by Congress for protection, *4948*
Vice presidential candidates from Maryland, *4626*
Year in which the congressional nominating caucus began to decline, *2976*
Year the public debt of the United States exceeded $100 million, *2126*

1817

Abolition newspaper, *3914*
Alabama territorial governor, *4859*
Child of a president to serve in a presidential cabinet, *1151*
College law school to be permanently organized, *2525*
First Lady to redecorate the White House, *3585*
Historical paintings in the Capitol, *1222*
Mississippi constitution, *4380*
Mississippi state capital, *4327*
Mississippi state governor, *4464*
Pan-American delegates from the United States, *2325*
President who had served in the Senate, *3481*
Presidential inauguration held outdoors in Washington, DC, *3650*
Use of the term "Era of Good Feelings", *1066*

1818

Architect of the Capitol who was born in the United States, *1223*
Federal flag act officially establishing an American flag, *1089*
Illinois constitution, *4381*
Illinois state capital, *4328*

Illinois state governor, *4465*
Increase in the travel expenses allowed to members of Congress, *1650*
State admitted to the Union with a population of less than 60,000, *4296*

1819

Alabama constitution, *4382*
Alabama state capital, *4329*
Alabama state governor, *4466*
Arkansas territorial governor, *4860*
Former president to head a university, *3482*
Land acquired by the United States from Spain, *4840*
Piracy law enacted by Congress, *4912*
President to ride on a steamboat, *3785*
President who was a bachelor, *3586*
State agricultural board, *4109*
Supreme Court decision on the power of states to tax federal assets, *4716*
Treaties establishing the United States as a transcontinental power, *2407*
Vice president who had served in both the House and the Senate, *4971*

1820

Antislavery magazine, *4243*
Bachelor tax enacted by a state, *4828*
Edition of the *Journal of the Senate of the United States of America*, *1691*
Federal law fixing term limits for civil service employees, *2022*
Maine constitution, *4383*
Maine state capital, *4330*
Maine state governor, *4467*
Missouri state governor, *4468*
Organized emigration of freed slaves to Africa, *4242*
Presidential election in which the candidates of a single party ran unopposed, *3181*
State political machine, *2911*
States with populations of more than 1 million, *3078*
United States warship assigned to capture slave ships, *2695*
Vice presidential candidate from Delaware, *4627*
Vice presidential candidate from New Jersey, *4628*
Wedding of a president's daughter in the White House, *5015*

1821

Artist to paint five presidents, *3537*
Diplomatic property owned by the United States, *2326*
Florida territorial governor, *4861*
Missouri constitution, *4384*
Missouri state capital, *4331*

1821—*continued*

President who had been governor of a territory, *3483*

Presidential inauguration to be postponed from Sunday to Monday, *3651*

Public college in Washington, DC, *1880*

State law to abolish imprisonment for debt, *2572*

State west of the Mississippi River to be admitted to the Union, *4297*

Supreme Court decision establishing its authority over state courts in matters of federal law, *4717*

1822

Governor of California under Mexican rule, *1431*

Latino to serve in Congress, *1589*

Latino to serve in the House of Representatives, *1493*

Mayor of Boston, MA, *1302*

President whose name was changed, *3484*

Recognition by the United States of a newly independent nation, *2253*

Washington news bureau, *3915*

1823

Articulation of the Monroe Doctrine, *2254*

Congressional representative to be refused a seat, *1590*

Congressman who was a Catholic priest, *1591*

Mayor of St. Louis, MO, *1303*

President pro tempore of the Senate to appoint committee members, *1692*

State birth registration law, *3949*

1824

Distinguished foreign personage to stay at the White House as a houseguest, *5016*

Foreigner to address a joint meeting of Congress, *1495*

Issue of *Register of Debates in Congress, 1494*

Manuscript by Abraham Lincoln, *3485*

Opinion poll, *2762*

Political snuffboxes, *2794*

Popular vote in a presidential election, *3183*

Presidential candidate from Kentucky, *4569*

Presidential candidate from Tennessee, *4568*

Presidential election in which all candidates were from the same political party, *3184*

State nominating convention, *4427*

Strike in which women participated, *2877*

Supreme Court decision establishing the power of the federal government to regulate commerce, *4718*

Treaty between the federal government and a South American nation, *2408*

Use of the term "national guard", *2664*

Vice presidential candidate from Kentucky, *4632*

Vice presidential candidate from North Carolina, *4629*

Vice presidential candidate from South Carolina, *4630*

Vice presidential candidate from Tennessee, *4631*

Vice presidential candidate to run with three presidential candidates simultaneously, *3182*

1825

Brothers to serve simultaneously as governors of their respective states, *4469*

Express mail, *3153*

First Lady to write an autobiography, *3587*

Former president who was elected to the House of Representatives, *3486*

International treaty rejected by the Senate, *2409*

Law code adopted by a state, *2519*

Police force in Washington, DC, *1881*

President of the Senate to abdicate his power to keep order, *1693*

President to wear long pants at his inauguration, *3652*

President who was a descendant of a signer of the Declaration of Independence, *3550*

President who was a former state governor and the son of a state governor, *3552*

President whose father was alive when he was inaugurated, *3551*

Presidential candidate nominated by a state legislature, *3228*

State tax enacted to support public schools, *3969*

Vice president from South Carolina, *4667*

Vice president who was born an American citizen, *4972*

Year in which more than 10,000 immigrants arrived in the United States, *3104*

Year in which the number of letters carried by the Post Office Department exceeded 10 million, *3154*

Year in which there was no mechanism for nominating presidential candidates, *2977*

1826

Commemoration of the birthday of Benjamin Franklin, *2192*

Conference of American republics, *2255*

First Lady born west of the Mississippi, *3589*

First Lady who had an occupation other than homemaking, *3588*

Funeral held at taxpayer expense, *1694*

Inheritance tax enacted by a state, *4829*

Mourning ribbons, *3524*

Official Jacksonian newspaper, *3916*

President who became a nonagenarian, *3525*

Stars and Stripes with the number "76", *1090*

1827

Anarchist, *2811*

Anti-Masonic Party, *2912*
Campaign biography, *2795*
Child of a president to attend West Point, *3553*
Federal law hostile to lotteries, *4000*
Mayor of Memphis, TN, *1304*
Political newspaper published by African-Americans, *3917*
President who learned reading and writing from his wife, *3826*

1828

Campaign newspapers, *3918*
Federal post office built for the purpose, *3155*
First Lady who died after her husband's election but before his inauguration, *3590*
Independent labor party, *2913*
Native American government modeled on that of the United States, *2739*
Native American newspaper, *2740*
President from the Democratic Party, *3709*
Presidential campaign of the modern type, *2763*
Presidential election won by the Democratic Party, *3185*
Scholarly political history of the United States, *1074*
Strike in which a militia was called out, *2477*
Supreme Court justice who had served as a federal judge, *4765*
Vice president from the Democratic Party, *5000*
Washington news correspondent, *3887*
Wedding of a president's son in the White House, *5017*
Year in which the Democratic Party controlled both houses of Congress, *1496*
Year in which the Democratic Party won control of the House of Representatives, *1556*
Year in which the Democratic Party won control of the Senate, *1695*

1829

Antislavery pamphlet by an African-American writer, *4244*
Bank deposit insurance law enacted by a state, *2105*
Kitchen cabinet of unofficial presidential advisors, *1152*
Labor union whose candidates won an election, *2486*
Landscaping of the Capitol grounds, *1224*
Mob scene at the White House, *3653*
Political cartoon produced by lithography, *3932*
Postmaster general to become a member of the president cabinet, *3156*
President born in South Carolina, *4600*
President from Tennessee, *4601*
President inaugurated in Washington in a ceremony open to the public, *3654*
President who had served in both the House of Representatives and the Senate, *3487*
Sanitary facilities in the Capitol, *1225*

Senate page, *1640*
Spoils system of presidential patronage on a large scale, *2023*
Use of the East Room in the White House, *5018*
Washington social scandal, *1882*

1830

Campaign assessments on government workers, *2781*
Census in which the national population exceeded 10 million, *3085*
Census that included deaf, mute, and blind people, *3086*
Character symbolizing the American people, *1132*
Commemoration of the birthday of Thomas Jefferson, *2193*
National convention of African-Americans, *2845*
Observatory established by the federal government, *2070*
Permanent Committee on Roads and Canals, *1697*
Post office building, *3157*
President who had served as mayor of a city, *3488*
Use of the term "lobbyist", *1497*
Year in which House seats were won by third parties, *1557*
Year in which Senate seats were won by a third party, *1696*

1831

Anti-Masonic Party presidential candidate, *3282*
Cabinet member who was Catholic, *1153*
Chaplain of the House of Representatives who was Catholic, *1558*
Commemoration of the Mecklenburg declaration of independence, *2194*
Congress in which 1,000 bills were introduced, *1498*
Convention city, *2978*
Independent Party presidential candidate, *3283*
Major antislavery periodical, *4245*
National nominating convention held by a political party, *2979*
National nominating convention held by a political party of importance, *2980*
President who had a stepmother, *3554*
Presidential candidate to be nominated in an open party convention, *3229*
Slave rebellion after the Revolution, *4246*
Supreme Court decision on the status of Native American tribes, *4719*
Treaty between the federal government and a foreign nation to provide for mutual reduction of import duties, *2410*
Use of the phrase "to the victor belong the spoils", *2024*

1832

Convention to renominate a sitting president, 2981
Democratic Party, 2914
Democratic Party national convention, 2982
Democratic Party presidential candidate, 3284
Former vice president to serve in the Senate, 4974
Library of the Supreme Court, 2063
Mayor of Buffalo, NY, 1305
National political convention to adopt the two-thirds rule, 2983
National reservation, 4146
Performance of "America the Beautiful", 1118
Politician to control a national convention, 2984
Presidential candidate of a major party to be nominated at a national convention, 3230
Presidential candidate to be nominated on the first ballot, 3231
Presidential candidate unanimously nominated by a national party convention, 3232
Presidential election in which all the candidates were nominated at party conventions, 3186
Presidential election in which the Whig Party participated, 3187
Symbol of the Democratic Party, 2915
Vaccination program by the federal government to protect Native Americans against smallpox, 4015
Vice president to resign, 4973

1833

First Lady who was the grandmother of a president, 3591
Interstate anticrime pact, 2527
President to ride on a railroad train, 3786
Public library established after the Revolution, 1259
Radical student leader, 2812
State aid to railroads, 4085
State bank to receive federal deposits, 2106
Treaty between the federal government and an Asian nation, 2411

1834

Cabinet appointee on record as having been rejected by the Senate, 1154
City mayor elected by popular vote, 1306
Labor newspaper, 3919
Political cartoon featuring Uncle Sam, 3933
President to be censured by Congress, 3511
Presidential protest to Congress, 3512
Use of federal troops to suppress a strike, 2478
Volume of Debates and Proceedings in the Congress of the United States, 1499
Whig Party, 2916

1835

Governor who was Catholic, 4470

Michigan state governor, 4471
Patent commissioner, 2600
President who was the target of an assassination attempt while in office, 3444
Presidential candidate from Ohio, 4570
Presidential candidate nominated in a church, 2985
Presidents who were related by marriage, 3555
Railroad to run trains to Washington, DC, 1883
Senate committee system empowering the majority party, 1698
Use of the term "Loco-Focos", 2917
Year in which the United States was free from debt, 2127

1836

Arkansas constitution, 4385
Arkansas state capitol, 4332
Arkansas state governor, 4472
Chief Justice to wear long pants at his inauguration, 4766
Child labor law enacted by a state that included an education requirement, 2454
Definitive edition of The Debates in the Several State Conventions on the Adoption of the Federal Constitution, 1831
Federal treasury surplus to be returned to the states, 4265
Gag rule in the House of Representatives, 1559
Numbering system for patents, 2601
Post office west of the Mississippi River, 3158
President of the Republic of Texas, 2374
Superintendent of schools hired by a city, 3970
Supreme Court chief justice who was Catholic, 4767
Supreme Court justice who had served as attorney general, 4768
Texas Independence Day, 2195
Vice presidential candidate named Johnson, 4975
Whig Party presidential candidate, 3285
Whig Party resolutions, 3034
Wisconsin territorial governor, 4862
Woman to become a union organizer, 2878

1837

Campaign torch, 2796
Mayor of Chicago, IL, 1307
Michigan constitution, 4386
Michigan state capital, 4333
Political cartoon showing the Democratic Party as a donkey, 3934
President from New York State, 4602
President to make extensive use of his constitutional power to remove officeholders, 3772
Presidential inauguration at which both the president and the chief justice had suffered earlier rejections by the Senate, 3655
Running water in the White House, 5019
San Jacinto Day, 2196

State board of education, *3971*
Vice president elected by the Senate, *4976*
Vice president from Kentucky, *4668*

1838

African-American to give antislavery lectures, *4247*
Alcohol prohibition law enacted by a state, *3943*
Iowa territorial governor, *4863*
Publication of *Democracy in America*, *3072*
State banking commission, *2107*
Steamboat inspection authorized by Congress, *4086*

1839

Antislavery political organization, *4248*
Dictionary of American law, *2520*
Liberty Party platform, *3035*
Liberty Party presidential candidate, *3286*
National political convention to adopt the unit rule, *2986*
President to attend West Point, *3696*
Single-issue political party, *2918*
Use of the name "Liberty Bell", *1111*

1840

Campaign banners, *2797*
Campaign newspaper of importance, *3920*
Campaign song, *2764*
Continent claimed for the United States, *2256*
Democratic presidential and vice presidential team to lose a bid for reelection, *3394*
Establishment of a treasury system, *2086*
Mayor of Austin, TX, *1308*
Official Whig administration newspaper, *3921*
Political party platform, *3036*
President and vice president to be born in the same county, *3465*
President elected from a state west of the Mississippi River, *3393*
President from the Whig Party, *3710*
President to travel to his inauguration by train, *3656*
Presidential candidate to make a campaign speech, *2765*
Presidential election won by the Whig Party, *3188*
Third party to participate in a presidential election, *3189*
Vice president from the Whig Party, *5001*
Year in which the Whig Party controlled both houses of Congress, *1500*
Year in which the Whig Party won control of the House of Representatives, *1560*
Year in which the Whig Party won control of the Senate, *1699*

1841

Continuous Senate filibuster, *1700*

Edition of *The New York Tribune*, *3922*
Factory workers' magazine, *3899*
First Lady who was widowed while her husband was in office, *3592*
Pension granted to the widow of a president, *3593*
President from Ohio, *4603*
President to bring slaves with him to Washington, DC, *4249*
President to die in office, *3526*
President to serve without a vice president, *3396*
President who did not deliver an annual message to Congress, *3753*
President whose grandson became president, *3556*
President without a party, *3711*
Secretary of state to serve in the State Department simultaneously with his son, *1155*
Senate press gallery, *1701*
State to be governed by two rival elected administrations, *4266*
Vice president to succeed to the presidency after the death of a president, *3397*
Year in which three presidents held office, *3395*

1842

Child labor law enacted by a state that regulated hours of employment, *2455*
First Lady who died while her husband was in office, *3594*
Girl born in the White House, *5020*
Narcotics tariff enacted by Congress, *4061*
Presidential commission whose creation was challenged by Congress, *1561*
State to repudiate a debt, *4267*
Tariff enacted by Congress to prevent the importation of obscene literature and pictures, *4949*
Temperance address by a future president, *2855*
Year in which more than 100,000 immigrants arrived in the United States, *3105*

1843

Attempt to bring impeachment proceedings against a president, *3630*
Consul to California, *2327*
Government on the Pacific Coast, *1432*
Photograph of a former president, *3538*
Use of the terms "Hunkers" and "Barnburners", *2919*
Vice presidential candidate from Ohio, *4633*

1844

Campaign hat, *2798*
Former First Lady to be granted a seat in the House of Representatives, *3595*
Incumbent president whose party refused to renominate him, *3398*

1844—*continued*

National Democratic Tyler Party presidential candidate, *3287*

Political news item transmitted by telegraph, *3871*

Politician to receive and decline a nomination by telegraph, *2987*

President to announce before his election that he would not run for reelection, *3399*

President to marry while in office, *3557*

President who narrowly escaped a fatal accident while in office, *3527*

Presidential candidate to be assassinated, *3235*

Presidential "dark horse" candidate, *3233*

Sentence of branding by a federal court, *2528*

Telegraph line to Washington, DC, *1884*

Telegraph message sent from the Capitol, *1226*

Treaty between the United States and China, *2412*

Use of the telegraph in politics, *2988*

Vice presidential nominee from a major party to decline the nomination, *3234*

1845

African-American lawyer formally admitted to the bar, *2585*

African-American vice consul, *2328*

Annexation of territory by joint resolution of Congress after failure to accomplish the same object by treaty, *4298*

Edition of the *United States Statutes at Large*, *2521*

Florida constitution, *4387*

Florida state capital, *4334*

Florida state governor, *4473*

Free church in Washington, DC, *1885*

Icebox in the White House, *5021*

Independent nation annexed by the United States, *4299*

Law book of federal laws then in force, *2522*

Mayor of Hannibal, MO, *1309*

Mayor of Peoria, IL, *1310*

National flag to become a state flag, *1091*

National labor congress, *2879*

Political photographer, *3888*

President born in North Carolina, *4604*

Presidential inauguration reported by telegraph, *3657*

Presidential veto to be overridden by Congress, *3844*

Senator of Jewish descent, *1763*

Speaker of the House who became president, *1633*

State police, *2529*

State to fix a time limit on legislative sessions, *4542*

Texas constitution, *4388*

Texas state capital, *4335*

Use of the term "manifest destiny", *2257*

Vice president from Pennsylvania, *4669*

1846

American republic on the West Coast, *4841*

Cracking of the Liberty Bell, *1112*

Democratic president whose party was in the minority in the House of Representatives, *3712*

Iowa constitution, *4389*

Iowa state capital, *4336*

Iowa state governor, *4474*

Mayor of Milwaukee, WI, *1311*

National art collection, *1886*

Photograph of the Capitol, *1227*

Senator elected on an antislavery ticket, *4250*

Smithsonian Institution, *1887*

State constitution to provide for election of judges, *4412*

State constitutional reform movement, *4268*

Texas state governor, *4475*

United States code of military justice for governing foreign territory, *2654*

Warehouse legislation enacted by Congress, *4913*

1847

Battle in which two future American presidents were combatants, *3697*

Gaslight illumination in the Capitol, *1228*

Mayor of New Bedford, MA, *1312*

Political speech on conservation, *4120*

Postage stamp depicting a president, *3164*

State law mandating a ten-hour workday, *2493*

State reformatory for boys, *2573*

1848

American to become president of an African republic, *2375*

California territorial governor, *4864*

Child labor law enacted by a state that restricted the age of the worker, *2456*

Congressional lobbyist who was a woman, *1501*

Credentials fight at a Democratic Party convention, *2989*

Election day for presidential voting held nationwide, *3190*

Father and son who were senators at the same session, *1764*

Free Soil Party platform, *3037*

Free Soil Party presidential candidate, *3289*

Gaslight illumination in the White House, *5022*

Journalist arrested by the Senate, *1703*

Liberty League presidential candidate, *3288*

Mayor of Syracuse, NY, *1313*

Political party run by a national committee, *2961*

President from Louisiana, *4605*

Presidential candidate from Louisiana, *4572*

Presidential candidate from Michigan, *4571*

Presidential candidate from New Hampshire, *4573*

Pure food and drug law established by Congress, *4016*

Speaker of the House to die in the Capitol, *1634*

State law giving property rights to married women, *1953*

Third party with an appeal broader than a single issue, *2920*

Treaty with Mexico, *2413*

Use of shorthand in the Senate, *1702*

Vice presidential candidate from Michigan, *4634*

Wisconsin constitution, *4390*

Wisconsin state capital, *4337*

Wisconsin state governor, *4476*

Women's rights convention, *2894*

1849

California state governor, *4477*

Conservationist document submitted to Congress, *4121*

Department of the Interior, *2038*

Mayor of Independence, MO, *1314*

Minnesota territorial governor, *4865*

Oregon territorial governor, *4866*

Photograph of a president in office, *3539*

Pioneer Day (Utah), *2197*

President who had received a patent, *3490*

President who was survived by his mother, *3528*

President whose party was in the minority in both houses of Congress, *3713*

President with no congressional experience, *3489*

Presidents who were cousins, *3558*

School desegregation lawsuit, *1918*

Secretary of the interior, *1156*

Senator to serve as unofficial president between two presidential terms, *3400*

Senator to serve three states, *1765*

Senator who was returned to the Senate after being defeated for the presidency, *1766*

State in the West to be denied admission to the Union, *4300*

Statement of the principles of the Greenback movement, *2813*

1850

Admission Day (California), *2198*

African-American captured under the Fugitive Slave Law of 1850, *4251*

American flag made on the Pacific Coast, *1092*

California constitution, *4391*

California state capital, *4338*

Community leader in the United States to exercise the authority of king and high priest, *4543*

Expansion of the Capitol, *1229*

First Lady to graduate from college, *3596*

Mayor of San Francisco, CA, *1315*

National convention for women's rights, *2895*

Secretary of state to serve more than once, *1157*

Senator to threaten another senator with a gun in the Senate chamber, *1767*

State constitution to recognize property rights for women, *1954*

State on the Pacific coast to be admitted to the Union, *4301*

Utah territorial governor, *4867*

1851

Brothers to serve as representatives in Congress simultaneously, *1592*

Insurance board established by a state government, *4050*

Issue of the *New York Times*, *3923*

Land-grant railroad, *4087*

Library in the White House, *5023*

New Mexico territorial governor, *4868*

Private mint authorized by the federal government, *2156*

Senator to serve as long-term head of a standing committee, *1768*

Senator to serve for 30 years, *1769*

Supreme Court justice with a university law degree, *4769*

1852

Campaign biography by a prominent author, *2799*

Fireproofing in the Library of Congress, *2064*

Immigration of Chinese nationals, *3106*

Incumbent senator to win a vice presidential nomination, *1771*

Mayor of Corpus Christi, TX, *1316*

Person to lie in state in the Capitol rotunda, *1230*

President from New Hampshire, *4606*

Presidential candidate from New Jersey, *4574*

Presidential candidate whose opponent had been his military commander, *3236*

Senator who was a practicing Jew, *1770*

State compulsory education law, *3972*

State law regulating women's work hours, *2494*

State temperance society of women, *2856*

Tax to limit immigration, *3107*

Vice president who served in both houses of Congress from different states, *4977*

Vice presidential candidate from Indiana, *4635*

1853

Attorney general to fill the position on a full-time basis, *1158*

Marriage of two descendants of the same president, *3559*

Mayor of Kansas City, KS, *1317*

Periodical of the women's rights movement, *2896*

1853—*continued*

President to be arrested, *3827*

President to deliver his inaugural address from memory, *3658*

President who was younger than 50 when he took office, *3401*

President whose oath of office did not include the word "swear", *3659*

Vice president born in North Carolina, *4670*

Vice president from Alabama, *4671*

Vice president sworn in on foreign soil, *4978*

Vice president to take the oath of office but never serve in office, *4979*

Washington territorial governor, *4869*

1854

Founding of the Republican Party, *2922*

Kansas territory governor, *4871*

Know-Nothing Party, *2921*

Nebraska territorial governor, *4870*

President to publish a book of poetry, *3491*

Speech by Abraham Lincoln denouncing slavery, *4252*

State governor to be removed from office by a state supreme court, *4478*

Symbol of the Republican Party, *2923*

Treaty between the United States and Japan, *2414*

1855

African-American to hold elective office, *1279*

City to build a comprehensive sewer system, *4017*

Claims by Native Americans for compensation for confiscated land, *2741*

Claims court established by the federal government, *1973*

Consul to Japan, *2329*

Frescoes in the Capitol, *1231*

Immigration receiving station, *3108*

Mayor of Los Angeles, CA, *1318*

Native Americans to become United States citizens, *2742*

Successful desegregation of public transportation, *1919*

1856

Beating in the Senate chamber, *1704*

Campaign poster showing the candidate and his wife, *2800*

Child of a president to decline a nomination for the presidency, *3560*

Clerical help for congressional committees, *1502*

Design for a statue for the raised Capitol dome, *1232*

Elected incumbent president whose party refused to renominate him, *3403*

Former president to run for reelection on a different party's ticket, *3402*

Intervention of federal troops in a territorial conflict over slavery, *4253*

Know-Nothing Party platform, *3038*

Know-Nothing Party presidential candidate, *3290*

North American Party presidential candidate, *3291*

Portrait of Abraham Lincoln, *3540*

President of a Central American country born in the United States, *2376*

Presidential candidate from California, *4575*

Presidential election in which the Republican Party participated, *3191*

Republican Party candidate to be nominated on the first ballot, *3237*

Republican Party platform, *3039*

Republican Party presidential candidate, *3292*

Salaries for consuls, *2330*

State fish commission, *4202*

State railroad safety law, *4088*

Third party to make a substantial showing in a presidential election, *3192*

1857

Congressional committee witness to be jailed for refusing to give testimony, *1562*

Federal law compelling the testimony of witnesses before the House and Senate, *1503*

Federal law giving property rights to married women, *1955*

Greenhouses at the White House, *5024*

Literacy qualification for voting, *4428*

Meeting of the House of Representatives in its present location, *1563*

National teachers' organization, *3973*

President from Pennsylvania, *4607*

President whose cabinet remained unchanged, *1159*

Presidential secretary to receive a governmental salary, *3740*

Senator to face allegations of corrupt election practices, *1772*

Vice president who was younger than 40, *4980*

1858

Congressional medal awarded to a physician, *1504*

Extension of mail service to the West Coast, *3159*

Minnesota constitution, *4392*

Minnesota state capital, *4339*

Minnesota state governor, *4479*

Overseas territory acquired by the United States, *4842*

Senator removed from a committee chairmanship against his will, *1773*

Year in which the Republican Party won control of the House of Representatives, *1564*

1861—*continued*

Paper money issued by the federal government, *2158*

Patent issued by the Confederate States of America, *2602*

Political cartoon with mass popularity, *3935*

Postmaster general of the Confederate States of America, *3160*

President born in Kentucky, *4609*

President-elect to require military protection at his inauguration, *3661*

President from the Republican Party, *3714*

President of the Confederacy, *1374*

President to function as an effective commander in chief, *3405*

Presidential call for volunteer troops to fight in the Civil War, *1378*

Press censorship by military authorities, *3856*

Published records of American diplomacy, *2331*

Senator to address the Senate in military uniform, *1709*

Session of the Confederate Congress, *1371*

Slave state to reject secession, *1367*

State governor to be impeached and acquitted, *4482*

State to hold a public referendum on secession, *1377*

Suspension of habeas corpus in wartime, *1380*

Tax levied by the Confederacy, *4802*

Transcontinental telegram of a political nature, *3857*

Union troops to arrive in Washington, DC, *1379*

Use of the Capitol as a war facility, *1234*

Vice president from Maine, *4672*

Vice president of the Confederacy, *1375*

Vice president to declare the election of the candidate who had opposed him for the presidency, *3197*

Year in which two presidents were elected, *3196*

1862

African-American unit organized during the Civil War, *1384*

African-American unit to fight in the Civil War, *1386*

American citizen hanged for treason, *2557*

Bill bearing the likeness of a president, *2161*

Bureau of Engraving and Printing, *2159*

Bureau of Internal Revenue, *4803*

Church disincorporated by Congress, *1949*

Department of Agriculture, *2039*

Draft law enacted by the Confederacy, *2633*

Emancipation proclamation, *4255*

Execution for slave trading carried out by the federal government, *2556*

First Lady of Mexico to reside in the United States, *2378*

Former president whose death was officially ignored, *3529*

Inheritance tax levied by Congress, *4804*

Land-grant college founded under the Morrill Act, *3974*

Large-scale free land distribution by the federal government, *4181*

Legal tender, *2160*

Military service by African-Americans to be authorized by Congress, *1385*

National cemeteries act, *2667*

Passport fee, *2259*

Polygamy ban enacted by Congress, *3950*

Postage stamps issued by the Confederacy, *3165*

Presidential executive order to be numbered, *3406*

Revenue stamps issued by the federal government, *4805*

Tobacco tax enacted by the federal government for internal revenue purposes, *4078*

1863

Arizona territorial governor, *4875*

Comptroller of the Currency, *2087*

Draft law enacted by Congress during wartime, *2634*

Draft riots, *2635*

Free mail delivery in cities, *3161*

Homestead grant under the Homestead Act, *4182*

Idaho territorial governor, *4876*

Model community for freed slaves founded by the federal government, *4256*

National code of the laws of war, *2655*

National scientific advisory body, *2071*

Oaths of allegiance to the United States taken by civilians, *1387*

Offer by a foreign power to mediate the Civil War, *1388*

Officer to preside over both of the branches of Congress, *1506*

Presidential amnesty granted during the Civil War, *3407*

Senator to draw a gun on the Senate sergeant at arms, *1775*

State founded within the borders of a seceded state, *4302*

Thanksgiving Day, *2242*

West Virginia constitution, *4395*

West Virginia Day, *2199*

West Virginia state capital, *4342*

West Virginia state governor, *4484*

Year the public debt of the United States exceeded $1 billion, *2128*

1864

Coin to use the motto "In God We Trust", *2162*

Federal cigarette tax, *4079*

Federal law giving African-American soldiers pay and benefits equal to those of white soldiers, *2656*

Independent Republican Party presidential candidate, *3295*

Montana territorial governor, *4877*

National hall of fame, *1067*

Native American general, *2744*

Nevada constitution, *4396*

Nevada state capital, *4343*

Nevada state governor, *4485*

Platform of the Independent Republicans, *3042*

Political figurals, *2802*

Presidential election in which a bloc of states did not participate, *3198*

Presidential election in which soldiers in the field were allowed to vote, *3199*

Soldier buried at Arlington National Cemetery, *2668*

State constitution telegraphed in its entirety, *4269*

State park, *4147*

Statue installed in National Statuary Hall in the Capitol, *1235*

1865

African-American allowed to enter the grounds of Congress, *1507*

African-American lawyer admitted to practice before the Supreme Court, *2586*

African-American preacher to deliver a sermon in the House of Representatives, *1566*

Capture of an American president by enemy troops, *1390*

Congressional directory, *1508*

Constitutional amendment that resulted from the Civil War, *1843*

Federal execution of a woman, *2558*

Former vice president to serve as an official of an enemy government, *4981*

Freedmen's Bureau, *1920*

Ku Klux Klan, *2814*

Labor cooperatives to be authorized by a state, *2487*

Nevada Day, *2200*

Peace conference during the Civil War, *1389*

President to be assassinated, *3446*

President to lie in state in the Capitol rotunda, *1236*

President who had neither military nor legal experience, *3493*

President whose grave was opened by thieves, *3530*

Presidential funeral cortege that included a caparisoned horse, *3447*

Presidential inauguration in which African-Americans formally participated, *3662*

Rewards offered by the federal government for suspects in the assassination of a president, *3448*

State environmental protection law enacted in connection with advertising, *4122*

State to ratify the 13th Amendment to the Constitution, *1842*

Town founded by African-Americans after the Civil War, *1260*

Trial of a war criminal by the federal government, *1391*

Vice president from Tennessee, *4673*

Vice president to succeed to the presidency after the assassination of a president, *3408*

1866

African-American state legislators, *4544*

American flag made of American bunting to fly over the Capitol, *1094*

Civil rights law enacted by Congress, *1921*

Commemoration of the birthday of Abraham Lincoln, *2201*

Congressional campaign committee, *1509*

Corrupt election practices law enacted by a state, *4429*

Delegate to a national political convention who was African-American, *2996*

Federal law prohibiting racial discrimination in housing, *4041*

General of the U.S. Army, *2625*

Interracial jury, *1974*

Irrigation law enacted by Congress, *4194*

Labor Reform Party, *2926*

National labor organization, *2880*

National organization to advocate universal voting rights, *2815*

National procedures for electing senators, *1710*

Newspaper reporter accredited to the White House, *3723*

Postage stamp honoring a dead president, *3166*

Queen to visit the United States, *2379*

Secretary of state to travel outside the United States while in office, *1160*

Soldiers' homes established by Congress, *2700*

State readmitted to the Union after the Civil War, *1392*

State to ratify the 14th Amendment to the Constitution, *1844*

Supreme Court decision setting limitations on the use of military force against American civilians, *4720*

Woman artist to be commissioned by the federal government, *2016*

1867

Alaska Day, *2202*

City housing code, *4042*

Commissioner of education of the United States, *3975*

Department of Education, *2040*

Design for the Statue of Liberty, *1123*

Federal law granting African-American men the right to vote, *1922*

1867—*continued*

Federal law regulating campaign finances, *2782*
Major city to be unincorporated, *1261*
Marshal of the Supreme Court, *4701*
Mayor of Minneapolis, MN, *1320*
National political organization of farmers, *2816*
Nebraska constitution, *4397*
Nebraska state capital, *4344*
Nebraska state governor, *4486*
Public university in Washington, DC, *1888*
Senate appropriations committee, *1711*
State constitution to ban bribery, *4270*
State forestry inquiry commission, *4137*
State governor who had previously been governor of a territory in which his state was not included, *4487*
State university supported by a direct property tax, *3976*
Territory annexed by the federal government beyond the nation's continental limits, *4844*
Territory annexed by the federal government that was noncontiguous, *4843*

1868

African-American woman to become a First Lady's confidante, *3597*
African-American women's rights activist who attempted to vote in a presidential election, *1956*
Chamber of commerce established by a state, *4914*
Federal law mandating an eight-hour workday, *2495*
Foreign city with the Confederate flag in its coat of arms, *1095*
Interracial jury, *1974*
Member of the House of Representatives to lie in state in the Capitol rotunda, *1237*
Memorial Day, *2203*
National definition of citizenship, *3109*
National labor organization for African-American workers, *2881*
Native American to win territorial concessions from the federal government, *2745*
President to be impeached, *3631*
Presidential amnesty granted during the Civil War, *3407*
Republican presidential candidate chosen unanimously on the first ballot, *3239*
Senate rules allowing the referral of nominations to appropriate committees, *1712*
Use of the word "male" in the Constitution, *1832*
Vice presidential candidate from Missouri, *4639*
Women to cast unofficial votes in a presidential election, *1957*

1869

African-American consul, *2332*
Emancipation Day (Texas), *2204*

Inaugural ball in the Treasury Building, *3663*
Indian Affairs commissioner who was Native American, *2746*
Labor bureau established by a state, *2441*
Labor Day, *2205*
Mayor of Seattle, WA, *1321*
Pensions for federal judges, *1975*
President whose parents were both alive at the time of his inauguration, *3664*
Prohibition Party, *2927*
Recognition by a European nation of the right of its subjects to acquire American citizenship, *2260*
Secretary of state to serve less than two weeks, *1161*
Speaker of the House who became vice president, *1635*
State board of health, *4018*
State to ratify the 15th Amendment to the Constitution, *1845*
Territory to grant full voting rights to women, *1958*
Transcontinental railroad, *4089*
Vice president from Indiana, *4674*
Voting machine, *1510*
Woman to practice law, *2587*
Woman to testify as a witness at a Senate hearing, *1713*
Wyoming territorial governor, *4878*

1870

African-American justice of a state supreme court, *4413*
African-American senator, *1776*
African-American to vote under authority of the 15th Amendment to the Constitution, *1923*
Census in which no slaves were counted, *3087*
Congressional legislation to control government expenditures, *2088*
Congressional representative who was African-American, *1594*
Department of Justice, *2041*
Federal law to protect fur seals, *4203*
Laws authorizing the use of force against the Ku Klux Klan, *1924*
Liberal Republican Party, *2928*
Major sale of land in the continental United States to a foreign consortium, *4271*
Pension granted to the widow of an assassinated president, *3598*
Political parties in Puerto Rico, *4887*
Solicitor general, *4702*
State governor to be impeached and convicted, *4488*
Woman to serve as justice of the peace, *1271*
Women to serve as jurors, *1270*

1871

Attorney general to head the Department of Justice, *1162*

Child of a president to attend West Point, *3553*
Crusading political cartoonist, *3936*
Federal law to reform the civil service, *2026*
Federal law withdrawing recognition of Native American tribal autonomy, *2747*
Federal office to protect U.S. fisheries, *4204*
Modernization of the infrastructure of Washington, DC, *1889*
National firearms lobby, *2817*
Political economy chair at a college, *3063*
Senate library, *1714*
Surgeon general, *4019*
Territorial government of Washington, DC, *1890*

1872

African-American vice presidential candidate, *3240*
African-American woman to practice law, *2588*
Bird refuge established by a state, *4206*
Civil Service Commission, *2027*
Congressional representative to serve a single day, *1595*
Federal fish hatchery, *4205*
Independent Liberal Republican Party presidential candidate, *3302*
Labor Reform Party platform, *3043*
Labor Reform Party presidential candidate, *3296*
Liberal Republican Convention of Colored Men, *3301*
Liberal Republican Party platform, *3045*
Liberal Republican Party presidential candidate, *3298*
Mail fraud law enacted by Congress, *3162*
National labor party, *2929*
National park, *4148*
National Working Men's Convention, *3299*
President who had been an executioner, *3494*
Presidential candidate to die during the election, *3243*
Presidential candidate who was Catholic, *3242*
Prohibition Party platform, *3044*
Prohibition Party presidential candidate, *3297*
State ban on sex discrimination in employment, *1959*
State governor who was African-American, *4489*
Straight-out Democratic Party platform, *3046*
Straight-out Democratic Party presidential candidate, *3300*
Woman to run as a presidential candidate, *3241*

1873

Abolition of the Senate franking privilege, *1715*
Anti-Monopoly Party, *2930*
Bonus paid to members of Congress by themselves, *1651*
Closing of the New York Stock Exchange, *2138*

Demonetization of silver, *2089*
Federal law encouraging settlers to grow trees, *4138*
Issue of the *Congressional Record*, *1511*
President to receive a salary raise, *3742*
Salary raise for the vice president, *3741*
Senator to resign in a case of a fraudulent election, *1777*
Vice president born in New Hampshire, *4675*
Woman to serve as a patent examiner, *2603*

1874

Case of child abuse brought to court, *3990*
Coins minted for a foreign government, *2163*
Confederate Memorial Day, *2206*
Development of the "Wisconsin Idea" of progressivism, *2818*
Elevators in the Capitol, *1238*
National temperance society of women, *2857*
Political cartoon showing the Republican Party as an elephant, *3937*
President born west of the Mississippi River, *3466*
Reigning king to visit the United States, *2380*
Republican president whose party was in the minority in the House of Representatives, *3715*
Salary cut for Congress, *1652*
Socialist Labor Party, *2931*

1875

African-American senator to serve a full term, *1778*
American National Party platform, *3047*
American National Party presidential candidate, *3303*
Centennial celebration of the Revolution, *1036*
Forestry association of national importance, *4139*
Homestead act for desert lands owned by the federal government, *4183*
Jim Crow law, *1925*
Popular image of the Minute Man, *1133*
President to serve as a senator both before and after his term in office, *3495*
Vice president to lie in state in the Capitol rotunda, *1239*

1876

Cabinet officer impeached by the House of Representatives, *1163*
Celluloid campaign buttons, *2803*
Colorado constitution, *4398*
Colorado state capital, *4345*
Colorado state governor, *4490*
Exhibition of part of the Statue of Liberty in the United States, *1124*
Forestry supervision by the federal government, *4141*

1876—*continued*

Greenback Party platform, *3048*

Greenback Party presidential candidate, *3304*

Lifesaving medal awarded by the Treasury Department, *2042*

Major defeat inflicted by Native Americans on regular U.S. Army troops, *2748*

Presidential election in which neither candidate received a majority of the electoral vote, *3200*

State forestry association, *4140*

Woman admitted to practice before the Court of Claims, *1976*

Woman to address a national political convention, *2998*

Year in which both major parties nominated incumbent governors for the presidency, *2997*

1877

African-American minister, *2333*

African-American town in continuous existence west of the Mississippi, *1262*

Arrangement of desks according to party, *1716*

Cabinet member who had served as a Confederate officer, *1164*

Colorado Day, *2209*

Federal law encouraging settlers to irrigate desert lands, *4195*

First Lady active in charitable causes, *3599*

First Lady to ban liquor in the White House, *3600*

Flag Day, *2208*

Kansas Day, *2207*

President and First Lady to celebrate their silver wedding anniversary in the White House, *3602*

President to take the oath of office twice in one year, *3665*

State reformatory for women, *2574*

Strike suppressed by federal troops in peacetime, *2479*

Use of the term "First Lady" to refer to the president's wife, *3601*

1878

Commission government for Washington, DC, *1891*

Easter Egg roll at the White House, *5026*

Federal lifesaving service, *4020*

Legal recognition of the term "District of Columbia", *1892*

National lawyers' society, *2589*

Political cartoons in color, *3938*

President to use a telephone, *3829*

Probation system for offenders, *2575*

Republican president whose party was in the minority in both houses of Congress, *3716*

1879

Ban enacted by a state on the employment of women in an occupation, *2458*

General to become president, *3698*

Public Lands Commission, *4184*

United States Geological Survey, *4185*

Woman lawyer admitted to practice before the Supreme Court, *2590*

1880

African-American to receive nominating votes for the vice presidency at the convention of a major party, *2999*

American Party presidential candidate, *3305*

Census in which the national population exceeded 50 million, *3088*

City with a population of more than 1 million, *3079*

Credentials fight at a Republican Party convention that determined the selection of the candidate, *3000*

President-elect who was simultaneously a senator-elect and a member of the House, *3513*

President to visit the West Coast of the United States while in office, *3787*

Presidential candidate from Iowa, *4578*

Presidential candidate from Maine, *4580*

Presidential candidate from Texas, *4579*

Presidential candidate from Vermont, *4577*

Presidential candidate to campaign throughout the country, *2766*

Presidential candidate who was present at the convention that nominated him, *3244*

Presidential election with a margin of difference of less than 1 percent of the popular vote, *3201*

Proponent of the Single Tax principle, *2819*

Single-tax proponent, *2820*

State with a population of more than 5 million, *3080*

Vice presidential candidate from Kansas, *4640*

1881

Act in the construction of the Statue of Liberty, *1125*

Date on which the Senate was equally divided between Republicans and Democrats, *1718*

Muckraking journalist, *3890*

National labor organization of importance, *2882*

President born in Vermont, *4610*

President to view his inaugural parade from a platform outside the White House, *3666*

President who was the son of a minister, *3562*

President whose mother lived at the White House, *3561*

Presidential candidate to make campaign speeches in a foreign language, *2767*

President's mother to attend her son's inauguration, *3667*

State pure food and drug law, *4021*
Statue cast by the federal government, *2707*
Telephone in the Senate, *1717*
Vice president born in Vermont, *4676*
Year in which more than 500,000 immigrants arrived in the United States, *3110*

1882

Federally mandated alcohol abuse programs in schools, *3944*
Immigration ban enacted by Congress, *3112*
Labor Day parade, *2210*
Naval attaché, *2334*
Restrictions by Congress on immigration of Chinese laborers, *3111*
Tariff commission established by Congress, *4950*

1883

Antitrust law enacted by a state, *4952*
Coronation on territory that would later become part of the United States, *2381*
Federal civil service reform law that was effective, *2028*
Korean embassy, *2261*
Mayor of Abilene, TX, *1322*
State to legalize labor unions, *2488*
Supreme Court decision on criminal jurisdiction on Native American reservations, *4721*
Woman appointed to a federal government job through the Civil Service, *2029*

1884

African-American to preside over the national political convention of a major party, *3001*
American Prohibition Party presidential candidate, *3307*
Anti-Monopoly Party platform, *3049*
Anti-Monopoly Party presidential candidate, *3306*
Brothers nominated for the presidency at the same convention, *3245*
Democratic president whose party was in the minority in the Senate, *3717*
Equal Rights Party platform, *3050*
Equal Rights Party presidential candidate, *3308*
Labor bureau of the federal government, *2442*
Naval war college, *2615*
Political cartoon to decisively influence a presidential election, *3939*
President elected after the Civil War who had not served in it, *3409*
President who had been a newspaper publisher, *3496*
Presidential candidate from Kansas, *4581*
Presidential candidate from the Democratic Party to be elected after the Civil War, *3247*
Presidential candidate from Washington, DC, *1893*

Use of the term "mugwump", *2932*
Vice presidential candidate from California, *4644*
Vice presidential candidate from Connecticut, *4643*
Vice presidential candidate from Illinois, *4642*
Vice presidential candidate from Mississippi, *4641*
Woman to argue for women's suffrage before a major committee of Congress, *1960*
Woman vice presidential candidate, *3246*

1885

Catalog of government publications, *2055*
Federal ban on fencing public lands, *4186*
Federal bird protection agency, *4207*
Gridiron Club, *3858*
Monument to George Washington authorized by the federal government, *2708*
President elected for two nonconsecutive terms, *3410*
Secretarial help for senators, *1719*
State forest commission, *4142*
State gas commission, *4129*
State legislator who was African-American to represent a constituency with a white majority, *4545*
Treaties withdrawn by a president after they were submitted to the Senate, *2415*
Vice president born in Ohio, *4677*

1886

Construction of the Statue of Liberty on site, *1127*
Dedication ceremony for the Statue of Liberty, *1128*
Drama about the Civil War, *1393*
Forest service of the United States, *4143*
Gubernatorial election in which two brothers were the opposing candidates, *4491*
Organization in charge of the Statue of Liberty, *1126*
President who held a doctorate in a field other than law, *3497*
President whose private life was harassed by reporters, *3724*
State arbitration board for labor disputes, *2450*
Ticker-tape parade, *2211*
Wedding of a president in the White House, *5027*

1887

Customs fee stamps, *4806*
Federal law dissolving Native American tribes as legal entities, *2749*
Federal regulatory agency, *2007*
Jewish minister and envoy, *2335*
Labor activists to be executed, *2559*
Librarian of the Supreme Court, *2065*

Federal immigration station, *3114*
Forest and fish reserve, *4145*
Kansas Day, *2215*
National environmental organization, *2823*
Oratory course, *3064*
Pledge of allegiance to the flag, *1097*
Populist Party platform, *3054*
President whose predecessor and successor were the same man, *3412*
Presidential election in which a socialist party participated, *3202*
Single tax adopted by a city for local revenue purposes, *4825*
Socialist Labor Party presidential candidate, *3313*
State to declare Lincoln's Birthday a legal holiday, *2216*
Supreme Court justice with no judicial or political experience, *4770*
Vice presidential candidate from Texas, *4646*
Voting machines used in an election, *1281*
Women to attend a national political convention as delegates, *3003*

1893

Ambassador of the United States, *2336*
American provincial government in Hawaii, *4274*
Child born in the White House to a president, *5030*
Federal road agency, *4092*
First Lady to give birth during her husband's term in office, *3603*
Lynching ban enacted by a state, *1926*
Muckraking journal of importance, *3900*
Railroad safety law enacted by Congress, *4091*
Secretarial help for congressional representatives, *1513*
Vice president from Illinois, *4678*

1894

Agricultural appropriation, *4110*
City employment office, *2463*
Democratic president whose party was in the minority in both houses of Congress, *3718*
Dog licensing ordinance, *4024*
Federal law forbidding hunting on national park land, *4149*
Income tax levied by Congress in peacetime, *4807*
Monument to a president's mother, *2710*
Patriots' Day, *2218*
Pension fund for teachers, *2472*
President protected by the Secret Service, *3413*
Protest march on Washington, *2824*
Reference book of American political history, *1075*
Senate investigating committee, *1722*
State law on union discrimination, *2489*
Women elected to a state legislature, *4546*

1895

Former vice president who became a state governor, *4982*
Judicial test of the Sherman Antitrust Act, *4954*
National anti-saloon league, *2858*
President who had been an engineer, *3498*
Standardized foreign service examinations, *2337*
Supreme Court decision invalidating a federal tax, *4723*

1896

Absentee voting law enacted by a state, *4431*
Audobon society, *4209*
National Party presidential candidate, *3314*
National political organization for African-American women, *2846*
National Silver Party convention, *3316*
National Silver Party platform, *3056*
Presidential candidate from Nebraska, *4583*
Presidential candidate to ride in a car, *3250*
Presidential candidate to run his campaign by telephone, *2769*
Rural free mail delivery, *3163*
Silverite presidential candidate, *3315*
Socialist Labor Party platform, *3055*
Sound Money Democratic Party, *2935*
Sound Money Democratic Party platform, *3057*
Sound Money Democratic Party presidential candidate, *3317*
Supreme Court decision validating the doctrine of "separate but equal" provisions for African-Americans, *4724*
Utah constitution, *4405*
Utah state capital, *4352*
Utah state governor, *4498*
Woman to serve as a state senator, *4547*

1897

American Flag Association, *1098*
Charter of autonomy for Puerto Rico, *4888*
Copyrights registrar of the United States, *2509*
First Lady to sit next to her husband at state dinners, *3604*
Library of Congress building, *2066*
Municipal milk station, *4025*
National parent-teacher association, *3977*
New Mexico territorial governor who was of Mexican ancestry, *4880*
Performance of *The Stars and Stripes Forever*, *1120*
State to adopt the use of the initiative and referendum, *4432*
Vice president from New Jersey, *4679*

1898

American flag raised over Puerto Rico, *4889*
Foreign service school in a college, *2338*
Island territory annexed by the federal government, *4845*

1898—*continued*

National anti-imperialist organization, *2825*
Presidential call for volunteer troops to fight in the Spanish-American War, *2642*
Social Democracy of America Party, *2936*
Vending machine law enacted by a city, *4916*

1899

Admiral of the Navy, *2696*
Census of Puerto Rico, *3090*
Child of a president to serve in the armed forces, *3563*
House majority leader, *1567*
House majority whip, *1568*
House minority leader, *1569*
Juvenile court, *1272*
Primary election law enacted by a state, *4434*
State law outlawing political caricatures, *3940*
Voting machines in congressional elections, *4433*

1900

Civil governor of Puerto Rico under the Foraker Act, *4891*
Comprehensive federal legislation to protect wildlife, *4210*
Electric power in the Capitol, *1240*
Hawaiian territorial governor, *4881*
Presidential candidate who had served a prison term, *3251*
Silver Republican Party platform, *3060*
Silver Republican Party presidential candidate, *3321*
Social Democratic Party of America platform, *3059*
Social Democratic Party of America presidential candidate, *3319*
Social Democratic Party of the United States platform, *3058*
Social Democratic Party of the United States presidential candidate, *3318*
Socialist Party, *2937*
Unincorporated territory of the United States, *4890*
Union Reform Party platform, *3061*
Union Reform Party presidential candidate, *3322*
United Christian Party presidential candidate, *3320*
Vice presidential candidate from Minnesota, *4647*
Vice presidential candidate from Rhode Island, *4648*
Woman to make a seconding speech at a national political convention, *3004*

1901

African-American to receive a White House dinner invitation, *5031*

Army war college, *2616*
City government using the commission plan, *1288*
Holding company worth a billion dollars, *4917*
House minority whip, *1570*
License plates for vehicles, *4093*
President with an environmental agenda, *4123*
Resident commissioner from Puerto Rico, *4892*
Rights of way on federal reserves, *4188*
Speeding driver law enacted by a state, *4094*
Statehouse with an all-marble dome, *4353*

1902

Census Bureau permanent organization, *3091*
Commemoration of the birthday of William McKinley, *2219*
Expansion and comprehensive renovation of the White House, *5032*
Federal penitentiary, *2576*
Fistfight in the Senate, *1723*
Large-scale federal irrigation legislation, *4196*
President to ride in a car, *3789*
President who had been president of a university, *3499*
Presidential yacht, *3788*
Reclamation service of the federal government, *4197*
United States case to be arbitrated in the Hague Permanent Court of Arbitration, *2264*
Workers' compensation insurance law enacted by a state, *2502*

1903

Antitrust Division in the Department of Justice, *4955*
Boycott law enacted by a state, *4918*
City to forbid the sale of firecrackers for Fourth of July celebrations, *2239*
Department of Commerce and Labor, *2043*
Federal bird reservation, *4211*
Federal wildlife refuge, *4212*
Mayor of Fairbanks, AK, *1325*
National political science society, *3073*
Secretary of commerce and labor, *1167*
State licensing law for nurses, *4026*
State to establish statewide primary elections, *4435*
Theater safety codes, *4043*

1904

Complete edition of *Journals of the Continental Congress*, *1049*
Continental Party presidential candidate, *3324*
Fingerprinting in federal penitentiaries, *2530*
Muckraking journalist who was a woman, *3891*
Native American state denied admission to the Union, *4304*
President since the Civil War who was a former cabinet member, *3500*

Presidential primary, *3203*
Socialist Party presidential candidate, *3323*
State licensing law for pharmacists, *4027*
Use of "American" as an adjective, *1068*
Vice president who succeeded to the presidency after a president's death and was then elected to a full term, *4983*
Vice presidential candidate from Nebraska, *4650*
Vice presidential candidate from West Virginia, *4649*

1905

Campaign finance reform proposal, *2783*
Industrial Workers of the World (Wobblies) convention, *2885*
International exchange of fingerprints, *2531*
Interstate Commerce Commission Medal of Honor, *4919*
Major American city founded in the 20th century, *1264*
National student socialist organization, *2826*
President to deliver his inaugural address bareheaded, *3668*
President to go underwater in a submarine, *3790*
President who advocated physical fitness, *3830*
President whose inaugural address did not include the word "I", *3669*
Year in which more than 1 million immigrants arrived in the United States, *3115*

1906

Cabinet member who was Jewish, *1169*
Consumer protection law enacted by Congress, *4920*
Criminal trial before the Supreme Court, *4703*
Employer's Liability Act enacted by Congress, *4052*
Federal law on product safety, *4028*
Labor union chartered by the federal government, *2490*
Muckraking novel of importance, *3892*
National monument designated by the federal government, *4150*
President to receive the Nobel Peace Prize, *3626*
President to visit a foreign country while in office, *3791*
Secretary of state to travel outside the United States on official business, *1168*
Travel expenses for the president, *3743*
Use of the term "muckraker", *3859*

1907

Air force, *2618*
Corrupt election practices law enacted by Congress, *2770*
Federal act regulating corporate contributions to election campaigns, *2784*

Federal horse farm, *4111*
Night court, *1273*
Oklahoma constitution, *4406*
Oklahoma state capital, *4354*
Oklahoma state governor, *4499*
Secret Service agent killed in the line of duty, *2581*
Senator of Native American descent, *1779*
Sterilization of humans by a state government as a matter of public policy, *3952*

1908

City government run by a city manager, *1289*
Environmental meeting for state governors, *4124*
Independence Party presidential candidate, *3325*
Municipal aviation tax, *4826*
National Conservation Commission, *4125*
Office buildings for U.S. senators and representatives, *1241*
Presidential candidate to appear in movie footage, *3252*
Price regulation law enacted by a state, *4956*
Senator who was the victim of an assassination attempt during a filibuster, *1780*
State law prohibiting discrimination against soldiers, *2657*
Vice presidential candidate from Iowa, *4651*
Vice presidential candidate from Nevada, *4652*
Workers' compensation insurance law enacted by Congress, *2503*

1909

Airplane owned by the United States, *1998*
Cherry trees planted in Washington, DC, *1894*
Child delinquency law enacted by a state, *3991*
Coin bearing the likeness of a president, *2164*
Corporation tax levied by Congress, *4808*
Credit union law enacted by a state, *2121*
Election using the preferential ballot system, *1282*
Federal hydroelectric plant, *4130*
First Lady to accompany her husband on the post-inauguration ride, *3670*
First Lady to attend all her husband's cabinet meetings, *3605*
International conservation conference, *4126*
Narcotics ban enacted by Congress, *4062*
National Association for the Advancement of Colored People, *2847*
Naturalized citizen to lie in state in the Capitol rotunda, *1242*
President to receive an annual salary of $75,000, *3744*
Senate permanent office building, *1724*
State-run old age home for pioneers, *4044*
State to ratify the 16th Amendment to the Constitution, *1846*

1910

Bureau of Mines, *4189*

Commerce court established by the federal government, *1977*

Federal act requiring congressional campaigns to disclose their finances, *2785*

Federal fine arts commission, *2017*

Former president to fly in an airplane, *3792*

New Hampshire presidential primary, *3204*

Pioneer Day (Idaho), *2220*

President to pitch a ball to open the baseball season, *3831*

Socialist mayor of a major city, *1326*

Supreme Court justice to be appointed and confirmed as chief justice, *4771*

Use of the term "dollar diplomacy", *2265*

1911

Airplane to land on the White House lawn, *5033*

City commissioner of Salt Lake City, UT, *1327*

Congressional representative to attend college after his term of service, *1598*

Congressional representative who was a Socialist, *1597*

Edition of the complete *Records of the Federal Convention of 1787*, *1833*

Federal act limiting campaign expenditures by candidates for Congress, *2786*

Federal cemetery containing the remains of both Union and Confederate soldiers, *2669*

Irrigation project authorized by the federal government, *4198*

Movie censorship board established by a state, *3860*

National anti-women's suffrage organization of importance, *2897*

National Parks Conference, *4151*

Senate majority leader, *1725*

Senate minority leader, *1726*

State-run adult education program, *3979*

State system of vocational, technical, and adult education, *3978*

State welfare payments, *3992*

Year that a substantial number of Socialists were elected to public office, *2938*

1912

Arizona constitution, *4408*

Arizona state capital, *4356*

Arizona state governor, *4501*

Children's Bureau, *3993*

City government using the manager plan, *1290*

Federal Bureau of Investigation, *2532*

Foreign and Domestic Commerce Bureau of the federal government, *4921*

Minimum wage law enacted by a state, *2496*

Movie censorship law enacted by Congress, *3861*

New Mexico constitution, *4407*

New Mexico state capital, *4355*

New Mexico state governor, *4500*

President whose government included all 48 contiguous states, *3414*

Presidential candidate wounded in an assassination attempt, *3253*

Presidential election in which two former presidents were defeated, *3205*

Progressive Party (Bull Moose), *2939*

Progressive Party (Bull Moose) presidential candidate, *3326*

Senator expelled from the Senate for corrupt election practices, *1781*

State to ratify the 17th Amendment to the Constitution, *1847*

Third party to win more than 25 percent of the popular vote in a presidential election, *3206*

Vice presidential candidate from Wisconsin, *4653*

Woman bailiff, *2533*

Year the Republican party renominated its entire ticket, *3005*

1913

Annual message delivered by a president in person since the 18th century, *3754*

Banking reform after the Civil War, *2108*

Bonding law enacted by a state, *4275*

Cabinet member to serve in five successive administrations, *1173*

Cabinet secretary to share the same last name as the president, *1170*

County public defender, *1275*

Democratic floor leader, *1727*

Department of Commerce, *2044*

Department of Labor, *2045*

Federal arbitration board for labor disputes, *2451*

Federal Office of Agricultural Markets, *4112*

First Lady to remarry after the death of her husband, *3606*

Governor of territorial Alaska, *4882*

Municipal small claims court, *1274*

Pension plan sponsored by a company, *2473*

Political cartoon entered in the *Congressional Record*, *1514*

President born in New Jersey, *4612*

President to advocate the creation of a national presidential primary, *3207*

President to hold regular press conferences, *3725*

Presidential press conference, *3862*

Rose garden planted at the White House, *5034*

Secretary of commerce, *1171*

Secretary of labor, *1172*

Senate majority whip, *1728*

Senator elected by popular vote under the 17th Amendment to the Constitution, *1782*

State court of small claims, *4414*

State law regulating chiropractic, *4029*

Strike settlement mediated by the federal Labor Department, *2480*

Transcontinental highway, *4276*

Veterans of Foreign Wars of the United States, *2701*

Woman mayor elected west of the Rocky Mountains, *1328*

1914

Alcohol prohibition vote taken in Congress, *3945*

Civilian government in the Panama Canal Zone, *4846*

Drug control law enacted by Congress, *4063*

Federal reserve banks, *2109*

Federal Trade Commission, *4922*

Filing date for 1040 tax forms, *4809*

First Lady to write a book published by a commercial publisher, *3607*

Railroad operated by the federal government, *4095*

Smoking ban in the Senate chambers, *1729*

Supreme Court decision concerning food additives, *4725*

War Risk Insurance Bureau, *4053*

White House Correspondents Association, *3726*

Year when the United States became a creditor nation, *2129*

1915

Arms sales to Russia, *2266*

Election using proportional representation, *1283*

Federal advisory committee on aeronautics, *4096*

Formal appeal for recognition of Native Americans as United States citizens, *2750*

Jurisdiction to provide for old-age pensions, *2474*

Missouri Day, *2221*

Movies in the Senate chambers, *1731*

President who was the child of divorced parents, *3564*

Senate minority whip, *1732*

Senate speech that lasted from sunset to sunrise, *1730*

State governor who was Jewish, *4502*

1916

American Indian Day, *2751*

Bird protection international treaty, *4213*

Birth control clinic, *3994*

Change in the method of allocating convention delegates, *3006*

Commemoration of the birthday of the Marquis de Lafayette, *2222*

Democratic presidential and vice presidential team to be reelected, *3415*

Election in which returns were broadcast on radio, *3208*

Federal child labor law, *2457*

Federal farm loan board, *4113*

Federal tax on war profits, *4810*

Grant-in-aid enacted by Congress to help the states build roads, *4190*

National Park Service, *4152*

Political news broadcast by radio, *3872*

Portrait of Uncle Sam to become famous, *1134*

Presidential election in which the wrong candidate was declared the winner by early newspaper editions, *3209*

President's flag, *1099*

Supreme Court justice who was Jewish, *4772*

Tax act to require publication of national tax statistics, *4811*

United States International Trade Commission, *4923*

Vice presidential candidate from Louisiana, *4654*

Year in which the Democratic party renominated its entire ticket, *3007*

Zoning ordinance, *1291*

1917

Constitutional amendment requiring ratification within seven years, *1848*

Federal propaganda bureau, *2643*

Federal tax on excess corporate profits, *4813*

Formal address by a president to the Senate in the Senate chamber, *1733*

Governor of Utah who was not a Mormon, *4503*

Liberty loans, *2091*

Loan made by the United States to a war ally, *2090*

New Mexico state governor of Latino ancestry, *4504*

Political cartoonist elected to Congress, *1571*

President who was born in the 20th century, *3467*

Senate rule allowing the limitation of debate, *1734*

State legislature to use an electric vote recorder, *4548*

Supreme Court decision barring racial segregation in housing, *4726*

War hero to lie in state in the Capitol rotunda, *1243*

Woman elected to the House of Representatives, *1599*

Year in which federal revenues from income taxes exceeded those from customs duties, *4812*

1918

Alcohol prohibition law enacted by Congress, *3946*

Cartoon unit run by a government, *3941*

Child of a president to die in combat, *3565*

Federal employment service, *2464*

1918—*continued*

Government operation of railroads, *4097*

National creed, *3074*

President to receive a passport while in office, *3793*

President to visit Europe while in office, *3794*

State of Income report released by the federal government, *4814*

States to ratify the 18th Amendment to the Constitution, *1849*

U.S. district attorney who was a woman, *1978*

Vice president to preside over a cabinet meeting, *4984*

White House china service that was made in the United States, *5035*

Year the public debt of the United States exceeded $10 billion, *2130*

1919

American Legion, *2702*

American woman to become a member of the British Parliament, *2268*

Armistice Day, *2223*

Bank wholly owned and operated by a state, *2110*

Communist Labor Party of America, *2940*

Communist Party of America, *2941*

Federal Trade Commission trade practice conference, *4924*

Gasoline tax levied by a state, *4830*

General association of nations promoted by a president, *2267*

General of the Armies of the United States, *2626*

National committee of a major political party to admit women as members, *2962*

National file on suspected political radicals, *2534*

National Parks Association, *4153*

President since Washington to submit a treaty to the Senate in person, *3514*

States to ratify the 19th Amendment to the Constitution, *1850*

Summer of national race riots, *2848*

Veterans Day, *2224*

Woman to act as unofficial president of the United States, *3416*

1920

Census in which the national population exceeded 100 million, *3092*

City to run an airport, *1265*

Constitutional amendment proposal to guarantee women the right to vote, *1962*

Effective state arbitration law, *2452*

Farmer Labor Party presidential candidate, *3327*

Federal statute to be printed on paper, *1515*

Incumbent senator to be elected president, *3501*

League of Women Voters, *2898*

Lithographed buttons, *2804*

Local election results to be announced on radio, *1284*

National civil liberties advocacy group, *2827*

Plymouth Rock monument, *2711*

President in whose honor an asteroid was named, *3627*

President who had been defeated in a earlier campaign for the vice presidency, *3417*

Presidential candidate from Missouri, *4584*

Presidential candidate from Utah, *4585*

Presidential candidate to run for office while in prison, *3255*

Presidential candidate who had been divorced, *3254*

Presidential election in which the candidates of both major parties were newspaper publishers, *3210*

Presidential election in which women voted, *3211*

Red scare, *2828*

Single Tax Party presidential candidate, *3328*

State with a population of more than 10 million, *3081*

Subcabinet member who was a woman, *1174*

Woman to serve as a judge in a general court, *4415*

Woman to serve as Civil Service commissioner, *2031*

Women's Bureau of the Labor Department, *2443*

Women's Equality Day, *2225*

Year when the urban population of the United States exceeded the rural population, *3082*

1921

Arms control conference held in the United States, *2269*

Burial at the Tomb of the Unknown Soldier, *2670*

Chicano civil rights organization, *2864*

Chief justice of the Supreme Court who had served as president of the United States, *4773*

Civil rights chair at a college, *2526*

Comptroller general of the United States, *2092*

Conference of great powers, *2270*

Death penalty imposed by a woman judge, *2561*

Father and son to occupy the same cabinet post, *1175*

Former president to become chief justice of the Supreme Court, *3502*

General Accounting Office, *1516*

Immigration quotas enacted by Congress, *3116*

Inaugural address broadcast to a crowd with loudspeakers, *3671*

President who came before the Senate to discourage action on a bill, *1735*

President who rode to his inauguration in a car, *3672*

Presidential inauguration broadcast over a public address system, 3673

Presidential inauguration speech read on radio at the same time that it was delivered in Washington, 3674

Sales tax enacted by a state, 4831

State cigarette tax, 4080

Treaty between the United States and Germany, 2416

Unknown soldier to lie in state in the Capitol rotunda, 1244

Vice president to regularly attend cabinet meetings, 4985

1922

Congresswoman who was a mother, 1600

Election campaign using radio, 2771

Massacre of strikebreakers by union members, 2886

National arbitration organization, 2591

National monument to Abraham Lincoln, 2712

National Radio Conference, 3873

President to make a radio broadcast, 3755

President to use a radio, 3832

White House Police Force, 5036

Woman to be appointed a senator, 1783

Woman to serve as a justice of a state supreme court, 4416

1923

City to own a National Football League franchise, 1266

Congresswoman elected to serve in the place of her husband, 1601

President and First Lady to die during the term for which he had been elected, 3531

President to visit Alaska while in office, 3795

President to visit Canada during his term in office, 3796

President who was sworn in by his father, 3675

President whose father outlived him, 3566

Presidential message to Congress that was broadcast on radio, 3756

Proposal for a constitutional amendment mandating equal legal rights for women and men, 1963

Radio broadcast of an open session of Congress, 1817

State law establishing English as an official language, 3117

State pension laws, 2475

U.S. Army Band, 2627

Weekly newsmagazine, 3901

Woman to serve as a federal internal revenue collector, 4815

1924

American political party funded and operated by a foreign nation, 2942

Bonus voting system, 3008

Citizenship and public affairs school at a college, 3065

Commonwealth Land Party presidential candidate, 3329

Comprehensive bill appropriating payments to legislative employees and clerks, 1653

Democratic congresswoman, 1602

Foreign Service of the United States, 2339

Law by which Native Americans became American citizens, 2752

Nationwide municipal reform organization, 1292

Newsreels showing presidential candidates, 3863

Nominating convention that required more than 100 ballots, 3010

Park planning agency with oversight of the capital city, 1895

Political convention to be broadcast on radio, 3009

President buried in Washington, DC, 3532

President to make a radio broadcast from the White House, 3757

President who was born in a hospital, 3468

Presidential candidate from Oregon, 4586

Presidential candidate from West Virginia, 4587

Presidential candidate from Wisconsin, 4588

Presidential election in which a communist party participated, 3212

Progressive Party (1924) presidential candidate, 3330

Progressive Party (of 1924), 2943

State to allow execution by lethal gas, 2562

Vice presidential candidate from Montana, 4655

Wilderness area to be formally named, 4154

Woman delegates to a Democratic convention, 3011

Woman to receive nominating votes for the vice presidency at the convention of a major party, 3012

Woman to serve as a state governor, 4505

Woman vice presidential candidate in the 20th century, 3256

1925

African-American labor union, 2887

Arbitration law enacted by Congress, 4945

Car insurance law enacted by a state, 4054

Congress whose members received a salary of $10,000, 1654

Congresswoman to serve 18 terms, 1603

Federal act regulating the receipt of gifts by candidates for Congress, 2787

Legal clash between evolutionists and creationists, 1950

President who was sworn in by a former president, 3676

Presidential inauguration to be broadcast on radio, 3677

1925—*continued*

Presidential voice to become nationally familiar, *3758*

Republican floor leader, *1736*

State supreme court in which all the judges were women, *4417*

Supreme Court nominee to testify before the Senate Judiciary Committee, *4774*

Vice president to receive the Nobel Peace Prize, *4986*

Woman to serve as legation secretary, *2341*

Woman vice consul, *2340*

1926

African-American woman lawyer admitted to practice before the Supreme Court, *2592*

Air force branch of the military, *2619*

Coin bearing the likeness of a living president, *2165*

Federal prison for women, *2577*

Major American city to elect a woman as mayor, *1329*

Mexican-American political newspaper, *3925*

Queen to visit the United States during her reign, *2382*

Senate election in which neither candidate was seated after a recount, *1737*

Senator unseated after a recount, *1784*

Survey of urban air pollution, *4160*

Woman sheriff, *2535*

1927

American executions to excite worldwide protest, *2563*

American flag displayed from the right hand of the Statue of Liberty, *1100*

Congress to enact more than 1,000 laws, *1517*

Federal agency to regulate broadcast media, *3875*

King born in the United States, *2383*

Monument to the American flag, *2713*

Propaganda course at a college, *3066*

Radio Commission of the United States, *3874*

Senate leader to occupy the party floor leader's desk, *1738*

Senator barred for spending too much on an election campaign, *1785*

State aviation department, *4277*

1928

Campaign bumper stickers, *2805*

Commemoration of the birthday of Woodrow Wilson, *2226*

Federal flood control legislation, *4191*

Latino elected to the Senate, *1786*

Physician to Congress, *1518*

Presidential candidate from a major party who was Catholic, *3258*

Presidential candidate killed in a rescue attempt, *3257*

Presidential nomination ceremony broadcast on radio, *3013*

Television broadcast of a presidential candidate accepting his nomination, *3259*

Woman justice on the federal bench, *1979*

1929

Air-conditioning in the Capitol, *1245*

Cabinet member convicted of a crime, *1177*

Congressman from a northern state who was African-American, *1604*

Currency of the standard size, *2166*

Federal farm board, *4114*

President born in Iowa, *4613*

President from California, *4614*

President to have a telephone on his desk in the White House, *3834*

President who had been a Boy Scout, *3833*

Radio broadcast from the Senate chamber, *1739*

Secretary of state to receive the Nobel Peace Prize, *1176*

State tax on chain stores, *4832*

Statewide Chicano civil rights organization, *2865*

Vice president from Kansas, *4680*

Vice president who had served as Senate majority leader, *4988*

Vice president who was of Native American ancestry, *4989*

Vice president's widow to receive a pension, *4987*

White House press secretary, *3727*

1930

Chief executive-elect of a foreign country to serve in a diplomatic position in Washington, *2342*

Chief justice of the Supreme Court to lie in state in the Capitol rotunda, *1246*

Consolidated federal agency for veterans' affairs, *2703*

County hydroelectric plant, *4131*

Grain stabilization corporation, *4115*

Large-scale repatriation program, *3118*

Police bureau of criminal alien investigation, *2536*

President buried in the National Cemetery, *3533*

Quack who almost became a state governor, *4506*

Secretary of labor who was not a member of the American Federation of Labor, *2444*

Supreme Court justice to be appointed, confirmed, and inaugurated twice, *4775*

Supreme Court nominee to be rejected by the Senate in the 20th century, *4776*

1931

Absolute monarch to visit the United States, *2384*

Pennsylvania Day, 2227

Resale price maintenance law enacted by a state, 4925

State to legalize casino gambling, 4001

Supreme Court decision invalidating a state law on First Amendment grounds, 4727

Woman to chair a House committee, 1605

1932

African-American vice presidential candidate in the 20th century, 3260

Bonus Army, 2829

Father-mother-son senatorial dynasty, 1787

Federal Home Loan Bank board, 2111

Gasoline tax levied by Congress, 4816

International friendship park, 2271

Jobless Party presidential candidate, 3331

Liberty Party (modern) presidential candidate, 3332

National union for public employees, 2491

Political party to nominate the same candidate six times, 3016

President to invite the president-elect to confer with him, 3419

President who came before the Senate unannounced, 1740

President whose mother was eligible to vote for him, 3567

Presidential candidate from Arkansas, 4589

Presidential candidate to accept his party's nomination in person, 3014

Presidential candidate to fly to a political convention, 3015

Reconstruction Finance Corporation, 2093

Republican presidential and vice presidential team to lose a bid for reelection, 3418

State to ratify the 20th Amendment to the Constitution, 1851

State unemployment insurance, 2465

Territory of the United States to win independence, 4847

Use of the term "New Deal", 3075

Vice presidential candidate from Oklahoma, 4656

Vice presidential candidate from Washington State, 4657

Woman elected to the Senate for a full term, 1788

Woman to take charge of an American legation, 2343

Wooden money, 2167

1933

Abrogation of the gold standard, 2095

Agricultural Adjustment Administration, 4118

Ambassador to the Soviet Union, 2345

Bank deposit insurance law enacted by Congress, 2112

Cabinet in which all members were sworn in at the same time and place, 1178

Central statistical board, 3093

Commodity credit corporation, 4929

Constitutional amendment ratified by state conventions rather than state legislatures, 1853

Constitutional amendment submitted to the states for repeal, 1854

Consumers' advisory board of the federal government, 4927

Delaware Day, 2229

Diplomatic relations between the United States and the Soviet Union, 2272

Electoral college members invited to a presidential inauguration, 3213

Electric power contract between a city and the federal government, 4132

Emergency housing corporation, 4046

Farm credit administration, 4116

Federal agency regulating labor relations, 2446

Federal Alcohol Control Administration, 3947

Federal Deposit Insurance Corporation, 2113

Federal Emergency Relief Administration, 2466

Federal industrial advisory board, 4928

Federal regulatory agency for agricultural lending, 4117

Federal trade policy executive committee, 4930

First Lady to hold a White House press conference, 3609

First Lady to undertake a career of public service, 3608

Gold hoarding order, 2094

Home owners' loan corporation, 4045

Income tax enacted by a state, 4833

Industrial Recovery Act, 4926

Interstate legislative conference, 4550

Labor advisory board of the federal government, 2445

Maritime Day, 2228

National emergency council, 2008

National employment system, 2467

President-elect who was the target of an assassination attempt, 3449

President to negotiate with the Soviet Union, 2273

President with a serious physical disability, 3420

Presidential fireside chat, 3759

Savings and loan association established by the federal government, 2114

Science and technology advisory board, 2072

Sit-down strike, 2481

State governor to be granted almost dictatorial power, 4507

State to ratify the 21st Amendment to the Constitution, 1852

Swimming pool in the White House, 5037

Vice president from Texas, 4681

Woman diplomat to hold the rank of minister, 2344

Woman to chair a Senate committee, 1789

Woman to serve in a presidential Cabinet, 1179

1933—*continued*
Woman to serve in a state legislature as speaker of the House, *4549*
Youth conservation corps, *4127*

1934

Archivist of the United States, *2067*
Community to fingerprint its citizens, *2537*
Convening of Congress under the 20th Amendment to the Constitution, *1519*
Credit union act passed by Congress, *2122*
Death penalty authorized by federal law, *2564*
Federal agency to regulate the securities markets, *2139*
Federal archiving agency, *2056*
Federal Communications Commission, *3876*
Federal corporation to encourage the purchase of electric appliances, *4931*
Federal credit union, *2123*
Federal Housing Administration, *4047*
Federal insurance program for bank deposits, *2115*
Federal theater project, *2018*
First Lady to travel in an airplane to a foreign country, *3610*
Mediation agency for railroads and commercial aviation, *4099*
National Mediation Board, *2453*
National Union for Social Justice, *2944*
Nationwide highway planning surveys authorized by Congress, *4098*
Negative election campaign run by media specialists, *2772*
President to conduct religious services as commander-in-chief of the Navy, *3734*
President to go through the Panama Canal while in office, *3798*
President to make a radio broadcast from a foreign country, *3760*
President to visit Hawaii while in office, *3799*
President to visit South America while in office, *3797*
Public Enemy Number 1, *2538*
Revenue stamp printed by the Post Office Department, *4817*
Soviet representative to the United States, *2346*
State legislature with a single chamber in the post-Revolutionary era, *4551*
State-run liquor stores, *4278*
Woman to head the state committee of a major political party, *2963*
Woman to serve as justice of the Circuit Court of Appeals, *1980*

1935

Bill to depict both sides of the Great Seal of the United States, *2169*
Currency note printed with the Great Seal of the United States, *2168*
Federal motor carrier legislation, *4100*

Large-scale federal jobs-creation programs, *2468*
National conference on crime, *2539*
National identification scheme for American citizens, *4068*
Native American tribal constitution, *2753*
Organized civil rights protest by people with disabilities, *2830*
President to read a veto message to Congress, *3761*
Session of the Supreme Court held in its own building, *4704*
Supreme Court decision striking down a major piece of New Deal legislation, *4728*

1936

African-American woman to serve as a federal administrator, *1999*
Day on which the president and the vice president were both out of the country, *3800*
Federal gold vault, *2096*
Federal law mandating a 40-hour work week, *2497*
Magazine of the federal government, *3902*
National Greenback Party presidential candidate, *3333*
National political convention to abrogate the two-thirds rule, *3017*
Nominating convention of a major party in which the delegates nominated a candidate without taking a ballot, *3018*
Pensions paid by the federal government to workers in private industry, *2476*
Pope to visit the United States before his election, *2385*
Presidential candidate from North Dakota, *4590*
Scientific public opinion polls, *2773*
Supreme Court decision banning coerced confessions, *4729*
Union Party, *2945*
Union Party presidential candidate, *3334*
Vice president's flag, *1101*

1937

Birth control clinic run by a state government, *3995*
Federal codification board, *2009*
Game preserve appropriation by the federal government, *4214*
Marijuana ban enacted by Congress, *4064*
Mayor of a major city to be recalled, *1330*
National seashore, *4155*
President inaugurated on January 20, *3678*
President to ride on a diesel train, *3801*
Senate parliamentarian, *1741*
Socialist Workers Party, *2946*
State to outlaw sit-down strikes, *2482*
Two joint sessions of Congress held on one day, *1520*

Woman to serve as foreman on a federal grand jury, *1981*

1938

African-American woman to serve as a state legislator, *4552*

Chicano labor convention, *2888*

Civil Aeronautics Authority, *4101*

Congresswoman who was not sworn in, *1606*

Federal Crop Insurance Corporation, *4119*

Gas regulation legislation passed by Congress, *4932*

Minimum wage law enacted by Congress, *2498*

Performance of "God Bless America", *1121*

Postage stamp issue depicting all the presidents, *3167*

State to require blood tests for marriage licenses, *3953*

Woman of American ancestry to become a queen, *2386*

1939

Administrative Office of the United States Courts, *1982*

African-American woman to be appointed a municipal judge, *1276*

Army officer to occupy the nation's highest military post and its highest nonelective civilian post, *2628*

British monarchs to visit the United States, *2387*

Child of a president to serve in the Senate, *1790*

Executive Office of the President, *3773*

Internal Revenue Code, *4818*

National Aviation Day, *2230*

Pinball ban enacted by a city, *4002*

President to deliver an address on television, *3762*

President to hold an airplane pilot's license, *3802*

Presidential campaign manager who was a woman, *2774*

Reorganization of the federal government in the 20th century, *2010*

Supreme Court decision affirming the right of Congress to set a time limit for the ratification of a constitutional amendment, *4730*

White House budget office, *3774*

1940

Air defense military organization, *2620*

Commissioner of Food and Drugs, *4030*

Congress in session a full year, *1818*

Draft law enacted by Congress during peacetime, *2636*

Draft number drawing, *2637*

Federal sedition law passed in peacetime since the Sedition Act of 1798, *3864*

Federal social security system, *4073*

Political convention to be televised, *3019*

President elected for third and fourth terms, *3421*

Registration of aliens by the federal government, *3119*

Speaker of the House of Representatives to serve longer than ten years, *1636*

Vice presidential candidate from Arizona, *4658*

1941

Congressional representative to vote twice against entry into war, *1608*

Declaration of U.S. alliance in World War II, *2644*

Federal attempt to address racial discrimination in employment, *1927*

Federal government airport, *1896*

Independent intelligence organization, *2671*

International oil embargo, *2275*

Large foreign aid package, *2274*

Member of Congress to enter active duty in the military during World War II, *1607*

Monument to four presidents, *2714*

Photographic pictorial biography of a president, *3541*

President who had been a military pilot, *3700*

President who had served in the U.S. Navy, *3699*

President whose second inauguration was attended by his mother, *3679*

President whose third inauguration was attended by his mother, *3680*

Presidential library, *3422*

Prime minister of Great Britain to address Congress in person, *2388*

Smoke control ordinance, *4161*

State to declare war on a foreign power before the U.S. government, *2645*

Vice president from Iowa, *4682*

1942

Citizenship granted on foreign soil, *3120*

Health insurance law enacted by a state, *4055*

National advocacy organization for people with physical disabilities of all kinds, *2831*

National guestworker program, *2469*

President to become a godfather to a member of the British royal family, *3568*

President to make a radio broadcast in a foreign language, *3763*

President to use Camp David as a retreat, *3835*

President who had served as a Navy pilot, *3701*

Presidential railroad car, *3803*

Price regulation law passed by Congress, *4933*

Wartime population relocation order, *2646*

1943

African-American to head a major congressional committee, *1609*

1943—*continued*

Ambassador to Canada, *2347*

Bill calling for independence for Puerto Rico, *4893*

Cabinet member to address a joint session of Congress, *1180*

Consolidated headquarters for the Department of Defense, *2606*

Doctrine of unconditional surrender by a foreign enemy of the United States, *2647*

Election law lowering the voting age in a state to 18, *4436*

Federal act regulating contributions by labor unions to congressional campaigns, *2788*

First Lady buried in Arlington National Cemetery, *3611*

Meeting of an American president and a Soviet leader, *2277*

National monument dedicated to an African-American, *2716*

National monument to Thomas Jefferson, *2715*

President in the 20th century to receive a medal for heroism, *3702*

President of a black African country to visit the United States, *2389*

President to fly in an airplane while in office, *3804*

President to visit a foreign country in wartime, *3805*

President to visit Africa during his term in office, *3806*

President to visit Asia during his term in office, *2276*

Presidential pet to star in a movie, *3569*

Statue of an American woman in uniform, *2717*

Woman to serve as presiding officer of the Senate, *1742*

Year the public debt of the United States exceeded $100 billion, *2131*

1944

African-American newspaper reporter accredited to the White House, *3893*

America First Party presidential candidate, *3335*

Congresswoman to visit a theater of war, *1610*

Federal execution of an organized crime boss, *2565*

Federal law providing for the education of veterans, *2704*

Meeting to establish the United Nations, *2430*

National organization of Native Americans, *2754*

Political action committee (PAC), *2832*

President who had been awarded the Distinguished Flying Cross, *3628*

President who had parachuted from an airplane, *3808*

Presidential airplane, *3807*

Public service symbol of the federal government, *1135*

Radiation experiments on human beings conducted by the federal government, *2073*

Republican presidential candidate to give his acceptance speech at the national convention, *3020*

Veteran of World War II to be elected to the Senate, *1791*

Woman to clerk for a Supreme Court justice, *4777*

Woman to serve as secretary of a major political party, *2964*

1945

African-American judge on the federal bench, *1983*

Civil rights anthem to achieve fame, *1122*

Congresswoman who had been an actress, *1611*

Defeated presidential and vice presidential candidates to die during the term they had sought, *3261*

Federal treaty signed by a woman, *2417*

First Lady appointed to a federal post after the death of her husband, *3612*

Fluoridation program for a city water supply, *4031*

Industrial and labor relations school at a college, *3067*

International Monetary Fund meeting, *2097*

President from Missouri, *4615*

President inaugurated at the White House, *3681*

President to attain the rank of 33rd-degree Mason, *3836*

President to have three vice presidents, *3423*

President to watch the swearing-in ceremony of a Supreme Court justice he appointed, *3424*

State agency for enforcing equal treatment in employment, *2459*

State in which all electricity came from public power plants, *4133*

Strike to last longer than a year, *2889*

United Nations conference, *2431*

United States representative to the United Nations, *2432*

Use of children's fiction as propaganda in occupied territory overseas, *2278*

Vice president from Missouri, *4683*

Woman cabinet member to serve under two presidents, *1181*

World bank, *2116*

1946

African-American territorial governor appointed by the president, *4883*

Ban-the-bomb demonstrations, *2833*

Council of Economic Advisers, *3775*

Defense Department think tank, *2672*

Full-time Spanish-language television station, *3877*

Law requiring registration of congressional lobbyists, *1521*

President to travel underwater in a submarine, *3809*

President who was a graduate of the United States Naval Academy, *3703*

President who was born after World War II, *3469*

Professional staffers on congressional committees, *1522*

Regulating agency of the nuclear industry, *4134*

Republican and Democratic policy committees in the Senate, *1743*

School for congressional pages, *1641*

United Nations General Assembly meeting, *2433*

Woman mayor of San Juan, PR, *4894*

1947

African-American newspaper reporter accredited to the congressional press gallery, *3894*

Air pollution control bureau, *4162*

Ambassador to India, *2348*

Armed Forces Day, *2231*

Central administration for all branches of the military, *2629*

Challenge to school segregation in the South, *1928*

Collective bargaining agency for the federal government, *2447*

Congressional opening session to be televised, *1819*

Congressional representative who received a Medal of Honor and was graduated from the U.S. Naval Academy, *1612*

"Daily Digest" of the Congressional Record, *1523*

Department of Defense, *2046*

Department of the Air Force, *2047*

Federal agency for the gathering of foreign intelligence, *2674*

Mutual-defense pact for the Western Hemisphere, *2418*

National Security Council, *2673*

Policy of containment of world communism, *2281*

President to address the National Association for the Advancement of Colored People, *1929*

President to pay a state visit to Canada, *3810*

President who had been president of a union, *3503*

Presidential address televised from the White House, *3765*

Regional agreement for collective defense under the U.N. Charter signed by the United States, *2420*

Regional cooperative in Oceania, *2419*

Secretary of defense, *1182*

State of the Union address, *3764*

State to ratify the 22nd Amendment to the Constitution, *1855*

U.S. aid program to contain the spread of communism, *2280*

United States delegation to the United Nations, *2434*

Woman to head a congressional mission abroad, *2279*

1948

Agency for disseminating information about the United States to foreign countries, *2282*

Ambassador to Israel, *2349*

Birth registration uniform numbering system, *3954*

Economic Cooperation Administration, *2283*

Federal law against threatening the president, *3450*

Governor of Puerto Rico to be elected, *4895*

Labor dispute in which the Taft-Hartley Act was invoked, *2483*

Monument to a Native American, *2718*

Order integrating the armed forces, *2658*

Political party convention at which spectators were charged an admission fee, *3022*

Presidential candidate who was renominated after a defeat, *3262*

Progressive Party (1948) presidential candidate, *3339*

Progressive Party (of 1948), *2947*

Senator to win a seat that had been occupied by his father and mother, *1793*

Socialist Workers Party presidential candidate, *3336*

States' Rights Democratic Party, *2948*

States' Rights Democratic Party presidential candidate, *3338*

Vegetarian Party presidential candidate, *3337*

Vice presidential candidate from Idaho, *4659*

Water pollution law enacted by Congress, *4163*

Woman elected to the Senate in her own right, *1792*

Woman to serve as secretary of the Republican National Convention, *3021*

1949

Congressional standing committee headed by an African-American, *1572*

Congresswoman to advance to the Senate, *1613*

Conservation park dedicated to Theodore Roosevelt, *4156*

General Services Administration, *2011*

National Chicano labor organization, *2890*

Peacetime alliance of European and North American nations, *2284*

President to receive an annual salary of $100,000, *3745*

President who had been divorced, *3613*

Presidential inauguration in which a rabbi participated, *3682*

Presidential inauguration to be televised, *3683*

1949—*continued*

Published federal guidelines for food toxicity, *4032*

Vice president known as "the Veep", *4990*

Vice president to marry during his term in office, *4991*

Vice president to receive a salary of $30,000, *3746*

Woman to hold the rank of ambassador, *2351*

Woman to serve as ambassador to the United States, *2350*

Woman treasurer of the United States, *2098*

1950

African-American delegate to the United nations, *2435*

African-American justice of the Circuit Court of Appeals, *1984*

Census in which the national population exceeded 150 million, *3094*

City to discontinue garbage collection, *4164*

Civil Defense director, *2675*

Federal agency to support civilian scientific research, *2074*

Husband and wife to be elected simultaneously to both chambers of a state legislature, *4553*

Uniform Code of Military Justice, *2659*

1951

Federal government office to be computerized, *2000*

First Lady to be received by the pope, *3614*

Gambling permit stamp issued by the federal government, *4003*

Large area of the United States contaminated by nuclear radiation, *4165*

Live atomic bomb explosion shown on television, *3878*

Peacetime death sentence for espionage, *2566*

Presidential press conference recorded on tape, *3728*

Senator who had been a newspaper reporter, *1794*

Television eyewitness allowed to testify in a federal court, *1985*

1952

African-American woman to run for vice president, *3263*

American Labor Party convention, *3342*

Campaign hosiery, *2806*

Church of God Party presidential candidate, *3341*

Commonwealth of the United States, *4897*

Constitution Party presidential candidate, *3343*

Cryptologic agency of the federal government, *2676*

Fireproofing in the White House, *5038*

Flag of the Commonwealth of Puerto Rico, *4896*

Microfilm editions of federal publications and documents, *2057*

Mother and son simultaneously elected to Congress, *1614*

National convention to require a pledge of party loyalty from its delegates, *3024*

National conventions to receive gavel-to-gavel television coverage, *3023*

Plastic skimmer campaign hats, *2807*

Political campaign based on talkathons, *2775*

Poor Man's Party presidential candidate, *3340*

Presidential candidate from Washington State, *4591*

Presidential election in which a computer was used to predict the outcome, *3214*

Televised speech that confirmed a candidate's place on the vice presidential ticket, *3264*

Television ad saturation campaign, *2777*

Year in which there were no reported lynchings of African-Americans, *1930*

1953

African-American with the rank of ambassador, *2354*

Book censorship board established by a state, *3865*

Cabinet conference to be televised, *1184*

Congresswoman to represent the United States in the United Nations, *2285*

Department of Health, Education, and Welfare, *2048*

Government agency promoting small business, *4934*

Internal Revenue Service, *4819*

President barred under the 22nd Amendment from running for a third term, *3425*

President born in Texas, *4616*

President-elect to attend a religious service along with his staff, *3735*

President to become a full communicant of a church during his term in office, *3736*

Presidential press conference that was entirely "on the record", *3866*

Secretary of health, education, and welfare, *1183*

Three brothers from one family to serve in the Senate, *1795*

Vice president from California, *4684*

White House official who was an African-American, *5039*

Woman career diplomat to advance to the rank of ambassador, *2353*

Woman to serve as ambassador to a major nation, *2352*

1954

Cabinet session to be broadcast on radio and television, *1186*

Civil defense test held nationwide, *2678*

Congressional hearings to be nationally tele-vised, *1524*

Federal execution for the killing of an FBI agent, *2567*

Military academy for Air Force officers, *2617*

Overthrow of a democratic foreign government arranged by the Central Intelligence Agency, *2677*

Political editorial broadcast on radio and televi-sion, *3879*

Secretary to the cabinet and presidential assis-tant, *1187*

Senator elected by a write-in vote, *1796*

State governor to appoint two United States senators in one year for interim terms, *4508*

State legislative hearing to be shown on televi-sion, *4554*

Subcabinet member who was African-American, *1185*

Terrorist shootings in the Capitol Building, *1247*

United States representative to the United Na-tions Educational, Scientific and Cultural Or-ganization, *2436*

1955

Cabinet session held at a place other than the seat of the federal government, *1188*

Federal government building built to withstand a nuclear attack, *2001*

IRS area service center, *4820*

Mass boycott by civil rights protesters, *2849*

Minimum hourly wage of one dollar, *2499*

Pioneer Party presidential candidate, *3344*

Prayer and meditation room in the Capitol, *1248*

President to appear on color television, *3766*

President who had served as Senate majority leader, *3504*

Presidential news conference filmed for televi-sion and newsreels, *3729*

Seat belt law enacted by a state, *4102*

Year in which the salary of members of Con-gress exceeded $20,000 per year, *1655*

1956

Alaska constitution, *4409*

Congressional representative of Asian ancestry, *1615*

Congressional representative reelected after serving a prison term, *1616*

Federal aid to libraries, *2068*

Federal education grants to the children of de-ceased veterans, *3980*

Liberal Party convention, *3345*

Mexican-American elected to the Texas state senate, *4555*

Motto of the United States, *3076*

Presidential candidate to run for office after suffering a heart attack, *3265*

Republican president to win reelection in the 20th century, *3426*

Republican presidential and vice presidential team to be reelected, *3427*

States' Rights Party presidential candidate, *3346*

Taxpayer usage study, *4821*

Texas Constitution Party presidential candidate, *3347*

Vice presidential candidate from Utah, *4660*

1957

Continental air defense alliance, *2607*

Federal civil rights agency, *1904*

Latino caucus of a major political party, *2965*

Mexican-American mayor of El Paso, TX, *1331*

National lobbying group for retirees, *2834*

President to fly in a helicopter, *3811*

President to go underwater in an atomic-powered submarine, *3812*

Senate solo filibuster to last for more than 24 hours, *1744*

Use of federal troops to enforce integration, *1931*

Year in which all the justices of the Supreme Court were graduates of a law school, *4778*

1958

Aerospace agency of the federal government, *2075*

African-American to become chief of a diplo-matic mission, *2355*

Democratic senator from Maine, *1797*

John Birch Society, *2835*

Moratorium on nuclear testing, *2286*

Pension for presidents and their widows, *3747*

Urban renewal program, *1267*

1959

Alaska state capital, *4357*

Alaska state governor, *4509*

Ambassador to Nepal, *2356*

American Nazi Party, *2950*

Captive Nations Week, *2287*

Crop recalled by order of the Food and Drug Administration, *4033*

Hawaii constitution, *4410*

Hawaii state governor, *4510*

President of all 50 states, *3428*

President whose party was in the minority in both houses of Congress during three con-gresses, *3719*

Senator of Asian ancestry, *1798*

Spy satellites, *2679*

State admitted to the Union that had no border with another state, *4305*

State admitted to the Union that was separated by a substantial body of water, *4306*

State capital that was the capital of a sovereign kingdom, *4358*

1959—*continued*

Statewide automotive emissions standards, *4103*

Workers World Party, *2949*

1960

African-American presidential candidate, *3266*

American flag to orbit the earth, *1102*

Civil rights sit-in, *2850*

Conservative Party of Virginia presidential candidate, *3349*

Federal undersea park, *4157*

Independent Afro-American Party presidential candidate, *3350*

National States' Rights Party presidential candidate, *3348*

Polynesian territory of the United States to adopt a constitution, *4848*

Presidential candidate from Alaska, *4593*

Presidential candidate from Mississippi, *4592*

Presidential election debates shown on television, *3215*

Senate election race in which both candidates were women, *1745*

Signal intelligence satellite, *2680*

State to ratify the 23rd Amendment to the Constitution, *1856*

Tax Cut Party presidential candidate, *3351*

Vice presidential candidate from Florida, *4661*

1961

Affirmative action order issued by the federal government, *1905*

African-American judge to serve on a federal district court, *1987*

Assassination planned by the U.S. government in peacetime, *2681*

Break between the United States and a member of the Organization of American States, *2289*

Cabinet member who was the brother of the president, *1189*

Consolidated federal agency to regulate maritime commerce, *4935*

Independent disarmament agency, *2609*

Member of the Foreign Service to hold the three top diplomatic posts in Europe, *2357*

Minimum wage law established by a city for public contract work, *2500*

Municipal air-raid shelter, *1268*

Openly homosexual individual to run for public office, *1285*

Peace Corps, *2288*

President who was Catholic, *3737*

Presidential inauguration to be televised in color, *3684*

Presidential news conference to be televised live, *3730*

President's Commission on the Status of Women, *1964*

Public disclosure of foreign travel expenditures by members of Congress, *1525*

Skyjacking law enacted by Congress, *4936*

Statewide land-use program, *4192*

Supreme Court decision extending the protection of the Bill of Rights to defendants in state courts, *4731*

Technical advisors sent to Vietnam, *2648*

U.S. district attorney who was African-American, *1986*

Use of the term "military-industrial complex", *2608*

Vice president to be sworn in by the speaker of the House, *4992*

Woman to serve as a president's personal physician, *3776*

1962

African-American woman to be elected to a judgeship, *1277*

Democratic governor of Vermont since the Civil War, *4511*

Federal laws requiring drug manufacturers to prove the effectiveness of their products, *4034*

First Lady to have a private audience with the pope, *3615*

Important Muslim American weekly, *3926*

Marriage of two descendants of different presidents, *3571*

Nuclear war confrontation, *2649*

President to switch parties in the 20th century, *3720*

President with a brother in the Senate, *3570*

Presidential hot line, *3837*

Republican governor of Oklahoma, *4512*

State to decriminalize homosexual acts between consenting adults in private, *1909*

State to have a state sport, *4279*

State to ratify the 24th Amendment to the Constitution, *1857*

Supreme Court decision on legislative apportionment, *4732*

Supreme Court decision on school prayer, *4733*

Woman ambassador to a Communist-bloc nation, *2358*

1963

Air pollution law of importance enacted by Congress, *4166*

Assassination of a president captured on film, *3451*

Commemorative postage stamp depicting a First Lady, *3168*

Commission appointed to investigate the assassination of a president, *3453*

Congressional ban on sex discrimination in wages, *1965*

Congressional representative sworn in before eight o'clock in the morning, *1617*

Homosexual rights demonstration in the United States, *2868*

Honorary citizenship authorized by Congress, *3121*

Nuclear arms-control treaty, *2421*

Office of the Special Representative for Trade Negotiations, *4937*

One-dollar Federal Reserve notes, *2170*

Photograph of the Senate in session, *1746*

President to witness the firing of a Polaris missile, *3838*

President whose father and mother both survived him, *3534*

Telephone hot line, *2290*

Television newswoman to report from Capitol Hill, *3880*

Trial by a panel of judges to determine the winner of a state election, *4437*

Vice president who was present at the assassination of the president he succeeded, *3452*

Woman to administer the presidential oath of office, *3685*

1964

Announcement that a U.S. embassy was bugged, *2359*

Comprehensive civil rights law enacted by Congress, *1932*

Comprehensive wilderness law, *4215*

Courtroom verdict to be televised, *3867*

Federal law mandating equal pay for women, *2460*

Federal law prohibiting discrimination in employment on the basis of sex, *1966*

Federal network of protected wilderness, *4158*

Former president to address the Senate, *3767*

Occupation of federal territory by Native American protesters in the modern era, *2755*

Office of Economic Opportunity, *3981*

Permanent Senate internal disciplinary committee, *1747*

Political ad raising fears of nuclear war, *2778*

Popular hoarding of a lower-denomination coin, *2171*

President and First Lady to receive honorary degrees at the same time, *3629*

President from a Southern state since the Civil War, *3429*

Presidential candidate from Arizona, *4594*

Presidential election in which the Republican Party earned a significant number of votes in the South, *3216*

Presidential election in which the state of Vermont was carried by a Democrat, *3217*

Presidential election in which votes were tallied electronically, *3218*

Shutdown of a college campus by student protesters, *2836*

State lottery in modern times, *4004*

Supreme Court decision giving protection to criticism of public officials, *4734*

United Nations permanent ambassador who was a woman, *2437*

Vice presidential candidate from Colorado, *4662*

Woman to receive nominating votes for the presidency at the convention of a major party, *3025*

Woman to serve on a federal government commission, *2002*

Year when citizens of Washington, DC, could vote in a presidential election, *1897*

1965

Act eliminating silver from most coinage, *2172*

African-American attorney to serve as solicitor general, *4705*

African-American woman to serve as a United States ambassador, *2360*

Cabinet meeting attended by a foreign national, *1190*

Consolidated arts funding agency, *2019*

Demonstration in Washington against the Vietnam War, *2859*

Department of Housing and Urban Development, *2049*

Federal aid program for primary and secondary schools, *3982*

Federal law requiring fair employment practices, *2461*

Federal law specifying penalties for the kidnappers and assassins of presidents, *3454*

Federal law to effectively protect the voting rights of African-Americans, *1933*

First Lady to hold the Bible at her husband's inauguration, *3686*

Government-funded health care program for the poor, *4056*

Health insurance plan enacted by Congress, *4057*

House page who was African-American, *1643*

Immigration quota applied to Mexico, *3122*

IRS Computing Center, *4822*

Nationwide consumer boycott in support of workers, *2891*

Pope to visit the United States, *2390*

President-elect to ride in an armored car at his inauguration, *3687*

President to meet with a pope in the United States, *3431*

President to view his inaugural parade from a heated reviewing stand, *3688*

Secret Service protection for former presidents and their families, *3430*

Senate page who was African-American, *1642*

State law to end de facto segregation in schools, *1934*

State narcotics ban, *4065*

State to ratify the 25th Amendment to the Constitution, *1858*

1965—*continued*

Supreme Court decision postulating a constitutional right to privacy, *4735*

Vice president born in South Dakota, *4685*

Vice president from Minnesota, *4686*

Woman to serve as chief justice of a state supreme court, *4418*

1966

African-American senator to be elected by popular vote, *1799*

African-American to serve in a presidential cabinet, *1191*

African-American woman to serve as judge of a federal district court, *1988*

Black Panther Party, *2951*

Black Power advocate, *2851*

Chicano radical nationalist movement, *2866*

Department of Transportation, *2050*

Federal endangered species list, *4216*

Freedom of Information Act, *2058*

Medicare identification cards, *4058*

National Organization for Women, *2899*

Official residence for the vice president, *4993*

Republican governor of Arkansas since Reconstruction, *4513*

Republican governor of Florida since Reconstruction, *4514*

Secretary of housing and urban development, *1192*

Space treaty signed by the United States, *2422*

1967

African-American to serve as chief executive of a major city, *1332*

Ambassadors in service to wed, *2361*

Attorney general whose father had also served as attorney general, *1194*

Ban on sex discrimination in hiring by the federal government, *1967*

Commissioner and council government of Washington, DC, *1898*

Federal Judicial Center, *1989*

Major city to elect an African-American as mayor, *1333*

National Chicano civil rights organization, *2867*

Plebiscite on the political status of Puerto Rico, *4898*

President who had college experience as a Senate staff member, *3505*

Presidential commission on overhauling the budgetary process, *2099*

Public defender hired by a state, *4419*

Salary review commission for elected officials, *1656*

Secretary of transportation, *1193*

State law legalizing abortion for medical reasons, *3955*

State ombudsman, *4280*

State to allow publicly traded corporations to obtain gambling licenses, *4005*

Supreme Court justice who was African-American, *4779*

Woman governor of Alabama, *4515*

1968

African-American to become chief of a State Department bureau, *2362*

African-American woman elected to the House of Representatives, *1618*

African-American woman to run for president, *3268*

Ambassador assassinated in office, *2363*

Ambassador killed by a terrorist attack, *2364*

American Independent Party, *2952*

American Independent Party presidential candidate, *3353*

American military massacre of political importance, *2650*

Choice of an island city for a convention, *3026*

Federal law creating Monday holidays, *2232*

Federal law granting equal access to disabled people, *1906*

Filibuster against a Supreme Court appointment, *1748*

Freedom and Peace Party presidential candidate, *3354*

Militant Native American civil rights organization, *2756*

National political convention to propose African-Americans for the offices of president and vice president, *3028*

Naturalization ceremony in the White House, *3123*

Nonproliferation treaty for weapons of mass destruction, *2423*

Peace and Freedom Party presidential candidate, *3352*

People's Constitutional Party presidential candidate, *3355*

Political convention to be televised in color, *3027*

Political interview aired on a television newsmagazine, *3881*

Politician to be assassinated while campaigning for his party's presidential nomination, *3267*

President who was a Rhodes Scholar, *3839*

Presidential candidate from Minnesota, *4595*

Roman Catholic clergyman sentenced to jail in the United States for political crimes, *2860*

Secret Service protection for major presidential and vice presidential candidates and nominees, *3269*

Supreme Court justice to participate in a television program, *4780*

U.S. balance of trade deficit in the 20th century, *2132*

Urban land-grant college, *3983*

Women to run as presidential candidates in the 20th century, *3270*

1969

African-American mayor of a major Southern city, *1334*

Council on Environmental Quality, *3777*

Federal agency for the support of economic development in Latin America and the Caribbean, *2291*

First Lady who was president of the student government at college, *3616*

Homosexual rights protest, *2870*

President to attend the launching of a manned space flight, *3840*

President to receive an annual salary of $200,000, *3748*

Radical homosexual organization, *2869*

Republican governor of Virginia since Reconstruction, *4516*

Senator to act in the movies, *1800*

Standardized criteria for federal incorporation, *2003*

State to mandate the votes of its presidential electors, *3219*

Vice president from Maryland, *4687*

Vice president to become president after a hiatus, *4994*

Vietnam War Moratorium Day demonstration, *2861*

1970

African-American mayor of a major Eastern city, *1335*

Cabinet member to serve in four different capacities, *1195*

Census compiled in part from statistics obtained by mail, *3096*

Census in which the national population exceeded 200 million, *3095*

City occupying more than 1,000 square miles, *1269*

Common Cause, *2837*

Congressional representative of Puerto Rican ancestry, *1620*

Congresswoman who was Jewish, *1621*

Earth Day, *2233*

Federal agency for administering credit unions, *2124*

Gay pride march, *2871*

National railroad, *4104*

Nationwide campus rioting, *2862*

No-fault car insurance law enacted by a state, *4059*

No-fault divorce law enacted by a state, *3956*

President who had served as ambassador to the United Nations, *3506*

Restoration of land to a Native American tribe, *2757*

Right to Life Party, *2953*

Roman Catholic priest to serve as a voting member of Congress, *1619*

School district to implement court-ordered busing to achieve racial integration, *1935*

Sky marshals, *2540*

Strike of postal employees, *2484*

United Nations Security Council resolution vetoed by the United States, *2438*

Woman to serve as director of a state bureau of corrections, *2578*

1971

Agency overseeing national elections, *2012*

Governor of the U.S. Virgin Islands, *4900*

House page who was female, *1644*

Law allowing corporations to form political action committees, *2838*

Libertarian Party, *2955*

Mandatory congressional 30-day summer recess, *1526*

Mass return of military decorations by war veterans, *2863*

National Women's Political Caucus, *2900*

Outdoor wedding held at the White House, *5040*

People's Party, *2954*

President to tape all his conversations in the White House, *3432*

Prior restraint of the press by order of the federal government, *3868*

Senate pages who were female, *1645*

State bottle bill, *4167*

State litter law, *4168*

State to ratify the 26th Amendment to the Constitution, *1859*

Supreme Court decision invalidating a state law on the grounds of gender discrimination, *4737*

Supreme Court decision upholding the power of Congress to outlaw racial discrimination in employment, *4736*

Vote in the House of Representatives to be tallied by machine, *1573*

Woman to serve as mayor of Oklahoma City, OK, *1336*

Women to become Secret Service agents, *2582*

1972

Attorney general to plead guilty to a criminal offense, *1196*

Campaign finance law that set limits on media spending, *2789*

Congressional candidate elected while missing, *1622*

Eagle Forum, *2839*

Federal agency chief to lie in state in the Capitol rotunda, *1249*

Federal agency to oversee consumer safety, *4938*

1972—*continued*

Income-tax checkoff to provide for the financing of presidential general election campaigns, *4823*

Large-scale presidential media event, *3731*

Libertarian Party presidential candidate, *3356*

Noise-control law enacted by a state, *4169*

People's Party presidential candidate, *3357*

President to address Soviet citizens on Soviet television, *3768*

President to visit a nation not recognized by the U.S. government, *3813*

President to visit the Soviet Union, *3814*

Presidential candidate from South Dakota, *4596*

Republican senator from North Carolina elected in the 20th century, *1801*

Strategic Arms Limitation Treaty, *2424*

Supreme Court decision barring the death penalty, *4738*

Vice presidential candidate from Washington, DC, *1899*

Vice presidential candidate of a major political party to resign before the election, *3271*

Woman to receive nominating votes for the presidency at a Democratic Party convention, *3029*

Woman to serve as chairman of a major political party, *2966*

1973

African-American congresswoman from a Southern state, *1623*

African-American mayor of Atlanta, GA, *1337*

African-American mayor of Detroit, MI, *1338*

African-American mayor of Los Angeles, CA, *1339*

Armed occupation by Native American protesters in the modern era, *2758*

Congresswoman to give birth while holding office, *1624*

Convictions in the Watergate case, *3517*

Curator of the Supreme Court, *4706*

Electoral vote cast for a woman presidential candidate, *3220*

Federal civil rights law for people with disabilities, *1907*

First Lady to earn a professional degree, *3617*

National homosexual rights organization, *2872*

National Right to Life Committee, *2840*

Native American tribe restored to federally recognized status after termination, *2759*

Oil embargo in peacetime, *2293*

Openly homosexual politican to win a municipal election, *1286*

President who had served as chairman of his political party, *3507*

Shuttle diplomacy, *2292*

State building located outside a state, *4281*

State governor of Asian ancestry, *4517*

Supreme Court decision giving equal legal status to men and women in the armed forces, *4740*

Supreme Court decision on the legality of abortion, *4739*

Televised Watergate hearings, *3882*

U.S. Labor Party, *2956*

Vice president appointed under the 25th Amendment to the Constitution, *4996*

Vice president born in Nebraska, *4688*

Vice president from Michigan, *4689*

Vice president to resign as a result of a criminal investigation, *4995*

Vote in the House of Representatives to be recorded electronically, *1574*

Woman to become an assistant secretary of state, *2365*

Women to serve as federal marshals, *2541*

1974

Congressional Budget Office, *1527*

Congresswoman who was a grandmother, *1625*

Democratic Party convention between presidential elections, *3030*

Homosexual civil rights legislation proposed at the federal level, *1910*

Incumbent president to testify before a committee of Congress, *1575*

Independent government agency to oversee political campaign contributions, *2790*

Policewomen to serve on the Capitol police force, *1250*

Politician who was openly homosexual to win a state election, *4438*

President and vice president elected together to resign their offices, *3434*

President and vice president to hold office together without either having been elected, *3437*

President born in Nebraska, *4617*

President from Michigan, *4618*

President to receive a presidential pardon, *3518*

President to resign, *3433*

President who came to the office through appointment rather than election, *3435*

Senate proceeding to be shown on television, *1749*

Senator who had been an astronaut, *1802*

Speed limit for highway traffic established by Congress, *4105*

Supreme Court ruling in a criminal case in which a United States president was named as a conspirator, *4741*

Vice president to succeed to the presidency after the resignation of the president, *3436*

Woman elected president of a state lawyers' association, *2593*

Woman governor elected in her own right, *4518*

Woman to serve as chairman of the Republican Party, *2967*

Woman to serve as mayor of a major city with a population over 500,000, *1340*

1975

African-American to serve as chief justice of a state supreme court, *4420*

Elected mayor of Washington, DC, in the 20th century, *1900*

Emperor of Japan to visit the United States, *2391*

Federal agency promoting safe transportation, *4106*

Federal law returning autonomy to Native American tribes, *2760*

Federal regulatory agency for futures trading, *2140*

Law limiting the use of Social Security numbers, *4069*

Limitations on senatorial earnings from honoraria, *1750*

President to make public the results of a routine medical examination, *3841*

President to survive two assassination attempts in one month, *3455*

President who had served as director of the Central Intelligence Agency, *3508*

Senate committee meetings open to the public, *1751*

Senate investigation of the FBI and the CIA, *2542*

Woman to serve as secretary of housing and urban development, *1197*

Year the public debt of the United States exceeded $500 billion, *2133*

1976

Congressional representatives to marry each other, *1626*

Law making misuse of Social Security numbers a federal crime, *4070*

Office of Science and Technology Policy, *3778*

Official etiquette for handling the American flag, *1103*

Radiation attacks against an American embassy, *2294*

Right-to-die law enacted by a state, *3958*

State dinner televised from the White House, *5041*

State voluntary sterilization regulation, *3957*

Televised presidential election debate between an incumbent president and a challenger, *3222*

U.S. Labor Party presidential candidate, *3358*

Woman governor of Washington, *4519*

Woman to deliver the keynote speech at a Democratic National Convention, *3031*

Woman to serve as ambassador to the Court of St. James, *2366*

Year in which abortion was mentioned in the national platforms of the major parties, *3221*

1977

African-American woman to serve in a presidential cabinet, *1198*

Attorney general to be incarcerated, *1200*

Department of Energy, *2051*

Judge who had served time in prison, *1278*

Office of Administration, *3779*

President from Georgia, *4619*

President to donate his papers to the federal government during his term in office, *3438*

President to make human rights a cornerstone of his foreign policy, *3439*

President to take the oath of office using a nickname, *3689*

President's mother to serve on a diplomatic mission, *3572*

Radio broadcast in which citizens telephoned the president, *3732*

Secretary of energy, *1201*

State to allow execution by lethal injection, *2568*

Woman to serve as secretary of commerce, *1199*

Woman to serve as under secretary of state, *2367*

1978

African-American militant to be elected mayor of a major American city, *1341*

Agency promoting ethical conduct in government, *2013*

Basketball star elected to the Senate, *1804*

Bilingual report of a congressional committee, *1576*

First Lady to pilot an airship, *3618*

Micronesian territory of the United States to adopt a constitution, *4849*

Middle East peace treaty brokered by an American president, *2425*

Republican governor of Texas since Reconstruction, *4520*

State plain-language law, *4282*

Woman elected to the Senate without prior experience in the House of Representatives, *1803*

Woman mayor of San Francisco, CA, *1342*

1979

African-American woman to serve as judge on the U.S. Court of Appeals, *1990*

Agency for administering federal personnel policies, *2032*

Citizens Party, *2957*

Coin to bear the depiction of an American woman, *2173*

Consolidated labor relations agency, *2448*

1979—*continued*

Department of Health and Human Services, *2052*

Diplomatic relations between the United States and the People's Republic of China, *2295*

Federal agency charged with protecting whistleblowers in the federal government, *2014*

Federal agency for national emergency management, *2015*

Large-scale hostage crisis, *2296*

Pope to visit the White House, *2392*

Secretary of education, *1203*

Secretary of health and human services, *1202*

State to declare sovereignty over a large tract of federal land, *4283*

Woman mayor of Chicago, IL, *1343*

1980

All-news television network, *3883*

American prisoner of war in Vietnam who was elected to Congress, *1806*

Boatlift of Cuban refugees, *3124*

Campaign finance law allowing members of the House to pocket leftover campaign funds, *1577*

Citizens Party presidential candidate, *3359*

Federal bailout of an auto manufacturer, *4939*

Federal Superfund for cleaning up toxic wastes, *4128*

Nuclear arms limitation treaty not approved by the Senate, *2426*

President who had been a professional actor, *3509*

Right to Life Party presidential candidate, *3360*

Televised debate among competitors for a party's presidential nomination, *2776*

Trade and Development Agency, *4940*

Vice presidential candidate from New Mexico, *4663*

Woman elected to the Senate whose political career owed nothing to a male relative, *1805*

Workers World Party presidential candidate, *3361*

1981

Mayor of a major American city who was of Mexican descent, *1344*

President inaugurated on the west front of the Capitol, *3690*

President to be wounded in an unsuccessful assassination attempt while in office, *3456*

Woman to become a Supreme Court justice, *4781*

Woman to serve as the United States representative to the United Nations, *2439*

Year the public debt of the United States exceeded $1 trillion, *2134*

1982

National monument to Vietnam veterans, *2719*

Year in which the salary of a Supreme Court justice topped $100,000, *4707*

1983

African-American mayor of Chicago, IL, *1345*

African-American mayor of Philadelphia, PA, *1347*

African-American to serve as chief sergeant-at-arms of a state legislature, *4556*

Latino mayor of a city without a large Latino population, *1346*

Presidential candidate who had been an astronaut, *3272*

Sex scandals involving congressional pages, *1646*

State teacher-testing requirement, *3984*

State to adopt a containership as its official ship, *4284*

U.S. embassy to be destroyed by a suicide bombing, *2368*

U.S. peacekeeping forces killed by suicide bombing, *2651*

Woman governor of Kentucky, *4521*

Woman to serve as secretary of transportation, *1204*

1984

City to extend domestic partnership benefits to homosexual employees, *1911*

Federal agency to promote the development of judicial administration in state courts, *4421*

Full diplomatic relations between the Vatican and the United States in the 20th century, *2297*

Green Party, *2958*

Initiative guaranteeing homeless people overnight shelter, *4048*

Presidential candidate from Colorado, *4597*

Presidential candidate in the 20th century to come within two percentage points of winning the entire electoral vote, *3274*

Presidential candidate to receive more than 50 million popular votes, *3275*

Soft-sell nostalgia ads, *2779*

United States Sentencing Commission, *1991*

Woman to run for vice president as the candidate of a major political party, *3273*

1985

Cabinet member indicted while in office, *1205*

Campaign funding organization for political candidates who support legal abortion, *2791*

Commercial-scale synthetic fuels plant owned by the federal government, *4135*

Inaugural parade cancelled in the 20th century, *3691*

President inaugurated in the Capitol rotunda, *3692*

President to formally transfer the presidency to an acting president, *3440*

Senator to fly in space, *1807*

Vice president to serve as acting president under the 25th Amendment, *4997*

Woman to head a regional bureau of the State Department, *2369*

1986

African-American ambassador to the Republic of South Africa, *2370*

Hawaii state governor of Hawaiian ancestry, *4522*

Hawaiian territorial governor who was of Hawaiian ancestry, *4884*

Martin Luther King Day, *2234*

National security advisor forced to resign, *1206*

Regular television coverage from the Senate chamber, *1752*

Woman governor of Nebraska, *4523*

1987

African-American mayor of Baltimore, MD, *1348*

City council composed entirely of Libertarian Party members, *1293*

Congressman to acknowledge that he was a homosexual, *1627*

Federal savings and loan bailout, *2125*

Parental leave law enacted by a state that applied to both mothers and fathers, *1968*

Session of Congress held outside Washington, DC, since 1800, *1820*

Treaty to reduce the number of nuclear missiles, *2427*

1988

African-American history trail, *4159*

Ban on surrogate motherhood enacted by a state, *3959*

Compensation paid to Japanese-Americans interned during World War II, *2652*

Consumer Party presidential candidate, *3363*

Federal agency with safety oversight of defense nuclear facilities, *2610*

Government official convicted of espionage for leaking secrets to the press, *2682*

Incumbent vice president to be elected president in the 20th century, *3441*

New Alliance Party presidential candidate, *3362*

Presidential candidate convicted in a federal criminal case, *3277*

Professional political consultant to head a major political party, *2968*

Smart-card welfare payments, *3996*

State ban on cheap handguns, *2543*

Supreme Court decision upholding the right to parody public figures, *4742*

Woman presidential candidate and African-American presidential candidate to get on the ballot in all 50 states, *3276*

1989

African-American mayor of New York City, *1351*

African-American mayor of Seattle, WA, *1350*

African-American state governor elected in his own right, *4524*

African-American to become director general of the Foreign Service, *2371*

African-American to serve as the chairman of a major political party, *2969*

Air bag requirement by the federal government, *4107*

Cabinet nomination by a newly elected president to be rejected, *1207*

Christian Coalition, *2841*

Department of Veterans Affairs, *2053*

Doomsday plan, *2683*

Father and daughter to serve simultaneously in the same house of representatives, *4557*

Federal drug control chief, *4067*

Incumbent African-American mayor of a major city to lose to a white candidate, *1349*

Latina elected to the House of Representatives, *1628*

Mercenaries arrested for planning terrorist acts on behalf of a foreign government, *2544*

Museum devoted solely to American political memorabilia, *1069*

Office of National Drug Control Policy, *4066*

Secretary of veterans affairs, *1208*

State to ration health care, *4035*

Summit conference on education by the nation's governors, *3985*

Supreme Court decision on the constitutionality of public religious displays, *4744*

Supreme Court decision on the right of a citizen to burn the American flag, *4743*

Woman to serve as surgeon general, *4039*

1990

African-American woman to serve as mayor of Washington, DC, *1901*

Alliance between the United States and the Soviet Union in an international crisis since World War II, *2299*

Census to count the homeless, *3097*

Chemical arms control treaty, *2428*

Comprehensive civil rights legislation for people with disabilities, *1908*

Electronic anti-counterfeiting features in U.S. currency, *2174*

Federal law to include the term "sexual orientation", *1912*

Mayor of a major American city arrested on drug charges, *1352*

Native American Day, *2235*

1990—*continued*

Post–Cold War summit of North American and European nations, *2298*

President to spend holidays with United States troops overseas, *3815*

Racial bias suit in which one African-American claimed discrimination by another African-American, *1936*

State taxation of religious goods, *4834*

State to elect two woman governors, *4525*

Treaty ending the Cold War, *2429*

Woman governor of Kansas, *4526*

Woman to serve as the police chief of a major city, *2545*

Year in which suburbanites outnumbered city and rural dwellers conbined, *3083*

1991

African–African-American Summit, *2300*

African-American mayor of Denver, CO, *1355*

African-American mayor of Kansas City, MO, *1354*

Alternate printing facility for U.S. currency, *2175*

British monarch to address Congress, *2393*

City to file for bankruptcy, *2135*

Ku Klux Klan leader to mount a credible campaign for state governor, *4440*

Mayoral election in a major city in which both candidates were African-Americans, *1356*

Modern proposal to ban lawyers from serving in state or local government, *2594*

Muslim mayor of an American city, *1353*

Muslim to offer the invocation to the House of Representatives, *1578*

Post–Cold War summit between the United States and the Soviet Union, *2301*

President whose body was exhumed, *3535*

State to have a gubernatorial runoff election, *4439*

State to have women serving simultaneously in the statehouse, House of Representatives, and Senate, *4285*

Statewide registration of assault weapons, *4036*

Supreme Court nominee accused of sexual harassment, *4782*

Woman governor of Oregon, *4527*

1992

African-American woman to serve as a senator, *1809*

Candidate for vice president who had been a prisoner of war in Vietnam, *3278*

Community service requirement for high school graduation, *3986*

Congresswoman who was a former welfare mother, *1629*

Constitutional amendment to be ratified two centuries after its proposal, *1860*

First Lady to deliver a major speech at a national political convention, *3619*

Grassroots Party presidential candidate, *3365*

Muslim to offer the invocation to the Senate, *1753*

Nationwide nutritional labeling standards, *4037*

Natural Law Party presidential candidate, *3366*

President and vice president in the 20th century who were both Southerners, *3442*

President from Arkansas, *4620*

Presidential election in which a Democratic winner failed to carry Texas, *3223*

Presidential nomination acceptance speech to mention homosexuals, *3032*

Secretary of state who was a former member of the Foreign Service, *1209*

State ban on the capture and display of whales and dolphins, *4217*

State law prohibiting specific civil rights protection for homosexuals, *1913*

State to be represented in the Senate by two women, *1808*

U.S. Taxpayers Party presidential candidate, *3364*

Woman mayor of Orlando, FL, *1357*

1993

African-American mayor of St. Louis, MO, *1358*

African-American to serve as secretary of agriculture, *1210*

African-American woman nominated to head the Justice Department's Civil Rights Division, *1937*

E-mail addresses for officials of the federal government, *2004*

Federal AIDS policy coordinator, *4038*

Federal government Web site on the Internet, *2005*

First Lady to be given an office in the West Wing of the White House, *3620*

First Lady who was also a federal official, *3621*

Homosexual rights protest of large scale, *2873*

House of Representatives that included a substantial number of African-American women, *1579*

Jewish woman to serve as a Supreme Court justice, *4783*

Library of U.S. foreign-policy papers on Africa and the Caribbean, *2069*

Outgoing president to order military action in the last week of his term, *3443*

Postwar President who had never served in the armed forces, *3704*

Recordings of Supreme Court proceedings released without the Court's approval, *4708*

State flag for Washington, DC, *1903*

Surgeon general who was African-American, *4040*

Vice president born in Washington, DC, *1902*
Woman governor of New Jersey, *4528*
Woman to head a branch of the United States military, *2611*
Woman to serve as attorney general, *1212*
Woman to serve as mayor of Minneapolis, MN, *1359*
Woman to serve as secretary of energy, *1211*

1994

Cold war enemy of the United States to join NATO, *2303*
Compensation paid to victims of mass racial violence, *1938*
County to file for bankruptcy, *2136*
Federal legislation recommending academic standards, *3987*
Federal protection against discrimination on the basis of sexual orientation, *1914*
Judicial decision allowing physicians to terminate the life of terminally ill patients at their request, *3961*
Law permitting doctor-assisted suicide, *3960*
Payment by the United States to a foreign nation for destroying nuclear weapons, *2302*
President to have a legal defense fund during his term in office, *3520*
Run-off election in the U.S. Virgin Islands, *4901*
Sexual harassment lawsuit against a president, *3519*
Summit of the Americas, *2304*
Visit by an American president to a country on the U.S. list of terrorist states, *3816*

1995

African-American mayor of Dallas, TX, *1360*
All-male march on Washington, *2852*
Attack by domestic terrorists on a federal facility resulting in large loss of life, *2006*
"Corrections Day", *1580*
Easing of trade limits on North Korea, *4941*
Full TV coverage of a state supreme court, *4422*
Independent agency for administering Social Security, *4074*
Municipal education program for men convicted of patronizing prostitutes, *2546*
National urban presidential primary, *3224*
Protest against the government of a black African country by African-Americans, *2305*
Reform Party presidential candidate, *3367*
Senate staff furlough, *1754*
Theory of fair division, *3077*
United States officials to die in the conflict in Bosnia, *2653*
White House Office for Women's Initiatives and Outreach, *3780*
Woman to preside over the Supreme Court, *4784*

1996

African-American mayor of Savannah, GA, *1361*
African-American to actively campaign for the presidential candidacy of the Republican Party, *3033*
African-American to serve as chief United States magistrate, *1992*
Capitol Hill employees to unionize, *2492*
Censorship of the Internet, *3869*
Convictions in the Whitewater case, *3521*
Executive Mayor of Miami–Dade County, FL, *1362*
Green Party presidential candidate, *3368*
Labor Party, *2959*
Postwar Democrat to win a second term as president, *3721*
Public information about the United States chemical arsenal, *2612*
State law banning corporate contributions to ballot question campaigns, *4441*
Talk-radio host to seek the presidential candidacy of a major party, *3884*
Vote on homosexual civil rights in the Senate, *1915*
Woman governor of New Hampshire, *4529*
Year the public debt of the United States exceeded $5 trillion, *2137*

1997

African-American congressman to deliver the Republican Party's official response to the State of the Union message, *1630*
African-American mayor of Houston, TX, *1364*
African-American mayor of Jackson, MS, *1363*
African-American to serve as secretary of labor, *1214*
Ambassador to Vietnam, *2372*
American citizen to become a Russian official, *2306*
City council with a majority of Green Party members, *1294*
City to ban products made in sweatshops, *2449*
Court decision preventing the enactment of term limits for state legislators, *4287*
Espionage budget made public, *2684*
Federal prosecution of a hate crime on the Internet, *1939*
Federal regulations restricting tobacco sales to minors, *4081*
First Lady to be depicted on a monument to a president, *3622*
International Conservative Congress, *2842*
IRS commissioner who was not an accountant or a lawyer, *4824*
Migration study jointly conducted by the United States and Mexico, *3125*
Non-NATO ally of the United States in the Western Hemisphere, *2308*
President to use the line-item veto, *3846*

1997—*continued*

Rules to prevent secret government-sponsored human experimentation, *2076*

Secretary of state to visit Vietnam, *2307*

Speaker who was punished by the House, *1637*

State in which two consecutive governors were forced to resign from office, *4530*

Statewide vote paid for by a single individual, *4286*

Supreme Court decisions invalidating three federal laws in three days, *4745*

United States coins depicting state symbols, *2176*

Voting rights in space, *4442*

White House Office of National AIDS Policy, *3781*

Woman governor of Arizona, *4531*

Woman to serve as secretary of state, *1213*

1998

African-American elected to a national leadership post in the Republican Party, *2960*

American Heritage Rivers, *4199*

Billion-dollar settlement in an environmental lawsuit, *4171*

Bounty of $5 million for an enemy of the United States, *2548*

Capitol Police Officers killed in the line of duty, *1251*

Deep underground nuclear waste storage site, *4170*

Detailed financial statement for the federal government, *2100*

Elected president to be impeached, *3632*

Federal judge to reduce a sentence as a protest against racial profiling, *1940*

Federal payment over the Internet, *2101*

Government report posted on the internet before its publication on paper, *2060*

Law making identity theft a federal crime, *4071*

Midterm election since World War II in which the president's party gained seats in the House of Representatives, *1581*

National DNA database, *2547*

President to attend a hockey game during his term in office, *3842*

President to give testimony before a grand jury during his term in office, *3522*

Reform Party candidate to win a governorship, *4443*

Ruling requiring retention of all electronic records of the federal government, *2059*

State appeals court decision ordering the extension of insurance benefits to homosexual partners of government employees, *1916*

State governor who had been a professional wrestler, *4532*

State in which women constituted more than 40 percent of the legislature, *4558*

Supreme Court decision on inclusion of candidates in televised political debates, *4746*

Woman governor of Ohio, *4533*

1999

Federal conviction for Internet piracy, *4942*

Former speaker of the House to become a television news commentator, *1638*

Internet camera showing the site of a presidential assassination, *3457*

Internet march on Washington, *2843*

President to participate in a live chat over the Internet, *3733*

President to visit Bulgaria, *3817*

Sex discrimination case to establish the rights of fathers of newborn babies, *1969*

Son of a Soviet premier to become an American citizen, *2394*

State criminal prosecution for the sale of confidential personal information, *4072*

State government to completely privatize its computer services, *4288*

State in which all of the top elected offices were held by women, *4289*

State police department to be monitored for racial profiling, *2549*

State to enact a school voucher plan, *3988*

Statewide school voucher program paid for with tax revenues, *3989*

Trial broadcast by the court over the Internet, *3870*

Woman appointed as chief White House counsel, *3782*

Year in which Medicare spending declined, *4060*

2000

Chaplain of the House of Representatives who was a Catholic priest, *1582*

Family Values Party presidential candidate, *3369*

First Lady elected to public office, *3623*

Multiracial census category, *3098*

Person to be counted in the 2000 census, *3099*

Presidential election in which all candidates and significant political parties operated sites on the Internet, *3225*

Senator elected posthumously, *1810*

State to enact a moratorium on executions, *2569*

State to establish civil unions for homosexual couples, *1917*

Vice president to chair the United Nations Security Council, *2440*

Vice presidential candidate who was Jewish, *3279*

Woman governor of Delaware, *4534*

Woman governor of Montana, *4535*

Woman governor of Puerto Rico, *4899*

Index by Month and Day

Following is a chronological listing of entries, arranged by month and day. (Many entries in the text are identified only by year, and so are listed only in the Index by Year.) To find an entry in the main body of the text, please search for the italicized number.

January 2—*continued*

1811	Senator to be censured, *1761*
1828	Washington news correspondent, *3887*
1854	State governor to be removed from office by a state supreme court, *4478*
1883	Mayor of Abilene, TX, *1322*
1890	Woman employed by the executive branch of the federal government for official duties, *2030*
1920	Red scare, *2828*
1934	State-run liquor stores, *4278*
1975	Elected mayor of Washington, DC, in the 20th century, *1900*
1996	African-American mayor of Savannah, GA, *1361*

January 3

1861	Slave state to reject secession, *1367*
1918	Federal employment service, *2464*
1933	Woman to serve in a state legislature as speaker of the House, *4549*
1934	Convening of Congress under the 20th Amendment to the Constitution, *1519*
1939	Child of a president to serve in the Senate, *1790*
1940	Congress in session a full year, *1818*
1945	Congresswoman who had been an actress, *1611*
1947	Congressional opening session to be televised, *1819*
	Congressional representative who received a Medal of Honor and was graduated from the U.S. Naval Academy, *1612*
1949	Congresswoman to advance to the Senate, *1613*
1953	Three brothers from one family to serve in the Senate, *1795*
1955	President who had served as Senate majority leader, *3504*
1956	Alaska constitution, *4409*
1959	Alaska state capital, *4357*
	President whose party was in the minority in both houses of Congress during three congresses, *3719*
	State admitted to the Union that had no border with another state, *4305*
1967	Ambassadors in service to wed, *2361*
1973	African-American congresswoman from a Southern state, *1623*
1976	Congressional representatives to marry each other, *1626*
1977	Judge who had served time in prison, *1278*

January 4

1836	Arkansas constitution, *4385*
1859	Meeting of the Senate in its present location, *1705*
	Senate session in the new Senate Chamber, *1706*
1896	Utah constitution, *4405*
	Utah state capital, *4352*
1915	State governor who was Jewish, *4502*
1971	Governor of the U.S. Virgin Islands, *4900*
1975	Federal law returning autonomy to Native American tribes, *2760*
1999	State in which all of the top elected offices were held by women, *4289*

January 5

1643	Legal divorce in the American colonies, *3948*
1776	Declaration of independence by a British colony, *1053*
	New Hampshire constitution, *4367*
	State legislature with a lower house known as the House of Representatives, *4539*
1802	Note-takers in the Senate, *1689*
1980	Televised debate among competitors for a party's presidential nomination, *2776*

January 6

1639	Colony to order surplus crops destroyed, *4108*
1759	First Lady, *3573*
1861	Northern city to consider secession during the Civil War, *1368*
1885	State legislator who was African-American to represent a constituency with a white majority, *4545*
1912	New Mexico constitution, *4407*
	New Mexico state capital, *4355*
1913	Woman mayor elected west of the Rocky Mountains, *1328*
1937	Two joint sessions of Congress held on one day, *1520*
1973	Electoral vote cast for a woman presidential candidate, *3220*

January 7

1935	Supreme Court decision striking down a major piece of New Deal legislation, *4728*

January 8

1783	State copyright law, *2505*
1790	Annual message, *3749*
1798	Constitutional amendment enacted after the passage of the Bill of Rights, *1839*

January 17—*continued*

1893 American provincial government in Hawaii, *4274*

1934 Federal corporation to encourage the purchase of electric appliances, *4931*

1961 Use of the term "military-industrial complex", *2608*

1969 President to receive an annual salary of $200,000, *3748*

1994 Federal protection against discrimination on the basis of sexual orientation, *1914*

January 18

1770 Attack on British soldiers by civilians in the Revolution, *1008*

1830 Permanent Committee on Roads and Canals, *1697*

1862 Former president whose death was officially ignored, *3529*

1949 Congressional standing committee headed by an African-American, *1572*

1966 Secretary of housing and urban development, *1192*

1990 Mayor of a major American city arrested on drug charges, *1352*

January 19

1840 Continent claimed for the United States, *2256*

1945 Defeated presidential and vice presidential candidates to die during the term they had sought, *3261*

1949 President to receive an annual salary of $100,000, *3745*

Vice president to receive a salary of $30,000, *3746*

1955 Presidential news conference filmed for television and newsreels, *3729*

1990 Woman to serve as the police chief of a major city, *2545*

January 20

1801 Supreme Court justice who had served in a presidential cabinet, *4761*

1869 Woman to testify as a witness at a Senate hearing, *1713*

1870 African-American senator, *1776*

1874 Salary cut for Congress, *1652*

1917 War hero to lie in state in the Capitol rotunda, *1243*

1937 President inaugurated on January 20, *3678*

1941 President whose second inauguration was attended by his mother, *3679*

President whose third inauguration was attended by his mother, *3680*

1945 President inaugurated at the White House, *3681*

President to have three vice presidents, *3423*

1949 Presidential inauguration in which a rabbi participated, *3682*

Presidential inauguration to be televised, *3683*

Vice president known as "the Veep", *4990*

1953 President barred under the 22nd Amendment from running for a third term, *3425*

President-elect to attend a religious service along with his staff, *3735*

1961 President who was Catholic, *3737*

Presidential inauguration to be televised in color, *3684*

Vice president to be sworn in by the speaker of the House, *4992*

1965 First Lady to hold the Bible at her husband's inauguration, *3686*

President-elect to ride in an armored car at his inauguration, *3687*

President to view his inaugural parade from a heated reviewing stand, *3688*

1966 Medicare identification cards, *4058*

1969 Vice president to become president after a hiatus, *4994*

1973 Convictions in the Watergate case, *3517*

1977 President to donate his papers to the federal government during his term in office, *3438*

President to make human rights a cornerstone of his foreign policy, *3439*

President to take the oath of office using a nickname, *3689*

1981 President inaugurated on the west front of the Capitol, *3690*

1985 Inaugural parade cancelled in the 20th century, *3691*

1986 Martin Luther King Day, *2234*

1993 First Lady to be given an office in the West Wing of the White House, *3620*

Postwar President who had never served in the armed forces, *3704*

1995 Easing of trade limits on North Korea, *4941*

1999 Internet march on Washington, *2843*

2000 Person to be counted in the 2000 census, *3099*

January 21

1895 Judicial test of the Sherman Antitrust Act, *4954*

1961 Cabinet member who was the brother of the president, *1189*

1985 President inaugurated in the Capitol rotunda, *3692*

1993 Woman to serve as secretary of energy, *1211*

1997 Speaker who was punished by the House, *1637*

January 22

1791 Use of the name "District of Columbia" and "Washington" for the federal city, *1867*

1917 Formal address by a president to the Senate in the Senate chamber, *1733*

1973 Supreme Court decision on the legality of abortion, *4739*

1996 Public information about the United States chemical arsenal, *2612*

January 23

1780 Town to be incorporated under the name of Washington, *1257*

1907 Senator of Native American descent, *1779*

1923 Congresswoman elected to serve in the place of her husband, *1601*

1973 Vote in the House of Representatives to be recorded electronically, *1574*

1977 African-American woman to serve in a presidential cabinet, *1198*

Woman to serve as secretary of commerce, *1199*

1997 Woman to serve as secretary of state, *1213*

January 24

1791 Presidential proclamation, *3373*

1943 Doctrine of unconditional surrender by a foreign enemy of the United States, *2647*

1972 Noise-control law enacted by a state, *4169*

January 25

1845 Annexation of territory by joint resolution of Congress after failure to accomplish the same object by treaty, *4298*

1929 Vice president's widow to receive a pension, *4987*

1945 Fluoridation program for a city water supply, *4031*

1951 Presidential press conference recorded on tape, *3728*

1961 Presidential news conference to be televised live, *3730*

Woman to serve as a president's personal physician, *3776*

1975 President to make public the results of a routine medical examination, *3841*

January 26

1695 Workers' compensation agreement, *2501*

1796 Associate Supreme Court justice to refuse elevation to the post of chief justice, *4757*

1826 First Lady born west of the Mississippi, *3589*

1837 Michigan constitution, *4386*

Michigan state capital, *4333*

1838 Alcohol prohibition law enacted by a state, *3943*

1907 Corrupt election practices law enacted by Congress, *2770*

1994 Cold war enemy of the United States to join NATO, *2303*

January 27

1863 Senator to draw a gun on the Senate sergeant at arms, *1775*

1900 Social Democratic Party of the United States platform, *3058*

Social Democratic Party of the United States presidential candidate, *3318*

1914 Civilian government in the Panama Canal Zone, *4846*

1975 Senate investigation of the FBI and the CIA, *2542*

January 28

1867 Major city to be unincorporated, *1261*

1915 Senate speech that lasted from sunset to sunrise, *1730*

1932 State unemployment insurance, *2465*

January 29

1802 Librarian of Congress, *2061*

1834 Use of federal troops to suppress a strike, *2478*

1861 Kansas state governor, *4483*

1874 Coins minted for a foreign government, *2163*

1877 Kansas Day, *2207*

1892 Kansas Day, *2215*

1902 Commemoration of the birthday of William McKinley, *2219*

1926 African-American woman lawyer admitted to practice before the Supreme Court, *2592*

January 29—continued

1951 Television eyewitness allowed to testify in a federal court, *1985*

1989 Office of National Drug Control Policy, *4066*

January 30

1798 Brawl in the House of Representatives, *1551*

Use of the mace of the House of Representatives to keep order, *1552*

1835 President who was the target of an assassination attempt while in office, *3444*

1942 Price regulation law passed by Congress, *4933*

January 31

1873 Abolition of the Senate franking privilege, *1715*

1940 Federal social security system, *4073*

2000 State to enact a moratorium on executions, *2569*

February

1741 Political magazine, *3895*

1757 Tolling of the Liberty Bell for an event of political importance, *1109*

1763 Use of the word "caucus", *1287*

1778 President who had made a transatlantic crossing, *3783*

1781 Broker to the Office of Finance of the United States, *2079*

1791 Difference of opinion among members of the cabinet, *1142*

1799 Death penalty in a tax riot, *2555*

1801 Meeting place of the Supreme Court in Washington, DC, *4699*

1804 Campaign committee appointed by a political party, *2761*

1853 Periodical of the women's rights movement, *2896*

1861 Capital of the Confederate States of America, *1370*

1906 Muckraking novel of importance, *3892*

1921 Civil rights chair at a college, *2526*

1933 State governor to be granted almost dictatorial power, *4507*

1972 Large-scale presidential media event, *3731*

1997 City to ban products made in sweatshops, *2449*

February 1

1775 Reconciliation plan to end the rebellion of the British colonies in America, *1014*

1790 Meeting place of the Supreme Court, *4693*

Session of the Supreme Court, *4694*

1860 Rabbi to open the House of Representatives with prayer, *1565*

1865 African-American lawyer admitted to practice before the Supreme Court, *2586*

State to ratify the 13th Amendment to the Constitution, *1842*

1904 President since the Civil War who was a former cabinet member, *3500*

1951 Live atomic bomb explosion shown on television, *3878*

1953 President to become a full communicant of a church during his term in office, *3736*

1960 Civil rights sit-in, *2850*

February 2

1790 Attorney general, *1139*

1848 Treaty with Mexico, *2413*

1870 African-American justice of a state supreme court, *4413*

1932 Reconstruction Finance Corporation, *2093*

February 3

1790 Clerk of the Supreme Court, *4695*

1803 Supreme Court decision declaring an act of Congress unconstitutional, *4712*

1809 Illinois territorial governor, *4857*

1836 Whig Party presidential candidate, *3285*

Whig Party resolutions, *3034*

1863 Offer by a foreign power to mediate the Civil War, *1388*

1865 Peace conference during the Civil War, *1389*

1933 Interstate legislative conference, *4550*

1947 African-American newspaper reporter accredited to the congressional press gallery, *3894*

1999 Sex discrimination case to establish the rights of fathers of newborn babies, *1969*

February 4

1789 President to receive the unanimous vote of the presidential electors, *3171*

1801 Supreme Court chief justice who had served in a presidential cabinet, *4762*

1861 Session of the Confederate Congress, *1371*

February 13

1799 Insurance regulation enacted by a state, *4049*

1861 Vice president to declare the election of the candidate who had opposed him for the presidency, *3197*

1889 Secretary of agriculture, *1165*

1930 Supreme Court justice to be appointed, confirmed, and inaugurated twice, *4775*

February 14

1790 President who had been a cabinet member, *3476*

Vice president who had served in a presidential cabinet, *4962*

1791 President to dispatch a personal envoy on an overseas mission, *2246*

1849 Photograph of a president in office, *3539*

1859 Oregon constitution, *4393*

Oregon state capital, *4340*

1865 Congressional directory, *1508*

1872 Bird refuge established by a state, *4206*

1883 State to legalize labor unions, *2488*

1899 Voting machines in congressional elections, *4433*

1903 Department of Commerce and Labor, *2043*

1912 Arizona constitution, *4408*

Arizona state capital, *4356*

Arizona state governor, *4501*

President whose government included all 48 contiguous states, *3414*

February 15

1799 Printed ballot, *4425*

1933 President-elect who was the target of an assassination attempt, *3449*

February 16

1903 Secretary of commerce and labor, *1167*

1938 Federal Crop Insurance Corporation, *4119*

February 17

1870 Woman to serve as justice of the peace, *1271*

1897 National parent-teacher association, *3977*

1936 Supreme Court decision banning coerced confessions, *4729*

1972 President to visit a nation not recognized by the U.S. government, *3813*

February 18

1688 Protest against slavery made by a religious group in the New World, *4226*

1834 Labor newspaper, *3919*

1841 Continuous Senate filibuster, *1700*

1856 Know-Nothing Party presidential candidate, *3290*

1861 First Lady of the Confederacy, *1376*

Inauguration of a rival president, *3660*

February 19

1807 Former vice president to be arrested, *4968*

1846 Texas state governor, *4475*

1942 Wartime population relocation order, *2646*

February 20

1781 Superintendent of finance under the Continental Congress, *2080*

1792 Postal service law enacted by Congress, *3146*

1809 Supreme Court decision on state recognition of federal court rulings, *4713*

1851 Private mint authorized by the federal government, *2156*

February 21

1828 Native American newspaper, *2740*

1862 Execution for slave trading carried out by the federal government, *2556*

1885 Monument to George Washington authorized by the federal government, *2708*

February 22

1791 Birthday visit made to a president by the entire Senate, *1679*

1819 Land acquired by the United States from Spain, *4840*

1842 Temperance address by a future president, *2855*

1846 Cracking of the Liberty Bell, *1112*

1847 Battle in which two future American presidents were combatants, *3697*

1856 Former president to run for reelection on a different party's ticket, *3402*

Know-Nothing Party platform, *3038*

1861 Assassination attempt on Abraham Lincoln, *3445*

1872 Labor Reform Party platform, *3043*

Labor Reform Party presidential candidate, *3296*

National labor party, *2929*
Prohibition Party platform, *3044*
Prohibition Party presidential candidate, *3297*

1886 Drama about the Civil War, *1393*
1888 Annual reading of George Washington's "Farewell Address" in the Senate, *1720*
1924 President to make a radio broadcast from the White House, *3757*

February 23

1848 Speaker of the House to die in the Capitol, *1634*
1861 President-elect to require military protection at his inauguration, *3661*
State to hold a public referendum on secession, *1377*
1883 Antitrust law enacted by a state, *4952*
1888 Industrial Reform Party presidential candidate, *3309*
1927 Radio Commission of the United States, *3874*

February 24

1855 Claims court established by the federal government, *1973*
1866 American flag made of American bunting to fly over the Capitol, *1094*
1868 President to be impeached, *3631*
1988 Supreme Court decision upholding the right to parody public figures, *4742*

February 25

1791 Bank of the United States, *2103*
Corporate body chartered by a special act of Congress, *4906*
Federal charter, *1995*
1799 Quarantine law enacted by Congress, *4011*
Shipbuilding law enacted by Congress, *2694*
1804 Political party to hold an open presidential nominating caucus, *2973*
1828 Wedding of a president's son in the White House, *5017*
1862 Bureau of Engraving and Printing, *2159*
Legal tender, *2160*
1885 Federal ban on fencing public lands, *4186*
1914 White House Correspondents Association, *3726*
1919 Gasoline tax levied by a state, *4830*

February 26

1940 Air defense military organization, *2620*
1991 State to have a gubernatorial runoff election, *4439*

February 27

1793 Nominee for associate justice of the Supreme Court to be rejected by the Senate, *4752*
1801 Congressional jurisdiction over Washington, DC, *1874*
1813 Vaccination law enacted by Congress, *4014*
1897 State to adopt the use of the initiative and referendum, *4432*
1922 National Radio Conference, *3873*
1973 Armed occupation by Native American protesters in the modern era, *2758*

February 28

1793 Senate election that was contested, *1757*
1815 Father and son to serve as U.S. ministers, *2324*
1844 President who narrowly escaped a fatal accident while in office, *3527*
1854 Founding of the Republican Party, *2922*
1861 Colorado territorial governor, *4873*
Confederate government bond, *2120*
1902 Fistfight in the Senate, *1723*
1997 Federal regulations restricting tobacco sales to minors, *4081*

February 29

1924 Commonwealth Land Party presidential candidate, *3329*
1944 Woman to serve as secretary of a major political party, *2964*

March

Pay for colonial legislators, *1472*
1638
1639 Political document printed in America, *1063*
1693 Trial of a printer for sedition, *3848*
1776 Independent government in an American colony, *1428*
1778 U.S. consular post, *2310*
1798 Use of sergeant at arms of the Senate to make an arrest, *1683*
1807 Withholding of a signed treaty by a president, *2406*
1860 Uniformed political marching group, *2801*
1861 Postmaster general of the Confederate States of America, *3160*

March—*continued*

1876	Cabinet officer impeached by the House of Representatives, *1163*
1881	Muckraking journalist, *3890*
1885	Treaties withdrawn by a president after they were submitted to the Senate, *2415*
1894	Protest march on Washington, *2824*
1909	Senate permanent office building, *1724*
1920	President in whose honor an asteroid was named, *3627*
1933	First Lady to undertake a career of public service, *3608*
1953	Book censorship board established by a state, *3865*
1959	American Nazi Party, *2950*
1991	African-American mayor of Kansas City, MO, *1354*

March 1

1642	City incorporated in the British colonies, *1253*
1781	President of the United States under the Articles of Confederation, *3370*
1792	Law establishing presidential succession, *3376*
1803	Ohio constitution, *4377*
	Ohio state capital, *4324*
	State admitted into the Union without a resolution of Congress, *4295*
	State in which slavery was illegal from the time it was admitted to the Union, *4240*
1867	Nebraska constitution, *4397*
	Nebraska state capital, *4344*
1869	State to ratify the 15th Amendment to the Constitution, *1845*
1872	National park, *4148*
1913	Bonding law enacted by a state, *4275*
1914	Filing date for 1040 tax forms, *4809*
1920	Federal statute to be printed on paper, *1515*
1927	Federal agency to regulate broadcast media, *3875*
1950	Civil Defense director, *2675*
1954	Terrorist shootings in the Capitol Building, *1247*
1975	Year the public debt of the United States exceeded $500 billion, *2133*

March 2

1642	Colonial ban on convicts holding public office, *1413*
1781	Congress to call itself "The United States in Congress Assembled", *1048*
1805	Vice president to be indicted while in office, *4967*

1807	Federal ban on the importation of African slaves, *4241*
1824	Supreme Court decision establishing the power of the federal government to regulate commerce, *4718*
1827	Federal law hostile to lotteries, *4000*
1833	State aid to railroads, *4085*
1836	Texas Independence Day, *2195*
1853	Washington territorial governor, *4869*
1861	Constitutional amendment proposal to bear the signature of a president, *1841*
	Copyright law on photographs enacted by Congress, *2507*
1867	Department of Education, *2040*
	Federal law regulating campaign finances, *2782*
1893	Railroad safety law enacted by Congress, *4091*
1955	Year in which the salary of members of Congress exceeded $20,000 per year, *1655*

March 3

1791	Internal revenue tax levied by Congress, *4797*
1797	President to serve two full terms, *3380*
1801	Land preemption act passed by Congress, *4178*
1803	Federal judge to be impeached, *1972*
	Grant of federal land to a foreigner, *4180*
1817	Alabama territorial governor, *4859*
1819	Piracy law enacted by Congress, *4912*
1842	Child labor law enacted by a state that regulated hours of employment, *2455*
1845	Florida constitution, *4387*
	Florida state capital, *4334*
	Law book of federal laws then in force, *2522*
	Presidential veto to be overridden by Congress, *3844*
1849	Department of the Interior, *2038*
1851	Library in the White House, *5023*
1857	President whose cabinet remained unchanged, *1159*
	Presidential secretary to receive a governmental salary, *3740*
1859	Oregon state governor, *4481*
1863	Draft law enacted by Congress during wartime, *2634*
	National scientific advisory body, *2071*
1865	Freedmen's Bureau, *1920*
1871	Federal law to reform the civil service, *2026*

Federal law withdrawing recognition of Native American tribal autonomy, *2747*

1873 Bonus paid to members of Congress by themselves, *1651*

Salary raise for the vice president, *3741*

1875 Homestead act for desert lands owned by the federal government, *4183*

1877 First Lady active in charitable causes, *3599*

First Lady to ban liquor in the White House, *3600*

1879 United States Geological Survey, *4185*

Woman lawyer admitted to practice before the Supreme Court, *2590*

1885 State forest commission, *4142*

1889 President to veto more than 100 bills in a single term, *3845*

1891 Federal foresting project, *4144*

1893 Federal road agency, *4092*

1899 Admiral of the Navy, *2696*

1903 State licensing law for nurses, *4026*

1915 Federal advisory committee on aeronautics, *4096*

1917 Federal tax on excess corporate profits, *4813*

1923 Weekly newsmagazine, *3901*

1943 Election law lowering the voting age in a state to 18, *4436*

1952 Flag of the Commonwealth of Puerto Rico, *4896*

1953 Woman to serve as ambassador to a major nation, *2352*

1971 Vote in the House of Representatives to be tallied by machine, *1573*

March 4

1789 Congressional representative appointed to a presidential cabinet, *1583*

Congressional representative who was Catholic, *1584*

Entry in *Journal of the House of Representatives of the United States*, *1532*

Meeting place of Congress, *1480*

Presidential candidate from Virginia, *4566*

Senate journal, *1661*

Session of Congress under the Constitution, *1811*

Session of the House of Representatives, *1533*

Session of the Senate, *1662*

Vice president who had served in the House of Representatives, *4960*

1791 Congressional representative who was Jewish, *1586*

President to govern more than the original 13 states, *3374*

Special session of the Senate, *1680*

State admitted to the Union after the ratification of the Constitution, *4291*

State of the Union that was formerly an independent republic, *4292*

Vermont state capital, *4321*

Vice president who had served in the Senate, *4963*

1793 President inaugurated in Philadelphia, *3642*

1797 Chief justice of the Supreme Court to administer the oath of office to a president, *4758*

Congressional representative to serve before his 25th birthday, *1587*

First Lady who was the daughter of a minister, *3582*

President who had served as vice president, *3381*

President who was older than 60 when he took office, *3382*

President who was sworn in by the chief justice of the Supreme Court, *3643*

President whose son became president, *3546*

1799 Supreme Court justice who had served in the House of Representatives, *4759*

1801 Chief justice of the Supreme Court to administer the oath of office to more than one president, *4763*

President from the Democratic-Republican Party, *3708*

President inaugurated in Washington, DC, *3644*

President who declined to attend the inauguration of his successor, *3645*

President who had served as secretary of state, *3478*

Presidential inauguration at which the Marine Band played music, *3646*

1805 President to have two vice presidents, *3389*

President who was younger than his vice president, *3390*

1809 First Lady to attend her husband's inauguration, *3584*

Inaugural ball held at Washington, DC, *3647*

President inaugurated in the Chamber of the House of Representatives, *3648*

President to be inaugurated in a suit of clothes entirely American-made, *3649*

March 4—*continued*

President who had served in the House of Representatives, *3480*

1817 First Lady to redecorate the White House, *3585*

President who had served in the Senate, *3481*

Presidential inauguration held outdoors in Washington, DC, *3650*

1823 Congressman who was a Catholic priest, *1591*

1825 Former president who was elected to the House of Representatives, *3486*

President to wear long pants at his inauguration, *3652*

President whose father was alive when he was inaugurated, *3551*

Vice president who was born an American citizen, *4972*

1829 Mob scene at the White House, *3653*

President inaugurated in Washington in a ceremony open to the public, *3654*

President who had served in both the House of Representatives and the Senate, *3487*

Spoils system of presidential patronage on a large scale, *2023*

1831 Chaplain of the House of Representatives who was Catholic, *1558*

1837 Presidential inauguration at which both the president and the chief justice had suffered earlier rejections by the Senate, *3655*

1845 Presidential inauguration reported by telegraph, *3657*

Speaker of the House who became president, *1633*

1849 President with no congressional experience, *3489*

Senator to serve as unofficial president between two presidential terms, *3400*

Senator to serve three states, *1765*

Senator who was returned to the Senate after being defeated for the presidency, *1766*

1851 Brothers to serve as representatives in Congress simultaneously, *1592*

1853 President to deliver his inaugural address from memory, *3658*

President who was younger than 50 when he took office, *3401*

President whose oath of office did not include the word "swear", *3659*

Vice president sworn in on foreign soil, *4978*

Vice president to take the oath of office but never serve in office, *4979*

1857 Vice president who was younger than 40, *4980*

1859 Child of a president to serve in the House of Representatives, *1593*

1861 Confederate States flag, *1093*

President from the Republican Party, *3714*

President to function as an effective commander in chief, *3405*

1863 Idaho territorial governor, *4876*

Officer to preside over both of the branches of Congress, *1506*

1865 Presidential inauguration in which African-Americans formally participated, *3662*

1869 Inaugural ball in the Treasury Building, *3663*

President whose parents were both alive at the time of his inauguration, *3664*

Speaker of the House who became vice president, *1635*

1873 President to receive a salary raise, *3742*

1875 African-American senator to serve a full term, *1778*

President to serve as a senator both before and after his term in office, *3495*

1881 President to view his inaugural parade from a platform outside the White House, *3666*

President whose mother lived at the White House, *3561*

President's mother to attend her son's inauguration, *3667*

1891 Congress to appropriate $1 billion, *1512*

Congressional representative elected by prohibitionists, *1596*

International copyright agreement, *2508*

1897 First Lady to sit next to her husband at state dinners, *3604*

1899 House majority leader, *1567*

House majority whip, *1568*

House minority leader, *1569*

1901 Resident commissioner from Puerto Rico, *4892*

1905 President to deliver his inaugural address bareheaded, *3668*

President who advocated physical fitness, *3830*

President whose inaugural address did not include the word "I", *3669*

1909 First Lady to accompany her husband on the post-inauguration ride, *3670*

First Lady to attend all her husband's cabinet meetings, *3605*

March 8

1756   Colonial legislature's mace still extant, *1479*

1783   First Lady who was born an American citizen, *3580*

1796   Supreme Court case challenging the validity of an act of Congress, *4711*

1849   Secretary of the interior, *1156*

1884   Woman to argue for women's suffrage before a major committee of Congress, *1960*

1894   Dog licensing ordinance, *4024*

1917   Senate rule allowing the limitation of debate, *1734*

1971   Supreme Court decision upholding the power of Congress to outlaw racial discrimination in employment, *4736*

March 9

1820   Wedding of a president's daughter in the White House, *5015*

1825   International treaty rejected by the Senate, *2409*

1829   Washington social scandal, *1882*

1907   Sterilization of humans by a state government as a matter of public policy, *3952*

1914   Smoking ban in the Senate chambers, *1729*

1964   Occupation of federal territory by Native American protesters in the modern era, *2755*

1989   Cabinet nomination by a newly elected president to be rejected, *1207*

March 10

1785   Minister plenipotentiary appointed after the Revolutionary War, *2316*

1821   President who had been governor of a territory, *3483*

1849   President who had received a patent, *3490*

1862   Bill bearing the likeness of a president, *2161*

1909   State-run old age home for pioneers, *4044*

1967   Attorney general whose father had also served as attorney general, *1194*

1970   Federal agency for administering credit unions, *2124*

1975   Woman to serve as secretary of housing and urban development, *1197*

March 11

1793   Supreme Court justice who had been a state governor, *4753*

Supreme Court justice who had served in the Senate, *4754*

1861   American national constitution to expressly legitimize slavery, *4254*

1930   Chief justice of the Supreme Court to lie in state in the Capitol rotunda, *1246*

President buried in the National Cemetery, *3533*

1941   Large foreign aid package, *2274*

1962   First Lady to have a private audience with the pope, *3615*

March 12

1804   Supreme Court justice to be impeached, *4764*

1849   State in the West to be denied admission to the Union, *4300*

1877   Cabinet member who had served as a Confederate officer, *1164*

1914   Railroad operated by the federal government, *4095*

1933   Presidential fireside chat, *3759*

1947   U.S. aid program to contain the spread of communism, *2280*

1993   Woman to serve as attorney general, *1212*

March 13

1638   Military organization established by a colony, *2663*

1770   Chamber of Commerce, *4903*

1955   Federal government building built to withstand a nuclear attack, *2001*

March 14

1792   Designs for the building of the Capitol, *1215*

Designs for the building of the White House, *5004*

1812   War bond issued by the federal government, *2118*

1820   Maine state capital, *4330*

1826   Conference of American republics, *2255*

1867   Commissioner of education of the United States, *3975*

1891   State seal designed by a woman, *4273*

1903   Federal bird reservation, *4211*

Federal wildlife refuge, *4212*

1936   Magazine of the federal government, *3902*

1964   Courtroom verdict to be televised, *3867*

1997   American citizen to become a Russian official, *2306*

March 15

1767 President from the working class, *3458*
1791 Supreme Court justice to resign, *4751*
1867 State university supported by a direct property tax, *3976*
1913 Municipal small claims court, *1274*
President to hold regular press conferences, *3725*
Presidential press conference, *3862*
State court of small claims, *4414*
1919 American Legion, *2702*
1937 Birth control clinic run by a state government, *3995*
1960 Federal undersea park, *4157*
1985 Cabinet member indicted while in office, *1205*
1989 Department of Veterans Affairs, *2053*
Secretary of veterans affairs, *1208*

March 16

1810 Supreme Court decision declaring a state law unconstitutional, *4714*
1827 Political newspaper published by African-Americans, *3917*
1929 State tax on chain stores, *4832*
1968 American military massacre of political importance, *2650*

March 17

1762 Saint Patrick's Day parade, *2181*
1776 Medal awarded by the Continental Congress, *1045*
1931 State to legalize casino gambling, *4001*
1947 "Daily Digest" of the Congressional Record, *1523*
1970 United Nations Security Council resolution vetoed by the United States, *2438*
1976 Woman to serve as ambassador to the Court of St. James, *2366*

March 18

1831 Supreme Court decision on the status of Native American tribes, *4719*
1890 Naval militia established by a state, *2665*
1913 State law regulating chiropractic, *4029*
1948 Birth registration uniform numbering system, *3954*
1954 Subcabinet member who was African-American, *1185*
1970 Strike of postal employees, *2484*

March 19

1906 Criminal trial before the Supreme Court, *4703*

1948 Labor dispute in which the Taft-Hartley Act was invoked, *2483*
1960 National States' Rights Party presidential candidate, *3348*
1965 State narcotics ban, *4065*

March 20

1816 Supreme Court decision upholding its authority to review state court decisions on appeal, *4715*
1833 Treaty between the federal government and an Asian nation, *2411*
1865 Labor cooperatives to be authorized by a state, *2487*
1925 Woman vice consul, *2340*
1990 Census to count the homeless, *3097*

March 21

1866 Soldiers' homes established by Congress, *2700*
1963 Trial by a panel of judges to determine the winner of a state election, *4437*

March 22

1630 Colonial gambling law for residents, *3998*
1765 Direct tax on Britain's American colonists without their consent, *1005*
1790 Secretary of state, *1140*
1872 State ban on sex discrimination in employment, *1959*

March 23

1867 State forestry inquiry commission, *4137*
1971 State to ratify the 26th Amendment to the Constitution, *1859*
1977 Woman to serve as under secretary of state, *2367*
2000 Chaplain of the House of Representatives who was a Catholic priest, *1582*

March 24

1629 Hunting law enacted by a colony, *4200*
1887 Jewish minister and envoy, *2335*
1890 Supreme Court decision invalidating a state economic regulation on grounds of substantive due process, *4722*

March 25

1634 Maryland Day, *2177*
1820 Maine constitution, *4383*
1900 Socialist Party, *2937*
1969 State to mandate the votes of its presidential electors, *3219*

March 26

1776	South Carolina constitution, *4360*
	State to set an age qualification for state senators, *4540*
1790	Naturalization act enacted by Congress, *3101*
1798	Mayor of Schenectady, NY, *1298*
1804	Orleans territorial governor, *4854*
1848	Journalist arrested by the Senate, *1703*
1866	Corrupt election practices law enacted by a state, *4429*
1962	Supreme Court decision on legislative apportionment, *4732*
1994	Federal legislation recommending academic standards, *3987*

March 27

1792	Congressional investigation, *1491*
1794	Ship constructed by the federal government, *2690*
	State to ratify the Eleventh Amendment to the Constitution, *1838*
	United States Navy, *2691*
1800	Contempt citation issued by the Senate to a journalist, *1685*
1807	Political newspaper using the word "Democratic" in its title, *3913*
1814	President who served in more than one war, *3694*
1929	President to have a telephone on his desk in the White House, *3834*
1933	Farm credit administration, *4116*
	Federal regulatory agency for agricultural lending, *4117*

March 28

1834	President to be censured by Congress, *3511*
1836	Chief Justice to wear long pants at his inauguration, *4766*
	Supreme Court chief justice who was Catholic, *4767*
	Supreme Court justice who had served as attorney general, *4768*
1848	Child labor law enacted by a state that restricted the age of the worker, *2456*
1865	State environmental protection law enacted in connection with advertising, *4122*
1978	Bilingual report of a congressional committee, *1576*
1997	Rules to prevent secret government-sponsored human experimentation, *2076*

March 29

1626	Colonial forestry law, *4136*
1790	President born during the administration of another president, *3461*
1812	Wedding in the White House, *5012*
1819	Former president to head a university, *3482*
1852	State law regulating women's work hours, *2494*

March 30

1893	Ambassador of the United States, *2336*
1981	President to be wounded in an unsuccessful assassination attempt while in office, *3456*

March 31

1790	Senator appointed by a governor, *1756*
1798	Mayor of Augusta, GA, *1299*
1854	Treaty between the United States and Japan, *2414*
1870	African-American to vote under authority of the 15th Amendment to the Constitution, *1923*
1933	Youth conservation corps, *4127*
1947	State to ratify the 22nd Amendment to the Constitution, *1855*
1979	Federal agency for national emergency management, *2015*
1995	Independent agency for administering Social Security, *4074*
1998	Detailed financial statement for the federal government, *2100*

April

1606	English colonial charter, *1433*
1692	Intercolonial postal system, *3132*
1789	Political cartoon lampooning President George Washington, *3931*
1791	Cabinet meeting, *1143*
1793	Regular cabinet meetings, *1145*
1795	Senate proceedings that were open to the public, *1681*
1802	Federal highway, *4084*
1822	Governor of California under Mexican rule, *1431*
1829	Kitchen cabinet of unofficial presidential advisors, *1152*
1841	President to bring slaves with him to Washington, DC, *4249*
1845	Mayor of Peoria, IL, *1310*
1862	Postage stamps issued by the Confederacy, *3165*
1871	Surgeon general, *4019*
1888	Woman mayor with a town council consisting entirely of women, *1324*

April 6—*continued*

1937 Woman to serve as foreman on a federal grand jury, *1981*

April 7

1789 Joint committee of the House and Senate, *1481*

Senate doorkeeper, *1666*

Standing rules adopted by the House of Representatives, *1537*

1798 Mississippi territorial governor, *4852*

1813 Senator to be appointed as a treaty negotiator, *1762*

1819 State agricultural board, *4109*

1826 Inheritance tax enacted by a state, *4829*

1972 Campaign finance law that set limits on media spending, *2789*

1997 White House Office of National AIDS Policy, *3781*

April 8

1834 City mayor elected by popular vote, *1306*

1866 Federal law prohibiting racial discrimination in housing, *4041*

1895 Supreme Court decision invalidating a federal tax, *4723*

1935 Large-scale federal jobs-creation programs, *2468*

April 9

1833 Public library established after the Revolution, *1259*

1847 State reformatory for boys, *2573*

1866 Civil rights law enacted by Congress, *1921*

1874 Case of child abuse brought to court, *3990*

1912 Children's Bureau, *3993*

1934 Woman to serve as justice of the Circuit Court of Appeals, *1980*

1937 State to outlaw sit-down strikes, *2482*

1963 Honorary citizenship authorized by Congress, *3121*

1966 Official residence for the vice president, *4993*

1998 Ruling requiring retention of all electronic records of the federal government, *2059*

April 10

1777 Lottery held by the Continental Congress, *1046*

1790 Patent law passed by Congress, *2597*

1933 State to ratify the 21st Amendment to the Constitution, *1852*

1976 State voluntary sterilization regulation, *3957*

1980 Citizens Party presidential candidate, *3359*

April 11

1640 Colonial election held in defiance of the Royal Courts, *1449*

1789 Select committee appointed by the House of Representatives, *1538*

1921 State cigarette tax, *4080*

1925 Woman to serve as legation secretary, *2341*

1953 Department of Health, Education, and Welfare, *2048*

Secretary of health, education, and welfare, *1183*

1954 State legislative hearing to be shown on television, *4554*

1965 Federal aid program for primary and secondary schools, *3982*

1989 Incumbent African-American mayor of a major city to lose to a white candidate, *1349*

April 12

1631 Militia, *2662*

1776 Colonial government to instruct its delegates to the Continental Congress to proclaim independence, *1054*

Halifax Resolutions Day, *2183*

1796 Presidential portrait of importance, *3536*

1892 Voting machines used in an election, *1281*

1900 Unincorporated territory of the United States, *4890*

1926 Senator unseated after a recount, *1784*

1933 Woman diplomat to hold the rank of minister, *2344*

1938 State to require blood tests for marriage licenses, *3953*

1945 Woman cabinet member to serve under two presidents, *1181*

1985 Senator to fly in space, *1807*

April 13

1789 House of Representatives election that was contested, *1539*

Standing committee of the House of Representatives that is still operating, *1540*

1801 Child of a president to be born in a foreign country, *3549*

1830 Commemoration of the birthday of Thomas Jefferson, *2193*

1920 Woman to serve as Civil Service commissioner, *2031*

1943 National monument to Thomas Jefferson, *2715*

April 22

1793 Proclamation of U.S. neutrality in time of war, *2638*

1794 State to ban the death penalty, *2554*

1856 Intervention of federal troops in a territorial conflict over slavery, *4253*

1864 Coin to use the motto "In God We Trust", *2162*

1970 Earth Day, *2233*

April 23

1775 Mobilization of American troops in the Revolutionary War, *1017*

1789 Contact between the president and the Congress, *1483*
Presidential mansion, *5003*

1860 National convention of a major party that failed to nominate a presidential candidate, *2990*

1872 African-American woman to practice law, *2588*

1898 Presidential call for volunteer troops to fight in the Spanish-American War, *2642*

1951 Senator who had been a newspaper reporter, *1794*

1971 Mass return of military decorations by war veterans, *2863*

April 24

1704 Newspaper published with government approval, *3904*

1783 College named after George Washington, *3964*

1863 National code of the laws of war, *2655*

April 25

1861 Union troops to arrive in Washington, DC, *1379*

1881 Statue cast by the federal government, *2707*

1901 License plates for vehicles, *4093*

1917 Loan made by the United States to a war ally, *2090*

1938 Postage stamp issue depicting all the presidents, *3167*

1945 United Nations conference, *2431*

1967 State law legalizing abortion for medical reasons, *3955*

1993 Homosexual rights protest of large scale, *2873*

April 26

1874 Confederate Memorial Day, *2206*

1954 State governor to appoint two United States senators in one year for interim terms, *4508*

2000 State to establish civil unions for homosexual couples, *1917*

April 27

1789 Chaplain of the Senate, *1670*

1805 American flag flown over a fortress of the Old World, *1086*

1816 Tariff passed by Congress for protection, *4948*

1822 President whose name was changed, *3484*

1861 Suspension of habeas corpus in wartime, *1380*

1938 Woman of American ancestry to become a queen, *2386*

April 28

1788 Maryland state capital, *4314*

1890 State employment service, *2462*

1909 Child delinquency law enacted by a state, *3991*
Naturalized citizen to lie in state in the Capitol rotunda, *1242*

1947 United States delegation to the United Nations, *2434*

April 29

1931 Absolute monarch to visit the United States, *2384*

1942 Health insurance law enacted by a state, *4055*

April 30

1789 Army organization under the Constitution, *2623*
Ceremony proposed for transmitting bills between houses of Congress, *1484*
Inaugural address, *3633*
Inaugural chintzes, *3634*
Inaugural tankards, *3635*
Political buttons, *2792*
President inaugurated in New York City, *3636*
President of the United States elected under the Constitution, *3371*
President to be inaugurated after his vice president, *3637*
President who owned slaves, *3822*
President whose mother was alive when he was inaugurated, *3638*
Presidential inauguration, *3639*
Religious service held as part of a presidential inauguration, *3640*
Response of the Senate to an inaugural address, *1671*

1798 Department of the Navy, *2037*
Military department of the federal government, *2605*

1802 Land subsidy by Congress for road improvements, *4179*

1803 Important exercise of an implied power of the government, *1997*

Territory annexed by the federal government, *4836*

1812 Louisiana state capital, *4325*

1820 Antislavery magazine, *4243*

1837 State board of education, *3971*

1889 National holiday, *2213*

1939 President to deliver an address on television, *3762*

1972 Attorney general to plead guilty to a criminal offense, *1196*

1997 African-American to serve as secretary of labor, *1214*

1999 State to enact a school voucher plan, *3988*

May

1539 Armed conflict between Europeans and Native Americans on American soil, *2720*

1772 Written constitution adopted by a community of American-born freemen, *1439*

1775 Independent postal service during the Revolution, *3137*

1776 Native American delegation to the Continental Congress, *2731*

1779 American general to engage in treason, *1034*

1789 Contact between the Congress and state governments, *4261*

Form of the enacting clause used in congressional bills, *1485*

Title formally proposed for the chief executive of the United States, *3372*

1796 Political party to hold a secret presidential nominating caucus, *2971*

1801 Location in Washington, DC, of the State Department, *1875*

Location in Washington, DC, of the Treasury Department, *1876*

1802 Federal patent office, *2599*

1812 American flag flown over a schoolhouse, *1087*

1827 Anarchist, *2811*

1832 Convention to renominate a sitting president, *2981*

Democratic Party presidential candidate, *3284*

1840 Political party platform, *3036*

1848 Presidential candidate from Michigan, *4571*

1860 National party convention to which the general public was admitted, *2991*

Presidential candidates from Illinois, *4576*

Republican presidential candidate to win an election, *3238*

Vice presidential candidate from Maine, *4636*

1884 Vice presidential candidate from Mississippi, *4641*

1886 Construction of the Statue of Liberty on site, *1127*

1888 Vice presidential candidate from Arkansas, *4645*

1891 Populist Party, *2934*

1894 Senate investigating committee, *1722*

1900 Vice presidential candidate from Minnesota, *4647*

1906 Use of the term "muckraker", *3859*

1912 Vice presidential candidate from Wisconsin, *4653*

1916 American Indian Day, *2751*

1920 Presidential candidate from Missouri, *4584*

1924 Presidential candidate from Oregon, *4586*

Vice presidential candidate from Montana, *4655*

1933 Income tax enacted by a state, *4833*

1945 Civil rights anthem to achieve fame, *1122*

1947 Armed Forces Day, *2231*

1987 Congressman to acknowledge that he was a homosexual, *1627*

1993 African-American woman nominated to head the Justice Department's Civil Rights Division, *1937*

May 1

1732 Tammany Day, *2179*

1772 Tammany political club, *2902*

1789 Chaplain of the House of Representatives, *1541*

1822 Mayor of Boston, MA, *1302*

1843 Consul to California, *2327*

1844 Incumbent president whose party refused to renominate him, *3398*

1850 Mayor of San Francisco, CA, *1315*

1857 Literacy qualification for voting, *4428*

1872 Liberal Republican Party platform, *3045*

Liberal Republican Party presidential candidate, *3298*

1900 Civil governor of Puerto Rico under the Foraker Act, *4891*

1904 Socialist Party presidential candidate, *3323*

1908 Vice presidential candidate from Iowa, *4651*

May 1—*continued*

1909 Federal hydroelectric plant, *4130*

1925 Car insurance law enacted by a state, *4054*

May 2

1837 Mayor of Chicago, IL, *1307*

1843 Government on the Pacific Coast, *1432*

1865 Rewards offered by the federal government for suspects in the assassination of a president, *3448*

1890 Oklahoma territorial governor, *4879*

1900 United Christian Party presidential candidate, *3320*

1917 Liberty loans, *2091*

1997 First Lady to be depicted on a monument to a president, *3622*

May 3

1845 African-American lawyer formally admitted to the bar, *2585*

1902 Workers' compensation insurance law enacted by a state, *2502*

1904 State licensing law for pharmacists, *4027*

1972 Federal agency chief to lie in state in the Capitol rotunda, *1249*

1994 Judicial decision allowing physicians to terminate the life of terminally ill patients at their request, *3961*

May 4

1865 President whose grave was opened by thieves, *3530*

1928 Woman justice on the federal bench, *1979*

1994 Compensation paid to victims of mass racial violence, *1938*

May 5

1682 Colony requiring rotation in public office, *1419*

1789 Bill passed by the Senate, *1672*

1832 Vaccination program by the federal government to protect Native Americans against smallpox, *4015*

1905 Major American city founded in the 20th century, *1264*

1908 State law prohibiting discrimination against soldiers, *2657*

May 6

1776 Virginia state governor, *4449*

1882 Restrictions by Congress on immigration of Chinese laborers, *3111*

1970 Nationwide campus rioting, *2862*

1994 Sexual harassment lawsuit against a president, *3519*

1995 African-American mayor of Dallas, TX, *1360*

May 7

1634 Colonial treason trial, *1411*

1789 Inaugural ball, *3641*

1800 Indiana territorial governor, *4853*

1930 Supreme Court nominee to be rejected by the Senate in the 20th century, *4776*

1946 African-American territorial governor appointed by the president, *4883*

1992 Constitutional amendment to be ratified two centuries after its proposal, *1860*

May 8

1783 Salute fired by Great Britain in honor of an officer of the United States, *2245*

1787 Prison reform society, *2808*

1789 Response by the House of Representatives to an inaugural address, *1542*

1792 Draft of civilians by Congress, *2632*

Federal revenue commissioner, *4798*

1812 Foreign aid bill, *2252*

Performance of "Hail to the Chief", *1117*

1866 Interracial jury, *1974*

1931 Resale price maintenance law enacted by a state, *4925*

1964 Former president to address the Senate, *3767*

May 9

1754 Political cartoon published in an American newspaper, *3928*

1796 Senators elected but not seated, *1758*

1860 Constitutional Union Party platform, *3040*

Constitutional Union Party presidential candidate, *3293*

1863 Comptroller of the Currency, *2087*

1997 Ambassador to Vietnam, *2372*

May 10

1775 Call for troops to fight in the Revolutionary War, *1018*

1797 Ship launched by the United States Navy, *2692*

1800 Cabinet secretaries to be fired, *1149*

1865 Capture of an American president by enemy troops, *1390*

1869 Transcontinental railroad, *4089*

1872 African-American vice presidential candidate, *3240*

Woman to run as a presidential candidate, *3241*

May 18—*continued*

1852 State compulsory education law, *3972*

1896 Supreme Court decision validating the doctrine of "separate but equal" provisions for African-Americans, *4724*

1931 Supreme Court decision invalidating a state law on First Amendment grounds, *4727*

1934 Death penalty authorized by federal law, *2564*

May 19

1643 Confederation of English colonies, *1414*

1796 Congressional protection of Native American hunting grounds, *2737*

1862 Large-scale free land distribution by the federal government, *4181*

1891 Populist Party presidential candidate, *3312*

1921 Immigration quotas enacted by Congress, *3116*

1964 Announcement that a U.S. embassy was bugged, *2359*

1998 Supreme Court decision on inclusion of candidates in televised political debates, *4746*

May 20

1639 Property tax established by a colony to support public schools, *4787*

1777 Treaty between states after the Declaration of Independence, *4257*

1785 Land set-aside for schools authorized by the Continental Congress, *3965*
Sale of federal land, *4174*
Survey of public lands, *4175*

1831 Commemoration of the Mecklenburg declaration of independence, *2194*

1835 Presidential candidate nominated in a church, *2985*

1868 Republican presidential candidate chosen unanimously on the first ballot, *3239*

1951 First Lady to be received by the pope, *3614*

May 21

1832 Democratic Party national convention, *2982*
National political convention to adopt the two-thirds rule, *2983*

1888 State-run crematory, *3951*

1901 Speeding driver law enacted by a state, *4094*

1909 Credit union law enacted by a state, *2121*

1928 Presidential candidate killed in a rescue attempt, *3257*

1934 Community to fingerprint its citizens, *2537*

1960 Presidential candidate from Alaska, *4593*

May 22

1649 Colonial law to control corrupt election practices, *1451*

1848 Credentials fight at a Democratic Party convention, *2989*

1856 Beating in the Senate chamber, *1704*

1902 United States case to be arbitrated in the Hague Permanent Court of Arbitration, *2264*

1912 State to ratify the 17th Amendment to the Constitution, *1847*

1933 Maritime Day, *2228*

1934 Woman to head the state committee of a major political party, *2963*

1935 President to read a veto message to Congress, *3761*

1943 First Lady buried in Arlington National Cemetery, *3611*

1972 President to visit the Soviet Union, *3814*

May 23

1788 South Carolina state capital, *4315*

1832 Politician to control a national convention, *2984*
Presidential candidate of a major party to be nominated at a national convention, *3230*
Presidential candidate to be nominated on the first ballot, *3231*
Presidential candidate unanimously nominated by a national party convention, *3232*

1872 National Working Men's Convention, *3299*

1988 State ban on cheap handguns, *2543*

May 24

1828 Federal post office built for the purpose, *3155*

1913 Strike settlement mediated by the federal Labor Department, *2480*

May 25

1789 Entry in the *Journal of the Executive Proceedings of the Senate of the United States of America*, *1673*
Treaties reviewed by the Senate, *1674*

1790 Copyright law enacted by Congress, *2506*

1844	Political news item transmitted by telegraph, *3871*
1964	Woman to serve on a federal government commission, *2002*
1998	President to attend a hockey game during his term in office, *3842*

May 26

1647	Ban on Jesuits, *1943*
1790	Governor of the Southwest Territory (Tennessee), *4851*
1836	Gag rule in the House of Representatives, *1559*
1864	Montana territorial governor, *4877*
1972	Strategic Arms Limitation Treaty, *2424*

May 27

1652	Minting act, *2143*
1825	Brothers to serve simultaneously as governors of their respective states, *4469*
1844	National Democratic Tyler Party presidential candidate, *3287*
1861	Dakota territorial governor, *4874*
1943	President of a black African country to visit the United States, *2389*

May 28

1734	Fish protection law enacted by a city, *4201*
1796	Federal law exempting debtors from prison, *2571*
1844	Telegraph message sent from the Capitol, *1226*
1879	Ban enacted by a state on the employment of women in an occupation, *2458*
1881	State pure food and drug law, *4021*
1896	National Party presidential candidate, *3314*
1913	Senate majority whip, *1728*
1932	African-American vice presidential candidate in the 20th century, *3260*
1972	President to address Soviet citizens on Soviet television, *3768*
1996	Convictions in the Whitewater case, *3521*

May 29

1790	Rhode Island constitution, *4374*
	Rhode Island state capitals, *4320*
1844	Politician to receive and decline a nomination by telegraph, *2987*
	President to announce before his election that he would not run for reelection, *3399*
	Presidential "dark horse" candidate, *3233*

	Use of the telegraph in politics, *2988*
	Vice presidential nominee from a major party to decline the nomination, *3234*
1848	Wisconsin constitution, *4390*
	Wisconsin state capital, *4337*
1908	Senator who was the victim of an assassination attempt during a filibuster, *1780*
1916	President's flag, *1099*
1917	President who was born in the 20th century, *3467*
1932	Bonus Army, *2829*

May 30

1644	Contested election in a colonial legislature, *1450*
1806	President who had killed a man in a duel, *3825*
1848	California territorial governor, *4864*
1854	Nebraska territorial governor, *4870*
1868	Memorial Day, *2203*
1908	Workers' compensation insurance law enacted by Congress, *2503*
1922	National monument to Abraham Lincoln, *2712*
1964	President and First Lady to receive honorary degrees at the same time, *3629*

May 31

1786	Strike benefit by a union, *2876*
1797	Test of presidential authority over the cabinet secretaries, *1147*
1864	Independent Republican Party presidential candidate, *3295*
	Platform of the Independent Republicans, *3042*
1870	Laws authorizing the use of force against the Ku Klux Klan, *1924*
1932	President who came before the Senate unannounced, *1740*
1978	State plain-language law, *4282*

June

1636	Settlement to welcome refugees of all faiths, *1941*
1754	Plan for the union of the British colonies, *1001*
1774	Character personifying the United States, *1129*
1778	Constitutional convention of a popular character, *4371*
1791	Design for Washington, DC, *1868*
1848	Presidential candidate from Louisiana, *4572*
	Vice presidential candidate from Michigan, *4634*

June—*continued*

1852 Presidential candidate from New Jersey, *4574*

1854 Kansas territory governor, *4871*

1856 Elected incumbent president whose party refused to renominate him, *3403*

Presidential candidate from California, *4575*

Republican Party candidate to be nominated on the first ballot, *3237*

1860 Southern Democratic Party, *2925*

Vice presidential candidate from Georgia, *4637*

1864 Federal law giving African-American soldiers pay and benefits equal to those of white soldiers, *2656*

1869 Woman to practice law, *2587*

1880 African-American to receive nominating votes for the vice presidency at the convention of a major party, *2999*

Presidential candidate from Iowa, *4578*

Presidential candidate from Texas, *4579*

Presidential candidate who was present at the convention that nominated him, *3244*

1884 Vice presidential candidate from Illinois, *4642*

1886 President who held a doctorate in a field other than law, *3497*

1888 Presidential candidate from Indiana, *4582*

1892 Candidate of a major party to be nominated for the presidency three times, *3248*

Vice presidential candidate from Texas, *4646*

1900 Vice presidential candidate from Rhode Island, *4648*

1902 Expansion and comprehensive renovation of the White House, *5032*

1905 Industrial Workers of the World (Wobblies) convention, *2885*

1908 National Conservation Commission, *4125*

1912 City government using the manager plan, *1290*

1916 Vice presidential candidate from Louisiana, *4654*

1918 Cartoon unit run by a government, *3941*

State of Income report released by the federal government, *4814*

1920 Presidential candidate from Utah, *4585*

1944 Presidential airplane, *3807*

1954 Overthrow of a democratic foreign government arranged by the Central Intelligence Agency, *2677*

1966 Black Power advocate, *2851*

1972 Libertarian Party presidential candidate, *3356*

1973 National Right to Life Committee, *2840*

1980 All-news television network, *3883*

1983 Latino mayor of a city without a large Latino population, *1346*

1991 City to file for bankruptcy, *2135*

1993 Library of U.S. foreign-policy papers on Africa and the Caribbean, *2069*

1994 President to have a legal defense fund during his term in office, *3520*

1995 White House Office for Women's Initiatives and Outreach, *3780*

1996 Labor Party, *2959*

1997 African-American mayor of Jackson, MS, *1363*

June 1

1779 President who had been governor of a state, *3474*

Vice president who had been governor of a state, *4958*

1785 Minister to Great Britain, *2317*

1786 Statehood Day (Tennessee), *2186*

1789 Congressional act, *1486*

1790 Congressional representative to die, *1585*

1792 Kentucky constitution, *4375*

Kentucky state capital, *4322*

State founded within the borders of an existing state, *4293*

Statehood Day (Kentucky), *2188*

1796 Tennessee constitution, *4376*

Tennessee state capital, *4323*

1801 Circulating library in Washington, DC, *1877*

1808 Land-grant university, *3967*

1886 State arbitration board for labor disputes, *2450*

1890 Census compiled by machines, *3089*

1923 Woman to serve as a federal internal revenue collector, *4815*

1964 Federal law mandating equal pay for women, *2460*

1990 Chemical arms control treaty, *2428*

June 2

1880 Credentials fight at a Republican Party convention that determined the selection of the candidate, *3000*

1886 President whose private life was harassed by reporters, *3724*

June 10—*continued*

1921   General Accounting Office, *1516*

1924   Bonus voting system, *3008*

      Political convention to be broadcast on radio, *3009*

1947   President to pay a state visit to Canada, *3810*

1963   Congressional ban on sex discrimination in wages, *1965*

June 11

1790   House of Representatives filibuster, *1547*

1878   Legal recognition of the term "District of Columbia", *1892*

1885   State gas commission, *4129*

1906   Employer's Liability Act enacted by Congress, *4052*

June 12

1775   Naval battle in the Revolutionary War, *1019*

1776   Bill of Rights, *1821*

      State legislature with an upper house known as the Senate, *4541*

      State to ban clergymen from serving in the legislature, *1947*

      Statement of the principle of inalienable rights, *1055*

      Virginia constitution, *4361*

1838   Iowa territorial governor, *4863*

1856   North American Party presidential candidate, *3291*

1871   Child of a president to attend West Point, *3553*

1920   Farmer Labor Party presidential candidate, *3327*

1942   President who had served as a Navy pilot, *3701*

1971   Outdoor wedding held at the White House, *5040*

June 13

1764   Committee of correspondence formed in a British colony in America, *1002*

1825   Law code adopted by a state, *2519*

1906   Consumer protection law enacted by Congress, *4920*

1913   County public defender, *1275*

1927   American flag displayed from the right hand of the Statue of Liberty, *1100*

1933   Home owners' loan corporation, *4045*

1967   Supreme Court justice who was African-American, *4779*

June 14

1642   Compulsory education law in a colony, *3962*

1775   Army of the United States, *2621*

1777   National flag to represent the United States, *1078*

1846   American republic on the West Coast, *4841*

1848   Liberty League presidential candidate, *3288*

1877   Flag Day, *2208*

1889   Flag salute, *1096*

1916   Year in which the Democratic party renominated its entire ticket, *3007*

1922   President to make a radio broadcast, *3755*

1927   Monument to the American flag, *2713*

1951   Federal government office to be computerized, *2000*

1954   Civil defense test held nationwide, *2678*

1993   Jewish woman to serve as a Supreme Court justice, *4783*

June 15

1775   General of the Continental Army, *2622*

1789   Presidential appointment, *3769*

1835   Patent commissioner, *2600*

1836   Arkansas state capitol, *4332*

1849   President who was survived by his mother, *3528*

1876   Woman to address a national political convention, *2998*

1910   Pioneer Day (Idaho), *2220*

1971   Prior restraint of the press by order of the federal government, *3868*

June 16

1789   Senate's use of its constitutional power to advise and consent, *1675*

1828   Supreme Court justice who had served as a federal judge, *4765*

1933   Bank deposit insurance law enacted by Congress, *2112*

      Federal Deposit Insurance Corporation, *2113*

      Industrial Recovery Act, *4926*

      Labor advisory board of the federal government, *2445*

1941   Federal government airport, *1896*

1970   African-American mayor of a major Eastern city, *1335*

June 17

1775   Major battle of the Revolutionary War, *1020*

June 22

1775 Continental money, *2146*
1870 Department of Justice, *2041*
1944 Federal law providing for the education of veterans, *2704*
1993 First Lady who was also a federal official, *3621*

June 23

1786 Treaty with a non-European nation, *2399*
1836 Federal treasury surplus to be returned to the states, *4265*
1844 Sentence of branding by a federal court, *2528*
1848 Congressional lobbyist who was a woman, *1501*
1860 Government Printing Office, *2054*
      Secret service established by the federal government, *2580*
      Vice presidential candidate from Oregon, *4638*
1869 Labor bureau established by a state, *2441*
1888 African-American to receive nominating votes for the presidency at the convention of a major party, *3002*
1906 Travel expenses for the president, *3743*
1938 Civil Aeronautics Authority, *4101*
1948 Political party convention at which spectators were charged an admission fee, *3022*
1960 State to ratify the 23rd Amendment to the Constitution, *1856*
1999 Son of a Soviet premier to become an American citizen, *2394*

June 24

1647 Woman to appeal for the right to vote, *2892*
1834 Cabinet appointee on record as having been rejected by the Senate, *1154*
1936 African-American woman to serve as a federal administrator, *1999*
1940 Political convention to be televised, *3019*
1948 Presidential candidate who was renominated after a defeat, *3262*
1970 Cabinet member to serve in four different capacities, *1195*
1980 Federal bailout of an auto manufacturer, *4939*
1997 Secretary of state to visit Vietnam, *2307*
1999 Internet camera showing the site of a presidential assassination, *3457*

June 25

1788 Virginia state capital, *4317*
1798 Deportation of aliens authorized by Congress, *3102*
      Federal immigration law requiring the collection of information on aliens, *3103*
1844 President to marry while in office, *3557*
1868 Federal law mandating an eight-hour workday, *2495*
1876 Major defeat inflicted by Native Americans on regular U.S. Army troops, *2748*
1936 National political convention to abrogate the two-thirds rule, *3017*
1938 Minimum wage law enacted by Congress, *2498*
1941 Federal attempt to address racial discrimination in employment, *1927*
1948 Federal law against threatening the president, *3450*
1962 Supreme Court decision on school prayer, *4733*
1999 State criminal prosecution for the sale of confidential personal information, *4072*

June 26

1848 Pure food and drug law established by Congress, *4016*
1860 Japanese diplomatic delegation to the United States, *2258*
1919 Bank wholly owned and operated by a state, *2110*
1920 Subcabinet member who was a woman, *1174*
1933 Consumers' advisory board of the federal government, *4927*
      Federal industrial advisory board, *4928*
1934 Credit union act passed by Congress, *2122*
1944 Republican presidential candidate to give his acceptance speech at the national convention, *3020*
1945 Federal treaty signed by a woman, *2417*

June 27

1652 Traffic law enacted by a colony, *4082*
1776 Execution by the Army, *2553*
1844 Presidential candidate to be assassinated, *3235*
1884 Labor bureau of the federal government, *2442*
1921 Comptroller general of the United States, *2092*

1934   Federal Housing Administration, 4047

1936   Nominating convention of a major party in which the delegates nominated a candidate without taking a ballot, 3018

1969   Homosexual rights protest, 2870

1979   African-American woman to serve as judge on the U.S. Court of Appeals, 1990

1988   Ban on surrogate motherhood enacted by a state, 3959

1997   Supreme Court decisions invalidating three federal laws in three days, 4745

June 28

1860   Southern Democratic Party platform, 3041

Southern Democratic Party presidential candidate, 3294

1892   Cabinet in which two secretaries had the same last name, 1166

1928   Presidential candidate from a major party who was Catholic, 3258

1940   Federal sedition law passed in peacetime since the Sedition Act of 1798, 3864

Registration of aliens by the federal government, 3119

1968   Federal law creating Monday holidays, 2232

1970   Gay pride march, 2871

June 29

1795   Supreme Court chief justice to resign, 4755

1956   Federal education grants to the children of deceased veterans, 3980

1972   Supreme Court decision barring the death penalty, 4738

June 30

1812   Treasury notes bearing interest, 2119

1841   Pension granted to the widow of a president, 3593

1853   Marriage of two descendants of the same president, 3559

1864   Federal cigarette tax, 4079

State park, 4147

1866   State to ratify the 14th Amendment to the Constitution, 1844

1886   Forest service of the United States, 4143

1906   Federal law on product safety, 4028

Labor union chartered by the federal government, 2490

1909   Coin bearing the likeness of a president, 2164

1921   Chief justice of the Supreme Court who had served as president of the United States, 4773

Former president to become chief justice of the Supreme Court, 3502

1936   Federal law mandating a 40-hour work week, 2497

1941   Presidential library, 3422

1948   Water pollution law enacted by Congress, 4163

1966   National Organization for Women, 2899

1974   Woman elected president of a state lawyers' association, 2593

1998   Federal payment over the Internet, 2101

July

1776   Proposals for the design of the Great Seal of the United States, 1104

1787   Suggestion that slaves be counted as full members of the population, 4235

1790   Instance of congressional "log-rolling" (vote-trading), 1548

1817   Pan-American delegates from the United States, 2325

1868   Vice presidential candidate from Missouri, 4639

1892   Single tax adopted by a city for local revenue purposes, 4825

1896   Presidential candidate from Nebraska, 4583

1904   Vice presidential candidate from West Virginia, 4649

1908   Vice presidential candidate from Nevada, 4652

1924   Presidential candidate from West Virginia, 4587

Presidential candidate from Wisconsin, 4588

1929   Currency of the standard size, 2166

1944   Political action committee (PAC), 2832

1946   Ban-the-bomb demonstrations, 2833

Professional staffers on congressional committees, 1522

1947   Policy of containment of world communism, 2281

1948   Vice presidential candidate from Idaho, 4659

1952   National conventions to receive gavel-to-gavel television coverage, 3023

1964   Presidential candidate from Arizona, 4594

Vice presidential candidate from Colorado, 4662

1970   Woman to serve as director of a state bureau of corrections, 2578

July—*continued*

1972 People's Party presidential candidate, *3357*

Presidential candidate from South Dakota, *4596*

Vice presidential candidate from Washington, DC, *1899*

1990 Racial bias suit in which one African-American claimed discrimination by another African-American, *1936*

July 1

1776 Congressional vote on a declaration of independence, *1056*

1835 Railroad to run trains to Washington, DC, *1883*

1847 Postage stamp depicting a president, *3164*

1851 Insurance board established by a state government, *4050*

1852 Person to lie in state in the Capitol rotunda, *1230*

1862 Bureau of Internal Revenue, *4803*

Inheritance tax levied by Congress, *4804*

Passport fee, *2259*

Polygamy ban enacted by Congress, *3950*

Revenue stamps issued by the federal government, *4805*

Tobacco tax enacted by the federal government for internal revenue purposes, *4078*

1863 Free mail delivery in cities, *3161*

Year the public debt of the United States exceeded $1 billion, *2128*

1871 Attorney general to head the Department of Justice, *1162*

1873 Woman to serve as a patent examiner, *2603*

1885 Federal bird protection agency, *4207*

1897 Copyrights registrar of the United States, *2509*

1907 Air force, *2618*

1918 Year the public debt of the United States exceeded $10 billion, *2130*

1921 Sales tax enacted by a state, *4831*

1924 Foreign Service of the United States, *2339*

1937 Senate parliamentarian, *1741*

1939 Executive Office of the President, *3773*

Reorganization of the federal government in the 20th century, *2010*

White House budget office, *3774*

1945 State agency for enforcing equal treatment in employment, *2459*

1961 Municipal air-raid shelter, *1268*

1968 Nonproliferation treaty for weapons of mass destruction, *2423*

1980 Trade and Development Agency, *4940*

July 2

1776 New Jersey constitution, *4362*

State to grant limited voting rights to women, *1952*

1777 State constitution to provide for emancipation from slavery, *4232*

Vermont constitution, *4370*

1788 Formal announcement that the Constitution was in effect, *1829*

1800 Federal district land office, *4177*

1862 Land-grant college founded under the Morrill Act, *3974*

1864 National hall of fame, *1067*

Statue installed in National Statuary Hall in the Capitol, *1235*

1890 Antitrust law enacted by Congress, *4953*

1892 Populist Party platform, *3054*

1908 Price regulation law enacted by a state, *4956*

1926 Air force branch of the military, *2619*

1932 Presidential candidate to accept his party's nomination in person, *3014*

Presidential candidate to fly to a political convention, *3015*

Use of the term "New Deal", *3075*

1934 Federal agency to regulate the securities markets, *2139*

1948 Ambassador to Israel, *2349*

Socialist Workers Party presidential candidate, *3336*

1964 Comprehensive civil rights law enacted by Congress, *1932*

Federal law prohibiting discrimination in employment on the basis of sex, *1966*

1965 Federal law requiring fair employment practices, *2461*

1971 State bottle bill, *4167*

State litter law, *4168*

July 3

1788 Post office west of the eastern seaboard, *3142*

1890 Idaho constitution, *4403*

Idaho state capital, *4350*

1968 African-American woman to run for president, *3268*

1989 Supreme Court decision on the constitutionality of public religious displays, *4744*

July 9—*continued*

1924 Nominating convention that required more than 100 ballots, *3010*

Woman delegates to a Democratic convention, *3011*

Woman to receive nominating votes for the vice presidency at the convention of a major party, *3012*

1953 Internal Revenue Service, *4819*

1965 African-American woman to serve as a United States ambassador, *2360*

July 10

1790 Vote to establish Washington, DC, *1865*

1795 Presidential amnesty issued to rebellious citizens, *3378*

1890 State to grant full voting rights to women, *1961*

Wyoming constitution, *4404*

Wyoming state capital, *4351*

1892 Defeated presidential candidate to be renominated by a major party, *3249*

1908 Presidential candidate to appear in movie footage, *3252*

1919 President since Washington to submit a treaty to the Senate in person, *3514*

1925 Legal clash between evolutionists and creationists, *1950*

1934 President to make a radio broadcast from a foreign country, *3760*

President to visit South America while in office, *3797*

1971 National Women's Political Caucus, *2900*

July 11

1767 First Lady who was the mother of a president, *3574*

1916 Grant-in-aid enacted by Congress to help the states build roads, *4190*

1934 President to go through the Panama Canal while in office, *3798*

1941 Independent intelligence organization, *2671*

July 12

1774 Declaration of independence by citizens of an American colony, *1050*

1856 President of a Central American country born in the United States, *2376*

1921 President who came before the Senate to discourage action on a bill, *1735*

1957 President to fly in a helicopter, *3811*

1965 State to ratify the 25th Amendment to the Constitution, *1858*

1974 Congressional Budget Office, *1527*

1976 Woman to deliver the keynote speech at a Democratic National Convention, *3031*

1984 Woman to run for vice president as the candidate of a major political party, *3273*

July 13

1787 Territory of the United States in which slavery was banned, *4236*

1836 Numbering system for patents, *2601*

1863 Draft riots, *2635*

1912 Senator expelled from the Senate for corrupt election practices, *1781*

1936 Pensions paid by the federal government to workers in private industry, *2476*

1972 Woman to receive nominating votes for the presidency at a Democratic Party convention, *3029*

1985 President to formally transfer the presidency to an acting president, *3440*

Vice president to serve as acting president under the 25th Amendment, *4997*

July 14

1778 Representative of a foreign country to the United States, *2311*

1798 Direct tax levied by Congress, *4800*

Federal law intended to intimidate the press, *3853*

1870 Pension granted to the widow of an assassinated president, *3598*

1911 Airplane to land on the White House lawn, *5033*

1918 Child of a president to die in combat, *3565*

1943 National monument dedicated to an African-American, *2716*

1972 Woman to serve as chairman of a major political party, *2966*

July 15

1779 Medal awarded by the Continental Congress to a foreigner, *1047*

1913 Senator elected by popular vote under the 17th Amendment to the Constitution, *1782*

1929 Federal farm board, *4114*

1964 Woman to receive nominating votes for the presidency at the convention of a major party, *3025*

July 16

1755 President who received a college education, *3819*

1789	Vice president to break a tie vote in the Senate, *4961*
1798	Health service established by the federal government, *4010*
1877	Strike suppressed by federal troops in peacetime, *2479*
1987	Session of Congress held outside Washington, DC, since 1800, *1820*
1992	Presidential nomination acceptance speech to mention homosexuals, *3032*

July 17

1861	Paper money issued by the federal government, *2158*
1862	African-American unit organized during the Civil War, *1384*
	Military service by African-Americans to be authorized by Congress, *1385*
	National cemeteries act, *2667*
1916	Federal farm loan board, *4113*
1948	States' Rights Democratic Party, *2948*
	States' Rights Democratic Party presidential candidate, *3338*
1959	Captive Nations Week, *2287*

July 18

1768	Patriotic song by an American, *1114*
1794	Silver coins issued by the Mint, *2153*
1985	Woman to head a regional bureau of the State Department, *2369*

July 19

1848	Women's rights convention, *2894*
1890	President during whose term more than five states were admitted to the Union, *3411*
1949	President who had been divorced, *3613*
1950	African-American justice of the Circuit Court of Appeals, *1984*

July 20

1831	Cabinet member who was Catholic, *1153*
1849	Mayor of Independence, MO, *1314*
1953	Woman career diplomat to advance to the rank of ambassador, *2353*

July 21

1828	Strike in which a militia was called out, *2477*
1861	Major battle of the Civil War, *1381*
1930	Consolidated federal agency for veterans' affairs, *2703*

1934	National Mediation Board, *2453*
1952	National convention to require a pledge of party loyalty from its delegates, *3024*

July 22

1790	Federal law regulating commerce with Native Americans, *2735*
1850	Secretary of state to serve more than once, *1157*
1896	Silverite presidential candidate, *3315*
1932	Federal Home Loan Bank board, *2111*
1934	Public Enemy Number 1, *2538*
1939	African-American woman to be appointed a municipal judge, *1276*
1953	African-American with the rank of ambassador, *2354*

July 23

1896	National Silver Party convention, *3316*
	National Silver Party platform, *3056*
1948	Progressive Party (1948) presidential candidate, *3339*
1967	Plebiscite on the political status of Puerto Rico, *4898*

July 24

1789	House Ways and Means Committee, *1544*
1824	Opinion poll, *2762*
1849	Pioneer Day (Utah), *2197*
1866	State readmitted to the Union after the Civil War, *1392*
1964	Permanent Senate internal disciplinary committee, *1747*
1974	Supreme Court ruling in a criminal case in which a United States president was named as a conspirator, *4741*
1998	Capitol Police Officers killed in the line of duty, *1251*

July 25

1866	General of the U.S. Army, *2625*
	National procedures for electing senators, *1710*
1916	Zoning ordinance, *1291*
1918	U.S. district attorney who was a woman, *1978*
1934	President to visit Hawaii while in office, *3799*
1952	Commonwealth of the United States, *4897*
1995	"Corrections Day", *1580*

July 26

1775	Postmaster general under the Continental Congress, *3138*
1788	New York state capital, *4318*
1797	President who was married overseas, *3547*
1866	Irrigation law enacted by Congress, *4194*
1923	President to visit Canada during his term in office, *3796*
1941	International oil embargo, *2275*
1947	Central administration for all branches of the military, *2629*
	National Security Council, *2673*
1948	Order integrating the armed forces, *2658*
1990	Comprehensive civil rights legislation for people with disabilities, *1908*

July 27

1789	Executive department authorized by Congress, *2033*
	Select committee appointed by the Senate, *1676*
1933	Central statistical board, *3093*

July 28

1777	State to grant universal voting rights to freemen, *4423*
1866	Woman artist to be commissioned by the federal government, *2016*
1868	Use of the word "male" in the Constitution, *1832*

July 29

1775	Treasurer of the United States, *2077*
1908	Independence Party presidential candidate, *3325*
1959	Senator of Asian ancestry, *1798*
1979	Coin to bear the depiction of an American woman, *2173*
1992	Community service requirement for high school graduation, *3986*

July 30

1619	Prayer offered at a session of a colonial legislature, *1468*
	Representative assembly in colonial America, *1469*
1943	Year the public debt of the United States exceeded $100 billion, *2131*
1956	Motto of the United States, *3076*
1965	Health insurance plan enacted by Congress, *4057*

July 31

1789	Standing committee of the Senate, *1677*

1790	Patent granted by the federal government, *2598*
1792	Federal building erected for public use, *1996*
1795	Return of coins to the Treasury, *2155*
1912	Movie censorship law enacted by Congress, *3861*
1918	White House china service that was made in the United States, *5035*
1933	Science and technology advisory board, *2072*
1968	African-American to become chief of a State Department bureau, *2362*
1972	Vice presidential candidate of a major political party to resign before the election, *3271*
1991	Post–Cold War summit between the United States and the Soviet Union, *2301*

August

1585	English colonial settlement, *1397*
1764	Colonial boycott of British goods, *1003*
1791	First Lady who had previously been divorced, *3581*
	Location of the Bank of the United States, *2104*
1824	State nominating convention, *4427*
1855	Consul to Japan, *2329*
1876	Exhibition of part of the Statue of Liberty in the United States, *1124*
1892	Pledge of allegiance to the flag, *1097*
1908	Municipal aviation tax, *4826*
1968	Presidential candidate from Minnesota, *4595*
1992	First Lady to deliver a major speech at a national political convention, *3619*
1993	Federal AIDS policy coordinator, *4038*

August 1

1787	Printed copies of the Constitution, *1823*
1790	Census of the population of the United States, *3084*
1861	Former president to serve as an official of an enemy government, *3492*
	Patent issued by the Confederate States of America, *2602*
1871	Senate library, *1714*
1876	Colorado constitution, *4398*
	Colorado state capital, *4345*
1877	Colorado Day, *2209*
1930	County hydroelectric plant, *4131*
1943	President in the 20th century to receive a medal for heroism, *3702*
1946	Regulating agency of the nuclear industry, *4134*

August 10—*continued*

1988 Compensation paid to Japanese-Americans interned during World War II, *2652*

August 11

1792 Supreme Court decision to be recorded, *4709*

Supreme Court dissent, *4697*

1852 Vice presidential candidate from Indiana, *4635*

1861 Senator to address the Senate in military uniform, *1709*

1924 Newsreels showing presidential candidates, *3863*

1928 Presidential nomination ceremony broadcast on radio, *3013*

1965 African-American attorney to serve as solicitor general, *4705*

1997 President to use the line-item veto, *3846*

August 12

1508 Capital of Puerto Rico, *4885*

European colonial settlement on Puerto Rico, *4886*

1585 Letters written by an English colonial governor in America, *1398*

1898 Island territory annexed by the federal government, *4845*

1954 Federal execution for the killing of an FBI agent, *2567*

1955 Minimum hourly wage of one dollar, *2499*

1961 Consolidated federal agency to regulate maritime commerce, *4935*

August 13

1868 Member of the House of Representatives to lie in state in the Capitol rotunda, *1237*

1970 No-fault car insurance law enacted by a state, *4059*

August 14

1888 American Party platform, *3052*

1934 Revenue stamp printed by the Post Office Department, *4817*

1935 National identification scheme for American citizens, *4068*

1941 Declaration of U.S. alliance in World War II, *2644*

1965 House page who was African-American, *1643*

August 15

1876 Forestry supervision by the federal government, *4141*

1936 Union Party presidential candidate, *3334*

1947 Ambassador to India, *2348*

August 16

1815 Pacifist society, *2810*

1824 Use of the term "national guard", *2664*

1916 Bird protection international treaty, *4213*

1999 Trial broadcast by the court over the Internet, *3870*

August 17

1790 Address to a president by a Jewish congregation, *3750*

1932 Jobless Party presidential candidate, *3331*

Liberty Party (modern) presidential candidate, *3332*

Presidential candidate from Arkansas, *4589*

Vice presidential candidate from Oklahoma, *4656*

Vice presidential candidate from Washington State, *4657*

1998 President to give testimony before a grand jury during his term in office, *3522*

August 18

1856 Salaries for consuls, *2330*

1911 Congressional representative to attend college after his term of service, *1598*

1913 Veterans of Foreign Wars of the United States, *2701*

1965 State law to end de facto segregation in schools, *1934*

1968 Peace and Freedom Party presidential candidate, *3352*

1978 First Lady to pilot an airship, *3618*

August 19

1861 Tax levied by the Confederacy, *4802*

1939 National Aviation Day, *2230*

1946 President who was born after World War II, *3469*

1995 United States officials to die in the conflict in Bosnia, *2653*

1999 Woman appointed as chief White House counsel, *3782*

August 20

1619 Africans in the English colonies, *4220*

1776 Artist's design for the Great Seal of the United States, *1105*

August 28—*continued*

1968 Ambassador killed by a terrorist attack, *2364*

August 29

1758 Reservation for Native Americans established by a state, *2727*
1817 Abolition newspaper, *3914*
1989 Latina elected to the House of Representatives, *1628*

August 30

1842 Narcotics tariff enacted by Congress, *4061*

Tariff enacted by Congress to prevent the importation of obscene literature and pictures, *4949*
1843 Vice presidential candidate from Ohio, *4633*
1890 Meat inspection law enacted by Congress, *4023*
1944 America First Party presidential candidate, *3335*
1962 Presidential hot line, *3837*
1997 Migration study jointly conducted by the United States and Mexico, *3125*

August 31

1904 Continental Party presidential candidate, *3324*
1919 Communist Labor Party of America, *2940*
1920 Local election results to be announced on radio, *1284*
1952 Constitution Party presidential candidate, *3343*

September

1789 Congressional vote on a location for the national capital, *1864*
1833 State bank to receive federal deposits, *2106*
1850 Expansion of the Capitol, *1229*
1864 State constitution telegraphed in its entirety, *4269*
1869 Prohibition Party, *2927*
1941 President who had served in the U.S. Navy, *3699*
1947 Regional agreement for collective defense under the U.N. Charter signed by the United States, *2420*
1952 Televised speech that confirmed a candidate's place on the vice presidential ticket, *3264*
1964 Shutdown of a college campus by student protesters, *2836*
1965 Nationwide consumer boycott in support of workers, *2891*

1997 International Conservative Congress, *2842*

September 1

1635 Grand jury, *1441*
1890 Single Tax League national conference, *2821*
1907 Night court, *1273*
1916 Federal child labor law, *2457*
1939 Army officer to occupy the nation's highest military post and its highest nonelective civilian post, *2628*
1989 Air bag requirement by the federal government, *4107*

September 2

1789 Department of the Treasury, *2035*
1896 Sound Money Democratic Party, *2935*

Sound Money Democratic Party platform, *3057*

Sound Money Democratic Party presidential candidate, *3317*
1914 War Risk Insurance Bureau, *4053*
1919 Communist Party of America, *2941*
1937 Game preserve appropriation by the federal government, *4214*
1944 President who had parachuted from an airplane, *3808*

September 3

1777 American flag flown in battle, *1080*
1783 Treaty between the federal government and a nation with which it had been at war, *2397*
1872 Presidential candidate who was Catholic, *3242*

Straight-out Democratic Party platform, *3046*

Straight-out Democratic Party presidential candidate, *3300*
1900 Union Reform Party platform, *3061*

Union Reform Party presidential candidate, *3322*
1964 Federal network of protected wilderness, *4158*
1997 State in which two consecutive governors were forced to resign from office, *4530*

September 4

1777 American flag flown on the high seas, *1081*
1919 General of the Armies of the United States, *2626*

September 5

1774 President of the Continental Congress, *1038*

September 13—*continued*

1948 Woman elected to the Senate in her own right, *1792*

September 14

1778 Minister plenipotentiary, *2312*
1814 Star-Spangled Banner, *1088*
1909 Election using the preferential ballot system, *1282*
1940 Draft law enacted by Congress during peacetime, *2636*

September 15

1736 Mayor of Norfolk, VA, *1297*
1965 Secret Service protection for former presidents and their families, *3430*

September 16

1776 President who had been wounded in action during a war, *3693*
1782 Impression made by the Great Seal of the United States, *1107*
1812 Vice presidential candidate from Massachusetts, *4625*
1833 Interstate anticrime pact, *2527*
1859 Senator killed in a duel during his term in office, *1774*
1940 Speaker of the House of Representatives to serve longer than ten years, *1636*
1974 Woman to serve as chairman of the Republican Party, *2967*

September 17

1774 Major action taken by the Continental Congress, *1044*
1778 Proposal to form a Native American state within the Union, *2732*
Treaty between the United States and a Native American nation, *2733*
1787 Constitution Day, *2187*
Constitution of the United States, *1825*
Regional compromise over the issue of slavery, *4237*
1789 Secretary of a federal executive department to take orders from Congress, *2036*
1796 Incumbent president to decline to run for reelection, *3379*
1947 Secretary of defense, *1182*

September 18

1793 Ceremony at the Capitol, *1219*
1850 African-American captured under the Fugitive Slave Law of 1850, *4251*

1851 Issue of the *New York Times*, *3923*
1883 Korean embassy, *2261*
1947 Department of Defense, *2046*
Department of the Air Force, *2047*
Federal agency for the gathering of foreign intelligence, *2674*
1978 Middle East peace treaty brokered by an American president, *2425*

September 19

1787 Newspaper to publish the Constitution, *1826*
Public copies of the Constitution, *1827*
1796 Farewell address by a president, *3751*
Isolationist address by a president, *2251*
Presidential warning against party politics, *2907*
1963 Homosexual rights demonstration in the United States, *2868*

September 20

1830 National convention of African-Americans, *2845*
1860 Prince of Wales to visit the United States, *2377*
1873 Closing of the New York Stock Exchange, *2138*
1881 Date on which the Senate was equally divided between Republicans and Democrats, *1718*
President who was the son of a minister, *3562*
1884 Equal Rights Party platform, *3050*
Equal Rights Party presidential candidate, *3308*
Presidential candidate from Washington, DC, *1893*
Vice presidential candidate from California, *4644*
Woman vice presidential candidate, *3246*
1895 Standardized foreign service examinations, *2337*
1973 Woman to become an assistant secretary of state, *2365*

September 21

1776 Delaware constitution, *4363*
1814 Library of Congress, *2062*

September 22

1656 Jury composed of women, *1443*
1776 American executed as a spy, *1028*
1789 Law setting pay rates for Congress, *1647*
Post Office Department, *3143*

Travel expenses for members of Congress, *1648*

1817 Child of a president to serve in a presidential cabinet, *1151*

1862 Emancipation proclamation, *4255*

1961 African-American judge to serve on a federal district court, *1987*

1975 President to survive two assassination attempts in one month, *3455*

September 23

1779 Naval hero, *1035*

1976 Televised presidential election debate between an incumbent president and a challenger, *3222*

September 24

1789 Chief justice of the Supreme Court, *4747*

Congressional act declared unconstitutional by the Supreme Court, *1488*

Creation of federal courts, *1970*

Salary established for the president, *3738*

Salary established for the vice president, *3739*

Salary of Supreme Court justices, *4690*

Supreme Court of the United States, *4691*

1906 National monument designated by the federal government, *4150*

1957 Use of federal troops to enforce integration, *1931*

1963 Photograph of the Senate in session, *1746*

1968 Political interview aired on a television newsmagazine, *3881*

September 25

1690 Newspaper suppressed by the government, *3903*

Political censorship of the press, *3847*

1789 Constitutional amendments to fail the ratification process, *1834*

1872 Liberal Republican Convention of Colored Men, *3301*

1981 Woman to become a Supreme Court justice, *4781*

September 26

1772 Medical licensing law enacted by a colony, *4009*

1789 Attorney of the United States, *1971*

Postmaster general of the United States, *3144*

1831 Anti-Masonic Party presidential candidate, *3282*

Convention city, *2978*

National nominating convention held by a political party, *2979*

Presidential candidate to be nominated in an open party convention, *3229*

1903 Boycott law enacted by a state, *4918*

1914 Federal Trade Commission, *4922*

1919 Woman to act as unofficial president of the United States, *3416*

1957 President to go underwater in an atomic-powered submarine, *3812*

1960 Presidential election debates shown on television, *3215*

1961 Independent disarmament agency, *2609*

1973 Federal civil rights law for people with disabilities, *1907*

September 27

1642 Monetary regulation act, *2142*

1919 National committee of a major political party to admit women as members, *2962*

1975 Law limiting the use of Social Security numbers, *4069*

September 28

1776 Pennsylvania constitution, *4364*

1915 Formal appeal for recognition of Native Americans as United States citizens, *2750*

1967 African-American to serve as chief executive of a major city, *1332*

Commissioner and council government of Washington, DC, *1898*

1989 Summit conference on education by the nation's governors, *3985*

September 29

1789 Commander-in-chief of the United States Army, *2624*

Pensions paid by the federal government, *2471*

1988 Federal agency with safety oversight of defense nuclear facilities, *2610*

September 30

1630 Execution in America, *2550*

1787 Ship to carry the American flag around the world, *1084*

1788 Senators elected to office, *1755*

State to elect senators to the United States Senate, *4260*

1791 Federal report on exports, *4907*

1847 Political speech on conservation, *4120*

September 30—*continued*

1975   Emperor of Japan to visit the United States, *2391*

1976   Right-to-die law enacted by a state, *3958*

1996   Year the public debt of the United States exceeded $5 trillion, *2137*

October

1664   North Carolina colonial governor, *1461*

1763   Strike of African-American laborers, *2875*

1770   Political cartoon to interfere with a trial, *3930*

1773   Protest against British taxation of tea shipments, *1010*

1791   Sale of building lots in Washington, DC, *1869*

1792   Delaware state governor, *4458*

Party endorsement of a presidential candidate, *2970*

1798   Prosecution under the Sedition Act, *3854*

1825   Presidential candidate nominated by a state legislature, *3228*

Year in which there was no mechanism for nominating presidential candidates, *2977*

1860   Royal personage to stay at the White House as a houseguest, *5025*

1915   Missouri Day, *2221*

1967   Presidential commission on overhauling the budgetary process, *2099*

1973   Shuttle diplomacy, *2292*

1988   Government official convicted of espionage for leaking secrets to the press, *2682*

1989   African-American to become director general of the Foreign Service, *2371*

Woman to serve as surgeon general, *4039*

1997   Non-NATO ally of the United States in the Western Hemisphere, *2308*

1999   Former speaker of the House to become a television news commentator, *1638*

October 1

1768   City to be occupied by the British before the Revolution, *1007*

1790   Political newspaper to carry partisanship to extremes, *3852*

1896   Rural free mail delivery, *3163*

1922   White House Police Force, *5036*

1924   President who was born in a hospital, *3468*

1934   Federal credit union, *2123*

1945   President to watch the swearing-in ceremony of a Supreme Court justice he appointed, *3424*

1946   Defense Department think tank, *2672*

1977   Department of Energy, *2051*

Secretary of energy, *1201*

1979   Pope to visit the White House, *2392*

1996   Capitol Hill employees to unionize, *2492*

Executive Mayor of Miami–Dade County, FL, *1362*

October 2

1889   Conference of American states initiated by the United States, *2262*

October 3

1632   Tobacco tax enacted by a colony, *4075*

1824   Treaty between the federal government and a South American nation, *2408*

1913   Political cartoon entered in the *Congressional Record*, *1514*

1919   Federal Trade Commission trade practice conference, *4924*

1924   Citizenship and public affairs school at a college, *3065*

October 4

1636   Law code of an American colony, *1471*

1854   Speech by Abraham Lincoln denouncing slavery, *4252*

1859   Kansas constitution, *4394*

1965   Pope to visit the United States, *2390*

President to meet with a pope in the United States, *3431*

1968   Filibuster against a Supreme Court appointment, *1748*

October 5

1947   Presidential address televised from the White House, *3765*

October 6

1884   Naval war college, *2615*

October 7

1763   Restriction by a European colonial power on settlements in Native American territory, *2728*

1935   Session of the Supreme Court held in its own building, *4704*

1997   Court decision preventing the enactment of term limits for state legislators, *4287*

October 20—_continued_

1862 Presidential executive order to be numbered, _3406_

1951 Gambling permit stamp issued by the federal government, _4003_

October 21

1639 Medical regulations enacted by a colony, _4006_

1968 Secret Service protection for major presidential and vice presidential candidates and nominees, _3269_

October 22

1962 Nuclear war confrontation, _2649_

1998 Billion-dollar settlement in an environmental lawsuit, _4171_

October 23

1850 National convention for women's rights, _2895_

1937 President to ride on a diesel train, _3801_

1946 United Nations General Assembly meeting, _2433_

1983 U.S. peacekeeping forces killed by suicide bombing, _2651_

October 24

1861 Transcontinental telegram of a political nature, _3857_

1881 Act in the construction of the Statue of Liberty, _1125_

1931 Pennsylvania Day, _2227_

October 25

1902 President who had been president of a university, _3499_

1929 Cabinet member convicted of a crime, _1177_

1954 Cabinet session to be broadcast on radio and television, _1186_

October 26

1850 Admission Day (California), _2198_
American flag made on the Pacific Coast, _1092_

1973 State building located outside a state, _4281_

October 27

1787 Issue of the _Federalist_ papers, _3071_

1994 Visit by an American president to a country on the U.S. list of terrorist states, _3816_

October 28

1862 African-American unit to fight in the Civil War, _1386_

1886 Dedication ceremony for the Statue of Liberty, _1128_
Ticker-tape parade, _2211_

1933 Emergency housing corporation, _4046_

1935 Native American tribal constitution, _2753_

1949 Woman to hold the rank of ambassador, _2351_

1964 United Nations permanent ambassador who was a woman, _2437_

1970 Sky marshals, _2540_

October 29

1835 Use of the term "Loco-Focos", _2917_

1845 African-American vice consul, _2328_

1940 Draft number drawing, _2637_

October 30

1884 Political cartoon to decisively influence a presidential election, _3939_

October 31

1791 Democratic-Republican (Jeffersonian) political newspaper, _3910_

1864 Nevada constitution, _4396_
Nevada state capital, _4343_

1865 Nevada Day, _2200_

November

1526 Escape of slaves from a colony in what is now United States territory, _4218_

1646 Law forbidding Native American religious rituals, _2725_

1796 Presidential election in which more than one candidate declared for the presidency, _3176_

1808 Vice president to serve under two presidents, _4969_

1846 Democratic president whose party was in the minority in the House of Representatives, _3712_

1854 Symbol of the Republican Party, _2923_

1870 Political parties in Puerto Rico, _4887_

1874 Republican president whose party was in the minority in the House of Representatives, _3715_

1878 Republican president whose party was in the minority in both houses of Congress, _3716_

1881 Presidential candidate to make campaign speeches in a foreign language, _2767_

November 2—*continued*

Presidential election in which the candidates of both major parties were newspaper publishers, *3210*

Presidential election in which women voted, *3211*

Single Tax Party presidential candidate, *3328*

1926 Senate election in which neither candidate was seated after a recount, *1737*

1945 Industrial and labor relations school at a college, *3067*

1954 Senator elected by a write-in vote, *1796*

1975 President who had served as director of the Central Intelligence Agency, *3508*

1993 Woman governor of New Jersey, *4528*

November 3

1840 Democratic presidential and vice presidential team to lose a bid for reelection, *3394*

President and vice president to be born in the same county, *3465*

President from the Whig Party, *3710*

President to travel to his inauguration by train, *3656*

Presidential election won by the Whig Party, *3188*

Third party to participate in a presidential election, *3189*

Vice president from the Whig Party, *5001*

1868 African-American women's rights activist who attempted to vote in a presidential election, *1956*

1896 Woman to serve as a state senator, *4547*

1907 Secret Service agent killed in the line of duty, *2581*

1911 State-run adult education program, *3979*

1945 African-American judge on the federal bench, *1983*

1964 President from a Southern state since the Civil War, *3429*

Presidential election in which the Republican Party earned a significant number of votes in the South, *3216*

Presidential election in which the state of Vermont was carried by a Democrat, *3217*

Presidential election in which votes were tallied electronically, *3218*

Year when citizens of Washington, DC, could vote in a presidential election, *1897*

1970 Congressional representative of Puerto Rican ancestry, *1620*

Congresswoman who was Jewish, *1621*

1980 Woman elected to the Senate whose political career owed nothing to a male relative, *1805*

1992 African-American woman to serve as a senator, *1809*

Natural Law Party presidential candidate, *3366*

President and vice president in the 20th century who were both Southerners, *3442*

Presidential election in which a Democratic winner failed to carry Texas, *3223*

1998 Midterm election since World War II in which the president's party gained seats in the House of Representatives, *1581*

Reform Party candidate to win a governorship, *4443*

State governor who had been a professional wrestler, *4532*

November 4

1646 Smoking ban in a colonial legislature, *1474*

1780 Consul to die in service, *2313*

1800 Defeated presidential candidate to run again successfully, *3387*

Party to continue in power in the White House for more than 20 years, *2908*

Presidential election that produced a change in the party in power, *3177*

Presidential election won by the Democratic-Republican Party, *3178*

1811 Speaker of the House who was simultaneously member, parliamentarian, and leader, *1632*

1828 President from the Democratic Party, *3709*

Presidential election won by the Democratic Party, *3185*

Vice president from the Democratic Party, *5000*

1856 Presidential election in which the Republican Party participated, *3191*

Third party to make a substantial showing in a presidential election, *3192*

1884 President elected after the Civil War who had not served in it, *3409*

Presidential candidate from the Democratic Party to be elected after the Civil War, *3247*

November 6—*continued*

President with a brother in the Senate, *3570*

Republican governor of Oklahoma, *4512*

1974 Woman to serve as mayor of a major city with a population over 500,000, *1340*

1983 Woman governor of Kentucky, *4521*

1984 Presidential candidate in the 20th century to come within two percentage points of winning the entire electoral vote, *3274*

Presidential candidate to receive more than 50 million popular votes, *3275*

1990 African-American woman to serve as mayor of Washington, DC, *1901*

November 7

1829 Labor union whose candidates won an election, *2486*

1848 Election day for presidential voting held nationwide, *3190*

1874 Political cartoon showing the Republican Party as an elephant, *3937*

1876 Presidential election in which neither candidate received a majority of the electoral vote, *3200*

1877 State reformatory for women, *2574*

1916 Democratic presidential and vice presidential team to be reelected, *3415*

Election in which returns were broadcast on radio, *3208*

Political news broadcast by radio, *3872*

Presidential election in which the wrong candidate was declared the winner by early newspaper editions, *3209*

1922 Congresswoman who was a mother, *1600*

1942 President to make a radio broadcast in a foreign language, *3763*

1950 Husband and wife to be elected simultaneously to both chambers of a state legislature, *4553*

1967 Major city to elect an African-American as mayor, *1333*

1972 Congressional candidate elected while missing, *1622*

1978 African-American militant to be elected mayor of a major American city, *1341*

Basketball star elected to the Senate, *1804*

1989 African-American mayor of New York City, *1351*

African-American state governor elected in his own right, *4524*

1995 National urban presidential primary, *3224*

2000 First Lady elected to public office, *3623*

Senator elected posthumously, *1810*

Woman governor of Delaware, *4534*

Woman governor of Montana, *4535*

Woman governor of Puerto Rico, *4899*

November 8

1701 Colony to change from a bicameral to a unicameral legislature, *1478*

1775 Mail franking privilege, *3139*

1811 Battle in the "Frontier War", *2738*

1864 Presidential election in which a bloc of states did not participate, *3198*

Presidential election in which soldiers in the field were allowed to vote, *3199*

1889 Montana constitution, *4401*

Montana state capital, *4348*

1892 President whose predecessor and successor were the same man, *3412*

Presidential election in which a socialist party participated, *3202*

1904 Vice president who succeeded to the presidency after a president's death and was then elected to a full term, *4983*

1932 Political party to nominate the same candidate six times, *3016*

President whose mother was eligible to vote for him, *3567*

Republican presidential and vice presidential team to lose a bid for reelection, *3418*

1938 African-American woman to serve as a state legislator, *4552*

1960 Conservative Party of Virginia presidential candidate, *3349*

Independent Afro-American Party presidential candidate, *3350*

Senate election race in which both candidates were women, *1745*

Tax Cut Party presidential candidate, *3351*

1962 African-American woman to be elected to a judgeship, *1277*

1966 African-American senator to be elected by popular vote, *1799*

Republican governor of Florida since Reconstruction, *4514*

1968 Roman Catholic clergyman sentenced to jail in the United States for political crimes, *2860*

1983 African-American mayor of Philadelphia, PA, *1347*

1988 Consumer Party presidential candidate, *3363*

Incumbent vice president to be elected president in the 20th century, *3441*

Woman presidential candidate and African-American presidential candidate to get on the ballot in all 50 states, *3276*

1999 President to participate in a live chat over the Internet, *3733*

November 9

1776 Maryland constitution, *4365*
1906 President to visit a foreign country while in office, *3791*
1921 Unknown soldier to lie in state in the Capitol rotunda, *1244*

November 10

1775 United States Marines, *2660*
1801 State ban on dueling, *4012*
1943 Statue of an American woman in uniform, *2717*

November 11

1647 Colonial law requiring towns to hire teachers and construct schools, *3963*
1887 Labor activists to be executed, *2559*
1889 State named for a person born in America, *4272*
Washington state capital, *4349*
Washington State constitution, *4402*
1919 Armistice Day, *2223*
Veterans Day, *2224*
1921 Burial at the Tomb of the Unknown Soldier, *2670*
1933 Electric power contract between a city and the federal government, *4132*
1938 Performance of "God Bless America", *1121*

November 12

1921 Arms control conference held in the United States, *2269*
Conference of great powers, *2270*
1932 President to invite the president-elect to confer with him, *3419*

November 13

1789 President to tour the country, *3784*
1839 Antislavery political organization, *4248*
Liberty Party platform, *3035*
Liberty Party presidential candidate, *3286*
Single-issue political party, *2918*

1933 Sit-down strike, *2481*
1997 IRS commissioner who was not an accountant or a lawyer, *4824*

November 14

1944 Veteran of World War II to be elected to the Senate, *1791*
1962 State to ratify the 24th Amendment to the Constitution, *1857*
1969 President to attend the launching of a manned space flight, *3840*
1995 Senate staff furlough, *1754*

November 15

1882 Naval attaché, *2334*
1898 Foreign service school in a college, *2338*
1944 National organization of Native Americans, *2754*

November 16

1676 Prison, *2570*
1700 Public library in an American city, *1254*
1776 American flag saluted by a foreigner, *1077*
Military pension awarded to a woman, *2698*
1798 Statement of the doctrine of nullification, *4262*
1907 Oklahoma constitution, *4406*
Oklahoma state capital, *4354*
1914 Federal reserve banks, *2109*
1933 Diplomatic relations between the United States and the Soviet Union, *2272*
President to negotiate with the Soviet Union, *2273*
1962 Marriage of two descendants of different presidents, *3571*
1963 President to witness the firing of a Polaris missile, *3838*

November 17

1777 Framework for a national government, *1032*
1800 Meeting place of the House of Representatives in Washington, DC, *1553*
Meeting place of the Senate in Washington, DC, *1686*
Session of Congress to meet in Washington, DC, *1815*
1871 National firearms lobby, *2817*
1933 National emergency council, *2008*
1947 President who had been president of a union, *3503*
1988 Professional political consultant to head a major political party, *2968*

November 18

1874 National temperance society of women, *2857*

1943 Ambassador to Canada, *2347*
Cabinet member to address a joint session of Congress, *1180*

1949 Vice president to marry during his term in office, *4991*

1998 African-American elected to a national leadership post in the Republican Party, *2960*

November 19

1794 Extradition treaty with a foreign country, *2403*

1806 Senator to take office despite being too young to serve, *1760*

1868 Women to cast unofficial votes in a presidential election, *1957*

1898 National anti-imperialist organization, *2825*

1990 Treaty ending the Cold War, *2429*

November 20

1771 Town named for George Washington, *1256*

1789 State to ratify the Bill of Rights, *1835*

1831 Independent Party presidential candidate, *3283*

1889 North Dakota state governor, *4495*

November 21

1789 North Carolina state capital, *4319*

1800 Senate quorum in Washington, DC, *1687*

1918 Alcohol prohibition law enacted by Congress, *3946*

1922 Woman to be appointed a senator, *1783*

1933 Ambassador to the Soviet Union, *2345*
Federal trade policy executive committee, *4930*

1946 President to travel underwater in a submarine, *3809*

1973 Women to serve as federal marshals, *2541*

1990 Post–Cold War summit of North American and European nations, *2298*

1999 President to visit Bulgaria, *3817*

November 22

1800 Joint session of Congress to meet in the Capitol, *1816*

1954 Secretary to the cabinet and presidential assistant, *1187*

1955 Cabinet session held at a place other than the seat of the federal government, *1188*

1963 Assassination of a president captured on film, *3451*
President whose father and mother both survived him, *3534*
Woman to administer the presidential oath of office, *3685*

1971 Supreme Court decision invalidating a state law on the grounds of gender discrimination, *4737*

November 23

1765 Local government to refuse to obey the Stamp Act, *1006*

1804 President born in the 19th century, *3463*

1814 President whose administration lost two vice presidents to death, *3392*
Vice president to be buried at Washington, DC, *1879*

1963 Vice president who was present at the assassination of the president he succeeded, *3452*

1968 Naturalization ceremony in the White House, *3123*

1973 Congresswoman to give birth while holding office, *1624*

November 24

1805 Vote of record in which participants of different races and both sexes were given an equal voice, *4839*

1896 Absentee voting law enacted by a state, *4431*

November 25

1715 English patent granted to a resident of America, *2596*

1875 Vice president to lie in state in the Capitol rotunda, *1239*

1897 Charter of autonomy for Puerto Rico, *4888*

1986 National security advisor forced to resign, *1206*

1997 Federal prosecution of a hate crime on the Internet, *1939*

November 26

1863 Thanksgiving Day, *2242*

1955 Pioneer Party presidential candidate, *3344*

November 27

1901 Army war college, *2616*

1918 President to receive a passport while in office, *3793*

December 5—_continued_

1791	Industrial report to Congress, _4908_
1831	Congress in which 1,000 bills were introduced, _1498_
1861	Kansas state capital, _4341_
1905	Campaign finance reform proposal, _2783_
	Interstate Commerce Commission Medal of Honor, _4919_
1927	King born in the United States, _2383_
	Senate leader to occupy the party floor leader's desk, _1738_
1933	Constitutional amendment ratified by state conventions rather than state legislatures, _1853_
	Constitutional amendment submitted to the states for repeal, _1854_

December 6

1787	State to ratify the federal Constitution, _1828_
1790	Meeting place of Congress that is still in existence, _1490_
	Session of Congress to meet in Philadelphia, _1813_
1824	Issue of _Register of Debates in Congress_, _1494_
1830	Observatory established by the federal government, _2070_
1915	Senate minority whip, _1732_
1923	Presidential message to Congress that was broadcast on radio, _3756_
1973	Vice president appointed under the 25th Amendment to the Constitution, _4996_
1974	Democratic Party convention between presidential elections, _3030_
1979	Secretary of education, _1203_
1994	County to file for bankruptcy, _2136_
1997	African-American mayor of Houston, TX, _1364_

December 7

1787	Delaware state capital, _4308_
1829	Senate page, _1640_
1835	Senate committee system empowering the majority party, _1698_
1848	Father and son who were senators at the same session, _1764_
1925	Congresswoman to serve 18 terms, _1603_
1927	Senator barred for spending too much on an election campaign, _1785_
1928	Latino elected to the Senate, _1786_
1933	Delaware Day, _2229_

December 8

1801	Annual message submitted by a president to Congress in writing, _3752_

1863	Presidential amnesty granted during the Civil War, _3407_
1928	Physician to Congress, _1518_
1941	Congressional representative to vote twice against entry into war, _1608_
1958	John Birch Society, _2835_
1987	Treaty to reduce the number of nuclear missiles, _2427_
1992	Secretary of state who was a former member of the Foreign Service, _1209_

December 9

1790	Newspapers provided to senators and representatives, _3909_
1819	President who was a bachelor, _3586_
1858	Senator removed from a committee chairmanship against his will, _1773_
1930	Secretary of labor who was not a member of the American Federation of Labor, _2444_
1994	Summit of the Americas, _2304_
1998	State appeals court decision ordering the extension of insurance benefits to homosexual partners of government employees, _1916_

December 10

1815	Military academy for naval officers, _2614_
1817	Mississippi constitution, _4380_
	Mississippi state capital, _4327_
1819	Vice president who had served in both the House and the Senate, _4971_
1824	Foreigner to address a joint meeting of Congress, _1495_
1869	Territory to grant full voting rights to women, _1958_
1918	Vice president to preside over a cabinet meeting, _4984_

December 11

1816	Indiana constitution, _4379_
	Indiana Day, _2191_
	Indiana state capital, _4326_
1872	State governor who was African-American, _4489_
1961	Technical advisors sent to Vietnam, _2648_
1970	President who had served as ambassador to the United Nations, _3506_
1971	Libertarian Party, _2955_
1980	Federal Superfund for cleaning up toxic wastes, _4128_

December 12

1787 Pennsylvania state capital, *4309*
1803 State to ratify the Twelfth Amendment to the Constitution, *1840*
1831 National nominating convention held by a political party of importance, *2980*
1870 Congressional representative who was African-American, *1594*
1906 Cabinet member who was Jewish, *1169*
1910 Supreme Court justice to be appointed and confirmed as chief justice, *4771*

December 13

1774 Attack against the British by a state militia, *1013*

December 14

1835 Presidential candidate from Ohio, *4570*
1961 President's Commission on the Status of Women, *1964*

December 15

1778 Arbitration law enacted by a state, *4944*
1791 Constitutional amendment, *1836*
      Statement of the principle of due process, *1837*
1795 Nominee for chief justice of the Supreme Court to be rejected by the Senate, *4756*
1814 Threat of secession by a regional group of states, *4264*
1874 Reigning king to visit the United States, *2380*
1931 Woman to chair a House committee, *1605*
1970 Restoration of land to a Native American tribe, *2757*
1971 Women to become Secret Service agents, *2582*

December 16

1773 Destruction of British tea shipments, *1011*
1857 Meeting of the House of Representatives in its present location, *1563*
1891 Committee on Irrigation and Reclamation, *1721*
      Immigration bureau superintendent, *3113*
1922 Woman to serve as a justice of a state supreme court, *4416*
1953 Presidential press conference that was entirely "on the record", *3866*

1988 Presidential candidate convicted in a federal criminal case, *3277*

December 17

1821 State law to abolish imprisonment for debt, *2572*
1883 Supreme Court decision on criminal jurisdiction on Native American reservations, *4721*
1895 National anti-saloon league, *2858*
1963 Air pollution law of importance enacted by Congress, *4166*

December 18

1776 North Carolina constitution, *4366*
1777 National day of thanksgiving, *2241*
1787 New Jersey state capital, *4310*
1865 Constitutional amendment that resulted from the Civil War, *1843*
1917 Constitutional amendment requiring ratification within seven years, *1848*
1935 Bill to depict both sides of the Great Seal of the United States, *2169*

December 19

1800 Former chief justice of the Supreme Court to refuse renomination, *4760*
1823 State birth registration law, *3949*
1945 First Lady appointed to a federal post after the death of her husband, *3612*
1966 Space treaty signed by the United States, *2422*
1974 President and vice president to hold office together without either having been elected, *3437*
      Senate proceeding to be shown on television, *1749*
1998 Elected president to be impeached, *3632*

December 20

1669 Rebellion by colonists against an English governor, *1417*
1780 Conscientious objectors, *2631*
1820 Bachelor tax enacted by a state, *4828*
1849 California state governor, *4477*
1860 Secession act at the start of the Civil War, *1365*
      State to secede from the Union, *1366*
1870 State governor to be impeached and convicted, *4488*
1893 Lynching ban enacted by a state, *1926*
1967 Federal Judicial Center, *1989*

December 21

1775 New Hampshire constitution, *4367*

December 22

1775 Commander-in-chief of the Continental Navy, *2688*

1807 Embargo by the federal government, *4910*

1828 First Lady who died after her husband's election but before his inauguration, *3590*

1914 Alcohol prohibition vote taken in Congress, *3945*

1973 Native American tribe restored to federally recognized status after termination, *2759*

December 23

1776 Foreign loan to the Continental Congress, *2078*

1814 Use of the Post Office to generate revenue in wartime, *3151*

1913 Banking reform after the Civil War, *2108*

1930 Police bureau of criminal alien investigation, *2536*

December 24

1963 Congressional representative sworn in before eight o'clock in the morning, *1617*

December 25

1862 Revenue stamps issued by the federal government, *4805*

1868 Interracial jury, *1974*

Presidential amnesty granted during the Civil War, *3407*

December 26

1799 Congressional eulogy for a president, *3523*

1941 Prime minister of Great Britain to address Congress in person, *2388*

1945 Strike to last longer than a year, *2889*

December 27

1677 Colonial postmaster, *3131*

1945 International Monetary Fund meeting, *2097*

World bank, *2116*

December 28

1832 Vice president to resign, *4973*

1846 Iowa constitution, *4389*

Iowa state capital, *4336*

State constitution to provide for election of judges, *4412*

1869 Labor Day, *2205*

1928 Commemoration of the birthday of Woodrow Wilson, *2226*

1992 Nationwide nutritional labeling standards, *4037*

December 29

1780 President who had served as minister to a foreign country, *3475*

Vice president who had served as minister to a foreign country, *4959*

1832 Former vice president to serve in the Senate, *4974*

1845 Independent nation annexed by the United States, *4299*

National flag to become a state flag, *1091*

Texas constitution, *4388*

Texas state capital, *4335*

1848 Gaslight illumination in the White House, *5022*

1961 Minimum wage law established by a city for public contract work, *2500*

December 30

1903 National political science society, *3073*

Theater safety codes, *4043*

December 31

1776 Price regulation law enacted by a colony, *4951*

1877 President and First Lady to celebrate their silver wedding anniversary in the White House, *3602*

1937 Socialist Workers Party, *2946*

1948 Senator to win a seat that had been occupied by his father and mother, *1793*

1981 Year the public debt of the United States exceeded $1 trillion, *2134*

1998 Woman governor of Ohio, *4533*

Index to Personal Names

Following is a listing of personal names to be found in the main body of the text, arranged alphabetically by last name. Each name is followed by a short description of the main entry where the person is mentioned, plus an italicized indexing number. To find the complete entry, please use the italicized indexing number to search the main body of the text.

Adams, John:—*continued*

Mourning ribbons, *3524*

National flag to represent the United States, *1078*

Party endorsement of a presidential candidate, *2970*

Peace conference during the American Revolution, *1027*

Political cartoon to interfere with a trial, *3930*

Political party to hold a secret presidential nominating caucus, *2971*

President elected by decision of the House of Representatives, *3179*

President from Massachusetts, *4599*

President of the Senate, *1669*

President to be inaugurated after his vice president, *3637*

President to be reelected, *3377*

President to have children, *3545*

President to have written a book, *3473*

President to reside in Washington, DC, *3386*

President who became a nonagenarian, *3525*

President who declined to attend the inauguration of his successor, *3645*

President who had been a schoolteacher, *3470*

President who had made a transatlantic crossing, *3783*

President who had served as minister to a foreign country, *3475*

President who had served as vice president, *3381*

President who had served in Congress, *3472*

President who received a college education, *3819*

President who was admitted to the bar, *3471*

President who was defeated for reelection by his own vice president, *3384*

President who was older than 60 when he took office, *3382*

President who was sworn in by the chief justice of the Supreme Court, *3643*

President who was younger than his vice president, *3390*

President whose ancestry was not British, *3460*

President whose father was alive when he was inaugurated, *3551*

President whose political party was not the same as the vice president's, *3707*

President whose son became president, *3546*

Presidential candidates from Massachusetts, *4564*

Presidential election in which a candidate was endorsed by a political party, *3173*

Presidential election in which both parties nominated candidates in secret caucus, *2972*

Presidential election in which more than one candidate declared for the presidency, *3176*

Presidential election in which the Democratic-Republican Party participated, *3175*

Presidential election that produced a change in the party in power, *3177*

Presidential election won by the Democratic-Republican Party, *3178*

Presidential election won by the Federalist Party, *3172*

Proposals for the design of the Great Seal of the United States, *1104*

Public celebration of national independence, *2236*

Reception held at the White House, *5008*

Response of the Senate to an inaugural address, *1671*

Senate president pro tempore, *1665*

Special session of Congress, *1814*

Supreme Court chief justice to resign, *4755*

Supreme Court chief justice who had served in a presidential cabinet, *4762*

Supreme Court decision declaring an act of Congress unconstitutional, *4712*

Test of presidential authority over the cabinet secretaries, *1147*

Treaty between the federal government and a nation with which it had been at war, *2397*

Treaty entered into by the federal government after independence, *2398*

Undeclared war, *2639*

United States Marines, *2660*

Use of the East Room in the White House, *5018*

Use of the word "caucus", *1287*

Vice president from Massachusetts, *4664*

Vice president from the Federalist Party, *4998*

Vice president to announce his own election as president, *4965*

Vice president to break a tie vote in the Senate, *4961*

Vice president who had served as minister to a foreign country, *4959*

Vice president who had served in the Continental Congress, *4957*

Wedding of a president's son in the White House, *5017*

Adams, John Quincy: Articulation of the Monroe Doctrine, *2254*

Campaign newspapers, *3918*

Chief justice of the Supreme Court to administer the oath of office to more than one president, *4763*

Child of a president to be born in a foreign country, *3549*

Child of a president to serve in a presidential cabinet, *1151*

Albright, Madeline Korbel: Secretary of state to visit Vietnam, *2307*
Woman to serve as secretary of state, *1213*

Alexander, Harold: President to pay a state visit to Canada, *3810*

Alexander, Joyce London: African-American to serve as chief United States magistrate, *1992*

Alexander, Moses: State governor who was Jewish, *4502*

Allen, Charles H.: Civil governor of Puerto Rico under the Foraker Act, *4891*

Allen, Florence Ellinwood: Death penalty imposed by a woman judge, *2561*
Woman to serve as a judge in a general court, *4415*
Woman to serve as a justice of a state supreme court, *4416*
Woman to serve as justice of the Circuit Court of Appeals, *1980*

Allen, Macon B.: African-American lawyer formally admitted to the bar, *2585*

Allen, Paul: Statewide vote paid for by a single individual, *4286*

Allen, Richard: National convention of African-Americans, *2845*

Allen, Stephen: Mayor of New York, NY, *1295*

Allgood, Howard Ray: Community to fingerprint its citizens, *2537*

Allison, William: Senator to serve as long-term head of a standing committee, *1768*

Altgeld, John Peter: Labor activists to be executed, *2559*

Ames, David: Arsenal of the federal government, *2604*

Ames, Mary Clemmer: Use of the term "First Lady" to refer to the president's wife, *3601*

Andersen, Elmer L.: Trial by a panel of judges to determine the winner of a state election, *4437*

Anderson, Eugenie Moore: Woman to hold the rank of ambassador, *2351*

Anderson, Helen Eugenie Moore: Woman ambassador to a Communist-bloc nation, *2358*

Anderson, John: Televised debate among competitors for a party's presidential nomination, *2776*

Anderson, Laurie B.: Women to become Secret Service agents, *2582*

Anderson, Mary: Women's Bureau of the Labor Department, *2443*

Anderson, Richard Clough: Conference of American republics, *2255*
Treaty between the federal government and a South American nation, *2408*

Anderson, Robert: Act inaugurating the Civil War, *1369*

Anderson, Violette Neatly: African-American woman lawyer admitted to practice before the Supreme Court, *2592*

André, John: American general to engage in treason, *1034*

Andrews, Thomas Coleman: States' Rights Party presidential candidate, *3346*

Andros, Edmund: Concealment of a colonial charter to prevent its revocation, *1438*
Tax revolt, *4793*

Andrus, Ethel: National lobbying group for retirees, *2834*

Anne, Queen of Great Britain: Native American envoys received as guests of the British crown, *2373*

Anthony, Susan B.: Coin to bear the depiction of an American woman, *2173*
League of Women Voters, *2898*
National organization to advocate universal voting rights, *2815*
State temperance society of women, *2856*
Woman to argue for women's suffrage before a major committee of Congress, *1960*

Apponyi, Geraldine: Woman of American ancestry to become a queen, *2386*

Arbenz Guzmán, Jacobo: Overthrow of a democratic foreign government arranged by the Central Intelligence Agency, *2677*

Argüello, Luis Antonio: Governor of California under Mexican rule, *1431*

Arias, Harmodio: President to go through the Panama Canal while in office, *3798*

Ariyoshi, George Ryoichi: State governor of Asian ancestry, *4517*

Arlin, Harold W.: Presidential inauguration speech read on radio at the same time that it was delivered in Washington, *3674*

Armas, Carlos Castillo: Overthrow of a democratic foreign government arranged by the Central Intelligence Agency, *2677*

Armstrong, Anne Legendre: Woman to serve as ambassador to the Court of St. James, *2366*
Woman to serve as chairman of the Republican Party, *2967*

Armstrong, James: Presidential candidate from Pennsylvania, *4561*

Arnett, Benjamin William: State legislator who was African-American to represent a constituency with a white majority, *4545*

Arnold, Benedict: American general to engage in treason, *1034*
Monument to a traitor, *2709*
Rhode Island colonial governor, *1460*

Arnold, Henry Harley "Hap": Defense Department think tank, *2672*

Arnold, Isaac N.: Mayor of Chicago, IL, *1307*

Arthur, Chester Alan: Date on which the Senate was equally divided between Republicans and Democrats, *1718*

Korean embassy, *2261*

President born in Vermont, *4610*

President who was the son of a minister, *3562*

President whose private life was harassed by reporters, *3724*

Restrictions by Congress on immigration of Chinese laborers, *3111*

Successful desegregation of public transportation, *1919*

Treaties withdrawn by a president after they were submitted to the Senate, *2415*

Vice president born in Vermont, *4676*

Arthur, William: President who was the son of a minister, *3562*

Ashburner, Charles Edward: City government run by a city manager, *1289*

Ashcroft, John: Senator elected posthumously, *1810*

Astor, Nancy Witcher Langhorne: American woman to become a member of the British Parliament, *2268*

Atcherson, Lucille: Woman to serve as legation secretary, *2341*

Atchison, David Rice: Senator to serve as unofficial president between two presidential terms, *3400*

Atherton, Ray: Ambassador to Canada, *2347*

Atkins, Henry A.: Mayor of Seattle, WA, *1321*

Atkinson, Eudora Clark: State reformatory for women, *2574*

Attucks, Crispus: Americans killed by British soldiers in the Revolution, *1009*

Commemoration of the Boston Massacre, *2182*

Atwater, Harvey Leroy "Lee": Professional political consultant to head a major political party, *2968*

Atwood, Harry Nelson: Airplane to land on the White House lawn, *5033*

Atwood, Margaret: President who was the child of divorced parents, *3564*

Atwood, N. E.: State fish commission, *4202*

Ayllón, Lucas Vazquez de: Escape of slaves from a colony in what is now United States territory, *4218*

Spanish colonial settlement, *1394*

B

Bache, Alexander Dallas: National scientific advisory body, *2071*

Bache, Benjamin Franklin: Political newspaper to carry partisanship to extremes, *3852*

Bacon, Augustus Octavius: Senator elected by popular vote under the 17th Amendment to the Constitution, *1782*

Bacon, Henry: National monument to Abraham Lincoln, *2712*

Badillo, Herman: Congressional representative of Puerto Rican ancestry, *1620*

Baer, John M.: Political cartoonist elected to Congress, *1571*

Bagley, Sarah George: Woman to become a union organizer, *2878*

Bailey, John: Congressional representative to be refused a seat, *1590*

Bailey, Theodorus: American citizen hanged for treason, *2557*

Bainbridge, William: Military academy for naval officers, *2614*

Ship launched by the United States Navy, *2692*

Baird, Spencer Fullerton: Federal office to protect U.S. fisheries, *4204*

Baker, Bobby: Permanent Senate internal disciplinary committee, *1747*

Baker, Edward Dickinson: Senator to address the Senate in military uniform, *1709*

Baker, Howard, Jr.: Televised debate among competitors for a party's presidential nomination, *2776*

Baker, Sue A.: Women to become Secret Service agents, *2582*

Balch, Colonel: Flag salute, *1096*

Baldwin, Harvey: Mayor of Syracuse, NY, *1313*

Baldwin, John: Abolition organization, *4231*

Baldwin, Roger Nash: National civil liberties advocacy group, *2827*

Baldwin, Simeon Eben: National lawyers' society, *2589*

Balley, Jacqueline P.: Women to serve as federal marshals, *2541*

Baltimore, Lord: Maryland Day, *2177*

Baltzell, Robert C.: Death penalty authorized by federal law, *2564*

Bamberger, Simon: Governor of Utah who was not a Mormon, *4503*

Banai, Eddie Benton: Militant Native American civil rights organization, *2756*

Bancroft, George: Commemoration of the birthday of Abraham Lincoln, *2201*

Military academy for naval officers, *2614*

Banks, Dennis: Armed occupation by Native American protesters in the modern era, *2758*

Militant Native American civil rights organization, *2756*

Banks, Nathaniel Prentice: North American Party presidential candidate, *3291*

Baranov, Aleksandr Andreyevich: Russian colonial governor of Alaska, *1430*

Barber, Amos W.: Wyoming state governor, *4497*

Barclay, Edwin James: President of a black African country to visit the United States, *2389*

Barclay, Thomas: Treaty with a non-European nation, *2399*

Barker, Bernard: Convictions in the Watergate case, *3517*

Barkley, Alben William: Vice president known as "the Veep", *4990*

Vice president to marry during his term in office, *4991*

Vice president to receive a salary of $30,000, *3746*

Barnard, Henry: Commissioner of education of the United States, *3975*

Barnes, William: Insurance department of a state, *4051*

Barnette, E. T.: Mayor of Fairbanks, AK, *1325*

Barney, Joshua: President to face enemy gunfire while in office, *3695*

Star-Spangled Banner, *1088*

Barnum, R. G.: Single Tax Party presidential candidate, *3328*

Barrett, George W.: Death penalty authorized by federal law, *2564*

Barrett, Joseph E.: President to fly in a helicopter, *3811*

Barrett, Nathaniel: Consuls appointed after the adoption of the Constitution, *2320*

Barry, Leonora: National labor organization to establish a women's division, *2884*

Barry, Marion S.: African-American militant to be elected mayor of a major American city, *1341*

Mayor of a major American city arrested on drug charges, *1352*

Barry, William Taylor: Postmaster general to become a member of the president cabinet, *3156*

Barstow, William Augustus: State governor to be removed from office by a state supreme court, *4478*

Bartelme, Mary Margaret: Juvenile court, *1272*

Bartholdi, Frédéric-Auguste: Dedication ceremony for the Statue of Liberty, *1128*

Design for the Statue of Liberty, *1123*

Exhibition of part of the Statue of Liberty in the United States, *1124*

Bartlett, George Arthur: Congressional representative to attend college after his term of service, *1598*

Bartlett, Josiah: New Hampshire state governor, *4444*

Bascom, John: Development of the "Wisconsin Idea" of progressivism, *2818*

Bashford, Coles: State governor to be removed from office by a state supreme court, *4478*

Bass, Charlotta A.: African-American woman to run for vice president, *3263*

American Labor Party convention, *3342*

Bass, Willie Isaac: Church of God Party presidential candidate, *3341*

Bassett, Ebenezer Don Carlos: African-American consul, *2332*

Bates, Frederick: Missouri territorial governor, *4858*

Bayard, James Asheton: Senator to be appointed as a treaty negotiator, *1762*

Bayard, Thomas F.: Ambassador of the United States, *2336*

Bayless, Betsey: State in which all of the top elected offices were held by women, *4289*

Beard, Frank: Political cartoon with mass popularity, *3935*

Beauregard, P. G. T.: Major battle of the Civil War, *1381*

Beckley, John James: Clerk of the House of Representatives, *1534*

Librarian of Congress, *2061*

Bedell, Grace: President to wear a beard, *3828*

Begin, Menachem: Middle East peace treaty brokered by an American president, *2425*

Belcher, Jonathan: Mason known to hold high government office in the colonies, *1422*

Belknap, William W.: Cabinet officer impeached by the House of Representatives, *1163*

Bell, Charles E.: African-American to serve as chief sergeant-at-arms of a state legislature, *4556*

Bell, John: Constitutional Union Party presidential candidate, *3293*

Presidential election in which more than 80 percent of eligible voters cast ballots, *3193*

Third party to win more than 10 percent of the electoral vote in a presidential election, *3195*

Vice president to declare the election of the candidate who had opposed him for the presidency, *3197*

Bellamy, Edward: Bellamy Nationalist Club, *2883*

Bellamy, Francis: Pledge of allegiance to the flag, *1097*

Bellecourt, Clyde: Militant Native American civil rights organization, *2756*

Bellmon, Henry: Republican governor of Oklahoma, *4512*

Bellows, Henry Adams: Radio Commission of the United States, *3874*

Belton, Sharon Sayles: Woman to serve as mayor of Minneapolis, MN, *1359*

Benjamin, Judah Philip: Senator who was a practicing Jew, *1770*

Bennett, Elbert Gladstone: Federal Deposit Insurance Corporation, *2113*

Bennett, James Gordon: Washington news correspondent, *3887*

Bennett, William J.: Federal drug control chief, *4067*

Benson, Ezra Taft: Cabinet conference to be televised, *1184*

Benson, Lucy Wilson: Woman to serve as under secretary of state, *2367*

Bentley, Alvin: Terrorist shootings in the Capitol Building, *1247*

Bentley, Charles Eugene: National Party presidential candidate, *3314*

Benton, Thomas Hart: Political cartoon featuring Uncle Sam, *3933*
  Senator to serve for 30 years, *1769*
  Senator to threaten another senator with a gun in the Senate chamber, *1767*

Berger, Victor Louis: Congressional representative who was a Socialist, *1597*
  Social Democratic Party of America presidential candidate, *3319*
  Socialist Party, *2937*

Bergh, Henry: Case of child abuse brought to court, *3990*

Bergstresser, Charles: Edition of the *Wall Street Journal*, *3924*

Bergstrom, George Edwin: Consolidated headquarters for the Department of Defense, *2606*

Berlin, Irving: Performance of "God Bless America", *1121*

Bernard, Francis: Reservation for Native Americans established by a state, *2727*

Berrigan, Philip: Roman Catholic clergyman sentenced to jail in the United States for political crimes, *2860*

Best, William Edward: Federal Home Loan Bank board, *2111*

Bethune, Mary Jane McLeod: African-American woman to serve as a federal administrator, *1999*

Bettman, Gary: President to attend a hockey game during his term in office, *3842*

Beundorf, Larry: President to survive two assassination attempts in one month, *3455*

Bialaski, Alexander Bruce: Federal Bureau of Investigation, *2532*

Bibb, William C.: Alabama territorial governor, *4859*

Bibb, William W.: Alabama state governor, *4466*

Biddle, Nicholas: American flag saluted by a foreigner, *1077*

Biggs, John F.: Federal Crop Insurance Corporation, *4119*

Bilal, Charles: Muslim mayor of an American city, *1353*

Billings, Theodore C.: Vice presidential candidate from Colorado, *4662*

Billings, William: Patriotic war song by an American, *1115*

Billington, John: Execution in America, *2550*

Bin Laden, Osama: Bounty of $5 million for an enemy of the United States, *2548*

Bingham, Mrs. William: Presidential portrait of importance, *3536*

Binns, John: Political newspaper using the word "Democratic" in its title, *3913*

Birch, John: John Birch Society, *2835*

Birney, Alice McLellan: National parent-teacher association, *3977*

Birney, James Gillespie: Antislavery political organization, *4248*
  Liberty Party presidential candidate, *3286*
  Single-issue political party, *2918*
  Third party to participate in a presidential election, *3189*

Black, Hugo Lafayette: Supreme Court decision extending the protection of the Bill of Rights to defendants in state courts, *4731*
  Supreme Court justice to participate in a television program, *4780*
  Year in which all the justices of the Supreme Court were graduates of a law school, *4778*

Black, James: Prohibition Party presidential candidate, *3297*

Blackfan, Joseph H.: Civil Service Commission, *2027*

Blackford, Isaac: Claims court established by the federal government, *1973*

Blackmun, Harry: Supreme Court decision on the legality of abortion, *4739*
  Woman to clerk for a Supreme Court justice, *4777*

Blaha, John: Voting rights in space, *4442*

Blaine, James Gillespie: Brothers nominated for the presidency at the same convention, *3245*
  Conference of American republics, *2255*
  Conference of American states initiated by the United States, *2262*
  Pan-American union, *2263*
  Political cartoon to decisively influence a presidential election, *3939*
  Symbol of the Republican Party, *2923*

Blair, Francis P.: Kitchen cabinet of unofficial presidential advisors, *1152*
  Official Jacksonian newspaper, *3916*

Blair, Francis Preston, Jr.: Vice presidential candidate from Missouri, *4639*

Blair, Izell: Civil rights sit-in, *2850*

Blair, John: Supreme Court justice with a university law degree, *4769*
  Supreme Court of the United States, *4691*

Bland, Theodore: Pan-American delegates from the United States, *2325*

Bland, Theodoric: Congressional representative to die, *1585*

Blasdel, Henry G.: Nevada state governor, *4485*

Blodget, Samuel: Location of the Bank of the United States, *2104*

Blodgett, Joseph R.: Native American tribal constitution, *2753*

Blount, William: Governor of the Southwest Territory (Tennessee), *4851*

Reporters at sessions of the Senate, *3886*

Senator to be impeached, *1759*

Senators elected but not seated, *1758*

Use of sergeant at arms of the Senate to make an arrest, *1683*

Bock, Audie: Green Party, *2958*

Bocock, Thomas Salem: Session of the Confederate Congress, *1371*

Bodfish, Morton: Federal Home Loan Bank board, *2111*

Boggs, Hale: Commission appointed to investigate the assassination of a president, *3453*

Boggs, Lindy: Session of Congress held outside Washington, DC, since 1800, *1820*

Boggs, Thomas Hale: Congressional candidate elected while missing, *1622*

Bolin, Jane Matilda: African-American woman to be appointed a municipal judge, *1276*

Bolton, Frances Payne: Congresswoman to represent the United States in the United Nations, *2285*

Congresswoman to visit a theater of war, *1610*

Mother and son simultaneously elected to Congress, *1614*

Woman to head a congressional mission abroad, *2279*

Bolton, Oliver Payne: Mother and son simultaneously elected to Congress, *1614*

Bond, Julian: National political convention to propose African-Americans for the offices of president and vice president, *3028*

Bond, Shadrach: Illinois state governor, *4465*

Bonner, James: Town named for George Washington, *1256*

Boone, Daniel M.: Missouri state capital, *4331*

Booth, John Wilkes: Federal execution of a woman, *2558*

President to be assassinated, *3446*

Vice president to succeed to the presidency after the assassination of a president, *3408*

Boreman, Arthur I.: West Virginia state governor, *4484*

Borglum, Gutzon: Monument to four presidents, *2714*

Bosley, Freeman, Jr.: African-American mayor of St. Louis, MO, *1358*

Botts, John Minor: Attempt to bring impeachment proceedings against a president, *3630*

Bouck, William: Vice presidential candidate from Washington State, *4657*

Boudinot, Elias: Lawyers admitted to practice before the Supreme Court, *2584*

Native American newspaper, *2740*

Standing rules adopted by the House of Representatives, *1537*

Bourne, Sylvanus: Consuls appointed after the adoption of the Constitution, *2320*

Boush, Samuel: Mayor of Norfolk, VA, *1297*

Boutwell, George Sewall: Bureau of Internal Revenue, *4803*

Bouvier, John: Dictionary of American law, *2520*

Bovay, Alvan Earle: Founding of the Republican Party, *2922*

Bowditch, Henry Ingersoll: State board of health, *4018*

Bowles, Carington: Map of the British colonies showing Native American lands, *2729*

Bowring, Eve: State governor to appoint two United States senators in one year for interim terms, *4508*

Boxer, Barbara: State to be represented in the Senate by two women, *1808*

Boyce, William: Patriotic song by an American, *1114*

Boyd, Alan Stephenson: Department of Transportation, *2050*

Secretary of transportation, *1193*

Boyington, William: Hall built to house a national party convention, *2992*

Boylston, Zabdiel: Political crusade by a newspaper, *3849*

Bradford, Andrew: Political magazine, *3895*

Bradford, Gamaliel: National anti-imperialist organization, *2825*

Bradford, Lawrence Wallace, Jr.: Senate page who was African-American, *1642*

Bradford, William: Governor of the Massachusetts Bay Colony, *1455*

Property tax levied by a colony, *4785*

Trial of a printer for sedition, *3848*

Bradley, Bill: Basketball star elected to the Senate, *1804*

Bradley, Stephen R.: Convention call, *2974*

Political party to hold an open presidential nominating caucus, *2973*

Bradley, Thomas: African-American mayor of Los Angeles, CA, *1339*

Bradley, Willis Winter, Jr.: Congressional representative who received a Medal of Honor and was graduated from the U.S. Naval Academy, *1612*

Bradstreet, Simon: Newspaper suppressed by the government, *3903*

Brady, Genevieve Garvan: Pope to visit the United States before his election, *2385*

Brady, James: Mayor of Hannibal, MO, *1309*

Brady, James S.: President to be wounded in an unsuccessful assassination attempt while in office, *3456*

Bryan, Charles Wayland: Nominating convention that required more than 100 ballots, *3010*

Bryan, William Jennings: Legal clash between evolutionists and creationists, *1950*
National Silver Party convention, *3316*
Presidential candidate from Nebraska, *4583*
Presidential candidate to appear in movie footage, *3252*
Presidential candidate to ride in a car, *3250*
Silver Republican Party presidential candidate, *3321*
Silverite presidential candidate, *3315*

Buchalter, Louis: Federal execution of an organized crime boss, *2565*

Buchanan, Franklin: Military academy for naval officers, *2614*

Buchanan, James: Copyright law on photographs enacted by Congress, *2507*
Elected incumbent president whose party refused to renominate him, *3403*
President from Pennsylvania, *4607*
President who was a bachelor, *3586*
Presidential election in which the Republican Party participated, *3191*
Presidential secretary to receive a governmental salary, *3740*
Royal personage to stay at the White House as a houseguest, *5025*
Senator removed from a committee chairmanship against his will, *1773*
Utah territorial governor, *4867*
Vice president to declare the election of the candidate who had opposed him for the presidency, *3197*

Buchanan, Patrick: U.S. Taxpayers Party presidential candidate, *3364*

Buckner, Simon Bolivar: Sound Money Democratic Party presidential candidate, *3317*

Buell, Abel: Continental coin, *2149*
Map of the United States, *1065*
Map to show the American flag, *1083*

Bulfinch, Charles: Architect of the Capitol who was born in the United States, *1223*
Dome on the Capitol, *1217*
Landscaping of the Capitol grounds, *1224*
Sanitary facilities in the Capitol, *1225*
Section of the Capitol to be completed, *1221*

Bullard, William Hannum Grubb: Radio Commission of the United States, *3874*

Bullitt, William Christian: Ambassador to the Soviet Union, *2345*
Diplomatic relations between the United States and the Soviet Union, *2272*

Bulloch, Archibald: Georgia state governor, *4446*

Bunker, Ellsworth: Ambassadors in service to wed, *2361*

Bunker, William: Prison, *2570*

Bunning, Jim: Woman governor of Kentucky, *4521*

Burchard, Anson W.: National arbitration organization, *2591*

Burger, Warren Earl: Supreme Court ruling in a criminal case in which a United States president was named as a conspirator, *4741*
Vice president to succeed to the presidency after the resignation of the president, *3436*

Burgoyne, John: Major American victory in the Revolutionary War, *1031*
National day of thanksgiving, *2241*

Burke, Mary: National labor organization of importance, *2882*

Burke, Yvonne Braithwaite: Congresswoman to give birth while holding office, *1624*

Burnett, Ida Wells: National Association for the Advancement of Colored People, *2847*

Burnett, Peter Hardeman: California state governor, *4477*
State on the Pacific coast to be admitted to the Union, *4301*

Burnside, Ambrose: National firearms lobby, *2817*

Burr, Aaron: Former vice president to be arrested, *4968*
Incumbent president who ran for reelection and was defeated, *3383*
Louisiana territorial governor, *4855*
President elected by decision of the House of Representatives, *3179*
President to be reelected, *3377*
President to have two vice presidents, *3389*
President to invoke executive privilege, *3391*
President who was younger than his vice president, *3390*
Presidential election in which both parties nominated candidates in secret caucus, *2972*
Presidential election in which more than one candidate declared for the presidency, *3176*
Presidential election in which the Democratic-Republican Party participated, *3175*
Presidential election won by the Democratic-Republican Party, *3178*
Presidential team from Virginia and New York, *3385*
Secret service established in a colony, *2579*
Vice president from New Jersey, *4679*
Vice president from New York, *4666*
Vice president to be indicted while in office, *4967*
Vice president to be reelected, *4964*

Burroughs, Edward: Roads improvement aid bill enacted by a state, *4090*

Burrows, William Ward: United States Marines, *2660*

Burt, Francis: Nebraska territorial governor, *4870*

Burton, Harold Hitz: President to watch the swearing-in ceremony of a Supreme Court justice he appointed, *3424*

Year in which all the justices of the Supreme Court were graduates of a law school, *4778*

Bush, Barbara Pierce: First Lady to deliver a major speech at a national political convention, *3619*

Bush, George Herbert Walker: Cabinet nomination by a newly elected president to be rejected, *1207*

Chemical arms control treaty, *2428*

Comprehensive civil rights legislation for people with disabilities, *1908*

Federal law to include the term "sexual orientation", *1912*

First Lady to deliver a major speech at a national political convention, *3619*

Incumbent vice president to be elected president in the 20th century, *3441*

Outgoing president to order military action in the last week of his term, *3443*

Post–Cold War summit between the United States and the Soviet Union, *2301*

Postwar President who had never served in the armed forces, *3704*

President to formally transfer the presidency to an acting president, *3440*

President to spend holidays with United States troops overseas, *3815*

President who had been awarded the Distinguished Flying Cross, *3628*

President who had parachuted from an airplane, *3808*

President who had served as a Navy pilot, *3701*

President who had served as ambassador to the United Nations, *3506*

President who had served as chairman of his political party, *3507*

President who had served as director of the Central Intelligence Agency, *3508*

Presidential candidate in the 20th century to come within two percentage points of winning the entire electoral vote, *3274*

Presidential election in which a Democratic winner failed to carry Texas, *3223*

Televised debate among competitors for a party's presidential nomination, *2776*

Vice president to serve as acting president under the 25th Amendment, *4997*

Butler, Albert: Beating in the Senate chamber, *1704*

Butler, Benjamin Franklin: American citizen hanged for treason, *2557*

Anti-Monopoly Party presidential candidate, *3306*

Butler, David: Nebraska state governor, *4486*

Butterfield, Alexander P.: President to tape all his conversations in the White House, *3432*

Byllinge, Edward: New Jersey colonial governor, *1464*

Byrd, Harry Flood: Constitution Party presidential candidate, *3343*

Byrne, Ethel: Birth control clinic, *3994*

Byrne, Jane Margaret Burke: African-American mayor of Chicago, IL, *1345*

Woman mayor of Chicago, IL, *1343*

C

Cabeza de Baca, Ezequiel: New Mexico state governor of Latino ancestry, *4504*

Cabot, George: Threat of secession by a regional group of states, *4264*

Caines, George: Law text published in the United States, *2516*

Calderon, Sila Maria: Woman governor of Puerto Rico, *4899*

Caldwell, Alexander: Senator to resign in a case of a fraudulent election, *1777*

Caldwell, James: Americans killed by British soldiers in the Revolution, *1009*

Caldwell, Orestes Hampton: Radio Commission of the United States, *3874*

Calhoun, Floride: Washington social scandal, *1882*

Calhoun, James S.: New Mexico territorial governor, *4868*

Calhoun, John Caldwell: Commemoration of the birthday of Thomas Jefferson, *2193*

Former vice president to serve in the Senate, *4974*

Independent nation annexed by the United States, *4299*

Official Jacksonian newspaper, *3916*

President and vice president in the 20th century who were both Southerners, *3442*

President of the Senate to abdicate his power to keep order, *1693*

Vice president from South Carolina, *4667*

Vice president from the Democratic Party, *5000*

Vice president to resign, *4973*

Vice president who was born an American citizen, *4972*

Vice presidential candidate from South Carolina, *4630*

Vice presidential candidate to run with three presidential candidates simultaneously, *3182*

Washington social scandal, *1882*

Year in which there was no mechanism for nominating presidential candidates, *2977*

Calley, William L., Jr.: American military massacre of political importance, *2650*

Calver, George Wehnes: Physician to Congress, *1518*

Calvert, Cecilius, Lord Baltimore: British colony whose charter guaranteed representative government, *1434*

Colonial charter of religious freedom for Christians, *1436*

Maryland colonial governor, *1456*

Calvert, Leonard: Maryland colonial governor, *1456*

Maryland Day, *2177*

Maryland state capital, *4314*

Cameron, Simon: Senator to face allegations of corrupt election practices, *1772*

Campbell, George Washington: Duel between representatives in Congress, *1588*

Campbell, John: Newspaper published with government approval, *3904*

Territory to grant full voting rights to women, *1958*

Campbell, John Archibald: Peace conference during the Civil War, *1389*

Wyoming territorial governor, *4878*

Campbell, Walter G.: Commissioner of Food and Drugs, *4030*

Cannon, Joseph G.: Office buildings for U.S. senators and representatives, *1241*

Cannon, Martha Hughes: Woman to serve as a state senator, *4547*

Capper, Arthur: Kansas state governor, *4483*

Caraway, Hattie Ophelia Wyatt: Woman elected to the Senate for a full term, *1788*

Woman to chair a Senate committee, *1789*

Woman to serve as presiding officer of the Senate, *1742*

Caraway, Thaddeus Horatio: Woman elected to the Senate for a full term, *1788*

Cardozo, Benjamin Nathan: Cabinet in which all members were sworn in at the same time and place, *1178*

Carey, Vincent: Right to Life Party, *2953*

Carhart, Arthur: Comprehensive wilderness law, *4215*

Wilderness area to be formally named, *4154*

Carleton, Cora G.: Women to attend a national political convention as delegates, *3003*

Carlin, John W.: Ruling requiring retention of all electronic records of the federal government, *2059*

Carlson, Grace: Socialist Workers Party presidential candidate, *3336*

Carmichael, Stokely: Black Power advocate, *2851*

Carnahan, Jean: Senator elected posthumously, *1810*

Carnahan, Mel: Senator elected posthumously, *1810*

Carnes, Burrell: Consuls appointed after the adoption of the Constitution, *2320*

Carr, Patrick: Americans killed by British soldiers in the Revolution, *1009*

Carrere, John: Office buildings for U.S. senators and representatives, *1241*

Carroll, Charles: Congressional representative who was Catholic, *1584*

Carroll, Daniel: Block of buildings constructed in Washington, DC, *1873*

Carroll, John: College in Washington, DC, *1871*

Carroll, William T.: Librarian of the Supreme Court, *2065*

Carson, Kit: Nevada state capital, *4343*

Carter, Chip: President's mother to serve on a diplomatic mission, *3572*

Carter, Jimmy: Affirmative action order issued by the federal government, *1905*

Diplomatic relations between the United States and the People's Republic of China, *2295*

Large-scale hostage crisis, *2296*

Middle East peace treaty brokered by an American president, *2425*

Nuclear arms limitation treaty not approved by the Senate, *2426*

Postwar President who had never served in the armed forces, *3704*

President from Georgia, *4619*

President to make human rights a cornerstone of his foreign policy, *3439*

President to take the oath of office using a nickname, *3689*

President who was a graduate of the United States Naval Academy, *3703*

President who was born in a hospital, *3468*

President's mother to serve on a diplomatic mission, *3572*

Radio broadcast in which citizens telephoned the president, *3732*

Televised presidential election debate between an incumbent president and a challenger, *3222*

Carter, John: Independent civil government in America, *1426*

Carter, Lillian Gordy: President's mother to serve on a diplomatic mission, *3572*

Carter, Reginald: African-American presidential candidate, *3266*

Independent Afro-American Party presidential candidate, *3350*

Carter, Rosalynn Smith: First Lady to pilot an airship, *3618*

Carver, George Washington: National monument dedicated to an African-American, *2716*

Carver, John: Governor of the Massachusetts Bay Colony, *1455*

Claiborne, William Charles Coles: Congressional representative to serve before his 25th birthday, *1587*
Louisiana state governor, *4461*
Louisiana territorial governor, *4855*
Orleans territorial governor, *4854*
State governor who had previously been governor of a territory, *4462*
Territorial government to borrow money from a city, *4838*
Clark, Edward E.: Libertarian Party presidential candidate, *3356*
Clark, Georgia Neese: Woman treasurer of the United States, *2098*
Clark, Kathryn I.: Women to become Secret Service agents, *2582*
Clark, Ramsey: Political interview aired on a television newsmagazine, *3881*
Clark, Thomas Campbell: Attorney general whose father had also served as attorney general, *1194*
Clark, Tom Campbell: Year in which all the justices of the Supreme Court were graduates of a law school, *4778*
Clark, William: Government-sponsored overland expedition to the Pacific Coast, *4837*
Missouri territorial governor, *4858*
Vote of record in which participants of different races and both sexes were given an equal voice, *4839*
Woman to serve as foreman on a federal grand jury, *1981*
Clark, William Ramsey: Attorney general whose father had also served as attorney general, *1194*
Clarke, Anne: Legal divorce in the American colonies, *3948*
Clarke, Denis: Legal divorce in the American colonies, *3948*
Clarke, Henry Deforest: Librarian of the Supreme Court, *2065*
Clarke, Walter: Court martial in a colony, *1444*
Clay, Henry: Campaign hat, *2798*
Incumbent president whose party refused to renominate him, *3398*
National Democratic Tyler Party presidential candidate, *3287*
National nominating convention held by a political party of importance, *2980*
Person to lie in state in the Capitol rotunda, *1230*
Popular vote in a presidential election, *3183*
President to be censured by Congress, *3511*
Presidential candidate from Kentucky, *4569*
Presidential election in which all candidates were from the same political party, *3184*
Presidential election in which all the candidates were nominated at party conventions, *3186*

Presidential election in which the Whig Party participated, *3187*
Recognition by the United States of a newly independent nation, *2253*
Senator to take office despite being too young to serve, *1760*
Senator who was returned to the Senate after being defeated for the presidency, *1766*
Speaker of the House who was simultaneously member, parliamentarian, and leader, *1632*
Symbol of the Republican Party, *2923*
Vice president from the Democratic Party, *5000*
Vice presidential candidate from Kentucky, *4632*
Vice presidential candidate to run with three presidential candidates simultaneously, *3182*
Whig Party presidential candidate, *3285*
Year in which the congressional nominating caucus began to decline, *2976*
Claypoole, David C.: Farewell address by a president, *3751*
Newspaper to publish the Constitution, *1826*
Clayton, Eva: House of Representatives that included a substantial number of African-American women, *1579*
Clayton, Joshua: Delaware state governor, *4458*
Cleaver, Eldridge: Peace and Freedom Party presidential candidate, *3352*
Cleaver, Emanuel: African-American mayor of Kansas City, MO, *1354*
Clements, William P., Jr.: Republican governor of Texas since Reconstruction, *4520*
Clemons, Lucian M.: Lifesaving medal awarded by the Treasury Department, *2042*
Cleveland, Esther: Child born in the White House to a president, *5030*
Cleveland, Frances Folsom: First Lady to give birth during her husband's term in office, *3603*
First Lady to remarry after the death of her husband, *3606*
Wedding of a president in the White House, *5027*
Cleveland, Grover: American provincial government in Hawaii, *4274*
Candidate of a major party to be nominated for the presidency three times, *3248*
Dedication ceremony for the Statue of Liberty, *1128*
Defeated presidential candidate to be renominated by a major party, *3249*
Democratic president whose party was in the minority in both houses of Congress, *3718*
Democratic president whose party was in the minority in the Senate, *3717*

First Lady to give birth during her husband's term in office, *3603*

First Lady to remarry after the death of her husband, *3606*

Political cartoon to decisively influence a presidential election, *3939*

President born in New Jersey, *4612*

President elected after the Civil War who had not served in it, *3409*

President elected for two nonconsecutive terms, *3410*

President protected by the Secret Service, *3413*

President to veto more than 100 bills in a single term, *3845*

President who had been an executioner, *3494*

President whose name was changed, *3484*

President whose predecessor and successor were the same man, *3412*

President whose private life was harassed by reporters, *3724*

Presidential candidate from the Democratic Party to be elected after the Civil War, *3247*

Sound Money Democratic Party, *2935*

Standardized foreign service examinations, *2337*

States admitted to the Union simultaneously, *4303*

Treaties withdrawn by a president after they were submitted to the Senate, *2415*

Wedding of a president in the White House, *5027*

Cline, Genevieve Rose: Woman justice on the federal bench, *1979*

Clinton, De Witt: Presidential election in which both candidates were nominated at open congressional caucuses, *2975*

State nominating convention, *4427*

Clinton, George: Coalition between Northern and Southern politicians, *2905*

Convention call, *2974*

New York state governor, *4451*

Party endorsement of a presidential candidate, *2970*

Political party to hold an open presidential nominating caucus, *2973*

President to be reelected, *3377*

President to have two vice presidents, *3389*

President who was younger than his vice president, *3390*

President whose administration lost two vice presidents to death, *3392*

Presidential candidates from New York State, *4565*

Presidential election in which a candidate was endorsed by a political party, *3173*

Presidential election in which candidates were separately nominated for the vice presidency, *3180*

Presidential election in which more than one candidate declared for the presidency, *3176*

Presidential team from Virginia and New York, *3385*

Salute fired by Great Britain in honor of an officer of the United States, *2245*

Vice president from New York, *4666*

Vice president to be reelected, *4964*

Vice president to die in office, *4970*

Vice president to serve under two presidents, *4969*

Vice president who was nominated specifically for that office, *4966*

Vice presidential candidate from New York State, *4621*

Clinton, Hillary Rodham: Convictions in the Whitewater case, *3521*

First Lady elected to public office, *3623*

First Lady to be given an office in the West Wing of the White House, *3620*

First Lady to earn a professional degree, *3617*

First Lady who was also a federal official, *3621*

First Lady who was president of the student government at college, *3616*

Clinton, William Jefferson: African-American congressman to deliver the Republican Party's official response to the State of the Union message, *1630*

African-American woman nominated to head the Justice Department's Civil Rights Division, *1937*

Captive Nations Week, *2287*

Convictions in the Whitewater case, *3521*

Elected president to be impeached, *3632*

Federal legislation recommending academic standards, *3987*

First Lady elected to public office, *3623*

First Lady to be given an office in the West Wing of the White House, *3620*

Midterm election since World War II in which the president's party gained seats in the House of Representatives, *1581*

Payment by the United States to a foreign nation for destroying nuclear weapons, *2302*

Postwar Democrat to win a second term as president, *3721*

Postwar President who had never served in the armed forces, *3704*

President and vice president in the 20th century who were both Southerners, *3442*

President from Arkansas, *4620*

President to attend a hockey game during his term in office, *3842*

President to give testimony before a grand jury during his term in office, *3522*

Clinton, William Jefferson:—*continued*

President to have a legal defense fund during his term in office, *3520*

President to participate in a live chat over the Internet, *3733*

President to use the line-item veto, *3846*

President to visit Bulgaria, *3817*

President who had college experience as a Senate staff member, *3505*

President who was a Rhodes Scholar, *3839*

President who was born after World War II, *3469*

Presidential election in which a Democratic winner failed to carry Texas, *3223*

Presidential nomination acceptance speech to mention homosexuals, *3032*

Rules to prevent secret government-sponsored human experimentation, *2076*

Senate staff furlough, *1754*

Sexual harassment lawsuit against a president, *3519*

Summit of the Americas, *2304*

Visit by an American president to a country on the U.S. list of terrorist states, *3816*

Clymer, George: Treasurer of the United States, *2077*

Cobb, Howell: Confederate constitution, *1372*

Cochrane, John: Independent Republican Party presidential candidate, *3295*

Cocke, William: Senators elected but not seated, *1758*

Coddington, William: Rhode Island state capitals, *4320*

Coffelt, Leslie: White House Police Force, *5036*

Coffin, Levi: Underground Railroad activities, *4234*

Coffin, Lorenzo S.: Vice presidential candidate from Iowa, *4651*

Cohen, P. J. and M. J.: Supreme Court decision establishing its authority over state courts in matters of federal law, *4717*

Cohn, Elizabeth: Woman to make a seconding speech at a national political convention, *3004*

Coiner, C. Benton: Conservative Party of Virginia presidential candidate, *3349*

Colby, William E.: President who had served as director of the Central Intelligence Agency, *3508*

Coleman, James V.: State forest commission, *4142*

Colfax, Schuyler: Officer to preside over both of the branches of Congress, *1506*

Speaker of the House who became vice president, *1635*

Vice president from Indiana, *4674*

Collbohm, Frank: Defense Department think tank, *2672*

Collins, Barbara-Rose: House of Representatives that included a substantial number of African-American women, *1579*

Collins, Cardiss: House of Representatives that included a substantial number of African-American women, *1579*

Collins, John: Rhode Island state governor, *4455*

Collins, Martha Layne: Woman governor of Kentucky, *4521*

Collins, Susan M.: State to be represented in the Senate by two women, *1808*

Colman, Norman Jay: Department of Agriculture, *2039*

Secretary of agriculture, *1165*

Columbus, Christopher: Columbus Day, *2189*

Colver, William Byron: Federal Trade Commission trade practice conference, *4924*

Colvin, John: Industrial Reform Party presidential candidate, *3309*

Commoner, Barry: Citizens Party presidential candidate, *3359*

Compton, Karl Taylor: Science and technology advisory board, *2072*

Conant, John A.: American Prohibition Party presidential candidate, *3307*

Vice presidential candidate from Connecticut, *4643*

Connally, John Bowden, Jr.: Televised debate among competitors for a party's presidential nomination, *2776*

Vice president who was present at the assassination of the president he succeeded, *3452*

Connor, Robert Digges Wimberley: Archivist of the United States, *2067*

Conway, James S.: Arkansas state governor, *4472*

Coolidge, Calvin: Campaign bumper stickers, *2805*

Coin bearing the likeness of a living president, *2165*

Congress whose members received a salary of $10,000, *1654*

Federal agency to regulate broadcast media, *3875*

Newsreels showing presidential candidates, *3863*

Organization in charge of the Statue of Liberty, *1126*

Political convention to be broadcast on radio, *3009*

Postage stamp issue depicting all the presidents, *3167*

President born in Vermont, *4610*

President to make a radio broadcast from the White House, *3757*

President who came before the Senate to discourage action on a bill, *1735*

President who had been defeated in a earlier campaign for the vice presidency, *3417*

President who was sworn in by a former president, *3676*

President who was sworn in by his father, *3675*

Presidential inauguration to be broadcast on radio, *3677*

Presidential message to Congress that was broadcast on radio, *3756*

Presidential voice to become nationally familiar, *3758*

Republican president to win reelection in the 20th century, *3426*

Vice president to regularly attend cabinet meetings, *4985*

Coolidge, Calvin, Jr.: Child of a president to die during his father's term in office, *3548*

Coolidge, John Calvin: President who was sworn in by his father, *3675*

Coolidge, Sherman: Formal appeal for recognition of Native Americans as United States citizens, *2750*

Coolidge, Victoria Josephine Moor: President who was sworn in by his father, *3675*

President whose mother was eligible to vote for him, *3567*

Cooper, George Marion: Birth control clinic run by a state government, *3995*

Cooper, John Sherman: Commission appointed to investigate the assassination of a president, *3453*

Cooper, Peter: Greenback Party presidential candidate, *3304*

Copley, L. G. A.: Kansas Day, *2207*

Copley, Sir Lionel: Maryland colonial governor, *1456*

Coppin, Fanny Jackson: National political organization for African-American women, *2846*

Corbin, Margaret: Military pension awarded to a woman, *2698*

Corcoran, Margaret: Woman to clerk for a Supreme Court justice, *4777*

Corcoran, William Wilson: National art collection, *1886*

Corley, D. B.: Mayor of Abilene, TX, *1322*

Cormier, Lucia Marie: Senate election race in which both candidates were women, *1745*

Cornbury, Lord: State to give its legislature sole power to determine the eligibility of legislators, *4537*

Cornell, Ezra: Telegraph line to Washington, DC, *1884*

Cornish, Samuel E.: Political newspaper published by African-Americans, *3917*

Cornwallis, Charles: American flag flown in battle, *1080*

Cornwallis, Lord: General of the Continental Army, *2622*

Cortelyou, George Bruce: Department of Commerce and Labor, *2043*

Department of Labor, *2045*

Secretary of commerce and labor, *1167*

Cosby, William: Legal precedent for freedom of the press, *3850*

Coughlin, Charles E.: Union Party, *2945*

Coughlin, Daniel: Chaplain of the House of Representatives who was a Catholic priest, *1582*

Courtney, Kent H.: Texas Constitution Party presidential candidate, *3347*

Vice presidential candidate from Louisiana, *4654*

Courville, Roy E.: Native American tribal constitution, *2753*

Cowdrey, Robert Hall: United Labor Party presidential candidate, *3311*

Cox, David C.: Civil Service Commission, *2027*

Cox, Edward: Outdoor wedding held at the White House, *5040*

Cox, James Middleton: President who had been defeated in a earlier campaign for the vice presidency, *3417*

Presidential candidate who had been divorced, *3254*

Presidential election in which the candidates of both major parties were newspaper publishers, *3210*

Presidential election in which women voted, *3211*

Cox, James Renshaw: Jobless Party presidential candidate, *3331*

Cox, William Wesley: Presidential candidate from Missouri, *4584*

Coxe, Tench: Federal revenue commissioner, *4798*

Coxey, Jacob S.: Protest march on Washington, *2824*

Craig, Minnie Davenport: Woman to serve in a state legislature as speaker of the House, *4549*

Cranch, William: Reporter of Supreme Court decisions, *4700*

Vice president to succeed to the presidency after the death of a president, *3397*

Crandall, F. A.: Government Printing Office, *2054*

Crane, Daniel B.: Sex scandals involving congressional pages, *1646*

Crane, Philip: Televised debate among competitors for a party's presidential nomination, *2776*

Cranfill, James Britton: Vice presidential candidate from Texas, *4646*

Craven, Charles: South Carolina colonial governor, *1462*

Crawford, Thomas: Design for a statue for the raised Capitol dome, *1232*

Crawford, William Harris: Popular vote in a presidential election, *3183*

Presidential election in which all candidates were from the same political party, *3184*

Vice president from the Democratic Party, *5000*

Vice presidential candidate to run with three presidential candidates simultaneously, *3182*

Year in which the congressional nominating caucus began to decline, *2976*

Crazy Horse: Major defeat inflicted by Native Americans on regular U.S. Army troops, *2748*

Monument to a Native American, *2718*

Creel, George: Federal propaganda bureau, *2643*

Cressingham, Clara: Women elected to a state legislature, *4546*

Creswell, John Angel James: Post Office Department, *3143*

Croasdale, William T.: Single Tax League national conference, *2821*

Crocker, Edwin S.: Woman to take charge of an American legation, *2343*

Crocker, Hans: State forestry inquiry commission, *4137*

Croker, Richard: Mayor of New York, NY, *1295*

Crommelin, John Geraerdt: National States' Rights Party presidential candidate, *3348*

Cronkite, Walter: National conventions to receive gavel-to-gavel television coverage, *3023*

Radio broadcast in which citizens telephoned the president, *3732*

Crosby, Robert: State governor to appoint two United States senators in one year for interim terms, *4508*

Cross, Julie Yvonne: Secret Service agent killed in the line of duty, *2581*

Crossley, Archibald: Scientific public opinion polls, *2773*

Crosswell, Harry: Satirical political magazine, *3896*

Crotty, Burke: President to deliver an address on television, *3762*

Crow Dog: Supreme Court decision on criminal jurisdiction on Native American reservations, *4721*

Crowell, Joseph T.: Government Printing Office, *2054*

Cruger, John: Chamber of commerce established by a state, *4914*

Cuffe, Paul: Black nationalist movement, *2844*

Cullom, Shelby M.: Senate majority leader, *1725*

Culotta, Samuel A.: African-American mayor of Baltimore, MD, *1348*

Cumming, Thomas: Mayor of Augusta, GA, *1299*

Cummings, Walter Joseph: Federal Deposit Insurance Corporation, *2113*

Cunningham, Ann Pamela: Presidential estate to be opened to the public, *3404*

Cunningham, Charles E.: Union Labor Party presidential candidate, *3310*

Vice presidential candidate from Arkansas, *4645*

Cunningham, Don: President to participate in a live chat over the Internet, *3733*

Curtis, Benjamin Robbins: Supreme Court justice with a university law degree, *4769*

Curtis, Charles: Republican floor leader, *1736*

Republican presidential and vice presidential team to lose a bid for reelection, *3418*

Senator of Native American descent, *1779*

Vice president from Kansas, *4680*

Vice president who had served as Senate majority leader, *4988*

Vice president who was of Native American ancestry, *4989*

Curtis, George William: Civil Service Commission, *2027*

Use of the term "mugwump", *2932*

Curtis, Merritt Barton: Tax Cut Party presidential candidate, *3351*

Curtis, William Eleroy: Pan-American union, *2263*

Cushing, Caleb: Attorney general to fill the position on a full-time basis, *1158*

Treaty between the United States and China, *2412*

Cushing, William: Associate Supreme Court justice to refuse elevation to the post of chief justice, *4757*

Chief justice of the Supreme Court to administer the oath of office to a president, *4758*

State to abolish slavery by a decision of the judiciary, *4233*

Supreme Court of the United States, *4691*

Custer, George Armstrong: Major defeat inflicted by Native Americans on regular U.S. Army troops, *2748*

Custis, Daniel Parke: First Lady, *3573*

D

Dale, Porter Hinman: Radio broadcast of an open session of Congress, *1817*

Daley, Richard M.: Incumbent African-American mayor of a major city to lose to a white candidate, *1349*

Dallas, Alexander James: Publication of Supreme Court decisions, *4692*

Reporter of Supreme Court decisions, *4700*

de Tocqueville, Alexis Charles-Henri-Maurice Clerel: Publication of *Democracy in America, 3072*

Dean, Howard: State to establish civil unions for homosexual couples, *1917*

Deane, Silas: Foreign officers recruited to the cause of the American Revolution, *1030*
Treaties entered into by the federal government, *2396*

Dearborn, Henry: Cabinet appointee to be rejected by the Senate, *1150*

Debel, Niels Henriksen: Sit-down strike, *2481*

DeBlois, Thomas A.: Naval militia established by a state, *2665*

Debs, Eugene Victor: Industrial Workers of the World (Wobblies) convention, *2885*
Presidential candidate to run for office while in prison, *3255*
Presidential candidate who had served a prison term, *3251*
Social Democratic Party of America platform, *3059*
Social Democratic Party of America presidential candidate, *3319*
Socialist Party, *2937*
Socialist Party presidential candidate, *3323*

Decatur, Stephen: Ship launched by the United States Navy, *2692*

Defrees, John Dougherty: Government Printing Office, *2054*

Deganawidah: Confederation in what is now the United States, *2721*

Degetau, Federico: Resident commissioner from Puerto Rico, *4892*

Delehanty, Thomas K.: President to be wounded in an unsuccessful assassination attempt while in office, *3456*

Demont, William: Traitor to the American cause during the Revolutionary War, *1029*

Denton, Jeremiah Andrew, Jr: American prisoner of war in Vietnam who was elected to Congress, *1806*

Derbigny, Pierre: Law code adopted by a state, *2519*

Derwinski, Edward Joseph: Department of Veterans Affairs, *2053*
Secretary of veterans affairs, *1208*

Desell, Paulette: Senate pages who were female, *1645*

Dewey, George: Admiral of the Navy, *2696*
War hero to lie in state in the Capitol rotunda, *1243*

Dewey, John: National civil liberties advocacy group, *2827*

Dewey, Nelson: Wisconsin state governor, *4476*

Dewey, Thomas Edmund: Defeated presidential candidate to be renominated by a major party, *3249*

President elected for third and fourth terms, *3421*

Presidential campaign manager who was a woman, *2774*

Presidential candidate who was renominated after a defeat, *3262*

Presidential election in which the wrong candidate was declared the winner by early newspaper editions, *3209*

Republican presidential candidate to give his acceptance speech at the national convention, *3020*

Dewitt, J. Doyle: Museum devoted solely to American political memorabilia, *1069*

DeWitt, John: Wartime population relocation order, *2646*

Dickerson, Nancy: Television newswoman to report from Capitol Hill, *3880*

Dickinson, Charles: President who had killed a man in a duel, *3825*

Dickinson, John: Patriotic song by an American, *1114*
Royal proclamation declaring Britain's colonies in America to be in open rebellion, *1021*

Dillinger, John: Public Enemy Number 1, *2538*

Dillon, John Forrest: Radio Commission of the United States, *3874*

Dinkins, David N.: African-American mayor of New York City, *1351*

Dirksen, Everett McKinley: Senator to act in the movies, *1800*

DiSiver, Albert: National civil liberties advocacy group, *2827*

Dix, Dorothea Lynde: Congressional lobbyist who was a woman, *1501*

Dix, John Adams: State political machine, *2911*

Dixon, Emmet: Session of the Confederate Congress, *1371*

Dixon, Jeremiah: Surveyed line separating North from South, *4172*

Dixon, Sharon Pratt: African-American woman to serve as mayor of Washington, DC, *1901*
State flag for Washington, DC, *1903*

Doak, Samuel: College named after George Washington, *3964*

Doak, William Nuckles: Secretary of labor who was not a member of the American Federation of Labor, *2444*

Dobbs, Farrell: Socialist Workers Party presidential candidate, *3336*

Dodds, Harold Willis: Use of the term "mugwump", *2932*

Dodge, Augustus Caesar: Father and son who were senators at the same session, *1764*

Dodge, David Low: Pacifist society, *2810*

Dunlap, John: Newspaper to publish the Constitution, *1826*
Printing of the Declaration of Independence, *1058*

Duvall, Gabriel: Supreme Court justice who had served in the House of Representatives, *4759*

Dykstra, Clarence Addison: Draft number drawing, *2637*

E

Eagleburger, Lawrence Sidney: Secretary of state who was a former member of the Foreign Service, *1209*

Eagleton, Thomas Francis: Vice presidential candidate of a major political party to resign before the election, *3271*

Early, Norm: African-American mayor of Denver, CO, *1355*
Mayoral election in a major city in which both candidates were African-Americans, *1356*

Eaton, Dorman B.: Federal civil service reform law that was effective, *2028*

Eaton, John Henry: Campaign biography, *2795*
Washington social scandal, *1882*

Eaton, Peggy: Washington social scandal, *1882*

Eaton, Theophilus: Colonial governor of Connecticut, *1459*

Eckert, J. Presper, Jr.: Federal government office to be computerized, *2000*

Edelin, Stanley: President to be arrested, *3827*

Edgerton, Sidney: Montana territorial governor, *4877*

Edison, Thomas Alva: Voting machine, *1510*

Edson, Susan Ann: Woman to serve as a president's personal physician, *3776*

Edwards, Edwin W.: Ku Klux Klan leader to mount a credible campaign for state governor, *4440*

Edwards, Emma Sarah: State seal designed by a woman, *4273*

Edwards, Ninian: Illinois territorial governor, *4857*

Egan, Shirley: Trial broadcast by the court over the Internet, *3870*

Egan, William A.: Alaska state governor, *4509*

Eggers, Otto R.: National monument to Thomas Jefferson, *2715*

Eisenberg, Sophie: Television eyewitness allowed to testify in a federal court, *1985*

Eisenhower, David: Marriage of two descendants of different presidents, *3571*
President to use Camp David as a retreat, *3835*

Eisenhower, Dwight David: Cabinet conference to be televised, *1184*
Cabinet session held at a place other than the seat of the federal government, *1188*
Campaign hosiery, *2806*
Captive Nations Week, *2287*
Child of a president to attend West Point, *3553*
Federal government building built to withstand a nuclear attack, *2001*
Federal undersea park, *4157*
Marriage of two descendants of different presidents, *3571*
Overthrow of a democratic foreign government arranged by the Central Intelligence Agency, *2677*
Peacetime alliance of European and North American nations, *2284*
Postwar President who had never served in the armed forces, *3704*
President barred under the 22nd Amendment from running for a third term, *3425*
President born in Texas, *4616*
President-elect to attend a religious service along with his staff, *3735*
President of all 50 states, *3428*
President to appear on color television, *3766*
President to become a full communicant of a church during his term in office, *3736*
President to fly in a helicopter, *3811*
President to go underwater in an atomic-powered submarine, *3812*
President to hold an airplane pilot's license, *3802*
President to use Camp David as a retreat, *3835*
President whose party was in the minority in both houses of Congress during three congresses, *3719*
Presidential candidate to run for office after suffering a heart attack, *3265*
Presidential election in which a computer was used to predict the outcome, *3214*
Presidential news conference filmed for television and newsreels, *3729*
Presidential press conference that was entirely "on the record", *3866*
Republican president to win reelection in the 20th century, *3426*
Republican presidential and vice presidential team to be reelected, *3427*
State admitted to the Union that had no border with another state, *4305*
State admitted to the Union that was separated by a substantial body of water, *4306*
Television ad saturation campaign, *2777*
United States representative to the United Nations Educational, Scientific and Cultural Organization, *2436*

Use of federal troops to enforce integration, *1931*

Use of the term "military-industrial complex", *2608*

White House official who was an African-American, *5039*

Year in which the salary of members of Congress exceeded $20,000 per year, *1655*

Eisenhower, John Sheldon Doud: Child of a president to attend West Point, *3553*

Ela, Jacob E.: Insurance board established by a state government, *4050*

Elders, Joycelyn: Surgeon general who was African-American, *4040*

Eliot, Charles William: Land trust, *4187*

Elizabeth II, Queen of England: British monarch to address Congress, *2393*

Woman to serve as ambassador to the Court of St. James, *2366*

Ellicott, Andrew: Authorized plan of the City of Washington, DC, *1870*

Design for Washington, DC, *1868*

Elliot, Jonathan: Definitive edition of *The Debates in the Several State Conventions on the Adoption of the Federal Constitution, 1831*

Elliott, Ezekiel Brown: Civil Service Commission, *2027*

Ellis, Seth Hockett: Union Reform Party presidential candidate, *3322*

Ellsberg, Daniel: Prior restraint of the press by order of the federal government, *3868*

Ellsworth, Henry Leavitt: Patent commissioner, *2600*

Ellsworth, Oliver: Chief justice of the Supreme Court to administer the oath of office to a president, *4758*

Creation of federal courts, *1970*

Former chief justice of the Supreme Court to refuse renomination, *4760*

President who was sworn in by the chief justice of the Supreme Court, *3643*

Presidential election in which more than one candidate declared for the presidency, *3176*

Session of the Senate, *1662*

Supreme Court chief justice to resign, *4755*

Elson, Edward L. R.: President-elect to attend a religious service along with his staff, *3735*

President to become a full communicant of a church during his term in office, *3736*

Ely, Richard T.: Development of the "Wisconsin Idea" of progressivism, *2818*

Emanuel, David: State governor who was Jewish, *4502*

Embree, Elihu: Antislavery magazine, *4243*

Emma, Queen of the Hawaiian Islands: Queen to visit the United States, *2379*

Emmett, Daniel Decatur: Song used as an anthem by the Confederacy, *1119*

Endecott, John: Ban on Quakers, *1945*

Engel, Steven: Supreme Court decision on school prayer, *4733*

Enlai, Zhou: Diplomatic relations between the United States and the People's Republic of China, *2295*

Enos, John L.: National teachers' organization, *3973*

Epton, Bernard: African-American mayor of Chicago, IL, *1345*

Ernst, Morris: National civil liberties advocacy group, *2827*

Ervin, Samuel James: Televised Watergate hearings, *3882*

Espy, Mike: African-American to serve as secretary of agriculture, *1210*

Estern, Neil: First Lady to be depicted on a monument to a president, *3622*

Estrich, Susan R.: Presidential campaign manager who was a woman, *2774*

Evans, George Henry: Labor newspaper, *3919*

Evans, Melvin H.: Governor of the U.S. Virgin Islands, *4900*

Evans, R. Wayne: U.S. Labor Party presidential candidate, *3358*

Evans, Rudolph: National monument to Thomas Jefferson, *2715*

Evans, Rudolph Martin: Federal Crop Insurance Corporation, *4119*

Evans, Samuel: Vice presidential candidate from Texas, *4646*

Evans, Timothy: Incumbent African-American mayor of a major city to lose to a white candidate, *1349*

Evarts, William M.: Dedication ceremony for the Statue of Liberty, *1128*

Eveleigh, Nicholas: Comptroller of the United States Treasury, *2081*

Everett, Edward: Constitutional Union Party presidential candidate, *3293*

Third party to win more than 10 percent of the electoral vote in a presidential election, *3195*

Evers, Charles: African-American mayor of a major Southern city, *1334*

Ewbank, Thomas: Conservationist document submitted to Congress, *4121*

Ewing, Thomas: Department of the Interior, *2038*

Secretary of the interior, *1156*

F

Fairbanks, Richard: Colonial post office established by law, *3127*

Fall, Albert Bacon: Cabinet member convicted of a crime, *1177*

Fallon, George: Terrorist shootings in the Capitol Building, *1247*

Falwell, Jerry: Supreme Court decision upholding the right to parody public figures, *4742*

Fanfani, Amintore: Cabinet meeting attended by a foreign national, *1190*

Faris, Herman Preston: Woman vice presidential candidate in the 20th century, *3256*

Farragut, David Glasgow: American citizen hanged for treason, *2557*

Statue cast by the federal government, *2707*

Farrakhan, Louis: All-male march on Washington, *2852*

Farrand, Max: Edition of the complete *Records of the Federal Convention of 1787*, *1833*

Faubus, Orval Eugene: National States' Rights Party presidential candidate, *3348*

Republican governor of Arkansas since Reconstruction, *4513*

Use of federal troops to enforce integration, *1931*

Fauset, Crystal Bird: African-American woman to serve as a state legislator, *4552*

Fechner, Robert: Youth conservation corps, *4127*

Feinstein, Dianne: State to be represented in the Senate by two women, *1808*

Woman mayor of San Francisco, CA, *1342*

Feline, Magdalen: Colonial legislature's mace still extant, *1479*

Felton, Rebecca Latimer: Woman to be appointed a senator, *1783*

Fenno, John: Political newspaper of national importance, *3908*

Fenoaltea, Sergio: Cabinet meeting attended by a foreign national, *1190*

Fenwick, Joseph: Consuls appointed after the adoption of the Constitution, *2320*

Fenwick, Millicent Hammond: Congresswoman who was a grandmother, *1625*

Ferguson, James Edward: American Party presidential candidate, *3305*

Ferguson, Miriam "Ma" Amanda Wallace: State to elect two woman governors, *4525*

Woman to serve as a state governor, *4505*

Fernow, Bernhard Eduard: Forest service of the United States, *4143*

Ferraro, Geraldine: Presidential candidate in the 20th century to come within two percentage points of winning the entire electoral vote, *3274*

Woman to run for vice president as the candidate of a major political party, *3273*

Ferry, Elisha Peyre: State named for a person born in America, *4272*

Washington state governor, *4494*

Ferry, Jules: Dedication ceremony for the Statue of Liberty, *1128*

Few, William: Session of the Senate, *1662*

Field, James Gaven: Populist Party presidential candidate, *3312*

Field, Pattie Hockaday: Woman vice consul, *2340*

Field, Stephen Johnson: Transcontinental telegram of a political nature, *3857*

Fielden, Samuel: Labor activists to be executed, *2559*

Fillmore, Abigail Powers: First Lady who had an occupation other than homemaking, *3588*

First Lady who was the daughter of a minister, *3582*

Library in the White House, *5023*

Fillmore, Millard: Expansion of the Capitol, *1229*

First Lady who had an occupation other than homemaking, *3588*

Former president to run for reelection on a different party's ticket, *3402*

Know-Nothing Party presidential candidate, *3290*

Library in the White House, *5023*

President who had a stepmother, *3554*

President whose party was in the minority in both houses of Congress, *3713*

Supreme Court justice with a university law degree, *4769*

Third party to make a substantial showing in a presidential election, *3192*

Utah territorial governor, *4867*

Findley, Paul: House page who was African-American, *1643*

Finley, Robert: Organized emigration of freed slaves to Africa, *4242*

Finney, Joan: State to have women serving simultaneously in the statehouse, House of Representatives, and Senate, *4285*

Woman governor of Kansas, *4526*

Finnie, William: Sergeant at arms of the Senate, *1682*

Fischer, Adolph: Labor activists to be executed, *2559*

Fishbourn, Benjamin: Presidential appointment to be rejected, *3770*

Fisher, Carl Graham: Transcontinental highway, *4276*

Fitzpatrick, Benjamin: Candidate to withdraw from the presidential race after the adjournment of his party's national convention, *2994*

Vice presidential candidate of a major political party to resign before the election, *3271*

Fitzsimons, Thomas: Congressional investigation, *1491*

Congressional representative who was Catholic, *1584*

Flagg, James Montgomery: Portrait of Uncle Sam to become famous, *1134*

Flannagan, Cope: War Risk Insurance Bureau, *4053*

Fleet, Henry: European to visit the future site of Washington, DC, *1862*

Fleming, Patricia S.: Federal AIDS policy coordinator, *4038*

Fleming, Tom: Political cartoon entered in the *Congressional Record*, *1514*

Flores, Irving: Terrorist shootings in the Capitol Building, *1247*

Flower, Roswell Pettibone: Agricultural appropriation, *4110*

Floyd, John: Independent Party presidential candidate, *3283*

Presidential election in which all the candidates were nominated at party conventions, *3186*

Flynt, Larry: Supreme Court decision upholding the right to parody public figures, *4742*

Fong, Hiram Leong: Senator of Asian ancestry, *1798*

Foote, Charles C.: Liberty League presidential candidate, *3288*

Vice presidential candidate from Michigan, *4634*

Foote, Henry: Senator to threaten another senator with a gun in the Senate chamber, *1767*

Forand, Aime: Government-funded health care program for the poor, *4056*

Forbes, Malcolm: State legislative hearing to be shown on television, *4554*

Forbes, Ralph: Supreme Court decision on inclusion of candidates in televised political debates, *4746*

Ford, Ebenezer: Labor union whose candidates won an election, *2486*

Ford, Gerald R.: Commission appointed to investigate the assassination of a president, *3453*

Ford, Gerald Rudolff: President who was the child of divorced parents, *3564*

Ford, Gerald Rudolph: Cabinet member to serve in four different capacities, *1195*

Incumbent president to testify before a committee of Congress, *1575*

Postwar President who had never served in the armed forces, *3704*

President and vice president to hold office together without either having been elected, *3437*

President born in Nebraska, *4617*

President from Michigan, *4618*

President to donate his papers to the federal government during his term in office, *3438*

President to make public the results of a routine medical examination, *3841*

President to receive a presidential pardon, *3518*

President to survive two assassination attempts in one month, *3455*

President who came to the office through appointment rather than election, *3435*

President who had been a Boy Scout, *3833*

President who had served as director of the Central Intelligence Agency, *3508*

President who was the child of divorced parents, *3564*

President whose name was changed, *3484*

Televised presidential election debate between an incumbent president and a challenger, *3222*

Vice president appointed under the 25th Amendment to the Constitution, *4996*

Vice president born in Nebraska, *4688*

Vice president from Michigan, *4689*

Vice president to succeed to the presidency after the resignation of the president, *3436*

Ford, James William: African-American vice presidential candidate in the 20th century, *3260*

Forrest, Nathan Bedford: Ku Klux Klan, *2814*

Forrestal, James Vincent: Department of Defense, *2046*

Secretary of defense, *1182*

Fort, Franklin William: Federal Home Loan Bank board, *2111*

Fortas, Abe: Filibuster against a Supreme Court appointment, *1748*

Forten, James: National convention of African-Americans, *2845*

Foster, Charles: Cabinet in which two secretaries had the same last name, *1166*

Foster, John Watson: Cabinet in which two secretaries had the same last name, *1166*

Foster, William Zebulon: African-American vice presidential candidate in the 20th century, *3260*

Presidential election in which a communist party participated, *3212*

Frank, Barney: Congressman to acknowledge that he was a homosexual, *1627*

Frankfurter, Felix: National civil liberties advocacy group, *2827*

Year in which all the justices of the Supreme Court were graduates of a law school, *4778*

Franklin, Benjamin: Artist's design for the Great Seal of the United States, *1105*

Colonial congress, *1423*

Commemoration of the birthday of Benjamin Franklin, *2192*

Continental coin, *2149*

Franklin, Benjamin:—*continued*

Independent postal service during the Revolution, *3137*

Minister plenipotentiary, *2312*

Peace conference during the American Revolution, *1027*

Pennsylvania constitution, *4364*

Pennsylvania state governor, *4456*

Plan for the union of the British colonies, *1001*

Political cartoon, *3927*

Political cartoon featuring Uncle Sam, *3933*

Political cartoon published in an American newspaper, *3928*

Political magazine, *3895*

Political newspaper to carry partisanship to extremes, *3852*

Postage stamp depicting a president, *3164*

Postmaster general under the Continental Congress, *3138*

President who had made a transatlantic crossing, *3783*

Proposal that senators should serve for free, *1658*

Proposals for the design of the Great Seal of the United States, *1104*

Public celebration of national independence, *2236*

Public figure lampooned in political cartoons, *3929*

Regulation allowing newspapers to be sent through the mails, *3907*

Tolling of the Liberty Bell for an event of political importance, *1109*

Treaties entered into by the federal government, *2396*

Treaty between the federal government and a nation with which it had been at war, *2397*

Treaty entered into by the federal government after independence, *2398*

Franklin, James: Political crusade by a newspaper, *3849*

Fraser, Alexander V.: Coast guard service, *2689*

Frasure, Robert C.: United States officials to die in the conflict in Bosnia, *2653*

Frazer, Victor O.: Run-off election in the U.S. Virgin Islands, *4901*

Freeman, Daniel: Homestead grant under the Homestead Act, *4182*

Frémont, Jessica Benton: Campaign poster showing the candidate and his wife, *2800*

Frémont, John Charles: American republic on the West Coast, *4841*

Campaign poster showing the candidate and his wife, *2800*

Independent Republican Party presidential candidate, *3295*

North American Party presidential candidate, *3291*

Presidential candidate from California, *4575*

Presidential election in which the Republican Party participated, *3191*

Republican Party candidate to be nominated on the first ballot, *3237*

Republican Party presidential candidate, *3292*

French, Daniel Chester: National monument to Abraham Lincoln, *2712*

Popular image of the Minute Man, *1133*

Freneau, Philip Morin: Conflict-of-interest case involving a journalist, *3885*

Democratic-Republican (Jeffersonian) political newspaper, *3910*

President to be stung by press criticism, *3722*

Friedan, Betty: National Organization for Women, *2899*

Friedman, Paul L.: Ruling requiring retention of all electronic records of the federal government, *2059*

Fries, John: Death penalty in a tax riot, *2555*

From, Al: President to participate in a live chat over the Internet, *3733*

Fromme, Lynette Alice "Squeaky": President to survive two assassination attempts in one month, *3455*

Fulani, Lenora B.: New Alliance Party presidential candidate, *3362*

Woman presidential candidate and African-American presidential candidate to get on the ballot in all 50 states, *3276*

Fulbright, J. William: President who had college experience as a Senate staff member, *3505*

Fuller, Alvan T.: American executions to excite worldwide protest, *2563*

Fuller, Ida May: Federal social security system, *4073*

Fuller, Melville W.: Judicial test of the Sherman Antitrust Act, *4954*

Supreme Court decision invalidating a federal tax, *4723*

G

Gaillard, John: Funeral held at taxpayer expense, *1694*

President pro tempore of the Senate to appoint committee members, *1692*

Gaines, Edmund P.: Former vice president to be arrested, *4968*

Gales, Joseph: Volume of *Debates and Proceedings in the Congress of the United States*, *1499*

Gallatin, Abraham Alfonse Albert: Senate election that was contested, *1757*

Gallatin, Albert: Senator to be appointed as a treaty negotiator, *1762*

Gallup, George: Scientific public opinion polls, 2773

Gardener, Helen Hamilton: Woman to serve as Civil Service commissioner, 2031

Gardenier, Barent: Duel between representatives in Congress, 1588

Gardiner, Julia: President to marry while in office, 3557

Gardner, Helen Hunt: Woman to serve as Civil Service commissioner, 2031

Gardner, John W.: Common Cause, 2837

Gardner, Susan: Consumer Party presidential candidate, 3363

Garey, A. E.: National union for public employees, 2491

Garfield, Elizabeth Ballou: President whose mother lived at the White House, 3561

President's mother to attend her son's inauguration, 3667

Garfield, James Abram: Credentials fight at a Republican Party convention that determined the selection of the candidate, 3000

Federal civil service reform law that was effective, 2028

Marriage of two descendants of different presidents, 3571

President-elect who was simultaneously a senator-elect and a member of the House, 3513

President to use a telephone, 3829

President to view his inaugural parade from a platform outside the White House, 3666

President whose mother lived at the White House, 3561

Presidential candidate to make campaign speeches in a foreign language, 2767

Presidential candidate who was present at the convention that nominated him, 3244

Presidential election with a margin of difference of less than 1 percent of the popular vote, 3201

President's mother to attend her son's inauguration, 3667

Woman to serve as a president's personal physician, 3776

Garfield, James Rudolph: Child of a president to serve in a presidential cabinet, 1151

Garfield, Newell: Marriage of two descendants of different presidents, 3571

Garn, Jake: Senator to fly in space, 1807

Garner, James Nance: President to have three vice presidents, 3423

Garner, John Nance: Day on which the president and the vice president were both out of the country, 3800

Republican presidential and vice presidential team to lose a bid for reelection, 3418

Vice president from Texas, 4681

Garnet, Henry Highland: African-American allowed to enter the grounds of Congress, 1507

African-American preacher to deliver a sermon in the House of Representatives, 1566

Garrard, James: Statement of the doctrine of nullification, 4262

Garrison, William Lloyd: Major antislavery periodical, 4245

Use of the name "Liberty Bell", 1111

Garvin, Florence: National Greenback Party presidential candidate, 3333

Gary, Elbert Henry: Holding company worth a billion dollars, 4917

Garza, Tony: Voting rights in space, 4442

Gasque, Elizabeth ("Bessie") Hawley: Congresswoman who was not sworn in, 1606

Gates, Horatio: Major American victory in the Revolutionary War, 1031

Gautier, Felisa Rincon de: Woman mayor of San Juan, PR, 4894

Geary, John White: Mayor of San Francisco, CA, 1315

State governor who had previously been governor of a territory in which his state was not included, 4487

Gebbie, Kristine M.: Federal AIDS policy coordinator, 4038

Gee Jon: State to allow execution by lethal gas, 2562

Genet, Edmond-Charles-Édouard: Regular cabinet meetings, 1145

George, Henry: Proponent of the Single Tax principle, 2819

Single-tax proponent, 2820

George III, King of England: Royal proclamation declaring Britain's colonies in America to be in open rebellion, 1021

George VI, King of England: British monarchs to visit the United States, 2387

Gérard, Conrad Alexandre: Representative of a foreign country to the United States, 2311

Gerry, Elbridge: Gerrymander, 1555

House of Representatives filibuster, 1547

President whose administration lost two vice presidents to death, 3392

Presidential election in which both candidates were nominated at open congressional caucuses, 2975

Treaty terminated by a joint resolution of Congress, 2404

Undeclared war, 2639

Vice president to be buried at Washington, DC, 1879

Vice president who had served in the House of Representatives, 4960

Vice presidential candidate from Massachusetts, 4625

Gerry, Elbridge T.: Case of child abuse brought to court, *3990*

Gertner, Nancy: Federal judge to reduce a sentence as a protest against racial profiling, *1940*

Gian-Cursio, Christopher: Vice presidential candidate from Florida, *4661*

Gibbons, Herbert Adams: Civil rights chair at a college, *2526*

Gibbons, William: Book advocating voting rights for women, *2893*

Gibley, H. Norman: Ambassadors in service to wed, *2361*

Gibson, John: Indiana territorial governor, *4853*

Gibson, John Michael: Capitol Police Officers killed in the line of duty, *1251*

Gibson, Kenneth A.: African-American mayor of a major Eastern city, *1335*

Gilchrist, John James: Claims court established by the federal government, *1973*

Gildersleeve, Virginia Crocheron: Federal treaty signed by a woman, *2417*

Gillette, William: Drama about the Civil War, *1393*

Gilmer, Thomas Walker: President who narrowly escaped a fatal accident while in office, *3527*

Gilmore, Gary: Supreme Court decision barring the death penalty, *4738*

Gilpin, William: Colorado territorial governor, *4873*

Gingrich, Newton Leroy "Newt": "Corrections Day", *1580*

Former speaker of the House to become a television news commentator, *1638*

Speaker who was punished by the House, *1637*

Ginsburg, Ruth Bader: Jewish woman to serve as a Supreme Court justice, *4783*

Gitlow, Benjamin: Presidential election in which a communist party participated, *3212*

Giuliani, Rudolph: First Lady elected to public office, *3623*

Glenn, John Herschel, Jr.: Presidential candidate who had been an astronaut, *3272*

Senator who had been an astronaut, *1802*

Glover, John: Navy of the United States, *2686*

Goddard, Mary Katherine: Woman to serve as a postmaster, *3136*

Goddard, Terry: State to have a gubernatorial runoff election, *4439*

Godkin, E. L.: Use of the term "mugwump", *2932*

Goethals, George W.: Civilian government in the Panama Canal Zone, *4846*

Goico, Pedro Gerónimo: Political parties in Puerto Rico, *4887*

Goldsborough, Louis Malesherbes: Observatory established by the federal government, *2070*

Goldwater, Barry Morris: Political ad raising fears of nuclear war, *2778*

Presidential candidate from Arizona, *4594*

Presidential election in which the Republican Party earned a significant number of votes in the South, *3216*

Presidential election in which the state of Vermont was carried by a Democrat, *3217*

Woman to receive nominating votes for the presidency at the convention of a major party, *3025*

Goler, George Washington: Municipal milk station, *4025*

Gonzales, Ron: President to participate in a live chat over the Internet, *3733*

Gonzalez, Henry B.: Mexican-American elected to the Texas state senate, *4555*

Gonzalez, Virgilio: Convictions in the Watergate case, *3517*

Goode, W. Wilson: African-American mayor of Philadelphia, PA, *1347*

Goodnow, Frank Johnson: National political science society, *3073*

Goodwin, John N.: Arizona territorial governor, *4875*

Arizona territorial governor, *4875*

Gorbachev, Mikhail S.: Chemical arms control treaty, *2428*

Post–Cold War summit between the United States and the Soviet Union, *2301*

Treaty to reduce the number of nuclear missiles, *2427*

Gordon, Nathaniel: Execution for slave trading carried out by the federal government, *2556*

Gore, Al *See* Gore, Albert, Jr.

Gore, Albert, Jr.: President and vice president in the 20th century who were both Southerners, *3442*

President to attend a hockey game during his term in office, *3842*

Vice president born in Washington, DC, *1902*

Vice president from Tennessee, *4673*

Vice president to chair the United Nations Security Council, *2440*

Vice presidential candidate who was Jewish, *3279*

Gorges, Ferdinando: City incorporated in the British colonies, *1253*

Waterpower development grant to a colonist, *4193*

Gorges, William: Chartered city in the United States, *1252*

Gosnold, Bartholomew: Colonial council, *1400*

Permanent English settlement, *1401*

Gould, Symon: Vegetarian Party presidential candidate, *3337*

Gould IV, William Benjamin: Federal agency regulating labor relations, *2446*

Grady, Henry F.: Ambassador to India, *2348*

Graeff, Abraham up den: Protest against slavery made by a religious group in the New World, *4226*

Graeff, Derick up den: Protest against slavery made by a religious group in the New World, *4226*

Graham, John: Pan-American delegates from the United States, *2325*

Granger, Gideon: President to introduce the spoils system into the civil service, *2021*

Granger, Gordon: Emancipation Day (Texas), *2204*

Grant, Frederick Dent: Child of a president to attend West Point, *3553*

Grant, Julia Boggs Dent: First Lady born west of the Mississippi, *3589*

First Lady to be received by the pope, *3614*

First Lady to be received by the pope, *3614*

Inaugural ball in the Treasury Building, *3663*

Grant, Ulysses Simpson: Centennial celebration of the Revolution, *1036*

Child of a president to attend West Point, *3553*

Credentials fight at a Republican Party convention that determined the selection of the candidate, *3000*

General of the U.S. Army, *2625*

Inaugural ball in the Treasury Building, *3663*

Laws authorizing the use of force against the Ku Klux Klan, *1924*

Liberal Republican Convention of Colored Men, *3301*

Liberal Republican Party, *2928*

National Working Men's Convention, *3299*

President to attend West Point, *3696*

President to function as an effective commander in chief, *3405*

President to receive a salary raise, *3742*

President to veto more than 100 bills in a single term, *3845*

President to visit the West Coast of the United States while in office, *3787*

President whose name was changed, *3484*

President whose parents were both alive at the time of his inauguration, *3664*

Reigning king to visit the United States, *2380*

Republican president whose party was in the minority in the House of Representatives, *3715*

Republican presidential candidate chosen unanimously on the first ballot, *3239*

Supreme Court nominee to die before taking office, *4750*

Grant, Ulysses Simpson, III: Swimming pool in the White House, *5037*

Grasso, Ella: Woman governor elected in her own right, *4518*

Gratz Brown, Benjamin: Independent Liberal Republican Party presidential candidate, *3302*

Liberal Republican Convention of Colored Men, *3301*

Liberal Republican Party, *2928*

Liberal Republican Party presidential candidate, *3298*

Straight-out Democratic Party presidential candidate, *3300*

Graves, John Temple: Independence Party presidential candidate, *3325*

Gray, Robert: Ship to carry the American flag around the world, *1084*

Gray, Samuel: Americans killed by British soldiers in the Revolution, *1009*

Graydon, William: Digest of American law, *2517*

Greeley, Horace: Edition of *The New York Tribune*, *3922*

Independent Liberal Republican Party presidential candidate, *3302*

Liberal Republican Convention of Colored Men, *3301*

Liberal Republican Party, *2928*

Liberal Republican Party presidential candidate, *3298*

Presidential candidate to die during the election, *3243*

Straight-out Democratic Party presidential candidate, *3300*

Green, Anne Catherine Hoof: Woman to serve as a postmaster, *3136*

Green, Bartholomew: Newspaper published with government approval, *3904*

Green, Bernard: Library of Congress building, *2066*

Green, Duff: Kitchen cabinet of unofficial presidential advisors, *1152*

Official Jacksonian newspaper, *3916*

Green, Theodore Francis: State law prohibiting discrimination against soldiers, *2657*

Greene, Nathanael: Statue installed in National Statuary Hall in the Capitol, *1235*

Greenleaf, James: Block of buildings constructed in Washington, DC, *1873*

Sale of building lots in Washington, DC, *1869*

Gregory, Dick: Freedom and Peace Party presidential candidate, *3354*

Gregory, William S.: Mayor of Kansas City, KS, *1317*

Gries, John Matthew: Federal Home Loan Bank board, *2111*

Griffiths, Martha: Federal law prohibiting discrimination in employment on the basis of sex, *1966*

Grimké, Charlotte Forten: National political organization for African-American women, *2846*

Griswold, Deirdre: Workers World Party presidential candidate, *3361*

Griswold, Roger: Brawl in the House of Representatives, *1551*

Use of the mace of the House of Representatives to keep order, *1552*

Groesbeck, William Slocum: Independent Liberal Republican Party presidential candidate, *3302*

Groves, John: Federal government airport, *1896*

Grundy, Joseph Ridgway: Senate election in which neither candidate was seated after a recount, *1737*

Gual, Pedro: Treaty between the federal government and a South American nation, *2408*

Guinier, Lani: African-American woman nominated to head the Justice Department's Civil Rights Division, *1937*

Gunnells, Leonard Blake: Birth registration uniform numbering system, *3954*

Gunter, Bill: Woman elected to the Senate whose political career owed nothing to a male relative, *1805*

H

Hadden, Briton: Weekly newsmagazine, *3901*

Hadfield, George: Superintendent of construction of the Capitol, *1218*

Hagelin, John: Natural Law Party presidential candidate, *3366*

Hagerty, Father Thomas J.: Industrial Workers of the World (Wobblies) convention, *2885*

Haionhwat'ha: Confederation in what is now the United States, *2721*

Hale, John Parker: Presidential candidate from New Hampshire, *4573*

Senator elected on an antislavery ticket, *4250*

Hale, Mrs. Stephen: American flag flown over a schoolhouse, *1087*

Hale, Nathan: American executed as a spy, *1028*

Hale, Sarah Josepha: Thanksgiving Day, *2242*

Hale, William: Mayor of Peoria, IL, *1310*

Hall, John Elihu: Law magazine, *3897*

Halleck, Henry W.: President to function as an effective commander in chief, *3405*

Hallet, Stephen: Superintendent of construction of the Capitol, *1218*

Hallinan, Vincent William: African-American woman to run for vice president, *3263*

American Labor Party convention, *3342*

Halprin, Lawrence: First Lady to be depicted on a monument to a president, *3622*

Halvorson, Kittel: Congressional representative elected by prohibitionists, *1596*

Hamilton, Alexander: Bank of the United States, *2103*

Department of the Treasury, *2035*

Difference of opinion among members of the cabinet, *1142*

Farewell address by a president, *3751*

Federal law intended to intimidate the press, *3853*

Industrial report to Congress, *4908*

Instance of congressional "log-rolling" (vote-trading), *1548*

Issue of the *Federalist* papers, *3071*

Loan to the United States, *2082*

Party tactics in Congress, *1487*

Political newspaper of national importance, *3908*

Political parties, *2903*

Proposals for the organization of the executive branch, *1993*

Revolutionary War national veterans' organization, *2699*

Secretary of a federal executive department to take orders from Congress, *2036*

Secretary of the treasury, *1138*

Tax rebellion against the federal government, *4799*

Vice president to be indicted while in office, *4967*

Hamilton, Andrew: Intercolonial postal system, *3132*

Legal precedent for freedom of the press, *3850*

Postmaster general of the English colonies, *3133*

Hamilton, John: Postmaster general of the British colonies, *3135*

Hamlet, James: African-American captured under the Fugitive Slave Law of 1850, *4251*

Hamlin, Hannibal: Presidential election won by the Republican Party, *3194*

Senator to draw a gun on the Senate sergeant at arms, *1775*

Vice president from Maine, *4672*

Vice president from the Republican Party, *5002*

Vice presidential candidate from Maine, *4636*

Hammer, Marion P.: National firearms lobby, *2817*

Hammond, George: British ambassador to the United States, *2247*

Hancock, John: Massachusetts state governor, *4454*

Harrison, Anna Tuthill Symmes:—*continued*

Pension granted to the widow of a president, *3593*

Harrison, Benjamin: Cabinet in which two secretaries had the same last name, *1166*

Child of a president to decline a nomination for the presidency, *3560*

First Lady who was the grandmother of a president, *3591*

Forest and fish reserve, *4145*

Former vice president who became a state governor, *4982*

Marriage of two descendants of different presidents, *3571*

President during whose term more than five states were admitted to the Union, *3411*

President from Indiana, *4611*

President whose father was a state governor, *3543*

President whose grandson became president, *3556*

President whose predecessor and successor were the same man, *3412*

Presidential candidate from Indiana, *4582*

States admitted to the Union simultaneously, *4303*

Woman employed by the executive branch of the federal government for official duties, *2030*

Harrison, Caroline Scott: Collection of White House china, *5028*

Daughters of the American Revolution, *2822*

First Lady who was the daughter of a minister, *3582*

Plan to enlarge the White House, *5029*

Harrison, Earl Grant: Registration of aliens by the federal government, *3119*

Harrison, Elizabeth Ramsey Irwin: First Lady who was the grandmother of a president, *3591*

Harrison, Francis Burton: Drug control law enacted by Congress, *4063*

Harrison, John Scott: Child of a president to decline a nomination for the presidency, *3560*

First Lady who was the grandmother of a president, *3591*

Harrison, Lucretia Knapp Johnson: First Lady who was the grandmother of a president, *3591*

Harrison, Richard: Lawyers admitted to practice before the Supreme Court, *2584*

Harrison, Robert Hanson: Presidential candidate from Maryland, *4560*

Supreme Court nominee to die before taking office, *4750*

Supreme Court of the United States, *4691*

Harrison, William Henry: Battle in the "Frontier War", *2738*

Campaign banners, *2797*

Campaign newspaper of importance, *3920*

Campaign song, *2764*

Child of a president to decline a nomination for the presidency, *3560*

Democratic presidential and vice presidential team to lose a bid for reelection, *3394*

First Lady who was the grandmother of a president, *3591*

Indiana territorial governor, *4853*

Louisiana territorial governor, *4855*

National political convention to adopt the unit rule, *2986*

Official Whig administration newspaper, *3921*

Pension granted to the widow of a president, *3593*

President and vice president to be born in the same county, *3465*

President from Ohio, *4603*

President from the Whig Party, *3710*

President to die in office, *3526*

President to travel to his inauguration by train, *3656*

President who did not deliver an annual message to Congress, *3753*

President who had been a medical student, *3477*

President who was a former state governor and the son of a state governor, *3552*

President whose father was a state governor, *3543*

President whose grandson became president, *3556*

Presidential candidate from Ohio, *4570*

Presidential candidate nominated in a church, *2985*

Presidential candidate to make a campaign speech, *2765*

Presidential election won by the Whig Party, *3188*

Third party to participate in a presidential election, *3189*

Vice president to succeed to the presidency after the death of a president, *3397*

Whig Party presidential candidate, *3285*

Year in which the Whig Party controlled both houses of Congress, *1500*

Year in which the Whig Party won control of the House of Representatives, *1560*

Year in which the Whig Party won control of the Senate, *1699*

Year in which three presidents held office, *3395*

Hart, Frederick: National monument to Vietnam veterans, *2719*

Hartly, Thomas: Lawyers admitted to practice before the Supreme Court, *2584*

Hartsfield, William Berry: Pinball ban enacted by a city, *4002*

Harvey, John: Colonial treason trial, *1411*

Hendrick:—*continued*

Plan for the union of the British colonies, *1001*

Hendricks, Thomas Andrew: Vice president born in Ohio, *4677*

Henenberg, Hattie L.: State supreme court in which all the judges were women, *4417*

Henry, James Buchanan: Presidential secretary to receive a governmental salary, *3740*

Henry, John: Presidential election in which more than one candidate declared for the presidency, *3176*

Henry, Joseph: Smithsonian Institution, *1887*

Henry, Patrick: Orator of the Revolution, *1004*

Statement of the principle of taxation with consent, *4786*

States-righters, *4259*

Virginia state governor, *4449*

Herer, Jack: Grassroots Party presidential candidate, *3365*

Hererra, Enrique Olaya: Chief executive-elect of a foreign country to serve in a diplomatic position in Washington, *2342*

Herman, Alexis: African-American to serve as secretary of labor, *1214*

Hernández, Joseph Marion: Latino to serve in Congress, *1589*

Latino to serve in the House of Representatives, *1493*

Hewitt, Don: Political interview aired on a television newsmagazine, *3881*

Hiawatha: Confederation in what is now the United States, *2721*

Hickey, Thomas: Execution by the Army, *2553*

Higgins, Daniel P.: National monument to Thomas Jefferson, *2715*

Hill, Anita F.: Supreme Court nominee accused of sexual harassment, *4782*

Hill, Thomas E.: Reference book of American political history, *1075*

Hillegas, Michael: Treasurer of the United States, *2077*

Hillenkoetter, Roscoe H.: Federal agency for the gathering of foreign intelligence, *2674*

Hillman, Sidney: Political action committee (PAC), *2832*

Hillquit, Morris: National civil liberties advocacy group, *2827*

Socialist Party, *2937*

Hills, Carla Anderson: Woman to serve as secretary of housing and urban development, *1197*

Hinckley, John Warnock, Jr.: President to be wounded in an unsuccessful assassination attempt while in office, *3456*

Hines, Frank T.: Consolidated federal agency for veterans' affairs, *2703*

Hirohito: Emperor of Japan to visit the United States, *2391*

Hisgen, Thomas Louis: Independence Party presidential candidate, *3325*

Hitz, William: Cabinet member convicted of a crime, *1177*

Hoban, James: Building erected in Washington, DC, by the federal government, *1872*

Designs for the building of the White House, *5004*

Superintendent of construction of the Capitol, *1218*

Hobart, Garret Augustus: Vice president from New Jersey, *4679*

Hobby, Oveta Culp: Cabinet conference to be televised, *1184*

Department of Health, Education, and Welfare, *2048*

Secretary of health, education, and welfare, *1183*

Hobson, Julius: People's Party presidential candidate, *3357*

Vice presidential candidate from Washington, DC, *1899*

Hobson, Richmond Pearson: Alcohol prohibition vote taken in Congress, *3945*

Hodges, Leonard B.: State forestry association, *4140*

Hoff, Philip H.: Democratic governor of Vermont since the Civil War, *4511*

Hoffman, Michael: State constitutional reform movement, *4268*

Hoffman, Paul Gray: Economic Cooperation Administration, *2283*

Hoge, David: Federal district land office, *4177*

Holcomb, Austin: Continental Party presidential candidate, *3324*

Holden, William Woods: State governor to be impeached and convicted, *4488*

Hollister, Nancy P.: Woman governor of Ohio, *4533*

Holly, Carrie: Women elected to a state legislature, *4546*

Holmes, David: Mississippi state governor, *4464*

Holmes, Joseph Austin: Bureau of Mines, *4189*

Holmes, Larry: Workers World Party presidential candidate, *3361*

Holmes, Oliver Wendell: Criminal trial before the Supreme Court, *4703*

Holton, Linwood: Republican governor of Virginia since Reconstruction, *4516*

Hong Yong Sik: Korean embassy, *2261*

Hood, Glenda: Woman mayor of Orlando, FL, *1357*

Hook, Sidney: National student socialist organization, *2826*

Hooker, Thomas: Colonial constitution, *1435*

Hull, Cordell:—*continued*

Day on which the president and the vice president were both out of the country, *3800*

Filing date for 1040 tax forms, *4809*

Hull, Isaac: Ship launched by the United States Navy, *2692*

Hull, Jane Dee: State in which all of the top elected offices were held by women, *4289*

Woman governor of Arizona, *4531*

Hull, John: Mint, *2144*

Minting act, *2143*

Hull, William: Michigan territorial governor, *4856*

Humphrey, G. K.: Internal Revenue Service, *4819*

Humphrey, George Magoffin: Cabinet conference to be televised, *1184*

Humphrey, Hubert Horatio: Presidential candidate from Minnesota, *4595*

Vice president born in South Dakota, *4685*

Vice president from Minnesota, *4686*

Humphreys, David: Political cartoon lampooning President George Washington, *3931*

President to dispatch a personal envoy on an overseas mission, *2246*

Hunt, E. Howard: Convictions in the Watergate case, *3517*

Hunt, George W. P.: Arizona state governor, *4501*

Hunt, John: Alabama state capital, *4329*

Hunte, William: Regulation allowing newspapers to be sent through the mails, *3907*

Hunter, David: Federal execution of a woman, *2558*

Hunter, Robert Mercer Taliaferro: Peace conference during the Civil War, *1389*

Session of the Confederate Congress, *1371*

Huntington, Samuel: Congress to call itself "The United States in Congress Assembled", *1048*

Presidential candidate from Connecticut, *4559*

Hurley, Edward Nash: Federal Trade Commission, *4922*

Hutt, Willard Andre: African-American history trail, *4159*

Hyatt, Thaddeus: Senate committee witness to be jailed for refusing to give testimony, *1707*

Hyde, Edward, Viscount Cornbury: New Jersey colonial governor, *1464*

Hyde, Henry J.: Elected president to be impeached, *3632*

I

Iacocca, Lee A.: Federal bailout of an auto manufacturer, *4939*

Ickes, Harold Le Claire: Emergency housing corporation, *4046*

Large-scale federal jobs-creation programs, *2468*

Native American tribal constitution, *2753*

Ide, William B.: American republic on the West Coast, *4841*

Ingersoll, Jared: Presidential election in which both candidates were nominated at open congressional caucuses, *2975*

Vice presidential candidate from Pennsylvania, *4624*

Iredell, James: Presidential candidates from North Carolina, *4567*

Presidential election in which more than one candidate declared for the presidency, *3176*

Supreme Court case challenging the validity of an act of Congress, *4711*

Supreme Court justices born outside the United States, *4749*

Supreme Court nominee to die before taking office, *4750*

Supreme Court of the United States, *4691*

Irons, Peter: Recordings of Supreme Court proceedings released without the Court's approval, *4708*

Irvine, Callender: Factory standardization to federal specification, *4911*

Isbell, Zachariah: Independent civil government in America, *1426*

Ives, Irving McNeil: Industrial and labor relations school at a college, *3067*

Iyotake, Tatanka: Major defeat inflicted by Native Americans on regular U.S. Army troops, *2748*

J

Jackson, Andrew: Cabinet appointee on record as having been rejected by the Senate, *1154*

Campaign biography, *2795*

Campaign medalets, *2793*

Campaign newspapers, *3918*

Chief justice of the Supreme Court to administer the oath of office to more than one president, *4763*

Commemoration of the birthday of Thomas Jefferson, *2193*

Convention to renominate a sitting president, *2981*

Jefferson, Thomas:—*continued*

Vice president who was nominated specifically for that office, *4966*

Withholding of a signed treaty by a president, *2406*

Year in which the Democratic-Republican Party controlled both houses of Congress, *1492*

Year in which the Democratic-Republican Party won control of the Senate, *1684*

Jenkins, Frank: Poor Man's Party presidential candidate, *3340*

Jenkins, Philip O.: Portrait of Abraham Lincoln, *3540*

Jenkins, Therese A.: Women to attend a national political convention as delegates, *3003*

Jenner, William Ezra: Texas Constitution Party presidential candidate, *3347*

Veteran of World War II to be elected to the Senate, *1791*

Jennings, Jonathan: Indiana state governor, *4463*

Jensen, Ben: Terrorist shootings in the Capitol Building, *1247*

John Paul II, Pope: Pope to visit the White House, *2392*

John XXIII, Pope: First Lady to have a private audience with the pope, *3615*

Johns, Frank T.: Presidential candidate from Oregon, *4586*

Presidential candidate killed in a rescue attempt, *3257*

Johnson, Andrew: Federal law granting African-American men the right to vote, *1922*

Federal law mandating an eight-hour workday, *2495*

Political cartoon showing the Democratic Party as a donkey, *3934*

President born in North Carolina, *4604*

President from a Southern state since the Civil War, *3429*

President to be impeached, *3631*

President to serve as a senator both before and after his term in office, *3495*

President to veto more than 100 bills in a single term, *3845*

President who had neither military nor legal experience, *3493*

President who had served as mayor of a city, *3488*

President who learned reading and writing from his wife, *3826*

Presidential amnesty granted during the Civil War, *3407*

Presidential candidate from the Democratic Party to be elected after the Civil War, *3247*

Rewards offered by the federal government for suspects in the assassination of a president, *3448*

Vice president born in North Carolina, *4670*

Vice president from Tennessee, *4673*

Vice president to succeed to the presidency after the assassination of a president, *3408*

Vice presidential candidate named Johnson, *4975*

Johnson, Anthony: African-American who was free, *4221*

Johnson, Ebenezer: Mayor of Buffalo, NY, *1305*

Johnson, Ed: Criminal trial before the Supreme Court, *4703*

Johnson, Eddie Bernice: House of Representatives that included a substantial number of African-American women, *1579*

Johnson, Eliza McCardle: President who learned reading and writing from his wife, *3826*

Johnson, Gregory Lee: Supreme Court decision on the right of a citizen to burn the American flag, *4743*

Johnson, Hale: Vice presidential candidate named Johnson, *4975*

Johnson, Harriet Lane: National art collection, *1886*

Johnson, Harvey: African-American mayor of Jackson, MS, *1363*

Johnson, Herschel Vespasian: Candidate to withdraw from the presidential race after the adjournment of his party's national convention, *2994*

Presidential election won by the Republican Party, *3194*

Vice presidential candidate from Georgia, *4637*

Vice presidential candidate named Johnson, *4975*

Johnson, Hiram Warren: Third party to win more than 25 percent of the popular vote in a presidential election, *3206*

Vice presidential candidate named Johnson, *4975*

Johnson, Hugh Samuel: Industrial Recovery Act, *4926*

Johnson, Lady Bird: First Lady to hold the Bible at her husband's inauguration, *3686*

President and First Lady to receive honorary degrees at the same time, *3629*

Woman to administer the presidential oath of office, *3685*

Johnson, Lyndon Baines: Affirmative action order issued by the federal government, *1905*

Ban on sex discrimination in hiring by the federal government, *1967*

Cabinet meeting attended by a foreign national, *1190*

Juneau, Solomon: Mayor of Milwaukee, WI, *1311*

Junior: Treaty between the United States and a Native American nation, *2733*

K

Kalakaua, David: Reigning king to visit the United States, *2380*

Kalakaua, King of the Hawaiian Islands: Coronation on territory that would later become part of the United States, *2381*

Kalb, Johann de: Foreign officers recruited to the cause of the American Revolution, *1030*

Kamehameha III, King of the Hawaiian Islands: State capital that was the capital of a sovereign kingdom, *4358*

Kapiolani, Queen of the Hawaiian Islands: Coronation on territory that would later become part of the United States, *2381*

Kassebaum, Nancy Landon: State to have women serving simultaneously in the statehouse, House of Representatives, and Senate, *4285*

Woman elected to the Senate whose political career owed nothing to a male relative, *1805*

Woman elected to the Senate without prior experience in the House of Representatives, *1803*

Katchatag, Stanton: Person to be counted in the 2000 census, *3099*

Kaufman, Irving Robert: Peacetime death sentence for espionage, *2566*

Television eyewitness allowed to testify in a federal court, *1985*

Kearse, Amalya Lyle: African-American woman to serve as judge on the U.S. Court of Appeals, *1990*

Keayne, Robert: Military organization established by a colony, *2663*

Keckley, Elizabeth Hobbs: African-American woman to become a First Lady's confidante, *3597*

Keegan, Lisa Graham: State in which all of the top elected offices were held by women, *4289*

Kefauver, Estes: Liberal Party convention, *3345*

Keller, Helen: National civil liberties advocacy group, *2827*

Kelley, Alfred: Mayor of Cleveland, OH, *1301*

Kelley, Oliver Hudson: National political organization of farmers, *2816*

Kellogg, Edward: Statement of the principles of the Greenback movement, *2813*

Kellogg, Frank Billings: Secretary of state to receive the Nobel Peace Prize, *1176*

Kelly, Sharon Pratt: African-American woman to serve as mayor of Washington, DC, *1901*

State flag for Washington, DC, *1903*

Kemmler, William: State to allow execution by electrocution, *2560*

Kemper, W. H.: State court of small claims, *4414*

Kendall, Amos: Kitchen cabinet of unofficial presidential advisors, *1152*

Political cartoon featuring Uncle Sam, *3933*

Kendall, George: Colonial council, *1400*

Rebellion in a British colony, *1402*

Kendrick, Captain: Ship to carry the American flag around the world, *1084*

Kennan, George Frost: Policy of containment of world communism, *2281*

Kennedy, Bernard Reilly: Federal codification board, *2009*

Kennedy, Edward Moore: President with a brother in the Senate, *3570*

Three brothers from one family to serve in the Senate, *1795*

Kennedy, John Fitzgerald: Affirmative action order issued by the federal government, *1905*

Cabinet member who was the brother of the president, *1189*

Internet camera showing the site of a presidential assassination, *3457*

Nuclear war confrontation, *2649*

Popular hoarding of a lower-denomination coin, *2171*

Postwar President who had never served in the armed forces, *3704*

President in the 20th century to receive a medal for heroism, *3702*

President to witness the firing of a Polaris missile, *3838*

President who had been a Boy Scout, *3833*

President who was born in the 20th century, *3467*

President who was Catholic, *3737*

President whose father and mother both survived him, *3534*

President with a brother in the Senate, *3570*

Presidential election debates shown on television, *3215*

Presidential hot line, *3837*

Presidential inauguration to be televised in color, *3684*

Presidential news conference to be televised live, *3730*

President's Commission on the Status of Women, *1964*

Skyjacking law enacted by Congress, *4936*

Technical advisors sent to Vietnam, *2648*

Three brothers from one family to serve in the Senate, *1795*

Vice president to become president after a hiatus, *4994*

Vice president who was present at the assassination of the president he succeeded, *3452*

Woman to administer the presidential oath of office, *3685*

Woman to serve as a president's personal physician, *3776*

Kennedy, Joseph Patrick: President whose father and mother both survived him, *3534*

Three brothers from one family to serve in the Senate, *1795*

Kennedy, Patrick Bouvier: Child of a president to die during his father's term in office, *3548*

Kennedy, Robert Francis: Assassination planned by the U.S. government in peacetime, *2681*

Cabinet member who was the brother of the president, *1189*

Politician to be assassinated while campaigning for his party's presidential nomination, *3267*

Secret Service protection for major presidential and vice presidential candidates and nominees, *3269*

Three brothers from one family to serve in the Senate, *1795*

Kennedy, Rose Elizabeth Fitzgerald: President whose father and mother both survived him, *3534*

Three brothers from one family to serve in the Senate, *1795*

Keppler, Joseph: Political cartoons in color, *3938*

Kern, John W.: Democratic floor leader, *1727*

Key, David McKendree: Cabinet member who had served as a Confederate officer, *1164*

Key, Francis Scott: Star-Spangled Banner, *1088*

Keyes, Alan L.: African-American to actively campaign for the presidential candidacy of the Republican Party, *3033*

Talk-radio host to seek the presidential candidacy of a major party, *3884*

Keys, Martha Elizabeth: Congressional representatives to marry each other, *1626*

Keyser, F. Ray, Jr.: Democratic governor of Vermont since the Civil War, *4511*

Khomeini, Ruhollah: Large-scale hostage crisis, *2296*

Khrushchev, Nikita: Nuclear war confrontation, *2649*

Son of a Soviet premier to become an American citizen, *2394*

Khrushchev, Sergei: Son of a Soviet premier to become an American citizen, *2394*

Kidd, William: Workers' compensation agreement, *2501*

Kieft, Willem: Smoking ban enacted by a colony, *4076*

Kill Buck, John: Treaty between the United States and a Native American nation, *2733*

Killebrew, Emmet Stephen: County hydroelectric plant, *4131*

King, A.: Continental Party presidential candidate, *3324*

King, Clarence: United States Geological Survey, *4185*

King, Claude Roy, Jr.: Republican governor of Florida since Reconstruction, *4514*

King, Clennon: African-American presidential candidate, *3266*

Independent Afro-American Party presidential candidate, *3350*

King, Coretta Scott: Vietnam War Moratorium Day demonstration, *2861*

King, Dorothy Ayer Gardner: President who was the child of divorced parents, *3564*

King, Leslie Lynch: President who was the child of divorced parents, *3564*

King, Martin Luther, Jr.: Comprehensive civil rights law enacted by Congress, *1932*

Federal law to effectively protect the voting rights of African-Americans, *1933*

Martin Luther King Day, *2234*

Mass boycott by civil rights protesters, *2849*

Supreme Court decision giving protection to criticism of public officials, *4734*

King, Rufus: Presidential election in which candidates were separately nominated for the vice presidency, *3180*

King, Samuel Wilder: Hawaiian territorial governor who was of Hawaiian ancestry, *4884*

King, William: Maine state governor, *4467*

King, William Rufus de Vane: Incumbent senator to win a vice presidential nomination, *1771*

Vice president born in North Carolina, *4670*

Vice president from Alabama, *4671*

Vice president sworn in on foreign soil, *4978*

Vice president to take the oath of office but never serve in office, *4979*

Vice president who served in both houses of Congress from different states, *4977*

Kingman, Elias: Washington news bureau, *3915*

Kinkead, John H.: Governor of territorial Alaska, *4882*

Kirby, Ephraim: Law report, *2513*

Kirby, Fred Morgan: Civil rights chair at a college, *2526*

Kirk, Ron: African-American mayor of Dallas, TX, *1360*

Kirkpatrick, Donald: American National Party presidential candidate, *3303*

Kirkpatrick, Jason: City council with a majority of Green Party members, *1294*

Kirkpatrick, Jeanne Duane Jordan: Woman to serve as the United States representative to the United Nations, *2439*

Kissinger, Henry Alfred: Secretary of state who was a former member of the Foreign Service, *1209*
Shuttle diplomacy, *2292*

Klein, Nelson Bernard: Death penalty authorized by federal law, *2564*

Kleindienst, Richard Gordon: Attorney general to plead guilty to a criminal offense, *1196*

Klock, Frances: Women elected to a state legislature, *4546*

Knapp, Joseph Gillett: State forestry inquiry commission, *4137*

Knox, Henry: Difference of opinion among members of the cabinet, *1142*
Entry in the *Journal of the Executive Proceedings of the Senate of the United States of America*, *1673*
Military academy established by the federal government, *2613*
Patent law passed by Congress, *2597*
Secretary of war, *1141*
Tennessee state capital, *4323*
Treaties reviewed by the Senate, *1674*
Treaty for which a president sought the Senate's advice and consent in person, *2400*

Knox, William: Consuls appointed after the adoption of the Constitution, *2320*

Knussman, Kevin: Sex discrimination case to establish the rights of fathers of newborn babies, *1969*

Koch, Edward: Homosexual civil rights legislation proposed at the federal level, *1910*

Koos-ta-ta, Paul: Native American tribal constitution, *2753*

Kościuszko, Tadeusz: Foreign officers recruited to the cause of the American Revolution, *1030*

Kozachenko, Kathy: Openly homosexual politican to win a municipal election, *1286*

Krajewski, Henry B.: Poor Man's Party presidential candidate, *3340*

Kreps, Juanita Morris: Woman to serve as secretary of commerce, *1199*

Kruzel, Joseph J.: United States officials to die in the conflict in Bosnia, *2653*

Kuskof, Ivan Alexandrovich: Russian colonial settlement, *1429*

L

La Follette, Philip: State unemployment insurance, *2465*

La Follette, Robert Marion: Development of the "Wisconsin Idea" of progressivism, *2818*
Newsreels showing presidential candidates, *3863*
Presidential candidate from Wisconsin, *4588*
Progressive Party (1924) presidential candidate, *3330*
Progressive Party (of 1924), *2943*
Senator who was the victim of an assassination attempt during a filibuster, *1780*

LaDuke, Winona: Green Party presidential candidate, *3368*

Lafayette, Marquis de: Commemoration of the birthday of the Marquis de Lafayette, *2222*
Distinguished foreign personage to stay at the White House as a houseguest, *5016*
Foreign officers recruited to the cause of the American Revolution, *1030*
Foreigner to address a joint meeting of Congress, *1495*
Grant of federal land to a foreigner, *4180*

Lahm, Frank Purdy: Airplane owned by the United States, *1998*

Laise, Carol Clendening: Ambassadors in service to wed, *2361*
Woman to become an assistant secretary of state, *2365*

Lamb, John: City employment office, *2463*

Lambert, Marie M.: Woman elected president of a state lawyers' association, *2593*

Landes, Bertha Knight: Major American city to elect a woman as mayor, *1329*

Landon, Alf: Woman elected to the Senate whose political career owed nothing to a male relative, *1805*

Lane, James H.: African-American unit to fight in the Civil War, *1386*

Lane, Joseph: Oregon territorial governor, *4866*
Southern Democratic Party presidential candidate, *3294*
Vice presidential candidate from Oregon, *4638*

Lane, Ralph: English colonial settlement, *1397*
Letters written by an English colonial governor in America, *1398*

Lane, Thomas Joseph: Congressional representative reelected after serving a prison term, *1616*

Lane, William Carr: Mayor of St. Louis, MO, *1303*

Langdon, John: President of the Senate, *1669*
Quorum of the Senate, *1664*
Senate president pro tempore, *1665*
Session of the Senate, *1662*
Vice presidential candidate from New Hampshire, *4622*
Vice presidential candidate to decline the nomination, *3227*

Langer, William: Pioneer Party presidential candidate, 3344

Langford, Nathaniel Pitt: National park, 4148

Langston, John Mercer: African-American minister, 2333

African-American to hold elective office, 1279

Lansky, Meyer: Major American city founded in the 20th century, 1264

Lapham, Increase Allen: State forestry inquiry commission, 4137

Larkin, Thomas Oliver: Consul to California, 2327

LaRouche, Lyndon: Presidential candidate convicted in a federal criminal case, 3277

U.S. Labor Party presidential candidate, 3358

Larrazola, Octaviano A.: Latino elected to the Senate, 1786

New Mexico state governor of Latino ancestry, 4504

Larsen, Paul J.: Civil Defense director, 2675

Lasswell, Harold Dwight: Propaganda course at a college, 3066

Lathrop, Julia Clifford: Children's Bureau, 3993

Latrobe, Benjamin Henry: Additions to the White House, 5010

Architect of the Capitol, 1216

Architect of the Capitol who was born in the United States, 1223

Hall of the House of Representatives in the Capitol, 1554

Sanitary facilities in the Capitol, 1225

Section of the Capitol to be completed, 1221

Latting, Patience Sewell: Woman to serve as mayor of Oklahoma City, OK, 1336

Laumer, Keith: Senator to act in the movies, 1800

Lawrence, Cornelius Van Wyck: City mayor elected by popular vote, 1306

Lawrence, Henry: City commissioner of Salt Lake City, UT, 1327

Lawrence, Richard: President who was the target of an assassination attempt while in office, 3444

Lazio, Rick: First Lady elected to public office, 3623

Le Moyne, Antoine, sieur de Sauvolle: French governor of the Louisiana Territory, 1420

Lebron, Lolita: Terrorist shootings in the Capitol Building, 1247

Lee, Ann: Conscientious objectors, 2631

Lee, Arthur: Treaties entered into by the federal government, 2396

Lee, Blair: Senator elected by popular vote under the 17th Amendment to the Constitution, 1782

Lee, Charles: Cabinet secretaries to be fired, 1149

Lee, Henry: Congressional eulogy for a president, 3523

Independent Party presidential candidate, 3283

Lee, Joseph Bracken: Texas Constitution Party presidential candidate, 3347

Vice presidential candidate from Utah, 4660

Lee, Mary Ann Randolph Custis: Soldier buried at Arlington National Cemetery, 2668

Lee, Richard Henry: Congressional vote on a declaration of independence, 1056

Lee, Robert E.: Soldier buried at Arlington National Cemetery, 2668

Leidesdorff, William A.: African-American vice consul, 2328

Leiserson, William Morris: National Mediation Board, 2453

Leisler, Jacob: Colonist hanged for treason, 2552

Lemke, William: National Union for Social Justice, 2944

Presidential candidate from North Dakota, 4590

Union Party presidential candidate, 3334

LeMoyne, Francis Julius: Liberty Party presidential candidate, 3286

L'Enfant, Pierre-Charles: Authorized plan of the City of Washington, DC, 1870

Design for the Washington Monument, 2705

Design for Washington, DC, 1868

Meeting place of Congress, 1480

Naturalized citizen to lie in state in the Capitol rotunda, 1242

Proposal for a national monument to George Washington, 2706

Lenox, Walter Scott: White House china service that was made in the United States, 5035

Leo XIII, Pope: First Lady to be received by the pope, 3614

Leonard, Jonah Fitz Randolph: United Christian Party presidential candidate, 3320

Leopold, Aldo: Comprehensive wilderness law, 4215

Wilderness area to be formally named, 4154

Lepke, Louis: Federal execution of an organized crime boss, 2565

LeRoux, Charles: Maces as symbols of royal authority, 1421

Levin, Lewis Charles: Congressional representative who was Jewish, 1586

Leviner, Alexander: Federal judge to reduce a sentence as a protest against racial profiling, 1940

Levy, Jeffrey Gerard: Federal conviction for Internet piracy, 4942

Levy, Simon Magruder: Military academy established by the federal government, 2613

Lorimer, William: Senator expelled from the Senate for corrupt election practices, *1781*

Lovelace, Francis: Overland mail service between colonies, *3130*

Lowery, Samuel L.: Woman admitted to practice before the Court of Claims, *1976*

Lowman, Mary D.: Woman mayor with a town council consisting entirely of women, *1324*

Lozano, Ignacio: Mexican-American political newspaper, *3925*

Lucas, Robert: Iowa territorial governor, *4863*
National political convention to adopt the two-thirds rule, *2983*

Luce, Clare Boothe: Woman to serve as ambassador to a major nation, *2352*

Luce, Henry: Weekly newsmagazine, *3901*

Luce, Stephen Bleecker: Naval war college, *2615*

Ludlow, Roger: Colonial constitution, *1435*
Connecticut constitution, *4373*

Lukash, William Matthew: President to make public the results of a routine medical examination, *3841*

Lundy, Benjamin: Abolition newspaper, *3914*

Lykins, Johnston: Mayor of Kansas City, KS, *1317*

Lynch, John Roy: African-American to preside over the national political convention of a major party, *3001*

Lyon, James: Circulating library in Washington, DC, *1877*

Lyon, Matthew: Brawl in the House of Representatives, *1551*
Federal law intended to intimidate the press, *3853*
Prosecution under the Sedition Act, *3854*
Use of the mace of the House of Representatives to keep order, *1552*

M

MacArthur, Douglas: Constitution Party presidential candidate, *3343*
Use of children's fiction as propaganda in occupied territory overseas, *2278*

Macauley, Robert Colvin: Single Tax Party presidential candidate, *3328*

MacBride, Roger Lea: Electoral vote cast for a woman presidential candidate, *3220*

Machado, Richard: Federal prosecution of a hate crime on the Internet, *1939*

Macías, Manuel: Charter of autonomy for Puerto Rico, *4888*

Maclay, William: Senators elected to office, *1755*
Session of the Senate, *1662*

State to elect senators to the United States Senate, *4260*
Travel expenses for members of Congress, *1648*

Macon, Nathaniel: Vice presidential candidate from North Carolina, *4629*

Madison, Dolley Todd: First Lady to attend her husband's inauguration, *3584*
Former First Lady to be granted a seat in the House of Representatives, *3595*
Object to be continuously the property of the White House since 1800, *5006*
Renovation of the White House that required the president to relocate, *5014*

Madison, James: Artist to paint five presidents, *3537*
Cabinet appointee to be rejected by the Senate, *1150*
Chief justice of the Supreme Court to administer the oath of office to more than one president, *4763*
Coalition between Northern and Southern politicians, *2905*
Congressional representative appointed to a presidential cabinet, *1583*
Constitutional amendment, *1836*
Convention call, *2974*
Democratic-Republican (Jeffersonian) political newspaper, *3910*
Edition of the complete *Records of the Federal Convention of 1787, 1833*
Farewell address by a president, *3751*
Inaugural ball held at Washington, DC, *3647*
Issue of the *Federalist* papers, *3071*
Party to continue in power in the White House for more than 20 years, *2908*
President inaugurated in the Chamber of the House of Representatives, *3648*
President to be inaugurated in a suit of clothes entirely American-made, *3649*
President to face enemy gunfire while in office, *3695*
President to sign a declaration of war against a European power, *2641*
President who had served in Congress, *3472*
President who had served in the House of Representatives, *3480*
President who was younger than his vice president, *3390*
President whose administration lost two vice presidents to death, *3392*
President whose ancestry was not British, *3460*
Presidential election in which both candidates were nominated at open congressional caucuses, *2975*
Presidential team from Virginia and New York, *3385*
Presidents who were cousins, *3558*

Renovation of the White House that required the president to relocate, *5014*

Response by the House of Representatives to an inaugural address, *1542*

Senator to be appointed as a treaty negotiator, *1762*

Statement of the doctrine of nullification, *4262*

Suggestion that slaves be counted as full members of the population, *4235*

Use of the term "cabinet", *1144*

Vice president to serve under two presidents, *4969*

Vice presidential candidates from Virginia, *4623*

Year the public debt of the United States exceeded $100 million, *2126*

Malcolm, Ellen: Campaign funding organization for political candidates who support legal abortion, *2791*

Manley, John: National naval force, *2685*

Mann, Horace: State board of education, *3971*

Mansfield, Arabella Aurelia Babb: Woman to practice law, *2587*

Mapp, Dollree: Supreme Court decision extending the protection of the Bill of Rights to defendants in state courts, *4731*

Marbury, William: Supreme Court decision declaring an act of Congress unconstitutional, *4712*

Marcy, William Learned: State political machine, *2911*

Use of the phrase "to the victor belong the spoils", *2024*

Marie, Queen of Rumania: Queen to visit the United States during her reign, *2382*

Markham, William: Pennsylvania colonial governor, *1458*

Marsh, George Perkins: Political speech on conservation, *4120*

Marshall, George Catlett: Army officer to occupy the nation's highest military post and its highest nonelective civilian post, *2628*

Marshall, John: Cabinet secretaries to be fired, *1149*

Casting of the Liberty Bell, *1108*

Chief justice of the Supreme Court to administer the oath of office to more than one president, *4763*

Federalist Party, *2904*

Former chief justice of the Supreme Court to refuse renomination, *4760*

Former vice president to be arrested, *4968*

Meeting place of the Supreme Court in Washington, DC, *4699*

President to invoke executive privilege, *3391*

Supreme Court chief justice who had served in a presidential cabinet, *4762*

Supreme Court decision declaring a state law unconstitutional, *4714*

Supreme Court decision establishing its authority over state courts in matters of federal law, *4717*

Supreme Court decision establishing the power of the federal government to regulate commerce, *4718*

Supreme Court decision on state recognition of federal court rulings, *4713*

Supreme Court decision on the power of states to tax federal assets, *4716*

Supreme Court decision on the status of Native American tribes, *4719*

Supreme Court justice who had served in the House of Representatives, *4759*

Treaty terminated by a joint resolution of Congress, *2404*

Undeclared war, *2639*

Marshall, Lois I. Kimsey: Vice president's widow to receive a pension, *4987*

Marshall, Robert: Comprehensive wilderness law, *4215*

Marshall, Thomas Riley: Democratic presidential and vice presidential team to be re-elected, *3415*

Vice president from Indiana, *4674*

Vice president to preside over a cabinet meeting, *4984*

Year in which the Democratic party renominated its entire ticket, *3007*

Marshall, Thurgood: African-American attorney to serve as solicitor general, *4705*

Supreme Court justice who was African-American, *4779*

Martin, Graham: Ambassador to Vietnam, *2372*

Martin, John: Colonial council, *1400*

Martin, Joseph W., Jr.: Prayer and meditation room in the Capitol, *1248*

Martin, Thomas S.: Senate minority leader, *1726*

Martinez, Eugenio: Convictions in the Watergate case, *3517*

Martz, Judy: Woman governor of Montana, *4535*

Mason, Charles: Surveyed line separating North from South, *4172*

Mason, George: Bill of Rights, *1821*

Statement of the principle of inalienable rights, *1055*

Mason, Stevens T.: Michigan state governor, *4471*

Massasoit: Treaty between English settlers and a Native American tribe, *2395*

Matchett, Charles Horatio: Presidential election in which a socialist party participated, *3202*

Socialist Labor Party presidential candidate, *3313*

Mather, Cotton: Political crusade by a newspaper, *3849*

Mather, Stephen Tyng: National Park Service, *4152*

Mathers, James: Senate doorkeeper, *1666*
Sergeant at arms of the Senate, *1682*
Use of sergeant at arms of the Senate to make an arrest, *1683*

Mauchly, John W.: Federal government office to be computerized, *2000*

Maury, James: Consuls appointed after the adoption of the Constitution, *2320*

Maverick, Samuel: Americans killed by British soldiers in the Revolution, *1009*

Maxwell, George Holmes: Citizenship and public affairs school at a college, *3065*

Maxwell, John: Vegetarian Party presidential candidate, *3337*

Maxwell, Lucien: Major sale of land in the continental United States to a foreign consortium, *4271*

Maxwell, William: American flag flown in battle, *1080*

May, Cornelis Jacobsen: New York colonial governor, *1454*
Permanent Dutch colony, *1407*

Mays, Melvin Edward: Mercenaries arrested for planning terrorist acts on behalf of a foreign government, *2544*

McAdoo, William Gibbs: Government operation of railroads, *4097*

McAfee, Henry H.: Forestry association of national importance, *4139*

McAlpin, Harry: African-American newspaper reporter accredited to the White House, *3893*

McBride, John: State employment service, *2462*

McCabe, Lorenzo Dow: President and First Lady to celebrate their silver wedding anniversary in the White House, *3602*

McCain, Franklin: Civil rights sit-in, *2850*

McCarl, John Raymond: Comptroller general of the United States, *2092*
General Accounting Office, *1516*

McCarthy, Eugene Joseph: Consumer Party presidential candidate, *3363*

McCarthy, Joseph Raymond: Congressional hearings to be nationally televised, *1524*
Political editorial broadcast on radio and television, *3879*

McCarthy, Timothy J.: President to be wounded in an unsuccessful assassination attempt while in office, *3456*

McClellan, George Brinton: Political figurals, *2802*
Presidential election in which soldiers in the field were allowed to vote, *3199*

McClintock, Mary: Women's rights convention, *2894*

McCloskey, Burr: Pioneer Party presidential candidate, *3344*

McCloy, John J.: Commission appointed to investigate the assassination of a president, *3453*

McClure, Samuel Sidney: Muckraking journal of importance, *3900*
Muckraking journalist who was a woman, *3891*

McConnell, Ellen: Senate pages who were female, *1645*

McCord, James W., Jr.: Convictions in the Watergate case, *3517*

McCormack, Ellen: Right to Life Party presidential candidate, *3360*

McCormack, Mary Ellen Wilson: Case of child abuse brought to court, *3990*

McCoy, William: Mayor of Independence, MO, *1314*

McCulloch, Hugh: Comptroller of the Currency, *2087*
Secret service established by the federal government, *2580*

McDonald, James Grover: Ambassador to Israel, *2349*

McDonald, Marshall: Federal office to protect U.S. fisheries, *4204*

McDonald, William C.: New Mexico state governor, *4500*

McDougal, James: Convictions in the Whitewater case, *3521*

McDougal, Susan: Convictions in the Whitewater case, *3521*

McDowell, Irvin: Major battle of the Civil War, *1381*

McGovern, George Stanley: Presidential candidate from South Dakota, *4596*

McGowan, John: Act inaugurating the Civil War, *1369*

McGuire, Peter J.: Labor Day parade, *2210*

McHenry, James: Cabinet secretaries to be fired, *1149*
Test of presidential authority over the cabinet secretaries, *1147*

McKean, Thomas: President of the United States under the Articles of Confederation, *3370*

McKenzie, Richard: Occupation of federal territory by Native American protesters in the modern era, *2755*

McKim, Charles F.: Expansion and comprehensive renovation of the White House, *5032*

McKinley, Ida Saxton: First Lady to sit next to her husband at state dinners, *3604*

McKinley, William: Commemoration of the birthday of William McKinley, *2219*
First Lady to sit next to her husband at state dinners, *3604*
Presidential call for volunteer troops to fight in the Spanish-American War, *2642*

Presidential candidate to run his campaign by telephone, 2769

McKinney, Cynthia Ann: Father and daughter to serve simultaneously in the same house of representatives, 4557

House of Representatives that included a substantial number of African-American women, 1579

McKinney, James Edward "Billy": Father and daughter to serve simultaneously in the same house of representatives, 4557

McLaurin, John: Fistfight in the Senate, 1723

McLean, John: Express mail, 3153

McMillan, James: School district to implement court-ordered busing to achieve racial integration, 1935

McNair, Alexander: Missouri state governor, 4468

McNamara, Robert S.: Prior restraint of the press by order of the federal government, 3868

McNamee, Graham: Political convention to be broadcast on radio, 3009

McNary, Charles: Senate leader to occupy the party floor leader's desk, 1738

McNeil, Joseph: Civil rights sit-in, 2850

McNutt, Paul Vories: State governor to be granted almost dictatorial power, 4507

McVeigh, Timothy: Attack by domestic terrorists on a federal facility resulting in large loss of life, 2006

McVickar, John: Political economy chair at a college, 3063

Mead, William R.: Expansion and comprehensive renovation of the White House, 5032

Means, Rice W.: Veterans of Foreign Wars of the United States, 2701

Means, Russell: Armed occupation by Native American protesters in the modern era, 2758

Militant Native American civil rights organization, 2756

Mecham, Evan: State in which two consecutive governors were forced to resign from office, 4530

State to have a gubernatorial runoff election, 4439

Medill, Joseph: Civil Service Commission, 2027

Medina, Ernest L.: American military massacre of political importance, 2650

Meek, Carrie: House of Representatives that included a substantial number of African-American women, 1579

Mein, John: Persecution of a newspaper editor by American revolutionaries, 3851

Mein, John Gordon: Ambassador assassinated in office, 2363

Ambassador killed by a terrorist attack, 2364

Mellette, Arthur Calvin: South Dakota state governor, 4493

States admitted to the Union simultaneously, 4303

Memminger, Christopher Gustavus: Confederate government bond, 2120

Tax levied by the Confederacy, 4802

Menéndez de Avilés, Pedro: French colonial settlement, 1395

Permanent Spanish colonial settlement, 1396

Meredith, Samuel: Treasurer of the United States, 2077

Merriam, Frank: Negative election campaign run by media specialists, 2772

Metcalf, Henry Brewer: Vice presidential candidate from Rhode Island, 4648

Meyers, Isaac: National labor organization for African-American workers, 2881

Meyers, Jan: State to have women serving simultaneously in the statehouse, House of Representatives, and Senate, 4285

Michikinikwa: Congressional investigation, 1491

Mickelson, Sig: National conventions to receive gavel-to-gavel television coverage, 3023

Middleton, Henry: President of the Continental Congress, 1038

Mifflin, Thomas: Pennsylvania state governor, 4456

Mikulski, Barbara Ann: Congresswoman to advance to the Senate, 1613

Woman elected to the Senate in her own right, 1792

Miles, Samuel: Electoral vote cast contrary to instructions, 3174

Miles, William Porcher: Confederate States flag, 1093

Miller, B. N.: Tax Cut Party presidential candidate, 3351

Miller, James: Arkansas territorial governor, 4860

Miller, John: North Dakota state governor, 4495

States admitted to the Union simultaneously, 4303

Milligan, Lambdin P.: Supreme Court decision setting limitations on the use of military force against American civilians, 4720

Milnor, George Sparks: Grain stabilization corporation, 4115

Milton, John: Presidential candidates from Georgia, 4563

Min Yong Ik: Korean embassy, 2261

Mindell, Fania: Birth control clinic, 3994

Minner, Ruth Ann: Woman governor of Delaware, 4534

Minuit, Peter: Delaware colonial governor, 1457

Dutch colonial settlement, 1405

Minuit, Peter:—*continued*

Pennsylvania colonial governor, *1458*

Permanent Dutch colony, *1407*

Miranda, Rafael Cancel: Terrorist shootings in the Capitol Building, *1247*

Mitchell, Arthur Wergs: Congressman from a northern state who was African-American, *1604*

Mitchell, Charlene: African-American woman to run for president, *3268*

Women to run as presidential candidates in the 20th century, *3270*

Mitchell, Charles Lewis: African-American state legislators, *4544*

Mitchell, Frank: House page who was African-American, *1643*

Mitchell, George: Militant Native American civil rights organization, *2756*

Mitchell, John Newton: Attorney general to be incarcerated, *1200*

Mitchell, Matthew: Colonial election held in defiance of the Royal Courts, *1449*

Mitchell, Michelle B.: Woman sheriff, *2535*

Mixon, Rhoda Holly Singleton: Town known to have been founded by a woman, *1258*

Moffat, John L.: Private mint authorized by the federal government, *2156*

Moffett, James Andrew: Federal Housing Administration, *4047*

Mohammed, Warith Deen: Muslim to offer the invocation to the Senate, *1753*

Mollison, Irvin Charles: African-American judge on the federal bench, *1983*

Mondale, Walter Frederick: Presidential candidate in the 20th century to come within two percentage points of winning the entire electoral vote, *3274*

Presidential candidate to receive more than 50 million popular votes, *3275*

Soft-sell nostalgia ads, *2779*

Vice president from Minnesota, *4686*

Woman to run for vice president as the candidate of a major political party, *3273*

Monroe, Elizabeth Kortwright: First Lady to redecorate the White House, *3585*

Monroe, James: Articulation of the Monroe Doctrine, *2254*

Artist to paint five presidents, *3537*

Chief justice of the Supreme Court to administer the oath of office to more than one president, *4763*

Distinguished foreign personage to stay at the White House as a houseguest, *5016*

Important exercise of an implied power of the government, *1997*

Pan-American delegates from the United States, *2325*

Party to continue in power in the White House for more than 20 years, *2908*

President during whose term more than five states were admitted to the Union, *3411*

President to receive the unanimous vote of the presidential electors, *3171*

President to ride on a steamboat, *3785*

President who had been wounded in action during a war, *3693*

President who had served in the Senate, *3481*

President whose ancestry was not British, *3460*

Presidential election in which the candidates of a single party ran unopposed, *3181*

Presidential inauguration held outdoors in Washington, DC, *3650*

Presidential inauguration to be postponed from Sunday to Monday, *3651*

Presidential team from Virginia and New York, *3385*

Territory annexed by the federal government, *4836*

Treaties establishing the United States as a transcontinental power, *2407*

Use of the term "Era of Good Feelings", *1066*

Vice presidential candidates from Virginia, *4623*

Wedding of a president's daughter in the White House, *5015*

Withholding of a signed treaty by a president, *2406*

Monroe, Maria Hester: Wedding of a president's daughter in the White House, *5015*

Monroney, A. S.: Prayer and meditation room in the Capitol, *1248*

Montgomery, John: Declaration of independence by citizens of an American colony, *1050*

Montoya, Alfred: National Chicano labor organization, *2890*

Moody, Blair: National convention to require a pledge of party loyalty from its delegates, *3024*

Senator who had been a newspaper reporter, *1794*

Moore, Annie: Federal immigration station, *3114*

Moore, James: Naval battle in the Revolutionary War, *1019*

South Carolina colonial governor, *1462*

Moore, Sara Jane: President to survive two assassination attempts in one month, *3455*

Moores, Frank Edward: Vending machine law enacted by a city, *4916*

Moos, Malcolm: Use of the term "military-industrial complex", *2608*

Moraga, José Joaquin: California state capital, *4338*

Moran, Mary: City to file for bankruptcy, *2135*

More, Nicolas: Judge to be impeached, *1445*

Morehead, John Motley: Woman to take charge of an American legation, *2343*

Moreland, Charles: State flag for Washington, DC, *1903*

Moreno, Luisa: Chicano labor convention, *2888*

Morgan, Arthur Ernest: Electric power contract between a city and the federal government, *4132*

Federal corporation to encourage the purchase of electric appliances, *4931*

Morgan, Harcourt Alexander: Federal corporation to encourage the purchase of electric appliances, *4931*

Morgan, John Pierpont: Holding company worth a billion dollars, *4917*

Morgenthau, Henry, Jr.: Farm credit administration, *4116*

Morison, Samuel Loring: Government official convicted of espionage for leaking secrets to the press, *2682*

Moro, Aldo: Cabinet meeting attended by a foreign national, *1190*

Morrey, Humphrey: Mayor of Philadelphia, PA, *1296*

Morrill, Justin: Statue installed in National Statuary Hall in the Capitol, *1235*

Morris, Esther Hobart: Woman to serve as justice of the peace, *1271*

Morris, Gouverneur: President to dispatch a personal envoy on an overseas mission, *2246*

Proposal for a presidential cabinet, *1136*

Morris, Kenneth: Civil rights anthem to achieve fame, *1122*

Morris, Robert: Block of buildings constructed in Washington, DC, *1873*

Broker to the Office of Finance of the United States, *2079*

Mint of the United States, *2151*

National flag to represent the United States, *1078*

Presidential mansion, *5003*

Sale of building lots in Washington, DC, *1869*

Senators elected to office, *1755*

Session of the Senate, *1662*

State to elect senators to the United States Senate, *4260*

Morris, Thomas: Vice presidential candidate from Ohio, *4633*

Morrow, Everett Frederic: White House official who was an African-American, *5039*

Morrow, Tracy L.: Racial bias suit in which one African-American claimed discrimination by another African-American, *1936*

Morse, Samuel Finley Breese: Political photographer, *3888*

Telegraph line to Washington, DC, *1884*

Telegraph message sent from the Capitol, *1226*

Morton, Levi Parsons: Act in the construction of the Statue of Liberty, *1125*

Former vice president who became a state governor, *4982*

Moscowitz, Henry: National Association for the Advancement of Colored People, *2847*

Moseley, William Dunn: Florida state governor, *4473*

Mosher, Eliza Maria: State reformatory for women, *2574*

Mosher, William Eugene: Citizenship and public affairs school at a college, *3065*

Motley, Constance Baker: African-American woman to serve as judge of a federal district court, *1988*

Mott, Lucretia: National organization to advocate universal voting rights, *2815*

Women's rights convention, *2894*

Moynihan, Daniel Patrick: First Lady elected to public office, *3623*

President to attend a hockey game during his term in office, *3842*

Muhlenberg, Frederick Augustus Conrad: Mace of the House of Representatives, *1529*

Response by the House of Representatives to an inaugural address, *1542*

Speaker of the House, *1631*

Use of the mace of the House of Representatives to keep order, *1552*

Muir, John: National environmental organization, *2823*

Mullett, Alexander: Modernization of the infrastructure of Washington, DC, *1889*

Mumford, William Bruce: American citizen hanged for treason, *2557*

Muñoz Marín, Luis: Governor of Puerto Rico to be elected, *4895*

Munson, Clara: Woman mayor elected west of the Rocky Mountains, *1328*

Murphy, Betty Southard: Federal agency regulating labor relations, *2446*

Murphy, Charles W.: State employment service, *2462*

Murphy, Ward E.: Woman to serve as director of a state bureau of corrections, *2578*

Murray, Peter: Public defender hired by a state, *4419*

Muskie, Edmund Sixtus: Democratic senator from Maine, *1797*

Myers, Henry: Strike benefit by a union, *2876*

Myers, Jacob H.: Voting machines used in an election, *1281*

Myers, Myer: Mace of the House of Representatives, *1529*

N

President to receive an annual salary of $200,000, *3748*

President to resign, *3433*

President to tape all his conversations in the White House, *3432*

President to visit a nation not recognized by the U.S. government, *3813*

President to visit the Soviet Union, *3814*

President who came to the office through appointment rather than election, *3435*

President who had served as ambassador to the United Nations, *3506*

Presidential election debates shown on television, *3215*

Republican presidential and vice presidential team to be reelected, *3427*

Strategic Arms Limitation Treaty, *2424*

Strike of postal employees, *2484*

Technical advisors sent to Vietnam, *2648*

Televised speech that confirmed a candidate's place on the vice presidential ticket, *3264*

Vice president appointed under the 25th Amendment to the Constitution, *4996*

Vice president from California, *4684*

Vice president to become president after a hiatus, *4994*

Vice president to succeed to the presidency after the resignation of the president, *3436*

Nixon, Tricia: Outdoor wedding held at the White House, *5040*

Noah, Mordecai Manuel: Jewish diplomat, *2323*

Noble, Elaine: Politician who was openly homosexual to win a state election, *4438*

Nolan, Beth: Woman appointed as chief White House counsel, *3782*

Nolan, John Ignatius: Congresswoman elected to serve in the place of her husband, *1601*

Nolan, Mae Ella: Congresswoman elected to serve in the place of her husband, *1601*

Norris, George William: Federal farm loan board, *4113*

North, Oliver: National security advisor forced to resign, *1206*

North, Simeon: Factory standardization to federal specification, *4911*

Norton, Eleanor Holmes: House of Representatives that included a substantial number of African-American women, *1579*

State flag for Washington, DC, *1903*

Norton, Mary Teresa Hopkins: Democratic congresswoman, *1602*

Woman to chair a House committee, *1605*

Woman to head the state committee of a major political party, *2963*

Nourse, Joseph: Free church in Washington, DC, *1885*

Novello, Antonia C.: Woman to serve as surgeon general, *4039*

Nugent, John: Journalist arrested by the Senate, *1703*

Nye, James W.: Nevada territorial governor, *4872*

O

O'Bannon, Presley Neville: American flag flown over a fortress of the Old World, *1086*

O'Brien, Jeremiah and John: Naval battle in the Revolutionary War, *1019*

O'Brien, Thomas Charles: National Union for Social Justice, *2944*

O'Brien, Timothy: Chaplain of the House of Representatives who was a Catholic priest, *1582*

O'Connor, James Francis Thaddeus: Federal Deposit Insurance Corporation, *2113*

O'Connor, Sandra Day: State in which all of the top elected offices were held by women, *4289*

Woman to become a Supreme Court justice, *4781*

Woman to preside over the Supreme Court, *4784*

O'Conor, Charles: Presidential candidate who was Catholic, *3242*

Straight-out Democratic Party presidential candidate, *3300*

Odlum, Jacqueline Cochran: Congressional representative of Asian ancestry, *1615*

Ogden, Aaron: Supreme Court decision establishing the power of the federal government to regulate commerce, *4718*

Ogden, William B.: Mayor of Chicago, IL, *1307*

Oglethorpe, James Edward: Colonial governor of Georgia, *1465*

Georgia Day, *2180*

O'Leary, Hazel: Woman to serve as secretary of energy, *1211*

Oliver, Henry Kemble: Labor bureau established by a state, *2441*

Olmsted, Frederick Law: Independent Liberal Republican Party presidential candidate, *3302*

Landscaping of the Capitol grounds, *1224*

Onassis, Jacqueline Lee Bouvier Kennedy: First Lady to have a private audience with the pope, *3615*

Woman to administer the presidential oath of office, *3685*

Oñate, Juan de: Spanish governor-general of New Mexico, *1399*

O'Neill, Thomas P.: President to formally transfer the presidency to an acting president, *3440*

Onis, Luis de: Land acquired by the United States from Spain, *4840*

Opper, Frederick: Character symbolizing the American people, *1132*

Orr, Kay: Woman governor of Nebraska, *4523*

Orr, Robert: Arsenal of the federal government, *2604*

Osborn, Charles: Abolition newspaper, *3914*

Osgood, Samuel: Postmaster general of the United States, *3144*
Presidential mansion, *5003*

O'Sullivan, John L.: Use of the term "manifest destiny", *2257*

Oswald, Lee Harvey: Commission appointed to investigate the assassination of a president, *3453*
Internet camera showing the site of a presidential assassination, *3457*

Otero II, Miguel Antonio: New Mexico territorial governor who was of Mexican ancestry, *4880*

Otis, James: Statement of the principle of taxation with consent, *4786*

Ovington, Mary White: National Association for the Advancement of Colored People, *2847*

Owen, Fred D.: Plan to enlarge the White House, *5029*

Owen, Robert: Independent labor party, *2913*

Owen, Ruth Bryan: Woman diplomat to hold the rank of minister, *2344*

Owen, William D.: Immigration bureau superintendent, *3113*

P

Page, William Tyler: National creed, *3074*

Pahlavi, Mohammed Reza: Large-scale hostage crisis, *2296*

Paine, Thomas: Anti-American satirical medalets, *2248*
Public call for independence to be published, *1025*

Palfrey, William: Consul to die in service, *2313*

Palisan, Johann: President in whose honor an asteroid was named, *3627*

Palmer, Alexander Mitchell: National file on suspected political radicals, *2534*
Red scare, *2828*

Palmer, John McAuley: Sound Money Democratic Party presidential candidate, *3317*

Pandit, Shrimati Vijaya Lakshmi: Woman to serve as ambassador to the United States, *2350*

Park, James Alan: Insurance law treatise, *2512*

Park, Maud Wood: League of Women Voters, *2898*

Parker, Arthur C.: American Indian Day, *2751*

Parker, Ely Samuel: Indian Affairs commissioner who was Native American, *2746*

Parker, George, Jr.: Election board game, *2768*

Parker, Joel: Labor Reform Party presidential candidate, *3296*

Parker, John: Clash of arms in the Revolutionary War, *1015*
War hero, *1016*

Parker, John J.: Supreme Court nominee to be rejected by the Senate in the 20th century, *4776*

Parker, John Milliken: Vice presidential candidate from Louisiana, *4654*

Parks, Rosa: Mass boycott by civil rights protesters, *2849*

Parrant, Pierre "Pig's Eye": Minnesota state capital, *4339*

Parry, Will H.: Federal Trade Commission, *4922*

Parsons, Albert: Labor activists to be executed, *2559*

Parsons, James Benton: African-American judge to serve on a federal district court, *1987*
African-American to serve as chief justice of a state supreme court, *4420*

Parsons, Lucy: Industrial Workers of the World (Wobblies) convention, *2885*

Parsons, Richard C.: Marshal of the Supreme Court, *4701*

Pass, Charles: Casting of the Liberty Bell, *1108*

Pastorius, Francis Daniel: Protest against slavery made by a religious group in the New World, *4226*

Paterson, William: Creation of federal courts, *1970*
Nominee for associate justice of the Supreme Court to be rejected by the Senate, *4752*
Prosecution under the Sedition Act, *3854*
Supreme Court case challenging the validity of an act of Congress, *4711*
Supreme Court justice who had been a state governor, *4753*
Supreme Court justice who had served in the Senate, *4754*
Supreme Court justices born outside the United States, *4749*

Paul, Alice: Proposal for a constitutional amendment mandating equal legal rights for women and men, *1963*

Paul, William M.: Naval militia established by a state, *2665*

Paul VI, Pope: Pope to visit the United States, *2390*

President to meet with a pope in the United States, *3431*

Paulding, James Kirke: Comic political history of the United States, *1073*

Payne, Sereno E.: House majority leader, *1567*

Payton, Carolyn Robertson: Peace Corps, *2288*

Peabody, Charles A.: Presidential executive order to be numbered, *3406*

Pearson, Levi: Challenge to school segregation in the South, *1928*

Pearson, Richmond Mumford: State governor to be impeached and convicted, *4488*

Pearsons, Hiram: Mayor of Chicago, IL, *1307*

Peek, George Nelson: Agricultural Adjustment Administration, *4118*

Federal trade policy executive committee, *4930*

Peers, William R.: American military massacre of political importance, *2650*

Pelz, Paul J.: Library of Congress building, *2066*

Peña, Federico Fabian: Latino mayor of a city without a large Latino population, *1346*

Pendleton, Florence: State flag for Washington, DC, *1903*

Pendleton, George H.: Federal civil service reform law that was effective, *2028*

Penelas, Alex: Executive Mayor of Miami–Dade County, FL, *1362*

Penn, William: Colonial legislature whose upper and lower houses had terms of differing lengths, *1476*

Colony requiring rotation in public office, *1419*

Colony to change from a bicameral to a unicameral legislature, *1478*

Mayor of Philadelphia, PA, *1296*

Pennsylvania colonial governor, *1458*

Pennsylvania Day, *2227*

Pennsylvania state capital, *4309*

Plan for the union of the British colonies, *1001*

Pennington, James W. C.: Successful desegregation of public transportation, *1919*

Pennypacker, Samuel Whitaker: Sterilization of humans by a state government as a matter of public policy, *3952*

Pepper, Claude D.: Latina elected to the House of Representatives, *1628*

Peralta, Pedro de: New Mexico state capital, *4355*

Public building in the United States that has been continuously occupied, *1403*

Percy, Charles: Senate pages who were female, *1645*

Perkins, Edward Joseph: African-American ambassador to the Republic of South Africa, *2370*

African-American to become director general of the Foreign Service, *2371*

Perkins, Frances: Woman cabinet member to serve under two presidents, *1181*

Woman to serve in a presidential Cabinet, *1179*

Perot, Ross: Reform Party presidential candidate, *3367*

Perry, Matthew C.: Treaty between the United States and Japan, *2414*

Pershing, John Joseph: General of the Armies of the United States, *2626*

U.S. Army Band, *2627*

Veterans Day, *2224*

Persons, William Frank: National employment system, *2467*

Peters, Richard: Law book of federal laws then in force, *2522*

Peterson, Peter: Ambassador to Vietnam, *2372*

Secretary of state to visit Vietnam, *2307*

Peterson-Mundy, Thomas: African-American to vote under authority of the 15th Amendment to the Constitution, *1923*

Phelps, John Wolcott: American Party presidential candidate, *3305*

Presidential candidate from Vermont, *4577*

Phillip, John: Colonial court to hear testimony from an African-American, *1440*

Phillips, Channing Emery: National political convention to propose African-Americans for the offices of president and vice president, *3028*

Phillips, Howard: U.S. Taxpayers Party presidential candidate, *3364*

Phillips, John: Mayor of Boston, MA, *1302*

Phillips, Wendell: National labor party, *2929*

Pickering, John: Federal judge to be impeached, *1972*

Pickering, Thomas: Cabinet secretaries to be fired, *1149*

Pickering, Timothy: Cabinet member to serve in two or more cabinet posts, *1146*

Foreign mail service of the United States Post Office, *3145*

Senator to be censured, *1761*

Test of presidential authority over the cabinet secretaries, *1147*

Pickersgill, Mary: Star-Spangled Banner, *1088*

Pickersgill, Mary Young: Flag flown by the Continental Army under Commander-in-Chief George Washington, *1076*

Pickle, James Jarrell ("Jake"): Congressional representative sworn in before eight o'clock in the morning, *1617*

Pierce, Franklin: Attorney general to fill the position on a full-time basis, *1158*

Campaign biography by a prominent author, *2799*

Claims court established by the federal government, *1973*

Pierce, Franklin:—*continued*

Democratic president whose party was in the minority in the House of Representatives, *3712*

Elected incumbent president whose party refused to renominate him, *3403*

Former president to run for reelection on a different party's ticket, *3402*

Incumbent senator to win a vice presidential nomination, *1771*

President born in the 19th century, *3463*

President from New Hampshire, *4606*

President to be arrested, *3827*

President to deliver his inaugural address from memory, *3658*

President who had been elected to Phi Beta Kappa, *3821*

President who was younger than 50 when he took office, *3401*

President whose cabinet remained unchanged, *1159*

President whose oath of office did not include the word "swear", *3659*

Presidential candidate whose opponent had been his military commander, *3236*

Pierce, Jane Means Appleton: First Lady who was the daughter of a minister, *3582*

Pierce, Richard: Political censorship of the press, *3847*

Pinchback, Pinckney Benton Stewart: Congressional representative to serve a single day, *1595*

State governor who was African-American, *4489*

Pinchot, Gifford: Environmental meeting for state governors, *4124*

National Conservation Commission, *4125*

Pinckney, Charles: Proposal in the Constitutional Convention for civil liberties, *1824*

Proposal that senators should serve for free, *1658*

Pinckney, Charles Cotesworth: Brothers who were candidates for the presidency simultaneously, *3226*

President elected by decision of the House of Representatives, *3179*

Presidential election in which both parties nominated candidates in secret caucus, *2972*

Presidential election in which candidates were separately nominated for the vice presidency, *3180*

Presidential election in which more than one candidate declared for the presidency, *3176*

Presidential election won by the Democratic-Republican Party, *3178*

Treaty terminated by a joint resolution of Congress, *2404*

Undeclared war, *2639*

Vice presidential candidate from South Carolina, *4630*

Pinckney, Thomas: Brothers who were candidates for the presidency simultaneously, *3226*

Minister plenipotentiary to Great Britain, *2321*

Minister to Great Britain, *2317*

Political party to hold a secret presidential nominating caucus, *2971*

Presidential election in which more than one candidate declared for the presidency, *3176*

Pinkerton, Allan: Assassination attempt on Abraham Lincoln, *3445*

Pinkney, John: Political satire, *1072*

Pinkney, William: Withholding of a signed treaty by a president, *2406*

Pintard, John Marsden: Consuls appointed after the adoption of the Constitution, *2320*

Pipe: Treaty between the United States and a Native American nation, *2733*

Pise, Charles Constantine: Chaplain of the House of Representatives who was Catholic, *1558*

Pitcairn, John: Clash of arms in the Revolutionary War, *1015*

Pitkin, Timothy: Scholarly political history of the United States, *1074*

Pitot, James: Mayor of New Orleans, LA, *1300*

Territorial government to borrow money from a city, *4838*

Pitt, William: Reconciliation plan to end the rebellion of the British colonies in America, *1014*

Pius XII, Pope: First Lady to be received by the pope, *3614*

Pope to visit the United States before his election, *2385*

Place, Martha M.: State to allow execution by electrocution, *2560*

Plessy, Homer Adolph: Supreme Court decision validating the doctrine of "separate but equal" provisions for African-Americans, *4724*

Plumbe, John, Jr.: Photograph of the Capitol, *1227*

Plume, Shirley: Indian Affairs commissioner who was Native American, *2746*

Plumer, William: President to receive the unanimous vote of the presidential electors, *3171*

Presidential election in which the candidates of a single party ran unopposed, *3181*

Poell, George H.: Interstate Commerce Commission Medal of Honor, *4919*

Poindexter, John M.: National security advisor forced to resign, *1206*

Q

R

Roosevelt, Eleanor:—_continued_

Presidents who were cousins, _3558_

Roosevelt, Franklin Delano: Cabinet in which all members were sworn in at the same time and place, _1178_

Compensation paid to Japanese-Americans interned during World War II, _2652_

Day on which the president and the vice president were both out of the country, _3800_

Declaration of U.S. alliance in World War II, _2644_

Diplomatic relations between the United States and the Soviet Union, _2272_

Doctrine of unconditional surrender by a foreign enemy of the United States, _2647_

Electoral college members invited to a presidential inauguration, _3213_

Federal industrial advisory board, _4928_

Federal law providing for the education of veterans, _2704_

First Lady appointed to a federal post after the death of her husband, _3612_

First Lady to be depicted on a monument to a president, _3622_

First Lady to undertake a career of public service, _3608_

Gold hoarding order, _2094_

Industrial Recovery Act, _4926_

Large foreign aid package, _2274_

Meeting of an American president and a Soviet leader, _2277_

Midterm election since World War II in which the president's party gained seats in the House of Representatives, _1581_

National identification scheme for American citizens, _4068_

Nominating convention of a major party in which the delegates nominated a candidate without taking a ballot, _3018_

President-elect who was the target of an assassination attempt, _3449_

President elected for third and fourth terms, _3421_

President inaugurated at the White House, _3681_

President inaugurated on January 20, _3678_

President to become a godfather to a member of the British royal family, _3568_

President to conduct religious services as commander-in-chief of the Navy, _3734_

President to deliver an address on television, _3762_

President to fly in an airplane while in office, _3804_

President to go through the Panama Canal while in office, _3798_

President to have three vice presidents, _3423_

President to invite the president-elect to confer with him, _3419_

President to make a radio broadcast from a foreign country, _3760_

President to make a radio broadcast in a foreign language, _3763_

President to negotiate with the Soviet Union, _2273_

President to read a veto message to Congress, _3761_

President to ride on a diesel train, _3801_

President to use Camp David as a retreat, _3835_

President to visit a foreign country in wartime, _3805_

President to visit Africa during his term in office, _3806_

President to visit Asia during his term in office, _2276_

President to visit Hawaii while in office, _3799_

President to visit South America while in office, _3797_

President who had been defeated in a earlier campaign for the vice presidency, _3417_

President whose mother was eligible to vote for him, _3567_

President whose second inauguration was attended by his mother, _3679_

President whose third inauguration was attended by his mother, _3680_

President with a serious physical disability, _3420_

Presidential candidate to accept his party's nomination in person, _3014_

Presidential candidate to fly to a political convention, _3015_

Presidential fireside chat, _3759_

Presidential library, _3422_

Presidential pet to star in a movie, _3569_

Presidents who were cousins, _3558_

Progressive Party (of 1948), _2947_

Republican president to win reelection in the 20th century, _3426_

Republican presidential and vice presidential team to lose a bid for reelection, _3418_

Scientific public opinion polls, _2773_

Use of the term "New Deal", _3075_

Wartime population relocation order, _2646_

Woman cabinet member to serve under two presidents, _1181_

Woman to serve in a presidential Cabinet, _1179_

Roosevelt, Franklin Delano, Jr.: Child of a president to serve in a presidential cabinet, _1151_

Federal law requiring fair employment practices, _2461_

Roosevelt, Quentin: Child of a president to die in combat, _3565_

Roosevelt, Sara Delano: President whose mother was eligible to vote for him, _3567_

President whose second inauguration was attended by his mother, *3679*

President whose third inauguration was attended by his mother, *3680*

Roosevelt, Theodore: African-American to receive a White House dinner invitation, *5031*

Antitrust Division in the Department of Justice, *4955*

Armed Forces Day, *2231*

Child of a president to die in combat, *3565*

Conservation park dedicated to Theodore Roosevelt, *4156*

Expansion and comprehensive renovation of the White House, *5032*

Federal bird reservation, *4211*

Federal law on product safety, *4028*

Federal wildlife refuge, *4212*

Former president to fly in an airplane, *3792*

International conservation conference, *4126*

Irrigation project authorized by the federal government, *4198*

Monument to four presidents, *2714*

National Conservation Commission, *4125*

National monument designated by the federal government, *4150*

President protected by the Secret Service, *3413*

President since the Civil War who was a former cabinet member, *3500*

President to deliver his inaugural address bareheaded, *3668*

President to go underwater in a submarine, *3790*

President to receive the Nobel Peace Prize, *3626*

President to ride in a car, *3789*

President to visit a foreign country while in office, *3791*

President who advocated physical fitness, *3830*

President whose inaugural address did not include the word "I", *3669*

President with an environmental agenda, *4123*

Presidential candidate wounded in an assassination attempt, *3253*

Presidential election in which two former presidents were defeated, *3205*

Presidential yacht, *3788*

Presidents who were cousins, *3558*

Progressive Party (Bull Moose), *2939*

Progressive Party (Bull Moose) presidential candidate, *3326*

Republican president to win reelection in the 20th century, *3426*

State law requiring candidates to file itemized accounts of campaign expenditures, *4430*

Third party to win more than 25 percent of the popular vote in a presidential election, *3206*

Use of the term "muckraker", *3859*

Vice president who succeeded to the presidency after a president's death and was then elected to a full term, *4983*

Roosevelt, Theodore, Jr.: Child of a president to die in combat, *3565*

Root, Elihu: Secretary of state to receive the Nobel Peace Prize, *1176*

Secretary of state to travel outside the United States on official business, *1168*

Roper, Elmo: Scientific public opinion polls, *2773*

Ros-Lehtinen, Ileana: Latina elected to the House of Representatives, *1628*

Rose, Ernestine: State law giving property rights to married women, *1953*

Rose, Frederick Henry: Congressional medal awarded to a physician, *1504*

Rosenberg, Ethel and Julius: Peacetime death sentence for espionage, *2566*

Rosenberg, Leo H.: Election in which returns were broadcast on radio, *3208*

Ross, Betsy: National flag to represent the United States, *1078*

Ross, Elizabeth Griscom: National flag to represent the United States, *1078*

Ross, George: National flag to represent the United States, *1078*

Ross, John: Native American government modeled on that of the United States, *2739*

Ross, Nellie Tayloe: Mint of the United States, *2151*

Woman to serve as a state governor, *4505*

Ross, William Bradford: Woman to serve as a state governor, *4505*

Rossotti, Charles: IRS commissioner who was not an accountant or a lawyer, *4824*

Rothstein, Barbara: Judicial decision allowing physicians to terminate the life of terminally ill patients at their request, *3961*

Rousseau, Lovell Harrison: Territory annexed by the federal government that was noncontiguous, *4843*

Routt, John: Colorado state governor, *4490*

Roy, Bill: Woman elected to the Senate without prior experience in the House of Representatives, *1803*

Rubenstein, Jacob L. *See* Ruby, Jack

Rublee, George: Federal Trade Commission, *4922*

Ruby, Jack: Commission appointed to investigate the assassination of a president, *3453*

Courtroom verdict to be televised, *3867*

Ruff, Charles F. C.: Woman appointed as chief White House counsel, *3782*

Ruggles, John: Numbering system for patents, *2601*

Rumsey, Mrs. Charles Cary: Consumers' advisory board of the federal government, *4927*

Rush, Benjamin: Abolition organization, *4231*

Rush, Richard: Year in which there was no mechanism for nominating presidential candidates, *2977*

Russell, Richard: Office buildings for U.S. senators and representatives, *1241*

Russell, Richard B.: Commission appointed to investigate the assassination of a president, *3453*

Russwurm, John Brown: Political newspaper published by African-Americans, *3917*

Rusticoat, Robert: Satirical political magazine, *3896*

Rutledge, Edmund: Peace conference during the American Revolution, *1027*

Rutledge, John: Independent government in an American colony, *1428*

Nominee for chief justice of the Supreme Court to be rejected by the Senate, *4756*

Presidential candidate from South Carolina, *4562*

South Carolina state governor, *4453*

Supreme Court justice to be appointed and confirmed as chief justice, *4771*

Supreme Court justice to be appointed, confirmed, and inaugurated twice, *4775*

Supreme Court justice to resign, *4751*

Supreme Court justice with a university law degree, *4769*

Supreme Court of the United States, *4691*

Ryan, Frank B.: Vote in the House of Representatives to be recorded electronically, *1574*

Ryan, George: State to enact a moratorium on executions, *2569*

S

Sacagawea: Vote of record in which participants of different races and both sexes were given an equal voice, *4839*

Sacco, Nicola: American executions to excite worldwide protest, *2563*

Sadat, Anwar: Middle East peace treaty brokered by an American president, *2425*

Salomon, Haym: Broker to the Office of Finance of the United States, *2079*

Salter, Susanna Medora: Woman elected mayor of a town, *1323*

Salvador, Francis: Jewish person elected to a public office in the New World, *1427*

Sampson, Edith Spurlock: African-American delegate to the United nations, *2435*

African-American woman to be elected to a judgeship, *1277*

Sanborn, Frank B.: Senate committee witness to be jailed for refusing to give testimony, *1707*

Sanchez, Alfonso: Chicano radical nationalist movement, *2866*

Sanders, Jared Young: Price regulation law enacted by a state, *4956*

Sanderson, James: Performance of "Hail to the Chief", *1117*

Sanger, Alice B.: Woman employed by the executive branch of the federal government for official duties, *2030*

Sanger, Margaret: Birth control clinic, *3994*

Santa Anna, Antonio López de: Battle in which two future American presidents were combatants, *3697*

San Jacinto Day, *2196*

Sargent, Winthrop: Alabama state governor, *4466*

Mississippi territorial governor, *4852*

Sarria, José: Openly homosexual individual to run for public office, *1285*

Saulsbury, Willard: Senator to draw a gun on the Senate sergeant at arms, *1775*

Saund, Dalip Singh: Congressional representative of Asian ancestry, *1615*

Saunders, William: National political organization of farmers, *2816*

Saunderson, Robert: Mint, *2144*

Sawyer, Eugene: Incumbent African-American mayor of a major city to lose to a white candidate, *1349*

Sayle, William: South Carolina colonial governor, *1462*

Scarborough, George P.: Claims court established by the federal government, *1973*

Schlafly, Phyllis: Eagle Forum, *2839*

Schlesinger, James Rodney: Department of Energy, *2051*

Secretary of energy, *1201*

Schmitz, John G.: American Independent Party presidential candidate, *3353*

Schmoke, Kurt L.: African-American mayor of Baltimore, MD, *1348*

Schrank, John Nepomuk: Presidential candidate wounded in an assassination attempt, *3253*

Schurz, Carl: Use of the term "mugwump", *2932*

Schwab, Harvey A.: Monument to the American flag, *2713*

Scopes, John Thomas: Legal clash between evolutionists and creationists, *1950*

Scott, Albert S.: Insurance board established by a state government, *4050*

Scott, Sir Walter: Performance of "Hail to the Chief", *1117*

Scott, Winfield: Former president to run for reelection on a different party's ticket, *3402*

Political cartoon with mass popularity, *3935*

Political figurals, *2802*

President-elect to require military protection at his inauguration, *3661*

Presidential candidate from New Jersey, *4574*

Press censorship by military authorities, *3856*

United States code of military justice for governing foreign territory, *2654*

Scriven, George Percival: Federal advisory committee on aeronautics, *4096*

Seale, Robert "Bobby": Black Panther Party, *2951*

Seaton, W. W.: Volume of *Debates and Proceedings in the Congress of the United States*, *1499*

Seidel, Emil: Socialist mayor of a major city, *1326*

Vice presidential candidate from Wisconsin, *4653*

Seixas, Moses: Address to a president by a Jewish congregation, *3750*

Sequoyah: Native American newspaper, *2740*

Sergeant, John: National nominating convention held by a political party of importance, *2980*

Sevareid, Eric: Supreme Court justice to participate in a television program, *4780*

Sevier, John: Independent civil government in America, *1426*

State denied admission into the Union, *4290*

Tennessee state governor, *4459*

Sewall, Arthur: National Silver Party convention, *3316*

Sewall, Samuel: Essay calling for the abolition of slavery to be published in the British colonies, *4227*

Seward, William Henry: National party convention to which the general public was admitted, *2991*

Offer by a foreign power to mediate the Civil War, *1388*

Published records of American diplomacy, *2331*

Secretary of state to travel outside the United States while in office, *1160*

Shaheen, Jeanne: President to participate in a live chat over the Internet, *3733*

Woman governor of New Hampshire, *4529*

Shallus, Jacob: Printed copies of the Constitution, *1823*

Shannon, Wilson: Kansas territory governor, *4871*

Shantz, Phyllis Frances: Women to become Secret Service agents, *2582*

Sharkey, William L.: Vice president sworn in on foreign soil, *4978*

Shaw, Frank: Mayor of a major city to be recalled, *1330*

Shaw, Samuel: Consul to take office under the Constitution, *2318*

Shays, Daniel: Rebellion against the federal government, *1994*

Shelby, Isaac: Kentucky state governor, *4457*

Shelikhov, Gregory: Russian colonial governor of Alaska, *1430*

Russian colonial settlement, *1429*

Shepherd, Alexander R.: Modernization of the infrastructure of Washington, DC, *1889*

Sherburne, Samuel, Jr.: Attorney of the United States, *1971*

Sheridan, George Augustus: Congressional representative to serve a single day, *1595*

Sherman, James S.: Year the Republican party renominated its entire ticket, *3005*

Sherman, John: Brothers nominated for the presidency at the same convention, *3245*

Island territory annexed by the federal government, *4845*

Sherman, Roger: Public celebration of national independence, *2236*

Sherman, William Tecumseh: Brothers nominated for the presidency at the same convention, *3245*

Confederate Memorial Day, *2206*

Shields, James: Senator to serve three states, *1765*

Shipp, Joseph F.: Criminal trial before the Supreme Court, *4703*

Shippee, Amasa: American flag flown over a schoolhouse, *1087*

Shippee, Lois: American flag flown over a schoolhouse, *1087*

Shippee, Rhoda: American flag flown over a schoolhouse, *1087*

Shiras, George, Jr: Supreme Court justice with no judicial or political experience, *4770*

Shoemaker, Thomas Buckman: Citizenship granted on foreign soil, *3120*

Shoemaker, Vaughn: Character symbolizing the American people, *1132*

Short, William: Presidential appointment, *3769*

Senate's use of its constitutional power to advise and consent, *1675*

Shotwell, Luman W.: Native American tribal constitution, *2753*

Shoup, George L.: Idaho state governor, *4496*

Shriver, Robert Sargent, Jr.: Office of Economic Opportunity, *3981*

Peace Corps, *2288*

Shuckburgh, Richard: Patriotic song to achieve popularity during the Revolution, *1113*

Shunk, Francis Rawn: Child labor law enacted by a state that restricted the age of the worker, *2456*

Sibley, Henry Hastings: Minnesota state governor, *4479*

Siebecker, Robert G.: Development of the "Wisconsin Idea" of progressivism, *2818*

Siegel, Benjamin "Bugsy": Major American city founded in the 20th century, *1264*

Sikwayi: Native American newspaper, *2740*

Silverman, Edward M.: Conservative Party of Virginia presidential candidate, *3349*

Simitière, Pierre Eugène Du: Artist's design for the Great Seal of the United States, *1105*

Simms, Ruth Hanna McCormick: Presidential campaign manager who was a woman, *2774*

Simonton, John W.: Congressional committee witness to be jailed for refusing to give testimony, *1562*

Sims, Julia Isabelle: Woman to serve as foreman on a federal grand jury, *1981*

Sinclair, Upton: Federal law on product safety, *4028*

Muckraking novel of importance, *3892*

National student socialist organization, *2826*

Sinclair, Upton Beall: Negative election campaign run by media specialists, *2772*

Sirhan, Sirhan Bishara: Politician to be assassinated while campaigning for his party's presidential nomination, *3267*

Sirica, John J.: Convictions in the Watergate case, *3517*

President to tape all his conversations in the White House, *3432*

Supreme Court ruling in a criminal case in which a United States president was named as a conspirator, *4741*

Sitting Bull: Major defeat inflicted by Native Americans on regular U.S. Army troops, *2748*

Skefos, Catherine Hetos: Curator of the Supreme Court, *4706*

Skipwith, Fulwar: Consuls appointed after the adoption of the Constitution, *2320*

Slater, Samuel: Child labor law enacted by a state that included an education requirement, *2454*

Smirnoff, Steve R.: American citizen to become a Russian official, *2306*

Smith, Alfred Emanuel: Effective state arbitration law, *2452*

Presidential candidate from a major party who was Catholic, *3258*

Television broadcast of a presidential candidate accepting his nomination, *3259*

Smith, Clyde Harold: Congresswoman to advance to the Senate, *1613*

Smith, Frank: Senator barred for spending too much on an election campaign, *1785*

Smith, Georgette: Trial broadcast by the court over the Internet, *3870*

Smith, Gerald Lyman Kenneth: America First Party presidential candidate, *3335*

Smith, Gerrit: Liberty League presidential candidate, *3288*

Smith, John: Book describing the government of a British colony in America, *1070*

Colonial council, *1400*

European to visit the future site of Washington, DC, *1862*

Smith, Joseph: Presidential candidate to be assassinated, *3235*

Smith, Kate: Performance of "God Bless America", *1121*

Smith, Margaret: Federal theater project, *2018*

Smith, Margaret Chase: Congresswoman to advance to the Senate, *1613*

Senate election race in which both candidates were women, *1745*

Woman elected to the Senate in her own right, *1792*

Woman elected to the Senate without prior experience in the House of Representatives, *1803*

Woman to receive nominating votes for the presidency at the convention of a major party, *3025*

Smith, Mary Louise: Woman to serve as chairman of the Republican Party, *2967*

Smith, Orren Randolph: Confederate States flag, *1093*

Smith, Samuel Francis: Performance of "America the Beautiful", *1118*

Smith, Samuel Harrison: Guide to parliamentary rules of order, *1688*

Library of Congress, *2062*

Political newspaper published in Washington, DC, *3912*

Smith, Seba: Character symbolizing the American people, *1132*

Smith, William: First Lady who was the daughter of a minister, *3582*

Smith, William Loughton: House of Representatives election that was contested, *1539*

House of Representatives filibuster, *1547*

Smithmeyer, John L.: Library of Congress building, *2066*

Smithson, James: Smithsonian Institution, *1887*

Smoot, Reed: Senate speech that lasted from sunset to sunrise, *1730*

Snowe, Olympia J.: State to be represented in the Senate by two women, *1808*

Solá, Pablo Vicente: Governor of California under Mexican rule, *1431*

Solberg, Thorvald: Copyrights registrar of the United States, *2509*

Soley, John Codman: Naval militia established by a state, *2665*

Sotheby, William: Law barring the importation of slaves into a British colony, *4229*

Soto, Hernando de: Armed conflict between Europeans and Native Americans on American soil, *2720*

Sousa, John Philip: Performance of *The Stars and Stripes Forever*, 1120

Southgate, James Haywood: National Party presidential candidate, 3314

Sowagonish: Court martial in a colony, 1444

Sparks, William Andrew Jackson: Federal ban on fencing public lands, 4186

Spencer, Sara Andrews: Woman to address a national political convention, 2998

Spies, August: Labor activists to be executed, 2559

Spilhaus, Frederick Athelstan: United States representative to the United Nations Educational, Scientific and Cultural Organization, 2436

Spock, Benjamin: Peace and Freedom Party presidential candidate, 3352

People's Party, 2954

People's Party presidential candidate, 3357

Spofford, Ainsworth: Library of Congress building, 2066

Springer, Carol: State in which all of the top elected offices were held by women, 4289

Springs, Lena Jones: Woman delegates to a Democratic convention, 3011

Woman to receive nominating votes for the vice presidency at the convention of a major party, 3012

Squanto: Treaty between English settlers and a Native American tribe, 2395

St. Clair, Arthur: Congressional investigation, 1491

Governor of the Northwest Territory, 4850

Territory owned by the federal government, 4835

Staehle, Albert: Public service symbol of the federal government, 1135

Stalin, Josef: Meeting of an American president and a Soviet leader, 2277

President to visit Asia during his term in office, 2276

Standing Bear, Henry: Monument to a Native American, 2718

Stanford, Leland: Transcontinental railroad, 4089

Stannard, William J.: U.S. Army Band, 2627

Stansbury, Abraham: Law text published in the United States, 2516

Stansbury, Arthur: Law text published in the United States, 2516

Stanton, Edwin McMasters: Political cartoon showing the Democratic Party as a donkey, 3934

President to function as an effective commander in chief, 3405

Supreme Court nominee to die before taking office, 4750

Stanton, Elizabeth Cady: League of Women Voters, 2898

National organization to advocate universal voting rights, 2815

State law giving property rights to married women, 1953

Woman to testify as a witness at a Senate hearing, 1713

Women's rights convention, 2894

Stanton, Frank: Political editorial broadcast on radio and television, 3879

Starr, Kenneth W.: Convictions in the Whitewater case, 3521

Elected president to be impeached, 3632

President to give testimony before a grand jury during his term in office, 3522

Stebbins, Henry Endicott: Ambassador to Nepal, 2356

Steck, Daniel Frederic: Senator unseated after a recount, 1784

Stedman, Seymour: Social Democratic Party of America presidential candidate, 3319

Steele, George W.: Oklahoma territorial governor, 4879

Steffens, Lincoln: Muckraking journal of importance, 3900

Stephens, Alexander Hamilton: Peace conference during the Civil War, 1389

Session of the Confederate Congress, 1371

Vice president of the Confederacy, 1375

Stettinius, Edward Reilly, Jr.: United States representative to the United Nations, 2432

Steuben, Baron von: Foreign officers recruited to the cause of the American Revolution, 1030

Stevens, Isaac Ingals: Washington territorial governor, 4869

Stevens, John: American provincial government in Hawaii, 4274

Stevens, Thaddeus: Member of the House of Representatives to lie in state in the Capitol rotunda, 1237

Stevenson, Adlai Ewing: Campaign hosiery, 2806

Liberal Party convention, 3345

Presidential election in which a computer was used to predict the outcome, 3214

Silver Republican Party presidential candidate, 3321

Vice president from Illinois, 4678

Stewart, Virginia Gladys: Woman of American ancestry to become a queen, 2386

Stimson, Henry Lewis: Draft number drawing, 2637

Presidential airplane, 3807

Stockdale, James Bond: Candidate for vice president who had been a prisoner of war in Vietnam, 3278

Reform Party presidential candidate, 3367

Stockton, John: National procedures for electing senators, 1710

Stockton, Richard: Vice presidential candidate from New Jersey, *4628*

Stoddard, Amos: Louisiana territorial governor, *4855*

Stoddert, Benjamin: Department of the Navy, *2037*

Navy regulation barring African-Americans, *2693*

Secretary of the navy, *1148*

United States Navy, *2691*

Stokes, Carl Burton: Major city to elect an African-American as mayor, *1333*

Stone, Harlan Fiske: Supreme Court nominee to testify before the Senate Judiciary Committee, *4774*

Stone, James: African-American to enlist in the United States armed forces during the Civil War, *1383*

Stone, Lucy: National organization to advocate universal voting rights, *2815*

Stone, Roy: Federal road agency, *4092*

Story, Joseph: Supreme Court decision upholding its authority to review state court decisions on appeal, *4715*

Stotler, Alicemarie H.: Federal prosecution of a hate crime on the Internet, *1939*

Stow, John: Casting of the Liberty Bell, *1108*

Stow, Marietta Lizzie Bell: Vice presidential candidate from California, *4644*

Woman vice presidential candidate, *3246*

Strachan, Paul A.: National advocacy organization for people with physical disabilities of all kinds, *2831*

Strang, James J.: Community leader in the United States to exercise the authority of king and high priest, *4543*

Straus, Oscar Solomon: Cabinet member who was Jewish, *1169*

Jewish minister and envoy, *2335*

Streeter, Alson Jenness: Union Labor Party presidential candidate, *3310*

Strickland, John: Star-Spangled Banner, *1088*

Strong, Caleb: Session of the Senate, *1662*

Strong, John F.: Governor of territorial Alaska, *4882*

Stuart, David: Use of the name "District of Columbia" and "Washington" for the federal city, *1867*

Stuart, Gilbert: Artist to paint five presidents, *3537*

Object to be continuously the property of the White House since 1800, *5006*

Presidential portrait of importance, *3536*

Studds, Gerry E.: Sex scandals involving congressional pages, *1646*

Sturgis, Frank: Convictions in the Watergate case, *3517*

Sturtevant, Brereton: Woman to serve as a patent examiner, *2603*

Sullivan, Charles Loten: Presidential candidate from Mississippi, *4592*

Tax Cut Party presidential candidate, *3351*

Sullivan, John: Attack against the British by a state militia, *1013*

Sullivan, L. B.: Supreme Court decision giving protection to criticism of public officials, *4734*

Summers, Rachael: Federal government employees who were women, *2020*

Sumner, Charles: African-American lawyer admitted to practice before the Supreme Court, *2586*

Beating in the Senate chamber, *1704*

School desegregation lawsuit, *1918*

Supina, Lauren: White House Office for Women's Initiatives and Outreach, *3780*

Surratt, Mary Eugenia: Federal execution of a woman, *2558*

Swaggart, Jimmy: State taxation of religious goods, *4834*

Swaine, John: Law book containing laws enacted by more than one session of Congress, *2514*

Swallow, Silas Comfort: United Christian Party presidential candidate, *3320*

Swann, Darius: School district to implement court-ordered busing to achieve racial integration, *1935*

Swann, James: School district to implement court-ordered busing to achieve racial integration, *1935*

Swann, Vera: School district to implement court-ordered busing to achieve racial integration, *1935*

Swarts, Gardner Taber: Health laboratory established by a city, *4022*

Swift, Joseph Gardner: Military academy established by the federal government, *2613*

Sykes, Eugene Octave: Federal Communications Commission, *3876*

Radio Commission of the United States, *3874*

Symington, J. Fife, III: State in which two consecutive governors were forced to resign from office, *4530*

State to have a gubernatorial runoff election, *4439*

Symmes, John Cleves: Land preemption act passed by Congress, *4178*

T

Ta-Sunko-Witko: Major defeat inflicted by Native Americans on regular U.S. Army troops, *2748*

Taft, Helen Herron: Cherry trees planted in Washington, DC, *1894*

Taylor, Zachary:—*continued*
Secretary of the interior, *1156*
Senator to serve as unofficial president between two presidential terms, *3400*
Teagle, Walter Clark: Federal industrial advisory board, *4928*
Teague, Raymond L.: Church of God Party presidential candidate, *3341*
Presidential candidate from Alaska, *4593*
Tecumseh: Battle in the "Frontier War", *2738*
Native American general, *2744*
Telfair, Edward: Presidential candidates from Georgia, *4563*
Telles, Raymond: Mexican-American mayor of El Paso, TX, *1331*
Tenskwatawa: Battle in the "Frontier War", *2738*
Terrell, Mary Church: National political organization for African-American women, *2846*
Terry, David: Senator killed in a duel during his term in office, *1774*
Teschemacher, H. F.: Transcontinental telegram of a political nature, *3857*
Thomas, Clarence: Supreme Court nominee accused of sexual harassment, *4782*
Thomas, Norman Mattoon: National civil liberties advocacy group, *2827*
Political party to nominate the same candidate six times, *3016*
Thompson, Smith: Supreme Court justice who had served in a presidential cabinet, *4761*
Thompson, Thomas: American flag flown on the high seas, *1081*
Thomson, Charles: Design for the Great Seal of the United States that was accepted, *1106*
Impression made by the Great Seal of the United States, *1107*
Signer of the Declaration of Independence, *1057*
Thornton, Matthew: New Hampshire state governor, *4444*
Thornton, William: Architect of the Capitol, *1216*
Architect of the Capitol who was born in the United States, *1223*
Designs for the building of the Capitol, *1215*
Dome on the Capitol, *1217*
Federal patent office, *2599*
Patent granted by the federal government, *2598*
Superintendent of construction of the Capitol, *1218*
Thurley, Richard: State toll bridge, *4083*
Thurman, Samuel: Presidential inauguration in which a rabbi participated, *3682*
Thurman, Sandra L.: White House Office of National AIDS Policy, *3781*

Thurmond, James Strom: National convention to require a pledge of party loyalty from its delegates, *3024*
President to formally transfer the presidency to an acting president, *3440*
Senate solo filibuster to last for more than 24 hours, *1744*
Senator elected by a write-in vote, *1796*
States' Rights Democratic Party presidential candidate, *3338*
Tibbles, Thomas Henry: Vice presidential candidate from Nebraska, *4650*
Tiffin, Edward: Ohio state governor, *4460*
Tijerina, Reies López: Chicano radical nationalist movement, *2866*
Tilden, Samuel Jones: Presidential election in which neither candidate received a majority of the electoral vote, *3200*
Year in which both major parties nominated incumbent governors for the presidency, *2997*
Tillman, Benjamin: Fistfight in the Senate, *1723*
Political cartoon entered in the *Congressional Record*, *1514*
Smoking ban in the Senate chambers, *1729*
Tisdal, V. C.: Jobless Party presidential candidate, *3331*
Vice presidential candidate from Oklahoma, *4656*
Tisquantum: Treaty between English settlers and a Native American tribe, *2395*
Tiyanoga: Native American envoys received as guests of the British crown, *2373*
Plan for the union of the British colonies, *1001*
Tobin, Mary Jane: Right to Life Party, *2953*
Todd, Thomas: Wedding in the White House, *5012*
Tomlinson, Homer Aubrey: Church of God Party presidential candidate, *3341*
Tompkins, Daniel D.: Presidential team from Virginia and New York, *3385*
Toole, Joseph K.: Montana state governor, *4492*
Topliff, Samuel: News agency to cover foreign politics, *3855*
Touro, Judah: Public library established after the Revolution, *1259*
Tower, John: Cabinet nomination by a newly elected president to be rejected, *1207*
Towne, Charles Arnette: Silver Republican Party presidential candidate, *3321*
Townsend, Francis Everett: Union Party presidential candidate, *3334*
Townsend, Kathleen Kennedy: President to participate in a live chat over the Internet, *3733*
Travell, Janet Graeme: Woman to serve as a president's personal physician, *3776*

Tree, Marietta Peabody: United Nations permanent ambassador who was a woman, *2437*

Trimble, Robert: Supreme Court justice who had served as a federal judge, *4765*

Trout, Robert: Presidential fireside chat, *3759*

Troyanovsky, Alexander Antonovich: Soviet representative to the United States, *2346*

Trueblood, Thomas Clarkson: Oratory course, *3064*

Truman, Bess Wallace: First Lady to be received by the pope, *3614*

Medicare identification cards, *4058*

Truman, Harry S.: African-American territorial governor appointed by the president, *4883*

Fireproofing in the White House, *5038*

First Lady appointed to a federal post after the death of her husband, *3612*

Former president to address the Senate, *3767*

Labor dispute in which the Taft-Hartley Act was invoked, *2483*

Medicare identification cards, *4058*

National convention to require a pledge of party loyalty from its delegates, *3024*

Order integrating the armed forces, *2658*

Overthrow of a democratic foreign government arranged by the Central Intelligence Agency, *2677*

President barred under the 22nd Amendment from running for a third term, *3425*

President elected for third and fourth terms, *3421*

President from Missouri, *4615*

President protected by the Secret Service, *3413*

President to address the National Association for the Advancement of Colored People, *1929*

President to have three vice presidents, *3423*

President to pay a state visit to Canada, *3810*

President to receive an annual salary of $100,000, *3745*

President to travel underwater in a submarine, *3809*

President to watch the swearing-in ceremony of a Supreme Court justice he appointed, *3424*

Presidential address televised from the White House, *3765*

Presidential election in which the wrong candidate was declared the winner by early newspaper editions, *3209*

Presidential inauguration in which a rabbi participated, *3682*

Presidential inauguration to be televised, *3683*

Presidential press conference recorded on tape, *3728*

President's flag, *1099*

Progressive Party (of 1948), *2947*

Renovation of the White House that required the president to relocate, *5014*

States' Rights Democratic Party, *2948*

U.S. aid program to contain the spread of communism, *2280*

United States delegation to the United Nations, *2434*

Vice president from Missouri, *4683*

White House Police Force, *5036*

Woman cabinet member to serve under two presidents, *1181*

Woman to serve as ambassador to the United States, *2350*

Trumbull, John: Historical paintings in the Capitol, *1222*

Trumbull, Jonathan, Sr.: Connecticut state governor, *4445*

Truth, Sojourner: African-American to give antislavery lectures, *4247*

African-American women's rights activist who attempted to vote in a presidential election, *1956*

Tubman, Harriet: National political organization for African-American women, *2846*

Underground Railroad activities, *4234*

Tucker, Jim Guy: Convictions in the Whitewater case, *3521*

Tucker, John: Clerk of the Supreme Court, *4695*

Tucker, St. George: Legal treatise analyzing the Constitution, *1830*

Treatise on common law written for the American legal profession, *2518*

Tumulty, Joseph Patrick: White House Correspondents Association, *3726*

Turner, Frederick Jackson: Development of the "Wisconsin Idea" of progressivism, *2818*

Turner, George A.: Federal education grants to the children of deceased veterans, *3980*

Turner, Henry C.: State agency for enforcing equal treatment in employment, *2459*

Turner, Nat: Slave rebellion after the Revolution, *4246*

Turner, Ted: All-news television network, *3883*

Turner, William G.: Federal education grants to the children of deceased veterans, *3980*

Tuscalossa: Armed conflict between Europeans and Native Americans on American soil, *2720*

Tuthill, Richard Stanley: Juvenile court, *1272*

Twain, Mark: Use of the term "New Deal", *3075*

Tweed, William Marcy "Boss": Crusading political cartoonist, *3936*

Twigg, Atrong: Civil rights anthem to achieve fame, *1122*

Tydings, Millard: Bill calling for independence for Puerto Rico, *4893*

Tyler, John: Annexation of territory by joint resolution of Congress after failure to accomplish the same object by treaty, *4298*

Attempt to bring impeachment proceedings against a president, *3630*

Campaign song, *2764*

Democratic presidential and vice presidential team to lose a bid for reelection, *3394*

First Lady who died while her husband was in office, *3594*

Former president to serve as an official of an enemy government, *3492*

Former president whose death was officially ignored, *3529*

Girl born in the White House, *5020*

Incumbent president whose party refused to renominate him, *3398*

National Democratic Tyler Party presidential candidate, *3287*

Official Whig administration newspaper, *3921*

President and vice president to be born in the same county, *3465*

President born during the administration of another president, *3461*

President to bring slaves with him to Washington, DC, *4249*

President to marry while in office, *3557*

President to serve without a vice president, *3396*

President who narrowly escaped a fatal accident while in office, *3527*

President who was a former state governor and the son of a state governor, *3552*

President without a party, *3711*

Presidential commission whose creation was challenged by Congress, *1561*

Presidential veto to be overridden by Congress, *3844*

Third party to participate in a presidential election, *3189*

Treaty between the United States and China, *2412*

Vice president from the Whig Party, *5001*

Vice president from Virginia, *4665*

Vice president to succeed to the presidency after the death of a president, *3397*

Year in which three presidents held office, *3395*

Tyler, Letitia Christian: First Lady who died while her husband was in office, *3594*

Girl born in the White House, *5020*

President to marry while in office, *3557*

U

Ulloa, Antonio de: Spanish governor of the Louisiana Territory, *1424*

Underwood, John Curtiss: Interracial jury, *1974*

Underwood, Oscar W.: House minority whip, *1570*

Upham, James: Pledge of allegiance to the flag, *1097*

Upshur, Abel Parker: President who narrowly escaped a fatal accident while in office, *3527*

Usher, Hezekiah: Law book of colonial laws, *2510*

Usher, John: Colonial copyright law, *2504*

V

Vail, Alfred: Telegraph message sent from the Capitol, *1226*

Van Buren, Abraham: Child of a president to attend West Point, *3553*

Van Buren, Hannah Hoes: First Lady who was born an American citizen, *3580*

Van Buren, Martin: Campaign song, *2764*

Child of a president to attend West Point, *3553*

Commemoration of the birthday of Thomas Jefferson, *2193*

Democratic Party national convention, *2982*

Democratic presidential and vice presidential team to lose a bid for reelection, *3394*

Establishment of a treasury system, *2086*

First Lady who was born an American citizen, *3580*

Free Soil Party presidential candidate, *3289*

Incumbent vice president to be elected president in the 20th century, *3441*

Political cartoon featuring Uncle Sam, *3933*

Political party platform, *3036*

Politician to control a national convention, *2984*

President born an American citizen, *3459*

President from New York State, *4602*

President who had been elected to Phi Beta Kappa, *3821*

Presidential candidate nominated in a church, *2985*

Presidential inauguration at which both the president and the chief justice had suffered earlier rejections by the Senate, *3655*

State political machine, *2911*

Third party with an appeal broader than a single issue, *2920*

Vice president elected by the Senate, *4976*

Vice presidential candidate named Johnson, *4975*

Washington social scandal, *1882*

Whig Party resolutions, *3034*

Year in which three presidents held office, *3395*

Van den Bogaert, Meyndertsz: Confederation in what is now the United States, *2721*

Van Houten, James J.: Patent issued by the Confederate States of America, *2602*

Vanderbilt, Cornelius: President of a Central American country born in the United States, *2376*

Vanzetti, Bartolomeo: American executions to excite worldwide protest, *2563*

Vare, William Scott: Senate election in which neither candidate was seated after a recount, *1737*

Ventura, Jesse "The Body": Reform Party candidate to win a governorship, *4443*

State governor who had been a professional wrestler, *4532*

Verhulst, Willem: Permanent Dutch colony, *1407*

Verniero, Peter G.: State police department to be monitored for racial profiling, *2549*

Verplanck, Gulian Crommelin: City mayor elected by popular vote, *1306*

Vespucci, Amerigo (Americus): Use of "America" as a geographical designation, *1062*

Vidal, Gore: People's Party, *2954*

Villard, Oswald Garrison: National Association for the Advancement of Colored People, *2847*

Virginia: Attempt to bring impeachment proceedings against a president, *3630*

von Knyphausen, Wilhelm: American flag flown in battle, *1080*

Vredenburgh, Dorothy McElroy: Woman to serve as secretary of a major political party, *2964*

W

Wadsworth, James Wolcott, Jr.: Senate minority whip, *1732*

Wagenknecht, Alfred: Communist Labor Party of America, *2940*

Wagner, George S.: Senate library, *1714*

Wagner, Robert Ferdinand: Federal agency regulating labor relations, *2446*

Minimum wage law established by a city for public contract work, *2500*

Wahhaj, Siraj: Muslim to offer the invocation to the House of Representatives, *1578*

Wahunsonacock: Capital to be located at the site of Washington, DC, *1861*

Waihee, John: Hawaii state governor of Hawaiian ancestry, *4522*

Wait, William E.: National labor congress, *2879*

Waldrake, Sarah: Federal government employees who were women, *2020*

Waldseemüller, Martin: Use of "America" as a geographical designation, *1062*

Walker, D. A.: Civil Service Commission, *2027*

Walker, David: Antislavery pamphlet by an African-American writer, *4244*

Walker, Edwin Garrison: African-American state legislators, *4544*

Walker, Frank Comerford: National emergency council, *2008*

Walker, James B.: American National Party presidential candidate, *3303*

Walker, Jane Harrison: Marriage of two descendants of different presidents, *3571*

Walker, John: International exchange of fingerprints, *2531*

Senator appointed by a governor, *1756*

Walker, Jonathan: Sentence of branding by a federal court, *2528*

Walker, Joseph A.: Secret Service agent killed in the line of duty, *2581*

Walker, Quork: State to abolish slavery by a decision of the judiciary, *4233*

Walker, William: President of a Central American country born in the United States, *2376*

Wallace, George Corley: American Independent Party, *2952*

American Independent Party presidential candidate, *3353*

Woman governor of Alabama, *4515*

Wallace, Henry Agard: Defeated presidential and vice presidential candidates to die during the term they had sought, *3261*

Father and son to occupy the same cabinet post, *1175*

Political party convention at which spectators were charged an admission fee, *3022*

President to have three vice presidents, *3423*

Progressive Party (1948) presidential candidate, *3339*

Progressive Party (of 1948), *2947*

Vice president from Iowa, *4682*

Wallace, Henry Cantwell: Father and son to occupy the same cabinet post, *1175*

Wallace, Lewis: Trial of a war criminal by the federal government, *1391*

Wallace, Lurleen B.: Woman governor of Alabama, *4515*

Wallace, Mike: Political interview aired on a television newsmagazine, *3881*

Wallace, William H.: Idaho territorial governor, *4876*

Wallace, William J.: Commonwealth Land Party presidential candidate, *3329*

Waller, Edwin: Mayor of Austin, TX, *1308*

Walling, William English: National Association for the Advancement of Colored People, *2847*

Walter, Thomas Ustick: Dome on the Capitol, *1217*

Expansion of the Capitol, *1229*

Ward, Hortense: State supreme court in which all the judges were women, *4417*

Warder, John Aston: Forestry association of national importance, *4139*

Warren, Earl: Commission appointed to investigate the assassination of a president, *3453*

Year in which all the justices of the Supreme Court were graduates of a law school, *4778*

Warren, Francis E.: Wyoming state governor, *4497*

Warren, Joseph: Major action taken by the Continental Congress, *1044*

Major battle of the Revolutionary War, *1020*

Warren, Josiah: Anarchist, *2811*

Warren, Mercy Otis: American woman to write political satire and history, *1071*

Washburn, Cadwallader Colden: Brothers to serve as representatives in Congress simultaneously, *1592*

Washburn, Israel, Jr.: Brothers to serve as representatives in Congress simultaneously, *1592*

Washburn, William Drew: Brothers to serve as representatives in Congress simultaneously, *1592*

Washburne, Elihu Benjamin: Brothers to serve as representatives in Congress simultaneously, *1592*

Secretary of state to serve less than two weeks, *1161*

Washington, Augustine: President whose mother was alive when he was inaugurated, *3638*

Washington, Booker Taliaferro: African-American to receive a White House dinner invitation, *5031*

Washington, George: Address to a president by a Jewish congregation, *3750*

Annual message, *3749*

Annual reading of George Washington's "Farewell Address" in the Senate, *1720*

Appeal from the justices of the Supreme Court to end circuit riding, *4696*

Artist to paint five presidents, *3537*

Authorized plan of the City of Washington, DC, *1870*

Biography of a president, *3823*

Birthday visit made to a president by the entire Senate, *1679*

Cabinet, *1137*

Cabinet meeting, *1143*

Cabinet member to serve in two or more cabinet posts, *1146*

Campaign expenditure of record, *2780*

Ceremony at the Capitol, *1219*

Ceremony at the White House, *5005*

Chief justice of the Supreme Court to administer the oath of office to a president, *4758*

Commemorative tree planted on the Capitol grounds, *1220*

Congressional act, *1486*

Congressional eulogy for a president, *3523*

Contact between the president and the Congress, *1483*

Copyright law enacted by Congress, *2506*

Democratic-Republican Party, *2906*

Democratic-Republican presidential candidate, *3280*

Department of Agriculture, *2039*

Design for the Washington Monument, *2705*

Entry in the *Journal of the Executive Proceedings of the Senate of the United States of America*, *1673*

Execution by the Army, *2553*

Farewell address by a president, *3751*

Federalist Party, *2904*

Federalist Party presidential candidate, *3281*

First Lady, *3573*

Flag flown by the Continental Army under Commander-in-Chief George Washington, *1076*

General of the Continental Army, *2622*

General to become president, *3698*

Honorary degree awarded to a president, *3624*

Impression made by the Great Seal of the United States, *1107*

Inaugural ball, *3641*

Inaugural ball held at Washington, DC, *3647*

Inaugural chintzes, *3634*

Inaugural tankards, *3635*

Incumbent president to decline to run for re-election, *3379*

Isolationist address by a president, *2251*

Joint meeting of the Senate and the House of Representatives, *1812*

Major battle lost by American forces, *1026*

Medal awarded by the Continental Congress, *1045*

Monument to a president's mother, *2710*

Monument to four presidents, *2714*

Monument to George Washington authorized by the federal government, *2708*

Mummers' play featuring George Washington instead of St. George, *2185*

National day of thanksgiving, *2241*

National flag to represent the United States, *1078*

National holiday, *2213*

Washington, George:—*continued*
Vote to establish Washington, DC, *1865*

Washington, Harold: African-American mayor of Chicago, IL, *1345*
Incumbent African-American mayor of a major city to lose to a white candidate, *1349*

Washington, John Augustine, Jr.: Presidential estate to be opened to the public, *3404*

Washington, Lucy Payne: Wedding in the White House, *5012*

Washington, Margaret Murray: National political organization for African-American women, *2846*

Washington, Martha Dandridge Custis: First Lady, *3573*
First Lady to receive free mail franking privileges, *3583*
Mail franking privilege, *3139*
Presidential estate to be opened to the public, *3404*
Warship named for a First Lady, *3577*

Washington, Mary Ball: Monument to a president's mother, *2710*
President whose mother was alive when he was inaugurated, *3638*

Washington, Walter Edward: African-American to serve as chief executive of a major city, *1332*
Commissioner and council government of Washington, DC, *1898*
Elected mayor of Washington, DC, in the 20th century, *1900*

Waters, Maxine: House of Representatives that included a substantial number of African-American women, *1579*

Watie, Stand: Native American general, *2744*

Watkins, Charles Lee: Senate parliamentarian, *1741*

Watson, Barbara M.: African-American to become chief of a State Department bureau, *2362*

Watson, Elizabeth M.: Woman to serve as the police chief of a major city, *2545*

Watterston, George: Librarian of Congress, *2061*

Watts, Julius Caesar, Jr.: African-American congressman to deliver the Republican Party's official response to the State of the Union message, *1630*
African-American elected to a national leadership post in the Republican Party, *2960*

Wayland, Julius Augustus: Social Democracy of America Party, *2936*

Weaver, James Baird: Greenback Party presidential candidate, *3304*
Populist Party presidential candidate, *3312*
Presidential candidate from Iowa, *4578*
Presidential candidate to campaign throughout the country, *2766*

Weaver, Robert Clifton: African-American to serve in a presidential cabinet, *1191*
Department of Housing and Urban Development, *2049*
Secretary of housing and urban development, *1192*

Webb, Wellington E.: African-American mayor of Denver, CO, *1355*
Mayoral election in a major city in which both candidates were African-Americans, *1356*

Webbe, John: Political magazine, *3895*

Webster, Daniel: Secretary of state to serve in the State Department simultaneously with his son, *1155*
Secretary of state to serve more than once, *1157*

Webster, Daniel Fletcher: Secretary of state to serve in the State Department simultaneously with his son, *1155*

Weeks, John W.: Naval militia established by a state, *2665*

Weems, Mason Locke: Biography of a president, *3823*

Weiner, Susan: African-American mayor of Savannah, GA, *1361*

Welch, Joseph: Congressional hearings to be nationally televised, *1524*

Welch, Robert H. W., Jr.: John Birch Society, *2835*

Wells, Heber M.: Utah state governor, *4498*

Wells, Tom: Family Values Party presidential candidate, *3369*

Wells-Barnett, Ida B.: National political organization for African-American women, *2846*

Welt, Theodore: Radical student leader, *2812*

Wentworth, John: Mayor of a major city to fire the entire police department, *1319*
New Hampshire state capital, *4316*

Werdel, Thomas Harold: States' Rights Party presidential candidate, *3346*

Wesberry, James: Book censorship board established by a state, *3865*

West, Absolom Madden: Vice presidential candidate from Mississippi, *4641*

West, John: Colonial treason trial, *1411*

West, Thomas, Baron De La Warr: Governor of the colony of Virginia, *1453*

Weston, Russell, Jr.: Capitol Police Officers killed in the line of duty, *1251*

Westwood, Frances Jean Miles: Woman to serve as chairman of a major political party, *2966*

Wharton, Clifton R.: African-American to become chief of a diplomatic mission, *2355*

Wharton, Thomas, Jr.: Pennsylvania state governor, *4456*

Wheatland, Henry: State fish commission, *4202*

Wheaton, Henry: Reporter of Supreme Court decisions, *4700*

Wheaton, Joseph: Sergeant at Arms of the House of Representatives, *1543*

Use of the mace of the House of Representatives to keep order, *1552*

Wheeler, Burton Kendall: Progressive Party (1924) presidential candidate, *3330*

Vice presidential candidate from Montana, *4655*

Wheeler, Etta: Case of child abuse brought to court, *3990*

Wheelwright, John: New Hampshire state capital, *4316*

White, Edward: Tax act to require publication of national tax statistics, *4811*

White, Edward Douglass: Governor who was Catholic, *4470*

Supreme Court decision concerning food additives, *4725*

Supreme Court justice to be appointed and confirmed as chief justice, *4771*

White, John: English colonial settlement, *1397*

White, Stanford: Expansion and comprehensive renovation of the White House, *5032*

White, William: Prison reform society, *2808*

White Eyes: Treaty between the United States and a Native American nation, *2733*

Whiteaker, "Honest John": Oregon state governor, *4481*

Whitman, Christine Todd: Woman governor of New Jersey, *4528*

Whitman, Walt: Japanese diplomatic delegation to the United States, *2258*

Whittaker, Charles Evans: Year in which all the justices of the Supreme Court were graduates of a law school, *4778*

Widnall, Sheila E.: Woman to head a branch of the United States military, *2611*

Wilder, L. Douglas: African-American state governor elected in his own right, *4524*

Wilkes, Charles: Continent claimed for the United States, *2256*

Wilkins, James Ernest: Subcabinet member who was African-American, *1185*

Wilkinson, James: Kentucky state capital, *4322*

Louisiana territorial governor, *4855*

Willett, Thomas: Mayor of New York, NY, *1295*

Willey, John: Mayor of Cleveland, OH, *1301*

Williams, Isaac: Neutrality regulation enacted by Congress that governed the actions of citizens, *2249*

Williams, James M.: African-American unit to fight in the Civil War, *1386*

Williams, Jonathan: Military academy established by the federal government, *2613*

Williams, Roger: Colonial charter of religious freedom for all faiths, *1437*

Document calling for religious toleration in America, *1942*

Rhode Island state capitals, *4320*

Settlement to welcome refugees of all faiths, *1941*

Willing, Thomas: Private bank chartered by Congress, *2102*

Willis, Frances Elizabeth: Woman career diplomat to advance to the rank of ambassador, *2353*

Woman to take charge of an American legation, *2343*

Willis, Francis: Colonial trial for slander against the government, *1442*

Willis, Sophia: American flag flown over a schoolhouse, *1087*

Willkie, Wendell Lewis: Defeated presidential and vice presidential candidates to die during the term they had sought, *3261*

Political convention to be televised, *3019*

President elected for third and fourth terms, *3421*

Wilson, Benjamin D.: Mayor of Los Angeles, CA, *1318*

Wilson, Dorilus: Mayor of Minneapolis, MN, *1320*

Wilson, Edith Bolling Galt: Woman to act as unofficial president of the United States, *3416*

Wilson, Ellen Louise Axson: First Lady who was the daughter of a minister, *3582*

Rose garden planted at the White House, *5034*

Wilson, Henry: Military service by African-Americans to be authorized by Congress, *1385*

National Working Men's Convention, *3299*

President whose name was changed, *3484*

Vice president born in New Hampshire, *4675*

Vice president to lie in state in the Capitol rotunda, *1239*

Wilson, James: Cabinet member to serve in five successive administrations, *1173*

Independence Day after the adoption of the Constitution, *2238*

Method of electing senators, *1657*

Supreme Court justices born outside the United States, *4749*

Supreme Court of the United States, *4691*

Wilson, Milburn Lincoln: Federal Crop Insurance Corporation, *4119*

Wilson, Samuel: Use of the term "Uncle Sam" as a reference to the United States, *1131*

Wilson, William Bauchop: Cabinet secretary to share the same last name as the president, *1170*

Department of Labor, *2045*

Secretary of labor, *1172*

685

Wilson, William Bauchop:—*continued*

Senate election in which neither candidate was seated after a recount, *1737*

Wilson, Woodrow: Annual message delivered by a president in person since the 18th century, *3754*

Armistice Day, *2223*

Bird protection international treaty, *4213*

Cabinet secretary to share the same last name as the president, *1170*

Civilian government in the Panama Canal Zone, *4846*

Democratic presidential and vice presidential team to be reelected, *3415*

Election in which returns were broadcast on radio, *3208*

Federal propaganda bureau, *2643*

Formal address by a president to the Senate in the Senate chamber, *1733*

General association of nations promoted by a president, *2267*

Political news broadcast by radio, *3872*

President buried in Washington, DC, *3532*

President since Washington to submit a treaty to the Senate in person, *3514*

President to advocate the creation of a national presidential primary, *3207*

President to hold regular press conferences, *3725*

President to receive a passport while in office, *3793*

President to visit Europe while in office, *3794*

President who had been president of a university, *3499*

President who held a doctorate in a field other than law, *3497*

Presidential election in which the wrong candidate was declared the winner by early newspaper editions, *3209*

Presidential election in which two former presidents were defeated, *3205*

President's flag, *1099*

Republican president to win reelection in the 20th century, *3426*

Vice president to preside over a cabinet meeting, *4984*

White House china service that was made in the United States, *5035*

White House Correspondents Association, *3726*

Woman to act as unofficial president of the United States, *3416*

Winchester, Boyd: International copyright agreement, *2508*

Winchester, Marcus: Mayor of Memphis, TN, *1304*

Wing, Simon: Presidential election in which a socialist party participated, *3202*

Socialist Labor Party presidential candidate, *3313*

Wingate, George: National firearms lobby, *2817*

Wingate, Paine: Session of the Senate, *1662*

Wingfield, Edward Maria: Colonial council, *1400*

Virginia colonial governor, *1452*

Winslow, Josiah: Colonial governor who was born in America, *1463*

Winslow, Samuel: Patent granted by a colony, *2595*

Winthrop, George: Monument to George Washington authorized by the federal government, *2708*

Winthrop, John: Colony with a bicameral legislature, *1473*

Document claiming a special spiritual mission for America, *3068*

Election held in a colony, *1447*

Governor of the Massachusetts Bay Colony, *1455*

Treatise on politics and government, *3069*

Winthrop, Robert C.: Use of the term "manifest destiny", *2257*

Wirt, William: Anti-Masonic Party presidential candidate, *3282*

National nominating convention held by a political party, *2979*

Presidential candidate to be nominated in an open party convention, *3229*

Presidential candidate unanimously nominated by a national party convention, *3232*

Presidential election in which all the candidates were nominated at party conventions, *3186*

Supreme Court decision on the status of Native American tribes, *4719*

Wirz, Henry: Trial of a war criminal by the federal government, *1391*

Wise, John: Document expressing American democratic ideals, *3070*

Tax revolt, *4793*

Wittenmyer, Annie T.: National temperance society of women, *2857*

Wolcott, Oliver, Jr.: Test of presidential authority over the cabinet secretaries, *1147*

Wollstonecraft, Mary: Book advocating voting rights for women, *2893*

Wolman, Leo: Labor advisory board of the federal government, *2445*

Wood, Fernando: Northern city to consider secession during the Civil War, *1368*

Transcontinental telegram of a political nature, *3857*

Wood, Walton J.: County public defender, *1275*

Wood, William M.: Naval militia established by a state, *2665*

Y

Z

Geographical Index

The following is a listing of key locations in the main body of the text, arranged alphabetically by state and city. To find an entry in the main body of the text, please search for the italicized indexing number.

ALABAMA

Alabama state governor, *4466*
Alabama territorial governor, *4859*
American Independent Party, *2952*
American Independent Party presidential candidate, *3353*
American prisoner of war in Vietnam who was elected to Congress, *1806*
Antitrust law enacted by a state, *4952*
Boycott law enacted by a state, *4918*
House minority whip, *1570*
Incumbent senator to win a vice presidential nomination, *1771*
State to ratify the 16th Amendment to the Constitution, *1846*
Summer of national race riots, *2848*
Treaties for postal routes through Native American territory, *3150*
Vice president from Alabama, *4671*
Vice president who served in both houses of Congress from different states, *4977*
Woman governor of Alabama, *4515*
Woman to serve as secretary of a major political party, *2964*

Birmingham

States' Rights Democratic Party, *2948*
States' Rights Democratic Party presidential candidate, *3338*

Cahaba

Vice president to take the oath of office but never serve in office, *4979*

Cahawba

Vice president sworn in on foreign soil, *4978*

Clarke County

Armed conflict between Europeans and Native Americans on American soil, *2720*

Huntsville

Alabama constitution, *4382*
Alabama state capital, *4329*

Mobile

African-American to serve as secretary of labor, *1214*

Montgomery

American national constitution to expressly legitimize slavery, *4254*
Attorney general to be incarcerated, *1200*
Capital of the Confederate States of America, *1370*
Confederate cabinet, *1373*
Confederate constitution, *1372*
Confederate States flag, *1093*
Inauguration of a rival president, *3660*
Mass boycott by civil rights protesters, *2849*
President of the Confederacy, *1374*
Session of the Confederate Congress, *1371*
Supreme Court decision giving protection to criticism of public officials, *4734*
Tax levied by the Confederacy, *4802*
Vice president of the Confederacy, *1375*

Prattville

Birth registration uniform numbering system, *3954*

Selma

Federal law to effectively protect the voting rights of African-Americans, *1933*

Wakefield

Former vice president to be arrested, *4968*

ALASKA

Alaska Day, *2202*

President who was born after World War II, *3469*

Jonesboro

Woman elected to the Senate for a full term, *1788*

Woman to chair a Senate committee, *1789*

Woman to serve as presiding officer of the Senate, *1742*

Little Rock

Arkansas constitution, *4385*

Arkansas state capitol, *4332*

Convictions in the Whitewater case, *3521*

Sexual harassment lawsuit against a president, *3519*

Use of federal troops to enforce integration, *1931*

Washington

President who had college experience as a Senate staff member, *3505*

CALIFORNIA

California state governor, *4477*

California territorial governor, *4864*

Campaign poster showing the candidate and his wife, *2800*

Congressional representative of Asian ancestry, *1615*

Congressional representative who received a Medal of Honor and was graduated from the U.S. Naval Academy, *1612*

Congresswoman elected to serve in the place of her husband, *1601*

Congresswoman who had been an actress, *1611*

Congresswoman who was a former welfare mother, *1629*

Corrupt election practices law enacted by a state, *4429*

Court decision preventing the enactment of term limits for state legislators, *4287*

Extension of mail service to the West Coast, *3159*

Governor of California under Mexican rule, *1431*

Homestead act for desert lands owned by the federal government, *4183*

Libertarian Party, *2955*

Libertarian Party presidential candidate, *3356*

Midterm election since World War II in which the president's party gained seats in the House of Representatives, *1581*

National environmental organization, *2823*

Nationwide consumer boycott in support of workers, *2891*

Negative election campaign run by media specialists, *2772*

No-fault divorce law enacted by a state, *3956*

Peace and Freedom Party presidential candidate, *3352*

President from California, *4614*

President inaugurated on the west front of the Capitol, *3690*

President to switch parties in the 20th century, *3720*

President who had been president of a union, *3503*

Presidential candidate from California, *4575*

Presidential election in which votes were tallied electronically, *3218*

Proponent of the Single Tax principle, *2819*

Republican Party presidential candidate, *3292*

Resale price maintenance law enacted by a state, *4925*

Right-to-die law enacted by a state, *3958*

Russian colonial settlement, *1429*

Secretary of education, *1203*

Senator killed in a duel during his term in office, *1774*

Spanish governor of California, *1425*

Spy satellites, *2679*

State constitution to recognize property rights for women, *1954*

State law outlawing political caricatures, *3940*

State on the Pacific coast to be admitted to the Union, *4301*

State taxation of religious goods, *4834*

State to be represented in the Senate by two women, *1808*

Statewide automotive emissions standards, *4103*

Statewide registration of assault weapons, *4036*

Supreme Court decision invalidating a state law on First Amendment grounds, *4727*

Tax to limit immigration, *3107*

U.S. district attorney who was a woman, *1978*

Vice president to become president after a hiatus, *4994*

Wartime population relocation order, *2646*

Arcata

City council with a majority of Green Party members, *1294*

Berkeley

City to extend domestic partnership benefits to homosexual employees, *1911*

Shutdown of a college campus by student protesters, *2836*

Contra Costa County

Grant-in-aid enacted by Congress to help the states build roads, *4190*

CALIFORNIA—*continued*
Hollywood

Presidential election debates shown on television, *3215*

Irvine

Federal prosecution of a hate crime on the Internet, *1939*

Loomis

Judge who had served time in prison, *1278*

Los Angeles

African-American mayor of Los Angeles, CA, *1339*
Air pollution control bureau, *4162*
Chicano labor convention, *2888*
Congresswoman to give birth while holding office, *1624*
County public defender, *1275*
Federal protection against discrimination on the basis of sexual orientation, *1914*
Green Party, *2958*
Live atomic bomb explosion shown on television, *3878*
Mayor of a major city to be recalled, *1330*
Mayor of Los Angeles, CA, *1318*
Mexican-American political newspaper, *3925*
Politician to be assassinated while campaigning for his party's presidential nomination, *3267*
President who had been a professional actor, *3509*
Secret Service agent killed in the line of duty, *2581*

Mariposa County

Private mint authorized by the federal government, *2156*

Monterey

California constitution, *4391*
Consul to California, *2327*

Mount Wilson

Live atomic bomb explosion shown on television, *3878*

Oakland

Bird refuge established by a state, *4206*
Black Panther Party, *2951*

Orange County

County to file for bankruptcy, *2136*

Palo Alto

Presidential nomination ceremony broadcast on radio, *3013*

Richmond

Grant-in-aid enacted by Congress to help the states build roads, *4190*

Sacramento

African-American to serve as chief sergeant-at-arms of a state legislature, *4556*
President to survive two assassination attempts in one month, *3455*
Transcontinental railroad, *4089*

San Diego

"Corrections Day", *1580*

San Francisco

Admission Day (California), *2198*
African-American vice consul, *2328*
American flag made on the Pacific Coast, *1092*
Defense Department think tank, *2672*
Equal Rights Party platform, *3050*
Equal Rights Party presidential candidate, *3308*
Federal treaty signed by a woman, *2417*
Immigration of Chinese nationals, *3106*
Mayor of San Francisco, CA, *1315*
Municipal education program for men convicted of patronizing prostitutes, *2546*
Occupation of federal territory by Native American protesters in the modern era, *2755*
Openly homosexual individual to run for public office, *1285*
President and First Lady to die during the term for which he had been elected, *3531*
President to survive two assassination attempts in one month, *3455*
President to visit the West Coast of the United States while in office, *3787*
President who had been defeated in a earlier campaign for the vice presidency, *3417*
Presidential candidate from Arizona, *4594*
Presidential candidate from Washington, DC, *1893*
Single-tax proponent, *2820*
State forest commission, *4142*
Televised presidential election debate between an incumbent president and a challenger, *3222*
Transcontinental highway, *4276*
Transcontinental telegram of a political nature, *3857*
U.S. district attorney who was African-American, *1986*
United Nations conference, *2431*

Vice presidential candidate from California, *4644*

Woman mayor of San Francisco, CA, *1342*

Woman to receive nominating votes for the presidency at the convention of a major party, *3025*

Woman vice presidential candidate, *3246*

San Jose

California state capital, *4338*

Woman to serve as mayor of a major city with a population over 500,000, *1340*

Santa Ana

Federal prosecution of a hate crime on the Internet, *1939*

Sonoma

American republic on the West Coast, *4841*

Stanford

President who had been an engineer, *3498*

Vandenberg

American flag to orbit the earth, *1102*

Yorba Linda

Vice president from California, *4684*

Yosemite

State park, *4147*

COLORADO

Child delinquency law enacted by a state, *3991*

Colorado Day, *2209*

Colorado state governor, *4490*

Colorado territorial governor, *4873*

Presidential candidate from Colorado, *4597*

State law legalizing abortion for medical reasons, *3955*

State law prohibiting specific civil rights protection for homosexuals, *1913*

Vice presidential candidate from Colorado, *4662*

Women elected to a state legislature, *4546*

Aurora

State criminal prosecution for the sale of confidential personal information, *4072*

Colorado Springs

Continental air defense alliance, *2607*

Military academy for Air Force officers, *2617*

Denver

African-American mayor of Denver, CO, *1355*

Colorado constitution, *4398*

Colorado state capital, *4345*

Latino mayor of a city without a large Latino population, *1346*

Libertarian Party presidential candidate, *3356*

Mayoral election in a major city in which both candidates were African-Americans, *1356*

Military academy for Air Force officers, *2617*

National organization of Native Americans, *2754*

Presidential candidate to run for office after suffering a heart attack, *3265*

Veterans of Foreign Wars of the United States, *2701*

Woman vice consul, *2340*

Grand Junction

Election using the preferential ballot system, *1282*

CONNECTICUT

Child labor law enacted by a state that regulated hours of employment, *2455*

Colonial law providing a fixed compensation for mail carriers, *3129*

Commissioner of education of the United States, *3975*

Connecticut state governor, *4445*

Federal fish hatchery, *4205*

License plates for vehicles, *4093*

President to run afoul of the law, *3515*

Presidential candidate from Connecticut, *4559*

Reservation for Native Americans, *2724*

Speeding driver law enacted by a state, *4094*

State to ratify the 14th Amendment to the Constitution, *1844*

Supreme Court decision postulating a constitutional right to privacy, *4735*

Vice presidential candidate from Connecticut, *4643*

Vice presidential candidate who was Jewish, *3279*

Woman governor elected in her own right, *4518*

Bridgeport

Arms sales to Russia, *2266*

City to file for bankruptcy, *2135*

Hartford

City to run an airport, *1265*

CONNECTICUT—Hartford—continued

Colonial constitution, *1435*
Concealment of a colonial charter to prevent its revocation, *1438*
Connecticut constitution, *4373*
Connecticut state capital, *4312*
Law book of federal laws, *2515*
Neutrality regulation enacted by Congress that governed the actions of citizens, *2249*
President to ride in a car, *3789*
State aviation department, *4277*
State copyright law, *2505*
State government to completely privatize its computer services, *4288*
Threat of secession by a regional group of states, *4264*
Uniformed political marching group, *2801*

Litchfield

Law report, *2513*
Temperance movement, *2854*

Middletown

Factory standardization to federal specification, *4911*

New Haven

Arbitration law enacted by a colony, *4943*
Connecticut state capital, *4312*
Continental coin, *2149*
Edition of the complete *Records of the Federal Convention of 1787*, *1833*
First Lady to earn a professional degree, *3617*
Map of the United States, *1065*
Sabbath laws published by a colony, *1412*
Scholarly political history of the United States, *1074*

New London

American general to engage in treason, *1034*

West Hartford

Museum devoted solely to American political memorabilia, *1069*

Westport

Black nationalist movement, *2844*

Wethersfield

Colonial election held in defiance of the Royal Courts, *1449*

DELAWARE

Consul to die in service, *2313*

Delaware colonial governor, *1457*
Delaware Day, *2229*
Delaware state governor, *4458*
Federal corporation to encourage the purchase of electric appliances, *4931*
President of the United States under the Articles of Confederation, *3370*
Rebellion by colonists against an English governor, *1417*
Senator to be appointed as a treaty negotiator, *1762*
Senator to draw a gun on the Senate sergeant at arms, *1775*
Slave state to reject secession, *1367*
State to ratify the federal Constitution, *1828*
Vice presidential candidate from Delaware, *4627*
Woman governor of Delaware, *4534*

Cooch's Bridge

American flag flown in battle, *1080*

New Castle

Delaware constitution, *4363*
Delaware state capital, *4308*

St. Mary's City

Colonial charter of religious freedom for Christians, *1436*

Wilmington

Woman to serve as a patent examiner, *2603*

DISTRICT OF COLUMBIA

Washington

Abolition of the Senate franking privilege, *1715*
Abrogation of the gold standard, *2095*
Act eliminating silver from most coinage, *2172*
Additions to the White House, *5010*
Administrative Office of the United States Courts, *1982*
Admiral of the Navy, *2696*
Aerospace agency of the federal government, *2075*
Affirmative action order issued by the federal government, *1905*
African-American allowed to enter the grounds of Congress, *1507*
African-American elected to a national leadership post in the Republican Party, *2960*
African-American history trail, *4159*
African-American lawyer admitted to practice before the Supreme Court, *2586*
African-American militant to be elected mayor of a major American city, *1341*

African-American newspaper reporter accredited to the congressional press gallery, *3894*

African-American newspaper reporter accredited to the White House, *3893*

African-American preacher to deliver a sermon in the House of Representatives, *1566*

African-American to become chief of a State Department bureau, *2362*

African-American to become director general of the Foreign Service, *2371*

African-American to serve as chief executive of a major city, *1332*

African-American to serve as the chairman of a major political party, *2969*

African-American to serve in a presidential cabinet, *1191*

African-American woman to become a First Lady's confidante, *3597*

African-American woman to practice law, *2588*

African-American woman to serve as a federal administrator, *1999*

African-American woman to serve as a United States ambassador, *2360*

African-American woman to serve as mayor of Washington, DC, *1901*

African-American woman to serve in a presidential cabinet, *1198*

Agency for administering federal personnel policies, *2032*

Agency for disseminating information about the United States to foreign countries, *2282*

Agency overseeing national elections, *2012*

Agency promoting ethical conduct in government, *2013*

Agricultural Adjustment Administration, *4118*

Air bag requirement by the federal government, *4107*

Air-conditioning in the Capitol, *1245*

Air pollution law of importance enacted by Congress, *4166*

Airplane to land on the White House lawn, *5033*

Alcohol prohibition law enacted by Congress, *3946*

Alcohol prohibition vote taken in Congress, *3945*

All-male march on Washington, *2852*

Ambassador to Canada, *2347*

Ambassador to Israel, *2349*

Ambassador to Nepal, *2356*

Ambassador to the Soviet Union, *2345*

American flag made of American bunting to fly over the Capitol, *1094*

American Party platform, *3052*

American passport, *2250*

Annual message delivered by a president in person since the 18th century, *3754*

Annual message submitted by a president to Congress in writing, *3752*

Annual reading of George Washington's "Farewell Address" in the Senate, *1720*

Annual salary for members of Congress, *1649*

Antitrust Division in the Department of Justice, *4955*

Antitrust law enacted by Congress, *4953*

Arbitration law enacted by Congress, *4945*

Architect of the Capitol, *1216*

Architect of the Capitol who was born in the United States, *1223*

Archivist of the United States, *2067*

Arms control conference held in the United States, *2269*

Army officer to occupy the nation's highest military post and its highest nonelective civilian post, *2628*

Army organization under the Constitution, *2623*

Army war college, *2616*

Arrangement of desks according to party, *1716*

Articulation of the Monroe Doctrine, *2254*

Attempt to bring impeachment proceedings against a president, *3630*

Attorney general to head the Department of Justice, *1162*

Attorney general to plead guilty to a criminal offense, *1196*

Attorney general whose father had also served as attorney general, *1194*

Authorized plan of the City of Washington, DC, *1870*

Ban on African-American slaves as mail carriers, *3149*

Ban on sex discrimination in hiring by the federal government, *1967*

Bank deposit insurance law enacted by Congress, *2112*

Banking reform after the Civil War, *2108*

Bankruptcy act, *4909*

Bathtubs in the Capitol, *1233*

Beating in the Senate chamber, *1704*

Bill bearing the likeness of a president, *2161*

Bill to depict both sides of the Great Seal of the United States, *2169*

Bird protection international treaty, *4213*

Block of buildings constructed in Washington, DC, *1873*

Bonus Army, *2829*

Bonus paid to members of Congress by themselves, *1651*

British monarch to address Congress, *2393*

Brothers to serve as representatives in Congress simultaneously, *1592*

Building erected in Washington, DC, by the federal government, *1872*

Bureau of Engraving and Printing, *2159*

Bureau of Internal Revenue, *4803*

Bureau of Mines, *4189*

Cabinet appointee on record as having been rejected by the Senate, *1154*

DISTRICT OF COLUMBIA—Washington—
continued

Cabinet appointee to be rejected by the Senate, *1150*

Cabinet conference to be televised, *1184*

Cabinet in which all members were sworn in at the same time and place, *1178*

Cabinet in which two secretaries had the same last name, *1166*

Cabinet meeting attended by a foreign national, *1190*

Cabinet member convicted of a crime, *1177*

Cabinet member to address a joint session of Congress, *1180*

Cabinet member to serve in four different capacities, *1195*

Cabinet member who was Catholic, *1153*

Cabinet member who was Jewish, *1169*

Cabinet member who was the brother of the president, *1189*

Cabinet nomination by a newly elected president to be rejected, *1207*

Cabinet officer impeached by the House of Representatives, *1163*

Cabinet secretary to share the same last name as the president, *1170*

Cabinet session to be broadcast on radio and television, *1186*

Campaign committee appointed by a political party, *2761*

Campaign finance law allowing members of the House to pocket leftover campaign funds, *1577*

Campaign finance reform proposal, *2783*

Campaign funding organization for political candidates who support legal abortion, *2791*

Capital to be located at the site of Washington, DC, *1861*

Capitol Hill employees to unionize, *2492*

Capitol Police Officers killed in the line of duty, *1251*

Cartoon unit run by a government, *3941*

Catalog of government publications, *2055*

Censorship of the Internet, *3869*

Census Bureau permanent organization, *3091*

Census compiled by machines, *3089*

Census compiled in part from statistics obtained by mail, *3096*

Census in which the national population exceeded 200 million, *3095*

Census that included deaf, mute, and blind people, *3086*

Central administration for all branches of the military, *2629*

Central statistical board, *3093*

Ceremony at the Capitol, *1219*

Ceremony at the White House, *5005*

Changes in the American flag to be authorized by Congress, *1085*

Chaplain of the House of Representatives who was a Catholic priest, *1582*

Chaplain of the House of Representatives who was Catholic, *1558*

Chemical arms control treaty, *2428*

Cherry trees planted in Washington, DC, *1894*

Chief executive-elect of a foreign country to serve in a diplomatic position in Washington, *2342*

Chief justice of the Supreme Court to lie in state in the Capitol rotunda, *1246*

Chief justice of the Supreme Court who had served as president of the United States, *4773*

Chief Justice to wear long pants at his inauguration, *4766*

Child born in the White House, *5009*

Child born in the White House to a president, *5030*

Child of a president to die during his father's term in office, *3548*

Child of a president to serve in a presidential cabinet, *1151*

Child of a president to serve in the House of Representatives, *1593*

Child of a president to serve in the Senate, *1790*

Children's Bureau, *3993*

Circulating library in Washington, DC, *1877*

Civil Aeronautics Authority, *4101*

Civil Defense director, *2675*

Civil rights law enacted by Congress, *1921*

Civil Service Commission, *2027*

Claims by Native Americans for compensation for confiscated land, *2741*

Claims court established by the federal government, *1973*

Clerical help for congressional committees, *1502*

Collection of White House china, *5028*

Collective bargaining agency for the federal government, *2447*

College in Washington, DC, *1871*

Commemoration of the birthday of Abraham Lincoln, *2201*

Commemoration of the birthday of Thomas Jefferson, *2193*

Commemorative postage stamp depicting a First Lady, *3168*

Commemorative tree planted on the Capitol grounds, *1220*

Commerce court established by the federal government, *1977*

Commission appointed to investigate the assassination of a president, *3453*

Commission government for Washington, DC, *1891*

Commissioner and council government of Washington, DC, *1898*

DISTRICT OF COLUMBIA—Washington—continued

Department of Education, *2040*

Department of Energy, *2051*

Department of Health and Human Services, *2052*

Department of Health, Education, and Welfare, *2048*

Department of Housing and Urban Development, *2049*

Department of Justice, *2041*

Department of Labor, *2045*

Department of the Air Force, *2047*

Department of the Interior, *2038*

Department of Transportation, *2050*

Department of Veterans Affairs, *2053*

Deportation of aliens authorized by Congress, *3102*

Design for a statue for the raised Capitol dome, *1232*

Design for the Great Seal of the United States that was accepted, *1106*

Design for the Washington Monument, *2705*

Design for Washington, DC, *1868*

Designs for the building of the Capitol, *1215*

Designs for the building of the White House, *5004*

Detailed financial statement for the federal government, *2100*

Distinguished foreign personage to stay at the White House as a houseguest, *5016*

Dome on the Capitol, *1217*

Doomsday plan, *2683*

Draft law enacted by Congress during peacetime, *2636*

Draft law enacted by Congress during wartime, *2634*

Draft number drawing, *2637*

Drug control law enacted by Congress, *4063*

E-mail addresses for officials of the federal government, *2004*

Easter Egg roll at the White House, *5026*

Economic Cooperation Administration, *2283*

Edition of the *United States Statutes at Large*, *2521*

Elected mayor of Washington, DC, in the 20th century, *1900*

Elected president to be impeached, *3632*

Electoral college members invited to a presidential inauguration, *3213*

Electric power in the Capitol, *1240*

Electronic anti-counterfeiting features in U.S. currency, *2174*

Elevators in the Capitol, *1238*

Emancipation proclamation, *4255*

Embargo by the federal government, *4910*

Emergency housing corporation, *4046*

Employer's Liability Act enacted by Congress, *4052*

Environmental meeting for state governors, *4124*

Espionage budget made public, *2684*

European to visit the future site of Washington, DC, *1862*

Executive Office of the President, *3773*

Expansion and comprehensive renovation of the White House, *5032*

Expansion of the Capitol, *1229*

Express mail, *3153*

Farm credit administration, *4116*

Father and son to occupy the same cabinet post, *1175*

Father and son who were senators at the same session, *1764*

Father-mother-son senatorial dynasty, *1787*

Federal advisory committee on aeronautics, *4096*

Federal agency charged with protecting whistleblowers in the federal government, *2014*

Federal agency chief to lie in state in the Capitol rotunda, *1249*

Federal agency for administering credit unions, *2124*

Federal agency for national emergency management, *2015*

Federal agency for the gathering of foreign intelligence, *2674*

Federal agency for the support of economic development in Latin America and the Caribbean, *2291*

Federal agency promoting safe transportation, *4106*

Federal agency regulating labor relations, *2446*

Federal agency to regulate broadcast media, *3875*

Federal agency to regulate the securities markets, *2139*

Federal agency to support civilian scientific research, *2074*

Federal agency with safety oversight of defense nuclear facilities, *2610*

Federal aid program for primary and secondary schools, *3982*

Federal aid to libraries, *2068*

Federal AIDS policy coordinator, *4038*

Federal Alcohol Control Administration, *3947*

Federal arbitration board for labor disputes, *2451*

Federal archiving agency, *2056*

Federal attempt to address racial discrimination in employment, *1927*

Federal ban on fencing public lands, *4186*

Federal ban on the importation of African slaves, *4241*

Federal bird protection agency, *4207*

Federal Bureau of Investigation, *2532*

Federal cemetery containing the remains of both Union and Confederate soldiers, *2669*

Income tax levied by Congress in peactime, *4807*

Increase in the travel expenses allowed to members of Congress, *1650*

Incumbent president to testify before a committee of Congress, *1575*

Incumbent vice president to be elected president in the 20th century, *3441*

Independent agency for administering Social Security, *4074*

Independent disarmament agency, *2609*

Independent government agency to oversee political campaign contributions, *2790*

Independent intelligence organization, *2671*

Indian Affairs commissioner who was Native American, *2746*

Industrial Recovery Act, *4926*

Industrial Reform Party presidential candidate, *3309*

Inheritance tax levied by Congress, *4804*

Initiative guaranteeing homeless people overnight shelter, *4048*

Internal Revenue Code, *4818*

Internal Revenue Service, *4819*

International conservation conference, *4126*

International Conservative Congress, *2842*

International Monetary Fund meeting, *2097*

International treaty rejected by the Senate, *2409*

Internet march on Washington, *2843*

Interstate legislative conference, *4550*

Irrigation law enacted by Congress, *4194*

IRS commissioner who was not an accountant or a lawyer, *4824*

Issue of *Register of Debates in Congress*, *1494*

Issue of the *Congressional Record*, *1511*

Jewish woman to serve as a Supreme Court justice, *4783*

Joint session of Congress to meet in the Capitol, *1816*

Journalist arrested by the Senate, *1703*

Judicial test of the Sherman Antitrust Act, *4954*

Kitchen cabinet of unofficial presidential advisors, *1152*

Labor bureau of the federal government, *2442*

Labor union chartered by the federal government, *2490*

Landscaping of the Capitol grounds, *1224*

Large-scale federal jobs-creation programs, *2468*

Large-scale hostage crisis, *2296*

Law limiting the use of Social Security numbers, *4069*

Law making identity theft a federal crime, *4071*

Law making misuse of Social Security numbers a federal crime, *4070*

Law requiring registration of congressional lobbyists, *1521*

Legal recognition of the term "District of Columbia", *1892*

Legal tender, *2160*

Letter written in the White House by a president, *5007*

Liberty loans, *2091*

Librarian of Congress, *2061*

Librarian of the Supreme Court, *2065*

Library in the White House, *5023*

Library of Congress, *2062*

Library of Congress building, *2066*

Library of the Supreme Court, *2063*

Library of U.S. foreign-policy papers on Africa and the Caribbean, *2069*

Limitations on senatorial earnings from honoraria, *1750*

Loan made by the United States to a war ally, *2090*

Location in Washington, DC, of the State Department, *1875*

Location in Washington, DC, of the Treasury Department, *1876*

Magazine of the federal government, *3902*

Mail franking privilege, *3139*

Mail fraud law enacted by Congress, *3162*

Mandatory congressional 30-day summer recess, *1526*

Marijuana ban enacted by Congress, *4064*

Marshal of the Supreme Court, *4701*

Mass return of military decorations by war veterans, *2863*

Mayor of a major American city arrested on drug charges, *1352*

Meat inspection law enacted by Congress, *4023*

Mediation agency for railroads and commercial aviation, *4099*

Meeting of the House of Representatives in its present location, *1563*

Meeting place of the House of Representatives in Washington, DC, *1553*

Meeting place of the Senate in Washington, DC, *1686*

Meeting place of the Supreme Court in Washington, DC, *4699*

Meeting to establish the United Nations, *2430*

Member of Congress to enter active duty in the military during World War II, *1607*

Member of the House of Representatives to lie in state in the Capitol rotunda, *1237*

Midterm election since World War II in which the president's party gained seats in the House of Representatives, *1581*

Military department of the federal government, *2605*

Military service by African-Americans to be authorized by Congress, *1385*

Minimum hourly wage of one dollar, *2499*

Minimum wage law enacted by Congress, *2498*

Mob scene at the White House, *3653*

Model community for freed slaves founded by the federal government, *4256*

Modernization of the infrastructure of Washington, DC, *1889*

DISTRICT OF COLUMBIA—Washington—
continued

President to invite the president-elect to confer with him, *3419*

President to lie in state in the Capitol rotunda, *1236*

President to make a radio broadcast from the White House, *3757*

President to make a radio broadcast in a foreign language, *3763*

President to make extensive use of his constitutional power to remove officeholders, *3772*

President to make human rights a cornerstone of his foreign policy, *3439*

President to negotiate with the Soviet Union, *2273*

President to participate in a live chat over the Internet, *3733*

President to pitch a ball to open the baseball season, *3831*

President to read a veto message to Congress, *3761*

President to receive a passport while in office, *3793*

President to receive a presidential pardon, *3518*

President to receive a salary raise, *3742*

President to receive an annual salary of $100,000, *3745*

President to receive an annual salary of $200,000, *3748*

President to receive an annual salary of $75,000, *3744*

President to request a handshake from visitors instead of a bow, *3824*

President to reside in Washington, DC, *3386*

President to resign, *3433*

President to review the nation's military forces, *3388*

President to ride on a diesel train, *3801*

President to serve without a vice president, *3396*

President to sign a declaration of war against a European power, *2641*

President to take the oath of office twice in one year, *3665*

President to take the oath of office using a nickname, *3689*

President to tape all his conversations in the White House, *3432*

President to travel to his inauguration by train, *3656*

President to use a radio, *3832*

President to use a telephone, *3829*

President to use the line-item veto, *3846*

President to veto more than 100 bills in a single term, *3845*

President to view his inaugural parade from a heated reviewing stand, *3688*

President to view his inaugural parade from a platform outside the White House, *3666*

President to visit a nation not recognized by the U.S. government, *3813*

President to visit Europe while in office, *3794*

President to watch the swearing-in ceremony of a Supreme Court justice he appointed, *3424*

President to wear long pants at his inauguration, *3652*

President who advocated physical fitness, *3830*

President who came before the Senate to discourage action on a bill, *1735*

President who came before the Senate unannounced, *1740*

President who came to the office through appointment rather than election, *3435*

President who declined to attend the inauguration of his successor, *3645*

President who did not deliver an annual message to Congress, *3753*

President who had been divorced, *3613*

President who had served as Senate majority leader, *3504*

President who had served in both the House of Representatives and the Senate, *3487*

President who narrowly escaped a fatal accident while in office, *3527*

President who was a bachelor, *3586*

President who was Catholic, *3737*

President who was sworn in by a former president, *3676*

President who was the son of a minister, *3562*

President who was the target of an assassination attempt while in office, *3444*

President who was younger than 50 when he took office, *3401*

President who was younger than his vice president, *3390*

President whose administration lost two vice presidents to death, *3392*

President whose ancestry was not British, *3460*

President whose cabinet remained unchanged, *1159*

President whose father and mother both survived him, *3534*

President whose father was alive when he was inaugurated, *3551*

President whose government included all 48 contiguous states, *3414*

President whose grandson became president, *3556*

President whose inaugural address did not include the word "I", *3669*

President whose mother lived at the White House, *3561*

President whose oath of office did not include the word "swear", *3659*

President whose parents were both alive at the time of his inauguration, *3664*

President whose party was in the minority in both houses of Congress, *3713*

Senate proceeding to be shown on television, *1749*

Senate quorum in Washington, DC, *1687*

Senate rule allowing the limitation of debate, *1734*

Senate rules allowing the referral of nominations to appropriate committees, *1712*

Senate session in the new Senate Chamber, *1706*

Senate speech that lasted from sunset to sunrise, *1730*

Senate staff furlough, *1754*

Senator expelled from the Senate for corrupt election practices, *1781*

Senator removed from a committee chairmanship against his will, *1773*

Senator to address the Senate in military uniform, *1709*

Senator to be appointed as a treaty negotiator, *1762*

Senator to draw a gun on the Senate sergeant at arms, *1775*

Senator to face allegations of corrupt election practices, *1772*

Senator to resign in a case of a fraudulent election, *1777*

Senator to serve as long-term head of a standing committee, *1768*

Senator to serve as unofficial president between two presidential terms, *3400*

Senator to serve for 30 years, *1769*

Senator to serve three states, *1765*

Senator to threaten another senator with a gun in the Senate chamber, *1767*

Senator who had been a newspaper reporter, *1794*

Sergeant at Arms of the House of Representatives, *1543*

Session of Congress to meet in Washington, DC, *1815*

Session of the Supreme Court held in its own building, *4704*

Sex scandals involving congressional pages, *1646*

Sky marshals, *2540*

Skyjacking law enacted by Congress, *4936*

Smithsonian Institution, *1887*

Smoking ban in the Senate chambers, *1729*

Solicitor general, *4702*

Soviet representative to the United States, *2346*

Speaker of the House of Representatives to serve longer than ten years, *1636*

Speaker of the House to die in the Capitol, *1634*

Speaker of the House who became president, *1633*

Speaker of the House who became vice president, *1635*

Speaker who was punished by the House, *1637*

Speed limit for highway traffic established by Congress, *4105*

Spoils system of presidential patronage on a large scale, *2023*

Standardized criteria for federal incorporation, *2003*

Standing Senate rule for the consideration of treaties, *2405*

State building located outside a state, *4281*

State dinner televised from the White House, *5041*

State flag for Washington, DC, *1903*

State of Income report released by the federal government, *4814*

State of the Union address, *3764*

State police department to be monitored for racial profiling, *2549*

State taxation of religious goods, *4834*

State to be represented in the Senate by two women, *1808*

State to cede land to the federal government, *1866*

Statue cast by the federal government, *2707*

Statue installed in National Statuary Hall in the Capitol, *1235*

Strike settlement mediated by the federal Labor Department, *2480*

Strike suppressed by federal troops in peacetime, *2479*

Subcabinet member who was a woman, *1174*

Subcabinet member who was African-American, *1185*

Summit conference on education by the nation's governors, *3985*

Superintendent of construction of the Capitol, *1218*

Supreme Court decision banning coerced confessions, *4729*

Supreme Court decision declaring a state law unconstitutional, *4714*

Supreme Court decision declaring an act of Congress unconstitutional, *4712*

Supreme Court decision giving equal legal status to men and women in the armed forces, *4740*

Supreme Court decision invalidating a state economic regulation on grounds of substantive due process, *4722*

Supreme Court decision invalidating a state law on First Amendment grounds, *4727*

Supreme Court decision invalidating a state law on the grounds of gender discrimination, *4737*

Supreme Court decision on criminal jurisdiction on Native American reservations, *4721*

Supreme Court decision on inclusion of candidates in televised political debates, *4746*

Supreme Court decision on state recognition of federal court rulings, *4713*

Vaccination program by the federal government to protect Native Americans against small-pox, *4015*

Veterans Day, *2224*

Vice president appointed under the 25th Amendment to the Constitution, *4996*

Vice president born in Washington, DC, *1902*

Vice president elected by the Senate, *4976*

Vice president from the Democratic Party, *5000*

Vice president known as "the Veep", *4990*

Vice president to be buried at Washington, DC, *1879*

Vice president to be indicted while in office, *4967*

Vice president to be sworn in by the speaker of the House, *4992*

Vice president to become president after a hiatus, *4994*

Vice president to declare the election of the candidate who had opposed him for the presidency, *3197*

Vice president to die in office, *4970*

Vice president to lie in state in the Capitol rotunda, *1239*

Vice president to preside over a cabinet meeting, *4984*

Vice president to receive a salary of $30,000, *3746*

Vice president to regularly attend cabinet meetings, *4985*

Vice president to resign as a result of a criminal investigation, *4995*

Vice president to succeed to the presidency after the assassination of a president, *3408*

Vice president to succeed to the presidency after the death of a president, *3397*

Vice president to succeed to the presidency after the resignation of the president, *3436*

Vice president who had served as Senate majority leader, *4988*

Vice president who had served in both the House and the Senate, *4971*

Vice president who had served in the Senate, *4963*

Vice president who served in both houses of Congress from different states, *4977*

Vice president who succeeded to the presidency after a president's death and was then elected to a full term, *4983*

Vice president who was younger than 40, *4980*

Vice presidential candidate from Washington, DC, *1899*

Vice presidential candidate to decline the nomination, *3227*

Vice presidential nominee from a major party to decline the nomination, *3234*

Vice president's flag, *1101*

Vice president's widow to receive a pension, *4987*

Vietnam War Moratorium Day demonstration, *2861*

Volume of *Debates and Proceedings in the Congress of the United States*, *1499*

Vote in the House of Representatives to be recorded electronically, *1574*

Vote in the House of Representatives to be tallied by machine, *1573*

Vote on homosexual civil rights in the Senate, *1915*

Vote to establish Washington, DC, *1865*

Voting machine, *1510*

Voting machines in congressional elections, *4433*

War bond issued by the federal government, *2118*

War hero to lie in state in the Capitol rotunda, *1243*

War Risk Insurance Bureau, *4053*

Warehouse legislation enacted by Congress, *4913*

Washington news bureau, *3915*

Washington social scandal, *1882*

Water pollution law enacted by Congress, *4163*

Wedding in the White House, *5012*

Wedding of a president in the White House, *5027*

Wedding of a president's daughter in the White House, *5015*

Wedding of a president's son in the White House, *5017*

White House budget office, *3774*

White House Correspondents Association, *3726*

White House Office for Women's Initiatives and Outreach, *3780*

White House Office of National AIDS Policy, *3781*

White House official who was an African-American, *5039*

White House Police Force, *5036*

White House press secretary, *3727*

Withholding of a signed treaty by a president, *2406*

Woman admitted to practice before the Court of Claims, *1976*

Woman appointed as chief White House counsel, *3782*

Woman appointed to a federal government job through the Civil Service, *2029*

Woman artist to be commissioned by the federal government, *2016*

Woman cabinet member to serve under two presidents, *1181*

Woman diplomat to hold the rank of minister, *2344*

Woman elected to the Senate in her own right, *1792*

Woman lawyer admitted to practice before the Supreme Court, *2590*

DISTRICT OF COLUMBIA—Washington—
continued

Woman to act as unofficial president of the United States, *3416*

Woman to argue for women's suffrage before a major committee of Congress, *1960*

Woman to become a Supreme Court justice, *4781*

Woman to chair a House committee, *1605*

Woman to chair a Senate committee, *1789*

Woman to hold the rank of ambassador, *2351*

Woman to preside over the Supreme Court, *4784*

Woman to serve as ambassador to a major nation, *2352*

Woman to serve as ambassador to the Court of St. James, *2366*

Woman to serve as ambassador to the United States, *2350*

Woman to serve as chairman of the Republican Party, *2967*

Woman to serve as Civil Service commissioner, *2031*

Woman to serve as presiding officer of the Senate, *1742*

Woman to serve as secretary of commerce, *1199*

Woman to serve as secretary of energy, *1211*

Woman to serve as secretary of state, *1213*

Woman to serve as secretary of transportation, *1204*

Woman to serve as the United States representative to the United Nations, *2439*

Woman to serve as under secretary of state, *2367*

Woman to serve in a presidential Cabinet, *1179*

Woman to serve on a federal government commission, *2002*

Woman to testify as a witness at a Senate hearing, *1713*

Women to become Secret Service agents, *2582*

Women to serve as federal marshals, *2541*

Women's Bureau of the Labor Department, *2443*

Workers' compensation insurance law enacted by Congress, *2503*

Year in which gross revenue from postage exceeded $100,000, *3147*

Year in which gross revenue from postage exceeded $1,000,000, *3152*

Year in which House seats were won by third parties, *1557*

Year in which Senate seats were won by a third party, *1696*

Year in which the Democratic Party controlled both houses of Congress, *1496*

Year in which the Democratic Party won control of the House of Representatives, *1556*

Year in which the Democratic Party won control of the Senate, *1695*

Year in which the Democratic-Republican Party controlled both houses of Congress, *1492*

Year in which the Democratic-Republican Party won control of the Senate, *1684*

Year in which the Republican Party controlled both houses of Congress, *1505*

Year in which the Republican Party won control of the House of Representatives, *1564*

Year in which the salary of a Supreme Court justice topped $100,000, *4707*

Year in which the salary of members of Congress exceeded $20,000 per year, *1655*

Year in which the Whig Party controlled both houses of Congress, *1500*

Year in which the Whig Party won control of the House of Representatives, *1560*

Year in which the Whig Party won control of the Senate, *1699*

Year in which three presidents held office, *3395*

Year the public debt of the United States exceeded $1 billion, *2128*

Year the public debt of the United States exceeded $1 trillion, *2134*

Year the public debt of the United States exceeded $10 billion, *2130*

Year the public debt of the United States exceeded $100 billion, *2131*

Year the public debt of the United States exceeded $100 million, *2126*

Year the public debt of the United States exceeded $5 trillion, *2137*

Year the public debt of the United States exceeded $500 billion, *2133*

Year when citizens of Washington, DC, could vote in a presidential election, *1897*

Youth conservation corps, *4127*

FLORIDA

Commemoration of the birthday of Jefferson Davis, *2217*

Family Values Party presidential candidate, *3369*

Florida constitution, *4387*

Florida state governor, *4473*

Florida territorial governor, *4861*

Latina elected to the House of Representatives, *1628*

Latino to serve in Congress, *1589*

Latino to serve in the House of Representatives, *1493*

President who had been governor of a territory, *3483*

President who served in more than one war, *3694*

Presidential primary, *3203*

Republican governor of Florida since Reconstruction, *4514*

Secretary of transportation, *1193*

Senator of Jewish descent, *1763*

GEORGIA—*continued*

Speaker who was punished by the House, *1637*
State birth registration law, *3949*
State railroad safety law, *4088*
State to abolish the laws of entail and primogeniture, *2511*
State to allow election of lower court judges, *4411*
State to ban clergymen from serving in the legislature, *1947*
Supreme Court decision barring the death penalty, *4738*
Supreme Court decision on the legality of abortion, *4739*
Supreme Court decision on the status of Native American tribes, *4719*
Supreme Court decision to be recorded, *4709*
Supreme Court dissent, *4697*
Vice president of the Confederacy, *1375*
Vice presidential candidate from Georgia, *4637*
Woman to be appointed a senator, *1783*

Atlanta

African-American mayor of Atlanta, GA, *1337*
African-American newspaper reporter accredited to the White House, *3893*
All-news television network, *3883*
Black Power advocate, *2851*
Federal penitentiary, *2576*
Martin Luther King Day, *2234*
Pinball ban enacted by a city, *4002*
Presidential candidate to run for office while in prison, *3255*
Racial bias suit in which one African-American claimed discrimination by another African-American, *1936*

Augusta

Mayor of Augusta, GA, *1299*

Crisp County

County hydroelectric plant, *4131*

Grover's Island

Shipbuilding law enacted by Congress, *2694*

Irwinville

Capture of an American president by enemy troops, *1390*

New Echota

Native American government modeled on that of the United States, *2739*
Native American newspaper, *2740*

Plains

President from Georgia, *4619*

Savannah

African-American mayor of Savannah, GA, *1361*
Georgia constitution, *4368*
Georgia state capital, *4311*
Maritime Day, *2228*
Patent issued by the Confederate States of America, *2602*
President to ride on a steamboat, *3785*
Presidential appointment to be rejected, *3770*

Wilkes County

Town to be incorporated under the name of Washington, *1257*

HAWAII

American provincial government in Hawaii, *4274*
Hawaii constitution, *4410*
Hawaii state governor, *4510*
Hawaii state governor of Hawaiian ancestry, *4522*
Hawaiian territorial governor, *4881*
Hawaiian territorial governor who was of Hawaiian ancestry, *4884*
Immigration of Chinese nationals, *3106*
Island territory annexed by the federal government, *4845*
President of all 50 states, *3428*
Senator of Asian ancestry, *1798*
State admitted to the Union that was separated by a substantial body of water, *4306*
State governor of Asian ancestry, *4517*
State ombudsman, *4280*
State to ratify the 23rd Amendment to the Constitution, *1856*
Statewide land-use program, *4192*

Hilo

President to visit Hawaii while in office, *3799*

Honolulu

Coronation on territory that would later become part of the United States, *2381*
State capital that was the capital of a sovereign kingdom, *4358*

IDAHO

Federal hydroelectric plant, *4130*
Idaho constitution, *4403*

Idaho state governor, *4496*
Idaho territorial governor, *4876*
Pioneer Day (Idaho), *2220*
Senate investigation of the FBI and the CIA, *2542*
State governor who was Jewish, *4502*
State seal designed by a woman, *4273*
Vice presidential candidate from Idaho, *4659*

Boise

Idaho state capital, *4350*
Municipal air-raid shelter, *1268*

Latah County

County created by federal law, *1263*

ILLINOIS

African-American to head a major congressional committee, *1609*
African-American to serve as chief justice of a state supreme court, *4420*
Anti-Monopoly Party, *2930*
Ban enacted by a state on the employment of women in an occupation, *2458*
Congressman from a northern state who was African-American, *1604*
Consumer Party presidential candidate, *3363*
Freedom and Peace Party presidential candidate, *3354*
Illinois state governor, *4465*
Portrait of Abraham Lincoln, *3540*
President from Illinois, *4608*
President from the Republican Party, *3714*
Seat belt law enacted by a state, *4102*
Secretary of veterans affairs, *1208*
Senate majority leader, *1725*
Senate majority whip, *1728*
Senate pages who were female, *1645*
Senator barred for spending too much on an election campaign, *1785*
Senator expelled from the Senate for corrupt election practices, *1781*
Senator removed from a committee chairmanship against his will, *1773*
Senator to act in the movies, *1800*
Sex scandals involving congressional pages, *1646*
State admitted to the Union with a population of less than 60,000, *4296*
State aid to railroads, *4085*
State ban on sex discrimination in employment, *1959*
State law establishing English as an official language, *3117*
State tax enacted to support public schools, *3969*
State to declare Lincoln's Birthday a legal holiday, *2216*

State to decriminalize homosexual acts between consenting adults in private, *1909*
State to enact a moratorium on executions, *2569*
State to ratify the 13th Amendment to the Constitution, *1842*
State to ratify the 24th Amendment to the Constitution, *1857*
State welfare payments, *3992*
States to ratify the 19th Amendment to the Constitution, *1850*
Vice president from Illinois, *4678*
Woman to serve as a federal internal revenue collector, *4815*

Alton

Eagle Forum, *2839*

Carthage

Presidential candidate to be assassinated, *3235*

Chicago

African-American judge to serve on a federal district court, *1987*
African-American mayor of Chicago, IL, *1345*
African-American to preside over the national political convention of a major party, *3001*
African-American to receive nominating votes for the vice presidency at the convention of a major party, *2999*
African-American vice presidential candidate in the 20th century, *3260*
African-American woman lawyer admitted to practice before the Supreme Court, *2592*
African-American woman to be elected to a judgeship, *1277*
African-American woman to run for vice president, *3263*
African-American woman to serve as a senator, *1809*
American Prohibition Party presidential candidate, *3307*
Anti-Monopoly Party platform, *3049*
Anti-Monopoly Party presidential candidate, *3306*
Brothers nominated for the presidency at the same convention, *3245*
Candidate of a major party to be nominated for the presidency three times, *3248*
City to build a comprehensive sewer system, *4017*
Civil rights anthem to achieve fame, *1122*
Communist Labor Party of America, *2940*
Communist Party of America, *2941*
Congressman from a northern state who was African-American, *1604*
Congresswoman who was a mother, *1600*
Continental Party presidential candidate, *3324*

ILLINOIS—Chicago—*continued*

Credentials fight at a Republican Party convention that determined the selection of the candidate, *3000*

Defeated presidential candidate to be renominated by a major party, *3249*

Farmer Labor Party presidential candidate, *3327*

Forestry association of national importance, *4139*

Hall built to house a national party convention, *2992*

Holding company worth a billion dollars, *4917*

Incumbent African-American mayor of a major city to lose to a white candidate, *1349*

Independence Party presidential candidate, *3325*

Industrial Workers of the World (Wobblies) convention, *2885*

Juvenile court, *1272*

Labor activists to be executed, *2559*

Labor Day, *2205*

Land-grant railroad, *4087*

Mayor of a major city to fire the entire police department, *1319*

Mayor of Chicago, IL, *1307*

Mercenaries arrested for planning terrorist acts on behalf of a foreign government, *2544*

Muckraking journalist, *3890*

National convention to require a pledge of party loyalty from its delegates, *3024*

National conventions to receive gavel-to-gavel television coverage, *3023*

National party convention to which the general public was admitted, *2991*

National political convention to propose African-Americans for the offices of president and vice president, *3028*

Political action committee (PAC), *2832*

Presidential candidate from Indiana, *4582*

Presidential candidate from Iowa, *4578*

Presidential candidate from Kansas, *4581*

Presidential candidate from Minnesota, *4595*

Presidential candidate from Nebraska, *4583*

Presidential candidate from Texas, *4579*

Presidential candidate from Utah, *4585*

Presidential candidate to accept his party's nomination in person, *3014*

Presidential candidate to fly to a political convention, *3015*

Presidential candidate who was present at the convention that nominated him, *3244*

Presidential candidates from Illinois, *4576*

Presidential election debates shown on television, *3215*

Progressive Party (Bull Moose), *2939*

Progressive Party (Bull Moose) presidential candidate, *3326*

Prohibition Party, *2927*

Propaganda course at a college, *3066*

Public Enemy Number 1, *2538*

Reference book of American political history, *1075*

Republican Party credentials dispute, *2993*

Republican presidential candidate chosen unanimously on the first ballot, *3239*

Republican presidential candidate to give his acceptance speech at the national convention, *3020*

Republican presidential candidate to win an election, *3238*

Single Tax Party presidential candidate, *3328*

Social Democracy of America Party, *2936*

Socialist Workers Party, *2946*

Summer of national race riots, *2848*

Theater safety codes, *4043*

Use of the term "New Deal", *3075*

Vice presidential candidate from Connecticut, *4643*

Vice presidential candidate from Illinois, *4642*

Vice presidential candidate from Louisiana, *4654*

Vice presidential candidate from Maine, *4636*

Vice presidential candidate from Rhode Island, *4648*

Woman mayor of Chicago, IL, *1343*

Woman reporter to cover a political convention, *3889*

Year the Republican party renominated its entire ticket, *3005*

Decatur

Presidential candidate to ride in a car, *3250*

East Peoria

Federal insurance program for bank deposits, *2115*

Herrin

Massacre of strikebreakers by union members, *2886*

Kaskaskia

Illinois constitution, *4381*

Illinois state capital, *4328*

Illinois territorial governor, *4857*

Moline

Agricultural Adjustment Administration, *4118*

Peoria

Mayor of Peoria, IL, *1310*

Speech by Abraham Lincoln denouncing slavery, *4252*

Treaty between the United States and Germany, *2416*

Treaty between the United States and Japan, *2414*

Treaty ending the Cold War, *2429*

Treaty entered into by the federal government after independence, *2398*

Treaty for which a president sought the Senate's advice and consent in person, *2400*

Treaty rejected by the Senate, *2402*

Treaty terminated by a joint resolution of Congress, *2404*

Treaty to reduce the number of nuclear missiles, *2427*

Treaty with a non-European nation, *2399*

Treaty with Mexico, *2413*

U.S. aid program to contain the spread of communism, *2280*

U.S. balance of trade deficit in the 20th century, *2132*

U.S. consular post, *2310*

U.S. embassy to be destroyed by a suicide bombing, *2368*

U.S. peacekeeping forces killed by suicide bombing, *2651*

Undeclared war, *2639*

United Nations conference, *2431*

United Nations General Assembly meeting, *2433*

United Nations permanent ambassador who was a woman, *2437*

United Nations Security Council resolution vetoed by the United States, *2438*

United States case to be arbitrated in the Hague Permanent Court of Arbitration, *2264*

United States code of military justice for governing foreign territory, *2654*

United States delegation to the United Nations, *2434*

United States International Trade Commission, *4923*

United States Navy, *2691*

United States officials to die in the conflict in Bosnia, *2653*

United States representative to the United Nations, *2432*

United States representative to the United Nations Educational, Scientific and Cultural Organization, *2436*

United States warship assigned to capture slave ships, *2695*

Use of "America" as a geographical designation, *1062*

Use of children's fiction as propaganda in occupied territory overseas, *2278*

Use of the term "dollar diplomacy", *2265*

Use of the term "manifest destiny", *2257*

Vice president to chair the United Nations Security Council, *2440*

Vice president who had served as minister to a foreign country, *4959*

Vietnam War Moratorium Day demonstration, *2861*

Visit by an American president to a country on the U.S. list of terrorist states, *3816*

Withholding of a signed treaty by a president, *2406*

Woman ambassador to a Communist-bloc nation, *2358*

Woman career diplomat to advance to the rank of ambassador, *2353*

Woman diplomat to hold the rank of minister, *2344*

Woman of American ancestry to become a queen, *2386*

Woman to become an assistant secretary of state, *2365*

Woman to head a congressional mission abroad, *2279*

Woman to head a regional bureau of the State Department, *2369*

Woman to hold the rank of ambassador, *2351*

Woman to serve as ambassador to a major nation, *2352*

Woman to serve as ambassador to the Court of St. James, *2366*

Woman to serve as ambassador to the United States, *2350*

Woman to serve as legation secretary, *2341*

Woman to serve as the United States representative to the United Nations, *2439*

Woman to serve as under secretary of state, *2367*

Woman to take charge of an American legation, *2343*

Woman vice consul, *2340*

World bank, *2116*

IOWA

Cabinet member to serve in five successive administrations, *1173*

Iowa state governor, *4474*

Iowa territorial governor, *4863*

Land-grant college founded under the Morrill Act, *3974*

President born in Iowa, *4613*

Presidential candidate from Iowa, *4578*

Senator to serve as long-term head of a standing committee, *1768*

Senator unseated after a recount, *1784*

State cigarette tax, *4080*

State constitution to provide for election of judges, *4412*

Vice presidential candidate from Iowa, *4651*

Woman to serve as chairman of the Republican Party, *2967*

IOWA—*continued*
Adair County

Vice president from Iowa, *4682*

Council Bluffs

Nebraska state capital, *4344*

Des Moines

Televised debate among competitors for a party's presidential nomination, *2776*

Dubuque

Post office west of the Mississippi River, *3158*

Iowa City

Iowa constitution, *4389*
Iowa state capital, *4336*

Mount Pleasant

Woman to practice law, *2587*

Oskaloosa

Community to fingerprint its citizens, *2537*

West Branch

President born west of the Mississippi River, *3466*

KANSAS

African-American unit to fight in the Civil War, *1386*
Kansas constitution, *4394*
Kansas Day, *2215*
Kansas state governor, *4483*
Kansas territory governor, *4871*
Presidential candidate from Kansas, *4581*
Quack who almost became a state governor, *4506*
Republican floor leader, *1736*
Senate minority whip, *1732*
Senator of Native American descent, *1779*
State governor to be impeached and acquitted, *4482*
State governor who had previously been governor of a territory in which his state was not included, *4487*
State law regulating chiropractic, *4029*
State to have women serving simultaneously in the statehouse, House of Representatives, and Senate, *4285*
Vice president who was of Native American ancestry, *4989*

Vice presidential candidate from Kansas, *4640*
Woman elected to the Senate without prior experience in the House of Representatives, *1803*
Woman governor of Kansas, *4526*
Woman to serve as secretary of transportation, *1204*
Woman treasurer of the United States, *2098*

Argonia

Woman elected mayor of a town, *1323*

El Dorado

Woman bailiff, *2533*

Haviland

Woman sheriff, *2535*

Kansas City

Mayor of Kansas City, KS, *1317*

Leavenworth

African-American unit organized during the Civil War, *1384*
Federal execution of an organized crime boss, *2565*
Fingerprinting in federal penitentiaries, *2530*

Nicodemus

African-American town in continuous existence west of the Mississippi, *1262*

Oskaloosa

Woman mayor with a town council consisting entirely of women, *1324*

Paola

Kansas Day, *2207*

Topeka

Congressional representatives to marry each other, *1626*
Kansas state capital, *4341*
State court of small claims, *4414*
Vice president from Kansas, *4680*

KENTUCKY

Kentucky state governor, *4457*
Presidential candidate from Kentucky, *4569*
Senator to take office despite being too young to serve, *1760*

Senator who was returned to the Senate after being defeated for the presidency, *1766*

State founded within the borders of an existing state, *4293*

State law to abolish imprisonment for debt, *2572*

Statehood Day (Kentucky), *2188*

Statement of the doctrine of nullification, *4262*

Vice president who had served in both the House and the Senate, *4971*

Vice presidential candidate from Kentucky, *4632*

Woman governor of Kentucky, *4521*

Danville

Kentucky constitution, *4375*

Floyd's Station

Vice president from Kentucky, *4668*

Fort Knox

Federal gold vault, *2096*

Frankfort

Kentucky state capital, *4322*

Hodgenville

President born beyond the boundaries of the original 13 states, *3464*

President born in Kentucky, *4609*

Lexington

Former vice president to serve as an official of an enemy government, *4981*

Presidents who were related by marriage, *3555*

Logan County

President who had killed a man in a duel, *3825*

Louisville

Liberal Republican Convention of Colored Men, *3301*

President whose body was exhumed, *3535*

Presidential candidate who was Catholic, *3242*

Secret ballot, *1280*

Straight-out Democratic Party platform, *3046*

Straight-out Democratic Party presidential candidate, *3300*

Supreme Court decision barring racial segregation in housing, *4726*

Washington

Speaker of the House who was simultaneously member, parliamentarian, and leader, *1632*

LOUISIANA

Congressional candidate elected while missing, *1622*

Father-mother-son senatorial dynasty, *1787*

Governor who was Catholic, *4470*

Important exercise of an implied power of the government, *1997*

Ku Klux Klan leader to mount a credible campaign for state governor, *4440*

Law code adopted by a state, *2519*

Louisiana constitution, *4378*

Louisiana state governor, *4461*

Louisiana territorial governor, *4855*

Orleans territorial governor, *4854*

President from Louisiana, *4605*

Presidential candidate from Louisiana, *4572*

Price regulation law enacted by a state, *4956*

Senator to win a seat that had been occupied by his father and mother, *1793*

State governor who had previously been governor of a territory, *4462*

State governor who was African-American, *4489*

State taxation of religious goods, *4834*

State to fix a time limit on legislative sessions, *4542*

Supreme Court decision validating the doctrine of "separate but equal" provisions for African-Americans, *4724*

Vice presidential candidate from Louisiana, *4654*

Baton Rouge

President elected from a state west of the Mississippi River, *3393*

Lake Providence

Congressional representative to serve a single day, *1595*

New Orleans

American citizen hanged for treason, *2557*

Commemoration of the birthday of the Marquis de Lafayette, *2222*

Confederate coin, *2157*

Express mail, *3153*

Jackson Day, *2190*

Louisiana state capital, *4325*

Mayor of New Orleans, LA, *1300*

National political science society, *3073*

Presidential campaign of the modern type, *2763*

Senator who was a practicing Jew, *1770*

Statue of an American woman in uniform, *2717*

Territorial government to borrow money from a city, *4838*

LOUISIANA—*continued*
Tangipahoa

Town known to have been founded by a woman, *1258*

MAINE

English colonial charter, *1433*
Patriots' Day, *2218*
Presidential candidate from Maine, *4580*
Senate election race in which both candidates were women, *1745*
State founded within the borders of an existing state, *4293*
State to be represented in the Senate by two women, *1808*
State to mandate the votes of its presidential electors, *3219*
State to ratify the 22nd Amendment to the Constitution, *1855*
States to ratify the 18th Amendment to the Constitution, *1849*
Vice president from the Republican Party, *5002*
Vice presidential candidate from Maine, *4636*
Woman to receive nominating votes for the presidency at the convention of a major party, *3025*

Augusta

Performance of *The Stars and Stripes Forever*, *1120*
Woman to serve as director of a state bureau of corrections, *2578*

Bucksport

Federal fish hatchery, *4205*

Machiasport

Naval battle in the Revolutionary War, *1019*

Paris

Vice president from Maine, *4672*

Portland

Maine constitution, *4383*
Maine state capital, *4330*

Rumford

Democratic senator from Maine, *1797*

Skowhegan

Congresswoman to advance to the Senate, *1613*

Woman elected to the Senate in her own right, *1792*

South Berwick

Waterpower development grant to a colonist, *4193*

Thomaston

Numbering system for patents, *2601*

Togus

Soldiers' homes established by Congress, *2700*

York

Chartered city in the United States, *1252*
City incorporated in the British colonies, *1253*

MARYLAND

African-American to actively campaign for the presidential candidacy of the Republican Party, *3033*
Biography of a president, *3823*
British colony whose charter guaranteed representative government, *1434*
Colonial ban on clergymen in the legislature, *1410*
Colonial legislature to use a mace as a symbol of authority, *1477*
Colonial naturalization law, *3100*
Community service requirement for high school graduation, *3986*
Constitutional amendment to be ratified two centuries after its proposal, *1860*
Consuls appointed after the adoption of the Constitution, *2320*
Contact between the Congress and state governments, *4261*
Maces as symbols of royal authority, *1421*
Maryland colonial governor, *1456*
Maryland constitution, *4365*
Maryland state governor, *4450*
Presidential candidate from Maryland, *4560*
Religious toleration law enacted by a colony, *1944*
Secretary of the navy, *1148*
Senator elected by popular vote under the 17th Amendment to the Constitution, *1782*
Sex discrimination case to establish the rights of fathers of newborn babies, *1969*
State ban on cheap handguns, *2543*
State constitution to ban bribery, *4270*
State to enact a conflict-of-interest law concerning its legislature, *4536*
State to have a state sport, *4279*
Supreme Court decision on the power of states to tax federal assets, *4716*

Supreme Court justice who was African-American, *4779*

Supreme Court nominee to die before taking office, *4750*

Surveyed line separating North from South, *4172*

Talk-radio host to seek the presidential candidacy of a major party, *3884*

Vice president to resign as a result of a criminal investigation, *4995*

Vice presidential candidates from Maryland, *4626*

Vote to establish Washington, DC, *1865*

Woman elected to the Senate in her own right, *1792*

Woman to appeal for the right to vote, *2892*

Workers' compensation insurance law enacted by a state, *2502*

Annapolis

Arbitration law enacted by a state, *4944*

Candidate for vice president who had been a prisoner of war in Vietnam, *3278*

Maryland state capital, *4314*

Military academy for naval officers, *2614*

President who was a graduate of the United States Naval Academy, *3703*

Baltimore

African-American mayor of Baltimore, MD, *1348*

Anti-Masonic Party, *2912*

Anti-Masonic Party presidential candidate, *3282*

Assassination attempt on Abraham Lincoln, *3445*

Candidate to withdraw from the presidential race after the adjournment of his party's national convention, *2994*

Congresswoman to advance to the Senate, *1613*

Constitutional Union Party platform, *3040*

Constitutional Union Party presidential candidate, *3293*

Convention city, *2978*

Convention to renominate a sitting president, *2981*

Credentials fight at a Democratic Party convention, *2989*

Democratic Party national convention, *2982*

Democratic Party presidential candidate, *3284*

Incumbent president whose party refused to renominate him, *3398*

Incumbent senator to win a vice presidential nomination, *1771*

Labor Reform Party, *2926*

Law magazine, *3897*

National Democratic Tyler Party presidential candidate, *3287*

National labor organization, *2880*

National labor organization for African-American workers, *2881*

National nominating convention held by a political party, *2979*

National nominating convention held by a political party of importance, *2980*

National political convention to adopt the two-thirds rule, *2983*

Political news item transmitted by telegraph, *3871*

Political party platform, *3036*

Politician to control a national convention, *2984*

President to announce before his election that he would not run for reelection, *3399*

President to make a radio broadcast, *3755*

President to travel to his inauguration by train, *3656*

President who held a doctorate in a field other than law, *3497*

Presidential candidate from Michigan, *4571*

Presidential candidate from New Jersey, *4574*

Presidential candidate nominated in a church, *2985*

Presidential candidate of a major party to be nominated at a national convention, *3230*

Presidential candidate to be nominated in an open party convention, *3229*

Presidential candidate to be nominated on the first ballot, *3231*

Presidential candidate unanimously nominated by a national party convention, *3232*

Presidential candidates from Illinois, *4576*

Presidential "dark horse" candidate, *3233*

Presidential inauguration reported by telegraph, *3657*

Roman Catholic clergyman sentenced to jail in the United States for political crimes, *2860*

Southern Democratic Party platform, *3041*

Southern Democratic Party presidential candidate, *3294*

Star-Spangled Banner, *1088*

Telegraph line to Washington, DC, *1884*

Telegraph message sent from the Capitol, *1226*

Union Reform Party platform, *3061*

Union Reform Party presidential candidate, *3322*

Use of the telegraph in politics, *2988*

Vice president from Maryland, *4687*

Vice presidential candidate from Georgia, *4637*

Vice presidential candidate from Oregon, *4638*

Woman to serve as a postmaster, *3136*

Bethesda

President to formally transfer the presidency to an acting president, *3440*

President to make public the results of a routine medical examination, *3841*

MARYLAND—*continued*
Bladensburg

Duel between representatives in Congress, *1588*
President to face enemy gunfire while in office, *3695*

Catonsville

Roman Catholic clergyman sentenced to jail in the United States for political crimes, *2860*

Chestertown

Honorary degree awarded to a president, *3624*

College Park

Airplane owned by the United States, *1998*

Cumberland

Federal highway, *4084*

Deer Park

President whose private life was harassed by reporters, *3724*

Ellicott's Mills

President to ride on a railroad train, *3786*

Frederick

Supreme Court chief justice who was Catholic, *4767*

Frederick County

Local government to refuse to obey the Stamp Act, *1006*

Ft. Meade

Cryptologic agency of the federal government, *2676*

Hyattsville

Single tax adopted by a city for local revenue purposes, *4825*

Patuxent

Jury composed of women, *1443*

St. Mary's City

Maryland state capital, *4314*

Thurmont

Middle East peace treaty brokered by an American president, *2425*
President to use Camp David as a retreat, *3835*

Williamsport

Use of federal troops to suppress a strike, *2478*

MASSACHUSETTS

African-American senator to be elected by popular vote, *1799*
African-American to give antislavery lectures, *4247*
African-American to serve as chief United States magistrate, *1992*
African-American unit organized during the Civil War, *1384*
Ban on Jesuits, *1943*
Ban on Quakers, *1945*
Beating in the Senate chamber, *1704*
Brothers to serve simultaneously as governors of their respective states, *4469*
Car insurance law enacted by a state, *4054*
Centennial celebration of the Revolution, *1036*
Child labor law enacted by a state that included an education requirement, *2454*
Child labor law enacted by a state that regulated hours of employment, *2455*
Child labor law enacted by a state that restricted the age of the worker, *2456*
Colonial ban on lawyers in the legislature, *1475*
Colonial law providing a fixed compensation for mail carriers, *3129*
Colonial law requiring towns to hire teachers and construct schools, *3963*
Colonial postmaster, *3131*
Colonial statute establishing religious qualifications for public office, *1416*
Colony to legalize slavery, *4222*
Colony with a bicameral legislature, *1473*
Compulsory education law in a colony, *3962*
Congressional representative reelected after serving a prison term, *1616*
Congresswoman to serve 18 terms, *1603*
Consul to take office under the Constitution, *2318*
Consuls appointed after the adoption of the Constitution, *2320*
Contested election in a colonial legislature, *1450*
Continental money, *2146*
Credit union law enacted by a state, *2121*
Document claiming a special spiritual mission for America, *3068*
Election board game, *2768*
Election held in a colony, *1447*
Father and son to serve as U.S. ministers, *2324*

Federal fish hatchery, *4205*

Free trade policy by the federal government, *4946*

Gerrymander, *1555*

Governor of the Massachusetts Bay Colony, *1455*

Horse racing ban, *3999*

Incumbent president who ran for reelection and was defeated, *3383*

Independence Day to be observed as a state holiday, *2237*

Insurance regulation enacted by a state, *4049*

Labor bureau established by a state, *2441*

Land trust, *4187*

Law against the celebration of Christmas, *2178*

Literacy qualification for voting, *4428*

Maine state governor, *4467*

Minimum wage law enacted by a state, *2496*

Mobilization of American troops in the Revolutionary War, *1017*

No-fault car insurance law enacted by a state, *4059*

Paper ballots, *1448*

Paper money, *2145*

Patent granted by a colony, *2595*

Patriots' Day, *2218*

Pay for colonial legislators, *1472*

Poll tax, *4789*

Postmarked mail, *3134*

President to have children, *3545*

President to have written a book, *3473*

President to publish a book of poetry, *3491*

President whose father was alive when he was inaugurated, *3551*

President whose political party was not the same as the vice president's, *3707*

President with a brother in the Senate, *3570*

Presidential candidates from Massachusetts, *4564*

Rebellion against the federal government, *1994*

Roman Catholic priest to serve as a voting member of Congress, *1619*

Secretary of war, *1141*

Senator to be censured, *1761*

Sex scandals involving congressional pages, *1646*

Smoking ban in a colonial legislature, *1474*

Speaker of the House to die in the Capitol, *1634*

Stamp tax, *4794*

State banking commission, *2107*

State board of education, *3971*

State board of health, *4018*

State compulsory education law, *3972*

State fish commission, *4202*

State gas commission, *4129*

State income tax, *4827*

State law to end de facto segregation in schools, *1934*

State seal, *4258*

State to abolish slavery by a decision of the judiciary, *4233*

State to ratify the 17th Amendment to the Constitution, *1847*

State vaccination law, *4013*

Statement of legislative independence by a colony, *1415*

Supreme Court decision invalidating a federal tax, *4723*

Territory of the United States in which slavery was banned, *4236*

Thanksgiving proclamation, *2240*

Treatise on politics and government, *3069*

Treaty between the United States and China, *2412*

Use of bullets as currency, *2141*

Vice president from the Federalist Party, *4998*

Vice president to be buried at Washington, DC, *1879*

Vice president to lie in state in the Capitol rotunda, *1239*

Vice president who had served in the Continental Congress, *4957*

Vice president who had served in the House of Representatives, *4960*

Vice presidential candidate from Massachusetts, *4625*

Voting registration law enacted by a state, *4426*

Voting requirements, *1446*

Boston

African-American state legislators, *4544*

African-American to hold a federal civil service job, *2025*

American woman to write political satire and history, *1071*

Americans killed by British soldiers in the Revolution, *1009*

Antislavery book, *4230*

Antislavery pamphlet by an African-American writer, *4244*

Architect of the Capitol who was born in the United States, *1223*

Artist to paint five presidents, *3537*

Audobon society, *4209*

Bellamy Nationalist Club, *2883*

Character personifying the United States, *1129*

City to be occupied by the British before the Revolution, *1007*

Colonial boycott of British goods, *1003*

Colonial copyright law, *2504*

Colonial gambling law for residents, *3998*

Colonial post office established by law, *3127*

Commemoration of the birthday of Benjamin Franklin, *2192*

Commemoration of the Boston Massacre, *2182*

Committee of correspondence formed in a British colony in America, *1002*

Confederation of English colonies, *1414*

MASSACHUSETTS—Boston—*continued*

Congressman to acknowledge that he was a homosexual, *1627*

Destruction of British tea shipments, *1011*

Draft law enacted by a colony, *2630*

Edition of the *United States Statutes at Large*, *2521*

Essay calling for the abolition of slavery to be published in the British colonies, *4227*

Federal judge to reduce a sentence as a protest against racial profiling, *1940*

John Birch Society, *2835*

Labor organization in a colony, *2874*

Law authorizing the penalty of death for blasphemy, *2551*

Law book of federal laws then in force, *2522*

Law forbidding Native American religious rituals, *2725*

Legal divorce in the American colonies, *3948*

Local political machine, *2901*

Major antislavery periodical, *4245*

Major battle of the Revolutionary War, *1020*

Mason known to hold high government office in the colonies, *1422*

Massachusetts state capital, *4313*

Mayor of Boston, MA, *1302*

Medal awarded by the Continental Congress, *1045*

Military organization established by a colony, *2663*

Militia, *2662*

Mint, *2144*

Minting act, *2143*

Monetary regulation act, *2142*

National anti-imperialist organization, *2825*

Naval militia established by a state, *2665*

News agency to cover foreign politics, *3855*

Newspaper published with government approval, *3904*

Newspaper suppressed by the government, *3903*

Overland mail service between colonies, *3130*

Patriotic song by an American, *1114*

Patriotic war song by an American, *1115*

Performance of "America the Beautiful", *1118*

Persecution of a newspaper editor by American revolutionaries, *3851*

Political cartoon to interfere with a trial, *3930*

Political censorship of the press, *3847*

Political crusade by a newspaper, *3849*

Politician who was openly homosexual to win a state election, *4438*

President who was admitted to the bar, *3471*

Probation system for offenders, *2575*

Reconciliation plan to end the rebellion of the British colonies in America, *1014*

School desegregation lawsuit, *1918*

Ship to carry the American flag around the world, *1084*

Supreme Court justice who was Jewish, *4772*

Tobacco tax enacted by a colony, *4075*

Urban renewal program, *1267*

Use of the name "Liberty Bell", *1111*

Use of the term "Era of Good Feelings", *1066*

Use of the word "caucus", *1287*

Brookline

President who was born in the 20th century, *3467*

Cambridge

College law school to be permanently organized, *2525*

Flag flown by the Continental Army under Commander-in-Chief George Washington, *1076*

Grand jury, *1441*

King born in the United States, *2383*

Law book of colonial laws, *2510*

Massachusetts constitution, *4359*

Political document printed in America, *1063*

Political economy chair at a college, *3063*

President who had been a college professor, *3479*

President who had been elected to Phi Beta Kappa, *3821*

President who received a college education, *3819*

State constitution to be submitted to the people for ratification, *4372*

Woman to head a branch of the United States military, *2611*

Canton

Congressional representative to be refused a seat, *1590*

Charlestown

Board of selectmen, *1409*

Military academy for naval officers, *2614*

Colrain

American flag flown over a schoolhouse, *1087*

Concord

Popular image of the Minute Man, *1133*

Dorchester

Property tax established by a colony to support public schools, *4787*

Town meeting, *1408*

Framingham

State reformatory for women, *2574*

Ipswich

Document expressing American democratic ideals, *3070*
Tax revolt, *4793*

Lexington

Clash of arms in the Revolutionary War, *1015*
War hero, *1016*

Lowell

Factory workers' magazine, *3899*
Woman to become a union organizer, *2878*

Marblehead

National naval force, *2685*

Melrose

Woman to serve as a patent examiner, *2603*

Nantucket

Prison, *2570*

New Bedford

Mayor of New Bedford, MA, *1312*

New Plymouth

Income tax levied by a colony, *4788*

Plymouth

Colonial forestry law, *4136*
Colonial governor who was born in America, *1463*
Colonial law to aid disabled veterans, *2697*
Execution in America, *2550*
Former president who was elected to the House of Representatives, *3486*
Law code of an American colony, *1471*
Plymouth Rock monument, *2711*
Property tax levied by a colony, *4785*
Statement of the principle of taxation with consent, *4786*
Thanksgiving Day, *2242*
Treaty between English settlers and a Native American tribe, *2395*

Quincy

First Lady who was the mother of a president, *3574*
Massachusetts state governor, *4454*
Minister to Great Britain, *2317*

Photograph of a former president, *3538*
President from Massachusetts, *4599*
President who became a nonagenarian, *3525*
Vice president from Massachusetts, *4664*

Rowley

State toll bridge, *4083*

South Braintree

American executions to excite worldwide protest, *2563*

Springfield

Arsenal of the federal government, *2604*
City to forbid the sale of firecrackers for Fourth of July celebrations, *2239*

Uxbridge

Woman whose vote was recorded, *1951*

Watertown

Supreme Court justice with a university law degree, *4769*

Wellesley

First Lady who was president of the student government at college, *3616*

Westborough

State reformatory for boys, *2573*

Weymouth

First Lady who was the daughter of a minister, *3582*

Worcester

African-American lawyer formally admitted to the bar, *2585*
National convention for women's rights, *2895*
President who had been a schoolteacher, *3470*

MICHIGAN

Ban on surrogate motherhood enacted by a state, *3959*
Federal law prohibiting discrimination in employment on the basis of sex, *1966*
Interracial jury, *1974*
Labor cooperatives to be authorized by a state, *2487*
Michigan state governor, *4471*

MICHIGAN—*continued*

Michigan territorial governor, *4856*
President to donate his papers to the federal government during his term in office, *3438*
Presidential candidate from Michigan, *4571*
State to ban the death penalty, *2554*
State to ratify the 21st Amendment to the Constitution, *1852*
States to ratify the 19th Amendment to the Constitution, *1850*
Tax Cut Party presidential candidate, *3351*
Vice president from Michigan, *4689*
Vice presidential candidate from Michigan, *4634*
Woman to serve as secretary of the Republican National Convention, *3021*

Ann Arbor

Microfilm editions of federal publications and documents, *2057*
Openly homosexual politican to win a municipal election, *1286*
Oratory course, *3064*
State university supported by a direct property tax, *3976*

Big Beaver Island

Community leader in the United States to exercise the authority of king and high priest, *4543*

Detroit

African-American mayor of Detroit, MI, *1338*
America First Party presidential candidate, *3335*
Congressman who was a Catholic priest, *1591*
Federal attempt to address racial discrimination in employment, *1927*
IRS Computing Center, *4822*
Local election results to be announced on radio, *1284*
Michigan constitution, *4386*
Michigan state capital, *4333*
National Right to Life Committee, *2840*
Prince of Wales to visit the United States, *2377*
Senator who had been a newspaper reporter, *1794*

Grand Rapids

African-American women's rights activist who attempted to vote in a presidential election, *1956*
Fluoridation program for a city water supply, *4031*
President from Michigan, *4618*

Highland Park

Federal bailout of an auto manufacturer, *4939*

Jackson

Founding of the Republican Party, *2922*

Royal Oak

National Union for Social Justice, *2944*

MINNESOTA

Congressional representative elected by prohibitionists, *1596*
Consumer Party presidential candidate, *3363*
Grassroots Party presidential candidate, *3365*
House majority whip, *1568*
Income tax enacted by a state, *4833*
Minnesota state governor, *4479*
Minnesota territorial governor, *4865*
Parental leave law enacted by a state that applied to both mothers and fathers, *1968*
Presidential candidate from Minnesota, *4595*
Primary election law enacted by a state, *4434*
Reform Party candidate to win a governorship, *4443*
Secretary of state to receive the Nobel Peace Prize, *1176*
State governor who had been a professional wrestler, *4532*
State to ratify the 26th Amendment to the Constitution, *1859*
Supreme Court decision invalidating a state economic regulation on grounds of substantive due process, *4722*
Trial by a panel of judges to determine the winner of a state election, *4437*
Vice president from Minnesota, *4686*
Vice presidential candidate from Minnesota, *4647*
Woman to serve as secretary of energy, *1211*

Austin

Sit-down strike, *2481*

Ceylon

Vice president from Minnesota, *4686*

Minneapolis

Mayor of Minneapolis, MN, *1320*
Militant Native American civil rights organization, *2756*
Woman to serve as mayor of Minneapolis, MN, *1359*
Women to attend a national political convention as delegates, *3003*

Ramsey County

Smart-card welfare payments, *3996*

Red Wing

Woman ambassador to a Communist-bloc nation, *2358*

St. Paul

Minnesota constitution, *4392*
Minnesota state capital, *4339*
Presidential election in which a communist party participated, *3212*
State forestry association, *4140*

MISSISSIPPI

African-American senator to serve a full term, *1778*
African-American to receive nominating votes for the vice presidency at the convention of a major party, *2999*
African-American to serve as secretary of agriculture, *1210*
Battle in which two future American presidents were combatants, *3697*
Federal flood control legislation, *4191*
Important exercise of an implied power of the government, *1997*
Mississippi state governor, *4464*
Mississippi territorial governor, *4852*
President of the Confederacy, *1374*
Presidential candidate from Mississippi, *4592*
Senator to threaten another senator with a gun in the Senate chamber, *1767*
State to repudiate a debt, *4267*
States to ratify the 18th Amendment to the Constitution, *1849*
Summer of national race riots, *2848*
Supreme Court decision banning coerced confessions, *4729*
Vice presidential candidate from Mississippi, *4641*

Fayette

African-American mayor of a major Southern city, *1334*

Jackson

African-American mayor of Jackson, MS, *1363*
Black Power advocate, *2851*

Natchez

African-American senator, *1776*
First Lady of the Confederacy, *1376*
First Lady who had previously been divorced, *3581*
Mississippi constitution, *4380*

Ocean Springs

French governor of the Louisiana Territory, *1420*

Tupelo

Electric power contract between a city and the federal government, *4132*
Federal corporation to encourage the purchase of electric appliances, *4931*

Washington

Mississippi state capital, *4327*

MISSOURI

Bachelor tax enacted by a state, *4828*
Brothers nominated for the presidency at the same convention, *3245*
Missouri Day, *2221*
Missouri state governor, *4468*
Missouri territorial governor, *4858*
Modern proposal to ban lawyers from serving in state or local government, *2594*
Presidential candidate from Missouri, *4584*
Secretary of agriculture, *1165*
Senator elected posthumously, *1810*
Senator to serve for 30 years, *1769*
Senator to threaten another senator with a gun in the Senate chamber, *1767*
State west of the Mississippi River to be admitted to the Union, *4297*
Vice presidential candidate from Missouri, *4639*
Vice presidential candidate of a major political party to resign before the election, *3271*

Fayette

National urban presidential primary, *3224*

Fulton

Presidential candidate from Alaska, *4593*

Hannibal

Mayor of Hannibal, MO, *1309*

Independence

Mayor of Independence, MO, *1314*
Medicare identification cards, *4058*

Jefferson City

Missouri state capital, *4331*

Kansas City

African-American mayor of Kansas City, MO, *1354*

MISSOURI—Kansas City—*continued*

Democratic Party convention between presidential elections, *3030*

IRS area service center, *4820*

Silver Republican Party platform, *3060*

Silver Republican Party presidential candidate, *3321*

Woman to make a seconding speech at a national political convention, *3004*

Lamar

President from Missouri, *4615*

Vice president from Missouri, *4683*

Newton County

National monument dedicated to an African-American, *2716*

Springfield

Federal cemetery containing the remains of both Union and Confederate soldiers, *2669*

St. Louis

African-American mayor of St. Louis, MO, *1358*

American Legion, *2702*

Commemoration of the birthday of the Marquis de Lafayette, *2222*

Extension of mail service to the West Coast, *3159*

Farmers' Alliance Party, *2933*

First Lady born west of the Mississippi, *3589*

Former president to fly in an airplane, *3792*

Government-sponsored overland expedition to the Pacific Coast, *4837*

International exchange of fingerprints, *2531*

Jobless Party presidential candidate, *3331*

Liberal Republican Party, *2928*

Liberty Party (modern) presidential candidate, *3332*

Mayor of St. Louis, MO, *1303*

Missouri constitution, *4384*

National Silver Party convention, *3316*

National Silver Party platform, *3056*

People's Party presidential candidate, *3357*

Presidential candidate from Arkansas, *4589*

Presidential inauguration in which a rabbi participated, *3682*

Silverite presidential candidate, *3315*

Smoke control ordinance, *4161*

Vice president to marry during his term in office, *4991*

Vice presidential candidate from Oklahoma, *4656*

Vice presidential candidate from Washington, DC, *1899*

Vice presidential candidate from Washington State, *4657*

Vice presidential candidate from West Virginia, *4649*

Year in which both major parties nominated incumbent governors for the presidency, *2997*

Year in which the Democratic party renominated its entire ticket, *3007*

MONTANA

Congressional representative to vote twice against entry into war, *1608*

Montana state governor, *4492*

Montana territorial governor, *4877*

State law banning corporate contributions to ballot question campaigns, *4441*

State pension laws, *2475*

Vice presidential candidate from Montana, *4655*

Woman elected to the House of Representatives, *1599*

Woman governor of Montana, *4535*

Dixon

Native American tribal constitution, *2753*

Fort Laramie

Native American to win territorial concessions from the federal government, *2745*

Helena

Montana constitution, *4401*

Montana state capital, *4348*

Little Bighorn

Major defeat inflicted by Native Americans on regular U.S. Army troops, *2748*

Virginia City

Montana state capital, *4348*

NEBRASKA

Nebraska state governor, *4486*

Presidential candidate from Nebraska, *4583*

State governor to appoint two United States senators in one year for interim terms, *4508*

State legislature with a single chamber in the post-Revolutionary era, *4551*

State to ratify the 25th Amendment to the Constitution, *1858*

Vice presidential candidate from Nebraska, *4650*

Woman governor of Nebraska, *4523*

Beatrice

Homestead grant under the Homestead Act, *4182*

Large-scale free land distribution by the federal government, *4181*

Grand Island

Interstate Commerce Commission Medal of Honor, *4919*

Lincoln

Nebraska constitution, *4397*

Omaha

Federal Trade Commission trade practice conference, *4924*
Nebraska state capital, *4344*
Nebraska territorial governor, *4870*
Populist Party platform, *3054*
President born in Nebraska, *4617*
President who was the child of divorced parents, *3564*
State in which all electricity came from public power plants, *4133*
Transcontinental railroad, *4089*
Vending machine law enacted by a city, *4916*
Vice president born in Nebraska, *4688*

Swan

Federal foresting project, *4144*

NEVADA

Gambling permit stamp issued by the federal government, *4003*
Large area of the United States contaminated by nuclear radiation, *4165*
Nevada Day, *2200*
Nevada state governor, *4485*
State narcotics ban, *4065*
State to allow publicly traded corporations to obtain gambling licenses, *4005*
State to declare sovereignty over a large tract of federal land, *4283*
State to legalize casino gambling, *4001*
State to ratify the 15th Amendment to the Constitution, *1845*
Vice presidential candidate from Nevada, *4652*

Carson City

Nevada constitution, *4396*
Nevada state capital, *4343*
Nevada territorial governor, *4872*
State constitution telegraphed in its entirety, *4269*
State to allow execution by lethal gas, *2562*

Frenchman Flat

Live atomic bomb explosion shown on television, *3878*

Las Vegas

Major American city founded in the 20th century, *1264*

Reno

Congressional representative to attend college after his term of service, *1598*

NEW HAMPSHIRE

Attorney of the United States, *1971*
Declaration of independence by a British colony, *1053*
Federal judge to be impeached, *1972*
Insurance board established by a state government, *4050*
New Hampshire presidential primary, *3204*
New Hampshire state governor, *4444*
Presidential candidate from New Hampshire, *4573*
Presidential candidate whose opponent had been his military commander, *3236*
Quorum of the Senate, *1664*
Secretary of state to serve more than once, *1157*
Senate president pro tempore, *1665*
Senator elected on an antislavery ticket, *4250*
State law mandating a ten-hour workday, *2493*
State legislature with a lower house known as the House of Representatives, *4539*
State lottery in modern times, *4004*
Vice presidential candidate from New Hampshire, *4622*
Woman governor of New Hampshire, *4529*

Concord

Constitutional convention of a popular character, *4371*
New Hampshire state capital, *4316*
State constitution to be submitted to the people for ratification, *4372*

Exeter

New Hampshire constitution, *4367*
New Hampshire state capital, *4316*

Farmington

Vice president born in New Hampshire, *4675*

Hillsboro

President born in the 19th century, *3463*
President from New Hampshire, *4606*

Peterborough

Public library established after the Revolution, *1259*

NEW HAMPSHIRE—*continued*

Portsmouth

Attack against the British by a state militia, *1013*
Colony to declare its independence, *1023*
Intercolonial postal system, *3132*
President to receive the Nobel Peace Prize, *3626*

Portsmouth Harbor

American flag displayed on a warship, *1079*

NEW JERSEY

Basketball star elected to the Senate, *1804*
Coin to use *E pluribus unum* as a motto, *2148*
Colonial law prohibiting slavery, *4225*
Colonial statute establishing religious toleration in public office, *1418*
Congresswoman who was a grandmother, *1625*
Holding companies authorized by a state, *4915*
Lawyers admitted to practice before the Supreme Court, *2584*
Mason known to hold high government office in the colonies, *1422*
Medical licensing law enacted by a colony, *4009*
National procedures for electing senators, *1710*
New Jersey colonial governor, *1464*
Noise-control law enacted by a state, *4169*
Nominee for associate justice of the Supreme Court to be rejected by the Senate, *4752*
Permanent Dutch colony, *1407*
Poor Man's Party presidential candidate, *3340*
Presidential candidate from New Jersey, *4574*
Public defender hired by a state, *4419*
Roads improvement aid bill enacted by a state, *4090*
State law on union discrimination, *2489*
State police department to be monitored for racial profiling, *2549*
State test of religious qualifications for public office, *1946*
State to give its legislature sole power to determine the eligibility of legislators, *4537*
State to grant limited voting rights to women, *1952*
State to legalize labor unions, *2488*
State to ratify the Bill of Rights, *1835*
Vice presidential candidate from New Jersey, *4628*
Woman governor of New Jersey, *4528*
Women to cast unofficial votes in a presidential election, *1957*

Caldwell

President born in New Jersey, *4612*

Elizabeth

Contact between the president and the Congress, *1483*

Evesham

Reservation for Native Americans established by a state, *2727*

Jersey City

Democratic congresswoman, *1602*
Woman to chair a House committee, *1605*

Long Branch

Vice president from New Jersey, *4679*

Morristown

First Lady who was widowed while her husband was in office, *3592*

Newark

African-American mayor of a major Eastern city, *1335*
Celluloid campaign buttons, *2803*
State legislative hearing to be shown on television, *4554*
Woman to serve as foreman on a federal grand jury, *1981*

Paterson

Strike in which a militia was called out, *2477*

Perth Amboy

African-American to vote under authority of the 15th Amendment to the Constitution, *1923*

Princeton

First Lady to remarry after the death of her husband, *3606*
New Jersey constitution, *4362*
New Jersey state capital, *4310*
New Jersey state governor, *4447*
President who had been president of a university, *3499*

Trenton

National conference on crime, *2539*
White House china service that was made in the United States, *5035*
Woman to head the state committee of a major political party, *2963*

NEW MEXICO

Chicano radical nationalist movement, *2866*
Latino elected to the Senate, *1786*
New Mexico state governor, *4500*
New Mexico state governor of Latino ancestry, *4504*
New Mexico territorial governor, *4868*
New Mexico territorial governor who was of Mexican ancestry, *4880*
People's Constitutional Party presidential candidate, *3355*
Restoration of land to a Native American tribe, *2757*
Vice presidential candidate from New Mexico, *4663*
Wilderness area to be formally named, *4154*
Women to run as presidential candidates in the 20th century, *3270*

Carlsbad

Deep underground nuclear waste storage site, *4170*

Colfax County

Major sale of land in the continental United States to a foreign consortium, *4271*

Espanola

Spanish governor-general of New Mexico, *1399*

Santa Fe

New Mexico constitution, *4407*
New Mexico state capital, *4355*
Public building in the United States that has been continuously occupied, *1403*

NEW YORK

African-American to give antislavery lectures, *4247*
Agricultural appropriation, *4110*
Anti-Masonic Party, *2912*
Audobon society, *4209*
Bank deposit insurance law enacted by a state, *2105*
Chief justice of the Supreme Court, *4747*
Coalition between Northern and Southern politicians, *2905*
Confederation in what is now the United States, *2721*
Congressional medal awarded to a physician, *1504*
Congressional representative of Puerto Rican ancestry, *1620*
Contact between the Congress and state governments, *4261*

Deadlocked senatorial election, *1660*
Defeated presidential and vice presidential candidates to die during the term they had sought, *3261*
Department of Housing and Urban Development, *2049*
Effective state arbitration law, *2452*
First Lady who had an occupation other than homemaking, *3588*
Former vice president who became a state governor, *4982*
House majority leader, *1567*
Insurance department of a state, *4051*
Intercolonial postal system, *3132*
Labor union to nominate its own political candidates, *2485*
Labor union whose candidates won an election, *2486*
Law code compiled in North America, *2722*
Lawyers admitted to practice before the Supreme Court, *2584*
License plates for vehicles, *4093*
Major battle lost by American forces, *1026*
National firearms lobby, *2817*
National labor organization to establish a women's division, *2884*
Native American symbols adopted for political purposes by colonial Americans, *1130*
New York colonial governor, *1454*
New York state governor, *4451*
Permanent Dutch colony, *1407*
Political party to nominate the same candidate six times, *3016*
Pope to visit the United States before his election, *2385*
President to make a radio broadcast from a foreign country, *3760*
President who was the son of a minister, *3562*
President with a serious physical disability, *3420*
Presidential campaign manager who was a woman, *2774*
Presidential candidates from New York State, *4565*
Presidential team from Virginia and New York, *3385*
Proposal for a presidential cabinet, *1136*
Secretary of commerce, *1171*
Secretary of defense, *1182*
Secretary of foreign affairs, *2315*
Senate minority whip, *1732*
Senate pages who were female, *1645*
Stamp tax, *4794*
State agency for enforcing equal treatment in employment, *2459*
State agricultural board, *4109*
State arbitration board for labor disputes, *2450*
State constitutional reform movement, *4268*
State environmental protection law enacted in connection with advertising, *4122*

NEW YORK—*continued*

State law giving property rights to married women, *1953*

State law requiring candidates to file itemized accounts of campaign expenditures, *4430*

State licensing law for pharmacists, *4027*

State plain-language law, *4282*

State pure food and drug law, *4021*

State superintendent of schools, *3968*

State to ratify the Eleventh Amendment to the Constitution, *1838*

State to require blood tests for marriage licenses, *3953*

State with a population of more than 10 million, *3081*

State with a population of more than 5 million, *3080*

States with populations of more than 1 million, *3078*

Supreme Court decision establishing the power of the federal government to regulate commerce, *4718*

Supreme Court decision on school prayer, *4733*

Supreme Court justice to be appointed, confirmed, and inaugurated twice, *4775*

Supreme Court nominee to testify before the Senate Judiciary Committee, *4774*

Third party to participate in a presidential election, *3189*

Use of the phrase "to the victor belong the spoils", *2024*

Use of the term "national guard", *2664*

Use of the terms "Hunkers" and "Barnburners", *2919*

Vice president from New York, *4666*

Vice president to become president after a hiatus, *4994*

Vice president who had served in the Senate, *4963*

Vice president who was nominated specifically for that office, *4966*

Vice presidential candidate from New York State, *4621*

Warship named for a First Lady, *3577*

Woman elected president of a state lawyers' association, *2593*

Woman justice on the federal bench, *1979*

Woman to run for vice president as the candidate of a major political party, *3273*

Year in which both major parties nominated incumbent governors for the presidency, *2997*

Albany

Colonial congress, *1423*

Dutch colonial settlement, *1405*

Patriotic song to achieve popularity during the Revolution, *1113*

Plan for the union of the British colonies, *1001*

Presidential candidate to fly to a political convention, *3015*

State political machine, *2911*

Television broadcast of a presidential candidate accepting his nomination, *3259*

Whig Party presidential candidate, *3285*

Whig Party resolutions, *3034*

Auburn

State to allow execution by electrocution, *2560*

Bronxville

President who had been a Boy Scout, *3833*

Buffalo

Free Soil Party platform, *3037*

Free Soil Party presidential candidate, *3289*

Liberty League presidential candidate, *3288*

Mayor of Buffalo, NY, *1305*

President elected after the Civil War who had not served in it, *3409*

President who had been an executioner, *3494*

Presidential candidate from New Hampshire, *4573*

Superintendent of schools hired by a city, *3970*

Vice presidential candidate from Michigan, *4634*

Vice presidential candidate from Ohio, *4633*

Chappaqua

First Lady elected to public office, *3623*

Easthampton

First Lady who was educated at a school, *3575*

Fishkill

Revolutionary War national veterans' organization, *2699*

Flushing Meadow

United Nations General Assembly meeting, *2433*

Hyde Park

Presidential library, *3422*

Ithaca

Industrial and labor relations school at a college, *3067*

Kinderhook

First Lady who was born an American citizen, *3580*

NEW YORK—New York—*continued*

Drawback legislation enacted by Congress, *4905*

Edition of the *Journal of the Senate of the United States of America, 1691*

Edition of *The New York Tribune, 3922*

Edition of the *Wall Street Journal, 3924*

Election in which returns were broadcast on radio, *3208*

Entry in *Journal of the House of Representatives of the United States, 1532*

Entry in the *Journal of the Executive Proceedings of the Senate of the United States of America, 1673*

Execution by the Army, *2553*

Execution for slave trading carried out by the federal government, *2556*

Executive department authorized by Congress, *2033*

Express mail, *3153*

Federal charter, *1995*

Federal education grants to the children of deceased veterans, *3980*

Federal execution of an organized crime boss, *2565*

Federal immigration station, *3114*

Federal law regulating commerce with Native Americans, *2735*

Federal theater project, *2018*

First Lady appointed to a federal post after the death of her husband, *3612*

First Lady of Mexico to reside in the United States, *2378*

First Lady to write a book published by a commercial publisher, *3607*

First Lady who was educated at a school, *3575*

Fish protection law enacted by a city, *4201*

Flag salute, *1096*

Form of the enacting clause used in congressional bills, *1485*

Formal announcement that the Constitution was in effect, *1829*

Gay pride march, *2871*

Holding company worth a billion dollars, *4917*

Homosexual civil rights legislation proposed at the federal level, *1910*

Homosexual rights demonstration in the United States, *2868*

Homosexual rights protest, *2870*

House of Representatives filibuster, *1547*

House Ways and Means Committee, *1544*

Immigration receiving station, *3108*

Inaugural address, *3633*

Inaugural ball, *3641*

Inaugural chintzes, *3634*

Independent Liberal Republican Party presidential candidate, *3302*

Interstate anticrime pact, *2527*

Issue of the *Federalist* papers, *3071*

Issue of the *New York Times, 3923*

Japanese diplomatic delegation to the United States, *2258*

Jewish minister and envoy, *2335*

Joint committee of the House and Senate, *1481*

Joint meeting of the Senate and the House of Representatives, *1812*

Joint rule of both houses of Congress, *1482*

Korean embassy, *2261*

Labor Day parade, *2210*

Labor newspaper, *3919*

Law book containing laws enacted by more than one session of Congress, *2514*

Law instruction at a college, *2523*

Law setting pay rates for Congress, *1647*

Law text published in the United States, *2516*

League of Women Voters, *2898*

Liberal Party convention, *3345*

Liquor reform movement, *2853*

Loan to the United States, *2082*

Mace of the House of Representatives, *1529*

Maces as symbols of royal authority, *1421*

Mayor of New York, NY, *1295*

Medical licensing law enacted by a city, *4008*

Meeting place of Congress, *1480*

Meeting place of the Supreme Court, *4693*

Method of choosing standing committees in the Senate, *1667*

Military pension awarded to a woman, *2698*

Minimum wage law established by a city for public contract work, *2500*

Muckraking journal of importance, *3900*

Narcotics ban enacted by Congress, *4062*

National arbitration organization, *2591*

National Association for the Advancement of Colored People, *2847*

National civil liberties advocacy group, *2827*

National homosexual rights organization, *2872*

National labor congress, *2879*

National Working Men's Convention, *3299*

Naturalization act enacted by Congress, *3101*

New Alliance Party presidential candidate, *3362*

New York state capital, *4318*

Night court, *1273*

Nominating convention that required more than 100 ballots, *3010*

Nominee for chief justice of the Supreme Court to be rejected by the Senate, *4756*

North American Party presidential candidate, *3291*

Northern city to consider secession during the Civil War, *1368*

Oath of office for members of Congress, *1530*

Object from the early House of Representatives still in use, *1531*

Organization in charge of the Statue of Liberty, *1126*

Organized civil rights protest by people with disabilities, *2830*

Overland mail service between colonies, *3130*

Pacifist society, *2810*

State temperance society of women, *2856*

Saratoga

Major American victory in the Revolutionary War, *1031*
Monument to a traitor, *2709*
National lawyers' society, *2589*

Schenectady

Mayor of Schenectady, NY, *1298*
Theory of fair division, *3077*

Schuylerville

National day of thanksgiving, *2241*

Seneca Falls

Women's rights convention, *2894*

Stony Point

Medal awarded by the Continental Congress to a foreigner, *1047*

Syracuse

Citizenship and public affairs school at a college, *3065*
Mayor of Syracuse, NY, *1313*

Troy

Use of the term "Uncle Sam" as a reference to the United States, *1131*

Utica

State nominating convention, *4427*

Warsaw

Antislavery political organization, *4248*
Liberty Party platform, *3035*
Liberty Party presidential candidate, *3286*
Single-issue political party, *2918*

Watervliet

Conscientious objectors, *2631*

West Point

American general to engage in treason, *1034*
Child of a president to attend West Point, *3553*
Military academy established by the federal government, *2613*
President to appear on color television, *3766*

President to attend West Point, *3696*

Westfield

President to wear a beard, *3828*

NORTH CAROLINA

American Heritage Rivers, *4199*
Commemoration of the Mecklenburg declaration of independence, *2194*
Governor of the Southwest Territory (Tennessee), *4851*
Independent civil government in America, *1426*
National seashore, *4155*
North Carolina colonial governor, *1461*
North Carolina state governor, *4448*
Petition to Congress by African-Americans, *4239*
Presidential candidates from North Carolina, *4567*
Republican senator from North Carolina elected in the 20th century, *1801*
Spanish colonial settlement, *1394*
State denied admission into the Union, *4290*
State governor to be impeached and convicted, *4488*
State licensing law for nurses, *4026*
State to enact a conflict-of-interest law concerning its legislature, *4536*
State to ratify the Twelfth Amendment to the Constitution, *1840*
Supreme Court nominee to be rejected by the Senate in the 20th century, *4776*
Televised Watergate hearings, *3882*
Vice president who served in both houses of Congress from different states, *4977*
Vice presidential candidate from North Carolina, *4629*
Written constitution adopted by a community of American-born freemen, *1439*

Chapel Hill

State university, *3966*

Charlotte

Civil rights sit-in, *2850*
School district to implement court-ordered busing to achieve racial integration, *1935*

Halifax

Colonial government to instruct its delegates to the Continental Congress to proclaim independence, *1054*
Halifax Resolutions Day, *2183*
North Carolina constitution, *4366*
North Carolina state capital, *4319*

NORTH CAROLINA—*continued*

Louisburg

Confederate States flag, *1093*

Pineville

President born in North Carolina, *4604*

Princeville

Town founded by African-Americans after the Civil War, *1260*

Raleigh

Birth control clinic run by a state government, *3995*
President born in North Carolina, *4604*

Roanoke Island

English colonial settlement, *1397*
Letters written by an English colonial governor in America, *1398*

Sampson County

Vice president born in North Carolina, *4670*

Washington

Town named for George Washington, *1256*

NORTH DAKOTA

Bonding law enacted by a state, *4275*
Dakota territorial governor, *4874*
International friendship park, *2271*
North Dakota state governor, *4495*
Political cartoonist elected to Congress, *1571*
Presidential candidate from North Dakota, *4590*
States admitted to the Union simultaneously, *4303*
Supreme Court decision on criminal jurisdiction on Native American reservations, *4721*

Beulah

Commercial-scale synthetic fuels plant owned by the federal government, *4135*

Bismarck

Bank wholly owned and operated by a state, *2110*
North Dakota constitution, *4399*
North Dakota state capital, *4346*

Esmond

Woman to serve in a state legislature as speaker of the House, *4549*

Medora

Conservation park dedicated to Theodore Roosevelt, *4156*

Portal

Absolute monarch to visit the United States, *2384*

OHIO

African-American to enlist in the United States armed forces during the Civil War, *1383*
Battle fought by federal troops after the formation of the Union, *2736*
Brothers nominated for the presidency at the same convention, *3245*
Commemoration of the birthday of William McKinley, *2219*
Congresswoman to represent the United States in the United Nations, *2285*
Congresswoman to visit a theater of war, *1610*
Expressions of official U.S. policy toward lands outside the 13 colonies, *4173*
Incumbent senator to be elected president, *3501*
Land preemption act passed by Congress, *4178*
Land set-aside for schools authorized by the Continental Congress, *3965*
Land subsidy by Congress for road improvements, *4179*
Mother and son simultaneously elected to Congress, *1614*
Nationwide campus rioting, *2862*
Ohio state governor, *4460*
President-elect who was simultaneously a senator-elect and a member of the House, *3513*
President from Ohio, *4603*
President from the Whig Party, *3710*
Presidential candidate from Ohio, *4570*
Presidential candidate to make campaign speeches in a foreign language, *2767*
Presidential candidate who had been divorced, *3254*
Presidential election in which votes were tallied electronically, *3218*
Sale of federal land to an individual, *4176*
Secretary of the interior, *1156*
Senator who had been an astronaut, *1802*
State admitted into the Union without a resolution of Congress, *4295*
State created from the Northwest Territory, *4294*
State employment service, *2462*
State in which slavery was illegal from the time it was admitted to the Union, *4240*
State law regulating women's work hours, *2494*
Survey of public lands, *4175*
Underground Railroad activities, *4234*
Vice president to receive the Nobel Peace Prize, *4986*

OHIO—*continued*

Marblehead

Lifesaving medal awarded by the Treasury Department, *2042*

Marion

President who had been a newspaper publisher, *3496*

Presidential election in which the candidates of both major parties were newspaper publishers, *3210*

Mount Pleasant

Abolition newspaper, *3914*

Muskingum County

Vice president born in Ohio, *4677*

New Concord

Presidential candidate who had been an astronaut, *3272*

North Olmsted

City to ban products made in sweatshops, *2449*

Steubenville

Federal district land office, *4177*

OKLAHOMA

African-American congressman to deliver the Republican Party's official response to the State of the Union message, *1630*

African-American elected to a national leadership post in the Republican Party, *2960*

Native American state denied admission to the Union, *4304*

Oklahoma state governor, *4499*

Oklahoma territorial governor, *4879*

Republican governor of Oklahoma, *4512*

State to allow execution by lethal injection, *2568*

Supreme Court nominee accused of sexual harassment, *4782*

Vice presidential candidate from Oklahoma, *4656*

Guthrie

Oklahoma constitution, *4406*

Oklahoma state capital, *4354*

Oklahoma City

Attack by domestic terrorists on a federal facility resulting in large loss of life, *2006*

Oklahoma state capital, *4354*

Woman to serve as mayor of Oklahoma City, OK, *1336*

OREGON

American Heritage Rivers, *4199*

Defeated presidential and vice presidential candidates to die during the term they had sought, *3261*

Gasoline tax levied by a state, *4830*

Husband and wife to be elected simultaneously to both chambers of a state legislature, *4553*

Labor Day, *2205*

Law permitting doctor-assisted suicide, *3960*

Libertarian Party presidential candidate, *3356*

Oregon state governor, *4481*

Oregon territorial governor, *4866*

Presidential candidate from Oregon, *4586*

Senate leader to occupy the party floor leader's desk, *1738*

Senator to address the Senate in military uniform, *1709*

State appeals court decision ordering the extension of insurance benefits to homosexual partners of government employees, *1916*

State bottle bill, *4167*

State litter law, *4168*

State to adopt the use of the initiative and referendum, *4432*

State to ration health care, *4035*

Vice presidential candidate from Oregon, *4638*

Vote of record in which participants of different races and both sexes were given an equal voice, *4839*

Woman governor of Oregon, *4527*

Bend

Presidential candidate killed in a rescue attempt, *3257*

Champoeg

Government on the Pacific Coast, *1432*

Eugene

Federal conviction for Internet piracy, *4942*

Oregon City

Oregon state capital, *4340*

Salem

Oregon constitution, *4393*

Oregon state capital, *4340*

Warrenton

Woman mayor elected west of the Rocky Mountains, *1328*

PENNSYLVANIA

Cabinet member to serve in two or more cabinet posts, *1146*

Cabinet secretary to share the same last name as the president, *1170*

Child labor law enacted by a state that restricted the age of the worker, *2456*

Colonial legislature whose upper and lower houses had terms of differing lengths, *1476*

Colony requiring rotation in public office, *1419*

Colony to change from a bicameral to a unicameral legislature, *1478*

Congressional representative who was Catholic, *1584*

Congressional representative who was Jewish, *1586*

Electoral vote cast contrary to instructions, *3174*

English patent granted to a resident of America, *2596*

Expressions of official U.S. policy toward lands outside the 13 colonies, *4173*

Federal revenue commissioner, *4798*

Flag Day, *2208*

Inheritance tax enacted by a state, *4829*

Law barring the importation of slaves into a British colony, *4229*

Lawyers admitted to practice before the Supreme Court, *2584*

Member of the House of Representatives to lie in state in the Capitol rotunda, *1237*

Movie censorship board established by a state, *3860*

Muckraking journalist who was a woman, *3891*

Pennsylvania colonial governor, *1458*

Pennsylvania Day, *2227*

President who had been a medical student, *3477*

Presidential candidate from Pennsylvania, *4561*

Printed ballot, *4425*

Secretary of labor, *1172*

Senate election in which neither candidate was seated after a recount, *1737*

Senate election that was contested, *1757*

Senator to face allegations of corrupt election practices, *1772*

Senators elected to office, *1755*

Speaker of the House, *1631*

State governor who had previously been governor of a territory in which his state was not included, *4487*

State-run liquor stores, *4278*

State to ban the death penalty, *2554*

State to elect senators to the United States Senate, *4260*

State with a unicameral legislature, *4538*

States with populations of more than 1 million, *3078*

Surveyed line separating North from South, *4172*

Tax rebellion against the federal government, *4799*

Vice presidential candidate from Pennsylvania, *4624*

Bethlehem

Death penalty in a tax riot, *2555*

Carlisle

Army war college, *2616*

Declaration of independence by citizens of an American colony, *1050*

Cove Gap

President from Pennsylvania, *4607*

Delaware County

Government assistance to the family of an insane person, *4007*

Easton

Civil rights chair at a college, *2526*

Germantown

Protest against slavery made by a religious group in the New World, *4226*

Gettysburg

Cabinet session held at a place other than the seat of the federal government, *1188*

Harrisburg

Digest of American law, *2517*

National political convention to adopt the unit rule, *2986*

Opinion poll, *2762*

Presidential candidate from Ohio, *4570*

Lancaster

Seat of the Continental Congress, *1039*

Lewisburg

Roman Catholic clergyman sentenced to jail in the United States for political crimes, *2860*

Philadelphia

Abolition organization, *4231*

Adoption of the dollar as the standard monetary unit, *2150*

PENNSYLVANIA—Philadelphia—*continued*

Proclamation of the unification of the colonies, *1052*

Progressive Party (1948) presidential candidate, *3339*

Proposal for a national capital, *1863*

Proposal for a presidential cabinet, *1136*

Proposal in the Constitutional Convention for civil liberties, *1824*

Proposal that senators should serve for free, *1658*

Proposals for the design of the Great Seal of the United States, *1104*

Prosecution under the Sedition Act, *3854*

Protest against British taxation of tea shipments, *1010*

Public call for independence to be published, *1025*

Public celebration of national independence, *2236*

Public figure lampooned in political cartoons, *3929*

Public reading of the Declaration of Independence, *1060*

Publication of Supreme Court decisions, *4692*

Publication of the Declaration of Independence in another language, *1061*

Quarantine law enacted by Congress, *4011*

Regional compromise over the issue of slavery, *4237*

Regular cabinet meetings, *1145*

Regulation allowing newspapers to be sent through the mails, *3907*

Representative of a foreign country to the United States, *2311*

Republican Party candidate to be nominated on the first ballot, *3237*

Republican Party platform, *3039*

Republican Party presidential candidate, *3292*

Seat of the Continental Congress, *1039*

Senate proceedings that were open to the public, *1681*

Sergeant at arms of the Senate, *1682*

Session of Congress held outside Washington, DC, since 1800, *1820*

Session of Congress to meet in Philadelphia, *1813*

Session of the Continental Congress, *1040*

Signer of the Declaration of Independence, *1057*

Silver coins issued by the Mint, *2153*

Special session of Congress, *1814*

Special session of the Senate, *1680*

State bank to receive federal deposits, *2106*

Strike benefit by a union, *2876*

Suggestion that slaves be counted as full members of the population, *4235*

Superintendent of finance under the Continental Congress, *2080*

Supreme Court case challenging the validity of an act of Congress, *4711*

Supreme Court decision to be overridden by an amendment to the Constitution, *4710*

Supreme Court decision to be recorded, *4709*

Tammany Day, *2179*

Tammany political club, *2902*

Televised presidential election debate between an incumbent president and a challenger, *3222*

Territory owned by the federal government, *4835*

Test of presidential authority over the cabinet secretaries, *1147*

Tobacco tax enacted by Congress, *4077*

Tolling of the Liberty Bell for an event of political importance, *1109*

Tolling of the Liberty Bell to announce a battle, *1110*

Treasurer of the United States, *2077*

Treatise on common law written for the American legal profession, *2518*

Treaty approved by the Senate that was held up for lack of funding, *2401*

Treaty terminated by a joint resolution of Congress, *2404*

Trial of a printer for sedition, *3848*

United States Marines, *2660*

United States Navy, *2691*

Use of sergeant at arms of the Senate to make an arrest, *1683*

Use of the mace of the House of Representatives to keep order, *1552*

Use of the name "United States" instead of "United Colonies", *1064*

Use of the term "cabinet", *1144*

Vice president from Pennsylvania, *4669*

Vice president to announce his own election as president, *4965*

Vice president to be reelected, *4964*

Vice president who had served in the Continental Congress, *4957*

Vice presidential candidate from Idaho, *4659*

Woman to serve as secretary of the Republican National Convention, *3021*

Year in which the Democratic-Republican Party won control of the House of Representatives, *1549*

Year in which the Federalist Party won control of both houses of Congress, *1489*

Year in which the Federalist Party won control of the House of Representatives, *1545*

Year in which the Federalist Party won control of the Senate, *1678*

Pittsburgh

American National Party platform, *3047*

American National Party presidential candidate, *3303*

RHODE ISLAND—Providence—*continued*

Statehouse with an all-marble dome, *4353*

Warwick

Colonial law to control corrupt election practices, *1451*

Colony to pass a slavery emancipation law, *4223*

SOUTH CAROLINA

African-American unit organized during the Civil War, *1384*

Beating in the Senate chamber, *1704*

Brothers who were candidates for the presidency simultaneously, *3226*

Colonial legislature's mace still extant, *1479*

Commemoration of the birthday of Woodrow Wilson, *2226*

Escape of slaves from a colony in what is now United States territory, *4218*

Federal act regulating corporate contributions to election campaigns, *2784*

Fistfight in the Senate, *1723*

Former vice president to serve in the Senate, *4974*

Funeral held at taxpayer expense, *1694*

House of Representatives election that was contested, *1539*

Laws authorizing the use of force against the Ku Klux Klan, *1924*

Minister plenipotentiary to Great Britain, *2321*

Political cartoon entered in the *Congressional Record*, *1514*

President from the working class, *3458*

President of the Senate to abdicate his power to keep order, *1693*

President pro tempore of the Senate to appoint committee members, *1692*

President who did not reside in the state of his birth, *3462*

President who served in more than one war, *3694*

President who was orphaned in childhood, *3542*

Presidential candidate from South Carolina, *4562*

Proposal that senators should serve for free, *1658*

Secession act at the start of the Civil War, *1365*

Senate solo filibuster to last for more than 24 hours, *1744*

Senator elected by a write-in vote, *1796*

Smoking ban in the Senate chambers, *1729*

South Carolina colonial governor, *1462*

South Carolina state governor, *4453*

State ban on the capture and display of whales and dolphins, *4217*

State to ratify the Articles of Confederation, *1033*

State to remove property ownership as a qualification for voting rights, *4424*

State to secede from the Union, *1366*

State to set an age qualification for state senators, *4540*

Vice president to resign, *4973*

Vice president who was born an American citizen, *4972*

Vice presidential candidate from South Carolina, *4630*

Woman to receive nominating votes for the vice presidency at the convention of a major party, *3012*

Year in which Senate seats were won by a third party, *1696*

Abbeville District

Vice president from South Carolina, *4667*

Beaufort

African-American justice of a state supreme court, *4413*

Charleston

Act inaugurating the Civil War, *1369*

Civil rights anthem to achieve fame, *1122*

Independent government in an American colony, *1428*

Independent Party presidential candidate, *3283*

Jewish person elected to a public office in the New World, *1427*

National convention of a major party that failed to nominate a presidential candidate, *2990*

Public library in an American city, *1254*

South Carolina constitution, *4360*

South Carolina state capital, *4315*

Strike of African-American laborers, *2875*

Dewitt's Corner

Treaty between states after the Declaration of Independence, *4257*

Florence

Congresswoman who was not sworn in, *1606*

Fort Sumter

Presidential call for volunteer troops to fight in the Civil War, *1378*

Georgetown

Congressional representative who was African-American, *1594*

Port Royal

French colonial settlement, *1395*

Summerton

Challenge to school segregation in the South, *1928*

Sumter

City government using the manager plan, *1290*

Waxhaw

President born in South Carolina, *4600*

SOUTH DAKOTA

Dakota territorial governor, *4874*
Native American Day, *2235*
Presidential candidate from South Dakota, *4596*
State to adopt the use of the initiative and referendum, *4432*
States admitted to the Union simultaneously, *4303*

Custer

Monument to a Native American, *2718*

Mount Rushmore

Monument to four presidents, *2714*

Pierre

South Dakota state capital, *4347*
South Dakota state governor, *4493*

Sioux Falls

South Dakota constitution, *4400*

Wallace

Vice president born in South Dakota, *4685*

Wounded Knee

Armed occupation by Native American protesters in the modern era, *2758*
Militant Native American civil rights organization, *2756*

TENNESSEE

Alcohol prohibition law enacted by a state, *3943*
Cabinet member who had served as a Confederate officer, *1164*
Congressional representative to serve before his 25th birthday, *1587*
Filing date for 1040 tax forms, *4809*

Governor of the Southwest Territory (Tennessee), *4851*
Governor of two different states, *4480*
Gubernatorial election in which two brothers were the opposing candidates, *4491*
House minority leader, *1569*
Jim Crow law, *1925*
President and vice president in the 20th century who were both Southerners, *3442*
President from Tennessee, *4601*
President to serve as a senator both before and after his term in office, *3495*
President who did not reside in the state of his birth, *3462*
President who had served in both the House of Representatives and the Senate, *3487*
Presidential candidate from Tennessee, *4568*
Presidential candidate from the Democratic Party to be elected after the Civil War, *3247*
Senator to be impeached, *1759*
Senators elected but not seated, *1758*
Speaker of the House who became president, *1633*
State readmitted to the Union after the Civil War, *1392*
State to hold a public referendum on secession, *1377*
Statehood Day (Tennessee), *2186*
Supreme Court decision on legislative apportionment, *4732*
Tennessee state governor, *4459*
Treaties for postal routes through Native American territory, *3150*
Use of sergeant at arms of the Senate to make an arrest, *1683*
Vice president from Tennessee, *4673*
Vice presidential candidate from Tennessee, *4631*

Chattanooga

Criminal trial before the Supreme Court, *4703*

Dayton

Legal clash between evolutionists and creationists, *1950*

Greeneville

President who had neither military nor legal experience, *3493*
President who had served as mayor of a city, *3488*
President who learned reading and writing from his wife, *3826*

Knoxville

State ban on dueling, *4012*
Tennessee constitution, *4376*

Former president to serve as an official of an enemy government, *3492*

Gambling law for ministers enacted by a colony, *3997*

Governor of the colony of Virginia, *1453*

Hunting law enacted by a colony, *4200*

Inheritance tax levied by a colony, *4792*

Maces as symbols of royal authority, *1421*

Medical regulations enacted by a colony, *4006*

Orator of the Revolution, *1004*

President from the Democratic-Republican Party, *3708*

President from the Federalist Party, *3705*

President of the Continental Congress, *1038*

President who had been governor of a state, *3474*

President who had served in the House of Representatives, *3480*

President who had served in the Senate, *3481*

President who was a former state governor and the son of a state governor, *3552*

President whose ancestry was not British, *3460*

President whose father was a state governor, *3543*

President whose mother was alive when he was inaugurated, *3638*

President whose political party was not the same as the vice president's, *3707*

Presidential candidate from Louisiana, *4572*

Presidential candidate from Virginia, *4566*

Presidential team from Virginia and New York, *3385*

Republican governor of Virginia since Reconstruction, *4516*

Secretary of energy, *1201*

Secretary of labor who was not a member of the American Federation of Labor, *2444*

Senate minority leader, *1726*

Senator appointed by a governor, *1756*

State founded within the borders of a seceded state, *4302*

State law mandating separation of church and state, *1948*

State legislature with an upper house known as the Senate, *4541*

State to ban clergymen from serving in the legislature, *1947*

State to hold a public referendum on secession, *1377*

State to ratify the 20th Amendment to the Constitution, *1851*

State voluntary sterilization regulation, *3957*

Statehood Day (Kentucky), *2188*

Statement of the principle of inalienable rights, *1055*

States-righters, *4259*

States with populations of more than 1 million, *3078*

Supreme Court decision upholding its authority to review state court decisions on appeal, *4715*

Vice president from the Democratic-Republican Party, *4999*

Vice president from the Whig Party, *5001*

Vice president who had been governor of a state, *4958*

Vice presidential candidates from Virginia, *4623*

Virginia colonial governor, *1452*

Virginia constitution, *4361*

Alexandria

Supreme Court justice to participate in a television program, *4780*

Tribute accorded by the populace to a president-elect, *3625*

Arlington

American Nazi Party, *2950*

Burial at the Tomb of the Unknown Soldier, *2670*

Consolidated headquarters for the Department of Defense, *2606*

First Lady buried in Arlington National Cemetery, *3611*

Memorial Day, *2203*

President buried in the National Cemetery, *3533*

Soldier buried at Arlington National Cemetery, *2668*

Charles City County

President and vice president to be born in the same county, *3465*

Charlottesville

Electoral vote cast for a woman presidential candidate, *3220*

Chesapeake

Christian Coalition, *2841*

Danville

American woman to become a member of the British Parliament, *2268*

Fairfax

National firearms lobby, *2817*

Fredericksburg

Monument to a president's mother, *2710*

Law school at a college, *2524*
Political economy course at a college, *3062*
Political satire, *1072*
Statehouse, *4307*
Televised presidential election debate between an incumbent president and a challenger, *3222*
Vice president to succeed to the presidency after the death of a president, *3397*
Virginia state capital, *4317*
Virginia state governor, *4449*

WASHINGTON

Full TV coverage of a state supreme court, *4422*
Presidential candidate from Washington State, *4591*
School for Native American children run by the Bureau of Indian Affairs, *2743*
State in which women constituted more than 40 percent of the legislature, *4558*
State named for a person born in America, *4272*
State to adopt a containership as its official ship, *4284*
Vice presidential candidate from Washington State, *4657*
Washington state governor, *4494*
Woman governor of Washington, *4519*

Olympia

Washington state capital, *4349*
Washington State constitution, *4402*
Washington territorial governor, *4869*

Seattle

African-American mayor of Seattle, WA, *1350*
City employment office, *2463*
Judicial decision allowing physicians to terminate the life of terminally ill patients at their request, *3961*
Major American city to elect a woman as mayor, *1329*
Major city to be unincorporated, *1261*
Mayor of Seattle, WA, *1321*
Statewide vote paid for by a single individual, *4286*

Tenino

Wooden money, *2167*

WEST VIRGINIA

Nominating convention that required more than 100 ballots, *3010*
Presidential candidate from West Virginia, *4587*

Rural free mail delivery, *3163*
Sales tax enacted by a state, *4831*
Slave state to reject secession, *1367*
State founded within the borders of a seceded state, *4302*
Vice presidential candidate from West Virginia, *4649*
West Virginia Day, *2199*
West Virginia state governor, *4484*

Alderson

Federal prison for women, *2577*

Pliny

Woman to serve on a federal government commission, *2002*

Wheeling

Post office west of the eastern seaboard, *3142*
West Virginia constitution, *4395*
West Virginia state capital, *4342*

WISCONSIN

Congressional hearings to be nationally televised, *1524*
Native American tribe restored to federally recognized status after termination, *2759*
Presidential candidate from Wisconsin, *4588*
Senator who was the victim of an assassination attempt during a filibuster, *1780*
State forestry inquiry commission, *4137*
State governor to be removed from office by a state supreme court, *4478*
State system of vocational, technical, and adult education, *3978*
State to establish statewide primary elections, *4435*
State unemployment insurance, *2465*
States to ratify the 19th Amendment to the Constitution, *1850*
Vice presidential candidate from Wisconsin, *4653*
Wisconsin state governor, *4476*
Woman artist to be commissioned by the federal government, *2016*

Belmont

Wisconsin state capital, *4337*

Green Bay

City to own a National Football League franchise, *1266*

Madison

Development of the "Wisconsin Idea" of progressivism, *2818*

WISCONSIN—Madison—*continued*

National union for public employees, *2491*
State legislature to use an electric vote recorder, *4548*
Wisconsin constitution, *4390*
Wisconsin state capital, *4337*
Wisconsin territorial governor, *4862*

Milwaukee

Congressional representative who was a Socialist, *1597*
Mayor of Milwaukee, WI, *1311*
Pioneer Party presidential candidate, *3344*
Presidential candidate wounded in an assassination attempt, *3253*
Socialist mayor of a major city, *1326*
Soldiers' homes established by Congress, *2700*

Racine

State-run adult education program, *3979*
Strike to last longer than a year, *2889*

Ripon

Founding of the Republican Party, *2922*

WYOMING

Constitutional amendment to be ratified two centuries after its proposal, *1860*
Federal law forbidding hunting on national park land, *4149*
National park, *4148*
National Parks Conference, *4151*
State to grant full voting rights to women, *1961*
Territory to grant full voting rights to women, *1958*
Woman to serve as a state governor, *4505*
Wyoming state governor, *4497*
Wyoming territorial governor, *4878*

Belle Fourche River

National monument designated by the federal government, *4150*

Cheyenne

Wyoming constitution, *4404*
Wyoming state capital, *4351*

Laramie

Women to serve as jurors, *1270*

South Pass

Woman to serve as justice of the peace, *1271*